W9-DBN-491

Alabama, Louisiana & Mississippi

Are we meeting your travel needs?

Send written comments to:

AAA Member Comments
1000 AAA Drive, Box 61
Heathrow, FL 32746-5063

Published by AAA Publishing
1000 AAA Drive
Heathrow, FL 32746-5063

Advertising Rate and Circulation Information
Call: (407) 444-8280

Printed in the USA by Quebecor World, Buffalo, NY

Photo Credit: (Cover & Title Page)
Stanton Hall, Natchez, MS
© age Fotostock / SuperStock

Printed on recyclable paper.
Please recycle whenever possible.

Mixed Sources
Product group from well-managed forests and other controlled sources
www.fsc.org Cert no. SW-COC-1610
© 1996 Forest Stewardship Council

Stock #4600

Alabama

Louisiana

Louisiana *continued*

Mississippi

Featured Information

Find Hotels As Easy As 1-2-3-4-5!

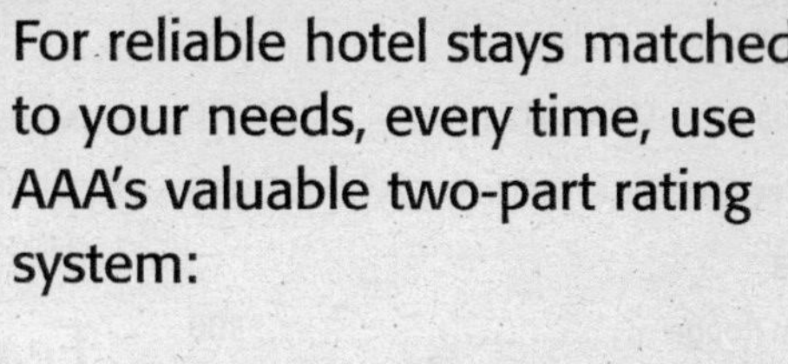

For reliable hotel stays matched to your needs, every time, use AAA's valuable two-part rating system:

- First, rest assured that *every* hotel designated **AAA Approved** upholds qualities important to members – cleanliness, service, and value.
- Focus your selection using the descriptive one-to-five **AAA Diamond Ratings** assigned exclusively to Approved properties to help you match your expectations.

Find AAA Approved and Diamond rated properties in the TourBook®, in print and on aaa.com. Look for the AAA logo on signage and billboards.

Read about **AAA Diamond Ratings** on page 20-21or visit aaa.com/Diamonds.

Attractions, lodgings and restaurants are listed on the basis of merit alone after careful evaluation and approval by one of AAA/CAA's full-time, professionally trained Tourism Editors. Evaluations are unannounced to ensure that we see an establishment just as you would see it.

An establishment's decision to advertise in the TourBook guide has no bearing on its evaluation or rating. Advertising for services or products does not imply AAA endorsement.

All information in this guide was reviewed for accuracy before publication. However, since changes inevitably occur between annual editions, we suggest you work with your AAA travel professional or check on AAA.com to confirm prices and schedules.

How the TourBook Guide is Organized

The TourBook guide is organized into three distinct sections.

The **Points of Interest** section helps you plan daily activities and sightseeing excursions and provides details about the city or attraction you are visiting.

The **Lodgings and Restaurants** section helps you select AAA Approved accommodations and dining facilities meeting your specific needs and expectations.

The **Reference** section provides indexes for locating information within this guide and items to aid the trip planning process.

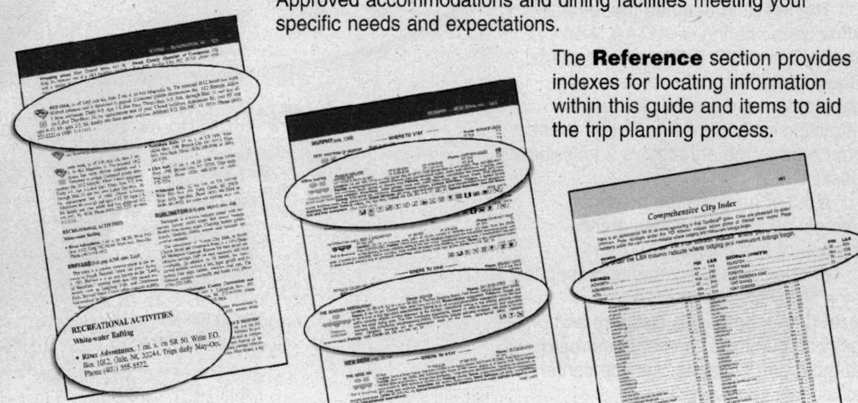

Locating the Attractions, Lodgings and Restaurants

Attractions, lodgings and restaurants are listed under the city in which they physically are located - or in some cases under the nearest recognized city. Most listings are alphabetically organized by state, province, region or island, then by city and establishment name.

A color is assigned to each state or province so that you can match the color bars at the top of the page to switch from the **Points of Interest** section to the **Lodgings and Restaurants** section.

Spotting maps help you physically locate points of interest, lodgings and restaurants in the major destinations.

The Comprehensive City Index located in the **Reference** section contains an A-to-Z list of cities.

Destination Cities and Destination Areas

Destination cities, established based on government models and local expertise, include metropolitan areas plus nearby vicinity cities. **Destination areas** are regions with broad tourist appeal; several cities will comprise the area.

If a city falls within a destination's vicinity, the city name will appear at its alphabetical location in the book, and a cross reference will give you the exact page on which listings for that city begin.

An orientation map appears at the beginning of each destination section to orient you to that destination.

Understanding the Points of Interest Listing

GEM Designation

A [GEM] indicates the attraction has been rated a AAA GEM, a "must see" point of interest that offers a *Great Experience for Members®*. These attractions have been judged to be of exceptional interest and quality by AAA Tourism Editors.

A GEM listing page with a brief description of individual GEM attractions follows the Orientation map near the beginning of each state or province Points of Interest section. Cross-references guide the reader to the attraction's listing page.

Discount Savings

The [SAVE] icon denotes those attractions offering AAA/CAA, AAA MasterCard, AAA VISA or international Show Your Card & Save discount cardholders a discount off the attraction's standard admission. Present your card at the attraction's admission desk.

A list of participating points of interest appears in the Reference section of this guide.

Shopping establishments preceded by a [SAVE] icon also provide to AAA/CAA members a discount and/or gift with purchase; present your card at the mall's customer service center to receive your benefit.

Exceptions

- Members should inquire in advance concerning the validity of the discount for special rates.
- The [SAVE] discount may not be used in conjunction with other discounts.
- Attractions that already provide a reduced senior or child rate may not honor the [SAVE] discount for those age groups.
- All offers are subject to change and may not apply during special events, particular days or seasons or for the entire validity period of the TourBook guide.

Shopping areas: Mast General Store, 630 W. King St., operates out of a 1913 building, stocked with a variety of goods...

[GEM] [SAVE] **RED OAK,** is off I-95 exit 4A, just n. to Dogwo... restored 1812 house has eight 60-foot columns and... Allow 1 hour minimum. Daily 9-5, Apr. 1-Labor D... Labor Day-Nov. 30; by appointment rest of year. C... 6-12, $5; ages 2-5, $4; family rate (two adults and two chi... 5555 or (800) 555-5555.

[GEM] [SAVE] **RED OAK,** is off I-95 exit 4A, just n. to Dogwood Dr., then 2 mi. e. to 610 Magnolia St. The restored 1812 house has eight 60-foot columns and is furnished in period. Costumed guides demonstrate the 1812 lifestyle. Allow 1 hour minimum. Daily 9-5, Apr. 1-Labor Day; Thurs.-Sun. 9-5, Feb.-Mar. 31 and day after Labor Day-Nov. 30; by appointment rest of year. Closed holidays. Admission $8; over 65 and ages 6-12, $5; ages 2-5, $4; family rate (two adults and two children) $12. DS, MC, VI. ($10). Phone (828) 555-5555 or (800) 555-5555.

RECREATIONAL ACTIVITIES

White-water Rafting

- **River Adventures,** 1 mi. s. on SR 50. Write P.O. Box 1012, Gale, NC 35244. Trips daily May-Oct. Phone (828) 555-5555.

BREVARD (F-3) pop. 6,789, elev. 2,229′

The town is a popular summer resort at the en... trance to Pisgah National Forest *(see place listin... p. 165)*. Brevard is in an area known as the "Lar... of Waterfalls," sporting more than 250 named w... terfalls such as Laughing Falls and Courthou... Falls. Brevard Music Center offers concerts night... last weekend in June to mid-August...

RECREATIONAL ACTIVI...

White-water Rafting

- **River Adventures,** 1 mi. s. ... Box 1012, Gale, NC 35244... Phone (828) 555-5555.

Directions

Unless otherwise specified, directions are given from the center of town, using the following highway designations:

I=interstate highway
SR=state route
FM=farm to market
Mex.=Mexican highway
US=federal highway
CR=county road
FR=forest road
Hwy.=Canadian or Caribbean highway

Prices and Dates of Operations

Admission prices are quoted without sales tax. Children under the lowest age specified are admitted free when accompanied by an adult. Days, months and age groups written with a hyphen are inclusive.

Prices pertaining to points of interest in the United States are quoted in U.S. dollars; points of interest in Canada are quoted in Canadian dollars; prices for points of interest in Mexico and the Caribbean are quoted as an approximate U.S. dollar equivalent.

Credit Cards Accepted

AX=American Express
CB=Carte Blanche
DC=Diners Club
DS=Discover
JC=Japan Credit Bureau
MC=MasterCard
VI=VISA

Bulleted Listings

Casino gambling establishments are visited by AAA personnel to ensure safety; casinos within hotels are presented for member information regardless of whether the lodging is AAA Approved.

Recreational activities of a participatory nature (requiring physical exertion or special skills) are not inspected.

Wineries are inspected by AAA Tourism Editors to ensure they meet listing requirements and offer tours.

All are presented in an abbreviated bulleted format for informational purposes.

Understanding the Lodging Listing

Official Appointment

[AAA] or [CAA] indicates our Official Appointment (OA) lodgings. These properties guarantee members the lowest public rate available at the time of booking for the dates of stay or a minimum 10% discount off the standard room rates published in TourBook guides. We highlight these properties with red and a [SAVE] icon to help you quickly identify them.

Diamond Rating

The number of diamonds informs you of the overall complexity of a lodging's amenities and service. Red indicates an Official Appointment lodging. An [fyi] in place of diamonds indicates the property has not been rated but is included as an "information only" service. A detailed description of each rating level appears on page 20.

Classification

All diamond rated lodgings are classified using three key elements: style of operation, overall concept and service level. See pages 22-23 for details on our classifications.

Online Reservations

This notation indicates AAA/CAA members can conveniently check room availability, validate room rates and make reservations for this property in a secure online environment at AAA.com.

Rates

Shown from left to right: dates the rates are effective; any meal plan included in the rates (see below); standard room rates for 1 person (1P) or 2 persons (2P); extra person charge (XP); and any applicable family plan indicator (see below).

Rates are provided to AAA by each lodging and represent the regular (rack) rate ranges for a standard room. Rates are rounded to the nearest dollar and do not include taxes. U.S., Mexican and Caribbean rates are in U.S. dollars; rates for Canadian lodgings are in Canadian dollars.

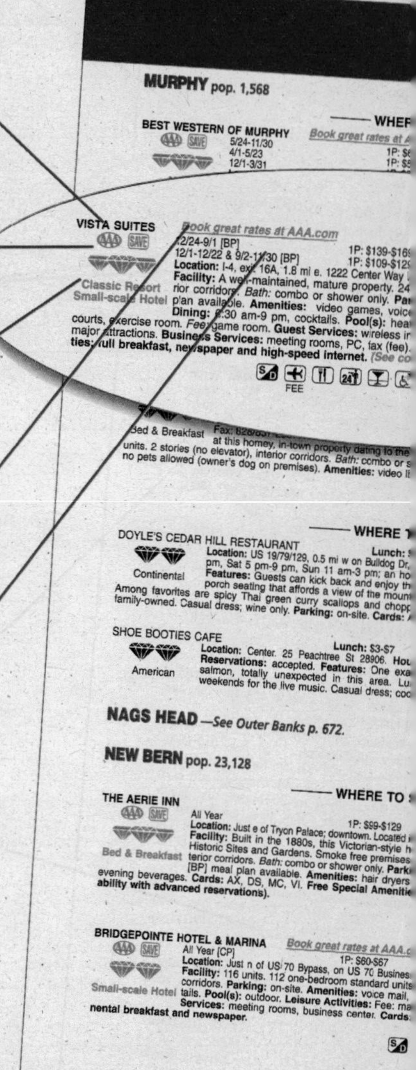

Meal Plan Indicators

AP = American Plan of three meals daily
BP = Breakfast Plan of full hot breakfast
CP = Continental Plan of pastry, juice and another beverage
ECP = Expanded Continental Plan, which offers a wider variety of breakfast items
MAP = Modified American Plan of two meals daily

See individual listing "Terms" for additional meal plans not included in the room rate.

Family Plan Indicators

F = Children stay free
D = Discounts for children
F17 = Children 17 and under stay free
D17 = Discount for children 17 or under

The number displayed will reflect the property's age policy.

Credit Cards Accepted

AX=American Express
CB=Carte Blanche
DC=Diners Club
DS=Discover
JC=Japan Credit Bureau
MC=MasterCard
VI=VISA

Spotting Symbol

Black ovals with white numbers are used to locate, or "spot," lodgings on maps we provide for larger cities.

Service Availability

Unit types, amenities and room features preceded by the word "Some" indicate the item is available on a limited basis, potentially within only one unit.

Free Special Amenities

Some OA properties offer special amenities such as Continental breakfast; expanded Continental breakfast or full breakfast; early check-in and late check-out; room upgrade or preferred room; local phone calls; or daily newspaper. This does not imply that only these properties offer these amenities.

Icons

Lodging icons represent some of the member values, services and facilities offered.

Discounts

- May offer discount
- Offers minimum 10% senior discount to members over 59

Member Services

- Airport transportation
- Pets allowed
- Restaurant on premises
- Restaurant off premises (walking distance)
- 24-hour room service
- Cocktail lounge
- Child care

Accessibility Features

- Accessible features
- Hearing-impaired equipment available
- Roll-in showers

In-Room Amenities

- Designated non-smoking rooms
- VCR
- Movies
- Refrigerator
- Microwave
- Coffee maker
- No air conditioning
- No TV
- No cable TV
- No telephones

Leisure Activities

- Full-service casino
- Pool
- Health club on premises
- Health club off premises
- Recreational activities

Safety Features (see page 24)

(Mexico and Caribbean only)

- Sprinklers
- Smoke detectors

SOME UNITS printed above the icons indicates the amenity is available on a limited basis, potentially in only one unit. **FEE** appearing below an icon indicates that an extra charge applies.

Understanding the Restaurant Listing

Official Appointment

(AAA) or (CAA) indicates our Official Appointment (OA) restaurants. The OA program permits properties to display and advertise the AAA or CAA emblem. We highlight these properties in red to help you quickly identify them. The AAA or CAA Approved sign helps traveling members find restaurants that want member business.

Diamond Rating

The number of diamonds informs you of the overall complexity of food, presentation, service and ambience. Red indicates an Official Appointment restaurant. A detailed description of each diamond level appears on page 21.

Cuisine Type

The cuisine type helps you select a dining facility that caters to your individual taste. AAA currently recognizes more than 90 different cuisine types.

Menus

This notation indicates AAA/CAA members can conveniently view the restaurant's menu in a secure online environment at AAA.com.

Credit Cards Accepted

AX=American Express

CB=Carte Blanche

DC=Diners Club

DS=Discover

JC=Japan Credit Bureau

MC=MasterCard

VI=VISA

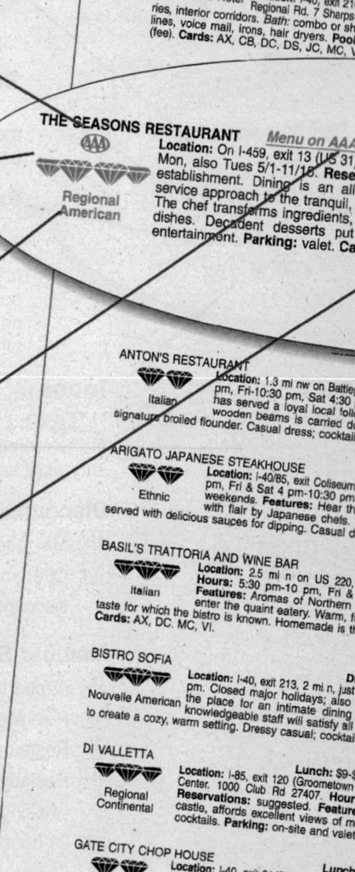

SLEEP INN Book at AAA.com
3/1-7/31 [ECP]
12/1-2/29 & 8/1-11/30 [ECP]
Small-scale Hotel Location: I-40, exit 210 wes
Regional Rd. 7 Sharps Airpa
ries, interior corridors. Bath: combo or shower
lines, voice mail, irons, hair dryers. Pool(s): s
(fee). Cards: AX, CB, DC, DS, JC, MC, VI.
THE SEASONS RESTAURANT Menu on AAA.co
Location: On I-459, exit 13 (US 31); 0.3
Mon, also Tues 5/1-11/15. Reservati
establishment. Dining is an all-arou
service approach to the tranquil, ocea
The chef transforms ingredients, base
dishes. Decadent desserts put an
entertainment. Parking: valet. Cards:
Regional American
ANTON'S RESTAURANT
Location: 1.3 mi nw on Battleground
pm, Fri-10:30 pm, Sat 4:30 pm-1
has served a loyal local following
wooden beams is carried downst
signature broiled flounder. Casual dress; cocktails. Pa
Italian
ARIGATO JAPANESE STEAKHOUSE
Location: I-40/85, exit Coliseum; at jc
pm, Fri & Sat 4 pm-10:30 pm, Sun
weekends. Features: Hear the siz
with flair by Japanese chefs. Watc
served with delicious sauces for dipping. Casual dress;
Ethnic
BASIL'S TRATTORIA AND WINE BAR
Location: 2.5 mi n on US 220, just
Hours: 5:30 pm-10 pm, Fri & Sat-
Features: Aromas of Northern Italia
enter the quaint eatery. Warm, freshl
taste for which the bistro is known. Homemade is the on
Cards: AX, DC, MC, VI.
Italian
BISTRO SOFIA
Location: I-40, exit 213, 2 mi n, just e on
pm. Closed major holidays; also Mon.
the place for an intimate dining expe
knowledgeable staff will satisfy all your
to create a cozy, warm setting. Dressy casual; cocktails. Pa
Dinner:
Nouvelle American
DI VALLETTA
Lunch: $9-$15
Location: I-85, exit 120 (Groometown Rd),
Center. 1000 Club Rd 27407. Hours: 6
Reservations: suggested. Features: T
castle, affords excellent views of manicu
cocktails. Parking: on-site and valet. Car
Regional Continental
GATE CITY CHOP HOUSE
Lunch: $9-
Location: I-40, exit 214B, 1.8 mi n to Holden
Fri & Sat 4:30 pm-10:30 pm. Closed;
Features: Visit the beautifully landscaped
room complete with a fireplace. Dine outs
housemade chocolate cake. Casual dress; cocktails. Parking:
American
GRAPEVINE CAFE & JUICE BAR
Lunch: $4
Location: Just s of W Friendly Ave; located beh
pm. Closed major holidays; also Sun. Feat
veggie chili and lasagna popular; internat
on-site. Cards: MC, VI.
Vegetarian

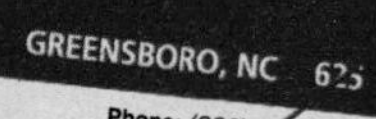

Prices

Rates shown represent the minimum and maximum entree cost per person. Exceptions may include one-of-a-kind or special market priced items. Rates are rounded to the nearest dollar and do not include taxes. U.S., Mexican and Caribbean rates are in U.S. dollars; rates for Canadian restaurants are in Canadian dollars.

Spotting Symbol

White ovals with black numbers serve as restaurant locators and are used to locate, or "spot," restaurants on maps we provide for larger cities.

Icons

Icons provide additional information about services and facilities.

- No air-conditioning
- Accessible features
- Cocktail lounge
- Designated smoking section available

Classifications

If applicable, a restaurant may be defined as:

Classic - renowned and/or landmark restaurant in business longer than 25 years, known for unique style and ambience.

Historic - properties must meet one of the following criteria:

- Listed on the U.S. National Register of Historic Places
- Designated a U.S. National Historic Landmark
- Located in a U.S. National Register Historic District

Separate criteria designate historic properties in Canada, Mexico and the Caribbean.

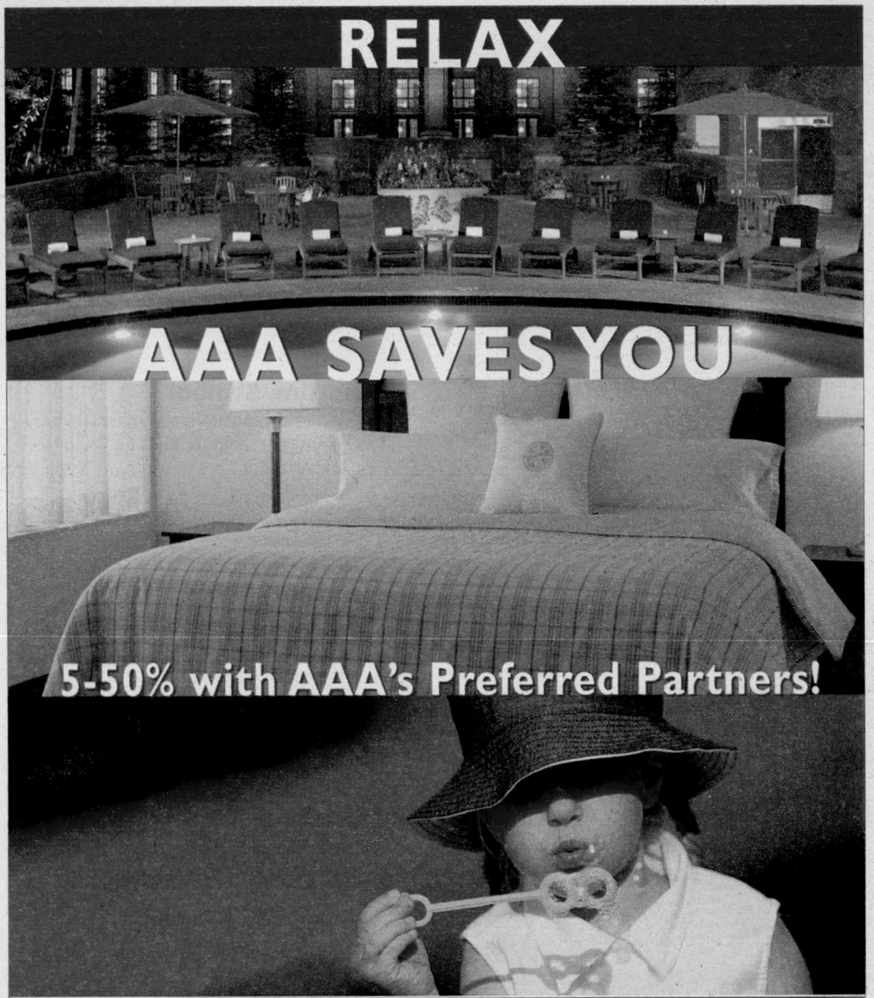

Lodging Rates Guaranteed

AAA/CAA members are guaranteed they will not be charged more than the maximum regular rate printed in the TourBook guide in each rate range for a standard room. Rates may vary within the range, depending on season and room type. Listed rates are based on last standard room availability. Obtain current AAA/CAA member rates and make reservations at AAA.com.

Discounts

Member discounts will apply to rates quoted within the rate range and are applicable at the time of booking. Special rates used in advertising, as well as special short-term promotional rates lower than the lowest listed rate in the range, are not subject to additional member discounts.

Exceptions

Rates for properties operating as concessionaires for the U.S. National Park Service are not guaranteed due to governing regulations. Rates in the Mexico TourBook are not guaranteed and may fluctuate based on the exchange rate of the peso.

Lodgings may temporarily increase room rates, not recognize discounts or modify pricing policies during special events. Examples of special events range from Mardi Gras and the Kentucky Derby (including pre-Derby events) to college football games, holidays, holiday periods and state fairs. Although some special events are listed in AAA/CAA TourBook guides and on AAA.com, it is always wise to check in advance with AAA travel professionals for specific dates.

Get the Room You Reserved

When making your reservation, identify yourself as a AAA or CAA member and request written confirmation to guarantee: type of room, rate, dates of stay, and cancellation and refund policies. At registration, show your membership card.

When you find your room is not as specified, and you have written confirmation of reservations for a certain type of accommodation, you should be given the option of choosing a different room or finding one elsewhere. Should you choose to go elsewhere and a refund is refused or resisted, submit the matter to AAA/CAA within 30 days, along with complete documentation, including your reasons for refusing the room and copies of your written confirmation and any receipts or canceled checks associated with this problem.

If you are charged more than the maximum rate listed in the TourBook guide for a standard

room, question the additional charge. If management refuses to adhere to the published rate, pay for the room and submit your receipt and membership number to AAA/CAA within 30 days. Include all pertinent information: dates of stay, rate paid, itemized paid receipts, number of persons in your party and the room number you occupied, and list any extra room equipment used. A refund of the amount paid in excess of the stated maximum will be made if our investigation indicates that unjustified charging occurred.

Deposit, Refund and Cancellation Policies

Most establishments give full deposit refunds if they have been notified at least 48 hours before the normal check-in time. Listing prose will note if more than 48 hours' notice is required for cancellation. Some properties may charge a cancellation or handling fee. When this applies, "cancellation fee imposed" will appear in the listing. If you cancel too late, you have little recourse if a refund is denied.

When an establishment requires full or partial payment in advance and your trip is cut short, a refund may not be given.

When canceling a reservation, phone the lodging immediately. Make a note of the date and time you called, the cancellation number if there is one, and the name of the person who handled the cancellation. If your AAA/CAA club made your reservation, allow them to make the cancellation for you as well, so you will have proof of cancellation.

Check-in and Check-out Times

Check-in and check-out times are shown in the lodging listings, under Terms, only if they are before 10 a.m. or after 3 p.m. respectively.

Members Save With Our Partners

These National Show Your Card & Save® partners provide the listed member benefits. Admission tickets that offer greater discounts may be available for purchase at the local AAA/CAA club. A maximum of six tickets is available at the discount price at the gate. Visit AAA.com to discover all the great Show Your Card & Save® discounts in your area.

SeaWorld/Busch Gardens AAA.com/SeaWorld

- Save $5 on 1-day gate admission at SeaWorld, Busch Gardens, and Sesame Place
- Save $3 on 1-day admission at Water Country USA and Adventure Island

- Save 10% on select up-close dining. Reservations are required; visit Guest Relations for details

AAA.com/BuschGardens

Six Flags Theme Parks

- 10% OFF Brunch with Bugs
- 10% OFF merchandise purchases of $15 or more at all Six Flags operated locations.

Universal Orlando AAA.com/Universal

- Save $4 on a 2-day/2-park pass at Universal Orlando's theme parks (savings apply to tickets purchased at the gate)

- Save 10% on select dining and souvenirs at both Universal Orlando theme parks and at select Universal CityWalk Orlando restaurants (excludes Emeril's)

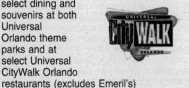

Universal Studios Hollywood

- Save $3 on a 1-day Universal Studios Hollywood pass (savings applies to tickets purchased at the gate) AAA.com/Universal
- Save 10% on select dining and souvenirs at Universal Studios Hollywood and Universal CityWalk

Gray Line

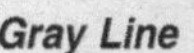

AAA.com/GrayLine

- Save 10% on sightseeing tours of 1 day or less

Landry's Seafood House, The Crab House, Chart House, Muer Seafood Restaurants, Joe's Crab Shack and Aquarium and Downtown Aquarium Restaurants

- 10% discount on food and non-alcoholic beverages at all of the above restaurants.
- 10% discount on novelty merchandise at Joe's Crab Shacks and Aquarium and Downtown Aquarium Restaurants.

Hard Rock Cafe

- Save 10% on food, beverage and merchandise at all U.S. and select Canadian and international locations

Restaurant Partner Savings applies to AAA/CAA members and up to five guests.

Tanger Outlet Centers www.tangeroutlet.com

- Save up to 20% on total purchase at select merchants with AAA/CAA coupon booklet
- Member BONUS: FREE $5 gift card for each additional Tanger Outlet Center visited after first within same calendar year
- Show membership card and register at the AAA customer service desk when you visit

Lodging Partners

SAVINGS. SELECTION. SATISFACTION.—When contacting one of these lodging partners, you will be given AAA/CAA's best rates for your dates of stay. Your valid membership card must be presented at check-in. Select the chain you want and have your membership card available when making a reservation and checking in. Let the property know if you are dissatisfied with any part of your stay. If the matter cannot be resolved, you are entitled to recompense (see page 17).

Offer good at time of publication; chains and offers may change without notice. Lodging partners offering discounts to AAA/CAA members may vary in Mexico and the Caribbean.

Visit
Over 1,000 AAA/CAA Offices
Click
AAA.com
Call
866-AAA-SAVE

CHOICE HOTELS INTERNATIONAL

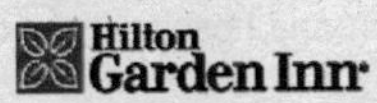

FOUR POINTS
BY SHERATON

Understanding the Diamond Ratings

AAA/CAA Tourism Editors have evaluated and rated each of the 60,000 lodging and restaurant establishments in the TourBook series to ensure quality travel information for our members. All properties must meet AAA's 27 minimum requirements (for lodgings) concerning cleanliness, comfort and security - or - AAA's 12 minimum requirements (for restaurants) pertaining to cleanliness, food preparation and service.

Eligible applicants receive an unannounced evaluation by a AAA/CAA Tourism Editor that includes two distinct components:

- AAA Approval: The Tourism Editor first must determine whether the property meets the criteria required to be AAA Approved. Every establishment that meets these strict guidelines offers AAA members the assurance that, regardless of the diamond rating, it provides acceptable quality, cleanliness, service and value.
- AAA Diamond Rating: Once an establishment becomes AAA Approved, it is then assigned a rating of one to five diamonds, indicating the extensiveness of its facilities, amenities and services, from basic to moderate to luxury. These diamond ratings guide members in selecting establishments appropriately matched to their needs and expectations.

LODGINGS

1 Diamond 

One diamond lodgings typically appeal to the budget-minded traveler. They provide essential, no-frills accommodations and basic comfort and hospitality.

2 Diamond 

Two diamond lodgings appeal to family travelers seeking affordable yet more than the basic accommodations. Facilities, decor and amenities are modestly enhanced.

3 Diamond 

Three diamond lodgings offer a distinguished style. Properties are multi-faceted, with marked upgrades in physical attributes, amenities and guest comforts.

4 Diamond 

Four diamond lodgings are refined and stylish. Physical attributes are upscale. The fundamental hallmarks at this level include an extensive array of amenities combined with a high degree of hospitality, service and attention to detail.

5 Diamond

Five diamond lodgings provide the ultimate in luxury and sophistication. Physical attributes are extraordinary in every manner. Service is meticulous, exceeding guest expectations and maintaining impeccable standards of excellence. Extensive personalized services and amenities provide first-class comfort.

fyi The lodging listings with fyi in place of diamonds are included as an *information only* service for members. The icon indicates that a property has not been rated for one or more of the following reasons: too new to rate, under construction, under major renovation, not evaluated, may not meet all AAA requirements.

A property not meeting all AAA requirements is included for either its member value or because it may be the only accommodation available in the area. Listing prose will give insight as to why the fyi designation was assigned.

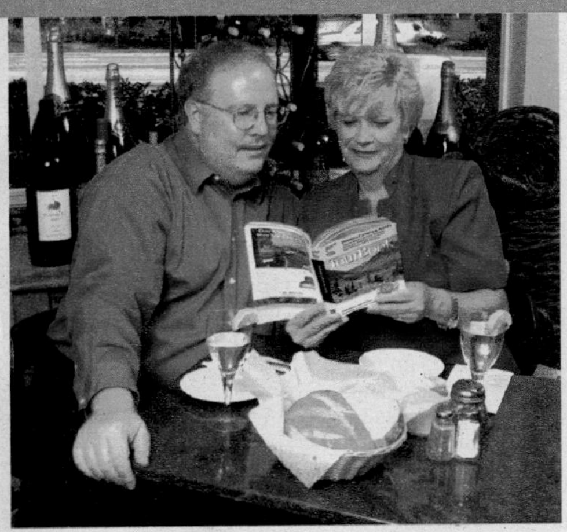

RESTAURANTS

1 Diamond 

One diamond restaurants provide simple, familiar specialty food (such as burgers, chicken, pizza or tacos) at an economical price. Often self-service, basic surroundings complement a no-nonsense approach.

2 Diamond 

Two diamond restaurants offer a familiar, family-oriented experience. Menu selection includes home-style foods and family favorites, often cooked to order, modestly enhanced and reasonably priced. Service is accommodating yet relaxed, a perfect complement to casual surroundings.

3 Diamond 

Three diamond restaurants convey an entry into fine dining and are often positioned as adult-oriented experiences. The atypical menu may feature the latest cooking trends and/or traditional cuisine. Expanded beverage offerings complement the menu. The ambience is well coordinated, comfortable and enhanced by a professional service staff.

4 Diamond 

Four diamond restaurants provide a distinctive fine-dining experience that is typically expensive. Surroundings are highly refined with upscale enhancements throughout. Highly creative chefs use imaginative presentations to augment fresh, top-quality ingredients. A proficient service staff meets or exceeds guest expectations. A wine steward may offer menu-specific knowledge to guide selection.

5 Diamond 

Five diamond restaurants are luxurious and renowned for consistently providing a world-class experience. Highly acclaimed chefs offer artistic menu selections that are imaginative and unique, using only the finest ingredients available. A maitre d' leads an expert service staff in exceeding guest expectations, attending to every detail in an effortless and unobtrusive manner.

fyi The restaurants with **fyi** in place of diamonds are included as an *information only* service for members. These listings provide additional dining choices but have not yet been evaluated.

Understanding the Lodging Classifications

To ensure that your lodging needs and preferences are met, we recommend that you consider an establishment's classification when making your travel choices. While the quality and comfort at properties with the same diamond rating should be consistent (regardless of the classification), there are differences in typical decor/theme elements, range of facilities and service levels.

Large-scale Hotel

A multistory establishment with interior room entrances. A variety of guest unit styles is offered. Public areas are spacious and include a variety of facilities such as a restaurant, fitness center, spa, business center, shops or meeting rooms.

Hotel Royal Plaza, Lake Buena Vista, FL

Small-scale Hotel

A multistory establishment typically with interior room entrances. A variety of guest unit styles is offered. Public areas are limited in size and/or the variety of facilities available.

Baymont Inn, Dallas Ft. Worth-Airport N, TX

Motel

A 1- to 3-story establishment typically with exterior room entrances facilitating convenient access to parking. The standard guest units have one bedroom with a bathroom and are typically similar in decor and design throughout. Public areas are limited in size and/or the variety of facilities available.

Best Western Deltona Inn, Deltona, FL

Country Inn

Similar in definition to a bed and breakfast but usually larger in scale, with spacious public areas offering a dining facility that serves at least breakfast and dinner.

Greenville Inn, Greenville, ME

Bed & Breakfast

Small-scale properties emphasizing a high degree of personal touches that provide guests an "at home" feeling. Guest units tend to be individually decorated. Rooms may not include some modern amenities such as televisions and telephones, and may have a shared bathroom. Usually owner-operated with a common room or parlor separate from the innkeeper's living quarters, where guests and operators can interact during evening and breakfast hours. Evening office closures are normal. A Continental or full, hot breakfast is served and is included in the room rate.

1884 Paxton House Inn, Thomasville, GA

Condominium

Vacation-oriented or extended-stay, apartment-style accommodations that are routinely available for rent through a management company. Units vary in design and decor and often contain one or more bedrooms, a living room, full kitchen and an eating area. Studio-type models combine the sleeping and living areas into one room. Typically, basic cleaning supplies, kitchen utensils and complete bed and bath linens are supplied. The guest registration area may be located off-site.

Sands of Kahana, Kahana, Maui, HI

Cabin/Cottage

Vacation-oriented, small-scale, freestanding houses or cabins. Units vary in design and decor and often contain one or more bedrooms, a living room, kitchen, dining area and bathroom. Studio-type models combine the sleeping and living areas into one room. Typically, basic cleaning supplies, kitchen utensils, and complete bed and bath linens are supplied. The guest registration area may be located off-site.

Desert Rose Inn, Bluff, UT

Ranch

Typically a working ranch with an obvious rustic, Western theme. In general, equestrian-related activities are featured, but ranches may include other animals and activities as well. A variety of guest unit styles is offered in a family-oriented atmosphere.

C Lazy U Ranch, Granby, CO

Vacation Home

Vacation-oriented or extended-stay, large-scale, freestanding houses that are routinely available for rent through a management company. Houses vary in design and decor and often contain two or more bedrooms, a living room, full kitchen, dining room and multiple bathrooms. Typically, basic cleaning supplies, kitchen utensils, and complete bed and bath linens are supplied. The guest registration area may be located off-site.

ResortQuest, Hilton Head Island, SC

Lodging Subclassifications

The following are subclassifications that may appear along with the classifications listed previously to provide a more specific description of the lodging.

Casino

Extensive gaming facilities are available such as blackjack, craps, keno and slot machines. Note: This subclassification will not appear beneath its diamond rating in the listing. It will be indicated by a icon and will be included in the row of icons immediately below the lodging listing.

Classic

Renowned and landmark properties, older than 50 years, well-known for their unique style and ambience.

Historic

These properties are typically over 75 years of age and exhibit many features of a historic nature with respect to architecture, design, furnishings, public record or acclaim. Properties must meet one of the following criteria:

- Maintained the integrity of the historical aspect
- Listed on the U.S. National Register of Historic Places
- Designated a U.S. National Historic Landmark
- Located in a U.S. National Register Historic District

Separate criteria designate historic properties in Canada, Mexico and the Caribbean.

Vacation Rental

Typically houses, condos, cottages or cabins; these properties are a "home away from home" offering more room and greater value for the money and generally provide the conveniences of home, such as full kitchens and washers/dryers. They are located in resort or popular destination areas within close proximity to major points of interest, attractions, or recreation areas. These properties may require a pre-arranged reservation and check-in at an off-site location. Housekeeping services may be limited or not included.

Resort

Recreation-oriented, geared to vacation travelers seeking a specific destination experience. Travel packages, meal plans, themed entertainment, and social and recreational programs are typically available. Recreational facilities are extensive and may include spa treatments, golf, tennis, skiing, fishing, water sports, etc. Larger resorts may offer a variety of guest accommodations.

Guest Safety

Room Security

In order to be approved for listing in AAA/CAA TourBook guides for the United States and Canada, accommodations must have dead-bolt locks on all guest room entry doors and connecting room doors.

If the area outside the guest room door is not visible from inside the room through a window or door panel, viewports must be installed on all guest room entry doors. Bed and breakfast properties and country inns are not required to have viewports. Ground floor and easily accessible sliding doors must be equipped with some type of secondary security locks.

Even with those approval requirements, AAA cannot guarantee guest safety. Tourism Editors view a percentage of rooms at each property since it is not feasible to evaluate every room in every lodging establishment. Therefore, AAA cannot guarantee that there are working locks on all doors and windows in all guest rooms.

Fire Safety

Because of the highly specialized skills needed to conduct professional fire safety inspections, AAA/CAA Tourism Editors cannot assess fire safety.

Properties must meet all federal, state and local fire codes. Each guest unit in all U.S. and Canadian lodging properties must be equipped with an operational, single-station smoke detector. A AAA/CAA Tourism Editor has evaluated a sampling of the rooms to verify this equipment is in place.

Mexico and the Caribbean

Requirements for some features, such as door locks and smoke detectors/sprinkler systems, differ in Mexico and the Caribbean. If a property met AAA's security requirements at the time of the evaluation, the phrase "Meets AAA guest room security requirements" appears in the listing.

Service Animals

The Americans with Disabilities Act (ADA) prohibits U.S. businesses that serve the public from discriminating against persons with disabilities. Some businesses have mistakenly denied access to persons who use service animals. Businesses must permit entry to guests and their service animals, as well as allow service animals to accompany guests to all public areas of a property.

A property is permitted to ask whether the animal is a service animal or a pet, and whether the guest has a disability. The property may not, however, ask questions about the nature of the disability, the service provided by the animal or require proof of a disability or certification that the animal is a service animal. These regulations may not apply in Canada, Mexico or the Caribbean.

No fees or deposits, even those normally charged for pets, may be charged for service animals. Service animals fulfill a critical need for their owners—they are not pets.

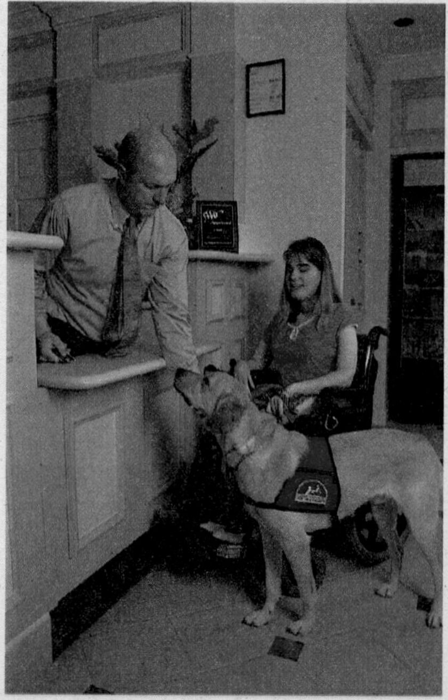

Savings for all Seasons

Hertz rents Fords and other fine cars. ® REG. U.S. PAT. OFF. © HERTZ SYSTEM INC., 1999/2006-99.

No matter the season, Hertz offers AAA members exclusive discounts and benefits.

Operating in 150 countries at over 8,100 locations, Hertz makes traveling more convenient and efficient wherever and whenever you go. Hertz offers AAA members discounts up to 20% on car rentals worldwide.

To receive your exclusive AAA member discounts and benefits, mention your AAA membership card at time of reservation and present it at time of rental. **In addition**, to receive a free one car class upgrade on daily, weekly or weekend rental in the United States and Canada, mention PC# 969194, and in Puerto Rico mention PC# 969183 at the time of reservation. Offer available through 12/15/07.

For reservations and program details, visit aaa.com/hertz, call your AAA Travel office or the Hertz/AAA Desk at **1-800-654-3080.**

Receive a free One Car Class Upgrade on a Hertz daily, weekly or weekend rental when reserving a compact two-door through full-size four door car (Class B-F) and take advantage of your AAA/CAA discount as well. Highest obtainable upgrade is to a Premium vehicle (Car Class G). This offer is available at participating Hertz locations in the U.S., Canada, and Puerto Rico. Advance reservations are required. Blackout periods may apply. Offer may be limited in some cities at some times, especially during periods of peak demand. This offer may only be used with a AAA/CAA CDP# and cannot be combined with any other CDP#, coupon, discount, rate or promotion. Hertz' standard age, driver and credit qualifications for the renting location apply and the car must be returned to that location. Taxes and optional services, such as refueling, are not included and are not subject to discount. Offer expires 12/15/2007.

Alabama

Sugar-white Beaches
Powdery sand borders the warm, emerald waters of the Gulf Coast

From the Civil War to Civil Rights
Historic sites evoke past struggles: the birth of the Confederacy and the fight to end racial discrimination

Golf to the Gulf
Golf courses abound; the Robert Trent Jones Golf Trail stretches from Huntsville to Mobile

The Land of Cotton
One crop was king in this center of Southern culture and heritage

A Mecca to Fishermen
Bass, crappie, catfish and deep-sea varieties attract anglers from far and wide

Shorter Mansion, Eufaula

the heart of Dixie

Bellingrath Gardens and Home, Theodore / Alabama Bureau of Tourism & Travel

The Deep South doesn't get any deeper than Alabama. This is where cotton was king, where the Confederacy was born and where Jefferson Davis' birthday is still a holiday.

But the state is more than just a cotton-belt cliché. In Huntsville you'll find NASA's Marshall Space Flight Center, where scientists developed the gee-whiz technology for sending men to the moon and where America's future in space continues to unfold. In Montgomery you'll encounter the nation's first memorial to the civil rights movement and those who perished in that historic struggle. And while Alabama might call to mind images of rural farmers, today most Alabamians live and work in cities.

You also might not expect to find covered bridges in Alabama, or canyons and swift-flowing rivers, or networks of caverns and caves, or subtropical gardens, or sugar-sand beaches, or snow-skiing or a venerable Mardi Gras celebration older than the one in New Orleans.

But Alabama offers all these things in addition to the antebellum homes, moss-draped oaks and Civil War monuments so often associated with the state. Visit, and you too will discover: The heart of Dixie beats strong in Alabama.

"T" minus 10 and counting. Sights set on the unknown, you're good to go. *Eight.* Excitement builds. *Six.* Imagination soars.

Three, two, one—Welcome to Alabama!

Yes, Alabama. Home of the U.S. Space and Rocket Center, where you can land a space shuttle, experience a simulated rocket liftoff or climb a Martian volcano. And if you're like most visitors who become space cadets for a day, you'll soon realize something you might not have suspected about this state: Alabama can really take you places.

You can chart a course from Huntsville's simulated space flights to the scenic splendor of the state's many forests. From the sleepy South of simpler times to the lively pulse of modern-day Birmingham. From relics of the past to lessons for the future.

The Final Frontier

Begin by surveying the terrain. Alabama in the north is a terminus of both the Cumberland Plateau and the Blue Ridge Mountains, and what plate tectonics wrought is now a perfect place to wander. Largely wooded and riddled with rivers, the region ranges from rocky mesas to rolling hills. The resulting waterfalls, rapids, canyons and caverns are generally modest enough to be accessible to even the marginally fit, pristine enough to be paradise to all who love nature.

Boldly go east, where Cheaha Mountain's chalk-white cliffs offer sweeping views of a carpet of green and gold treetops.

Or set your coordinates to the southwest, where waves wash pure white sands and gulls scream and frolic. Just off the coast, Dauphin Island's dunes are a touchdown point for thousands of migrating birds intent on journeys of their own.

Canvass the state's mid-section and you'll surely find cotton. It's no longer king, though. Alabama evolved from a one-crop economy after boll weevils devastated much of 1915's harvest. Now peanuts, soybeans, corn and such share the soil. But all is not flat farmland. Alien forms cover the landscape in places, courtesy of the shape-morphing effects of kudzu—often called "the vine that ate the South." Growing up to a foot a day, this Asian import quickly creates distorted topiaries out of telephone poles, trees, shrubs and just about anything else that stands still too long.

Explorer Alonso Alvarez de Piñeda sails into Mobile Bay.
1519
Alabama is admitted as the 22nd state.
1819
Montgomery becomes the first capital of the Confederacy.
1861

Library of Congress

1763
The Treaty of Paris ending the French and Indian War gives Mobile to Britain.

1915
The boll weevil devastates the state's one-crop cotton economy and forces a diversification in agriculture.

Alabama Historical Timeline

These are the Voyages

Kudzu's hardly the first wanderer to become attached to Alabama. At Russell Cave National Monument, near Bridgeport, evidence suggests prehistoric man made this his first home in the region—some 10,000 years ago.

American Indians left their legacy in place names from Tuskegee to Tuscaloosa. Spanish, French and British settlers imprinted the coastal region's culture and architecture with their influences. Their fierce struggles for territorial control shaped the state's history, and its people.

A zest for friendlier competition lives on. While allegiance to church and family may nourish an Alabamian's soul, it is college football that warms the heart of the state. Visit in the fall and you just might find yourself transported to a modern-day battlefield where war cries still fill the air, though flags and first downs have replaced muskets and mortar.

A love of sports is just one tradition people here proudly perpetuate. Hospitality is another. Should your itinerary call for sampling "the Deep South," Alabama will serve it up with a smile. In Mobile, tour the Oakleigh neighborhood of varied historic homes. In Montgomery, sit down to supper at Sahara, where portraits of state politicians cover the walls, and sugared Southern accents fill the air.

Or are you seeking newer civilizations? Be sure to trek to Birmingham's Five Points South district. With its restaurants, nightclubs and modern boutiques, the gathering spot draws an eclectic mix of the pierced and the professional.

More than anything, you'll find this state is proud of its progress. For proof, look to Enterprise's Boll Weevil Monument, honoring that insect's role as "herald of prosperity." Or visit the Birmingham Civil Rights Institute, where you can step into settings that unflinchingly re-create past conflicts, then access archives and educational programs dedicated to protecting future human rights.

Where else can Alabama take you? How about atop the deck of a World War II battleship in Mobile? Down to a spelunkers' favorite stomping grounds in one of its many caves? Or off to the races at what many call "the world's fastest speedway" in Talladega?

From caves to cliffs to coast, the controls are in your hands.

1955

The Montgomery bus boycott is launched when Rosa Parks is arrested for refusing to surrender her bus seat to a white passenger.

Library of Congress

1960

The George C. Marshall Space Flight Center is established in Huntsville.

1965

Despite violent opposition, Dr. Martin Luther King Jr. leads a march from Selma to Montgomery to protest voting inequities.

1989

The nation's first memorial to the civil rights movement and those who died during the struggle is dedicated in Montgomery.

2002

Birmingham native Vonetta Flowers is the first African-American to win a gold medal in a Winter Olympic Games sport—bobsledding.

©Reuters NewMedia Inc/Corbis

2005

Hurricane Katrina, the nation's most extensive and costly natural disaster, strikes the Gulf Coast.

©Dan Anderson/epa/Corbis

Recreation

Ready to have some fun? Well, put on your play clothes and pack a lunch, because Alabama is to recreation what summer vacation is to third-graders. Whether you plan to explore a forest or play 18, cast for a keeper or scope out stalactites—once you get outdoors in Alabama, you won't want to come in till the fireflies fade.

On Your Feet

There's **hiking,** for starters. From Conecuh's soggy bottomlands in the south to William B. Bankhead's unspoiled Sipsey Wilderness in the northwest, Alabama's national forests alone offer enough preserved habitats to soothe any soul. But to really appreciate the state's wild side, try imagining the American Indians who for centuries worshipped, played, hunted and fought here. You will certainly be walking in their footsteps.

Take Indian House Trail, at Buck's Pocket State Park north of Grove Oak. Along this craggy spine of the Cumberland Plateau, where a thin layer of topsoil works wonders with wildflowers, you'll find jagged rock overhangs that once sheltered Cherokees. At Cheaha State Park, near Anniston, Bald Rock Nature Trail delivers you to an awesome overlook well worth the uphill effort. As you stand and scout surrounding foothills, remember that the Creek Confederacy once claimed this land.

To really give your imagination a boost, head to 320-acre Moundville Archaeological Park, about 15 miles outside of Tuscaloosa. The site, once the center of the formidable Moundville Indian civilization, has life-size figures posed to depict inhabitants' activities. Go **walking** on nature trails and graded paths, or **climb** atop a 60-foot-high earthen mound to overlook the grounds below.

All three parks offer **camping** facilities, making it easy to top off a day of active envisioning with a night under the stars.

Golfers will want to follow footsteps of a different kind on the state's renowned Robert Trent Jones Golf Trail, which counts Auburn/Opelika's Grand National—a PGA championship course—among its 26 stops at 10 locations.

Enhancing the trail's challenging designs is an emphasis on natural elements, evident in the native wiregrass of Dothan's Highland Oaks and the wetlands and dense woods of Mobile's Magnolia Grove. You'll find seven premier courses in the Gulf Shores/Orange Beach area and fine courses at several state parks, too, from Lakepoint in Eufaula to Oak Mountain in Pelham.

Sunken Treasure

Prefer **fishing** to fairways? You've come to the right place. But first, a riddle: What do ships and tanks left over from World War II, Korea and Vietnam have to do with plentiful populations of red snapper?

The answer: Everything, when the decommissioned vessels becomes an artificial reef off the coast of Orange Beach. Other fish species that now call the equipment home include grouper, amberjack and triggerfish.

To get out to where they're biting, look for **saltwater fishing** charters at Orange Beach. Or head to Dauphin Island where a deep-water fishing pier extends more than 800 feet into the Gulf.

If **freshwater fishing** is what you're after, keep this in mind: They don't call Weiss Lake in Cherokee County "Crappie Capital of the World" for nothing. Its unofficial title notwithstanding, the lake also offers plenty of bass and catfish as well as great **boating** opportunities. At 30,200 acres, it's plenty big enough for wide-open **water skiing.** Or simply go **swimming** if that's more your speed.

Still more adventure can be found underground. Caves formed in the limestone and sandstone landscape of northeastern Alabama are a mecca for **spelunking** enthusiasts with experience in subterranean exploration—in fact, Huntsville is home to the National Speleological Society. For guided cave tours, visit Sequoyah Caverns in Valley Head, where lighted pools of water reflect an otherworldly array of overhead formations. Or tour DeSoto Caverns Park in Childersburg, where you'll be dwarfed by the Great Onyx Chamber—larger than a football field and taller than a 12-story building. And be sure to bring a sweater; the caves stay cool.

Recreational Activities

Throughout the TourBook, you may notice a Recreational Activities heading with bulleted listings of recreation-oriented establishments listed underneath. Similar operations also may be mentioned in Destination City recreation sections. Since normal AAA inspection criteria cannot be applied, these establishments are presented only for information. Age, height and weight restrictions may apply. Reservations often are recommended and sometimes are required. Addresses and/or phone numbers are provided so visitors can contact the attraction for additional information.

Fast Facts

POPULATION: 4,447,100.

AREA: 51,998 square miles; ranks 28th.

CAPITAL: Montgomery.

HIGHEST POINT: 2,407 ft., Cheaha Mountain.

LOWEST POINT: Sea level, Gulf of Mexico.

TIME ZONE(S): Central. DST.

MINIMUM AGE FOR UNRESTRICTED DRIVER'S LICENSE: 17.

SEAT BELT/CHILD RESTRAINT LAWS: All front-seat occupants are required to use a seat belt or a child safety restraint. Ages 6-13 must wear a seat belt regardless of seat position. Child restraints are required for under age 6.

HELMETS FOR MOTORCYCLISTS: Required for all riders.

RADAR DETECTORS: Permitted.

FIREARMS LAWS: Vary by state and/or county. Contact Alabama Department of Public Safety, 500 Dexter Ave., Montgomery, AL 36130; phone (334) 242-4445.

HOLIDAYS: Jan. 1; Martin Luther King Jr. Day and Robert E. Lee's Birthday, Jan. (3rd Mon.); Washington's Birthday, Feb. (3rd Mon.); Confederate Memorial Day, Apr. (4th Mon.); Memorial Day, May (last Mon.); Jefferson Davis' Birthday, June (1st Mon.); July 4; Labor Day; Columbus Day, Oct. (2nd Mon.); Veterans Day, Nov. 11; Thanksgiving; Christmas, Dec. 25.

TAXES: Alabama's statewide sales tax is 4 percent with local options to impose additional increments. There also is an occupancy tax on lodgings.

INFORMATION CENTERS: State welcome centers are on I-65 southbound, about 3 mi. s. of the Tennessee border south of Ardmore; I-10 westbound, 1 mi. w. of the Florida border north of Seminole; I-10 eastbound, 1 mi. e. of the Mississippi border west of Grand Bay; I-85 southbound, 1 mi. w. of the Georgia border near Lanett; I-59 southbound, at the Georgia border northeast of Hammondville; I-59 northbound and I-20 eastbound, at the Mississippi border near Cuba; US 231 northbound, 1 mi. n. of the Florida border south of Madrid; and I-20 westbound, near the Georgia border east of Heflin. Welcome center restrooms are open 24 hours. Travel and routing information is dispensed 8-5.

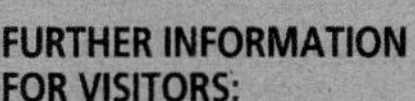

FURTHER INFORMATION FOR VISITORS:

Bureau of Tourism
and Travel
401 Adams Ave.
P.O. Box 4927
Montgomery, AL 36103
(800) 252-2262

RECREATION INFORMATION:

Division of State Parks
Department of Conservation and
Natural Resources
64 N. Union St.
Montgomery, AL 36130
(800) 252-7275 (reservations and
information)

FISHING AND HUNTING REGULATIONS:

Division of Game & Fish
Department of Conservation and Natural
Resources
64 N. Union St., Suite 457
Montgomery, AL 36130
(334) 242-3829

NATIONAL FOREST INFORMATION:

National Forest Service
2946 Chestnut St.
Montgomery, AL 36107
(334) 832-4470

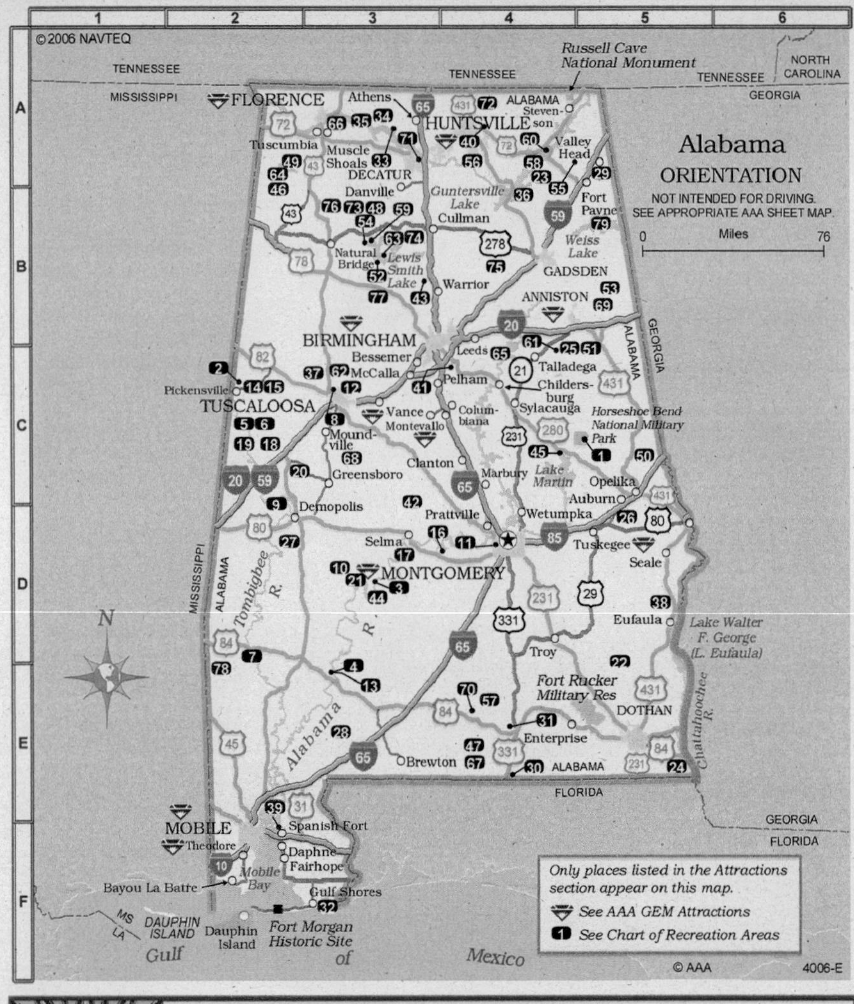

Alabama Temperature Averages Maximum / Minimum

From the records of the National Weather Service

	JAN	FEB	MAR	APR	MAY	JUNE	JULY	AUG	SEPT	OCT	NOV	DEC
Birmingham	56 35	58 37	65 42	74 50	82 58	89 67	91 70	90 69	86 63	76 51	64 40	56 35
Huntsville	52 33	55 35	63 41	74 50	83 58	91 67	92 70	92 69	87 62	76 50	63 39	53 34
Mobile	61 41	65 45	69 49	77 57	84 64	89 71	91 73	90 72	86 68	79 59	69 47	63 43
Montgomery	57 36	61 40	67 45	76 52	84 61	90 69	92 72	92 71	88 66	79 55	66 42	59 38

Points of Interest Offering A *Great Experience for Members*®

Anniston (B-4)

ANNISTON MUSEUM OF NATURAL HISTORY—Minerals, fossils and rare animals in open dioramas are among the many exhibits one can encounter at this museum. See p. 39.

Birmingham (B-3)

ARLINGTON ANTEBELLUM HOME AND GARDENS—This fully restored 1840s mansion houses an impressive collection of antiques and decorative arts. See p. 48.

BIRMINGHAM CIVIL RIGHTS INSTITUTE—Man's inhumanity to man is compellingly depicted in this museum devoted to the ongoing struggle for human rights. See p. 48.

BIRMINGHAM MUSEUM OF ART—More than 21,000 multicultural pieces on three levels include paintings, Mexican artifacts, Chinese gold jewelry and Japanese ceramics. See p. 49.

VULCAN PARK—Look up at the 56-foot-high statue or down on the city. See p. 50.

Florence (A-2)

FRANK LLOYD WRIGHT ROSENBAUM HOUSE MUSEUM—This 1940 home is a Usonian masterpiece. See p. 59.

Huntsville (A-4)

U.S. SPACE AND ROCKET CENTER—With its huge collection of rockets and space hardware, the center offers space enthusiasts the chance to have a first-hand and hands-on encounter with America's space program. See p. 64.

Mobile (F-2)

MOBILE MUSEUM OF ART—More than 2,000 years of cultural history are represented among such collections as 19th- and 20th-century American art; Southern decorative arts and furniture; African art; and contemporary crafts. See p. 67.

MOBILE'S HISTORIC DISTRICTS—Explore the city's diverse architectural styles on a walking tour of its six historic neighborhoods. See p. 67.

USS *ALABAMA* BATTLESHIP MEMORIAL PARK—Dedicated to Alabama's veterans, this park features the World War II-era battleship USS *Alabama*. See p. 69.

Montevallo (C-3)

THE AMERICAN VILLAGE—Stroll through replicas of historic buildings and take part in reenactments devoted to America's journey for liberty and independence. See p. 52.

Montgomery (D-3)

ALABAMA SHAKESPEARE FESTIVAL—Despite its name, this festival features a variety of plays, both classical and modern, presented in two theaters. See p. 70.

FIRST WHITE HOUSE OF THE CONFEDERACY—This 1835 Italianate house was the home of Jefferson Davis and his family while Montgomery was the capital of the Confederacy. See p. 70.

OLD ALABAMA TOWN—See more than 50 buildings representing a range of 19th-century lifestyles as you stroll through this restored village. See p. 71.

Theodore (F-2)

BELLINGRATH GARDENS AND HOME—Meander through this estate's 65 landscaped acres resplendent with camellias, azaleas, roses, chrysanthemums and numerous other flowering plants. See p. 77.

Tuskegee (D-5)

CARVER MUSEUM—Visit the laboratory where scientist George Washington Carver produced many agricultural innovations that were important to the economy of the South. See p. 80.

Vance (C-3)

THE MERCEDES-BENZ VISITOR CENTER—The history of the German automobile manufacturer is depicted through vintage vehicles and racing, sports and concept cars. See p. 80.

RECREATION AREAS

	MAP LOCATION	CAMPING	PICNICKING	HIKING TRAILS	BOATING	BOAT RAMP	BOAT RENTAL	FISHING	SWIMMING	PETS ON LEASH	BICYCLE TRAILS	NATURE PROGS.	VISITOR CENTER	LODGE/CABINS	FOOD SERVICE
NATIONAL FORESTS *(See place listings)*															
Conecuh 84,000 acres on the Alabama-Florida border.		●	●	●	●	●		●	●	●	●				
Talladega 389,000 acres. Central Alabama.		●	●	●	●	●		●	●	●					
Tuskegee 11,054 acres n.e. of Tuskegee.		●	●	●						●		●			
William B. Bankhead 180,000 acres. Northwestern Alabama.		●	●	●	●	●		●	●	●	●				
NATIONAL MILITARY PARKS *(See place listings)*															
Horseshoe Bend (C-4) 2,040 acres 12 mi. n. of Dadeville on SR 49.	1		●	●	●	●		●	●	●			●		
ARMY CORPS OF ENGINEERS															
Bigbee Valley Campground (C-2) 22 acres 2.6 mi. w. of jct. SRs 14 and 86, near Pickensville.	2	●	●	●	●	●		●		●					
Chilatchee Creek Park (D-3) 552 acres 9 mi. e. of Alberta off CR 29.	3	●	●		●	●		●		●					
Claiborne Lake (E-3) 5,930 acres 20 mi. n.w. of Monroeville via SR 41 to Claiborne Lock and Dam on the Alabama River.	4	●	●	●	●	●		●	●	●			●		
Cochrane Campground (C-2) 40 acres 10 mi. s. of Aliceville on SR 17.	5	●	●		●	●		●		●					
Cochrane Recreation Area (C-2) 395 acres 10 mi. w. of Aliceville via SR 17 on the Tennessee-Tombigbee Waterway.	6	●	●	●	●	●		●		●					
Coffeeville Lake (D-2) 8,300 acres 3.5 mi. w. of Coffeeville on US 84.	7	●	●		●	●		●		●					
Deerlick Creek Recreation Area (C-3) 300 acres 12 mi. n.e. of Tuscaloosa on US 82 and Rice Mine Rd.	8	●	●	●		●		●	●	●					
Demopolis (D-2) 10,000 acres 6 mi. w. of Demopolis on US 80 to Lock and Dam Rd.	9	●	●	●	●	●		●		●			●		
East Bank Park (D-3) 60 acres 12 mi. n.w. of Camden on SR 28.	10	●	●		●	●		●	●	●					
Gunter Hill Park (D-4) 422 acres 9 mi. w. of Montgomery on Booth Rd.	11	●		●	●	●		●		●					
Holt Lake (C-3) 2,300 acres 10 mi. n. of Tuscaloosa on SR 216 to Lock and Dam Rd.	12	●	●	●	●	●		●	●				●		
Isaac Creek Park (E-3) 713 acres 20 mi. n.w. of Monroeville off SR 41 and CR 17 at Claiborne Lock and Dam.	13	●	●	●	●	●		●		●					
Pickensville Recreation Area (C-2) 310 acres 1 mi. w. of Pickensville via SR 86 on the Tennessee-Tombigbee Waterway.	14		●	●	●	●		●	●						
Pickensville Day Use Area (C-2) 15 acres in Pickensville, 1 mi. w. of jct. SRs 14 and 86.	15		●	●	●	●		●	●	●					
R.E. "Bob" Woodruff Lake (D-3) 12,510 acres 25 mi. w. of Montgomery via US 80 to Robert F. Henry Lock and Dam on the Alabama River.	16	●	●	●	●	●		●	●	●			●	●	
Six Mile Creek Park (D-3) 95 acres 6 mi. s. of Selma via SR 41 and CR 152.	17	●	●		●	●		●		●					
Sumter Landing (C-2) 350 acres 8 mi. n.w. of Gainesville via CR 85 on the Tennessee-Tombigbee Waterway.	18		●		●	●		●							
S.W. Taylor (C-2) 127 acres 9 mi. n.w. of Gainesville via CR 85 on the Tennessee-Tombigbee Waterway.	19		●	●	●	●		●							
Warrior Lake (C-2) 9,200 acres 3 mi. e. of Eutaw on SR 14 to Lock and Dam Rd.	20	●	●		●	●		●							
William "Bill" Dannelly Reservoir (D-3) 17,000 acres 45 mi. s.w. of Selma on the Alabama River via SR 28.	21	●	●		●	●		●	●	●			●	●	
STATE															
Blue Springs (E-5) 103 acres 6 mi. e. of Clio off SR 10. Tennis; playground.	22	●	●					●	●	●					●
Buck's Pocket (A-4) 2,000 acres 2 mi. n. of Grove Oak off SR 227. Playground.	23	●	●	●	●	●		●		●					●

RECREATION AREAS

	MAP LOCATION	CAMPING	PICNICKING	HIKING TRAILS	BOATING	BOAT RAMP	BOAT RENTAL	FISHING	SWIMMING	PETS ON LEASH	BICYCLE TRAILS	NATURE PROGS.	VISITOR CENTER	LODGE/CABINS	FOOD SERVICE
Chattahoochee (E-5) 596 acres 11 mi. s.e. of Gordon via SR 95.	24	●	●	●	●		●	●		●					
Cheaha (C-4) 2,799 acres 29 mi. s. of Anniston off SR 49. Playground. No pets permitted in lodging facilities.	25	●	●	●	●			●	●	●		●	●	●	●
Chewacla (D-5) 696 acres 4 mi. s. off US 29. Tennis; playground. *(See Auburn p. 42)*	26	●	●	●	●		●	●	●	●			●	●	●
Chickasaw (D-2) 520 acres 4 mi. n. of Linden on US 43. Playground.	27	●	●	●						●					
Claude D. Kelley (E-3) 960 acres 11 mi. n. of Atmore on SR 21. Playground.	28	●	●	●	●	●	●	●	●	●				●	
DeSoto (A-5) 5,067 acres. Scenic. Tennis; playground, pool. *(See Fort Payne p. 60)*	29	●	●	●				●	●	●		●	●	●	●
Florala (E-4) 40 acres off US 331 in Florala. Playground.	30	●	●		●	●		●	●	●					●
Frank Jackson (E-4) 2,050 acres 3 mi. n. of Opp off US 331. Playground.	31		●	●	●			●	●						●
Gulf (F-3) 6,150 acres 10 mi. s. of Foley off SR 59. Golf (18 holes), tennis; playground.	32	●	●	●	●	●	●	●	●	●	●	●	●		●
Joe Wheeler															
Elk River (A-3) 80 acres 15 mi. w. of Athens off US 72. Playground.	33		●		●	●	●	●		●					
First Creek (A-3) 1,800 acres 2 mi. w. of Rogersville via US 72. Golf (18 holes), tennis; playground.	34	●	●	●	●	●	●	●	●		●		●	●	●
Joe Wheeler Dam (A-3) 420 acres 9 mi. n. of Town Creek off SR 101. Tennis; playground.	35		●		●	●		●						●	
Lake Guntersville (B-4) 5,559 acres 6 mi. n.e. of Guntersville off SR 227. Golf (18 holes), tennis; playground.	36	●	●	●	●	●	●	●	●	●	●	●	●	●	●
Lake Lurleen (C-2) 1,625 acres 12 mi. n.w. of Tuscaloosa off US 82. Playground.	37	●	●	●	●	●	●	●	●	●		●	●		●
Lakepoint Resort (D-5) 1,220 acres 7 mi. n. of Eufaula off SR 431. Golf (18 holes), tennis; horse rental, playground.	38	●	●	●	●	●	●	●	●	●	●	●	●	●	●
Meaher (F-2) 1,327 acres 2 mi. w. of Spanish Fort on US 90. CLOSURE INFORMATION: The campground was damaged in the 2004 and 2005 hurricane seasons and is closed; as of June 2006, a reopening date had not been set.	39	●	●	●	●	●		●							
Monte Sano (A-4) 2,140 acres 4 mi. e. of Huntsville. Playground.	40	●	●	●						●				●	●
Oak Mountain (C-3) 9,940 acres 3 mi. e. of US 31 from Pelham off I-65 exit 246. Scenic. Golf, tennis; horse rental, playground. *(See Pelham p. 53)*	41	●	●	●	●	●	●	●	●	●	●	●	●	●	●
Paul M. Grist (D-3) 1,080 acres 15 mi. n. of Selma off SR 22. Playground.	42	●	●	●	●	●	●	●	●	●					●
Rickwood Caverns (B-3) 380 acres. Horse rental, playground. *(See Warrior p. 53)*	43	●	●	●					●	●					●
Roland Cooper (D-3) 236 acres 6 mi. n.e. of Camden off SR 41. Golf (9 holes); playground.	44	●	●	●	●	●		●		●		●		●	●
Wind Creek (C-4) 1,445 acres 7 mi. s.e. of Alexander City off SR 63. Playground.	45	●	●	●	●	●	●	●	●	●	●	●			●
OTHER															
Bear Creek (B-2) 670 acres 30 mi. s.w. of Russellville via US 43 and SR 172.	46	●	●		●	●		●	●	●					
Blue Pond (E-4) 11 acres 13 mi. s.w. of Andalusia on SR 137.	47		●	●	●			●	●	●					
Brushy Lake (B-3) 150 acres 12 mi. s. of Moulton on FR 245.	48	●	●	●	●	●		●		●					
Cedar Creek (A-2) 4,300 acres 10 mi. w. of Russellville via SR 24 and CR 41.	49	●	●		●	●	●	●	●	●					●
Chambers County Lake (C-5) 183 acres 5 mi. s.e. of Lafayette on CR 55.	50		●	●	●	●	●	●							

RECREATION AREAS

Recreation Area	Map Location	Camping	Picnicking	Hiking Trails	Boating	Boat Ramp	Boat Rental	Fishing	Swimming	Pets on Leash	Bicycle Trails	Nature Progs.	Visitor Center	Lodge/Cabins	Food Service
Clay County Lake (C-5) 74 acres 1 mi. s.w. of Delta off SR 9.	51	•	•		•	•	•	•							
Clear Creek (B-3) 600 acres 5 mi. n. of Jasper via SR 195 to Manchester, then n. on CR 27.	52	•	•	•	•	•		•	•	•	•				
Coleman Lake (B-5) 250 acres 10 mi. n. of Heflin via US 78, CR 61 and FRs 553 and 500.	53	•	•	•	•	•		•	•	•					
Corinth (B-3) 500 acres 7 mi. e. of Double Springs via US 278, CR 33 and FR 113.	54	•	•		•	•		•	•	•					
DeKalb County Lake (B-4) 120 acres off SR 75 at Sylvania.	55	•	•		•	•	•	•							•
Ditto's Landing (A-4) 214 acres 12 mi. s. of Huntsville via US 231 on Hobbs Island Rd. Tennis; softball field.	56	•	•		•	•		•		•					
Gantt Lake (E-4) 2,747 acres 11 mi. n. of Andalusia on US 29. Water skiing.	57				•	•		•	•	•					
Goose Pond Colony (A-4) 365 acres 6 mi. s. of Scottsboro via SR 79. Golf (18 holes); amphitheater.	58	•	•	•	•	•		•	•	•			•	•	•
Houston (B-3) 1,000 acres 6 mi. s.e. of Double Springs via US 278, CRs 33 and 63 and FR 118.	59	•	•		•	•		•	•	•					
Jackson County Park (A-4) 63 acres 2 mi. s. of Scottsboro on County Park Rd. Playground.	60	•	•		•	•		•	•						•
Lake Chinnabee (C-4) 250 acres 13 mi. n.e. of Talladega on SR 42.	61	•	•	•	•	•		•		•					
Lake Tuscaloosa (C-3) 5,885 acres 10 mi. n. of Tuscaloosa off SR 69/43.	62		•		•	•		•		•					
Lewis Smith Lake (B-3) 21,200 acres 7 mi. s.w. of Cullman on CR 22.	63	•	•	•	•	•	•	•	•				•	•	•
Little Bear (A-2) 1,680 acres 12 mi. w. of Russellville via SR 24.	64	•	•		•	•		•	•	•					•
Logan Martin Lake (C-4) 18,000 acres w. of Talladega on the Coosa River.	65	•	•		•	•	•	•	•	•				•	•
McFarland (A-3) 325 acres in Florence on SR 20 below O'Neal Bridge.	66	•	•		•	•		•		•					
Open Pond (E-4) 150 acres 15 mi. s.w. of Andalusia via US 29 and SR 137.	67	•	•	•	•	•		•		•					
Payne Lake (C-3) 800 acres 16 mi. n.e. of Greensboro on SR 25.	68	•	•	•	•	•		•	•	•					
Pine Glen (B-5) 5 acres 6 mi. n. of Heflin via US 78 and FR 500.	69	•	•	•				•		•					
Point A Lake (E-4) 700 acres 5 mi. n.w. of Andalusia off US 29.	70	•	•		•	•		•	•	•					
Point Mallard Park (A-3) 750 acres at the e. end of 8th St. S.E. in Decatur. Golf (18 holes); ice rink. *(See Decatur p. 56)*	71	•	•	•				•	•	•	•				
Sharon Johnston (A-4) 250 acres 6 mi. n.e. of Huntsville on Coldman Rd. Pool, shooting range.	72	•	•					•	•	•					
Sipsey River (B-3) 6 acres 9 mi. n.e. of Haleyville via CR 23 and FR 26.	73		•	•				•		•					
Smith Lake Park (B-3) 172 acres s.w. of Cullman via SR 69 and CR 222. Miniature golf, playground.	74	•	•		•	•		•	•	•	•			•	
Sportsman Lake Park (B-4) 160 acres 1 mi. s. on US 31 in Cullman. Paddleboat rental. No motor boats.	75	•	•		•	•	•	•		•		•			
Upper Bear (B-3) 1,860 acres 16 mi. s. of Russellville via US 43, near Bear Creek.	76	•	•		•	•		•	•	•					
Walker County Lake (B-3) 163 acres 3 mi. s.e. of Jasper off Old US 78.	77		•	•	•	•	•	•							
Washington County Lake (E-2) 84 acres 2 mi. w. of Millry off CR 34.	78	•	•		•	•	•	•							
Weiss Lake (B-5) 30,200 acres just n.e. of Centre on SR 9 along the Coosa River.	79	•	•	•	•	•	•	•	•	•			•	•	•

Points of Interest

ANNISTON (B-4) pop. 24,276, elev. 745′

Samuel Noble and Daniel Tyler established textile mills and blast furnaces in Anniston to help launch the South into the mainstream of the Industrial Revolution after the devastating effects of the Civil War. In 1879 the owners hired several Eastern architects to build a modern company town, which opened to the public in 1883. Many historic structures from this model city remain.

West of town is Anniston Army Depot, one of the nation's largest ordnance and reclamation depots. The highest point in the state, 2,407-foot Cheaha Mountain, is south of town in Cheaha State Park *(see Recreation Chart and the AAA Southeastern CampBook).*

Calhoun County Convention and Visitors Bureau: 1330 Quintard Ave., Anniston, AL 36201; phone (256) 237-3536 or (800) 489-1087.

GEM SAVE **ANNISTON MUSEUM OF NATURAL HISTORY** is at 800 Museum Dr., at jct. SR 21 and US 431 in Lagarde Park. The Design For Living Exhibit Hall features more than 400 specimens of North American birds, including extinct and endangered species collected by 19th-century naturalist William Werner.

Other highlights are the Lagarde Africa Hall, containing more than 100 African animals displayed in simulated natural settings; a cave-dwelling creatures exhibit; Egyptian mummies; and changing art exhibits. The Dynamic Earth depicts the planet's formation and includes minerals, fossils, gemstones and dinosaurs. Nature Space offers a large learning area with hands-on activities. On the grounds are nature trails, picnic facilities and the Berman Museum of World History *(see attraction listing).*

Allow 2 hours minimum. Mon.-Sat. 10-5, Sun. 1-5, Memorial Day-Labor Day; Tues.-Sat. 10-5, Sun. 1-5, rest of year. Closed Thanksgiving and Dec. 24-25. Admission $4.50; over 60 and military with ID $4; ages 4-17, $3.50; free to all Thurs. 1-5. MC, VI. Phone (256) 237-6766.

SAVE **BERMAN MUSEUM OF WORLD HISTORY,** jct. US 431 and SR 21 at 840 Museum Dr., contains more than 3,000 objects, including an array of rare weapons and armor, and an art collection with bronzes by Frederic Remington. Many of the items belonged to historical figures such as Napoleon I and Jefferson Davis. A jeweled royal Persian scimitar and Asian art are other highlights.

You are invited to relax on Alabama's beautiful Gulf beaches, shop in specialty stores, dine in restaurants where locals eat, or just visit friends and family. Hundreds of special shows are open during The Year of Alabama Arts, including a major folk-art exhibition in downtown Birmingham.

Children are invited to play with hundreds of butterflies at the Huntsville Botanical Gardens. Play golf on the Robert Trent Jones Golf Trail in 10 cities. Welcome the return of Mobile's legendary 1908 Battle House hotel and enjoy the 75th anniversary florals at world-famous Bellingrath Gardens. Make plans today to visit.

Renaissance Battle House Hotel
Mobile
rsabattlehouse.com

Nation's Largest Seasonal Butterfly House
Huntsville Botanical Garden
hsvbg.org

Kentuck Art Galleries
Northport
kentuck.org

Hank Williams Trail
Montgomery - Georgiana
hankwilliamstrail.com

Allow 1 hour minimum. Mon.-Sat. 10-5, Sun. 1-5, Memorial Day-Labor Day; Tues.-Sat. 10-5, Sun. 1-5, rest of year. Closed Jan. 1, Thanksgiving and Dec. 24-25. Admission $3.50; over 60 and military with ID $3; ages 4-17, $2.50. AX, DS, MC, VI. Phone (256) 237-6261.

CHURCH OF ST. MICHAEL AND ALL ANGELS is at W. 18th St. and Cobb Ave. The 1888 church, built in the Norman style, has a 95-foot tower housing 12 bells. The interior is noteworthy for its 12-foot-long white Carrara marble altar, alabaster reredos, stained-glass windows and hand-carved woodwork. Daily 8-noon and 1-4. Free. Phone (256) 237-4011.

ATHENS (A-3) pop. 18,967, elev. 720′

ALABAMA VETERANS MUSEUM AND ARCHIVES is at 100 W. Pryor St. in the old L& N Freight Depot. This museum relates the stories of local military personnel from the Civil War to the present through the display of uniforms and other military artifacts. Guided tours are given by veterans who talk about their experiences in the military. Allow 1 hour minimum. Wed. and Fri.-Sat. 9-3, and by appointment; closed Jan. 1, Thanksgiving and Dec. 25. Donations. Phone (256) 771-7578.

AUBURN (C-4) pop. 42,987, elev. 698′

Auburn is the home of Auburn University, which was ceded to the state in 1872 as a land-grant college and is now the largest university in Alabama; its enrollment exceeds 20,000. The Old Main, Church Street and Auburn University historic districts encompass many buildings dating from 1847 to 1927. Of interest is the Auburn University Chapel, an 1850 Gothic Revival structure at Thach Avenue and S. College Street.

Four miles south of town off US 29 is Chewacla State Park, comprising 696 acres that include a 23-acre fishing and swimming lake with boat rentals. Other amenities include vacation cabins, campsites, hiking and bicycle trails, tennis courts, picnic areas and a playground; phone (334) 887-5621 or (800) 252-7275. *See Recreation Chart and the AAA Southeastern CampBook.*

Auburn-Opelika Convention and Visitors Bureau: 714 E. Glenn Ave., Auburn, AL 36830; phone (334) 887-8747 or (866) 880-8747.

AUBURN UNIVERSITY, on S. College St., was founded in 1856 by the Methodist Church and envisioned as a religious, educational and cultural center for men. A walking tour of campus includes Haley Center and the university chapel, the oldest building on campus. Maps are available in the Foy Union lobby. Free. Phone (334) 844-4244.

JULE COLLINS SMITH MUSEUM OF FINE ARTS is off I-85 exit 51, then 2 mi. n. on US 29/SR 147. American and European art from the 19th and 20th centuries is displayed in eight galleries. The permanent collection includes works by Marc Chagall, Salvador Dalí, Henri Matisse, Joan Miró, Pablo Picasso and Pierre-Auguste Renoir. Traveling exhibits also are featured. The modernistic building is on manicured grounds.

Guided tours are available. Food is available. Allow 1 hour minimum. Tues.-Sat. 10-5, Sun. 11-5; closed Jan. 1, Easter, Thanksgiving and Dec. 25. Admission $5; over 54, $4; students with ID and under 17 free. MC, VI. Phone (334) 844-3081.

BAYOU LA BATRE (F-1) pop. 2,313, elev. 7′

Although the Maubilla Indians were the first people to settle in the area, Bayou La Batre was officially founded by Joseph Bosarge in 1786 as part of a Spanish land grant. The city's main street is the bayou where trawlers are often three or four abreast on both sides of the tributary as it enters the Mississippi Sound. Bayou La Batre's boat-building, seafood and petroleum industries are among the largest on the Gulf Coast.

Bayou La Batre Chamber of Commerce: 12745 Padgett Switch Rd., P.O. Box 486, Bayou La Batre, AL 36509; phone (251) 824-4088.

BEATRICE pop. 412, elev. 269′

RIKARD'S MILL is at 4116 SR 265N. This restored 1845 water-powered gristmill in the piney woods along Flat Creek grinds corn into meal and grits. Blacksmithing and cane syrup making demonstrations also are presented. Guided tours are available. Allow 1 hour minimum. Picnicking is permitted. Open Thurs.-Sun. 11 a.m.-dusk, Apr.-Dec. Admission $5; over 64 and under 12, $3. Phone (251) 789-2781.

BESSEMER—*see Birmingham p. 52.*

Birmingham

City Population: 242,820 **Elevation:** 1,200 ft.

Editor's Picks:

© Gibson Stock Photography

Alabama's largest city also is one of its youngest. Since its founding in 1871, Birmingham has transformed itself from empty farmland to steel boomtown to major commercial and service center. Despite the bustle found in any metropolitan center, traditional Southern hospitality is still characteristic of the city's residents.

The Jones Valley's rare abundance of the essential ingredients for steel production—iron ore, coal and limestone—was known as early as the 1850s, contributing to the settlement's early growth. Small furnaces were erected in the area during the Civil War to produce munitions for the Confederate Army.

However, the lack of rail lines to move iron and steel products thwarted any major industrial effort. In 1871, when two railroad lines converged, the plans for Birmingham were drawn and capitalists from around the state rushed in to exploit the new city's resources. Within decades Birmingham was established as a major manufacturing center.

This initial vigor paled after World War II. Cheaper and higher quality iron ore imported from abroad as well as diminished steel orders combined to close several factories, resulting in widespread unemployment. The smog and smoke accumulated from years of heavy industry further dimmed prospects for the "Pittsburgh of the South."

In the 1960s an even darker cloud formed over the city when the racial unrest that had been building across the South erupted in violence. In 1963 civil rights movement leaders sponsored sit-ins, marches and pickets to protest segregation and force local businesses to employ more African-Americans. Kelly Ingram Park (formerly West Park) occupies a square block between 16th and 17th Streets and between 5th and 6th Avenues North and was the assembly point for participants in the Christian Leadership Conference's sit-ins, boycotts and marches.

The police response to the civil unrest during this period was swift and sometimes brutal, including the use of high-pressure water hoses and police dogs. Thousands were arrested, including Dr. Martin Luther King Jr. It was during his incarceration that King wrote his widely read essay, "Letter from a Birmingham Jail." In June 1963 business and civil rights leaders reached an agreement, and Birmingham residents soon rallied around the common goal of peaceful resolution.

The Birmingham of the 21st century is strikingly different from the city of the past generation. Gone are the pollution-spewing smokestacks of manufacturers; the city's renovated central business district boasts a smog-free skyline. Racial tensions have likewise dissipated.

Having experienced the pitfalls of a single-industry economy, Birmingham has diversified to include medical, engineering, educational, financial and technological industries among its top resources. Medicine and medical research figure prominently in its future; the city has 21 hospitals. While the largest single employer is the University of Alabama

Getting There — *starting on p. 45*

Getting Around — *starting on p. 45*

What To See — *starting on p. 48*

What To Do — *starting on p. 50*

Where To Stay — *starting on p. 218*

Where To Dine — *starting on p. 219*

at Birmingham, one out of every 10 people in the work force is involved in health care.

The medical center of the University of Alabama specializes in open-heart surgery and diabetes treatment. The Kirklin Clinic at the University of Alabama, 2000 Sixth Ave. S., is a 430,000-square-foot health-care clinic designed by I.M. Pei.

Samford University is Alabama's largest private college and includes the Howard College of Arts and Sciences, the Cumberland School of Law and professional schools of pharmacy, nursing, business, music, education and divinity.

Birmingham's extensive public park system provides a wealth of opportunities for recreation and relaxation. Lovers of art and history will find the murals and Rucker Agee map collection at the Linn-Henley Research Library, 2100 Park Pl., worth their while; phone (205) 226-3665. The city's lively arts groups and wide variety of cultural offerings add to the enjoyment this modern metropolis provides residents and visitors alike.

McWane Science Center / © Jeff Greenberg / Alamy

Getting There

By Car

Several major highways intersect in Birmingham, providing easy access from all directions. North-south I-65 cuts straight through the city, affording direct routes from Montgomery and Nashville. From Chattanooga, Tenn., and other points northeast, I-59 runs through the Appalachian foothills before merging with I-20, intersecting I-65 near the city center and continuing southwest into Mississippi.

I-459 branches off from I-59 just east of the city limits and loops southward to bypass downtown traffic, rejoining I-20/59 near McCalla. Approaching from due east, I-20 meets the I-459 bypass before merging with I-59 downtown.

Getting Around

Street System

Laid out in an orderly grid pattern, Birmingham is fairly easy to navigate. The downtown area is bounded by I-20/59 to the north, I-65 to the west and US 31, the Red Mountain Expressway, to the east. North-south thoroughfares are designated as streets, while east-west routes are avenues. Both streets and avenues are numbered, although some also have names, such as University Boulevard (Eighth Avenue South).

Unless otherwise posted, a right turn on red is permitted after a complete stop.

Parking

With numerous public and private lots, parking is not a problem in Birmingham. Garages generally

Destination Birmingham

A city evolved. A step back in time. Birmingham's mix of trend and tradition reveals a dynamic destination still very much in touch with its Southern charm.

Here medical research is state of the art, while a grand antebellum home holds its own. Civil rights struggles are recounted so they may serve as stepping stones. And a designated historic district is the hippest place to hang out.

Alabama Bureau of Tourism & Travel

Barber Vintage Motorsports Museum, Leeds.
Skid lids are not required for viewing five floors of bikes and a smattering of classic vintage autos. (See listing page 52)

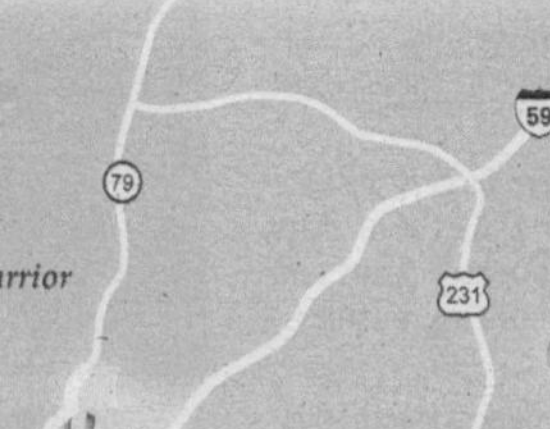

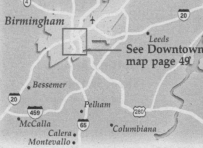

Birmingham Civil Rights Institute.
Immerse yourself in settings that preserve the hard lessons learned from past struggles. (See listing page 48)

Karim Shamsi-Basha
Alabama Bureau of Tourism & Travel

© McWane Science Center

McWane Science Center, Birmingham.
Indulge your curiosity and sense of adventure through hands-on exhibits and larger-than-life images on screen. (See listing page 49)

Birmingham Zoo.
Wildlife enthusiasts of all ages can view many species of animals at one of the South's largest zoos. (See listing page 49)

© Birmingham Zoo

Places included in this AAA Destination City:

The Informed Traveler

Sales Tax: State, county and city sales taxes total 9 percent in Birmingham. A lodging tax of 14 percent also is levied.

WHOM TO CALL

Emergency: 911

Police (non-emergency): (205) 328-9311

Time and Temperature: (205) 916-0021

Hospitals: Carraway Methodist Medical Center, (205) 502-6000; Medical Center East, (205) 838-3000; University of Alabama Hospital, (205) 934-4011.

WHERE TO LOOK

Newspapers

Birmingham has two major newspapers, *The Birmingham News* in the morning and the *Birmingham Post-Herald* in the afternoon. Smaller daily and weekly papers cater to the suburbs and special interests.

Radio

Birmingham radio station WERC (960 AM) is an all-news/weather station; WBHM (90.3 FM) is a member of National Public Radio.

Visitor Information

Greater Birmingham Convention and Visitors Bureau: 2200 Ninth Ave. N., Birmingham, AL 35203; phone (205) 458-8000 or (800) 458-8085.

Birmingham Area Chamber of Commerce: 505 N. 20th St., Suite 200, Birmingham, AL 35203; phone (205) 324-2100.

TRANSPORTATION

Air Travel

Birmingham International Airport is served by major domestic carriers and regional commuter lines. Most major hotels provide shuttle service, usually free, to and from the airport. Taxi fare from the airport to downtown is about $10 one way.

Rental Cars

One of the largest car rental agencies in the city, Hertz, (205) 591-6090 or (800) 654-3080, offers discounts to AAA members. Check the telephone directory for other car rental agencies.

Rail Service

Amtrak trains destined for New York and New Orleans depart from the station at 1819 Morris Ave.; phone (205) 324-3033.

Buses

Greyhound Lines Inc., at 618 19th St. N., provides commercial bus service to and from the city; phone (205) 252-7190 or (800) 231-2222.

Taxis

Taxis are on the meter system; the typical charge is $1.75 for the first mile and $1.60 for each additional mile. The two largest companies are Homewood, (205) 871-4684, and Yellow, (205) 252-1131. Other companies are listed in the telephone directories.

Public Transport

Birmingham-Jefferson County Transit Authority provides bus service around town and into the outlying suburbs. The authority also manages DART, a system of free minibuses serving the downtown area. Basic bus fare is $1. Exact change is required. Phone (205) 521-0101 for schedule and route information.

charge from $4 to $7 per day; on-street metered parking is available downtown.

What To See

ALABAMA JAZZ HALL OF FAME is off I-20/59 exit 125A eastbound, s.e. on 17th St. to 1631 Fourth Ave. N. The museum, in the 1935 Carver Theatre for the Performing Arts, spotlights jazz greats who have links to Alabama. Photographs, instruments, costumes and other artifacts belonging to such legends as Nat King Cole, Duke Ellington, Ella Fitzgerald and Lionel Hampton are exhibited. Jazz performances are scheduled March through November; phone for schedule.

Guided tours are available. Allow 1 hour minimum. Tues.-Sat. 10-5; closed major holidays. Admission $2. Guided tour $3. Phone (205) 254-2731.

SAVE **ALABAMA SPORTS HALL OF FAME MUSEUM** is next to the Birmingham-Jefferson Convention Complex at 2150 Richard Arrington Jr. Blvd. N. In addition to various sports-related displays, films highlight memorable sports moments and the athletic achievements of Alabama sports champions. Mon.-Sat. 9-5. Admission $5, senior citizens $4, students with ID $3, under 6 free, family rate $14. AX, MC, VI. Phone (205) 323-6665.

GEM **ARLINGTON ANTEBELLUM HOME AND GARDENS,** 331 Cotton Ave. S.W., dates from the 1840s and is a fine example of Greek Revival architecture. The house, on a 6-acre estate in old Elyton, was built by one of the 10 founders of Birmingham and is furnished with a collection of 19th-century decorative arts. Tues.-Sat. 10-4, Sun. 1-4; closed major holidays. Last tour begins 1 hour before closing. Admission $5; over 54, $4.50; ages 6-18, $3. Phone (205) 780-5656.

BIRMINGHAM BOTANICAL GARDENS, 2612 Lane Park Rd., comprises 67.5 acres of flowers, trees and shrubs. More than 230 species of birds can be observed. The grounds also contain a conservatory and a Japanese garden as well as 24 landscaped gardens and plant collections. A free horticultural lending library contains books, CD ROMS and videotapes.

Picnicking is permitted in designated locations. Food is available. Pets are not permitted. Allow 2 hours minimum. Garden open daily dawn-dusk. Growing houses open daily 7-3. Free. Phone (205) 414-3900.

GEM SAVE **BIRMINGHAM CIVIL RIGHTS INSTITUTE,** 520 16th St. N., contains permanent exhibits describing the Birmingham civil rights movement and worldwide human rights struggles. A 3-minute introductory movie details class struggles and violent labor strikes occurring in the early 20th century between wealthy Birmingham steel industrialists and coal miners. Touch screen monitors offer access to an audiovisual history library.

Allow 2 hours minimum. Tues.-Sat. 10-5, Sun. 1-5; closed major holidays. Last admission is 30 minutes before closing. Admission $9; over 64, $5;

Kelly Ingram Park / © Andre Jenny / Alamy

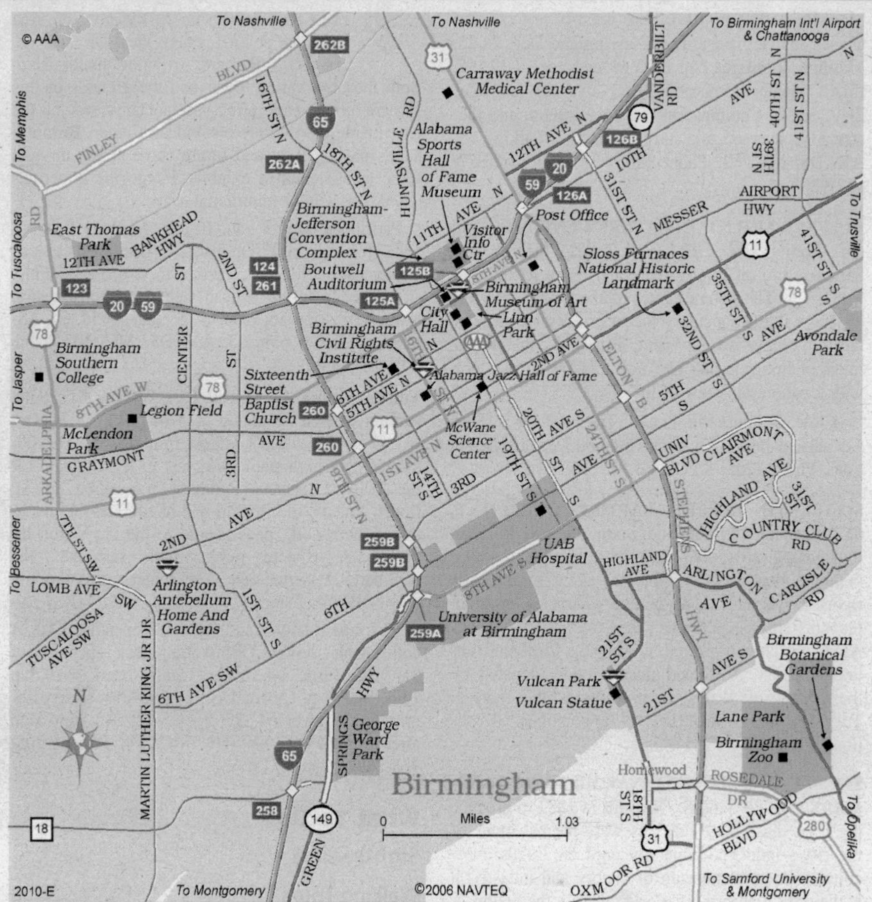

college students with ID $4; under 17 free; free to all Sun. AX, DS, MC, VI. Phone (205) 328-9696 or (866) 328-9696.

GEM **BIRMINGHAM MUSEUM OF ART,** 2000 Eighth Ave. N., features a permanent collection of more than 21,000 pieces of American and European art. Exhibits include the Kress Collection of Renaissance Art; pre-Columbian, Asian, African and American Indian art and artifacts; European silver, porcelain and glass; an extensive Wedgwood pottery collection; and photographs. Handheld, automated phone-like devices give detailed information on the exhibits and can be carried throughout the museum.

Allow 1 hour minimum. Tues.-Sat. 10-5, Sun. noon-5; closed city holidays. Free. Phone (205) 254-2565.

BIRMINGHAM ZOO, s. on US 280 in Lane Park, is one of the South's largest zoos. Birds, reptiles and mammals from around the world, including a rare black rhinoceros and a Siberian white tiger, dwell in simulated natural settings. A children's zoo and a predator display are featured along with daily educational programs. A train and carousel also are available.

Food is available. Daily 9-5 (also Tues. and Fri.-Sat. 5-7), Memorial Day-Labor Day; 9-5, rest of year. Closed Thanksgiving and Dec. 25. Admission $11; over 64 and ages 2-12, $6. Admission half-price Tues. Train and carousel each $2. AX, DS, MC, VI. Phone (205) 879-0409.

SAVE **McWANE SCIENCE CENTER,** downtown at jct. Second Ave. N. and 19th St. N. at 200 19th St. N., offers four levels of science adventures and interactive exhibits. Children under 6 can explore Just Mice Size, where everything appears 10 times larger than normal. ScienceQuest has hands-on exhibits about motion, energy, light and sound, while World of Water takes a look at aquatic life from around the globe. Films at the IMAX theater surround visitors with action. Traveling exhibits also are featured.

Food is available. Allow 2 hours minimum. Museum Mon.-Sat. 10-6, Sun. noon-6, June-Aug.;

Mon.-Fri. 9-5, Sat. 10-6, Sun. noon-6, rest of year. Closed Jan. 1, Easter, Thanksgiving and Dec. 24-25. Museum admission $9; over 65 and ages 2-12, $8. IMAX theater admission $7.50; over 65 and ages 2-12, $6.50. Combination rate for museum and theater $14; over 65 and ages 2-12, $12. Parking $3. AX, DS, MC, VI. Phone (205) 714-8300 or (877) 462-9263.

RUFFNER MOUNTAIN NATURE CENTER is 8 mi. n.e.; from I-59 exit 132 go e. 1 blk., then e. onto 83rd St., s.e. on Rugby Ave., and .7 mi. e. to 1214 S. 81st St. The nature center of this 1,000-acre forest and wildlife sanctuary focuses on Ruffner Mountain's biology, geology and history. There are 11 miles of hiking trails; one trail ends at an overlook with a panoramic view of the city.

Allow 2 hours minimum. Tues.-Sat. 9-5, Sun. 1-5; closed Jan. 1, Thanksgiving and Dec. 25. Donations. Phone (205) 833-8264.

SIXTEENTH STREET BAPTIST CHURCH is downtown at 16th St. and Sixth Ave. N. In 1963 four young girls died here in a Sunday morning bombing that became a pivotal event in the civil rights movement. A 45-minute videotape program recounts the event and the role this African-American church played in shaping local and national history. A stained-glass window donated by the people of Wales commemorates the tragedy. Tues.-Fri. 10-4, Sat. 10-1 by appointment. Donations. Phone (205) 251-9402.

SLOSS FURNACES NATIONAL HISTORIC LANDMARK is at 20 32nd St. N. Built in 1882 to produce pig iron, these blast furnaces were the backbone of the city's industrial economy until the 1970s. Now converted into a museum of history and industry, it is the only such preservation project in the nation. A 32-acre park surrounds the site. A brochure for self-guiding tours interprets history and describes the furnaces' operations.

Allow 30 minutes minimum. Tues.-Sat. 10-4, Sun. noon-4; closed city holidays. Guided tours are offered Sat.-Sun. at 1, 2 and 3. Tour schedule may vary; phone ahead. Free. Phone (205) 324-1911.

SOUTHERN MUSEUM OF FLIGHT/ALABAMA AVIATION HALL OF FAME, off I-59/20 at airport exit, following signs to 4343 73rd St. N., presents eight decades of aviation history. The hall of fame honors aviators with ties to the state, including the Wright brothers who flew from an airfield that became part of Maxwell Air Force Base in Montgomery. Military, commercial and experimental aircraft are displayed. Other exhibits feature the Tuskegee Airmen, women in aviation, photographs and aircraft from the Cold War Era.

Allow 1 hour minimum. Tues.-Sat. 9:30-4:30, Sun. 1-4:30; closed major holidays. Admission $3, senior citizens and students with ID $2, under 5 free. Phone (205) 833-8226.

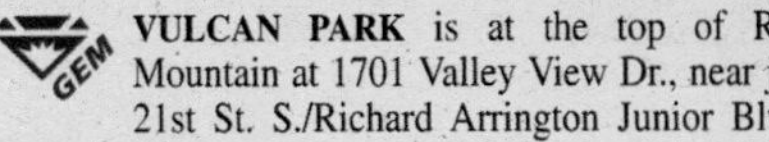

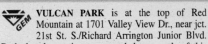

VULCAN PARK is at the top of Red Mountain at 1701 Valley View Dr., near jct. 21st St. S./Richard Arrington Junior Blvd. Both the observation tower and the grounds of this 10-acre urban park offer spectacular views of the city. Inside the interpretive Vulcan Center, Birmingham's past, present and future come to life through static and interactive exhibits. Picnicking is permitted. Allow 1 hour minimum.

Park open daily 7 a.m.-10 p.m. (open 1-10 Jan. 1 and Thanksgiving). Observation deck and Vulcan Center open Mon.-Sat. 10-6, Sun. 1-6. Park admission free. Inclusive Vulcan Center and observation tower admission $6; over 64, $5; ages 5-12, $4. Admission after 6 p.m. $3. AX, DS, MC, VI. Phone (205) 933-1409.

Vulcan Statue, in Vulcan Park off US 31 at the summit of Red Mountain at 1701 Valley View Dr., is one of the world's largest iron figures. The 60-ton, 56-foot-high statue was cast in Birmingham for the 1904 Louisiana Purchase Exposition in St. Louis. Vulcan, the Roman god of fire and the inventor of metalwork, pays tribute to the city's iron industry. A 10-acre public park surrounds the landmark. A visitor education center traces the history of Birmingham.

Park open daily 7 a.m.-10 p.m. (open 1-10 Jan. 1 and Thanksgiving). Observation deck open Mon.-Sat. 10-6, Sun. 1-6. Visitor center open Mon.-Sat. 10-6, Sun. 1-6. Closed Dec. 24-25. All-inclusive admission $6; over 64, $5; ages 5-12, $4. Admission after 6 p.m. $3. AX, DS, MC, VI. Phone (205) 933-1409.

What To Do

Sightseeing

Walking Tours

Brochures detailing self-guiding tours of historic sites along the Black Heritage Tour are available from the Greater Birmingham Convention and Visitors Bureau, 2200 Ninth Ave. N., Birmingham, AL 35203-1100; phone (205) 458-8000 or (800) 458-8085.

Sports and Recreation

Alabama's unofficial status as "Football Capital of the South" is largely the legacy of University of Alabama coach Paul "Bear" Bryant, who led his Crimson Tide **football** team to more than 300 victories. For Crimson Tide sports tickets phone (205) 348-2262.

The University of Alabama at Birmingham, (205) 975-8221; Samford University, (205) 726-2966; Miles College, (205) 929-1615; and Birmingham-Southern College, (205) 226-4935, also have competitive sports teams. The Birmingham Barons, AA **baseball** affiliates of the Chicago White Sox, play their home games at Hoover Metropolitan Stadium; phone (205) 988-3200. Baseball fans will want to take a free self-guiding tour of the restored 1910

Rickwood Field at 2031 11th Ave. S., where among others, Ty Cobb, Babe Ruth, Satchel Paige and Willie Mays swung for center field; phone (205) 458-8161.

Auto racing attracts legions of fans to the Birmingham International Raceway, off I-459; phone (205) 781-2471. Nearby, the Talladega Superspeedway *(see Talladega p. 76)* holds two NASCAR Winston Cup events as well as the Busch Grand National and ARCA events. The Birmingham Race Course, 1000 John Rogers Dr., offers on-site greyhound **dog racing;** phone (205) 838-7500.

Note: Policies concerning admittance of children to pari-mutuel betting facilities vary. Phone for information.

Tennis courts can be found at most city parks, along with facilities for **hiking** and **bicycling.** City **golf** courses include Highland Park, 3300 Highland Ave., and Roebuck, 8920 Roebuck Blvd. For information about other public golf courses and tennis courts, phone the convention and visitor bureau, (205) 458-8000 or (800) 458-8085.

Shopping

Downtown warehouses that once produced America's oldest soft drink, Dr. Pepper, now comprise the upscale Pepper Place, which is one of the region's better-known interior design centers. The Riverchase Galleria, I-459 and US 31S, is *the* place to shop in Birmingham. Topped by one of the largest glass skylights in the Western Hemisphere, the Galleria includes a JCPenney, Macy's, McRae's, Parisian, Proffitt's, Sears, more than 200 specialty stores, an office tower and a sizable hotel.

Other retail centers include Century Plaza, I-20 and Oporto-Madrid Boulevard, with JCPenney and Sears; Colonial Brookwood Village, US 280E and Lakeshore Drive, with anchor stores Macy's and Parisian; The Summit, at US 280E and I-459, which has Parisian and Saks as well as many upscale specialty shops. Window-shoppers and novelty hunters will want to visit the antique shops and trendy boutiques of Five Points South, off 20th Street S. and Highland Avenue.

Performing Arts

Birmingham has maintained strong ties to theater and the arts. This commitment was rewarded in 1989, when it was selected by the U.S. Conference of Mayors as America's Most Livable City, an award based in part on a city's commitment to and support of the arts.

The University of Alabama at Birmingham Department of Theatre presents dramatic productions in the Alys Robinson Stephens Performing Arts Center late September through May; phone (205) 975-2787 or (877) 278-8457. The Terrific New Theatre, open year-round, features off-Broadway shows; phone (205) 328-0868. The Birmingham Children's Theatre, one of the largest professional children's theaters in the country, presents nine different shows during its September through May season; phone (205) 458-8181.

Contemporary and experimental drama are hallmarks of the Birmingham Festival Theatre, which features new playwrights and local talent; phone (205) 933-2383.

The Alabama Ballet stages most of its performances at the Birmingham-Jefferson Convention Complex Concert Hall; phone (205) 322-4300. Opera Birmingham sponsors performances throughout the year; phone (205) 322-6737.

Special concerts, big-name entertainment and shows are presented at the Alys Robinson Stephens Performing Arts Center in Birmingham October through May; phone (205) 975-2787.

Special Events

Birmingham heralds spring with the Birmingham International Festival in April, a tribute to international culture that focuses on a different country or culture each year.

City Stages, held in mid-May, is a large downtown festival celebrating Birmingham's rich musical heritage with crafts and children's activities as well as performances by local and nationally known musicians. Other city events include an Oktoberfest in mid-October and the Greek Food Festival in late September.

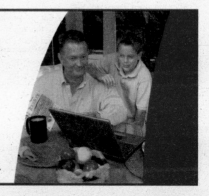

The Birmingham Vicinity

BESSEMER (C-3) pop. 29,672, elev. 515'

BESSEMER HALL OF HISTORY MUSEUM, 1905 Alabama Ave., is in a restored railroad depot. Fossils, American Indian artifacts, pioneer items, Civil War memorabilia and a collection of old telephones and business machines—including a typewriter from Adolf Hitler's hideaway, Eagle's Nest—are among the items displayed. Changing exhibits include pieces pertinent to the industrial history of Jefferson County. Allow 30 minutes minimum. Tues.-Sat. 9-noon and 1-4; closed holidays. Donations. Phone (205) 426-1633.

ALABAMA ADVENTURE is at 4599 Visionland Pkwy. The grounds contain Magic City USA Theme Park and Splash Beach Water Park. Magic City USA Theme Park is home to thrill rides such as the Zoomerang triple loop steel roller coaster and Space Shot, a 185-foot free fall ride. Marvel City has children's rides. Splash Beach's offering include the nine-story Acapulco Drop Speed Ride, a lazy river, wave pool and a sand beach.

Food is available. Allow 3 hours minimum. Mon.-Fri. 10-8, Sat. 10-10, Sun. 11-8, Memorial Day weekend-Labor Day. Hours may vary; phone ahead. Admission to Magic City USA Theme Park or Splash Beach Water Park $25.95; over age 61 or under 48 inches tall $16.95. Combination admission to both parks $29.95; over age 61 or under 48 inches tall $19.95. Parking $7. AX, DS, MC, VI. Phone (205) 481-4750.

CALERA (C-3) pop. 3,158, elev. 497'

HEART OF DIXIE RAILROAD MUSEUM is at 1919 Ninth St. This museum features operating standard- and narrow-gauge railways, two restored depots, a collection of railroad artifacts and memorabilia, and an outdoor collection of railroad locomotives, cars and cabooses. A 45-minute ride aboard a standard-gauge train, and a 10-minute ride aboard a narrow-gauge train are offered. Picnicking is permitted. Allow 1 hour minimum.

Museum open Tues.-Sat. 9-4; closed major holidays. Train rides at 11, 1 and 2, last Sat. in Apr.-last Sat. in Sept.; schedule varies late Mar. through mid-Apr., in Oct. and late Nov. through mid-Dec. Phone to verify all schedules. Museum by donations. Fare for 45-minute trip $10; over 64, $8; ages 2-12, $7. Locomotive ride $25; caboose ride $15. Fare for 10-minute ride $3. Combination tickets are available. Phone (205) 668-3435 or (800) 943-4490.

COLUMBIANA (C-4) pop. 3,316, elev. 524'

KARL C. HARRISON MUSEUM OF GEORGE WASHINGTON is at 50 Lester St. The museum, encouraged by a sixth-generation granddaughter of Martha Washington, contains letters, china, 18th- and 19th-century wooden furniture, books and other personal effects of the first family and their descendents. Guided tours are available. Allow 1 hour minimum. Mon.-Fri. 10-3; closed holidays. Free. Phone (205) 669-8767.

LEEDS (C-4) pop. 10,455, elev. 622'

BARBER VINTAGE MOTORSPORTS MUSEUM is off I-20E exit 140, e. on US 78, s. on Rex Lake Rd., then w. to 6030 Barber Motorsports Pkwy. The museum presents what is considered to be the country's largest collection of motorcycles, with more than 650 of the nearly 1,000 machines displayed; the earliest example dates to 1904. Vintage race cars also are showcased.

Allow 1 hour minimum. Mon.-Sat. 10-6, Sun. noon-6, Apr.-Sept.; Mon.-Sat. 10-5, Sun. noon-5, rest of year. Closed major holidays. Admission $10; ages 4-12, $6. Phone (205) 699-7275.

McCALLA (C-3) elev. 475'

TANNEHILL IRONWORKS HISTORICAL STATE PARK is 2 mi. e. of I-20/59 exit 100 (Bucksville), following signs. These 1,500 acres of wooded hills preserve ironworks that operated 1829-65. A major Confederate munitions supplier during the Civil War, the ironworks were destroyed by Union forces in 1865. The Alabama Iron and Steel Museum displays artifacts of the industry. Walking trails trace historic roadways. Crafts demonstrations are held weekends March through November.

Picnicking is permitted. Camping is available. Park daily 7 a.m.-dusk. Museum Tues.-Fri. 9-5, Sat. 10-5, Sun. 1-5. A gristmill operates the third weekend of the month. Park admission $3; over 61, $2; ages 6-11, $1. Museum $2; ages 6-11, $1. Phone (205) 477-5711.

MONTEVALLO (C-3) pop. 4,825, elev. 430'

GEM **THE AMERICAN VILLAGE** is at 3727 SR 119. Costumed interpreters re-enact Colonial times and events that shaped American history. Catch the Spirit of Liberty presents the story of American independence with freedom rallies, patriot parades and cannon firings. Interpreters assuming the roles of Ben Franklin, Patrick Henry, Betsy Ross other historical figures interact with guests.

The park also contains replicas of the White House Oval Office, a Colonial courthouse, the Liberty Bell and Constitution Green. Washington Hall is patterned after Mount Vernon. The President's House is similar to country's first presidential residence and beginning in late 2007 is to be furnished in the period of the late 1700s.

The Pettus Randall Miniature Museum of American History presents a collection of American presidents and first ladies as well as some 35 historical dioramas. Guided tours are available. Allow 1 hour,

30 minutes minimum. Mon.-Fri. 10-4, day after Labor Day-Memorial Day; Tues.-Sat. 10-4, rest of year. Programs may vary; phone ahead. Admission $8.50; senior citizens, students with ID and ages 5-17, $8. AX, MC, VI. Phone (205) 665-3535 or (877) 811-1776.

PELHAM (C-4) pop. 14,369, elev. 460′

OAK MOUNTAIN STATE PARK is 3 mi. e. of US 31 off I-65 exit 246. This 9,940-acre park is at the southernmost part of the Appalachian chain and offers a scenic drive to the top of Double Oak Mountain. The park also has a wildlife center, an 18-hole golf course, a beach, nature and hiking trails, horseback riding, a BMX track, tennis courts, pedal boats and canoes.

Picnicking is permitted. Camping is available. Daily 7 a.m.-dusk. Admission Mon.-Fri. $2; over 61 and ages 6-11, $1. Admission Sat.-Sun. and holidays $3; over 61 and ages 6-11, $1. Phone (205) 620-2524 or (800) 252-7275. *See Recreation Chart and the AAA Southeastern CampBook.*

WARRIOR (B-4) pop. 3,169, elev. 504′

RICKWOOD CAVERNS STATE PARK is off I-65 exit 284 (northbound) or exit 289 (southbound), then w., following signs. The caverns contain an interesting display of stalactites and stalagmites. A miniature train meanders through the grounds on a half-mile track.

Picnicking and swimming are permitted. Camping is available. Grounds daily 8 a.m.-dusk. Park facilities daily 10-6, Memorial Day-Labor Day. Cave tours are offered daily 10-5, Memorial Day-Labor Day; Sat.-Sun. 10-5, Mar. 1-day before Memorial Day and day after Labor Day-Oct. 31. Last cave tour leaves at closing. Park $1, under 6 free. Cave tours $8; ages 6-11, $5. Swimming $3, under 3 free. Train ride $1. AX, MC, VI. Phone (205) 647-9692. *See Recreation Chart and the AAA Southeastern CampBook.*

© Rob Lagerstrom / Birmingham Botanical Gardens

This ends listings for the Birmingham Vicinity.
The following page resumes the alphabetical listings of cities in Alabama.

BREWTON (E-3) pop. 5,498, elev. 84′

THOMAS E. McMILLAN MUSEUM is in the Fine Arts Center at Jefferson Davis Community College, s. just off US 31, following signs. This small museum offers archeological artifacts and historical exhibits. Permanent displays include prehistoric American Indian and Early American military and civilian items; other exhibits interpret the heritage of the southwestern Alabama region. Temporary exhibits also are presented.

Guided tours are available. Tues. and Thurs. 9-3 and by appointment; closed first week of June, first week of Sept. and last 2 weeks of Dec. Free. Phone (251) 809-1528.

CALERA—*see Birmingham p. 52.*

CENTRE (B-5) pop. 3,216, elev. 663′

CHEROKEE HISTORICAL MUSEUM is at 101 E. Main St. An eclectic mix of more than 7,000 artifacts fills this 1919 three-storey former department store which itself provides an interesting glimpse into the past. Offering include vintage cars and tractors, photographs, a doll collection, housewares and cowboy bathtubs. Allow 1 hour minimum. Tues. 9:30-4, Wed.-Sat. 8:30-4; closed major holidays. Donations. Phone (256) 927-7835.

CHILDERSBURG (C-4) pop. 4,927, elev. 412′

On this site in 1540 Hernando de Soto discovered Coosa, a Creek Indian capital and sacred peace town. Since European settlement in the early 19th century, Childersburg has evolved into a lumber and farm community with paper manufacturing and recycling as its major industry. Just north is Kymulga Grist Mill Park and the 105-foot Kymulga Covered Bridge, which was built in the 1860s and spans the Talladega Creek.

Childersburg Chamber of Commerce: 805 Third St. S.W., P.O. Box 527, Childersburg, AL 35044; phone (256) 378-5482.

DESOTO CAVERNS PARK, 5 mi. e. on SR 76 to 5181 DeSoto Caverns Pkwy., covers 80 acres surrounding the historic onyx-marble caverns named for Hernando DeSoto. Hour-long guided tours include a laser light and water show in the Great Onyx Chamber, which is larger than a football field and higher than a 12-story building. The park also offers such activities as gemstone panning, a squirt-gun maze, water-balloon activities, archery, cave-wall climbing and a playground.

Picnicking is permitted. Camping is available. Mon.-Sat. 9-5:30, Sun. 1-5:30, Apr.-Oct.; Mon.-Sat. 9-4:30, Sun. 1-4:30, rest of year. Closed Thanksgiving and Dec. 25. Park free. Cave tours $14.99; ages 4-11, $11.99. Activities $4.49 each. Special festivals $10. DS, MC, VI. Phone (256) 378-7252 or (800) 933-2283. *See the AAA Southeastern CampBook.*

CLANTON (C-3) pop. 7,800, elev. 600′

THE WATER COURSE is off I-65 exit 205, then .5 mi. w. to 2030 Seventh St. S. As a project of the Alabama Power Co., interactive exhibits, two game shows and educational displays about the state's water resources are offered. Visitors can take a simulated helicopter flight over Alabama's waterways, learn how hydroelectricity is generated and view aquariums containing native fish from rivers, streams and swamps. Mon.-Sat. 9-4; closed holidays. Free. Phone (205) 280-4442 or (800) 280-4442.

COLUMBIANA—*see Birmingham p. 52.*

CONECUH NATIONAL FOREST

Elevations in the forest range from 200 ft. in the swamp areas to 320 ft. at Open Pond Tower. Refer to AAA maps for additional elevation information.

On the Alabama-Florida border, Conecuh National Forest covers almost 84,000 acres. Backpacking is permitted along the 20-mile Conecuh Trail, which offers 5- and 10.5-mile loops through the forest. Deer, squirrels, rabbits and quails are commonly sighted; alligators and wild turkeys also can be seen. The trail offers five different starting points, including Open Pond, which has year-round facilities for camping, fishing and boating.

Bicycling is permitted on the North Loop Trail. Blue Pond, 13 miles southwest of Andalusia via US 29 and SR 137, offers hiking, picnicking and swimming. Trail maps can be purchased from the district ranger's office in Andalusia. Developed recreation areas are open daily 6 a.m.-10 p.m., Apr.-Sept.; dawn-dusk, rest of year. Free. Parking $3. For more information contact the District Ranger, 16375 US 29, Andalusia, AL 36420; phone (334) 222-2555. *See Recreation Chart and Andalusia in the AAA Southeastern CampBook.*

CULLMAN (B-4) pop. 13,995, elev. 802′

Cullman was the vision of John G. Cullmann, a German immigrant who bought a tract of land in 1872, upon which he hoped to establish a self-sustaining colony of his countrymen. Beginning with only five German families, the project was so successful that 6 years later the Alabama legislature designated Cullman the seat of the newly created county, also named for its founder.

An abundance of timber and coal created such prosperity that Queen Wilhelmina of the Netherlands gave her backing to the Dutch company organized to develop the community's resources. World War I prevented the full materialization of the project, and the town's economic base shifted to electrical equipment production and poultry processing.

Clarkson Covered Bridge, 7 miles west of I-65 on US 278, then 2 miles north following signs, is one of Alabama's largest. The surrounding wooded area contains picnic facilities, hiking paths and a non-operating gristmill.

Cullman Area Chamber of Commerce, Convention and Tourism Bureau: 301 2nd Ave.

S.W., Cullman, AL 35055; phone (256) 734-0454 or (800) 313-5114.

SAVE **AVE MARIA GROTTO,** off I-65 exit 308 then 4 mi. e. on US 278, is on the grounds of St. Bernard Abbey and its preparatory school. Using pictures as a guide, over a period of 50 years, Benedictine monk Brother Joseph decorated the main grotto with dioramas depicting biblical events and created nearly 125 miniatures of famous churches, buildings and shrines from many parts of the world. Construction materials range from bits of discarded glass and jewelry to native stone and marble.

Food is available. Picnicking is permitted. Allow 1 hour minimum. Daily 8-6, Apr.-Sept.; daily 8-5, rest of year. Closed Jan. 1 and Dec. 25. Admission $7; over 55, $5; ages 6-12, $4.50. AX, DS, MC, VI. Phone (256) 734-4110.

SAVE **CULLMAN COUNTY MUSEUM,** 211 2nd Ave. N.E., is in a replica of the home of founder John Cullmann. Displays representative of the town's rural past and its German heritage include antique clothing, American Indian artifacts and a street scene with various historical items displayed in storefront windows. There also is a life-size bronze statue of Cullmann.

Mon.-Fri. 9-noon and 1-4, Sun. 1:30-4:30; closed major holidays. Admission $4; under 12, $2. Phone (256) 739-1258 or (800) 533-1258.

THE EVELYN BURROW MUSEUM is at 1315 CR 222. The eclectic objects displayed are part of the personal collection amassed by a local couple over a 65-year period. They include a 600-pound, bronze double-mermaid fountain pond, historical Biblical scenes made of fine china, Tiffany lamps, Faberge eggs and Dresden porcelain. The collection of horse sculptures is said to be the largest known. Allow 1 hour minimum. Mon.-Fri. 9-4; closed major holidays. Free. Phone (256) 775-7477.

DANVILLE (B-3) elev. 600'

JESSE OWENS MEMORIAL PARK AND MUSEUM is 1.5 mi. e. of jct. SR 157 and CR 187 to CR 203, then just e. to 7019 CR 203. At the 1936 Olympic games in Nazi era Berlin, this African-American track star won four gold medals. The park features a replica of Owens' Alabama boyhood home as well as an 8-foot bronze sculpture of Owens, a replica of the 1936 broad jump area and a 1936 Olympic torch, a baseball field, and a playground. The museum contains a collection of memorabilia and interactive video activities.

Guided tours are available. Picnicking is permitted. Allow 1 hour minimum. Tues.-Sat. 11-4, Sun. 1-4 (open Memorial Day, July 4 and Labor Day 1-4). Closed Jan. 1, Thanksgiving and Dec. 25. Free. Phone (256) 974-3636.

DAPHNE (F-2) pop. 16,581, elev. 157'

Now a resort and recreational area on Mobile Bay, Daphne had its beginnings in the early 18th century when it served as a gathering spot for European fur traders. A popular legend claims that Gen. Andrew Jackson directed his troops during the War of 1812 from a fork in one of Daphne's live oaks.

Owing to a prime location on the Eastern Shore, Daphne is sometimes called "Jubilee City." The name refers to the harvesting and celebrating in which the residents indulge when a natural convergence of summer tidal and weather conditions forces multitudes of fish and crustaceans into shallow shoreline waters, where they easily become the catch-of-the-day.

The city is home to the United States Sports Academy, 1 mile east on US 98, a graduate school devoted to sports education. The American Sport Art Museum and Archives, a part of the academy, celebrates the world of sports through artistic interpretation. A large collection of sculpture, paintings and other media are complemented by an archive of sports history.

Bayfront Park, on Bayfront Drive, and May Day Park, on the west side of College Street, are pleasant places to picnic and enjoy views of the water. A boat launch is available at May Day Park.

Eastern Shore Chamber of Commerce & Visitor Center—Daphne: 29750 Larry Dee Cawyer Dr., P.O. Box 310, Daphne, AL 36526-0310; phone (251) 621-8222.

MALBIS MEMORIAL CHURCH (Greek Orthodox), on CR 27, is a copy of a Byzantine church in Athens, Greece. The mosaic-adorned church contains several striking murals and a hand-carved, white marble wall. The freestanding wall serves as a backdrop for the altar, marble pulpit and bishop's throne, all of which were imported from Greece. Tours are offered daily 10-4. Free. Phone (251) 626-3050.

DAUPHIN ISLAND (F-2) pop. 1,371, elev. 6'

Early in the 1700s the French established the first European settlement in the Louisiana Territory on Dauphin (DOFF-in) Island, which they originally named Massacre because of the many human skeletons they found. When the group realized the island's potential as a defense post, the name was changed to Dauphin, the title of the eldest son of Louis XIV, and the settlement was moved to the mainland. For 2 centuries the island served military purposes only.

Today much of the island is a bird sanctuary. The Dauphin Island Park and Recreation Board, in partnership with the National Audubon Society and the Friends of the Dauphin Island Audubon Bird Sanctuary, maintains 160 acres with walking trails that are free and open to the public.

A bridge that forms part of SR 193 provides an especially scenic entrance to the island, which also is accessible by ferry from the Fort Morgan Peninsula, Orange Beach and Gulf Shores. The Gulf shores and a large freshwater lake provide many opportunities for recreation. Chartered fishing trips may be arranged at Dauphin Isle Marina. A nearby fishing pier and a boat ramp also are available. Bienville Beach offers swimming.

Dauphin Island Chamber of Commerce: P.O. Box 5, Dauphin Island, AL 36528; phone (251) 861-5524 or (877) 532-8744.

SAVE **THE ESTUARIUM AT THE DAUPHIN ISLAND SEA LAB,** just past the ferry landing at 101 Bienville Blvd., focuses on the four key ecosystems of coastal Alabama—the swamps of the Mobile-Tensaw River delta, Mobile Bay, the barrier islands and the Gulf of Mexico. Interactive exhibits and 27 aquariums depict one of the country's largest estuary systems.

Mon.-Sat. 9-6, Sun. noon-6, Mar.-Aug.; Mon.-Sat. 9-5, Sun. 1-5, rest of year. Closed Jan. 1, Easter, Thanksgiving and Dec. 24-25 and 31. Admission $6; over 50, $5; ages 5-18, $3. AX, DS, MC, VI. Phone (251) 861-7500.

FORT GAINES HISTORIC SITE, 51 Bienville Blvd., was one of two fortifications guarding Mobile Bay during the Civil War. Directly opposite on Mobile Point, Fort Morgan *(see Gulf Shores p. 62)* guarded the eastern entrance to the bay. The two forts overlook the site of the Battle of Mobile Bay. The structure, completed by the Confederacy in 1861, is a five-sided brick rampart with bastions. A museum contains Civil War artifacts. Allow 30 minutes minimum. Daily 9-6, June-Aug.; 9-5, rest of year. Closed Thanksgiving and Dec. 25. Admission $5; ages 5-12, $3; under 4 free. MC, VI. Phone (251) 861-6992.

DECATUR (A-3) pop. 53,929, elev. 573′

Reduced to four buildings by the end of the Civil War and blighted by a yellow fever epidemic in 1888, Decatur survived and then prospered when chemical companies were established in the 1950s. Wheeler Lake, one of the Tennessee Valley Authority reservoirs spread across northern Alabama, is just northwest. The city's waterfront supports both industry and recreation.

One of the best-preserved Victorian-era neighborhoods in Alabama, the Old Decatur District between the Tennessee River and Lee Street is most easily explored on a walking tour. This historic district occupies the original townsite settled in 1820. The tree-lined neighborhood contains late 19th-century houses, shops and the restored 1833 Old State Bank *(see attraction listing)*, which survived the Civil War.

Equally interesting is the Albany Heritage District north of Delano Park on US 31. Once known as the new Chicago of the South because of its development by Northern industrialists, this Victorian neighborhood enjoyed a boom period prior to the yellow fever epidemic. Fine examples of Queen Anne, Shingle and Eastlake architectural styles are concentrated along Gordon Drive and Sherman and Jackson streets. Several of the houses in both historic districts are open during the Christmas Tour of Homes in early December.

Decatur/Morgan County Convention and Visitors Bureau: 719 6th Ave. S.E., P.O. Box 2349, Decatur, AL 35602; phone (256) 350-2028 or (800) 524-6181.

Self-guiding tours: Maps outlining walking tours through Old Decatur and the Albany Heritage District are distributed by the convention and visitors bureau. Also available is a brochure for a 13-block Civil War walking tour through the Old Decatur district, which includes important sites from the 1864 battle for Decatur.

COOK'S NATURAL SCIENCE MUSEUM, 412 13th St. S.E., contains displays of mounted wildlife, an extensive insect exhibit, live snakes, shells, coral, and a rock and mineral collection. Wildlife films are shown in the auditorium. Allow 1 hour minimum. Mon.-Sat. 9-noon and 1-5, Sun. 2-5; closed Jan. 1, Thanksgiving and Dec. 24-25. Free. Phone (256) 350-9347.

THE OLD STATE BANK, 925 Bank St. N.E., opened in 1833 as a branch of the Alabama state bank system. During the Civil War the building served as a military hospital and guardhouse. Guided tours are available. Allow 30 minutes minimum. Mon.-Fri. 9:30-noon and 1:30-4:30; closed major holidays. Free. Phone (256) 350-5060.

POINT MALLARD PARK, at the e. end of 8th St. S.E., is a 500-acre recreation park on the Tennessee River featuring an aquatic center with a wave pool, an Olympic-size diving pool, a waterslide, a flume ride, a duck pond and a beach. Other facilities include lighted tennis courts, a playground, a recreation center, 25-acre campground, nature and bicycle trails, an 18-hole championship golf course and a year-round ice skating complex.

Grounds daily 24 hours. Aquatic center daily 10-6 (also Tues. and Thurs. 6-9 p.m.), Memorial Day weekend-Labor Day. Park free. Aquatic center $15; ages 5-11, $10. MC, VI. Phone (256) 341-4900. *See Recreation Chart and the AAA Southeastern CampBook.*

WHEELER NATIONAL WILDLIFE REFUGE occupies approximately 34,500 acres surrounding the middle third of Wheeler Reservoir, between the cities of Decatur and Huntsville. The refuge, one of Alabama's largest and oldest, attracts a variety of migratory waterfowl. Habitats include pine uplands, mud flats, tupelo swamps, bottomland hardwoods and agricultural fields. The Wildlife Visitor Center, on SR 67 between Decatur and I-65, offers displays about conservation and the Tennessee River. Nature trails are available.

Boating, fishing, hunting and picnicking are permitted. Hunting permits are available at the visitor center. Daily 9-5, Oct.-Feb.; Tues.-Sat. 9-4, rest of year. Free. Phone (256) 350-6639.

DEMOPOLIS (D-2) pop. 7,540, elev. 117′

A small band of Napoleonic exiles founded Demopolis (dem-AH-po-lis), "city of the people," in 1817. They optimistically attempted to establish vineyards and olive groves, but being unaccustomed to farming, the French Emigrants for the Cultivation of the Vine and Olive soon deserted the four townships Congress had granted them.

In the 1820s American planters settled on the banks of the Tombigbee River and launched the era of the Black Belt's cotton prosperity. Although cotton continues its reign, the products of cattle ranches, dairy farms and soybean fields also contribute to the area's economy.

Demopolis Area Chamber of Commerce: 102 E. Washington St., P.O. Box 667, Demopolis, AL 36732; phone (334) 289-0270.

BLUFF HALL, overlooking the Tombigbee River at 405 Commissioners Ave., exemplifies two major architectural trends in the antebellum South. Built in 1832 as a Federal townhouse, the brick structure was later remodeled in Greek Revival style when a colonnaded portico, a large rear wing and a louvered gallery were added.

The restored house contains period clothing, Empire and Victorian furniture and local history displays. Tours are offered Tues.-Sat. 10-5, Sun. 2-5, Mar.-Dec.; Tues.-Sat. 10-4, Sun. 2-4, rest of year. Closed Jan. 1, July 4, Thanksgiving and Dec. 25. Admission $5; students with ID, $4; ages 6-18, $3. MC, VI. Phone (334) 289-9644.

SAVE **GAINESWOOD,** at 805 S. Cedar Ave., is a historic mansion featuring original furnishings, domed ceilings and fluted columns. Built in 1821 as a dogtrot cabin, the house gradually grew to more than 6,200 square feet as Gaineswood became the center of a cotton plantation in the mid-1800s. Altered and modified in the century following the Civil War, the property has been restored to its 1860s appearance by the Alabama Historical Commission.

Allow 30 minutes minimum. Guided tours are given on the hour Tues.-Fri. 9-4. Other times are available by appointment; phone ahead. Closed state holidays. Last tour begins 1 hour before closing. Admission $5; ages 6-18, $3. Phone (334) 289-4846.

DOTHAN (E-5) pop. 57,737, elev. 355'

When the railroad came to Dothan (DO-thin) in 1889, the rustic settlement was populated only by rowdy lumberjacks and turpentine workers. By 1910 mechanized farming brought new economic vigor to the rolling terrain of Wiregrass country.

Almost equidistant from Atlanta, Birmingham, Mobile and Tallahassee, Fla., modern Dothan is a natural marketing center involved in the cultivation of peanuts.

Part of Alabama's Robert Trent Jones Golf Trail, Highland Oaks Golf Course, 800 Royal Pkwy., offers a choice of four nine-hole courses.

Lawn and garden tours are the focus of the Dothan Azalea Trail, held in April. Noteworthy historic attractions in town include the Dothan Opera House, built as a city auditorium in 1915. People, places and events prominent in Dothan's history are spotlighted courtesy of a series of 14 murals painted on buildings in the city's historic downtown area.

Robert Trent Jones Golf Trail

Alabama's Robert Trent Jones Golf Trail features a network of 432 holes at ten facilities stretching from north Alabama to the Gulf of Mexico. All the courses along the golf trail were designed by golf course architect Robert Trent Jones Sr., and each was intended to give golfers a challenging experience in country-club elegance at public course prices.

© Michael Clemmer Golf Landscape Photography

Most facilities include two 18-hole championship courses or three nine-hole championship courses, in addition to an 18- or nine-hole (respectively) short course. The course at Capitol Hill has three championship 18-hole courses, while the Ross Bridge in Hoover has one 18-hole course covering 330 acres, making it the third-longest course in the world.

Sites include Oxmoor Valley in Birmingham, (205) 942-1177; Ross Bridge in Hoover, (205) 949-3085; Hampton Cove in Huntsville, (256) 551-1818; Magnolia Grove in Mobile, (251) 645-0075; The Shoals in Muscle Shoals, (256) 446-5111; Grand National in Auburn/Opelika, (334) 749-9042; Highland Oaks in Dothan, (334) 712-2820; Cambrian Ridge in Greenville, (334) 382-9787; Capitol Hill in Prattville, (334) 285-1114; and Silver Lakes in Calhoun County, (256) 892-3268.

Fees at each course range $35-$67 for 18 holes ($15 for the 18-hole short course), or $7.50 for the nine-hole short course. Cart rentals are $15 per person.

For additional information, to verify rates or to reserve a tee time phone (800) 949-4444.

Dothan Area Convention & Visitors Bureau: 3311 Ross Clark Cir., P.O. Box 8765, Dothan, AL 36304; phone (334) 794-6622 or (888) 449-0212.

Shopping areas: Wiregrass Commons, with Dillard's, JCPenney and Parisian, is a major mall in the Ross Clark Circle area off US 231.

SAVE **LANDMARK PARK** is 3 mi. n. of Ross Clark Cir. on US 431. This 100-acre living-history park includes a restored 1895 house and a late 19th-century farm complete with farm animals, a sugar cane mill and smokehouse. Also featured are a 1908 church, a schoolhouse, a general store, a drugstore, a doctor's office and a marsh containing native wildlife. An interpretive center offers planetarium shows, nature displays and art exhibits.

Special events are held throughout the year. Picnicking is permitted. Mon.-Sat. 9-5, Sun. noon-6; closed Jan. 1, Thanksgiving and Dec. 25. Planetarium shows are offered Sat. at 11, 1 and 3, Sun. at 1 and 3. Shows are not recommended for under 4. Park admission $3; ages 4-15, $2. Planetarium $1. MC, VI. Phone (334) 794-3452. *See color ad starting on p. 40.*

WATER WORLD, 1 blk. w. of Ross Clark Cir. in Westgate Park, has a wave pool, waterslides, a children's pool, a video arcade and a children's play area. Picnic facilities and food are available. Only persons wearing swimsuits are allowed in the water. Mon.-Fri. 10-6 (also Tues. and Thurs. 6-9 p.m.), Sat. 10-7, Sun. noon-7, Memorial Day weekend-last weekend in Aug.; schedule varies May 1-day before Memorial Day weekend and in Sept. Ages 13-59, $10; ages 3-12, $7; over 59 free; half-price to all Tues. and Thurs. 5-9. Tube rentals $2. MC, VI. Phone (334) 615-3750.

WIREGRASS MUSEUM OF ART is at 126 Museum Ave., off US 84E just e. of the civic center. The museum has seven galleries with changing exhibits that feature national and regional decorative arts. A children's area with hands-on activities is featured. Lectures and seminars are offered periodically. Allow 1 hour minimum. Tues.-Sat. 10-5 (also some Sun. 1-5 for special events); closed major holidays. Donations. Phone (334) 794-3871.

ENTERPRISE (E-4) pop. 21,178, elev. 349′

Enterprise's economy was at a standstill in 1915 after the voracious, snouted boll weevil arrived in Coffee County from Mexico. The half-inch beetle systematically began destroying the area's cotton crop, the sole base of Coffee County's economy. Though farmers bombarded the insect with chemicals and poisons, it succeeded in reducing the crop to one-tenth its usual size.

Out of necessity farmers planted a number of cash crops. Included among them were peanuts, which flourished. The transition to diversified farming was so successful that the town is credited with playing a significant role in the agricultural revolution of the South. The gate city to Fort Rucker Military Reservation *(see place listing p. 60)*, Enterprise today is a blend of agriculture, industry and military interests.

Enterprise Chamber of Commerce: 553 Glover Ave., P.O. Box 310577, Enterprise, AL 36331; phone (334) 347-0581 or (800) 235-4730.

BOLL WEEVIL MONUMENT, in the center of town, may well be the country's only tribute to an insect. Erected in 1919, it memorializes the destructive beetle that crippled cotton farming throughout the South. The resulting economic shift from agriculture to industry ushered in a new era. An inscription on the statue reads, "In profound appreciation of the Boll Weevil and what it has done as the herald of prosperity."

EUFAULA (D-5) pop. 13,908, elev. 200′

Antebellum houses are the hallmark of Eufaula, named after a tribe of the Creek Confederacy that lived in the region. The Seth Lore Historic District contains 19th-century structures embodying Greek Revival, Italianate and Victorian styles. Many can be seen during the Pilgrimage of Homes held every spring.

Fishing, boating and water skiing are enjoyed on Lake Eufaula, formed by the Walter F. George Lock and Dam on the Chattahoochee River.

Eufaula-Barbour County Chamber of Commerce: 333 E. Broad St., Eufaula, AL 36027; phone (334) 687-6664 or (800) 524-7529.

Self-guiding tours: Driving-tour maps that highlight Eufaula's outstanding antebellum houses as well as information about the Pilgrimage of Homes are available at the Shorter Mansion *(see attraction listing)* and the chamber of commerce.

EUFAULA NATIONAL WILDLIFE REFUGE, 7 mi. n. on US 431, then 2 mi. e. on SR 165, is an 11,184-acre refuge on the Chattahoochee River that provides a feeding and resting habitat for migratory waterfowl. It contains more than 280 species of birds, including ducks, geese, egrets and herons. Woodland mammals include beavers, foxes, deer and bobcats. The refuge has a nature trail and two observation towers as well as nature displays in the administrative office.

Refuge daily dawn-dusk. Office Mon.-Fri. 8-4:30; closed holidays. Free. Phone (334) 687-4065.

SAVE **FENDALL HALL** is 1 mi. w. off US 231 at 917 W. Barbour St. Built around 1860, the Italianate-style Fendall Hall was home to four generations of the Young family. Now a house museum, the structure has been restored to depict the 1880-1916 period. Highlights include hand-painted murals in three of the first-floor rooms, a black and white marble entrance floor and Italian marble fireplaces.

Guided tours are available. Allow 30 minutes minimum. Mon.-Tues. and Thurs.-Sat. 10-4; closed state holidays. Admission $5; ages 6-18, $3. Phone (334) 687-8469.

SAVE **SHORTER MANSION,** on US 431 at 340 N. Eufaula Ave., is an outstanding example of neoclassic architecture. Built in 1884 by wealthy cotton planter Eli Sims Shorter II, the mansion was enlarged and completed in 1906. The restored house is furnished with antiques. Mon.-Sat. 10-4 (Central Time); closed Jan. 1, Memorial Day, July 4, Labor Day, Thanksgiving and Dec. 24-25. Admission $5; ages 5-12, $3. Phone (334) 687-3793 or (888) 383-2852.

FAIRHOPE (F-2) pop. 12,480, elev. 125′

Founded upon utopian ideals, Fairhope was established in 1894 by Henry George and several families who funded the colony with a Single Tax System. Under the plan, residents hold a renewable 99-year lease on their land and own all improvements. The single tax colony pays all taxes. Civic pride and idealism still prevail as evidenced by the city's attractively landscaped streets and profusion of flowering gardens. An artistic migration accounts for the resort's many unusual downtown shops, galleries and restaurants.

On a bluff above Mobile Bay, Fairhope's 2 miles of beach are the setting for local yachting competitions in the summer. Flounder, crab and shrimp can be caught easily during Jubilee, Mobile Bay's natural late-summer phenomenon in which bottom-dwelling marine life, delirious because of a sudden lack of oxygen in the water, head toward the shore. When alarms sound, every available bucket, cooking pot and washbasin is enlisted to harvest this seafood bonanza.

At the marina, the Fairhope Pier extends a quarter of a mile into the bay, providing good fishing and panoramic views of the surrounding area. Although the structure was damaged in the 2004 and 2005 hurricane seasons, repairs were expected to be complete by mid-summer of 2006.

Eastern Shore Chamber of Commerce & Visitor Center—Fairhope: 327 Fairhope Ave., P.O. Box 310, Fairhope, AL 36532; phone (251) 928-6387 or (251) 621-8222.

Shopping areas: Downtown Fairhope features art galleries and numerous antique, book, craft, clothing and gift shops.

EASTERN SHORE ART CENTER, 401 Oak St., has four galleries presenting exhibits that change monthly. Displays include paintings, photographs, sculpture, pottery, baskets and canvas art. Visitors also can view artists working in the center's fine arts academy classes. Allow 30 minutes minimum. Mon.-Fri. 10-4, Sat. 10-2; closed federal holidays. Free. Phone (251) 928-2228.

WEEKS BAY NATIONAL ESTUARINE RESEARCH RESERVE, 14 mi. e. on US 98 to 11300 US 98, is a 3,028-acre estuary providing a rich, diverse habitat for a variety of fish and crustaceans. Its broad, shallow waters are fed by tributaries branching off from Mobile and Weeks bays. An interpretive center displays a collection of regional plants and live animals. Self-guiding nature trails wind through wetlands, marshes and forests.

Guided tours are available. Allow 1 hour minimum. Mon.-Sat. 9-5, Sun. 1-5; interpretive center closed state and federal holidays. Free. Phone (251) 928-9792.

FLORENCE (A-2) pop. 36,264, elev. 580′

Florence is the largest of the four cities in the Muscle Shoals area *(see place listing p. 73)*. Incorporated in 1818—a year before Alabama became a state—Florence began as a trading post on a westbound stagecoach route.

Ferdinand Sannoner, an Italian engineer commissioned to design the new city, named it after his birthplace in Italy. Florence's parks and plazas express Sannoner's vision while accommodating an expanding industrial base. Major electrometallurgical and aluminum-, rubber- and steel-fabricating plants are in the area.

Wilson Dam, east of Florence on SR 133, possesses one of the world's highest single-lift navigation locks, which lift commercial and pleasure boats up to 100 feet in a single operation. Under Tennessee Valley Authority (TVA) control since 1933, the dam, 4,541 feet long and 137 feet high, also boasts the largest hydroelectric generating capacity of all the TVA dams.

Oscar DePriest, the first African-American man to serve in Congress, and William C. Handy, famed blues composer, were born in Florence. Handy earned the title "Father of the Blues" through such compositions as "St. Louis Blues" and "Memphis Blues." Handy is honored by jazz and blues artists during the 7-day W.C. Handy Festival, held in late July.

Florence/Lauderdale Tourism Office: One Hightower Pl., Florence, AL 35630; phone (256) 740-4141 or (888) 356-8687.

Shopping areas: Florence's leading retail center is Regency Square Mall, 1.25 miles west of US 43. It has Dillard's, JCPenney, Parisian and Sears.

SAVE **CHILDREN'S MUSEUM OF THE SHOALS** is at 2810 Darby Dr. at the entrance to Diebert Park; from jct. SRs 133 and 72 continue n. on SR 133 then go w. on Darby Dr. The hands-on exhibits, mainly about the local area, encourage young visitors to learn using their imaginations and creativity. On the grounds are a playground and walking trails. Picnicking is permitted. Allow 2 hours minimum. Tues.-Sat. 10-5; closed major holidays. Admission $4; under 2 free. MC, VI. Phone (256) 765-0500.

GEM **FRANK LLOYD WRIGHT ROSENBAUM HOUSE MUSEUM** is at 601 Riverview Dr.; take Hicks Blvd. to Riverview Dr. Houses in Frank Lloyd Wright's Usonian genre were designed to provide low-cost yet elegant suburban homes for individual middle income families, homes that would grow and evolve as the family grew and evolved. The flat, multilevel roof and overhanging eaves, the board-and-batten walls, the expanses of glass, the flowing space and the hot-water heating system embedded in the concrete floor are Usonian hallmarks.

Originally 1,540 square feet, the cypress, glass and brick Rosenbaum house was completed in 1940; two Wright-designed wings, totaling 1,080 square feet, were added in 1948. The Rosenbaums lived in the house until 1999 when the city purchased it and its Wright-designed furniture, and began a meticulous restoration.

Allow 1 hour minimum. Guided tours as needed Tues.-Sat. 10-4; closed major holidays. Last tour leaves 30 minutes before closing. Fee $8, over 62 and students with ID $5. Phone (256) 740-8899.

INDIAN MOUND AND MUSEUM, 1028 S. Court St., is one of the largest domiciliary Indian mounds in the Tennessee Valley. The pre-Columbian mound measures 43 feet high with a summit that is 145 feet by 94 feet. A museum features 10,000-year-old artifacts. Guided 30-minute tours are available. Tues.-Sat. 10-4; closed major holidays. Admission $2, students with ID 50c. Phone (256) 760-6427.

POPE'S TAVERN MUSEUM, 203 Hermitage Dr., was a stagecoach stop and inn during the early 1800s and later a hospital for Confederate and Union soldiers during the Civil War. The museum has Civil War memorabilia and rare antiques. Guided tours are available. Allow 30 minutes minimum. Tues.-Sat. 10-4; closed major holidays. Admission $2, students with ID 50c. Phone (256) 760-6439.

W.C. HANDY HOME AND MUSEUM, 620 W. College St. at Marengo St., is the birthplace of composer and musician William C. Handy. Known as "Father of the Blues," Handy was born in the log cabin on Nov. 16, 1873. The house contains his piano, trumpet, memorabilia and tributes from renowned people. Guided tours are available. Allow 30 minutes minimum. Tues.-Sat. 10-4; closed major holidays. Admission $2; under 18, 50c. Phone (256) 760-6434.

FORT MORGAN STATE HISTORIC SITE—*see Gulf Shores p. 62.*

FORT PAYNE (B-5) pop. 12,938, elev. 897′

Fort Payne is associated with interesting geological formations and American Indian history, the latter embodied in the nearby Cherokee town of Willston, established in 1779. The town of Fort Payne was established in the late 19th century around the stockade that held the Cherokees prior to their forced westward migration on the Trail of Tears.

Fort Payne's Opera House, in the center of town, was built in 1889 and is the oldest active theater in Alabama. Restored as a cultural arts center, the opera house can be toured by appointment.

South of town, Little River Canyon National Preserve's 14,000 acres offer recreational opportunities to suit most any taste. Kayaking, picnicking, rock climbing, bird-watching, mountain biking, hiking, swimming and canoeing are among the outdoor pursuits to be enjoyed. The Little River, which flows atop Lookout Mountain, has created waterfalls, canyons and sandstone cliffs, all of which can be appreciated from numerous overlooks along a scenic rim drive. DeSoto State Park *(see attraction listing)* is within the preserve. For additional information contact the preserve's headquarters at 2141 Gault Ave. N.; phone (256) 845-9605.

DeKalb County Tourist Association: 1503 Glenn Blvd. S.W., P.O. Box 681165, Fort Payne, AL 35968; phone (256) 845-3957 or (888) 805-4740.

ALABAMA FAN CLUB AND MUSEUM, 101 Glenn Blvd., is at jct. SR 35 and US 11, 1 mi. e. of I-59 exit 218. The museum traces the career of the country music band Alabama and displays costumes, musical instruments and awards, including the group's gold and platinum records. Allow 30 minutes minimum. Mon.-Sat. 8-4:30, Sun. noon-4:30. Admission $3; over 55, $2; under 12, $1.50. AX, DS, MC, VI. Phone (256) 845-1646.

DEPOT MUSEUM, off US 11 at 105 5th St. N.E., is in an 1891 Richardsonian Romanesque-style railroad depot. Exhibits include American Indian artifacts, 19th-century farm and office equipment, photographs and household items from the late 1800s and early 1900s, a caboose and more than 90 dioramas depicting nursery rhymes and historic events. Allow 30 minutes minimum. Mon., Wed. and Fri. 10-4, Sun. 2-4; closed major holidays. Donations. Phone (256) 845-5714.

DeSOTO STATE PARK is off I-59, 8 mi. n.e. The range known as Lookout Mountain runs through the park, which is situated along the Little River Canyon, one of the deepest canyons east of the Mississippi. Also within the park is DeSoto Falls, which drops 100 feet. Hiking and nature trails extend throughout the park. A swimming pool operates Memorial Day through Labor Day. Lookout Mountain Trail, a scenic road with overlooks, follows the west rim for 20 miles.

Picnicking is permitted. Camping is permitted. Food is available. Daily 7 a.m.-dusk. Park free. Picnic area $1 per person. Swimming pool $2. Phone (256) 845-5380 or (800) 568-8840. *See Recreation Chart and the AAA Southeastern CampBook.*

FORT RUCKER MILITARY RESERVATION (E-4) pop. 6,052

U.S. ARMY AVIATION MUSEUM is on SR 249, 10 mi. s. of US 231 at the Fort Rucker Army Post, Building 6000. The museum contains an extensive collection of U.S. Army aircraft, with emphasis on the evolution of the helicopter. Many one-of-a-kind planes are displayed.

Exhibits include an R4-B, the first military production helicopter; an AH-64 Apache combat helicopter; and several World War I aircraft. Allow 1 hour, 30 minutes minimum. Mon.-Sat. 9-4, Sun. noon-4; closed Jan. 1, Thanksgiving and Dec. 24-25 and 31. Free. Phone (334) 255-2893 or (888) 276-9286.

GADSDEN (B-4) pop. 38,978, elev. 558′

This town in the foothills of Lookout Mountain is one of Alabama's largest industrial centers. Industry began to flourish in Gadsden as early as 1895, not long after William P. Lay built an electrical plant in hopes of enticing investors into the area. Today local industries produce steel, rubber, fabricated metal, electrical equipment and electronic devices.

Gadsden Chamber of Commerce: One Commerce Sq., P.O. Box 185, Gadsden, AL 35902; phone (256) 543-3472.

Shopping areas: Nineteen miles north of town on US 431 is the Boaz Outlet complex, a factory outlet mall with stores selling Gap, Polo/Ralph Lauren, Tommy Hilfiger, Vanity Fair and other name-brand products at discounted prices. Colonial Mall of Gadsden, on US 411, contains McRae's, Sears and many smaller stores.

EMMA SANSOM MONUMENT, First and Broad sts., is a memorial to the 15-year-old Alabama girl who guided Confederate Gen. Nathan Bedford Forrest as he pursued 2,000 Federal troops. The statue depicts Emma pointing to a shortcut across Black Creek, which enabled Forrest to capture the Union forces. The night of his victory Forrest sent his "highest regards to Emma Sansom for her gallant conduct" and asked for a lock of her hair as a keepsake.

GADSDEN MUSEUM OF ART, 515 Broad St., displays a permanent collection of paintings, sculpture, decorative arts and historical artifacts. Allow 30 minutes minimum. Mon.-Fri. 10-4, Sun.-Sun. by appointment; closed holidays. Free. Phone (256) 546-7365 to verify schedule.

MARY G. HARDIN CENTER FOR CULTURAL ARTS, 501 Broad St., features exhibits by local and national artists. The Imagination Place Children's Museum has hands-on exhibits as well as a child-size city complete with a grocery store, a bank and a doctor's office. The center has a working 72-foot model railroad depicting 1940s Gadsden. Concerts are presented summer weekends.

Food is available. Allow 1 hour minimum. Mon.-Fri. 9-6 (also Tues. 6-9 p.m.), Sat. 10-6, Sun. 1-5. Children's museum Mon.-Fri. 9-5, Sat. 10-5, Sun. 1-5. Closed Jan. 1, Easter, July 4, Labor Day, Thanksgiving and Dec. 25. Admission $3; ages 2-12, $2. Phone (256) 543-2787.

NOCCALULA FALLS PARK is 2.5 mi. n. of the business district and 2 mi. e. from I-59. Creek waters plummet 95 feet from a limestone ledge within the park. Highlights include a covered bridge, botanical garden and a pioneer village of split-log buildings, complete with accessories. A petting zoo

Spanish Moss

It's not Spanish and it's not moss; it is uniquely American and related to the pineapple. Spanish moss, the silver-green tresses that adorn trees from North Carolina to South America, is one of nature's more picturesque oddities.

Spanish moss is not a parasite but an epiphyte, a type of plant that has no roots but lives off moisture in the atmosphere. Tiny scales on the moss's tendrils trap rain for easy absorption and also keep internal moisture from evaporating. The plants are nourished by mineral-rich cells that wash off the host tree; the greater the number of cells, the more prolific the moss, which is why masses of moss are often found on very old or decaying trees. Also called long moss or vegetable horsehair, Spanish moss covers more trees than any other type of epiphyte. It does not bear fruit like its spiny distant cousin the pineapple, but it sometimes produces small yellow flowers.

Digital Archives

Spanish moss stems can grow as long as 25 feet, with threadlike leaves 1 to 3 inches long sprouting from them. Primarily decorative, the moss sometimes is used as packing material and upholstery stuffing.

and animal habitat house also are available. A 1-mile train ride departs from the park's train station, passing the falls en route to the pioneer village.

Picnicking is permitted. Park and amenities open daily 9 a.m.-dusk, Mar.-Oct. Christmas on the Rocks light display open daily 5-9 p.m., day after Thanksgiving-Jan. 1. Park free. Combined admission for garden, village, petting zoo, animal habitat and train ride $6; over 54, $4; ages 4-12, $3. Phone (256) 549-4663.

GREENSBORO (C-3) pop. 2,731, elev. 220′

MAGNOLIA GROVE HISTORIC HOUSE MUSEUM is at 1002 Hobson St., at the w. end of Greensboro's historic district at Main St. and US 14. This two-story Greek Revival structure was built about 1840 by the wealthy planter Col. Isaac Croom and later was the boyhood home of Croom's nephew, Richmond Pearson Hobson, a hero of the Spanish-American War. The house is furnished with original pieces belonging to the Croom and Hobson families.

Allow 30 minutes minimum. Mon.-Fri. (also first and third Sat. of the month) 10-4; closed state holidays. Admission $5; senior citizens, students and military with ID $4; ages 6-18, $3. Phone (334) 624-8618.

GULF SHORES (F-3) pop. 5,044, elev. 2′

Since its connection to the mainland by the Intracoastal Waterway in 1933, Gulf Shores on the Gulf of Mexico's Pleasure Island has attracted vacationers with its beaches, excellent fishing and scenic golf courses. This area was nearly destroyed by Hurricane Frederick in 1979 when 100 mph winds flattened sand dunes and caused more than $2 billion in damage.

Gulf Shores recovered, however, and once again boasts resort facilities as well as offering sailing, parasailing, swimming and fishing in the waters of the Gulf. Charter boat fishing can be arranged at Orange Beach. The Alabama Gulf Coast Convention and Visitors Bureau visitor information office in Orange Beach is at 23685 Perdido Beach Blvd.

Alabama Gulf Coast Convention and Visitors Bureau: 3150 Gulf Shores Pkwy., P.O. Box 457, Gulf Shores, AL 36547; phone (251) 974-1510 or (800) 745-7263.

Shopping areas: More than 120 factory outlet stores, including Banana Republic, Brooks Brothers, Gap Outlet, Polo/Ralph Lauren, Seiko and Tommy Hilfiger, comprise Riviera Centre Factory Stores, on SR 59 south of nearby Foley.

BON SECOUR NATIONAL WILDLIFE REFUGE, 8 mi. w. of SR 59 on SR 180, consists of 6,700 acres of coastal land with geographic features ranging from sand dunes to woodlands. Many types of wildlife, including some endangered species, can be seen. Nature and hiking trails are available. Pets are not permitted. Daily dawn-dusk. Office Mon.-Fri. 7-3:30. Closed holidays. Free. Phone (251) 540-7720.

FORT MORGAN STATE HISTORIC SITE, 21 mi. w. on SR 180 at the entrance to Mobile Bay, shared strategic importance with Fort Gaines *(see Dauphin Island p. 56)* during the Civil War. After a 14-day siege in 1864, this Confederate stronghold surrendered following the Battle of Mobile Bay. The fort was reactivated during the Spanish-American War and World Wars I and II. A museum and artillery pieces also are featured. Ferry service links Fort Morgan to Dauphin Island. Brochures for walking tours are available.

Allow 1 hour minimum. Fort daily 8-7, June-Sept.; 8-6, Mar.-May; 8-5, rest of year. Museum daily 9-5. Closed Jan. 1, Thanksgiving and Dec. 25. Admission $5; ages 6-18, $3. Phone (251) 540-7127.

HORSESHOE BEND NATIONAL MILITARY PARK (C-5)

Twelve miles north of Dadeville on SR 49, the 2,040-acre Horseshoe Bend National Military Park commemorates Andrew Jackson's decisive victory over the Creek Nation. The battle broke the Indian nation's power and ended the Creek War of 1813-14.

In August 1813 hostilities between the Upper Creek Indians and frontiersmen erupted with a massacre at Fort Mims in which 250 men, women and children died. On March 27, 1814, Jackson's force of Tennessee Militia, Regular U.S. Infantry and Lower Creek and Cherokee allies destroyed Chief Menawa's Red Stick band. The Indians had gathered in the "horseshoe bend" of the Tallapoosa River to defend their lands. The victory opened much of central Alabama and southern Georgia to settlement and gave Jackson national fame.

Creek Indian history and military weapons are among the exhibits in the park museum; a 10-minute slide presentation about the conflict is presented. Six stops along a 3-mile road through the battlefield interpret the encounter. A 2.8-mile nature trail also offers views of the battlefield. Museum daily 9-4:30; battlefield road daily 8-5. Closed Jan. 1, Thanksgiving and Dec. 25. Free. Phone (256) 234-7111. *See Recreation Chart.*

HUNTSVILLE (A-3) pop. 158,216, elev. 750′

Huntsville was the site of the first English-speaking settlement in Alabama. In 1819 the first constitutional convention and state legislature met in Huntsville, and Alabama became the 22nd state of the Union.

The nation's space program began in Huntsville in 1950. Spearheaded by the development of the Saturn V moon rocket by Dr. Wernher von Braun and his team of German scientists, space technology and exploration have gained increasing momentum through the advances made at the NASA George C. Marshall Space Flight Center, established in 1960.

Originally created to design NASA's rocket propulsion systems, the Marshall Center later became involved in all aspects of the space program, including research in microgravity as well as spacecraft and experimental research and development. The Marshall Center developed the engines and rockets used to launch the space shuttle.

The Tennessee River and its many adjoining lakes provide a variety of recreational opportunities, including water skiing and fishing. A number of parks beautify downtown and the environs.

Big Spring International Park, west of Courthouse Square, is on the site where John Hunt founded the city in 1805. It also is the location of the Fearn Canal, which was used in the 19th century to transport cotton to the river. Throughout the park are gifts from foreign countries; of special interest is a sculptured bridge from Japan. Various festivals are held in the park throughout the year.

The Madison County Nature Trail, 12 miles from downtown on Green Mountain, includes a 16-acre lake, a covered bridge and a wildlife sanctuary.

The Twickenham Historic District, downtown and south and east of Courthouse Square, is one of Alabama's largest antebellum residential districts. Descendants of the original owners live in many of the houses. The district is a living museum of 19th-century architecture. Guided walking tours of Twickenham are provided by the convention and visitors bureau on Saturday during the summer months.

The Old Town Historic District, east and north of Courthouse Square, contains 19th- and early 20th-century houses, some still in the process of restoration. Restored bungalows dominate the Five Points Historic District.

The Huntsville Pilgrimage, held the first weekend in May, offers a tour of some of the city's most beautiful and historically interesting residences. Additional information can be obtained from the Huntsville Pilgrimage Association, 500 Church St., Huntsville, AL 35801; phone (256) 533-5723.

Huntsville/Madison County Convention and Visitors Bureau: 500 Church St., Huntsville, AL 35801; phone (256) 551-2370 or (800) 772-2348. *See color ad.*

Self-guiding tours: Maps outlining tours of Huntsville's three historic areas and brochures detailing points of interest in the city and county are available from the convention and visitors bureau.

Shopping areas: More than 120 stores, including Belk, Dillard's, JCPenney, Parisian and Sears, offer opportunities for browsing and bargain hunting at Madison Square Mall, US 72W at Research Park Boulevard. Parkway Place, at Bob Wallace and Drake avenues, includes Dillard's and Parisian.

In high-tech Huntsville the Historic Huntsville Foundation operates Harrison Brothers Hardware at 124 South Side Sq. Established in 1879 and moved to this site in 1897, clerks at this old-fashioned hardware store ring sales of vintage tools, housewares and other items on a hand-cranked cash register.

For the more adventurous or thrifty, the Unclaimed Baggage Center, 30 miles away at 509 West Willow St. in Scottsboro, is open Monday through Friday 9-6 and Saturday 8-6 CST. Their merchandise consists of unclaimed cargo and the contents of unclaimed luggage, and ranges through nearly everything that can be packed in baggage or shipped by air. The building covers a city block.

ALABAMA CONSTITUTION VILLAGE, 109 Gates Ave., marks the site of the 1819 constitutional convention by which Alabama entered the Union. Eight reconstructed buildings depict Southern life in the early 1800s. Costumed guides demonstrate crafts and domestic skills typical of 19th-century Alabama.

Allow 1 hour minimum. Wed.-Sat. 10-4, Mar.-Oct.; daily 5-9 p.m., day after Thanksgiving-Dec. 22. Admission $7; over 54 and ages 4-17, $6. Combination tickets with EarlyWorks Children's Museum and Historic Huntsville Depot are available. MC, VI. Phone (256) 564-8100.

BURRITT ON THE MOUNTAIN—A LIVING MUSEUM, atop Round Top Mountain at 3101 Burritt Dr., features an 11-room mansion containing antique furnishings, archeological artifacts, a rock and mineral display and exhibits about local history. A historic park contains restored 19th-century rural homes furnished in period. Nature trails also are offered.

Picnicking is permitted. Allow 1 hour minimum. Tues.-Sat. 9-5, Sun. noon-5, Apr.-Oct.; Tues.-Sat. 10-4, Sun. noon-4, rest of year. Closed Jan. 1, Thanksgiving and Dec. 24-25. Last admission is 30 minutes before closing. Admission $5; senior citizens, military and students with ID $4; ages 2-12, $3. Additional fees may apply during special events. MC, VI. Phone (256) 536-2882.

EARLYWORKS CHILDREN'S MUSEUM is downtown at 404 Madison St. A film, narrated by native Alabamian Bo Jackson, serves as an introduction to this interactive museum. Visitors explore Southern history and learn about the people, agriculture, mining and politics. Children can hear stories from a talking tree, try on 19th-century clothing, explore a 46-foot keel boat and turn the handle on a cotton gin to separate seeds from the bolls.

Allow 1 hour minimum. Tues.-Sat. 9-4; closed Jan. 1, Thanksgiving and Dec. 24-25. Admission $10; over 54 and ages 4-17, $8; ages 1-3, $4. Combination tickets with Alabama Constitution Village and Historic Huntsville Depot are available. MC, VI. Phone (256) 564-8100.

HISTORIC HUNTSVILLE DEPOT is at 320 Church St.. Highlights include an extensive collection of locomotives and railway cars, a multimedia presentation about railroad history and an HO model train exhibit. After Union forces captured the building in 1862, it served as a military prison. Graffiti scratched into the building's walls by Confederate and Union soldiers still are visible. Life-size robotic figures tell about 1912 railroad operations.

Wed.-Sat. 10-4, Mar.-Dec.; closed Thanksgiving and Dec. 24-25. Admission $7; senior citizens and ages 4-17, $6. Combination tickets with Alabama Constitution Village and EarlyWorks Children's Museum are available. MC, VI. Phone (256) 564-8100.

HUNTSVILLE BOTANICAL GARDEN, off I-565 exit 15 then .5 mi. e. to 4747 Bob Wallace Ave., offers 112 acres of year-round gardens including perennials, day lilies, roses, wildflowers, ferns, herbs, vegetables and aquatic plants. Constitution Walk offers a reflection pond encircled by red maples planted in honor of the nation's founders. Also on the grounds is a garden to children and the Tessmann Butterfly House, open May through September. Seasonal festivals are held throughout the year.

Picnicking is permitted. Allow 1 hour minimum. Mon.-Sat. 9-8, Sun. 1-8, Memorial Day-Labor Day; Mon.-Sat. 9-5, Sun. 1-5, rest of year. Closed Jan. 1, Thanksgiving and Dec. 25. Admission $10; over 54 and military with ID $8; ages 3-18, $3. Admission may be higher during seasonal festivals. Phone (256) 830-4447.

SAVE **HUNTSVILLE MUSEUM OF ART,** downtown at 300 Church St. S. in Big Spring Park, features major traveling exhibitions and works by nationally and regionally acclaimed artists, and a gallery of works by local children. Food is available Tues.-Sun. Allow one hour minimum. Mon.-Sat. 10-5 (also Thurs. 5-8), Sun. 1-5; closed Jan. 1, Easter, Thanksgiving and Dec. 25.

Admission $7; over 60, students and military with ID $6; ages 6-11, $3. Half price to all Thurs. 5-8. MC, VI. Phone (256) 535-4350 or (800) 786-9095.

SCI-QUEST is at 102-D Wynn Dr. This hands-on learning experience explores the mysteries of science. Visitors learn about electricity, light and sound, experience an earthquake or enter a tornado chamber. The Immersive Theater presents interactive 3-D science films. Allow 1 hour minimum. Tues.-Fri. 9-4, Sat. 10-6, Sun. 1-5; closed holidays. Hours may vary; phone ahead. Last admission is 1 hour before closing.

Admission $7; over 65, $6.50; ages 3-18, $6. Combined Sci-Quest and theater admission $11.75; over 65, $11.25; ages 3-18, $10.75. Theater admission $5.75. Additional fees may apply during special events. AX, DS, MC, VI. Phone (256) 837-0606.

GEM SAVE **U.S. SPACE AND ROCKET CENTER,** One Tranquility Base just off I-565, is an exposition center featuring one of the world's largest collections of space and rocket hardware. Interactive exhibits simulate the experience of space flight, including travel aboard the space shuttle.

The Spacedome IMAX Theater presents space and science films projected on a 67-foot dome screen that surrounds viewers. Other attractions include the Mars climbing wall, Spacewalk, Space Shot, Kids' Cosmos and a G-Force accelerator. The U.S. Space Camp and Aviation Challenge adjoin the museum. The Rocket Park displays NASA rockets and Army defense missiles, including a full-scale shuttle exhibit and the Saturn V moon rocket.

Picnicking is permitted. Food is available. Daily 9-5; closed Jan. 1, Thanksgiving and Dec. 24-25 and 31. Admission (includes museum, IMAX Theater and Rocket Park) $18.95; ages 6-12, $12.95. AX, DS, MC, VI. Phone (256) 837-3400 or (800) 637-7223.

SAVE **WEEDEN HOUSE MUSEUM,** 300 Gates Ave. S.E., preserves furniture and architecture of the Federal period. Birthplace of artist-poet Maria

Howard Weeden, the 1819 house features hand-carved mantels and a leaded-glass fanlight as well as her 19th-century watercolors. Weeden's written works are read during guided tours. Allow 1 hour minimum. Tours are given Mon.-Fri. 11-4. Admission $5; under 12, $4. Phone (256) 536-7718.

WHEELER NATIONAL WILDLIFE REFUGE—*see Decatur p. 56.*

LEEDS—*see Birmingham p. 52.*

MARBURY (C-4) elev. 520'

CONFEDERATE MEMORIAL PARK, 437 CR 63, contains two of the few cemeteries dedicated exclusively to Confederate soldiers. From 1902-1939, the Old Soldiers Home operated here, giving care to elderly Confederate Civil War veterans. A museum displays Civil War uniforms, equipment and artifacts. Nature trails traverse the 102-acre park.

Picnicking is permitted. Allow 30 minutes minimum. Park daily 6 a.m.-dusk. Museum daily 9-5; closed holidays. Reservations are required for use of pavilion. Free. Phone (205) 755-1990.

McCALLA—*see Birmingham p. 52.*

MOBILE (F-2) pop. 198,915, elev. 8'

Mobile was founded in 1702 by Jean Bienville le Moyne, and was named after the Mauvilla Indians, who had a settlement on the site. A much-coveted port throughout its history, Mobile was particularly important to the Confederacy.

In 1864 the Union captured the CSS *Tennessee* in the Battle of Mobile Bay but lost the monitor *Tecumseh.* The subsequent surrender of Fort Gaines and Fort Morgan *(see Dauphin Island p. 56 and Gulf Shores p. 62)* on Mobile Point, coupled with the siege of Fort Blakely and Spanish Fort on the east side of the bay 6 months later, wore down the Confederates' resistance. Federal forces occupied Mobile on April 12, 1865. Relics of the battles are still evident.

Alabama's only seaport, Mobile is on the west side of the Mobile River near the mouth of Mobile Bay. The city's river channel, only 10 feet deep in 1826, has been dredged over the years to accommodate oceangoing vessels of 40-foot draft. The discovery of large natural gas deposits also has brought drilling rigs to the bay.

Meetings, conventions and cultural activities take place in the Mobile Municipal Auditorium, a huge waterfront civic center and entertainment complex.

Mobile's Mardi Gras, though smaller in size than the celebration in New Orleans, is said to be the original American pre-Lenten carnival. First observed in 1703 and suspended during the Civil War, the festivities have been held continually since 1866. During the 2 weeks before Lent, mystic societies parade through the streets each evening, and on the Sunday before Mardi Gras day, several thousand revelers turn out to celebrate Joe Cain Day, named for the man who revived Mardi Gras after the Civil War.

Mobile also is the site of the Senior Bowl football game in January, played by the nation's best senior collegiate football players, while the GMAC Bowl is held in December. Teenage girls from throughout the nation compete for scholarships and awards at the America's Junior Miss Pageant in June.

Bay City Convention and Tours offers historic homes tours and azalea tours in mid-March and early April as well as year-round van tours of historic Mobile. Tours depart from the Fort Condé Welcome Center; reservations are required. For additional information write Bay City Convention and Tours, P.O. Box 304, Mobile, AL 36601; phone (251) 479-9970.

Mobile Greyhound Park is 10 miles west off I-10 at the Dawes Theodore Road exit; racing season runs January through mid-December; phone (251) 653-5000.

Note: Policies concerning admittance of children to pari-mutuel betting facilities vary. Phone for information.

Mobile Bay Convention & Visitors Bureau: One S. Water St., Mobile, AL 36602; phone (251) 208-2000 or (800) 566-2453. *See color ad p. 65.*

Self-guiding tours: Mobile is most beautiful during azalea season, mid-March through early April. Fort Condé Welcome Center provides maps that show where visitors can best see azaleas in bloom; phone (800) 566-2453. Mobile's historic districts also can be seen on walking and driving tours *(see attraction listing p. 67).*

Shopping areas: Colonial Mall Bel Air at Airport Boulevard and I-65 has Dillard's, JCPenney, Parisian and Sears. Across the street is Springdale Mall, which features McRae's.

GEM **BELLINGRATH GARDENS AND HOME**—*see Theodore p. 77.*

BIENVILLE SQUARE, bounded by Dauphin, St. Joseph, St. Francis and Conception sts. in the business district, is a park planted with many live oaks and azaleas.

BRAGG-MITCHELL MANSION is 2.4 mi. e. of I-65 at 1906 Spring Hill Ave. A combination of Greek Revival and Italianate architectural styles, it is said to be one of Mobile's finest antebellum mansions. Stately oaks surrounding the house were cut down to allow Confederate artillery free range to shell Federal troops. The owner, Judge John Bragg, replanted using acorns from the original trees.

Allow 30 minutes minimum. Tues.-Fri. 10-4. Last tour begins 30 minutes before closing. Hours may vary; phone ahead. Admission $5, senior citizens $4.50, students $3, under 6 free. Phone (251) 471-6364.

CATHEDRAL OF THE IMMACULATE CONCEPTION, on Claiborne St. between Conti and Dauphin sts., is one of the oldest churches in the city. Built in 1829, it occupies the site used by Mobile's first settlers as a burial ground. Daily 8:30-3. Free. Phone (251) 434-1565.

SAVE **CONDÉ-CHARLOTTE MUSEUM HOUSE,** 104 Theatre St., is in an 1822 building that was Mobile's first jail and courthouse. The museum displays European and American furnishings from the 18th and 19th centuries. There also is a Spanish garden. Guided tours are available. Allow 30 minutes minimum. Tues.-Sat. 10-4; closed holidays. Last admission is 30 minutes before closing. Admission $5; ages 6-18, $2. Phone (251) 432-4722.

FORT CONDÉ, 150 S. Royal St. at Church St., served as an administrative and military center of the Louisiana Territory. The fort, partially restored to its 1702 appearance, was occupied successively by French, English and Spanish troops. A museum displays artifacts recovered from on-site archeological excavations. Exhibit rooms contain equipment once necessary for the fort's operation. Fort Condé also is the official welcome center for the city of Mobile.

Allow 1 hour minimum. Daily 8-5; closed major holidays. Free. Phone (251) 208-7658.

SAVE **GULF COAST EXPLOREUM SCIENCE CENTER AND IMAX DOME THEATER,** 65 Government St. at the corner of Water St., features three venues. The permanent exhibit, Hands On Hall, has 57 interactive stations that teach basic science principles. Internationally recognized traveling exhibits, updated several times each year, explore scientific themes. Science-based films are shown at the IMAX theater.

Allow 1 hour, 30 minutes minimum. Mon.-Fri. 9-5, Sat. 10-5, Sun. noon-5; closed major holidays. Hours may vary with featured exhibits; phone ahead. Science center or theater admission $7.75; over 60 and ages 13-18, $6.50; ages 2-12, $6. Combination ticket $12; over 60 and ages 13-18, $11;

ages 2-12, $9.75. Rates may increase for special exhibits. Reservations are recommended for the theater. AX, DS, MC, VI. Phone (251) 208-6873 or (877) 625-4386.

MALBIS MEMORIAL CHURCH—
see Daphne p. 55.

MOBILE BOTANICAL GARDENS is at 5151 Museum Dr. next to Langan Park; from I-65 exit 5A go 1.5 mi. w. on Springhill Ave., just s. on Pfc. John New St., then .6 mi. w. on Museum Dr. This 100-acre site contains 7 distinct areas in a woodland setting: The Herb Garden; The Founders Fragrance & Texture Garden; The Rhododendron Garden; The John Allen Smith Japanese Maple Garden; The Fern Glade; the 60-acre Longleaf Pine Forest; The Camellia Winter Garden. Picnicking is permitted. Allow 1 hour minimum. Daily dawn-dusk. Donations. Phone (251) 342-0555.

SAVE **MOBILE CARNIVAL MUSEUM** is at 355 Government St. This museum presents the history of Mobile's Mardi Gras celebration through memorabilia and interactive exhibits, including two floats. The showpiece is the extensive collection of elaborate gowns, trains, crowns and scepters of carnival royalty dating from 1921. Allow 1 hour minimum. Mon., Wed. and Fri.-Sat. 9-4; closed Jan. 1 and Dec. 25. Admission $5; under 12, $2. Phone (251) 432-3324.

MOBILE MEDICAL MUSEUM is at 1664 Springhill Ave. This collection of more than 50,000 medical artifacts dates from the late 1700s to the present. Exhibits include an apothecary, the ophthalmology collection of J. William Rosenthal, M.D., and archives documenting medical practices in the South. Guided tours are available. Allow 1 hour minimum. Mon.-Fri. 9-4; closed holidays. Admission $5, senior citizens and students with ID $4. Phone (251) 415-1109.

GEM **MOBILE MUSEUM OF ART** is off Springhill Ave. in Langan Park at 4850 Museum Dr. This art museum, one of the Gulf Coast's largest, has a permanent collection of more than 6,000 works spanning more than 2,000 years of cultural history. Exhibits include American art; Southern decorative arts and furniture; African, Asian and European art; and contemporary crafts. Touring exhibitions from other prestigious museums and collections also are presented.

Allow 1 hour minimum. Mon.-Sat. 10-5, Sun. 1-5; closed Jan. 1, Thanksgiving and Dec. 25. Admission $6; over 50, $5; students with ID $4; under 7 free. Additional fees may be charged for special exhibits. Phone (251) 208-5200.

MOBILE'S HISTORIC DISTRICTS are within a 2 mi. radius of Oakleigh Historic Complex at 300 Oakleigh Pl. The districts are a cross section of the city's architectural heritage and can be explored on self-guiding walking or driving tours designed by the Mobile Historic Development Commission. Brochures are available at most downtown hotels or the Fort Condé Welcome Center, 150 S. Royal St. at Church Street.

Church Street East, extending from Water St. to Broad St., is the city's most diverse historic district. The original structures built during Mobile's colonial French, Spanish and English eras were destroyed by fires in 1827 and 1839. Present buildings, dating from the late 19th century, represent Federal, Greek Revival, Italianate, Queen Anne and Victorian architectural styles. Tours begin at the restored City Hall, 111 S. Royal St.

De Tonti Square, 9 blks. n. of the central business area, is characterized by dignified brick townhouses, iron-lace fences, antique gaslights and flagstone sidewalks. These residences, built in the 1850s and '60s, reflect the city's prosperity as a cotton-shipping port. The resulting affluence gave rise to fashionable houses constructed in the Federal, Greek Revival, Italianate, Victorian and Gulf Coast Cottage styles.

Lower Dauphin Street Commercial District, Dauphin St. between Water and Broad sts., is the only predominantly 19th-century commercial district in Mobile. It is characterized by a high concentration of closely spaced, two- and three-story brick structures built in the Federal, Italianate, Victorian and 20th-century Revival styles. The district's eastern end features early skyscrapers and buildings dating from the 1920s and '30s.

Oakleigh Garden District, surrounding Oakleigh Mansion and Washington Sq., contains some of the city's finest late 19th-century residences. The district is characterized by architectural details that followed individual tastes rather than an adherence to strict stylistic designs. The result is a mix of newer mansions set amid modest cottages and simple houses. Government Street is known for its canopy of oaks.

Old Dauphin Way, adjacent to downtown, was one of the first preservation neighborhoods in Alabama. During the 19th century many of these Gulf Coast cottages and Victorian-style structures housed middle-class merchants. The smaller cottages were the homes of servants who worked in the grand houses along Government Street. In the district's west end are examples of the 20th-century bungalow style.

Spring Hill, about 6.5 miles w. of the waterfront, was founded in the 1820s as a wooded summer retreat far from the inner city, which was ravaged by yellow fever. Greek Revival houses dating from the 1850s can be seen. Also in this area is Spring Hill College, established in 1830 and said to be the first institution of higher learning in Alabama.

THE MUSEUM OF MOBILE is near the historic district at Government and Royal sts. Housed in an 1855 landmark building, this museum presents more than 300 years of local history and culture. Exhibits chronologically detail Mobile's development from early settlement to modern times. Destructive hurricanes, yellow fever epidemics and an 1860s explosion that nearly leveled the city also are documented. The children's Discovery Room features hands-on activities.

Guided tours are available. Allow 1 hour minimum. Mon.-Sat. 9-5, Sun. 1-5; closed major holidays. Admission $5; over 54, $4; ages 7-17, $3;. Phone (251) 208-7569.

NATIONAL AFRICAN-AMERICAN ARCHIVES & MUSEUM is at 564 Dr. Martin Luther King, Jr. Ave., in the Davis Ave. branch of the Mobile Public Library. This small museum houses biographies of African-Americans who made significant contributions to the history of the nation, such as Rosa Parks and Willie Mays. Artifacts include slavery and Civil War memorabilia. Allow 1 hour minimum. Tues.-Fri. 8-4, Sat. 10-2, Sun. by appointment; closed major holidays. Donations. Phone (251) 433-8511.

SAVE **OAKLEIGH HISTORIC COMPLEX,** 300 Oakleigh Pl., features three museums. Cox-Deasy Cottage is a raised Gulf Coast cottage typical of Mobile's 19th-century middle class. The Oakleigh Period House Museum is in an 1833 Greek Revival villa furnished with antiques of the Empire, Regency and early Victorian periods. Mardi Gras Cottage includes exhibits depicting 200 years of the celebration. Tours are conducted by costumed guides.

Allow 30 minutes minimum. Complex open Tues.-Sat. 9-3; closed Mardi Gras Day, July 4, Thanksgiving and Dec. 25. Admission $7. MC, VI. Phone (251) 432-1281.

PHOENIX FIRE MUSEUM, 203 S. Claiborne St., is in the restored home of the Phoenix Volunteer Fire Company No. 6. This building houses turn-of-the-20th-century horse-drawn steam engines and early motorized vehicles. The upstairs gallery recounts the history of the volunteer fire companies of Mobile from their organization in 1819. Allow 30 minutes minimum. Tues.-Sat. 9-5, Sun. 1-5; closed city holidays. Free. Phone (251) 208-7554.

RICHARDS DAR HOUSE, 256 N. Joachim St. in De Tonti Sq., is a restored townhouse built in 1860 by Charles G. Richards, a steamboat captain. The

Italianate house features iron-lace trim and lavish early Victorian and Empire furnishings. A formal garden is on the grounds. Guided tours are available. Allow 30 minutes minimum. Mon.-Fri. 11-3:30, Sat. 10-4, Sun. 1-4; closed Jan. 1, Mardi Gras parade days, Easter, July 4 and Dec. 23-26 and 31. Admission $5; under 12, $2. Phone (251) 208-7320.

SOLDIERS AND SAILORS MEMORIAL PARK, between Government and Houston sts., was created in memory of men killed in World War I. The half-acre park contains an azalea-bordered pool that mirrors a memorial arch.

GEM SAVE **USS *ALABAMA* BATTLESHIP MEMORIAL PARK,** 2703 Battleship Pkwy., is a 175-acre park dedicated to the Alabamians who served in the armed forces during World War II, the Korean War, the Vietnam War, Operation Desert Storm and Operation Iraqi Freedom. The battleship earned its 12 battle stars while part of a World War II strike force in the Pacific. The submarine USS *Drum* undertook 13 missions in the Pacific Theater in WW II.

The battleship's decks, turrets, mess, berth compartments, bridge, wardroom and captain's cabin are open for tours, as are the USS *Drum's* torpedo rooms and the crew's quarters. The park also displays 24 historic aircraft.

Allow 1 hour, 30 minutes minimum. Daily 8-6, Apr.-Sept.; 8-4, rest of year. Closed Dec. 25. Admission (includes both vessels) $12; ages 6-11, $6. Parking $2. AX, DS, MC, VI. Phone (251) 433-2703 or (251) 432-5951. *See color ad p. 68.*

MONTEVALLO—*see Birmingham p. 52.*

MONTGOMERY (D-3)

pop. 201,568, elev. 191′

See map page 70.

Montgomery was chartered in 1817 and named after Gen. Richard Montgomery, a Revolutionary War Hero who died in 1775 during the battle of Quebec. Prior to the Civil War, it flourished as a cotton market and transportation center. The town's volume of commerce and its central location led to the transfer of the state government from Tuscaloosa in 1846.

In February 1861, Jefferson Davis arrived in Montgomery and was sworn in as president of the Confederate States of America. On Apr. 11, 1861, he sent a telegraph commanding troops to remove Northern aggressors from Fort Sumter, culminating in the first shots of the Civil War.

Montgomery's status as capital of the Confederacy was short-lived; within months the Confederate government moved to more strategically located Richmond, Va. Montgomery was spared devastation during the war, although prosperity ended abruptly when the town was surrendered to Union troops. Recovery began when railroad lines came through in the 1880s. Union Station was completed in 1898 and served as the city's rail station until the late 1970s; it is now the Montgomery Area Visitor Center.

Montgomery was the nation's first city to introduce an electric streetcar system to local travel. The Lightning Route operated from 1886 to 1936, when it was replaced by the bus system.

Today Montgomery is one of the largest livestock markets and dairy centers in the Southeast. The development of nearby hydroelectric power has spurred manufacturing growth; an important product is Victorian-style furniture.

Maxwell Air Force Base, where the Wright Brothers' Flight School once stood, is the site of the Air University, the Air Force's center of professional military education. The Air Force Senior NCO Academy and the Extension Course Institute are at nearby Gunter Annex to Maxwell Air Force Base.

Completed in 1989, the Civil Rights Memorial stands in the front plaza of the Southern Poverty Law Center, 400 Washington Ave., as a monument to those who died in the struggle for racial equality. The memorial features the top of a circular marble table covered with a thin sheet of flowing water and inscribed with dates of key events and names of people involved in the civil rights movement. It is set against a 40-foot curved waterfall flowing over inscribed words from Martin Luther King Jr.'s "I Have a Dream" speech.

The Hank Williams Memorial honors the country singer, who is perhaps best known for his lovesick ballad, "Your Cheatin' Heart." The memorial is downtown at 1305 Upper Wetumpka Rd. in the Oakwood Cemetery Annex and is open daily dawn-dusk; phone (334) 262-3200.

Weekdays the W.A. Gayle Planetarium, 1010 Forest Ave., presents sky shows and science programs; phone (334) 241-4799.

Trolleys resembling those used at the turn of the 20th century travel through the downtown Montgomery area, providing transportation to government buildings, historical sites, the Riverfront Amphitheatre and Riverwalk Stadium, home to the Class AA Montgomery Biscuits. The trolleys run continually, stopping every 40 minutes 9-6, Monday through Saturday.

Montgomery Area Visitor Center in Historic Union Station: 300 Water St., Montgomery, AL 36104; phone (334) 262-0013 or (800) 240-9452. *See color ad starting on p. 40 & p. 43 & p. 71.*

Self-guiding tours: The 30-Page *Visitor Guide to Montgomery* is available from the visitor bureau. Available on-line from the National Park Service is information about the 54-mile Selma to Montgomery National Historical Trail. The trail runs from the Brown Chapel AME Church in Selma to the state capitol in Montgomery.

Shopping areas: Eastdale Mall, at the intersection of US 231 and US 80 Bus. Rte., has Dillard's, JCPenney, Sears and more than 90 other stores and restaurants. Montgomery Mall, at the intersection of US 231 and US 82 on Southern Boulevard, offers 100 stores including Parisian. The Shoppes at East Chase, off I-85 between Taylor Road and Chantilly Parkway, include such upscale retailers as Abercrombie & Fitch, Banana Republic and Williams-Sonoma. The Mulberry District, off I-85N exit 2, offers boutique shopping and casual restaurants in a neighborhood setting.

ALABAMA SHAKESPEARE FESTIVAL, in the Carolyn Blount Theatre, e. on Woodmere Blvd. via East Blvd. to 1 Festival Dr., presents classical and contemporary plays. The professional repertory company performs in two theaters, the 750-seat Festival Stage and the 274-seat Octagon. Meet-the-cast parties, pre-show and after-theater discussions, and a landscaped park are additional features.

Picnicking is permitted in the park. The 2005-2006 season runs Nov. 20-Aug. 20. The 2006-2007 season runs Oct. 13-June 24. Performances are held Tues.-Sun. at 7:30 p.m. Weekend matinees are held Sat.-Sun. at 2. Schedule may vary; phone ahead. Tickets $15-$37. AX, DS, MC, VI. Phone (334) 271-5353 or (800) 841-4273. *See color ad starting on p. 40.*

ALABAMA STATE CAPITOL, on Capitol (Goat) Hill at the e. end of Dexter Ave., is a Greek Revival-style structure with a 90-foot white dome. The 1851 building, capitol of the Confederacy during the first 3 months of the Civil War, is where Jefferson Davis was elected president. A three-story spiral stairway and murals depicting Alabama history adorn the rotunda; a Confederate soldiers memorial is on the south lawn.

Guided tours on the hour Mon.-Fri. 9-4, Sat. at 9, 11, 1 and 3; closed major holidays. Free. Phone (334) 242-3935.

DEXTER AVENUE KING MEMORIAL BAPTIST CHURCH, 454 Dexter Ave., had the Rev. Dr. Martin Luther King Jr. as its pastor 1954-60. It was in this church that the leaders of the desegregation movement met for the first time in 1955 and decided to institute a bus boycott as a form of peaceful protest. The church contains a detailed mural chronicling Dr. King's nonviolent crusade against racial oppression.

Guided tours depart Tues.-Thurs. at 10 and 2, self-guiding tours are permitted Fri. at 10, and guided tours by appointment only are given Sat. 10:30-1:30. Reservations should be made a week in advance. Admission $3; ages 1-18, $2. Phone (334) 263-3970. *See color ad p. 71.*

FIRST WHITE HOUSE OF THE CONFEDERACY, at 644 Washington Ave. across from the capitol, was the home of Jefferson Davis and his family when Montgomery was the Confederate capital. Designed in the Italianate style, the two-story wooden house, built 1832-35, was moved 10 blocks to its present site in the early 20th century.

Period furnishings, war relics and some of Davis' personal property are displayed. The restored house features reception halls, double parlors and a library. Mon.-Fri. 8-4:30; closed state holidays. Donations. Phone (334) 242-1861.

HANK WILLIAMS MUSEUM, downtown next to the Tuskegee Bank Building at 118 Commerce St., honors the country music legend. The acclaimed singer and songwriter is remembered

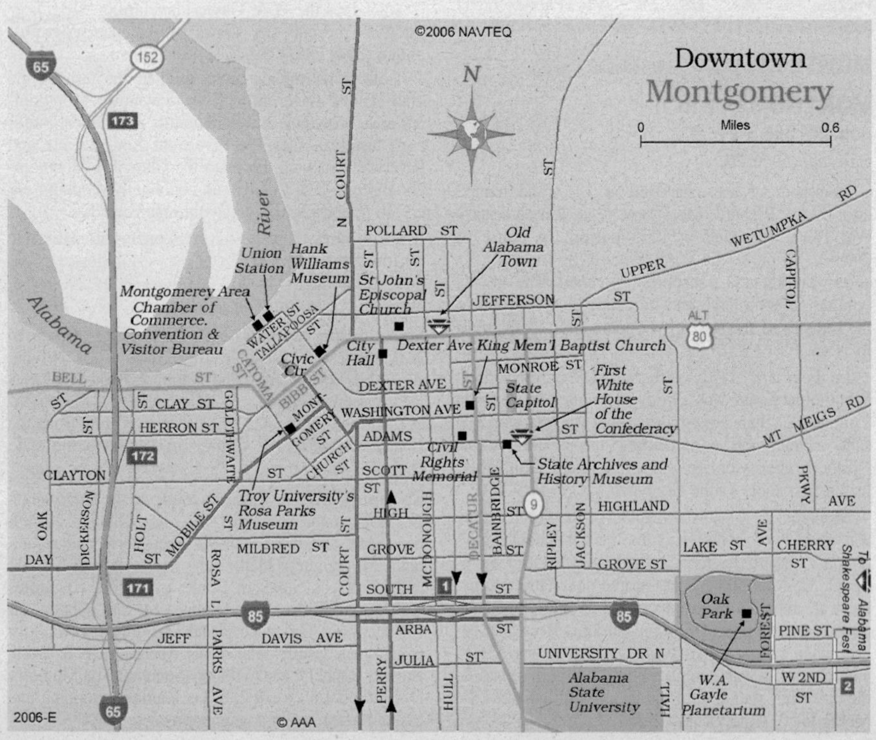

through exhibits that include his 1952 baby blue Cadillac, a Steinway piano, autographed albums, costumes and an operating Wurlitzer jukebox that plays favorite country ballads.

Allow 1 hour minimum. Mon.-Sat. 9-4:30, Sun. 1-4; phone for holiday schedules. Admission $8; ages 3-11, $3. AX, MC, VI. Phone (334) 262-3600.

MANN WILDLIFE LEARNING MUSEUM is at 325 Vandiver Blvd., next to the Montgomery Zoo. Conservation is the theme of this natural history museum, which features mounted native North American animals and aquatic creatures. Hands-on displays allow visitors to touch moose and other large mammals. Detailed fossil exhibits include woolly mammoth bones and mastodon tusks.

Daily 9-5; closed Jan. 1, Thanksgiving and Dec. 25. Admission $6; over 65 and ages 3-12, $4. Combination ticket with the Montgomery Zoo $10; over 65 and ages 3-12, $7. DS, MC, VI. Phone (334) 240-4900.

MONTGOMERY MUSEUM OF FINE ARTS, in Wynton M. Blount Cultural Park off Woodmere Blvd./Vaughn Rd., has a permanent collection noted for American paintings and sculpture, Old Master prints, Southern regional art and 19th-century American decorative arts. Such artists as Robert Henri, John Singer Sargent, James McNeill Whistler, Rembrandt and Edward Hopper are represented. The hands-on ARTWORKS gallery encourages creativity while educating children of all ages about the elements of art.

Tues.-Sat. 10-5 (also Thurs. 5-9), Sun. noon-5; closed Jan. 1, Thanksgiving and Dec. 25. Guided tours are offered Thurs. at 6:30 p.m. by appointment and Sat.-Sun. at 1. Free. Phone (334) 244-5700.

SAVE **MONTGOMERY ZOO,** off North Blvd. between Coliseum Blvd. and Lower Wetumpka Rd., contains approximately 900 birds, mammals and reptiles from around the world, including rare and endangered species. The animals are grouped geographically in outdoor, barrier-free settings. Zoo Weekend, held in April, features stage shows and activities for all.

Allow 1 hour minimum. Daily 9-5; closed Jan. 1, Thanksgiving and Dec. 25. Admission $6; over 65 and ages 3-12, $4. Train rides $2. Combination ticket with the Mann Wildlife Learning Museum $10; over 65 and ages 3-12, $7. DS, MC, VI. Phone (334) 240-4900.

GEM SAVE **OLD ALABAMA TOWN,** downtown at 301 Columbus St., is a collection of 50 restored buildings representing life in 19th- and early 20th-century central Alabama. The village depicts living and working conditions ranging from the simple existence of rural pioneers to the elegant surroundings of the urban gentry.

Included are a three-story, 1850 Italianate townhouse that retains its original kitchen, slave quarters and well; a country doctor's office, with period medical equipment and implements; an 1892 corner grocery whose shelves are stocked with goods common to that time; a log cabin; a cotton gin; a blacksmith shop; a gristmill; and shotgun and dogtrot houses. Drugstore and print shop museums depict those occupations.

Audiotapes are available for self-guiding tours. Allow 2 hours minimum. Mon.-Sat. 9-3; closed Jan. 1, Thanksgiving and Dec. 24-25 and 31. Admission $8; ages 6-18, $4. MC, VI. Phone (334) 240-4500 or (888) 240-1850.

ST. JOHN'S EPISCOPAL CHURCH, 113 Madison Ave. at N. Perry St., was built in 1834 and is the oldest Episcopal church in the city. The pew in which Jefferson Davis sat is marked. Mon.-Fri. 9-4. Free. Phone (334) 262-1937.

SCOTT AND ZELDA FITZGERALD MUSEUM, 919 Felder Ave., is in the house the Fitzgeralds occupied during the 1930s while Scott wrote "Tender is the Night" and Zelda penned "Save Me the Waltz." The noted couple's lives are featured in a videotape presentation. Photographs, letters and other memorabilia are displayed. Many exhibits pertain to Zelda, who was born and raised in Montgomery.

Allow 1 hour minimum. Wed.-Fri. 10-2, Sat.-Sun. 1-5. Donations. Phone (334) 264-4222.

STATE ARCHIVES AND HISTORY MUSEUM, in the Alabama Department of Archives and History at 624 Washington Ave., explore the development of Alabama through American Indian, pioneer and military artifacts; portrait galleries; and a children's gallery. An exhibit about 19th-century life features the Official State Bible used by Jefferson Davis when he took the oath of office. A photograph display traces the Selma-to-Montgomery Civil Rights March and the voting-rights struggle of the 1960s.

Museum open Mon.-Fri. and first Sat. of the month 8:30-4:30. Reference room Tues.-Fri. and first Sat. of the month 8:30-4:30. Closed federal and state holidays. Free. Phone (334) 242-4363, or (334) 242-4435 for the reference room.

SAVE **TROY UNIVERSITY'S ROSA PARKS MUSEUM** is at 252 Montgomery St., on the Troy University campus. This interactive museum honors Rosa Parks, whose 1955 arrest for refusing to give up her seat on a public bus led to the Montgomery bus boycott. The protest precipitated the U.S. Supreme Court decision that banned bus segregation. Exhibits tell the story of the struggle for civil rights in the 1950s.

Guided tours are available. Allow 1 hour minimum. Mon.-Fri. 9-5, Sat. 9-3; closed holidays. Admission $5.50; under 13, $3.50. Phone (334) 241-8616. *See color ad p. 71.*

MOUNDVILLE (C-3) pop. 1,809, elev. 164′

One of the country's best preserved prehistoric mound groups lies on the south bank of the Black Warrior River in Moundville. The agrarian American Indian culture, which built the mounds, developed from A.D. 1000 to 1500 into what is considered one of the most advanced prehistoric civilizations north of Mexico.

Possessing considerable artistic skill, the people advanced pottery making, copper working and stone carving to high levels of refinement. Moundville served as the civic and cultural center for many small villages up and down the river.

SAVE **MOUNDVILLE ARCHAEOLOGICAL PARK,** .5 mi. w. of SR 69 at the edge of town, preserves the ceremonial center of Moundville Indian culture. Remnants of this 300-acre city, dating from A.D. 1000, consist of 28 mounds once used as lodges and religious sites. Steps lead to the summit of the largest, which stands 60 feet high. A re-created temple depicts ceremonies. Museum artifacts illustrate village life. Models of aboriginal dwellings and earthworks also are presented.

Picnicking is permitted. Camping is available. Allow 1 hour minimum. Park daily 8-dusk. Museum daily 9-5, Mar.-Oct.; 9-4, rest of year. Closed Jan. 1, Easter, Thanksgiving and Dec. 24-25 and 31. Admission $4; senior citizens and ages 6-17, $2. MC, VI. Phone (205) 371-2234.

MUSCLE SHOALS AREA (A-3)

The region known as Muscle Shoals in northwestern Alabama includes the Quad-Cities of Muscle Shoals, Florence *(see place listing p. 59)*, Sheffield and Tuscumbia *(see place listing p. 78)*; two dams on the Tennessee River; and more than 1,200 miles of scenic lakeshore.

A 650-mile navigation channel and the hydroelectric-generating facilities created by a system of Tennessee Valley Authority (TVA) dams ensure economic potential for the Muscle Shoals area and the Tennessee River Valley. Industries include the TVA's National Fertilizer Development Center and the adjacent International Fertilizer Development Center; both have free lobby displays. Across Wheeler Dam in Rogersville is Joe Wheeler State Park Resort *(see Recreation Chart and the AAA Southeastern CampBook)*.

In 1965 a local disc jockey set up a recording studio in the small community of Muscle Shoals. When local singer Percy Sledge recorded "When a Man Loves a Woman," which sold more than a million copies, the soulful Muscle Shoals sound began. Other artists followed, including Aretha Franklin, Peggy Lee, Liza Minnelli, Bob Seger and the Rolling Stones.

Colbert County Tourism—Muscle Shoals Area: 719 US 72W, P.O. Box 740425, Tuscumbia, AL 35674; phone (256) 383-0783 or (800) 344-0783.

NATCHEZ TRACE PARKWAY—

see place listing in Mississippi p. 190.

NATURAL BRIDGE (B-3)

On US 278 approximately 1 mile west of the junction with SRs 5 and 13, Natural Bridge is in a scenic area. Formed some 200 million years ago, the rock arch is 148 feet long and towers 60 feet above winding pathways. The natural gardens are adorned with mountain laurel, snowball bushes and giant magnolias. Picnicking is permitted. Daily 8 a.m.-dusk. Admission $2.50; ages 6-12, $1.50. Phone (205) 486-5330.

OPELIKA (C-5) pop. 23,498, elev. 822′

Opelika was founded in 1837 and is known for its mixture of fine Greek Revival and Victorian houses. From late March through early April the Azalea/Dogwood Trail, a self-guiding driving tour, leads visitors past many of these houses during the peak blooming season of these perennials. A different kind of driving tour can be taken on the 54 holes of the Grand National, a course on the Robert Trent Jones Golf Trail.

Auburn-Opelika Convention and Visitors Bureau: 714 E. Glenn Ave., P.O. Box 2216, Auburn, AL 36831; phone (334) 887-8747 or (866) 880-8747.

Shopping areas: USA Factory Outlet Stores at 1220 Fox Run Pkwy. offers major-brand bargains in more than 20 establishments.

PELHAM—*see Birmingham p. 53.*

PICKENSVILLE (C-2) pop. 662, elev. 232′

TENN-TOM WATERWAY/TOM BEVILL VISITOR CENTER is .5 mi. s. of SR 86 on SR 14 at the Tom Bevill Lock and Dam. By connecting the Tennessee and Tombigbee rivers with a system of locks, this 234-mile canal provides a shortcut to the Gulf of Mexico. The visitor center, built in 19th-century Greek Revival style and furnished in period, features displays about river travel and wildlife. Photographs, models and audiovisual presentations also are presented. A 19th-century cast-iron fountain dominates the garden.

Daily 9-5, Mar.-Oct.; 8-4, rest of year. Visitor center closed holidays except Memorial Day, July 4 and Labor Day. Phone to verify schedule. Free. Phone (205) 373-8705.

U.S. Snagboat *Montgomery*, at the Tom Bevill Visitor Center .5 mi. s. of SR 86 on SR 14 at the Tom Bevill Lock and Dam, is one of the last steam-powered stern-wheelers used in the South. The snagboat, which for nearly 60 years removed debris from nearby rivers, has exhibits that chronicle maintenance operations on the South's major waterways. Daily 9-5, Mar.-Oct.; 8-4, rest of year. Closed holidays except Memorial Day, July 4 and Labor Day. Free. Phone (205) 373-8705.

PRATTVILLE (D-4) pop. 24,303, elev. 193′

Established in the late 1830s by Daniel Pratt of New Hampshire, Prattville has the feel of its founder's native New England. The town's historic district has more than 150 buildings, many predating the Civil War.

Prattville Area Chamber of Commerce: 131 N. Court St., Prattville, AL 36067; phone (334) 365-7392.

PRATTAUGAN MUSEUM AND HERITAGE CENTER, corner of Main and Chestnut sts. at 102 E. Main St., is in the McWilliams-Smith-Rice house, built in 1848. Items belonging to town founder Daniel Pratt and Autauga County artifacts are displayed, as are historic pieces from the families who occupied the home. An archive contains genealogical information. Mon.-Fri. 10-4; closed holidays. Free. Phone (334) 361-0961.

RUSSELL CAVE NATIONAL MONUMENT (A-4)

Eight miles northwest of Bridgeport via CRs 75 and 98, Russell Cave National Monument is a 310-acre archeological site first investigated in 1953. The focal point of the site is a cave shelter where the Tennessee River Valley traverses the Cumberland Plateau. This cave, continuously occupied by various cultures for 10,000 years, is part of a larger cavern that extends about 7 miles into the side of a limestone mountain.

Excavations have uncovered, layer by layer, the story of the people who inhabited the cave from approximately 10,000 B.C. to A.D. 1650. Artifacts found in the area chart societal progress from the Paleo period through the Mississippian period when residents used pottery and more sophisticated weapons and tools, buried their dead in mounds and developed a primitive form of agriculture.

Using objects recovered from the excavations, the visitor center portrays these prehistoric people. In the nearby shelter visitors can see exposed cave wall rock layers. Nature trails wind through the site. Interpreters demonstrate the prehistoric people's tools and weapons. Audiovisual programs are presented in the visitor center. Daily 8-4:30-5; closed Jan. 1, Thanksgiving and Dec. 25. Free. Phone (256) 495-2672.

SEALE (D-5) elev. 340'

FORT MITCHELL NATIONAL CEMETERY, on SR 165, 6 mi. s. of US 431, contains the graves of military personnel from World War I to Operation Desert Storm. Five archeological sites, including prehistoric upland campsites, historic Creek settlements, the Fort Mitchell Military Post area, a Creek trading house and a log school building, are in and around the cemetery. Cemetery daily 8 a.m.-dusk. Office Mon.-Fri. 8-4:30. Free. Phone (334) 855-4731.

SELMA (D-3) pop. 20,512, elev. 139'

Selma first drew national attention during the Civil War when it was second only to Richmond as an arsenal of the Confederacy. The Selma Ordnance Works manufactured one of the most powerful muzzle-loading cannons ever built as well as the ironclad ships including the CSS *Tennessee*, remembered for its historic role in the Battle of Mobile Bay *(see Mobile p. 65)*.

The destruction of Selma's shot and shell foundry, powder mill and navy yard became a Union imperative that was fulfilled when Gen. J.H. Wilson and his Union forces destroyed nearly two-thirds of the city during the Battle of Selma in April 1865. A monument to those who fought and died stands in the historic Old Live Oak Cemetery.

The five blocks of Water Avenue that survived the Civil War constitute one of the few remaining antebellum riverfront business districts in the South. Built in 1837, the St. James Hotel at 1200 Water Ave. is a rare example of an early riverfront hotel. It served as quarters for Confederate officers as well as arsenal and foundry personnel.

Selma's Old Town Historic District includes more than 1,250 historic structures. Among its notable residences is the two-story frame home of Sen. John Tyler Morgan, one of Alabama's most honored political and military leaders. In late March several private homes are opened to the public during Spring Historic Pilgrimage.

In the 1960s battles of another sort took place in Selma, including a watershed event that forever linked its name to the civil rights struggle. On Mar. 21, 1965, Martin Luther King Jr. began his legendary voting rights march at the Brown Chapel AME Church, 410 Martin Luther King Jr. St. Five days later, he and thousands of marchers arrived in the state capital to demand equal voting rights. The Selma to Montgomery National Historical Trail memorializes the 54-mile walk; it includes the Edmund Pettus Bridge and other landmarks that figured prominently in the demonstration.

Selma and Dallas Centre for Commerce: 912 Selma Ave., Selma, AL 36701; phone (334) 875-7241 or (800) 457-3562.

Self-guiding tours: The Selma Windshield Tour leads drivers through a historic district that includes Martin Luther King, Jr. St. and Old Live Oak Cemetery. Brochures for this and other tours can be obtained at the Selma and Dallas Centre for Commerce or from the Visitor Information Center at 2207 Broad St., Selma, AL 36701; phone (334) 875-7485. Available on-line from the National Park Service is information about the 54-mile Selma to Montgomery National Historical Trail. The trail runs from the Brown Chapel AME Church in Selma to the state capitol in Montgomery.

NATIONAL VOTING RIGHTS MUSEUM AND INSTITUTE, 1012 Water Ave., is w. of the Edmund Pettus Bridge, a historic landmark from the Selma-to-Montgomery voting-rights march. The museum houses a variety of displays depicting the struggles and accomplishments of the voting-rights movement. Allow 1 hour minimum. Mon.-Fri. 9-5, Sat.

10-3, Sun. by appointment; closed major holidays. Admission $6, students with ID $4, under 6 free. Phone (334) 418-0800.

OLD CAHAWBA ARCHAEOLOGICAL STATE PARK is 9 mi. s.w. on SR 22, then 5 mi. s. on CR 9, at the confluence of the Cahaba and Alabama rivers. Once a thriving antebellum river town, the site served as the state capital 1820-26. The town was an important prison site during the Civil War, but all that remains today are a one-story frame townhouse, a two-story brick slave building and some ruins. Streets and building sites are marked with interpretive signs.

Park open daily 8-5. Welcome center open daily 9-5. Closed Jan. 1, Thanksgiving and Dec. 25. Grounds free. Phone (334) 872-8058.

OLD DEPOT MUSEUM, 4 blks. e. of US 80 on the corner of Water Ave. and Martin Luther King, Jr. St., is a restored brick railroad depot. Displays depict local history and include Civil War and African-American history exhibits. A rail car and caboose contain railroad exhibits, and a museum houses antique fire trucks. An archive reference room is available.

Allow 1 hour minimum. Mon.-Sat. 10-4, Sun. by appointment; closed holidays. Admission $4; over 55, $3; college students with ID $2; ages 5-17, $1. Phone (334) 874-2197.

STURDIVANT HALL, 713 Mabry St., is a restored 1852 mansion that exemplifies neoclassic architecture. Furnished with period antiques, the building epitomizes the South's golden age of the 1850s. A display of antique dolls is noteworthy. Guided tours are available. Tues.-Sat. 10-4; closed holidays. Admission $5; ages 6-18, $2. Phone (334) 872-5626.

VAUGHN-SMITHERMAN MUSEUM, 109 Union St., is a 19th-century antebellum structure that has served as a Confederate hospital, a courthouse and a military school. The three-story Greek revival building houses Civil War artifacts, antique furniture, exhibits about local hospitals and politics, and various displays depicting Selma's history. Tues.-Sat. 9-4; closed major holidays. Admission $3, under 12 free. Phone (334) 874-2174.

SPANISH FORT (F-2) pop. 5,423, elev. 158'

Spanish Fort sits on a hill directly opposite the bay from Mobile. True to its name, the site served as an active fort during the Revolutionary War, the War of 1812 and the Civil War. Preserved Civil War breastplates still are visible throughout town.

Meaher State Park is 1,327 acres of wetlands on Mobile Bay offering a boat launch, elevated fishing pier, a nature trail and limited overnight camping facilities; only the campground is closed due to damages sustained during the 2004 and 2005 hurricane seasons. The park is at 5200 Battleship Pkwy. E./US 90/US 98. Phone (251) 626-5529.

Eastern Shore Chamber of Commerce & Visitor Center—Spanish Fort: 29750 Larry Dee Cawyer Dr., P.O. Box 310, Daphne, AL 36526; phone (251) 621-8222.

HISTORIC BLAKELEY STATE PARK is off I-10 exit 35A, 1 blk. n. on US 98, then .2 mi. e. on US 31 and 4.5 mi. n. on SR 225. This 3,800-acre site was the scene of the last major battle of the Civil War; the engagement ended hours after the surrender by Gen. Robert E. Lee at Appomattox Courthouse in Virginia, Apr. 9, 1865. The battle is reenacted every other year in April. More than 10 miles of nature trails are offered. Bicycling, camping, fishing and horseback riding are permitted. Daily 9-5; closed Dec. 24-25. Admission $3; ages 6-12, $1.50. Phone (251) 626-0798.

STEVENSON (A-4) pop. 1,770, elev. 628'

STEVENSON RAILROAD DEPOT MUSEUM, 2 mi. n. of US 72 on SR 117, displays photographs, memorabilia and Civil War relics. During the Civil War this railroad junction and its depot were strategically vital to the South. Allow 30 minutes minimum. Mon.-Sat. 8-4; closed state holidays. Free. Phone (256) 437-3012.

SYLACAUGA (C-4) pop. 12,616, elev. 600'

Sylacauga (sil-a-COG-a), known as the Marble City, is built on a foundation of solid marble. This translucent white stone, in some places only 12 feet below the surface, has been used since the 1840s to construct notable buildings, one of which is the U.S. Supreme Court Building in Washington, D.C. Sylacauga's quarries also produce crushed and ground marble.

Sylacauga Chamber of Commerce: 17 W. Fort Williams St., P.O. Box 185, Sylacauga, AL 35150; phone (256) 249-0308.

ISABEL ANDERSON COMER MUSEUM & ARTS CENTER, 711 N. Broadway Ave., displays local archeological finds and historical artifacts as well as changing exhibits of works by Southeastern artists. Tues.-Fri. 10-5; closed major holidays. Free. Phone (256) 245-4016.

TALLADEGA (C-4) pop. 15,143, elev. 553'

In November 1813 Andrew Jackson led his men to the aid of a besieged pioneer fort and in the ensuing Battle of Talladega (tal-ah-DIG-ah) defeated a large band of Creek Indians. His route, the Jackson Trace, is designated by a marker 5 miles south of Talladega on SR 77.

Talladega was founded along the Appalachian foothills in 1834 and is one of the state's oldest inland towns. The city is home to the Alabama Institute for the Deaf and Blind and to Talladega College. Some of the largest motor sports events in Alabama are held at the Talladega Superspeedway *(see attraction listing).*

Six miles southeast of the city is the Waldo Covered Bridge, one of the state's oldest. The 115-foot bridge was built in the 1850s of a Howe and Queenspost combination design.

Greater Talladega Area Chamber of Commerce: 210 East St. S., Talladega, AL 35160; phone (256) 362-9075.

SAVE **INTERNATIONAL MOTORSPORTS HALL OF FAME AND MUSEUM,** off I-20 exit 173 or 168, is next to the Talladega Superspeedway on Speedway Blvd. This five-building complex houses more than 100 racing vehicles as well as racing-related memorabilia and a research library. Allow 1 hour minimum. Daily 9-5; closed Jan. 1, Easter, Thanksgiving and Dec. 25. Admission $10; ages 7-17, $5. Phone (256) 362-5002.

TALLADEGA SUPERSPEEDWAY is at 3366 Superspeedway Blvd. The stands of this 2.66-mile tri-oval track seat more than 140,000 and the 212-acre infield accommodates thousands more. The 45-minute bus tour includes the pit area. The two major events at Talladega are the Aaron's 499 NASCAR NEXTEL Cup Race in April and the UAW-Ford 500 in October. For more information and tickets write Talladega Superspeedway, P.O. Box 777, Talladega, AL 35161.

Track tour daily 9-4; no tours race week and the week following race week. Tour $5; ages 6-17, $4. Phone (256) 362-2261 or (877) 462-3342, or TDD (866) 472-8725.

© International Speedway Corporation

AAA is the Official Auto Club of Talladega Superspeedway

TALLADEGA NATIONAL FOREST

Elevations in the forest range from 578 ft. at Big Wills Lake to 2,407 ft. at Cheaha Mountain. Refer to AAA maps for additional elevation information.

Divided into two nearly equal sections, the Talladega in eastern Alabama near the Georgia border and the Oakmulgee just southeast of Tuscaloosa in west-central Alabama, Talladega National Forest consists of 389,000 acres. Within the Oakmulgee Division is the 45,000-acre Oakmulgee Wildlife Management Area surrounding Payne Lake.

The Talladega Division contains two wildlife management areas: 39,320-acre Choccolocco in the northern portion and 31,943-acre Hollins in the southern portion. Also in the Talladega Division is the Pinhoti Trail system, which traverses the highest terrain in Alabama, providing a 102-mile hike through rugged but scenic country between the towns of Piedmont and Sylacauga. Sometime in the future the trail will connect through Georgia to the Appalachian trail. Several miles of marked side trips and loop trails branch off the main trail. Also within this division is the Cheaha Wilderness, comprising 7,245 acres and the 9,200-acre Dugger Mountain Wilderness.

The Talladega Scenic Drive runs through 23 miles of the forest, following the crest of Horseblock Mountain along SRs 49 and 281. For more information contact the Talladega National Forest, Forest Service Office, 1001 North St. (SR 21N), Talladega, AL 35160; phone (256) 362-2909. *See Recreation Chart and the AAA Southeastern CampBook.*

THEODORE (F-2) pop. 6,811, elev. 50′

GEM SAVE **BELLINGRATH GARDENS AND HOME** are off CR 59. The 900-acre estate includes 65 acres of cultivated and landscaped gardens that surround the 1935 mansion. The original gardens were patterned after the grand gardens of Italy, France and England by Walter D. Bellingrath, a pioneer in the Coca-Cola bottling industry. The Asian garden melds cultural concepts of landscape art. The grounds bloom with more than 3 million lights and animated displays during Magic Christmas in Lights.

The brick and wrought-iron mansion contains Bessie Morse Bellingrath's collection of furniture; Dresden, Meissen, Royal Dalton and Sèvres porcelain; china; crystal; sterling silver; and Oriental rugs. The Delchamps Gallery of Boehm Porcelain, in the center of the gardens, houses one of the largest public exhibits of Boehm porcelain in existence.

Food is available. Allow 1 hour, 30 minutes minimum. Gardens daily 8-5 (also 5-9, day after Thanksgiving-Dec. 31). House daily 9-4 (also 4-9, day after Thanksgiving-Dec. 31). Combination ticket for house, gardens and cruise $26; ages 5-11, $17. Combination ticket for house and gardens or gardens and cruise $18; ages 5-11, $11. Gardens only $10; ages 5-11, $5.50. Discount applies only to gardens admission.. AX, DC, DS, MC, VI. Phone (251) 973-2217 or (800) 247-8420. *See color ad p. 66.*

Alabama Cruises at Bellingrath Gardens, at Bellingrath Gardens and Home off CR 59, offers 45-minute cruises along the River of Birds. Native vegetation and wildlife, including ospreys, pelicans and songbirds, are featured. Dinner cruises are available on weekends. Sightseeing cruises depart from the gardens at the River Pavilion boat dock daily at 10, noon and 2, Feb. 15-Nov. 30.

Fare (includes Bellingrath gardens) $18; ages 5-12, $11. Combination ticket for cruise, gardens and home $26; ages 5-12, $17. Tickets are purchased at the gardens. AX, DS, MC, VI. Phone (251) 973-1244.

TROY (D-4) pop. 13,935, elev. 581′

PIONEER MUSEUM OF ALABAMA, 2 mi. n. on US 231, is a multibuilding village depicting rural 19th- and early 20th-century Southern life. More

AAA and Motorsports

AAA, a pioneer in the development and growth of auto racing during the first half of the 20th century, has returned to the racetrack. Today the association is the "Official Auto Club" and "Official Roadside Assistance Provider" of 11 tracks owned and operated by the International Speedway Corporation (ISC), which hosts the NASCAR NEXTEL Cup Series and Indy Racing League (IRL) events.

As part of an agreement with ISC, AAA's widely recognized logo appears on track safety and recovery vehicles as well as on track signs, in racing programs and at other promotional venues. ISC, a leading promoter of motorsports activities in the United States, conducts more than 100 events annually. ISC/AAA facilities include California Speedway in Fontana, Calif.; Darlington Raceway in Darlington, S.C.; Daytona International Speedway in Daytona Beach, Fla.; Homestead-Miami Speedway in Homestead, Fla.; Kansas Speedway in Kansas City, Kan.; Martinsville Speedway in Martinsville, Va.; Michigan International Speedway in Cambridge Junction, Mich.; Phoenix International Raceway in Phoenix, Ariz.; Richmond International Raceway in Richmond, Va.; Talladega Superspeedway in Talladega, Ala.; and Watkins Glen International in Watkins Glen, N.Y.

than 18,000 artifacts are presented in the main building. Set on 35 acres are a corn crib and barn, a re-created covered bridge, a working smokehouse, an 1881 locomotive and 1894 depot, log cabins, a tenant house, a gristmill and general stores. Allow 1 hour minimum. Mon.-Sat. 9-5; closed major holidays. Admission $5; over 60, $3; ages 5-18, $2. MC, VI. Phone (334) 566-3597.

TUSCALOOSA (C-2) pop. 77,906, elev. 225′

In the Choctaw language *tusko* means "warrior" and *loosa* means "black." By permission of the U.S. Government, Creek Indians established the Black Warrior Town in 1809; 4 years later it was burned after a revolt. Defeated, these American Indians were forced to move westward, and new settlers who came from South Carolina called their community Tuscaloosa (tus-ka-LOO-sa).

Tuscaloosa was the state capital 1826-46. Although the University of Alabama was established in 1831, it was not until 1896 that the efforts of educator Julia Strudwick Tutwiler resulted in the admission of women. Stillman College, founded in 1876, offers liberal arts studies to 1,200 students.

Today's Tuscaloosa offers an array of cultural and historic attractions, year-round events and many opportunities for shopping and dining. Several of the city's graceful antebellum houses still stand, especially in the Druid City District near Queen City Avenue. The Mildred Warner House on Eighth Street is a Georgian residence occupied 1820-1962.

Holt Lake *(see Recreation Chart)* offers many water sports, as does Lake Lurleen State Park *(see Recreation Chart and the AAA Southeastern CampBook)*. Outdoor enthusiasts and bird-watchers enjoy walking trails along the Warrior River.

Tuscaloosa Convention and Visitors Bureau: 1305 Greensboro Ave., P.O. Box 3167, Tuscaloosa, AL 35403; phone (205) 391-9200 or (800) 538-8696.

Shopping areas: Tuscaloosa's major shopping center is University Mall at McFarland Boulevard and 15th Street. It includes JCPenney, McRae's, Parisian and Sears.

BATTLE-FRIEDMAN HOUSE, 1010 Greensboro Ave., is a Greek Revival mansion built in 1835. Late 19th-century chandeliers grace the parlor while other furnishings date from the early 1800s. Plaster stucco made to look like Italian pink marble distinguishes the mansion's facade. Allow 30 minutes minimum. Tues.-Sat. 10-noon and 1-4, Sun. 1-4. Admission $5. Phone (205) 758-6138.

CHILDREN'S HANDS-ON MUSEUM, 2213 University Blvd., is in a three-story building containing a variety of participatory exhibits for children ages 2-12. The interactive programs are designed to stimulate children's curiosity and promote an understanding of their world. Among the highlights are a Choctaw Indian village, farmers market, Beaver's Bend, hospital and general store.

Allow 1 hour, 30 minutes minimum. Mon.-Fri. 9-5, Sat. 10-4; closed major holidays. Admission $5, under 2 free. AX, DS, MC, VI. Phone (205) 349-4235.

UNIVERSITY OF ALABAMA, 1 mi. s. of US 82 on University Blvd., offers an art gallery, a 50-acre arboretum and a pre-Civil War classroom. The campus also contains the Alabama Museum of Natural History, the Gorgas House and the Paul W. Bryant Museum. An information desk is in the Ferguson Center/Student Union. Guided tours of the campus leave from room 203 of the Student Services Center Mon.-Fri. at 10 and 2, Sat. at 10. Reservations are suggested. Guided tours free. To reserve a tour phone (205) 348-5666 or (800) 933-2262. For Crimson Tide sports tickets phone (205) 348-2262.

Alabama Museum of Natural History, University of Alabama, is in Smith Hall on 6th Ave. at the n.e. corner of the University of Alabama campus quadrangle. Exhibits include fossils and minerals from the Coal Age, Dinosaur Age and ice ages. Of special interest is the Hodges meteorite, which gained distinction in 1954 when it crashed through the roof of a Sylacauga house and struck the napping occupant, thus making it the only known meteorite to have hit a human. Tues.-Sat. 10-4:30; closed holidays. Admission $2, senior citizens and students with ID $1, under 6 free. Phone (205) 348-7550.

Gorgas House is at 810 Capstone Dr. on the n.w. corner of the University of Alabama campus quadrangle. Built in 1829, the house was designed as a student dining hall. It is one of only four structures to have survived the burning of the university during the Civil War. In 1879 the house became the residence of Gen. Josiah B. Gorgas, Chief of Ordnance for the Confederacy and later president of the university. Now open for tours, the house contains some of Gorgas' personal effects. Tues.-Fri. 10-4; closed university holidays. Admission $2. Phone (205) 348-5906.

Paul W. Bryant Museum is at 300 Paul W. Bryant Dr. across from the Coleman Coliseum on the University of Alabama campus. The museum illustrates the University of Alabama football tradition from its 1892 beginning to the present. There is a special exhibit about coach Paul "Bear" Bryant as well as photographs, audiovisual displays, a research library and a games film library. Allow 1 hour minimum. Daily 9-4; closed major holidays. Admission $2; over 62 and ages 6-17, $1. Phone (205) 348-4668.

TUSCUMBIA (A-2) pop. 7,856, elev. 453′

During the 1830s a canal was built around the rapids of the Tennessee River, and the first railway west of the Alleghenies connected the canal landing to Tuscumbia. Belle Mont Mansion, reminiscent of Thomas Jefferson's Palladian style of architecture, was one of Alabama's first plantation houses. Built about 1830, the U-shaped brick house was designed around a courtyard. Belle Mont is open by appointment; phone (256) 637-8513. Big Spring, for which the town was originally named, is in a park at the foot of N. Main Street; it produces 55 million gallons of cold spring water daily.

An unusual nearby attraction is the Key Underwood Coon Dog Memorial Graveyard west of town. In the Freedom Hills, a popular hunting area of the Cumberland Mountain Range, lie graves bearing touching epitaphs to prized coonhounds. A small park with picnic facilities adjoins the cemetery; phone (256) 383-0783.

Colbert County Tourism—Tuscumbia: 719 US 72W, P.O. Box 740425, Tuscumbia, AL 35674; phone (256) 383-0783 or (800) 344-0783.

SAVE **ALABAMA MUSIC HALL OF FAME,** 2 mi. w. of US 43 on US 72W, displays clothing, contracts and memorabilia associated with noted Alabama musicians. Included in the collection are Elvis Presley's original contract with Sun Records, the tour bus that belonged to the group Alabama and wax figures depicting Nat King Cole and Hank Williams. Allow 1 hour minimum. Mon.-Sat. 9-5, Sun. 1-5; closed Jan. 1, Thanksgiving and Dec. 20-31. Admission $8; over 55 and ages 13-18, $7; ages 6-12, $5. AX, MC, VI. Phone (256) 381-4417 or (800) 239-2643. *See color ad starting on p. 40.*

SAVE **HELEN KELLER BIRTHPLACE AND SHRINE,** 2 mi. n. of US 72 via N. Main St. to Keller Ln., is a 10-acre site that includes Helen Keller's early home. Deaf and blind from the age of 18 months, Keller succeeded in graduating cum laude from Radcliffe College in 1904 and became a world-renowned author and lecturer. Keller's indomitable spirit led Mark Twain to liken her to Joan of Arc. The biographical play "The Miracle Worker" is presented mid-summer.

Allow 30 minutes minimum. Mon.-Sat. 8:30-4, Sun. 1-4. Admission $6; senior citizens $5; ages 5-18, $2. Phone (256) 383-4066 or (888) 329-2124. *See color ad starting on p. 40.*

TUSKEGEE (D-5) pop. 11,846, elev. 459'

Named for the Creek Indian village Taskigi, Tuskegee was settled by the French, who built a fort nearby. The fort changed hands in 1763 when France surrendered the territory to England. It assumed a significant role when Andrew Jackson's troops used it to launch a campaign against the Creek Confederacy, ultimately leading to the tribe's defeat.

The seat of Macon County, Tuskegee is the home of Tuskegee University, formerly known as Tuskegee Institute. The school was designated a national historic landmark in 1965 for its great contributions in education for African-Americans. As head of the school's agricultural department, George Washington Carver's accomplishments helped the South's economic recovery after boll weevil infestations destroyed cotton farming. Today Tuskegee University enrolls some 3,000 students in liberal arts, education, business and engineering degree programs. Campus tours are available; phone (334) 727-8347.

Tuskegee Area Chamber of Commerce: 121 S. Main St., Tuskegee, AL 36083; phone (334) 727-6619.

Self-guiding tours: The Black Heritage Trail features many sites that figure prominently in African-American history. Brochures featuring a map and descriptions of the sites are available from the chamber of commerce.

TUSKEGEE INSTITUTE NATIONAL HISTORIC SITE, on SR 126 (W. Montgomery Rd.) s. of I-85 exit 32, honors the school founded in 1881 by noted educator Booker T. Washington. Originally established to train African-American teachers, the institute gained prominence in the early 1900s thanks to agricultural innovations developed by George Washington Carver. A walking tour includes the Booker T. Washington Monument and the University Chapel.

Walking tour maps are available at the Carver Museum and the National Park Service Headquarters, 1212 W. Montgomery Rd.; phone (334) 727-6390.

GEM **Carver Museum,** near the entrance to Tuskegee University on SR 126 (W. Montgomery Rd.) s. of I-85 exit 32, follows Carver's careers as an artist, teacher and scientist. His preserved laboratory depicts experiments that resulted in some 400 extractions from peanuts and 175 by-products from sweet potatoes. Among his inventions were a paint formulated from Alabama clay and a synthetic marble made from wood pulp. Daily 9-4:30; closed Jan. 1, Thanksgiving and Dec. 25. Free. Phone (334) 727-3200.

The Oaks, on W. Montgomery Rd. at Tuskegee University, is the former home of Booker T. Washington, who lived here from 1900 until his death in 1915. Dignitaries who visited the home included presidents Howard Taft and Theodore Roosevelt as well as philanthropist Andrew Carnegie. The restored 1899 Queen Anne-style house is furnished with period items and contains his study.

Allow 30 minutes minimum. Daily 9-4:30; closed Jan. 1, Thanksgiving and Dec. 25. Tours begin at the Carver Museum. Last tour begins 1 hour before closing. Free. Phone (334) 727-3200.

TUSKEGEE NATIONAL FOREST

Elevations in the forest range from 260 ft. to 510 ft. Refer to AAA maps for additional elevation information.

Northeast of Tuskegee, the 11,054-acre Tuskegee National Forest permits fishing and hunting in season with an Alabama state license. The Bartram National Recreation Trail offers hiking and mountain biking through an 8.5-mile section of mostly secluded woodland. The forest also has a 14-mile horse and hiking trail, rustic campsites and a replica of Booker T. Washington's childhood home. The home is at the Taska Recreational Area on US 29.

The district headquarters, off SR 186 near Tuskegee, is open Mon.-Fri. 7:30-4. For more information contact Tuskegee National Forest, District Office, 125 National Forest Rd. 949, Tuskegee, AL 36083; phone (334) 727-2652. *See Recreation Chart.*

VALLEY HEAD (A-4) pop. 611, elev. 1,026′

In the early 19th century Dr. John S. Gardner, a Methodist minister, attempted to transform the Valley Head region into a silk-producing center. He planted mulberry trees and imported silkworms, but the valley's unsuitable climate doomed the project to failure.

Gardner's home, Winston House, served as headquarters in 1863 for Union colonel Jefferson C. Davis from Kentucky, a cousin of the Confederate president. Local legend recalls a *faux pas* made by an old-timer who stumbled on the Union encampment. Upon hearing that the commander was Jeff Davis, the befuddled man cornered the colonel and asked, "Which pays you the most? Colonelin' the Bluecoats or Presidentin' the Confederates?" The home is now a bed and breakfast inn.

SEQUOYAH CAVERNS, 6 mi. n. off I-59 and US 11, then 1.5 mi. w., following signs, is named for the inventor of the Cherokee alphabet. Features include waterfalls, creeks and the lighted underground Looking Glass Lakes, which reflect thousands of formations. Picnicking and camping are permitted.

Guided tours are offered Mon.-Sat. 9-5, Sun. 11-5, Mar.-Nov.; Sat. 9-5, Sun. 11-5, rest of year. Closed Thanksgiving and Dec. 25. Last tour leaves 1 hour before closing. Fee $10.95; ages 4-12, $5.95. DS, MC, VI. Phone (256) 635-0024 or (800) 843-5098.

VANCE (C-3) pop. 500, elev. 516′

GEM **THE MERCEDES-BENZ VISITOR CENTER,** off I-59 exit 89, traces the German company's earliest days as a motorcycle manufacturer in the 1880s to its current standing as a world-renowned automaker. Vehicle displays include vintage automobiles, 1950s racing and sports cars, and concept models. Engineering techniques are highlighted with videotape presentations and exhibits.

The visitor center is located on the grounds of the company's only U.S. manufacturing plant. A 90-minute factory tour showing the assembly of M-Class sport-utility vehicles is available.

Note: Factory tours are temporarily discontinued until early 2007 due to manufacturing plant expansion. Visitor center/museum open Mon.-Fri. 9-5; closed major holidays. Phone for tour schedule. Free. AX, DS, MC, VI. Phone (205) 507-2253 or (888) 286-8762.

WARRIOR—*see Birmingham p. 53.*

WETUMPKA (D-4) pop. 5,726, elev. 191′

The Coosa River flows through the middle of Wetumpka, creating opportunities for tourism and outdoor recreation. Nature trails, including the Swayback Ridge Trail, wind through the nearby Appalachian foothills, and Lake Martin—one of the world's largest man-made lakes—and Lake Jordan attract fishing and boating enthusiasts. These attributes help explain why Wetumpka also is known as "The City of Natural Beauty."

Upriver are remnants of the western rim of the Wetumpka Meteor Impact Crater, unusual rock formations rising out of the water. The 4-mile-wide crater was formed some 83 million years ago when a meteor more than 1,100 feet in diameter crashed into the Earth's surface; today's city sits right on the bull's-eye of what is said to be the greatest natural disaster in Alabama history.

Crossing the Coosa is the Bibb Graves Bridge, built in 1937 and one of only two known bridges south of the Mason-Dixon line that are suspended by reinforced concrete arches. Cruises aboard the *Betsy Ann* Riverboat are another way to enjoy the river. Wetumpka also abounds in antebellum churches, historic homes and landmarks such as the Greek Renaissance-style Elmore County Courthouse. Annual events include the Coosa River Whitewater Festival in early June, Riverfest in mid-August and Christmas on the Coosa in December.

Wetumpka Area Chamber of Commerce: 110 East Bridge St., P.O. Box 785, Wetumpka, AL 36092; phone (334) 567-4811.

AL HOLMES WILDLIFE MUSEUM is 5 mi. s. on US 231, 1.5 mi. e. on Redland Rd., then 1.5 mi. s.e. to 1723 Rifle Range Rd. The museum exhibits more than 900 species of mounted wildlife and offers a touch-and-feel board that allows visitors to feel different animal skins. Allow 30 minutes minimum. Mon.-Fri. 9-5. Admission $4; ages 2-12, $2. DS, MC, VI. Phone (334) 567-7966.

FORT TOULOUSE-JACKSON PARK, 3 mi. w. of US 231, is a wildlife sanctuary. Archeological excavations provided information for the reconstruction of forts Toulouse and Jackson. The 1825 Graves House Museum serves as an interpretive center. Nature trails, an arboretum, an Indian mound and a boat ramp are featured. Living-history demonstrations are offered the third weekend of the month, April through November.

Guided tours are available. Picnicking and camping are permitted. Park daily dawn-dusk; museum daily 8-5. Closed Jan. 1, Thanksgiving and Dec. 25. Admission $2; over 62 and ages 6-12, $1. Camping fees $11-$14. MC, VI. Phone (334) 567-3002.

WILLIAM B. BANKHEAD NATIONAL FOREST

Elevations in the forest range from 510 ft. at Lewis Smith Lake to 1,074 ft. at Penitentiary Mountain. Refer to AAA maps for additional elevation information.

In northwestern Alabama, the 180,000-acre William B. Bankhead National Forest encompasses lakes, limestone canyons and a natural bridge as well as the 25,986-acre Sipsey Wilderness Area. Recreation areas within the forest include Sipsey River, Corinth, Houston and Brushy lakes and Clear Creek. Hunting for deer, wild turkeys, squirrels and quails is permitted in season. The office in Double Springs is open Mon.-Fri. 7:30-4, Sat. 8-5.

For more information contact William B. Bankhead National Forest, District Office, P.O. Box 278, Double Springs, AL 35553; phone (205) 489-5111. See Recreation Chart and the AAA Southeastern CampBook.

AAA
2006
ATLAS
More Roads · More Cities · Better Atlas

AAA

Louisiana

Cobblestones & Lacy Wrought Iron
New Orleans' eclectic French Quarter exudes Gallic charm

Bayous, Swamps & Marshlands
See alligators, herons and other wildlife on boat tours through Louisiana's waterways

Mansions & Plantations
The days of hoop skirts and magnolias live on along the Great River Road

Sportsman's Paradise
The bass are always biting at Louisiana's lakes, rivers and bayous

Blackened Redfish, Gumbo & Po-boys
Call it Cajun, Creole or down-home—it's just plain good

Oak Alley Plantation, Vacherie

like a good gumbo

New Orleans / © Richard Cummins / SuperStock

Louisiana is different things to different people, yet its irresistible allure beckons all of us in some way. This is a state of contrasts, with enticements that can be flamboyant or sedate, raucous or discreet.

With a heritage that incorporates an intriguing blend of American Indian, Spanish, French, English and African cultures, Louisiana is like a good gumbo—a hearty concoction of ingredients with enough variations to suit individual tastes.

Louisiana offers you the solitude of a wilderness lake or the excitement of landing a record catch in offshore Gulf waters, the bawdiness and excess of Mardi Gras or the quiet reverence of ancient Indian mounds. Riches come from

oil fields or, with a little luck, from casinos and Thoroughbred race tracks.

You can explore mysterious, moss-draped bayous with a Cajun guide on a swamp tour or visit New Orleans' elegant garden district courtesy of a historic streetcar.

Nineteenth-century grandeur and opulence—exemplified by stately River Road mansions along the Mississippi—contrast with the barns, blacksmith shop and re-creations of everyday plantation life of that era at Baton Rouge's Rural Life Museum.

Louisiana is jambalaya and zydeco, breakfast at Brennan's and jazz at Preservation Hall. Come enjoy the spice, the gentility, the worldly sophistication and the Southern hospitality.

If Louisiana's list of official symbols included a food category, gumbo would probably be its emblem. Although the state's signature dish is closely associated with Cajun or Creole heritage, it is likely the product of a cultural simmering that began more than 300 years ago with the meeting of American Indians and European explorers in the Mississippi River basin.

First You Make a Roux. . .

Roux is a mixture of flour and oil—the first ingredients in a traditional gumbo. French-speaking Acadians get the credit for this simple yet flavorful foundation. However, there are as many opinions about how gumbo originated as there are recipes for it in a Louisiana cookbook.

One theory has it that local American Indians created a soupy facsimile with vegetables, meats and seafood. Fact is, they did introduce an ingredient that has stood the test of time: To prepare gumbo today without adding a pinch of ground sassafras leaves—or *filé* (FEE-lay)—is to commit a culinary *faux pas.*

Filé aside, there are ancient cooking artifacts at Poverty Point State Historic Site, near Epps, that reveal how native cultures fixed food as early as 1700 B.C.

French Acadians exiled from Nova Scotia in the mid-1700s found refuge in southern Louisiana, bringing with them secrets of Old World cooking that later defined a culinary genre—Cajun cuisine. You can taste the French heritage here in everything from shrimp *étouffée* to alligator *sauce piquant.*

Flavor your pilgrimage to the Cajuns' adopted homeland with a reading of Henry Wadsworth Longfellow's "Evangeline," a love story based on the historic disbursement of the French Acadian people. St. Martinville has several sites commemorating the event. Don't miss the Acadians' mother church, St. Martin de Tours, which was built around 1844 for the congregation established in 1765 by the earliest arrivals to the territory.

Enjoy generous helpings of the Cajun lifestyle at Acadian Village and Vermilionville, two living-history settlements in Lafayette. Hungry for more ambience? Try eating *écrevisses boilli* (boiled crawfish) off a newsprint tablecloth in the bayou country. Now that's Cajun. *Aiyee!*

Louisiana Historical Timeline

1682

Explorer René-Robert Cavelier, Sieur de La Salle, claims the territory for France.

© Corbis

1762

Louis XV gives the province to his cousin, Charles III of Spain.

1764

The first French-speaking Acadians settle in the region after being expelled from Nova Scotia.

Library of Congress

1803

Three years after Napoleon regains Louisiana, the U.S. purchases it for $15 million. Statehood is granted in 1812.

Library of Congress

1815

Gen. Andrew Jackson's troops defeat the British in the Battle of New Orleans.

Another word for gumbo is okra. The sticky pod that creates a gummy texture when cooked comes from Africa, but African-Americans brought much more than food to Louisiana's ethnic table.

As a child, trumpeter Louis Armstrong followed brass bands through the streets of New Orleans. Satchmo's jazzy sounds still blow through the French Quarter, from Jackson Square banquettes to the venerable Preservation Hall.

In Melrose, folk artist Clementine Hunter worked her way from the cotton fields to the kitchen to the canvas while living at Melrose Plantation for most of her 100 years; today, her acclaimed paintings garnish its walls.

. . .and the Rest is History

In the early 1700s French colonists set up a trading post on the Red River in northern Louisiana. The fickle river changed course, but the outpost named Natchitoches stayed put. That it predates New Orleans by 4 years makes Natchitoches the oldest permanent French settlement in the Louisiana Purchase, a heritage the city jealously guards in a 33-block historic district and with a reconstruction of a 1732 fort.

A visit to New Orleans is like stepping into the late 18th century. You can spend days studying architecture that spans more than 250 years. Cabildo. Presbytère. St. Louis Cathedral. Make a vow to inspect one of the Vieux Carré's oldest buildings: The Old Ursuline Convent, built in 1745, was a nunnery that miraculously escaped the 1788 fire that destroyed most of the city. Saints and sinners have passed through these doors.

Federal troops tried to burn Baton Rouge's Old State Capitol during the Civil War. This indestructible bastion now is a museum focused on Louisiana's colorful political history. Exhibits recall one of the state's darkest hours—the assassination of Gov. Huey P. Long, a.k.a. the "Kingfish"—as well as brighter moments courtesy of Jimmie Davis, the candidate who sang his way through two successful gubernatorial campaigns and into the Country Music Hall of Fame.

There's so much more of Louisiana waiting to be savored. Whatever you desire is just up the nearest road, river or bayou.

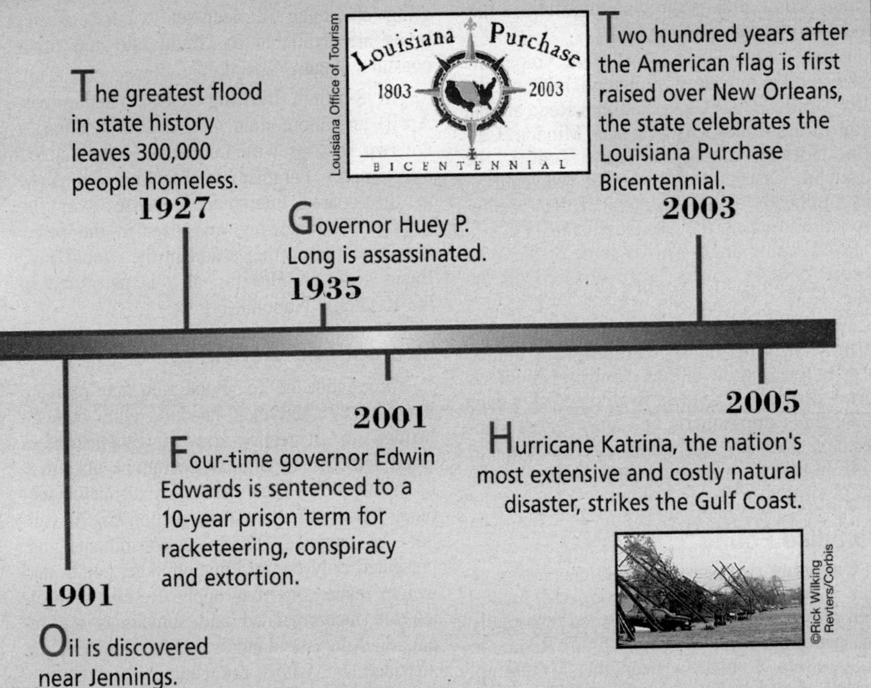

1927
The greatest flood in state history leaves 300,000 people homeless.
Louisiana Office of Tourism
Louisiana Purchase
1803
2003
BICENTENNIAL
1935
Governor Huey P. Long is assassinated.
2003
Two hundred years after the American flag is first raised over New Orleans, the state celebrates the Louisiana Purchase Bicentennial.
1901
Oil is discovered near Jennings.
2001
Four-time governor Edwin Edwards is sentenced to a 10-year prison term for racketeering, conspiracy and extortion.
2005
Hurricane Katrina, the nation's most extensive and costly natural disaster, strikes the Gulf Coast.
©Rick Wilking Reuters/Corbis

Recreation

You don't have to be from the Pelican State to realize its potential for outdoor enjoyment. Snow skiing is out of the question, but almost anything else you fancy is available *carte blanche.*

The One and Only Kisatchie

The Kisatchie, Louisiana's only national forest, is a vast playground for recreation seekers. Actually, it's a composite of six units scattered around the central and northern sections of the state. Topography ranges from flat to rolling, with dense forests and wetlands throughout.

More than 100 miles of trails invite **hiking, bicycling** and **horseback riding.** The Evangeline District (south of Alexandria) offers seven hiking trails of varying lengths, most of which intersect. Here's the long and short of it:

Wild Azalea National Recreational Trail is a hiker's springtime favorite for its blossoms. You can cover a small section in a few hours or make the 31-mile journey over mildly rolling terrain in 2-3 days. Overnight camping is permitted, but there are no facilities. Lakeshore Trail, the more scenic of two 10-mile hiking paths around Kincaid Lake, is canopied with oak, beech and hickory trees; it starts near the eastern shore boat ramp. Valentine Trail's 3-mile loop is the way to go if you like to do your walking in circles.

Want a little more slant while you pant? Take a hike or ride a mountain bike on the hilly 8-mile Sugar Cane National Recreational Trail in the Caney District, near Minden. Caroline Dormon Hiking and Horse Trail, in the Kisatchie District (northwest of Alexandria), has trailheads at the Kisatchie Bayou campground and along the Longleaf Trail (FR 59), a paved scenic drive. This is some of the most rugged country in the forest—indeed, in the state.

Whether you plan to commune with nature or frolic with the family, **camping** is available at primitive and developed campsites in all six forest districts. Excellent water access ramps make the campgrounds at Caney Lakes (Upper and Lower) and Kincaid Lake popular with **boaters; swimming** and **water skiing** are permitted.

Paradise Found

Canoeing is a peaceful experience on more than 1,400 miles of state-designated natural and scenic streams recommended especially for paddling. The Bogue Chitto River, in southeastern Louisiana near the Mississippi border, tops the list; a public boat ramp at Franklinton provides easy access. Navigability, accessibility and availability of outfitters near Six Mile Creek, north of Lake Charles, make this section of Whiskey Chitto Creek a favorite destination.

State parks cater to outdoors enthusiasts. North Toledo Bend State Park, west of Natchitoches, lures **anglers** to Toledo Bend Reservoir, a 186,000-acre basin of the Sabine River. If the bass or sak-a-lait (crappie) are biting, you could drift into Texas waters before you know it! Speaking of bass, try for brag-size specimens in False River (truthfully, it's an oxbow lake) near New Roads, or in Black Lake (north of Natchitoches). From the marshes of Bayou Segnette State Park (south of New Orleans) you can hook fresh- or saltwater fish in lakes and bayous that connect to the Gulf of Mexico.

The only state park with direct Gulf access is Grand Isle, where **surf fishing** for speckled trout is superb. A 400-foot fishing pier—open to the public daily 8-7 and only to paid campground guests after 7 p.m.—is the pride of the park. Some of the best **offshore fishing** for snapper, mackerel and cobia is near production rigs in the oil fields about 4-5 miles out. The mighty tarpon provides the ultimate angling challenge in deep-sea waters; charter boats are available in Grand Isle and other coastal villages.

An 8-month **hunting** season (September-April) and more than 45 wildlife sanctuaries are two reasons why Louisiana is nicknamed Sportsman's Paradise. You'll find waterfowl in the coastal marshlands, geese over the southwestern prairies, and deer in the piney woods of the northeast and in the Atchafalaya Basin swamps. Hunting also is permitted in the Kisatchie National Forest.

Recreational Activities

Throughout the TourBook, you may notice a Recreational Activities heading with bulleted listings of recreation-oriented establishments listed underneath. Similar operations also may be mentioned in Destination City recreation sections. Since normal AAA inspection criteria cannot be applied, these establishments are presented only for information. Age, height and weight restrictions may apply. Reservations often are recommended and sometimes are required. Addresses and/or phone numbers are provided so visitors can contact the attraction for additional information.

Fast Facts

POPULATION: 4,468,976.

AREA: 48,523 square miles; ranks 31st.

CAPITAL: Baton Rouge.

HIGHEST POINT: 535 ft., Driskill Mountain.

LOWEST POINT: -5 ft., New Orleans.

TIME ZONE(S): Central. DST.

MINIMUM AGE FOR UNRESTRICTED DRIVER'S LICENSE: 17.

MINIMUM AGE FOR GAMBLING: 21.

SEAT BELT/CHILD RESTRAINT LAWS: Seat belts are required for driver and all front-seat passengers. Children ages 6-12 and at least 60 lbs. are required to be in a child restraint or seat belt; child restraints are required for under age 6 or under 60 lbs.

HELMETS FOR MOTORCYCLISTS: Required for all riders.

RADAR DETECTORS: Permitted.

FIREARMS LAWS: Vary by state and/or parish. Contact Louisiana State Police Headquarters, 11117 Airline Hwy., Baton Rouge, LA 70816; phone (225) 754-8500.

HOLIDAYS: Jan. 1; Martin Luther King Jr. Day, Jan. (3rd Mon.); Mardi Gras Day, Shrove Tuesday; Good Friday; Memorial Day, May (last Mon.); July 4; Labor Day, Sept. (1st Mon.); Election Day, Nov. (even years); Veterans Day, Nov. 11; Thanksgiving; Christmas.

TAXES: Louisiana's statewide sales tax is 4 percent; local parish and city taxes can be as much as 5.5 percent.

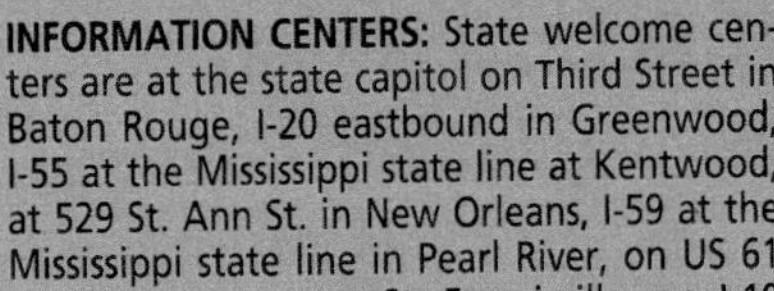

INFORMATION CENTERS: State welcome centers are at the state capitol on Third Street in Baton Rouge, I-20 eastbound in Greenwood, I-55 at the Mississippi state line at Kentwood, at 529 St. Ann St. in New Orleans, I-59 at the Mississippi state line in Pearl River, on US 61 at St. Francisville, on I-10 westbound at Slidell, I-20 westbound near the Mississippi state line at Tallulah, US 84 at Vidalia and I-10 eastbound at Vinton. All state welcome centers are open daily 8:30-5, except New Orleans (9-5) and Baton Rouge (8-4:30); closed Jan. 1, Easter, Thanksgiving and Dec. 25.

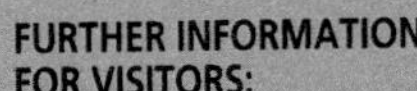

FURTHER INFORMATION FOR VISITORS:

Louisiana Department of Culture, Recreation and Tourism
P.O. Box 94291
Baton Rouge, LA 70804-9291
(225) 342-8119
(800) 677-4082
See color ad card insert

RECREATION INFORMATION:

Louisiana Office of State Parks
P.O. Box 44426
Baton Rouge, LA 70804-4426
(225) 342-8111
(888) 677-1400

FISHING AND HUNTING REGULATIONS:

Louisiana Department of Wildlife and Fisheries
2000 Quail Dr.
Baton Rouge, LA 70808
(225) 765-2800

NATIONAL FOREST INFORMATION:

Kisatchie National Forest
Supervisor's Office
2500 Shreveport Hwy.
Pineville, LA 71360
(318) 473-7160

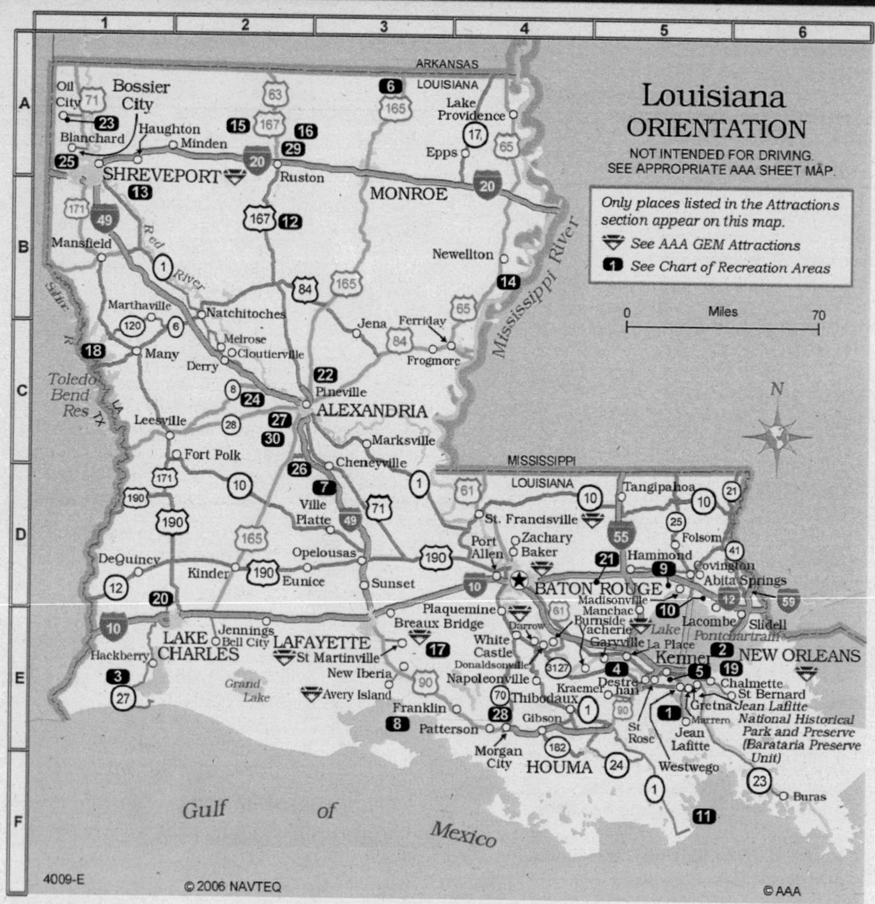

Louisiana Temperature Averages Maximum / Minimum

From the records of the National Weather Service

	JAN	FEB	MAR	APR	MAY	JUNE	JULY	AUG	SEPT	OCT	NOV	DEC
Baton Rouge	63/42	65/45	71/50	78/58	81/64	90/70	91/72	91/72	88/67	81/56	70/46	64/43
Lake Charles	62/44	65/47	70/51	78/58	85/66	90/72	92/74	92/74	89/69	82/59	70/49	64/45
New Orleans	62/43	67/46	71/50	78/56	84/63	90/70	91/74	91/72	87/68	80/60	70/49	65/45
Shreveport	57/38	60/41	67/47	75/55	83/63	91/71	93/73	94/73	89/67	79/55	66/45	59/40

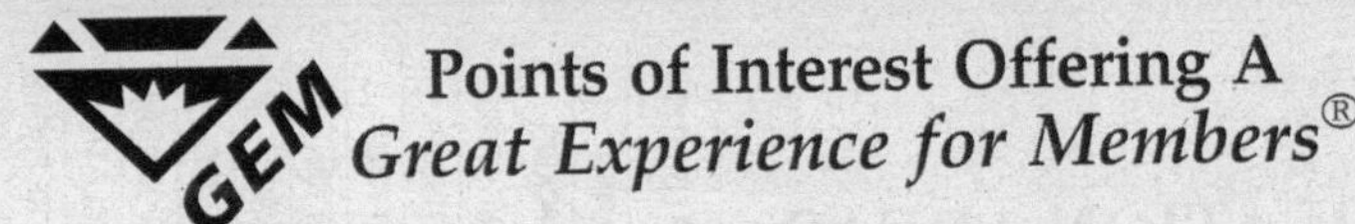

Points of Interest Offering A *Great Experience for Members®*

Avery Island (E-3)

JUNGLE GARDENS—More than just Tabasco sauce comes from Avery Island; camellias, azaleas and snowy egrets flourish at this lush tropical garden. See p. 94.

Baton Rouge (D-4)

LOUISIANA STATE CAPITOL—Overlooking the Mississippi River, this 34-story Art Deco building with marble interior offers scenic views as well as state information. See p. 96.

LSU MUSEUM OF ART—English and American portrait paintings and early Creole furniture exemplify this museum's extensive fine art and decorative art collections, with an accent on regional works. See p. 97.

LSU RURAL LIFE MUSEUM—Rural life on an 1800s Louisiana plantation is re-created at this outdoor museum. See p. 97.

SHAW CENTER FOR THE ARTS—The center has stunning views both inside and out; inside are the LSU Museum of Art, a sculpture garden, a theater and art galleries, while outside one can gaze at the Mississippi River and downtown Baton Rouge. See p. 97.

Darrow (E-4)

HOUMAS HOUSE—Once called The Sugar Palace, this exquisite 23-room mansion with lush gardens demonstrates how its 19th-century owners lived in the lap of luxury. See p. 98.

New Orleans (E-6)

AUDUBON AQUARIUM OF THE AMERICAS—Up-close and personal encounters with marine life found throughout the Americas abound at this aquarium. See p. 127.

AUDUBON ZOO—This urban zoo's animals reside in habitats resembling their native lands. See p. 128.

THE NATIONAL WORLD WAR II MUSEUM—A vast collection of artifacts, personal effects, diaries and oral histories tell the stories of World War II soldiers. See p. 131.

NEW ORLEANS MUSEUM OF ART—This museum's 46 galleries contain a comprehensive collection of paintings, sculptures, prints, photographs, decorative arts and glassware. See p. 129.

THE OGDEN MUSEUM OF SOUTHERN ART—Four centuries of art reflecting the heritage of the South are on display; crafts, paintings, photographs and sculpture are included in the mix. See p. 132.

PRESERVATION HALL—Long lines and limited seating only add to the atmosphere of the traditional jazz played here nightly. See p. 124.

ST. LOUIS CATHEDRAL—This venerable 18th-century cathedral in Jackson Square is a French Quarter landmark. See p. 125.

SYDNEY AND WALDA BESTHOFF SCULPTURE GARDEN—A luxurious garden highlights a collection of contemporary sculptures created by internationally renowned artists. See p. 129.

St. Francisville (D-4)

ROSEDOWN PLANTATION STATE HISTORIC SITE—This 1835 plantation showcases many original furnishings; its 28 acres of formal gardens were modeled after the great gardens of 17th-century France. See p. 156.

St. Martinville (E-3)

LONGFELLOW-EVANGELINE STATE HISTORIC SITE—Evangeline and Gabriel would feel right at home in this area set aside to memorialize the state's French-speaking bayou cultures. See p. 157.

ST. MARTIN DE TOURS CATHOLIC CHURCH—One of the oldest Catholic churches in Louisiana, the present building dates to 1844. See p. 158.

Shreveport (A-1)

R.W. NORTON ART GALLERY—Classic examples of American and European art grace the walls of this art museum. See p. 159.

Vacherie (E-5)

OAK ALLEY PLANTATION—Majestic 300-year-old live oaks line a quarter-mile corridor leading to this Greek Revival mansion, built 1837-39. See p. 153.

White Castle (E-4)

NOTTOWAY PLANTATION—Built to be the grandest plantation home along the Mississippi River, Nottoway does not disappoint. See p. 161.

RECREATION AREAS

	MAP LOCATION	CAMPING	PICNICKING	HIKING TRAILS	BOATING	BOAT RAMP	BOAT RENTAL	FISHING	SWIMMING	PETS ON LEASH	BICYCLE TRAILS	NATURE PROGS.	VISITOR CENTER	LODGE/CABINS	FOOD SERVICE
NATIONAL FORESTS *(See place listings)*															
Kisatchie 600,000 acres. Central and northern Louisiana. Water skiing; horse rental.		•	•	•	•	•		•	•	•					
NATIONAL PRESERVES															
Barataria (E-5) 20,000 acres. Canoeing. *(See Jean Lafitte National Historical Park and Preserve p.150)*	1		•	•	•	•	•	•				•	•		
NATIONAL WILDLIFE REFUGES															
Bayou Sauvage (E-5) 23,000 acres. *(See New Orleans p. 128)*	2		•	•	•	•		•		•	•				
Sabine (E-1) 125,000 acres. CLOSURE INFORMATION: Due to the effects of the 2005 hurricane season, this refuge is closed and no reopening date has been set. *(See Hackberry p. 100)*	3			•	•	•		•		•			•		
ARMY CORPS OF ENGINEERS															
Bonnet Carre Spillway (E-5) 8,000 acres. 6 mi. w. of Destrehan off SR 48. Bicycling, horseback riding.	4	•	•		•	•		•		•					
STATE															
Bayou Segnette (E-5) 580 acres in Westwego off US 90. CLOSURE INFORMATION: Due to the effects of the 2005 hurricane season, this park is closed; phone (888) 677-1400 for updates. *(See Westwego p. 153)*	5	•	•	•	•	•		•	•	•			•	•	
Chemin-A-Haut (A-3) 503 acres 10 mi. n.e. of Bastrop on SR 139. Playground.	6	•	•	•	•	•	•	•	•	•			•	•	
Chicot (D-3) 6,400 acres 8 mi. n. of Ville Platte off SR 3042.	7	•	•	•	•	•	•	•	•	•		•		•	
Cypremort Point (E-3) 185 acres 24 mi. s. of Jeanerette off SR 319. Crabbing, water skiing, windsurfing.	8		•		•	•		•	•	•				•	
Fairview-Riverside (D-5) 98 acres 2 mi. e. of Madisonville on SR 22. Historic. Water skiing.	9	•	•	•	•			•		•					
Fontainebleau (D-5) 2,809 acres 3 mi. s.e. of Mandeville on US 190. CLOSURE INFORMATION: Due to the effects of the 2005 hurricane season, day-use facilities and group camp areas are closed; phone (888) 677-1400 for updates.	10	•	•	•	•	•		•	•	•	•			•	
Grand Isle (F-5) 140 acres at Grand Isle off SR 1. CLOSURE INFORMATION: Due to the effects of the 2005 hurricanes, beach camping is closed; the beach is open for day use. Birdwatching.	11	•	•		•			•	•	•			•		
Jimmie Davis (B-2) 296 acres 4 mi. w. of Chatham via SRs 4 and 1209.	12	•	•	•	•	•		•	•	•				•	
Lake Bistineau (B-1) 750 acres 8 mi. s. of Doyline on SR 163.	13	•	•	•	•	•	•	•	•	•				•	
Lake Bruin (B-4) 53 acres 3 mi. n.e. of St. Joseph via SRs 605 and 604. Water skiing.	14	•	•		•	•	•	•	•	•					
Lake Claiborne (A-2) 620 acres 7 mi. s.e. of Homer on SR 146. Water skiing.	15	•	•	•	•	•	•	•	•	•				•	
Lake D'Arbonne (A-2) 655 acres 5 mi. w. of Farmerville on SR 2.	16	•	•	•	•	•		•		•			•	•	
Lake Fausse Pointe (E-3) 6,127 acres 18 mi. s.e. of St. Martinville off the West Atchafalaya Protection Levee road. Water skiing.	17	•	•	•	•	•	•	•		•			•	•	
North Toledo Bend (C-1) 990 acres 9 mi. w. of Zwolle off SR 3229. Nature trails.	18	•	•	•	•	•		•	•	•	•		•	•	
St. Bernard (E-5) 358 acres 18 mi. s.e. of New Orleans on SR 39. CLOSURE INFORMATION: Due to the effects of the 2005 hurricane season, the park is closed and no reopening date has been set; phone (888) 677-1400 for updates. Nature trails.	19	•	•	•					•	•					

RECREATION AREAS

RECREATION AREAS	MAP LOCATION	CAMPING	PICNICKING	HIKING TRAILS	BOATING	BOAT RAMP	BOAT RENTAL	FISHING	SWIMMING	PETS ON LEASH	BICYCLE TRAILS	NATURE PROGS.	VISITOR CENTER	LODGE/CABINS	FOOD SERVICE
Sam Houston Jones (D-1) 1,087 acres 9 mi. n. of Lake Charles off SR 378. CLOSURE INFORMATION: Due to the effects of the 2005 hurricane season, a limited number of cabins are available; phone (888) 677-1400 for updates. Bird-watching; nature trails, playground.	20	•	•	•	•	•	•	•		•				•	
Tickfaw (D-5) 1,200 acres 32 mi. e. of Baton Rouge off I-12. Canoeing.	21	•	•	•	•		•	•		•	•	•	•	•	
OTHER															
Buhlow Lake (C-3) 73 acres in Pineville off US 71. Water skiing.	22		•	•	•	•		•	•				•		
Caddo Lake (A-1) 40,000 acres 12 mi. n.w. of Shreveport off SR 1. Water skiing.	23	•	•		•	•	•	•	•						•
Cotile Reservoir (C-2) 2,000 acres 20 mi. w. of Alexandria via SRs 1 and 1200.	24	•	•	•	•	•		•	•		•				
Cross Lake (A-1) 8,575 acres. Water skiing.	25		•		•	•	•	•	•						•
Indian Creek Reservoir (D-2) 2,250 acres 10 mi. s. of Alexandria off US 165.	26	•	•	•	•	•		•	•	•	•	•			
Kincaid Lake (C-2) 2,000 acres e. of Gardner on SR 28.	27		•	•	•	•	•	•						•	•
Lake End (E-4) 30 acres in Morgan City off SR 70.	28	•	•		•	•		•	•						
Lincoln Parish Park (A-2) 260 acres 4 mi. n. of Ruston on SR 33.	29	•	•	•	•	•		•	•		•				
Valentine Lake (C-2) 80 acres s.w. of Gardner off SR 28.	30	•	•	•	•			•	•	•					

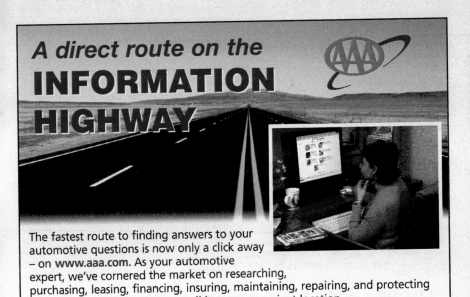

Points of Interest

ABITA SPRINGS—*see New Orleans p. 147.*

ALEXANDRIA (C-3) pop. 46,342, elev. 77'

Alexandria is at the geographical center of Louisiana. The area lost most of its homes, cotton gins, courthouse records, churches and libraries in 1864 when Union troops burned Alexandria and nearby Pineville *(see place listing p. 154)*. St. Francis Xavier Cathedral was built in 1898 on the corner of Fourth and Beauregard streets, the 1865 site of a mutiny by troops under the command of Gen. George Armstrong Custer.

During World War II some 7 million troops trained in the Alexandria vicinity under Gens. Dwight Eisenhower, Mark Clark and George Patton. Much overseas military strategy was planned in the Hotel Bentley in downtown Alexandria.

Modern Alexandria is the commercial, educational and military center of central Louisiana. Many lakes, several state parks and two nearby districts of the Kisatchie National Forest *(see place listing p. 102)* provide opportunities for outdoor activity. Alexandria Park on Masonic Drive has recreational facilities and a zoo.

Alexandria/Pineville Area Convention and Visitors Bureau—Alexandria: 707 Main St., Alexandria, LA 71301; phone (318) 442-9546 or (800) 551-9546.

SAVE **ALEXANDRIA MUSEUM OF ART** is at 933 Main St. This 1898 building, on the site of the first European settlement in the region, displays fine arts, including collections of northern Louisiana folk arts and crafts. Tues.-Fri. 10-5, Sat. 10-4; closed major holidays. Admission $4; senior citizens, active military and students with ID $3; under 13, $2. AX, MC, VI. Phone (318) 443-3458.

ALEXANDRIA ZOO is .9 mi. n.e. of jct. US 71 and US 165 at 3016 Masonic Dr. The zoo contains some 500 wild animals including 20 endangered species. The Louisiana Habitat Exhibit features a Cajun cabin and native wildlife. Miniature train tours are available. Allow 1 hour minimum. Daily 9-5; closed Jan. 1, Thanksgiving and Dec. 25. Admission $3; ages 4-12, $2; over 65, $1.50. Train $1.50. Phone (318) 473-1143.

KENT PLANTATION HOUSE is at 3601 Bayou Rapides Rd. Built 1796-1800, the house is a mixture of French and Spanish Colonial architecture. The 4-acre plantation and gardens have been restored to their early 19th-century appearance. Outbuildings include a slave cabin, milk house, blacksmith house, dependency, barn, sugar mill, carriage house and kitchen.

Allow 1 hour minimum. Guided tours depart on the hour Mon.-Sat. 9-11 and 1-3; closed Jan. 1, Thanksgiving, day after Thanksgiving, Dec. 24-25 and Dec. 31. Admission $6; over 65, $5; ages 6-12, $2. Phone (318) 487-5998.

AVERY ISLAND (E-3) elev. 50'

Avery Island, reached by toll bridge, is underlaid by a great salt dome that in places is within 12 feet of the surface. The rock salt mine on the island is said to have been the first discovered in the Western Hemisphere. During the Civil War the salt it produced was used as a food preservative throughout the South. No motorcycles are permitted on the island.

GEM **JUNGLE GARDENS** is off SR 329. Subtropical flora, aged live oaks, mirror pools and sunken gardens cover 200 acres. Thousands of camellias, azaleas and irises are usually in bloom November through June. The Bird City sanctuary, established to protect the nearly extinct snowy egret, is home to more than 20,000 herons and egrets during nesting.

Alligators and deer also are part of the gardens' abundant wildlife. The Chinese Garden contains bamboo stands and a Buddha dating from A.D. 1000. Allow 1 hour minimum. Daily 9-5. Admission $6.25; ages 6-12, $4.50. MC, VI. Phone (337) 369-6243.

McILHENNY COMPANY is off SR 329. Company founder Edmund McIlhenny, who received a special variety of red capsicum pepper seeds from Central America as a gift from a friend in 1868, developed the fiery Tabasco brand pepper sauce that is still produced on Avery Island by his descendants. Guests may view factory operations, a 10-minute film, multimedia displays and historical artifacts. Allow 1 hour minimum. Guided factory tours daily 9-4; closed major holidays. Free. Phone (337) 365-8173 or (800) 634-9599.

BAKER (D-4) pop. 13,793, elev. 80'

HERITAGE MUSEUM is at 1606 Main St. Housed in a 1906 Victorian home, the museum offers displays pertaining to area history. The Heritage Village features reconstructed turn-of-the-20th-century buildings. Allow 30 minutes minimum. Mon.-Fri. 10-4. Free. Phone (225) 774-1776.

BATON ROUGE (D-4) pop. 227,818, elev. 60'

The flags of seven nations have flown over Baton Rouge—those of France, England, Spain, West Florida, the Sovereign State of Louisiana, the Confederacy and the United States. Despite this, the original name bestowed by a French explorer in 1699 has endured. Meaning "red stick" or "red staff," the name referred to a tall cypress tree, stripped of its bark and draped with freshly killed animals, that marked the boundary between the hunting grounds of two American Indian tribes.

In 1849 Baton Rouge became the state capital. As the battlefront moved north through Louisiana during the Civil War, the capital shifted to Opelousas, then Alexandria and finally Shreveport. Union troops occupied Baton Rouge during most of the war.

The Battle of Baton Rouge State Monument, North Boulevard and Riverside Street, is on the site of the 4-hour bloody attempt by Confederate soldiers to retake the city in April 1862. The city again became state capital in the early 1880s when home rule was restored.

Baton Rouge is the second largest city in Louisiana and one of the largest ports in the nation. It is at the northern end of the "Petrochemical Gold Coast"—the industrial belt that flanks the Mississippi for 100 miles downriver to New Orleans. Across the river from Baton Rouge great sugar plantations form an area known as the "Sugar Bowl of America."

The profusion of magnolia and cypress trees and antebellum homes belies the city's industrial image. Baton Rouge also is home to two major universities: Louisiana State University *(see attraction listing)* and Southern University. The latter overlooks the Mississippi in north Baton Rouge off US 61 and is home to the Red Stick Monument. Campus tours can be arranged.

Baton Rouge's oldest church, St. Joseph Cathedral, is at 412 North St. Built in 1853, the cathedral stands upon the site of two earlier churches, the first dating to 1790. The Gothic Revival-style St. James Episcopal Church, with three Tiffany glass windows over the altar, is at 208 N. 4th St.

The Mississippi River Road Corridor, a 70-mile stretch of the Great River Road, winds through eight parishes from Baton Rouge to New Orleans and offers travelers scenic views of the Mississippi River as well as the chance to visit historical sites, museums, small towns and old cemeteries along the way.

Baton Rouge Area Convention and Visitors Bureau: 730 North Blvd., Baton Rouge, LA 70802; phone (225) 383-1825 or (800) 527-6843. *See color ad card insert.*

Shopping areas: The Cortana Mall, 9401 Cortana Rd., features Dillard's and Sears. The Mall of Louisiana, 6401 Bluebonnet Blvd., counts Dillard's, JCPenney, Belk and Sears among its 200 stores. SAVE Tanger Outlet Center, 2200 Tanger Blvd. off I-10 exit 177 in Gonzales, offers some 56 outlet stores. The Perkins Road area is home to antique shops. Towne Center at Cedar Lodge, Corporate Boulevard and Jefferson Highway, is a main-street style shopping village with such shops as Ann Taylor Loft, Gap and Talbots.

BATON ROUGE ZOO is 1 mi. e. of SR 19 at 3601 Thomas Rd. Most of the zoo's 1,400 animals and birds reside in naturalistic outdoor habitats. L'aquarium de Louisiane highlights the region's fish, reptiles and amphibians. Tropical birds are featured at Parrot Paradise. A children's zoo is on the grounds.

Food is available. Mon.-Fri. 9:30-5, Sat.-Sun. 9:30-6, first Sun. in Apr.-last Sat. in Oct.; daily 9:30-5, rest of year. Closed Jan. 1, Thanksgiving and Dec. 24-25. Admission $5; senior citizens $4; ages 2-12, $2; free to all Wed. 3-5. Train and tram rides $1.50. Phone (225) 775-3877.

BLUE BAYOU WATERPARK AND DIXIE LANDIN' THEME PARK is at 18142 Perkins Rd. Five waterslides, a water play area and a wave pool are the

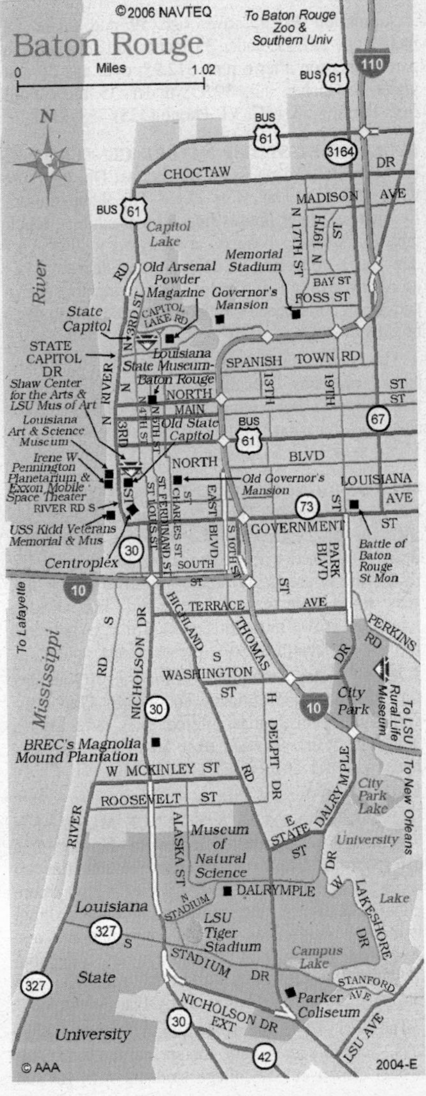

highlights of the water park. A lagoon features diving, volleyball and a gator and lily pad walk. Dixie Landin' is an amusement park with 24 rides, including a roller coaster with a 14-story drop and a flume ride with drops of 26 and 50 feet. A children's section includes a carousel and a biplane ride.

Note: Restrictions apply to clothing and items that may be carried in; phone ahead for specific details. Picnicking is permitted. Food is available. Wagon, wheelchair and locker rentals are available. Pets are not permitted. Allow 1 hour minimum. Water park daily 10-6, mid-May to early Aug.; Sat.-Sun 10-6, early May to mid-May. Theme park Sun.-Thurs. 2-9, Fri.-Sat. 2-10, mid-May to early Aug.; Sat. noon-7, early Apr.-late Apr.; Sat.-Sun. 2-8, late Apr. to mid-May.

Admission $32.95, over age 59 and under 48 inches tall $27.95, under 35 inches tall free. Theme park admission after 6 p.m. $12.95; over age 59 and under 48 inches tall, $9.95; under 35 inches tall free. Parking $5. MC, VI. Phone (225) 753-3333.

BLUEBONNET SWAMP NATURE CENTER is off I-10 exit 162, 2.5 mi. s. on Bluebonnet Dr., then just w. to 10503 N. Oak Hills Pkwy. The 9,500-square-foot nature center houses live-animal exhibits, touch tables, a working beehive, a backyard wildlife garden and a collection of duck-hunting decoys. Visitors may explore a 65-acre cypress-tupelo swamp and a magnolia-beech hardwood forest via trails and boardwalks.

The site's inhabitants include herons, owls, hawks, raccoons, bobcats, snakes, turtles and alligators. Allow 1 hour minimum. Tues.-Sat. 9-5, Sun. noon-5. Admission $2; over 64 and students with ID $1.50; ages 3-17, $1. Phone (225) 757-8905.

BREC'S MAGNOLIA MOUND PLANTATION is at 2161 Nicholson Dr. The 1791 French-Creole home once was the centerpiece of a 950-acre cotton plantation. Furnished with Federal-style pieces from the 1800s, the house is surrounded by 16 acres of oak trees, some more than 200 years old. The working plantation grows much of the food that is prepared during open-hearth cooking presentations.

Allow 1 hour minimum. Mon.-Sat. 10-4, Sun. 1-4; closed major holidays and Mardi Gras Day. Cooking demonstrations offered Tues. and Thurs., Oct.-May. Admission $8; over 50 and college students with ID $6; ages 5-17, $3. MC, VI. Phone (225) 343-4955.

SAVE **LOUISIANA ART & SCIENCE MUSEUM** is downtown at 100 S. River Rd. Housed in a historic train station, the museum features fine art exhibitions, a sculpture gallery, a creative playroom with art activities, and an Egyptian tomb exhibit. Permanent exhibitions include contemporary and Civil War photographs, a Southern art collection, 18th- to 20th-century paintings by American and European artists, and sculptures by Ivan Mestrovic.

Tues.-Fri. 10-4, Sat. 10-5, Sun. 1-5; closed holidays. Schedule may vary for special exhibits. Admission $6; over 65, college students with ID and ages 2-12, $5; free to all first Sun. of the month. Admission may increase for special exhibits. AX, DS, MC, VI. Phone (225) 344-5272.

Irene W. Pennington Planetarium & ExxonMobil Space Theater is in the Louisiana Art & Science Museum. Planetarium programs, large-format films and laser shows are shown on a 60-foot domed screen. Three galleries showcase the solar system, the planets and the universe. Exhibits include a 40-foot solar system clock and nine built-to-scale planet models, including the 15-foot-wide rings of Saturn.

Allow 1 hour minimum. Tues.-Fri. 10-4, Sat. 10-8, Sun. 1-5; closed major holidays. Show schedule varies, phone ahead. Galleries $6; over 65 and ages 4-12, $5. Galleries and one planetarium show $8; over 65 and ages 4-12, $7. Galleries and two planetarium shows $16; over 65 and ages 4-12, $14. Galleries and three planetarium shows $24; over 65 and ages 4-12, $21. Under 3 are not permitted in the theater. AX, DS, MC, VI. For schedule information phone (225) 344-5272.

GEM **LOUISIANA STATE CAPITOL** is on State Capitol Dr. at Third St. The 34-story-high building is said to be the nation's tallest state capitol. Flanking the front steps are the statues "The Patriots" and "The Pioneers" by Lorado Taft. Some 26 varieties of marble adorn the interior. Statuary, murals and a polished lava floor are inside Memorial Hall, which opens to the House and Senate chambers. Also on the first floor is a state visitor information center.

An observation deck on the 27th floor offers a panoramic view of Baton Rouge. Zachary Taylor's former home site is marked on the grounds not far from the sunken garden where Huey P. Long is buried. Long, who spearheaded construction of the capitol as governor of Louisiana, was assassinated in its corridors in 1935. Allow 30 minutes minimum. Daily 8-4:30. Observation deck 8-4. Free. Phone (225) 342-7317.

Old Arsenal Powder Magazine is on the e. side of the Capitol grounds. Built in 1838, the compound supplied weapons and ammunition to Confederate troops at the onset of the Civil War. The arsenal was seized in 1862 during the Union occupation of the city. Hands-on exhibits dealing with the storage and usage of gunpowder are included along with historical displays. Tues.-Sat. 9-4; closed holidays. Admission $1, over 60 and under 18 free. Phone (225) 342-0401.

LOUISIANA STATE MUSEUM—BATON ROUGE is at 660 N. Fourth St. Items that make up the cultural, industrial and historical fabric of Louisiana are on display, including Napoleon's death mask and a Confederate submarine. The 69,000-square-foot museum also features exhibits about African-American history, Mardi Gras, and the state's musical past. Tues.-Sat. 10-5, Sun. noon-5; closed holidays. Admission $6; senior citizens, active military and students with ID $5; under 13 free. Phone (225) 342-5428.

LOUISIANA STATE UNIVERSITY is 3 mi. s. at jct. Highland Rd. and Dalrymple Dr. The university was established near Alexandria in 1860 and transferred to Baton Rouge in 1869. Campus maps are available at the visitor center. On the grounds are American Indian mounds believed to be more than 1,600 years old. LSU's mascot, a Bengal tiger named Mike, lives in a cage outside Tiger Stadium. Phone (225) 578-5030.

LSU Museum of Natural Science is in Foster Hall. A zoology collection includes dioramas depicting Louisiana wildlife and some 350 mounted native birds. Mon.-Fri. 8-4; closed state and school holidays. Free. Phone (225) 578-2855.

GEM **LSU RURAL LIFE MUSEUM** is e. on I-10 to Essen Lane exit (exit 160). This outdoor folk museum is a re-creation of an 1800s plantation with more than 15 relocated or re-created buildings on 5 acres. The cultures and lifestyles of pre-industrial Louisianans are recalled through collections of tools, household utensils, furniture and farming implements.

The museum is divided into three areas. The Barn area contains rural life artifacts from prehistory to the early 1900s, including tools and vehicles. The Plantation area is a complex of nine buildings authentically furnished to re-create the plantation's major activities and includes a gristmill and blacksmith shop. The Folk Architecture area showcases the diverse construction techniques of seven buildings to illustrate the various cultures of Louisiana settlers. Other highlights include the 25-acre Windrush Gardens.

Allow 1 hour, 30 minutes minimum. Daily 8:30-5; closed Jan. 1, Easter, Thanksgiving and Dec. 24-25. Admission $7; over 61, $6; ages 5-11, $4. Phone (225) 765-2437.

OLD GOVERNOR'S MANSION is at 502 North Blvd. between Royal and St. Charles sts. This Georgian mansion was constructed in 1930 for Gov. Huey Long and is said to be a copy of the White House as designed by Thomas Jefferson. The mansion was replaced as the official governor's residence in 1961. Docent-led tours allow visitors to see the state dining room, the governor's office and living quarters, and keepsakes from the mansion's political families.

Allow 1 hour minimum. Tues.-Fri. 10-4; closed holidays. Last tour departs 1 hour before closing. Admission $6; senior citizens $5; grades K-12, $4. MC, VI. Phone (225) 387-2464.

OLD STATE CAPITOL is at 100 North Blvd. and River Rd. The Gothic Revival castle was built in 1847. Burned by the Union Army, the castle was repaired in 1882 and served as the state capitol until 1932. Particularly interesting is the large skylight of colored glass panes. The building, which now houses hands-on exhibits about Louisiana politics and history, also contains the state film and video archives. Tues.-Sat. 10-4, Sun. noon-4; closed holidays. Admission $4; over 55, $3; students with ID $2; under 6 free. Phone (225) 342-0500 or (800) 488-2968.

GEM **SHAW CENTER FOR THE ARTS,** 100 Lafayette St., is home to the LSU Museum of Art, the LSU School of Art Gallery, the Manship Theatre, the Irene W. Pennington Rooftop Terrace and Sculpture Garden and an art gallery. The LSU School of Art Gallery features works from the faculty and students of Louisiana State University. The 125,000-square-foot building, covered with translucent channel glass, overlooks and reflects the Mississippi River.

Visitors may see a panoramic vista of the river and the Old State Capitol District from the sixth-floor terrace. Food is available. Mon. 9-5, Tues.-Wed. 9 a.m.-10 p.m., Thurs.-Sat. 9 a.m.-11 p.m., Sun. 11-5. Free. Phone (225) 346-5001.

GEM **LSU Museum of Art** is in the Shaw Center for the Arts at 100 Lafayette St. The museum contains permanent collections focusing on fine arts and decorative arts. Notable collections include 17th to 20th-century portrait paintings; Newcomb pottery and crafts; pre-electricity lighting; locally crafted 19th-century silver; Inuit sculpture; early Creole and American furnishings made in Louisiana; and jade *objets d'art* from the Ming and Qing dynasties. Changing exhibitions feature national and international art collections.

Educational programs and gallery tours are available. Tues.-Sat. 10-5 (also Thurs. 5-8), Sun. 1-5. Admission $8; senior citizens and students with ID $6; ages 6-17, $4. Phone (225) 389-7200.

USS *KIDD* VETERANS MEMORIAL AND MUSEUM is on the Mississippi River across from the Baton Rouge Centroplex at 305 S. River Rd. The memorial consists of an observation tower, a museum complex and the USS *Kidd,* a World War II destroyer. Exhibits include a model ship collection, maritime artifacts and a replica of the Vietnam Veterans Memorial Wall. Outside the museum are two fighter planes, a P-40 Flying Tiger and a Corsair A-7E.

Allow 1 hour minimum. Daily 9-5; closed Thanksgiving and Dec. 25. Admission $7; over 59, $6; military with ID $5; ages 5-12, $4. AX, DS, MC, VI. Phone (225) 342-1942.

CASINOS

- **Belle of Baton Rouge**, 103 France St. Daily 24 hours. Phone (225) 378-6000 or (800) 676-4847.
- **Casino Rouge**, 1717 N. River Rd. Daily 24 hours. Phone (225) 709-7777 or (800) 447-6843.

BELL CITY (E-2) elev. 8'

CAMERON PRAIRIE NATIONAL WILDLIFE REFUGE is 6 mi. w. on SR 14, then 12 mi. s. on SR 27. More than 200 migrating and wintering bird species inhabit the 25,548-acre refuge, which includes fresh and salt marsh, coastal prairie and old rice fields.

The refuge comprises two separate units, the freshwater Gibbstown area and East Cove, a salt marsh open only to boats. The Gibbstown visitor center offers a bird checklist, hands-on exhibits and an alligator pond.

Allow 1 hour minimum. Mon.-Fri. 8-4, Sat. 10-4; closed major holidays. Free. Phone (337) 598-2216.

BOSSIER CITY (A-1) pop. 56,461, elev. 175′

Across the Red River from Shreveport and near Barksdale Air Force Base, Bossier City is the industrial hub of Bossier Parish and an entertainment center for the area. Thoroughbred racing takes place Thursday through Sunday at Harrah's Louisiana Downs from April through October; phone (318) 742-5555 or (318) 747-7223. The highlight of the racing season, the Isle of Capri Super Derby in September, is accompanied by a month-long festival with a variety of events and entertainment.

Note: Policies concerning admittance of children to pari-mutuel betting facilities vary. Phone for information.

A marker at Airline and Shed roads commemorates the 9-mile covered road built in 1874. Because cotton wagons often became mired in axle-deep mud, a corduroy road of split logs was constructed. Later a shed was added above the road to divert rainfall to drainage ditches beside the roadway.

Shreveport-Bossier Convention and Tourist Bureau—Bossier City: 100 John Wesley Blvd., Bossier City, LA 71112; phone (318) 226-8884 or (800) 551-8682.

8TH AIR FORCE MUSEUM is 2.8 mi. e. on Barksdale Blvd., .4 mi. s. on Access Rd., .2 mi. n. on Langley Dr., .1 mi. w. on Rickenbacker Ave., then .1 mi. e. to 88 Shreveport Rd. on Barksdale Air Force Base. The museum captures the periods of World Wars I and II through its exhibits of aircraft, uniforms, art, sculpture and aviation memorabilia. Aircraft on display include the B-17 Flying Fortress and the KC-97 Stratofreighter. Air Force films are presented in a reproduction of a World War II briefing room.

Note: Photo ID is required to enter the museum. All vehicles are subject to search. Backpacks, briefcases and large bags are not permitted. Allow 1 hour minimum. Daily 9:30-4; closed Jan. 1, Thanksgiving and Dec. 25. Free. Phone (318) 456-5553 or (318) 456-3065.

CASINOS

- **Boomtown Casino**, 300 Riverside Dr. Daily 24 hours. Phone (318) 746-0711 or (877) 762-4420.
- **Horseshoe Riverboat Casino**, 711 Horseshoe Blvd. Daily 24 hours. Phone (318) 742-0711 or (800) 895-0711.
- **Isle of Capri Casino**, I-20 exit 20A, then s. to 77 Hamilton Ln. Daily 24 hours. Phone (318) 678-7777 or (800) 843-4753.

BREAUX BRIDGE (E-3) pop. 7,281, elev. 15′

Named for Aricole Breaux, an Acadian who built a bridge over Bayou Teche, Breaux Bridge was an important shipping center when steamboats plied the river. The town now touts itself as Crawfish Capital of the World.

Bayou Teche Visitors Center: 314 E. Bridge St., Breaux Bridge, LA 70517; phone (337) 332-8500 or (888) 565-5939.

BURAS—*see New Orleans p. 148.*

CHALMETTE—*see New Orleans p. 148.*

CHENEYVILLE (C-3) pop. 901, elev. 63′

LOYD HALL PLANTATION is w. on US 71, s. on US 167, then 1 mi. e. to 292 Loyd Bridge Rd. **CLOSURE INFORMATION:** The plantation is closed due to damage from the 2005 hurricane season and has no plans to reopen.

CLOUTIERVILLE (C-2) elev. 109′

KATE CHOPIN HOUSE-BAYOU FOLK MUSEUM is .2 mi. e. of SR 1 on SR 495. An original edition of "Bayou Folk," a collection of Kate Chopin's short stories, is the focal point of the museum. The home of Oscar and Kate Chopin is typical of early 1800s Louisiana: The lower story is handmade brick; the upper story is heart cypress mortised with wood pegs. There are no inside stairs to the second floor. Behind the house are a blacksmith's shop, a country doctor's office and displays of early farm equipment.

Allow 1 hour minimum. Mon.-Sat. 10-5, Sun. 1-5; closed Jan. 1, Easter, Thanksgiving and Dec. 25. Admission $5; ages 6-18, $3. Phone (318) 379-2233.

COVINGTON—*see New Orleans p. 148.*

DARROW (E-4) elev. 21′

GEM SAVE **HOUMAS HOUSE** is at 40136 River Rd. (SR 942). Once the seat of a 20,000-acre sugar plantation, the French- and Spanish-style rear house was built in the late 1700s. A Greek Revival mansion was added in 1840. The restored mansion is furnished with early 19th-century antiques, including a Parisian mantel clock rumored to have belonged to Marie Antoinette and Limoges china emblazoned with the Houmas name.

A mural depicting a sugar cane field greets guests in the main hall and a graceful spiral staircase winds its way through the manse's three stories. Formal gardens, fountains and live oaks surround the house, which has been the setting for several films, including "Hush Hush Sweet Charlotte" with Bette Davis. Guides in period dress provide historical background.

Food is available. Allow 1 hour minimum. Guided tours Mon.-Wed. 10-5, Thurs.-Sun. 10-8;

closed Jan. 1, Thanksgiving and Dec. 25. Mansion and gardens $20; ages 13-18, $15; ages 6-12, $10. Gardens $10. MC, VI. Phone (225) 473-9380.

DEQUINCY (D-1) pop. 3,398, elev. 85′

The first European settlers to arrive in this area were startled to find the local American Indians wearing ornaments of gold. Thus began the persistent rumors of the "Lost Mine of Wyndham Creek." The Indians never divulged the source of their treasure.

Southwest Louisiana/Lake Charles Convention & Visitors Bureau—DeQuincy: 1205 N. Lakeshore Dr., Lake Charles, LA 70601; phone (337) 436-9588 or (800) 456-7952.

DEQUINCY RAILROAD MUSEUM is at 400 Lake Charles Ave. Housed in a restored 1923 train depot of Mission Revival architecture, the museum exhibits railroad memorabilia and equipment including a 1913 steam locomotive, a 1929 caboose and a 1947 passenger coach. Mon.-Fri. 9-4, Sat.-Sun. noon-4; closed Jan. 1, Thanksgiving and Dec. 25. Donations. Phone (337) 786-2823.

DERRY (C-2) elev. 109′

SAVE **MAGNOLIA PLANTATION HOME** is off I-49 exit 119, 4 mi. w. on SR 1, then 2.4 mi. n. on SR 493 to 5487 SR 119. This working plantation has remained in the same family since a 1753 French land grant. The house was rebuilt in 1896 using the foundation, walls and columns of an 1830s building burned during the Civil War. The two-and-a-half story, 27-room home is furnished in Southern Empire period and includes a chapel. Allow 1 hour minimum. Mon.-Sat. 1-4; closed Jan. 1 and Dec. 25. Admission $7; ages 12-18, $5; ages 6-11, $3. Phone (318) 379-2221.

DESTREHAN—*see New Orleans p. 148.*

DONALDSONVILLE (E-4) pop. 7,605

HISTORIC DONALDSONVILLE MUSEUM, 318 Mississippi St., is in a building that was once home to B. Lemann & Bro., reportedly the oldest family-owned department store in Louisiana. Galleries of the Past highlights life in the 1800s in Donaldsonville. Galleries also feature exhibits about the State Capitol, the Lemann store, the corner grocery, the theater, commercial life and the Civil War. Allow 30 minutes minimum. Mon.-Fri. 9-5, Sat. 10-3; closed Easter, Thanksgiving and Dec. 25. Admission $2. Phone (225) 746-0004.

EPPS (A-3) pop. 1,153, elev. 100′

Epps lies between the Boeuf River and Bayou Macon. The rich Macon Ridge soil of this region supports lush fields of cotton, rice and soybeans.

POVERTY POINT NATIONAL MONUMENT is 4.25 mi. e. on SR 134, then 1 mi. n. on SR 577. The 400-acre site is one of the earliest and largest prehistoric settlements discovered in North America. The complex of earthen mounds dates 1700-700 B.C. The central structure is an octagonal array of concentric ridges three-quarters of a mile in diameter. An outlying bird-shaped mound is 70 feet high. The site has a museum and walking trails. Visitors can watch excavations in progress.

Picnicking is permitted. Allow 2 hours minimum. Daily 9-5; closed Jan. 1, Thanksgiving and Dec. 25. Admission $2, over 61 and under 13 free. Phone (318) 926-5492 or (888) 926-5492.

EUNICE (D-2) pop. 11,499, elev. 49′

The rich, prairie soil surrounding Eunice enticed the early Acadians to settle in the area in 1894. The Acadian influence can still be seen in the historic buildings around town. Cajun organizations preserve Acadian heritage and provide educational programming about the French/Cajun language.

The Rendez Vous des Cajuns, held every Saturday night at the Liberty Center for Performing Arts, features a 2-hour live broadcast of Cajun and zydeco music.

Eunice Tourist Information Center: 200 S. C.C. Duson Dr., Eunice, LA 70535; phone (337) 457-2565.

THE EUNICE MUSEUM is at 220 S. C.C. Duson Dr. Housed in an old train depot, the museum recounts the history of local Cajun and American Indian cultures, area railroads and farming. A videotape chronicling the history of Cajun country zydeco music is shown. Allow 30 minutes minimum. Guided tours Tues.-Sat. 9-5; closed major holidays. Free. Phone (337) 457-6540.

PRAIRIE ACADIAN CULTURAL CENTER is at 250 W. Park Ave. Part of the Jean Lafitte National Historical Park and Preserve *(see place listing p. 150)*, the center houses exhibits depicting the Acadian migration and culture. Quilting, craft and cooking demonstrations also are presented. A live radio show featuring Cajun music and stories is broadcast from the center every Saturday evening. Allow 1 hour minimum. Tues.-Fri. and holidays 8-5, Sat. 8-6; closed Dec. 25. Free. Phone (337) 457-8499.

FERRIDAY (B-3) pop. 3,723, elev. 63′

DELTA MUSIC MUSEUM is at 218 Louisiana Ave. Exhibits concentrate on the lives and music of native sons Jerry Lee Lewis, Mickey Gilley, Jimmie Davis and PeeWee Whittaker. Other musicians noted for their contributions to the Delta region, such as Fats Domino, Aaron Neville and Percy Sledge, also are featured. Live performances take place throughout the year. Allow 30 minutes minimum. Mon.-Fri. 9-4; closed holidays. Free. Phone (318) 757-9999.

FOLSOM—*see New Orleans p. 148.*

FORT POLK (C-2)

FORT POLK MILITARY MUSEUM is 5 mi. s. on US 171 to the Fort Polk exit, following the entrance road to the main gate, in Building 917 on South Carolina Ave. Exhibits include uniforms, insignia and small arms of the 12 U.S. divisions that have served at the fort. A 2.5-acre park displays artillery pieces, tanks, helicopters and other vehicles. Picnic facilities are available. Allow 2 hours minimum. Wed.-Fri. 10-2, Sat.-Sun. 9-4; closed Jan. 1, Thanksgiving and Dec. 25. Free. Phone (337) 531-7905.

FRANKLIN (E-3) pop. 8,354, elev. 16′

In 1800 Pennsylvanian Guinea Lewis founded the town and named it for his home state's preeminent statesman and philosopher, Benjamin Franklin. Most early settlers came from the Northeast, and their strong Union sympathies saved Franklin from the destruction other towns in Louisiana suffered at the hands of the Union Army during the Civil War. On Bayou Teche in the Atchafalaya Basin, Franklin is presently a center for salt production, sugar-refining and carbon-black operations.

Cajun Coast Visitors & Convention Bureau—Franklin: 15307 US 90W, Franklin, LA 70538; phone (337) 828-2555 or (800) 256-2931. *See color ad card insert.*

Self-guiding tours: Brochures describing a self-guiding walking tour of Franklin's historic district are available from the visitors and convention bureau.

SAVE **GREVEMBERG HOUSE MUSEUM** is just s. of jct. SRs 182 and 322 at 407 Sterling Rd. The restored 1851 Greek Revival home is furnished with period antiques. Among the local artifacts displayed are newspapers, kitchen implements and children's toys. Allow 30 minutes minimum. Daily 10-4; closed major holidays. Admission $6; over 62 and ages 12-18, $5; ages 3-11, $4. Phone (337) 828-2092.

OAKLAWN MANOR is w. off SR 182 via US 90 exit 3211. This 1837 Greek Revival mansion was the center of one of the area's first sugar cane plantations. A virtual fortress, it has 20-inch-thick walls. Inside is an extensive collection of rare prints and oil paintings by John James Audubon and an assortment of hand-painted carvings of waterfowl that winter in southern Louisiana. The manor grounds were fashioned after the Gardens of Versailles.

Daily 10-4; closed major holidays. Admission $10; ages 7-17, $5. Phone (337) 828-0434.

FROGMORE (C-3) elev. 61′

FROGMORE COTTON PLANTATION is at 11054 US 84. An orientation videotape precedes a guided tour of the plantation's original steam cotton gin, slave quarters and antebellum structures. Slave customs, music and daily life are detailed. Visitors can see the contrast between an 1850s steam cotton gin and a modern, computerized, 900-bale-per-day operation by touring the 1,800-acre working plantation.

Allow 1 hour, 30 minutes minimum. Mon.-Fri. 9-3, Sat. 10-2, Mar. 8-May 31 and Sept. 1-Nov. 15; Mon.-Fri. 9-noon, June-Aug.; schedule varies rest of year. Closed July 4. Historic tour $10. Modern tour $5. Combination tour $12; ages 6-18, $5. DS, MC, VI. Phone (318) 757-2453 or (318) 757-3333.

GARYVILLE—*see New Orleans p. 149.*

GIBSON (E-4) elev. 5′

SAVE **WILDLIFE GARDENS** is s. of jct. US 90 and SR 20; cross Bayou at Greenwood School bridge, then 2 mi. w. following signs to 5306 N. Bayou Black Dr. A self-guiding walking tour of the gardens, which surround a natural swamp, offers a view of native plants and animals, including raccoons, alligators and deer. Allow 1 hour, 30 minutes minimum. Tues.-Sat. 9-3; closed major holidays. Admission $5; ages 2-12, $3. Phone (985) 575-3676.

GRETNA—*see New Orleans p. 149.*

HACKBERRY (E-1) pop. 1,699, elev. 6′

SABINE NATIONAL WILDLIFE REFUGE is 8 mi. s. on SR 27. **CLOSURE INFORMATION:** Due to the effects of the 2005 hurricane season, the refuge is closed and no reopening date has been set. Phone (337) 762-3816. *See Recreation Chart.*

HAMMOND (D-5) pop. 17,639, elev. 47′

SAVE **KLIEBERT'S TURTLE AND ALLIGATOR TOURS** is off I-55 exit 22W (Springfield), 1 mi. n. on frwy. service rd. to Hoffman Rd., then w. to 41083 W. Yellow Water Rd. The 45-minute guided walking tour of this commercial farm is through compounds housing tens of thousands of turtles and past a large pond with 250 alligators, some weighing more than 1,400 pounds. Allow 1 hour minimum. Daily noon-dusk, Mar.-Oct. Fee $6; over 61, $4; ages 2-11, $3. MC, VI. Phone (985) 345-3617 or (800) 854-9164.

HAUGHTON (A-1) pop. 2,792, elev. 237′

TOUCHSTONE'S WILDLIFE AND ART MUSEUM is at 3386 US 80E. Dioramas featuring more than 1,000 animals from around the world are displayed at the museum, which also features American Indian artifacts and memorabilia from the Civil War and World Wars I and II. Allow 1 hour minimum. Tues.-Sat. 9-5. Admission $2.50, under 6 free with adult. Phone (318) 949-2323.

HOUMA (F-4) pop. 32,393, elev. 14′

Laced with waterways spanned by 52 bridges, the delta city of Houma (HO-ma) is often likened to Venice, Italy. Seven bayous converge, and the Intracoastal Waterway and Houma Navigational Canal provide ready access to the Gulf where saltwater fishing is popular.

Boat trips into the deep swamp and bayou country of southern Louisiana's Atchafalaya Basin are offered by Annie Miller's Son's Swamp and Marsh

Tours, Bayou Neuf and Munson's Cypress Bayou Swamp Tours. Another tour company, Atchafalaya Basin Backwater Adventure, leads trips from nearby Gibson. In the backwater areas, sharp eyes can often spot herons, ducks, alligators, raccoons, nutrias and other wildlife. Spring and summer are best for viewing alligators and nesting waterbirds.

A scenic 140-mile stretch of US 90, beginning in Lafayette and ending in Paradis, intersects with SRs 24 and 57 in Houma. Just south of town SRs 56 and 57 form an 80-mile circular driving tour through bayou country.

Houma Area Convention and Visitors Bureau: 114 Tourist Dr., Gray, LA 70359; phone (985) 868-2732 or (800) 688-2732. *See color ad card insert.*

Self-guiding tours: Brochures describing a 2-hour self-guiding walking tour of the Houma historic district are available from the convention and visitors bureau.

BAYOU TERREBONNE WATERLIFE MUSEUM is at 7910 W. Park Ave. A 46-foot-long mural demonstrating how flora and fauna change through 10 different ecosystems weaves through the museum. Interactive exhibits allow visitors to drive a shrimping boat, practice oyster-tonging and view models of boats. Other exhibits demonstrate fishing and trapping industries. A 13.5-foot-long alligator is displayed.

Allow 1 hour minimum. Tues.-Fri. 10-5, Sat. noon-4. Admission $3; over 65, $2.50; ages 2-13, $2. AX, DS, MC, VI. Phone (985) 580-7200.

A CAJUN MAN'S SWAMP CRUISE departs 10 mi. w. on SR 182 to Antill Ln. Alligators, deer, opossums, raccoons and waterfowl can be seen on this narrated tour of the Louisiana swamps. Allow 2 hours minimum. Trips depart Tues.-Sat. at 10 and 2, Mon. at 2, Mar.-Nov.; Mon.-Sat. at 2, rest of year (weather permitting). Closed Jan. 1, Thanksgiving and Dec. 25. Schedule may vary; phone ahead. Fare $20; under 13, $10. Reservations are required. Phone (985) 868-4625.

SAVE **CAJUN TOURS AND CRUISES** is at 709 May Ave. The Cajun way of life on Louisiana's bayous is reflected in several tours, which can include a visit to a seafood factory, bayou community, American Indian fishing village and Cajun village. Alligators, egrets, herons and pelicans are just some of the wildlife that can be seen. Tours range from 1.5 to 5.5 hours; multiday tours also are available. Open daily at 9. Fare $15-$100; under 12, $10-$80. Reservations are suggested. MC, VI. Phone (985) 872-6157.

SAVE **SOUTHDOWN PLANTATION/TERREBONNE MUSEUM** is at 1208 Museum Dr., 9 mi. s. of US 90 via SR 311 near jct. SR 664 (St. Charles St.). The first floor of this pink Victorian manor house was built in 1859; a second story was added in 1893. Original Minor family furniture and Boehm and Doughty porcelain are among the items displayed on a 12-room guided tour. Exhibits recount the history and culture of Terrebonne Parish, including its sugar plantations, Cajun heritage, art, literature, industry and local crafts.

Allow 1 hour minimum. Guided tours depart on the hour Tues.-Sat. 10-3; closed holidays. Admission $5; over 65 and college students with ID $4; ages 6-18, $2. Phone (985) 851-0154.

JEAN LAFITTE—*see New Orleans p. 149.*

JEAN LAFITTE NATIONAL HISTORICAL PARK AND PRESERVE—*see New Orleans p. 150.*

JENA (C-3) pop. 2,971, elev. 157′

CATAHOULA NATIONAL WILDLIFE REFUGE is 12 mi. e. on US 84. Nature trails, a 9-mile wildlife drive and an observation tower are part of the refuge, which protects 14,750 acres of natural habitat for native and migratory waterfowl and such animals as alligators, beavers, deer, bobcats and otters. Allow 1 hour minimum. Daily dawn-dusk. Free. Phone (318) 992-5261.

JENNINGS (E-2) pop. 10,986, elev. 28′

Founded in 1884, free homesteads and rich prairie land lured Midwestern wheat farmers, who soon switched to growing rice. The Mermentau River, its banks lined with moss-draped trees, flows through this island in an ocean of rice paddies.

In 1901 Louisiana's first oil well came in 5 miles northeast of Jennings, touching off a rush of oil developers to the area. The Louisiana Oil and Gas Park on SR 26 at I-10 houses an information center, live alligator displays and a replica of the state's first oil derrick. Oil and rice are still the mainstays of Jennings' economy. Many wells, streams and canals supply the water needed to grow the rice, and airplanes are often used to plant the crops.

Jeff Davis Parish Tourist Commission: 100 Rue de l'Acadie, Jennings, LA 70546; phone (337) 821-5521 or (800) 264-5521.

W.H. TUPPER GENERAL MERCHANDISE MUSEUM is at 311 N. Main St. This museum houses the entire inventory of a rural store that closed in 1949. The collection includes toys and games, period fashions, fabric, patent medicines, antique automobile parts and hardware. Many items are in unopened packages and original displays. Within the same building is the Louisiana Telephone Pioneer Museum, which chronicles a century of telephone communication.

Allow 1 hour minimum. Mon.-Fri. 9-5; closed holidays. Admission (including Louisiana Telephone Pioneer Museum) $3, students with ID $1. Phone (337) 821-5532.

ZIGLER MUSEUM is at 411 Clara St. A converted brick Colonial home contains wildlife artwork,

American and European art from medieval to contemporary periods, Louisiana art and changing exhibits. Tues.-Sat. 9-5, Sun. 1-4; closed holidays. Admission $2; under 17, $1. Phone (337) 824-0114.

KENNER—*see New Orleans p. 150.*

KINDER (D-2) pop. 2,148, elev. 49′

CASINOS

- **Grand Casino Coushatta**, 5 mi. n. on US 165 at 777 Coushatta Dr. Daily 24 hours. Phone (337) 738-7300 or (800) 584-7263.

KISATCHIE NATIONAL FOREST

Elevations in the forest range from 80 ft. along the banks of the forest's rivers and creeks to 400 ft. in the Kisatchie Hills. Refer to AAA maps for additional elevation information.

Kisatchie National Forest extends across the central and northern parts of the state. The terrain of Louisiana's only national forest, comprised of six districts and more than 600,000 acres, varies from swamps of hardwood and cypress trees draped with Spanish moss to sandstone hills covered with longleaf pine. Farming and lumbering in the early 1900s had left much of this land unproductive, but most of the area revived after the forest's establishment in 1930.

The forest offers more than 40 developed recreation areas. Most are open all year; swimming sites are open seasonally. The 31-mile Wild Azalea National Recreation Trail, near Alexandria off FR 273, offers floral displays in spring and brilliant colors in fall. Castor Creek Scenic Area, reached on foot from the Wild Azalea Trail, has many old, moss-covered hardwoods.

Near Minden the 8-mile Sugar Cane National Recreation Trail mixes history, nature and lakeside scenery as it winds across rolling hills. Among the many other trails within the forest is the 10-mile Big Branch Trail near Leesville. Kisatchie Hills Wilderness Area, also known as Louisiana's Little Grand Canyon, is an area of mesas, cliffs and canyons.

The forest can be enjoyed by car as well as by foot. The 17-mile Longleaf Scenic Byway, beginning at the junction of FR 337 and SR 117 and ending on SR 119, winds through some of Louisiana's most rugged forest land.

Kisatchie Bayou, off FR 366, offers 6 miles of canoe routes and probably the best fishing in the district. Saline Bayou, a national scenic river off FR 513, is good for wildlife viewing and can be canoed for 13 miles. Edible wild foods in Kisatchie include huckleberries, blackberries, elderberries and mayhaw fruit.

Ranger offices for the various districts are in Natchitoches *(see place listing p. 107)*, Leesville *(see place listing p. 104)*, Alexandria *(see place listing p. 94)*, Homer, Winnfield and Bentley. For further information contact the Supervisor, Kisatchie National Forest, 2500 Shreveport Highway, Pineville, LA 71360; phone (318) 473-7160. *See Recreation Chart and the AAA Southeastern CampBook.*

KRAEMER (E-4) elev. 4′

TORRES' CAJUN SWAMP TOURS departs from 101 Torres Rd. (SR 307). Guided 1.5-hour boat tours are offered through local swamps and bayous, affording views of area wildlife. A small zoo features various animal exhibits. Allow 2 hours minimum. Daily 9-6. Fare $15; over 65, $13.50; ages 1-12, $8. Phone (985) 633-7739.

ZAM'S BAYOU SWAMP TOURS departs from 135 Kraemer Bayou Rd. Narrated boat tours of Bayou Boeuf offer glimpses of blue herons, turtles, snakes, nutrias, raccoons, minks and alligators as passengers cruise beneath the swamp's moss-draped cypress and oak trees. A collection of local wildlife—both preserved and living—also can be seen. Allow 2 hours minimum. Daily 9:30-4. Fare $15; ages 6-12, $7.50. MC, VI. Phone (985) 633-7881.

LACOMBE—*see New Orleans p. 150.*

LAFAYETTE (E-3) pop. 110,257, elev. 40′

When expelled from Nova Scotia by the British in the 1700s, the French Acadian farmers settled around Lafayette, a region of 22 parishes that would come to be known as Acadiana. Their descendants, commonly called Cajuns, still speak a French dialect and observe the traditions of their ancestors. Like gumbo, the staple of Cajun cuisine, Acadiana has become a melting pot of cultures. French is still the dominant influence, with traces of Spanish, African, American Indian, German and English.

Agriculture and cattle raising were the key occupations around Vermilionville, as the town was first called. During the 1850s highly organized rustlers caused the ranchers to band together into an army of 4,000 vigilantes that drove the rustlers out.

The Civil War and yellow fever hindered Vermilionville's growth, but in 1881 prosperity rode into town on an iron horse when the railroad was extended from New Orleans to Houston. Three years later the town changed its name to honor Marquis de Lafayette, a French general who served in the Continental army during the American Revolution.

Like many southern Louisiana towns, Lafayette was transformed by the discovery of offshore oil. Presently it is the center of the Gulf oil and gas industry; many company offices are housed in the Heymann Oil Center. The town also is the home of the University of Louisiana at Lafayette.

The Live Oak Society has its headquarters in Lafayette. This group was organized to preserve the live oak, an evergreen shade tree. Membership is limited to live oaks at least 100 years old. Annual membership dues are 25 acorns. One of the society's venerable members stands in front of St. John's Cathedral, 915 St. John St.; it is more than 450 years old.

Thoroughbred races are held Thursday through Saturday and Monday at Evangeline Downs on US 167N April through Labor Day. Quarter horse racing takes place Thursday through Sunday from mid-September through October; phone (337) 896-7223.

Note: Policies concerning admittance of children to pari-mutuel betting facilities vary. Phone for information.

A year-round attraction is Acadiana Park, off East Alexander Street in the north part of town, where a nature trail winds through 3.5 miles of woodland. A scenic stretch of US 90 begins in Lafayette at the I-10 junction and runs 140 miles east to Paradis.

Lafayette Convention and Visitors Commission: 1400 N.W. Evangeline Thruway, P.O. Box 52066, Lafayette, LA 70501; phone (337) 232-3737, or (800) 346-1958 out of La., or (800) 543-5340 in Canada and United States. *See color ad card insert.*

ACADIAN CULTURAL CENTER is off I-10 exit 103A, 5 mi. s. to Surrey St., then .5 mi. e. to 501 Fischer Rd. Part of the Jean Lafitte National Historical Park and Preserve *(see place listing p. 150)*, the center offers exhibits detailing the various aspects of Cajun culture and a 40-minute film, "The Cajun Way: Echoes of Acadia." Allow 1 hour minimum. Daily 8-5; closed Mardi Gras Day and Dec. 25. Film shown on the hour 9-4. Free. Phone (337) 232-0789.

ACADIAN VILLAGE is 10 mi. s. of I-10 exit 100, then w. onto Ridge Rd., following signs. This restored bayou town depicts the early 19th-century lifestyle of Acadians in southern Louisiana. Buildings relocated to the site include a general store, barn, chapel and several houses. The village also includes 10 acres of gardens and woodlands. Allow 30 minutes minimum. Daily 10-4; closed major holidays. Admission $7; over 62, $6; ages 6-14, $4. MC, VI. Phone (337) 981-2364.

ALEXANDRE MOUTON HOUSE is at 1122 Lafayette St. The oldest part of this structure was built about 1800 by Jean Mouton, founder of Lafayette, for use as a town or Sunday house. Furnished in period, the house operates as a museum; displays include heirlooms, local historical memorabilia and Mardi Gras costumes. Tues.-Sat. 9-4:30, Sun. 1-4; closed holidays. Admission $3, senior citizens $2, students with ID $1. Phone (337) 234-2208.

CHILDREN'S MUSEUM OF ACADIANA is at 201 E. Congress St. The museum offers activities for children from preschool age to fourth grade. Hands-on displays include an operating room, ambulance, television newsroom, grocery store and bank. Allow 1 hour minimum. Tues.-Sat. 10-5; closed holidays. Admission $5, under 1 free. AX, DS, MC, VI. Phone (337) 232-8500.

LAFAYETTE NATURAL HISTORY MUSEUM & PLANETARIUM, 433 Jefferson St., houses exhibits relating to science, technology and math. Children's activities and workshops add to the fun at the interactive center, with changing collections offering a variety of learning experiences. Allow 1 hour minimum. Museum Tues.-Fri. 9-5, Sat. 10-6, Sun. 1-6. Planetarium shows Wed. at 4, Sat. at 11, 1:30, 2:45 and 4, Sun. at 1:30, 2:45 and 4. Closed major holidays. Admission $5; over 62, $3; ages 4-17, $2. Phone (337) 291-5544.

UNIVERSITY ART MUSEUM is at 710 E. St. Mary Blvd. on the University of Louisiana campus. Changing exhibits of 18th-century through present-day artworks fill 11,000 square feet of gallery space. The museum's furnishings include pieces by such 20th-century designers as Harry Bertoia, Isamu Noguchi and Eero Saarinen. Allow 1 hour minimum. Tues.-Sat. 10-5; closed holidays. Admission $5; over 50, $4; ages 5-17, $3. AX, MC, VI. Phone (337) 482-2278.

VERMILIONVILLE is 5 mi. s. of I-10 exit 103A, then .5 mi. e. to 300 Fisher Rd. This heritage and folklife park brings to life the early days of Cajun and Creole settlers from the mid-1700s to late 1800s. Costumed craftspeople, cooking demonstrations, live music and art are featured. Self-guiding tours include five original homes and 12 reproduction buildings that contain period furnishings and artifacts.

Food is available. Allow 2 hours minimum. Tues.-Sun. 10-4; closed Jan. 1, Mardi Gras Day, Thanksgiving and Dec. 24-25 and 31. Admission $8; over 65, $6.50; ages 6-18, $5. AX, MC, VI. Phone (337) 233-4077 or (866) 992-2968.

LAKE CHARLES (E-2) pop. 71,757, elev. 18′

Lake Charles owes its early development to a happy combination of Capt. J.B. Watkins, natural resources and a deepwater port. In 1887 Watkins moved his New York newspaper to Lake Charles and started an advertising program that, with the terminus of a railroad at New Orleans, resulted in the establishment of a 17-mill lumber industry.

An abundance of pine and cypress led to a building frenzy at the turn of the 19th century. There were not enough architects to meet construction demands, so carpenters built houses from book plans that they modified for individual homeowners. These distinct designs now define the historic Charpentier (French for carpenter) District.

Lake Charles' Contraband Days, which takes place the first 2 weeks in May, is one of Louisiana's largest festivals; it centers on the legend of the "Gentleman Pirate," Jean Lafitte, who supposedly hid his treasures along the shores of Lake Charles.

The Creole Nature Trail National Scenic Byway (SRs 27 and 82), 9 miles west of Lake Charles, runs south from I-10 and passes through several refuges.

Southwest Louisiana/Lake Charles Convention & Visitors Bureau—Lake Charles: 1205 N. Lakeshore Dr., Lake Charles, LA 70601; phone (337) 436-9588 or (800) 456-7952. *See color ad card insert.*

Self-guiding tours: Brochures for a 180-mile driving tour of the Creole Nature Trail National Scenic Byway and a riding/walking tour of the historic district are available from the convention and visitors bureau.

Shopping areas: Prien Lake Mall, off I-210 Lake Street exit on W. Prien Lake Road, features Dillard's and Sears among its more than 80 stores.

IMPERIAL CALCASIEU MUSEUM is at 204 W. Sallier St. at Ethel St. The museum features historical displays, an art gallery and a library with a collection of Audubon prints. Re-creations of late 19th-century rooms include a pharmacy, Victorian bedroom, parlor, country store and barbershop. The adjacent Gibson-Barham Gallery houses fine arts exhibits. On the grounds is a 300-year-old oak tree.

Allow 30 minutes minimum. Tues.-Sat. 10-5; closed Jan. 1, Mardi Gras Day, Easter, Memorial Day, Labor Day, Thanksgiving and Dec. 24-25 and 31. Admission $2; ages 6-18, $1. MC, VI. Phone (337) 439-3797.

CASINOS

- **Harrah's Lake Charles Casino**, 505 N. Lakeshore Dr. **CLOSURE INFORMATION:** The casino is closed due to the effects of the 2005 hurricane season and has no plans to reopen. Phone (337) 437-1500 or (800) 977-7529.

- **Isle of Capri Casino**, off I-10 exit 19A to 711 Isle Capri Blvd. Daily 24 hours. Phone (318) 678-7777 or (800) 843-4753.

LA PLACE—*see New Orleans p. 150.*

LAKE PROVIDENCE (A-4) pop. 5,104, elev. 106′

LOUISIANA STATE COTTON MUSEUM is 1 mi. s. on US 65. Housed in a rural plantation setting, this museum commemorates the history and heritage of cotton cultivation in Louisiana. Hands-on exhibits and outdoor displays include a collection of blues music and instruments, an authentic sharecropper's cabin and an original Gullet Cotton Gin, circa 1920. A cotton field is cultivated on the grounds. Picnicking is permitted. Allow 1 hour minimum. Mon.-Sat. 9-4:30, Apr.-Oct.; Mon.-Fri. 9-4, rest of year; closed holidays. Free. Phone (318) 559-2041.

LEESVILLE (C-1) pop. 6,753, elev. 238′

Leesville, named for Gen. Robert E. Lee, was founded in 1871. Horse racing was once the chief avocation of this section of western Louisiana. The cotton-picking machine, invented by two Mississippians, was first demonstrated nearby. Forestry is the mainstay of Leesville's economy.

Vernon Parish Tourist Commission: P.O. Box 349, Leesville, LA 71496; phone (337) 238-0783.

MADISONVILLE—*see New Orleans p. 151.*

MANCHAC (D-5) elev. 96′

SAVE **MOCKINGBIRD SWAMP TOURS** is off I-55 exit 15, then 1.25 mi. s.e. on US 51 to departure point at Gator's Den. Cruising through the lush semitropical wetlands of the Manchac Swamp, passengers can see egrets, raccoons, nutrias, turtles, water snakes and alligators. Allow 2 hours minimum. Tours depart daily at 10, noon and 2. Fare $25; under 12, $15. Reservations are required. Phone (985) 748-7637.

MANSFIELD (B-1) pop. 5,582, elev. 331′

One of the few major Civil War engagements in Louisiana was fought near Mansfield in 1864. Gen. Richard Taylor drew up his battle plans under a large water oak that once stood at the east end of Polk Street. The nearby buildings of Old Mansfield Female College, a pioneer in the education of women 1852-1929, were used as a barracks and hospital.

DeSoto Parish Tourist Bureau: 101 N. Washington Ave., Mansfield, LA 71052; phone (318) 872-1177.

MANSFIELD STATE HISTORIC SITE is 4 mi. s.e. at 15149 SR 175. The 177-acre site commemorates the climactic battle of the Red River campaign of April 8, 1864, when Gen. Richard Taylor and his Confederate troops drove Union forces back to Alexandria. The battle saved Shreveport and the Red River territory for the South and prevented the war from moving onward toward Texas. A museum features exhibits and battle relics.

Picnicking is permitted. Allow 1 hour minimum. Daily 9-5; closed Jan. 1, Thanksgiving and Dec. 25.

Admission $2, over 62 and under 12 free. Phone (318) 872-1474 or (888) 677-6267.

MANY (C-1) pop. 2,889, elev. 242′

Named for the commander of nearby Fort Jesup, Many was established as a trading post in 1843 in an area settled by Belgians. The old San Antonio Trace (now SR 6) passes through town. Spanish influence remains from the days when Spain ruled the narrow strip of land along the Sabine River. Los Adaes, northeast of Many, was capital of the Spanish Province of Texas and is now a state historic site. It serves as a reminder of the blending of French, Spanish and American Indian cultures.

Sabine Parish Tourist Commission: 920 Fisher Rd., Many, LA 71449; phone (318) 256-5880 or (800) 358-7802.

FORT JESUP STATE HISTORIC SITE is 6 mi. n.e. on SR 6 at 32 Geoghagan Rd. The 21-acre site was established in 1822 in the event of a dispute with Spain over the western limits of the Louisiana Purchase. First commanded by Gen. Zachary Taylor, the fort became known as the "Cradle of the Mexican War," serving as the embarkation point for troops sent to Texas. Artifacts and exhibits are housed in a log kitchen and an officers' barracks.

Picnic facilities are available. Allow 1 hour minimum. Daily 9-5; closed Jan. 1, Thanksgiving and Dec. 25. Admission $2, over 62 and under 12 free. Phone (318) 256-4117 or (888) 677-5378.

HODGES GARDENS is 12 mi. s. on US 171 in Florien. Winding roads take visitors past 70 acres of gardens, a 225-acre lake, greenhouses, an island memorial to the Louisiana Purchase and pastures with deer, sheep and buffaloes. Hiking and bicycling trails, picnic facilities, food, fishing and boat rentals are available. Allow 3 hours minimum. Daily 8-5; closed Jan. 1, Thanksgiving and Dec. 24-25. Last admission is 30 minutes before closing. Admission $6.50; over 65, $5.50; ages 6-17, $3. Phone (318) 586-3523 or (800) 354-3523.

MARKSVILLE (C-3) pop. 5,537, elev. 85′

Marksville was settled by Acadians in the late 18th century. The town was originally on the Red River, but over the years the river has shifted its course so that it now runs 5 miles north of town. The area around Marksville saw much fighting during the Civil War. Fort De Russy, a Confederate stronghold north of Marksville, fell to Union forces on March 14, 1864.

Avoyelles Parish Commission of Tourism: 208 S. Main St., P.O. Box 24, Marksville, LA 71351; phone (318) 253-0585 or (800) 833-4195.

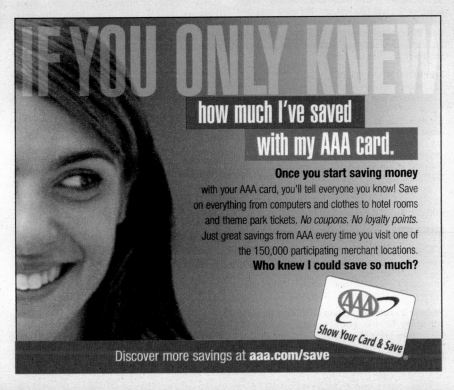

HYPOLITE BORDELON HOME AND VISITOR CENTER is .5 mi. w. on SR 1. Circa 1820, the Creole cottage contains furnishings representative of the early 19th century. A chapel and other smaller buildings also are on the grounds. Allow 30 minutes minimum. Mon.-Tues. and Thurs.-Fri. 9-5, Wed. and Sat. 9-3; closed Jan. 1, July 4 and Thanksgiving. Admission $2; ages 3-12, $1. Phone (318) 253-0284.

CASINOS

- **Paragon Casino and Resort**, 711 Paragon Pl. Daily 24 hours. Phone (318) 253-1946 or (800) 946-1946.

MARRERO—*see New Orleans p. 151.*

MARTHAVILLE (B-1) elev. 260′

REBEL STATE HISTORIC SITE is 3 mi. n.w. to 1260 SR 1221. This site was named in honor of an unknown Confederate soldier, or Rebel, killed during the Civil War and buried by a local family. A focal point of the park is the Louisiana Country Music Museum, which has exhibits about the development of regional folk music. Bluegrass, gospel and country music concerts are given throughout the year.

Picnicking is permitted. Allow 30 minutes minimum. Daily 9-5; closed Jan. 1, Thanksgiving and Dec. 25. Admission $2, over 62 and under 13 free. Phone (318) 472-6255 or (888) 677-3600.

MELROSE (C-2) elev. 109′

The town of Melrose on Cane River Lake lies in an area known as La Côte Joyeuse, meaning "happy coast" in French. SRs 494 and 119 cross back and forth over the Cane, which is an old course of the Red River. Many homes and gardens dating from the mid-19th century are scattered throughout this section of Natchitoches Parish.

MELROSE PLANTATION is e. on CR 493 to CR 119. Marie Therese Coincoin, a freed slave, and her sons received land grants on which they built Yucca House in 1796, the African House in 1800 and the Big House in 1833. In 1898 Melrose became the home of John Hampton Henry and his wife, Cammie. Mrs. Henry patronized and hosted many artists, including Clementine Hunter, whose work is on display, and writers such as William Faulkner and John Steinbeck.

Daily noon-4; closed major holidays and Fri. preceding events. Admission $7; ages 13-17, $4; ages 6-12, $3. MC, VI. Phone (318) 379-0055.

MINDEN (A-2) pop. 13,027, elev. 181′

Charles Hance Veeder founded Minden in 1836, naming it after a town on the Weser River in Germany where his parents were born. Besides being a productive agricultural region, the area around Minden is rich in petroleum and natural gas.

Webster Parish Convention & Visitors Bureau: 101 Sibley Rd., P.O. Box 819, Minden, LA 71058-0819; phone (318) 377-4240 or (800) 264-6336.

GERMANTOWN COLONY AND MUSEUM is 7 mi. n. on Germantown Rd. (Webster Parish Rd. 114) to 120 Museum Rd. The colony was founded by German settlers in 1835 and operated under a communal system for 37 years. The original kitchen, dining hall and one cabin remain. The smokehouse and blacksmith shop have been restored. The buildings contain artifacts used by the settlers.

Allow 1 hour, 30 minutes minimum. Wed.-Sat. 10-3. Admission $3; under 12, 50c. Phone (318) 377-6061.

MONROE (B-3) pop. 53,107, elev. 77′

Monroe, on the banks of the Ouachita River, is the trade center of northeast Louisiana and home to the University of Louisiana at Monroe. Recreational facilities can be found at Chennault and Forsythe parks, Lazarre Point, on a bend of the river, and at Kiroli Park. The parks surrounding 3,600-acre Cheniere Lake permit fishing and hunting.

Monroe-West Monroe Convention and Visitors Bureau: 601 Constitution Dr., West Monroe, LA 71292; phone (318) 387-5691 or (800) 843-1872.

Shopping areas: The Pecan Land Mall, with more than 90 stores, features Dillard's, JCPenney, Belk and Sears.

EMY-LOU BIEDENHARN FOUNDATION is at 2006 Riverside Dr. The complex contains the Bible Museum, the Biedenharn Home and ELsong Gardens and Conservatory. The nondenominational museum's collection of Bibles includes a 1560 Geneva Bible and a 1611 King James Bible. The 1914 house, which contains china, crystal, silver and soft drink memorabilia, was built by the first bottler of Coca-Cola, Joseph Biedenharn. The gardens were named after his daughter Emy-Lou.

Guided 45-minute tours are offered on the hour Mon.-Sat. 10-5, Sun. 2-5; closed Jan. 1, Easter, July 4 (garden open), Thanksgiving and Dec. 24-25. Last tour departs 1 hour before closing. Free. Phone (318) 387-5281 or (800) 362-0983.

LOUISIANA PURCHASE GARDENS AND ZOO is at 1405 Bernstein Dr. This 100-acre site is home to more than 750 animals. The moated animal confines are surrounded by landscaped gardens. Boat rides through the habitats are available April through September. Daily 10-5; closed Jan. 1 and Dec. 25. Admission $4.50; over 65 and ages 3-12, $3. Rides $2 each. MC, VI. Phone (318) 329-2400.

MASUR MUSEUM OF ART is at 1400 S. Grand St. The Masur family donated their home for use as a free public art museum in 1963. Displays include a collection of paintings, prints, photographs and sculptures as well as changing monthly exhibits. Allow 30 minutes minimum. Tues.-Thurs. 9-5, Fri.-Sun. 2-5. Free. Phone (318) 329-2237.

NORTHEAST LOUISIANA CHILDREN'S MUSEUM is at 323 Walnut St. At this hands-on museum, children can explore restaurant jobs in the Kids' Café, drive an ambulance at Health Hall, solve puzzles in the Think Tank and blow bubbles at the

Bubble Works. Toddler Town features soft blocks and educational toys for young visitors. Allow 1 hour minimum. Tues.-Fri. 9-2, Sat. 10-5. Admission $5, under 1 free. Phone (318) 361-9611.

MORGAN CITY (E-4) pop. 12,703, elev. 6′

The Chitimacha Indians were the first to settle in the area, but the character of the region was shaped by the 18th-century Acadian refugees from Canada. Better known as Cajuns, their culture is evident in the food, language, music and architecture found in this region. Two scenic highways, US 90 and SR 70, intersect at Morgan City.

On the banks of the Atchafalaya River, Morgan City once called itself the Jumbo Shrimp Capital of the World. But since offshore oil was discovered in 1947, the petroleum industry has far surpassed the shrimp market in economic importance. Morgan City annually celebrates both industries with its Shrimp and Petroleum Festival during Labor Day weekend.

Morgan City Tourist Information Center: 727 Myrtle St., Morgan City, LA 70380; phone (985) 384-3343.

Self-guiding tours: Morgan City's historic downtown district can be explored courtesy of a walking tour brochure available at the information center on Myrtle Street or at businesses in the downtown area.

BROWNELL MEMORIAL PARK & CARILLON TOWER is 4 mi. n.e. on SR 70. Visitors to the park, which covers 9.5 acres along the ridges of a swamp, can see native wild plants and numerous species of resident and migratory birds. The 106-foot tower, one of the largest cast-bell carillons in the world, has 61 bronze bells that chime every 30 minutes. Daily 9-5, Apr.-Oct.; 9-4, rest of year. Closed major holidays. Free. Phone (985) 384-2283.

CYPRESS MANOR AND MARDI GRAS MUSEUM is at 715 Second St. The 1906 two-story house contains antiques and Mardi Gras costumes dating from 1928 to the present. Tues.-Sat. 10-4:30, Sun. 1-5; closed holidays. Admission $3; ages 5-17, $2. Phone (985) 380-4651.

SWAMP GARDENS, 725 Myrtle St., focuses on the lifestyle of the Cajuns. During guided walking tours of the 3.5-acre cypress grove, visitors can see live alligators, bears, deer and other swamp creatures along with displays about the Cajun people. Picnicking is permitted. Allow 1 hour minimum. Guided tours depart daily at 10, 11, 1, 2, 3 and 4, May-Oct.; at 10, 11, 1, 2 and 3, rest of year. Closed Jan. 1, Mardi Gras Day, Thanksgiving and Dec. 25. Admission $4; ages 3-18, $2. Phone (985) 384-3343.

NAPOLEONVILLE (E-4) pop. 686, elev. 15′

Napoleonville's name was bestowed by a French settler who had fought under the "Little Colonel." The town is the site of an enormous salt dome, which is used by Mobil Oil for storing natural gas-liquids.

Christ Episcopal Church on the edge of town dates from 1853. During the Civil War Union troops stabled horses in the church and used the stained-glass window above the altar for target practice. After the war the window was sent to the Tiffany Studios in New York for repairs, only to be shattered by a storm in 1909 and repaired again.

MADEWOOD PLANTATION HOUSE is 2 mi. s. on SR 308. Designed in 1846 by Henry Howard, a prominent New Orleans architect, Madewood resembles a Greek temple. Its furnishings reflect an elegant antebellum lifestyle and include a Meissen mirror, a Mathew Brady photograph of Gen. Robert E. Lee and an unsupported, curved staircase. On the grounds are a carriage house, an 1822 riverboat captain's home and a cottage. A guided tour lasts 45 minutes.

Daily 10-4; closed Jan. 1, Thanksgiving and Dec. 25. Admission $10; ages 3-12, $6. AX, DS, MC, VI. Phone (985) 369-7151.

NATCHITOCHES (B-2) pop. 17,865, elev. 120′

Natchitoches (NAK-a-tish) is the oldest permanent settlement in the Louisiana Purchase. From 1714 until about 1825 when the Red River channel retreated 5 miles east, Natchitoches was an important trading center.

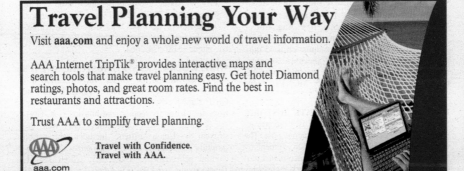

Interesting old homes and plantations can be seen in the Cane River Creole National Historic Park south of town. Nearby facilities within the historic park include the Kate Chopin House-Bayou Folk Museum in Cloutierville *(see attraction listing p. 98)*, Fort St. Jean Baptiste State Historic Site *(see attraction listing)*, Oakland Plantation and Los Adaes State Historic Site. Tours of the nearby 1818 Oakland Plantation on SR 494 are available. Special lectures and cultural demonstrations are also offered; phone (318) 356-8441. Los Adaes State Historic Site, 10 miles west off SR 6, is the site of a fort built in 1721 to protect Spanish territory from the French.

Cane River Lake, a 32-mile-long meandering waterway that flows through downtown Natchitoches and into plantation country, is open for fishing, boating, skiing and swimming. The lake is home to ducks, nutria and many varieties of birds, including kingfishers, snowy and great egrets and great blue herons.

Among the city's annual events is the Christmas Festival of Lights, held from late November through early January. The festival includes, in addition to 300,000 holiday lights, fireworks, a lighted barge parade, music, arts and crafts, food, a festival parade, a living history encampment and a special children's festival area.

Natchitoches Parish Tourist Commission: 781 Front St., Natchitoches, LA 71457; phone (318) 352-8072 or (800) 259-1714.

Self-guiding tours: The St. Denis Walk of Honor, beginning at the corner of Second Street and Rue St. Denis, honors people who have brought recognition to the community. Granite squares embedded in the sidewalk bear the names and professions of such famous people as John Ford, John Wayne and Julia Roberts.

A map detailing a walking tour of the Natchitoches historic district and a driving tour of the surrounding area is available from the tourist commission.

SAVE **BAYOU PIERRE ALLIGATOR PARK** is 8 mi. n. on SR 1 to 380 Old Bayou Pierre Rd. About 1,000 alligators of all sizes live at the park in natural habitats that are accessible by raised walkways. Feedings and informative shows are offered.

Food is available. Allow 1 hour minimum. Daily 10-6, Apr. 15-Aug. 15; Sat.-Sun. 10-6, Aug. 16-Oct. 15 and Labor Day. Shows are given hourly 11:30-4:30 (weather permitting). Last admission is 45 minutes before closing. Phone ahead to confirm schedule; alligators are inactive on cold days. Admission $6.95; ages 3-12, $4.95. MC, VI. Phone (318) 354-0001 or (877) 354-7001.

FORT ST. JEAN BAPTISTE STATE HISTORIC SITE is at 130 Moreau St. The site is a reconstruction of the 1732 French fort and trading post. The original fort was built to prevent encroachment by the Spanish from east Texas into French-held Louisiana. Local materials and 18th-century technology were used in the re-creation. The fort includes a barracks, warehouse, chapel and a commandant's house.

Allow 1 hour minimum. Daily 9-5; closed Jan. 1, Thanksgiving and Dec. 25. Admission $2, over 62 and under 13 free. For guided tours phone (318) 357-3101 or (888) 677-7853 at least 2 weeks in advance.

IMMACULATE CONCEPTION CATHOLIC CHURCH is at 2nd and Church sts. The church dates from 1717 when a Franciscan walked 21 miles from the Spanish mission at Los Adaes to say Mass in Natchitoches—the first public religious service in the town. Except for the pews and the American- and Austrian-made stained-glass windows, all fittings and furnishings in the church were imported from France. Allow 30 minutes minimum. Mon.-Fri. 8-4. Free. Phone (318) 352-3422.

NATCHITOCHES NATIONAL FISH HATCHERY is at 615 SR 1S. This facility raises fish for stocking in coastal and inland waters. A 16-tank aquarium displays different species of fish from the Southeast, including striped and large-mouth bass, channel catfish, redear sunfish and bluegill. Also on display are alligators and turtles. Allow 30 minutes minimum. Daily 8-3; closed federal holidays. Free. Phone (318) 352-5324.

TRINITY PARISH CHURCH is at 533 2nd St. The first services were held in this Norman Gothic building on Ash Wednesday 1858, when only the walls, floor and ceiling were complete. The church was the first non-Catholic church in Natchitoches. The tower bell is said to be one-third silver. Allow 30 minutes minimum. Open daily 24 hours. Free. Phone (318) 352-3113.

NEWELLTON (B-4) pop. 1,482, elev. 70'

Newellton lies at the northwest end of Lake St. Joseph, between the Great River Road (US 65) and the Mississippi River. Lake Bruin State Park *(see Recreation Chart and the AAA Southeastern CampBook)*, 10 miles south near St. Joseph via SRs 608, 605 and 604, offers boating, swimming and water skiing. An outstanding natural feature of Lake Bruin is the cypress growth that lines the shore. For park information phone (318) 766-3530.

Fishing, hiking and wildlife observation can be enjoyed at the 57,000-acre Tensas River National Wildlife Refuge, 15 miles northwest off US 65. Exhibits and brochures are available at the visitor center; phone (318) 574-2664.

WINTER QUARTERS STATE HISTORIC SITE is 8 mi. s.e. on SR 608. Dr. Haller Nutt's mansion was built in 1805 as a winter hunting camp. During the Civil War, Mrs. Nutt saved the 2,000-acre plantation from destruction by feeding and housing Gen. Ulysses S. Grant's troops; outbuildings later were destroyed by Union drifters. Included are period furniture and displays about Nutt's medical and agricultural achievements. Daily 9-5; closed Jan. 1, Thanksgiving and Dec. 25. Admission $2, over 61 and under 12 free. Phone (318) 467-9750 or (888) 677-9468.

NEW IBERIA (E-3) pop. 32,623, elev. 20′

The area around New Iberia was settled by French Acadians who fled Nova Scotia. In 1779 they were joined by a group of Spaniards under the leadership of Lt. Col. Francisco Bouligny. The Spaniards called their settlement Nueva Iberia, and it is one of the few Spanish town names remaining in southern Louisiana. The majority of the present population is of French and Spanish descent. New Iberia was incorporated in 1839 due to the efforts of Frederic H. Duperier, a plantation owner who also donated the land on which St. Peter's Catholic church was built.

New Iberia is on Bayou Teche, which flows through the Evangeline country and takes its name from an American Indian word *teche,* meaning "snake." The Teche country is known as the "Sugar Bowl of Louisiana."

A white marble statue of the Roman emperor Hadrian stands near the corner of Weeks and St. Peter streets. The 7-foot-tall statue, sculpted in Rome about A.D. 130, represents justice, wisdom and community development. Bouligny Plaza on West Main Street honors the town's founder; the central feature of the square is a bust of Francisco Bouligny.

Iberia Parish Convention and Visitors Bureau: 2704 SR 14, New Iberia, LA 70560; phone (337) 365-1540 or (888) 942-3742. *See color ad card insert*

Self-guiding tours: The convention and visitors bureau offers free walking tour maps of New Iberia.

JOSEPH JEFFERSON HOME AND RIP VAN WINKLE GARDENS is 6 mi. s. from jct. US 90 and SR 14, then 1.5 mi. w. to 5505 Rip Van Winkle Rd. Joseph Jefferson was an acclaimed actor in the late 1800s known for his role as Rip Van Winkle; his home was built as a winter respite from his stage performances. The 22-room mansion features a cupola, period paintings and fine furnishings. Camellias, day lilies, roses and magnolias are among the many flowers that blossom year-round in 20 acres of interlocking gardens.

Allow 1 hour minimum. Daily 9-4; closed Jan. 1, Good Friday, Easter, July 4, Dec. 25. House tours are given daily on the hour 9-4. Admission $10; over 65 and ages 9-17, $8. AX, DS, MC, VI. Phone (337) 359-8525.

KONRICO RICE MILL is at 309 Ann St. Open since 1912, Konrico is said to be the nation's oldest rice mill still in operation. A 20-minute slide show about the history of the mill and the region precedes the guided tour. Allow 1 hour minimum. Tours Mon.-Sat. at 10, 11, 1, 2 and 3; closed Jan. 1, July 4, Thanksgiving and Dec. 25. Phone to confirm hours around holidays. Admission $4; over 62, $3.50; under 12, $2.25. AX, DS, MC, VI. Phone (337) 364-7242 or (800) 551-3245.

SAVE **SHADOWS-ON-THE-TECHE** is at 317 E. Main St. (SR 182). Built in 1834 by David Weeks, a prominent sugar planter, this white-pillared mansion remained in the family for four generations. A door in the art studio bears autographs of the guests of great-grandson William Weeks Hall, including those of D.W. Griffith, Cecil B. DeMille and Henry Miller. The gardens are filled with azaleas, camellias and huge, moss-draped live oaks.

Allow 1 hour minimum. Guided tours are given Mon.-Sat. 9-4:30, Sun. noon-4:30; closed Jan. 1, Easter, Thanksgiving and Dec. 25. Admission $7; over 62, $6.25; ages 6-11, $4. Phone (337) 369-6446.

New Orleans

City Population: 484,674 **Elevation:** 11 ft.

Editor's Picks:

Audubon Aquarium of the Americas .... *(see p. 127)*

Audubon Zoo .... *(see p. 128)*

Preservation Hall .... *(see p. 124)*

Bourbon Street, French Quarter
© Visions of America / SuperStock

Inexorably altered by deadly Hurricane Katrina in 2005, New Orleans was once called "The City that Care Forgot," a nickname that aptly described its *bon vivant* atmosphere. It was always a melting pot of peoples and cultures, with diversity not merely recognized, but celebrated. Out of this eclectic blend of French, Spanish and African influences came jazz, Cajun cooking and Mardi Gras. Built in an improbable location—on a swamp in a bend between the Mississippi River and a large lake—the Crescent City nonetheless became a popular vacation destination.

Today, New Orleans is a city in recovery. The storm displaced nearly half a million people, and questions about rebuilding in a flood plain have yet to be answered. More attractions, restaurants, galleries, historic sights and hotels seem to reopen weekly—sometimes with reduced hours or services. It remains imperative for travelers to call ahead to verify the evolving conditions in the hospitality sector of a rebuilding city economy.

Residents display a kind of determined resolve not be overwhelmed by their troubles. In the words of the Cajun swamplanders, *Laissez les bon temps rouler!* Let the good times roll, indeed. Pierre and Jean-Baptiste Le Moyne, sieurs d'Iberville and de Bienville, arrived in 1699 with the purpose of settling the region for France. Bienville founded Nouvelle-Orléans less than 20 years later, naming it after the French regent Phillippe, Duc d'Orléans. To express its gratitude, the French government rounded up thieves, prostitutes and other undesirables and shipped them across the Atlantic to populate the fledgling city. When this policy proved less than successful, the French lured German immigrants to Bienville's settlement in the hope of creating a more stable citizenry. Within 5 years New Orleans had become the capital of the French territory, which included all lands drained by the Mississippi River.

Slavery was introduced to the area almost immediately; by 1724 city leaders instituted the Code Noir. Although this policy was designed to regulate African-American's behavior and activities, it had the contradictory effect of guaranteeing somewhat lenient treatment of slaves and protecting the rights of free people of color.

The next few decades were marked by the city's growth, economically and otherwise. The cultivation of cotton and sugar began in the mid-1700s, giving rise to the plantation era and a wealthy upper class. This heyday ended abruptly in 1762, when France ceded the city to Spain in the secret Treaty of Fontainbleau.

In 1768 some of New Orleans' leading citizens attempted to overthrow Don Antonio de Ulloa, the Spanish governor. Ulloa fled to Havana and Spain promptly sent Irish-born Gen. Alexander O'Reilly to

Getting There — *starting on p. 116*

Getting Around — *starting on p. 116*

What To See — *starting on p. 118*

What To Do — *starting on p. 135*

Where To Stay — *starting on p. 348*

Where To Dine — *starting on p. 370*

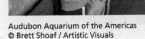

Audubon Aquarium of the Americas
© Brett Shoaf / Artistic Visuals

end the rebellion. He had five of the conspirators executed and another seven imprisoned, a record which earned him the unwanted moniker "Bloody O'Reilly." Despite this controversial incident, he became the colonial governor, thus cementing Spain's rule.

During this period the ancestors of the present-day Cajuns began to arrive, driven from their colony in Nova Scotia by the British and an impending civil war. The French Acadian settlers slowly made their way south, arriving in New Orleans in a trickle through the 1770s. In 1785 a large group of Acadians settled in southern Louisiana, concentrating along the bayous where they farmed and kept to themselves, developing the distinctive culture their descendants still practice.

Two devastating fires in 1788 and 1794 destroyed almost every building in the city. Spanish architecture predominated during the rebuilding process, much to the chagrin of the beleaguered French. Because of the friction between the two peoples, a distinct Spanish culture existed in tandem with the firmly established French community.

Within a month in late 1803 ownership of Louisiana passed from Spain to France and then to the United States through the Louisiana Purchase. The city's transfer to American rule was calm politically, if not socially. A clash of cultures soon commenced, with the French keeping to the Vieux Carré (VOO cah-RAY), or French Quarter, and the Americans populating the Garden District and Faubourg Ste. Marie. A second wave of Germans arrived early in the 19th century, adding to the city's newfound status as one of Louisiana's major cities sporting a cosmopolitan atmosphere.

Less than a decade after New Orleans became an American city, the United States and Great Britain were again at war. The invading army greatly coveted the port and nearly captured it during the famous Battle of New Orleans, which pitted British Gen. Edward Pakenham against U.S. Gen. Andrew Jackson in a surprising American victory. It was a pivotal moment in New Orleans' history, underscoring the city's political and economic importance.

Within the first half of the 19th century, lucrative sugar and cotton enterprises, combined with the port's success, placed New Orleans among the wealthiest Southern cities. But plantations depended on slave labor for profitability, and Northerners could no longer condone the institution of slavery. This ideological conflict swiftly escalated, and by the end of the decade, Southern leaders sounded the call to leave the Union.

As the Civil War spread west, the same port that made the city so prosperous became a major liability, for once again it was a key military target. New Orleans was captured in late April 1862, 1 year after the fighting began.

Destination New Orleans

New Orleans never rolls up the welcome mat, or the sidewalks. There's always some excuse to let the good times roll.

Sugar Bowl festivities kick off in January; Mardi Gras, perhaps the biggest free show in the country, rides fast on its heels; then the Jazz and Heritage Festival ushers in spring. And that's only the beginning.

Jeff Strout
© New Orleans
Metropolitan CVB

Mardi Gras, New Orleans. A profusion of color, a sea of people and a string of seemingly unending parades are what you'll find here on Fat Tuesday. (See mention page 146)

Carl Purcell / © New Orleans Metropolitan CVB

St. Louis Cathedral, New Orleans. The cathedral, flanked by the Cabildo and the Presbytère, overlooks the statue of Andrew Jackson and the square named for the general. (See listing page 125)

Places included in this AAA Destination City:

© Gibson Stock Photography

Longue Vue House and Gardens, New Orleans.
Landscape architect Ellen Biddle Shipman designed the gardens of this 8-acre estate for philanthropists Edgar and Edith Stern.
(See listing page 130)

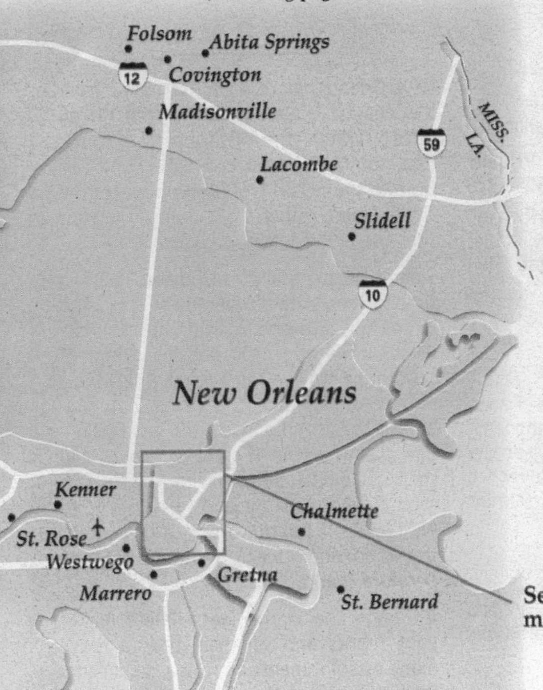

© Audubon Aquarium of the Americas

Audubon Zoo, New Orleans.
Asian elephants, Malayan sun bears and Bengal tigers are among the rare and endangered animals at this 58-acre oasis on the banks of the Mississippi.
(See listing page 128)

Louisiana Office of Tourism

Jackson Square, New Orleans.
The sidewalks around Jackson Square, in the Vieux Carré, are open-air stages for the arts, both visual and performing.
(See listing page 121)

The Informed Traveler

Sales Tax: Louisiana's statewide sales tax is 4 percent; an additional 5 percent is levied in the New Orleans metro area, and Orleans Parish has a .5 percent tax on food and beverages. The city has an 11 percent lodging tax, plus an occupancy tax of 50c-$1 per night.

WHOM TO CALL

Emergency: 911

Police (non-emergency): (504) 821-2222

Fire: (504) 581-3473

Time and Temperature: (504) 828-4000

Information for the Mobility and Visually Impaired: (504) 523-7325 or (800) 695-7325

Hospitals: Ochsner Foundation Hospital, (504) 842-3000; Touro Infirmary, (504) 897-7011; Tulane University Hospital, (504) 588-5263.

WHERE TO LOOK

Newspapers

The main daily paper is *The Times-Picayune,* published throughout the day. *Clarion Herald,* a Catholic weekly, enjoys wide circulation. Smaller journals cover the French Quarter and suburbs. *Gambit Weekly* highlights entertainment.

Radio

New Orleans radio station WWL (870 AM) is an all-news/weather station; WWNO (89.9 FM) is a member of National Public Radio.

Visitor Information

New Orleans Metropolitan Convention and Visitors Bureau: 2020 St. Charles Ave., New Orleans, LA 70130; phone (504) 566-5011 or (800) 672-6124. *See color ad card insert.*

New Orleans Tourism Marketing Corporation: 365 Canal St., Suite 1120, New Orleans, LA 70130; phone (504) 524-4784 or (800) 810-3200.

WHAT TO PACK

New Orleans, more than 100 miles from the nearest ocean, is surrounded on all sides by water—the Mississippi River to the east, south and west and Lake Pontchartrain to the north. This position makes the city's climate rather moist during much of the year.

Summer is generally the hottest, wettest time of year, with temperatures averaging in the low 80s and relative humidity almost always above 60 percent. Frequent rainstorms provide some relief. The winter season also tends to be damp, but temperatures rarely dip below the low 50s, negating any threat of sleet or snow. Cold snaps are mild and short-lived. The fog created by the moisture and heat interferes with aviation, but only mildly affects street traffic. *For additional information see temperature chart p. 90.*

Although the warm, wet climate makes light fabrics and summer styles a must, many establishments impose a dress code. Bring casual clothes for daytime and switch to a dressier style for nighttime. Rain gear is essential year-round.

U.S. Gen. Benjamin Butler led the occupying forces, who were vilified by the bitter New Orleanians. Women especially made it a point to show their distaste for the Yankee invaders. Their contemptuous behavior, which included spitting on Union soldiers, was so disruptive that Butler issued General Order 28, stating that any lady found guilty of such behavior would be considered a prostitute and treated as such. The citizenry was outraged, and Butler soon was replaced by Gen. Nathaniel P. Banks, who was liked no better but avoided further controversy.

New Orleans remained under Union rule until 1876, when Rutherford B. Hayes' election to the presidency was tainted by vote fraud. Louisiana's electoral body held a decisive vote, which they would cast for Hayes only if government troops were withdrawn. The deal was honored on both ends, effectively ending Reconstruction. By the close of the 19th century New Orleans regained something of its former luster, although it would never recapture its prewar glory. Ironically, much of its renewed economic stability was due mainly to the efforts of the hated Northern carpetbaggers.

The gains African-Americans made during Reconstruction eroded after its end, as the Louisiana Legislature enacted the legal institution of segregation. This was cemented by the Supreme Court decision in the Plessy v. Ferguson case, which was first tried in New Orleans. In that landmark decision the highest court in the land decreed that "separate but equal" facilities for both races were constitutionally acceptable.

The 20th century ushered in the Martin Behrman era. New Orleans' only five-term mayor, Behrman was the center of a Democratic political machine known as the New Orleans Ring. Although corrupt, the politico and his successors ruled the Crescent City through the 1920s, when Huey P. Long won the Louisiana governor's seat in the 1928 election. Long despised the ring and did everything in his power to destroy it; in the process he stripped the city of most of its governing powers. In 1936 Long's successor made peace with the city and restored its self-rule.

The Depression was particularly difficult for New Orleans. Isolated by the Mississippi River and sprawling Lake Pontchartrain, stripped of its government and still struggling with the aftermath of the Civil War, the Big Easy suffered hard times. World War II eased the economic burden of the Depression by establishing a manufacturing base in the city, but social ills still ran rampant. A reform platform propelled a young veteran named deLesseps Morrison into the mayor's office in 1946. During his administration NASA established a plant to build rocket boosters and later, external tanks for the space shuttle; Lockheed Martin Michoud Space Systems would become one of the city's largest employers

The Port of New Orleans bustled with international trade, serving thousands of ships from more than 60 countries. Petroleum, steel, rubber, coffee and fertilizer remain major imports. More than 750,000 cruise passengers added to the port's annual statistics, and riverboat gambling provided a boost to tourism.

Jackson Square / © Brett Shoaf / Artistic Visuals

Although suburban migration led to a declining city population, metro growth continued. The city's first African-American mayor, Ernest "Dutch" Morial, was elected in 1978; his son Marc returned the family name to city hall in 1994. The elder Morial's support of airport expansion brought an additional million passengers to New Orleans during his first term, and neighborhood restoration programs created renewed interest in urban living. Clarence Ray Nagin, running as a reformer with no prior political experience, won the mayoral race in 2002 and again in 2006.

Building its first flood levee as early as 1719, New Orleans fought a continuous battle against the tides. A complex system of levees, drainage canals and pumps kept the city dry but also caused it to sink. By 2004, New Orleans was 6 feet below sea level. Hurricanes throughout the 20th century—particularly Betsy in 1965—caused severe flooding, and experts warned that a direct hit would cripple the city. The predictions came true on August 29, 2005, when Hurricane Katrina made landfall. The levees holding back Lake Pontchartrain crumbled, leaving parts of New Orleans under 20 feet of water. Thousands of survivors were stranded in horrific conditions, and the slow emergency response prompted national outrage.

Getting There

By Car

Two major automobile routes enter New Orleans from the north. I-59, a four-lane controlled-access freeway, comes from Hattiesburg, Miss.; it is paralleled by two-lane US 11. North of Slidell US 11 becomes I-10, an east-west route linking New Orleans with Baton Rouge to the west and Mississippi's Gulf of Mexico beaches to the east. No damage was sustained from Hurricane Katrina.

From Jackson, Miss., I-55 leads south between lakes Maurepas and Pontchartrain. It then connects with I-10 at La Place for the final 26 miles into New Orleans. The 24-mile, four-lane Lake Pontchartrain Causeway, a scenic route into the city, is accessible from both I-55 and I-59 via I-12; the toll is $3.

I-10 and US 90 are the main east-west approaches, running parallel east of New Orleans. US 90 passes through a series of beach communities; I-10 affords faster travel. US 90 follows Claiborne Avenue through the city, crossing the Mississippi River via the Huey P. Long Bridge.

Near the Superdome, US 90 Bus. Rte. follows the Pontchartrain Expressway across The Crescent City Connection bridge. Then, as West Bank Expressway, it runs through the suburbs to rejoin US 90 near Bridge City; the inbound toll is $1. I-10 offers expressway travel through the heart of the city and is the direct link to Louis Armstrong New Orleans International Airport via a four-lane airport access road.

From the west, I-10 and US 90 are parallel or combined routes to Lafayette. From there US 90 takes a scenic, southerly swing through bayou country, and I-10, which is the shorter and faster route, heads for New Orleans via Baton Rouge.

Air Travel

Louis Armstrong New Orleans International Airport is about 21 miles west of downtown New Orleans in Kenner and is served by nearly all major domestic and foreign carriers. Citybound traffic exits the airport in two directions.

To connect with the expressway, exit the airport to the east and take Airport Road (not Airline Highway) north to I-10 east. After about 10 miles I-10 moves southward into town. Exiting to I-610 east will lead to the eastern leg of I-10. Another route into New Orleans is via US 61 east (Airline Highway), which is accessed just south of the terminal building.

The average taxicab fare from the airport to the French Quarter is $28 for one or two people and $12 per person for additional riders. Limousine service is available at $40 to $50 an hour. The Airport Shuttle has a booth at the airport luggage pickup. Vans depart every 15 minutes from the airport and provide transportation into the city for $13 one way; phone (504) 465-9780. Jefferson Parish Transit Co. operates an express bus from the airport to Carrollton and Tulane avenues. Fare is $1.10; phone (504) 818-1077.

New Orleans is served by several major car rental agencies. Arrangements should be made before you leave on your trip. Your local AAA club can provide this service or additional information. Hertz, (504) 568-1645 or (800) 654-3080, offers discounts to AAA members.

Rail Service

Amtrak uses the Union Passenger Terminal at 1001 Loyola Ave. Daily service is offered. Phone (504) 528-1631 or (800) 872-7245 for further information.

Buses

The Greyhound Lines Inc. bus terminal is at 1001 Loyola Ave.; phone (504) 525-6075 or (800) 231-2222 for schedule and fares.

Getting Around

Street System

Though many streets were under water after Hurricane Katrina, the only lasting damage was to the electrical streetcar line. All roads were open within a few weeks of the storm.

The street system is determined by the natural boundaries of the Mississippi River and Lake Pontchartrain. North-south streets are usually perpendicular to the lakeshore or riverbank, while east-west routes are more or less parallel to them.

Uptown means upstream and generally toward the river. Lakeside indicates the general direction toward the lake; riverside denotes the direction toward the river. Downtown, which encompasses the central business district, is east and northeast of Lee Circle.

The river-oriented part of the city falls within the triangle formed by Carrollton and Esplanade avenues and the Mississippi. Canal Street, Tulane Avenue and the Pontchartrain Expressway are the main thoroughfares. New Orleans' principal routes across the city are Tchoupitoulas Street and St. Charles, Claiborne and Broad avenues.

Above the Carrollton-Esplanade apex, roads run approximately northward to Lake Pontchartrain. In addition to Pontchartrain Expressway, the main routes are Wisner Boulevard and Elysian Fields Avenue. Major crosstown routes through New Orleans are Airline Highway, City Park Avenue, Gentilly Boulevard and Lakeshore Drive.

Canal Street, which runs northwest, divides north from south. Thus, street numbering moves outward from it as well as lakeward from the Mississippi. Streets also change names as they cross Canal. For example, Royal Street becomes St. Charles Avenue, and Bourbon Street becomes Carondelet Street. Except for divided thoroughfares such as Canal, Tulane, Basin and St. Charles, most streets downtown and in the French Quarter are one-way.

Few left turns are permitted from major arteries or moderately traveled downtown streets. It is easier to loop to the right back around the block than to drive a mile or more in search of a legal left turn. Right and left turns on red at one-way intersections are permitted unless otherwise posted.

The speed limit is 30 mph on most streets and 35 mph on boulevards, or as posted. However, on many streets these limits will rarely be reached. Heat, humidity and a water table that lies only 2 to 3 feet below the surface make street maintenance a continuing problem. A buckle of pavement may be the closest thing to a hill you see in New Orleans.

Rush hours are from 7 to 9 a.m. and 3 to 6 p.m. Avoid driving during these hours whenever possible. Congestion is greatest on bridges, I-10, I-610 and on the narrow streets of the French Quarter, several of which are blocked off for pedestrian use.

Parking

Parking lots and garages can be found throughout the downtown business area; fees range from $3 to $10 for the first hour and from $5 to $15 per day. Parking fees at the Riverwalk and in areas of the French Quarter are higher: $5 and up for 3-4 hours at the Riverwalk and $5.50 to $6.50 for 2 hours in the French Quarter (the closer to Bourbon Street, the higher the rates).

On-street parking is scarce and is prohibited in most central sections. Visitors should read—*and heed*—the rather small signs that tell where and when parking is legal, as the regulations are strictly enforced by prompt towing and heavy fines.

French Quarter

Taxis

Cabs are plentiful in the main business and tourist areas. Average fare is $3.50 initially and ranges from $1.60 to $2 for each additional mile. The largest companies are Checker/Yellow, (504) 943-2411; Metry, (504) 835-4242; and United, (504) 522-9771. Information about taxi service also can be obtained from the Taxicab Bureau; phone (504) 658-7102.

Public Transportation

New Orleans' city bus system is inexpensive and efficient. On regular runs within the city limits the bus fare is $1.25 and transfers are 25c; express fare is $1.50 or 25c with a transfer from a regular bus. The VisiTour pass, $5 for 1 day or $12 for 3 days, allows unlimited rides on all Regional Transit Authority buses and streetcars; exact change is required. Many fares were reduced or suspended after Hurricane Katrina.

The clanging streetcars that ply the city's last line of its kind up St. Charles Avenue are part of the transit system *(see attraction listing p. 136)*. **CLOSURE INFORMATION:** The storm destroyed the line's overhead electrical system; partial service in the downtown central business district is reported to resume by early 2007 and service in all areas is expected to resume by late 2007. In the interim, bus service is available on the same route.

Another line along Canal Street, with red streetcars, runs from Esplanade Avenue to Canal Street, then along Canal Street from the Mississippi River to the City Park Avenue terminal. Canal Street connects to City Park at Beauregard Circle via a line along North Carrollton Avenue. **Note:** The red streetcars have been temporarily replaced by the olive-green streetcars due to damage caused by Hurricane Katrina.

The Riverfront Streetcar provides transportation along the Mississippi River from Thalia Street to Esplanade Avenue; fare is $1.50. All streetcar fares have been suspended at least through August 5, 2006. The Regional Transit Authority can provide more information about both bus and streetcar routes and fares; phone (504) 248-3900.

Buses marked "Vieux Carré" make a complete circuit of the French Quarter as well as a portion of the business district Monday through Friday from 6 a.m. to 6:45 p.m. Maps outlining tourist-related transit routes are available at the New Orleans Metropolitan Convention and Visitors Bureau welcome center at 529 St. Ann St., next to Jackson Square.

Outlying parishes are served by other bus companies. East Jefferson Parish, including the airport, is served by Jefferson Parish Transit Co., (504) 818-1077. Westside Transit Lines Inc., (504) 367-7433, operates buses to Gretna, Harvey and other suburbs across the river.

A ferry system connects New Orleans with the West Bank and provides excellent views of the downtown skyline. The 10-minute trips depart from the Canal Street and Jackson Avenue docks and cost $1 per automobile. Pedestrians are transported free of charge.

What To See

The French Quarter

The French Quarter—some 90 blocks between Canal Street, Rampart Street, Esplanade Avenue and the Mississippi River—represents the original French Colonial settlement of Nouvelle Orleans. Known as the Vieux Carré (VOO cah-RAY) or "old square," the Quarter was laid out by military engineers in a simple gridiron pattern with straight, narrow streets.[8]

In many ways the French Quarter remains the true heart of the city, not only because of its historical nature, but also because it is still very much

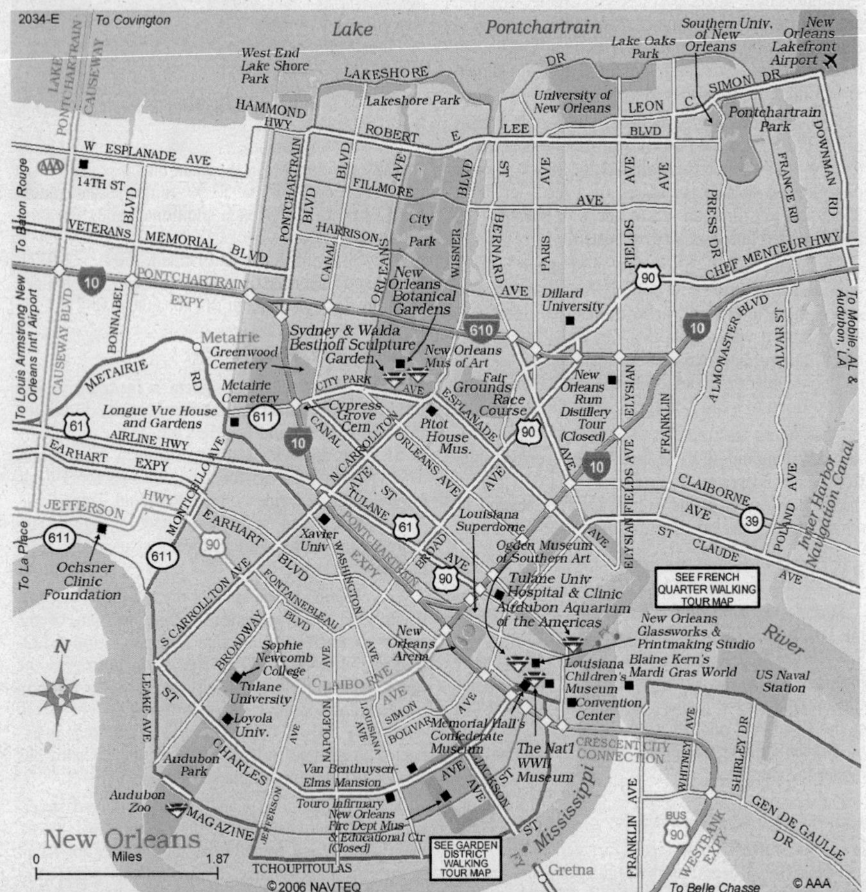

alive. People from all walks of life reside in this historic area and guard its iron-embroidered architectural treasures with fierce pride, enjoying the Quarter's endless variety with as much gusto as first-time tourists. Hurricane Katrina did little permanent damage in the Quarter, which stands on the city's highest ground and avoided flooding.

Typical of the contradictions of the Quarter is that its architecture is not French, but Spanish. Disastrous fires in 1788 and 1794 destroyed all but a handful of the original French structures. Street names have changed from French to Spanish to mainly French again; the gold and blue signs on the corner buildings indicate the street names that prevailed under earlier régime.

In every doorway lingers the memory of some famous character. Legend has it that on Bourbon Street, near the demure Royal Street and its antique stores, once stood the shop Jean Lafitte and his brother Pierre operated as a clearinghouse for their contraband. Marie Laveau, most powerful of a succession of voodoo queens, frequented the St. Louis Cathedral, Jackson Square and, in her waning years, the parish prison where she consoled the condemned.

Maspero's Exchange on Chartres Street was a scheming ground for the filibusters. Often financed by state and local politicians, these swashbuckling adventurers launched elaborate campaigns for power and land in revolution-ripe countries which were at peace with the United States. One of the most famous was William Walker, self-styled "liberator" of Nicaragua and Honduras. As the country became more industrialized after the Civil War, the hunger for land diminished, and filibustering came to an end.

Although it is only one facet of New Orleans, the French Quarter is the city's great drawing card. Visitors throng to its restaurants and luxurious hotels. They hunt antiques on Royal Street and carouse on Bourbon Street. The Quarter contains enough of the proper and the improper, the sacred and the profane, and the conventional and the unconventional to keep any visitor happy.

SAVE **BEAUREGARD-KEYES HOUSE** is at 1113 Chartres St. Built in 1826, this Greek Revival house was the residence of Confederate General Pierre G. Beauregard 1866-68. The house and its walled garden were restored by novelist Frances Parkinson Keyes. Guided tours provide views of Mrs. Keyes' apartment and study and the general's bedroom. Allow 1 hour minimum. Tours are given on the hour Mon.-Sat. 10-3. Admission $5; senior citizens and students with ID $4; ages 2-12, $2. Phone (504) 523-7257.

THE CABILDO OF THE LOUISIANA STATE MUSEUM faces Jackson Square on the uptown side of St. Louis Cathedral at 701 Chartres St. The Spanish governor and the governing body, the Very Illustrious Cabildo, ruled Louisiana from this statehouse.

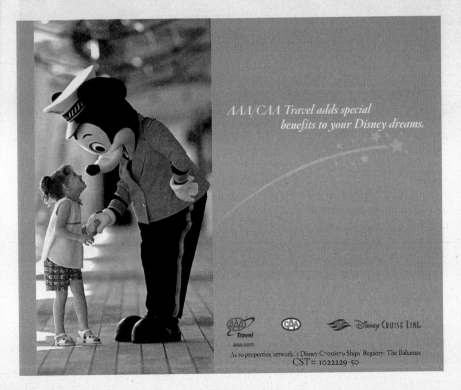

The structure, third on the site, dates from 1799. Exhibits portray the history and culture of Louisiana from European settlement to Reconstruction. The Arsenal, which in 1865 replaced an original building of the Spanish occupation, features exhibits about the importance of the city as a Mississippi River port.

Allow 2 hours, 30 minutes minimum. Tues.-Sun. 10-4; closed holidays. Admission $6, senior citizens and students with ID $5, under 13 free. MC, VI. Phone (504) 568-6968 or (800) 568-6968.

FRENCH MARKET is at 1001 Decatur St. between St. Ann and Barracks sts. Reputedly the oldest open-air market in the country, the market had its beginnings as a Choctaw trading post. Later markets on the site were destroyed by fires and hurricanes; the city constructed more permanent buildings in the early 1800s. The complex includes a farmers' market; a flea market; gift shops; clothing boutiques; coffee stands, including Café du Monde; and cafés. **Note:** The farmers' market was damaged by hurricanes in 2005 and is being renovated; some vendors are open. Daily 9-8. Free. Phone (504) 522-2621.

FRENCH QUARTER VISITOR CENTER—JEAN LAFITTE NATIONAL HISTORICAL PARK is at 419 Decatur St. Information about the six sites of the Jean Lafitte National Historical Park and Preserve *(see place listing p. 150)* is provided at the New Orleans center, which interprets the city's history and multicultural heritage. Guided 90-minute walking tours of the French Quarter are offered. Daily 9-5; closed Mardi Gras Day and Dec. 25. French Quarter walking tours daily at 9:30; passes become available at 9 on a first-come-first-served basis. Free. Phone (504) 589-2636.

SAVE **GALLIER HOUSE MUSEUM** is at 1118-32 Royal St. Designed by the noted New Orleans architect James Gallier Jr. as his home, this Victorian residence has been restored and refurnished to its 1860s appearance. Guided tours depart Mon.-Fri. at 10, 11, noon, 2 and 3; closed major holidays. Admission $6; over 65, college students with ID and ages 8-18, $5. Phone (504) 525-5661.

SAVE **HERMANN-GRIMA HOUSE** is at 820 St. Louis St. This restored 1831 Georgian-style mansion includes a Creole kitchen, slave quarters, a stable and courtyards. Creole cooking demonstrations are given every Thursday, October through May. Allow 30 minutes minimum. Guided tours depart Mon.-Fri. at 10, 11, noon, 2 and 3; closed holidays. Admission $6; over 65, college students with ID and ages 8-18, $5. Phone (504) 525-5661.

THE HISTORIC NEW ORLEANS COLLECTION is at 533 Royal St. The complex of restored 18th- and 19th-century buildings includes a French Quarter bank, a courthouse, a mansion, a Creole cottage and courtyards. Galleries in the 1792 Merieult House present exhibits dedicated to different periods in the history of New Orleans. A research center is at 410 Chartres St.

Allow 1 hour, 30 minutes minimum. Complex open Tues.-Sat. 9:30-4:30; closed holidays. Guided gallery tours conducted Tues.-Sat. at 10, 11, 2 and 3. Complex free. Guided gallery tours $5; rates may vary per exhibit. Phone (504) 523-4662. *See color ad p. 123.*

Williams Residence is behind the main building at the rear of the courtyard. French Quarter preservationists Gen. and Mrs. L. Kemper Williams purchased and restored the buildings that comprise The Historic New Orleans Collection. Their home is furnished in various periods and depicts the opulence of mid-20th-century New Orleans. Allow 30 minutes minimum. Guided tours conducted Tues.-Sat. at 10, 11, 2 and 3. Admission $5.

JACKSON SQUARE is in the heart of the French Quarter between Decatur and Chartres sts. Called the Plaza de Armas by the Spanish, the place for public meetings and celebrations was renamed for Gen. Andrew Jackson, hero of the Battle of New Orleans, in 1848. His equestrian statue stands at the center; on the northwestern side is St. Louis Cathedral, flanked by The Cabildo, the Pontalba Buildings and the Presbytère *(see attraction listings)*.

The Native Tongue

Beignets (ben-YAYS)—square, fluffy pastries, deep-fried and covered with powdered sugar. Locals refer to them as doughnuts; they're *de rigeur* with café au lait.

Café au Lait—coffee blended with chicory and hot milk.

Cajun—a descendant of the French Acadians who fled Canada in the mid-1700s and settled in the Louisiana bayous.

Chartres (CHAR-ters)—speaking a second language won't help with some street names, as in Burgundy (ber-GUN-dee), Conti (KON-tye) and Calliope (CAL-lee-ope) streets.

Digital Archives

Chèr—a Cajun endearment.

Creole—strictly speaking, the original French and Spanish families who formed the elite of New Orleans society, as opposed to English-speaking settlers who came later.

Fais do-do (fay doh-doh)—a Cajun street dance that lasts all night.

Lagniappe (lan-yap)—an elusive term for "a little something extra," like a baker's dozen.

Laissez les bons temps rouler (lay-zay leh bawn tawn roo-LAY)—Let the good times roll.

Pirogue (pee-ROW)—a long, narrow swamp boat, originally made from a hollowed cypress log.

Praline (PRAW-leen)—a Creole candy made with brown sugar, cream, butter and pecans.

Tchoupitoulas (chop-a-TOO-liss)—pronouncing this street is the true test of a native.

Vieux Carré (VOO cah-RAY)—the "Old Square," or the French Quarter.

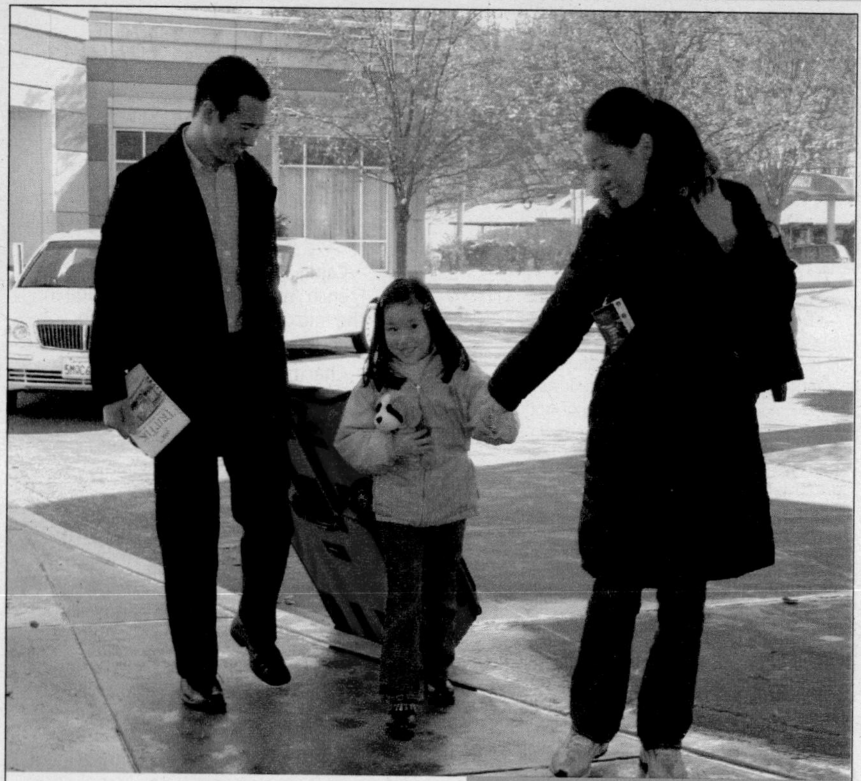

The historic center of the city, Jackson Square also is the Quarter's unofficial Left Bank. Sidewalk artists, palm readers and street performers draw daily crowds. The perimeter streets are blocked to traffic, and no dogs are allowed.

LOUISIANA STATE MUSEUM comprises eight historic buildings in the French Quarter. Local and state heritage, the Creole lifestyle and the city's cultural traditions are reflected in the museum collection. Sites include the Cabildo and the Arsenal, Madame John's Legacy, the Old U.S. Mint, 1850 House (The Lower Pontalba) and the Presbytère *(see attractions listed separately)*. Creole House and Jackson House are closed to the public.

Other members of the museum group are the Louisiana State Museum–Patterson *(see attraction listing p. 154)* and the Louisiana State Museum–Baton Rouge *(see attraction listing p. 96)*. Phone (504) 568-6968 or (800) 568-6968.

MADAME JOHN'S LEGACY is at 632 Dumaine St. Operated by the Louisiana State Museum, this restored 1789 Creole home is one of the few surviving examples of French Colonial architecture in the French Quarter. Folk art and history exhibits are offered. **CLOSURE INFORMATION:** Due to the effects of Hurricane Katrina, the home is closed for renovations; phone for scheduled reopening date. Phone (504) 568-6968 or (800) 568-6968.

SAVE **MUSÉE CONTI WAX MUSEUM** is at 917 Conti St. Costumed, life-size wax figures are displayed in historically accurate settings depicting New Orleans' history from 1699 to the present. Figures include Louis Armstrong, Napoleon Bonaparte, Andrew Jackson and Jean Lafitte. The Haunted Dungeon contains scenes from famous horror stories.

A 2.5-hour self-guiding walking tour to Jackson Square is available. **CLOSURE INFORMATION:** As a result of the 2005 hurricane season, the museum is not open to the public; plans are to reopen in fall 2006 and visitors are advised to phone ahead for schedule and rates. Phone (504) 581-1993 or (800) 233-5405.

SAVE **NEW ORLEANS PHARMACY MUSEUM** is at 514 Chartres St. Built in 1823 by Louis J. Dufilho Jr., the nation's first licensed pharmacist, this building displays old apothecary items and medical equipment dating from the 1820s. The museum also has a collection of voodoo potions and a garden of medicinal herbs. **Note:** Due to the effects of Hurricane Katrina, the museum is only open by appointment; plans are to reopen fully sometime in 2006. Phone ahead for rates and schedule. Phone (504) 565-8027.

SAVE **NEW ORLEANS SCHOOL OF COOKING** is at 524 St. Louis St., between Decatur and Chartres sts. Two-and-a-half-hour cooking demonstrations are offered in an early 19th-century renovated molasses warehouse. Chefs teach Creole/Cajun cuisine including dishes such as gumbo, jambalaya and pralines and flavor lessons with local history and legends. Classes include meals and recipes.

Note: The school is on a limited schedule due to the effects of the 2005 hurricane season. Phone ahead for updates. Two-and-a-half-hour class Wed.-Sun. at 10; closed Mardi Gras Day, Easter, Thanksgiving and Dec. 25. Fee $27. Reservations are required. AX, MC, VI. Phone (504) 525-2665 or (800) 237-4841.

OLD URSULINE CONVENT is at 1112 Chartres St. One of the oldest buildings in the Mississippi Valley, the 1745 convent was built for Ursuline nuns who came from France. Here they cared for the city's indigent and taught the children of the plantation aristocracy. An adjoining chapel was constructed in 1845 for the Catholic archbishop who took up residence after the nuns relocated in 1824.

CLOSURE INFORMATION: The convent is closed due to the effects of the 2005 hurricane season and plans are to reopen in early 2007; visitors are advised to phone ahead for hours and rates. Phone (504) 529-3040.

OLD U.S. MINT is at 400 Esplanade Ave. A Federal mint 1838-61, the building was the Confederacy's only mint for a few months in 1861. It continued as a U.S. mint until 1909. The site was renovated in the 1850s and blends Classical Revival and Victorian styles. **CLOSURE INFORMATION:** Due to damage caused by Hurricane Katrina, the building is expected to remain closed for renovations through 2008. Phone (504) 568-6968 or (800) 568-6968.

PONTALBA BUILDINGS flank Jackson Square on St. Peter and St. Ann sts. The red brick apartment houses were erected in 1849 by the Baroness Micaela Almonester de Pontalba, who is credited with transforming the dusty parade ground into a handsome garden park. The Renaissance-style buildings were intended to stem the uptown flow of business. Although they failed in that, for many years they were among New Orleans' most desirable addresses.

1850 House (The Lower Pontalba) is at 523 St. Ann St. From parlor to kitchen to servant's quarters in this Louisiana State Museum house, each room is furnished with period pieces made in New Orleans. The Friends of the Cabildo conducts daily guided tours of the French Quarter departing from the 1850 House *(see What to Do, Guided Walking Tours p. 142)*. **CLOSURE INFORMATION:** Due to the effects of Hurricane Katrina, the building is closed; phone for scheduled reopening date, hours and rates. Phone (504) 568-6968 or (800) 568-6968.

THE PRESBYTÈRE faces Jackson Square on the e. side of the basilica at 751 Chartres St. Begun in 1793 as an ecclesiastical house, the building was completed for use as court chambers in 1813. Although the Presbytère never served the function indicated by its name, it remained church property until 1853. Now part of the Louisiana State Museum complex, the building houses the Louisiana Portrait Gallery, a Mardi Gras collection and changing exhibits about Louisiana history and culture.

Allow 1 hour, 30 minutes minimum. **Note:** Due to the effects of Hurricane Katrina, the building is open on a limited schedule; phone ahead for updates. Fri.-Sun. 10-4; closed holidays. Admission $6; senior citizens, active military and students with ID $5; under 13 free. Phone (504) 568-6968 or (800) 568-6968.

GEM **PRESERVATION HALL** is at 726 St. Peter St. Traditional jazz is presented here in its truest form. Each night one of five or six bands takes its turn performing. Food and beverages are not permitted on the premises. Seating is limited; expect to wait in line at the door and stand throughout the performance. Tape recording is not permitted.

Allow 30 minutes minimum. Daily 8 p.m.-midnight; closed Mardi Gras Day. Music begins at 8:15; sets start approximately every 45 minutes with a brief intermission. Admission $8, students under 26 with ID $5. Phone (504) 522-2841 or (800) 785-5772.

RIPLEY'S BELIEVE IT OR NOT! is at 620 Decatur St. A large piece of the Berlin Wall, a replica of the London Tower Bridge composed of 264,345 matches and a Chinese dragon ship sculpted from more than 1,000 pounds of jade are just a few of the 500 exhibits on display in 14 galleries. Daily noon-9. Hours may vary; phone ahead. Admission

$13.95; senior citizens and students with ID $11.95; ages 7-12, $9.95. MC, VI. Phone (504) 586-1233.

ST. LOUIS CATHEDRAL is at 615 Pere Antoine Alley, facing Jackson Square. One of the oldest and most photographed churches in the country, the cathedral was the third house of worship to be built on this site. It was completed in 1794 as part of the beneficence of Don Andres Almonester de Roxas, who spent a substantial part of his fortune rebuilding New Orleans after the second great fire. Don Andres is among the distinguished Frenchmen and Spaniards interred in the church. St. Anthony's Garden behind the church was once a notorious dueling ground.

To the outrage of modern critics and historians, remodeling in 1851 modified the Spanish style of the church with steeples and a Greek Revival portico. The basilica remains an active force in the life of New Orleans. Visitors are welcome between services. Mon.-Sat. 9-5, Sun. 1-5. Free. Phone (504) 525-9585.

Other Points of Interest

Other New Orleans points of interest are in the city's more or less distinct districts or neighborhoods and outlying suburbs. The part of the city known as **Downtown,** extending roughly from the river to Claiborne Avenue between Poydras and Canal streets, is the central business area. The term downtown also is a general name for that part of the city downstream from Canal Street and lakeward from the river.

The **Warehouse District** is bounded by Canal Street, St. Charles Avenue, the Pontchartrain Expressway and the river. Old storage buildings have been converted into upscale lofts, galleries and museums such as the National World War II Museum *(see attraction listing p. 131)* and The Ogden Museum of Southern Art *(see attraction listing p. 132)*.

Uptown refers to areas upriver from Canal Street; the Garden District and the various university sections are in this locale. Most of this area was spared from major flooding.

More a historic than a distinct geographical area is the **Irish Channel,** in the vicinity of St. Thomas Street. Once a brawling waterfront neighborhood, it was named for the many Irish immigrants who settled there during the 1840s.

Though all parts of the city were hit by hurricane-force winds and rain, it was flooding from the levee breaches that caused catastrophic damage. Beyond the high ground along the river, New Orleans' low-lying neighborhoods were hardest hit; vast sections may be razed. **Gentilly,** a section of homes and smaller businesses, centers on Gentilly Boulevard (US 90) from the Fair Grounds Race Track to the Inner Harbor Navigation Canal. **East New Orleans,**

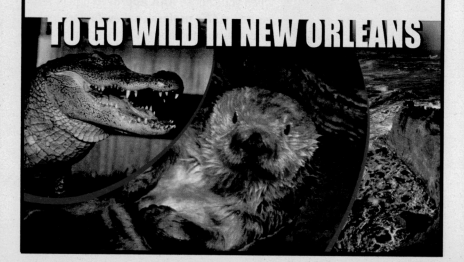

flanked by lakes Borne and Pontchartrain, extends eastward from the Inner Harbor Navigation Canal. The **Lakeshore** included the West End, Lake Vista and other subdivisions around the north end of City Park.

Across the river is the **West Bank,** comprising the suburban communities of Algiers, Gretna *(see place listing p. 149)*, Harvey, Marrero *(see place listing p. 151)* and Westwego *(see place listing p. 153)*.

AUDUBON AQUARIUM OF THE AMERICAS is on the Mississippi River at 1 Canal St. More than 15,000 specimens represent some 530 species of marine life found throughout the Americas. Visitors can see sharks, stingrays, red-bellied piranhas, white alligators, black-footed and rockhopper penguins, sea otters and endangered sea turtles.

Aquatic habitats include the 400,000-gallon Gulf of Mexico exhibit, the Caribbean Reef tunnel, the Amazon Rainforest and the Mississippi River. Other displays include the Seahorse Gallery and one of the largest jellyfish collections in the world. The aquarium's Entergy IMAX Theatre immerses visitors in larger-than-life nature films shown on a five-and-one-half-story screen. Adjacent to the aquarium, Woldenberg Riverfront Park is the location of cultural and educational facilities.

Food is available. Allow 2 hours minimum for the aquarium, 30 minutes minimum for the theater. Aquarium Tues.-Sun. 10-5; closed Mardi Gras Day, Thanksgiving and Dec. 25. Last admission 1 hour before closing. Theater show hours vary; phone ahead.

Aquarium admission $16; over 64, $13; ages 2-12, $9.50. Theater $8; over 64, $7; ages 2-12, $5. Combination ticket with theater $20; over 64, $17; ages 2-12, $12. Combination ticket with Audubon Zoo $22; over 64, $18; ages 2-12, $14. Combination ticket with theater and zoo $28; over 64, $24; ages 2-12, $18. Parking $4. Reservations are recommended for the theater. AX, DS, MC, VI. Phone (504) 581-4629 or (800) 774-7394. *See color ad p. 126.*

AUDUBON INSECTARIUM is at 423 Canal St. Exhibits at this nature museum devoted to the insect world include Butterflies in Flight, which includes a replica of a Japanese garden where butterflies flutter freely; Prehistoric Wonders, featuring the world's earliest insects; Awards Night, an interactive theater presentation with animatronics and special effects; and Life Underground, in which guests are reduced to the size of bugs.

Insects of New Orleans, Metamorphosis, Louisiana Swamp and a roach race arena also are highlights. Live cooking shows instruct visitors how to cook insects. **Note:** The museum is scheduled to open in summer 2007. Phone ahead for schedule and rates. AX, MC, VI. Phone (800) 774-7394.

AUDUBON LOUISIANA NATURE CENTER is s. off I-10 exit 244 (Read Blvd.) to Nature Center Dr.

in Joe W. Brown Memorial Park. This nature preserve includes a science museum, planetarium, greenhouse, butterfly gardens and forest life exhibit. The science center emphasizes the relationship between man and nature in Louisiana. The 86 acres of ponds and woods surrounding the center can be explored along self-guiding nature trails.

CLOSURE INFORMATION: The nature center will remain closed indefinitely due to damage caused by Hurricane Katrina; phone ahead for schedule and rates. Phone (504) 581-4629 or (800) 774-7394. *See color ad p. 126.*

AUDUBON PARK borders the Mississippi River between Exposition Blvd., Walnut St. and St. Charles Ave. In 1884-85 the area was the scene of the World's Industrial and Cotton Exposition, which startled the world with electric lighting indoors and out. The park has tree-shaded lagoons, gardens, a labyrinth, bridle paths and a golf course. Picnicking is permitted. Park open daily 5 a.m.-11 p.m. Free. Phone (504) 581-4629.

GEM **Audubon Zoo** is at 6500 Magazine St. just s. of the park. Encompassing 58 acres of realistic habitats and more than 1,500 animals, the zoo is home to many rare and endangered species. Exhibits include the African Savanna, Australian Outback, Asian Domain, Embraceable Zoo, World of Primates and Reptile Encounter, home to a Komodo dragon. Mayan temples and ruins are the setting for Jaguar Jungle.

The Louisiana Swamp Exhibit recreates the culture and wildlife of a 1930s Cajun settlement. The Swamp Train takes passengers on a tour of the zoo. Guests may go for a whirl on the Endangered Species Carousel while riding such creatures as zebras and giraffes. Narrated feedings and elephant shows are offered daily. The zoo can be visited via the Aquarium/Zoo Cruise *(see What To Do, Boat Tours p. 135).*

Note: Due to the effects of Hurricane Katrina, the following schedule is in effect; phone ahead or check AAA.com for updates. Allow 3 hours minimum. Tues.-Fri. 10-4, Sat.-Sun. 10-5. Closed Mardi Gras Day, the first Fri. in May and Dec. 25. Last admission 1 hour before closing.

Admission $12; over 64, $9; ages 2-12, $7. Train $4. Carousel rides $2. AX, DS, MC, VI. Phone (504) 581-4629 or (800) 774-7394. *See color ad p. 126.*

BAYOU SAUVAGE NATIONAL WILDLIFE REFUGE is 16 mi. e. on I-10 to exit 246A, 2 mi. s. on I-510, then 4 mi. e. on US 90. One of the largest urban wildlife refuges in the country, Bayou Sauvage contains 23,000 acres of marshland, bayous, lagoons and hardwood forest. More than 340 bird species visit the area. Boardwalks, nature trails and picnic facilities are available.

The refuge is also open to boating and fishing; guided canoe trips and bird-watching tours are offered by reservation. Refuge open daily dawn-dusk. Free. Phone (985) 882-2000. *See Recreation Chart.*

SAVE **BLAINE KERN'S MARDI GRAS WORLD** is on the west bank of the Mississippi River, across from downtown New Orleans in historic Algiers Point at 233 Newton St. A free ferry leaves Canal St. on the hour and half-hour and is met by a Mardi Gras World shuttle bus. This designer and builder of Mardi Gras floats, costumes, props and figures offers guided tours through workshops where artists and sculptors work on their creations.

Allow 1 hour minimum. Daily 9:30-4:30; closed Mardi Gras Day, Easter, Thanksgiving and Dec. 25. Admission $15; over 62 and students with ID $11; ages 4-11, $7.25. AX, DC, DS, MC, VI. Phone (504) 361-7821 or (800) 362-8213. *See color ad.*

CITY PARK is at the n. end of Esplanade Ave. The 1,500-acre municipal park is among the largest in the country. The park contains the New Orleans Museum of Art, the Sydney and Walda Besthoff Sculpture Garden, a botanical garden, two miniature trains, a 1906 wooden carousel and a fairy tale theme park. Golf, tennis and picnic facilities are on the grounds. Canoes and paddleboats can be rented for rides on 8 miles of scenic lagoons. **Note:** The park was damaged by Hurricane Katrina and some activities, including canoes and paddleboats, were not available as of June 2006; phone ahead for updates. Fishing is allowed with a permit. Phone (504) 482-4888.

New Orleans Botanical Garden is on Victory Ave. in City Park. Designed during the Art Deco and WPA periods, the garden is arranged in a series of rooms, some of which are accented with fountains and statuary. Plantings include azaleas, bamboo, camellias, magnolias, palms and roses. The train garden presents a miniature replica of New Orleans. A conservatory showcases a tropical rain forest and a living fossil exhibit.

Allow 30 minutes minimum. Tues.-Sat. 10-4:30, Sun. noon-5; closed major holidays. Admission $5; ages 5-12, $2. DS, MC, VI. Phone (504) 483-9386.

GEM SAVE **New Orleans Museum of Art** is at 1 Collins Diboll Cir. in City Park. Funded by millionaire sugar broker Isaac Delgado in 1910, the Greek Revival building is home to 46 galleries. The collection includes a comprehensive survey of Western and non-Western art from the pre-Christian era to the present. An entire floor is dedicated to Asian, African, Oceanic, Pre-Columbian and Native American art.

The museum also houses a treasury of work by French artists, including Edgar Degas, Raoul Dufy, Joan Miró, Claude Monet and Pablo Picasso. Other displays include sculpture, photography, decorative arts and an extensive Fabergé collection.

Note: The museum is open on a reduced schedule as a result of Hurricane Katrina; phone ahead to confirm hours. Food is available. Allow 1 hour, 30 minutes minimum. Wed.-Sun. 10-4:30; closed major holidays and Mardi Gras Day. Admission $8; over 54 and students with ID $7; ages 3-17, $4. Admission may increase for special exhibits. MC, VI. Phone (504) 658-4100. *See color ad p. 130.*

GEM **Sydney and Walda Besthoff Sculpture Garden** is at 1 Collins Diboll Cir. in City Park. Next to the New Orleans Museum of Art, the sculpture garden contains 50 sculptures on 5 landscaped acres. Sculptures by such artists as Jacques Lipchitz, Renè Magritte, Henry Moore, Pierre Auguste Renoir, George Rickey and George Segal are surrounded by pine and live oak trees, camellias and magnolias.

Well-placed pools, footbridges and paved paths highlight the collection. Azaleas, Japanese yews, wax myrtles, sago and windmill palms, and aquatic plants such as Louisiana iris and spider lilies mingle throughout the garden. **Note:** The sculpture garden is open on a reduced schedule as a result of Hurricane Katrina; phone ahead to confirm hours. Picnicking is not permitted. Allow 1 hour minimum. Wed.-Sun. 10-4:30; closed major holidays and Mardi Gras Day. Free. Phone (504) 488-2631.

FORT PIKE STATE HISTORIC SITE is 23 mi. e. via US 90. The fort was established in 1819 to defend the city's water approaches. Two moats surrounded the fort; within were a citadel, service buildings and soldiers' quarters. Named for Gen. Zebulon Montgomery Pike, the fort served in various capacities during the Seminole Wars, the Mexican War and the Civil War; it was abandoned in the 1890s. **CLOSURE INFORMATION:** Fort Pike suffered severe damage as a result of Hurricane Katrina and is closed indefinitely.

JACKSON BARRACKS MILITARY MUSEUM is at 6400 St. Claude Ave. Displayed are weapons and artifacts used in wars dating from the American Revolution and including such 20th-century conflicts as Desert Storm. Tableaux with life-size figures depict soldiers in realistic wartime settings, while personal memorabilia offers accounts of life in the trenches. On the grounds of the 1833 military complex are tanks, fighter planes and other examples of American firepower. **CLOSURE INFORMATION:** The museum is closed temporarily due to the effects of the 2005 hurricane season; check AAA.com for updates to schedule and rates.

JEAN LAFITTE NATIONAL HISTORICAL PARK AND PRESERVE—*see place listing p. 150.*

LAKE PONTCHARTRAIN CAUSEWAY is off I-10 on Causeway Blvd. The world's longest overwater highway bridge crosses 24 miles of open water, taking passengers out of sight of land for 8 miles. The bridge supports a four-lane divided highway with pullover areas for sightseeing and an opening span at mile marker 16 to accommodate ships. **Note:** Emergency call boxes are at half-mile intervals. Toll $3 southbound. Phone (504) 835-3118.

SAVE **LONGUE VUE HOUSE AND GARDENS** is off I-10 exit Metairie Rd. at 7 Bamboo Rd. This Greek Revival mansion was the home of philanthropists Edgar Bloom Stern and his wife Edith, daughter of Sears magnate Julius Rosenwald. The mansion is furnished with 18th- and 19th-century American and English antiques and surrounded by 8 acres of landscaped gardens and fountains. An interactive half-acre children's garden also is included.

Grounds Mon.-Sat. 10-4. Children's garden Mon.-Sat. 10-4, Sun. 1-4. Guided tours of the house are offered Mon.-Sat. 10-4, Sun. 1-4; closed holidays. Hours may vary; phone ahead. Admission $10; over 62, $9; ages 6-16, $5. Phone (504) 488-5488.

LOUISIANA CHILDREN'S MUSEUM is at 420 Julia St. between Magazine and Tchoupitoulas sts. Hands-on exhibits are offered for children between 2 and 12 years old. Highlights include a math and physics lab, a waterworks area, a role-play café, a theater and a physical fitness exhibit featuring a rock climbing wall. Children also can shop in a mini supermarket, stand inside a giant bubble, pilot a tugboat down the Mississippi River or anchor a news program.

Tues.-Sat. 9:30-4:30, Sun. noon-4:30; closed Jan. 1, Mardi Gras Day, Easter, July 4, Thanksgiving and Dec. 25. Hours may vary; phone ahead. Admission $7, under 1 free. Under 16 must be with an adult. AX, DS, MC, VI. Phone (504) 523-1357.

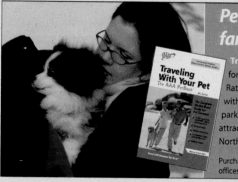

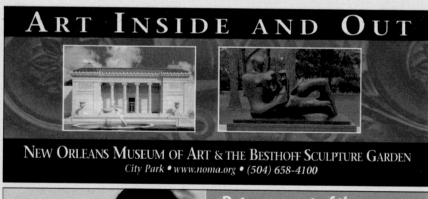

MEMORIAL HALL'S CONFEDERATE MUSEUM is at 929 Camp St. The museum displays uniforms, flags, weapons, paintings, currency and other Civil War relics as well as some personal effects of Jefferson Davis and Robert E. Lee. **Note:** The museum is operating on a limited schedule due to the effects of the 2005 hurricane season. Allow 30 minutes minimum. Thurs.-Sat. 10-4; closed holidays. Hours may vary; phone ahead. Admission $5; over 65 and students with ID $4; under 13, $2. MC, VI. Phone (504) 523-4522.

GEM SAVE **THE NATIONAL WORLD WAR II MUSEUM** is at 945 Magazine St. The stories of World War II soldiers are told through a vast collection of artifacts, film footage, photographs, personal effects, diaries and oral histories. New Orleans was chosen as the site of the museum, a Smithsonian Institution affiliate, to honor Andrew Higgins, a local boatbuilder whose amphibious landing craft was credited by Dwight Eisenhower with winning the war. On display is a replica of a Higgins Boat used at Normandy.

Interactive galleries take visitors from the early days of the war and the planning of the Normandy invasion, the massive air and sea assault on June 6, 1944, through the road to victory in Europe. Photographs, video presentations, Japanese artifacts and a 60-foot-square animated map are displayed. The film "D-Day Remembered" is shown.

Food is available. Allow 2 hours, 30 minutes minimum. Tues.-Sun. 9-5 (also Thurs. 5-7); closed Jan. 1, Mardi Gras Day, Thanksgiving and Dec. 25. Admission $14; over 65, students and active or retired military with ID $8; ages 5-12, $6; military in uniform free. Last admission 30 minutes before closing. Parking $6 at the visitor lot adjacent to the museum on Camp St. AX, DS, MC, VI. Phone (504) 527-6012. *See color ad.*

NEW ORLEANS FIRE DEPARTMENT MUSEUM AND EDUCATIONAL CENTER is at 1135 Washington Ave. This restored 1850s firehouse features antique firefighting vehicles, including an 1838 hand pumper and an 1860 hand-drawn ladder truck. Uniforms, insignia and equipment are displayed along with photographs paying tribute to firefighters in action. **CLOSURE INFORMATION:** The museum is temporarily closed due to the effects of the 2005 hurricane season; phone ahead or check AAA.com for schedule and rates. Phone (504) 896-4756.

NEW ORLEANS GLASSWORKS AND PRINTMAKING STUDIO is between Girod and Julia sts. at 727 Magazine St. Visitors may observe glassblowing master craftsmen, metal sculptors and printmakers in a spacious, open working studio. The processes of silver alchemy, copper enameling, paper marbling, glass bead making and bookbinding also are demonstrated. The adjoining New Orleans ArtWorks Gallery exhibits the finished works by local and international artisans.

Allow 30 minutes minimum. Mon.-Sat. 11-5, Sept.-May; Mon.-Fri. 11-5, rest of year. Closed Jan.

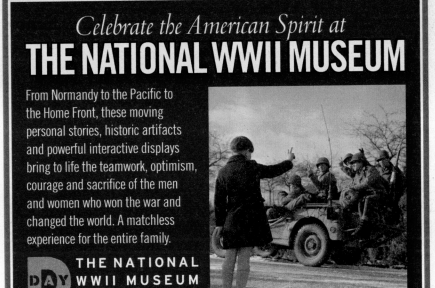

1, Mardi Gras Day and Dec. 25. Free. Phone (504) 529-7277.

NEW ORLEANS RUM DISTILLERY TOUR is at 2815 Frenchmen St. Several varieties of rum are made from Louisiana sugar cane and blackstrap molasses in this distillery. Tours include tastings and a behind-the-scenes look at the distillation and filtration processes. **CLOSURE INFORMATION:** The tour is temporarily suspended due to the effects of the 2005 hurricane season; check AAA.com for scheduled reopening date and rates.

GEM **THE OGDEN MUSEUM OF SOUTHERN ART** is at 925 Camp St. Southern art from the 1700s to the present is represented in a permanent collection amassed by New Orleans entrepreneur Roger Ogden. The museum displays more than 2,700 works in 22 galleries, including paintings, sculpture, ceramics, crafts and glass. Featured artists include Walter Anderson, Benny Andrews, Nene Humphrey, Clarence Millet and Will Henry Stevens.

Several galleries are devoted to contemporary photography as well as photography from the 1930s to the 1950s. Permanent exhibitions include Southern Crafts: Clay, Wood and Metal; Impressionism and Tonalist Landscapes; and Florida: The American Riviera.

Note: The museum is operating on a reduced schedule due to the effects of the 2005 hurricane season. Guided tours are available. Allow 1 hour, 30 minutes minimum. Fri.-Sun. 11-4, Thurs. 6-8 p.m. Hours may vary; phone ahead. Admission $10; over 64 and students with ID $8; ages 5-17, $5. AX, DS, MC, VI. Phone (504) 539-9600.

OLD CEMETERIES are scattered throughout the city. Because water filled the graves before coffins could be lowered, tombs were built above ground. Mausoleums, 100 or more feet long and four tiers high, are of solid masonry. Most burials still are above ground, custom rather than necessity.

Note: New Orleans' cemeteries have become victims of their own architecture; the lavish tombs provide cover for the disreputable, and vandalism is not uncommon. Those planning to visit inner city cemeteries should be aware of these problems and travel in groups. For more information, phone (504) 525-3377 or (888) 721-7493.

Cypress Grove Cemetery is at 120 City Park Ave. at the foot of Canal St. Many of the city's firemen are buried at the cemetery, which was founded in 1840. Gates open daily 8-4.

Greenwood Cemetery is at Metairie Rd. and City Park Ave. at the foot of Canal St. Some 20,500 tombs include guild and organization mausoleums and a monument to the Confederate dead. Daily 8-4.

Lafayette Cemetery No. 1 is in the Garden District between Washington Ave. and Prytania, Sixth and Coliseum sts. The architecture here is somewhat simpler than that of the Creole cemeteries. The pillars of early American society repose in tombs that are as graciously proportioned as the mansions they built. Mon.-Fri. 7:30-2:30, Sat. 7:30-noon.

Metairie Cemetery is off I-10 at 5100 Pontchartrain Blvd. at the foot of Canal St. The largest cemetery in New Orleans, Metairie is a showplace of tomb architecture. Established in 1873 on the site of an antebellum racetrack, it contains fine military memorials; the tomb of Gov. William C. Claiborne, first American governor of Louisiana; and graves of many leading families. Among the elaborate tombs is one built for Josie Arlington, the leading madam of Storyville. Daily 8:30-5.

St. Louis Cemetery No. 1 is at Basin and St. Louis sts., just n. of the French Quarter. The oldest and best known of the city's above-ground cemeteries opened in 1789. New Orleans' first African-American mayor, Ernest "Dutch" Morial, is interred here; the remains of Voodoo queen Marie Laveau are said to rest in the Glapion family tomb, though there is no proof. Daily 8-3.

St. Louis Cemetery No. 3 is at 3421 Esplanade Ave. near the entrance to City Park. The tombs of some of the old Creole families are found here. Daily 8-3.

PITOT HOUSE MUSEUM is at 1440 Moss St. This West Indies-style plantation was built in the late 18th-century. The house was moved to its present site and meticulously restored and furnished with period Louisiana and American antiques. A guided tour offers insight into Southern life in the early 1800s. Allow 1 hour minimum. Tours depart Wed.-Sat. 10-2; closed major holidays and Mardi Gras Day. Admission $5; over 65, $4; under 12, $3. Phone (504) 482-0312.

Creole Queen / © Brett Shoaf / Artistic Visuals

SIX FLAGS NEW ORLEANS, e. on I-10 and I-510 at 12301 Six Flags Pkwy. (exit 246A), is a 140-acre theme park.

CLOSURE INFORMATION: Due to damage sustained as a result of the 2005 hurricane season, Six Flags New Orleans was closed for the 2006 season and at press time did not have a scheduled opening date or hours of operation for the 2007 season. Phone (504) 253-8000.

VAN BENTHUYSEN-ELMS MANSION is at 3029 St. Charles Ave. Built in 1869, the Greek Revival and Italianate mansion features ornate architecture and decorative accents, including hand-carved oak and mahogany woodwork, Carrara marble fireplaces, 24-karat gold sconces and Irish tapestry wall coverings. The mansion was home to a German baron 1931-41; it was later discovered that he was a spy.

Allow 1 hour minimum. Mon.-Fri. 10-2; closed Jan. 1, Mardi Gras Day, July 4, Labor Day, Thanksgiving and Dec. 25. Admission $5, under 11 free. Phone (504) 895-5493.

CASINOS

- **Harrah's New Orleans Casino**, 8 Canal St. Daily 24 hours. Phone (504) 533-6000 or (800) 427-7247.

What To Do

Sightseeing

Boat Tours

Perhaps the best and easiest way to experience the sounds, scents and strange beauty of Louisiana is by boat. Tours take passengers through swamps and bayous and past city skylines and historical areas; many tours provide information and insight into the history and ecosystem of this region. In addition to your camera, take along insect repellent. Reservations, always a good idea, can be arranged at most hotel transportation desks or at the boats; phone to confirm departure times. Boarding for all tours listed begins 30 minutes before departure.

AQUARIUM/ZOO CRUISE offers departures from both the Audubon Aquarium of the Americas on Canal St. and the Audubon Zoo at Audubon Landing in Audubon Park. The riverboat *John James Audubon* takes passengers for a 7-mile narrated cruise along the Mississippi River between the aquarium and the zoo.

Food is available. The riverboat departs the aquarium Tues.-Sun. at 10, noon, 2 and 4. Return-trip departures from the zoo are at 11, 1, 3 and 5. Closed Mardi Gras Day, Thanksgiving and Dec. 25. Hours may vary; phone ahead. One-way fare (cruise only) $13; ages 2-12, $6.50. Round trip (cruise only) $17; ages 2-12, $8.50. Combination cruise, aquarium and zoo admission $38.25; ages 2-12, $21.25. Other combination tickets are available. AX, DS, MC, VI. Phone (504) 586-8777 or (800) 233-2628.

CAJUN QUEEN departs from the Audubon Aquarium of the Americas dock on Canal St. This 600-passenger riverboat takes passengers down the Mississippi River on a narrated 1-hour harbor cruise past the French Quarter and through one of the world's busiest ports. A 2-hour jazz cruise with optional dinner also is offered.

Food is available. **Note:** Due to the effects of Hurricane Katrina, the following temporary schedule is in effect; phone ahead or check AAA.com for updates. Jazz cruise boards Fri.-Sun. at 7 and departs at 8. Harbor cruise departs Fri.-Sun. at 10:30 and 2:30; boarding is 15 minutes prior to departure. Closed Mardi Gras Day and Dec. 25. Jazz cruise fare with dinner $53; ages 6-20, $28. Jazz cruise fare without dinner $30; ages 6-20, $20. Harbor cruise fare $20; over 65, $18; ages 3-12, $12. AX, MC, VI. Phone (504) 524-0814 or (800) 445-4109.

CREOLE QUEEN departs from the Canal Street dock at Riverwalk. This 1,000-passenger paddle-wheeler offers a 2-hour jazz cruise on the Mississippi River with optional dinner. A narrated 1-hour harbor cruise also is available.

Note: Due to the effects of Hurricane Katrina, the following temporary schedule is in effect; phone ahead or check AAA.com for updates. Food is available. Jazz cruise boards Fri.-Sun. at 7 and departs at 8. Harbor cruise departs Fri.-Sun. at 10:30 and 2:30; boarding is 15 minutes prior to departure. Closed Mardi Gras Day and Dec. 25. Jazz cruise fare with dinner $53; ages 6-20, $28. Jazz cruise fare without dinner $30; ages 6-20, $20. Harbor cruise fare $20; over 65, $18; ages 3-12, $12. AX, MC, VI. Phone (504) 524-0814 or (800) 445-4109.

NEW ORLEANS SWAMP TOURS AT BAYOU SAUVAGE is 17 mi. e. on I-10 to exit 251 (US 11). Passengers embark on a narrated boat tour of Bayou Sauvage National Wildlife Refuge *(see attraction listing p. 128)*, home to alligators, deer, otters, nutria and 340 bird species. Native guides provide a colorful account of swamp life and Cajun folklore. **CLOSURE INFORMATION:** Due to the effects of the 2005 hurricane season, the tours are suspended indefinitely; phone ahead for schedule and rates. Phone (504) 236-3143.

STEAMBOAT *NATCHEZ* docks at the Toulouse St. Wharf at Jackson Square. This stern-wheel steamboat features live jazz and narrated 2-hour Mississippi River tours of the port of New Orleans. A dinner jazz cruise is also available. Narrated river tours depart Wed.-Sun. at 2:30 (also Fri.-Sun. at 11:30) and board 30 minutes before departure; closed Mardi Gras Day, Thanksgiving and Dec. 25. Hours may vary; phone ahead. Fare $18.50; ages 6-12, $9.25. AX, DS, MC, VI. Phone (504) 586-8777 or (800) 233-2628.

Bus, Carriage and Streetcar Tours

The best way to become acquainted with New Orleans is to take an organized bus tour. These range from a 2-hour trip through the city to a 6.5-hour tour of the entire metropolitan area and a local plantation.

Some companies also conduct visits to hot spots on New Orleans' nightclub circuit. Passengers are picked up from and returned to motels and hotels throughout the metropolitan area. Reservations are advised. Many downtown hotels have sightseeing booths, and motel managers can often provide information and reservations.

One of the major sightseeing companies is SAVE Gray Line of New Orleans Inc.; phone (504) 569-1401. Consult the telephone directory for other companies.

Horse-drawn carriages leave continuously from Jackson Square for narrated tours of the French Quarter. The waiting time varies; most tours require a minimum of six passengers and depart when the carriage is full.

ST. CHARLES AVENUE STREETCAR can be boarded at stops along St. Charles Ave. and Canal St. The oldest continuously running street railway, the streetcar is now part of the municipal transit system. The 35 olive-green trolley cars date 1923-24.

From Canal Street (near the French Quarter) the line runs up St. Charles Avenue, past the Garden District, the campuses of Tulane and Loyola universities and Audubon Park. The Canal Street stop is at the corner of Carondelet Street.

Note: The system's overhead electrical lines were destroyed by Hurricane Katrina; full service is expected to resume by late 2007. In the interim, buses are operating on the same route. Fare $1.25 each way (exact change required). Phone (504) 248-3900.

Walking Tours

AAA Walking Tour: The French Quarter

Refer to the map following. This walking tour begins at **Jackson Square,** but you can start at any point convenient to your hotel. If you enter the Quarter by car, parking is available in three lots on Decatur Street near Jackson Brewery, with entrances at Conti, Toulouse and St. Peter streets. Providing a good transportation alternative for visitors staying at hotels outside the Quarter is the air-conditioned Riverfront Streetcar, which travels for 2 miles along the levee from Thalia Street (Inbound) to Esplanade (Outbound) at the downriver boundary of the French Quarter. Stops include the New Orleans Convention Center, the Riverwalk, the Aquarium of the Americas, Jackson Brewery and the French Market. Get off the trolley at Dumaine to reach **Jackson Square,** your starting point.

The names of sites that are printed in bold type are described in greater detail in the What to See/The French Quarter section. Even if you do not tour a listed site, reading the listing when you reach that point should make the tour more interesting.

One really needs several days to fully explore the Quarter, although some might wager that a lifetime is not long enough to truly know this eclectic locale. If you have only a day, slip into your most comfortable walking shoes and prepare to experience the heart and soul of New Orleans. The tour takes up to 2 hours.

Known as the Place d'Armes by the French and Plaza de Armas by the Spanish, Jackson Square was renamed in 1848 in honor of Gen. Andrew Jackson, the hero of the Battle of New Orleans during the War of 1812. Standing near the imposing statue of Old Hickory, you are in what has been called the finest architectural setting in the United States.

On St. Peter and St. Ann streets—beyond the verdant plantings, the painting-adorned iron fence and the cheery umbrellas of the sidewalk artists—rise the stately **Pontalba Buildings.**

Diagonally across Chartres Street from the Pontalbas is another set of twins, **The Cabildo** and **The**

Presbytère. In turn, these elegant structures frame the crown jewel of the square, the **St. Louis Cathedral.** On a sunny morning, surrounded by flowers and pigeons and lulled by the De Gaulle Fountain, you might be tempted to end your walking tour right here, before you have even begun.

Do not—there is too much to see and do. On the St. Ann side of the square in the Lower Pontalba is the Louisiana Tourism Office, a good place to pick up maps and brochures. If time permits, take a tour of the **1850 House** for a glimpse of what life in a middle-class Creole town house was like in the 19th century.

Cross Decatur Street and experience a New Orleans tradition, Café du Monde *(see color ad p. 132)*. Except for facade renovations, not much has changed at this coffee stand since steaming *café au lait* (a blend of chicory coffee and half hot milk) and fried, confectioners' sugar-dusted doughnuts, or beignets, were first served in 1862.

The cafe anchors the north end of the historic **French Market** *(see attraction listing p. 120)*, which had its origins as a Choctaw trading ground even before the city was established by Jean-Baptiste LeMoyne in 1718. Among the Indian trade goods was a finely ground powder made from sassafras leaves—the filé (FEE-lay) sought by Creole cooks to thicken gumbo.

The market complex consists of a series of colonnaded buildings stretching along Decatur and N. Peters streets from St. Ann to Barracks streets, with gift shops and bazaars, clothing stores, a candy cookery, more coffee stands and informal eateries. The sweet smell of pralines may entice you to stop and buy a walking snack. A small courtyard tucked behind these buildings contains several lifeline statues, including a bronze girl reclining on a fountain.

Stroll along Decatur and cross N. Peters. Note the 13-foot-tall gilded statue of Joan of Arc on the Place de France, a tiny wedge of ground forming a point where N. Peters diverges from Decatur. A gift from the people of France, the Maid of Orleans stands as another reminder of the city's French connection.

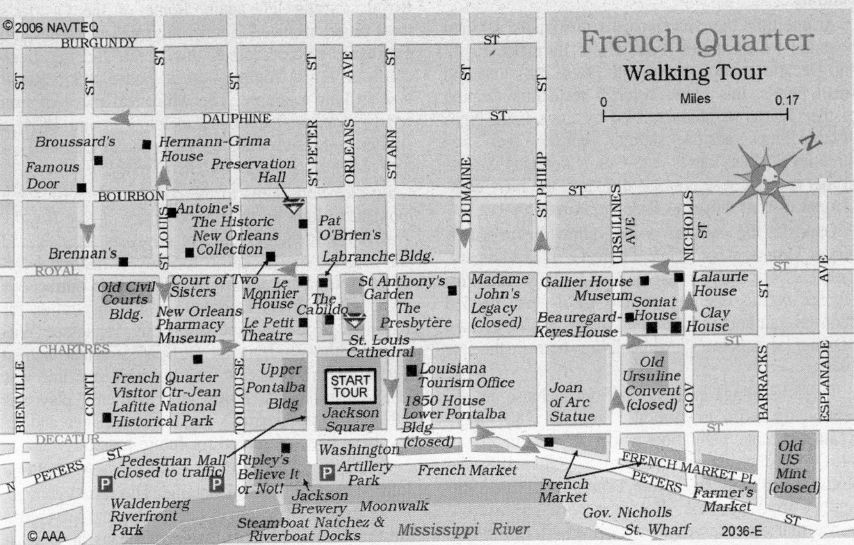

The visitor center for the New Orleans Jazz National Historical Park at 916 N. Peters features exhibits about America's most famous indigenous musical art form.

Stop at the corner of Ursulines Avenue and French Market Place. The last pavilions house the open-air farmer's market, once a riot of color and aromas. In recent years, flea market bargains have replaced fresh produce in many stalls. Beyond the French Market on Esplanade Avenue is the **Old U.S. Mint**, which lost its roof to Hurricane Katrina in 2005. The red brick building served as the Confederacy's only mint for a few months during the Civil War and continued as a federal mint until 1909.

Turn left on Ursulines, passing the shaded seating area of Latrobe Park and crossing Decatur. This street was aptly named for the historic site beyond the high walls on your right; a quick right at Chartres brings you to old doors that open onto the courtyard of the Archbishop Antoine Blanc Memorial complex, which contains the **Old Ursuline Convent.** Constructed in 1745 during the French occupation, the convent is one of the city's oldest buildings.

At one time the convent walls surrounded all land bounded by Ursulines Avenue and Barracks, Royal and Decatur streets. Along with house museums and small hotels, this quiet, colorful residential section of the Quarter is characterized by three main types of dwellings: narrow shotgun houses, two- and three-level town houses, and Creole cottages. Streets in this area are less populated than in the busy commercial district closer to Jackson Square.

Opposite the convent is the yellow **Beauregard-Keyes House,** where Gen. Pierre G. T. Beauregard, hailed as the "Great Creole" after defending Fort Sumter at the opening of the Civil War, resided 1866-68; author Frances Parkinson Keyes penned "Dinner at Antoine's" while living here in the late 1940s.

Three buildings away is the Soniat House, an exceptionally large town house built in 1829 by a wealthy Creole plantation owner for his family of 14. One of many quaint hotels in the Quarter, Soniat House is fronted by a fine example of mid-19th-century iron lacework. Note the *porte-cochere* entrance that once served as a carriageway and watch for other examples of this architectural amenity throughout the district.

Cross to the far side of Gov. Nicholls Street and turn left. From this side, you can see over the brick wall at 618-620 and into the courtyard of the Clay House, the 1828 home of statesman Henry Clay's brother, John, who was married to Mrs. Soniat's sister.

Turn left on Royal Street, the Vieux Carré's premier shopping address, especially for antiques. Facing you on the corner at 1140 Royal will be the three-story Lalaurie House, one of the most mysterious sites in the Big Easy. Legend has it that the mistress of this house, Delphine Lalaurie, tortured her slaves, then set fire to the building when she was discovered, escaping to Europe through the Clay garden and out the Soniat carriageway. Many locals maintain the house is haunted; it's a favorite stop on ghost tours.

At 1132 Royal is the stately **Gallier House,** residence of James Gallier Jr., the son of a prominent 19th-century New Orleans architect, who followed successfully in his father's footsteps. Gallier Sr.'s works include the handsome Greek Revival old city hall (Gallier Hall) on St. Charles Avenue facing Lafayette Square. Besides his home, the younger Gallier designed the Creole's beloved French Opera House, which occupied the corner of Bourbon and Toulouse streets until it burned in 1919.

When you reach St. Philip, turn right and walk up the block past the McDonogh School to Bourbon Street. On the northwest corner is one of the oldest surviving buildings in the French Quarter. Lafitte's Blacksmith Shop, now a tavern, dates to 1772. The privateer Lafitte brothers were said to run the shop as a front for their smuggling enterprises.

Turn left on Bourbon and continue along this quiet stretch—away from the bars, jazz halls and adults-only clubs—to Dumaine. Go left to return to Royal, turning left again. Some of the Quarter's most ornate ironwork adorns the small balconies and expansive galleries along this street, and the green cornstalk fence fronting a guest house at 915 Royal is a striking example. The whimsical piece of iron artistry was crafted in Philadelphia around 1834; a similar fence surrounds a Fourth Street Garden District mansion *(see Garden District Walking Tour)*.

Retrace your steps to the corner and pause for a moment to look up the long corridor of *Rue Royale*. This is the French Quarter of novelists, satirists and playwrights: the backdrop for Keyes' historical fiction, a setting for John Kennedy Toole's outrageous "A Confederacy of Dunces" and the inspiration for a Pulitzer Prize-winning drama by Tennessee Williams. Although Blanche DuBois' streetcar named Desire doesn't pass this way anymore (the line was removed in the late 1940s, after Williams' play was published), the Quarter's mystique, romance and allure have been preserved for future literati.

Turn left, taking a slight detour to see **Madame John's Legacy** at 632 Dumaine. The raised cottage, a rare example of French Creole design, survived a fire that destroyed most of New Orleans in 1794. It takes its name from native New Orleanian George Washington Cable's 19th-century short story "Tite Poulette," in which an heirless Creole named John bequeaths his house to a quadroon with a beautiful daughter. Cable's depictions of Creole lifestyles were disdained by the community. Moviegoers who follow author Anne Rice's vampire series may recall seeing exterior shots of this house in "Interview With the Vampire."

Return to Royal Street to continue your walking tour. In the next block between Pere Antoine's and Pirates alleys is St. Anthony's Garden. The sedate backyard of the cathedral once rang with the clashing blades of challenged Creoles. On Pirates Alley, a byway both portrayed and inhabited by Quarter artists and authors, look for 624, a bookstore named for the building's famous 1930s resident—William Faulkner.

Get out the camera. Just past Pirates Alley on the corner at St. Peter, you will walk under the balconies of the Labranche Building, one of the Quarter's most photographed structures for its lacy acorn and oak leaf grillwork.

Turn right on St. Peter for a glimpse through gated entries of two popular nightspots, Pat O'Brien's and **Preservation Hall**. Pat O's, as the locals call it, reverberates nightly with sing-alongs in the piano bar. Next door, Preservation Hall musicians only jam evenings, usually to a packed house.

Backtrack to Royal. On the uptown riverside corner (that's the one across the street on the right side of St. Peter) is the four-story, 1811 structure conceived as the first "skyscraper." Protests that the subsoil would not support such a tall edifice halted it at three floors; the fourth was added 65 years later. The "YLM" in the ironwork is the monogram of the first owner, Yves Le Monnier. Another of Cable's Creole tales is set in this house.

The next four blocks form the main commercial area. Several fine old restaurants, a pastry shop, cool courtyard taverns, two large hotels and the greatest concentration of antique stores in the Quarter line the street. Rows of horsehead hitching posts, art studios, galleries and gift shops add to the charm.

Amble uptown on Royal. Midway up the block is The Court of Two Sisters restaurant, occupying the 1832 building where Creole siblings sold Paris clothing and notions in the late 1880s. It has one of the Quarter's largest dining courtyards.

Continuing toward Canal Street, cross Toulouse to the 500 block of Royal, where you will pass **The Historic New Orleans Collection**, a seven-building museum that includes the **Williams Residence**.

Turn right on St. Louis Street. In the middle of the block on your right is Antoine's, one of New Orleans' oldest family-operated restaurants. French-born founder Antoine Alciatore's son created the establishment's signature dish, oysters Rockefeller—so named for its rich sauce—here in the late 1800s.

Cross Bourbon and look for the **Hermann-Grima House**, built in 1831. Now the property of the Christian Women's Exchange, it has a lovely courtyard and the only stable in the Quarter. This handsome Colonial structure exemplifies the American impact on Creole New Orleans.

Turn left at Dauphine and left again toward the river, following Conti to Bourbon Street. On the way you'll pass Broussard's, established in 1920 by Parisian-trained chef Joseph Broussard.

At the corner of Bourbon on the right is the Famous Door. Jazz greats have played this stage since 1934, and a roster of the luminaries who have entered to be entertained frames the portal.

Continue on Conti and turn left at Royal. Two buildings dominate the river side of the street. The oversized 1910 Beaux Arts-style structure on the 400 block first housed district and state courts, then

the Wildlife and Fisheries Commission. The Louisiana Supreme Court now resides in the newly refurbished old Civil Courts Building. This intersection was once the city's financial hub; the grand old Bank of Louisiana building at 334 Royal now serves as the French Quarter 8th District Police Station.

Commanding though they may be, don't allow these architectural landmarks to steal your attention away from the culinary giant across the street—Brennan's, oldest of the Brennan clan's renowned New Orleans restaurants. Put breakfast at Brennan's on your must-do list and don't miss their original dessert, bananas Foster. Built as a residence in the late 18th century, the building was converted around 1805 for the Louisiana Bank, the first financial institution in the Louisiana Purchase territory. Note the letters "LB" in the wrought-iron balcony.

On the far side of the police station on Chartres is another culinary institution, K-Paul's Louisiana Kitchen. Chef Paul Prudhomme helped make Cajun cooking a household name with the opening of his restaurant in 1979.

A right on St. Louis then a left on Chartres will take you back to the heart of the Vieux Carré, cathedral spires in view. On the way note the 1823 apothecary shop of Louis Dufilho at 514 Chartres, home of the **New Orleans Pharmacy Museum**. The devastating 1788 fire started in the home of a Spanish official at the Toulouse Street intersection. At the corner of Chartres and St. Peter streets is Le Petit Theatre du Vieux Carré, an active element in the city's cultural life.

Back at Jackson Square you can enter the quadrangle from any side for a well-earned rest. But why stop now? You're in New Orleans, where excess is a lifestyle; where locals embrace an old Acadian concept called lagniappe—a reference to getting a little something extra, like a bonus. Your lagniappe is just across Decatur Street, where one more great photo opportunity awaits.

Mount the steps at Washington Artillery Park for a panorama of the historic plaza. Camera in hand, align General Jackson with the cathedral and capture a postcard-worthy image. *Click.* Now turn around and face the mighty, muddy Mississippi. With a little luck you just might get a shot of the **Steamboat *Natchez*** taking on passengers at the Toulouse Street Wharf; the sternwheeler's melodious steam calliope puffs out tunes. *Click.* And from this wide vantage point of the river you'll see why New Orleans is called the Crescent City. *Click.*

AAA Walking Tour: The Garden District

Refer to the map following. The fine old homes of the Garden District, bounded by Jackson and Louisiana avenues and St. Charles Avenue and Magazine Street, preserve traces of the era of cotton and sugar empires, when grand antebellum plantations dominated the landscape. This was primarily the American section of town, named for the lush garden estates.

The district owes its luxuriant vegetation to an 1816 flood caused by the overflowing Mississippi River. Although many plantations between Carrollton and the emerging American sector were destroyed, a rich deposit of alluvial silt created a very desirable feature for future development—higher ground. In the early 1830s Jacques Livaudais sold his sugar cane plantation, which was soon subdivided, later incorporated as the city of Lafayette and subsequently annexed to New Orleans, when it became known as the Garden District.

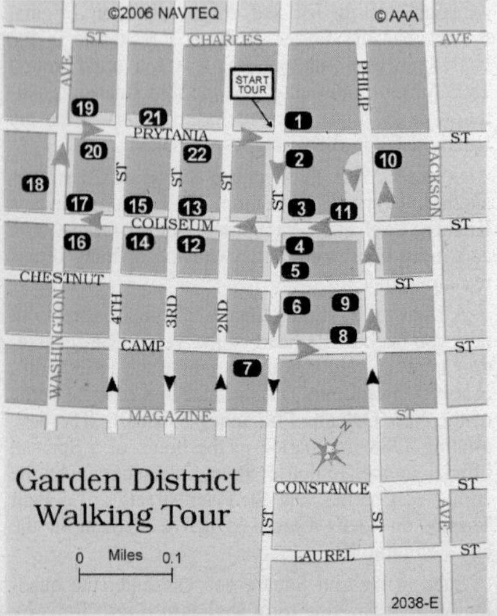

In addition to thriving indigenous and exotic plantings and magnolia trees rivaling oaks in size, the neighborhood boasts a variety of building styles, including Gothic, Greek Revival and Renaissance. Many homes are embellished with iron lacework, a hallmark of New Orleans architecture.

The Garden District is easy to tour, but not necessarily easy to walk. Because some of the sidewalks have become warped by the roots of old oak trees, it is recommended that you wear comfortable shoes and watch your step. Also, look out for the occasional marble carriage step near the curb in front of some residences, remnants of a bygone era.

Please keep in mind that these are private residences, closed to the public. In conjunction with the Spring Fiesta, a 2-week celebration that usually begins in March, tours through select homes are given. For information phone Spring Fiesta Headquarters, (504) 581-1367.

There are no public parking lots in the Garden District and many parking spaces on the one-way cross streets are occupied by residents' vehicles. Your best bet is to take the St. Charles Avenue bus, which travels from Canal Street to the Garden District. The ride takes up to 15 minutes; the walking tour lasts about 1 hour and 30 minutes.

When your bus stops on Jackson Avenue, disembark and walk one block south toward the river to Prytania Street, then 2 blocks west (left) to your starting point at First Street. On the right facing Prytania is the **1** Bradish Johnson House, a Second Empire-style mansion erected in 1872 by New Orleans architect James Freret for a wealthy sugar planter. Louise S. McGehee School for girls has occupied this ornately appointed house since 1929. Like many other Garden District residences, this one is surrounded by an iron fence and shaded by large trees—in this case, mimosa, magnolia and oak. Cross Prytania for another look.

You are standing in front of **2** Toby's Corner, 2340 Prytania St., the district's oldest house. This austere 1838 Greek Revival raised plantation features square columns rising to a Greek cornice. Note the herringbone pattern of the brick sidewalk.

Continue down First. The **3** two-story Greek facade supported by four massive columns at 1407 forms the imposing veranda on a frame house that probably dates from the 1840s.

Cross Coliseum. Two Italianate mansions built simultaneously in 1869 by architect Samuel Jamison anchor both ends of this block. But the **4** Morris House, 1331 First St., and the **5** Carroll House, 1315 First St. at Chestnut, have something else in common: identical ironwork.

Leaving Carroll House, cross Chestnut. The **6** elegant double-galleried town house framed by two curbside oak trees at 1239 First St. was originally the Brevard House, but locals know it as Rosegate, author Anne Rice's former home. A combination of Greek Revival and Italianate styles, the 1857 mansion is noted for its cast-iron adornments. Tread carefully here: The guardian oaks' gnarly roots have corrupted the sidewalk.

Walk to the end of the block. Diagonally across Camp Street is the 7 Payne House, historically significant as the home where Jefferson Davis, President of the Confederacy, died in 1889. A large marble slab near the curb is engraved with highlights of Davis' illustrious military and political career. The Greek Revival structure is one of the most outstanding examples of Garden District antebellum architecture.

Turn left at Camp, then go left again at Philip. As you make your way toward Chestnut, note the 8 frame Italianate behind a large magnolia tree at 1220 Philip. Owned by sugar broker Samuel Delgado, the house was occupied at one time by his nephew Isaac, who amassed an art collection that he donated to the city in 1911. This was the foundation for the New Orleans Museum of Art, formerly Delgado Museum, located in City Park.

A few doors down on the left at 9 1238 Philip St., at the corner of Chestnut, is a single town house dating from 1853. The use of Doric columns on the lower veranda and composite ones on the upper balcony is characteristic of the period. The octagonal wing facing Chestnut was added around 1869, a reflection of Victorian preferences.

Continue on Philip, crossing Chestnut and Coliseum. A 10 quaint raised American cottage stands in the middle of the block at 1433. A spacious front gallery distinguishes this from the Creole version.

Double back to Coliseum and turn right. Starting from the corner, the 11 series of eight shotgun houses at 2301-29 Coliseum is misnamed the Seven Sisters; the origin of this moniker is dubious. Modest in scale when compared to the grandeur of their neighbors seen thus far on the tour, the single-story and camelback (having a second story atop the rear section) dwellings are believed to be early "spec" houses.

Walk down to the Third Street intersection. On your left at 1331 Third is the 12 Musson House, built around 1853. It was the home of Creole cotton factor Michel Musson, uncle of Edgar Degas. Degas' painting "A Cotton Office in New Orleans" depicts activities at his uncle's office, which he visited regularly during his 1872-73 stay at the Musson family's Esplanade Avenue home.

Across Coliseum facing Third is the 13 Robinson House, one of the area's largest residences. Completed for a Virginia businessman just after the Civil War, the structure is executed in the more expansive style of the later antebellum period. The architect was Henry Howard, designer of Nottoway Plantation in White Castle, Madewood Plantation in Napoleonville and several other Garden District homes. Especially notable is the graceful curved portico.

Cross Third and continue on Coliseum. Just outside the arched gates of the 14 1840s Greek Revival house at 2618 Coliseum is another stately oak tree and another bumpy banquet. Careful as you head toward Fourth Street.

Garden District / © AAA / A.R. Lockwood

The gables, ironwork galleries and gingerbread trim on the 15 chalet-style Koch mansion at 2627 Coliseum make for an interesting architectural contrast to the otherwise classic Garden District fare. The house was built 1860-70.

On the left in the next block of Coliseum, 16 starting with 2700 and ending with 2726, are five double-galleried town houses known as Freret's Folly. The story goes that architect William A. Freret's venture was not the success he had hoped for; hence the nickname.

Now turn your attention to the aqua-colored, turreted Victorian that wraps around Washington Avenue just ahead on the right. This is 17 Commander's Palace, one of New Orleans' finest dining destinations and catalyst for the careers of popular chefs Paul Prudhomme and Emeril Lagasse. Although it is now operated by the Brennan family, this landmark restaurant dates from 1880; it was named for founder Emile Commander.

Sorry, you usually can't get in without a reservation, but with a little advance planning you can recount the highlights of your walking tour another day over lunch, a jazz brunch (Saturdays and Sundays only) or dinner. Try the bread pudding soufflé, Commander's Palace's twist on an old New Orleans favorite.

Round the corner and walk along Washington. Just across from Commander's beyond dreary brick walls is one of the "cities of the dead" that New

Orleans is known for. 18 Lafayette Cemetery No. 1 was established in 1833 when the Garden District was within the city of Lafayette. Gates are open every day except Sunday, but we recommend that you enter with a guide.

Take a sharp right at Prytania, where you'll pass 19 The Rink, an 1884 skating rink that now contains upscale shops. There's also a coffee shop inside. If you've already taken the French Quarter walking tour you're sure to experience *dèjá vu* as you stroll down Prytania alongside the cornstalk-motif fence enclosing 20 Col. Short's Villa, 1448 Fourth St. The handsome 1859 Italianate residence is another of Henry Howard's architectural legacies. A bronze plate on the fence details the seizure and occupation of the house during the Civil War.

The 21 unique Gothic Revival house at 2605 Prytania St. has a matching guest house on the grounds. This is said to be the only residence of its type in the Garden District. Across Third and a little farther down on the right is 22 2504 Prytania, home of the Women's Opera Guild. This 1865 Greek Revival by William A. Freret features a later Italianate addition. The elaborately furnished house can be toured by appointment; phone (504) 899-1945.

Cross Second, First and Philip streets and proceed to Jackson Avenue. From this point it is only 1 block left to St. Charles Avenue and the bus stop. Beyond Washington is the Lower Garden District, and beyond that, Uptown, which embraces both sides of St. Charles Avenue. What began as a series of plantations between Lafayette and Carrollton is now home to several neighborhoods as well as Loyola University, Tulane University and historic Audubon Park.

Guided Walking Tours

Park rangers from the Jean Lafitte National Historical Park and Preserve conduct 90-minute walking tours of the French Quarter daily at 9:30. Tours depart from the French Quarter Visitor Center *(see attraction listing p. 121)*; free tickets become available at 9 and are offered on a first-come, first-served basis. Tours are limited to 25 people. Phone (504) 589-2636.

The Friends of the Cabildo, (504) 523-3939, conduct guided 2-hour tours of the French Quarter Tues.-Sun. at 10 and 1:30, and Mon. at 1:30. Tours begin at the 1850 House (The Lower Pontalba). Fee $12; over 61 and ages 13-20, $10; under 13 free when accompanied by a family member. Fee includes admission to the 1850 House (The Lower Pontalba) and Madame John's Legacy.

SAVE **HAUNTED HISTORY TOURS INC.** departs from various locations in the French Quarter. Theatrical guides recount history and folklore on these 2-hour walking tours through the streets and alleys of New Orleans.

The Voodoo-Cemetery Tour departs at 10 a.m. and 1:15 p.m., Garden District Tour at 10 a.m. and 1:30 p.m., Witchcraft-Voodoo Tour at 7:30 p.m., Haunted History Ghost Tour at 2, 6 and 8 p.m., and Vampire Tour at 8:30 p.m. Tours are offered daily except Mardi Gras Day, rain or shine; phone for departure locations. Fee $20; senior citizens $17; under 13, $10. Reservations are required. Phone (504) 861-2727 or (888) 644-6787.

HISTORIC NEW ORLEANS WALKING TOURS depart from various locations in the French Quarter. Various 2-hour walking tours impart the flavor of New Orleans and the French Quarter. Guides entertain and inform guests about such topics as architecture, history, celebrity homes, literature, voodoo, hauntings and music.

Allow 2 hours minimum. Garden District/Cemetery Tour departs daily at 11 a.m. and 1:45 p.m.; Cemetery/Voodoo Tour Mon.-Sat. at 10 a.m. and 1 p.m., Sun. at 10 a.m.; French Quarter History Tour daily at 10:30 a.m.; Haunted French Quarter Walk daily at 7:30 p.m. Closed Mardi Gras Day, Thanksgiving and Dec. 25.

Cemetery/Voodoo Tour $15; over 62 and students with ID $13; ages 6-12, $7. Haunted French Quarter Walk $15; over 62 and students with ID $13; ages 6-12, $7. Garden District/Cemetery Tour $15; over 62 and students with ID $13; ages 6-12, $7. French Quarter History Tour $12; over 62 and students with ID $10; ages 6-12, $7. Phone (504) 947-2120.

Self-guiding Walking Tours

The compactness of New Orleans makes it a natural city to explore on foot. Of special interest, visitors can take self-guiding walking tours of the Civic Center, a complex of five buildings surrounded by a plaza along Loyola Avenue between Poydras Street and Tulane Avenue. The 11-story City Hall faces the Garden of the Americas and has statues of Simón Bolívar, Benito Juárez and Francisco Morazán. Other structures are the Civil Courts Building, State Supreme Court Building, State Office Building and the New Orleans Public Library.

The U.S. Customs House, Decatur and Canal streets, was once the site of old Fort St. Louis. Built in 1848 under the guidance of Gen. Pierre G. Beauregard, it combines two revival styles—Egyptian outside and Greek inside. The building is open to the public Mon.-Fri. 8-4:30.

In addition to the tours described above, self-guiding driving and walking tour brochures are available at the New Orleans Metropolitan Convention and Visitors Bureau at 2020 St. Charles Ave.; phone (504) 566-5011.

Remember that New Orleans is a port city with many types of people and all of the problems inherent in such urban areas. Wandering should be tempered with the same awareness and common sense appropriate in any large city: Limit it to daylight hours and well-traveled routes, leave conspicuous wallets and handbags in your hotel safe and do not go alone.

Spectator Sports

From professional football to pirogue races, there always is something exciting to watch. For listings of coming contests see the sports and events columns in the daily papers and in the monthly *New Orleans* magazine.

Baseball

Baseball fans can catch the **New Orleans Zephyrs** at **Zephyr Stadium** on Airline Highway in Metairie. Affiliated with the Houston Astros, the AAA minor league team takes to the field April through August; phone (504) 734-5155 for tickets.

Basketball

The **New Orleans Hornets**, (800) 462-2849, give NBA aficionados something to cheer about at the **New Orleans Arena.** The arena, across from the Louisiana Superdome, also is home to the **Tulane University Green Wave,** phone (504) 865-5810 for university tickets. The **University of New Orleans Privateers,** also an NCAA Division I team, hold court at the campus arena; phone (504) 280-7222 for tickets. **CLOSURE INFORMATION:** The university arena is temporarily closed due to damage sustained during Hurricane Katrina; phone ahead for updates.

Football

Football ranks as the favorite spectator sport. The **New Orleans Saints** of the National Football League go marching into the **Louisiana Superdome** from August to December, with games generally starting at noon; for tickets phone (504) 731-1700 or 598-4653.

Tulane University's Green Wave football team frequents the Superdome, which becomes a collegiate battlefield every November for the Bayou Classic, a gridiron clash between rival universities **Grambling State** and **Southern**. The Nokia Sugar Bowl game is played in the Superdome in early January.

Horse Racing

One of the city's most enduring sports, Thoroughbred racing can be enjoyed at **Fair Grounds Race Course,** 1751 Gentilly Blvd., where the mechanical starting gate was introduced. Racing takes place Thursday through Monday from Thanksgiving Day through March. When the live racing season ends, visitors still can partake in the facility's off-track wagering, offered year-round. **Note:** The track is closed for renovations due to the effects of the 2005 hurricane season. It is scheduled to reopen in November 2006. For information phone (504) 944-5515.

Note: Policies concerning admittance of children to pari-mutuel betting facilities vary. Phone for information.

Recreation

It is easy to see why Louisiana is often called the Sportsman's Paradise. The semitropical climate provides another benefit: It is possible to participate in outdoor activities year-round. From bicycling to tennis, there are a multitude of places in and around the metropolitan area to enjoy your sport of choice.

Bicycling

A paved bicycle path running some 5.4 miles along the **Mississippi River levee** starts at Colonial Club Drive in Harahan and ends at the Orleans Parish line. **Lakeshore Drive,** on the south shore of Lake Pontchartrain, offers scenery and light traffic. Skirting the Metairie section of the south shore is **Linear Park,** a converted road.

Tammany Trace, a rails-to-trails path on the north shore of Lake Pontchartrain, runs from Abita Springs through Covington, Mandeville, Lacombe and into Slidell. Horseback riding, in-line skating, running and walking also are permitted. For information phone (985) 867-9490.

Fishing

Bluegill, crappie and large-mouth bass are taken from freshwater lakes and rivers. Fishing is permitted at several area state parks, including **Bayou Segnette**, **Fairview-Riverside, Fontainebleau** and **St. Bernard**. **CLOSURE INFORMATION:** Bayou Segnette, Fontainebleau and St. Bernard sustained damage from the 2005 hurricane season and have closed indefinitely; for information, contact the Office of State Parks, Department of Culture, Recreation and Tourism, P.O. Box 44426, Baton Rouge, LA 70804 or phone (225) 342-8111.

Just 2 hours southwest of New Orleans on the Gulf of Mexico, **Grand Isle** offers both freshwater and saltwater fishing. Bluefish, cobia, channel bass, pompano and red snapper range the coastal waters. Game fish such as marlin, tarpon, tuna and sailfish run from late spring through fall in the Gulf.

Boats can be chartered for offshore fishing; for details phone Louisiana Department of Wildlife and Fisheries, (504) 568-5636. A fishing license is required for persons over 16 and costs $15 for residents; the 1-day fee for non-residents is $5 for freshwater and $15 for saltwater. A non-resident license valid for 4 consecutive days is $15 for freshwater and $45 for saltwater. An annual license for non-residents, good for both freshwater and saltwater, costs $90.

Golf

The New Orleans area provides several locations for duffers to engage in their favorite activity. The following courses have 18 holes and are open to the public year-round: Audubon Park Course, (504) 865-8260, 473 Walnut St.; Bayou Oaks Golf Course, (504) 483-9397, 1040 Filmore Ave.; English Turn Golf & Country Club, (504) 392-2200, 1 Clubhouse Dr.; and Lakewood Country Club, (504) 393-1010, 4801 Gen. DeGaulle Ave.

CLOSURE INFORMATION: Bayou Oaks and Lakewood sustained damage during the 2005 hurricane season and are closed as of June 2006; Lakewood plans to reopen in late 2007 and visitors are advised to phone ahead for updates.

Jogging and Walking

In a city as lively as New Orleans, walking may be the only way to ensure you are not missing anything. A stroll through the ***Vieux Carré*** or the **Garden District** reveals the city's eclectic history and

Riverwalk Marketplace / © AAA / A.R. Lockwood

provides an in-depth look at New Orleans' colorful street life as well. Use good sense and keep all city walking to daylight hours.

Parks are scattered throughout the Big Easy. Audubon and City parks in particular are good spots for a stroll or jog, and the sea wall along Lake Pontchartrain makes for a particularly eye-catching exercise site. In Metairie, **Lafreniere Park** offers 155 landscaped acres complete with lagoons encircled by exercise paths.

Picnicking

Picnicking in and around New Orleans can be quite a treat, especially if the picnic basket contains some of the local concoctions. Municipal parks, the levee, and the lakefront are good spots. At certain times of the year insect repellent is a prudent accessory for any outing.

Tennis

Courts are open to the public at most of the facilities administered by the New Orleans Recreation Department; phone (504) 658-3000. Mid-City's 1,500-acre **City Park Tennis Center** has 10 hard courts that may be reserved for $5 an hour; phone (504) 482-4888. Players will find 10 courts for $6 an hour in Audubon Park; phone (504) 861-2537. **CLOSURE INFORMATION:** The tennis courts at Audubon Park are closed temporarily due to the effects of the 2005 hurricane season; phone ahead for updates.

Water Sports

Sailing regattas are held throughout the year on Lake Pontchartrain. **Audubon** and **City** parks offer a variety of water-related activities, including canoeing. For rental information phone (504) 581-4629 and 482-4888, respectively. Waterways are accessible at several nearby state parks, including **Bayou Segnette** in Westwego, **Fairview-Riverside** in Madisonville and **Fontainebleau** in Mandeville. **CLOSURE INFORMATION:** Bayou Segnette and Fontainebleau are temporarily closed due to the effects of the 2005 hurricane season.

Shopping

Join the locals for a day of window shopping or a weekend of bargain hunting along some of the most picturesque streets in the South. Antiquing is one of the most popular and interesting types of shopping. But be on the lookout for such equally sought after wares as detailed papier-mâché Mardi Gras masks, colorful jazz posters and used books. The Quarter is a great place to pick up pralines, spicy condiments, coffee and other packaged local fare.

Antiques

New Orleans' distinctive European heritage has made the area a treasure chest for antique hunters. Eighteenth- and 19th-century furnishings, rare coins, weapons and estate pieces of all kinds are showcased at the many curio shops throughout the area. In addition to Victorian and art deco items, there are ancient relics from countries across the globe, including African tribal artifacts and Oriental pieces.

The best places for good finds are just about anywhere in the ***Vieux Carré***—especially along **Royal Street**—as well as 6 miles of **Magazine Street** from Sixth Street in the **Garden District** running to Henry Clay Avenue just before Audubon Park.

Malls

One of New Orleans' premier malls is found in the very heart of the downtown business district. **New Orleans Centre,** 1400 Poydras St. next to the Louisiana Superdome, offers a convenient and affordable multilevel parking garage connected to the building. Lord & Taylor and Macy's are among the upscale merchants at this tri-level, glass-roofed structure. Small boutiques and restaurants add a charming touch. **CLOSURE INFORMATION:** New Orleans Centre sustained damage from the 2005 hurricane season and is closed indefinitely.

At the foot of Canal Street is **The Shops at Canal Place,** a vertical mall housing Brooks Brothers, Gucci, Saks Fifth Avenue and an array of other stores and cafes. Downtown stores are open Monday through Saturday from 10 to 6, Sunday from noon to 6.

The main suburban shopping centers are **Clearview Shopping Mall,** 4436 Veterans Memorial Blvd.; **The Esplanade Mall,** off West Esplanade Avenue in Kenner; **Lakeside Shopping Centers,** at Veterans Memorial Boulevard and N. Causeway Boulevard; **Oakwood Shopping Center** on the West Bank Expressway, about a mile past the Gretna end of the Crescent City Connection; and **The Plaza Mall** in Lake Forest, 5700 Read Blvd. **CLOSURE INFORMATION:** Oakwood Shopping Center and The Plaza Mall sustained damage during the 2005 hurricane season and are closed indefinitely.

Specialty Districts

New Orleans is truly a shopper's haven, with offerings running the gamut from top-name designers to funky locally owned boutiques. Nowhere is this diversity better illustrated than in The French Quarter, which offers much more than antiques. A typical block along Royal Street might also hold an Oriental gift shop, a very select clothing boutique, a praline shop, a famed restaurant or two and an art market.

The **French Market** *(see attraction listing p. 120)*, in the *Vieux Carré* along Decatur Street between St. Ann Street and Ursulines Avenue, houses shops, informal restaurants and open-air produce stands within its centuries-old arcades.

Canal Street is the original downtown shopping thoroughfare. Many establishments are still family-owned, some with their roots in the early part of the 20th century. Other stores are tucked along **Gravier and Common streets** and the side streets between them.

Jackson Brewery, a complex of shops and eateries overlooking the Mississippi River and the dock of the Steamboat *Natchez*, is at Decatur and St. Peter streets in a former turn-of-the-20th-century brewery. Topped by bold letters proclaiming "Home of Jax Beer," it is a favorite spot for browsing and sampling New Orleans cuisine. A memorabilia collection on the second floor chronicles the brewery's history.

Riverwalk Marketplace, along the Mississippi River at the foot of Poydras Street, is on the site of the 1984 Louisiana World's Fair in the historic Warehouse District. In addition to Abercrombie & Fitch, The Disney Store, The Sharper Image and **Cookin' Cajun Cooking School**, this sprawling riverside shopping mecca contains about 140 emporiums and includes a marketplace, food court, dockside promenade and Spanish plaza.

A variety of smart clothing and specialty shops is scattered along **St. Charles Avenue** between Lee Circle and Jackson Avenue; many are in old houses. **The Rink,** a Garden District shopping niche, is a renovated 19th-century skating rink.

Riverbend, at St. Charles and Carrollton avenues, presents a tempting array of goods ranging from jewelry to gourmet food to home decor, all housed in renovated residential and commercial buildings. There are some good restaurants in the area as well.

Performing Arts

Although New Orleans is known primarily as the cradle of jazz, other forms of entertainment are an important part of the cultural scene. Its orchestra, which is managed by its members, presents a full season of classical pieces and a summer pops series. Community theater has been a French Quarter institution since 1916, and the cutting edge of arts is explored by **Warehouse District** groups, in keeping with that area's bohemian reputation.

Dance

The **New Orleans Ballet Association** sponsors several international touring dance groups, from major professional companies to smaller avant-garde groups. Performances are given at the **Mahalia Jackson Theatre of the Performing Arts** in Louis Armstrong Park on St. Ann Street. For information and tickets phone the association, (504) 522-0996, or Ticketmaster, (504) 522-5555.

The same venue hosts the **Delta Festival Ballet,** Louisiana's largest resident professional troupe. Performances are offered October through April. **CLOSURE INFORMATION:** Delta Festival Ballet sustained damage during the 2005 hurricane season; phone the Mahalia Jackson Theatre, (504) 218-0150, for updates.

Film

Landmark Canal Place Cinema, at Canal Place, offers critically acclaimed films along with standard movie theater fare; for schedule phone (504) 581-5400. Originally built in 1915 as a tent show for short films, the restored **Prytania Theater,** 5339 Prytania St. in the Garden District, now shows feature, foreign and independent films as well as Hollywood classics; phone (504) 891-2787.

The **New Orleans AMC Theater,** a megaplex movie theater at 1200 Elmwood Park Blvd. in Metairie, features 20 movie screens, 36 concession stands and valet parking; phone (504) 734-2020.

Blaine Kern's Mardi Gras World / © Brett Shoaf / Artistic Visuals

Music

From September through May, New Orleans' calendar is filled with symphony and chamber music concerts, recitals and other programs. The **Louisiana Philharmonic Orchestra** is a professional regional ensemble that offers a full series of classical works as well as pops concerts, often featuring guest appearances by international artists and conductors. Performances are given at the **Orpheum** on University Place. Special programs are offered at other area venues, including the **Pontchartrain Center** in Kenner; phone (504) 523-6530.

Chamber music concerts are sponsored by the **New Orleans Friends of Music,** a volunteer organization that brings several touring groups to the city.

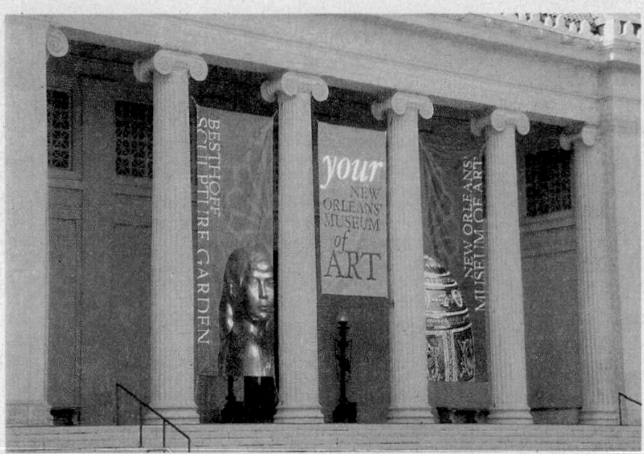

New Orleans Museum of Art / © AAA / A.R. Lockwood

Performances are generally held at **Dixon Hall** on the Tulane University campus. For recital and ticket information phone (504) 895-0690.

Jazz at **Preservation Hall** *(see attraction listing p. 124)* is a concert in every sense of the word. The New Orleans Jazz Club sponsors several programs during the year, and sometimes big names in non-Dixieland areas of jazz do pass through; phone (504) 523-8939.

A variety of musical performances is held in the Mahalia Jackson Theatre of the Performing Arts. The **New Orleans Arena,** across from the Louisiana Superdome, hosts popular concerts and center-stage events; phone (504) 587-3663.

Opera

Opera was first performed in New Orleans in 1796. The **New Orleans Opera Association,** founded in 1943, presents four productions each season; phone (504) 529-3000 or (800) 881-4459. Performances are held at various venues in the city, including the McAlister Auditorium at Tulane University and the Ernest Morial Convention Center Theater.

Theater

Of the many very good theatrical groups, New Orleans' pride is **Le Petit Theatre du Vieux Carré,** 616 St. Peter St. Begun in 1916, it is considered the oldest continuously active community theater in the country. A full season of five traditional productions lasts from September through June and may include musicals, dramas and classic plays; phone (504) 522-2081.

Southern playwrights are celebrated September through May at the **Southern Repertory Theatre** at Canal Place; phone (504) 522-6545. The company, which occasionally includes Equity artists, produces shows exploring the South and regional themes.

Avant-garde theater is centered in the Warehouse District, a funky enclave of both the performing and visual arts. The **Contemporary Arts Center,** 900 Camp St., presents various cultural offerings, including theater, performance art, dance and music; phone (504) 528-3800.

The **Saenger Theatre,** at Canal and Rampart streets, sponsors a Broadway series, bringing major touring companies to the Big Easy each year. Completed in 1927, the restored opulent Italian Renaissance theater gives patrons an outdoors feeling with a ceiling of stars and clouds and a special effects machine that simulates sunrises and sunsets. Additional features include chandeliers from the Palace of Versailles and a 778-pipe organ; phone (504) 525-1052. **CLOSURE INFORMATION:** The theater sustained damage during the 2005 hurricane season and is closed for renovations; phone ahead for updates.

The **Rivertown Repertory Theatre** in nearby Kenner showcases family productions; phone (504) 468-7221. Also in Jefferson Parish is the **Jefferson Performing Arts Center,** 400 Phlox St.; phone (504) 885-2000. Affiliate organizations of the Jefferson Performing Arts Society present Broadway musicals, opera, ballet, orchestral concerts, choral works and children's productions at the center and other locations.

Special Events

Traditionally labeled the "City that Care Forgot," New Orleans pursues its fun with an enthusiasm rarely found elsewhere. In part this is probably why there are so many parades. At one time or another nearly everyone—from the small, old-time funeral bands to the largest convention group—marches down Canal Street, and others watch with unjaded pleasure.

Sugar Bowl activities kick off New Orleans' events season with a series of major contests in basketball, sailing, soccer, tennis and track; the grand finale is the Sugar Bowl football game played in early January in the Louisiana Superdome.

The one event that is synonymous with the city and into which it pours its whole soul is **Mardi Gras.** Meaning "Fat Tuesday," Mardi Gras is Shrove Tuesday, the last day before Lent. Mardi Gras also refers to the 2 weeks before Ash Wednesday. This period is only about the last third of the entire Carnival season, which begins January 6. In a sense Mardi Gras lasts all year, as planning for next year's fete begins as soon as the last one fades.

The Carnival season starts with a series of glittering private balls. During the last 2 weeks the tempo increases, and parades presented throughout the city are staged by Carnival organizations called krewes. The first organized parade, the Mistick Krewe of Comus, entered the scene in 1857. The King of Carnival, Rex made his first appearance in 1872 when the Russian Grand Duke Alexis Romanoff visited. Rex was the first daytime parade and introduced the official Mardi Gras colors of green, purple and gold. In 1909 the first black krewe, Zulu, was introduced. Iris, the first woman's krewe, was founded in 1917.

Today more than 60 parades are featured with themed floats bearing costumed krewe royalty. Maskers toss "throws" from moving floats to the shouting, pleading crowd. Throws can include anything from beads and doubloons to stuffed animals and plastic cups. Of all the throws tossed from the floats, the Zulu coconut or "Golden Nugget" is the most sought after.

The weekend before Mardi Gras features two of the largest and most elaborate parades, the Krewe of Endymion on Saturday night and Bacchus on Sunday night. The affair culminates on Fat Tuesday. Through narrow streets surge masses of laughing, pranking, drinking, dancing people, most costumed. On Lundi Gras, Fat Monday, the night before Mardi Gras, the city hosts a big bash at Spanish Plaza complete with entertainment, fireworks and the arrival of Rex by riverboat; a mask is required for admission.

The two Mardi Gras Day parades—Rex, King of Carnival and Monarch of Merriment, in the morning and Comus, God of Revelry, by torchlight that evening—wend through the crush. So long as there is no threat to safety almost anything goes on this maddest, most intoxicating of all Tuesdays.

A large parade is staged by the Krewe of Argus in suburban Metairie, where the holiday also is celebrated with costuming and merriment. Neighborhood parades also are held during the Carnival season. In retrospect, Mardi Gras is believable only because it happens every year.

Just how this citywide party manages to evade commercialism and still thrive can be traced to the fact that New Orleanians stage it for their own enjoyment and out of their own pockets. Some say that even if not one tourist dime from Mardi Gras clinked into the city's strongbox, the celebration would continue unchanged. It is this genuineness that helps to make Mardi Gras one of the nation's great attractions.

Spring Fiesta, in early March, features ladies in antebellum gowns as well as two weekends of pageants, plays, art shows and concerts. Of interest are the tours, which include visits to French Quarter homes and patios, Garden District mansions and plantation homes. For more information contact the Spring Fiesta Headquarters, 529 St. Ann St., New Orleans, LA 70116; phone (504) 581-1367.

In mid-April the **French Quarter Festival** brings the more boisterous segment back to the city. Music and games are naturally part of the merrymaking, but the big draw is the more than 50 food booths set up by local restaurants in Jackson Square.

The **Jazz and Heritage Festival,** with concerts, food and craft booths, is the last weekend in April through the first weekend in May. Internationally known musicians perform on 10 stages at the Fair Grounds Race Course daily from 11-7; additional performances are given citywide. Tickets can be purchased from Ticketmaster; phone (504) 522-5555.

Celebration in the Oaks transforms City Park *(see attraction listing p. 128)* into a festive holiday wonderland from the Friday after Thanksgiving through the first Sunday in January. A 2-mile driving tour allows visitors to thoroughly enjoy more than a million lights and displays decorating the park. Other sightseeing options include horse-drawn carriage rides, tour buses that depart from area hotels and a self-guiding walking tour encompassing several of the park's most popular areas. **A New Orleans Christmas,** in December, offers historic house tours.

On **New Year's Eve** Jackson Square is the place to be when a huge, glittering ball begins to descend the pole atop Jackson Brewery 10 seconds before midnight.

The New Orleans Vicinity

ABITA SPRINGS (D-5) pop. 1,957, elev. 33'

Choctaw Indians were among the first to discover the supposed curative properties of Abita's artesian springs. The pure water was bottled for public consumption as early as 1896 and was served at the 1904 World's Fair. Chartered in 1912, the town of Abita Springs became a popular summer resort for residents of New Orleans.

St. Tammany Parish Tourist and Convention Commission—Abita Springs: 68099 SR 59, Mandeville, LA 70471; phone (985) 892-0520 or (800) 634-9443.

SAVE **ABITA MYSTERY HOUSE AT THE UCM MUSEUM** is at 22275 SR 36. Paint-by-number masterpieces, postcards, pocket combs and more than 250,000 bottlecaps are among the unusual displays at this folk art museum, which is housed in a vintage filling station, a 90-year-old Creole cottage and the House of Shards, a building covered in mosaics. Highlights include animated scenes of Southern life created by Louisiana artist John Preble from found and recycled objects.

Allow 30 minutes minimum. Daily 10-5; closed Jan. 1, Mardi Gras Day, Easter, Thanksgiving and Dec. 25. Admission $3, under 3 free. MC, VI. Phone (985) 892-2624 or (888) 211-5731.

BURAS (F-6) elev. 2′

FORT JACKSON is 6 mi. s.e. on SR 23. Built 1822-32 to defend the mouth of the Mississippi River, the fort was named after Gen. Andrew Jackson. Fort Jackson was used during the Civil War and was modified in 1898 at the onset of the Spanish-American War. The fortification later served as a World War I training base. **CLOSURE INFORMATION:** The fort was heavily flooded and damaged by hurricanes in 2005 and is closed indefinitely; for updates, check AAA.com or contact Plaquemines Parish. Phone (504) 392-6690.

CHALMETTE (E-6) pop. 32,069, elev. 7′

On the east bank of the Mississippi River, Chalmette is the seat of St. Bernard Parish. The town's main industries include oil and gas production as well as commercial fishing. Locals and visitors alike enjoy fishing and hunting in the surrounding wetlands.

St. Bernard Parish Office of Tourism—Chalmette: 8201 W. Judge Perez Dr., Chalmette, LA 70043; phone (504) 278-4242.

CHALMETTE BATTLEFIELD AND NATIONAL CEMETERY is on SR 46, 6 mi. downriver from the New Orleans French Quarter. Part of the Jean Lafitte National Historical Park and Preserve *(see place listing p. 150)*, this 141-acre park preserves the site of the Battle of New Orleans. On Jan. 8, 1815, Gen. Andrew Jackson and 4,000 militiamen defeated a force of British regulars, securing the Mississippi River and America's claim to the Louisiana Territory.

The Chalmette National Cemetery, the Malus-Beauregard House and a visitor center are on the grounds. **CLOSURE INFORMATION:** The park is closed indefinitely due to hurricane damage; phone ahead for schedule and rates. Phone (504) 589-2133.

COVINGTON (D-5) pop. 8,483, elev. 26′

North of Lake Pontchartrain, Covington is a favorite recreation area for New Orleanians. It lies in the "Ozone Belt," a section of southern Louisiana so nicknamed because of its thick pine forests which improve the quality of the air. After the Civil War Covington gained repute as a health resort, where people came to take advantage of not only the air but also the mineral waters at nearby Abita Springs.

Some of Louisiana's finest horse farms, where quarter horses, Thoroughbreds and Arabian horses are raised, can be found in the area. The Lake Pontchartrain Causeway provides a scenic 24-mile shortcut to New Orleans across Lake Pontchartrain, beginning near the I-12 junction in Covington.

St. Tammany Parish Tourist and Convention Commission—Covington: 68099 SR 59, Mandeville, LA 70471; phone (985) 892-0520 or (800) 634-9443.

H.J. SMITH & SONS OLDTIME COUNTRY STORE & MUSEUM is at 308 N. Columbia St. The Smith family has operated this store continuously since 1876. A museum contains such items as a hand-operated washing machine, farm tools and a 1920s gas pump. Allow 30 minutes minimum. Mon.-Tues. and Thurs.-Fri. 8:30-5, Wed. 8:30-noon, Sat. 8:30-1; closed major holidays. Free. Phone (985) 892-0460.

SAVE **INSTA-GATOR RANCH & HATCHERY,** 5.1 mi. n. of US 190 on SR 21, 1.5 mi. s.e. on SR 1084, 1 mi. s. on SR 1083, then w. to 23440 Lowe Davis Rd., is home to some 2,000 American and Louisiana alligators. On a 1.5-hour guided tour, visitors learn how eggs are harvested, incubated and hatched; the brave may touch a live 4-foot gator.

Allow 1 hour, 30 minutes minimum. Tours are offered Tues.-Sat. 9:30-3, Sun. at 1 and 2:30; closed Jan. 1, Easter, Thanksgiving and Dec. 25. Hours may vary; phone ahead. Admission $14; over 62 and military with ID $12; ages 3-12, $9. Reservations are required for tours. AX, DS, MC, VI. Phone (985) 892-3669 or (888) 448-1560.

DESTREHAN (E-5) pop. 11,260, elev. 10′

An oil refinery town founded in 1914, Destrehan is on the site of the plantation established by Jean Noel Destrehan, a wealthy Creole merchant, planter and legislator.

SAVE **DESTREHAN PLANTATION,** 13034 River Rd. (SR 48), is one of the oldest plantation homes in the lower Mississippi Valley. The central portion of the house was built 1787-90, and the wings, or *garçonnières,* were added about 1812. Pirate Jean Lafitte's frequent visits gave rise to stories of hidden treasure in the walls.

Visitors can observe the continuing restoration of the exterior Greek-style architecture and explore the various outbuildings. Guides in period costumes conduct tours of the house. Allow 1 hour minimum. Mon.-Sat. 9-4, Sun. noon-4; closed Jan. 1, Mardi Gras Day, Easter, Thanksgiving and Dec. 24-25. Admission $10; ages 6-17, $5. MC, VI. Phone (985) 764-9315.

ORMOND PLANTATION is off I-310 exit 6, then .9 mi. w. on SR 48 to 13786 River Rd. Built before 1790, Ormond is the oldest Louisiana Colonial-style plantation on the Mississippi River. The house is modeled after the great sugar plantations of the West Indies. Allow 30 minutes minimum. Guided tours offered daily 10-3; closed major holidays. Admission $7; senior citizens $6; ages 13-17, $5; ages 6-12, $3. AX, CB, MC, VI. Phone (985) 764-8544.

FOLSOM (D-5) pop. 525, elev. 150′

GLOBAL WILDLIFE CENTER is w. on SR 40. Zebras, giraffes, bison, camels and eland are among the more than 3,000 animals that roam this 900-acre preserve in natural settings. Visitors may feed the animals on a 1.5-hour covered wagon safari tour. Allow 2 hours minimum. Daily 8-5; closed Jan. 1,

Thanksgiving and Dec. 24-25 and 31. Admission $14; over 62, $11; ages 2-11, $8. DS, MC, VI. Phone (985) 624-9453.

GARYVILLE (E-5) pop. 2,775, elev. 14′

SAN FRANCISCO PLANTATION is 3.25 mi. w. at 2646 River Rd. (SR 44). The 1856 house is one of the finest examples of Steamboat Gothic architecture in southern Louisiana. Authentically restored, the galleried house features five hand-painted mural ceilings, period antiques and vivid colors. An 1830s slave cabin and 1840s schoolhouse are shaded by 300-year-old live oaks. Tours are led by storytelling guides in period costume.

Daily 9:40-4:40, Apr.-Oct.; 10-4, rest of year. Closed Jan. 1, Mardi Gras Day, Easter, Thanksgiving and Dec. 25. Admission $10; ages 4-17, $5. Phone (985) 535-2341 or (888) 322-1756.

GRETNA (E-5) pop. 17,423, elev. 5′

The German settlement of Mechanikham was established in 1836. Later renamed Gretna in honor of a Scottish village, the town was incorporated in 1913. Gretna's historic district includes Creole cottages, a blacksmith shop and an 1841 firehouse.

City of Gretna Visitor Center: Huey P. Long Avenue at Fourth Street, P.O. Box 404, Gretna, LA 70054; phone (504) 363-1580 or (888) 447-3862. *See color ad p. 124.*

GERMAN-AMERICAN CULTURAL CENTER is off US 90 Bus. Rte. exit 7 at 519 Huey P. Long Ave. This museum chronicles the German settlers who came from the Rhine River valley to the French colony of Louisiana in the 1720s. Lured by the promises of rich fields and gold, some 1,600 Germans set sail from France; only 300 survived the journey and their first year in Louisiana.

Allow 30 minutes minimum. Wed.-Sat. 10-3; closed Jan. 1, Mardi Gras Day and Thanksgiving. Admission $3; over 60 and ages 10-17, $2; under 10, $1. Phone (504) 363-4202.

JEAN LAFITTE (E-5) pop. 2,137, elev. 2′

Jean Lafitte Tourist Commission: 4707 Jean Lafitte Blvd., Lafitte, LA 70067; phone (504) 689-4754 or (800) 689-3525.

LIL' CAJUN SWAMP TOURS is n. on SR 45, .5 mi. n. on SR 3134, then 3.5 mi. w. on SR 301, following signs. Narrated boat cruises take passengers through the swamps, bayous and marshes of "Cajun Country." In addition to plantation ruins and an above-ground cemetery, sights include an abundance of wetland wildlife including alligators and a variety of birds. Evening shrimp trawling trips are available.

CLOSURE INFORMATION: The attraction is closed indefinitely due to the effects of the 2005 hurricane season. For updates, contact Jefferson Convention and Visitors Bureau; phone (504) 731-7083.

Jean Lafitte

Smuggler, privateer and unlikely patriot, Jean Lafitte left an enduring mark on Louisiana lore. By the early 1800s the native of France had established a lucrative smuggling business, run from a blacksmith shop in New Orleans' French Quarter. He later assumed command of the disorganized bands of privateers based in Barataria Bay south of the city.

In 1814 the British failed to sway Lafitte's allegiance with a bribe of $30,000 in gold and a captaincy in the Royal Navy. Instead, Lafitte revealed the British plans to attack New Orleans to Gov. William Claiborne, who responded by dispatching Federal forces against Lafitte's Baratarian colony. Lafitte refused to fire on the American flag, and the Federals destroyed the smugglers' haven.

Digital Archives

Undaunted, Lafitte offered to help Andrew Jackson defend New Orleans in exchange for a full pardon for himself and his men. Jackson accepted, and the battle-seasoned buccaneers fought honorably against the British.

Lafitte became the toast of the town, but the lure of his old life prevailed. In 1817 he established the pirate village of Campeche on Galveston Island, Texas, and resumed plundering Spanish ships. But when one of his captains attacked an American vessel, Lafitte was forced at gunpoint to leave Galveston. After throwing a raucous final party and burning Campeche, Lafitte boarded *The Pride* and sailed away, leaving behind only his legend and rumors of buried treasure.

JEAN LAFITTE NATIONAL HISTORICAL PARK AND PRESERVE (E-6)

Comprising six sites in the Mississippi Delta region, the Jean Lafitte National Historical Park and Preserve was established to preserve some of the state's richest natural and historic resources.

The park includes the Acadian Cultural Center in Lafayette *(see place listing p. 103)*; Barataria Preserve; Chalmette Battlefield and National Cemetery *(see attraction listing p. 148)*; the French Quarter Visitor Center in New Orleans *(see attraction listing p. 121)*; the Prairie Acadian Cultural Center in Eunice *(see place listing p. 99)*; and the Wetlands Acadian Cultural Center in Thibodaux *(see place listing p. 160)*.

BARATARIA PRESERVE is on SR 45 on the West Bank of the Mississippi River in Jefferson Parish. Established to maintain and preserve important coastal wetlands, the 20,000-acre unit of hardwood forest, cypress swamp and marsh is home to alligators, herons, egrets and nutria. Archeological sites contain the remains of the ancient Troyville, Marksville and Tchefuncte cultures.

On the grounds are a visitor center and 9 miles of boardwalks and trails. Canoeing and fishing (with a state license) are permitted. Allow 2 hours minimum. Daily 9-5; closed Mardi Gras Day and Dec. 25. Free. Phone (504) 589-2330.

KENNER (E-5) pop. 70,517, elev. 9′

Kenner lies on the Mississippi River just west of New Orleans. Minor Kenner and his brother William Butler Kenner founded the town in 1852 in a successful attempt to lure the builders of the New Orleans, Jackson and Great Northern Railroad to run the railway near their sugar plantations. Currently, oil and gas are the largest industries. Louis Armstrong New Orleans International Airport is in Kenner.

Kenner Tourist Information Center: 2828 Loyola Dr., Kenner, LA 70062; phone (504) 468-7527 or (800) 473-6789.

Self-guiding tours: A brochure outlining a walking tour of Rivertown, the city's historic district, is available from the Rivertown Welcome Center, 405 Williams Blvd., Kenner, LA 70062; phone (504) 468-7231.

Shopping areas: The Esplanade Mall, 1401 W. Esplanade Ave. off Williams Boulevard, is one of the largest local shopping areas; stores include Dillard's, Macy's and Mervyn's.

RIVERTOWN, bounded by Kenner Avenue, Minor and Felix sts. and the Mississippi River, is Kenner's historic preservation district. The 16-block area embraces many restored late 19th- and early 20th-century structures and features museums, a fine arts gallery, shops and theaters.

Museums include the Cannes Brûlée Native American Village; Daily Living Science Center; Louisiana Toy Train Museum; Louisiana Wildlife Museum and Aquarium; Mardi Gras Museum; Saints Hall of Fame; and Space Station Kenner.

CLOSURE INFORMATION: Louisiana Toy Train Museum and Space Station Kenner are closed for renovations due to damage from the 2005 hurricane season and plan to reopen in fall 2006; phone ahead for rates and schedule. The multi-museum pass price will go into effect when all museums are open.

Museum hours Tues.-Sat. 9-5; closed holidays and Mardi Gras Day. Cannes Brûlée Native American Village $5; ages 2-12 and over 59, $3. Saints Hall of Fame $3; over 60, $2.50; ages 2-12, $2. Multi-museum pass $15; over 55, $11; ages 2-12, $9. Rates vary for other museums; phone ahead. Phone (504) 468-7231.

Daily Living Science Center is at 409 Williams Blvd. The center offers hands-on exhibits and experiments, planetarium shows, an observatory and a full-scale model of the NASA space station.

Louisiana Toy Train Museum is at 519 Williams Blvd. A collection of toy trains, working layouts and a children's half-scale caboose are displayed.

Louisiana Wildlife Museum and Aquarium is at 303 Williams Blvd. The museum exhibits more than 700 preserved specimens of native Louisiana wildlife. Displays include fish, reptiles, mammals, birds and butterflies. A 15,000-gallon freshwater aquarium holds a variety of aquatic life from local waters.

CASINOS

- **Treasure Chest Casino**, I-10 exit 223, then 2 mi. n. to 5050 Williams Blvd. Sun.-Thurs. 11 a.m.-3 a.m.; Fri.-Sat. 11 a.m.-5 a.m. Hours may vary; phone ahead. Phone (504) 443-8000 or (800) 298-0711.

LACOMBE (E-5) pop. 7,518, elev. 17′

BIG BRANCH MARSH NATIONAL WILDLIFE REFUGE is off I-12 exit 74 then s. to 61389 SR 434. On the north shore of Lake Pontchartrain, the 17,094-acre refuge consists of beaches, grass beds, swamps, hardwood hammocks and pine ridges. These varied habitats invite a variety of fowl as well as deer, minks, otters, nutrias and raccoons. Visitors may view exhibits and a wildlife demonstration garden at the visitor center.

Fishing, hiking, hunting and picnicking are permitted. Allow 1 hour minimum. Daily 8-4:30; closed Jan. 1, Mardi Gras Day, Thanksgiving and Dec. 25. Free. Phone (985) 882-2000.

LA PLACE (E-5) pop. 27,684, elev. 13′

AIRBOAT ADVENTURES is off I-10 exit 209, then 8.4 mi. n. to the public boat landing; pick-up service is available from local hotels. Two- or six-passenger airboat tours cover 11 acres. Passengers can spot hawks, owls, alligators, egrets, nutria, wildflowers and even the remains of a late 19th-century railroad.

Allow 2 hours, 30 minutes minimum. Tours daily at 7, 9:45, noon, 2:15 and 4:15, Feb.-Oct.; at 9:45, noon and 2:15, rest of year. Closed Jan. 1, Mardi Gras Day, Easter, Thanksgiving and Dec. 25. Fare $65; under 13, $45. Hotel pick-up fee $25 per person. Reservations are required. AX, MC, VI. Phone (504) 885-7325 or (888) 467-9267.

CAJUN PRIDE SWAMP TOURS is off I-10 exit 209 to I-55 exit 1, then .25 mi. e. to departure point, following signs. Steel swamp boats glide through the Manchac Swamp, as experienced guides relate facts about the area's history. Alligators, nutria, hawks, raccoons, turtles and swamp vegetation may be seen. Passengers may touch a small live alligator.

Food is available. Picnicking is permitted. Allow 2 hours minimum. Tours depart daily at 9:30, noon, 2:15 and 4:15, Apr.-Oct.; at 9:30, noon and 2:15, rest of year. Fare $23; senior citizens and military with ID $21; ages 4-12, $16. AX, DC, DS, MC, VI. Phone (504) 467-0758, (985) 651-4269 or (800) 467-0758.

MADISONVILLE (D-5) pop. 677, elev. 7′

Madisonville is beside the Tchefuncte River, a busy 18th- and 19th-century waterway for shipping goods to New Orleans via Lake Pontchartrain. A public boat launch and Fairview-Riverside State Park *(see Recreation Chart)* within 2 miles of town provide opportunities for water sports and outdoor recreation.

Madisonville Chamber of Commerce: P.O. Box 746, Madisonville, LA 70447; phone (985) 845-9824.

LAKE PONTCHARTRAIN BASIN MARITIME MUSEUM is at 133 Mabel Dr. Exhibits celebrating Madisonville's maritime heritage highlight Tchefuncte River shipbuilding and other north shore industries that contributed to the development of nearby New Orleans. Featured are a reproduction of a small steamboat, a diorama depicting life in a river settlement, vintage outboard motors, a Fresnel lens and an orientation film. Allow 1 hour minimum. Tues.-Sat. 10-4, Sun. noon-4; closed holidays. Admission $3, under 6 free. MC, VI. Phone (985) 845-9200.

OTIS HOUSE is at 119 Fairview Dr. in the 99-acre Fairview-Riverside State Park. Facing the Tchefuncte River and surrounded by moss-draped oak trees, Otis House was built in the 1880s as part of a lumber mill, then purchased and renovated in the 1920s by Frank Otis, a mahogany importer. The Queen Anne-style house contains antiques and family memorabilia.

Visitors learn about local industries and culture from knowledgeable tour guides. Allow 1 hour minimum. Wed.-Sun. 9-5; closed Jan. 1, Thanksgiving and Dec. 25. Admission $2, over 61 and under 13 free. AX, DS, MC, VI. Phone (985) 792-4652.

MARRERO (E-5) pop. 36,165, elev. 6′

Jefferson Convention & Visitors Bureau: 1221 Elmwood Park Blvd., Suite 300, Jefferson, LA 70123; phone (504) 731-7083 or (877) 572-7474. *See color ad p. 129.*

JEAN LAFITTE SWAMP TOURS is 3.5 mi. s. on Barataria Blvd. (SR 45) to SR 3134 (Lafitte LaRose Hwy.), then 5 mi. e. Tour guides narrate the history of the Louisiana swamps as a boat winds through the bayou. Visitors can view moss-draped cypress trees and native wildlife. Allow 2 hours minimum. Trips daily at 10 and 2 (weather permitting); closed Mardi Gras Day, Thanksgiving and Dec. 25. Fare $24; over 65, $23; ages 3-12, $15. AX, MC, VI. Phone (504) 689-4186 or (800) 445-4109.

ST. BERNARD (E-6) elev. 5′

St. Bernard is named after Bernardo de Galvez, the leader of the area's original colonists from the Canary Islands off the coast of Africa. Plantation ruins can be seen along the San Bernardo Scenic Byway on SR 46. The town's proximity to the Mississippi River and the Intracoastal Waterway provide access to such recreational opportunities as bass and saltwater fishing and boating.

St. Bernard Parish Office of Tourism—St. Bernard: 8201 W. Judge Perez Dr., Chalmette, LA 70043; phone (504) 278-4242.

LOS ISLEÑOS MUSEUM is at 1357 Bayou Rd. The history of the Canary Islands and its inhabitants (known as Isleños) who established a colony in southeastern Louisiana is depicted through exhibits which include arts, crafts and photo displays. The Ducros Museum and Library, the Coconut Island Bar and the late 18th-century Estopinal House are on the museum grounds. **CLOSURE INFORMATION:** The museum is closed for renovations indefinitely due to hurricane damage; phone ahead for scheduled reopening date and rates. Phone (504) 682-0862.

ST. ROSE (E-5) pop. 6,540, elev. 10′

LA BRANCHE PLANTATION DEPENDENCY HOUSE is at 11244 River Rd. Built about 1792 by a German family, this house was once used as the *garçonnière*, or bachelor quarters, of the prosperous La Branche Sugar Plantation. Features include antique furnishings, Federal woodwork, slave quarters, a gazebo and a bathtub owned by Zachary Taylor.

Allow 30 minutes minimum. **Note:** Due to the effects of the 2005 hurricane season, hours may vary; phone ahead to confirm. Sat.-Sun. 10-4; closed holidays. Admission $5; ages 13-17, $3; ages 6-12, $2. Phone (504) 468-8843.

SLIDELL (E-5) pop. 25,695, elev. 11′

Slidell is the industrial center of St. Tammany Parish. Brick and tile manufacturers, sawmills, creosoting plants and shipyards contribute to the city's economy.

The area around Slidell is known for water sports, hunting and other outdoor activities. At Pearl River Wildlife Management Area, about 7 miles northeast of Slidell, adventurers may go boating, camping, canoeing and fishing in its 34,896 acres while observing wildlife, including deer, turkeys, bald and golden eagles, swallowtail kites and ospreys.

Visitors may engage in bicycling, horseback riding, in-line skating, running and walking at Tammany Trace, a rails-to-trails path on the north shore of Lake Pontchartrain which treads its way from Slidell into Abita Springs.

St. Tammany Parish Tourist and Convention Commission—Slidell: 1000 Caruso Blvd., Suite 197, Slidell, LA 70461; phone (985) 643-1409.

Shopping areas: North Shore Square Mall, I-12 at North Shore Boulevard (exit 80), contains more than 80 stores including Dillard's, JCPenney, Mervyn's and Sears.

SAVE **CAJUN ENCOUNTERS SWAMP TOUR** is 7.3 mi. e. on US 190, then .3 mi. e. on US 90 to departure point. Tours are guided by a native who imparts detailed information about swamp wildlife. Passengers view the bayou and its environs, including a Cajun village, from small boats that seat 14-25 people.

Note: The tour is running on a reduced schedule due to the 2005 hurricane season. Allow 2 hours minimum. Departures daily at noon; closed Mardi Gras Day. Phone ahead for schedule updates. Fare $23; over 65, $21; ages 3-12, $15. Transportation to the departure point is available for a fee. AX, MC, VI. Phone (504) 834-1770 or (866) 928-6877.

HONEY ISLAND SWAMP TOURS is 2 mi. e. on US 190 to SR 1090/Military Rd., 1 mi. n. to Crawford Landing/I-10 Frontage rds., then 1.5 mi. e. to departure point. The ecologist-guided, 2-hour flatboat tours emphasize the ecology and natural history of Honey Island Swamp, one of the country's least altered river swamps. The small cypress-lined bayous and sloughs are home to alligators, bears, deer, eagles, herons, nutrias, owls and other wildlife.

Morning and afternoon trips are offered daily; phone for schedule. Closed major holidays. Fare $23; under 12, $15. Van transportation from New Orleans is offered for an additional charge. Reservations are required. Phone (985) 641-1769, or (504) 242-5877 in New Orleans.

VACHERIE (E-5) elev. 16′

Vacherie (va-sha-REE) is an old settlement on the west bank of the Mississippi where SR 20 from Thibodaux meets the river. In French it means a "place where cows are kept." About 2 miles downstream the Lutcher-Vacherie Ferry makes a scenic crossing of the river every half-hour from 5 a.m. to midnight. The crossing takes about 15 minutes.

River Region Chamber of Commerce: P.O. Box 1443, La Place, LA 70069; phone (985) 359-9777.

SAVE **LAURA: A CREOLE PLANTATION** is off I-10 exit 194, 5 mi. s. on SR 641 to Veterans Memorial Bridge, then 4 mi. w. to 2247 SR 18. The 1805 main house and original outbuildings of this sugar cane plantation provide the setting for true accounts about four generations of its Creole owners, based on the memoirs of the original owner's great-granddaughter, Laura Locoul. The Br'er Rabbit tales made popular by Joel Chandler Harris are said to have originated in the slave quarters. Guided tours are offered in English and French.

Note: In August 2004, the plantation was damaged by fire. Restoration is under way and the interior of the house is available for tours, although it is not fully restored. Renovations are expected to be completed by December 2006. Tours begin with a discussion of Creole and plantation history in front of the main house and include a tour of the slave cabins. Food is available. Allow 1 hour minimum.

Tours are given daily at 10, 11:15, 12:30, 1:45, 3 and 4; closed Jan. 1, Mardi Gras Day, Easter, Thanksgiving and Dec. 25. Admission $10; ages 6-17, $5. DS, MC, VI. Phone (225) 265-7690 or (888) 799-7690.

GEM SAVE **OAK ALLEY PLANTATION** is 3 mi. w. off SR 20 on SR 18. The Greek Revival mansion was named for the two rows of live oaks, planted in the early 1700s, that form a quarter-mile alley from the Mississippi River to the house. Built 1837-39, Oak Alley has been restored and decorated with period furniture. Mansion tours are provided by knowledgeable guides dressed in period costume. Guests may stroll the plantation grounds; a map is provided.

Allow 1 hour minimum. Guided tours daily 10-4; closed Jan. 1, Thanksgiving and Dec. 25. Schedule may vary; phone ahead. Admission $10; ages 13-18, $5; ages 6-12, $3. Phone (225) 265-2151 or (800) 442-5539.

WESTWEGO (F-5) pop. 10,763, elev. 5'

Westwego was founded in 1870 by the Texas and Pacific Railroad, which was compensated by the state to build a westward railroad. Travelers heard rail workers yell "West we go!" as trains departed, which is how the town got its unusual name, according to legend. Cajun artifacts and an early 1900s grocery store are showcased in the Westwego Historical Museum, 275 Sala Ave.; phone (504) 341-3161.

The town's chief industries are marine-based, including fisheries and boat- and shipbuilding. Recreational activities can be found at Bayou Segnette State Park off US 90 *(see Recreation Chart and the AAA Southeastern CampBook)*.

Westwego Tourist Information Center: 10 Westbank Expwy., Westwego, LA 70094; phone (504) 436-0812.

CAJUN CRITTERS SWAMP TOUR is at 363 Louisiana Ave. Two-hour swamp cruises depart from the end of Bayou Segnette. A Cajun guide shepherds passengers through the backwaters of New Orleans, dispensing knowledge about cypress trees, wildflowers, waterfowl, otters, minks, nutria, deer, alligators and armadillos.

Allow 2 hours minimum. Departures daily at 9:30, 1:30 and 3:30, early Apr.-late Oct.; at 9:30 and 1:30, rest of year. Fare $20; ages 6-12, $15. Transportation to the departure point is available for a fee. Reservations are suggested. Phone (504) 347-0962 or (800) 575-5578.

This ends listings for the New Orleans Vicinity.
The following page resumes the alphabetical listings of cities in Louisiana.

OIL CITY (A-1) pop. 1,219, elev. 204′

LOUISIANA STATE OIL AND GAS MUSEUM is off SR 1 exit Savage St., then .25 mile e. to jct. Land Ave. The museum, housed in the city's old railroad depot, displays early oil field equipment, railroad memorabilia, early 1900s postcards and photographs, and Caddo Indian relics. Allow 30 minutes minimum. Mon.-Fri. 9-4; closed holidays. Free. Phone (318) 995-6845.

OPELOUSAS (D-3) pop. 22,860, elev. 59′

Established as a French trading post in 1720, Opelousas takes its name from the original settlers, the Opelousas Indians. Jim Bowie, inventor of the Bowie knife, lived in Opelousas in the early 1800s and was married in the town. After a cholera epidemic killed his wife and children, Bowie joined the fight for Texas independence and died at the Alamo in 1836.

Opelousas claims another noted person—Louis Garriques. The son of a field marshal in the court of Louis XVI, Garriques was a general in Napoleon Bonaparte's army. A shipwreck brought him to Louisiana, where he was a hero in the Battle of New Orleans. Garriques became a member of the Louisiana Senate and House of Representatives. He is buried on the grounds of the St. Landry Catholic Church.

Weir House, an example of classic Federal architecture at 106 N. Union St., serves as the Opelousas Museum of Art. Works by artists from across the country are featured in rotating exhibits; phone (337) 942-4991 or (800) 424-5442.

Opelousas Tourist Information Center: 828 E. Landry St., Opelousas, LA 70570; phone (337) 948-6263 or (800) 424-5442.

Self-guiding tours: The historic sites and homes of Opelousas are outlined on a driving-tour map and brochure available at the tourist information center.

OPELOUSAS MUSEUM AND INTERPRETIVE CENTER is at 315 N. Main St. This museum explores Opelousas from prehistoric times to the present. Exhibits include the Civil War Room, the Geraldine Smith Welch Doll Collection, the Louisiana Video Library and the Zydeco Music Festival archives. Allow 1 hour minimum. Mon.-Sat. 9-5; closed major holidays. Free. Phone (337) 948-2589.

PATTERSON (E-4) pop. 5,130, elev. 9′

At the close of the 18th century a Captain Patterson established several plantations on Bayou Teche. The community that sprang up was named Pattersonville. The area's early planters, most of whom were English, built plantations along the bayou to the northwest. The town, its name shortened to Patterson, was for years an important lumbering center. An old sugar plantation district contains many restored homes and historic landmarks.

Cajun Coast Visitors & Convention Bureau—Patterson: 112 Main St., Patterson, LA 70392; phone (985) 395-4905 or (800) 256-2931.

LOUISIANA STATE MUSEUM–PATTERSON is at 118 Cotton Rd. Louisiana's aviation history is chronicled at the museum, which honors aviation pioneers Jimmy Wedell and Harry Williams. The men designed and built record-setting racing planes and founded the state's first commercial airline. On display are a Delta Stearman crop-duster, President Dwight Eisenhower's Aero-Commander and a replica of a Mercury space capsule.

Allow 30 minutes minimum. Mon.-Sat. 9-5; closed holidays. Admission $3; over 62, $2; under 13 free. Phone (985) 399-1268.

PINEVILLE (C-3) pop. 13,829, elev. 104′

Much of Pineville was destroyed in 1864 when retreating Union forces burned the town. One survivor was the Mount Olivet Church on Main Street. Dedicated in 1854, the church served as a barracks for the bluecoats during the town's Union occupation.

At Bailey's Dam near O.K. Allen Bridge, a marker indicates the site of a dam constructed by Union troops to move gunboats over the Red River rapids. Nearby are the earthworks of Fort Buhlow, a Confederate stronghold built and abandoned before the invaders arrived.

More recent wars are memorialized at the Alexandria National Cemetery on Shamrock Street, one of four national cemeteries in Louisiana. Established in 1867, it has graves of soldiers who fought in the Indian, Mexican, Civil and Spanish-American wars and World Wars I and II.

Modern activity along the Red River is of a more peaceful nature. Pineville shares the recreational and cultural resources of neighboring Alexandria *(see place listing p. 94)*. Pineville Park on SR 28 on the east side of town provides additional leisure pursuits. Catahoula National Wildlife Refuge *(see attraction listing in Jena p. 101)*, 32 miles northeast, is a 5,308-acre day-use area with year-round fishing, hiking trails and an observation tower.

Alexandria/Pineville Area Convention and Visitors Bureau—Pineville: 707 Main St., Alexandria, LA 71301; phone (318) 442-9546 or (800) 551-9546.

PLAQUEMINE (D-4) pop. 7,064, elev. 20′

The town of Plaquemine bears the name of the nearby bayou in the Atchafalaya Basin. Early French explorers found the banks of the stream lined with persimmon trees and dined with the local American Indians on *pliakmine,* a bread made from the fruit of the trees.

Plaquemine Bayou, a distributary of the Mississippi River, was a navigable waterway for centuries until after the Civil War when a levee built to prevent flooding sealed off the mouth of the bayou. In 1909 the Plaquemine Locks were completed, and this shortcut from the Mississippi into the interior of Louisiana was restored. After 52 years of service the locks closed in 1961, their operations taken over by a larger set of locks upriver at Port Allen.

Iberville Department of Tourism: 58050 Meriam St., P.O. Box 389, Plaquemine, LA 70765-0389; phone (225) 687-5190, ext. 177.

PLAQUEMINE LOCK STATE HISTORIC SITE is downtown at 57730 Main St. The 1909 lock structure and lockhouse are preserved at this site; the lockhouse now is a museum and tourist information center. Allow 30 minutes minimum. Daily 9-5; closed Jan. 1, Thanksgiving and Dec. 25. Admission $2, over 61 and under 13 free. Phone (225) 687-7158 or (877) 987-7158.

PORT ALLEN (D-4) pop. 5,278, elev. 25′

Port Allen, across the Mississippi River from Baton Rouge *(see place listing p. 94)*, was named after Henry Watkins Allen, Louisiana's last Confederate governor. The Port Allen Lock, located off SR 1 just south of I-10, connects the Mississippi to the Intracoastal Waterway. From atop the lock wall, visitors can view the river and barges being locked through; phone (225) 343-3752. A scenic portion of SR 1 extends 35 miles southeast from Port Allen to Donaldsonville and the intersection with SR 70.

West Baton Rouge Tourist Commission: 2855 I-10 Frontage Rd., Port Allen, LA 70767; phone (225) 344-2920 or (800) 654-9701.

WEST BATON ROUGE MUSEUM is at 845 N. Jefferson Ave. Local history exhibits include a 22-foot model of a 1904 sugar mill and a restored American Empire-style bedroom. Various 19th-century documents, tools and memorabilia also are featured. Two relocated buildings are on the premises: an antebellum slave cabin from Allendale Plantation and the Aillet House, a French Creole cottage built around 1830.

Allow 30 minutes minimum. Tues.-Sat. 10-4:30, Sun. 2-5; closed holidays. Admission $4; over 65 and ages 3-18, $2. Phone (225) 336-2422.

RUSTON (A-2) pop. 20,546, elev. 319′

With the completion of a railroad across northern Louisiana in the mid-1880s, area merchants, farmers and cotton growers converged on a rail shipping townsite established by Robert E. Russ. Today I-20 is the primary transportation artery to points east and west of Ruston, and natural gas, oil and a respectable peach crop sustain the economy. Ruston is home to both Louisiana Tech University and Grambling State University.

The Louisiana Tech Horticulture Center, US 80 and Tech Farm Road, displays tropical plants; phone (318) 257-2918. The 1849 Absalom Autrey House, 15 miles north on SR 152, is a hand-hewn log dogtrot house.

Recreational opportunities are available at nearby Lake Claiborne State Park *(see Recreation Chart and Homer in the AAA Southeastern CampBook)*. Lincoln Parish Park *(see Recreation Chart)*, 3.5 miles north on SR 33, is known for its challenging 10-mile mountain bicycle trail, complete with jumps. Swimming, fishing, boating and camping also are available; phone (318) 251-5156.

Ruston-Lincoln Parish Convention & Visitors Bureau: 104 E. Mississippi St., Ruston, LA 71273; phone (318) 255-2031 or (800) 392-9032.

LINCOLN PARISH MUSEUM is at 609 N. Vienna St. Housed in the 1886 Kidd-Davis mansion, the museum features artifacts and memorabilia from the area. Allow 30 minutes minimum. Tues.-Fri. 10-noon and 1-4; closed major holidays. Free. Phone (318) 251-0018.

NORTH LOUISIANA MILITARY MUSEUM is at 201 Memorial Dr. American participation in military conflicts dating from the Civil War is chronicled with a collection of weapons, heavy artillery, uniforms, insignia and such personal items as diaries and medals. Allow 1 hour minimum. Mon.-Fri. 10-6:30, Sat. 10-5, Sun. 1-5; closed Jan. 1, Thanksgiving and Dec. 25. Admission $2, under 12 free. Phone (318) 251-5099 or (318) 255-3196.

ST. BERNARD—*see New Orleans p. 151.*

ST. FRANCISVILLE (D-4) pop. 1,712, elev. 115′

One of the oldest towns in Louisiana, St. Francisville was established near the site of a monastery built in 1785 on land granted to Capuchine friars by the King of Spain. The monastery was soon destroyed by fire, but the name remained.

When the United States purchased Louisiana in 1803, West Florida, a section along the Gulf Coast, was retained by Spain. The inhabitants, descendants of the original Anglo-Saxon settlers, did not want Spanish rule. They waited 7 years for the United States to decide if this region was indeed part of the Louisiana Purchase.

Finally a group of planters attacked the fort at Baton Rouge, captured the Spanish governor and set up their own republic. In 1810 St. Francisville became the capital of the Free and Independent Republic of West Florida, a small but spunky nation. After 74 days the U.S. Army marched into St. Francisville and finally claimed West Florida as part of the original Louisiana Purchase.

West Feliciana Parish Tourist Commission: 11757 Ferdinand St., P.O. Box 1548, St. Francisville, LA 70775; phone (225) 635-6769 or (800) 789-4221.

Self-guiding tours: A driving/walking-tour map of St. Francisville is available from the information center at the historical society museum, 11757 Ferdinand St.

AFTON VILLA GARDENS is 4 mi. n. on US 61. This 20-acre park is beside the ruins of a villa destroyed by fire in 1963. The gardens are approached through a Gothic gate house with a wrought-iron arch. Live oaks and azaleas line the avenue for a half mile. Stone steps lead to a formal boxwood garden. A ravine planted with daffodils and azaleas is especially colorful in the spring.

Daily 9-4:30, Mar. 1-July 1 and Oct. 1-Dec. 1; closed Thanksgiving. Admission $5, under 12 free. Phone (225) 635-6773.

AUDUBON STATE HISTORIC SITE is 3 mi. e. off US 61 on SR 965. On this 100-acre woodland site is the 1806 Oakley Plantation House, where John James Audubon lived as an art teacher in 1821 while working on "Birds of America." A collection of his first-edition prints is displayed. Guided tours of the house are offered. On the grounds are a plantation barn, formal and kitchen gardens, two slave cabins, nature trails and picnic facilities.

Allow 1 hour minimum. Daily 9-5; closed Jan. 1, Thanksgiving and Dec. 25. House tours are offered 10-4. Admission $2, over 62 and under 13 free. Phone (225) 635-3739 or (888) 677-2838.

BUTLER GREENWOOD is at 8345 US 61. Built in 1796, this English-style plantation house still is run by descendants of the original owners. The house has a formal Victorian parlor furnished with gilded French pier mirrors and Louis XV rosewood pieces. Surrounded by more than 100 oaks on 50 acres, the formal garden dates from the 1840s and is one of the few remaining antebellum gardens in the state. Daily 9-5. Admission $5, under 12 free. AX, MC, VI. Phone (225) 635-6312.

THE COTTAGE PLANTATION is 5 mi. n. of jct. US 61 and SR 10, at 10528 Cottage Ln. The plantation tour allows visitors to see a virtually complete plantation as it stood in the early 1800s. Buildings include the main house with many original furnishings, the law office (later used as a schoolhouse), milk house, kitchen, carriage house, smoke house, commissary, tack room, greenhouses, horse barn and slave cabins. Gardens feature azaleas, camellias, crape myrtles, dogwoods and live oaks.

Allow 1 hour minimum. Daily 9:30-4:30; closed holidays. Admission $6, under 13 free. Phone (225) 635-3674.

GREENWOOD PLANTATION is 3 mi. w. of SR 66 at 6838 Highland Rd. The 1830 Greek Revival mansion burned in 1960 and was restored in the 1980s. Its period decor includes ladies' parlor furniture, portraits and silver doorknobs and hinges. Allow 1 hour minimum. Daily 9-5, Mar.-Oct.; 10-4, rest of year. Closed Jan. 1, Easter, Thanksgiving and Dec. 25. Admission $7; ages 6-11, $2. AX, DS, MC, VI. Phone (225) 655-4475.

LOCUST GROVE STATE HISTORIC SITE is just n.e. off US 61 at CR 10 and Bains-Ristroph Rd. A 1-acre cemetery contains the graves of personages from the War of 1812 and Civil War periods. Among the notable people buried is Jefferson Davis' first wife. Daily 9-5. Free. Phone (225) 635-3739 or (888) 677-2838.

THE MYRTLES PLANTATION is 1 mi. n. of jct. US 61 and SR 10, at 7747 US 61. During a tour of the 1796 plantation, guests may view such features as Baccarat crystal chandeliers, a stained-glass entrance door, gilded French furniture, Aubusson tapestries, Carrara marble mantles and a 10-acre garden with live oaks. A guided mystery tour in which guests are regaled with legends of apparitions also is available; the plantation is reputedly haunted.

Food is available. Allow 1 hour minimum. Daily 9-5; closed Jan. 1, Thanksgiving and Dec. 24-25. Guided mystery tours depart on the hour Fri.-Sat. 6-8 p.m. Admission $8; under 12, $4. Mystery tours $10. AX, MC, VI. Phone (225) 635-6277 or (800) 809-0565.

GEM **ROSEDOWN PLANTATION STATE HISTORIC SITE** is just e. of SR 10 and US 61. Daniel Turnbull, a wealthy cotton planter, built the 16-room house approached by a live-oak avenue in 1835. Inspired by their honeymoon to the great gardens of Europe, including Versailles, his wife created 28 acres of formal gardens in the Louisiana wilderness. The gardens feature camellias, azaleas, medicinal herbs and century-old shrubs and trees and are dotted with Italian statuary and gazebos.

Thirteen historic buildings are located on the 371-acre site, including a doctor's office, kitchen, hothouse, milk house and barn. Guided tours offer a glimpse of 19th-century plantation life. Many of the original furnishings imported from Europe are on display. The main staircase is crafted from imported mahogany and Italian marble fireplaces are featured.

Picnicking is permitted. Allow 1 hour, 30 minutes minimum. Site open daily 9-5; closed Jan. 1, Thanksgiving and Dec. 25. Guided tours depart on the hour 10-4. Admission $10; over 61, $8; ages 6-17, $4. Phone (225) 635-3332 or (888) 376-1867.

ST. MARTINVILLE (E-3)

pop. 6,989, elev. 19'

In 1760 the first settler of the St. Martinville area purchased land along Bayou Teche from the Attakapa Indians. By 1764 a Frenchman had established an indigo plantation. After Spanish occupation in 1769 the settlement became a military post, Poste de Attakapas. St. Martinville's early Acadian settlers were joined by refugees—many with titles—driven from France when the revolution began.

Some of the French supported the new Republic of France and clashed with the Royalists when Spain returned Louisiana to France. More tension arose when Louisiana was bought by the United States. The language, customs and crafts of the French and the French Acadians have survived 2 centuries.

Legends of Evangeline, the character immortalized by Henry Wadsworth Longfellow, are encountered everywhere. It was in this town that the real-life Evangeline came in search of her lover Gabriel, only to find he had married another. The focal point of St. Martinville is the St. Martin de Tours Catholic Church square on Main Street. Next to the church is the 1857 Greek Revival-style Presbytère.

St. Martinville Tourist Information Center: 215 Evangeline Blvd., P.O. Box 436, St. Martinville, LA 70582; phone (337) 394-2233.

ACADIAN MEMORIAL is at 121 S. New Market St. The story of the Acadian exile from Nova Scotia is preserved at the memorial, which documents the mid-18th century arrival in Louisiana with a mural depicting ancestors of area Cajuns. Acadian family names, taken from ships' manifests or regional civil records, are displayed on bronze plaques arranged by arrival year. A multimedia history center also is available for research.

Allow 30 minutes minimum. Memorial daily 10-4. History center Mon.-Fri. 10-4. Closed Jan. 1, Sunday before Mardi Gras Day, Easter, Mother's Day, Father's Day, Thanksgiving and Dec. 25. Donations. Phone (337) 394-2258.

AFRICAN AMERICAN MUSEUM is at 123 S. New Market St. in the St. Martinville Cultural Heritage Center. Exhibits such as a 26-foot mural, interactive displays and oral history videos chronicle the history of African-Americans in Louisiana. Allow 30 minutes minimum. Daily 10-4; closed major holidays. Admission $2; ages 6-11, $1. Phone (337) 394-2273.

EVANGELINE OAK is on the bayou at the end of Port St. Evangeline and her lover are supposed to have met beneath this oak, which is said to be the most photographed tree in America.

GEM **LONGFELLOW-EVANGELINE STATE HISTORIC SITE** is n. on SR 31. The 157-acre site borders Bayou Teche in a region settled by Acadians from Nova Scotia. The plantation home, Maison Olivier, was built around 1815 of cypress, brick and *bousillage*, a mix of mud and moss packed between beams. Guided tours are offered of the house, where exhibits depict Creole plantation life.

Surrounding the house is a landscape of fruit, nut and shade trees and vegetable and herb gardens. An outdoor kitchen, storehouse and a reproduction of an Acadian cabin also are on the grounds. Allow 1 hour minimum. Daily 9-5; closed Jan. 1, Thanksgiving and Dec. 25. Last tour begins 1 hour before closing. Admission $2, over 62 and under 12 free. Phone (337) 394-3754 or (888) 677-2900.

PETIT PARIS MUSEUM is at 103 S. Main St. This building on Church Square houses elaborate costumes created for the local Rotary Club's annual Mardi Gras Ball. The highlight of the museum is The Durand Wedding Exhibit, which displays detailed reproductions of the wedding finery once worn by the family of a wealthy 19th-century plantation owner. Allow 30 minutes minimum. Mon.-Sat. 9:30-4:30. Admission $1; over 60, 75c; ages 6-14, 50c. Phone (337) 394-7334.

Audubon Golf Trail

Louisiana's legacy as the Sportsman's Paradise is reflected in the Audubon Golf Trail, a network of seven world-class golf courses across the state. Each public course is a registered member of the Audubon Cooperative Sanctuary Program, which promotes ecological land management and the conservation of natural resources.

The trail honors naturalist and artist John James Audubon, who painted many of his bird studies in Louisiana. Member courses are committed to the preservation of wildlife habitat, providing a total of 135 holes that combine challenge with natural beauty.

Audubon Golf Trail, Tamahka Trails Golf Club, Marksville / Peter A. Mayer Advertising Inc.

The members of the Audubon Golf Trail are Calvert Crossing in Calhoun, (318) 397-0064; Carter Plantation in Springfield, (225) 294-9855; Cypress Bend Resort in Many, (318) 590-1500; Gray Plantation in Lake Charles, (337) 562-1663; The Island in Plaquemine, (225) 685-0808; OakWing Golf Club in Alexandria, (318) 561-0260; Olde Oaks Golf Club in Shreveport-Bossier City, (318) 742-0333; Tamahka Trails Golf Club in Marksville, (318) 240-6300; and TPC of Louisiana at Fairfield in New Orleans, (504) 436-8721. **CLOSURE INFORMATION:** TPC of Louisiana at Fairfield is closed due to the effects of Hurricane Katrina; it is scheduled to reopen in September 2006.

Each course is open year-round. Fees range $35-$160 for 18 holes, including cart rental. Reservations are accepted up to a year in advance; a non-refundable fee of $5 per player is charged.

For further information, to verify rates or to reserve a tee time, phone (866) 248-4652.

GEM **ST. MARTIN DE TOURS CATHOLIC CHURCH** is at 133 S. Main St. One of the oldest churches in the state, it was established in 1765. The present edifice, built in 1844, has an 1883 replica of the Grotto of Lourdes. Jean Francois Mouchet's painting of St. Martin of Tours forms part of the main altar. The baptismal font was a gift from Louis XVI. Behind the left wing of the church is the grave of Emmeline Labiche, thought to be the heroine of Henry Wadsworth Longfellow's poem "Evangeline." A statue of Evangeline stands in the churchyard.

Mon.-Sat. 8:30-4:30. Church free. Guided tours of the church and the Petit Paris Museum $2; over 60, $1.50; ages 6-14, $1. Tour reservations are required. Phone (337) 394-7334.

ST. MARTIN PARISH COURTHOUSE is at 415 S. Main St. Built in 1838 in Greek Revival style with massive Ionic columns, the courthouse contains records dating from 1760 as well as changing exhibits. Mon.-Fri. 8:30-4:30; closed holidays. Free. Phone (337) 394-2210.

ST. ROSE—*see New Orleans p. 152.*

SHREVEPORT (A-1) pop. 200,145, elev. 206′

Before Capt. Henry Miller Shreve arrived in northwest Louisiana in 1833, it was possible to walk across the Red River without getting wet. Shreve spent more than 5 years clearing the Great Raft—a logjam that choked the river for 165 miles. The bustling frontier settlement on the river at Bennett and Cane's Bluff benefited immensely from the opening of the channel. When incorporated in 1839, the town honored Shreve by taking his name.

Cotton was king in northwest Louisiana, and Shreveport became the hub of its domain. Shreveport remained in Confederate hands throughout the war and was therefore spared destruction. The steamboat commerce that had built the town succumbed to competition from the railroads, but Shreveport weathered the transition smoothly.

In 1906 the first of several oil strikes in the region was made, and Shreveport's economic course was set. Besides being a major producer of oil and gas, the state's third largest city is developing a broad industrial base. Cotton remains important but is no longer the commercial mainstay it once was.

Although Shreveport, with its distinctly Texan affinities, differs in flavor from cities in southern Louisiana, the desire to balance progress with preservation is equally strong. The restored Strand Theater, downtown on Louisiana Avenue, opened in 1925 and presents a wide variety of performing arts.

Nearby Cross Lake is a major recreation area *(see Recreation Chart)*. A beautiful drive along the south shore of the lake leads to Ford Municipal Park. Other areas within the city offering a variety of recreational pursuits include C. Bickham Dixon Park in southeast Shreveport and the Clyde Fant Parkway beside the Red River.

Several major events take place in Shreveport. The Red River Revel, an 8-day open-air festival of the visual and performing arts, is held in early October, and the Independence Bowl football game at Independence Stadium takes place in December.

Shreveport-Bossier Convention and Tourist Bureau—Shreveport: 629 Spring St., Shreveport, LA 71101; phone (318) 222-9391 or (800) 551-8682. *See color ad.*

Self-guiding tours: A brochure detailing a walking tour of the city's historical sites is available at the convention and tourist bureau.

AMERICAN ROSE CENTER is off I-20 exit 5W, then n. to 8877 Jefferson Paige Rd. Pathways weave through the 118-acre research facility of the American Rose Society, where roses bloom from April through October. Christmas in Rose Land features millions of lights and animated scenes.

Gardens open Mon.-Fri. 9-5, Sat. 9-6, Sun. 1-6, Apr.-Oct. Christmas in Rose Land 5:30-10 p.m., day after Thanksgiving-Dec. 24 and Dec. 26-30. Admission $4; over 62, $3; under 12 free. Christmas admission $10 per private vehicle (over 4 people $15 per private vehicle) or $4 per person. Phone (318) 938-5402 or (318) 938-5534.

ARK-LA-TEX ANTIQUE & CLASSIC VEHICLE MUSEUM is off I-20 exit 19A to 601 Spring St. Vintage vehicles, period costumes and memorabilia are displayed at the museum, where exhibits change twice a year. Allow 1 hour minimum. Wed.-Sat. 10-5. Admission $6; over 54 and military with ID $5; ages 6-12, $4. MC, VI. Phone (318) 222-0227.

BARNWELL MEMORIAL GARDEN AND ART CENTER is at 601 Clyde Fant Pkwy. This dome-shaped conservatory houses the Shreveport Botanical Gardens and art and flower displays, including a fragrance garden. A 166-foot gallery across the rear of the facility offers a panorama of the Red River. Mon.-Fri. 9-4:30, Sat.-Sun. 1-5. Free. Phone (318) 673-7703.

LOUISIANA STATE EXHIBIT MUSEUM is at 3015 Greenwood Rd. The museum houses murals and displays about Louisiana history, agriculture, industry, natural resources, wildlife and recreation. An exceptionally large and detailed relief map of the state is recessed in the rotunda floor. Around the rotunda are 22 dioramas depicting post-Depression economic activities, while four exterior frescoes illustrate Louisiana's 1930s labor force.

Allow 1 hour minimum. Mon.-Fri. 9-4, Sat.-Sun. noon-4; closed major holidays. Admission $5; ages 6-17, $1. Special events $5. Phone (318) 632-2020.

MEADOWS MUSEUM OF ART is at 2911 Centenary Blvd. on the campus of Centenary College. Featured is a 360-piece collection of Jean Despujols' paintings and drawings of Indochina in the 1930s. A documentary entitled "Indochina Revisited" is shown regularly. The museum also displays changing exhibits. Allow 1 hour minimum. Tues.-Wed. and Fri. noon-4, Thurs. noon-5, Sat.-Sun. 1-4. Free. Phone (318) 869-5169.

GEM **R.W. NORTON ART GALLERY** is off I-49 Pierremont Ave. exit, .25 mi. e. to Creswell Ave., then 1 blk. n. to 4747 Creswell Ave. European and American paintings, sculpture and decorative arts are displayed. Galleries are devoted to Flemish tapestries from the late 16th century, works by Auguste Rodin, rare books, antique dolls, Wedgwood pottery and silver pieces by Paul Revere. Other permanent exhibits contain works by Frederic Remington and Charles Russell.

Allow 1 hour, 30 minutes minimum. Tues.-Fri. 10-5, Sat.-Sun. 1-5; closed Jan. 1, July 4, Thanksgiving and Dec. 25. Free. Phone (318) 865-4201.

SCI-PORT DISCOVERY CENTER is downtown between Lake and Crockett sts. at 820 Clyde Fant Pkwy. Children can crawl through an ant colony at this interactive center, which features more than 200 programs and exhibits for visitors of all ages. Eight discovery areas explore the body, technology, space, the environment and science in everyday life. Films are shown daily in the five-story IMAX Dome Theater. A planetarium is scheduled to open November 2006.

Food is available. Allow 1 hour, 30 minutes minimum. Mon.-Sat. 10-6, Sun. 1-6, Memorial Day-Labor Day; Mon.-Fri. 10-5, Sat. 10-6, Sun. 1-6, rest of year. IMAX film schedule varies; phone ahead. Closed Easter, Thanksgiving and Dec. 25.

Admission to discovery areas $8.50; over 59, military with ID and ages 3-12, $7; $1 for all first Tues. of the month 10-noon. IMAX Theater $8.50; over 59, military with ID and ages 3-12, $7; $5 for all first Tues. of the month 10-noon. Combination ticket $13; over 59 and military with ID $11; ages 3-12, $11. Rates may vary; phone ahead. AX, MC, VI. Phone (318) 424-3466 or (877) 724-7678.

WALTER B. JACOBS MEMORIAL NATURE PARK is at 8012 Blanchard-Furrh Rd. More than 160 acres of wilderness are maintained as a preserve for bird-watching, hiking, nature walks, photography and picnicking. Five nature trails, ranging from a quarter-mile to 2.5 miles, allow visitors to explore gently rolling hills replete with wildlife and native trees. An interpretive building provides exhibits and classroom facilities for special programs.

Allow 1 hour minimum. Wed.-Sat. 8-5, Sun. 1-5; closed Jan. 1, Easter, Thanksgiving and Dec. 25. Free. Phone (318) 929-2806.

WATERTOWN USA is s. off I-20 exit 8S following signs to 7670 W. 70th St. The water park includes pools and waterslides, a playground and a section for small children. Lockers, showers and picnic facilities are available. Mon.-Fri. 11-6 (also Fri. 6-8 p.m., mid-June to mid-Aug.), Sat. 10-8, Sun. noon-6, Memorial Day to mid-Aug.; Sat.-Sun. in May and early Sept. Admission $17.95, over 62 and under 3 free. Reduced rates after 4. AX, DS, MC, VI. Phone (318) 938-5475.

CASINOS

- **Sam's Town Shreveport Casino**, 315 Clyde Fant Pkwy. at the riverfront. Daily 24 hours. Phone (318) 424-7777 or (877) 429-0711.

SLIDELL—*see New Orleans p. 152.*

SUNSET (D-3) pop. 2,352, elev. 44'

SAVE **CHRETIEN POINT PLANTATION** is 5 mi. s. on SR 93, w. 1 blk. on SR 356, then 1 mi. n. to 665 Chretien Point Rd. following signs. Hypolite Chretien built the 12-room brick mansion in 1831 on his 10,000-acre cotton plantation. Now on 20 acres, the restored house is fronted with six Tuscan columns and features lunettes over doors and windows. Guided tours give visitors a view of an interior staircase that is said to have been copied for use on the set of "Gone With the Wind."

Allow 1 hour minimum. Mon.-Fri. 1-5, Sat.-Sun. 10-5; closed Jan. 1, Easter, Thanksgiving and Dec. 25. Last tour departs 1 hour before closing. Admission $10; over 64, $8; ages 6-12, $5; military with ID $3; military in uniform free. Phone (337) 662-5876 or (800) 880-7050.

TANGIPAHOA (D-5) pop. 747, elev. 179'

Tangipahoa is unusual in that its first settlers were women. In 1806 Mrs. Rhoda Holly Singleton

Mixon arrived from South Carolina with her young daughter and a retinue of slaves. She bought a large parcel of land that her family owned until after the Civil War.

The Tangipahoa River, which runs through the parish from the Mississippi line to Lake Pontchartrain, provides opportunities for camping, canoeing and tubing. The countryside surrounding Tangipahoa is largely devoted to truck farming and dairying.

CAMP MOORE CONFEDERATE MUSEUM & CEMETERY is off I-55 exit 57, 1.5 mi. e. on SR 440, then .2 mi. n. on US 51, following signs. Camp Moore was a training camp for Civil War soldiers, many of whom died of malaria without ever facing battle. Exhibits feature currency, weapons, uniforms, medical equipment, photographs, personal effects and musical instruments. A cemetery is on the site and a research library is available.

Allow 1 hour minimum. Tues.-Sat. 10-3; closed major holidays. Admission $2, students with ID $1, under 6 free. AX, DS, MC, VI. Phone (985) 229-2438.

THIBODAUX (E-4) pop. 14,431, elev. 15′

Thibodaux (TIB-o-dough) is a sugar belt town on Bayou Lafourche. The oil and gas industry is important but agriculture is the town's economic mainstay, with sugar cane the principal crop. Thibodaux has its own Mardi Gras, complete with carnival balls and parades.

St. John's Episcopal Church on Jackson Street dates from 1844. It was the church of the Confederacy's "Fighting Bishop," Leonidas Polk, founder of Lafourche Parish. Across the bayou is Rienzi, a plantation built in 1796 by order of the Queen of Spain; she intended to use it as a sanctuary in the event that Napoleon Bonaparte defeated Spain. Rienzi is not open to the public.

Lafourche Parish Tourist Commission: 4484 SR 1, P.O. Box 340, Raceland, LA 70394; phone (985) 537-5800 or (877) 537-5800. *See color ad card insert.*

Self-guiding tours: A walking tour brochure detailing points of interest in the city, and a driving tour brochure for the surrounding area are available from the Thibodaux Chamber of Commerce, 1058 Canal Blvd., Thibodaux, LA 70302; phone (985) 446-1187.

LAUREL VALLEY VILLAGE is 2 mi. e. on SR 308 to 230 Laurel Valley Rd. Comprised of 70 buildings, the village is said to be the largest surviving sugar plantation in the United States. Built in the late 1800s, the small, Acadian-style cabins on the site have housed sharecroppers, German prisoners of war and Civilian Conservation Corps (CCC) laborers.

A general store displays antique tools, farm implements and local arts and crafts. Wed.-Fri. 10-3, Sat.-Sun. noon-3; closed holidays. Free. Phone (985) 446-7456.

WETLANDS ACADIAN CULTURAL CENTER is at 314 St. Marys St. Part of the Jean Lafitte National Historical Park and Preserve *(see place listing in New Orleans p. 150)*, the center traces the history and culture of the Cajuns from the 1600s to the present. Craft demonstrations and videotape and film presentations also are offered. Allow 1 hour, 30 minutes minimum. Mon.-Thurs. 9-6 (also Mon. 6-8 p.m.), Fri.-Sun. 9-5; closed Dec. 25. Free. Phone (985) 448-1375.

VACHERIE—*see New Orleans p. 152.*

VILLE PLATTE (D-3) pop. 8,145, elev. 75′

LOUISIANA STATE ARBORETUM is 8 mi. n. on SR 3042. More than 150 species of native labeled trees and plants are represented at the 300-acre arboretum. Wild deer, foxes, opossums, raccoons and other species may be sighted along a 2.5-mile nature trail. Allow 1 hour minimum. Daily 9-5; closed Jan. 1, Thanksgiving and Dec. 25. Free. Phone (337) 363-6289 or (888) 677-6100.

WESTWEGO—*see New Orleans p. 153.*

WHITE CASTLE (E-4) pop. 1,946, elev. 25′

Not a trace is left of the plantation house for which White Castle is named. The gabled 19th-century manor fell victim to the whims of the mighty Mississippi. The encroaching river forced owners to move the house four times, and each time a section of the building was lost. The "castle" was ultimately reduced to two cottages; today all that remains is its name. A scenic stretch of SR 1 passes through White Castle, intersecting SR 404.

GEM **NOTTOWAY PLANTATION** is 2 mi. n. off SR 1 via signs. Nottoway was considered one of the wonders of the antebellum South. John H. Randolph, a wealthy sugar cane planter, commissioned New Orleans architect Henry Howard to design and build the most palatial home on the Mississippi. When completed in 1859, Nottoway, the center of a self-sufficient 7,000-acre plantation, was the largest house in Louisiana.

The three-story, 64-room mansion, a blend of Greek Revival and Italianate styles, offered such conveniences as gas lamps, indoor bathrooms and an intercom system that employed silver call bells in every room—all unusual and advanced amenities for the 19th century. Spared from destruction during the Civil War, Nottoway has been restored and furnished in period. Its 200 windows command views of the river, lawns and old live oaks.

Food is available. Allow 1 hour, 30 minutes minimum. Tours daily 9-5; closed Dec. 25. Admission $10; under 12, $4. AX, DS, MC, VI. Phone (225) 545-2730.

ZACHARY (D-4) pop. 11,275, elev. 101′

PORT HUDSON STATE HISTORIC SITE is 6 mi. w. on SR 64, then 4 mi. n. on US 61 to 756 W. Plains/Port Hudson Rd. Included in the 899-acre park is the site of a Civil War battle said to be the longest siege in American military history—the fight for Port Hudson and control of the Mississippi River. Interpretive exhibits, a museum, outdoor cannon displays and an observation tower also are on the grounds. Allow 30 minutes minimum. Daily 9-5; closed Jan. 1, Thanksgiving and Dec. 25. Admission $2, over 62 and under 13 free. Phone (225) 654-3775 or (888) 677-3400.

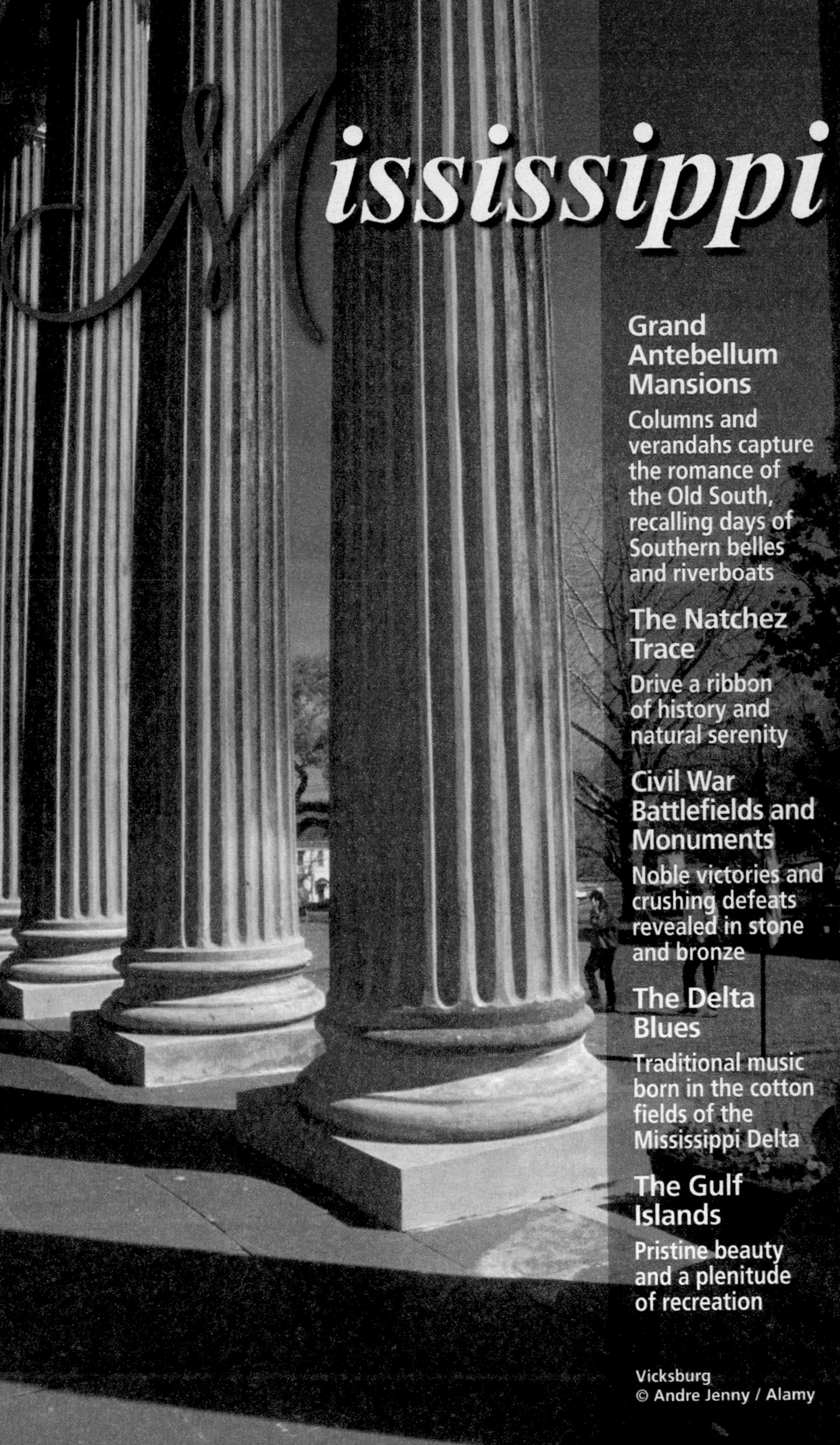

Mississippi
Grand Antebellum Mansions
Columns and verandahs capture the romance of the Old South, recalling days of Southern belles and riverboats
The Natchez Trace
Drive a ribbon of history and natural serenity
Civil War Battlefields and Monuments
Noble victories and crushing defeats revealed in stone and bronze
The Delta Blues
Traditional music born in the cotton fields of the Mississippi Delta
The Gulf Islands
Pristine beauty and a plenitude of recreation

Vicksburg
© Andre Jenny / Alamy

Tutwiler / © age fotostock / SuperStock

A warm welcome awaits you in Mississippi, whether you're exploring the ancient Natchez Trace, frolicking on the sugar-white sand along the Gulf Coast or touring a magnificent antebellum mansion.

Venture 8,000 years back in time on the scenic Natchez Trace, a path originally traced by buffalo and early natives. Split-rail fences and rolling fields blend with ancient mounds built by nomadic Indian tribes. Beginning at Natchez, the road makes a northeastern diagonal all the way to the Mississippi-Alabama state line. Giant oak trees shade picnic spots along the way. You won't find billboards and neon lights here—just miles of unspoiled nature and stirring history.

Mississippi's eclectic mix of culture and heritage is reflected in its landscape.

a legacy of Southern grace

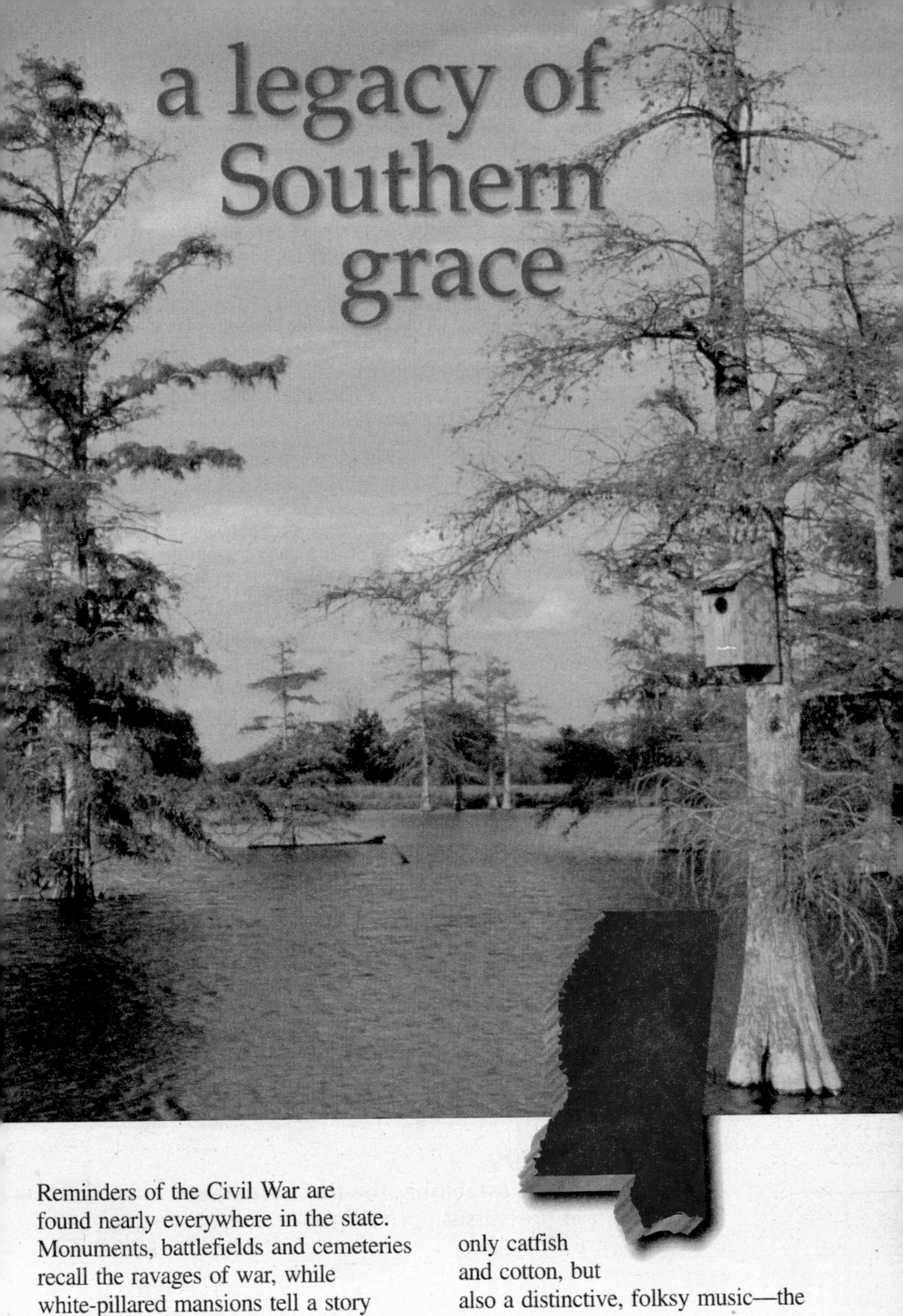

Reminders of the Civil War are found nearly everywhere in the state. Monuments, battlefields and cemeteries recall the ravages of war, while white-pillared mansions tell a story of prosperity brought about by cotton and river commerce.

You'll find echoes of a Southern legacy in the fertile Mississippi Delta, a lush, green region that cultivated not only catfish and cotton, but also a distinctive, folksy music—the Delta blues.

You'll experience it in the sweet smell of magnolias, in restored plantations and in Southern neighborhoods and river port towns.

Union artillery shells rained down upon the Confederate-held city, screaming through the air and blasting houses into kindling. Men and women who hadn't fled the fighting huddled in caves hollowed out of their backyards and nearby hills, praying that explosions would not bury them alive. During lulls, they scurried through cratered streets, desperately searching for food. Mule meat became a staple, supplemented later—as things grew worse—by rats. This was life in Vicksburg for 47 days during the Civil War.

Union forces under Gen. Ulysses S. Grant eventually triumphed. The prize: control of the Mississippi River, effectively cleaving the Confederacy in two. But the price for winning was a devastating loss of life on both sides; battle scars are still visible within Vicksburg National Military Park.

You don't have to be a Civil War buff to be impressed with the hundreds of ornate monuments lining the park's 16-mile loop road. To best enjoy a drive among the reconstructed forts and trenches, hire a guide or rent an audiotape at the visitor center. Vicksburg National Cemetery, also within the park, serves as final resting place for nearly 17,000 Civil War soldiers. Here, a vista of grave markers stretching toward the horizon in neatly ordered rows vividly illustrates how many soldiers perished.

Jackpot!

Fortunately, winning in Mississippi nowadays is no longer a harrowing endeavor. The soldiers of yesteryear have been replaced by armies of gamblers. Since gaming was legalized in 1990, grand and glitzy Vegas-style casinos have popped up like neon-lit wildflowers in Vicksburg and the Tunica-Robinsonville area.

Cannon fire and rebel yells have given way to the felt-muffled rattle of dice, the clatter of roulette wheels and the joyful hoots from jackpot winners. The similarity to Las Vegas doesn't end there. You'll also find an array of restaurants and golf courses as well as shows ranging from small-time lounge acts to big-name celebrity appearances. Following the destruction of the 2005 hurricane season, the casinos of the Gulf Coast were among the first structures repaired or rebuilt and reopened—providing employment to residents sorely in need of income.

If lady luck turns her back on you, head for the nearest casino theater and odds are good you'll be treated to a taste of the blues. The songs may be about losing, but blues hounds are big winners in the state that gave

Mississippi Historical Timeline

1541 Hernando de Soto discovers the Mississippi River.

1699 Pierre le Moyne establishes the first permanent settlement in the Mississippi Valley.

1861 Mississippi secedes from the Union; Senator Jefferson Davis is elected President of the Confederate States of America.

Library of Congress

1906 A tropical storm destroys a large portion of the Gulf Coast's timber industry.

1960-64 Mississippi is the site of violence during the Civil Rights Movement.

Library of Congress

birth to this distinctively American musical genre. Just a stone's throw from the Tunica-Robinsonville gaming center is Clarksdale, once home to blues legends W.C. Handy, Muddy Waters, John Lee Hooker and Ma Rainey. Known as the Delta, the surrounding countryside once rang with the woeful tunes of African slaves toiling in cotton fields. Their descendants still gather in juke joints to savor what is known worldwide as the Delta blues. If you hunger for this soulful music, then missing Clarksdale's Sunflower River Blues Festival in early August would be a crying shame.

Without the blues there would be no rock 'n' roll, and without Mississippi there would be no "King of Rock 'n' Roll." Elvis Presley was born in a small shotgun house in Tupelo that is now part of the Elvis Presley Center and Museum.

And music lovers aren't the only winners in the Magnolia State. Bibliophiles have Mississippi to thank for writers John Grisham, Willie Morris, Eudora Welty and Richard Wright, historian Shelby Foote and Nobel Prize-winning native William Faulkner. Get closer to the literary legend at Rowan Oak, his former home in Oxford. Faulkner memorabilia are enshrined here, and an outline for his final novel is scrawled on one room's walls.

This Old House

Preserving historic homes is a constant struggle against wear and weather, but towns like Natchez and Biloxi are winning the battle. During its antebellum heyday, Natchez's well-heeled merchants and planters built palatial homes that today exemplify the town's victory over time. Stanton Hall in particular—with its white marble mantles, gold-leaf mirrors and antique rosewood furnishings—still flaunts its 19th-century extravagance.

In Biloxi, Confederate president Jefferson Davis' last residence, Beauvoir, has been carefully maintained and restored to appear as it did when he retired there in the 1870s. Stroll along the house's square-pillared gallery overlooking the Gulf of Mexico and you'll see why Davis selected this peaceful site as a writer's retreat. Beauvoir is closed to repair damage incurred during the 2005 hurricane season; it is scheduled to reopen June 3, 2008.

Even once-defeated Vicksburg has won its latter-day fight against decay, showing off fine pre-Civil War houses like trophies on a shelf. And during annual pilgrimages, these homes are opened to the public—proof that Mississippians are willing to share their winnings.

1962

James Meredith becomes the first African-American to attend the University of Mississippi.

Library of Congress

1969

Hurricane Camille hits the Gulf Coast, resulting in extensive property damage.

1983

Lenore Prather becomes the state's first woman Supreme Court Justice.

1990

Mississippi legalizes gambling, spurring the development of casinos and gaming resorts that boost the state's economy.

2003

Nissan opens the state's first automobile manufacturing plant—in Canton.

2005

Hurricane Katrina, the nation's most extensive and costly natural disaster, strikes the Gulf Coast.

©Jim Reed/Corbis

Recreation

The outdoors beckons you in Mississippi. Myriad lakes, rivers and offshore waters, lush green forests and tranquil back roads offer diversions difficult to resist. Thanks to the Magnolia State's mild climate, these temptations can be enjoyed year-round.

Hooked on Fishing

Fishing is taken very seriously by Mississippians—in fact it's said to be the most popular outdoor activity. And no wonder, considering the options available. Which will it be—freshwater or saltwater, the Gulf of Mexico or miles of lakes, bayous, streams, rivers or marshes?

The excitement of **deep-sea fishing** along the Gulf Coast draws anglers hoping to bring home a trophy-size catch. Mississippi Sound and Gulf of Mexico waters teem with amberjack, cobia, flounder, grouper, mackerel, red drum, red snapper and trout, to name just a few. Half-, full-day and overnight fishing charters are easy to arrange; check the harbors and marinas along the coast, particularly in Biloxi and Gulfport. Seasoned captains know the waters and which spots to try.

If you prefer **freshwater fishing,** you're in luck—more than 150 species can be found in Mississippi's inland waterways. And if a native offers to share the location of his favorite fishin' hole, now that's true Southern hospitality.

Crappie are biting at the Ross Barnett Reservoir northeast of Jackson and at lakes Arkabutla, Enid, Grenada and Sardis in northern Mississippi. If Sardis is your destination, expand your water sports itinerary by **boating, swimming** and **water skiing** at nearby John W. Kyle State Park. Locals say the bass are best at Lake Ross Barnett, southwest of Mize. But if it's catfish you're after, head to Lake Tom Bailey east of Meridian and the Big Black, Mississippi, Noxubee and Pearl rivers.

If your travels take you to the coast, Gulf Islands National Seashore is good for **beachcombing.** Ship Island, one of the seashore's three barrier islands, is about 10 miles offshore. Cruise on over by excursion boat from Biloxi or Gulfport. Take along plenty of sunscreen and a picnic lunch and plan on spending a day swimming in the azure Gulf waters, shelling, birding and exploring Fort Massachusetts, manned during the 19th century for coastal defense.

On the Wilder Side

Mississippi is a **hunting** paradise. Forests, fields and wetlands are well populated with deer and wild turkeys. Those in the know say the western counties bordering Ole Man River are the best places to find deer, and the state's location on the Mississippi flyway makes migratory ducks and geese fair game, especially in the fertile Delta region. But before you pack your suitcase, phone the Mississippi Department of Wildlife, Fisheries and Parks at (601) 432-2400 for information about hunting and fishing seasons and license requirements.

History and the beauty of nature draw many fans of **bicycling, hiking** and **horseback riding** to the Natchez Trace. Originally a footpath used by American Indians, then by pioneers, soldiers and tradesmen traveling between Natchez and Nashville, the trail now is a two-lane parkway retracing those 450 miles. Lined with dogwoods, magnolias and moss-draped cypresses, the trace is similar to a quiet country road and invites slow, leisurely travel. Short side trips lead to Civil War battlefields, scenic overlooks, plantations, nature trails and down-home Southern cooking. Contact the Natchez Trace Parkway, 2680 Natchez Trace, Tupelo, MS 38801, (800) 305-7417, for additional information.

A trek on the Black Creek Trail, which runs along the creek between Fairley Bridge and Big Creek landings, will introduce you to the piney woods of southeastern Mississippi. This 40-mile-long trail, which meanders over rolling hill country and more than 90 bridges, is part of the De Soto National Forest's Black Creek Wilderness. A welcome respite might include a relaxing **float trip** by canoe on scenic Black Creek, a stream with sandbars perfect for **picnicking** and **camping.**

Recreational Activities

Throughout the TourBook, you may notice a Recreational Activities heading with bulleted listings of recreation-oriented establishments listed underneath. Similar operations also may be mentioned in Destination City recreation sections. Since normal AAA inspection criteria cannot be applied, these establishments are presented only for information. Age, height and weight restrictions may apply. Reservations often are recommended and sometimes are required. Addresses and/or phone numbers are provided so visitors can contact the attraction for additional information.

Fast Facts

POPULATION: 2,844,658.

AREA: 47,689 square miles; ranks 32nd.

CAPITAL: Jackson.

HIGHEST POINT: 806 ft., Woodall Mountain.

LOWEST POINT: Sea level, Gulf of Mexico.

TIME ZONE(S): Central.

MINIMUM AGE FOR UNRESTRICTED DRIVER'S LICENSE: 16.

MINIMUM AGE FOR GAMBLING: 21.

SEAT BELT/CHILD RESTRAINT LAWS: Seat belts or child passenger restraint systems are required for driver and all front-seat occupants. Children 4-8 are required to use a seat belt; child passenger restraint systems are required for under age 4.

HELMETS FOR MOTORCYCLISTS: Required.

RADAR DETECTORS: Permitted.

FIREARMS LAWS: Vary by state or county. Contact the Mississippi Department of Public Safety, 412 E. Woodrow Wilson Ave., Jackson, MS 39213; phone (601) 987-1572.

HOLIDAYS: Jan. 1; Martin Luther King Jr. Day and Robert E. Lee's Birthday, Jan. (3rd Mon.); Washington's Birthday, Feb. (3rd Mon.); Confederate Memorial Day, Apr. (last Mon.); Memorial Day and Jefferson Davis' Birthday, May (last Mon.); July 4; Labor Day; Veterans Day, Nov. 11; Thanksgiving; Christmas, Dec. 25.

TAXES: Mississippi's statewide sales tax is 7 percent. Localities may impose taxes on lodgings and restaurants.

INFORMATION CENTERS: State welcome centers are near Greenville on US 82 at Reed Road; US 78 at Tremont; I-55N between Chatawa and Osyka; Hernando on I-55; Natchez on US 61S at Sergeant Prentiss Drive; Nicholson on I-59; Pascagoula on I-10; Toomsuba on I-20; Vicksburg on I-20; and Waveland on I-10. The centers are open Mon.-Sat. 8-5, Sun. 1-5.

FURTHER INFORMATION FOR VISITORS:

Mississippi Division of Tourism
P.O. Box 1705
Ocean Springs, MS 39566-1705
(800) 927-6378
(866) 733-6477

RECREATION INFORMATION:

Department of Wildlife, Fisheries and Parks
Parks Information
P.O. Box 451
Jackson, MS 39205-0451
(601) 432-2400
(800) 467-2757

FISHING AND HUNTING REGULATIONS:

Department of Wildlife, Fisheries and Parks
1505 Eastover Dr.
Jackson, MS 39211
(601) 432-2400

NATIONAL FOREST INFORMATION:

U.S. Department of Agriculture
Forest Service
100 W. Capitol St.
Suite 1141, McCoy Federal Bldg.
Jackson, MS 39269
(601) 965-4391
(877) 444-6777 (reservations)
TTY (877) 833-6777

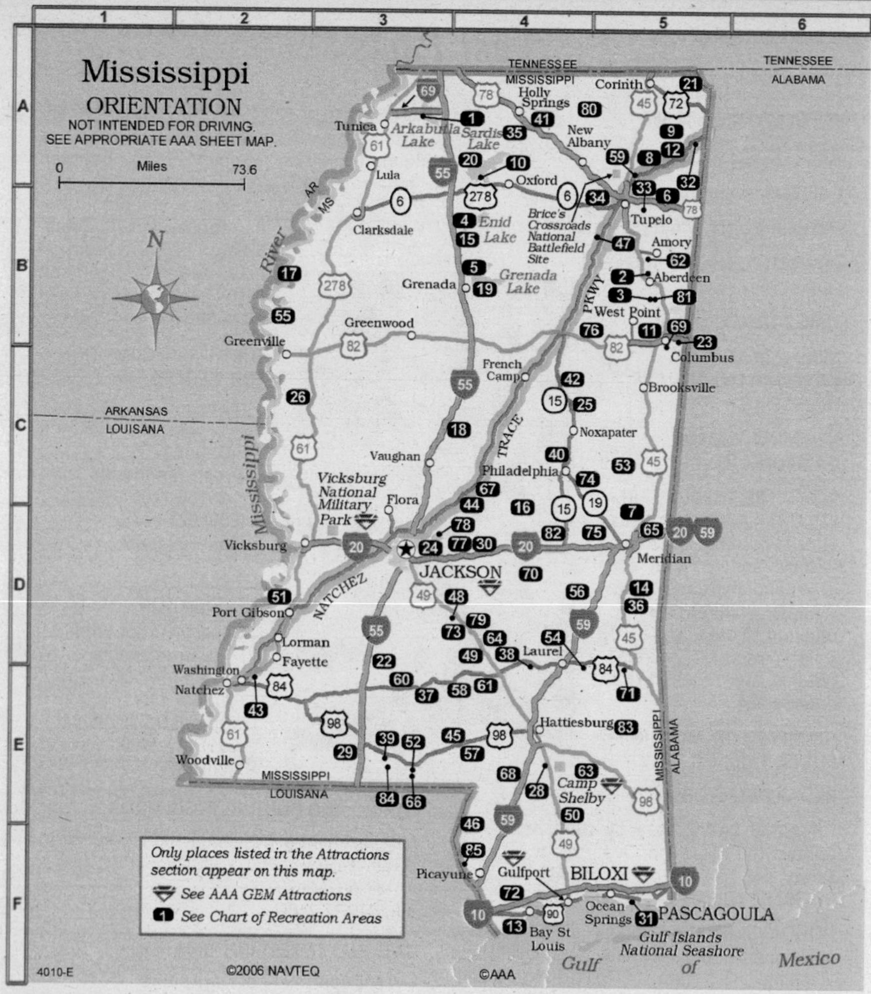

Mississippi Temperature Averages Maximum / Minimum

From the records of the National Weather Service

	JAN	FEB	MAR	APR	MAY	JUNE	JULY	AUG	SEPT	OCT	NOV	DEC
Jackson	57/35	62/40	68/45	76/53	84/61	90/68	93/68	92/70	88/65	79/54	67/43	60/38
Meridian	59/37	62/39	69/44	77/52	85/60	91/68	93/70	93/70	88/64	79/52	67/41	60/36
Vicksburg	57/41	61/43	67/48	75/56	83/64	89/71	90/73	91/73	86/67	77/58	66/47	59/42

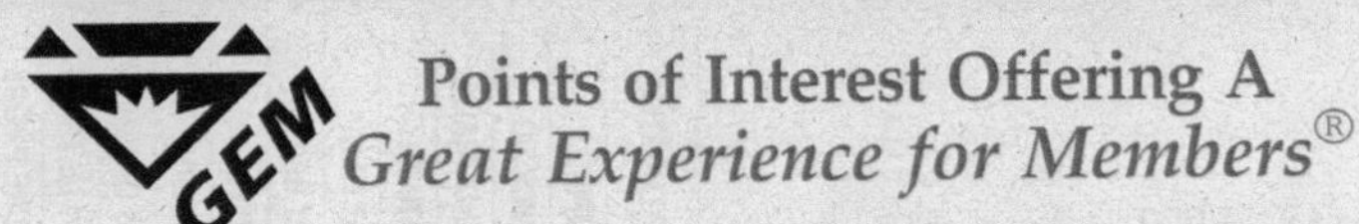

GEM
Points of Interest Offering A
Great Experience for Members®

Biloxi (F-5)

BEAUVOIR—JEFFERSON DAVIS HOME AND PRESIDENTIAL LIBRARY—The 1853 house and pavilions are restored and furnished with original pieces once belonging to the president of the Confederate States of America. Closed because of 2005 hurricane season damage; scheduled to reopen June 3, 2008. See p. 176.

Gulfport (F-4)

LYNN MEADOWS DISCOVERY CENTER—Pick carrots, play the part of news reporter, explore a tree house or paint a self-portrait—the center's stimulating exhibits cater to wee ones. Even the restrooms are child-size. See p. 182.

Hattiesburg (E-4)

ARMED FORCES MUSEUM—More than 17,000 artifacts pertinent to the history of the United States military retrace the steps of soldiers. See p. 183.

Jackson (D-3)

MISSISSIPPI AGRICULTURE AND FORESTRY/ NATIONAL AGRICULTURAL AVIATION MUSEUM—Exhibits at the complex trace technological and economic events of the lumber and agricultural industries. See p. 185.

MISSISSIPPI MUSEUM OF NATURAL SCIENCE—Displays in this large, modern facility focus on plants, wildlife and environments indigenous to Mississippi. See p. 186.

MISSISSIPPI SPORTS HALL OF FAME AND MUSEUM—Interactive exhibits bring to life the careers of great sports legends who called Mississippi home. See p. 186.

Vicksburg National Military Park (C-3)

VICKSBURG NATIONAL MILITARY PARK—Union and Confederate avenues parallel actual battle lines of the Vicksburg siege. Scenes of combat activity and unit positions are illustrated. See p. 196.

RECREATION AREAS

RECREATION AREAS	MAP LOCATION	CAMPING	PICNICKING	HIKING TRAILS	BOATING	BOAT RAMP	BOAT RENTAL	FISHING	SWIMMING	PETS ON LEASH	BICYCLE TRAILS	NATURE PROGS.	VISITOR CENTER	LODGE/CABINS	FOOD SERVICE
NATIONAL FORESTS *(See place listings)*															
Bienville 179,402 acres. Central Mississippi. Horse trail.		•	•	•	•	•	•	•	•	•			•		
Delta 59,553 acres. West-central Mississippi.		•	•					•							
De Soto 500,487 acres. Southeastern Mississippi. Horse rental.		•	•	•	•	•		•	•						
Holly Springs 154,654 acres. Northern Mississippi.		•	•	•	•	•		•	•						
Homochitto 188,994 acres. Southwestern corner of Mississippi.		•	•	•	•			•	•						
Tombigbee 66,576 acres. East-central Mississippi. Horse rental.		•	•	•	•	•		•	•						
NATIONAL SEASHORES *(See place listings)*															
Gulf Islands 135,000 acres. Southern Mississippi.		•	•		•	•		•	•	•		•	•		•
ARMY CORPS OF ENGINEERS															
Arkabutla Lake (A-3) 12,730 acres 15 mi. w. of Hernando off SR 304. Sailing, water skiing.	1	•	•	•	•	•		•	•	•					
Blue Bluff (B-5) 65 acres 1 mi. n. of Aberdeen off US 45. Water skiing; playground.	2	•	•	•	•	•		•	•						
DeWayne Hayes (Columbus Lake) (B-5) 6 acres 6 mi. n.e. of Columbus off SR 373.	3	•	•	•	•	•		•	•	•					
Enid Lake (B-4) 15,500 acres 12 mi. s. of Batesville on I-55. Tennis, water skiing.	4	•	•	•	•	•		•	•	•				•	•

RECREATION AREAS

RECREATION AREAS	MAP LOCATION	CAMPING	PICNICKING	HIKING TRAILS	BOATING	BOAT RAMP	BOAT RENTAL	FISHING	SWIMMING	PETS ON LEASH	BICYCLE TRAILS	NATURE PROGS.	VISITOR CENTER	LODGE/CABINS	FOOD SERVICE
Grenada Lake (B-4) 35,820 acres 3 mi. n.e. of Grenada. Tennis, water skiing; fitness trail.	5	•	•	•	•	•	•	•	•	•			•	•	•
Jamie Whitten Historical Center and Park (B-5) 12 acres 2 mi. n. of Fulton off SR 78. Historical center.	6	•	•	•	•	•		•	•				•		
Okatibbee Lake (D-5) 3,800 acres 7 mi. n.w. of Meridian off SR 19. Water skiing; waterslide.	7	•	•	•	•	•	•	•	•	•		•	•	•	•
Old Bridge Beach (Bay Springs Lake) (A-5) 12 acres 20 mi. e. of Booneville off SR 4.	8		•					•	•	•					
Piney Grove (A-5) 25 acres 15 mi. e. of Booneville, then s. off SR 30 on Bay Springs Lake. Water skiing; playground.	9	•	•	•	•	•		•	•						
Sardis Lake and Dam (A-4) 32,100 acres 5 mi. e. off I-55 at Sardis. Water skiing; fitness trail.	10	•	•	•	•	•	•	•	•	•				•	•
Waverly Ferry Park (B-5) On Columbus Lake, off SR 50. Historic railroad bridge.	11	•	•	•	•	•		•							
West Dam Site (Bay Springs Lake) (A-5) 23 acres 20 mi. e. of Booneville off SR 4.	12		•			•		•		•					
STATE															
Buccaneer (F-4) 398 acres off US 90 at Waveland. Tennis; wave pool. CLOSURE INFORMATION: The park was damaged in the 2005 hurricane season; it was expected to reopen in late 2006 or early 2007. Phone (800) 467-2757.	13	•	•	•				•	•	•			•		•
Clarkco (D-5) 815 acres 5 mi. n. of Quitman on US 45. Tennis, water skiing.	14	•	•	•	•	•	•	•	•	•		•	•	•	•
George Payne Cossar (B-4) 982 acres 5 mi. n.e. of Oakland on SR 32. Water skiing.	15	•	•	•	•	•	•	•	•	•		•	•	•	•
Golden Memorial (C-4) 107 acres 5 mi. e. of Walnut Grove off SR 492.	16		•	•	•		•	•	•	•		•	•		
Great River Road (B-2) 731 acres off SR 1 near Rosedale.	17	•	•	•	•	•	•	•		•		•	•		•
Holmes County (C-4) 436 acres 4 mi. s. of Durant off I-55 exit 150.	18	•	•	•	•	•	•	•	•	•		•	•	•	•
Hugh White (B-4) 1,256 acres 5 mi. e. of Grenada off SR 8. Tennis, water skiing.	19	•	•	•	•	•	•	•	•	•		•	•	•	•
John W. Kyle (A-4) 740 acres 9 mi. e. of Sardis on SR 315. Tennis, water skiing.	20	•	•	•	•	•	•	•	•	•		•	•	•	•
J.P. Coleman (A-5) 637 acres 13 mi. n. of Iuka off SR 25.	21	•	•	•	•	•	•	•	•	•		•	•	•	•
Lake Lincoln (D-3) 550 acres 6 mi. e. of Wesson. Nature trails, pavilion.	22	•	•		•	•	•	•	•				•		
Lake Lowndes (B-5) 750 acres 6 mi. s.e. of Columbus off SR 69. Tennis. *(See Columbus p. 179)*	23	•	•	•	•	•	•	•	•	•		•	•	•	•
LeFleur's Bluff (D-3) 310 acres off I-55 n. at E. Lakeland exit in Jackson. Golf, tennis; driving range, playground.	24	•	•	•	•	•	•	•	•	•		•	•		•
Legion (C-4) 420 acres on old SR 25 in Louisville.	25	•	•	•	•	•	•	•	•	•			•	•	
Leroy Percy (C-2) 2,371 acres 6 mi. w. of Hollandale on SR 12.	26	•	•	•	•		•	•	•	•		•	•	•	•
Natchez (E-2) 3,411 acres 10 mi. n. of Natchez off US 61. Nature trails.	27	•	•	•	•	•	•	•		•			•	•	
Paul B. Johnson (E-4) 744 acres 15 mi. s. of Hattiesburg off US 49. Water skiing. CLOSURE INFORMATION: As a result of the hurricane season of 2005, as of June 2006 one-third of the camping spaces were occupied by FEMA temporary housing trailers; phone (601) 582-7721 for campsite availability.	28	•	•	•	•	•	•	•	•	•		•	•	•	•
Percy Quin (E-3) 1,700 acres 5 mi. s.w. of McComb off I-55. Water skiing. CLOSURE INFORMATION: As a result of the hurricane season of 2005, as of June 2006 only 30 of the 122 camping spaces were not occupied by FEMA temporary housing trailers and were available on a first-come, first-served basis; phone (601) 684-3938 for updated information.	29	•	•	•	•	•	•	•	•	•		•	•	•	•
Roosevelt (D-4) 540 acres off I-20 exit 25. Tennis.	30	•	•	•	•	•	•	•	•	•		•	•	•	•

RECREATION AREAS

RECREATION AREAS	MAP LOCATION	CAMPING	PICNICKING	HIKING TRAILS	BOATING	BOAT RAMP	BOAT RENTAL	FISHING	SWIMMING	PETS ON LEASH	BICYCLE TRAILS	NATURE PROGS.	VISITOR CENTER	LODGE/CABINS	FOOD SERVICE
Shepard (F-5) 306 acres 3 mi. w. of Pascagoula off US 90. CLOSURE INFORMATION: As a result of the hurricane season of 2005, as of June 2006 all the camping spaces were occupied by FEMA temporary housing trailers, but the park was expected to reopen to the general public in late 2006 or early 2007; phone (228) 497-2244 for updated information.	31	•	•	•		•		•		•	•		•		
Tishomingo (A-5) 1,340 acres 2 mi. e. of Tishomingo off SR 25.	32	•	•	•	•	•	•	•	•	•		•	•	•	•
Tombigbee (B-5) 602 acres 6 mi. s.e. of Tupelo off SR 6. Tennis.	33	•	•	•	•	•	•	•	•	•		•	•	•	•
Trace (B-5) 1,980 acres 10 mi. e. of Pontotoc off SR 6.	34	•	•	•	•	•	•	•	•	•	•		•	•	
Wall Doxey (A-4) 749 acres 7 mi. s. of Holly Springs off SR 7.	35	•	•	•	•	•	•	•	•	•		•	•	•	•
OTHER															
Archusa Creek Water Park (D-5) 1,000 acres 1 mi. e. of Quitman on SR 18. Water skiing.	36	•	•	•	•	•	•	•	•	•				•	
Atwood Water Park (E-3) 78 acres 2 mi. e. of Monticello off US 84. Tennis; pavilion, playground.	37	•	•	•	•	•		•					•		
Big Creek Water Park (D-4) 800 acres 10 mi. w. of Laurel off US 84.	38	•	•	•	•	•	•	•	•	•				•	
Bogue Chitto Water Park (E-3) 230 acres 12 mi. e. of McComb on US 98. Pavilion, playground.	39	•	•	•	•	•		•	•				•		
Burnside Lake Park (C-4) 115 acres 2 mi. n.e. of Philadelphia on SR 15. Ball fields, pavilion, playground.	40	•	•	•	•	•		•					•		
Chewalla Lake (A-4) 260 acres 7 mi. e. of Holly Springs off SR 4 on FR 611.	41	•	•	•	•	•		•	•	•		•			
Choctaw Lake (C-4) 100 acres 5 mi. s. of Ackerman off SR 15.	42	•	•	•	•	•		•	•	•					
Clear Springs (E-2) 13 acres 7 mi. w. of Meadville off US 84/98 on FR 104. No boats with motors permitted.	43	•	•	•	•			•	•	•			•		
Coal Bluff Park (D-4) 60 acres 10 mi. n.e. of Sandhill. Tennis.	44	•	•	•	•	•		•	•	•	•				
Columbia Water Park (E-4) 60 acres 2 mi. n. of Columbia off SR 35. Pavilion.	45		•		•	•		•							
Crossroads Water Park (E-4) 50 acres e. of Bogalusa on SR 26 at Crossroads.	46		•	•	•	•		•							
Davis Lake (B-5) 200 acres 13 mi. n.e. of Houston off SR 15. Water skiing; horse trail.	47	•	•	•	•	•		•	•	•	•				
D'Lo Water Park (D-4) 72 acres 2 mi. n. of Mendenhall off old US 49. Mapped float trips; pavilion, playground.	48	•	•	•	•	•	•	•	•				•		
Dry Creek Water Park (D-4) 800 acres 5 mi. w. of Mount Olive off US 49.	49	•	•	•	•	•	•	•	•	•					
Flint Creek Water Park (E-4) 1,900 acres 1 mi. e. of Wiggins on SR 29. Water skiing; waterslides.	50	•	•	•	•	•	•	•	•					•	
Grand Gulf Military Park (D-2) 400 acres 7 mi. n.w. of Port Gibson on SR 462. *(See Port Gibson p. 193)*	51	•	•	•						•			•		
Holmes Water Park (E-3) 43 acres off SR 27 in Tylertown on Magee's Creek. Ball fields, pavilion, playground.	52		•	•	•	•		•							
Kemper (C-5) 652 acres 3 mi. n.w. of DeKalb off SR 397.	53				•	•	•	•							•
Lake Bogue Homa (D-4) 1,200 acres 6 mi. e. of Laurel on US 84.	54		•		•	•	•	•	•						•
Lake Bolivar (B-2) 512 acres 15 mi. s. of Rosedale off SR 1.	55	•	•			•	•	•							•
Lake Claude Bennett (D-4) 71 acres 20 mi. e. of Bay Springs off SR 18.	56	•	•		•	•	•	•	•						•
Lake Columbia and Lake Bill Waller (E-4) 90 and 200 acres 12 mi. s.e. of Columbia in the Marion County Management Area.	57	•	•		•	•	•	•	•						•
Lake Jeff Davis (E-4) 164 acres 3 mi. s. of Prentiss on SR 42.	58	•	•		•	•	•	•	•						•

RECREATION AREAS

	MAP LOCATION	CAMPING	PICNICKING	HIKING TRAILS	BOATING	BOAT RAMP	BOAT RENTAL	FISHING	SWIMMING	PETS ON LEASH	BICYCLE TRAILS	NATURE PROGS.	VISITOR CENTER	LODGE/CABINS	FOOD SERVICE
Lake Lamar Bruce (A-5) 330 acres 1.5 mi. n.e. of Saltillo.	59	•	•		•	•	•	•	•						•
Lake Mary Crawford (E-3) 135 acres 5 mi. w. of Monticello on US 84.	60	•	•		•	•	•	•	•						•
Lake Mike Conner (E-4) 88 acres 8 mi. w. of Collins off US 84.	61	•	•		•	•	•	•	•						•
Lake Monroe (B-5) 111 acres n. of Aberdeen off US 45.	62	•	•		•	•	•	•	•						•
Lake Perry (E-5) 125 acres 3 mi. w. of Beaumont.	63	•	•		•	•	•	•	•						•
Lake Ross Barnett (D-4) 87 acres 4 mi. s.w. of Mize off SR 35.	64	•	•		•	•	•	•	•						•
Lake Tom Bailey (D-5) 234 acres 8 mi. e. of Meridian on US 11.	65	•	•		•	•	•	•	•						•
Lake Walthall (E-3) 62 acres 8 mi. s.e. of Tylertown.	66		•		•	•		•							
Leake County Water Park (C-4) 100 acres 16 mi. n.e. of Sandhill off SR 25.	67	•	•	•	•	•		•							
Little Black Creek Water Park (E-4) 1,100 acres 5 mi. n.w. of Lumberton on Old Purvis-Lumberton Hwy.	68	•	•	•	•	•	•	•	•	•				•	
Luxapalila Creek (B-5) 334 acres 5 mi. s.e. of Columbus off SR 69. Water skiing.	69		•	•	•	•		•							
Marathon Lake (D-4) 70 acres 12 mi. s.e. of Forest off SR 501 on FR 506. No boats with motors permitted.	70	•	•	•	•	•		•	•	•					
Maynor Creek Water Park (E-5) 1,000 acres 4 mi. w. of Waynesboro on US 84W. Water skiing; waterslides.	71	•	•	•	•	•	•	•	•	•				•	
McLeod Park (F-4) 328 acres off Texas Flat Rd. in Kiln. Pavilion.	72	•	•	•	•	•	•	•	•				•		
Merit Water Park (D-4) 25 acres 3 mi. s. of Mendenhall via SR 43. Waterfall.	73		•	•					•						
Neshoba Legion Lake (C-4) 225 acres 8 mi. s.e. of Philadelphia.	74	•	•		•	•	•	•	•						•
Okatibbee Water Park (D-5) 360 acres 7 mi. n.w. of Meridian off SR 19. Waterslides.	75	•	•	•	•	•	•	•	•	•	•			•	•
Oktibbeha County Lake (B-5) 479 acres 9 mi. w. of Starkville on US 82, then 2 mi. n. on a county road. Water skiing.	76	•	•	•	•	•	•	•	•						•
Pelahatchie Lake (D-4) 25 mi. e. of Jackson off I-20 on SR 43.	77	•			•	•		•	•				•		
Ross Barnett Reservoir (D-3) 30,000 acres 7 mi. n. of Jackson on I-55, then 3 mi. e. on Natchez Trace Pkwy. Water skiing.	78	•	•		•	•	•	•	•						•
Simpson County Legion Lake (D-4) 94 acres 5 mi. n. of Magee on US 49.	79	•	•					•							•
Tippah County Lake (A-4) 165 acres 2.5 mi. n. of Ripley on SR 15, then 2.5 mi. w. on a paved road.	80	•	•		•	•	•	•	•						•
Town Creek (B-5) 27 acres 8 mi. w. of Columbus off SR 50.	81	•		•	•	•		•	•	•					
Turkey Creek Water Park (D-4) 600 acres in Decatur.	82	•	•	•	•	•	•	•	•	•				•	
Turkey Fork Lake (E-5) 250 acres 25 mi. e. of Richton via SRs 42 and 63.	83	•	•	•	•	•		•	•	•					
Walker's Bridge Water Park (E-3) 5 acres 3 mi. w. of Tylertown off SR 48. Pavilion.	84		•		•	•		•							
Walkiah Bluff Water Park (F-4) 18 acres 4 mi. w. of Picayune on SR 43. Pavilion.	85	•	•		•	•		•							

Points of Interest

ABERDEEN (B-5) pop. 6,415, elev. 230'

By 1850 Aberdeen was a major port, shipping cotton from a large part of northern Mississippi and selling goods from the east and south. Cotton prosperity continued into the early part of the 20th century, with trains replacing steamboats as freight carriers.

During that time merchants and plantation owners competed with one another to build and furnish the most impressive house in the area. As a result, the town offers fine examples of various architectural styles. Some of the houses are open by appointment all year. Also of interest is the Old Aberdeen Cemetery.

Scenic Blue Bluff Recreation Area is on the 4,000-acre Aberdeen Lake section of the Tennessee-Tombigbee Waterway. Two miles north on Meridian Street, this 55-acre site offers boating, camping, fishing, hiking and hunting. *See Recreation Chart and the AAA Southeastern CampBook.*

Aberdeen Visitors Bureau: 125 W. Commerce St., P.O. Box 288, Aberdeen, MS 39730; phone (662) 369-9440 or (800) 634-3538.

Self-guiding tours: The visitor bureau offers an illustrated pamphlet that outlines an architectural driving tour including more than 50 restored properties.

THE MAGNOLIAS is at 732 W. Commerce St. This Greek Revival antebellum home was built in 1850 by plantation owner William A. Sykes. The property features an original three-level mahogany and walnut staircase and period furnishings. Allow 1 hour minimum. Mon.-Fri. 10-2, Sat.-Sun. by appointment; closed major holidays. Admission $5, under 6 free. Phone (662) 369-7956 Mon.-Fri., or (662) 634-3538 Sat.-Sun.

AMORY (B-5) pop. 6,956, elev. 241'

Commerce in Amory is supported by rail and by sail: The town was founded by the K.C.M. & B. Railroad in 1887; now it serves as a port on the Tennessee-Tombigbee Waterway.

Monroe County Chamber of Commerce: 601 Second Ave., P.O. Box 128, Amory, MS 38821; phone (662) 256-7194.

AMORY REGIONAL MUSEUM is at 715 S. Third St. at Eighth Ave. Displays include furnishings, photographs, medical equipment, a restored railroad car, a military room with items dating from WWII and assorted memorabilia relating to Monroe County's history. A two-story log cabin built about 1840 is furnished in period. Guided tours are available. Allow 30 minutes minimum. Tues.-Fri. 9-5, Sat.-Sun. 1-5; closed major holidays. Free. Phone (662) 256-2761.

BAY ST. LOUIS (F-4) pop. 8,209, elev. 28'

Until hurricane Katrina struck the Gulf Coast on Aug. 29, 2005, Bay St. Louis was a community where visitors could browse in the many art and antiques shops along the bay, and wonder at the lives of the original owners of the Victorian houses lining the streets.

Katrina damaged or destroyed more than 60 percent of the structures and infrastructure in Bay Saint Louis, and more than 90 percent in its sister city of Waveland. Some of the older buildings on higher ground and sheltered by larger buildings survived the storm and its storm surge.

Today the community is rebuilding and restoring its infrastructure and its lives, with the grace and tenacity born of its Deep South roots.

Mississippi Gulf Coast Convention and Visitors Center—Bay St. Louis: P.O. Box 6128, Gulfport, MS 39506-6128; phone (228) 896-6699 or (800) 237-9493.

JOHN C. STENNIS SPACE CENTER is on SR 607, 2.5 mi. n. of I-10 exit 2. Research at this 13,480-acre space shuttle main-engine testing center includes space, oceanographic and environmental studies by NASA and other agencies. A visitor center offers lectures, films, a motion simulator, exhibits and tours of the shuttle complex. A moon rock and the Apollo 4 command module are displayed.

A photo ID is required for visitors over 17. Guided tours are available. Allow 30 minutes minimum. Wed.-Sat. 10-3; closed Jan. 1, Easter, July 4, Thanksgiving and Dec. 25. Last admission 1 hour before closing. Free. Phone (228) 688-2370 or (800) 237-1821, option 1.

CASINOS

- **Hollywood Casino Bay St. Louis** is s. off I-10 exit 607, then e. on US 90; exit n. on Blue Meadow Rd. and follow signs. **CLOSURE INFORMATION:** The casino was damaged in the 2005 hurricane season and was expected to reopen in September of 2006. Daily 24 hours. Phone (228) 467-9257 or (800) 562-4425.

BELZONI (C-3) pop. 2,663, elev. 112'

Belzoni is the self-proclaimed Catfish Capital of the World, producing tons of the farm-raised variety of this finny Southern staple. For those seeking a different example of Mother Nature's bounty, there is Wister Gardens 3 miles north. on US 7 to 500 Henry Rd. Plantings at this 7-acre botanical garden offer year-round enjoyment with azaleas, fruit trees, crape myrtles, roses, a gazebo, a fountain, a garden house, water gardens, swans and ducks. The gardens of this private residence are open Mon.-Fri. 9-5 except on holidays.

THE CATFISH CAPITOL is at 111 Magnolia St. In a renovated railroad depot whose grounds are dotted with innovative sculptures fashioned from catfish farming and fishing related items, this visitor center offers exhibits about this industry and about the region, its history and its people. Allow 30 minutes minimum. Mon.-Fri. 9-5; closed Jan. 1, July 4, Thanksgiving and Dec. 25. Free. Phone (662) 247-4838 or (800) 408-4838.

BIENVILLE NATIONAL FOREST

Elevations in the forest range from 340 ft. at the creek bottoms to 570 ft.

In central Mississippi, Bienville's 179,402 acres of pine and hardwood forest were once the depleted holdings of four large lumber companies. Bienville Pines Scenic Area, a mile south of the community of Forest on SR 501, features a nature trail in a stand of virgin pine. Shockaloe National Recreation Trail, 5 miles west of Forest on US 80, offers 23 miles of hiking and horseback riding trails. Other recreational activities possible within the forest include camping, fishing, hunting and swimming.

For further information contact the Forest Supervisor, Bienville National Forest, Route 2, 3473 SR 35S, Forest, MS 39074; phone (601) 469-3811. The Ranger's District office is on the west side of SR 35, about 1.5 miles south of I-20. *See Recreation Chart and the AAA Southeastern CampBook.*

BILOXI (F-5) pop. 50,644, elev. 22'

The hurricane season of 2005 badly damaged or destroyed much of this delightful resort town. Displaying Biloxi moxie, some businesses, attractions and casinos have reopened and others are rebuilding or planning to rebuild on the original sites.

The city's history began in 1699 when Pierre Lemoyne first entered what is today Biloxi. The city's culture and customs have been influenced by the six flags that have flown over the region. Biloxi, an American Indian word for "first people," has been governed by France, Spain, Great Britain, the West Florida Republic, the Confederacy and the United States. Biloxi was the first capital of the Louisiana Territory

The mild climate, white sandy beaches, championship golf courses, deep-sea fishing, tours of antebellum houses, art galleries and antiques shops made Biloxi a resort town. In the 1990s casino gambling arrived to add glitz and the long shot of instant wealth to this genteel city's Old World charm.

The Old Lighthouse, US 90 and Porter Avenue, was built in 1847 in Baltimore and shipped to Biloxi on a brig in 1848. The lighthouse is temporarily closed in order to repair damage from the 2005 hurricane season; phone (228) 435-6308. Originally bordered by water on three sides, the lighthouse now stands 100 yards north of the shoreline. Sightseeing bus tours of the Gulf Coast offered by Gray Line have been indefinitely suspended because of damage caused by the 2005 hurricane season; phone (800) 565-8913.

Mississippi Gulf Coast Convention and Visitors Center—Biloxi: P.O. Box 6128, Gulfport, MS 39506-6128; phone (228) 575-4297 896-6699 or (800) 237-9493.

GEM **BEAUVOIR—JEFFERSON DAVIS HOME AND PRESIDENTIAL LIBRARY** is off I-110; 5.5 mi. w. on US 90 (Beach Blvd.) to Beauvoir Rd. This 1853 estate was the last home of Jefferson Davis, U.S. senator and secretary of war, and president of the Confederate States of America. The house and the pavilions are restored and are on 51 picturesque acres; furnishings are mostly original Davis pieces. The Palladian-style Jefferson Davis Presidential Library contains a theater, exhibit gallery and research library. A 15-minute historical film is shown.

The Confederate Museum, in the Confederate Veterans' Hospital building, displays guns, uniforms and other personal items belonging to Confederate soldiers. A cemetery contains more than 700 Confederate graves, including that of Samuel Emory Davis, and the Tomb of the Unknown Soldier of the Confederate States of America.

CLOSURE INFORMATION: The 2005 hurricane season caused extensive damage to the property; Beauvoir is scheduled to reopen June 3, 2008.(228) 388-1313, (228) 388-9074 or (800) 570-3818.

SAVE **BILOXI SCHOONERS THE *GLENN L. SWETMAN* AND THE *MIKE SEKUL*** are at Point Cadet Marina on US 90E, 1 mi. e. of I-110. Harbor and beachfront cruises lasting 2.5 hours are offered. The vessels are replicas of the Biloxi schooners that harvested seafood in the late 1800s and early 1900s. Damage from the 2005 hurricane season has been repaired and a normal schedule resumed. Afternoon and evening cruises are available. Fare $25; ages

DID YOU KNOW

Elvis Presley, the King of Rock 'n' Roll, was born in Tupelo.

3-12, $10. Phone (228) 435-6320 for schedule and reservations.

BILOXI SHRIMPING TRIP, LLC is at US 90 and Main St. at the Biloxi Small Craft Harbor. The 70-minute trip allows passengers a look at the variety of sea life caught on a real shrimping expedition in the calm, protected waters between Deer Island and the Biloxi shoreline. Aboard the *Sailfish*, a guide sets the net out with an explanation of how to make it operate correctly. When the net is retrieved about 20 minutes later, all the species caught are identified.

Damage from the 2005 hurricane season has been repaired and a normal schedule resumed. Trips are offered daily late Feb.-Nov. 30 (weather permitting). Phone for schedule. 2006 fare $12; ages 4-12, $8. 2007 fare $15; ages 4-12, $10. Phone (228) 385-1182 for schedule or (800) 289-7908.

J.L. SCOTT MARINE EDUCATION CENTER AND AQUARIUM is just s. of US 90 at 115 Beach Blvd. The center contains a variety of exhibits relating to native Mississippi and Gulf of Mexico marine life. A 42,000-gallon aquarium is home to sharks, sea turtles and eels; smaller tanks display fish and various animals. Live snakes, turtles, alligators and other swamp dwellers also are displayed. Educational audiovisual presentations are shown continuously in the auditorium.

CLOSURE INFORMATION: In 2005 the center was destroyed by Hurricane Katrina; plans call for rebuilding it in the distant future. It now operates a greatly simplified program for school groups in Ocean Springs. Mon.-Sat. 9-4; closed Jan. 1, Sat. before Easter, Thanksgiving and Dec. 25. Admission $5; over 64, $4; ages 3-12, $3. Phone (228) 818-8890.

MARITIME & SEAFOOD INDUSTRY MUSEUM is n. on US 90 to Myrtle St. then e. to Point Cadet Plaza at 115 First St. **CLOSURE INFORMATION:** The museum was destroyed in the 2005 hurricane season; plans call for rebuilding it. Phone (228) 435-6320.

OHR-O'KEEFE MUSEUM OF ART is off US 90 at 136 G.E. Ohr St. The museum displays more than 250 works by George E. Ohr (1857-1918), whose innovative ceramic designs and flamboyant personality led him to proclaim himself "The Mad Potter of Biloxi." Two other galleries feature rotating exhibits. **CLOSURE INFORMATION:** Damaged during the 2005 hurricane season, the museum plans to reopen in spring of 2008. Phone (228) 374-5547.

SHIP ISLAND EXCURSIONS—*see Gulfport p. 182.*

TULLIS-TOLEDANO MANOR was 1.2 mi. e. on US 90 at 360 Beach Blvd. **CLOSURE INFORMATION:** The manor was destroyed during the 2005 hurricane season and will not be rebuilt.

CASINOS

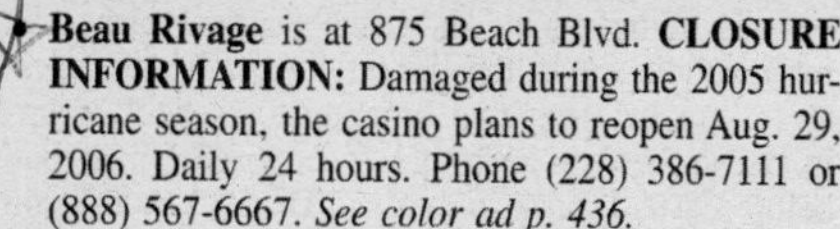

- **Beau Rivage** is at 875 Beach Blvd. **CLOSURE INFORMATION:** Damaged during the 2005 hurricane season, the casino plans to reopen Aug. 29, 2006. Daily 24 hours. Phone (228) 386-7111 or (888) 567-6667. *See color ad p. 436.*
- **Boomtown Casino** is e. of I-110 at 676 Bayview Ave. Daily 24 hours. Phone (228) 435-7000 or (800) 627-0777.
- **Casino Magic** is at 195 Beach Blvd. **CLOSURE INFORMATION:** Damaged during the 2005 hurricane season, there are no plans to reopen. Daily 24 hours. Phone (228) 435-2559 or (800) 562-4425.
- **Grand Casino Biloxi** is at 265 Beach Blvd. **CLOSURE INFORMATION:** Damaged during the 2005 hurricane season, the casino plans to reopen in mid- to late summer 2006. Daily 24 hours. Phone (228) 436-2946 or (800) 946-2946.
- **Imperial Palace** is at 850 Bayview Ave. **Note:** Damage from the 2005 hurricane season has been repaired and a normal schedule resumed. Daily 24 hours. Phone (228) 436-3000 or (800) 436-3000.
- **Isle of Capri Casino** is 1.5 mi. e. of I-110 on US 90 in the Isle of Capri Crown Plaza at 151 Beach Blvd. **Note:** Damage from the 2005 hurricane season has been repaired and a normal schedule resumed. Daily 24 hours. Phone (228) 435-5400 or (800) 843-4753.
- **Palace Casino Resort** is at 158 Howard Ave. **Note:** Damage from the 2005 hurricane season has been repaired and a normal schedule resumed. Daily 24 hours. Phone (228) 432-8888 or (800) 725-2239.
- **President Casino Broadwater Resort** is at 2110 Beach Blvd. **CLOSURE INFORMATION:** The Casino was destroyed in the 2005 hurricane season; there are no plans to rebuild.
- **Treasure Bay Casino** is at 1980 Beach Blvd. **CLOSURE INFORMATION:** Damaged during the 2005 hurricane season, the casino plans to reopen by November of 2006. Daily 24 hours. Phone (228) 385-6000 or (800) 747-2839.

BRICES CROSS ROADS NATIONAL BATTLEFIELD SITE (B-4)

Six miles west of Baldwyn on SR 370, the 1-acre Brices Cross Roads National Battlefield Site is a memorial site to the Civil War battle fought June 10, 1864. Despite superiority in numbers, Union troops under Gen. Samuel D. Sturgis were forced to retreat at the end of the all-day encounter. The Confederate force led by Gen. Nathan B. Forrest captured all Federal supplies, 18 pieces of artillery, arms and ammunition.

Granite markers along SR 370 show the progress of the battle, starting 1.5 miles east of the site, and a 1-mile walking trail with interpretive signs traverses the property. A cemetery next to the site contains the graves of 99 Confederate soldiers, 98 of whom are identified by name and unit.

The nearby by town of Baldwyn operates the Brices Cross Roads Visitor Center at 607 Grisham St., near the junction of SR 370 and US 45. The center offers exhibits, a 22-minute videotape presentation, a battlefield model and a flag memorial. Audiotapes for a driving tour of the site are available.

Site open daily dawn-dusk. Visitor center open Tues.-Sat. 9-5, Sun. 12:30-5. Site admission free. Visitor center admission $3; under 13, $1. Phone (662) 365-3969.

CLARKSDALE (B-3) pop. 20,645, elev. 180′

Clarksdale/Coahoma County Chamber of Commerce: 1540 DeSoto Ave., P.O. Box 160, Clarksdale, MS 38614; phone (662) 627-7337.

DELTA BLUES MUSEUM is at 1 Blues Alley. One of B.B. King's "Lucille" guitars, harmonicas played by Sonny Boy Williams II and a cabin belonging to Muddy Waters help relate the history and influence of the Delta blues in Mississippi. Self-guiding tours are available. Allow 1 hour minimum. Mon.-Sat. 9-5, Mar.-Oct.; 10-5, rest of year. Admission $7, senior citizens and students with ID $5. MC, VI. Phone (662) 627-6820.

COLUMBUS (B-5) pop. 25,944, elev. 221′

Now an agricultural and trade center, Columbus was spared the Civil War destruction suffered by many other towns. Although it housed a Confederate arsenal and briefly became the state capital in 1863, it was never attacked by Union forces.

Both Confederate and Union soldiers who died in the 1862 Battle of Shiloh are buried in Friendship Cemetery at 14th Avenue and Fourth Street. On April 25, 1866, war widows noticed the forgotten graves of the Union soldiers. The women, joined by their friends and families, decided to decorate the graves of both Confederate and Union soldiers. This impartial gesture of compassion later evolved into the observance of Memorial Day.

In 1911 Thomas Lanier Williams was born in Columbus. Better known as Tennessee Williams, his dramatic characterizations of the South made him one of America's leading playwrights. The gingerbread-adorned house at 300 Main St., where he spent the first four years of his life, is now a Mississippi state visitor information center. Phone (662) 328-0222.

The country's first state-supported college for women, the Mississippi University for Women, was founded in Columbus in 1884. Tours of the campus are available; phone (662) 329-7106. Columbus Air Force Base, north on SR 373, is one of three pilot-training bases in the United States.

Many of the city's antebellum mansions and gardens are open to the public in April during the Columbus Pilgrimage. Costumed interpreters welcome guests and 19th-century history is recounted. Other tours are offered throughout the year; phone (662) 329-3533.

The Tennessee-Tombigbee Waterway flows beneath the town's bluff and has excellent fishing and boating opportunities as well as recreational and camping areas. Nearby Lake Lowndes State Park offers camping, boating, tennis and fishing opportunities. *See Recreation Chart and the AAA Southeastern CampBook.*

Columbus Convention and Visitors Bureau: 321 Seventh St. N., P.O. Box 789, Columbus, MS 39703; phone (662) 329-1191 or (800) 327-2686.

Self-guiding tours: Pamphlets and information, including the African-American Heritage Guide, are available at the Tennessee Williams Home/Welcome Center at 300 Main St.; phone (662) 328-0222.

CORINTH (A-5) pop. 14,054, elev. 436'

During the Civil War Corinth was occupied by both Union and Confederate troops. In October 1862 forces clashed in the Battle of Corinth, one of the war's more intense engagements. Some historians consider it to have been the bloodiest battle in the Western Hemisphere. Battery Robinette is a reconstruction of the part of the Federal inner line of defense that was the most contested position in the battle.

The Corinth National Cemetery, a segment of the Corinth Civil War Battlefield, is the final resting place for more than 5,600 soldiers. Historic buildings dating from before and after the war line city streets.

Corinth Area Visitors Center: 602 E. Waldron St., Corinth, MS 38835; phone (662) 287-8300 or (800) 748-9048.

Self-guiding tours: A pamphlet detailing a tour of historic home sites is available from the Corinth Area Visitor Center.

CORINTH CIVIL WAR INTERPRETIVE CENTER is at 501 Linden St. W. at Battery Robinette. This site, which is a unit of the Shiloh National Military Park in Tennessee, chronicles the Battle of Corinth and its significance in Civil War history. Exhibits and multimedia presentations examine topics such as slavery, the military importance of railroads, battlefield defense fortifications and Reconstruction. An outdoor water sculpture chronicles events in U.S. history 1770-1870.

Daily 8:30-4:30. Hours may vary; phone ahead. Free. Phone (662) 287-9273.

CROSSROADS MUSEUM is at Wick and Fillmore sts. Civil War articles, Chickasaw artifacts and other exhibits tracing Corinth's history are displayed. A research room with genealogical records also is on the premises. Guided tours are available. Allow 30 minutes minimum. Mon.-Sat. 10-5, Sun. 11-5, Mar.-Oct.; Tues.-Sat. 10-4:30, Sun. 11-4:30, rest of year. Closed major holidays. Admission $5, over 65, military and students with ID $3, under 16 free. Phone (662) 287-3120.

DELTA NATIONAL FOREST

Elevations in the forest range from 85 ft. south of Dummyline Road to 100 ft. at the north end of the forest.

In west-central Mississippi, Delta National Forest covers 59,553 acres of hardwood bottomlands. The forest lies within the most productive hardwood region in North America.

For further information contact the District Manager, Delta National Forest, 402 US 61N, Rolling Fork, MS 39159; phone (662) 873-6256. *See Recreation Chart.*

DE SOTO NATIONAL FOREST

Elevations in the forest range from 140 ft. to 370 ft.

In southeastern Mississippi, De Soto National Forest arches across 500,487 acres from Laurel to the Gulf of Mexico near Biloxi. Two wilderness areas, the Black Creek and the Leaf, are within the mostly pinewood forest.

A 32-mile float trip on Black Creek can begin from several landing sites; a 41-mile hiking trail parallels the creek. The creek has been designated a National Wild and Scenic River.

The Ashe Forest Tree Nursery near Brooklyn is one of the larger Forest Service tree nurseries in the nation. The nursery grounds are open daily 9-5.

For further information contact the Forest Supervisor, De Soto National Forest, 418 S. Magnolia,

Laurel, MS 39440; phone (601) 428-0594. *See Recreation Chart.*

FAYETTE (D-2) pop. 2,242

SPRINGFIELD PLANTATION is 8 mi. w. on US 61. The plantation was built 1786-91 by wealthy Virginia planter Thomas Marston Green Jr. Andrew Jackson and Rachel Robards were married at the plantation in 1791. The 1,000-acre grounds still are farmed. Picnicking is permitted. Allow 30 minutes minimum. Thirty-minute guided tours are given daily 9:30-dusk; closed Dec. 25. Admission $10; ages 2-11, $5. Phone (601) 786-3802.

FLORA (D-3) pop. 1,546

A small trading center for surrounding farms, Flora has wide streets and large old houses. One of the town's oldest houses, built in the early 1850s on a county road just east of the railroad depot, was the birthplace of Belle Kearney, a prominent activist in the Prohibition and women's suffrage movements. In 1922 she became the first woman to be elected to the Mississippi State Senate.

SAVE **MISSISSIPPI PETRIFIED FOREST** is 2.5 mi. s.w. of jct. US 49 and SR 22, following signs to 124 Forest Park Rd. A self-guiding nature trail leads past 36-million-year-old petrified logs. An earth science museum displays rocks, minerals, fossils and petrified woods; a visitor center has exhibits and dioramas. Picnicking is permitted. Daily 9-6, Apr. 1-Labor Day; 9-5, rest of year. Closed Dec. 25. Admission $5; over 65 and grades 1-12, $4. AX, DS, MC, VI. Phone (601) 879-8189.

FRENCH CAMP (C-4) pop. 393

One of the oldest settlements in Mississippi, French Camp was inhabited by the Natchez, Choctaw and Chickasaw Indians before Louis LeFleur arrived about 1812. LeFleur built an inn on the Natchez Trace, and because of his nationality, local travelers named the place French Camp. LeFleur married a Choctaw woman; their son, who renamed himself Greenwood Leflore, became a state senator and the chief of the Choctaw tribe.

FRENCH CAMP HISTORICAL AREA is at French Camp Academy, off the Natchez Trace Pkwy. at 1 Fine Pl. The area comprises the 1840 dogtrot-style Huffman Log Cabin, now a crafts gallery and visitor center, and the 1846 Col. James Drane House. The Federal-style Drane House was built by one of the area's earliest settlers. Restored in Civil War period, the house is furnished with antiques.

Food is available. Mon.-Sat. 8:30-5; closed Jan. 1, July 4, Labor Day, Thanksgiving and Dec. 25-Dec. 31. Free. Phone (662) 547-6657.

GREENVILLE (B-2) pop. 41,633, elev. 126′

One of the Mississippi River's largest ports, Greenville was once in constant danger of being washed away. In 1927 the town was under water for 70 days. The problem was solved in 1935 by the construction of levees, which forced the river 6 miles to the west and created Lake Ferguson. The levees are now sites for riverboat gambling casinos.

Greenville has produced a number of noteworthy literary and artistic figures including Muppets creator Jim Henson; poet William Alexander Percy; novelists Ellen Douglas, Shelby Foote and Walker Percy; and Pulitzer Prize winning journalist Hodding Carter.

On the west side of town at US 82 and Reed Road is the Mississippi Welcome Center of Greenville, also known as the River Road Queen. As an exhibit at the 1986 Louisiana World Exposition, the structure was built to look like a 19th-century sternwheeler; phone (662) 332-2378.

Greenville/Washington County Convention and Visitors Bureau: 410 Washington Ave., Greenville, MS 38702; phone (662) 334-2711 or (800) 467-3582.

WINTERVILLE MOUNDS STATE PARK AND MUSEUM is 5 mi. n at 2415 SR 1N. The site is a restoration of the original ceremonial gathering place of the Lower Mississippi Valley Indians. The museum contains artifacts, jewelry, pottery, utensils and art of the Moundbuilders. Several mounds remain intact nearby, remnants of a culture that lived and farmed in the area around the year 1000.

Allow 1 hour minimum. Grounds daily dawn-dusk. Museum Mon.-Sat. 9-5, Sun. 1:30-5; closed Jan. 1, Thanksgiving, day after Thanksgiving and Dec. 25. Free. Phone (662) 334-4684.

CASINOS

- **Bayou Caddy's Jubilee Casino** is at 211 S. Lakefront Rd. Daily 24 hours. Phone (662) 335-1111.

- **Light House Point Casino** is at 199 Lakefront Rd. Daily 24 hours. Phone (662) 334-7711 or (800) 878-1777.

GREENWOOD (B-3) pop. 18,425, elev. 136′

Relying upon such natural resources as the Yazoo River and its delta's fertile soil, Greenwood is one of the largest cotton markets in the United States. The city is at its busiest during the harvest season, August through December.

Greenwood Convention and Visitors Bureau: P.O. Box 739, Greenwood, MS 38935-0739; phone (662) 453-9197 or (800) 748-9064.

SAVE **COTTONLANDIA MUSEUM** is .5 mi. w. of the Yazoo River Bridge at 1608 US 82W bypass. Displays relate to the history of cotton production and the inhabitants of the Mississippi River Delta. Included are pre-Columbian pottery, a mastodon skeleton, a collection of Mississippi artworks and geological and military history exhibits. Local American Indian artifacts include photographs of and relics belonging to the last chief of the Choctaw Nation east of the Mississippi River.

Allow 1 hour minimum. Mon.-Fri. 9-5, Sat.-Sun. 2-5; closed major holidays and holiday weekends. Admission $5; over 64, $3.50; ages 4-18, $2. Phone (662) 453-0925.

GREENWOOD BLUES HERITAGE MUSEUM is at 222 Howard St., at jct. Washington St. The exhibits of photographs and memorabilia chronicle the history of the Delta Blues. Mon.-Sat. 10-5; closed major holidays. Donations. Phone (662) 451-7800.

GRENADA (B-3) pop. 14,879, elev. 193′

Grenada was formed when two rival towns, Pittsburgh and Tullahoma, were united in a symbolic wedding ceremony July 4, 1836. The union of the towns was prompted by the wedding of a Tullahoma bride and a Pittsburgh groom.

Grenada County Chamber of Commerce and Tourism Commission: 95 S.W. Frontage Rd., P.O. Box 1824, Grenada, MS 38902; phone (662) 226-2571 or (800) 373-2571.

Self-guiding tours: Brochures detailing driving and walking tours are available from the chamber of commerce.

GRENADA LAKE VISITOR CENTER is off I-55 exit 206, 4 mi. e. on SR 8 to Scenic Loop 333 at the beginning of the dam. The center provides information about Grenada Lake and the Grenada Lake Dam. An 18-minute, multimedia presentation tells about the building of the dam and the recreational facilities at the lake. Exhibits focus on the Native American, civil war and natural history of the region, and a balcony provides a scenic view of the lake. There are fishing, boating and other water-related recreational opportunities.

Allow 30 minutes minimum for the visitor center. Center open daily 9-noon and 1:30-5:30; closed Jan. 1, Thanksgiving and Dec. 25. Center free. Phone (662) 226-1679. *See Recreation Chart and the AAA Southeastern CampBook.*

GULF ISLANDS NATIONAL SEASHORE (F-5)

Stretching 160 miles from Fort Walton Beach, Fla., to Gulfport, the Gulf Islands National Seashore covers 137,000 acres, more than 80 percent of which are underwater. The Mississippi section comprises four barrier islands—Ship, Horn, Cat and Petit Bois—which extend from Gulfport to Pascagoula *(see place listings p. 181 and p. 192)* as well as the Davis Bayou Area, on the mainland near Ocean Springs.

Note: Damage from the 2004 and 2005 hurricane seasons was severe. Although most areas have reopened to the public, the National Park Service, in an advisory issued May 3, 2006, advises that "Visitors should watch out for hazardous debris when visiting the islands." Most of interior marshes of Petit Bois Island are filled with sand. Davis Bayou Campground is closed.

The long, narrow islands, which lie about 10 miles offshore, are moving westward each year as the forces of wind and waves that created them transfer land from eastern tips to western ends. Dunes dotted with sea oats, salt grass and pennywort line their shores, and there are extensive marsh areas with lagoons. Inland vegetation includes bush goldenrod, live oak, palmetto, prickly pear and slash pine.

Horn Island and Petit Bois Island are wildlife sanctuaries; residents include snakes, alligators, raccoons and rabbits. Migrating terns, herons, egrets and other sea birds nest there in winter. Horn Island is open to wilderness camping and is accessible by private or licensed charter boat.

The Davis Bayou Area is entered off US 90 east of Ocean Springs. The area contains the Mississippi District Seashore headquarters, a temporary visitor center next to the William M. Colmer Visitor Center which was damaged by the 2005 hurricanes, and recreational facilities such as a fishing pier, boat launch, playground, nature trail, boardwalks and a 51-site campground. The Davis Bayou Campground is closed. The temporary visitor center is open daily 8:30-4:30. Phone (228) 875-9057. The Ocean Springs Chamber of Commerce *(see place listing p. 190)* can provide information about guided kayaking tours in the national seashore; phone (228) 875-4424.

For further information contact the Superintendent, Gulf Islands National Seashore, 3500 Park Rd., Ocean Springs, MS 39564; phone (228) 875-9057. *See Recreation Chart and the AAA Southeastern CampBook. For member discount information, see the "National Parks Pass/Golden Passports" page under the Featured Information section in the back of this guide.*

SHIP ISLAND is accessible by a ferry that departs from Gulfport *(see attraction listing p. 182)*. The island was a staging ground for the British during the War of 1812 and for Union troops in 1862 prior to Adm. David Farragut's successful expedition against New Orleans. Fort Massachusetts is on the island and dates from 1859; it is one of many 19th-century coastal defense forts.

Note: On West Ship Island all the buildings except Fort Massachusetts and the ranger tower were destroyed during the 2005 hurricane season. The pier and boardwalk have been rebuilt. The island has no public restrooms or potable water. Allow 5 hours minimum. Transportation and tours of the fort daily early Mar.-Oct. 31. The island closes at sunset. Fort admission free.

GULFPORT (F-4) pop. 71,127, elev. 19′

Gulfport, the state's second most populous city, is an important seaport for shipping of lumber, cotton and seafood; it is reputed to be the largest banana port in North America. Following the devastation wrought by hurricane Katrina in 2005, the city is rebuilding and redefining itself.

Mississippi Gulf Coast Convention and Visitors Center—Gulfport: P.O. Box 6128, Gulfport, MS 39506-6128; phone (228) 896-6699 or (800) 237-9493.

Shopping areas: After repairing the damage sustained during the 2005 hurricane season, Prime Outlets at Gulfport, 10000 Factory Shops Blvd., offers nearly 50 outlet stores open Monday through Saturday 10-9, Sunday 11-6.

CEC/SEABEE MUSEUM is 1 mi. n. of SR 90 on Broad Ave.; ask directions at the Naval Construction Battalion Center main gate. The museum contains photographs and artifacts relating the history of the Seabees (CB's, or Construction Battalions) and the Navy's Civil Engineer Corps. A model U-boat and weapons and uniforms from World War II, the Korean War, Vietnam War and Desert Storm are displayed.

Note: The museum's building was destroyed during the 2005 hurricane season; parts of the museum's collections that survived the storms are temporarily displayed in a smaller facility. Rebuilding is contemplated, with a completion date of 2008 or 2009. **Note:** A photo ID, vehicle registration and proof of auto insurance are required of non-military personnel for admittance to the base. Mon.-Fri. 10-4; closed holidays. Donations. Phone (228) 871-3619.

GEM **LYNN MEADOWS DISCOVERY CENTER** is at 246 Dolan Ave. In this hands-on children's museum "where learning and laughter go hand in hand" visitors can tromp in treehouses, understand a pulley fully, cross a creek, sort seafood, touch a tornado, crank a crane and much more.

Picnic tables and a toddlers' outdoor play area also are available on the oak-canopied, 6-acre grounds of this renovated 1914 school. Tues.-Sat. 10-5, Sun. noon-5; closed Jan. 1, Mardi Gras Day, Easter, Thanksgiving and Dec. 24-25. Admission $7, under age 1 free. MC, VI. Phone (228) 897-6039.

SHIP ISLAND EXCURSIONS depart Gulfport Small Craft Harbor. These boat tours to Ship Island take about 1 hour. **Note:** Tickets for the ferry are sold on a first-come, first-served basis beginning 1 hour before each scheduled departure. Tickets tend to sell out quickly holidays and summer weekends. Allow 3 hours minimum.

Note: The 2006 Ship Island Excursions schedule was a reduced one because of damage to the island's facilities in the 2005 hurricane season; the expanded full schedule may be resumed in 2007. The 2006 schedule is Good Friday-Fri. before Memorial Day and Aug. 7-Aug. 20, departures Wed.-Fri. at 9 (return at 2:30), Sat. at 9 and noon (returns at 2:30 and 5), Sun. at noon (return at 5); Sat. before Memorial Day-Aug. 6, departures daily at 9 and noon (returns at 2:30 and 5); Aug. 21-Oct. 29, departures Wed.-Sat. at 9 (return at 2:30), Sun. at noon (return at 5); Labor Day weekend schedule is Sat.-Sun. at 9 and noon (returns at 2:30 and 5), Mon. at 9 (return at 2:30).

Round-trip fare $20; over 61 and military with ID $18; ages 3-10, $10. A fuel surcharge may be assessed. If a minimum of 25 tickets is not sold, the trip is canceled and the fare is refunded. MC, VI. To verify schedule and fares phone (228) 864-1014 or (866) 466-7386.

SHIP ISLAND—
see Gulf Islands National Seashore p. 181.

CASINOS

- **Copa Casino** was at 777 Copa Blvd., s. of jct. US 90/49 in the port of Gulfport. **CLOSURE INFORMATION:** The casino was destroyed during the 2005 hurricane season; there are no plans to rebuild.

- **Grand Casino Gulfport** is at 3215 W. Beach Blvd. **CLOSURE INFORMATION:** The casino was destroyed during the 2005 hurricane season; there are no plans to rebuild.

HATTIESBURG (E-4) pop. 44,779, elev. 143'

Capt. William H. Hardy, a pioneer lumberman and engineer, founded Hattiesburg in 1882 and named it after his wife. Despite being in the longleaf pine belt, the city's industries were diverse, so it escaped economic disaster when a 1920s lumber boom eventually ended. Hattiesburg is the home of the University of Southern Mississippi and William Carey College.

Houses and public buildings in the Hattiesburg historic districts date 1884-1930. Various architectural styles are displayed in the Hub City, North Main, Oaks and Mobile Street districts.

Hattiesburg Convention and Visitors Center: 6443 US 49, P.O. Box 16122, Hattiesburg, MS 39404-6122; phone (601) 268-3220 or (800) 638-6877. *See color ad.*

Self-guiding tours: To obtain brochures detailing driving and walking tours or information about outdoor activities, contact the convention and visitors bureau.

GEM **ARMED FORCES MUSEUM** is off US 49, 4.2 mi. s. of jct. US 98, then 1.5 mi. e. on South Gate Rd. to Bldg. 850. Exhibits include more than 17,000 pieces of military memorabilia such as weapons, uniforms and incidentals used during the major wars fought by the United States. The museum is at one of the largest National Guard training sites in the country. The Library contains 4,500 works about United States military history as well as documents about World War II German Prisoner of War Camps in Mississippi.

Allow 1 hour minimum. Tues.-Sat. 9-4:30; closed major holidays. Free. Phone (601) 558-2757 or (800) 638-6877.

HATTIESBURG ZOO AT KAMPER PARK is at 107 17th Ave. S. This 12-acre zoo presents a variety of indigenous and exotic animals, including antelopes, hawks, jaguars, monkeys, ostriches, prairie dogs, Siberian tigers and zebras. Walking trails, a playground, a carousel and a miniature-train also are offered. Picnicking is permitted. Food is available. Allow 1 hour minimum.

Daily 10-4; closed Jan. 1, Thanksgiving and Dec. 24-25 and 31. Admission $2; over 61 and ages 4-12, $1. Carousel and train $1.25 per ride. Phone (601) 545-4576.

HOLLY SPRINGS (A-4) pop. 7,957, elev. 601'

Holly Springs was established during the great antebellum cotton boom. Gen. Ulysses S. Grant set up a supply depot here in 1862 before moving his Union forces to Vicksburg. The town was recaptured by Confederate general Earl Van Dorn, who took about 1,500 Union prisoners and destroyed Grant's supplies. By the war's end Holly Springs had experienced 62 raids.

Holly Springs is the birthplace of artist Kate Freeman Clark, who showed enough talent at 16 to be sent to the New York School of Art. Clark signed her works "Freeman Clark" so no one would know they were painted by a woman. She returned to Holly Springs in 1923 after her mother died, leaving more than 1,000 paintings in storage in New York. After Clark's death in 1957, the Kate Freeman Clark Art Gallery was built; it reputedly contains the world's largest collection of works by a given artist.

During the 3-day Holly Springs Pilgrimage beginning the third Thursday in April, the Kate Freeman Clark Art Gallery is open for free tours. Also open during the pilgrimage are such historic 19th-century houses as Cedarhurst, Dunvegan, Greenwood, Grey Gables, Hamilton Place, Magnolias and Walter Place.

Holly Springs Tourism and Recreation Bureau: 104 E. Gholson Ave., Holly Springs, MS 38635; phone (662) 252-2515.

Self-guiding tours: The Holly Springs Square encompasses nearly 100 19th-century buildings, including many historic houses. For tour information contact the tourism bureau, or the chamber of commerce at 148 E. College Ave. Free driving tour maps are available.

SAVE **MARSHALL COUNTY HISTORICAL MUSEUM** is temporarily located at 111 Van Dorn Ave. After Sept. 2006 the location is 220 E. College Ave. The museum houses exhibits about Marshall County history; Civil War items from the 62 Union raids on Holly Springs; a military uniform collection; an old doctor's office; women's clothing from the 1870s; and antique furniture, tools and machinery.

Note: The museum was scheduled to return to its renovated facilities at 220 E. College Ave. at the corner of Randolph St. in October of 2006. Phone ahead to verify location. Allow 1 hour minimum. Mon.-Fri. 10-5; closed major holidays. Admission $2. Phone (662) 252-3669 to verify location and admission.

HOLLY SPRINGS NATIONAL FOREST

Elevations in the forest range from 400 ft. to 600 ft.

In north-central Mississippi almost extending to the Tennessee border, the Holly Springs National Forest covers 154,654 acres. The Puskus Lake Hiking Trail is an environmental learning trail with interpretive signs.

Chewalla Lake Hiking Trail offers nearly 4.5 miles of primitive and fairly difficult hiking. The trail takes a southern route from the recreation area and circles the lake to a point on the northeast side where it terminates at Johnston Mill Pond. Camping, bass fishing (state license required) and picnic areas are available at 260-acre Chewalla Lake. The forest contains more than 40 man-made lakes.

For further information contact the Forest Supervisor, Holly Springs National Forest, P.O. Box 400, Holly Springs, MS 38635; phone (601) 965-4391. *See Recreation Chart and the AAA Southeastern CampBook.*

HOMOCHITTO NATIONAL FOREST

Elevations in the forest range from 175 ft. on the Homochitto River to 460 ft. on the ridges at the northern edge of the forest.

Lying mostly in the Homochitto River watershed in the southwestern corner of the state, the Homochitto National Forest encompasses 188,994 acres. The Pipes Lake Trail, a narrow 2-mile hiking trail, meanders around the lake. Other popular recreational pursuits in the forest are camping, boating, swimming and hunting.

For further information contact the Forest Supervisor, Homochitto National Forest, Route 1 Box 1, Meadville, MS 39653; phone (601) 384-5876. *See Recreation Chart and the AAA Southeastern CampBook.*

JACKSON (D-3) pop. 184,256, elev. 286'

Jackson, the state capital and most populous city, was once a trading post called LeFleur's Bluff. Many Virginians and Carolinians passed through the area as they followed the Old Natchez Trace toward the Southwest. Named for Andrew Jackson, the city earned the rueful nickname Chimneyville when Gen. William Tecumseh Sherman burned it in July 1863. The Confederate trenches can still be seen in Battlefield Park.

Jackson's central location has made it a prime trade and distribution center for Mississippi and the rest of the Deep South. The city also is a leading educational and medical center. On Capitol Street overlooking the business district is the Governor's Mansion. Free guided tours of the 1841 Greek Revival mansion are given Tues.-Fri. at 9:30, 10, 10:30 and 11; the mansion may be closed for state events, so phone (601) 359-6421 to confirm accessibility.

Several esteemed American writers have ties to Jackson. Pulitzer Prize winning novelist Eudora Welty was a lifelong resident. Guided tours of the Eudora Welty House and gardens at 1119 Pinehurst St. are available by reservation Wednesday through Friday at 11, 1 and 3; phone (601) 353-7762. Willie Morris, author of "My Dog Skip," was born here in

1934, and African-American writer Richard Wright attended classes in the mid-1920s at Smith Robertson School, now a city museum and cultural center *(see attraction listing)*.

Northeast of Jackson off I-55 is the Natchez Trace Parkway *(see place listing p. 190)*. This scenic highway follows the historic trade route that once ran from Natchez to Nashville.

Metro Jackson Convention and Visitors Bureau: 921 N. President St., P.O. Box 1450, Jackson, MS 39215-1450; phone (601) 960-1891 or (800) 354-7695.

Self-guiding tours: Brochures, available from the convention and visitors bureau, outline tours of Jackson's historic neighborhoods as well as key sites from the 1960s civil rights movement.

Shopping areas: The Metrocenter Mall, 3645 US 80W, has Belk's and Sears as its anchor stores. The Northpark Center Mall, 1200 E. County Line Rd., which contains more than 100 specialty stores, features Belk's, Dillard's, JCPenney and McRae's.

CITY HALL is at 219 S. President St., 4 blks. s. of the Capitol. The building was one of few left standing after Gen. William Tecumseh Sherman's troops set fire to the city in July 1863. Allow 30 minutes minimum. Mon.-Fri. 8-5. Free. Phone (601) 960-1084.

JACKSON ZOOLOGICAL PARK is at 2918 W. Capitol St. More than 500 animals from around the world, including elephants, giraffes, monkeys, sea lions and rhinoceroses populate the zoo. Another highlight is a children's petting zoo. Allow 1 hour minimum. Mon.-Thurs. 9-5, Fri.-Sun. 9-6, Memorial Day-Labor Day; daily 9-5, rest of year. Closed Jan. 1, Thanksgiving and Dec. 25. Admission $5.30; over 64, $3.25; ages 2-12, $2.70. Train ride $2. Parking $1, during special events $2. Phone (601) 352-2585.

MANSHIP HOUSE MUSEUM is at 420 E. Fortification St. at Congress St. This Gothic Revival house was built in 1857 by Charles Henry Manship, a merchant and decorative painter, and has been restored and furnished to its 1888 appearance. A film describes techniques used to restore the house's original faux woodgraining and marbling. An adjoining visitor center displays family memorabilia and 19th-century decorative arts.

Allow 1 hour minimum. One-hour guided tours are offered Tues.-Fri. 9-4, Sat. 10-4; closed holidays. Donations. Phone (601) 961-4724.

GEM **MISSISSIPPI AGRICULTURE AND FORESTRY/NATIONAL AGRICULTURAL AVIATION MUSEUM** is .2 mi. e. of I-55 exit 98B, following signs, at 1150 Lakeland Dr./SR 15 next to the Smith-Wills Stadium. The four exhibit areas of this 39-acre complex trace technological and economic events that changed American life.

The exhibits span three eras of transportation and tell the story of Mississippi's farmers and lumbermen with such items as presses, experimental cotton

The Meandering Mississippi

Like a daydreaming youngster dawdling on the way home from school, the Mississippi River takes far longer and travels much farther than it really needs to. Before the Army Corps of Engineers began a concerted effort in the 1940s to tame the river's meandering ways, its constantly changing course wreaked havoc upon the bordering land.

A glance at a Louisiana or Mississippi map hints at the scope of the problem. Though the river officially separates the two states, bits of both cling to opposite banks, grafted there as the river shifted in favor of shorter routes. The former river channels often remain as horseshoe-shaped oxbow lakes.

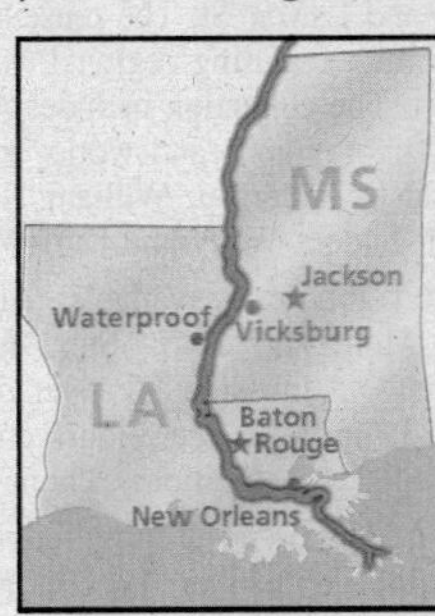

Digital Archives

The river's waters frequently gnawed away plantation land. Sometimes whole towns had to be moved or left to drown. Despite its name, Waterproof, La., was relocated four times. Other towns were left high and dry. When the river wore through the neck of land where Vicksburg, Miss., stood, the flow of the nearby Yazoo River had to be diverted for the city to remain a river port. Work by the Army Corps of Engineers prevented the Atchafalaya River from capturing the course of the lower Mississippi and stranding New Orleans and Baton Rouge.

Concrete mattes, jetties and a series of levees longer than the Great Wall of China now largely control the flow of the river. Although it has been tamed, the mighty Mississippi will likely never be mastered.

pickers, log wagons, steel-wheeled tractors and 19th-century cotton gins. The National Agricultural Aviation Museum and Hall of Fame displays crop-dusting aircraft and equipment.

The main house, smokehouse, chicken house and 11 other buildings of the Fortenberry-Parkman Farm illustrate farm life in the 1920s. A nearby crossroads town also is representative of the 1920s, with a general store, filling station, doctor's office, sawmill, church and school.

Bus tours are available. Allow 2 hours minimum. Mon.-Sat. 9-5; closed Jan. 1, Thanksgiving and Dec. 24-25 and 31. Admission $4; over 59, $3; ages 6-18, $2; ages 3-5, 50c. Bus tour $3. Phone (601) 713-3365.

MISSISSIPPI MUSEUM OF ART is at 201 E. Pascagoula St. until May 2007, when it moves into the Mississippi Arts Pavilion across the parking lot at jct. Pascagoula St. and LaMar St. The museum presents changing exhibits featuring regional, national and international art. The collection includes African American folk art, photographs and works by Mississippi natives Walter Anderson, William Hollingsworth, Marie Hull, Eudora Welty and Karl Wolfe.

Guided tours and food are available. Allow 2 hours minimum. Mon.-Sat. 10-5, Sun. noon-5; closed major holidays. Admission $5; over 59, $4; students with ID $3; under 6 free. Hours and fees may vary during special exhibitions. Phone (601) 960-1515 or (866) 843-9278.

GEM **MISSISSIPPI MUSEUM OF NATURAL SCIENCE** is at 2148 Riverside Dr. The museum contains ecological exhibits, mounted wildlife specimens and a technical library. Graphic and interactive displays offer detailed views of the environment. Exhibits focus on plants, animals, fossils, insects, natural habitats and extinct and endangered species native to Mississippi. A 100,000-gallon, 20-aquarium system contains 200 species of native fish, reptiles and amphibians. Alligators and turtles live in "The Swamp," a greenhouse with a garden and aquarium.

Audiovisual programs about nature are presented in a large theater; 2.5 miles of interpretive trails are on the 300-acre grounds. Hands-on educational programs are offered. Allow 1 hour minimum. Mon.-Fri. 8-5, Sat. 9-5, Sun. 1-5; closed major holidays. Admission $5; over 60, $4; ages 3-18, $2. Phone (601) 354-7303.

GEM **MISSISSIPPI SPORTS HALL OF FAME AND MUSEUM** is at 1152 Lakeland Dr., .3 mi. e. of I-55 exit 98B, next to the Smith-Wills Stadium. The museum, the columns of which are shaped like squared-off bowling pins topped by huge sports balls, presents interactive displays, films and artifacts honoring prominent Mississippi sports personalities.

Guided tours are available. Allow 1 hour minimum. Mon.-Sat. 10-4; closed Jan. 1, Memorial Day, Labor Day, Thanksgiving and Dec. 24-25 and 31. Admission $5; over 59 and ages 6-17, $3.50; under 6 free. MC, VI. Phone (601) 982-8264 or (800) 280-3263.

MUNICIPAL ART GALLERY is at 839 N. State St. This gallery in a restored 1860s house displays a small collection of contemporary paintings and offers monthly changing exhibits. Allow 30 minutes minimum. Tues.-Sat. 9-5, Sun. 2-5; closed holidays. Free. Phone (601) 960-1582.

THE OAKS HOUSE MUSEUM is at 823 N. Jefferson St. Built in 1846, the Greek Revival cottage was occupied by Gen. William Tecumseh Sherman during the siege of Jackson in June 1863; it was one of only 11 structures left standing after he burned the city. The house is furnished with period antiques, including an original rocker and a horsehide couch from Abraham Lincoln's law office.

Allow 30 minutes minimum. Tues.-Sat. 10-3; closed Jan. 1, Thanksgiving and Dec. 25. Admission $4.50; over 64, $4; students with ID $3.50; under 10 free. Phone (601) 353-9339.

OLD CAPITOL MUSEUM is at N. State and Capitol sts. Completed in 1839, it served as the seat of Mississippi government until 1903. Inside this restored Greek Revival structure with interesting design elements are exhibits about Mississippi from prehistory through the Civil War, Reconstruction, the cotton culture and the civil rights movement. **CLOSURE INFORMATION:** The museum was damaged in the 2005 hurricane season and is closed until 2008. Phone (601) 576-6920.

RUSSELL C. DAVIS PLANETARIUM/RONALD McNAIR SPACE THEATER is at 201 E. Pascagoula St., next to the Mississippi Museum of Art. The complex offers programs that examine aspects of astronomy, science, travel and the arts. Sky shows, laser-light shows and films are shown on a 60-foot-wide dome screen in the McNair Space Theater.

Allow 1 hour minimum. Sky shows are offered Fri. at 8:30, Sat. at 3 and 8:30, Sun. at 3. Laser-light show schedule varies; phone ahead. Films are shown Tues.-Thurs. at 10 and noon, Fri. at 10, noon and 7:30, Sat. at noon, 2 and 7:30, Sun. at 2 and 4, Sept.-May; Mon.-Fri. at noon and 2, Sat. at 2, 4 and 7:30, Sun. at 2 and 4, rest of year. Closed Jan. for annual maintenance, Easter, Memorial Day, July 4, Labor Day, Thanksgiving and Dec. 24-25.

Admission $5.50; over 64, $4.50; ages 4-12, $3. Laser-light show or film $1 extra. Prices may vary, phone ahead. Phone (601) 960-1550.

SMITH ROBERTSON MUSEUM AND CULTURAL CENTER is at 528 Bloom St. Housed in Jackson's first public school building for African-Americans, the museum features exhibits portraying their lives, history and culture. Allow 30 minutes minimum. Mon.-Fri. 9-5, Sat. 10-1, Sun. 2-5; closed major holidays. Admission $4.50; over 62, $3; under 18, $1.50. Phone (601) 960-1457.

STATE CAPITOL is on the grounds bordered by High, Mississippi, President and West sts. This dignified Beaux-arts structure, built 1901-03, houses the executive and legislative branches of state government and the Hall of Governors portraits.

Guided and self-guiding tours are available. Allow 1 hour minimum. Mon.-Fri. 8-5; closed holidays. Guided tours are given Mon.-Fri. on the hour 9-11 and on the half-hour 1:30-3:30. Free. Reservations are required for guided tours. Phone (601) 359-3114.

LAUREL (D-4) pop. 18,393, elev. 243′

Established as a lumber camp on the Southern Railroad, Laurel began to grow in the 1890s with the arrival of lumber companies from Iowa. These companies encouraged employees to build houses and churches and to remain when timber operations ended. Laurel is a major industrial city, home of the Masonite Corp. and an important oil field supply center.

Jones County Chamber of Commerce: P.O. Box 527, Laurel, MS 39441; phone (601) 428-0574.

LAUREN ROGERS MUSEUM OF ART is at 565 Fifth Ave. at Seventh St. Exhibits emphasizing American art from the 19th century to the present include works by Mary Cassatt, Winslow Homer and James McNeill Whistler. The museum also has Georgian silver, baskets from American Indian cultures and 18th- and 19th-century Japanese woodblock prints. Traveling exhibits and a library complement the permanent collections.

Guided tours are available Tues.-Fri. Allow 1 hour minimum. Tues.-Sat. 10-4:45, Sun. 1-4 (library closed Sun.); closed holidays. Donations. Phone (601) 649-6374.

LORMAN (D-2)

About 10 miles northwest on SR 552 are the ruins of Windsor, which was among the houses in the Port Gibson area *(see place listing p. 192)* spared from Gen. Ulysses S. Grant's torch during his march on Vicksburg. Built about 1860 by some 600 slaves at a cost of $175,000, the four-story mansion was used during the war as a Confederate observation tower and a Federal hospital.

Ironically, the house was destroyed by a fire caused by a careless smoker in 1890. All that remains are the 23 columns that once graced one of the most beautiful mansions in the South.

Another historic highlight is the Natchez Trace Parkway *(see place listing p. 190)*, which lies just west of town. This especially scenic highway follows the old Natchez-to-Nashville trade route.

Port Gibson/Claiborne County Chamber of Commerce—Lorman: P.O. Box 491, Port Gibson, MS 39150; phone (601) 437-4351.

LULA (A-3) pop. 370, elev. 180′

CASINOS

- **Isle of Capri Casino and Entertainment Resort** is 8 mi. w. on US 49 from US 61 at the Helena Bridge. Daily 24 hours. Phone (662) 363-2250 or (800) 789-5825.

MERIDIAN (D-5) pop. 39,968, elev. 329′

Meridian was conceived in the early 1830s when a wealthy plantation owner began offering free land to settlers he thought would make good neighbors. Plans were made to have the state's two major railroads intersect on the plantation, which was subsequently sold to two railroad developers. The town was incorporated in 1860 by the developers and named Meridian, which they thought meant "junction."

During the Civil War, Meridian became a division headquarters for the Confederate Army. In 1864 approximately 10,000 Union troops blazed through the town, leveling it. Despite other setbacks such as a yellow fever epidemic in 1878 and a hurricane in 1906, manufacturing, trade, timber and cattle industries were established.

On Sept. 8, 1897, Jimmie Rodgers, The Singing Brakeman, was born in Meridian, where he lived on and off during his childhood; Rodgers is buried in Oak Grove Cemetery. Take exit 154A off I-59/20 going south on SR 19; at the second traffic light go left (east) then take an immediate right (south) onto Azalea Drive. At the fork in the road veer left (east) onto Oak Grove.

Rose Hill Cemetery on 40th Avenue is the burial site of Emil and Kelly Mitchell, early 20th-century King and Queen of the Gypsies in the United States.

Meridian/Lauderdale County Tourism Bureau: 212 Constitution Ave, P.O. Box 5313, Meridian, MS 39302; phone (601) 482-8001 or (888) 868-7720.

Shopping areas: Bonita Lakes Mall is on Bonita Dr. Among the 70 stores, restaurants and cinemas are Dillard's, Goody's, JCPenney, McRae's and Sears.

DENTZEL CAROUSEL is in Highland Park on 41st Ave. between 19th St. and State Blvd. Built in 1896 by German immigrant Gustav Dentzel, this gaily ornate merry-go-round is one of the country's oldest, and is the only two-row, stationary Dentzel menagerie known to exist. The carousel arrived in town in 1909 and was installed in a structure built according to Dentzel blueprints.

Allow 30 minutes minimum. Daily 1-5, day after Memorial Day-early Aug.; Sat.-Sun. 1-5, mid-Aug. through Oct. 31 and early Apr.-Memorial Day; Sat. 1-5, rest of year. Fare 50c. Phone (601) 485-1904.

JIMMIE RODGERS MEMORIAL AND MUSEUM is off I-20 exit 153, then 2 mi. n.w. following signs. The center is devoted to the Father of Country Music. Exhibits include the guitar, personal items, concert clothing, sheet music and correspondence of this hometown legend. Railroad equipment used by Rodgers, who also was known as The Singing Brakeman, is displayed.

Allow 1 hour minimum. Mon.-Sat. 10-4, Sun. 1-5; closed Jan. 1, Thanksgiving and Dec. 25. Admission $5, under 10 free with adult. Phone (601) 485-1808.

MERIDIAN MUSEUM OF ART is at 628 25th Ave. at Seventh St. Four galleries of rotating exhibits and collections include 18th- and 19th-century English portraits, 20th-century and contemporary American photographs, sculptures and decorative artworks. Allow 30 minutes minimum. Tues.-Sun. 1-5; closed major holidays. Free. Phone (601) 693-1501.

MERIDIAN STATE FISH HATCHERY is 1.5 mi. s. of I-20 on US 11. The hatchery has raising ponds containing indigenous fish. Each year the hatchery raises up to 2.5 million warm-water sport fish. Allow 30 minutes minimum. Daily 7-4. Reservations are recommended. Free. Phone (601) 483-7019.

MERREHOPE AND F.W. WILLIAMS HOUSES are at 905 Martin Luther King Jr. Memorial Dr. The original 1858 Merrehope, the back section of the present building, was one of six buildings left standing after Sherman's troops destroyed Meridian in 1864. Expanded in 1868, the present 20-room Victorian mansion features etched ruby glass framing the front door. The Queen Anne-style Williams House features leaded, beveled stained-glass windows and gingerbread trim.

Allow 1 hour, 30 minutes minimum. Guided tours are given Mon.-Sat. 10-4, April 1-day before Thanksgiving; Mon.-Sat. 9-4, Sun. 1-4, day after Thanksgiving-Dec. 30; Tues.-Sat. 10-3, rest of year. Closed Jan. 1, July 4, Labor Day, Thanksgiving and Dec. 24-25. Last tour begins 45 minutes before closing. Admission (includes both houses) $10; over 55, $9; ages 6-12, $5. Phone (601) 483-8439.

NATCHEZ (E-2) pop. 18,464, elev. 202'

French colonizer Jean Baptiste le Moyne, established Fort Rosalie in what is now Natchez (NATCH-ez) in 1716. The town's golden era came in the 19th century, when cotton growing was a leading industry, and Natchez was an important river port. Fortunes were made and vast plantations with magnificent houses reflected the prosperity of the period. Many of these houses are open to the public during the spring and autumn Natchez Pilgrimage *(see attraction listing).*

After the Civil War Natchez entered a stagnant period that lasted until the discovery of oil and the coming of industry. This inactivity might have helped preserve the approximately 500 antebellum houses and other buildings that still grace city streets; most are within an area bounded by Broadway, Washington, Union and High streets.

Other points of interest include the 1822 Greek Revival Trinity Episcopal Church, 305 S. Commerce St., with its two stained-glass windows by Louis Comfort Tiffany. The Federal-style First Presbyterian Church, 117 S. Pearl St., was built 1828-29. The 1841, Gothic Revival St. Mary's Catholic Church, 107 S. Union St., was the first cathedral built in Mississippi. North of the city via US 61 is the Natchez Trace Parkway *(see place listing p. 190).*

The area known as Natchez Under-the-Hill, on Silver Street overlooking the Mississippi River, was once a lair for gamblers, thieves and riverboat roughnecks. The settlement was built on a steep slope and caves were dug into the bluff to hide stolen goods. These hideaways caused landslides in the already erosion-prone area. Although eventually abandoned after a series of natural disasters, some of the original buildings have been restored and contain shops and restaurants.

The Natchez Pilgrimage: Natchez is noted for its yearly pilgrimages. Antebellum houses are open for the Spring Pilgrimage Mar. 10-Apr. 14, 2007. The Fall Pilgrimage will be held Sept. 30-Oct.14, 2006, and Sept. 29-Oct. 13, 2007.

Spring Pilgrimage events include the Confederate Pageant, held Monday, Wednesday, Friday and Saturday evenings, and the humorous "Southern Exposure," a satire of the pilgrimage, on Tuesday, Thursday, Friday, Saturday and Sunday nights. Southern Road to Freedom, a musical history of the African-American experience in Natchez, is presented Tuesday, Thursday and Saturday nights. An American Indian Fair takes place, and carriage rides are available.

The Mississippi Medicine Show and the Voices of Hope Singers are included in the Fall Pilgrimage, a celebration featuring craft fairs and regional food and music. Also in fall is the Great Mississippi River Balloon Race.

An organized program featuring two daily tours is available for the pilgrimages. To tour all the houses, which can be visited only as scheduled, four days are required for the Spring Pilgrimage and three days for the Fall Pilgrimage. Information and tickets can be obtained from Natchez Pilgrimage Tours *(see attraction listing p. 189).* Transportation for the spring and fall tours also is available at an additional cost. For details phone Natchez Pilgrimage Tours at (800) 647-6742.

Natchez Convention and Visitors Bureau: 640 S. Canal St., Box C, Natchez, MS 39120; phone (601) 446-6345 or (800) 647-6724. *See color ad p. 465.*

Self-guiding tours: The Deep South Antique & Wine Trail begins in Natchez and travels 200 miles southeast to Slidell, La. In all, some 100 antiques stores are highlighted, including those on Antique Row at Franklin and Main streets.

AUBURN is in Duncan Park at 400 Duncan Ave. This 1812 Federal- and Georgian-style two-story, redbrick mansion, with white Corinthian columns supporting a portico, was one of the most elaborate houses of its time. A freestanding spiral stairway accentuates the interior, which has undergone careful restoration. The house is furnished with period antiques and reproductions.

Allow 1 hour minimum. Guided tours are given as needed Wed.-Sat. 10-2; closed major holidays. Last tour begins 30 minutes before closing. Fee $8; ages 6-18, $4. Phone (601) 442-5981.

DUNLEITH is at 84 Homochitto St. This 1856 Greek Revival mansion contains furnishings from

1850, French Zuber wallpaper and carpets made by V'soske of Puerto Rico. The 40-acre estate also has a carriage house, dairy barn and poultry house. Allow 30 minutes minimum. Daily 9-4:30; closed Thanksgiving and Dec. 25. Admission $7 ($8 during Natchez Pilgrimages); over 54, $6; ages 6-17, $4. Phone (601) 446-8500 or (800) 433-2445. *See color ad p. 465.*

GRAND VILLAGE OF THE NATCHEZ INDIANS is off US 61S at 400 Jefferson Davis Blvd. From 1682 this 128-acre village was the ceremonial center and chief settlement of the Natchez Indians. After the tribe attacked a French fort in 1729, the French retaliated and destroyed the village. A museum displays excavated artifacts, renovated mounds, a reconstructed hut and other interpretive exhibits that illustrate the daily life of the Natchez Indians. Wooded nature trails traverse the area. Allow 30 minutes minimum. Mon.-Sat. 9-5, Sun. 1:30-5. Donations. Phone (601) 446-6502.

HISTORIC JEFFERSON COLLEGE—
see Washington p. 197.

THE HOUSE ON ELLICOTT'S HILL is at 211 Canal St. at Jefferson St. Built in 1798 on the site where Maj. Andrew Ellicott raised the American flag in defiance of Spain in 1797, the house is furnished in period and includes an attached kitchen. The architectural features of this western frontier house show West Indies influence.

Allow 30 minutes minimum. **Note:** Until completion of restoration in Sept. 2006, the house is open by appointment only. Guided tours are given daily every 30 minutes 9-4 beginning in Oct. 2006; abbreviated schedule during pilgrimages. Last tour begins 30 minutes before closing. Admission $8; ages 6-17, $4. MC, VI. Phone (601) 442-2011 to confirm the house has reopened.

LONGWOOD is at 140 Lower Woodville Rd. Reputedly the largest octagonal house in the country, the brick house—topped with a large onion-shaped dome—was begun in 1858 for Dr. Haller Nutt. Due to a lack of skilled labor, the only interior area that was finished was the basement, where the family lived. The rest of the interior was never finished. The living quarters are furnished with heirlooms.

Guided tours are given daily every 30 minutes 9-4:30; abbreviated schedule during pilgrimages. Closed Thanksgiving and Dec. 25. Admission $8; ages 6-17, $4. Phone (601) 442-5193.

MONMOUTH is at 36 Melrose Ave. at jct. John A. Quitman Pkwy. Gen. John Quitman, a hero of the Mexican War, Mississippi governor and U.S. congressman, bought this mansion in 1826. Built in 1818, the house is furnished with period and original Quitman pieces and is on 26 landscaped acres.

Allow 30 minutes minimum. Guided tours are given daily 9:30-11:45 and 2-4:15, except during pilgrimages; closed Jan. 1, Easter, Thanksgiving and Dec. 25. Fee $8; ages 6-17, $4. AX, DS, MC, VI. Phone (601) 442-5852 or (800) 828-4531.

NATCHEZ CARRIAGE TOURS depart the Canal Street Depot at 201 S. Canal St. Three companies offer narrated horse-drawn carriage tours lasting 30-45 minutes. Tours are available daily on a walk-in basis or by reservation. Fare $10; under 12, $5. Phone (601) 442-4518 for Magnolia Carriage Co. or (601) 442-2151 for Southern Carriage Co.

NATCHEZ NATIONAL HISTORICAL PARK is 1 mi. w. of US 61, at 1 Melrose-Montebello Pkwy. Created in 1988, this park is composed of three properties: the 80-acre Melrose Estate; the William Johnson House, which is open Thurs.-Sun. 9-4:30; and the 18th-century, French-built Fort Rosalie. The fort is not yet open to the public. Visitor center open Mon.-Sat. 8-5, Sun. 9-4; closed Jan. 1, Thanksgiving and Dec. 25. Hours may be extended in the summer. Free. Phone (601) 446-5790.

Melrose Estate is at 1 Melrose-Montebello Pkwy. A blend of Greek Revival and Georgian architecture, the house was completed in 1845 and is surrounded by outbuildings and gardens. The house, accessible only by guided tour, contains hand-carved early Victorian furniture, Italian marble fireplaces and two rare, painted English floorcloths.

Allow 30 minutes minimum. Estate open daily 8:30-5. Guided tours of the mansion are given daily on the hour 9-4; closed Jan. 1, Thanksgiving and Dec. 25. Grounds free. Guided tour $8; over 62 and ages 6-17, $4. Phone (601) 446-5790.

NATCHEZ PILGRIMAGE TOURS depart 640 S. Canal St. Tickets are available for pilgrimage tours and individual or combination tours of seven 19th-century antebellum houses: Auburn, Longwood, Magnolia Hall, Melrose, Monmouth, Rosalie and Stanton Hall. The depot is a year-round tour information and planning center for area attractions.

Spring pilgrimage daily 8-5:30, Mar. 10-Apr. 14, 2006. Fall Pilgrimage daily Sept. 30-Oct.14, 2006, and Sept. 29-Oct. 13, 2007; Mon.-Sat. 9-5, rest of year. Closed Dec. 25. Spring pilgrimage half-day tour $28; ages 6-17, $14. Fall pilgrimage half-day tour $21; ages 6-17, $10. Three-house bus tour ticket with pickup from the Natchez Welcome Center $33; ages 6-17, $25. Self-guiding tour ticket rest of year $8; ages 6-17, $4. AX, MC, VI. Phone (601) 446-6631 or (800) 647-6742.

ROSALIE is at 100 Orleans St. This large brick Federal-style mansion was built around 1820 near the former site of the French Fort Rosalie. The house served as the local headquarters for the Union Army during the Civil War and is furnished with its original 1850s furniture. Surrounding the mansion are the 4-acre, formal Rosalie Historic Gardens, which back up to a 6-acre meadow overlooking the Mississippi River.

Allow 30 minutes minimum. Guided tours are given daily every 30 minutes 9-4; closed Easter, Thanksgiving and Dec. 25. Schedule is abbreviated during pilgrimages. Last tour begins at closing. Admission $8; ages 6-17, $4. Gardens admission $3, under 18 free. Phone (601) 445-4555.

STANTON HALL is at 401 High St. at Pearl St. Built around 1857 on an entire city block, the house is one of America's largest antebellum mansions. Stanton Hall is furnished with Natchez antiques and art objects. Allow 30 minutes minimum. Tours are given daily every half-hour 10-4. Abbreviated schedule during pilgrimages. Last tour begins at closing. Admission $8, students with ID $4. Phone (601) 446-6631 or (800) 647-6742.

CASINOS

- **Isle of Capri Casino** is at 70 Silver St. Daily 24 hours. Phone (601) 445-0605 or (800) 722-5825.

WINERIES

- **Old South Winery** is at 65 S. Concord Ave., 5 blks. off US 61 Bus. Rte. Guided 15-minute tours on demand Mon.-Sat. 10-5, Sun. 1-5; closed Jan. 1, Easter, July 4, Thanksgiving and Dec. 25. Phone (601) 445-9924.

NATCHEZ TRACE PARKWAY (C-4)

The Natchez Trace Parkway angles southwest to northeast for 444 miles across Mississippi, Alabama and Tennessee. The road commemorates the Old Natchez Trace, which began as an American Indian footpath leading between the Chickasaw and Choctaw Nations. Later this path evolved into a post road and pioneer trail. Commonly known as the Old Southwest Road, it was instrumental in linking the lower Mississippi and southern Ohio river valleys.

Wayside exhibits, self-guiding nature trails and interpretive signs highlight locations that illustrate the history of the parkway. Emerald Mound, said to be the second largest ceremonial mound in the country, is 11 miles northeast of Natchez, Miss., on a road about a mile off the parkway at Milepost 10.3. A 12-minute video presentation about the Natchez Trace and displays are offered at the visitor center in Tupelo, Miss., at Milepost 266. It is open daily 8-5; closed Dec. 25.

The parkway extends from Natchez, Miss., to just south of Nashville, with a short detour in Jackson, Miss. Drivers should follow posted detour information. There are picnic areas along the route. Gas is available on the trace at Milepost 193 or in neighboring communities

For further information contact the Supervisor, Natchez Trace Parkway, 2680 Natchez Trace, Tupelo, MS 38801; phone (662) 680-4027 or (800) 305-7417.

Note: The points of interest along the parkway are listed in Milepost order, from south to north. Because often it is difficult to reach the rangers at the individual sites, the best phone numbers by which to reach any of these points of interest are the two listed above.

MOUNT LOCUST is 15 mi. n.e. of Natchez at Milepost 15.5. The inn was built in 1779 and was a popular stop for travelers on the Natchez Trace in the mid-1800s. It now contains historical exhibits. Rangers give informative talks regarding Mount Locust, the Old Trace and its modern counterpart, the Natchez Trace Parkway. Allow 1 hour minimum. Grounds daily 8:30-5. Inn daily 8:30-5, Feb.-Nov. Free. Phone (800) 305-7417.

CHICKASAW VILLAGE SITE is n.w. of Tupelo between US 78 and SR 6 at Milepost 261.8. The area was the location of a fortified Chickasaw Indian village. Foundation markers and interpretive panels explain the site. An exhibit shelter and audio station tell the story of the Chickasaw; a nature trail identifies some of the plants they used for food and medicine. Allow 30 minutes minimum. Daily 24 hours; closed Dec. 25. Free. Phone (662) 680-4027 or (800) 305-7417.

MERIWETHER LEWIS SITE is at Milepost 385.9 at jct. SR 20 and the parkway, 7.5 mi. e. of Hohenwald. The 800-acre site is a tribute to the Western explorer, who, with Capt. William Clark, led the first expedition through the Rocky Mountains to the Pacific Ocean. He also served as governor of the Louisiana Territory. An exhibit area has information about his life, the Natchez Trace and the Louisiana Purchase.

The park contains 7 miles of hiking trails, picnic areas, streams and primitive campsites amid rolling hills. Allow 30 minutes minimum. Museum daily 8-5; closed Dec. 25. Free. Phone (931) 796-2675 or (800) 305-7417.

NEW ALBANY (A-5) pop. 7,607, elev. 364′

On Sept. 25, 1897, William Cuthbert Faulkner was born in New Albany, where he lived until his family moved to Oxford shortly before his fifth birthday. The original spelling of the family name was without the "u", which crept into spelling in 1918 when he briefly worked at the Winchester Repeating Arms Company in New Haven, Conn.

Union County Development Association: P.O. Box 125, New Albany, MS 38652; phone (662) 534-4354 or (888) 534-8232.

UNION COUNTY HERITAGE MUSEUM is at 114 Cleveland St. Exhibits spotlight notable events in Union County from the Cretaceous period to the present. A William Faulkner display retraces the Mississippi native's life. Guided and self-guiding tours are available. Allow 30 minutes minimum. Mon.-Fri. 10-5, Sat. by appointment; closed federal holidays. Donations. Phone (662) 538-0014 or (888) 534-8232.

OCEAN SPRINGS (F-5)

pop. 17,225, elev. 22′

The first permanent European settlement in the Mississippi Valley was established in the Ocean Springs area in 1699. The community was christened Ocean Springs in 1854 by a physician who established a sanatorium in town; he took advantage of the same purported health-giving spring waters that local American Indians used for medicinal purposes.

On Aug. 29, 2005, hurricane Katrina and its storm surge roared ashore destroying almost every building along the waterfront, and many inland structures. While many inland commercial areas were spared destruction and resumed normal operations by the summer of 2006, many homes and public areas remained to be rebuilt or repaired.

In the last half of the 20th century this Gulf Coast resort became something of an artists' colony where visitors could observe people at work in their shops. Shearwater Pottery was established here in 1928 by Peter Anderson and continues as a family enterprise. Of the pottery's 15 building, 11 were completely destroyed or rendered irreparable by Katrina. The pottery plans to open a temporary small-scale production facility at the Mary C. O'Keefe Cultural Center, and modest retail facility somewhere in Ocean Springs. More detailed information was not available in June 2006.

The town's historic churches are worth more than a quick once-over. The wood-shingled St. John's Episcopal Church at Porter and Rayburn avenues was designed in 1892 by Louis Sullivan, the Father of American Architecture. The church sustained relatively minor damage during Katrina.

Outdoor recreation can be found just east of town in the Davis Bayou Area of Gulf Islands National Seashore *(see place listing p. 181)*. The area is entered off US 90 east of town. The area contains the Mississippi District Seashore headquarters, a temporary visitor center next to the William M. Colmer Visitor Center which was damaged by the 2005 hurricanes, and recreational facilities such as a fishing pier, boat launch, playground, nature trail, boardwalks and a 51-site campground. As of June 2006, the Davis Bayou Campground was still closed because of hurricane Katrina. The temporary visitor center is open daily 8:30-4:30. Phone (228) 875-9057. The Ocean Springs Chamber of Commerce can provide information about guided fresh- and saltwater kayaking tours in the national seashore.

Ocean Springs Chamber of Commerce Main Street Visitors Center: 1000 Washington Ave., Ocean Springs, MS 39564; phone (228) 875-4424.

Self-guiding tours: Brochures available at the chamber of commerce include the Walking and Driving Tour, the Shopping and Dining Guide, and the Live Oaks Bicycle Route.

Shopping areas: Many of the 50-plus shops and galleries downtown offer the works of the growing number of craftspersons, artisans and artists in the area.

WALTER ANDERSON MUSEUM OF ART is at 510 Washington Ave. Changing displays include this mid-20th-century artist's watercolors, oils, drawings, sculpture, block prints, pottery and murals. The adjacent Community Center contains Anderson's largest mural. Other works include pieces by his brothers, master potter and founder of Shearwater Pottery Peter Anderson (1901-1984), and James McConnell Anderson (1907-1998), painter and ceramist.

Allow 1 hour, 30 minutes minimum. Tues.-Sat. 9:30-4:30, Sun. 12:30-4:30; closed Jan. 1, Easter, Thanksgiving and Dec. 24-25. Admission $7; over 62, military and students with ID $6; ages 6-15, $5. MC, VI. Phone (228) 872-3164.

OXFORD (A-4) pop. 11,756, elev. 458'

Oxford is built on land bought in 1836 from a Chickasaw woman named Ho-kah. The town's founders chose the name Oxford in hopes of getting the state university established in town. The plan worked: The University of Mississippi, or Ole Miss, opened its doors in 1848. When the Civil War broke out, students fought under the name University Greys.

On the University of Mississippi campus is the Center for the Study of Southern Culture. Housed in the 1848 Barnard Observatory building, the center contains changing exhibits of Southern literature, art and photography. The Ole Miss Blues Archive, a collection of blues music and memorabilia, is next door in Farley Hall.

Antebellum houses grace the town where writer William Cuthbert Faulkner primarily lived and worked from shortly before his fifth birthday in 1902 until his death in 1962. Renamed Jefferson in his fiction, the town provided a backdrop for many of his novels. Best-selling author John Grisham, reared in Southaven, graduated from the Ole Miss law school in 1981.

Oxford Tourism Council: 107 Courthouse Sq., Suite 1, Oxford, MS 38655; phone (662) 234-4680 or (800) 758-9177.

Self-guiding tours: Information about driving and walking tours is available Mon.-Fri. 8-5 at the Tourist Information Center in City Hall on the Square, (662) 232-2477, and Sat. 10-4 and Sun. 1-4 next door in Skipwith Hall, (662) 232-2415.

ROWAN OAK is .5 mi. s. of the town square off Old Taylor Rd. Once the home of William Faulkner, the white clapboard house is where the Nobel Prize-winning author wrote most of his works. Faulkner bought and restored Rowan Oak in 1930.

The two-story house has been preserved to look as it did at the time of Faulkner's death at the age of 64 in 1962. The plot outline of his novel "A Fable" is scribbled on the walls. Allow 1 hour minimum. Tues.-Sat. 10-4, Sun. 1-4. Grounds daily dawn-dusk. Hours may vary; phone ahead. Admission $5; free to all Wed. Phone (662) 234-3284.

UNIVERSITY MUSEUMS are 5 blks. e. of the University of Mississippi campus on University Ave. at Fifth St. The museums house a permanent collection of more than 16,000 objects, including Greek and Roman antiquities; African, Caribbean and Southern American folk art; American paintings; 19th-century physical science instruments; Civil War artifacts;

and collections of dolls, porcelain and silver. Other exhibits are changed periodically.

Guided tours are available. Allow 1 hour, 30 minutes minimum. Tues.-Sat. 9:30-4:30, Sun. 1-4:30; closed major holidays and some university holidays. Free. Reservations are required for guided tours. Phone (662) 915-7073.

PASCAGOULA (F-5) pop. 26,200

Pascagoula is an industrial center and the 1946 birthplace of singer/songwriter Jimmy Buffett. The Pascagoula River is called the Singing River because of its occasional eerie sound, best heard on still evenings in late summer and autumn. It is said to be the death chant of a Pascagoula tribe that committed mass suicide in the river's waters rather than submit to defeat at the hands of the Biloxi Indians.

Pascagoula continues rebuilding following the devastation wreaked upon it in the 2005 hurricane season.

Jackson County Chamber of Commerce: 720 Krebs Ave., P.O. Box 480, Pascagoula, MS 39568-0480; phone (228) 762-3391.

OLD SPANISH FORT MUSEUM is n. off US 90; take Pascagoula St. to Lake Ave., following signs. Although not really a Spanish fort, the 1718 building is believed to be the oldest structure still standing in the Mississippi Valley. An adjacent museum houses 18th-century items, American Indian artifacts and a children's hands-on exhibit. The grounds, a picnic area and a cemetery overlook Krebs Lake.

CLOSURE INFORMATION: The museum was damaged in the 2005 hurricane season and is closed until spring of 2007. Phone for schedule; closed major holidays. Phone for prices. Phone (228) 769-1505.

SCRANTON NATURE CENTER is .5 mi. s. of US 90, following signs. Exhibits include fossils, minerals, plants and wildlife native to the Gulf Coast. **CLOSURE INFORMATION:** The museum was damaged in the 2005 hurricane season and is expected to reopen Aug. 8, 2006. Picnicking is permitted. Guided and self-guiding tours are available. Allow 30 minutes minimum. Tues.-Sat. 10-4, Sun. 1-4; closed holidays. Donations. Phone (228) 938-6612.

PHILADELPHIA (C-4) pop. 7,303, elev. 424′

CASINOS

- **Pearl River Resort and Casino** is at 39350 US 16W in the Silver Star hotel. Daily 24 hours. Phone (601) 650-1234 or (866) 447-3275.

PICAYUNE (F-4) pop. 10,535, elev. 64′

Picayune was named by Eliza Jane Poitevent Nicholson, who owned and edited a New Orleans newspaper that sold for a picayune, a half dime. Portraits and antiques owned by a wealthy local family are displayed in the Margaret Reed Crosby Memorial Library at 900 Goodyear Blvd.; phone (601) 798-5081.

Greater Picayune Chamber of Commerce: 201 US 11N, P.O. Box 448, Picayune, MS 39466; phone (601) 798-3122.

THE CROSBY ARBORETUM is e. on SR 43S, then s. on Ridge Rd., following signs 1.2 mi. to 1986 Ridge Rd. The paths in this 64-acre native plant center, which has more than 300 species, meander through natural areas such as bogs, swamps, hammocks, savannas and woodlands. A 12-minute orientation videotape is offered.

The pavilion was designed by Fay Jones, a student of Frank Lloyd Wright and designer of the award-winning Thorncrown Chapel in Eureka Springs, Ark. Picnicking is permitted. Allow 1 hour minimum. Wed.-Sun. 9-5; closed Thanksgiving and Dec. 24-Jan. 1. Admission $4; under 12, $2. Phone (601) 799-2311.

PORT GIBSON (D-2) pop. 1,840, elev. 116′

Port Gibson was named for its founder, Samuel Gibson, who received a land grant of 820 acres from the Spanish in the mid-1700s. The town was spared destruction on Gen. Ulysses S. Grant's march to Vicksburg in 1863; legend has it that Grant said the town resting in the curve of Bayou Pierre was "too beautiful to burn." One of the nearby houses that escaped the general's torch was Windsor *(see Lorman p. 187)*.

St. Joseph Catholic Church, 909 Church St., was completed in 1851 and is a fine example of the Gothic Revival style. The altarpiece is a copy of Rubens' "The Crucifixion" executed by noted portraitist Thomas Healy. The communion rail and seven walnut panels were carved by 17-year-old Daniel Foley, son of the St. Louis contractor who built the church.

Port Gibson/Claiborne County Chamber of Commerce Tourist Information Center: 1601 Church St., P.O. Box 491, Port Gibson, MS 39150; phone (601) 437-4351.

Self-guiding tours: Three tours have been developed by the Bureau of Recreation and Parks. The tours, which have color-coded interpretive markers at important historical sites, cover Port Gibson, the Windsor ruins, battlefields and the Grand Gulf area. Brochures are available at the tourist information center at 1601 Church St.

FIRST PRESBYTERIAN CHURCH is at 605 Church St. at jct. and Walnut St. The steeple is topped with a gold-leaf hand pointing the way to Heaven—the original was carved by a 17-year-old in 1859. After years of damage by weather and woodpeckers it was replaced with a metal hand that measures 12 feet from the base to the tip of the finger and is 165 feet above the ground. Chandeliers from a steamboat adorn the Romanesque Revival church's interior. Allow 30 minutes minimum. Daily 9-5. Free. Phone (601) 437-4351.

GRAND GULF MILITARY PARK is 7 mi. n.w. across the Bayou Pierre Bridge. The site of the shelling of Confederate forts Cobun and Wade by Union ironclad gunboats, the 400-acre park includes the forts, hiking trails, a cemetery, an observation tower and several restored buildings. A museum in the visitor center contains photographs, scale models and items commemorating local history.

Picnicking is permitted. Allow 30 minutes minimum. Grounds daily dawn-dusk; closed Jan. 1, Thanksgiving and Dec. 25. Museum daily 8-5; closed major holidays. Park and museum admission $3; over 59, $2; grades K-12, $1. Phone (601) 437-5911. *See Recreation Chart.*

OAK SQUARE is at 1207 Church St. The 1850 Greek Revival mansion sits on landscaped grounds and is furnished with antiques. The house has Corinthian columns, elaborate millwork and ceiling medallions. Allow 30 minutes minimum. **Note:** The main house is undergoing restoration and is expected to reopen in late 2006. Guided tours are given Mon.-Sat. 9-5, Sun. 1-5. Last tour begins at closing. Admission $6; under 12, $3. AX, DS, MC, VI. Phone (601) 437-4350 to verify schedule.

STARKVILLE pop. 21,869, elev. 374′

NOXUBEE NATIONAL WILDLIFE REFUGE is 7 mi. s. on SR 25. Primarily a waterfowl refuge, the area has nature trails and picnic grounds. More than 250 bird species have been recorded at the 48,000-acre refuge, which is one of the last strongholds of the endangered red-cockaded woodpecker. Deer, coyotes, raccoons and alligators are among the permanent non-flying residents. Fishing is permitted Mar.-Oct.; hunting is permitted in season.

For further information contact the Refuge Manager, 2970 Bluff Lake Rd., Brooksville, MS 39739. Refuge daily dawn-dusk. Visitor Center Mon.-Fri. 8-4:30, Sat.-Sun. 10-4. Office Mon.-Fri. 8-4:30. Free. Phone (662) 323-5548.

TOMBIGBEE NATIONAL FOREST

Elevations in the forest range from 400 ft. to 700 ft.

In east-central Mississippi, Tombigbee National Forest gets its name (pronounced tom-BECK-bee) from a Choctaw word meaning "coffin makers." The 66,576-acre forest consists mainly of pine and hardwood trees. Several developed sites offer recreational facilities.

For further information contact the Forest Supervisor, Tombigbee National Forest, Route 1 Box 98A, Ackerman, MS 39735; phone (662) 285-3264. *See Recreation Chart and the AAA Southeastern CampBook.*

TUNICA (A-3) pop. 1,132, elev. 190′

The center of the local cotton industry for more than a century, Tunica has recently reinvented itself as a rapidly growing gambling destination. The first casino here opened on the banks of the Mississippi in 1992 and since then the town has become the third largest gaming destination in America. Large casino resorts offer glitzy Las Vegas-style accommodations and big-name entertainment, while museums preserve the area's Southern heritage and blues music history. Outdoor recreational opportunities include golfing, tennis, fishing, hunting and water sports.

Shuttles provide transportation between Tunica's nine casinos and the attractions at Tunica RiverPark *(see attraction listings)*; the service operates Sun.-Thurs. 10 a.m.-11 p.m., Fri.-Sat. 10 a.m.-3 a.m. A fee of $1 is charged. For a schedule and information phone (901) 577-7700.

Tunica Convention & Visitors Bureau: 13625 US 61, P.O. Box 2739, Tunica, MS 38676; phone (662) 363-3800 or (888) 488-6422.

Shopping areas: Casino Factory Shoppes, on US 61 at Grand Casino Parkway S., is an outlet mall featuring 40 stores, including Gap, G.H. Bass, Nautica, OshKosh B'Gosh and Reebok. The shops are open Mon.-Thurs. 10-7, Fri.-Sat. 10-8, Sun. noon-6.

BLUES & LEGENDS HALL OF FAME MUSEUM is in the Horseshoe Casino Hotel complex at 1021 Casino Center Dr. The museum celebrates this American musical form, which had its beginnings in the 19th-century Mississippi Delta cotton fields. Blues history is depicted through memorabilia such as guitars, harmonicas, concert posters and photographs, exhibits about Beale Street and the Chicago and West Coast blues scenes as well as colorful portraits of more than 20 blues legends.

The museum is closed for remodeling and is scheduled to reopen in July 2006. Allow 30 minutes minimum. Daily 9 a.m.-10 p.m. Free. Phone (901) 521-0086.

TUNICA MUSEUM is 2 mi. n. on US 61, across from the Paul Battle Jr. Arena & Exposition Center at One Museum Blvd. Exhibits trace county history from its American Indian habitation, through European exploration, early settlement, plantation life, the Civil War, Reconstruction, sharecropping, the struggles of the Civil Rights era and desegregation, and the arrival of the casinos. Interpretive trails wind through the adjacent 15-acre Walter D. and Dorothy K. Wills Nature Conservancy.

Allow 1 hour minimum. Mon.-Sat. 10-5; closed Jan. 1, July 4, Labor Day, Thanksgiving and Dec. 24-25. Free. Phone (662) 363-6631.

TUNICA RIVERPARK is 10 mi. n. on US 61, 1.8 mi. w. on SR 304 (Casino Strip Resorts Blvd.), n. on Fitzgeralds Blvd. then w. on RiverPark Dr., following signs. This 168-acre complex on the banks of the Mississippi comprises a grouping of river-related activities—nature trails along the riverfront, a river overlook, a paddle-wheel riverboat offering cruises, and a museum and interpretive center dedicated to the river and its history. Daily 24 hours. Free.

***Tunica Queen* Riverboat** departs from Tunica RiverPark Landing, 10 mi. n. on US 61, 1.8 mi. w. on SR 304 (Casino Strip Resorts Blvd.), n. on Fitzgeralds Blvd. then w. on RiverPark Dr., following signs. Scenic cruises are aboard a triple-deck, 300-passenger paddlewheeler and include a 90-minute sightseeing cruise with an optional deli lunch; a 1-hour sightseeing and River Lore cruise; a 2-hour dinner-dance cruise with riverboat-style musical entertainment; and Thanksgiving dinner cruises and a New Year's Eve cruise.

Food is available. Allow 1 hour, 30 minutes minimum. Sightseeing cruise departs Tues.-Sun. at 11, 1 and 3, Apr.-Oct.; Sat. at 1 and 3 in Mar. and Nov. River Lore cruise departs Tues.-Sun. at 3, Apr.-Oct.; Sat. at 3 in Nov. Dinner-dance cruise leaves Tues.-Sat. at 6:30, Apr.-Oct.; Sat. at 6:30 in Nov. Boarding begins 30 minutes before departure.

Fare for either sightseeing cruise $12; over 64, $11; ages 3-11, $7. Dinner cruise $39.50; over 64, $37.50. Reservations are recommended. AX, DS, MC, VI. Phone (662) 363-7622 or (866) 805-3535.

Tunica RiverPark Museum & Interpretive Center is in Tunica RiverPark next to Fitzgeralds Casino. Go 10 mi. n. on US 61, 1.8 mi. w. on SR 304 (Casino Strip Resorts Blvd.), n. on Fitzgeralds Blvd. then w. on RiverPark Dr., following signs. In a strikingly contemporary building on a levee of the Mississippi River, the museum depicts river history and ecology and the economic impact the river has had on the area. Several aquariums feature examples of native river life, and interactive exhibits include an opportunity to pilot a riverboat. An ecology trail, outdoor observation deck and rocking chairs provide relaxing ways to view the river.

Allow 1 hour minimum. Daily 9-5. Last admission 1 hour before closing. Admission $5; over 65 and under 12, $4. AX, DS, MC, VI. Phone (662) 357-0050 or (866) 517-4837.

CASINOS

- **Bally's Casino** is 2.5 mi. w. of jct. US 61 at 1450 Bally Blvd. Daily 24 hours. Phone (662) 357-1500 or (800) 382-2559.
- **Fitzgerald's Casino** is at 711 Lucky Ln. Daily 24 hours. Phone (662) 363-5825 or (800) 766-5825.
- **Gold Strike Casino** is w. of US 61 at 1010 Casino Center Dr. Daily 24 hours. Phone (662) 357-1111.
- **Grand Casino Tunica** is at 13615 Old Hwy. 61N. Daily 24 hours. Phone (662) 363-2788 or (800) 946-4946.
- **Hollywood Casino** is at 1150 Casino Strip Blvd. Daily 24 hours. Phone (662) 357-7700 or (800) 871-0711.
- **Horseshoe Casino** is at 1021 Casino Center Dr. Daily 24 hours. Phone (662) 357-5500 or (800) 303-7463.
- **Resorts Casino** is at 1100 Casino Strip Blvd. Daily 24 hours. Phone (662) 363-7777 or (800) 427-7247.
- **Sam's Town Gambling Hall** is at 1477 Casino Strip Blvd. in the Sam's Town Hotel. Daily 24 hours. Phone (662) 363-0711 or (800) 456-0711.
- **Sheraton Casino** is off US 61 s. at 1107 Casino Center Dr. Daily 24 hours. Phone (662) 363-4900 or (800) 391-3777.

TUPELO (B-5) pop. 34,211, elev. 270'

The Tupelo region was once the homeland of the Chickasaw Indians. Hernando de Soto and company made camp with the tribe in 1540 but were driven out after a few months. During the 1736 Battle of Ackia the French Army tried to rout the Chickasaw but was forced instead to retreat, thus crippling French efforts to dominate the region. The area also was the site of a fierce and strategic Civil War battle.

Originally a railroad town, the city was named for the tupelo gum trees early settlers used to construct their houses. It was in Tupelo that Elvis Presley, the King of Rock 'n' Roll, was born Jan. 8, 1935.

The Natchez Trace Parkway *(see place listing p. 190)* passes through Tupelo following the historic trade route to Nashville.

Tupelo Convention and Visitors Bureau: 399 E. Main St., P.O. Drawer 47, Tupelo, MS 38802; phone (662) 841-6521 or (800) 533-0611.

Self-guiding tours: The Elvis Presley Driving Tour points out local sites that figured prominently in the entertainer's early years. Included is the hardware store where he bought his first guitar and a drive-in restaurant that he frequented with friends. Maps and brochures are available from the visitor bureau.

Shopping areas: Discount outlets for major clothing and housewares retailers are featured at the Factory Stores of America on Eason Boulevard. The Mall at Barnes Crossing, at US 78 and US 45, includes JCPenney, McRae's, Parisian, Sears and some 100 specialty shops.

ELVIS PRESLEY BIRTHPLACE is off US 78 Veteran's Blvd. exit, following signs to 306 Elvis Presley Dr. The site features the two-room, white frame house where Presley was born. A museum contains personal effects and memorabilia. The surrounding 15-acre Elvis Presley Park includes a meditation chapel, landscaped walkways, a memorial fountain and granite markers that denote events from his early years in Tupelo. A life-size bronze statue depicts the entertainer as a hometown boy.

Allow 30 minutes minimum. Mon.-Sat. 9-5:30, Sun. 1-5, May-Sept.; Mon.-Sat. 9-5, Sun. 1-5, rest of year. Closed Thanksgiving and Dec. 25. Museum $6; ages 7-12, $3. House $2.50; ages 6-12, $1.50. Combination ticket $7; ages 7-12, $3.50. Phone (662) 841-1245.

TUPELO NATIONAL BATTLEFIELD is off SR 6, 1.3 mi. w. of jct. US 45. The battlefield was the site of the Battle of Tupelo, the last major Civil War battle fought in Mississippi. On July 14-15, 1864, Confederate troops led by Gen. Nathan Bedford Forrest attacked Gen. Andrew Jackson Smith's Union forces in an attempt to cut the Union supply line. A granite marker commemorates the dead of both armies. Allow 30 minutes minimum. Daily 24 hours. Free.

VICKSBURG (D-2) pop. 26,407, elev. 177'

Although today riverboat casinos dock here, Vicksburg's location on the Mississippi River once was of such strategic importance during the Civil War that the city was called the Gibraltar of the Confederacy. In 1863, after a 47-day siege pitting Gen. Ulysses S. Grant and Adm. David Dixon Porter against the Confederate forces of Gen. John Pemberton, the city was surrendered. Vicksburg National Military Park *(see place listing p. 196)* outlines the positions of both armies.

Still a trade center, Vicksburg offers history, industry, science and the arts. Historical theater is presented by The Dixie Showboat Players, whose melodrama "Gold in the Hills" is performed Friday and Saturday evenings March through early April and in July at the Parkside Playhouse on Frontage Road/Confederate Avenue; phone (601) 636-0471.

Anchuca, a Greek Revival mansion at 1010 First East St., is furnished with 18th- and 19th-century antiques and artifacts. Next to the main house are landscaped gardens, brick courtyards and former slave quarters. Confederate president Jefferson Davis once addressed townspeople from the balcony. Guided tours generally are available daily 9:30-3; phone (601) 661-0111 or (888) 686-0111 to verify that the house is not closed for a private event.

During Vicksburg's pilgrimages many of the city's 19th-century houses and buildings are open to the public for morning, afternoon and candlelight tours. The Spring Pilgrimage usually begins the third Saturday in March and continues through the first full week of April; the event is scheduled Mar. 17-Apr. 7, 2007. The Fall Pilgrimage lasts for 3 weeks usually beginning the first Saturday in October and is scheduled Oct. 7-28, 2006, and Oct. 5-20, 2007. For more pilgrimage information contact the convention and visitors bureau.

Vicksburg Convention and Visitors Bureau: P.O. Box 110, Vicksburg, MS 39180; phone (601) 636-9421, or (800) 221-3536 out of Miss. There are two walk-in visitor centers: downtown at 1221 Washington at the corner of Clay St.; and 3300 Clay St. at Old Hwy. 27, across from Vicksburg National Military Park. *See color ad.*

Self-guiding tours: Most of Vicksburg's antebellum and late 19th-century buildings are downtown; some are open to the public. Maps and brochures detailing tours are available at the convention and visitors bureau. Additional information is available at the state visitor center at I-20 and Washington Street; phone (601) 638-4269.

Shopping areas: Pemberton Square, 3505 Pemberton Blvd., features Belk's, Dillard's and JCPenney. Vicksburg Factory Outlets, 4000 S. Frontage Rd., offers 30 discount retailers. Downtown's historic Washington Street is a great place for antique shopping.

SAVE **BIEDENHARN COCA-COLA MUSEUM** is at 1107 Washington St. The museum is in the restored late 19th-century candy store and soda fountain where Joseph Biedenharn first bottled Coca-Cola in 1894. Coca-Cola memorabilia, a bottle collection and antique bottling equipment are displayed. Food is available. Allow 30 minutes minimum. Mon.-Sat. 9-5, Sun. 1:30-4:30; closed Jan. 1, Easter, Thanksgiving and Dec. 25. Admission $3; ages 6-12, $2. AX, DS, MC, VI. Phone (601) 638-6514.

CEDAR GROVE is at 2200 Oak St. The mansion was built on the banks of the Mississippi River 1840-58 and was damaged by shells from Union gunboats during the siege of Vicksburg: A cannonball remains lodged in a parlor wall. The house has a collection of period antiques and original furnishings, including a hidden safe and a Regina music box. Gazebos, fountains and courtyards are also on the 4 acres of formal grounds.

Allow 30 minutes minimum. Thirty-minute guided tours are given daily at 10. Self-guiding tours daily 1-4. Closed Dec. 25. Guided tour $6; under 12, $3. Self-guiding tour $4; under 12, $2. Phone (601) 636-1000 or (800) 862-1300.

DUFF GREEN MANSION is at 1114 First East St. Built in 1856 by Duff Green, a wealthy merchant, the mansion was used simultaneously as a Confederate and Union hospital during the siege of Vicksburg. During one of five attacks on the house, Mary Green gave birth to a son in a nearby shelter and named him Siege. The restored Palladian mansion, now a bed and breakfast, is furnished with antiques, including a chandelier from 1730.

Allow 30 minutes minimum. Guided tours are given daily noon-5. Last tour begins at closing. Admission $6, students with ID $4, under 6 free. AX, DS, MC, VI. Phone (601) 636-6968 or (800) 992-0037.

SAVE **MARTHA VICK HOUSE** is at 1300 Grove St. This Greek Revival mansion was built in 1830 for the spinster daughter of the city's founder, Newitt Vick. It is furnished with late 18th- and early 19th-century antiques and decorated with a collection of post-Impressionist paintings by Frederick Ragot. Allow 30 minutes minimum. Mon.-Sat. 9-5, Sun. 1-5; closed Jan. 1 and Dec. 25. Admission $5, under 12 free. Phone (601) 638-7036.

McRAVEN is at 1445 Harrison St. Built in three sections, the house includes the original 1797 brick structure, the 1836 American Empire section and the 1849 Greek Revival segment. The furnishings include antique tools, period art, period weaponry and Civil War items. The 3-acre gardens, once a Confederate campsite, now are the site of battle reenactments in May and on the July 4 weekend.

Damaged during the 2005 hurricane season, repairs have been completed but the hours open have been temporarily reduced. Allow 1 hour, 30 minutes minimum. Temporary schedule is daily 10-2, Mar.-Nov. The usual schedule, Mon.-Sat. 9-5, Sun. 10-5, Mar.-Nov., may be resumed in late 2006. Admission $5; over 64, $4.50; ages 12-18, $3; ages 6-11, $2.50. Phone (601) 636-1663 to verify schedule.

OLD COURT HOUSE MUSEUM is at jct. Cherry, Jackson, Monroe and Grove sts. The structure was built 1858-60 by slaves. Thirty-foot columns support porticos on each of the building's four sides. A restored courtroom contains original iron grillwork. Southern antebellum items are displayed. Allow 30 minutes minimum. Mon.-Sat. 8:30-4:30, Sun. 1:30-4:30; closed Jan. 1, Thanksgiving and Dec. 24-25. Admission $5; over 64, $4.50; grades K-12, $3. Phone (601) 636-0741.

SAVE **VICKSBURG BATTLEFIELD MUSEUM** is off I-20 exit 4B, then w. on Clay St. to 4139 I-20 (Frontage Rd.). Through the use of paintings, reference materials, maps, model ships and other artifacts, exhibits at the museum present the land and naval history of the Civil War. A 30-minute slide show presented every 45 minutes relates the hardships of daily life during the 47-day siege.

Allow 30 minutes minimum. Open daily 9-5; closed Jan. 1, Easter, Thanksgiving and Dec. 25. First slide show begins at 9:15. Last admission 1 hour before closing. Admission $5.50; grades 1-12, $3.25; ages 3-5, $1.10; family rate $20. AX, DS, MC, VI. Phone (601) 638-6500.

CASINOS

- **Harrah's Casino** is in the Harrah's Casino Hotel at 1310 Mulberry St. Daily 24 hours. Phone (601) 636-3423 or (800) 427-7247.
- **Isle of Capri Casino** is off I-20 exit 1A to 3990 Washington St. Daily 24 hours. Phone (601) 636-5700 or (800) 946-4753.
- **Rainbow Hotel Casino** is at 1380 Warrenton Rd. Daily 24 hours. Phone (601) 636-7575 or (800) 503-3777.

GEM VICKSBURG NATIONAL MILITARY PARK (C-3)

Entered via I-20 exit 4B, then .2 mi. w. on Clay St./US 80, Vicksburg National Military Park adjoins Vicksburg on two sides and covers more than 1,700 acres. The military operations of the Vicksburg siege in 1863 can be visualized and understood by following a 16-mile driving tour marked by signs. Union and Confederate avenues parallel actual battle lines.

Forts, trenches and artillery positions, visible both within and outside the park boundaries, have been re-created on actual sites. The original Federal siege line and the Confederate defense perimeter were destroyed shortly after the capture of Vicksburg.

More than 1,260 memorials, monuments, statues, tablets, bronze portraits and markers honor the officers and enlisted men who participated in the Vicksburg campaign.

The park drive-through gates open daily at 8 and close at 5 during Standard Time, at 6 during most of Daylight Saving Time, and at 7 during the summer. The park is closed Dec. 25.

PARK TOURS are available through licensed guides who ride along in guests' private vehicles. Reservations are recommended for the 2-hour tours. For self-guiding tours, various audiotapes, including the TravelBrains Vicksburg Field Guide, are available for purchase at the national park visitor center. For information, phone (601) 636-0583.

ADMISSION to Vicksburg National Military Park is $8 per private vehicle for a pass good for 7 days. Licensed guide service $35 per private vehicle. Audiotape tours $6.50-$29.95. *For member discount information, see the "National Parks Pass/Golden Passports" page under the Featured Information section in the back of this guide.*

USS *CAIRO* MUSEUM is opposite the national cemetery entrance at Milepost 7.8 in Vicksburg National Military Park. Displays include items recovered from the Union ironclad USS *Cairo*, which was sunk in the Yazoo River north of Vicksburg in 1862. The vessel is believed to have been the first sunk by an electrically detonated mine. A 6-minute audiovisual program explains the salvage of the gunboat, which has been restored and is next to the museum.

Picnic facilities are available. Allow 30 minutes minimum. Daily 9:30-6, Apr.-Oct.; 8:30-5, rest of year. Closed Dec. 25. Free. Phone (601) 636-2199.

VICKSBURG NATIONAL CEMETERY is at the northern end of Vicksburg National Military Park at Tour Stop 8 and can be entered via Connecting and Union aves. In its 116 acres are the graves of nearly 17,000 Civil War Union soldiers and more than 1,200 veterans of later wars. The 5,000 Confederate dead were buried in the "Soldier's Rest" plot in the Vicksburg city cemetery, Cedar Hill Cemetery. Allow 30 minutes minimum. Daily 8-5. Free.

VISITOR CENTER is at the entrance to Vicksburg National Military Park at 3201 Clay St. An 18-minute film presents an introduction to the Vicksburg campaign. Exhibits illustrate the effects of the siege upon soldiers and civilians. Allow 30 minutes minimum. Daily 8-5; closed Dec. 25. Phone (601) 636-0583.

WASHINGTON (E-2)

HISTORIC JEFFERSON COLLEGE is off US 61 near US 84E. The college was incorporated in 1802 as the first chartered educational institution in the Mississippi Territory. In 1817 it hosted the first constitutional convention in the state. The school is being restored as a historic landmark and several buildings are open to the public. On weekdays a resident artisan demonstrates the making of cypress shingles and white oak baskets.

Nature trails and picnic facilities are on the grounds. Allow 30 minutes minimum. Grounds daily dawn-dusk. Buildings Mon.-Sat. 9-5, Sun. 1-5. Closed major holidays. Donations. Phone (601) 442-2901.

WEST POINT (B-5) pop. 12,145, elev. 238′

The Granary of Dixie, as the West Point area was later called, was sold to James Robertson in 1844 by two American Indians. The town was a battleground during the Civil War, but some Union officers enjoyed the area so much they settled in West Point after the war.

WAVERLEY is 9 mi. e. on SR 50, then 1 mi. s. The 1852 house has four self-supporting curved stairways that connect cantilevered balconies in an octagonal cupola. Some furnishings have remained since antebellum days. Daily 9-5. Admission $7.50. Phone (662) 494-1399.

WOODVILLE (E-2) pop. 1,192, elev. 382′

Settled in the 18th century, Woodville was incorporated into the Mississippi Territory in 1811. Overlooking the Mississippi River from a high hill 16 miles west is the town of Fort Adams. A fort built there in 1799 was the setting for Edward Everett Hale's 1863 novel "The Man Without a Country."

Self-guiding tours: Many antebellum houses and churches are open to the public. A brochure that outlines a walking tour and lists historic structures is available from the Woodville Civic Club, P.O. Box 1055, Woodville, MS 39669; phone (601) 888-3998.

ROSEMONT PLANTATION is 1 mi. e. of US 61 on SR 24. In 1810 the plantation became the family home of 2-year-old Jefferson Davis, later president of the Confederate States of America. Originally called Poplar Grove, the cottage was renamed for the rose garden planted by Davis' mother. Forty-five-minute guided tours include audiotape narratives about Davis' life and the history of the house, which contains many original furnishings.

Tues.-Sat. 10-4:30 (also Sun. during the Natchez pilgrimages), first week in Mar.-second week in Dec.; otherwise by appointment. Last tour begins at closing. Fee $10, students with ID $5. Phone (601) 888-6809.

Alabama

Shorter Mansion, Eufaula

ABBEVILLE pop. 2,987

WHERE TO STAY

BEST WESTERN-ABBEVILLE INN *Book great rates at AAA.com* **Phone:** (334)585-5060

Motel

All Year 1P: $59-$79 2P: $59-$79 XP: $5 F16

Location: Jct SR 27. 1237 US Hwy 431 36310. Fax: 334/585-5060. **Facility:** 40 one-bedroom standard units, some with whirlpools. 2 stories (no elevator), exterior corridors. **Parking:** on-site. **Terms:** pets ($8 extra charge). **Amenities:** high-speed Internet, irons, hair dryers. **Pool(s):** small outdoor. **Guest Services:** wireless Internet. **Cards:** AX, DC, DS, MC, VI.

SOME UNITS

FEE

ALBERTVILLE pop. 17,247

WHERE TO STAY

JAMESON INN *Book at AAA.com* **Phone:** (256)891-2600

Small-scale Hotel

All Year [ECP] 1P: $54-$120

Location: On US 431, just e of SR 75. 315 Martling Rd 35950. Fax: 256/891-2674. **Facility:** 42 one-bedroom standard units, some with whirlpools. 2 stories (no elevator), exterior corridors. **Parking:** on-site. **Terms:** cancellation fee imposed, small pets only. **Amenities:** high-speed Internet, hair dryers. *Some:* irons. **Pool(s):** small outdoor. **Leisure Activities:** exercise room. **Guest Services:** valet laundry, wireless Internet. **Business Services:** PC. **Cards:** AX, DC, DS, MC, VI.

SOME UNITS

ASK

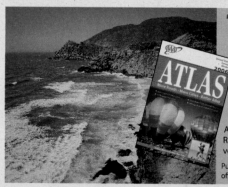

ALEXANDER CITY pop. 15,008

WHERE TO STAY

BEST WESTERN HORSESHOE INN *Book great rates at AAA.com* **Phone:** (256)234-6311

AAA SAVE

Motel

All Year [ECP] 1P: $69-$75 2P: $69-$75 XP: $5 F12

Location: Jct US 280 and SR 22. 3146 US Hwy 280 35010. Fax: 256/234-6314. **Facility:** 64 units. 62 one-bedroom standard units. 2 one-bedroom suites. 1-2 stories (no elevator), exterior corridors. **Parking:** on-site. **Amenities:** voice mail, irons, hair dryers. *Some:* high-speed Internet. **Pool(s):** outdoor. **Guest Services:** wireless Internet. **Business Services:** meeting rooms, fax (fee). **Cards:** AX, CB, DC, DS, MC, VI. **Free Special Amenities: expanded continental breakfast and local telephone calls.**

(See color ad below)

SOME UNITS

HOLIDAY INN EXPRESS *Book at AAA.com* **Phone:** 256/234-5900

Small-scale Hotel

Property failed to provide current rates

Location: US 280, just ne of jct SR 22. 2945 US Hwy 280 35010. Fax: 256/234-5918. **Facility:** 42 one-bedroom standard units, some with whirlpools. 2 stories (no elevator), interior corridors. **Parking:** on-site. **Amenities:** high-speed Internet, irons, hair dryers. **Pool(s):** outdoor. **Guest Services:** valet and coin laundry, wireless Internet. **Business Services:** PC, fax (fee).

SOME UNITS

JAMESON INN *Book at AAA.com* **Phone:** (256)234-7099

Small-scale Hotel

All Year [ECP] 1P: $54-$120

Location: US 280, just s of jct SR 22; just w of jct SR 63. 4335 US Hwy 280 35010. Fax: 256/234-9807. **Facility:** 62 one-bedroom standard units, some with whirlpools. 2 stories (no elevator), exterior corridors. *Bath:* combo or shower only. **Parking:** on-site. **Terms:** cancellation fee imposed, small pets only ($10 extra charge). **Amenities:** hair dryers. **Pool(s):** outdoor. **Leisure Activities:** exercise room. **Guest Services:** wireless Internet. **Business Services:** PC, fax (fee). **Cards:** AX, DC, DS, MC, VI.

SOME UNITS

FEE

WHERE TO DINE

BURKE'S LAKE HILL RESTAURANT **Lunch:** $4-$16 **Dinner:** $6-$16 **Phone:** 256/215-5400

American

Location: US 280 at bridge; s of jct SR 63. 8751 US Hwy 280 35010. **Hours:** 11 am-8 pm, Fri & Sat-9 pm, Sun-3 pm. Closed: Mon. **Features:** The friendly, family-run restaurant is a local favorite, and it's no wonder. Perched atop a bluff overlooking a lake, it offers not only beautiful views and spectacular sunsets but also outstanding seafood. Try the battered, deep-fried seafood platter, the lunch buffet or the Thursday "all-you-can-eat" special: raw oysters on the shell. The meat-and-potatoes crowd isn't forgotten either. The decor is welcoming but modest. Casual dress. **Parking:** on-site. **Cards:** AX, MC, VI.

CECIL'S PUBLIC HOUSE **Lunch:** $7-$18 **Dinner:** $7-$18 **Phone:** 256/329-0732

American

Location: Jct N Central St, just n of downtown. 2432 Green St 35010. **Hours:** 11 am-2 & 5-9 pm, Sat from 5 pm. Closed: 1/1, 11/22, 12/25, 12/26; also Sun. **Reservations:** accepted. **Features:** Downtown in a converted house that was built circa 1900, the restaurant features a decor accented with stained glass windows and an antique plate collection. Steak, seafood, chicken and pasta are served in hearty portions. Casual dress; cocktails. **Parking:** on-site. **Cards:** AX, MC, VI.

ANDALUSIA pop. 8,794

WHERE TO STAY

COMFORT INN *Book great rates at AAA.com* **Phone:** 334/222-8891

Motel

All Year 1P: $65-$70 2P: $65-$70 XP: $10 F18

Location: On US 84 Bypass. 1311 Dr. MLK Jr Expwy 36420. Fax: 334/222-8891. **Facility:** 48 units. 47 one-bedroom standard units, some with whirlpools. 1 one-bedroom suite ($85-$95). 2 stories (no elevator), exterior corridors. **Parking:** on-site. **Terms:** cancellation fee imposed. **Amenities:** high-speed Internet, irons, hair dryers. **Pool(s):** outdoor. **Leisure Activities:** exercise room. **Guest Services:** coin laundry, wireless Internet. **Business Services:** meeting rooms. **Cards:** AX, DC, DS, MC, VI.

SOME UNITS

DAYS INN *Book great rates at AAA.com* **Phone:** 334/427-0050

Motel

Property failed to provide current rates

Location: On US 84 Bypass. 1604 Dr. MLK Jr Expwy 36420. Fax: 334/222-2718. **Facility:** 43 units. 42 one-bedroom standard units, some with whirlpools. 1 one-bedroom suite with kitchen (no utensils). 2 stories (no elevator), exterior corridors. **Parking:** on-site. **Terms:** pets ($10 extra charge). **Amenities:** video library, high-speed Internet, irons, hair dryers. *Some:* DVD players (fee). **Pool(s):** outdoor. **Guest Services:** area transportation, wireless Internet. **Business Services:** meeting rooms.

SOME UNITS

FEE FEE

SCOTTISH INN *Book great rates at AAA.com* **Phone:** (334)222-7511

AAA SAVE

Motel

All Year 1P: $45-$60 2P: $45-$60 XP: $4 F12

Location: On US 84 Bypass. 1421 Dr. MLK Jr Expwy 36420. Fax: 334/222-9705. **Facility:** 57 one-bedroom standard units. 2 stories (no elevator), exterior corridors. **Parking:** on-site. **Terms:** cancellation fee imposed, package plans, pets ($4-$10 extra charge). **Amenities:** hair dryers. *Some:* irons. **Pool(s):** outdoor. **Guest Services:** wireless Internet. **Cards:** AX, DS, MC, VI.

SOME UNITS

FEE

ANNISTON pop. 24,276

WHERE TO STAY

LONG LEAF LODGE AT MCCLELLAN **Phone:** 256/820-9494

Motel

All Year [ECP] 1P: $60-$75 2P: $60-$75 XP: $20 F12

Location: I-20, exit 185, 10 mi n on SR 21, then 1.5 mi e into McClellan-Ballzell Gate. 74 Exchange Ave 36205 (PO Box 5854). Fax: 256/820-8388. **Facility:** 50 one-bedroom standard units with efficiencies. 2 stories (no elevator). **Parking:** on-site. **Terms:** cancellation fee imposed, weekly rates available, pets ($25 fee). **Amenities:** voice mail. *Some:* irons, hair dryers. **Guest Services:** area transportation, wireless Internet. **Business Services:** meeting rooms, fax (fee). **Cards:** DS, MC, VI.

SOME UNITS

ASK FEE

SUPER 8 MOTEL *Book at AAA.com* **Phone:** (256)820-1000

Motel

All Year 1P: $50-$70 2P: $55-$75 XP: $5 F16

Location: I-20, exit 185, 10 mi n on SR 21. 6220 McClellan Blvd 36206. Fax: 256/820-5862. **Facility:** 44 units. 43 one-bedroom standard units. 1 one-bedroom suite with kitchen. 1 story, exterior corridors. **Parking:** on-site. **Terms:** package plans. **Amenities:** high-speed Internet, irons, hair dryers. **Pool(s):** outdoor. **Guest Services:** coin laundry, wireless Internet. **Business Services:** fax (fee). **Cards:** AX, CB, DC, DS, MC, VI.

SOME UNITS

ASK

THE VICTORIA, A COUNTRY INN *Book at AAA.com* **Phone:** 256/236-0503

Historic Country Inn

All Year [BP] 1P: $99 2P: $99 XP: $10 F17

Location: I-20, exit 185, 4 mi n on SR 21/US 431. 1600 Quintard Ave 36202 (PO Box 2213). Fax: 256/236-1138. **Facility:** In a convenient location, the property has individually decorated rooms, a courtyard and an upscale restaurant. 60 units. 56 one-bedroom standard units. 3 one-bedroom suites ($149-$229). 1 cottage. 2-3 stories, interior/exterior corridors. **Parking:** on-site and valet. **Terms:** package plans, small pets only (except in main building). **Amenities:** voice mail, irons, hair dryers. *Some:* DVD players, CD players. **Dining:** The Victoria Restaurant, see separate listing. **Pool(s):** small outdoor. **Leisure Activities:** *Fee:* massage. **Guest Services:** gift shop, valet laundry, wireless Internet. **Business Services:** meeting rooms, business center. **Cards:** AX, DC, DS, MC, VI.

SOME UNITS

ASK VCR

WHERE TO DINE

THE VICTORIA RESTAURANT **Dinner:** $16-$32 **Phone:** 256/236-0503

Continental

Location: I-20, exit 185, 4 mi n on SR 21/US 431; in The Victoria, A Country Inn. 1600 Quintard Ave 36202. **Hours:** 6 am-9 & 6-9 pm, Fri-10 pm, Sat 7 am-11 & 6-10 pm, Sun 7 am-11 & 6-9 pm. Closed major holidays. **Reservations:** suggested. **Features:** Set in a mansion listed on the National Register of Historic Places, The Victoria Restaurant presents excellent dishes served in intimate surroundings brimming with Victorian elegance. They offer a four-course dinner and feature fresh seasonal desserts daily. Dressy casual; cocktails. **Parking:** valet. **Cards:** AX, DC, DS, MC, VI. **Historic**

ARAB pop. 7,174

WHERE TO STAY

JAMESON INN *Book at AAA.com* **Phone:** (256)586-5777

Small-scale Hotel

All Year [ECP] 1P: $54-$120

Location: On US 231, 0.5 mi n of jct SR 69. 706 N Brindlee Mountain Pkwy 35016. Fax: 256/586-1314. **Facility:** 42 one-bedroom standard units, some with whirlpools. 2 stories (no elevator), exterior corridors. *Bath:* combo or shower only. **Parking:** on-site. **Terms:** cancellation fee imposed, small pets only ($10 extra charge). **Amenities:** hair dryers. **Pool(s):** outdoor. **Leisure Activities:** exercise room. **Guest Services:** wireless Internet. **Business Services:** PC, fax (fee). **Cards:** AX, DC, DS, MC, VI.

SOME UNITS

ASK

FEE

WHERE TO DINE

THE ORIGINAL GOLDEN RULE BAR-B-Q AND GRILL **Lunch:** $6-$10 **Dinner:** $6-$12 **Phone:** 256/586-1174

Barbecue

Location: US 69, Brindlee Mountain Pkwy, 3.2 mi n. 2433 N Brindlee Mountain Pkwy 35016. **Hours:** 11 am-8 pm, Sun-7 pm. **Features:** Alabamians long have been adhering to the Golden Rule for succulent real pit barbecue. Now a local chain, this place cooks up a variety of Southern favorites and serves sinful desserts. Casual dress. **Parking:** on-site. **Cards:** MC, VI.

SAN PEDRO MEXICAN GRILL **Lunch:** $5-$9 **Dinner:** $5-$9 **Phone:** 256/931-2488

Mexican

Location: On US 231, 0.5 mi n of jct SR 69; in Town Plaza Shopping Center. 183 N Brindlee Mountain Pkwy 35016. **Hours:** 11 am-9 pm, Fri-10 pm, Sat noon-10 pm. Closed major holidays. **Reservations:** accepted. **Features:** Varied Mexican dishes—including preparations of beef, chicken, seafood and pork—are made in house and served in generous portions. The simple, cozy atmosphere and large, comfortable booths make this a good place for families. Casual dress; cocktails. **Parking:** on-site. **Cards:** MC, VI.

ARDMORE pop. 1,034

WHERE TO STAY

The following lodging was either not evaluated or did not meet AAA rating requirements but is listed for your information only.

BUDGET INN **Phone:** 256/423-6699

fyi

Not evaluated. **Location:** I-65, exit 365, just se. I-65 & Hwy 53 35739 (28555 Boyds Chapel Rd, ELKMONT, 35620). Facilities, services, and decor characterize a mid-range property.

ATHENS pop. 18,967

WHERE TO STAY

BEST WESTERN ATHENS INN *Book great rates at AAA.com* **Phone:** (256)233-4030

AAA SAVE

Small-scale Hotel

All Year [BP] 1P: $69-$109 2P: $69-$109 XP: $5 F16

Location: I-65, exit 351, just w. 1329 Hwy 72 35611 (PO Box 1168, 35612). Fax: 256/233-4554. **Facility:** 85 one-bedroom standard units. 2 stories (no elevator), exterior corridors. **Parking:** on-site. **Terms:** 7 day cancellation notice, small pets only ($10 extra charge). **Amenities:** high-speed Internet, irons, hair dryers. **Pool(s):** outdoor. **Guest Services:** coin laundry, wireless Internet. **Business Services:** PC. **Cards:** AX, CB, DC, DS, JC, MC, VI. **Free Special Amenities: local telephone calls and high-speed Internet.**

SOME UNITS

FEE

COMFORT INN *Book great rates at AAA.com* **Phone:** 256/232-2704

Small-scale Hotel

All Year 1P: $69-$89 2P: $69-$89

Location: I-65, exit 351, just e on US 72, then just s. 1218 Kelli Dr 35613. Fax: 256/230-3783. **Facility:** 63 one-bedroom standard units, some with whirlpools. 2 stories (no elevator), exterior corridors. *Bath:* combo or shower only. **Parking:** on-site. **Terms:** package plans. **Amenities:** voice mail, irons, hair dryers. **Pool(s):** outdoor. **Guest Services:** coin laundry, wireless Internet. **Cards:** AX, CB, DC, DS, JC, MC, VI.

SOME UNITS

ASK

COUNTRY HEARTH INN *Book great rates at AAA.com* **Phone:** (256)232-1520

AAA SAVE

Small-scale Hotel

All Year 1P: $53-$79 2P: $53-$79 XP: $5 F

Location: I-65, exit 351, just e on US 72. 1500 Hwy 72 E 35611. Fax: 256/233-8525. **Facility:** 49 one-bedroom standard units, some with whirlpools. 2 stories (no elevator), exterior corridors. **Parking:** on-site. **Terms:** weekly rates available, small pets only ($5 extra charge). **Amenities:** irons, hair dryers. **Pool(s):** small outdoor. **Guest Services:** coin laundry, wireless Internet. **Business Services:** meeting rooms. **Cards:** AX, DC, DS, MC, VI. **Free Special Amenities: continental breakfast and local telephone calls.**

SOME UNITS

FEE

HAMPTON INN ATHENS *Book great rates at AAA.com* **Phone:** 256/232-0030

Small-scale Hotel

Property failed to provide current rates

Location: I-65, exit 351, just ne. 1488 Thrasher Blvd 35611. Fax: 256/233-7006. **Facility:** 56 one-bedroom standard units, some with whirlpools. 2 stories (no elevator), exterior corridors. **Parking:** on-site. **Terms:** small pets only ($25 fee). **Amenities:** voice mail, irons, hair dryers. **Pool(s):** heated outdoor. **Guest Services:** valet and coin laundry, wireless Internet. **Business Services:** meeting rooms, PC.

SOME UNITS

FEE

VCR

WHERE TO DINE

LAWLERS BARBEQUE **Lunch:** $3-$10 **Dinner:** $3-$10 **Phone:** 256/233-1818

Barbecue

Location: I-65, exit 351, just e on US 72. 1506 Hwy 72 E 35611. **Hours:** 10 am-8:30 pm. Closed major holidays; also Sun. **Features:** Locals know and love the casual eatery for good, old-fashioned pit barbecue. Casual dress. **Parking:** on-site. **Cards:** AX, DS, MC, VI.

ATMORE pop. 7,676

—— WHERE TO STAY ——

BEST WESTERN OF ATMORE Book great rates at AAA.com **Phone:** 251/368-8182

SAVE

Small-scale Hotel

All Year 1P: $55 2P: $61 XP: $6 F12

Location: I-65, exit 57, just e. 6141 Hwy 21 36502. Fax: 251/368-1035. **Facility:** 88 one-bedroom standard units, some with kitchens. 2 stories (no elevator), interior corridors. *Bath:* combo or shower only. **Parking:** on-site. **Terms:** cancellation fee imposed. **Amenities:** irons, hair dryers. *Some:* high-speed Internet. **Dining:** 6 am-9 pm. **Pool(s):** outdoor. **Guest Services:** wireless Internet. **Business Services:** meeting rooms, fax (fee). **Cards:** AX, DC, DS, MC, VI. **Free Special Amenities: local telephone calls and high-speed Internet.**

SOME UNITS

ATTALLA pop. 6,592

—— WHERE TO STAY ——

AMERICAS BEST VALUE INN & SUITES Book at AAA.com **Phone:** (256)570-0117

Small-scale Hotel

4/30-10/8 [CP] 1P: $150 2P: $180 XP: $10 F12

12/1-4/29 & 10/9-11/30 [CP] 1P: $40-$45 2P: $50-$60 XP: $10 F12

Location: I-59, exit 183 southbound, just e; exit northbound, through first set of lights, then just e. 915 E 5th Ave 35954. Fax: 256/570-0751. **Facility:** 45 one-bedroom standard units. 2 stories (no elevator), exterior corridors. **Parking:** on-site. **Terms:** weekly rates available, small pets only ($10 deposit). **Amenities:** voice mail, hair dryers. **Business Services:** fax (fee). **Cards:** AX, CB, DC, DS, JC, MC, VI.

SOME UNITS

FEE

DAYS INN ATTALLA Book great rates at AAA.com **Phone:** (256)538-7861

Small-scale Hotel

All Year [BP] 1P: $54-$60 2P: $60-$65 XP: $6 F12

Location: I-59, exit 183 northbound, just e; exit southbound, through first set of lights, then just e. 801 Cleveland Ave 35954. Fax: 256/538-1010. **Facility:** 141 units. 139 one-bedroom standard units. 2 one-bedroom suites. 2 stories (no elevator), exterior corridors. *Bath:* combo or shower only. **Parking:** on-site. **Terms:** package plans, pets ($10 fee). **Amenities:** voice mail, irons, hair dryers. **Pool(s):** outdoor. **Guest Services:** valet laundry, wireless Internet. **Business Services:** meeting rooms, PC, fax (fee). **Cards:** AX, CB, DC, DS, MC, VI.

SOME UNITS

ASK FEE

ECONO LODGE Book great rates at AAA.com **Phone:** (256)538-9925

Small-scale Hotel

All Year [BP] 1P: $54-$150 2P: $59-$150 XP: $5 F

Location: I-59, exit 183, just w. 507 Cherry St 35954. Fax: 256/538-5000. **Facility:** 108 one-bedroom standard units, some with whirlpools. 2 stories (no elevator), interior corridors. **Parking:** on-site. **Terms:** small pets only ($25 deposit). **Amenities:** voice mail. *Some:* hair dryers. **Pool(s):** outdoor. **Guest Services:** coin laundry, wireless Internet. **Business Services:** meeting rooms, fax (fee). **Cards:** AX, CB, DC, DS, MC, VI.

SOME UNITS

ASK FEE

AUBURN pop. 42,987

—— WHERE TO STAY ——

BEST WESTERN UNIVERSITY CONVENTION CENTER Book great rates at AAA.com **Phone:** (334)821-7001

SAVE

Small-scale Hotel

All Year 1P: $81-$225 2P: $81-$225

Location: I-85, exit 51, 1.4 mi n on US 29/SR 147. 1577 S College St 36830. Fax: 334/821-7008. **Facility:** 118 units. 110 one-bedroom standard units. 8 one-bedroom suites. 2-3 stories (no elevator), exterior corridors. **Parking:** on-site. **Amenities:** voice mail, irons, hair dryers. **Pool(s):** outdoor. **Leisure Activities:** limited exercise equipment. **Guest Services:** wireless Internet. **Business Services:** conference facilities. **Cards:** AX, CB, DC, DS, JC, MC, VI. **Free Special Amenities: expanded continental breakfast and high-speed Internet.**

SOME UNITS

THE CRENSHAW GUEST HOUSE **Phone:** (334)821-1131

SAVE

Historic Bed & Breakfast

All Year [BP] 1P: $65-$100 2P: $85-$150 XP: $10 F12

Location: I-85, exit 51, 4 mi n on US 29/SR 147. Located in the historic district. 371 N College St 36830. Fax: 334/826-8123. **Facility:** This gracious, restored Victorian home is located just northeast of the university. Smoke free premises. 8 units. 7 one-bedroom standard units. 1 one-bedroom suite ($100-$200). 2 stories (no elevator), interior/exterior corridors. **Parking:** on-site. **Terms:** 3 day cancellation notice, weekly rates available. **Amenities:** CD players. **Guest Services:** valet laundry, wireless Internet. **Business Services:** meeting rooms. **Cards:** AX, MC, VI. **Free Special Amenities: full breakfast and high-speed Internet.**

SOME UNITS

VCR

HAMPTON INN Book great rates at AAA.com **Phone:** 334/821-4111

Small-scale Hotel

9/1-11/30 1P: $91-$250 2P: $91-$250

12/1-8/31 1P: $89-$109 2P: $89-$109

Location: I-85, exit 51, just s on US 29. 2430 S College St 36832. Fax: 334/821-2146. **Facility:** 104 one-bedroom standard units. 3 stories, interior corridors. *Bath:* combo or shower only. **Parking:** on-site. **Terms:** cancellation fee imposed. **Amenities:** voice mail, irons, hair dryers. **Pool(s):** outdoor. **Guest Services:** valet and coin laundry, wireless Internet. **Business Services:** meeting rooms. **Cards:** AX, DC, DS, MC, VI.

SOME UNITS

ASK FEE

HOLIDAY INN EXPRESS HOTEL & SUITES AUBURN Book at AAA.com Phone: 334/502-1090

Property failed to provide current rates

Small-scale Hotel

Location: I-85, exit 51, 0.6 mi n on US 29/SR 147. 2013 S College St 36832. Fax: 334/502-7090. **Facility:** 82 units. 80 one-bedroom standard units, some with whirlpools. 2 one-bedroom suites. 3 stories, interior corridors. *Bath:* combo or shower only. **Parking:** on-site. **Amenities:** dual phone lines, voice mail, irons, hair dryers. **Pool(s):** heated outdoor. **Leisure Activities:** whirlpool, exercise room. **Guest Services:** valet and coin laundry, wireless Internet. **Business Services:** meeting rooms, PC.

SOME UNITS

THE HOTEL AT AUBURN UNIVERSITY & DIXON CONFERENCE CENTER Book great rates at AAA.com **Phone:** (334)821-8200

Large-scale Hotel

All Year 1P: $89-$119

Location: I-85, exit 51, 3.5 mi n on US 29/SR 147. Located across from Auburn University. 241 S College St 36830. Fax: 334/826-8755. **Facility:** 248 units. 245 one-bedroom standard units. 3 one-bedroom suites. 6 stories, interior corridors. **Parking:** on-site. **Terms:** cancellation fee imposed. **Amenities:** voice mail, irons, hair dryers. *Some:* DVD players, honor bars. **Dining:** Ariccia Italian Trattoria & Bar, see separate listing. **Pool(s):** outdoor. **Leisure Activities:** jogging, exercise room. **Guest Services:** valet laundry, wireless Internet. **Business Services:** conference facilities, PC (fee). **Cards:** AX, CB, DC, DS, JC, MC, VI. **Free Special Amenities: local telephone calls and newspaper.**

SOME UNITS

JAMESON INN Book at AAA.com **Phone:** (334)502-5020

Motel

All Year [ECP] 1P: $54-$120

Location: I-85, exit 58, 1.5 mi n on US 280 W, then 2.1 mi s on US 29/SR 14. 1212 Mall Pkwy 36831. Fax: 334/502-5021. **Facility:** 42 one-bedroom standard units, some with whirlpools. 2 stories (no elevator), exterior corridors. **Parking:** on-site. **Terms:** cancellation fee imposed, small pets only ($10 extra charge). **Amenities:** hair dryers. *Some:* irons. **Pool(s):** outdoor. **Leisure Activities:** exercise room. **Guest Services:** wireless Internet. **Business Services:** PC. **Cards:** AX, DC, DS, MC, VI.

SOME UNITS

FEE

MICROTEL INN & SUITES Book great rates at AAA.com **Phone:** (334)826-1444

Small-scale Hotel

All Year 1P: $55-$200 2P: $55-$200 XP: $5 F16

Location: I-85, exit 51, just n. 2174 S College St 36832 (1870 Hillton Ct, 36830). Fax: 334/826-5456. **Facility:** 42 one-bedroom standard units, some with whirlpools. 2 stories (no elevator), interior corridors. *Bath:* combo or shower only. **Parking:** on-site. **Terms:** 14 day cancellation notice-fee imposed, [CP] meal plan available, small pets only ($10 fee). **Amenities:** high-speed Internet, voice mail, safes. *Some:* irons, hair dryers. **Guest Services:** wireless Internet. **Cards:** AX, DC, DS, MC, VI. **Free Special Amenities: continental breakfast and local telephone calls.**

SOME UNITS

FEE

WHERE TO DINE

ARICCIA ITALIAN TRATTORIA & BAR **Lunch:** $8-$10 **Dinner:** $8-$24 **Phone:** 334/844-5140

Italian

Location: I-85, exit 51, 3.5 mi n on US 29/SR 147; in The Hotel at Auburn University & Dixon Conference Center. 241 S College St 36830. **Hours:** 6:30 am-10:30 pm, Sun 6:30-10 am, 11-2 & 4:30-10 pm. **Reservations:** suggested. **Features:** For the most part, the Italian fare served here is pretty traditional but there are a few more interesting and creative choices on the menu and there's quite a bit of emphasis put on presentation. The restaurant is attractive with a semi-open kitchen and is very much like a modern trattoria. Casual dress; cocktails. **Parking:** on-site. **Cards:** AX, DC, DS, MC, VI.

AUBURN CITY LIMITS **Lunch:** $6-$8 **Dinner:** $15-$30 **Phone:** 334/821-3330

American

Location: On SR 14; 1 mi w of jct SR 267. 2450 Hwy 14 W 36830. **Hours:** 11 am-2 & 5:30-10 pm. Closed: Sun. **Reservations:** accepted. **Features:** An Asian-infused pork tenderloin entree, a hot daily soup and a luscious dessert are just a sample of the many creative dishes you can enjoy at this casual and upscale eatery. Dressy casual; cocktails. **Parking:** on-site. **Cards:** AX, DS, MC, VI.

GOOD OL' BOYS **Lunch:** $7-$16 **Dinner:** $7-$16 **Phone:** 334/826-3900

American

Location: I-85, exit 51, 2 mi e to Sandhill Rd, then 1.5 mi n. 1843 Sandhill Rd 36830. **Hours:** 5 pm-10 pm, Fri & Sat from 4:30 pm, Sun 11:30 am-9 pm. Closed major holidays; also Mon. **Features:** Fried catfish reigns at the homey restaurant, but other Southern favorites find their way onto the menu. Although this place doesn't offer much to the health-conscious diner, the salad bar could step in to fill that need. Traditional decor has a down-home feel. Casual dress. **Parking:** on-site. **Cards:** AX, DS, MC, VI.

J. WILLIAMS **Lunch:** $6-$13 **Dinner:** $19-$30 **Phone:** 334/501-5656

American

Location: I-85, exit 51, 3.5 mi n on US 29/SR 147, just e on Sanford, then just n. 277 S Gay St 36830. **Hours:** 11 am-2 & 5-9 pm, Fri-10 pm, Sat 5 pm-10 pm, Mon 5 pm-9 pm. Closed major holidays; also Sun. **Reservations:** accepted. **Features:** Decor is on the formal side but the atmosphere manages to remain one of relaxed comfort. Service is very pleasant and the cuisine can be classified as creative American. Their grilled Chilean sea bass was voted one of the top 100 dishes in Alabama by the Alabama Travel Bureau, and there is an extensive wine list. Dressy casual; cocktails. **Parking:** on-site. **Cards:** AX, DS, MC, VI.

OLDE AUBURN ALE HOUSE **Dinner:** $10-$22 **Phone:** 334/821-6773

American

Location: Between S College and Gay sts, in alley near parking deck; downtown. 124 Tichenor Ave 36830. **Hours:** 3:30 pm-10 pm. Closed: 12/25; also Sun. **Reservations:** accepted. **Features:** This eatery serves up sumptuous fare, such as pork tenderloin, and a good selection of beers which are brewed in house. Casual dress; cocktails. **Parking:** on-site. **Cards:** AX, DS, MC, VI.

PROVINO'S ITALIAN RESTAURANT **Dinner:** $9-$19 **Phone:** 334/826-7360

Italian

Location: I-85, exit 57, just w. 2575 Hilton Garden Dr 36831. **Hours:** 4:30 pm-10 pm, Sun 11 am-9 pm. Closed major holidays; also 12/24. **Reservations:** accepted, Sun-Thurs. **Features:** Menu includes traditional Italian favorites served in a "neighborhood diner" atmosphere of red-and-white checkered tablecloths and baskets of fruit. Of special note is the unique house salad and delicious desserts like homemade cheesecake. Casual dress; beer & wine only. **Parking:** on-site. **Cards:** AX, DS, MC, VI.

BAY MINETTE pop. 7,820

WHERE TO STAY

WINDWOOD INN *Book great rates at AAA.com* **Phone:** (251)937-8800

Motel

All Year [CP] 1P: $55-$85 2P: $55-$85 XP: $5 F18

Location: I-65, exit 34, 5.7 mi s on SR 59. 610 McMeans Ave 36507. Fax: 251/937-9414. **Facility:** 48 one-bedroom standard units, some with whirlpools. 2 stories (no elevator), exterior corridors. *Bath:* combo or shower only. **Parking:** on-site. **Pool(s):** outdoor. **Business Services:** fax (fee). **Cards:** AX, DS, MC, VI.

SOME UNITS

BAYOU LA BATRE pop. 2,313

WHERE TO STAY

BAYOU LA BATRE INN & SUITES *Book at AAA.com* **Phone:** (251)824-2020

Motel

All Year 1P: $60-$90 2P: $60-$90

Location: 0.8 mi w on US 188. Located in a rural area. 13155 N Wintzell Ave 36509. Fax: 251/824-1153. **Facility:** 40 one-bedroom standard units, some with kitchens (no utensils) and/or whirlpools. 2 stories (no elevator), exterior corridors. *Bath:* combo or shower only. **Parking:** on-site. **Terms:** cancellation fee imposed, package plans. **Amenities:** *Some:* irons. **Pool(s):** small outdoor. **Business Services:** meeting rooms. **Cards:** AX, CB, DC, DS, JC, MC, VI.

SOME UNITS

BESSEMER

—*See Birmingham p. 229.*

Destination Birmingham

pop. 242,820

Birmingham's a delight for any traveler looking to find that certain "sense of place." It's part big city, part small town, and 100 percent Southern.

Museums showcase flight, art, sports and more. Just blocks from downtown's skyscrapers, pedestrian-friendly Five Points South beckons browsers. And outlying areas offer great spots for canoeing, hiking and scenic drives.

© Gibson Stock Photography

Sloss Furnaces National Historic Landmark, Birmingham. Towering pig-iron furnaces dwarf their surroundings. (See listing page 50)

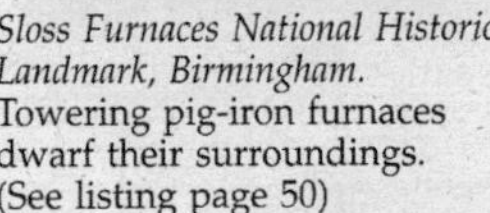

© Gibson Stock Photography

Downtown, Birmingham. Stately churches and contemporary office buildings harmoniously blend in downtown.

© R. Krubner / Robertstock

Birmingham City Hall. The city hall looks out onto peaceful Linn Park.

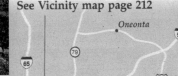

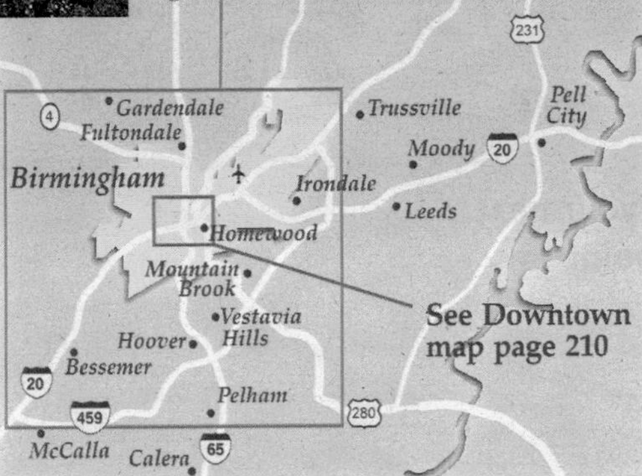

P*laces included in this AAA Destination City:*

Greater Birmingham CVB

The Summit, Birmingham. Shoppers stroll the streets seeking rare finds and big bargains. (See mention page 51)

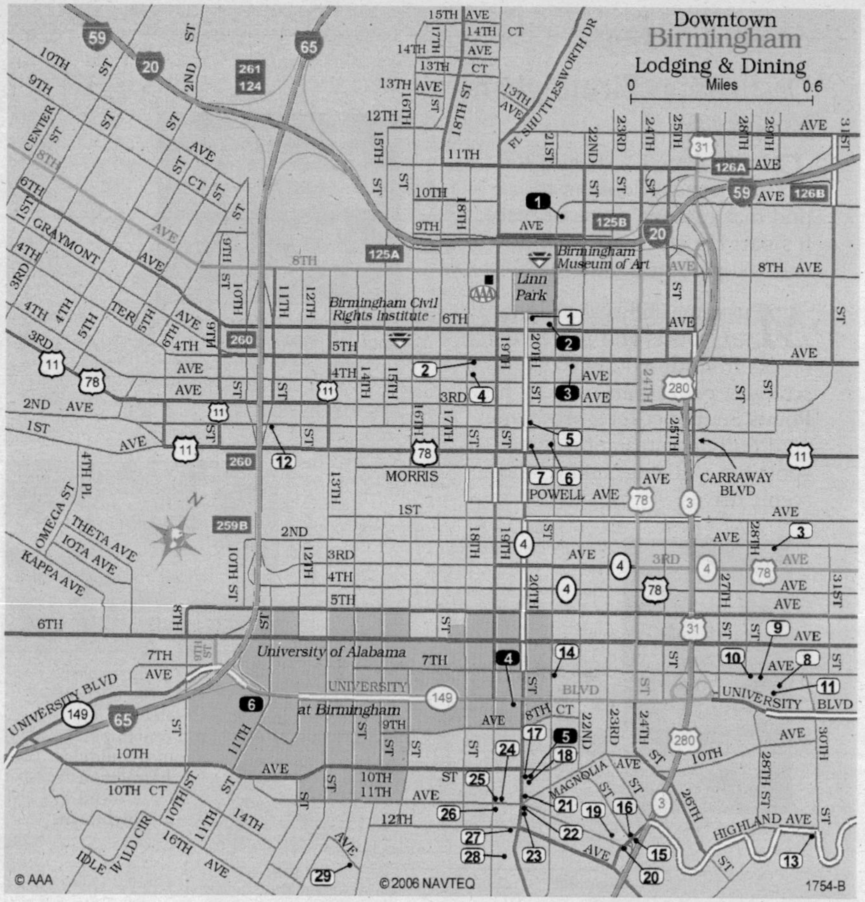

Downtown Birmingham Lodging & Dining

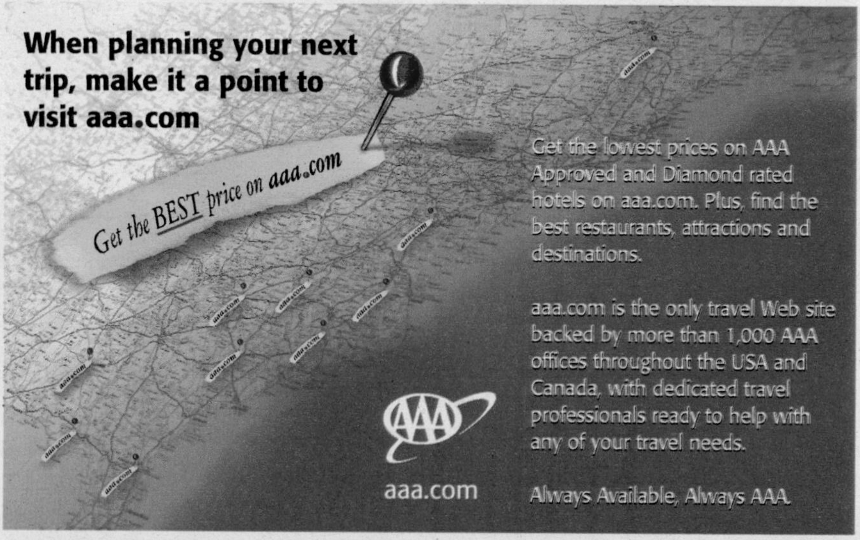

© AAA

© 2006 NAVTEQ

1754-B

Downtown Birmingham

This index helps you "spot" where approved accommodations and restaurants are located on the corresponding detailed maps. Lodging rate ranges are for comparison only and show the property's high season; rates are per night, unless only weekly (W) rates are available. Restaurant rate range is for dinner, unless only lunch (L) is served. Turn to the listing page for more detailed rate information and consult display ads for special promotions.

Spotter/Map Page Number	OA	**DOWNTOWN BIRMINGHAM - Lodgings**	Diamond Rating	Rate Range High Season	Listing Page
1 / p. 210	AAA	**Sheraton Birmingham Hotel** - see color ad p 218	◆◆◆	$109-$249 SAVE	219
2 / p. 210	AAA	**The Tutwiler-A Wyndham Historic Hotel**	◆◆◆	$152 SAVE	219
3 / p. 210		Historic Redmont Hotel	◆◆◆	$89-$115	218
4 / p. 210		DoubleTree Hotel Birmingham	fyi	$169-$209	218
5 / p. 210		Pickwick Hotel & Conference Center	◆◆◆	Failed to provide	218
6 / p. 210		Medical Center Inn	◆◆	$69-$139	218
		DOWNTOWN BIRMINGHAM - Restaurants			
1 / p. 210		The Grille At The Tutwiler	◆◆	$15-$30	220
2 / p. 210		Zoes Kitchen	◆	$7-$10(L)	222
3 / p. 210		Cantina	◆	$5-$8	219
4 / p. 210	AAA	**Restaurant G**	◆◆◆	$23-$28	221
5 / p. 210		Pita Loco	◆	$3-$14	221
6 / p. 210		John's City Diner	◆◆	$10-$25	220
7 / p. 210		Cafe Dupont	◆◆◆◆	$25-$34	219
8 / p. 210		Lakeview Oyster House	◆◆	$9-$25	221
9 / p. 210		Bombay Cafe	◆◆	$8-$27	219
10 / p. 210		Sol y Luna	◆◆	$8-$16	221
11 / p. 210		Sneaky Pete's Cafe	◆◆	$5-$10	221
12 / p. 210		Niki's Downtown	◆	$6-$10	221
13 / p. 210		Rojo	◆	$6-$15	221
14 / p. 210		La Cocina	◆◆	$5-$20	220
15 / p. 210		Highland Coffee Company	◆	$3-$7	220
16 / p. 210		Bottega Cafe	◆◆◆	$9-$22	219
17 / p. 210		Sakura Japanese Restaurant	◆◆	$9-$16	221
18 / p. 210		Five Points Grill	◆◆	$12-$20	220
19 / p. 210		Hot and Hot Fish Club	◆◆◆	$20-$50	220
20 / p. 210		Bottega Restaurant	◆◆◆◆	$16-$30	219
21 / p. 210		Cosmo's Pizza	◆	$11-$20	220
22 / p. 210		Chez Fon Fon	◆◆◆	$18-$30	219
23 / p. 210		Highlands Bar & Grill	◆◆◆◆	$19-$30	220
24 / p. 210		Surin West	◆◆	$9-$18	221
25 / p. 210		Jim N' Nick's Bar-B-Q	◆◆	$7-$17	220
26 / p. 210		Golden Temple Vegetarian Cafe	◆◆	$4-$8(L)	220
27 / p. 210	AAA	**Ocean**	◆◆◆◆	$15-$38	221
28 / p. 210		Cobb Lane Restaurant	◆◆◆	$12-$31	219
29 / p. 210		Dreamland Bar-B-Que Ribs	◆	$6-$18	220

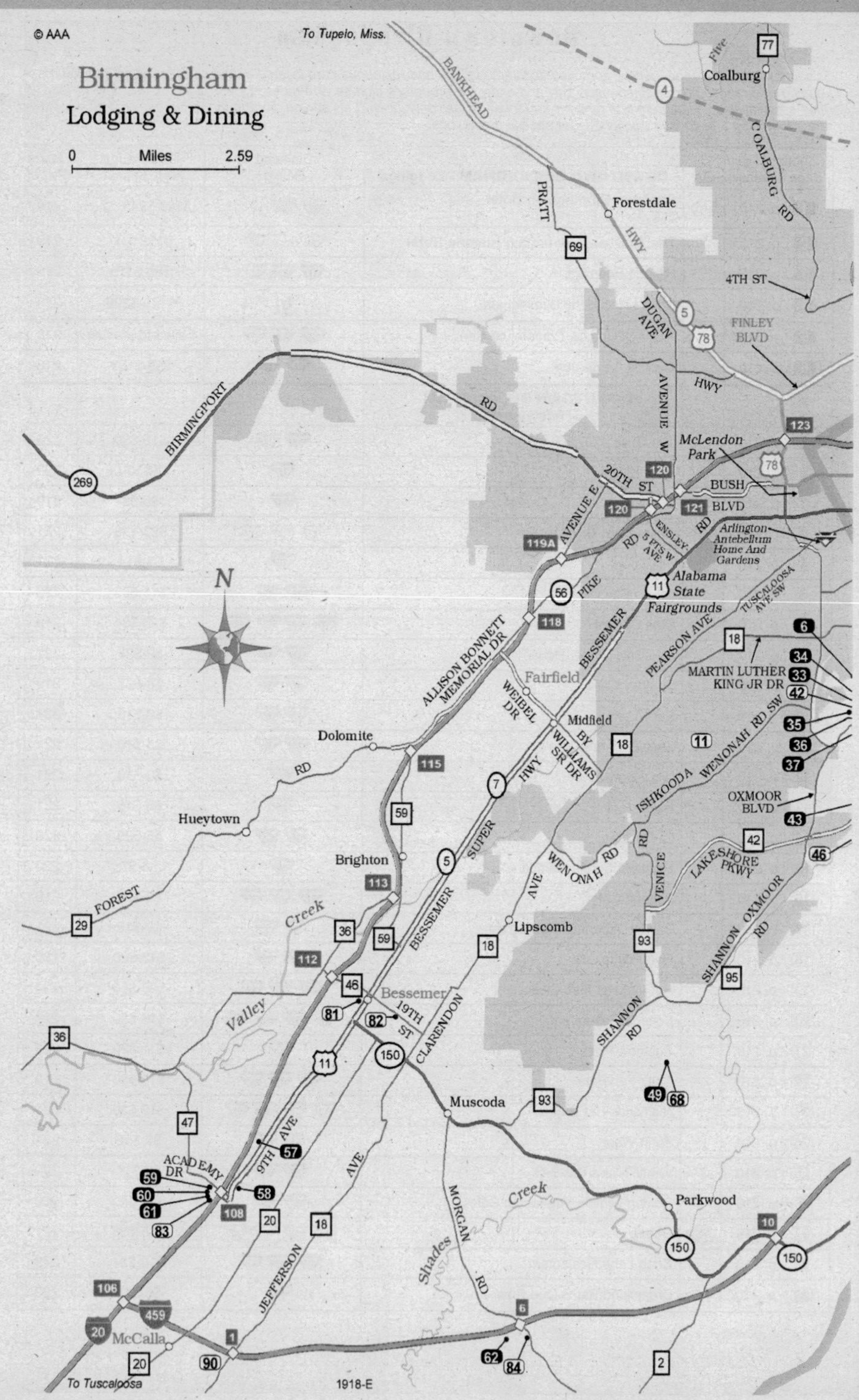
© AAA
To Tupelo, Miss.
Birmingham
Lodging & Dining
0 Miles 2.59
N
Coalburg
Forestdale
Dolomite
Hueytown
Brighton
Fairfield
Midfield
Bessemer
Lipscomb
Muscoda
Parkwood
McCalla
McLendon Park
Arlington Antebellum Home And Gardens
Alabama State Fairgrounds
To Tuscaloosa
1918-E

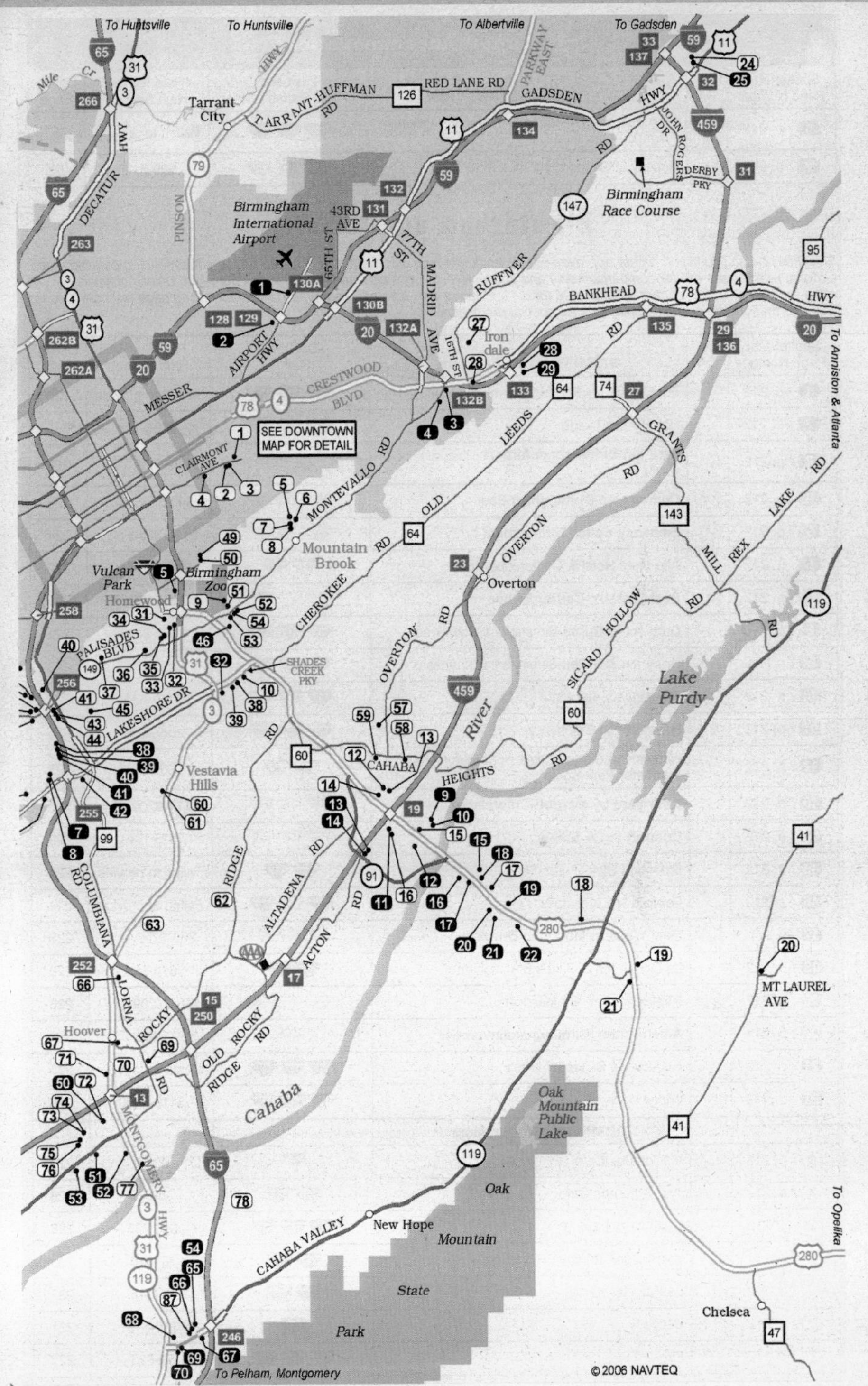
To Huntsville
To Huntsville
To Albertville
To Gadsden
Tarrant City
TARRANT-HUFFMAN RD
RED LANE RD
GADSDEN HWY
PARKWAY EAST
DECATUR HWY
PINSON
Birmingham International Airport
43RD AVE
65TH ST
77TH ST
MADRID AVE
16TH ST
AIRPORT HWY
JOHN ROGERS DR
DERBY PKY
Birmingham Race Course
RUFFNER RD
BANKHEAD HWY
Iron dale
MESSER
CRESTWOOD BLVD
SEE DOWNTOWN MAP FOR DETAIL
CLAIRMONT AVE
MONTEVALLO RD
LEEDS
OLD LEEDS RD
GRANTS MILL RD
Mountain Brook
CHEROKEE RD
OVERTON RD
Overton
LAKE REX RD
HOLLOW RD
SICARD HOLLOW RD
Vulcan Park
Homewood
Birmingham Zoo
PALISADES BLVD
SHADES CREEK PKY
LAKESHORE DR
Lake Purdy
River
CAHABA HEIGHTS RD
Vestavia Hills
COLUMBIANA RD
RIDGE RD
ALTADENA RD
ACTON RD
MT LAUREL AVE
LORNA RD
Hoover
ROCKY RIDGE RD
OLD ROCKY RIDGE RD
Cahaba
MONTGOMERY HWY
Oak Mountain Public Lake
Oak Mountain State Park
CAHABA VALLEY RD
New Hope
Chelsea
To Anniston & Atlanta
To Opelika
To Pelham, Montgomery
© 2006 NAVTEQ

Airport Accommodations

Spotter/Map Page Number	OA	BIRMINGHAM INTERNATIONAL	Diamond Rating	Rate Range High Season	Listing Page
1 / p. 212		Four Points by Sheraton Birmingham Airport, 1.3 mi s of terminal	◆◆◆	Failed to provide	225
2 / p. 212		Holiday Inn-Airport, 1.5 mi s of terminal	◆◆◆	$99-$119	225

Birmingham and Vicinity

This index helps you "spot" where approved accommodations and restaurants are located on the corresponding detailed maps. Lodging rate ranges are for comparison only and show the property's high season; rates are per night, unless only weekly (W) rates are available. Restaurant rate range is for dinner, unless only lunch (L) is served. Turn to the listing page for more detailed rate information and consult display ads for special promotions.

Spotter/Map Page Number	OA	BIRMINGHAM - Lodgings	Diamond Rating	Rate Range High Season	Listing Page
1 / p. 212		Four Points by Sheraton Birmingham Airport	◆◆◆	Failed to provide	225
2 / p. 212		Holiday Inn-Airport	◆◆◆	$99-$119	225
3 / p. 212	AAA	**Park Inn Birmingham Airport** - see color ad p 226	◆◆	$69-$79 SAVE	226
4 / p. 212	AAA	**Comfort Inn Birmingham East**	◆◆◆	$90-$155 SAVE	223
5 / p. 212	AAA	**Embassy Suites Birmingham**	◆◆◆	$139-$359 SAVE	224
6 / p. 212		Alta Vista Hotel & Conference Center	◆◆	$89-$189	222
7 / p. 212	AAA	**Best Western Carlton Suites**	◆◆◆	$109-$198 SAVE	223
8 / p. 212		Drury Inn & Suites-Birmingham Southwest	◆◆◆	$80-$140	224
9 / p. 212		Drury Inn & Suites-Birmingham Southeast	◆◆◆	$85-$140	223
10 / p. 212		Birmingham Marriott	◆◆◆	$119-$214	223
11 / p. 212		Hampton Inn-Colonnade	◆◆◆	$99-$169	225
12 / p. 212		Homestead Studio Suites Hotel-Birmingham Perimeter Park South	◆◆	$60-$95	225
13 / p. 212	AAA	**Courtyard by Marriott-Colonnade**	◆◆◆	$174-$209 SAVE	223
14 / p. 212	AAA	**Comfort Inn & Suites**	◆◆◆	$85 SAVE	223
15 / p. 212		Extended Stay Studio Plus	◆◆	Failed to provide	224
16 / p. 212		Fairfield Inn Inverness	◆◆◆	Failed to provide	224
17 / p. 212	AAA	**Best Western Mountain Brook**	◆◆◆	$80-$200 SAVE	223
18 / p. 212		La Quinta Inn & Suites Birmingham	◆◆	$70-$94	226
19 / p. 212	AAA	**Residence Inn By Marriott**	◆◆◆	$164-$209 SAVE	226
20 / p. 212	AAA	**AmeriSuites (Birmingham/Inverness)**	◆◆◆	$99-$205 SAVE	222
21 / p. 212		Homewood Suites by Hilton	◆◆◆	Failed to provide	225
22 / p. 212		Wingate Inn	◆◆◆	$119-$160	226
		BIRMINGHAM - Restaurants			
1 / p. 212		V. Richards Cafe	◆	$6-$9	229
2 / p. 212		The Silvertron Cafe	◆◆	$8-$22	228
3 / p. 212		Little Savannah	◆◆◆	$30-$35	228
4 / p. 212		Los Amigos Mexican Restaurant	◆◆	$7-$13	228
5 / p. 212		La Paz Restaurant	◆◆	$6-$15	227
6 / p. 212		Bacca	◆	$10-$19	227
7 / p. 212		Fire	◆◆◆	$9-$23	227

Spotter/Map Page Number	OA	**BIRMINGHAM** - Restaurants (continued)	Diamond Rating	Rate Range High Season	Listing Page
8 / p. 212		Mauby's	♦♦♦	$23-$31	228
9 / p. 212		Cafe de France	♦♦	$5-$13(L)	227
10 / p. 212		McCormick & Schmick's	♦♦♦	$15-$25	228
11 / p. 212		Taj India	♦♦	$9-$19	228
12 / p. 212		The Grape at the Summit	♦♦	$8-$20	227
13 / p. 212		Tavern on the Summit	♦♦	$7-$22	228
14 / p. 212		Village Tavern	♦♦♦	$11-$25	229
15 / p. 212		Kobe Japanese Steak House & Sushi Bar	♦♦	$12-$25	227
16 / p. 212		Edgar's Bakery	♦	$5-$7(L)	227
17 / p. 212		Full Moon Bar-B-Que	♦	$6-$12	227
18 / p. 212		Lloyd's Restaurant	♦	$8-$24	228
19 / p. 212		Zapata's Mexican Restaurant	♦♦	$8-$12	229
20 / p. 212		Standard Bistro	♦♦♦	$17-$28	228
21 / p. 212		Taste Bud Organics	♦	$6-$12	228
		TRUSSVILLE - Lodgings			
25 / p. 212		Hampton Inn Birmingham/Trussville	♦♦♦	$89-$129	241
		TRUSSVILLE - Restaurant			
24 / p. 212		Zapata's Mexican Restaurant	♦♦	$6-$13	241
		IRONDALE - Lodgings			
28 / p. 212		Holiday Inn Express Inn and Suites Birmingham East	♦♦♦	$77-$250	237
29 / p. 212		Hampton Inn Birmingham East/Irondale	♦♦♦	$89-$102	236
		IRONDALE - Restaurants			
27 / p. 212		Irondale Cafe	♦	$5-$9	237
28 / p. 212		Hamburger Heaven	♦	$5-$8	237
		HOMEWOOD - Lodgings			
32 / p. 212	AAA	**Courtyard By Marriott**	♦♦♦	$99-$229 SAVE	231
33 / p. 212		Super 8 Motel	♦♦	$44-$63	232
34 / p. 212		Red Roof Inn	♦♦	Failed to provide	232
35 / p. 212	AAA	**Ramada Inn**	♦♦♦	$59-$199 SAVE	232
36 / p. 212		Oxmoor Inn	♦♦♦	$62-$159	232
37 / p. 212	AAA	**Comfort Inn-Oxmoor**	♦♦	$67-$77 SAVE	231
38 / p. 212	AAA	**Residence Inn by Marriott**	♦♦♦	$108-$189 SAVE	232
39 / p. 212		La Quinta Inn & Suites Birmingham (Homewood)	♦♦♦	$99-$125	232
40 / p. 212		StudioPLUS	♦♦	Failed to provide	232
41 / p. 212		Hampton Inn - Lakeshore	♦♦♦	Failed to provide	231
42 / p. 212	AAA	**TownePlace Suites by Marriott**	♦♦♦	$149-$159 SAVE	233
43 / p. 212		Hilton Garden Inn Birmingham-Lake Shore	♦♦♦	Failed to provide	232
		HOMEWOOD - Restaurants			
31 / p. 212		De Vinci's	♦♦	$10-$16	233
32 / p. 212		Franklin's Homewood Gourmet	♦	$6-$10	233

Spotter/Map Page Number	OA	HOMEWOOD - Restaurants (continued)	Diamond Rating	Rate Range High Season	Listing Page
33 / p. 212		Demetri's B.B.Q.	◆	$5-$19	233
34 / p. 212		Dave's Pizza	◆◆	$6-$30	233
35 / p. 212		O' Carr's	◆	$5-$8(L)	234
36 / p. 212		Nabeel's Cafe and Taverna	◆◆	$5-$17	233
37 / p. 212		New York Pizza	◆	$7-$15	234
38 / p. 212		Copper Grill Lobster & Steak House	◆◆◆	$24-$42	233
39 / p. 212		Brio Tuscan Grille	◆◆◆	$11-$22	233
40 / p. 212		The Original Steakhouse & Sports Theater	◆◆	$12-$19	234
41 / p. 212		Acapulco Bar and Grill	◆◆	$7-$13	233
42 / p. 212		The Restaurant at Culinard	◆◆◆	$35	234
43 / p. 212		Paw Paw Patch	◆	$4-$7	234
44 / p. 212		Pho Que Huong	◆◆	$6-$10	234
45 / p. 212		Gian Marco's	◆◆◆	$15-$25	233
46 / p. 212		San San Trio	◆◆	$6-$21	234
		MOUNTAIN BROOK - Lodgings			
46 / p. 212		Hampton Inn-Mountain Brook	◆◆◆	Failed to provide	238
		MOUNTAIN BROOK - Restaurants			
49 / p. 212		Chez Lulu & Continental Bakery	◆◆	$6-$18	238
50 / p. 212		Cafe Ciao	◆◆	$7-$16	238
51 / p. 212		Browdy's	◆	$7-$10	238
52 / p. 212		Daniel George Restaurant & Bar	◆◆◆	$20-$32	238
53 / p. 212		Gilchrist Drug Co	◆	$3-$5(L)	238
54 / p. 212		Olexa's	◆◆	$5-$12(L)	238
		HOOVER - Lodgings			
49 / p. 212		Renaissance Ross Bridge Golf Resort & Spa - see color ad p 200	◆◆◆◆	Failed to provide	235
50 / p. 212	AAA	**The Wynfrey Hotel** - see color ad p 225	◆◆◆◆	$169-$239 SAVE	235
51 / p. 212	AAA	**Best Western Riverchase Inn**	◆◆	$69-$140 SAVE	234
52 / p. 212	AAA	**Courtyard by Marriott-Hoover**	◆◆◆	$164 SAVE	235
53 / p. 212	AAA	**AmeriSuites (Birmingham/Riverchase)**	◆◆◆	$99-$205 SAVE	234
54 / p. 212		La Quinta Inn & Suites Birmingham (Hoover/Riverchase)	◆◆◆	$99-$125	235
		HOOVER - Restaurants			
66 / p. 212		The Olive Tree	◆◆	$9-$20	236
67 / p. 212		Full Moon Bar-B-Que	◆	$6-$16	236
68 / p. 212		Brock's	◆◆◆	$18-$35	235
69 / p. 212		Costa's Mediterranean Cafe	◆◆	$8-$20	235
70 / p. 212		The Fish Market	◆	$9-$18	236
71 / p. 212		Guadalajara Restaurant	◆◆	$7-$15	236
72 / p. 212	AAA	**Shula's Steak House**	◆◆◆	$25-$55	236
73 / p. 212		Cambridge Coffee	◆	$4-$6	235
74 / p. 212		Qdoba Mexican Grill	◆	$5-$8	236

Spotter/Map Page Number	OA	HOOVER - Restaurants (continued)	Diamond Rating	Rate Range High Season	Listing Page
75 / p. 212		Firebirds Rocky Mountain Grill	3 diamonds	$12-$24	236
76 / p. 212		Cajun Steamer Bar and Grill	2 diamonds	$8-$20	235
77 / p. 212		La Dolce Vita Cucina Italiana	2 diamonds	$12-$25	236
78 / p. 212		Tin Roof BBQ	1 diamond	$4-$17	236
		BESSEMER - Lodgings			
57 / p. 212		Motel 6 #426	1 diamond	$42-$58	230
58 / p. 212		Hampton Inn	3 diamonds	$110-$170	229
59 / p. 212		Jameson Inn	2 diamonds	$54-$120	229
60 / p. 212	AAA	**Best Western Hotel & Suites**	3 diamonds	$89-$250 SAVE	229
61 / p. 212		Comfort Inn	3 diamonds	Failed to provide	229
62 / p. 212		Sleep Inn	2 diamonds	$59-$139	230
		BESSEMER - Restaurants			
81 / p. 212		Bob Sykes Bar-B-Q	1 diamond	$7-$12	230
82 / p. 212		The Bright Star	2 diamonds	$12-$25	230
83 / p. 212		Golden Rule Bar-B-Q and Grill	2 diamonds	$6-$14	230
84 / p. 212		Johnny Ray's	1 diamond	$5-$12	230
		PELHAM - Lodgings			
65 / p. 212	AAA	**Quality Inn**	2 diamonds	$89-$160 SAVE	240
66 / p. 212		Ramada Limited	2 diamonds	$62-$149	240
67 / p. 212	AAA	**Best Western at Oak Mountain**	3 diamonds	$109-$199 SAVE	239
68 / p. 212		Sleep Inn	2 diamonds	$80-$285	240
69 / p. 212		Holiday Inn Express	3 diamonds	Failed to provide	239
70 / p. 212		Hampton Inn & Suites Pelham	3 diamonds	$95-$175	239
		PELHAM - Restaurant			
87 / p. 212		Pollo Volador	2 diamonds	$7-$16	240
		VESTAVIA HILLS - Restaurants			
57 / p. 212		Mudtown Eat & Drink	2 diamonds	$7-$14	242
58 / p. 212		Miss Myra's Pit Bar-B-Q	1 diamond	$5-$16	241
59 / p. 212		Satterfield's	3 diamonds	$20-$33	242
60 / p. 212		Sekisui	2 diamonds	$8-$31	242
61 / p. 212		Nonnas	3 diamonds	$15-$25	242
62 / p. 212		Leonardo's Italian Restaurant	2 diamonds	$8-$25	241
63 / p. 212		Diplomat Deli	1 diamond	$4-$15	241
		MCCALLA - Restaurant			
90 / p. 212		Momma's Ice Cream & Coffee Inc	1 diamond	$3-$6	237

DOWNTOWN BIRMINGHAM (See map and index starting on p. 210)

WHERE TO STAY

DOUBLETREE HOTEL BIRMINGHAM Phone: (205)933-9000 **4**

fyi All Year 1P: $169-$209 2P: $169-$209 XP: $10 F18

Large-scale Hotel Under major renovation, scheduled to be completed June 2006. **Last rated:** ◆◆◆ **Location:** 0.8 mi s of downtown; jct University Blvd. 808 20th St S 35205. Fax: 205/933-0920. **Facility:** 298 units. 296 one- and 2 two-bedroom standard units. 14 stories, interior corridors. *Bath:* combo or shower only. **Parking:** on-site. **Terms:** 5 day cancellation notice-fee imposed, package plans. **Amenities:** high-speed Internet, voice mail, irons, hair dryers. **Pool(s):** outdoor. **Leisure Activities:** exercise room. **Guest Services:** valet laundry. **Business Services:** conference facilities, fax (fee). **Cards:** AX, CB, DC, DS, JC, MC, VI.

SOME UNITS / VCR / FEE

HISTORIC REDMONT HOTEL *Book at AAA.com* Phone: (205)324-2101 **3**

◆◆◆ All Year 1P: $89-$115 2P: $89-$115

Historic Large-scale Hotel **Location:** Corner of Fifth Ave and Richard Arlington Blvd. 2101 Fifth Ave N 35203. Fax: 205/324-0610. **Facility:** A jewel in downtown Birmingham, this is the oldest hotel in the area; with its beautiful rooms as well as pubic areas, some say the hotel is haunted. Smoke free premises. 114 units. 113 one- and 1 two-bedroom standard units. 14 stories, interior corridors. **Parking:** on-site (fee) and valet. **Terms:** [AP], [BP], [CP] & [ECP] meal plans available, package plans, 14% service charge. **Amenities:** video games (fee), high-speed Internet, dual phone lines, voice mail, irons, hair dryers. **Leisure Activities:** exercise room. **Guest Services:** valet laundry. **Business Services:** conference facilities, business center. **Cards:** AX, CB, DC, DS, JC, MC, VI.

ASK

MEDICAL CENTER INN *Book at AAA.com* Phone: (205)933-1900 **6**

◆◆ All Year 1P: $69-$139 2P: $69-$139 XP: $4 F

Small-scale Hotel **Location:** I-65, exit 259A northbound; exit 259B southbound, just e. Located within easy access to University of Alabama Birmingham. 800 11th St S 35205. Fax: 205/933-8476. **Facility:** 190 one-bedroom standard units. 4 stories, exterior corridors. **Parking:** on-site. **Terms:** 3 day cancellation notice, weekly rates available. **Amenities:** high-speed Internet, voice mail, irons, hair dryers. **Pool(s):** outdoor. **Guest Services:** coin laundry, area transportation, wireless Internet. **Cards:** AX, CB, DC, DS, JC, MC, VI.

SOME UNITS

ASK / /

PICKWICK HOTEL & CONFERENCE CENTER *Book at AAA.com* Phone: 205/933-9555 **5**

◆◆◆ Property failed to provide current rates

Small-scale Hotel **Location:** 1.5 mi s of downtown (Five Points area). 1023 20th St S 35205. Fax: 205/933-6918. **Facility:** 63 units. 35 one-bedroom standard units. 28 one-bedroom suites with efficiencies (no utensils). 7 stories, interior corridors. *Bath:* combo or shower only. **Parking:** on-site. **Terms:** small pets only ($75 extra charge). **Amenities:** high-speed Internet, voice mail, safes (fee), irons, hair dryers. **Leisure Activities:** limited exercise equipment. **Guest Services:** valet laundry, area transportation. **Business Services:** meeting rooms, business center.

SOME UNITS / / FEE

(See map and index starting on p. 210)

SHERATON BIRMINGHAM HOTEL *Book great rates at AAA.com* **Phone:** (205)324-5000 1

AAA SAVE

1/1-11/30	1P: $109-$249	2P: $109-$249	XP: $20	F16
12/1-12/31	1P: $89-$229	2P: $89-$229	XP: $20	F16

Large-scale Hotel

Location: I-20/59, exit 22nd St. Located adjacent to civic center. 2101 Richard Arrington Blvd N 35203. Fax: 205/307-3045. **Facility:** 770 units. 764 one-bedroom standard units. 6 one-bedroom suites. 16 stories, interior corridors. **Parking:** on-site (fee) and valet. **Terms:** cancellation fee imposed. **Amenities:** dual phone lines, voice mail, irons, hair dryers. *Fee:* video games, high-speed Internet. *Some:* fax. **Dining:** 2 restaurants, 6 am-2 am, cocktails. **Pool(s):** small heated indoor. **Leisure Activities:** saunas, whirlpool, exercise room, spa. **Guest Services:** gift shop, valet laundry. **Business Services:** conference facilities, business center. **Cards:** AX, DC, DS, MC, VI. **Free Special Amenities: newspaper.** *(See color ad p 218)*

SOME UNITS

FEE

THE TUTWILER-A WYNDHAM HISTORIC HOTEL *Book great rates at AAA.com* **Phone:** (205)322-2100 2

AAA SAVE

All Year [ECP]	1P: $152	2P: $152	XP: $15	F17

Historic Large-scale Hotel

Location: Between Richard Arrington Jr Blvd and 20th St; just s of Woodrow Wilson Park. 2021 Park Pl N 35203. Fax: 205/325-1183. **Facility:** This restored historic hotel features elegant public areas and many large rooms. 147 units. 96 one-bedroom standard units. 50 one- and 1 two-bedroom suites. 8 stories, interior corridors. *Bath:* combo or shower only. **Parking:** on-site (fee) and valet. **Terms:** package plans, pets ($100 fee). **Amenities:** CD players, high-speed Internet (fee), dual phone lines, voice mail, irons, hair dryers. **Dining:** The Grille At The Tutwiler, see separate listing. **Leisure Activities:** pool privileges. **Guest Services:** valet laundry. **Business Services:** meeting rooms, fax. **Cards:** AX, CB, DC, DS, JC, MC, VI. **Free Special Amenities: expanded continental breakfast and newspaper.**

SOME UNITS

FEE FEE FEE

WHERE TO DINE

BOMBAY CAFE **Lunch:** $7-$24 **Dinner:** $8-$27 **Phone:** 205/322-1930 9

American

Location: Corner of 7th Ave and 28th St. 2839 7th Ave S 35233. **Hours:** 11 am-2 & 5:30-9:30 pn, Fri & Sat-10:30 pm. Closed major holidays. **Reservations:** suggested. **Features:** The menu changes daily to highlight Continental preparations of seafood, prime steaks, lamb and veal. An expansion of the property includes The Canteen, an upscale martini bar. Casual dress; cocktails. **Parking:** valet and street. **Cards:** AX, MC, VI.

BOTTEGA CAFE **Lunch:** $9-$22 **Dinner:** $9-$22 **Phone:** 205/939-1000 16

Italian

Location: Just w of US 31/SR 3; in Five Points area. 2240 Highland Ave S 35205. **Hours:** 11 am-11 pm. Closed major holidays; also Sun. **Features:** The popular trattoria sustains a casual atmosphere without compromising quality. Community tables and a frenetic pace make for an enjoyable dining experience. On the seasonal menu are fresh gulf seafood, organic vegetables and flatbreads and pizza cooked over a wood fire. Weeknight specials deserve a look. Casual dress; cocktails. **Parking:** valet and street. **Cards:** AX, DS, MC, VI.

BOTTEGA RESTAURANT **Dinner:** $16-$30 **Phone:** 205/939-1000 20

Italian

Location: Southside. 2240 Highland Ave 35205. **Hours:** 5:30 pm-10 pm, Fri & Sat-10:30 pm. Closed major holidays; also Sun. **Reservations:** suggested. **Features:** Here you will find gourmet dishes served in a tasteful atmosphere. A friendly, attentive staff makes for a very pleasant experience as you sample creative meat, foul and seafood dishes, a wide selection of appetizers and many tasty desserts. Dressy casual; cocktails. **Parking:** valet and street. **Cards:** AX, DS, MC, VI.

CAFE DUPONT **Lunch:** $16-$22 **Dinner:** $25-$34 **Phone:** 205/322-1282 7

Regional American

Location: Corner of Morris Ave and 20th St N. 113 20th St N 35203. **Hours:** 11 am-2 & 5:30-9 pm, Sat from 5:30 pm, Tues 11 am-2 pm. Closed: Sun & Mon. **Reservations:** suggested. **Features:** Chef/owner Dupont combines his special touches with foods from around the region, such as Georgia quail and gulf shrimp. He also dabbles in other meat and seafood preparations. The dining room offers a warm and soothing atmosphere in which to enjoy the nicely presented creations. Dressy casual; beer & wine only. **Parking:** valet. **Cards:** MC, VI.

CANTINA **Lunch:** $5-$8 **Dinner:** $5-$8 **Phone:** 205/323-6980 3

Mexican

Location: Jct 2nd Ave and 29th St S; in Martin Biscuit Building. 2901 2nd Ave S 35233. **Hours:** 11 am-9 pm, Mon-3 pm, Fri & Sat-10 pm. Closed major holidays; also Sun. **Features:** As its name suggests, Cantina sustains a casual, laid-back atmosphere. Customers order and pay at the counter, then find a table and wait for their food to be delivered. While the menu is limited, each flavorful item is prepared with care. Casual dress; cocktails. **Parking:** on-site. **Cards:** AX, MC, VI.

CHEZ FON FON **Dinner:** $18-$30 **Phone:** 205/939-3221 22

French

Location: I-65, exit 259 (University Blvd), 1 mi e to 20th St, then just s; at Five Points South. 2007 11th Ave S 35205. **Hours:** 5 pm-10 pm. Closed major holidays; also Mon & Sun. **Reservations:** not accepted. **Features:** Delicious food is served in a wonderful atmosphere that's upscale in every way. French style infuses all aspects of the food and design at the amazing local favorite. Dressy casual; cocktails. **Parking:** valet and street. **Cards:** AX, DS, MC, VI.

COBB LANE RESTAURANT **Lunch:** $10-$17 **Dinner:** $12-$31 **Phone:** 205/933-0462 28

Continental

Location: Just n of jct 13th Ave S. 1 Cobb Ln 35205. **Hours:** 11 am-2 & 5:30-9 pm, Sun-2 pm. Closed: Mon. **Features:** Established in 1948, the historic district restaurant has been a Birmingham tradition for years. It is tucked away on a cobblestone street and nurtures an Old World ambience. The mood is inviting both in the interior dining area and in the summer courtyard. This place is known for its she-crab soup, as well as moderately priced entrees executed with a Southern flair. Among interesting items are fried green tomatoes, Southern fried catfish fillet and the scrumptious chocolate roulage. Casual dress; cocktails. **Parking:** on-site. **Cards:** MC, VI.

(See map and index starting on p. 210)

COSMO'S PIZZA **Lunch:** $6-$15 **Dinner:** $11-$20 **Phone:** 205/930-9971 (21)

Pizza

Location: Corner of 20th St S and Magnolia Ave; behind Pickwick Hotel & Conference Center. 2012 Magnolia Ave 35205. **Hours:** 11 am-11 pm, Fri & Sat-midnight, Sun noon-11 pm. Closed: 12/25. **Features:** The groovy neighborhood pizza joint whips up an array of salads, appetizers, sandwiches and, of course, pizza by the slice or the pie. For starters, antipasti, alligator medallions and spinach salad are good choices. More than 35 pizza toppings allow for myriad combinations, and a variety of beers complement the customized thin-crust pies. Casual dress; cocktails. **Parking:** street. **Cards:** AX, DS, MC, VI.

DREAMLAND BAR-B-QUE RIBS **Lunch:** $6-$18 **Dinner:** $6-$18 **Phone:** 205/933-2133 (29)

Barbecue

Location: I-65, exit 259, 0.7 mi e on University Blvd, then s on 15th St S. 1427 14th Ave S 35205. **Hours:** 10 am-10 pm, Fri & Sat-11 pm, Sun 11 am-9 pm. Closed: 11/22. **Features:** Ain't nothing like 'em nowhere: this is the best place to go for ribs. Stacks of white bread and pools of BBQ sauce keep locals coming here day after day. Casual dress; beer only. **Parking:** on-site. **Cards:** AX, DC, DS, MC, VI.

FIVE POINTS GRILL **Lunch:** $7-$15 **Dinner:** $12-$20 **Phone:** 205/933-6363 (18)

American

Location: In Five Points South. 1035 20th St S 35205. **Hours:** 6 am-1 am, Thurs-Sat to 2 am, Sun 9 am-2 am. Closed major holidays. **Features:** In the center of Five Points, the restaurant has a large area for outdoor seating from which the people-watching doesn't get any better. The relaxed spot is a favorite for good food, including a large assortment of breads and beers. Casual dress; cocktails; entertainment. **Parking:** street. **Cards:** AX, MC, VI.

GOLDEN TEMPLE VEGETARIAN CAFE **Lunch:** $4-$8 **Phone:** 205/933-8933 (26)

Vegetarian

Location: In Five Points area of Southside. 1901 11th Ave S 35205. **Hours:** 11 am-3 pm, Sat-2:30 pm. Closed major holidays; also Sun. **Features:** Serving Magic City for 32 years, the cafe lets vegetarians and non-vegetarians alike load up on sandwiches, salads, chips, guacamole, quesadillas (particularly the delicious spinach one), smoothies, juices, teas and many tofu offerings. A health food store adjoins. Casual dress. **Parking:** on-site. **Cards:** AX, DS, MC, VI.

THE GRILLE AT THE TUTWILER **Lunch:** $8-$17 **Dinner:** $15-$30 **Phone:** 205/322-2100 (1)

American

Location: Between Richard Arrington Jr Blvd and 20th St; just s of Woodrow Wilson Park; in The Tutwiler-A Wyndham Historic Hotel. 2021 Park Pl N 35203. **Hours:** 6-11 am, 11:30-2:30 & 5:30-9 pm. **Reservations:** accepted. **Features:** In one of downtown's most historic hotels, The Grille prepares such American favorites as steak, chops and sandwiches. Floor-to-ceiling windows and dark mahogany lend to a warm and relaxed, yet upscale, atmosphere. Dressy casual; cocktails. **Parking:** valet and street. **Cards:** AX, DS, MC, VI.

HIGHLAND COFFEE COMPANY **Lunch:** $3-$7 **Dinner:** $3-$7 **Phone:** 205/933-0600 (15)

Coffee/Espresso

Location: Southside. 2255 Highland Ave 35205. **Hours:** 6:30 am-9 pm, Thurs-Sat to 11 pm. Closed: 11/22. **Reservations:** not accepted. **Features:** Diners can sip a smooth cup of coffee with an assortment of breads and pastries or order a sandwich at the casual deli-style counter attached to the main coffeehouse. Casual dress; cocktails. **Parking:** street. **Cards:** AX, DS, MC, VI.

HIGHLANDS BAR & GRILL **Dinner:** $19-$30 **Phone:** 205/939-1400 (23)

American

Location: Just w of jct US 31/280 and Highland Ave exit; Five Points area. 2011 11th Ave S 35205. **Hours:** 6 pm-10 pm, Fri & Sat-10:30 pm. Closed major holidays; also Sun & Mon. **Reservations:** required. **Features:** A refined, yet unstuffy, atmosphere makes this place popular with local professionals and business people. The daily changing menu always offers fresh, in-season dishes, a fine wine selection and impeccably prepared desserts. Dressy casual; cocktails. **Parking:** valet and street. **Cards:** AX, MC, VI.

HOT AND HOT FISH CLUB **Dinner:** $20-$50 **Phone:** 205/933-5474 (19)

New World

Location: Just off US 31. 2180 11th Ct S 35205. **Hours:** 5:30 pm-10 pm, Fri & Sat-10:30 pm. Closed: Sun & Mon. **Reservations:** suggested. **Features:** A classic theater kitchen embellishes the cozy, intimate setting. The well-trained staff creates artistic dishes. Recommended is the flounder roll, crispy duck confit and the spectacular combination cheese tray. Dressy casual; cocktails. **Parking:** valet and street. **Cards:** AX, CB, DC, MC, VI.

JIM N' NICK'S BAR-B-Q **Lunch:** $7-$17 **Dinner:** $7-$17 **Phone:** 205/320-1060 (25)

Barbecue

Location: I-65, exit 259 (University Blvd), 1 mi e, then just s on 20th St; in Five Points area of Southside. 1908 11th Ave S 35209. **Hours:** 10:30 am-9 pm, Fri & Sat-10 pm. Closed: 11/22, 12/25. **Features:** Put a little South in your mouth! This restaurant offers the freshest tastes of what the South is all about, including delicious BBQ and scrumptious desserts. Casual dress; cocktails. **Parking:** street. **Cards:** AX, DC, MC, VI.

JOHN'S CITY DINER **Lunch:** $6-$10 **Dinner:** $10-$25 **Phone:** 205/322-6014 (6)

American

Location: Between 1st and 2nd aves N. 112 Richard Arrington Blvd 35203. **Hours:** 11 am-3:30 & 5-9 pm, Fri-10 pm, Sat 5 pm-10 pm. Closed major holidays; also Sun. **Features:** John's has been a popular "down-home" eatery in the Birmingham historic district since 1944. The decor is nautical and nostalgic. The menu offers many fresh seafood dishes and country-style vegetables, as well as their famous coleslaw. Casual dress; cocktails. **Parking:** on-site. **Cards:** AX, DS, MC, VI.

LA COCINA **Lunch:** $5-$20 **Dinner:** $5-$20 **Phone:** 205/252-7626 (14)

Mexican

Location: Corner of 7th Ave and 20th St; University Area. 2117 7th Ave S 35233. **Hours:** 11 am-9 pm, Mon from 4 pm, Sat from 5 pm. Closed major holidays. **Reservations:** not accepted. **Features:** Friendly, helpful staff members serve ample portions of traditional Mexican cuisine. The informal dining room is suited for a casual dining experience. Casual dress; cocktails. **Parking:** street. **Cards:** AX, DC, DS, MC, VI.

(See map and index starting on p. 210)

LAKEVIEW OYSTER HOUSE **Lunch:** $6-$18 **Dinner:** $9-$25 **Phone:** 205/252-5888 (8)

Seafood

Location: Between 28th and 32nd sts. 731 29th St S 35233. **Hours:** 11 am-2 & 5-9 pm, Fri-11 pm, Sat 5 pm-10 pm. Closed: Sun. **Features:** In a restored downtown Victorian home, the restaurant serves everything from po' boy sandwiches and mahi mahi to grilled, fried and raw oysters and jerk chicken. Casual dress; cocktails. **Parking:** on-site. **Cards:** AX, MC, VI.

NIKI'S DOWNTOWN **Lunch:** $6-$10 **Dinner:** $6-$10 **Phone:** 205/251-1972 (12)

Location: I-65, exit 260B (3rd Ave N), just n, just e on 12th St N, then just s. 1101 2nd Ave N 35203. **Hours:** 6 am-6 pm. Closed major holidays; also Sat & Sun. **Features:** A city landmark, the restaurant serves delicious home-cooked meals in a relaxed setting. Police officers, lawyers, professionals and locals have been mingling here for more than 50 years. Daily offerings include 13 meats and 32 vegetables, along with traditional Greek dishes. Despite its nondescript appearance, this place is a hot spot. Casual dress. **Parking:** on-site. **Cards:** AX, DC, DS, MC, VI.

OCEAN **Dinner:** $15-$38 **Phone:** 205/933-0999 (27)

AAA

Seafood

Location: Between 12th (Highland Ave) and 13th aves S; in Five Points area. 1218 20th St S 35205. **Hours:** 5:30 pm-10 pm. Closed: 11/22; also Sun & Mon. **Reservations:** required. **Features:** The award-winning restaurant focuses on fresh seafood from around the world, a raw bar with an array of oyster species and sushi rolls. Lending excitement to the contemporary atmosphere are many textures, designs and accent lighting. The seafood tower for two is popular, as are fresh catches prepared any of eight ways. Casual dress; cocktails. **Parking:** valet and street. **Cards:** AX, DS, MC, VI.

THE ORIGINAL PANCAKE HOUSE **Lunch:** $4-$10 **Phone:** 205/933-8837

American

Location: I-65, exit 259 (University Blvd), 1 mi e, then just s on 20th St S; at Five Points South. 1931 11th Ave S 35205. **Hours:** 6:30 am-2 pm, Sat & Sun 7 am-2:30 pm. Closed major holidays. **Features:** Freshly squeezed orange juice and real cheese grits go great with the many breakfast choices at this popular spot. The Dutch Baby is fluffy and one of a kind, and if you are really hungry try their famous apple pancakes. Large portions are served up daily from the "most copied menu". Casual dress. **Parking:** street. **Cards:** AX, DC, DS, MC, VI.

PITA LOCO **Lunch:** $3-$14 **Dinner:** $3-$14 **Phone:** 205/252-4899 (5)

International

Location: Between 20th and 21st sts; in lobby of Frank Nelson Building. 2000 2nd Ave N 35203. **Hours:** 8 am-7 pm. Closed major holidays; also Sun. **Features:** In the lobby of a downtown office building, the small restaurant specializes in Middle Eastern cuisine and treats patrons to the best hummus around. Those whose tastes are less adventurous can opt for American staples, such as burgers and sandwiches. This place opens for breakfast. Casual dress. **Parking:** street. **Cards:** AX, DS, MC, VI.

RESTAURANT G **Lunch:** $9-$15 **Dinner:** $23-$28 **Phone:** 205/323-1820 (4)

AAA

American

Location: Corner of 4th Ave N and 19th St. 1820 4th Ave N 35203. **Hours:** 11 am-2 & 5-9 pm, Fri-10 pm, Sat 5 pm-10 pm, Mon 11 am-2 pm. Closed major holidays. **Reservations:** accepted. **Features:** The distinctive downtown spot has a contemporary feel. An "uptown" influence punctuates offerings of Southern food, which are prepared with local organic produce. Guests can peruse an extensive wine list and ponder an impressive array of martinis. Dressy casual; cocktails. **Parking:** valet. **Cards:** AX, DS, MC, VI.

ROJO **Lunch:** $6-$15 **Dinner:** $6-$15 **Phone:** 205/328-4733 (13)

Mexican

Location: Jct 30th St S and Highland Ave S. 2921 Highland Ave S 35205. **Hours:** 11 am-10 pm. Closed major holidays; also Mon. **Features:** Upon entering the hot spot, guests walk to the counter to order their favorite Latin or Mexican dish, such as sizzling fajitas, steak- or chicken-filled burritos and nacho platters smothered in cheese. Minutes later, it's brought to their table. No one leaves here hungry. Casual dress; cocktails. **Parking:** street. **Cards:** AX, DS, MC, VI.

SAKURA JAPANESE RESTAURANT **Dinner:** $9-$16 **Phone:** 205/933-1025 (17)

Japanese

Location: 1.5 mi s of downtown; next to Pickwick Hotel. 1025 20th St S 35205. **Hours:** 5 pm-10:30 pm, Thurs-2 am, Fri & Sat-3 am, Sun-9:30 pm. Closed major holidays. **Features:** Guests unwind in a casual setting for a meal of Japanese cuisine. From Thursday through Saturday, the atmosphere transforms into a popular late-night party place in which midnight sushi is a big draw. Casual dress; beer & wine only. **Parking:** street. **Cards:** AX, MC, VI.

SNEAKY PETE'S CAFE' **Lunch:** $5-$10 **Dinner:** $5-$10 **Phone:** 205/327-5414 (11)

American

Location: US 31, exit 8th Ave, just e. 744 29th St S 35233. **Hours:** 10:30 am-10 pm, Sat & Sun-midnight. **Features:** Much more than hotdogs, this quick lunch spot located in the heart of the Lakeview district is popular with the medical crowd and offers patio seating. Casual dress; cocktails. **Parking:** on-site. **Cards:** AX, DS, JC, MC.

SOL Y LUNA **Lunch:** $8-$16 **Dinner:** $8-$16 **Phone:** 205/322-1186 (10)

Southwestern

Location: Between 28th and 29th sts; in Lakeview District. 2811 7th Ave S 35233. **Hours:** 11 am-2 & 5-10 pm, Wed-Sat to midnight; Sunday brunch. Closed major holidays; also for dinner Sun. **Reservations:** accepted. **Features:** Both the decor and the Mexican and Southwestern food put patrons in a Taos or Santa Fe state of mind. Tomatillo soft lobster is an example of the succulent food options, which pair with a nice selection of premium tequilas. Servers are knowledgeable. Casual dress; cocktails. **Parking:** on-site. **Cards:** AX, CB, DC, DS, JC, MC, VI.

SURIN WEST **Lunch:** $7-$18 **Dinner:** $9-$18 **Phone:** 205/324-1928 (24)

Thai

Location: I-65, exit 259 (University Blvd), 1 mi e, then just s on 20th St S; in Five Points South. 1918 11th Ave S 35205. **Hours:** 11 am-2:30 & 5:30-9:45 pm, Fri 5:30 pm-10:30 pm, Sat 11:30 am-2:30 & 5:30-10:30 pm, Sun 11:30 am-2:30 pm. Closed major holidays. **Reservations:** accepted. **Features:** Located in the eccentric Five Points area, the restaurant offers thai dishes, lunch specials, and sushi in a dark atmosphere. Casual dress; cocktails. **Parking:** street. **Cards:** AX, MC, VI.

(See map and index starting on p. 210)

ZOES KITCHEN **Lunch:** $7-$10 **Phone:** 205/252-5200 (2)

American

Location: Between 19th and 20th sts; across from courthouse; in One Federal Place Building. 1819 5th Ave N 35203. **Hours:** 10 am-4 pm. Closed major holidays; also Sat & Sun. **Features:** Fresh and tasty food makes up this restaurant's menu. At lunchtime, this place is popular with the business crowd for its convenient location and in-and-out speed. Casual dress. **Parking:** street. **Cards:** AX, DS, MC, VI.

BIRMINGHAM pop. 242,820 (See map and index starting on p. 212)

WHERE TO STAY

ALTA VISTA HOTEL & CONFERENCE CENTER *Book at AAA.com* **Phone:** (205)290-8000 6

Small-scale Hotel

All Year [BP] 1P: $89-$189 2P: $89-$189 XP: $10 F18

Location: I-65, exit 256 northbound; exit 256A southbound, just w on Oxmoor Rd, 1 mi n on Vulcan Rd and Bagby Dr, then just e. 260 Goodwin Crest Dr 35209. Fax: 205/290-8001. **Facility:** 181 units. 166 one-bedroom standard units. 15 one-bedroom suites. 7 stories, interior corridors. *Bath:* combo or shower only. **Parking:** on-site. **Terms:** cancellation fee imposed. **Amenities:** voice mail, irons, hair dryers. **Pool(s):** outdoor. **Leisure Activities:** exercise room. **Guest Services:** valet and coin laundry, wireless Internet. **Business Services:** meeting rooms. **Cards:** AX, DS, MC, VI.

SOME UNITS

ASK / /

p

AMERISUITES (BIRMINGHAM/INVERNESS) *Book great rates at AAA.com* **Phone:** (205)995-9242 20

AAA SAVE

Small-scale Hotel

All Year 1P: $99-$205 2P: $99-$205 XP: $10 F17

Location: I-459, exit 19 (US 280), 1.7 mi e, just s to Inverness Pkwy. 4686 Hwy 280 E 35242. Fax: 205/995-2226. **Facility:** 128 one-bedroom standard units. 6 stories, interior corridors. *Bath:* combo or shower only. **Parking:** on-site. **Terms:** cancellation fee imposed, small pets only ($10 extra charge). **Amenities:** video games (fee), high-speed Internet, voice mail, irons, hair dryers. **Pool(s):** heated outdoor. **Leisure Activities:** exercise room. **Guest Services:** valet and coin laundry, area transportation-within 5 mi, wireless Internet. **Business Services:** meeting rooms. **Cards:** AX, CB, DC, DS, JC, MC, VI. **Free Special Amenities: full breakfast and high-speed Internet.**

SOME UNITS

FEE / /

(See map and index starting on p. 212)

BEST WESTERN CARLTON SUITES *Book great rates at AAA.com* **Phone:** (205)940-9990 **7**

AAA SAVE

Small-scale Hotel

All Year 1P: $109-$198 2P: $109-$198 XP: $10 F12

Location: I-65, exit 255 (Lakeshore Pkwy), just w to Wildwood Pkwy, then just n. 140 State Farm Pkwy 35209. Fax: 205/940-9930. **Facility:** 104 units. 49 one-bedroom standard units, some with whirlpools. 55 one-bedroom suites ($109-$198), some with whirlpools. 4 stories, interior corridors. *Bath:* combo or shower only. **Parking:** on-site. **Terms:** [BP] meal plan available, small pets only ($10 extra charge). **Amenities:** high-speed Internet, voice mail, irons, hair dryers. *Some:* DVD players. **Pool(s):** heated indoor. **Leisure Activities:** exercise room. **Guest Services:** complimentary evening beverages: Mon-Thurs, valet and coin laundry. **Business Services:** meeting rooms, business center. **Cards:** AX, CB, DC, DS, MC, VI. **Free Special Amenities: full breakfast and high-speed Internet.**

SOME UNITS

FEE

BEST WESTERN MOUNTAIN BROOK *Book great rates at AAA.com* **Phone:** (205)991-9977 **17**

AAA SAVE

Motel

All Year 1P: $80-$200 XP: $5 F17

Location: I-459, exit 19 (US 280), 1.4 mi e. 4627 Hwy 280 E 35242. Fax: 205/995-0570. **Facility:** 102 one-bedroom standard units. 3 stories, exterior corridors. *Bath:* combo or shower only. **Parking:** on-site. **Terms:** [ECP] meal plan available, small pets only ($20 fee). **Amenities:** irons, hair dryers. **Pool(s):** outdoor. **Leisure Activities:** sauna, whirlpool, steamroom. **Guest Services:** valet laundry. **Business Services:** meeting rooms, fax (fee). **Cards:** AX, CB, DC, DS, JC, MC, VI. **Free Special Amenities: expanded continental breakfast and high-speed Internet.**

SOME UNITS

FEE

BIRMINGHAM MARRIOTT *Book great rates at AAA.com* **Phone:** 205/968-3775 **10**

Large-scale Hotel

All Year 1P: $119-$214

Location: I-459, exit 19 (US 280), 0.6 mi e on US 280, then just n. Located in a modern commercial area. 3590 Grandview Pkwy 35243. Fax: 205/968-3742. **Facility:** 295 one-bedroom standard units. 8 stories, interior corridors. *Bath:* combo or shower only. **Parking:** on-site. **Terms:** cancellation fee imposed. **Amenities:** voice mail, irons, hair dryers. **Pool(s):** heated indoor. **Leisure Activities:** exercise room. **Guest Services:** gift shop, valet and coin laundry, wireless Internet. **Business Services:** conference facilities, business center. **Cards:** AX, CB, DC, DS, JC, MC, VI.

SOME UNITS

FEE FEE

COMFORT INN & SUITES *Book great rates at AAA.com* **Phone:** (205)968-3700 **14**

AAA SAVE

Small-scale Hotel

All Year 1P: $85 2P: $85 XP: $10 F

Location: I-459, exit 19 (US 280), 1.6 mi w on southwest frontage road. 4400 Colonnade Pkwy 35243. Fax: 205/968-0997. **Facility:** 67 units. 63 one-bedroom standard units. 4 one-bedroom suites ($90-$131). 2 stories, interior corridors. **Parking:** on-site. **Terms:** 7 day cancellation notice, [CP] meal plan available. **Amenities:** high-speed Internet, voice mail, safes (fee), irons, hair dryers. **Pool(s):** small outdoor. **Guest Services:** complimentary evening beverages: Mon-Thurs, valet laundry. **Business Services:** meeting rooms, PC, fax. **Cards:** AX, CB, DC, DS, JC, MC, VI.

SOME UNITS

COMFORT INN BIRMINGHAM EAST *Book great rates at AAA.com* **Phone:** 205/957-0084 **4**

AAA SAVE

Small-scale Hotel

All Year 1P: $90-$150 2P: $95-$155 XP: $10 F15

Location: I-20, exit 132B, just s. 4965 Montevallo Rd 35210. Fax: 205/314-2400. **Facility:** 83 one-bedroom standard units, some with whirlpools. 3 stories, interior corridors. *Bath:* combo or shower only. **Parking:** on-site. **Terms:** cancellation fee imposed. **Amenities:** high-speed Internet, dual phone lines, voice mail, safes (fee), irons, hair dryers. **Pool(s):** outdoor. **Leisure Activities:** exercise room. **Guest Services:** coin laundry, wireless Internet. **Business Services:** meeting rooms. **Cards:** AX, CB, DC, DS, MC, VI. **Free Special Amenities: continental breakfast and high-speed Internet.**

SOME UNITS

FEE

COURTYARD BY MARRIOTT-COLONNADE *Book great rates at AAA.com* **Phone:** (205)967-4466 **13**

AAA SAVE

Small-scale Hotel

All Year 1P: $174-$199 2P: $174-$209

Location: I-459, exit 19 (US 280), 1.6 mi w on southwest frontage road. 4300 Colonnade Pkwy 35243. Fax: 205/967-2499. **Facility:** 122 units. 118 one-bedroom standard units, some with whirlpools. 4 one-bedroom suites. 4 stories, interior corridors. *Bath:* combo or shower only. **Parking:** on-site. **Terms:** cancellation fee imposed, package plans. **Amenities:** high-speed Internet, voice mail, irons, hair dryers. **Pool(s):** heated indoor. **Leisure Activities:** whirlpool. **Guest Services:** sundries, valet and coin laundry, wireless Internet. **Business Services:** meeting rooms, business center. **Cards:** AX, DC, DS, JC, MC, VI. **Free Special Amenities: preferred room (subject to availability with advance reservations) and high-speed Internet.**

SOME UNITS

FEE

DRURY INN & SUITES-BIRMINGHAM SOUTHEAST *Book at AAA.com* **Phone:** (205)967-2450 **9**

Small-scale Hotel

All Year [BP] 1P: $85-$130 2P: $95-$140 XP: $10 F18

Location: I-459, exit 19, just e on US 280; in Grandview. 3510 Grandview Pkwy 35243. Fax: 205/967-6455. **Facility:** 150 units. 107 one-bedroom standard units. 43 one-bedroom suites ($125-$170). 6 stories, interior corridors. *Bath:* combo or shower only. **Parking:** on-site. **Amenities:** high-speed Internet, voice mail, irons, hair dryers. **Pool(s):** heated indoor/outdoor. **Leisure Activities:** whirlpool, exercise room. **Guest Services:** complimentary evening beverages: Mon-Sat, valet and coin laundry. **Business Services:** meeting rooms, PC. **Cards:** AX, CB, DC, DS, MC, VI.

SOME UNITS

(See map and index starting on p. 212)

DRURY INN & SUITES-BIRMINGHAM SOUTHWEST *Book at AAA.com* **Phone:** (205)940-9500 8

Small-scale Hotel

All Year [BP] 1P: $80-$130 2P: $90-$140 XP: $10 F18

Location: I-65, exit 255, 0.5 mi on northwest frontage road. 160 State Farm Pkwy 35209. Fax: 205/940-9500. **Facility:** 138 units. 118 one-bedroom standard units. 20 one-bedroom suites ($120-$145), some with whirlpools. 5 stories, interior corridors. *Bath:* some combo or shower only. **Parking:** on-site. **Amenities:** high-speed Internet, dual phone lines, voice mail, irons, hair dryers. **Pool(s):** heated indoor/outdoor. **Leisure Activities:** whirlpool, exercise room. **Guest Services:** sundries, valet and coin laundry. **Business Services:** meeting rooms, business center. **Cards:** AX, CB, DC, DS, MC, VI.

SOME UNITS

EMBASSY SUITES BIRMINGHAM *Book great rates at AAA.com* **Phone:** (205)879-7400 5

SAVE

Large-scale Hotel

All Year [BP] 1P: $139-$359 2P: $139-$359 XP: $10 F18

Location: Just n of jct US 31 and 280, exit 21st Ave southbound, then 0.3 mi s. Located on Red Mountain. 2300 Woodcrest Pl 35209. Fax: 205/870-4523. **Facility:** 242 units. 228 one- and 14 two-bedroom suites. 8 stories, interior corridors. *Bath:* combo or shower only. **Parking:** on-site. **Terms:** package plans, small pets only ($50 fee, $300 deposit). **Amenities:** video games (fee), high-speed Internet, dual phone lines, voice mail, irons, hair dryers. **Dining:** 11 am-11 pm, cocktails. **Pool(s):** heated indoor. **Leisure Activities:** sauna, whirlpool. **Guest Services:** complimentary evening beverages, valet and coin laundry, area transportation-within 5 mi. **Business Services:** conference facilities, fax (fee). **Cards:** AX, CB, DC, DS, JC, MC, VI. **Free Special Amenities: full breakfast and newspaper.**

SOME UNITS

FEE FEE

EXTENDED STAY STUDIO PLUS *Book at AAA.com* **Phone:** 205/408-0107 15

Small-scale Hotel

Property failed to provide current rates

Location: I-459, exit 19 (US 200), 1.9 mi se, then just n. 101 Cahaba Park Cir 35242. Fax: 205/408-6072. **Facility:** 72 units. 71 one-bedroom standard units with kitchens. 1 one-bedroom suite. 3 stories (no elevator), interior corridors. *Bath:* combo or shower only. **Parking:** on-site. **Terms:** pets ($75 fee). **Amenities:** high-speed Internet, voice mail, irons, hair dryers. **Pool(s):** small outdoor. **Guest Services:** valet and coin laundry. **Business Services:** fax (fee).

SOME UNITS

FEE

FAIRFIELD INN INVERNESS *Book great rates at AAA.com* **Phone:** 205/991-1055 16

Small-scale Hotel

Property failed to provide current rates

Location: I-459, exit 19 (US 280), 1.3 mi e. 707 Key Dr 35242. Fax: 205/991-2066. **Facility:** 63 one-bedroom standard units. 3 stories, interior corridors. *Bath:* combo or shower only. **Parking:** on-site. **Amenities:** high-speed Internet, irons, hair dryers. **Pool(s):** heated indoor. **Leisure Activities:** exercise room. **Guest Services:** valet laundry, wireless Internet. **Business Services:** fax (fee).

SOME UNITS

(See map and index starting on p. 212)

FOUR POINTS BY SHERATON BIRMINGHAM AIRPORT *Book great rates at AAA.com* **Phone:** 205/591-7900 **1**

Property failed to provide current rates

Small-scale Hotel **Location:** I-20/59, exit 129, just n. 5216 Airport Hwy 35212. Fax: 205/591-6004. **Facility:** 196 units. 191 one-bedroom standard units. 5 one-bedroom suites. 4 stories, interior corridors. *Bath:* combo or shower only. **Parking:** on-site. **Amenities:** high-speed Internet, voice mail, irons, hair dryers. *Fee:* video games, safes. **Pool(s):** outdoor. **Leisure Activities:** sauna, exercise room. **Guest Services:** valet laundry. **Business Services:** meeting rooms, business center.

SOME UNITS

HAMPTON INN-COLONNADE *Book great rates at AAA.com* **Phone:** (205)967-0002 **11**

All Year 1P: $99-$149 2P: $109-$169

Small-scale Hotel **Location:** I-459, exit 19 (US 280), 0.5 mi w on south frontage road. 3400 Colonnade Pkwy 35243. Fax: 205/969-0901. **Facility:** 133 one-bedroom standard units. 5 stories, interior corridors. *Bath:* combo or shower only. **Parking:** on-site. **Amenities:** voice mail, irons, hair dryers. *Some:* high-speed Internet. **Pool(s):** outdoor. **Leisure Activities:** exercise room. **Guest Services:** valet laundry, area transportation, wireless Internet. **Business Services:** meeting rooms, business center. **Cards:** AX, DC, DS, MC, VI.

SOME UNITS

HOLIDAY INN-AIRPORT *Book at AAA.com* **Phone:** (205)591-6900 **2**

All Year 1P: $99-$119 2P: $99-$119

Small-scale Hotel **Location:** I-20/59, exit 129, just s. 5000 Richard Arrington Blvd 35212. Fax: 205/591-2093. **Facility:** 226 one-bedroom standard units. 9 stories, interior corridors. *Bath:* combo or shower only. **Parking:** on-site. **Terms:** cancellation fee imposed, [AP], [BP], [CP] & [ECP] meal plans available. **Amenities:** high-speed Internet, voice mail, irons, hair dryers. **Pool(s):** outdoor. **Leisure Activities:** exercise room. **Guest Services:** valet laundry, area transportation. **Business Services:** meeting rooms. **Cards:** AX, CB, DC, DS, JC, MC, VI.

SOME UNITS

HOMESTEAD STUDIO SUITES HOTEL-BIRMINGHAM PERIMETER PARK SOUTH *Book at AAA.com* **Phone:** (205)967-3800 **12**

All Year 1P: $60-$90 2P: $65-$95 XP: $5 F17

Small-scale Hotel **Location:** I-459, exit 19 (US 280), 0.5 mi e, then just s. 12 Perimeter Park S 35243. Fax: 205/967-0025. **Facility:** 137 one-bedroom standard units with efficiencies. 2 stories (no elevator), exterior corridors. *Bath:* combo or shower only. **Parking:** on-site. **Terms:** small pets only ($25 fee). **Amenities:** high-speed Internet (fee), voice mail, irons. **Guest Services:** coin laundry. **Business Services:** fax (fee). **Cards:** AX, DC, DS, MC, VI.

SOME UNITS

FEE

HOMEWOOD SUITES BY HILTON *Book at AAA.com* **Phone:** 205/995-9823 **21**

Property failed to provide current rates

Small-scale Hotel **Location:** I-459, exit 19 (US 280), 1.8 mi e, then just s. 215 Inverness Center Dr 35242. Fax: 205/995-9843. **Facility:** 95 units. 45 one-bedroom standard units with efficiencies. 39 one- and 11 two-bedroom suites with kitchens. 4 stories, interior corridors. *Bath:* combo or shower only. **Parking:** on-site. **Terms:** pets ($75 fee). **Amenities:** video library (fee), DVD players, high-speed Internet, dual phone lines, voice mail, irons, hair dryers. **Pool(s):** small outdoor. **Leisure Activities:** whirlpool, exercise room, sports court. **Guest Services:** sundries, complimentary evening beverages: Mon-Thurs, valet and coin laundry. **Business Services:** meeting rooms, business center.

SOME UNITS

FEE

(See map and index starting on p. 212)

LA QUINTA INN & SUITES BIRMINGHAM *Book great rates at AAA.com* **Phone:** (205)995-9990 18

Small-scale Hotel

All Year 1P: $70-$90 2P: $74-$94 XP: $6 F18

Location: I-459, exit 19 (US 280), 1.2 mi e. 513 Cahaba Park Cir 35242. Fax: 205/995-0563. **Facility:** 100 one-bedroom standard units. 3 stories, interior corridors. **Parking:** on-site. **Terms:** [ECP] meal plan available, small pets only. **Amenities:** video games (fee), high-speed Internet, voice mail, irons, hair dryers. **Leisure Activities:** exercise room. **Guest Services:** valet laundry. **Business Services:** fax (fee). **Cards:** AX, CB, DC, DS, MC, VI.

SOME UNITS

PARK INN BIRMINGHAM AIRPORT *Book great rates at AAA.com* **Phone:** 205/951-0700 3

Small-scale Hotel

All Year 1P: $69 2P: $79 XP: $5 F15

Location: I-20, exit 132, just sw. 7901 Crestwood Blvd 35210. Fax: 205/313-3701. **Facility:** 101 one-bedroom standard units. 2 stories (no elevator), exterior corridors. **Parking:** on-site. **Terms:** cancellation fee imposed. **Amenities:** high-speed Internet (fee), voice mail, irons, hair dryers. **Pool(s):** small outdoor. **Guest Services:** coin laundry. **Business Services:** meeting rooms, fax. **Cards:** AX, CB, DC, DS, MC, VI. **Free Special Amenities: continental breakfast and high-speed Internet.** *(See color ad below)*

SOME UNITS

FEE

RESIDENCE INN BY MARRIOTT *Book great rates at AAA.com* **Phone:** (205)991-8686 19

Small-scale Hotel

All Year [BP] 1P: $164-$209 2P: $164-$209

Location: I-459, exit 19 (US 280), 2 mi e. Located in a modern commercial area. 3 Greenhill Pkwy 35242. Fax: 205/991-8729. **Facility:** 128 units. 120 one-bedroom standard units with kitchens. 8 two-bedroom suites ($154) with kitchens. 2 stories (no elevator), exterior corridors. *Bath:* combo or shower only. **Parking:** on-site. **Terms:** pets ($75 fee). **Amenities:** high-speed Internet, voice mail, irons, hair dryers. **Pool(s):** outdoor. **Leisure Activities:** whirlpool, limited exercise equipment, basketball, volleyball. **Guest Services:** sundries, complimentary evening beverages: Mon-Thurs, valet and coin laundry, wireless Internet. **Business Services:** meeting rooms, PC, fax (fee). **Cards:** AX, CB, DC, DS, JC, MC, VI. **Free Special Amenities: expanded continental breakfast and high-speed Internet.**

SOME UNITS

FEE

WINGATE INN *Book at AAA.com* **Phone:** (205)995-8586 22

Small-scale Hotel

All Year 1P: $119-$160 2P: $119-$160

Location: I-459, exit 19 (US 280), 2.6 mi e. Located in Meadow Brook Corporate Park. 800 Corporate Ridge Dr 35242. Fax: 205/995-2124. **Facility:** 100 units. 97 one-bedroom standard units. 3 one-bedroom suites ($135-$175). 4 stories, interior corridors. *Bath:* combo or shower only. **Parking:** on-site. **Amenities:** high-speed Internet, dual phone lines, voice mail, safes, irons, hair dryers. **Pool(s):** small outdoor. **Leisure Activities:** whirlpool, exercise room. **Guest Services:** complimentary evening beverages: Wed, valet laundry, wireless Internet. **Business Services:** meeting rooms, business center. **Cards:** AX, CB, DC, DS, MC, VI.

SOME UNITS

(See map and index starting on p. 212)

WHERE TO DINE

BACCA **Lunch:** $8-$15 **Dinner:** $10-$19 **Phone:** 205/802-2222 (6)

Pizza

Location: Crestline Village. 4 Dexter Ave 35213. **Hours:** 11 am-9 pm. Closed major holidays. **Reservations:** accepted. **Features:** The family-friendly eatery lets patrons choose from more than 35 pizza toppings, including typical ingredients and such exotic choices as pine nuts, fennel sausage, peach chutney and Cambozola cheese. Those not in the mood for pizza can select from full-size entrees, a large selection of salads and gourmet sandwiches. Casual dress; beer & wine only. **Parking:** on-site. **Cards:** AX, MC, VI.

BARNHILL'S BUFFET **Lunch:** $5-$9 **Dinner:** $7-$10 **Phone:** 205/836-4001

American

Location: I-59, exit Roebuck Pkwy, 1 mi n on SR 75. 9540 Parkway E 35215. **Hours:** 10:45 am-8:45 pm, Fri-9 pm, Sat 7 am-9 pm, Sun 7 am-8:45 pm. Closed: 12/25. **Features:** Casual dress. **Parking:** on-site. **Cards:** AX, DS, MC, VI.

CAFE DE FRANCE **Lunch:** $5-$13 **Phone:** 205/871-1000 (9)

French

Location: US 280, exit Hollywood Blvd, just n, then just nw; in Birmingham Botanical Gardens. 2612 Lane Park Rd 35223. **Hours:** 10 am-2 pm. Closed: 11/22, 12/25; also Sun. **Reservations:** accepted. **Features:** The elegant surroundings overlook Birmingham Botanical Gardens. On the menu of French cuisine are chicken, beef and seafood dishes, as well as salads and sandwiches. Casual dress; cocktails. **Parking:** on-site. **Cards:** AX, DS, MC, VI.

THE CHEESECAKE FACTORY **Lunch:** $8-$18 **Dinner:** $10-$20 **Phone:** 205/262-1800

International

Location: Just n of jct US 280 and I-459; at Summit Shopping Complex. 236 Summit Blvd 35224. **Hours:** 11 am-11 pm, Fri & Sat-12:30 am, Sun 10 am-11 pm. **Reservations:** accepted. **Features:** Casual dress; cocktails. **Parking:** on-site. **Cards:** AX, CB, DC, DS, JC, MC, VI.

EDGAR'S BAKERY **Lunch:** $5-$7 **Phone:** 205/968-0150 (16)

Deli/Subs Sandwiches

Location: I-459, exit 19 (US 280), 0.5 mi w on south frontage road; in The Shops of Colonnade. 3439 Colonnade Pkwy 35243. **Hours:** 6:30 am-6 pm. Closed major holidays; also Sun. **Features:** Delicious bread and light lunches are affordable and fast at this local bakery chain. Casual dress. **Parking:** on-site. **Cards:** AX, DS, MC, VI.

FIRE **Lunch:** $9-$23 **Dinner:** $9-$23 **Phone:** 205/802-1410 (7)

Regional American

Location: In Crestline Village at Mountain Brook; just s of clock tower. 212 Country Club Park 35213. **Hours:** 11 am-2 & 5:30-9 pm, Fri-10 pm, Sat 5:30 pm-10 pm, Sun 10:30 am-2 pm. Closed: 11/22, 12/24, 12/25; also Mon. **Reservations:** accepted. **Features:** The talented chef/owner treats diners to excellent and distinctive cuisine prepared in the Creole tradition. Featured items include turtle soup, fried green tomatoes, seven-hour lamb and fresh catch in crawfish maque choux with scallions and fresh dill. Nightly specials also merit a look. Casual dress; cocktails. **Parking:** street. **Cards:** AX, DS, MC, VI.

FOX AND HOUND PUB & GRILLE **Lunch:** $6-$18 **Dinner:** $6-$18 **Phone:** 205/968-3823

American

Location: I-459, exit 19 (US 280), 0.5 mi w on south frontage road. 3425 Colonnade Pkwy 35243. **Hours:** 11 am-2 am. Closed: 12/25. **Features:** Casual dress; cocktails. **Parking:** on-site. **Cards:** AX, DS, MC, VI.

FULL MOON BAR-B-QUE **Lunch:** $6-$12 **Dinner:** $6-$12 **Phone:** 205/991-7328 (17)

Barbecue

Location: Between Key Dr and Inverness Pkwy. 4635 Hwy 280 E 35242. **Hours:** 10 am-9 pm, Fri & Sat-10 pm. Closed: 1/1, 12/25; also Sun. **Features:** A Birmingham-area chain, the much-loved pork house is known for its half-moon cookies. Patrons savor barbecue ribs, pork and chicken, which are slow-cooked over real hickory wood in brick fire pits. Casual dress; beer only. **Parking:** on-site. **Cards:** AX, CB, DC, DS, JC, MC, VI.

THE GRAPE AT THE SUMMIT **Lunch:** $6-$12 **Dinner:** $8-$20 **Phone:** 205/970-7777 (12)

Gourmet Grocery

Location: I-459, exit 19, just ne; in Summit Shopping Center. 214 Summit Blvd 35243. **Hours:** 11 am-11 pm, Fri & Sat-midnight, Sun noon-9 pm. **Features:** The restaurant's staff imparts knowledge about the many wine selections and helps guests narrow down the selection most suited to them. The options pair well with selections from the menu. Casual dress; wine only. **Parking:** on-site. **Cards:** MC, VI.

KOBE JAPANESE STEAK HOUSE & SUSHI BAR **Lunch:** $7-$18 **Dinner:** $12-$25 **Phone:** 205/298-0200 (15)

Japanese

Location: I-459, exit 106, just e on US 280. 3501 Grandview Pkwy 35243. **Hours:** 11 am-2 & 5-10 pm, Fri 11 am-2 & 4:30-11 pm, Sat 4:30 pm-11 pm, Sun 11 am-2 & 4:30-10 pm. Closed major holidays. **Reservations:** accepted. **Features:** Watch as food is prepared right before the many diners' eyes. Cooks have several tricks up their sleeves as they prepare an assortment of Japanese dishes as well as hand rolled sushi. Casual dress; cocktails. **Parking:** on-site. **Cards:** AX, CB, DC, DS, JC, MC, VI.

LA PAZ RESTAURANT **Lunch:** $5-$12 **Dinner:** $6-$15 **Phone:** 205/879-2225 (5)

Mexican

Location: Just w of Church St. 99 Euclid Ave 35213. **Hours:** 11 am-10 pm, Fri & Sat-11 pm. Closed: 11/22, 12/25. **Reservations:** not accepted. **Features:** Traditional Mexican and Southwestern dishes—including seafood choices, stuffed peppers, great margaritas and fresh salsa made on the premises daily—are served in a casual and lively dining area decorated with Mexican handicrafts. Casual dress; cocktails. **Parking:** street. **Cards:** AX, MC, VI.

(See map and index starting on p. 212)

LITTLE SAVANNAH Dinner: $30-$35 Phone: 205/591-1119 (3)

American

Location: Between 38th and 39th sts S; near Highland Golf Course. 3811 Clairmont Ave 35222. **Hours:** 5:30 pm-9:30 pm. Closed major holidays; also Sun & Mon. **Features:** In a historic neighborhood, the restaurant allows for cozy, intimate dining. The menu changes frequently to take advantage of the availability of seasonal ingredients. Tantalizing starters range from fried blue crab dumplings to black tiger shrimp over creamy polenta. Hearty entrees run the gamut from house-smoked duck to wild boar. Such seafood as Nantucket scallops and Hawaiian prawns is always on the menu. Tempting dessert selections and varied wines round out a fine meal. Dressy casual; cocktails. **Parking:** street. **Cards:** AX, DS, MC, VI.

LLOYD'S RESTAURANT **Lunch:** $4-$15 **Dinner:** $8-$24 **Phone:** 205/991-5530 (18)

American

Location: I-459, exit 19 (US 280/Mountain Brook), 4 mi s. 5301 Hwy 280 S 35242. **Hours:** 11 am-9 pm. **Features:** The menu was made to satisfy the hungry, and locals swear by the hamburger steak with gravy. Other options include ribs, barbecue chicken, steak and fried whole catfish and fillets. The atmosphere is friendly and casual. Casual dress. **Parking:** on-site. **Cards:** DS, MC, VI.

LOS AMIGOS MEXICAN RESTAURANT **Lunch:** $5-$12 **Dinner:** $7-$13 **Phone:** 205/324-5896 (4)

Mexican

Location: US 31, exit 8th Ave S, 8.7 mi ne at jct Clairmont/University aves; in Piggly Wiggly Shopping Center. 3324 Clairmont Ave 35222. **Hours:** 11 am-2 & 5-9:30 pm, Sat 11:30 am-10 pm, Sun 11:30 am-9 pm. Closed major holidays. **Features:** There is always at fiesta at Los Amigos, where the service is quick and friendly and the traditional Mexican favorites are tasty. Choices include burritos, tacos and enchiladas. Casual dress; cocktails. **Parking:** on-site. **Cards:** MC, VI.

MAUBY'S **Dinner:** $23-$31 **Phone:** 205/870-7115 (8)

Continental

Location: Just n of Country Club Blvd. 121 Oak St 35213. **Hours:** 5 pm-10 pm, Sun also 11 am-2 pm. Closed: 1/1. **Reservations:** suggested. **Features:** The mood is casually sophisticated in the main dining room and more relaxed on the garden deck. The daily changing menu lists hand-cut steaks, fresh seafood, lamb, pork and chicken entrees prepared with a French Cajun flair. Dressy casual; cocktails. **Parking:** street. **Cards:** MC, VI.

MCCORMICK & SCHMICK'S **Lunch:** $7-$12 **Dinner:** $15-$25 **Phone:** 205/871-5171 (10)

Seafood

Location: US 280 E, exit Homewood/Mountain Brook (SR 149), just s; in Colonial Brookwood Village. 719 Shades Creek Pkwy 35209. **Hours:** 11 am-11 pm, Sun-9 pm. **Reservations:** accepted. **Features:** Serving seafood in a dressy casual setting, the restaurant features a large bar and a unique rotunda and architecture. Dressy casual; cocktails. **Parking:** on-site. **Cards:** AX, CB, DC, DS, JC, MC, VI.

THE SILVERTRON CAFE **Lunch:** $8-$14 **Dinner:** $8-$22 **Phone:** 205/591-3707 (2)

American

Location: US 280 W and 31 N, 0.3 mi e on University Blvd, then 0.7 mi w. 3813 Clairmont Ave 35222. **Hours:** 11 am-10 pm, Sun-9 pm. Closed major holidays. **Features:** On a residential street, the popular gathering spot features an extensive array of fresh salads, pasta dishes and wonderful burgers and steaks, as well as favorable wrap-style sandwiches. Among other choices are Mexican specialties of chicken or steak quesadillas and fajitas, Cajun-style blackened tenderloin filet, rib-eye steak and mahi mahi. Casual dress; cocktails. **Parking:** street. **Cards:** AX, MC, VI.

STANDARD BISTRO **Lunch:** $8-$12 **Dinner:** $17-$28 **Phone:** 205/995-0512 (20)

Regional American

Location: Jct US 280/Dunnavant Valley Rd (CR 41), 3.3 mi ne on Dunnavant Valley Rd (CR 41). 3 Mt Laurel Ave 35242. **Hours:** 11 am-2 & 5:30-10:30 pm, Tues from 5:30 pm. Closed: 1/1, 11/22, 12/25; also Sun & Mon. **Reservations:** accepted. **Features:** Contemporary Southern cuisine is served in a casually comfortable open dining room. Offerings center on organic vegetables and free-range meats, fowl and lamb. Favorites of duck two ways, roast pheasant breast and varied selections of grilled seafood pair with choices from the comprehensive wine list. The chef's tasting menu merits consideration. Casual dress; cocktails. **Parking:** street. **Cards:** AX, DS, MC, VI.

TAJ INDIA **Lunch:** $5-$11 **Dinner:** $9-$19 **Phone:** 205/939-3805 (11)

Indian

Location: In Five Points area of Southside. 2226 Highland Ave 35205. **Hours:** 11 am-2 & 5-10 pm, Fri & Sat 11:30 am-2:30 & 5-11 pm, Sun 11:30 am-2:30 & 5-9 pm. Closed major holidays. **Reservations:** accepted. **Features:** A touch of India graces both the menu and the decor. The enormous array of choices spans from tandoori and curry dishes to vegetarian options. Servers are informed and attentive. Casual dress; cocktails. **Parking:** on-site. **Cards:** AX, CB, DC, DS, JC, MC, VI.

TASTE BUD ORGANICS **Lunch:** $6-$12 **Dinner:** $6-$12 **Phone:** 205/995-8888 (21)

Natural/Organic

Location: Jct SR 119 and US 280, just s; in Greystone Center. 5510 Hwy 280, Suite 116 35242. **Hours:** 9 am-6:30 pm, Fri-3:30 pm. Closed major holidays; also Sat & Sun. **Features:** Most diners order "to go" at the small natural and organic food outlet, but a few tables allow for on-site dining. Great vegetarian selections include veggie burgers, which pair with smoothies and juices. Counter service is the mode here. A fresh produce section is available. Casual dress. **Parking:** on-site. **Cards:** AX, MC, VI.

TAVERN ON THE SUMMIT **Lunch:** $7-$22 **Dinner:** $7-$22 **Phone:** 205/298-1222 (13)

American

Location: I-459, exit 19 (US 280), 0.5 mi n. 225 Summit Blvd 35243. **Hours:** 11 am-11 pm, Sun-10 pm. Closed major holidays. **Features:** Nestled in a mall with ample parking, the combination watering hole and restaurant is a favorite for an after-work drink and sandwich or a nice steak or seafood dinner. The dining room has a warm and cozy feel, and the bar is busy and lively most nights. Casual dress; cocktails. **Parking:** on-site. **Cards:** AX, DS, MC, VI.

(See map and index starting on p. 212)

VILLAGE TAVERN Lunch: $8-$10 Dinner: $11-$25 Phone: 205/970-1640 (14)

American

Location: I-459, exit 19 (US 280), just n; in Summit Complex. 101 Summit Blvd 35243. Hours: 11 am-midnight, Sun 10 am-10 pm. Closed: 11/22, 12/25. Reservations: accepted. Features: A large stone fireplace complements the woods throughout the dining room, giving this place an old-time tavern feel. On the menu are fresh fish, steaks, sandwiches and other comfort foods. Service is friendly and attentive. Cocktails. Parking: on-site and valet. Cards: AX, DC, MC, VI.

V. RICHARDS CAFE Lunch: $6-$9 Dinner: $6-$9 Phone: 205/591-7000 (1)

American

Location: US 31, exit 8th Ave, 1 mi e. 3916 Clairmont Ave 35222. Hours: 11 am-7 pm, Sun-6 pm. Closed major holidays. Features: A recent offshoot of a gourmet market, the quaint cafe prepares fresh and delicious food, including soups, salads and sandwiches. Casual dress. Parking: on-site. Cards: AX, DS, MC, VI.

ZAPATA'S MEXICAN RESTAURANT Lunch: $5-$10 Dinner: $8-$12 Phone: 205/991-0002 (19)

Mexican

Location: I-459, exit 19, 0.5 mi se. 5479 Hwy 280 35242. Hours: 11 am-10 pm, Sun-9 pm. Features: On a busy highway, this Mexican spot gets it right. The restaurant lures crowds all day long. Casual dress; cocktails. Parking: on-site. Cards: AX, DS, MC, VI.

The Birmingham Vicinity

BESSEMER pop. 29,672 (See map and index starting on p. 212)

WHERE TO STAY

BEST WESTERN HOTEL & SUITES Book great rates at AAA.com Phone: (205)481-1950 (60)

AAA SAVE

Small-scale Hotel

All Year [ECP] 1P: $89-$250 2P: $89-$250 XP: $5 F17

Location: I-20/59, exit 108, just sw. 5041 Academy Ln 35022. Fax: 205/481-2597. **Facility:** 70 one-bedroom standard units, some with efficiencies (no utensils). 3 stories, interior corridors. *Bath:* combo or shower only. **Parking:** on-site. **Terms:** pets ($10 extra charge). **Amenities:** high-speed Internet, irons, hair dryers. **Pool(s):** outdoor. **Leisure Activities:** whirlpool, exercise room. **Guest Services:** valet and coin laundry, wireless Internet. **Business Services:** fax (fee). **Cards:** AX, CB, DC, DS, MC, VI. **Free Special Amenities: expanded continental breakfast and local telephone calls.**

SOME UNITS

FEE

COMFORT INN Book great rates at AAA.com Phone: 205/428-3999 (61)

Small-scale Hotel

Property failed to provide current rates

Location: I-20/59, exit 108, just sw. 5051 Academy Ln 35022. Fax: 205/428-8053. **Facility:** 59 units. 57 one-bedroom standard units, some with kitchens and/or whirlpools. 2 one-bedroom suites, some with kitchens. 3 stories, interior corridors. *Bath:* combo or shower only. **Parking:** on-site. **Amenities:** high-speed Internet, voice mail, irons, hair dryers. *Some:* dual phone lines. **Pool(s):** small outdoor. **Leisure Activities:** exercise room. **Guest Services:** valet and coin laundry. **Business Services:** meeting rooms, fax.

SOME UNITS

COUNTRY INN & SUITES Phone: 256/547-9700

fyi

Small-scale Hotel

Property failed to provide current rates

Too new to rate, opening scheduled for August 2006. **Location:** I-20/59, exit 108 (Academy), just sw. Academy Way 35022. **Amenities:** 66 units, coffeemakers, microwaves, refrigerators, pool.

FAIRFIELD INN BY MARRIOTT

fyi

Small-scale Hotel

Property failed to provide current rates

Too new to rate. **Location:** I-20/59, exit 108 (Academy), just sw. 5001 Academy Ln 35022. **Amenities:** 80 units, coffeemakers, pool.

HAMPTON INN Book great rates at AAA.com Phone: (205)425-2010 (58)

Small-scale Hotel

All Year [ECP] 1P: $110-$150 2P: $120-$170

Location: I-20/59, exit 108, 0.5 mi ne. 4910 Civic Ln 35022. Fax: 205/425-1630. **Facility:** 84 units. 78 one-bedroom standard units, some with whirlpools. 6 one-bedroom suites. 4 stories, interior corridors. *Bath:* combo or shower only. **Parking:** on-site. **Amenities:** video games (fee), high-speed Internet, voice mail, irons, hair dryers. **Pool(s):** outdoor. **Leisure Activities:** exercise room. **Guest Services:** coin laundry, wireless Internet. **Business Services:** meeting rooms, fax (fee). **Cards:** AX, DS, MC, VI.

SOME UNITS

ASK

JAMESON INN Book at AAA.com Phone: (205)428-3194 (59)

Small-scale Hotel

All Year [ECP] 1P: $54-$120

Location: I-20/59, exit 108, just sw. Located in a modern, light-commercial area. 5021 Academy Ln 35022. Fax: 205/428-2690. **Facility:** 60 one-bedroom standard units, some with whirlpools. 2 stories (no elevator), exterior corridors. *Bath:* combo or shower only. **Parking:** on-site. **Terms:** cancellation fee imposed, small pets only ($10 fee). **Amenities:** high-speed Internet, hair dryers. *Some:* irons. **Pool(s):** outdoor. **Leisure Activities:** exercise room. **Business Services:** PC, fax (fee). **Cards:** AX, DC, DS, MC, VI.

SOME UNITS

ASK

FEE

(See map and index starting on p. 212)

MOTEL 6 #426 Book at AAA.com **Phone:** 205/426-9646 57

Motel

4/13-11/30	1P: $42-$52	2P: $48-$58	XP: $3	F17
12/1-4/12	1P: $39-$49	2P: $45-$55	XP: $3	F17

Location: I-20/59, exit 108, 1 mi ne on US 11. 1000 Shiloh Ln 35020. Fax: 205/426-9305. **Facility:** 121 one-bedroom standard units. 2 stories (no elevator), exterior corridors. *Bath:* combo or shower only. **Parking:** on-site. **Terms:** small pets only. **Pool(s):** outdoor. **Guest Services:** coin laundry. **Cards:** AX, CB, DC, DS, MC, VI.

SOME UNITS

SLEEP INN Book great rates at AAA.com **Phone:** (205)424-0000 62

Small-scale Hotel

All Year	1P: $59-$139	2P: $59-$139	XP: $5	F16

Location: I-459, exit 6, just e, then just s. 1259 Greenmor Dr 35022. Fax: 205/424-1971. **Facility:** 73 one-bedroom standard units. 3 stories, interior corridors. *Bath:* shower or tub only. **Parking:** on-site. **Terms:** small pets only ($10 extra charge). **Amenities:** high-speed Internet, voice mail, irons, hair dryers. **Pool(s):** small outdoor. **Business Services:** PC, fax (fee). **Cards:** AX, CB, DC, DS, JC, MC, VI.

SOME UNITS

FEE

WHERE TO DINE

BOB SYKES BAR-B-Q **Lunch:** $4-$8 **Dinner:** $7-$12 **Phone:** 205/426-1400 81

Barbecue

Location: I-59/20, exit 112 (19th/18th St), 0.7 mi e, then just s. 1724 9th Ave 35020. **Hours:** 10:30 am-9 pm, Fri & Sat-10 pm. Closed: Sun. **Features:** In the family since 1957, the restaurant builds on its fine tradition of treating guests to succulent ribs and pulled pork, as well as barbecue chicken and burgers. A number of sides complement the offerings. Also good here are the pies. Casual dress. **Parking:** on-site. **Cards:** AX, DS, MC, VI.

THE BRIGHT STAR **Lunch:** $7-$20 **Dinner:** $12-$25 **Phone:** 205/426-1861 82

South Greek

Location: I-65, exit 112, 1 mi e; downtown. 304 19th St N 35020. **Hours:** 10:45 am-3:15 & 4:30-9 pm, Thurs-Sat to 10 pm. Closed: 1/1, 12/25, 12/26. **Features:** American cuisine. Family owned and operated since 1914. Memorabilia of local area displayed. Casual dress; cocktails. **Parking:** valet and street. **Cards:** AX, DC, DS, MC, VI.

GOLDEN RULE BAR-B-Q AND GRILL **Lunch:** $5-$11 **Dinner:** $6-$14 **Phone:** 205/426-5188 83

Barbecue

Location: I-20/59, exit 108 (Academy), just sw. 5060 Academy Ln 35022. **Hours:** 11 am-9 pm, Fri & Sat-10 pm. Closed: 11/22, 12/25 & Easter. **Features:** Claiming the South's most famous barbeque, this eatery has been treating Alabamians to the delicious flavors of real pit BBQ since its beginning in 1891. Now a local chain, Golden Rule cooks up a variety of southern favorites. Casual dress; beer only. **Parking:** on-site. **Cards:** AX, DS, MC, VI.

JOHNNY RAY'S **Lunch:** $3-$9 **Dinner:** $5-$12 **Phone:** 205/422-6639 84

Barbecue

Location: I-459, exit 6, just s. 2910 Morgan Rd 35022. **Hours:** 11 am-9 pm, Mon & Tues-8:30 pm. Closed: Sun. **Features:** Johnny Ray knows barbecue, and it shows on diners' faces. Plenty of finger-licking sauce drenches the delicious offerings, which are sweetly topped off by such Southern-favorite desserts as coconut cream and lemon ice-box pie. Casual dress. **Parking:** on-site. **Cards:** MC, VI.

CALERA pop. 3,158

WHERE TO STAY

HOLIDAY INN EXPRESS Book at AAA.com **Phone:** (205)668-3641

Small-scale Hotel

All Year	1P: $85	2P: $85	XP: $10	F18

Location: I-65, exit 231, just se. 357 Hwy 304 35040. Fax: 205/668-3102. **Facility:** 65 one-bedroom standard units. 2 stories (no elevator), exterior corridors. *Bath:* combo or shower only. **Parking:** on-site. **Terms:** pets ($20 extra charge). **Amenities:** dual phone lines, voice mail, irons, hair dryers. **Pool(s):** outdoor. **Guest Services:** valet and coin laundry. **Business Services:** meeting rooms, business center. **Cards:** AX, DC, DS, MC, VI.

SOME UNITS

FEE

WHERE TO DINE

WILDFIRE BARBEQUE & GRILL **Lunch:** $6-$12 **Dinner:** $6-$15 **Phone:** 205/621-6887

Barbecue

Location: I-65, exit 234, just w. 100 Hwy 87 35040. **Hours:** 10:30 am-9 pm, Sun 11 am-8 pm. Closed major holidays. **Features:** Steaks and barbecue are the name of the game. There's a lively lounge, and service is friendly. Pulled pork barbecue is one example of the enjoyable, well-prepared food. Casual dress; cocktails. **Parking:** on-site. **Cards:** AX, DS, MC, VI.

FULTONDALE pop. 6,595

WHERE TO STAY

COMFORT SUITES Book great rates at AAA.com **Phone:** (205)259-2160

Small-scale Hotel

All Year	1P: $109-$154	XP: $10	F

Location: I-65, exit 267, just e to Park St, then just s. 1325 Old Walker Chapel Rd 35068. Fax: 205/259-2170. **Facility:** 70 one-bedroom standard units. 3 stories, interior corridors. *Bath:* combo or shower only. **Parking:** on-site. **Terms:** cancellation fee imposed, weekly rates available, [CP] meal plan available. **Amenities:** high-speed Internet, voice mail, irons, hair dryers. **Pool(s):** small indoor. **Leisure Activities:** whirlpool, limited exercise equipment. **Guest Services:** sundries, valet and coin laundry, wireless Internet. **Business Services:** meeting rooms, business center. **Cards:** AX, DC, DS, MC, VI.

SOME UNITS

FAIRFIELD INN & SUITES Book great rates at AAA.com Phone: 205/849-8484

Property failed to provide current rates

Small-scale Hotel **Location:** I-65, exit 267, 0.7 mi s. 1795 Morris Ave 35068. Fax: 205/849-7373. **Facility:** 75 units. 72 one-bedroom standard units, some with whirlpools. 3 one-bedroom suites. 3 stories, interior corridors. *Bath:* combo or shower only. **Parking:** on-site, winter plug-ins. **Amenities:** video games (fee), high-speed Internet, voice mail, irons, hair dryers. *Some:* CD players, dual phone lines. **Pool(s):** heated indoor. **Leisure Activities:** whirlpool, limited exercise equipment. **Guest Services:** sundries, valet and coin laundry, wireless Internet. **Business Services:** meeting rooms, business center.

SOME UNITS

HAMPTON INN Book great rates at AAA.com Phone: 205/439-6700

All Year 1P: $116 2P: $116

Small-scale Hotel **Location:** I-65, exit 267, just e. 1716 Fulton Rd 35068. Fax: 205/439-6701. **Facility:** 65 one-bedroom standard units. 4 stories, interior corridors. *Bath:* combo or shower only. **Parking:** on-site. **Amenities:** high-speed Internet, voice mail, irons, hair dryers. **Pool(s):** small outdoor. **Business Services:** business center. **Cards:** AX, DC, DS, MC, VI.

SOME UNITS

ASK

HOLIDAY INN EXPRESS FULTONDALE Book at AAA.com Phone: 205/439-6300

Property failed to provide current rates

Small-scale Hotel **Location:** I-65, exit 267, just e. 1733 Fulton Rd 35068. Fax: 205/439-6301. **Facility:** 67 one-bedroom standard units, some with whirlpools. 3 stories, interior corridors. *Bath:* combo or shower only. **Parking:** on-site. **Amenities:** high-speed Internet, voice mail, irons, hair dryers. **Pool(s):** small outdoor. **Leisure Activities:** exercise room. **Business Services:** fax (fee).

SOME UNITS

GARDENDALE pop. 11,626

WHERE TO STAY

BEST WESTERN GARDENDALE Book great rates at AAA.com Phone: (205)631-1181

AAA SAVE

All Year 1P: $67-$155

Small-scale Hotel **Location:** I-65, exit 271, 0.6 mi w, then just s. 842 Thompson St 35071. Fax: 205/631-1066. **Facility:** 59 one-bedroom standard units, some with whirlpools. 3 stories, interior corridors. *Bath:* combo or shower only. **Parking:** on-site. **Amenities:** high-speed Internet, voice mail, irons, hair dryers. **Pool(s):** small outdoor. **Leisure Activities:** exercise room. **Business Services:** meeting rooms, business center. **Cards:** AX, DC, DS, MC, VI. **Free Special Amenities: expanded continental breakfast and high-speed Internet.**

SOME UNITS

MICROTEL INN & SUITES-BIRMINGHAM NORTH-GARDENDALE Phone: 205/631-6320

fyi

All Year 1P: $49-$89 2P: $59-$109 XP: $10 F17

Small-scale Hotel Too new to rate. **Location:** I-65, exit 271. 850 Odum Rd 35071. Fax: 205/631-6450. **Amenities:** 81 units, coffeemakers, microwaves, refrigerators, pool. **Cards:** AX, CB, DC, DS, MC, VI.

HOMEWOOD pop. 25,043 (See map and index starting on p. 212)

WHERE TO STAY

COMFORT INN-OXMOOR Book great rates at AAA.com Phone: (205)941-0990 37

AAA SAVE

4/1-7/31	1P: $67-$77	2P: $67-$77	XP: $10	F16
12/1-3/31 & 8/1-11/30	1P: $61-$71	2P: $61-$71	XP: $10	F16

Small-scale Hotel **Location:** I-65, exit 256 northbound; exit 256A southbound, 0.3 mi w. 195 Oxmoor Rd 35209. Fax: 205/941-1527. **Facility:** 153 units. 69 one- and 82 two-bedroom standard units. 2 one-bedroom suites. 2 stories (no elevator), exterior corridors. *Bath:* combo or shower only. **Parking:** on-site. **Amenities:** voice mail, irons, hair dryers. **Pool(s):** outdoor. **Leisure Activities:** exercise room. **Guest Services:** valet laundry, wireless Internet. **Business Services:** meeting rooms, fax (fee). **Cards:** AX, CB, DC, DS, JC, MC, VI. **Free Special Amenities: expanded continental breakfast and high-speed Internet.**

SOME UNITS

COURTYARD BY MARRIOTT Book great rates at AAA.com Phone: (205)879-0400 32

AAA SAVE

All Year 1P: $99-$229 2P: $99-$229

Small-scale Hotel **Location:** On SR 149, just e of jct US 31. Located across from the Brookwood Village Mall. 500 Shades Creek Pkwy 35209. Fax: 205/879-6324. **Facility:** 140 units. 126 one-bedroom standard units. 14 one-bedroom suites. 3 stories, interior corridors. *Bath:* combo or shower only. **Parking:** on-site. **Terms:** 3 day cancellation notice, [BP] meal plan available. **Amenities:** high-speed Internet, voice mail, irons, hair dryers. **Dining:** 6:30-10 am, Sat & Sun 7-11 am. **Pool(s):** outdoor. **Leisure Activities:** whirlpool, exercise room. **Guest Services:** sundries, valet and coin laundry. **Business Services:** meeting rooms, business center. **Cards:** AX, DC, DS, JC, MC, VI. **Free Special Amenities: newspaper and high-speed Internet.**

SOME UNITS

HAMPTON INN - LAKESHORE Book great rates at AAA.com Phone: 205/313-2060 41

Property failed to provide current rates

Small-scale Hotel **Location:** I-65, exit 256, just w. (30 Statefarm Pkwy, 35209). Fax: 205/313-2070. **Facility:** 97 one-bedroom standard units. 6 stories, interior corridors. *Bath:* combo or shower only. **Parking:** on-site. **Amenities:** high-speed Internet, dual phone lines, voice mail, irons, hair dryers. **Pool(s):** small outdoor. **Leisure Activities:** exercise room. **Guest Services:** valet and coin laundry. **Business Services:** meeting rooms, business center.

SOME UNITS

(See map and index starting on p. 212)

HILTON GARDEN INN BIRMINGHAM-LAKE SHORE *Book great rates at AAA.com* **Phone:** 205/314-0274 43

Small-scale Hotel

Property failed to provide current rates

Location: I-65, exit 255 (Lakeshore Pkwy), just w to Wildwood Cir, then n. 520 Wildwood Circle N 35209. Fax: 205/314-0275. **Facility:** 95 units. 90 one-bedroom standard units. 5 one-bedroom suites with whirlpools. 6 stories, interior corridors. *Bath:* combo or shower only. **Parking:** on-site. **Amenities:** video games (fee), high-speed Internet, dual phone lines, voice mail, irons, hair dryers. **Pool(s):** small heated indoor. **Leisure Activities:** whirlpool, exercise room. **Guest Services:** complimentary evening beverages: Wed, valet and coin laundry. **Business Services:** meeting rooms, business center.

SOME UNITS

LA QUINTA INN & SUITES BIRMINGHAM (HOMEWOOD) *Book great rates at AAA.com* **Phone:** (205)290-0150 39

Small-scale Hotel

All Year [ECP] 1P: $99-$115 2P: $109-$125 XP: $10 F18

Location: I-65, exit 255, 0.9 mi on northwest frontage road. 60 State Farm Pkwy 35209. Fax: 205/290-0850. **Facility:** 129 units. 121 one-bedroom standard units. 8 one-bedroom suites ($115-$135). 5 stories, interior corridors. *Bath:* combo or shower only. **Parking:** on-site. **Terms:** small pets only. **Amenities:** video games (fee), high-speed Internet, dual phone lines, voice mail, irons, hair dryers. **Pool(s):** heated outdoor. **Leisure Activities:** whirlpool, exercise room. **Guest Services:** valet and coin laundry. **Business Services:** meeting rooms, fax (fee). **Cards:** AX, CB, DC, DS, MC, VI.

SOME UNITS

ASK

OXMOOR INN **Phone:** (205)942-2041 36

Small-scale Hotel

All Year 1P: $62-$159 XP: $10 F

Location: I-65, exit 256A, just w. 260 Oxmoor Rd 35209. Fax: 205/942-6183. **Facility:** 192 units. 191 one-bedroom standard units. 1 one-bedroom suite. 4 stories, interior corridors. *Bath:* combo or shower only. **Parking:** on-site. **Terms:** 7 day cancellation notice. **Amenities:** voice mail, irons, hair dryers. **Pool(s):** outdoor. **Leisure Activities:** limited exercise equipment. **Guest Services:** valet laundry. **Business Services:** meeting rooms, business center. **Cards:** AX, DS, MC, VI.

SOME UNITS

ASK

RAMADA INN *Book great rates at AAA.com* **Phone:** (205)916-0464 35

AAA SAVE

Small-scale Hotel

All Year [ECP] 1P: $59-$199 XP: $5 F18

Location: I-65, exit 256 northbound; exit 256A southbound, just w. 226 Summit Pkwy 35209. Fax: 205/916-0298. **Facility:** 115 one-bedroom standard units. 5 stories, interior corridors. **Parking:** on-site. **Terms:** small pets only ($25 fee). **Amenities:** voice mail, irons, hair dryers. **Pool(s):** small outdoor. **Guest Services:** valet and coin laundry, wireless Internet. **Business Services:** meeting rooms, business center. **Cards:** AX, CB, DC, DS, JC, MC, VI. **Free Special Amenities: expanded continental breakfast and high-speed Internet.**

SOME UNITS

FEE

RED ROOF INN *Book at AAA.com* **Phone:** 205/942-9414 34

Motel

Property failed to provide current rates

Location: I-65, exit 256 northbound; exit 256A southbound, just nw. 151 Vulcan Rd 35209. Fax: 205/942-9499. **Facility:** 96 one-bedroom standard units. 2-3 stories (no elevator), exterior corridors. **Parking:** on-site. **Terms:** small pets only. **Amenities:** video games (fee), voice mail. **Business Services:** fax (fee).

SOME UNITS

RESIDENCE INN BY MARRIOTT *Book great rates at AAA.com* **Phone:** (205)943-0044 38

AAA SAVE

Small-scale Hotel

All Year 1P: $108-$189

Location: I-65, exit 255, 1 mi on northwest frontage road. 50 State Farm Pkwy 35209. Fax: 205/943-0668. **Facility:** 120 units. 96 one- and 24 two-bedroom standard units with kitchens. 3 stories, interior corridors. *Bath:* combo or shower only. **Parking:** on-site. **Terms:** cancellation fee imposed, [BP] meal plan available, pets ($75 fee). **Amenities:** high-speed Internet, voice mail, irons, hair dryers. **Pool(s):** heated outdoor. **Leisure Activities:** whirlpool, exercise room, sports court. **Guest Services:** complimentary evening beverages, valet and coin laundry. **Business Services:** meeting rooms, fax (fee). **Cards:** AX, DC, DS, MC, VI. **Free Special Amenities: full breakfast and high-speed Internet.**

SOME UNITS

FEE

STUDIOPLUS *Book at AAA.com* **Phone:** 205/290-0102 40

Motel

Property failed to provide current rates

Location: I-65, exit 256, just w. 40 Statefarm Pkwy 35209. Fax: 205/912-2092. **Facility:** 71 one-bedroom standard units with kitchens. 3 stories (no elevator), interior corridors. *Bath:* combo or shower only. **Parking:** on-site. **Terms:** office hours 7 am-11 pm, pets ($25 fee). **Amenities:** voice mail, irons, hair dryers. **Pool(s):** small outdoor. **Guest Services:** coin laundry, wireless Internet. **Business Services:** fax (fee).

SOME UNITS

FEE

SUPER 8 MOTEL *Book at AAA.com* **Phone:** (205)945-9888 33

Small-scale Hotel

All Year 1P: $44-$63 2P: $44-$63 XP: $5 F12

Location: I-65, exit 256 northbound; exit 256A southbound, just nw. 140 Vulcan Rd 35209. Fax: 205/945-9928. **Facility:** 96 one-bedroom standard units. 3 stories (no elevator), interior corridors. **Parking:** on-site. **Terms:** weekly rates available, [ECP] meal plan available, small pets only ($5 extra charge). **Amenities:** voice mail. *Some:* irons, hair dryers. **Leisure Activities:** exercise room. **Guest Services:** coin laundry. **Business Services:** fax (fee). **Cards:** AX, CB, DC, DS, JC, MC, VI.

SOME UNITS

ASK

FEE

(See map and index starting on p. 212)

TOWNEPLACE SUITES BY MARRIOTT Book great rates at AAA.com **Phone:** 205/943-0114 42

AAA SAVE

Small-scale Hotel

All Year [CP] 1P: $149-$159 2P: $149-$159

Location: I-65, exit 255, 0.6 mi w, then just n. Located adjacent to Lowes. 500 Wildwood Cir 35209. Fax: 205/943-0115. **Facility:** 127 units. 89 one-bedroom standard units with kitchens. 6 one- and 32 two-bedroom suites with kitchens. 4 stories, interior corridors. *Bath:* combo or shower only. **Parking:** on-site. **Terms:** pets ($75 deposit). **Amenities:** high-speed Internet, voice mail, irons, hair dryers. **Pool(s):** small outdoor. **Leisure Activities:** exercise room. **Guest Services:** valet and coin laundry. **Business Services:** PC, fax. **Cards:** AX, CB, DC, DS, JC, MC, VI. **Free Special Amenities: high-speed Internet.**

FEE SOME UNITS

WHERE TO DINE

ACAPULCO BAR AND GRILL **Lunch:** $6-$12 **Dinner:** $7-$13 **Phone:** 205/941-1183 41

Mexican

Location: I-65, exit 256A, just se. 430 Green Springs Hwy 35209. **Hours:** 11 am-9:30 pm, Fri-10:30 pm, Sat-10 pm, Sun 11:30 am-9 pm. Closed major holidays. **Features:** Happy hour, lunch specials and quick service are hallmarks of this spot. Freshly made chips and salsa prime the palate for traditional Mexican favorites or something a little different, such as chicken soup. Cocktails. **Parking:** on-site. **Cards:** AX, MC, VI.

BRIO TUSCAN GRILLE **Lunch:** $10-$15 **Dinner:** $11-$22 **Phone:** 205/879-9177 39

Italian

Location: US 280, w on Shades Creek Pkwy, just s; in Brookwood Village Mall. 591 Brookwood Village 35209. **Hours:** 11 am-10 pm, Fri & Sat-11 pm, Sun 10:30 am-10 pm. Closed: 11/22, 12/25. **Reservations:** accepted. **Features:** The restaurant's cuisine, including many traditional and creative dishes, takes a cue from Tuscany. A large, open dining room and extensive menu contribute to a comfortable and sophisticated dining experience. The service style is casual, and the staff is pleasant and attentive. Dressy casual; cocktails. **Parking:** on-site and valet. **Cards:** AX, DS, MC, VI.

COPPER GRILL LOBSTER & STEAK HOUSE **Dinner:** $24-$42 **Phone:** 205/414-1411 38

Steak & Seafood

Location: Just e of US 31; just w of US 280; in Brookwood Village Mall. 595 Brookwood Village 35209. **Hours:** 5:30 pm-10 pm, Fri & Sat 5 pm-11 pm, Sun 5 pm-10 pm. **Reservations:** suggested. **Features:** Although lobster and steak get top billing, they don't say it all. Diners have a broad choice of Certified Angus beef and fresh, super-large lobsters, but the veal chop and lamb chops also entice. Lending to the soothing atmosphere are twinkling lights that resemble stars. Dressy casual; cocktails. **Parking:** on-site and valet. **Cards:** MC, VI.

DAVE'S PIZZA **Lunch:** $6-$30 **Dinner:** $6-$30 **Phone:** 205/871-3283 34

Pizza

Location: Jct US 31, just w. 1819 29th Ave S 35209. **Hours:** 11 am-10 pm, Sun from 5 pm. Closed: 12/25. **Features:** Gourmet pizza and sandwiches make up the menu at the family-friendly hot spot, a local favorite. During colder months, the dining room is enclosed and heated, but it becomes an open-air spot in the summer. Heaters and warmed blankets allow for year-round al fresco dining on the patio. Casual dress. **Parking:** street. **Cards:** MC, VI.

DEMETRI'S B.B.Q. **Lunch:** $5-$19 **Dinner:** $5-$19 **Phone:** 205/871-1581 33

Barbecue

Location: US 31 and 28th Ave S, just w. 1901 28th Ave S 35209. **Hours:** 6 am-8:30 pm. Closed major holidays; also Sun. **Features:** Known for great barbecue pulled pork, chicken and tender and moist spare ribs, this place also serves a wonderful breakfast of omelets, hot cakes and French toast that the staff describes as "unimaginably great." Completing the menu are numerous salads and homemade pies. Casual dress. **Parking:** on-site. **Cards:** AX, MC, VI.

DE VINCI'S **Lunch:** $6-$16 **Dinner:** $10-$16 **Phone:** 205/879-1455 31

Italian

Location: US 31 and Rosedale Dr, just w, then just s. 2707 18th St S 35209. **Hours:** 11 am-11 pm. Closed: 11/22, 12/25 & Easter. **Features:** The family-operated eatery's owner takes pride in providing well-prepared dishes, including calzones, pizza, pasta and traditional Italian specialties. The small dining rooms have a residential feel. Stuffed olives make a good starter course. Casual dress; beer & wine only. **Parking:** on-site. **Cards:** AX, DS, MC, VI.

FRANKLIN'S HOMEWOOD GOURMET **Lunch:** $6-$10 **Dinner:** $6-$10 **Phone:** 205/871-1620 32

Deli/Subs Sandwiches

Location: Jct US 31 and 28th Ave S, just w. 1919 28th Ave S 35209. **Hours:** 10:30 am-7 pm, Sat-5 pm. Closed major holidays; also Sun. **Features:** Chef Franklin Biggs brings gourmet style to specialty deli-style sandwiches, as well as pasta, poultry, seafood and meat dishes. Signature items include baby blue salad and Carlene's plate, which adds barbecue salmon to the salad. Also worth consideration are turkey and cranberry roll-ups, Santa Fe beef with pepper jack, pesto chicken salad and the beef and blue sandwich. Casual dress. **Parking:** on-site. **Cards:** AX, DS, MC, VI.

GIAN MARCO'S **Lunch:** $10-$20 **Dinner:** $15-$25 **Phone:** 205/871-9622 45

Italian

Location: I-65, exit 256B, just s to Green Springs Hwy, just e to Carr Ave, then 0.4 mi e. 721 Broadway St 35209. **Hours:** 5 pm-10 pm, Wed-Fri also 11 am-2 pm. Closed major holidays; also Sun. **Reservations:** suggested. **Features:** Tuscan influences weave throughout the menu at the lively and ever-so-popular neighborhood restaurant. This is the place to be for those who can secure a reservation. Dressy casual; cocktails. **Parking:** on-site. **Cards:** MC, VI.

NABEEL'S CAFE AND TAVERNA **Lunch:** $5-$17 **Dinner:** $5-$17 **Phone:** 205/879-9292 36

Greek

Location: Jct Central Ave and Oxmoor Rd. 1706 Oxmoor Rd 35209. **Hours:** 9:30 am-9:30 pm. Closed major holidays; also Sun. **Reservations:** accepted. **Features:** Greek food, including pita sandwiches, cold plates and salads, is the primary focus at the cafe, which has a full bar and grocery mart on site. The strong entree selection lists moussaka, pastitsio and spanakopita. Rounding out the menu are baklava and kataifi. Casual dress; cocktails. **Parking:** street. **Cards:** AX, CB, DC, DS, JC, MC, VI.

(See map and index starting on p. 212)

NEW YORK PIZZA Lunch: $7-$15 Dinner: $7-$15 Phone: 205/871-4000 (37)

Pizza

Location: I-65, exit 256 A, 1 mi ne; in Edgewood Shopping Center. 1010 Oxmoor Rd 35209. **Hours:** 11 am-9:30 pm, Fri & Sat-10 pm, Sun 4 pm-9:30 pm. Closed major holidays. **Features:** The local pizzeria bakes made-to-order pizzas, calzones and sandwiches. Families can relax and share a meal at a great price. Casual dress; beer only. **Parking:** on-site. **Cards:** MC, VI.

O' CARR'S Lunch: $5-$8 Phone: 205/879-2196 (35)

Deli/Subs Sandwiches

Location: US 31, just w on 29th Ave S, then just s. 2909 18th St S 35209. **Hours:** 10 am-4 pm. Closed major holidays; also Sun & Mon. **Features:** Patrons will find a lengthy list of salads and sandwiches at the popular lunch spot. Homemade cheesecake is a must. Casual dress. **Parking:** on-site.

THE ORIGINAL STEAKHOUSE & SPORTS THEATER Lunch: $7-$19 Dinner: $12-$19 Phone: 205/944-1011 (40)

Steak House

Location: I-65, exit 256, just e, then just s. 150 Green Springs Hwy 35209. **Hours:** 11 am-11 pm, Fri & Sat-midnight, Sun-10 pm. Closed: 11/22, 12/24, 12/25. **Features:** The restaurant specializes in grilled steaks but also serves other standard selections. Television sets line the ceiling, and the back wall comprises enormous-screen TVs that show sports programming magnified to movie proportions. Brick walls and woods help give the dining room its steakhouse look. Casual dress; cocktails. **Parking:** on-site. **Cards:** AX, DS, MC, VI.

PAW PAW PATCH Lunch: $4-$7 Dinner: $4-$7 Phone: 205/942-6640 (43)

American

Location: I-65, exit 256A, just e. 410 Green Springs Hwy 35209. **Hours:** 11 am-8 pm. Closed major holidays; also Sat & Sun. **Features:** The fare centers on basic country cooking: meatloaf, fried chicken, string beans, black-eyed peas, cheesy macaroni and cheese and desserts of cobbler or warm banana pudding. Portions are large, and tasty rolls are part of the tastes-like-home food. Casual dress. **Parking:** on-site. **Cards:** DS, MC, VI.

PHO QUE HUONG Lunch: $6-$10 Dinner: $6-$10 Phone: 205/942-5400 (44)

Vietnamese

Location: I-65, exit 255, 0.3 mi e to Green Springs Hwy, then just s. 430 Green Springs Hwy, Suite 15 35209. **Hours:** 11 am-3 & 5-10 pm, Sun-9 pm. Closed major holidays. **Features:** The modestly appointed Vietnamese eatery specializes in pho (pronounced "fuh"), chicken- or beef-based broths with accompanying meat, bean sprouts, basil, jalapenos and lime. Offerings are aromatic, healthy and satisfying. Other options also find their way onto the menu. Casual dress. **Parking:** on-site. **Cards:** AX, DS, MC, VI.

THE RESTAURANT AT CULINARD Lunch: $15 Dinner: $35 Phone: 205/271-8228 (42)

Continental

Location: I-65, exit 256A, just w on Oxmoor Rd, then just n. 195 Vulcan Rd 35209. **Hours:** 11 am-1 & 6-9 pm. **Features:** The fine-dining establishment offers some of the best food to be found in the area. Senior-level chefs from the Culinary Institute of Virginia College show off their talent in such choices as grilled buffalo meatloaf, venison osso buco with braised mirepoix, grilled hanger steak au poivre with eggplant caviar and Asian glazed salmon with sesame-broccoli fried rice. The delightful four-course meal is reasonably priced. Dressy casual; cocktails. **Parking:** on-site. **Cards:** MC, VI.

SAN SAN TRIO Lunch: $6-$16 Dinner: $6-$21 Phone: 205/942-7099 (46)

Sushi

Location: I-65, exit 255 (Lakeshore Dr), 0.8 mi w. 227 Lakeshore Pkwy 35209. **Hours:** 11 am-3 & 4:30-10 pm, Fri 4:30 pm-11 pm, Sat noon-11 pm, Sun noon-10 pm. Closed: 11/22, 12/25. **Reservations:** accepted. **Features:** Japanese and French influences set the restaurant apart from the rest of the crowd. Beautiful artistic displays of sushi and sashimi and tenderloins of beef and salmon tartare are just the beginning. Among tempting entrees are grilled rack of lamb, Chilean sea bass and grilled lobster. Casual dress; beer only. **Parking:** on-site. **Cards:** AX, DS, MC, VI.

HOOVER pop. 62,742 (See map and index starting on p. 212)

WHERE TO STAY

AMERISUITES (BIRMINGHAM/RIVERCHASE) Book great rates at AAA.com Phone: (205)988-8444 (53)

SAVE

Small-scale Hotel

All Year 1P: $99-$205 2P: $99-$205 XP: $10 F17

Location: I-459, exit 13, 0.5 mi s on US 31, then 0.8 mi w on SR 150. 2980 John Hawkins Pkwy 35244. Fax: 205/988-8407. **Facility:** 128 one-bedroom standard units. 6 stories, interior corridors. *Bath:* combo or shower only. **Parking:** on-site. **Terms:** cancellation fee imposed, small pets only ($10 extra charge). **Amenities:** voice mail, irons, hair dryers. *Fee:* video games, safes. **Pool(s):** heated outdoor. **Leisure Activities:** exercise room. **Guest Services:** valet and coin laundry, wireless Internet. **Business Services:** meeting rooms, fax (fee). **Cards:** AX, CB, DC, DS, JC, MC, VI. **Free Special Amenities: expanded continental breakfast and high-speed Internet.**

SOME UNITS

FEE

BEST WESTERN RIVERCHASE INN Book great rates at AAA.com Phone: (205)985-7500 (51)

SAVE

Small-scale Hotel

All Year [ECP] 1P: $69-$140 2P: $69-$140

Location: I-459, exit 13, 0.5 mi s on US 31, then 0.4 mi w on SR 150. 1800 Riverchase Dr 35244. Fax: 205/733-8122. **Facility:** 137 one-bedroom standard units. 2 stories (no elevator), exterior corridors. **Parking:** on-site. **Terms:** check-in 4 pm. **Amenities:** video games (fee), voice mail, irons, hair dryers. *Some:* high-speed Internet. **Pool(s):** outdoor. **Leisure Activities:** limited exercise equipment. **Guest Services:** complimentary and valet laundry, area transportation-within 3 mi. **Business Services:** business center. **Cards:** AX, CB, DC, DS, MC, VI. **Free Special Amenities: expanded continental breakfast and high-speed Internet.**

SOME UNITS

(See map and index starting on p. 212)

COURTYARD BY MARRIOTT-HOOVER *Book great rates at AAA.com* **Phone:** (205)988-5000 52

SAVE Small-scale Hotel

All Year 1P: $164 2P: $164

Location: I-459, exit 13B, 1 mi s on US 31. 1824 Montgomery Hwy S 35244. Fax: 205/988-4659. **Facility:** 153 units. 140 one-bedroom standard units. 13 one-bedroom suites. 3 stories, interior corridors. *Bath:* combo or shower only. **Parking:** on-site. **Terms:** package plans. **Amenities:** high-speed Internet, voice mail, irons, hair dryers. **Dining:** 6:30-10 am, Sat & Sun 7-11 am. **Pool(s):** outdoor. **Leisure Activities:** whirlpool, exercise room. **Guest Services:** valet and coin laundry. **Business Services:** meeting rooms, business center. **Cards:** AX, CB, DC, DS, JC, MC, VI. **Free Special Amenities: high-speed Internet.**

SOME UNITS

LA QUINTA INN & SUITES BIRMINGHAM (HOOVER/RIVERCHASE) *Book great rates at AAA.com* **Phone:** (205)403-0096 54

Small-scale Hotel

All Year [ECP] 1P: $99-$115 2P: $109-$125 XP: $10 F18

Location: I-65, exit 247 (Valleydale Rd), just w. 120 Riverchase Pkwy E 35244. Fax: 205/403-0380. **Facility:** 133 units. 129 one-bedroom standard units. 4 one-bedroom suites ($115-$135). 4 stories, interior corridors. *Bath:* combo or shower only. **Parking:** on-site. **Terms:** package plans, small pets only. **Amenities:** video games (fee), high-speed Internet, dual phone lines, voice mail, irons, hair dryers. **Pool(s):** heated outdoor. **Leisure Activities:** whirlpool, exercise room. **Guest Services:** valet and coin laundry. **Business Services:** meeting rooms, fax (fee). **Cards:** AX, CB, DC, DS, MC, VI.

SOME UNITS

ASK

RENAISSANCE ROSS BRIDGE GOLF RESORT & SPA *Book great rates at AAA.com* **Phone:** 205/916-7677 49

Large-scale Hotel

Property failed to provide current rates

Location: I-459, exit 10, 1.6 mi w on SR 150, 4 mi n on Ross Bridge Pkwy, then just w. 4000 Grand Ave 35216. Fax: 205/949-3031. **Facility:** Escape the hustle and bustle of the city and retreat to the rolling hills of Alabama. Here, guests can enjoy fine dining and modern spa treatments. This is a very unique setting that will not disappoint; don't miss the resident bagpiper at sundown. Smoke free premises. 259 units. 251 one-bedroom standard units. 8 one-bedroom suites with kitchens. 6 stories, interior corridors. *Bath:* combo or shower only. **Parking:** valet and street. **Terms:** check-in 4 pm. **Amenities:** CD players, dual phone lines, voice mail, safes, irons, hair dryers. *Fee:* video games, high-speed Internet. **Dining:** Brock's, see separate listing. **Pool(s):** heated outdoor, heated indoor. **Leisure Activities:** saunas, whirlpools, waterslide, jogging, exercise room, spa. *Fee:* golf-18 holes. **Guest Services:** gift shop, valet laundry, wireless Internet. **Business Services:** conference facilities, business center. ***(See color ad p 200)***

SOME UNITS

FEE

THE WYNFREY HOTEL *Book great rates at AAA.com* **Phone:** (205)987-1600 50

SAVE Large-scale Hotel

All Year 1P: $169-$239 2P: $169-$239 XP: $20 F18

Location: I-459, exit 13 (US 31), adjacent to the Riverchase Galleria. 1000 Riverchase Galleria 35244. Fax: 205/988-4597. **Facility:** Contributing to this hotel's aura of luxury are an attentive staff, well-appointed rooms and an upscale restaurant. 329 units. 327 one-bedroom standard units. 2 one-bedroom suites with whirlpools. 14 stories, interior corridors. *Bath:* combo or shower only. **Parking:** on-site (fee) and valet. **Terms:** cancellation fee imposed, package plans, pets ($250 deposit). **Amenities:** dual phone lines, voice mail, honor bars, irons, hair dryers. *Fee:* video games, high-speed Internet. *Some:* CD players, safes. **Dining:** 2 restaurants, 6 am-10 pm, cocktails, also, Shula's Steak House, see separate listing, entertainment. **Pool(s):** outdoor. **Leisure Activities:** saunas, whirlpool, exercise room. **Guest Services:** valet laundry, area transportation-within 3 mi, wireless Internet. **Business Services:** conference facilities, business center. **Cards:** AX, CB, DC, DS, MC, VI. **Free Special Amenities: newspaper.** Affiliated with A Preferred Hotel. ***(See color ad p 225)***

SOME UNITS

VCR

FEE

WHERE TO DINE

BROCK'S **Lunch:** $10-$15 **Dinner:** $18-$35 **Phone:** 205/949-3051 68

Mediterranean

Location: I-459, exit 10, 1.6 mi w on SR 150, 4 mi n on Ross Bridge Pkwy, then just w; in Renaissance Ross Bridge Golf Resort & Spa. 4000 Grand Ave 35216. **Hours:** 6:30-10:30 am, 11:30-2 & 5-10 pm, Fri-11 pm, Sat 6:30 am-10:30 & 5-10 pm. **Reservations:** suggested. **Features:** Seafood, beef and poultry are prepared with Mediterranean flair in the subdued, romantic atmosphere. Men must wear jackets, and jeans and T-shirts are not permitted. Dressy casual; cocktails. **Parking:** on-site and valet. **Cards:** AX, DS, MC, VI.

CAJUN STEAMER BAR AND GRILL **Lunch:** $8-$20 **Dinner:** $8-$20 **Phone:** 205/985-7785 76

Cajun

Location: I-459, exit Galleria, just e; in Patton Creek Shopping Center. 180 Main St, Suite 200 35244. **Hours:** 11 am-10 pm, Fri & Sat-11 pm, Sun-9 pm. Closed major holidays. **Features:** Guests can take a seat on the balcony or inside the air-conditioned dining area. Either way, this place evokes the feel of the Big Easy. Crescent City food is whipped up in the Magic City style. Casual dress; cocktails. **Parking:** on-site. **Cards:** MC, VI.

CAMBRIDGE COFFEE **Lunch:** $4-$6 **Dinner:** $4-$6 **Phone:** 205/988-3838 73

Coffee/Espresso

Location: I-459, exit 13A; in Patton Creek Shopping Center. 160 Main St 35244. **Hours:** 7 am-10 pm, Fri & Sat-11 pm, Sun from 8 am. Closed: 11/22, 12/25 & Easter. **Features:** Relax, surf the net and sip a cup of joe; live music makes this a happening place after work. Casual dress; beer only. **Parking:** on-site. **Cards:** AX, DS, MC, VI.

COSTA'S MEDITERRANEAN CAFE **Lunch:** $5-$19 **Dinner:** $8-$20 **Phone:** 205/978-1603 69

Mediterranean

Location: I-65, exit 252, just s to Lorna Rd, then 1.5 mi se. 3443 Lorna Rd 35216. **Hours:** 11 am-9 pm, Fri-10 pm, Sun noon-10 pm. Closed: 11/22, 12/25. **Features:** The popular Greek and Italian restaurant dishes up Mediterranean standards in huge portions. Fresh warm garlic loaves accompany each entree. Among Italian offerings are baked ziti, baked lasagna and veal parmigiana, while Greek selections range from moussaka and pastitsio to preparations of lamb, chicken and pork. Homemade sauces are incomparable. Casual dress; cocktails. **Parking:** on-site. **Cards:** MC, VI.

(See map and index starting on p. 212)

FIREBIRDS ROCKY MOUNTAIN GRILL **Lunch:** $7-$14 **Dinner:** $12-$24 **Phone:** 205/733-2002 (75)

Location: I-459, exit 13A, just s; in Patton Creek Shopping Center. 191 Main St 35244. **Hours:** 11 am-10 pm, Fri & Sat-11 pm. Closed major holidays. **Features:** Casual dress; cocktails. **Parking:** on-site. **Cards:** AX, DS, MC, VI.

THE FISH MARKET **Lunch:** $6-$11 **Dinner:** $9-$18 **Phone:** 205/823-3474 (70)

Seafood

Location: I-65, exit 252 (Montgomery Hwy S), 1.4 mi s. 1681 Montgomery Hwy 35216. **Hours:** 10 am-9 pm, Fri & Sat-10 pm, Sun 10:30 am-8 pm. **Features:** Fresh fish is the promise at this spot, which touts the motto: "If it's not fresh, it won't be sold." The walls in the large dining room display an ocean mural and some mounted fish. Fish selections are plentiful, but those who prefer land-based fare also have a range of choices. Casual dress; cocktails. **Parking:** on-site. **Cards:** AX, DS, MC, VI.

FULL MOON BAR-B-QUE **Lunch:** $4-$12 **Dinner:** $6-$16 **Phone:** 205/822-6666 (67)

Barbecue

Location: I-65, exit 252, 1.2 mi s on US 31 S. 2000 Patton Chapel Rd 35216. **Hours:** 10 am-9 pm, Fri & Sat-10 pm. Closed major holidays; also Sun. **Features:** Known as Alabama's best little pork house and famous for their half-moon cookies, this chain found throughout the Birmingham area offers barbecue ribs, pork and chicken, slow-cooked over real hickory wood in brick fire pits. Casual dress; beer only. **Parking:** on-site. **Cards:** AX, DS, MC, VI.

GUADALAJARA RESTAURANT **Lunch:** $5-$12 **Dinner:** $7-$15 **Phone:** 205/823-9549 (71)

Mexican

Location: I-459, exit 13, just n on US 31; in Centre at Riverchase. 1694 Montgomery Hwy 35216. **Hours:** 11 am-9:30 pm, Fri-10:30 pm, Sat-10 pm. Closed major holidays. **Features:** Seating is plentiful at this spot, where the hot, fresh chips and salsa keep coming. Yummy offerings, including kids' choices, line the menu. Casual dress; cocktails. **Parking:** on-site. **Cards:** AX, DS, MC, VI.

LA DOLCE VITA CUCINA ITALIANA **Dinner:** $12-$25 **Phone:** 205/985-2909 (77)

Italian

Location: I-459, exit 13B, 1 mi s on US 31. 1851 Montgomery Hwy 35244. **Hours:** 5 pm-9 pm, Fri & Sat-10 pm. Closed major holidays. **Features:** In a shopping plaza, the restaurant serves traditional Italian favorites, such as meat-filled ravioli, veal scaloppine and calamari. An intimate atmosphere makes for a pleasurable dining experience. Casual dress; cocktails. **Parking:** on-site. **Cards:** AX, DS, MC, VI.

THE OLIVE TREE **Lunch:** $7-$9 **Dinner:** $9-$20 **Phone:** 205/823-5825 (66)

Greek

Location: I-65, exit 252 southbound, just s on Lorna Rd, then just e; exit northbound, just s on US 31, then se. 2030 Little Valley Rd 35216. **Hours:** 11 am-midnight, Sat 5 pm-10 pm. Closed major holidays; also Mon. **Reservations:** accepted. **Features:** Home-style Greek and Southern dishes come together at the mountaintop restaurant. Casual dress; cocktails. **Parking:** on-site. **Cards:** AX, DS, MC, VI.

QDOBA MEXICAN GRILL **Lunch:** $5-$8 **Dinner:** $5-$8 **Phone:** 205/987-7108 (74)

Mexican

Location: I-459, exit 13A; in Patton Creek Shopping Center. 160 Main St, Suite 140 35244. **Hours:** 11 am-7 pm. Closed major holidays. **Features:** You can have your burrito prepared any way you like it at this quick-serve eatery. Casual dress. **Parking:** on-site. **Cards:** AX, DS, MC, VI.

SHULA'S STEAK HOUSE **Dinner:** $25-$55 **Phone:** 205/987-1600 (72)

Steak & Seafood

Location: I-459, exit 13 (US 31), adjacent to the Riverchase Galleria; in The Wynfrey Hotel. 1000 Riverchase Galleria 35244. **Hours:** 5:30 pm-10 pm, Sun-9 pm. Closed major holidays. **Reservations:** suggested. **Features:** Boasting an upscale atmosphere and excellent American cuisine, the fine dining establishment is the ideal setting for a special, intimate dinner. Its newly renovated dining rooms offer an elegant setting for a truly memorable meal. Dressy casual; cocktails. **Parking:** on-site and valet. **Cards:** AX, DC, DS, MC, VI.

TIN ROOF BBQ **Lunch:** $4-$17 **Dinner:** $4-$17 **Phone:** 205/987-4002 (78)

Barbecue

Location: I-65, exit 247 (Valleydale Rd), 0.5 mi e; in Southlake Village Shopping Center. 4524 Southlake Pkwy, Suite 20 35244. **Hours:** 11 am-8 pm, Fri & Sat-9 pm. Closed: 11/22, 12/25 & Easter; also Sun. **Features:** This locally popular barbecue joint with an eclectic decor serves huge portions of tasty food. For starters, try the brunswick stew, then move on to the slow cooked ribs, complete with four types of housemade sauce. Be sure to save room for a slice of their famous icebox pie. Casual dress; cocktails. **Parking:** on-site. **Cards:** AX, DS, MC, VI.

IRONDALE pop. 9,813 (See map and index starting on p. 212)

WHERE TO STAY

HAMPTON INN BIRMINGHAM EAST/IRONDALE *Book great rates at AAA.com* **Phone:** (205)956-4100 (29)

Motel

All Year [ECP] 1P: $89-$98 2P: $94-$102

Location: I-20, exit 133, just e. 3910 Kilgore Memorial Dr 35210. Fax: 205/956-0906. **Facility:** 70 one-bedroom standard units. 2 stories, exterior corridors. **Parking:** on-site. **Amenities:** high-speed Internet, voice mail, irons, hair dryers. **Pool(s):** outdoor. **Guest Services:** valet laundry. **Business Services:** meeting rooms, PC, fax. **Cards:** AX, CB, DC, DS, JC, MC, VI.

SOME UNITS

(See map and index starting on p. 212)

HOLIDAY INN EXPRESS INN AND SUITES BIRMINGHAM EAST Book at AAA.com Phone: (205)957-0555 28

Small-scale Hotel

All Year 1P: $77-$250 2P: $109-$250 XP: $8 F

Location: I-20, exit 133, just sw on Crescent, then just s. 811 Old Grants Mill Rd 35210. Fax: 205/957-0559. **Facility:** 100 one-bedroom standard units. 4 stories, interior corridors. *Bath:* combo or shower only. **Parking:** on-site. **Terms:** [ECP] meal plan available, package plans. **Amenities:** high-speed Internet, dual phone lines, voice mail; irons, hair dryers. **Pool(s):** outdoor. **Leisure Activities:** exercise room. **Guest Services:** complimentary evening beverages: Tues, Wed & 7/1-7/31, valet and coin laundry, wireless Internet. **Business Services:** meeting rooms, business center. **Cards:** AX, DC, DS, MC, VI.

SOME UNITS

WHERE TO DINE

HAMBURGER HEAVEN Lunch: $5-$8 Dinner: $5-$8 Phone: 205/951-3570 28

American

Location: I-20, exit 132B, just s on Montevallo Rd, then 0.5 mi e. 1703 Crestwood Blvd 35210. **Hours:** 10 am-9 pm. Closed major holidays. **Features:** The restaurant's name says it all. Birmingham loves this burger joint, and newcomers will, too. Casual dress. **Parking:** on-site.

IRONDALE CAFE Lunch: $5-$8 Dinner: $5-$9 Phone: 205/956-5258 27

American

Location: I-20, exit 133, 0.7 mi nw on 20th St S. 1906 1st Ave N 35210. **Hours:** 10:45 am-2:30 & 4:30-7:30 pm, Sun-2:30 pm; Sat 10:45 am-2:30 pm 5/1-8/31. Closed major holidays; also Sat 9/1-4/30. **Features:** Do not miss the original whistle stop cafe, famous for its good home cooking and known for having an inspirational part in the book and movie "Fried Green Tomatoes." The food is as southern as its gets and the price is right. Casual dress. **Parking:** on-site. **Cards:** AX, MC, VI.

LEEDS pop. 10,455

WHERE TO STAY

COMFORT INN & SUITES Book great rates at AAA.com Phone: (205)640-6600

Small-scale Hotel

All Year 1P: $80-$200 2P: $80-$200 XP: $5 F13

Location: I-20, exit 144A westbound; exit 144B eastbound, just ne. 1951 Village Dr 35094. Fax: 205/640-6600. **Facility:** 45 one-bedroom standard units, some with whirlpools. 2 stories (no elevator), interior corridors. **Parking:** on-site. **Terms:** 3 night minimum stay - seasonal, [CP] meal plan available. **Amenities:** high-speed Internet, irons, hair dryers. **Pool(s):** outdoor. **Leisure Activities:** exercise room. **Business Services:** meeting rooms, fax (fee). **Cards:** AX, CB, DC, DS, MC, VI. **Free Special Amenities: continental breakfast and high-speed Internet.**

SOME UNITS

DAYS INN OF LEEDS Book great rates at AAA.com Phone: (205)699-9833

Motel

All Year 1P: $59-$200 2P: $59-$200 XP: $5 F13

Location: I-20, exit 144A eastbound; exit 144B westbound, just s. 1838 Ashville Rd 35094. **Facility:** 52 one-bedroom standard units, some with whirlpools. 2 stories (no elevator), exterior corridors. **Parking:** on-site. **Terms:** 3 night minimum stay - seasonal, [CP] meal plan available, small pets only ($7 extra charge). **Amenities:** hair dryers. *Some:* irons. **Pool(s):** outdoor. **Guest Services:** coin laundry. **Business Services:** fax (fee). **Cards:** AX, CB, DC, DS, MC, VI. **Free Special Amenities: continental breakfast and high-speed Internet.**

SOME UNITS

FEE

MCCALLA (See map and index starting on p. 212)

WHERE TO DINE

MOMMA'S ICE CREAM & COFFEE INC Lunch: $3-$6 Dinner: $3-$6 Phone: 205/281-9481 90

American

Location: I-459, exit 1, just s; in Shops at Letson Farms. 4761 Eastern Valley Rd 35111. **Hours:** 7 am-9 pm, Sun from 1 pm. Closed major holidays. **Features:** Patrons visit to unwind and let Momma treat them to something sweet. Soups, sandwiches, freshly made desserts, hot coffee and cool ice cream all take off the edge at the cute little cafe. Casual dress. **Parking:** on-site. **Cards:** MC, VI.

MOODY pop. 8,053

WHERE TO STAY

SUPER 8 MOTEL Book at AAA.com Phone: 205/640-7091

Motel

Property failed to provide current rates

Location: I-20, exit 144, 1 mi n on US 411. 2451 Moody Pkwy 35004. Fax: 205/640-7410. **Facility:** 50 one-bedroom standard units, some with whirlpools. 2 stories (no elevator), exterior corridors. **Parking:** on-site. **Terms:** small pets only ($10 extra charge).

SOME UNITS

FEE

MOUNTAIN BROOK pop. 20,604 (See map and index starting on p. 212)

WHERE TO STAY

HAMPTON INN-MOUNTAIN BROOK Book great rates at AAA.com Phone: 205/870-7822 46

Property failed to provide current rates

Small-scale Hotel

Location: Jct US 31, just e. 2731 US Hwy 280 35223. Fax: 205/871-7610. **Facility:** 130 one-bedroom standard units. 5 stories, interior corridors. **Parking:** on-site. **Amenities:** video games (fee), voice mail, irons, hair dryers. **Pool(s):** outdoor. **Guest Services:** valet laundry. **Business Services:** meeting rooms, fax (fee).

SOME UNITS

WHERE TO DINE

BROWDY'S **Lunch:** $7-$10 **Dinner:** $7-$10 **Phone:** 205/879-8585 51

American

Location: Just e of jct Cahaba Rd. 2713 Culver Rd 35223. **Hours:** 11 am-7 pm, Mon-1:30 pm. **Features:** A local favorite for more than 50 years, the casual family-owned-and-operated restaurant employs a friendly service staff who bring out all kinds of hand-made sandwiches and bakery items. Also on the menu are such entrees as yummy Southern fried chicken. Casual dress. **Parking:** on-site. **Cards:** MC, VI.

CAFE CIAO **Lunch:** $7-$16 **Dinner:** $7-$16 **Phone:** 205/871-2423 50

Italian

Location: Jct Fairway Dr; in Olde English Village. 2031 Cahaba Rd 35223. **Hours:** 11 am-10 pm. **Features:** The casual eatery in Olde English Village puts forth a menu of Italian-themed salads, sandwiches, burgers, pizzas and pasta dishes. Among selections made from homemade sauces and pasta are chicken and spinach saute, farfalle and pesto cream sauce with shrimp and bay scallops, chicken parmigiana and eggplant with penne. Casual dress; cocktails. **Parking:** street. **Cards:** MC, VI.

CHEZ LULU & CONTINENTAL BAKERY **Lunch:** $6-$18 **Dinner:** $6-$18 **Phone:** 205/870-7011 49

French

Location: Jct 20th Ave S; in Olde English Village. 1909 Cahaba Rd 35223. **Hours:** 7 am-6:30 pm. **Features:** In the quaint and charming area of shops known as Olde English Village, the bistro-style restaurant presents a French-themed menu that lists tartes, salads, sandwiches and soups. Imported cheeses and homemade spreads go into such interesting choices as pan bagna, goat cheese with fresh pear, organic lettuce and roasted walnuts on sourdough and French brie with roasted red pepper, organic lettuces and kalamata olives on focaccia. The bakery turns out homemade European-style breads and pastries. Casual dress. **Parking:** street. **Cards:** MC, VI.

DANIEL GEORGE RESTAURANT & BAR **Dinner:** $20-$32 **Phone:** 205/871-3266 52

American

Location: US 280, exit Hollywood Blvd, just ne on Montevallo Rd, just s on Cahaba Rd, then just nw. 2837 Culver Rd 35223. **Hours:** 5:30 pm-9:30 pm, Fri & Sat-10 pm. Closed: 11/22, 12/25; also Sun & Mon. **Reservations:** suggested. **Features:** Diners sit down to creative American cuisine in a casually elegant setting. Representative of seafood, wild and domestic game, meats and poultry prepared with flair are such entrees as bourbon-molasses pork tenderloin and pan-seared black tuna. The wine list is extensive. Dressy casual; cocktails. **Parking:** street. **Cards:** AX, MC, VI.

GILCHRIST DRUG CO **Lunch:** $3-$5 **Phone:** 205/871-2181 53

Deli/Subs Sandwiches

Location: US 280, exit Hollywood Blvd, just ne on Montevallo Rd, then just s. 2805 Cahaba Rd 35223. **Hours:** 8 am-5 pm, Sat from 8:30 am. Closed major holidays; also Sun. **Features:** The tiny sandwich shop does bustling business at lunchtime. Its claims to fame are freshly squeezed, tangy-sweet limeade and an old-fashioned soda shop atmosphere. Sandwiches include delicatessen favorites, including tasty pimiento cheese, BLTs and tuna, ham and chicken salad. Casual dress. **Parking:** street. **Cards:** MC, VI.

OLEXA'S **Lunch:** $5-$12 **Phone:** 205/871-2060 54

American

Location: US 280; ramp toward Mountain Brook, 0.4 mi e, then just s; in Mountain Brook Village. 2838 Culver Rd 35223. **Hours:** 10 am-4 pm. Closed: Sun. **Features:** Guests enjoy a taste of heaven upon ordering wedding cake by the slice at the wonderfully cute lunch spot. The menu comprises delicious salads and light sandwiches. Casual dress. **Parking:** street. **Cards:** AX, MC, VI.

ONEONTA pop. 5,576

WHERE TO STAY

BEST WESTERN COLONIAL INN Book great rates at AAA.com **Phone:** (205)274-2200

AAA SAVE

3/1-10/31	1P: $77-$150	2P: $85-$150	XP: $8	F16
12/1-2/28 & 11/1-11/30	1P: $73	2P: $79	XP: $8	F16

Small-scale Hotel

Location: On SR 75, 0.5 mi n of jct US 231. 293 Valley Rd 35121. Fax: 205/274-2660. **Facility:** 35 one-bedroom standard units, some with whirlpools. 2 stories (no elevator), exterior corridors. *Bath:* combo or shower only. **Parking:** on-site. **Terms:** 7 day cancellation notice, small pets only ($8 extra charge). **Amenities:** high-speed Internet, dual phone lines, irons, hair dryers. **Pool(s):** small outdoor. **Business Services:** PC. **Cards:** AX, DS, MC, VI. **Free Special Amenities: continental breakfast and high-speed Internet.**

SOME UNITS

FEE

WHERE TO DINE

CHINA WOK **Lunch:** $5-$9 **Dinner:** $7-$10 **Phone:** 205/625-6668

Chinese

Location: Just s of jct 231. 410 2nd Ave E 35121. **Hours:** 11 am-10 pm, Fri & Sat-10:30 pm. **Features:** The new restaurant prepares typical Chinese selections, and its buffet lunch specials are a steal. Casual dress. **Parking:** on-site. **Cards:** AX, CB, DC, DS, JC, MC, VI.

Pick a destination. Any destination.

Wherever you're headed, there's always a Choice hotel that fits your travel plans and budget. And, as a AAA/CAA member, you'll save at over 4,000 Choice hotels across the U.S. Plus, it's easy to earn nights or flights with our reward programs.* Just contact your local AAA/CAA office, call 800.228.1222 or visit choicehotels.com to book.

choicehotels.com
800.228.1222

We'll see you there.

CHOICE HOTELS INTERNATIONAL®

*Visit choicehotels.com for complete reward program details.

We'll see you there.
CHOICE HOTELS INTERNATIONAL®

 TourBookMark

Lodging Listing Symbols

Member Values (see pgs. 12-13)

- Official Appointment
- Offers lowest public rate or minimum 10% discount
- May offer discount
- Offers senior discount
- Informational listing only

Member Services

- Airport transportation
- Pets allowed
- Restaurant on premises
- Restaurant off premises (walking distance)
- 24-hour room service
- Cocktail lounge
- Child care

Accessibility Features

- Accessibility features
- Roll-in showers
- Hearing impaired equipment

Leisure Activities

- Full service casino
- Pool
- Health club on premises
- Health club off premises
- Recreational activities

In-Room Amenities

- Non-smoking rooms
- VCR
- Movies
- Refrigerator
- Microwave
- Coffee maker
- No air conditioning
- No TV
- No cable TV
- No telephones

Safety Features (see page 24) (Mexico and Caribbean only)

- S Sprinklers
- D Smoke detectors

Call property for detailed information about fees & restrictions relating to the lodging listing symbols.

CHOICE HOTELS INTERNATIONAL®

PELHAM pop. 14,369 (See map and index starting on p. 212)

WHERE TO STAY

BEST WESTERN AT OAK MOUNTAIN *Book great rates at AAA.com* **Phone:** (205)982-1113 67

AAA SAVE

Small-scale Hotel

All Year 1P: $109-$199 2P: $109-$199

Location: I-65, exit 246, just sw, then just s on State Park Rd. 100 Bishop Cir 35124. Fax: 205/982-0452. **Facility:** 60 one-bedroom standard units, some with whirlpools. 3 stories, interior corridors. *Bath:* combo or shower only. **Parking:** on-site. **Terms:** [CP] meal plan available, small pets only ($10 extra charge). **Amenities:** irons, hair dryers. **Pool(s):** outdoor. **Guest Services:** wireless Internet. **Business Services:** meeting rooms, business center. **Cards:** AX, DS, MC, VI. **Free Special Amenities: expanded continental breakfast and high-speed Internet.**

SOME UNITS

FEE

HAMPTON INN & SUITES PELHAM *Book great rates at AAA.com* **Phone:** (205)313-9500 70

Small-scale Hotel

All Year [BP] 1P: $95-$175 2P: $95-$175 XP: $10 F18

Location: I-65, exit 246, 0.6 mi w on SR 119. 232 Cahaba Valley Rd 35124. Fax: 205/313-9600. **Facility:** 85 one-bedroom standard units, some with whirlpools. 3 stories, interior corridors. *Bath:* combo or shower only. **Parking:** on-site. **Terms:** cancellation fee imposed. **Amenities:** video games (fee), high-speed Internet, dual phone lines, voice mail, irons, hair dryers. **Pool(s):** outdoor. **Leisure Activities:** exercise room. **Guest Services:** sundries, complimentary evening beverages: Wed, valet and coin laundry, wireless Internet. **Business Services:** meeting rooms, business center. **Cards:** AX, CB, DC, DS, JC, MC, VI.

SOME UNITS

ASK

HOLIDAY INN EXPRESS *Book at AAA.com* **Phone:** 205/987-8888 69

Small-scale Hotel

Property failed to provide current rates

Location: I-65, exit 246, 0.5 mi w on SR 119. 260 Cahaba Valley Rd 35124. Fax: 205/987-5878. **Facility:** 81 one-bedroom standard units, some with whirlpools. 3 stories, interior corridors. *Bath:* combo or shower only. **Parking:** on-site. **Amenities:** dual phone lines, voice mail, irons, hair dryers. **Pool(s):** heated indoor. **Leisure Activities:** exercise room. **Guest Services:** valet and coin laundry, wireless Internet. **Business Services:** meeting rooms, business center.

SOME UNITS

(See map and index starting on p. 212)

QUALITY INN Book great rates at AAA.com **Phone:** (205)444-9200 65

SAVE

Small-scale Hotel

All Year 1P: $89-$160 2P: $89-$160 XP: $10 F

Location: I-65, exit 246, just nw. 110 Cahaba Valley Pkwy 35124. Fax: 205/444-9846. **Facility:** 62 one-bedroom standard units, some with whirlpools. 2 stories (no elevator), exterior corridors. **Parking:** on-site. **Terms:** 14 day cancellation notice-fee imposed, pets ($25 deposit, $10 extra charge). **Amenities:** high-speed Internet, irons, hair dryers. **Pool(s):** outdoor. **Guest Services:** valet laundry, wireless Internet. **Business Services:** fax (fee). **Cards:** AX, CB, DC, DS, MC, VI. **Free Special Amenities: full breakfast and high-speed Internet.**

SOME UNITS

FEE

RAMADA LIMITED Book at AAA.com **Phone:** (205)987-0444 66

Small-scale Hotel

All Year 1P: $62-$149 2P: $62-$149 XP: $4 F18

Location: I-65, exit 246, just nw. 113 Cahaba Valley Pkwy E 35124. Fax: 205/987-4816. **Facility:** 48 one-bedroom standard units, some with whirlpools. 2 stories (no elevator), exterior corridors. **Parking:** on-site. **Amenities:** high-speed Internet, voice mail, irons, hair dryers. **Pool(s):** outdoor. **Leisure Activities:** exercise room. **Guest Services:** coin laundry. **Business Services:** fax (fee). **Cards:** AX, DC, DS, MC, VI.

SOME UNITS

ASK

SLEEP INN Book great rates at AAA.com **Phone:** (205)982-9800 68

Small-scale Hotel

All Year 1P: $80-$275 2P: $85-$285 XP: $10 F18

Location: I-65, exit 246, 0.4 mi w on SR 119. 200 Southgate Dr 35124. Fax: 205/982-0525. **Facility:** 80 one-bedroom standard units. 3 stories, interior corridors. *Bath:* combo or shower only. **Parking:** on-site. **Terms:** check-in 4 pm. **Amenities:** voice mail, irons, hair dryers. **Pool(s):** outdoor. **Guest Services:** valet laundry, wireless Internet. **Business Services:** meeting rooms, fax (fee). **Cards:** AX, CB, DC, DS, JC, MC, VI.

SOME UNITS

ASK

WHERE TO DINE

BUFFALO'S SOUTHWESTERN CAFE' **Lunch:** $6-$14 **Dinner:** $6-$14 **Phone:** 205/989-0005

Southwest American

Location: I-65, exit 246, 0.6 mi w on SR 119. 234 Cahaba Valley Rd 35124. **Hours:** 11 am-10 pm, Fri & Sat-11 pm. Closed: 11/22, 12/25. **Reservations:** accepted. **Features:** The restaurant takes guests out West for sizzling steak, Santa Fe cheese steak and Buffalo chicken wings. Fajitas are out of this world. The cantina serves magnificent margaritas, in keeping with the original Southwestern look of the dining room. Casual dress; cocktails. **Parking:** on-site. **Cards:** AX, DC, DS, MC, VI.

POLLO VOLADOR **Lunch:** $5-$16 **Dinner:** $7-$16 **Phone:** 205/682-9535 87

Mexican

Location: I-65, exit 246, 0.4 mi w. 557 Cahaba Valley Rd 35124. **Hours:** 11 am-9:30 pm, Fri & Sat-10:30 pm. Closed major holidays. **Features:** Mexican food draws diners to the popular eating place. Among items served are whole chickens, including the not-to-be-missed pollo asados. Also noteworthy are the lunch specials and tempting desserts big enough for two. Casual dress; cocktails. **Parking:** on-site. **Cards:** AX, DC, MC, VI.

PELL CITY pop. 9,565

WHERE TO STAY

HAMPTON INN Book great rates at AAA.com **Phone:** (205)814-3000

Small-scale Hotel

All Year [ECP] 1P: $89-$94 2P: $94-$99 XP: $5 F18

Location: I-20, exit 158 eastbound; exit 158A westbound, just ne. 220 Vaughan Ln 35125. Fax: 205/814-3001. **Facility:** 75 one-bedroom standard units. 4 stories, interior corridors. *Bath:* combo or shower only. **Parking:** on-site. **Amenities:** high-speed Internet, dual phone lines, voice mail, irons, hair dryers. **Pool(s):** small outdoor. **Leisure Activities:** exercise room. **Guest Services:** valet and coin laundry. **Business Services:** meeting rooms, business center. **Cards:** AX, CB, DC, DS, JC, MC, VI.

SOME UNITS

ASK

HOLIDAY INN EXPRESS PELL CITY **Phone:** 205/884-0047

fyi

Small-scale Hotel

All Year 1P: $94-$109 2P: $94-$109 XP: $10 F

Too new to rate. **Location:** I-20, 158 eastbound; 158A westbound, just ne. 240 Vaughn Ln 35125. Fax: 205/884-0015. **Amenities:** 91 units, coffeemakers, microwaves, refrigerators, pool. **Terms:** 14 day cancellation notice-fee imposed. **Cards:** AX, CB, DC, DS, JC, MC, VI.

WHERE TO DINE

GOLDEN RULE BAR-B-QUE AND GRILL **Lunch:** $4-$12 **Dinner:** $6-$15 **Phone:** 205/338-1443

Barbecue

Location: I-20, exit 158 eastbound; exit 158A westbound, just n. 1700 Martin St N 35125. **Hours:** 10:30 am-9 pm. Closed major holidays. **Features:** Alabamians have been adhering to the Golden Rule for succulent real pit barbecue since its beginning in 1891. Now a local chain, this place cooks up a variety of Southern favorites. Casual dress. **Parking:** on-site. **Cards:** AX, MC, VI.

TRUSSVILLE pop. 12,924 (See map and index starting on p. 212)

WHERE TO STAY

COMFORT INN & SUITES Book great rates at AAA.com **Phone:** (205)661-3636

Small-scale Hotel

All Year 1P: $99-$100 2P: $99-$100 XP: $8 F13

Location: I-59, exit 141, just e on Chalkville Rd, then just n. 4740 Norrell Dr 35173. Fax: 205/661-3646. **Facility:** 66 units. 64 one-bedroom standard units. 2 one-bedroom suites ($100-$145) with whirlpools. 3 stories, interior corridors. *Bath:* combo or shower only. **Parking:** on-site. **Terms:** 15 day cancellation notice-fee imposed, [CP] meal plan available. **Amenities:** high-speed Internet, voice mail, irons, hair dryers. **Pool(s):** outdoor. **Leisure Activities:** limited exercise equipment. **Guest Services:** valet and coin laundry. **Business Services:** meeting rooms, business center. **Cards:** AX, CB, DC, DS, JC, MC, VI.

ASK SOME UNITS

HAMPTON INN BIRMINGHAM/TRUSSVILLE Book great rates at AAA.com **Phone:** (205)655-9777 25

Small-scale Hotel

All Year 1P: $89-$129 2P: $89-$129 XP: $10 F

Location: I-459, exit 32, just e on US 11, then just n. 1940 Edwards Lake Rd 35235. Fax: 205/655-0181. **Facility:** 78 one-bedroom standard units. 4 stories, interior corridors. *Bath:* combo or shower only. **Parking:** on-site. **Terms:** 3 day cancellation notice, [BP] meal plan available. **Amenities:** dual phone lines, voice mail, irons, hair dryers. **Pool(s):** outdoor. **Leisure Activities:** limited exercise equipment. **Guest Services:** valet laundry, wireless Internet. **Business Services:** meeting rooms, PC, fax (fee). **Cards:** AX, CB, DC, DS, JC, MC, VI.

ASK SOME UNITS FEE

HOLIDAY INN EXPRESS HOTEL & SUITES Book great rates at AAA.com **Phone:** (205)655-2700

AAA SAVE

Small-scale Hotel

All Year 1P: $104-$195 2P: $109-$195

Location: I-59, exit 141, just e on CR 10, then just s. 5911 Valley Rd 35173. Fax: 205/655-5500. **Facility:** 64 units. 61 one-bedroom standard units. 3 one-bedroom suites ($109-$155), some with whirlpools. 3 stories, interior corridors. *Bath:* combo or shower only. **Parking:** on-site. **Terms:** cancellation fee imposed, [ECP] meal plan available, package plans. **Amenities:** high-speed Internet, voice mail, irons, hair dryers. **Pool(s):** outdoor. **Leisure Activities:** exercise room. **Guest Services:** valet and coin laundry. **Business Services:** meeting rooms. **Cards:** AX, CB, DC, DS, JC, MC, VI. **Free Special Amenities: expanded continental breakfast and local telephone calls.**

SOME UNITS

JAMESON INN Book at AAA.com **Phone:** (205)661-9323

Small-scale Hotel

All Year [ECP] 1P: $54-$120

Location: I-59, exit 141, just e on Chalkville Rd, then just n. 4730 Norrell Dr 35173. Fax: 205/655-9331. **Facility:** 60 one-bedroom standard units, some with whirlpools. 2 stories (no elevator), exterior corridors. *Bath:* combo or shower only. **Parking:** on-site. **Terms:** cancellation fee imposed, small pets only ($10 fee). **Amenities:** hair dryers. *Some:* irons. **Pool(s):** outdoor. **Leisure Activities:** exercise room. **Guest Services:** wireless Internet. **Business Services:** PC, fax (fee). **Cards:** AX, DC, DS, MC, VI.

ASK FEE SOME UNITS

WHERE TO DINE

ZAPATA'S MEXICAN RESTAURANT **Lunch:** $5-$12 **Dinner:** $6-$13 **Phone:** 205/661-0904 24

Mexican

Location: I-459, exit 32, just e on US 11, then just n. 1930 Edwards Lake Rd 35235. **Hours:** 11 am-10 pm, Sun-9 pm. Closed major holidays. **Features:** Inexpensive lunch specials entice groups small and large to congregate at the popular, busy restaurant. The large bar area is great for relaxing, while the dining room fills with the tempting aromas of traditional burritos, tacos and fajitas. Casual dress; cocktails. **Parking:** on-site. **Cards:** AX, DS, MC, VI.

VESTAVIA HILLS pop. 24,476 (See map and index starting on p. 212)

WHERE TO DINE

DIPLOMAT DELI **Lunch:** $4-$15 **Dinner:** $4-$15 **Phone:** 205/979-1515 63

Deli/Subs Sandwiches

Location: I-65, exit 252 (Vestavia Hills), 1 mi n. 1425 Montgomery Hwy 35216. **Hours:** 11 am-8 pm, Fri & Sat-9 pm, Sun noon-3 pm. Closed major holidays. **Features:** Hot sandwiches—Reubens, muffulettas and the New York double deli of pastrami and corned beef—share menu space with New York submarine sandwiches and the ever-favorite club. Also popular are daily made soups and wonderfully tasty and freshly made Italian and chicken salads. Roulage, silk pie and baklava satisfy a sweet tooth. Casual dress; beer & wine only. **Parking:** on-site. **Cards:** MC, VI.

LEONARDO'S ITALIAN RESTAURANT **Lunch:** $6-$15 **Dinner:** $8-$25 **Phone:** 205/979-6996 62

Italian

Location: 3 mi s of US 280. 2520 Rocky Ridge Rd 35243. **Hours:** 11 am-2 & 5-9 pm, Fri-10 pm, Sat 5 pm-10 pm. Closed major holidays; also Sun. **Features:** Walking into the restaurant, diners can't help but notice the famous faces on the walls in the entryway. They are among the many who have enjoyed homemade garlic rolls with such flavorful dishes as veal Marsala, fettuccine Alfredo, spaghetti and numerous seafood dishes. Casual dress; cocktails. **Parking:** on-site. **Cards:** AX, DS, MC, VI.

MISS MYRA'S PIT BAR-B-Q **Lunch:** $5-$16 **Dinner:** $5-$16 **Phone:** 205/967-6004 58

Barbecue

Location: I-459, exit 19 (US 280), w on US 280, 0.8 mi n on Summit Blvd, then w; corner of Cahaba Heights Rd and White Oak Dr. 3278 Cahaba Heights Rd 35243. **Hours:** 10 am-9 pm, Fri & Sat-10 pm, Sun 10:30 am-8 pm. Closed major holidays. **Features:** Miss Myra brings her Mississippi barbecue style to Alabama. She infuses her sauce with a bit of both states. Inside the store-like atmosphere, patrons need not be bashful about ordering, and she'll come right out and ask how much they want. Casual dress. **Parking:** on-site. **Cards:** AX, DS, MC, VI.

(See map and index starting on p. 212)

MUDTOWN EAT & DRINK **Lunch:** $7-$14 **Dinner:** $7-$14 **Phone:** 205/967-3300 (57)

American

Location: Just e of US 280. 3144 Green Valley Rd 35243. **Hours:** 11 am-9:30 pm, Fri & Sat-10:30 pm. Closed major holidays. **Features:** It's worth traveling off the beaten path to experience the creative cuisine at this Mudtown establishment. Guests unwind in a warm and cozy environment to sample grilled fish with fried green tomatoes or a BLT iceberg salad with blue cheese crumbles and toasted pecans. The menu lists something for everyone. Limited seating may mean a wait, but that shouldn't be any concern. Casual dress; cocktails. **Parking:** on-site. **Cards:** AX, DS, MC, VI.

NONNAS **Lunch:** $9-$12 **Dinner:** $15-$25 **Phone:** 205/978-1212 (61)

Italian

Location: Between Canyon Rd and Mountain View Dr. 700 Montgomery Hwy 35216. **Hours:** 11 am-2 & 5-9 pm, Thurs & Fri-10 pm, Sat 5 pm-10 pm. Closed major holidays; also Sun. **Reservations:** suggested. **Features:** The well-regarded restaurant continues to grow in popularity due in part to its service-oriented staff and comfortable atmosphere. Representative of the Italian-Mediterranean cuisine are such dishes as roasted game hen, lemon-rosemary shrimp and veal Marsala, as well as the petite pan pizza starter and the award-winning bread pudding dessert. Dressy casual; cocktails. **Parking:** on-site. **Cards:** AX, CB, DC, DS, JC, MC, VI.

SATTERFIELD'S **Lunch:** $7-$18 **Dinner:** $20-$33 **Phone:** 205/969-9690 (59)

Continental

Location: US 280; ramp toward Cahaba Heights, then 0.8 mi e. 3161 Cahaba Heights Rd 35243. **Hours:** 11 am-2 & 5:30-10 pm, Fri-10:30 pm, Sat 5:30 pm-10:30 pm, Mon 5:30 pm-10 pm. Closed: Sun. **Reservations:** suggested. **Features:** In the heart of historic Cahaba Heights, the loud, fun European bistro invites fine dining. Locally grown vegetables and nightly specials built around fresh seafood factor on the constantly changing menu. Dressy casual; cocktails. **Parking:** valet. **Cards:** AX, MC, VI.

SEKISUI **Lunch:** $8-$31 **Dinner:** $8-$31 **Phone:** 205/978-7775 (60)

Japanese

Location: Just w of US 31 on Canyon Rd. 700 Montgomery Hwy 35216. **Hours:** 11:30 am-2 & 5-9:30 pm. **Features:** The contemporary restaurant presents a Japanese-themed menu with such items as chicken or beef teriyaki, lamb and strip loin, fried squid legs, baked green mussels, sauteed lobster and grilled stuffed trout, as well as combination entrees, tempura, kushiyaki and box dishes. The sushi bar turns out an extensive variety of seafood rolls, nigiri, sashimi and raw fish. Casual dress; cocktails. **Parking:** on-site. **Cards:** MC, VI.

This ends listings for the Birmingham Vicinity.
The following page resumes the alphabetical listings of cities in Alabama.

BOAZ pop. 7,411

WHERE TO DINE

REIDS CHICKEN STOP — American — **Lunch:** $5-$7 **Dinner:** $5-$7 **Phone:** 256/840-1500

Location: Just w of jct US 431 and SR 168 (Mill Ave). 10775 Alabama Hwy 168 35957. **Hours:** 10 am-8 pm. **Features:** The laid-back spot employs true Southern cooks who fry crispy, golden chicken to perfection. **Parking:** on-site. **Cards:** MC, VI.

CALERA —See Birmingham p. 230.

CHICKASAW pop. 6,364 (See map and index starting on p. 266)

WHERE TO STAY

AMERICA'S BEST INN — Motel — Book at AAA.com — **Phone:** 251/457-4006 — 25

Property failed to provide current rates

Location: I-65, exit 10, just e. 370 W Lee St 36611. Fax: 251/457-8239. **Facility:** 58 one-bedroom standard units, some with whirlpools. 2 stories (no elevator), exterior corridors. **Parking:** on-site. **Amenities:** hair dryers. **Pool(s):** outdoor. **Leisure Activities:** exercise room. **Guest Services:** wireless Internet.

SOME UNITS

CHILDERSBURG pop. 4,927

WHERE TO STAY

DAYS INN — Small-scale Hotel — Book great rates at AAA.com — **Phone:** (256)378-6007

All Year 1P: $50-$100 2P: $55-$100 XP: $5 F16

Location: 0.8 mi s of jct SR 76. 33669 US Hwy 280 35044. Fax: 256/378-3535. **Facility:** 40 one-bedroom standard units. 2 stories (no elevator), exterior corridors. **Parking:** on-site. **Terms:** pets ($10 fee). **Amenities:** hair dryers. *Some:* irons. **Pool(s):** outdoor. **Cards:** AX, CB, DC, DS, MC, VI.

ASK — FEE — SOME UNITS

CLANTON pop. 7,800

WHERE TO STAY

BEST WESTERN INN — AAA SAVE — Small-scale Hotel — Book great rates at AAA.com — **Phone:** 205/280-1006

All Year [ECP] 1P: $60-$65 2P: $75-$85 XP: $10 F12

Location: I-65, exit 205, 0.5 mi e. Located on hilltop. 801 Bradberry Ln 35046. Fax: 205/280-1387. **Facility:** 53 one-bedroom standard units, some with whirlpools. 2 stories (no elevator), exterior corridors. *Bath:* combo or shower only. **Parking:** on-site. **Terms:** 5 day cancellation notice, pets ($6 fee, $20 deposit). **Amenities:** irons, hair dryers. **Pool(s):** outdoor. **Guest Services:** sundries, wireless Internet. **Business Services:** fax (fee). **Cards:** AX, DC, DS, MC, VI. **Free Special Amenities: expanded continental breakfast and high-speed Internet.**

FEE — SOME UNITS

GUESTHOUSE INTERNATIONAL INN — AAA SAVE — Small-scale Hotel — Book great rates at AAA.com — **Phone:** (205)280-0306

All Year 1P: $55-$65 2P: $61-$71

Location: I-65, exit 208, just w. 946 Lake Mitchell Rd 35045. Fax: 205/755-8113. **Facility:** 74 one-bedroom standard units. 2 stories (no elevator), exterior corridors. **Parking:** on-site. **Terms:** package plans, pets ($20 deposit). **Amenities:** hair dryers. *Some:* irons. **Pool(s):** outdoor. **Guest Services:** valet laundry. **Business Services:** meeting rooms, PC, fax (fee). **Cards:** AX, CB, DC, DS, MC, VI.

FEE — SOME UNITS

HOLIDAY INN EXPRESS/CLANTON — Small-scale Hotel — Book at AAA.com — **Phone:** 205/280-1880

All Year [ECP] 1P: $89 2P: $89 XP: $10 F12

Location: I-65, exit 205, 0.5 mi e. 815 Bradberry Ln 35046. Fax: 205/280-1882. **Facility:** 63 one-bedroom standard units. 3 stories, interior corridors. *Bath:* combo or shower only. **Parking:** on-site. **Terms:** 5 day cancellation notice. **Amenities:** high-speed Internet, voice mail, irons, hair dryers. **Pool(s):** heated indoor. **Leisure Activities:** whirlpool, limited exercise equipment. **Guest Services:** coin laundry, wireless Internet. **Business Services:** meeting rooms, business center. **Cards:** AX, DC, DS, MC, VI.

ASK — SOME UNITS

CULLMAN pop. 13,995

WHERE TO STAY

BEST WESTERN FAIRWINDS INN — AAA SAVE — Small-scale Hotel — Book great rates at AAA.com — **Phone:** (256)737-5009

All Year 1P: $55-$125 2P: $55-$125

Location: I-65, exit 310, just e. 1917 Commerce Ave NW 35055. Fax: 256/737-5009. **Facility:** 50 one-bedroom standard units, some with whirlpools. 2 stories (no elevator), exterior corridors. **Parking:** on-site. **Terms:** small pets only ($9 extra charge). **Amenities:** high-speed Internet, voice mail, irons, hair dryers. **Pool(s):** outdoor. **Leisure Activities:** exercise room. **Guest Services:** coin laundry, wireless Internet. **Business Services:** fax. **Cards:** AX, CB, DC, DS, MC, VI. **Free Special Amenities: expanded continental breakfast and high-speed Internet.**

FEE — SOME UNITS

COMFORT INN *Book great rates at AAA.com* **Phone:** 256/734-1240

Small-scale Hotel

Property failed to provide current rates

Location: I-65, exit 310, just e. 5917 Alabama Hwy 157 NW 35058. Fax: 256/734-3318. **Facility:** 50 one-bedroom standard units, some with whirlpools. 2 stories (no elevator), exterior corridors. **Parking:** on-site. **Terms:** small pets only ($20 fee). **Amenities:** irons, hair dryers. **Pool(s):** outdoor. **Guest Services:** wireless Internet. **Business Services:** meeting rooms, PC.

SOME UNITS

FEE

DAYS INN *Book great rates at AAA.com* **Phone:** (256)739-3800

Motel

All Year 1P: $53-$80 2P: $61-$80 XP: $5 F12

Location: I-65, exit 308, just e. 1841 4th St SW 35055. Fax: 256/739-3123. **Facility:** 119 one-bedroom standard units. 2 stories (no elevator), exterior corridors. **Parking:** on-site. **Terms:** [BP] meal plan available, pets ($5 extra charge). **Amenities:** hair dryers. *Some:* irons. **Pool(s):** outdoor. **Guest Services:** wireless Internet. **Business Services:** business center. **Cards:** AX, CB, DC, DS, JC, MC, VI.

SOME UNITS

ASK FEE

ECONO LODGE *Book great rates at AAA.com* **Phone:** (256)734-2691

AAA SAVE

Motel

3/1-8/31	1P: $55-$60	2P: $65-$75	XP: $10	D15
12/1-2/28 & 9/1-11/30	1P: $50-$55	2P: $60-$70	XP: $10	D15

Location: I-65, exit 304, just e. 1655 CR 437 35055. Fax: 256/734-4778. **Facility:** 60 one-bedroom standard units. 2 stories (no elevator), exterior corridors. **Parking:** on-site. **Terms:** 7 day cancellation notice, package plans, pets ($6 fee). **Guest Services:** coin laundry, wireless Internet. **Cards:** AX, DC, MC, VI.

SOME UNITS

FEE

HAMPTON INN *Book great rates at AAA.com* **Phone:** (256)739-4444

Small-scale Hotel

All Year [BP] 1P: $82-$159 2P: $88-$159

Location: I-65, exit 310, just e. 6100 Alabama Hwy 157 35058. Fax: 256/739-4437. **Facility:** 83 one-bedroom standard units, some with whirlpools. 3 stories, interior corridors. *Bath:* combo or shower only. **Parking:** on-site. **Terms:** 3 day cancellation notice, package plans. **Amenities:** high-speed Internet, dual phone lines, voice mail, irons, hair dryers. **Pool(s):** outdoor. **Leisure Activities:** limited exercise equipment. **Guest Services:** valet and coin laundry, wireless Internet. **Business Services:** meeting rooms, business center. **Cards:** AX, CB, DC, DS, MC, VI.

SOME UNITS

ASK

HOLIDAY INN EXPRESS HOTEL & SUITES *Book at AAA.com* **Phone:** (256)736-1906

Small-scale Hotel

All Year 2P: $94-$150 XP: $6 F18

Location: I-65, exit 310, just ne. 2052 Hayes Dr 35058. Fax: 256/734-2728. **Facility:** 78 one-bedroom standard units, some with whirlpools. 3 stories, interior corridors. *Bath:* combo or shower only. **Parking:** on-site. **Terms:** [ECP] meal plan available. **Amenities:** high-speed Internet, dual phone lines, voice mail, irons, hair dryers. **Pool(s):** small heated indoor. **Leisure Activities:** exercise room. **Guest Services:** sundries, valet and coin laundry, wireless Internet. **Business Services:** meeting rooms, business center. **Cards:** AX, CB, DC, DS, JC, MC, VI.

SOME UNITS

ASK

WHERE TO DINE

ALL STEAK RESTAURANT **Lunch:** $5-$10 **Dinner:** $8-$29 **Phone:** 256/734-4322

AAA

American

Location: I-65, exit 308 (US 278), e to US 31, then just n; downtown. 314 2nd Ave SW; Cullman Bank 4th Floor 35055. **Hours:** 6 am-9 pm, Thurs-Sat to 10 pm, Sun 6:30 am-3 pm. Closed major holidays. **Reservations:** accepted. **Features:** Established in 1934, this local landmark recently moved to a new location. The menu features quality steak and seafood choices, as well as their famous, complimentary orange roll. There is a buffet on Sunday, and outdoor dining is available. Casual dress. **Parking:** on-site. **Cards:** MC, VI.

BAXTER'S STEAKHOUSE **Lunch:** $5-$16 **Dinner:** $7-$16 **Phone:** 256/739-9899

American

Location: I-65, exit 310, just e. 6092 AL Hwy 157 35057. **Hours:** 11 am-9 pm, Fri & Sat-10 pm. Closed major holidays. **Features:** The restaurant offers an array of freshly prepared favorites such as sirloin, mashed potatoes and green beans. Casual dress. **Parking:** on-site. **Cards:** AX, DS, MC, VI.

THE DOG HOUSE **Lunch:** $2-$7 **Phone:** 256/775-2400

AAA

American

Location: I-65, exit 308, 1.2 mi sw. 1202 4th St SW 35055. **Hours:** 10:30 am-2:30 pm. Closed: Sun. **Features:** Serving up Chicago style dogs and homemade fries and chips, this is a great place to grab a quick "bite" to eat. Casual dress. **Parking:** on-site. **Cards:** AX, DS, MC, VI.

JOHNNY'S BAR-B-Q **Lunch:** $5-$12 **Dinner:** $5-$12 **Phone:** 256/734-8539

AAA

Regional American

Location: I-65, exit 308 (US 278), 1.2 mi e. 1401 4th St SW 35055. **Hours:** 10 am-9 pm. Closed major holidays; also Sun & Mon. **Features:** Popular with the locals, the restaurant specializes in pork and chicken barbecue but also offers some tasty seafood dishes. The atmosphere is friendly and laid-back. Casual dress. **Parking:** on-site. **Cards:** AX, DS, MC, VI.

DAPHNE pop. 16,581

WHERE TO STAY

HAMPTON INN MOBILE-EAST BAY DAPHNE Book great rates at AAA.com Phone: 251/626-2220

Small-scale Hotel. All Year [ECP] 1P: $129-$174 2P: $139-$184 XP: $10 F18

Location: I-10, exit 35A eastbound; exit 35 westbound, just s. 29451 US Hwy 98 36526. Fax: 251/626-2218. **Facility:** 135 one-bedroom standard units. 6 stories, interior corridors. *Bath:* combo or shower only. **Parking:** on-site. **Amenities:** video library, high-speed Internet, voice mail, irons, hair dryers. *Some:* DVD players. **Pool(s):** small outdoor. **Leisure Activities:** whirlpool, exercise room. **Guest Services:** complimentary evening beverages: Mon-Thurs, valet and coin laundry. **Business Services:** meeting rooms, PC. **Cards:** AX, DC, DS, MC, VI. ***(See color ad p 269)***

SOME UNITS

HILTON GARDEN INN Book great rates at AAA.com Phone: 251/625-0020

Small-scale Hotel. Property failed to provide current rates

Location: I-10, exit 35A eastbound; exit 35 westbound, just s. 29546 N Main St 36526. Fax: 251/626-3856. **Facility:** 124 units. 123 one-bedroom standard units. 1 two-bedroom suite with whirlpool. 5 stories, interior corridors. *Bath:* combo or shower only. **Parking:** on-site. **Amenities:** high-speed Internet, dual phone lines, voice mail, irons, hair dryers. **Leisure Activities:** whirlpool, exercise room. **Guest Services:** sundries, valet and coin laundry. **Business Services:** meeting rooms, business center. ***(See color ad p 269)***

SOME UNITS

MICROTEL INN & SUITES Book at AAA.com Phone: (251)621-7807

Small-scale Hotel. All Year 1P: $83-$130 2P: $83-$130 XP: $5 F16

Location: I-10, exit 35A eastbound; exit 35 westbound, 0.5 mi s. 29050 US 98 36526. Fax: 251/625-1252. **Facility:** 71 one-bedroom standard units. 4 stories, interior corridors. *Bath:* combo or shower only. **Parking:** on-site. **Terms:** [ECP] meal plan available. **Amenities:** high-speed Internet, voice mail, irons. **Guest Services:** coin laundry. **Business Services:** meeting rooms, PC. **Cards:** AX, CB, DC, DS, MC, VI.

SOME UNITS

WHERE TO DINE

LONGHORN STEAKHOUSE Lunch: $6-$13 Dinner: $10-$20 Phone: 251/625-8960

Steak House

Location: I-10, exit 35A eastbound; exit 35 westbound, 0.5 mi e. 6870 US Hwy 90 36526. **Hours:** 11 am-10 pm, Fri & Sat-11 pm. Closed: 11/22, 12/25. **Features:** A nicely varied menu lists selections of steak, prime rib, chicken, ribs and seafood. The relaxed atmosphere has a decidedly Western feel. Casual dress; cocktails. **Parking:** on-site. **Cards:** AX, DC, DS, MC, VI.

THE NAUTILUS RESTAURANT Lunch: $6-$10 Dinner: $9-$17 Phone: 251/626-3972

Seafood

Location: I-10, exit 35A eastbound; exit 35 westbound, 0.5 mi s. 29249 US 98 36526. **Hours:** 11 am-9 pm, Fri & Sat-10 pm. Closed: 11/22, 12/25. **Features:** Enjoy the sunset over Mobile Bay as you sample fresh gulf seafood and steak. House specialties include seafood scampi and baked oysters. The restaurant's nautical decor features diving helmets and lovely carved figureheads from sailing ships. Live piano music Saturday and Sunday 6 pm-9 pm. Casual dress; cocktails. **Parking:** on-site. **Cards:** AX, DC, DS, MC, VI.

DAUPHIN ISLAND pop. 1,371

WHERE TO DINE

LIGHTHOUSE BAKERY Lunch: $3-$6 Phone: 251/861-2253

Bakery/Desserts

Location: Just e of SR 193. 919 Chaumont Ave 36528. **Hours:** 6 am-3 pm, Sat-4 pm, Sun 9 am-3 pm. Closed major holidays; also Mon & Tues. **Features:** Start off your day with a great cup of coffee and a freshly baked cinnamon roll or cheese danish. Or drop in for a light lunch and a great tasting sandwich. Everything here is homemade from scratch. Casual dress. **Parking:** on-site. **Cards:** MC, VI.

DECATUR pop. 53,929

WHERE TO STAY

BEST WESTERN RIVER CITY HOTEL Book great rates at AAA.com Phone: (256)301-1388

Small-scale Hotel. All Year [ECP] 1P: $79-$89 XP: $10 F12

Location: I-65, exit 334, 8 mi n. 1305 Front Ave 35603. Fax: 256/355-8775. **Facility:** 59 one-bedroom standard units, some with whirlpools. 3 stories, interior corridors. *Bath:* combo or shower only. **Parking:** on-site, winter plug-ins. **Terms:** small pets only ($25 fee). **Amenities:** high-speed Internet, irons, hair dryers. **Pool(s):** small outdoor. **Guest Services:** coin laundry. **Business Services:** PC, fax (fee). **Cards:** AX, CB, DC, DS, MC, VI.

SOME UNITS

FEE FEE

COMFORT INN & SUITES Book great rates at AAA.com Phone: (256)355-1999

AAA SAVE

Small-scale Hotel. All Year 1P: $71-$91 2P: $71-$91 XP: $10 F18

Location: SR 67, jct Beltline Rd SW. 2212 Danville Rd SW 35601. Fax: 256/350-2773. **Facility:** 103 units. 92 one-bedroom standard units. 11 one-bedroom suites. 3 stories, interior corridors. *Bath:* combo or shower only. **Parking:** on-site. **Terms:** [ECP] meal plan available, small pets only ($10 fee, $35 deposit). **Amenities:** high-speed Internet, voice mail, safes (fee), irons, hair dryers. *Some:* dual phone lines. **Pool(s):** outdoor. **Guest Services:** complimentary evening beverages: Mon-Thurs, valet laundry, wireless Internet. **Business Services:** meeting rooms, business center. **Cards:** AX, CB, DC, DS, MC, VI. **Free Special Amenities: expanded continental breakfast and local telephone calls.**

SOME UNITS

FEE FEE

COUNTRY INN & SUITES BY CARLSON *Book at AAA.com* **Phone:** (256)355-6800

Small-scale Hotel

All Year 1P: $87 2P: $87 XP: $5 F18

Location: US 31 to Church St, just w. Located in the downtown historic district. 807 Bank St NE 35601. Fax: 256/350-0965. **Facility:** 110 units. 36 one-bedroom standard units. 74 one-bedroom suites, some with whirlpools. 3 stories, interior corridors. *Bath:* combo or shower only. **Parking:** on-site. **Terms:** package plans. **Amenities:** high-speed Internet, voice mail, irons, hair dryers. **Pool(s):** outdoor. **Leisure Activities:** sauna, whirlpool, exercise room. **Guest Services:** coin laundry, wireless Internet. **Business Services:** meeting rooms. **Cards:** AX, DC, DS, MC, VI.

SOME UNITS

COURTYARD BY MARRIOTT *Book great rates at AAA.com* **Phone:** (256)355-4446

Small-scale Hotel

All Year 1P: $99 2P: $99

Location: SR 67, 4 mi w of jct US 31. 1209 Courtyard Cir 35603. Fax: 256/355-1793. **Facility:** 113 units. 109 one-bedroom standard units, some with whirlpools. 4 one-bedroom suites. 4 stories, interior corridors. *Bath:* combo or shower only. **Parking:** on-site. **Terms:** package plans. **Amenities:** video games (fee), high-speed Internet, dual phone lines, voice mail, irons, hair dryers. **Pool(s):** small heated indoor. **Leisure Activities:** whirlpool, exercise room. **Guest Services:** sundries, valet and coin laundry. **Business Services:** meeting rooms, business center. **Cards:** AX, CB, DC, DS, MC, VI.

SOME UNITS

HAMPTON INN *Book great rates at AAA.com* **Phone:** 256/355-5888

Small-scale Hotel

Property failed to provide current rates

Location: SR 67, 1.5 mi e of jct US 72A, 4 mi w of jct US 31, then 8 mi w on I-65. 2041 Beltline Rd SW 35601. Fax: 256/355-8434. **Facility:** 90 one-bedroom standard units, some with whirlpools. 4 stories, interior corridors. *Bath:* combo or shower only. **Parking:** on-site, winter plug-ins. **Amenities:** voice mail, irons, hair dryers. **Pool(s):** outdoor. **Leisure Activities:** exercise room. **Guest Services:** valet laundry, wireless Internet. **Business Services:** meeting rooms, PC.

SOME UNITS

HOLIDAY INN HOTEL & SUITES *Book at AAA.com* **Phone:** (256)355-3150

Small-scale Hotel

All Year 1P: $70-$119 2P: $70-$119 XP: $5 F19

Location: Just w of jct US 31, 72A and SR 20. 1101 6th Ave NE 35601. Fax: 256/350-5262. **Facility:** 205 units. 183 one-bedroom standard units. 22 one-bedroom suites. 5 stories, interior/exterior corridors. **Parking:** on-site. **Terms:** package plans, small pets only ($15 fee). **Amenities:** voice mail, irons, hair dryers. **Pool(s):** heated indoor/outdoor. **Leisure Activities:** whirlpool, exercise room. **Guest Services:** valet and coin laundry, wireless Internet. **Business Services:** conference facilities, business center. **Cards:** AX, CB, DC, DS, JC, MC, VI.

SOME UNITS

FEE FEE FEE

JAMESON INN *Book at AAA.com* **Phone:** (256)355-2229

Small-scale Hotel

All Year [ECP] 1P: $54-$120

Location: SR 67, 1.6 mi s of jct US 72A; 3.9 mi n of jct US 31. 2120 Jameson Pl SW 35603. Fax: 256/341-9056. **Facility:** 58 one-bedroom standard units, some with whirlpools. 2 stories (no elevator), exterior corridors. *Bath:* combo or shower only. **Parking:** on-site. **Terms:** cancellation fee imposed, small pets only ($10 fee). **Amenities:** hair dryers. **Pool(s):** outdoor. **Leisure Activities:** exercise room. **Guest Services:** valet laundry, wireless Internet. **Business Services:** meeting rooms, PC. **Cards:** AX, DC, DS, MC, VI.

SOME UNITS

FEE

MICROTEL INN & SUITES *Book at AAA.com* **Phone:** (256)301-9995

Small-scale Hotel

All Year 1P: $49-$69 2P: $49-$89

Location: On SR 67, 4 mi w of jct US 31. 2226 Beltline Rd SW 35601 (PO Box 5015). Fax: 256/301-9742. **Facility:** 77 one-bedroom standard units. 3 stories, interior corridors. *Bath:* combo or shower only. **Parking:** on-site. **Terms:** small pets only ($15 fee). **Amenities:** voice mail. *Some:* irons, hair dryers. **Pool(s):** small outdoor. **Leisure Activities:** exercise room. **Guest Services:** coin laundry, wireless Internet. **Business Services:** meeting rooms, fax. **Cards:** AX, DC, DS, MC, VI.

SOME UNITS

FEE

WHERE TO DINE

BARNHILL'S BUFFET **Lunch:** $5-$9 **Dinner:** $7-$10 **Phone:** 256/351-1680

American

Location: Jct Danville Rd SW, just sw on SR 67. 1702 Beltline Rd SW 35601. **Hours:** 10:45 am-8:45 pm, Fri-9 pm, Sat 7 am-9 pm, Sun 7 am-8:45 pm. Closed: 12/25. **Features:** Casual dress. **Parking:** on-site. **Cards:** AX, DS, MC, VI.

BIG BOB GIBSON'S-BBQ **Lunch:** $4-$9 **Dinner:** $4-$9 **Phone:** 256/350-6969

Barbecue

Location: On US 31; 1.2 mi n of jct SR 67. 1715 6th Ave SE 35601. **Hours:** 7 am-8 pm. Closed major holidays. **Features:** Family owned since 1925, this place is heaven for barbecue lovers. The food has been praised in countless magazines and reviews. One bite of the delicious smoked barbecue coated in tangy sauce, and guests understand what all the fuss is about. Casual dress. **Parking:** on-site. **Cards:** AX, MC, VI.

CAFE 113 **Dinner:** $15-$30 **Phone:** 256/351-1400

Continental

Location: Center. 113 Grant St 35601. **Hours:** 5 pm-10 pm, Sat from 6 pm. Closed: Sun. **Reservations:** accepted. **Features:** The downtown cafe has an eclectic decor that is as interesting as the food is good. A varied selection of red meat, fish and fowl is offered. The casual, friendly wait staff provides professional service. Casual dress; cocktails. **Parking:** street. **Cards:** AX, DC, DS, MC, VI.

SIMP MCGHEE'S **Dinner:** $16-$26 **Phone:** 256/353-6284

American

Location: Historic downtown. 725 Bank St 35601. **Hours:** 5:30 pm-9 pm. Closed major holidays; also Sun. **Features:** Antiques abound in converted 1890s dry goods building. Cajun and seafood specialties. Many beef entrees as well as pork and fowl. Metal ceilings, hard wood floors and old time pictures help guests step back in time over one hundred years. Casual dining on first floor and more formal dining on second floor. Casual dress; cocktails. **Parking:** street. **Cards:** AX, DC, DS, MC, VI.

TASTE OF CHINA **Lunch:** $6-$10 **Dinner:** $6-$12 **Phone:** 256/340-3443

Chinese

Location: I-65, exit 334, 1 mi w; in Mallard Shopping Plaza. 2941 Point Mallard Pkwy 35603. **Hours:** 10:30 am-9:30 pm, Fri & Sat-10:30 pm. **Features:** The compact restaurant serves up big taste and ample portions for a small price. Casual dress. **Parking:** on-site. **Cards:** MC, VI.

DEMOPOLIS pop. 7,540

WHERE TO STAY

HOLIDAY INN EXPRESS *Book at AAA.com* **Phone:** 334/289-9595

Small-scale Hotel

Property failed to provide current rates

Location: On US 80, 0.9 mi w of jct US 43 N. 943 Hwy 80 W 36732. Fax: 334/289-9570. **Facility:** 51 one-bedroom standard units, some with whirlpools. 3 stories, interior corridors. *Bath:* combo or shower only. **Parking:** on-site. **Amenities:** high-speed Internet, dual phone lines, voice mail, irons, hair dryers. **Pool(s):** outdoor. **Guest Services:** valet and coin laundry, wireless Internet. **Business Services:** meeting rooms, business center.

SOME UNITS

DOTHAN pop. 57,737

WHERE TO STAY

AMERICAS BEST VALUE INN & SUITES *Book great rates at AAA.com* **Phone:** (334)793-5200

Motel

All Year 1P: $45-$85 2P: $47-$99 XP: $5 F18

Location: 0.8 mi s of jct US 84; west end of town. 2901 Ross Clark Cir 36301. Fax: 334/678-1670. **Facility:** 122 units. 105 one-bedroom standard units, some with kitchens. 16 one- and 1 two-bedroom suites with kitchens. 3 stories, exterior corridors. **Parking:** on-site. **Terms:** small pets only ($10 fee). **Amenities:** *Some:* high-speed Internet, irons, hair dryers. **Pool(s):** small outdoor. **Leisure Activities:** barbecue grills, picnic tables. **Guest Services:** coin laundry, wireless Internet. **Cards:** AX, DS, MC, VI. **Free Special Amenities: continental breakfast and high-speed Internet.**

SOME UNITS

FEE

BEST WESTERN DOTHAN INN & SUITES *Book great rates at AAA.com* **Phone:** (334)793-4376

Small-scale Hotel

All Year [ECP] 1P: $66-$95 2P: $66-$95 XP: $5 F12

Location: 0.3 mi n of Ross Clark Cir. 3285 Montgomery Hwy 36303. Fax: 334/793-7720. **Facility:** 150 units. 134 one-bedroom standard units, some with efficiencies and/or whirlpools. 16 one-bedroom suites with efficiencies and whirlpools. 2 stories (no elevator), interior/exterior corridors. **Parking:** on-site. **Terms:** 3 day cancellation notice, weekly rates available, package plans. **Amenities:** high-speed Internet, voice mail, irons, hair dryers. **Pool(s):** small outdoor. **Leisure Activities:** charcoal grill. **Guest Services:** valet and coin laundry, wireless Internet. **Business Services:** meeting rooms, PC. **Cards:** AX, CB, DC, DS, JC, MC, VI. **Free Special Amenities: continental breakfast and local telephone calls.**

SOME UNITS

COMFORT INN *Book great rates at AAA.com* **Phone:** (334)793-9090

Small-scale Hotel

All Year [ECP] 1P: $85-$106 2P: $85-$106 XP: $5 F18

Location: Just w of jct US 231; northwest part of town. 3593 Ross Clark Cir 36303 (PO Box 9311, 36304). Fax: 334/793-4367. **Facility:** 122 one-bedroom standard units, some with whirlpools. 5 stories, interior corridors. **Parking:** on-site. **Terms:** package plans, small pets only ($10 extra charge). **Amenities:** voice mail, irons, hair dryers. **Pool(s):** outdoor. **Leisure Activities:** exercise room. **Guest Services:** valet laundry, wireless Internet. **Business Services:** meeting rooms, PC. **Cards:** AX, CB, DC, DS, JC, MC, VI. **Free Special Amenities: expanded continental breakfast and high-speed Internet.**

SOME UNITS

FEE

DAYS INN *Book great rates at AAA.com* **Phone:** (334)793-2550

Motel

All Year 1P: $40-$45 2P: $46-$51 XP: $6 F17

Location: 0.9 mi s of jct US 84; west end of town. 2841 Ross Clark Cir 36301. Fax: 334/793-7962. **Facility:** 118 units. 117 one-bedroom standard units. 1 one-bedroom suite with efficiency. 2 stories (no elevator), exterior corridors. **Parking:** on-site. **Terms:** package plans, pets ($5 extra charge). **Amenities:** safes, hair dryers. *Some:* irons. **Pool(s):** outdoor. **Leisure Activities:** whirlpool, putting green. **Guest Services:** coin laundry, wireless Internet. **Cards:** AX, DC, DS, MC, VI.

SOME UNITS

FEE

ECONO LODGE *Book great rates at AAA.com* **Phone:** (334)673-8000

Motel

All Year [CP] 1P: $35-$85 2P: $40-$90 XP: $5 F18

Location: 0.8 mi s of jct US 84; west end of town. 2910 Ross Clark Cir 36301. Fax: 334/671-0037. **Facility:** 41 one-bedroom standard units. 2 stories (no elevator), exterior corridors. *Bath:* combo or shower only. **Parking:** on-site. **Amenities:** high-speed Internet, irons, hair dryers. **Pool(s):** outdoor. **Cards:** AX, CB, DC, DS, JC, MC, VI. **Free Special Amenities: continental breakfast and high-speed Internet.**

SOME UNITS

FAIRFIELD INN BY MARRIOTT *Book great rates at AAA.com* **Phone:** 334/671-0100

Small-scale Hotel

Property failed to provide current rates

Location: Just s of jct US 84; west end of town. 3038 Ross Clark Cir 36301. Fax: 334/671-8608. **Facility:** 63 one-bedroom standard units. 3 stories, interior corridors. *Bath:* combo or shower only. **Parking:** on-site. **Amenities:** irons, hair dryers. **Pool(s):** small heated indoor. **Guest Services:** valet laundry.

SOME UNITS

HOLIDAY INN EXPRESS *Book great rates at AAA.com* **Phone:** (334)671-3700

AAA SAVE

Motel

All Year 1P: $80-$90

Location: Just s of jct US 84; west end of town. 3071 Ross Clark Cir 36301. Fax: 334/702-4102. **Facility:** 112 one-bedroom standard units. 2 stories (no elevator), exterior corridors. *Bath:* combo or shower only. **Parking:** on-site. **Terms:** [CP] meal plan available, small pets only ($15 fee). **Amenities:** voice mail, irons, hair dryers. **Leisure Activities:** pool privileges. **Guest Services:** valet laundry, wireless Internet. **Business Services:** meeting rooms. **Cards:** AX, CB, DC, DS, JC, MC, VI.

SOME UNITS

FEE

HOLIDAY INN-SOUTH *Book at AAA.com* **Phone:** 334/794-8711

Small-scale Hotel

All Year [BP] 1P: $60-$125 2P: $60-$125 XP: $10 F17

Location: Just e of US 231; in south part of town. 2195 Ross Clark Cir 36301. Fax: 334/671-3781. **Facility:** 143 units. 129 one-bedroom standard units. 14 one-bedroom suites. 2 stories (no elevator), exterior corridors. *Bath:* combo or shower only. **Parking:** on-site. **Terms:** package plans, small pets only ($15 extra charge). **Amenities:** voice mail, irons, hair dryers. *Some:* DVD players. **Pool(s):** outdoor. **Leisure Activities:** exercise room. **Guest Services:** valet and coin laundry, wireless Internet. **Business Services:** meeting rooms. **Cards:** AX, DS, MC, VI.

SOME UNITS

FEE

HOWARD JOHNSON EXPRESS INN *Book at AAA.com* **Phone:** (334)792-3339

Motel

All Year 1P: $62-$75 2P: $62-$75

Location: 1.4 mi s of jct SR 52; west end of town. 2244 Ross Clark Cir 36301. Fax: 334/792-3339. **Facility:** 60 units. 52 one-bedroom standard units, some with whirlpools. 8 one-bedroom suites ($100-$135) with kitchens. 2 stories (no elevator), exterior corridors. **Parking:** on-site. **Terms:** package plans, pets ($10-$20 extra charge). **Amenities:** high-speed Internet, voice mail, irons, hair dryers. **Pool(s):** small outdoor. **Leisure Activities:** basketball. **Guest Services:** coin laundry. **Cards:** AX, CB, DC, DS, JC, MC, VI.

SOME UNITS

FEE

MOTEL 6 #1233 *Book at AAA.com* **Phone:** 334/793-6013

Motel

5/25-11/30 1P: $35-$45 2P: $41-$51 XP: $3 F17

12/1-5/24 1P: $33-$43 2P: $39-$49 XP: $3 F17

Location: 0.8 mi s of jct US 84; west end of town. 2907 Ross Clark Cir 36301. Fax: 334/793-2377. **Facility:** 101 one-bedroom standard units, some with efficiencies (no utensils). 2 stories (no elevator), exterior corridors. *Bath:* combo or shower only. **Parking:** on-site. **Terms:** small pets only. **Pool(s):** small outdoor. **Guest Services:** coin laundry. **Cards:** AX, CB, DC, DS, MC, VI.

SOME UNITS

QUALITY INN *Book great rates at AAA.com* **Phone:** (334)794-6601

AAA SAVE

Motel

All Year 1P: $65-$85 2P: $65-$85

Location: Just s of jct US 84, west end of town. 3053 Ross Clark Cir 36301. Fax: 334/794-9032. **Facility:** 102 one-bedroom standard units. 2 stories (no elevator), exterior corridors. *Bath:* combo or shower only. **Parking:** on-site. **Terms:** pets ($25 fee). **Amenities:** voice mail, irons, hair dryers. **Dining:** 6 am-1:30 & 5-9 pm, Sat 7 am-10:30 & 5-9 pm, Sun 7-10:30 am, cocktails. **Pool(s):** outdoor, wading. **Guest Services:** valet laundry. **Business Services:** meeting rooms. **Cards:** AX, CB, DC, DS, JC, MC, VI.

SOME UNITS

FEE

SLEEP INN & SUITES *Book great rates at AAA.com* **Phone:** (334)671-2086

AAA SAVE

Small-scale Hotel

All Year [BP] 1P: $79-$109 2P: $82-$112 XP: $3 F18

Location: On US 231, 1.7 mi n of Ross Clark Cir Bypass. 4654 Montgomery Hwy 36303. Fax: 334/671-2087. **Facility:** 67 one-bedroom standard units. 3 stories, interior corridors. *Bath:* combo or shower only. **Parking:** on-site. **Terms:** package plans. **Amenities:** high-speed Internet, voice mail, irons, hair dryers. **Dining:** 11 am-10 pm, cocktails. **Pool(s):** small outdoor. **Leisure Activities:** limited exercise equipment. **Guest Services:** valet and coin laundry, wireless Internet. **Business Services:** meeting rooms. **Cards:** AX, CB, DC, DS, JC, MC, VI. **Free Special Amenities: full breakfast and local telephone calls.**

SOME UNITS

SUPER 8 MOTEL *Book at AAA.com* **Phone:** (334)792-3232

Motel

All Year [CP] 1P: $50-$75 2P: $55-$75 XP: $5 F12

Location: Just w of US 231; in south part of town. 2215 Ross Clark Cir 36301. Fax: 334/792-3232. **Facility:** 44 one-bedroom standard units, some with kitchens and/or whirlpools. 2 stories (no elevator), exterior corridors. **Parking:** on-site. **Terms:** cancellation fee imposed. **Amenities:** high-speed Internet, hair dryers. *Some:* irons. **Pool(s):** outdoor. **Cards:** AX, DS, MC, VI.

SOME UNITS

WHERE TO DINE

BARNHILL'S BUFFET **Lunch:** $5-$9 **Dinner:** $7-$10 **Phone:** 334/712-1760

American

Location: Jct SR 210, 0.7 mi n on US 231. 3562 Montgomery Way 36303. **Hours:** 10:45 am-8:45 pm, Fri-9 pm, Sat 7 am-9 pm, Sun 7 am-8:45 pm, Closed: 12/25. **Features:** Casual dress. **Parking:** on-site. **Cards:** AX, DS, MC, VI.

CRYSTAL RIVER SEAFOOD **Lunch:** $6-$10 **Dinner:** $9-$24 **Phone:** 334/794-4153

Seafood

Location: Just w of jct US 231; northwest part of town. 3460 Ross Clark Cir 36303. **Hours:** 11 am-9 pm, Fri & Sat-10 pm. Closed: 11/22, 12/25. **Features:** For generous portions, good service and reasonably priced fresh seafood, the restaurant doesn't disappoint. Casual dress; beer & wine only. **Parking:** on-site. **Cards:** AX, DS, MC, VI.

LARRY'S REAL PIT BAR-B-Q **Lunch:** $6-$8 **Dinner:** $6-$10 **Phone:** 334/792-5211

Barbecue

Location: Just n of jct US 84; west end of town. 3115 Ross Clark Cir 36301. **Hours:** 10:30 am-9 pm. Closed: 1/1, 11/22, 12/25. **Features:** Prompt and friendly service complement the large portions of tasty barbecue. Casual dress. **Parking:** on-site. **Cards:** AX, MC, VI.

OLD MEXICO **Lunch:** $4-$6 **Dinner:** $6-$13 **Phone:** 334/712-1434

Mexican

Location: 0.8 mi s of jct US 84; west end of town. 2920 Ross Clark Cir 36301. **Hours:** 11 am-10 pm, Sun-9 pm. Closed: 1/1, 11/22, 12/25. **Reservations:** accepted. **Features:** Old Mexico offers authentic Mexican cuisine in a nifty atmosphere. Start with tortilla chips and salsa served on arrival, then mix and match choices from an excellent selection of your favorite entrees. There is a full bar and an attentive staff. Casual dress; cocktails. **Parking:** on-site. **Cards:** AX, DS, MC, VI.

OLD MILL RESTAURANT **Dinner:** $9-$22 **Phone:** 334/794-8530

American

Location: Jct Ross Clark Cir Bypass, 1.4 mi n on US 231, then just w. 2557 Murphy Mill Rd 36303. **Hours:** 4:30 pm-9:30 pm, Fri & Sat-10 pm. Closed major holidays; also 12/24 & Sun. **Features:** This upscale establishment specializes in steak and seafood. Their fish selections are filleted on the premises, and include grouper, snapper, tuna and amberjack. The beef is also cut in-house and marinated in the Old Mill's own special sauce. Casual dress; cocktails. **Parking:** on-site. **Cards:** AX, MC, VI.

THE RIVER NILE BISTRO **Lunch:** $6-$7 **Dinner:** $8-$10 **Phone:** 334/702-9111

Basque

Location: Just w of jct Cherokee Ave; Crepe Myrtle Shopping Center. 2620 N Montgomery Hwy 36303. **Hours:** 11 am-9 pm. Closed: 11/22, 12/25; also Sun. **Features:** With a name like The River Nile one would expect Egyptian food; however, this little cafe-style restaurant serves up light foods, mostly sandwiches like The Sweet Pepper Mummy, The Cleopatra, The Sphinx, King Tut or The Great Pyramids. The funky little downtown restaurant also features ecclectic decor: colorful artwork, brightly-coloured tables and walls, a mish-mash of chairs; nothing matches but somehow it works. Casual dress. **Parking:** street. **Cards:** AX, DS, MC, VI.

ENTERPRISE pop. 21,178

WHERE TO STAY

COMFORT INN *Book great rates at AAA.com* **Phone:** (334)393-2304

All Year [ECP] 1P: $70 2P: $70 XP: $5 F17

Motel

Location: On US 84 Bypass. 615 Boll Weevil Cir 36330. Fax: 334/347-5954. **Facility:** 78 units. 72 one-bedroom standard units. 6 one-bedroom suites ($140) with kitchens. 2 stories (no elevator), exterior corridors. **Parking:** on-site. **Terms:** pets ($25 fee). **Amenities:** high-speed Internet, safes, irons, hair dryers. **Pool(s):** small outdoor. **Leisure Activities:** picnic area with charcoal grill. **Guest Services:** valet and coin laundry. **Business Services:** meeting rooms. **Cards:** AX, DC, DS, MC, VI. **Free Special Amenities: expanded continental breakfast and high-speed Internet.**

SOME UNITS

FEE

DAYS INN-ENTERPRISE *Book great rates at AAA.com* **Phone:** (334)393-3297

All Year 1P: $50-$75 2P: $50-$75 XP: $5 F12

Motel

Location: On US 84 Bypass. 714 Boll Weevil Cir 36330. Fax: 334/393-3297. **Facility:** 41 one-bedroom standard units, some with whirlpools. 2 stories (no elevator), exterior corridors. **Parking:** on-site. **Terms:** [CP] meal plan available. **Amenities:** high-speed Internet, safes (fee), irons, hair dryers. **Pool(s):** outdoor. **Guest Services:** coin laundry, wireless Internet. **Business Services:** PC. **Cards:** AX, CB, DC, DS, JC, MC, VI.

SOME UNITS

ASK

WHERE TO DINE

EURO-ITALIAN BISTRO **Lunch:** $6-$17 **Dinner:** $6-$17 **Phone:** 334/348-9900

Italian

Location: Just e on SR 248 from jct US 84 Bypass; in Morgan Square Plaza. 913 Rucker Blvd 36330. **Hours:** 11 am-9 pm, Fri & Sat-10 pm. Closed major holidays. **Features:** Enjoy an international menu with offerings such as custom made pizza, lobster ravioli, filet mignon and lobster bolognese. Each of the four dining rooms has a different theme. Casual dress; cocktails. **Parking:** on-site. **Cards:** AX, DC, DS, MC, VI.

EUFAULA pop. 13,908

WHERE TO STAY

EUFAULA COMFORT SUITES *Book great rates at AAA.com* **Phone:** (334)616-0114

All Year [ECP] 1P: $69-$129 2P: $69-$129 XP: $5 F17

Small-scale Hotel

Location: 1.7 mi s on US 431 from jct US 82 E, then just e. 12 Paul Lee Pkwy 36027. Fax: 334/616-7217. **Facility:** 54 one-bedroom standard units, some with whirlpools. 2 stories, interior corridors. *Bath:* combo or shower only. **Parking:** on-site. **Terms:** 30 day cancellation notice, pets ($25 fee). **Amenities:** voice mail, irons, hair dryers. **Pool(s):** heated indoor. **Leisure Activities:** sauna, whirlpool, exercise room. **Guest Services:** valet laundry, wireless Internet. **Business Services:** meeting rooms. **Cards:** AX, DC, DS, JC, MC, VI.

SOME UNITS

ASK

FEE

JAMESON INN *Book at AAA.com* **Phone:** (334)687-7747

Motel

All Year [ECP] 1P: $54-$120

Location: On US 431, 1 mi s of US 82 E. 136 Towne Center Blvd 36027. Fax: 334/687-7101. **Facility:** 40 units. 38 one-bedroom standard units. 2 two-bedroom suites with whirlpools. 2 stories (no elevator), exterior corridors. **Parking:** on-site. **Terms:** cancellation fee imposed, small pets only ($10 extra charge). **Amenities:** irons, hair dryers. **Pool(s):** small outdoor. **Leisure Activities:** exercise room. **Guest Services:** wireless Internet. **Business Services:** PC. **Cards:** AX, DC, DS, MC, VI.

SOME UNITS

FEE

SUPER 8 MOTEL **Phone:** (334)687-3900

Motel

6/1-8/31	1P: $49-$65	2P: $55-$79	XP: $6	F12
3/1-5/31	1P: $45-$55	2P: $49-$65	XP: $6	F12
12/1-2/28 & 9/1-11/30	1P: $42-$49	2P: $49-$59	XP: $6	F12

Location: On US 431, 1.1 mi s of jct US 82 E. 1375 S Eufaula Ave 36027. Fax: 334/687-6870. **Facility:** 42 one-bedroom standard units, some with whirlpools. 2 stories (no elevator), exterior corridors. **Parking:** on-site. **Terms:** [CP] meal plan available, package plans. **Amenities:** high-speed Internet, irons, hair dryers. **Pool(s):** outdoor. **Cards:** AX, DC, DS, MC, VI.

SOME UNITS

EVERGREEN pop. 3,630

WHERE TO STAY

COMFORT INN *Book great rates at AAA.com* **Phone:** (251)578-4701

AAA SAVE

Motel

All Year 1P: $60-$100 2P: $60-$110 XP: $10 F13

Location: I-65, exit 96, just w. I-65 Hwy 83 Bates Rd 36401 (PO Box 564). Fax: 251/578-3180. **Facility:** 60 one-bedroom standard units. 2 stories (no elevator), exterior corridors. **Parking:** on-site. **Terms:** pets ($10 extra charge). **Amenities:** high-speed Internet, irons, hair dryers. **Pool(s):** outdoor. **Guest Services:** wireless Internet. **Cards:** AX, CB, DC, DS, JC, MC, VI.

FEE

DAYS INN OF EVERGREEN *Book great rates at AAA.com* **Phone:** (251)578-2100

Motel

All Year 1P: $55 2P: $70 XP: $10 F13

Location: I-65, exit 96, just w. Rt 2 36401 (Rt 2, Box 389). Fax: 251/578-2100. **Facility:** 40 one-bedroom standard units. 2 stories (no elevator), exterior corridors. **Parking:** on-site. **Terms:** [CP] meal plan available, pets ($10 extra charge). **Amenities:** high-speed Internet, irons, hair dryers. **Guest Services:** wireless Internet. **Cards:** AX, DC, DS, MC, VI.

SOME UNITS

FEE

FAIRHOPE pop. 12,480

WHERE TO STAY

HOLIDAY INN EXPRESS *Book great rates at AAA.com* **Phone:** 251/928-9191

AAA SAVE

Small-scale Hotel

All Year 1P: $108 2P: $108

Location: On US 98, 2.2 mi s of jct SR 104. 19751 Greeno Rd 36532. Fax: 251/990-7824. **Facility:** 65 one-bedroom standard units. 3 stories, interior corridors. *Bath:* combo or shower only. **Parking:** on-site. **Amenities:** voice mail, irons, hair dryers. **Pool(s):** heated outdoor. **Guest Services:** valet and coin laundry. **Business Services:** meeting rooms. **Cards:** AX, CB, DC, DS, JC, MC, VI. **Free Special Amenities: continental breakfast and local telephone calls.**

SOME UNITS

FEE

KEY WEST INN *Book at AAA.com* **Phone:** (251)990-7373

Motel

9/1-11/30 [CP]	1P: $89-$99	2P: $89-$99	XP: $5	F12
5/1-8/31 [CP]	1P: $79-$89	2P: $79-$89	XP: $5	F12
12/1-4/30 [CP]	1P: $69-$79	2P: $69-$79	XP: $5	F12

Location: On US 98, 1.9 mi s of jct SR 104. 231 S Greeno Rd 36532. Fax: 251/990-9671. **Facility:** 55 one-bedroom standard units. 2 stories (no elevator), exterior corridors. *Bath:* combo or shower only. **Parking:** on-site. **Terms:** package plans, pets ($10 extra charge). **Amenities:** high-speed Internet, irons, hair dryers. **Pool(s):** small outdoor. **Guest Services:** coin laundry. **Cards:** AX, DS, MC, VI.

SOME UNITS

FEE

WHERE TO DINE

THE FAIRHOPE INN RESTAURANT **Lunch:** $10-$12 **Dinner:** $24-$29 **Phone:** 251/928-6226

Regional American

Location: Just s of Fairhope Ave; center. 63 S Church St 36532. **Hours:** 11 am-2 & 5-9 pm, Fri & Sat-10 pm. Closed: 1/1, 12/25; also Mon. **Reservations:** suggested. **Features:** The contemporary cuisine here has a Louisiana influence and features seafood, beef, pork, veal, chicken and duck. The restaurant's attractive bed-and-breakfast-style setting includes an enclosed verandah and decor featuring gilt mirrors and antiques. Dressy casual; cocktails. **Parking:** on-site. **Cards:** AX, DS, MC, VI.

GAMBINO'S **Lunch:** $6-$11 **Dinner:** $9-$20 **Phone:** 251/928-5444

Italian

Location: 1.4 mi w on Fairhope Ave from jct US 98, then 0.8 mi s on Mobile St. 18 Laurel Ave 36532. **Hours:** 11 am-3 & 5-9:30 pm, Fri-10:30 pm, Sat 5 pm-9:30 pm. Closed: 1/1, 12/25. **Reservations:** accepted, except weekends. **Features:** Since 1976, the restaurant has served certified black Angus beef, seafood and pasta dishes to a loyal, local clientele. At peak times there may be a line to get in to dine. Casual dress; cocktails. **Parking:** on-site. **Cards:** AX, DS, MC, VI.

MARY ANN'S

Deli/Subs Sandwiches

Lunch: $5-$13 **Phone:** 251/928-3663

Location: Between Fairhope Ave and De La Mare St; downtown. 7 S Church St 36532. **Hours:** 11 am-2:30 pm. Closed major holidays; also Sun & week of Labor Day. **Features:** Lunch is the only meal this bright, cheery place serves, and chances are Mary Ann will be wandering around greeting guests. Offerings include homemade soup, quiche and hearty deli sandwiches that can be built to order. Casual dress; beer & wine only. **Parking:** street. **Cards:** AX, DS, MC, VI.

FAYETTE pop. 4,922

WHERE TO STAY

ROSE HOUSE INN

Historic Bed & Breakfast

Phone: (205)932-7673

All Year 1P: $59-$79 2P: $59-$99 XP: $10 F6

Location: 0.3 mi w on SR 18, then 0.3 mi n. Located in a residential area. 325 2nd Ave NW 35555. Fax: 205/932-5559. **Facility:** This restored historic home and adjacent, more modern guest house, is set on a large landscaped yard among mature oak trees. Smoke free premises. 10 one-bedroom standard units. 2 stories (no elevator), interior corridors. *Bath:* combo or shower only. **Parking:** on-site. **Terms:** package plans. **Amenities:** high-speed Internet, voice mail, irons, hair dryers. **Cards:** AX, DS, MC, VI.

SOME UNITS

/ VCR /

FLORENCE pop. 36,264

WHERE TO STAY

COMFORT INN *Book great rates at AAA.com*

AAA SAVE

Small-scale Hotel

Phone: (256)740-0444

All Year 1P: $69-$120 2P: $74-$130 XP: $5 F17

Location: US 43/72, just se of jct SR 133 (Cox Creek Pkwy). 150 Etta Gray Dr 35630. Fax: 256/740-6965. **Facility:** 48 one-bedroom standard units. 2 stories (no elevator), interior corridors. **Parking:** on-site, winter plug-ins. **Terms:** [CP] meal plan available. **Amenities:** high-speed Internet, irons, hair dryers. **Pool(s):** outdoor. **Leisure Activities:** exercise room. **Guest Services:** coin laundry, wireless Internet. **Business Services:** meeting rooms, business center. **Cards:** AX, CB, DC, DS, JC, MC, VI. **Free Special Amenities: expanded continental breakfast and newspaper.**

SOME UNITS

HAMPTON INN-FLORENCE MIDTOWN *Book great rates at AAA.com*

AAA SAVE

Small-scale Hotel

Phone: (256)764-8888

All Year 1P: $71-$107 2P: $71-$107

Location: On US 43/72, 0.4 mi nw of jct SR 133 (Cox Creek Pkwy). 2281 Florence Blvd 35630. Fax: 256/760-1930. **Facility:** 90 one-bedroom standard units, some with whirlpools. 4 stories, interior corridors. *Bath:* combo or shower only. **Parking:** on-site, winter plug-ins. **Terms:** 3 day cancellation notice-fee imposed, [BP] meal plan available, package plans. **Amenities:** video games (fee), high-speed Internet, dual phone lines, voice mail, irons, hair dryers. **Pool(s):** outdoor. **Leisure Activities:** exercise room. **Guest Services:** valet and coin laundry. **Business Services:** meeting rooms, fax (fee). **Cards:** AX, DC, DS, MC, VI. **Free Special Amenities: full breakfast and local telephone calls.**

SOME UNITS

JAMESON INN *Book at AAA.com*

Small-scale Hotel

Phone: (256)764-5326

All Year [ECP] 1P: $54-$120

Location: On US 43/72, just nw of jct SR 133 (Cox Creek Pkwy). Located behind Shoney's Restaurant. 115 Ana Dr 35630. Fax: 256/764-4433. **Facility:** 64 one-bedroom standard units. 2 stories (no elevator), exterior corridors. *Bath:* combo or shower only. **Parking:** on-site. **Terms:** cancellation fee imposed, small pets only ($10 fee). **Amenities:** *Some:* irons. **Pool(s):** outdoor. **Leisure Activities:** exercise room. **Guest Services:** valet laundry, wireless Internet. **Business Services:** meeting rooms, PC. **Cards:** AX, DC, DS, MC, VI.

SOME UNITS

ASK FEE

KNIGHTS INN FLORENCE *Book at AAA.com*

Motel

Phone: (256)766-2620

All Year 1P: $38-$61 2P: $43-$66 XP: $5 F13

Location: 2 mi w; jct Cox Creek Pkwy (SR 133) and US 72. 1915 Florence Blvd (US 72) 35630. Fax: 256/246-2228. **Facility:** 77 one-bedroom standard units. 1 story, exterior corridors. **Parking:** on-site. **Terms:** [CP] meal plan available, small pets only ($10 deposit). **Amenities:** hair dryers. *Some:* irons. **Pool(s):** outdoor. **Guest Services:** wireless Internet. **Business Services:** fax (fee). **Cards:** AX, CB, DC, DS, JC, MC, VI.

SOME UNITS

ASK FEE

MARRIOTT SHOALS HOTEL AND SPA *Book great rates at AAA.com*

Resort Large-scale Hotel

Phone: 256/246-3600

Property failed to provide current rates

Location: From US 72, 7.9 mi n on SR 133 (SE Wilson Dam Rd). 800 Cox Creek Pkwy S 35630. **Facility:** 200 units. 194 one-bedroom standard units. 3 one- and 3 two-bedroom suites, some with whirlpools. 6 stories, interior corridors. *Bath:* combo or shower only. **Parking:** on-site, winter plug-ins. **Terms:** small pets only ($75 fee). **Amenities:** video games (fee), CD players, high-speed Internet, dual phone lines, voice mail, safes, irons, hair dryers. *Some:* DVD players. **Dining:** 360 Grille, see separate listing. **Pool(s):** heated indoor/outdoor. **Leisure Activities:** whirlpools, waterslide, golf-36 holes, exercise room, spa. **Guest Services:** gift shop, valet and coin laundry, area transportation. **Business Services:** conference facilities, business center. ***(See color ad p 200)***

SOME UNITS

24 FEE

SUPER 8 MOTEL Book great rates at AAA.com Phone: (256)757-2167

Motel

All Year 1P: $51-$110 XP: $10 F17

Location: 3.8 mi e on US 43/72 from jct SR 133 (Cox Creek Pkwy). Located at Shoal Creek Bridge. 101 Hwy 72 & 43 E 35631-1457 (PO Box 1457). Fax: 256/757-1282. **Facility:** 34 one-bedroom standard units, some with efficiencies (no utensils). 1 story, exterior corridors. **Parking:** on-site, winter plug-ins. **Terms:** pets ($5 fee, $10 deposit). **Amenities:** *Some:* DVD players. **Pool(s):** outdoor. **Guest Services:** coin laundry, wireless Internet. **Cards:** AX, DC, DS, MC, VI. **Free Special Amenities: continental breakfast and high-speed Internet.**

SOME UNITS

FEE

WHERE TO DINE

360 GRILLE Dinner: $18-$44 Phone: 256/246-3660

Continental

Location: From US 72, 7.9 mi n on SR 133 (SE Wilson Dam Rd); in Marriott Shoals Hotel and Spa. 800 Cox Creek Pkwy S 35630. **Hours:** 5 pm-11 pm. Closed: Sun & Mon. **Reservations:** suggested. **Features:** Diners are treated to breathtaking views of the Tennessee valley as they sample creatively prepared dry-aged steaks and chops, fresh fish and Sunday brunch dishes. Cocktails; entertainment. **Parking:** on-site. **Cards:** AX, DC, DS, JC, MC, VI.

BARNHILL'S BUFFET Lunch: $5-$9 Dinner: $7-$10 Phone: 256/718-3766

American

Location: Jct US 43, just n on SR 133. 201 Cox Creek Pkwy 35630. **Hours:** 10:45 am-8:45 pm, Fri-9 pm, Sat 7 am-9 pm, Sun 7 am-8:45 pm. Closed: 12/25. **Features:** Casual dress. **Parking:** on-site. **Cards:** AX, DS, MC, VI.

BAYOU BLUE Lunch: $6-$12 Dinner: $8-$15 Phone: 256/766-3227

Seafood

Location: Between SR 18 and Sweetwater Ave. 2151 Florence Blvd 35630. **Hours:** 11 am-10 pm, Fri & Sat-11 pm. Closed major holidays; also Sun & Mon. **Features:** Diners spice up their trip with great Cajun food. The large bar area invites relaxation, and friendly service furthers that mood. Casual dress; cocktails. **Parking:** on-site. **Cards:** MC, VI.

DALE'S STEAKHOUSE Dinner: $11-$29 Phone: 256/766-4961

Steak House

Location: On US 43/72, 0.5 mi se of downtown. 1001 Mitchell Blvd 35630. **Hours:** 5 pm-10 pm. Closed major holidays; also Sun. **Reservations:** suggested. **Features:** The steakhouse's food and atmosphere make up for what is absent on the outside. A fixture on grocery shelves, the signature steak sauce tastes delicious on the many cuts of beef tenderloin, prime rib, pork chops, beef kebab and beef ribs. The old-fashioned service and menu won't let customers down. Dressy casual; cocktails. **Parking:** on-site. **Cards:** AX, DC, MC, VI.

FOLEY pop. 7,590

WHERE TO STAY

BEST WESTERN RIVIERA INN Book great rates at AAA.com Phone: (251)943-8600

Motel

3/1-8/31	1P: $89-$139	2P: $89-$139
12/1-2/28 & 9/1-11/30	1P: $79-$99	2P: $79-$99

Location: On SR 59, 1.1 mi s of jct US 98. 1504 S McKenzie St 36535. Fax: 251/943-8600. **Facility:** 42 units. 40 one-bedroom standard units. 2 one-bedroom suites ($129-$159) with whirlpools. 2 stories (no elevator), exterior corridors. **Parking:** on-site. **Amenities:** irons, hair dryers. *Some:* high-speed Internet. **Pool(s):** outdoor. **Guest Services:** coin laundry. **Cards:** AX, CB, DC, DS, JC, MC, VI.

SOME UNITS

ASK

HOLIDAY INN EXPRESS Book great rates at AAA.com Phone: (251)943-9100

Small-scale Hotel

5/25-9/2 [CP]	1P: $111-$187	2P: $111-$187	XP: $5	F18
3/1-5/24 [CP]	1P: $95-$164	2P: $95-$164	XP: $5	F18
9/3-11/30 [CP]	1P: $95-$137	2P: $95-$137	XP: $5	F18
12/1-2/28 [CP]	1P: $95-$130	2P: $95-$130	XP: $5	F18

Location: On SR 59, 1.9 mi s of jct US 98. 2682 S McKenzie St 36535. Fax: 251/943-9421. **Facility:** 83 one-bedroom standard units, some with whirlpools. 3 stories, exterior corridors. *Bath:* combo or shower only. **Parking:** on-site. **Terms:** package plans, small pets only ($20 fee). **Amenities:** voice mail, irons, hair dryers. *Some:* high-speed Internet. **Pool(s):** heated outdoor, wading. **Leisure Activities:** whirlpool, limited exercise equipment. **Guest Services:** valet and coin laundry, airport transportation-Foley Airport, area transportation-within 10 mi. **Business Services:** meeting rooms, PC. **Cards:** AX, DC, DS, MC, VI.

SOME UNITS

FEE FEE

KEY WEST INN Book at AAA.com Phone: (251)943-1241

Motel

All Year [CP]	1P: $60-$120	2P: $60-$120	XP: $10	F12

Location: On SR 59, 1.8 mi s of jct US 98. 2520 S McKenzie St 36535. Fax: 251/943-1561. **Facility:** 44 one-bedroom standard units. 2 stories (no elevator), exterior corridors. **Parking:** on-site. **Terms:** 2-4 night minimum stay - seasonal, cancellation fee imposed, pets ($10 extra charge). **Pool(s):** small outdoor. **Guest Services:** coin laundry. **Cards:** AX, DC, DS, MC, VI.

SOME UNITS

ASK

FEE

SUPER 8 MOTEL *Book great rates at AAA.com* **Phone:** (251)943-3297

5/19-9/5 [CP]	1P: $69-$149	2P: $69-$149	XP: $10	F12
3/1-5/18 [CP]	1P: $59-$99	2P: $59-$99	XP: $10	F12
9/6-11/30 [CP]	1P: $49-$99	2P: $49-$99	XP: $10	F12
12/1-2/28 [CP]	1P: $45-$89	2P: $45-$89	XP: $10	F12

Motel

Location: On SR 59, 1.2 mi s of jct US 98. 1517 S McKenzie St 36535. Fax: 251/943-7548. **Facility:** 84 units. 82 one-bedroom standard units. 2 one-bedroom suites. 2 stories (no elevator), interior corridors. **Parking:** on-site. **Amenities:** irons. **Pool(s):** outdoor. **Leisure Activities:** exercise room. **Guest Services:** coin laundry. **Business Services:** meeting rooms. **Cards:** AX, DS, MC, VI. **Free Special Amenities: continental breakfast and local telephone calls.**

SOME UNITS

WHERE TO DINE

THE GIFT HORSE RESTAURANT **Lunch:** $10 **Dinner:** $13 **Phone:** 251/943-3663

Southern

Location: On US 98, just w of jct SR 59. 209 W Laurel Ave 36535. **Hours:** 11 am-9 pm. Closed: 12/25. **Reservations:** accepted. **Features:** Experience true Southern hospitality and cuisine at this 1912 landmark restaurant, with its "groaning" 28-foot mahogany table from 1840. Diners help themselves to seafood gumbo, praline sweet potatoes and perhaps fried chicken. The daily changing menu always offers great value for hearty appetites. Casual dress. **Parking:** street. **Cards:** MC, VI. **Historic**

LAMBERT'S CAFE III **Lunch:** $9-$19 **Dinner:** $9-$19 **Phone:** 251/943-7655

American

Location: SR 59, 2.4 mi s of jct US 98. 2981 S McKenzie St 36535. **Hours:** 10:30 am-9 pm. Closed: 1/1, 11/22, 12/25. **Features:** Tired of the same old approach to serving dinner rolls? Then perhaps the "Home of Throwed Rolls" is for you! With its rural American decor, home cooking menu and bread literally thrown to you from across the room, Lambert's is definitely a novelty. Casual dress. **Parking:** on-site.

SONNY'S REAL PIT BAR-B-Q **Lunch:** $6-$8 **Dinner:** $8-$13 **Phone:** 251/945-7675

Barbecue

Location: Jct US 98, 3 mi s on SR 59. 3177 S McKenzie St 36535. **Hours:** 11 am-9 pm, Fri & Sat-10 pm. Closed: 11/22, 12/25. **Features:** House specialties include barbecue ribs, pork and chicken grilled over an open pit and fresh, homemade pie. Rustic and comfortable, the atmosphere is perfect for family meals.The salad bar is always a popular choice also. Casual dress; beer only. **Parking:** on-site. **Cards:** AX, DS, MC, VI.

FORT PAYNE pop. 12,938

WHERE TO STAY

DAYS INN *Book great rates at AAA.com* **Phone:** (256)845-2085

4/1-11/30 [ECP]	1P: $74-$129	2P: $79-$134	XP: $5	F16
12/1-3/31 [ECP]	1P: $60-$90	2P: $65-$95	XP: $5	F16

Motel

Location: I-59, exit 218, just w. 1416 Glenn Blvd SW 35968 (PO Box 680655). Fax: 256/845-7745. **Facility:** 65 one-bedroom standard units. 2 stories (no elevator), exterior corridors. **Parking:** on-site. **Amenities:** high-speed Internet, irons, hair dryers. **Pool(s):** outdoor. **Guest Services:** valet and coin laundry. **Business Services:** meeting rooms, fax (fee). **Cards:** AX, CB, DC, DS, MC, VI. **Free Special Amenities: expanded continental breakfast and high-speed Internet.**

SOME UNITS

FEE

HAMPTON INN *Book great rates at AAA.com* **Phone:** 256/304-2600

Property failed to provide current rates

Small-scale Hotel

Location: I-59, exit 218, just w. 1201 Jordan Rd SW 35968. Fax: 256/304-2601. **Facility:** 56 one-bedroom standard units. 4 stories, interior corridors. *Bath:* combo or shower only. **Parking:** on-site. **Amenities:** high-speed Internet, voice mail, irons, hair dryers. **Pool(s):** heated indoor. **Leisure Activities:** exercise room. **Guest Services:** valet and coin laundry, wireless Internet. **Business Services:** meeting rooms, business center.

SOME UNITS

HOLIDAY INN EXPRESS HOTEL & SUITES *Book great rates at AAA.com* **Phone:** (256)997-1020

4/2-5/2 & 9/4-11/30	1P: $99-$159	2P: $99-$159	XP: $9	F18
5/3-9/3	1P: $80-$100	2P: $80-$100	XP: $9	F18
12/1-4/1	1P: $75-$95	2P: $75-$95	XP: $9	F18

Small-scale Hotel

Location: I-59, exit 218, just w. 112 Airport Rd W 35968. Fax: 256/997-1080. **Facility:** 60 units. 59 one-bedroom standard units, some with whirlpools. 1 one-bedroom suite ($80-$160) with whirlpool. 3 stories, interior corridors. *Bath:* combo or shower only. **Parking:** on-site. **Terms:** [ECP] meal plan available, package plans. **Amenities:** dual phone lines, voice mail, irons, hair dryers. **Pool(s):** small heated outdoor. **Guest Services:** valet and coin laundry, wireless Internet. **Business Services:** meeting rooms, business center. **Cards:** AX, DC, DS, JC, MC, VI. **Free Special Amenities: expanded continental breakfast and high-speed Internet.**

SOME UNITS

FULTONDALE —*See Birmingham p. 230.*

GADSDEN pop. 38,978

WHERE TO STAY

BEST WESTERN GADSDEN HOTEL & SUITES *Book great rates at AAA.com* **Phone:** (256)570-0569

All Year	1P: $89-$109	2P: $95-$115

Small-scale Hotel

Location: I-59, exit 181, just w. 205 Enterprise Dr 35904. Fax: 256/570-6344. **Facility:** 67 one-bedroom standard units, some with whirlpools. 3 stories, interior corridors. *Bath:* combo or shower only. **Parking:** on-site. **Amenities:** high-speed Internet, voice mail, irons, hair dryers. *Some:* DVD players. **Pool(s):** small outdoor. **Leisure Activities:** exercise room, volleyball. **Guest Services:** complimentary evening beverages, valet and coin laundry. **Business Services:** business center. **Cards:** AX, DC, DS, MC, VI. **Free Special Amenities: expanded continental breakfast and high-speed Internet.**

SOME UNITS

GADSDEN INN & SUITES

Phone: 256/543-7240

Small-scale Hotel

4/1-9/1	1P: $46-$64	2P: $54-$74	XP: $5	F3
12/1-3/31 & 9/2-11/30	1P: $46-$54	2P: $54-$60	XP: $5	F3

Location: Jct US 411 and 431/278; enter on 2nd St off US 431. 200 Albert Rains Blvd 35901 (PO Box 1051, 35902). Fax: 256/543-7240. **Facility:** 83 units. 75 one-bedroom standard units, some with efficiencies and/or whirlpools. 8 one-bedroom suites ($90-$119) with kitchens and whirlpools. 1-2 stories (no elevator), exterior corridors. *Bath:* combo or shower only. **Parking:** on-site, winter plug-ins. **Terms:** 2 night minimum stay - seasonal, [ECP] meal plan available. **Amenities:** high-speed Internet, voice mail, irons. **Pool(s):** outdoor. **Leisure Activities:** exercise room, game room. **Guest Services:** valet and coin laundry. **Business Services:** meeting rooms. **Cards:** AX, CB, DC, DS, MC, VI.

SOME UNITS

ASK / /

HAMPTON INN *Book great rates at AAA.com*

Phone: (256)546-2337

AAA SAVE

Small-scale Hotel

All Year 1P: $89-$104

Location: I-759, exit 4B, just n on US 411. 129 River Rd 35901. Fax: 256/547-5124. **Facility:** 100 one-bedroom standard units. 3 stories, interior corridors. *Bath:* combo or shower only. **Parking:** on-site. **Amenities:** high-speed Internet, voice mail, irons, hair dryers. **Pool(s):** outdoor. **Leisure Activities:** exercise room. **Guest Services:** valet laundry. **Business Services:** meeting rooms, fax (fee). **Cards:** AX, CB, DC, DS, MC, VI. **Free Special Amenities: expanded continental breakfast and high-speed Internet.**

SOME UNITS

/ /

MOTEL 6 #1495 *Book at AAA.com*

Phone: 256/543-1105

Small-scale Hotel

4/20-8/30	1P: $37-$47	2P: $43-$53	XP: $3	F17
12/1-4/19 & 8/31-11/30	1P: $35-$45	2P: $41-$51	XP: $3	F17

Location: I-759, exit 4A, 0.8 mi s on US 411. 1600 Rainbow Dr 35901. Fax: 256/543-7836. **Facility:** 104 one-bedroom standard units. 2 stories (no elevator), exterior corridors. *Bath:* combo or shower only. **Parking:** on-site. **Pool(s):** outdoor. **Guest Services:** coin laundry. **Business Services:** meeting rooms, fax (fee). **Cards:** AX, CB, DC, DS, MC, VI.

SOME UNITS

/ /

WHERE TO DINE

OLIVES CAFE

Lunch: $7-$11 Dinner: $11-$25 Phone: 256/547-8673

American

Location: I-759, exit 4B, 0.6 mi n on Rainbow Dr, then 0.8 mi nw on 3rd St. 504 Broad St 35901. **Hours:** 11 am-2 & 5-10 pm, Sun-Tues to 2 pm. Closed major holidays. **Features:** The downtown dinner-style cafe dishes out Southern hospitality and delicious meals. Mama Corleone's meatballs are representative of the Mediterranean fare. Desserts are homemade. Casual dress; cocktails. **Parking:** on-site. **Cards:** DC, MC, VI.

TOP O'THE RIVER

Dinner: $10-$15 Phone: 256/547-9817

Seafood

Location: I-759, exit 4A, 0.8 mi s on US 411. 1606 Rainbow Dr 35901. **Hours:** 5 pm-9 pm, Fri-10 pm, Sat 4 pm-10 pm, Sun noon-8 pm. Closed major holidays; also 12/24. **Features:** Folks line up to get into this restaurant which features generous portions of catfish, chicken, shrimp and steak. The fresh baked cornbread, still warm in its own skillet, is a real treat. Also worth a try: the unusual fried dill pickles. Casual dress; cocktails. **Parking:** on-site. **Cards:** AX, DS, MC, VI.

GARDENDALE —See Birmingham p. 231.

GREENVILLE pop. 7,228

WHERE TO STAY

BEST WESTERN INN *Book great rates at AAA.com*

Phone: (334)382-9200

AAA SAVE

Motel

All Year [CP] 1P: $55-$80 2P: $55-$85 XP: $6 F18

Location: I-65, exit 130, just n on SR 185. 56 Cahaba Rd 36037. Fax: 334/382-9200. **Facility:** 45 one-bedroom standard units. 2 stories (no elevator), exterior corridors. **Parking:** on-site. **Amenities:** irons, hair dryers. **Pool(s):** outdoor. **Guest Services:** valet laundry, wireless Internet. **Cards:** AX, CB, DC, DS, JC, MC, VI. **Free Special Amenities: continental breakfast and high-speed Internet.**

SOME UNITS

/ /

COMFORT INN *Book great rates at AAA.com*

Phone: 334/383-9595

AAA SAVE

Small-scale Hotel

All Year [CP] 1P: $55-$80 2P: $55-$85 XP: $6 F12

Location: I-65, exit 130, n on SR 185. 1029 Fort Dale Rd 36037. Fax: 334/382-2813. **Facility:** 54 one-bedroom standard units, some with whirlpools. 3 stories, interior corridors. *Bath:* combo or shower only. **Parking:** on-site. **Terms:** 7 day cancellation notice, small pets only ($5 extra charge). **Amenities:** irons, hair dryers. **Pool(s):** outdoor. **Leisure Activities:** exercise room. **Guest Services:** valet laundry, wireless Internet. **Business Services:** meeting rooms. **Cards:** AX, CB, DC, DS, JC, MC, VI. **Free Special Amenities: continental breakfast and newspaper.**

SOME UNITS

FEE / /

DAYS INN *Book great rates at AAA.com*

Phone: (334)382-3118

AAA SAVE

Motel

All Year [CP] 1P: $55-$75 2P: $60-$80 XP: $5 F15

Location: I-65, exit 130, just s on SR 185. 946 Fort Dale Rd 36037. Fax: 334/382-2578. **Facility:** 39 one-bedroom standard units. 2 stories (no elevator), exterior corridors. **Parking:** on-site. **Terms:** pets ($10 extra charge). **Amenities:** high-speed Internet, irons, hair dryers. **Pool(s):** outdoor. **Guest Services:** valet laundry, wireless Internet. **Cards:** AX, CB, DC, DS, MC, VI. **Free Special Amenities: continental breakfast and high-speed Internet.**

SOME UNITS

FEE / /

HAMPTON INN-GREENVILLE *Book great rates at AAA.com* **Phone:** 334/382-9631

Small-scale Hotel

Property failed to provide current rates

Location: I-65, exit 130, just n on SR 185. 219 Interstate Dr 36037. Fax: 334/383-9029. **Facility:** 69 one-bedroom standard units. 3 stories, interior corridors. *Bath:* combo or shower only. **Parking:** on-site. **Terms:** check-in 4 pm. **Amenities:** dual phone lines, voice mail, irons, hair dryers. **Pool(s):** outdoor. **Guest Services:** valet and coin laundry, wireless Internet. **Business Services:** meeting rooms.

SOME UNITS

JAMESON INN *Book at AAA.com* **Phone:** (334)382-6300

Motel

All Year [ECP] 1P: $54-$120

Location: I-65, exit 130, just n on SR 185, then just w on Cahaba Rd. 71 Jameson Ln 36037. Fax: 334/382-9394. **Facility:** 40 one-bedroom standard units, some with whirlpools. 2 stories (no elevator), exterior corridors. **Parking:** on-site. **Terms:** cancellation fee imposed, small pets only ($10 fee). **Amenities:** irons, hair dryers. **Pool(s):** outdoor. **Leisure Activities:** exercise room. **Guest Services:** wireless Internet. **Business Services:** PC. **Cards:** AX, DC, DS, MC, VI.

SOME UNITS

FEE

WHERE TO DINE

BATES HOUSE OF TURKEY RESTAURANT **Lunch:** $5-$7 **Phone:** 334/382-6123

American

Location: I-65, exit 130, just w. 1001 Fort Dale Rd 36037. **Hours:** 10 am-6 pm. Closed major holidays. **Features:** Turkey and all the fixins are served up just like a Thanksgiving feast at this family-owned restaurant; you can even take home one of their organic birds. Casual dress. **Parking:** on-site. **Cards:** MC, VI.

OLD MEXICO **Lunch:** $5-$10 **Dinner:** $5-$10 **Phone:** 334/383-9950

Mexican

Location: I-65, exit 130, just s on SR 185. 941 Fort Dale Rd 36037. **Hours:** 11 am-2 & 5-10 pm. Closed: 7/4, 12/25; also Sun. **Reservations:** accepted. **Features:** Standard, but successfully-prepared Mexican cuisine is served here; locals come for the fajitas and delicious half-priced margaritas on Wednesday nights. The place has quite a bit of charm in terms of decor. Casual dress; cocktails. **Parking:** on-site. **Cards:** AX, DC, DS, MC, VI.

GULF SHORES pop. 5,044

WHERE TO STAY

BEST WESTERN ON THE BEACH **Phone:** 251/948-2711

fyi

Small-scale Hotel

Property failed to provide current rates

Under major renovation, scheduled to be completed May 2007. **Last rated:** **Location:** On SR 182, just e of jct SR 59. 337 E Beach Blvd 36542 (PO Box 481, 36547). Fax: 251/948-7339. **Facility:** 101 units. 100 one-bedroom standard units, some with efficiencies or kitchens. 1 one-bedroom suite with kitchen. 3-6 stories, interior/exterior corridors. **Parking:** on-site. **Amenities:** voice mail, irons, hair dryers. **Pool(s):** outdoor, heated indoor, wading. **Leisure Activities:** whirlpools, fishing, exercise room. **Guest Services:** coin laundry. **Business Services:** meeting rooms, fax (fee).

SOME UNITS

COURTYARD BY MARRIOTT *Book great rates at AAA.com* **Phone:** (251)968-1113

AAA SAVE

Small-scale Hotel

5/18-8/18	1P: $98-$152	2P: $98-$152
2/9-5/17 & 8/19-11/30	1P: $89-$116	2P: $89-$116
12/1-2/8	1P: $80	2P: $80

Location: SR 59, 2.4 mi n of jct SR 180. 3750 Gulf Shores Pkwy 36542. Fax: 251/968-1112. **Facility:** 90 units. 87 one-bedroom standard units, some with whirlpools. 3 one-bedroom suites. 3 stories, interior corridors. *Bath:* combo or shower only. **Parking:** on-site. **Terms:** package plans. **Amenities:** high-speed Internet, dual phone lines, voice mail, irons, hair dryers. **Dining:** 6-10 am, Sat & Sun-11 am. **Pool(s):** outdoor. **Leisure Activities:** whirlpool, exercise room. **Guest Services:** valet and coin laundry. **Business Services:** meeting rooms. **Cards:** AX, DC, DS, MC, VI. **Free Special Amenities: newspaper and early check-in/late check-out.**

SOME UNITS

THE GULF SHORES PLANTATION *Book great rates at AAA.com* **Phone:** (251)540-5000

AAA SAVE

Resort Condominium

5/22-8/11	1P: $119-$209	2P: $119-$232
8/12-11/30	1P: $89-$165	2P: $89-$215
3/1-5/21	1P: $99-$172	2P: $99-$197
12/1-2/28	1P: $75-$129	2P: $75-$145

Location: Oceanfront. On SR 180, 12.4 mi w of SR 59. 805 Plantation Rd 36542 (PO Box 1299, 36547). Fax: 251/540-6055. **Facility:** On the Gulf of Mexico and off the beaten path, this resort features many different styles of rooms. 320 units. 50 one-bedroom standard units with efficiencies. 56 one-, 199 two- and 15 three-bedroom suites with kitchens. 3-9 stories, interior/exterior corridors. **Parking:** on-site. **Terms:** check-in 4 pm, 2-7 night minimum stay - seasonal, 7 day cancellation notice, weekly rates available. **Amenities:** voice mail, irons, hair dryers. *Some:* DVD players, CD players. **Dining:** 11 am-10 pm; closed 3/1-9/4, cocktails. **Pool(s):** 6 outdoor, heated indoor, 3 wading. **Leisure Activities:** saunas, whirlpools, steamroom, rental sailboats in summer, putting green, 8 tennis courts (7 lighted), exercise room, basketball, horseshoes, shuffleboard, volleyball. *Fee:* game room. **Guest Services:** gift shop, coin laundry. **Business Services:** meeting rooms. **Cards:** AX, DS, MC, VI. *(See color ad p 256)*

SOME UNITS

VCR

LA QUINTA INN Book great rates at AAA.com Phone: 251/967-3500

Small-scale Hotel

Property failed to provide current rates

Location: On SR 180, just w of jct SR 59. 213 W Fort Morgan Rd 36542. Fax: 251/967-4766. **Facility:** Smoke free premises. 54 one-bedroom standard units, some with whirlpools. 2 stories, interior corridors. *Bath:* combo or shower only. **Parking:** on-site. **Amenities:** voice mail, irons, hair dryers. **Pool(s):** heated indoor. **Leisure Activities:** sauna, whirlpool, game room. **Guest Services:** coin laundry. **Business Services:** meeting rooms. ***(See color ad p 386)***

SOME UNITS

MICROTEL INN Phone: 251/967-3000

Small-scale Hotel

All Year	1P: $40-$100	2P: $50-$120	XP: $5	F18

Location: On SR 59, 2.2 mi n of jct SR 180. 3600 Gulf Shore Pkwy 36542 (PO Box 4107, 36547). Fax: 251/967-2363. **Facility:** 61 one-bedroom standard units. 2 stories (no elevator), interior corridors. *Bath:* combo or shower only. **Parking:** on-site. **Terms:** 2-3 night minimum stay - seasonal. **Pool(s):** small outdoor. **Cards:** AX, DS, MC, VI.

SOME UNITS

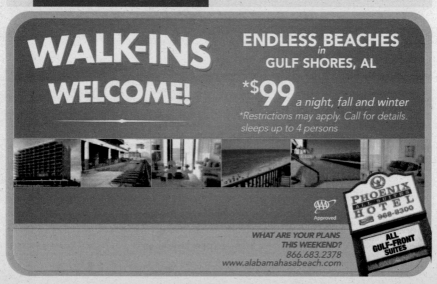

PHOENIX ALL SUITES HOTEL **Phone:** 251/968-8300

5/2-8/5	1P: $160-$260	2P: $160-$260
2/1-5/1	1P: $144-$209	2P: $144-$209
8/6-11/30	1P: $100-$141	2P: $100-$141
12/1-1/31	1P: $78-$108	2P: $78-$108

Condominium

Location: Oceanfront. On SR 182, just e of SR 59. 201 E Beach Blvd 36542 (PO Box 4009). Fax: 251/968-5785. **Facility:** This new property offers modernly furnished one-bedroom suites with (gulf-view) balconies, fully equipped kitchens and covered parking. Smoke free premises. 84 one-bedroom suites with kitchens. 9 stories, exterior corridors. **Parking:** on-site. **Terms:** 7 day cancellation notice-fee imposed. **Amenities:** DVD players, CD players, high-speed Internet, voice mail, safes, irons, hair dryers. **Pool(s):** wading, lap. **Guest Services:** coin laundry. **Cards:** AX, DS, MC, VI. **Free Special Amenities: high-speed Internet.** *(See color ad p 256)*

WHERE TO DINE

GULF SHORES BISTRO & BAKERY **Lunch:** $6-$15 **Dinner:** $6-$20 **Phone:** 251/967-4646

Regional Creole

Location: 0.4 mi n on SR 59 from jct SR 180, then just w. 200 Club House Dr 36542. **Hours:** 7:30 am-9 pm, Sat & Sun 8 am-2 pm. Closed: 11/22, 12/25. **Features:** This relaxed eatery with its open kitchen provides a New Orleans and Caribbean inspired cuisine, such as barbecue shrimp, paneed catfish, crab and mango pastry and cedar plank mahi. A long list of appetizers, sandwiches, pastas and salads round out the menu. The bakery case that greets you as you enter will remind you to save some room for dessert. Casual dress; cocktails. **Parking:** on-site. **Cards:** AX, DC, DS, MC, VI.

LUCY BUFFETT'S LULU'S AT HOMEPORT MARINA **Lunch:** $6-$15 **Dinner:** $6-$15 **Phone:** 251/967-5858

Seafood

Location: From north end of Intracoastal Waterway bridge, just e on E 29th Ave, then just s. 200 E 25th Ave 36542. **Hours:** 11 am-10 pm. Closed: 1/1, 11/22, 12/24, 12/25. **Features:** The open-air waterfront restaurant has a fun Caribbean resort feel to it and serves very simple, local seafoods such as fried crab claws, fried oysters or peel-and-eat shrimp. They also feature live music every night, a sand dune playground area for children and boat dockage. This place is all about fun. Casual dress; cocktails. **Parking:** on-site. **Cards:** AX, DS, MC, VI.

ORIGINAL OYSTER HOUSE **Lunch:** $6-$9 **Dinner:** $9-$16 **Phone:** 251/948-2445

Seafood

Location: On SR 59, 0.7 mi s of SR 180; in Bayou Village. 701 Gulf Shores Pkwy 36542. **Hours:** 11 am-10 pm, Fri & Sat-11 pm. Closed: 11/22, 12/25 & Easter. **Features:** This family oriented restaurant is popular with locals and visitors alike, and it is easy to see why. Fresh seafood is served in generous portions and by the friendliest servers you can find, and the salad bar lets you get all the greens you need before you fill up. Casual dress; cocktails. **Parking:** on-site. **Cards:** AX, DC, DS, MC, VI.

GUNTERSVILLE pop. 7,395

WHERE TO STAY

HAMPTON INN LAKE GUNTERSVILLE *Book great rates at AAA.com* **Phone:** 256/582-4176

All Year 1P: $89-$104 2P: $94-$109 XP: $5 F17

Small-scale Hotel

Location: On US 431, 1.9 mi s of jct SR 69. 14451 Hwy 431 S 35976. Fax: 256/264-7111. **Facility:** 79 one-bedroom standard units. 4 stories, interior corridors. *Bath:* combo or shower only. **Parking:** on-site. **Amenities:** high-speed Internet, dual phone lines, voice mail, irons, hair dryers. **Pool(s):** heated outdoor. **Leisure Activities:** fishing, limited exercise equipment. **Guest Services:** valet and coin laundry. **Business Services:** meeting rooms, business center. **Cards:** AX, DS, MC, VI.

SOME UNITS

WHERE TO DINE

BISTRO LA LUNA **Lunch:** $6-$10 **Dinner:** $20-$25 **Phone:** 256/582-0930

Southwestern

Location: 1.2 mi e on Wyeth Dr from jct US 431, follow signs. 7001 Val Monte Dr 35976. **Hours:** 5 pm-9 pm, Fri-10 pm, Sat 11 am-2 & 5-10 pm. Closed: 12/25; also Sun & Mon. **Reservations:** suggested. **Features:** Who would have thought that one could find such creativity in a little town like Guntersville? The restaurant is the place to go if you're looking for a step up from the usual. The ambiance is upscale casual, the service polished and the Southwestern menu delightfully eclectic. Try the gator wrap for lunch or, for dinner, savor every bite of the "The Big Mammou," an extra spicy blend of chicken, andouille sausage, garlic and green onion in a zesty tomato sauce over fettucine. Casual dress; cocktails. **Parking:** on-site. **Cards:** AX, DS, MC, VI.

KC'S COYOTE CAFE **Dinner:** $12-$30 **Phone:** 256/582-1676

American

Location: Just w of jct US 431 and Taylor St; downtown. 410 Old Town St 35976. **Hours:** 5 pm-10 pm. Closed: Sun & Mon. **Features:** Housed in a funky little building in the old part of town, the restaurant serves steak and seafood and is dedicated to offering only the highest quality products without use of preservatives, additives or artificial ingredients. Casual dress; cocktails. **Parking:** on-site. **Cards:** MC, VI.

TOP O' THE RIVER **Lunch:** $8-$17 **Dinner:** $8-$17 **Phone:** 256/582-4567

Seafood

Location: 1.1 mi e on Wyeth Dr from jct US 431, follow signs. 7004 Val Monte Dr 35976. **Hours:** 5 pm-9 pm, Fri-10 pm, Sat 4 pm-10 pm, Sun noon-8 pm. Closed major holidays; also 12/24. **Features:** With military precision, the large and popular family restaurant can welcome and serve over 700 people at a time. It is known locally for its excellent catfish and delicious homemade cornbread and coleslaw. Also high on most people's list are the fried dill pickles and mustard greens. Casual dress; cocktails. **Parking:** on-site. **Cards:** AX, DS, MC, VI.

HAMILTON pop. 6,786

WHERE TO STAY

DAYS INN Book great rates at AAA.com **Phone:** (205)921-1790

Small-scale Hotel

All Year	1P: $65	2P: $65	XP: $5	F

Location: US 78, exit 14, 1 mi n, then 1 mi w on US 43. 1849 Military St S 35570. Fax: 205/921-1790. **Facility:** 38 one-bedroom standard units, some with whirlpools. 2 stories (no elevator), exterior corridors. *Bath:* combo or shower only. **Parking:** on-site. **Terms:** pets ($10 extra charge). **Amenities:** high-speed Internet, irons, hair dryers. **Pool(s):** outdoor. **Guest Services:** coin laundry, wireless Internet. **Business Services:** fax (fee). **Cards:** AX, DC, DS, MC, VI. **Free Special Amenities: continental breakfast and high-speed Internet.**

SOME UNITS FEE

ECONO LODGE INN & SUITES Book great rates at AAA.com **Phone:** 205/921-7831

Small-scale Hotel

Property failed to provide current rates

Location: US 78, exit 14, 1 mi n, then 1 mi w on US 43. 2031 Military St S 35570. Fax: 205/921-7831. **Facility:** 80 one-bedroom standard units. 2 stories (no elevator), exterior corridors. **Parking:** on-site. **Terms:** pets ($25 deposit). **Amenities:** hair dryers. *Some:* high-speed Internet, irons. **Pool(s):** outdoor. **Guest Services:** valet and coin laundry. **Business Services:** meeting rooms, fax (fee).

SOME UNITS FEE

HANCEVILLE pop. 2,951

WHERE TO STAY

COMFORT INN Book great rates at AAA.com **Phone:** 256/352-0151

Small-scale Hotel

All Year	1P: $65-$110	2P: $65-$110	XP: $5	F

Location: I-65, exit 287, 16 mi n on US 31. 810 Main St NE 35077. Fax: 256/352-4151. **Facility:** 42 one-bedroom standard units, some with whirlpools. 2 stories (no elevator), interior corridors. *Bath:* combo or shower only. **Parking:** on-site. **Amenities:** high-speed Internet, voice mail, irons, hair dryers. **Pool(s):** small outdoor. **Leisure Activities:** limited exercise equipment. **Guest Services:** coin laundry. **Business Services:** fax. **Cards:** AX, CB, DC, DS, MC, VI.

SOME UNITS

HOMEWOOD —See Birmingham p. 231.

HOOVER —See Birmingham p. 234.

HUNTSVILLE pop. 158,216

Airport Accommodations

HUNTSVILLE INT'L-CARL T JONES FIELD	Diamond Rating	Rate Range High Season	Listing Page
Hampton Inn-Huntsville/Madison, 0.5 mi e of airport	3 diamonds	$84-$94	264
Holiday Inn Huntsville-West, 0.5 mi n of airport	3 diamonds	$109	264
Motel 6 - 1087, 0.5 mi e of airport	1 diamond	$39-$55	264
Radisson Inn Huntsville Airport, 2 mi n of airport	3 diamonds	$107-$139	265
Ramada Inn & Conference Center, 2 mi n of airport	2 diamonds	Failed to provide	265

WHERE TO STAY

AMERICA'S BEST INNS Book great rates at AAA.com **Phone:** (256)539-9671

Motel

All Year	1P: $59-$79	2P: $59-$79	XP: $4	F16

Location: I-565, exit 19B, 0.5 mi n on US 231/431, Cook Ave exit. 1304 N Memorial Pkwy 35801. Fax: 256/539-6514. **Facility:** 90 one-bedroom standard units, some with whirlpools. 2 stories (no elevator), exterior corridors. **Parking:** on-site. **Terms:** small pets only. **Amenities:** irons, hair dryers. **Pool(s):** small outdoor. **Guest Services:** coin laundry, wireless Internet. **Business Services:** fax. **Cards:** AX, DS, MC, VI. **Free Special Amenities: continental breakfast and high-speed Internet.**

SOME UNITS

BEST WESTERN ROCKET CITY INN & SUITES Book great rates at AAA.com **Phone:** (256)837-7412

Small-scale Hotel

All Year	1P: $79-$89	2P: $79-$89	XP: $5	D12

Location: I-565, exit 14B, 2.6 mi n on Research Park Blvd, then 0.6 mi w on US 72. 6200 Torok Cir 35806. Fax: 256/830-4978. **Facility:** 63 units. 57 one-bedroom standard units, some with whirlpools. 6 one-bedroom suites with efficiencies (no utensils). 3 stories, interior corridors. **Parking:** on-site. **Terms:** cancellation fee imposed. **Amenities:** high-speed Internet, voice mail, irons, hair dryers. *Some:* DVD players. **Pool(s):** small outdoor. **Leisure Activities:** limited exercise equipment. **Business Services:** meeting rooms, business center. **Cards:** AX, CB, DC, DS, MC, VI.

SOME UNITS

COUNTRY INN & SUITES BY CARLSON Book at AAA.com Phone: (256)837-4070

Small-scale Hotel All Year [ECP] 1P: $99-$129 2P: $109-$139 XP: $10 F12

Location: I-565, exit 14B, 2.6 mi n on Research Park Blvd, then 1 mi e on US 72. 4880 University Dr 35816. Fax: 256/837-4535. **Facility:** 170 units. 60 one-bedroom standard units. 110 one-bedroom suites, some with whirlpools. 3 stories, interior corridors. *Bath:* combo or shower only. **Parking:** on-site. **Terms:** cancellation fee imposed. **Amenities:** high-speed Internet, voice mail, irons, hair dryers. **Pool(s):** outdoor. **Leisure Activities:** sauna, whirlpool, exercise room. **Guest Services:** valet and coin laundry, area transportation, wireless Internet. **Business Services:** meeting rooms, fax (fee). **Cards:** CB, JC.

SOME UNITS

COURTYARD BY MARRIOTT-HUNTSVILLE Book great rates at AAA.com Phone: (256)837-1400

AAA SAVE

Small-scale Hotel All Year 1P: $80-$189 2P: $80-$199 XP: $10 F18

Location: I-565, exit 14B, 1.5 mi e. 4804 University Dr 35816. Fax: 256/837-3582. **Facility:** 149 units. 137 one-bedroom standard units. 12 one-bedroom suites. 3 stories, interior corridors. *Bath:* combo or shower only. **Parking:** on-site. **Terms:** cancellation fee imposed. **Amenities:** high-speed Internet, voice mail, irons, hair dryers. **Dining:** 6:30-10 am, Sat & Sun 7-10:30 am. **Pool(s):** small outdoor. **Leisure Activities:** whirlpool, limited exercise equipment. **Guest Services:** sundries, valet and coin laundry. **Business Services:** meeting rooms, business center. **Cards:** AX, DC, DS, MC, VI. **Free Special Amenities: high-speed Internet.**

SOME UNITS

DAYS INN & SUITES Book great rates at AAA.com Phone: (256)971-0208

Small-scale Hotel All Year 1P: $70-$90 2P: $70-$90 XP: $6 F12

Location: I-565, exit 14B, 2.6 mi n on Research Park Blvd, 0.8 mi w on US 72, then just s. Located adjacent to Westside Center Mall. 1145 McMurtrie Dr 35806. Fax: 256/971-1099. **Facility:** 45 one-bedroom standard units, some with whirlpools. 2 stories, interior corridors. **Parking:** on-site. **Terms:** cancellation fee imposed. **Amenities:** high-speed Internet, dual phone lines, irons, hair dryers. **Pool(s):** small outdoor. **Guest Services:** coin laundry. **Business Services:** meeting rooms, fax (fee). **Cards:** AX, DC, DS, MC, VI.

SOME UNITS

EMBASSY SUITES HOTEL Phone: 256/539-7373

fyi

Large-scale Hotel All Year 1P: $119-$189 2P: $119-$189

Too new to rate. **Location:** I-565, exit 19C; downtown; in Von Braun Center. 800 Monroe St SW 35801. **Amenities:** 300 units, restaurant, coffeemakers, microwaves, refrigerators, pool. **Cards:** AX, CB, DC, DS, JC, MC, VI. ***(See color ad below)***

EXTENDED STAYAMERICA HUNTSVILLE-U.S. SPACE AND ROCKET CENTER Book at AAA.com Phone: (256)830-9110

Motel All Year 1P: $59-$74 2P: $64-$79 XP: $5 F17

Location: I-565, exit 17A, just s, then 0.5 mi w. 4751 Govenors House Dr 35805. Fax: 256/830-4935. **Facility:** 108 one-bedroom standard units with efficiencies. 3 stories, exterior corridors. *Bath:* combo or shower only. **Parking:** on-site. **Terms:** office hours 7 am-11 pm, pets ($25 fee). **Amenities:** voice mail, irons. **Guest Services:** coin laundry, wireless Internet. **Business Services:** fax (fee). **Cards:** AX, CB, DC, DS, MC, VI.

FEE SOME UNITS

FAIRFIELD INN BY MARRIOTT Book great rates at AAA.com Phone: 256/971-0921

Small-scale Hotel All Year 1P: $82-$89 2P: $82-$89

Location: I-565, exit 14B (US 72), 0.4 mi w of jct SR 255. 1385 Enterprise Way 35806. Fax: 256/971-2072. **Facility:** 79 one-bedroom standard units. 3 stories, interior corridors. *Bath:* combo or shower only. **Parking:** on-site. **Amenities:** high-speed Internet, irons, hair dryers. **Pool(s):** small heated indoor. **Leisure Activities:** whirlpool, exercise room. **Guest Services:** valet laundry, wireless Internet. **Cards:** AX, CB, DC, DS, JC, MC, VI.

SOME UNITS

GUESTHOUSE SUITES PLUS *Book great rates at AAA.com* **Phone:** (256)837-8907

Small-scale Hotel

All Year 1P: $90 2P: $90 XP: $10 F17

Location: I-565, exit 17A, 1.1 mi n on SR 53 (Jordan Ln), just w on US 72, then just n. 4020 Independence Dr 35816. Fax: 256/837-5435. **Facility:** 112 one-bedroom standard units with kitchens. 2 stories (no elevator), exterior corridors. **Parking:** on-site. **Terms:** check-in 4 pm, package plans. **Amenities:** high-speed Internet, voice mail, irons, hair dryers. **Pool(s):** small outdoor. **Guest Services:** valet and coin laundry. **Business Services:** meeting rooms, fax. **Cards:** AX, DC, DS, MC, VI. *(See color ad below)*

SOME UNITS

HAMPTON INN-ARSENAL/SOUTH PARKWAY *Book great rates at AAA.com* **Phone:** (256)882-2228

Small-scale Hotel

All Year 1P: $75-$81

Location: I-565, exit 19A, 5 mi s on US 231, then just w. 501 Boulevard S 35802. Fax: 256/882-1129. **Facility:** 90 one-bedroom standard units, some with whirlpools. 5 stories, interior corridors. *Bath:* combo or shower only. **Parking:** on-site. **Terms:** cancellation fee imposed. **Amenities:** video games (fee), high-speed Internet, dual phone lines, voice mail, irons, hair dryers. **Pool(s):** small outdoor. **Leisure Activities:** exercise room. **Guest Services:** valet laundry. **Business Services:** meeting rooms, fax (fee). **Cards:** AX, DS, MC, VI. **Free Special Amenities: expanded continental breakfast and local telephone calls.**

SOME UNITS

HAMPTON INN HUNTSVILLE *Book great rates at AAA.com* **Phone:** (256)830-9400

Small-scale Hotel

All Year [ECP] 1P: $77-$87 2P: $82-$92 XP: $5 F18

Location: I-565, exit 14B, 2.6 mi n on Research Park Blvd, then 1 mi e on US 72. 4815 University Dr 35816. Fax: 256/830-0978. **Facility:** 159 one-bedroom standard units, some with whirlpools. 3 stories, interior/exterior corridors. *Bath:* combo or shower only. **Parking:** on-site. **Amenities:** high-speed Internet, dual phone lines, voice mail, irons, hair dryers. **Pool(s):** heated outdoor. **Leisure Activities:** whirlpool. **Guest Services:** valet laundry. **Business Services:** PC, fax (fee). **Cards:** AX, CB, DC, DS, MC, VI.

SOME UNITS

HOLIDAY INN EXPRESS HOTEL & SUITES *Book at AAA.com* **Phone:** (256)721-1000

Small-scale Hotel

All Year [ECP] 1P: $72-$85 2P: $72-$85

Location: I-565, exit 17A, just e. 3808 University Dr 35816. Fax: 256/722-2016. **Facility:** 146 units. 118 one-bedroom standard units. 28 one-bedroom suites ($89-$119). 2 stories (no elevator), interior corridors. *Bath:* combo or shower only. **Parking:** on-site. **Terms:** pets ($25 fee). **Amenities:** video games (fee), high-speed Internet, dual phone lines, voice mail, irons, hair dryers. *Some:* CD players. **Pool(s):** small outdoor. **Leisure Activities:** exercise room. **Guest Services:** complimentary evening beverages: Mon-Thurs, valet laundry, area transportation, wireless Internet. **Business Services:** meeting rooms, business center. **Cards:** AX, CB, DC, DS, JC, MC, VI.

SOME UNITS

FEE

HOLIDAY INN HUNSTVILLE DOWNTOWN *Book great rates at AAA.com* **Phone:** (256)533-1400

Large-scale Hotel

All Year 1P: $88-$100 2P: $88-$100

Location: Just w of Church St; downtown. Located across from Von Braun Civic Center. 401 Williams Ave SW 35801. Fax: 256/536-5568. **Facility:** 271 one-bedroom standard units. 4 stories, interior corridors. *Bath:* combo or shower only. **Parking:** on-site. **Terms:** cancellation fee imposed, small pets only ($25 fee). **Amenities:** video games (fee), dual phone lines, voice mail, irons, hair dryers. **Dining:** 6 am-11 pm, cocktails. **Pool(s):** outdoor. **Leisure Activities:** whirlpool, exercise room. **Guest Services:** valet and coin laundry, area transportation-within 3 mi, wireless Internet. **Business Services:** conference facilities, business center. **Cards:** AX, DC, DS, MC, VI. **Free Special Amenities: local telephone calls and newspaper.** *(See color ad below)*

SOME UNITS

FEE

HOLIDAY INN RESEARCH PARK *Book at AAA.com* **Phone:** (256)830-0600

Large-scale Hotel

All Year 1P: $94-$104 2P: $94-$104

Location: I-565, exit 14B, 2.6 mi n on Research Park Blvd, then just e on US 72. Located at the Madison Square Mall. 5903 University Dr 35806. Fax: 256/830-9576. **Facility:** 200 one-bedroom standard units. 5 stories, interior corridors. *Bath:* combo or shower only. **Parking:** on-site. **Terms:** check-in 4 pm, [BP] meal plan available, package plans. **Amenities:** video games (fee), high-speed Internet, voice mail, irons, hair dryers. *Some:* CD players. **Pool(s):** indoor/outdoor. **Leisure Activities:** sauna, whirlpool, exercise room. **Guest Services:** valet and coin laundry, area transportation, wireless Internet. **Business Services:** conference facilities, business center. **Cards:** AX, CB, DC, DS, JC, MC, VI.

SOME UNITS

LA QUINTA INN & SUITES HUNTSVILLE *Book great rates at AAA.com* **Phone:** (256)830-8999

Small-scale Hotel

All Year 1P: $74-$94 2P: $74-$94 XP: $6 F18

Location: I-565, exit 14B, 2.6 mi n on Research Park Blvd, then 1 mi e on US 72. 4890 University Dr SE 35816. Fax: 256/837-5720. **Facility:** 99 units. 96 one-bedroom standard units. 2 two- and 1 three-bedroom suites, some with kitchens. 3 stories, interior corridors. **Parking:** on-site. **Terms:** [ECP] meal plan available, pets (in smoking units). **Amenities:** video games (fee), high-speed Internet, voice mail, irons, hair dryers. **Pool(s):** outdoor. **Guest Services:** valet laundry, wireless Internet. **Cards:** AX, CB, DC, DS, MC, VI. ***(See color ad p 386)***

SOME UNITS

LA QUINTA INN HUNTSVILLE (RESEARCH PARK) *Book great rates at AAA.com* **Phone:** (256)830-2070

Small-scale Hotel

All Year [ECP] 1P: $80-$90 2P: $86-$96 XP: $6 F18

Location: I-565, exit 14B, 2.6 mi n on Research Park Blvd, then 1 mi e on US 72. 4870 University Dr NW 35816-1847. Fax: 256/830-4412. **Facility:** 130 one-bedroom standard units. 2 stories (no elevator), exterior corridors. **Parking:** on-site. **Amenities:** video games (fee), voice mail, irons, hair dryers. *Some:* dual phone lines. **Pool(s):** outdoor. **Guest Services:** valet and coin laundry, wireless Internet. **Business Services:** fax. **Cards:** AX, CB, DC, DS, MC, VI. ***(See color ad p 386)***

SOME UNITS

LA QUINTA INN HUNTSVILLE (SPACE CENTER) *Book great rates at AAA.com* **Phone:** (256)533-0756

Small-scale Hotel

All Year [ECP] 1P: $70-$80 2P: $76-$86 XP: $6 F18

Location: I-565, exit 17A, 1.1 mi n on SR 53 (Jordan Ln), then 0.6 mi e on US 72. 3141 University Dr (Hwy 72) 35816. Fax: 256/539-5414. **Facility:** 130 one-bedroom standard units. 2 stories (no elevator), exterior corridors. **Parking:** on-site. **Amenities:** video games (fee), voice mail, irons, hair dryers. **Pool(s):** outdoor. **Guest Services:** valet laundry, wireless Internet. **Business Services:** meeting rooms. **Cards:** AX, CB, DC, DS, MC, VI. ***(See color ad p 386)***

SOME UNITS

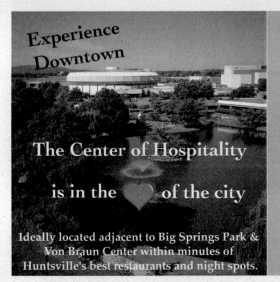

MARRIOTT HUNTSVILLE Book great rates at AAA.com Phone: (256)830-2222

Large-scale Hotel

All Year 1P: $200-$210 2P: $200-$210 XP: $10 F18

Location: I-565, exit 15, just sw. Located adjacent to Space and Rocket Center. 5 Tranquility Base 35805. Fax: 256/895-0904. **Facility:** 290 one-bedroom standard units. 7 stories, interior corridors. **Parking:** on-site. **Terms:** [AP] meal plan available, package plans. **Amenities:** dual phone lines, voice mail, irons, hair dryers. *Fee:* video games, high-speed Internet. **Pool(s):** heated indoor/outdoor. **Leisure Activities:** sauna, whirlpool, hiking trails, exercise room. **Guest Services:** gift shop, valet and coin laundry, wireless Internet. **Business Services:** conference facilities, business center. **Cards:** AX, CB, DC, DS, JC, MC, VI.

SOME UNITS

RADISSON SUITE HOTEL Book at AAA.com Phone: (256)882-9400

Large-scale Hotel

All Year 1P: $99 2P: $99 XP: $10 F17

Location: I-565, exit 19A, 5 mi sw on US 231/431. 6000 Memorial Pkwy S 35802. Fax: 256/882-9684. **Facility:** 152 one-bedroom suites, some with kitchens and/or whirlpools. 3 stories, interior corridors. **Parking:** on-site. **Terms:** [AP] & [BP] meal plans available, package plans. **Amenities:** video games (fee), dual phone lines, voice mail, irons, hair dryers. **Pool(s):** heated outdoor. **Leisure Activities:** whirlpool. **Guest Services:** valet and coin laundry, area transportation. **Business Services:** meeting rooms, fax (fee). **Cards:** AX, CB, DC, DS, JC, MC, VI.

SOME UNITS

FEE

SUBURBAN EXTENDED STAY Book great rates at AAA.com Phone: (256)830-2500

Small-scale Hotel

All Year 1P: $46-$90 2P: $46-$90

Location: I-565, exit 14B, 2.6 mi n on Research Park Blvd, then 1 mi e on US 72. 1565 The Boardwalk 35816. Fax: 256/830-2500. **Facility:** 132 units. 124 one-bedroom standard units with efficiencies. 8 one-bedroom suites with efficiencies. 3 stories, interior corridors. *Bath:* combo or shower only. **Parking:** on-site. **Amenities:** high-speed Internet, voice mail. **Leisure Activities:** exercise room. **Guest Services:** coin laundry, wireless Internet. **Business Services:** fax. **Cards:** AX, DC, DS, MC, VI.

SOME UNITS

VCR

WHERE TO DINE

BARNHILL'S BUFFET **Lunch:** $5-$9 **Dinner:** $7-$10 **Phone:** 256/535-4423

American

Location: I-565, exit 17A, 1.1 mi n on SR 53 (Jordan Ln), then 0.4 mi e. 3801 University Dr 35816. **Hours:** 10:45 am-8:45 pm, Fri-9 pm, Sat 7 am-9 pm, Sun 7 am-8:45 pm. Closed: 12/25. **Features:** Casual dress. **Parking:** on-site. **Cards:** AX, DS, MC, VI.

CAFE BERLIN **Lunch:** $7-$11 **Dinner:** $10-$22 **Phone:** 256/880-9920

German

Location: I-565, exit 19A, 3.4 mi s on US 231, exit Airport Rd, then 0.3 mi e; in Piedmont Station Plaza. 964 Airport Rd 35802. **Hours:** 11 am-9 pm, Fri & Sat-10 pm. Closed major holidays. **Features:** The small, pleasantly-decorated restaurant with its light lime walls, warm woods and bistro-style chairs and tables offers an interesting selection of German- and French-inspired cuisine. The smartly attired wait staff in their ruffled tuxedo shirts and long black aprons add to the modern Euro look. Casual dress; cocktails. **Parking:** on-site. **Cards:** AX, DS, MC, VI.

GREEN HILLS GRILLE **Lunch:** $7-$16 **Dinner:** $7-$16 **Phone:** 256/837-8282

American

Location: I-565, exit 14B, 2.6 mi n on Research Park Blvd, 1 mi e on US 72, then just s on Wynn Dr. 5100 Sanderson St NW 35805. **Hours:** 10:45 am-10 pm, Fri & Sat-11 pm. Closed: 11/22, 12/25. **Reservations:** accepted. **Features:** The restaurant's wood-fired grill prepares dishes with a Southwestern flair. Regular menu offerings combine with hearty daily specials to please patrons. Portions are generous and servers are efficient and friendly. Casual dress; cocktails. **Parking:** on-site. **Cards:** AX, DC, DS, MC, VI.

LITTLE PAUL'S GIBSON BARBECUE **Lunch:** $4-$8 **Dinner:** $4-$8 **Phone:** 256/536-7227

Barbecue

Location: Downtown; across from Huntsville Hospital. 815 Madison St 35801. **Hours:** 10 am-8 pm. Closed major holidays; also Sun. **Features:** Tasty, down-home barbecue and friendly service keep loyal customers coming back to the popular, family-owned restaurant. Save room for the scrumptious homemade pies. Casual dress. **Parking:** on-site. **Cards:** AX, CB, DC, DS, MC, VI.

LUCIANO ITALIAN RESTAURANT **Lunch:** $7-$10 **Dinner:** $11-$20 **Phone:** 256/885-0505

Italian

Location: I-565, exit 19A, 3.4 mi s on US 231, exit Airport Rd, then 0.3 mi e; in Piedmont Station Plaza. 964 Airport Rd 35802. **Hours:** 11 am-2 & 5-9 pm, Fri & Sat 5 pm-10 pm. **Reservations:** suggested. **Features:** Soft music and delightful artwork contribute to the relaxing dining experience. Italian dishes are served in generous portions. The setting is perfect for a romantic dinner for two. Service is always friendly and attentive, even when the restaurant is busy, which is often. Casual dress; cocktails. **Parking:** on-site. **Cards:** AX, DS, MC, VI.

MAIN ST CAFE & BAKERY **Lunch:** $5-$7 **Phone:** 256/881-0044

American

Location: I-565, SR 53 (S Memorial Pkwy), exit onto US 231, 3.4 mi s. 7500 S Memorial Pkwy 35802. **Hours:** 7 am-5 pm, Sat 8 am-2 pm. Closed: Sun. **Features:** Cakes, soups and sandwiches are light and tasty standbys at the little bakery, while upscale fare, such as filet medallions with garlic mashed potatoes, tempts diners at the popular Italian bistro. The house salad is delicious. Venture up to the second level to check out a second dining area and full bar. A good selection of wines is available. Casual dress. **Parking:** on-site. **Cards:** MC, VI.

OL' HEIDELBERG RESTAURANT **Lunch:** $7-$9 **Dinner:** $10-$18 **Phone:** 256/922-0556

German

Location: I-565, exit 14B, 2.6 mi n on Research Park Blvd, then 0.3 mi w on US 72; in University Place Shopping Center. 6125 University Dr 35806. **Hours:** 11 am-9 pm, Fri & Sat-10 pm. Closed major holidays. **Features:** From the traditionally-costumed staff to the cuckoo clocks on the wall, the restaurant is true to its traditions. Authentic German dishes are offered using good, quality ingredients. Generous portions and simple preparations are the standards of a menu that features sandwiches, sausages and wiener schnitzel. Casual dress; beer & wine only. **Parking:** on-site. **Cards:** AX, DS, MC, VI.

ROSIE'S MEXICAN CANTINA **Lunch:** $6-$9 **Dinner:** $7-$14 **Phone:** 256/922-1001

Mexican

Location: I-565, exit 14B, 2.6 mi n on Research Park Blvd, then 0.3 mi w on US 72; in University Place Shopping Center. 6125 University Dr 35816. **Hours:** 11 am-9:30 pm, Fri & Sat-10:30 pm. Closed major holidays; also Sun. **Features:** A lively atmosphere and energetic staff create the feeling of a Mexican fiesta. Diners feast on generous portions of south-of-the-border cuisine, including fajitas, chiles rellenos and Mexican lasagna. Casual dress; cocktails. **Parking:** on-site. **Cards:** AX, DC, DS, MC, VI.

IRONDALE —*See Birmingham p. 236.*

JACKSON pop. 5,419

WHERE TO STAY

ECONO LODGE *Book great rates at AAA.com* **Phone:** (251)246-4111

Motel

All Year 1P: $58-$68

Location: On US 43. 3680 N College Ave 36545. Fax: 251/246-0099. **Facility:** 36 one-bedroom standard units. 2 stories (no elevator), exterior corridors. **Parking:** on-site. **Terms:** package plans, small pets only. **Guest Services:** valet laundry. **Business Services:** meeting rooms, fax (fee). **Cards:** AX, DS, MC, VI. **Free Special Amenities: expanded continental breakfast and local telephone calls.**

SOME UNITS

JASPER pop. 14,052

WHERE TO STAY

HOLIDAY INN EXPRESS HOTEL & SUITES *Book at AAA.com* **Phone:** 205/302-6400

Small-scale Hotel

Property failed to provide current rates

Location: On SR 118, 3 mi w of jct SR 69. 202 Oakhill Rd 35501. Fax: 205/302-0880. **Facility:** 64 one-bedroom standard units, some with whirlpools. 3 stories, interior corridors. *Bath:* combo or shower only. **Parking:** on-site. **Amenities:** dual phone lines, voice mail, irons, hair dryers. **Pool(s):** outdoor. **Leisure Activities:** exercise room. **Guest Services:** valet and coin laundry. **Business Services:** meeting rooms, fax (fee).

SOME UNITS

JAMESON INN *Book at AAA.com* **Phone:** (205)387-7710

Small-scale Hotel

All Year [ECP] 1P: $54-$120

Location: SR 118, 1.8 mi w of jct SR 69. 1100 Hwy 118 35501. Fax: 205/387-7703. **Facility:** 60 one-bedroom standard units, some with whirlpools. 2 stories (no elevator), exterior corridors. *Bath:* combo or shower only. **Parking:** on-site. **Terms:** cancellation fee imposed, small pets only ($10 fee). **Amenities:** high-speed Internet, hair dryers. *Some:* irons. **Pool(s):** outdoor. **Leisure Activities:** exercise room. **Business Services:** PC, fax (fee). **Cards:** AX, DC, DS, MC, VI.

SOME UNITS

ASK

FEE

WHERE TO DINE

PERICO'S AUTHENTIC MEXICAN RESTAURANT **Lunch:** $6-$12 **Dinner:** $8-$15 **Phone:** 205/387-8800

Mexican

Location: Just n of jct 69. 2201 Hwy 78 E 35501. **Hours:** 11 am-10 pm, Sat-9:30 pm, Sun-8:30 pm. Closed major holidays. **Features:** The locally owned restaurant boasts a fine happy hour and quick traditional Mexican meals. Homemade tortillas and tamales spice things up. Casual dress; cocktails. **Parking:** on-site. **Cards:** MC, VI.

LANETT pop. 7,897

WHERE TO STAY

ECONO LODGE Book great rates at AAA.com Phone: 334/768-3500

Motel

All Year 1P: $50-$80 2P: $59-$89 XP: $10 F12

Location: I-85, exit 79, just w. 12 E 22nd St 36863. Fax: 334/768-3500. **Facility:** 40 one-bedroom standard units. 2 stories (no elevator), exterior corridors. **Parking:** on-site. **Cards:** AX, CB, DS, MC, VI.

SOME UNITS

LEEDS —*See Birmingham p. 237.*

LINCOLN pop. 4,577

WHERE TO STAY

DAYS INN LINCOLN Book great rates at AAA.com Phone: (205)763-8080

Small-scale Hotel

All Year 1P: $57-$75 2P: $57-$180 XP: $6 F12

Location: I-20, exit 168, just s. 945 Speedway Industrial Dr 35096. Fax: 205/763-8062. **Facility:** 41 one-bedroom standard units, some with whirlpools. 2 stories (no elevator), interior corridors. **Parking:** on-site. **Terms:** [CP] meal plan available. **Amenities:** irons, hair dryers. **Pool(s):** small outdoor. **Guest Services:** coin laundry, wireless Internet. **Business Services:** fax (fee). **Cards:** AX, DC, DS, MC, VI.

SOME UNITS

MADISON pop. 29,329

WHERE TO STAY

HAMPTON INN-HUNTSVILLE/MADISON Book great rates at AAA.com Phone: (256)464-8999

Small-scale Hotel

All Year 1P: $84-$89 2P: $89-$94 XP: $5 F18

Location: I-565, exit 8, just n on Wall Triana Hwy, then 0.6 mi w. 9225 Madison Blvd 35758 (PO Box 1217). Fax: 256/464-5313. **Facility:** 103 one-bedroom standard units. 3 stories, interior corridors. *Bath:* combo or shower only. **Parking:** on-site. **Terms:** [ECP] meal plan available. **Amenities:** video games (fee), dual phone lines, voice mail, irons, hair dryers. *Some:* high-speed Internet. **Pool(s):** heated outdoor. **Leisure Activities:** whirlpool, exercise room. **Guest Services:** valet laundry, area transportation, wireless Internet. **Business Services:** business center. **Cards:** AX, CB, DC, DS, JC, MC, VI.

SOME UNITS

HOLIDAY INN HUNTSVILLE-WEST Book at AAA.com Phone: 256/772-7170

Small-scale Hotel

All Year 1P: $109 2P: $109

Location: I-565, exit 8, just nw. 9035 Madison Blvd 35758 (PO Box 6290, HUNTSVILLE, 35824). Fax: 256/464-0762. **Facility:** 167 one-bedroom standard units. 2 stories, interior/exterior corridors. *Bath:* some combo or shower only. **Parking:** on-site. **Terms:** [BP] meal plan available. **Amenities:** high-speed Internet, dual phone lines, voice mail, irons, hair dryers. **Dining:** Port of Madison Steak House, see separate listing. **Pool(s):** small outdoor. **Leisure Activities:** whirlpool, exercise room. **Guest Services:** valet laundry, area transportation, wireless Internet. **Business Services:** meeting rooms, business center. **Cards:** AX, DC, DS, MC, VI.

SOME UNITS

FEE FEE

MOTEL 6 - 1087 Book at AAA.com Phone: 256/772-7479

Motel

5/25-11/30	1P: $39-$49	2P: $45-$55	XP: $3	F17
12/1-5/24	1P: $37-$47	2P: $43-$53	XP: $3	F17

Location: I-565, exit 8, just n on Wall Triana Hwy, then just w. 8995 Madison Blvd 35758 (PO Box 6123, HUNTSVILLE, 35824). Fax: 256/772-9771. **Facility:** 90 one-bedroom standard units. 2 stories (no elevator), exterior corridors. *Bath:* combo or shower only. **Parking:** on-site. **Terms:** small pets only. **Pool(s):** small outdoor. **Guest Services:** coin laundry. **Cards:** AX, CB, DC, DS, MC, VI.

SOME UNITS

FEE FEE

RADISSON INN HUNTSVILLE AIRPORT Book at AAA.com Phone: (256)772-8855

Small-scale Hotel

All Year [BP] 1P: $107-$139 2P: $107-$139 XP: $10 F12

Location: I-565, exit 8, just n on Wall Triana Hwy, then 0.4 mi e. 8721 Madison Blvd 35758. Fax: 256/464-0783. **Facility:** 136 units. 133 one-bedroom standard units, some with whirlpools. 3 one-bedroom suites. 2 stories (no elevator), interior corridors. **Parking:** on-site. **Terms:** cancellation fee imposed, package plans. **Amenities:** video games (fee), dual phone lines, voice mail, irons, hair dryers. *Some:* high-speed Internet. **Pool(s):** outdoor. **Leisure Activities:** whirlpool, exercise room. **Guest Services:** valet laundry, area transportation, wireless Internet. **Business Services:** meeting rooms, fax (fee). **Cards:** AX, DC, DS, MC, VI.

SOME UNITS

RAMADA INN & CONFERENCE CENTER Book at AAA.com Phone: 256/772-0701

Large-scale Hotel

Property failed to provide current rates

Location: I-565, exit 8, just n on Wall Triana Hwy, then 0.4 mi e. 8716 Madison Blvd 35758. Fax: 256/772-8900. **Facility:** 153 one-bedroom standard units. 2 stories (no elevator), interior corridors. *Bath:* combo or shower only. **Parking:** on-site. **Terms:** pets ($10-$15 fee). **Amenities:** video games (fee), voice mail, irons, hair dryers. *Some:* dual phone lines. **Pool(s):** outdoor. **Leisure Activities:** lighted tennis court. **Guest Services:** valet laundry, area transportation, wireless Internet. **Business Services:** meeting rooms, business center.

SOME UNITS

FEE

WHERE TO DINE

GREENBRIER BAR-B-Q **Lunch:** $5-$12 **Dinner:** $5-$12 **Phone:** 256/355-6062

Regional American

Location: I-565, exit 3, 0.5 mi sw on north service road. 15050 Hwy 20 W 35758. **Hours:** 10:30 am-9 pm, Sun-8 pm. Closed: 11/22, 12/24, 12/25; also Mon. **Features:** A local favorite for simple family dining, the restaurant offers a basic menu of mostly barbecued meats and some seafood dishes. Casual dress. **Parking:** on-site. **Cards:** AX, DC, DS, MC, VI.

GUADALAJARA JALISCO **Lunch:** $4-$6 **Dinner:** $5-$11 **Phone:** 256/774-1401

Mexican

Location: I-565, exit 8, 0.3 mi n on Wall Triana Hwy, then 0.8 mi e. 8572 Madison Blvd 35758. **Hours:** 10:30 am-9 pm, Wed & Thurs-9:30 pm, Fri & Sat-10 pm. Closed: 1/1, 12/25. **Reservations:** accepted. **Features:** The festive little restaurant offers traditional Mexican fare. Come on a Monday night and be treated to great live Mariachi music. Casual dress; cocktails. **Parking:** on-site. **Cards:** AX, DC, DS, MC, VI.

PAULI'S BAR & GRILL **Dinner:** $22-$27 **Phone:** 256/722-2080

AAA

American

Location: I-565, exit 14 (Research Park Blvd NW), 3.4 mi n to US 72, then 3 mi w. 7143 C-Hwy 72 W 35758. **Hours:** 5 pm-11 pm. Closed: Sun. **Reservations:** suggested. **Features:** This family owned and operated restaurant offers fine dining in a casual atmosphere; an impressive wine collection features over 45 different types that can be enjoyed by the glass. Dressy casual; cocktails. **Parking:** on-site. **Cards:** MC, VI.

PORT OF MADISON STEAK HOUSE **Lunch:** $7-$13 **Dinner:** $9-$24 **Phone:** 256/772-7170

American

Location: I-565, exit 8, just nw; in Holiday Inn Huntsville-West. 9035 Madison Blvd 35758. **Hours:** 6-9 am, 11-2 & 6-10 pm, Sat 7 am-10 & 6-9 pm, Sun 7-10 am. **Reservations:** accepted. **Features:** Variety is key at this popular establishment. The daily lunch buffet includes items such as Jamaican chicken, fried catfish, barbecue pork and vegetable dishes, in addition to salads and tempting desserts. Casual dress; cocktails. **Parking:** on-site. **Cards:** AX, CB, DC, DS, JC, MC, VI.

MCCALLA —*See Birmingham p. 237.*

MILLBROOK pop. 10,386

WHERE TO STAY

COUNTRY INN & SUITES Book at AAA.com Phone: 334/495-3000

Small-scale Hotel

All Year [ECP] 1P: $69-$99 2P: $69-$99 XP: $5 F

Location: I-65, exit 179, just e. 1925 Cobbs Ford Rd 36054. Fax: 334/285-8940. **Facility:** 63 units. 54 one-bedroom standard units, some with whirlpools. 9 one-bedroom suites ($79-$119). 3 stories, interior corridors. *Bath:* some combo or shower only. **Parking:** on-site. **Amenities:** high-speed Internet, voice mail, irons, hair dryers. **Pool(s):** heated indoor. **Leisure Activities:** whirlpool, limited exercise equipment. **Guest Services:** valet and coin laundry, wireless Internet. **Business Services:** PC. **Cards:** AX, DC, DS, MC, VI.

SOME UNITS

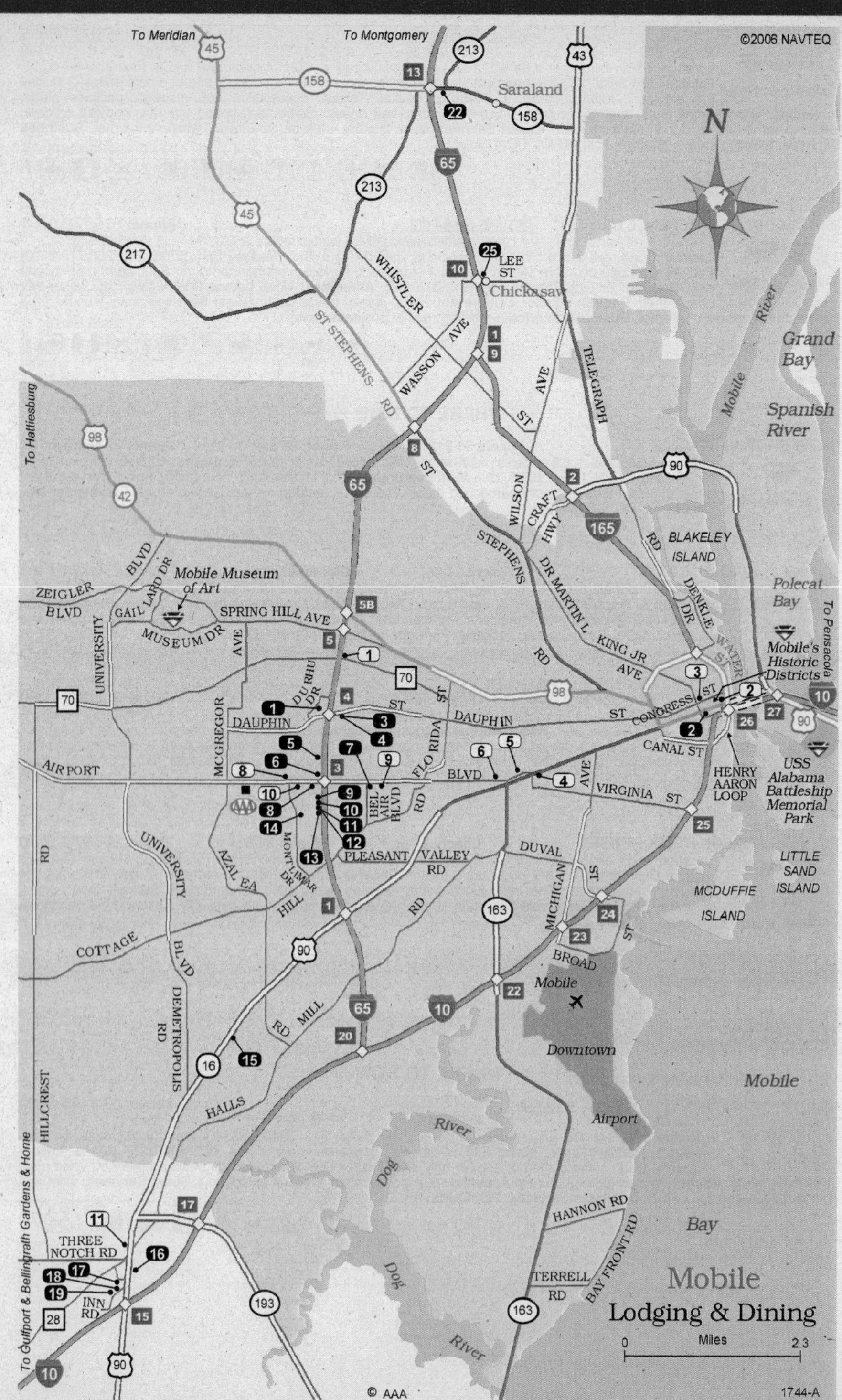

Mobile
Lodging & Dining
©2006 NAVTEQ
© AAA
1744-A
To Meridian
To Montgomery
To Hattiesburg
To Pensacola
To Gulfport & Bellingrath Gardens & Home
Saraland
Chickasaw
Grand Bay
Spanish River
Mobile River
Polecat Bay
BLAKELEY ISLAND
MCDUFFIE ISLAND
LITTLE SAND ISLAND
Mobile Museum of Art
Mobile's Historic Districts
USS Alabama Battleship Memorial Park
Mobile Downtown Airport
Mobile Bay
Dog River
Miles
0
2.3

Mobile

This index helps you "spot" where approved accommodations and restaurants are located on the corresponding detailed maps. Lodging rate ranges are for comparison only and show the property's high season; rates are per night, unless only weekly (W) rates are available. Restaurant rate range is for dinner, unless only lunch (L) is served. Turn to the listing page for more detailed rate information and consult display ads for special promotions.

Spotter/Map Page Number	OA	MOBILE - Lodgings	Diamond Rating	Rate Range High Season	Listing Page
1 / p. 266		Americas Best Value Inn & Suites	2	$60-$100	268
2 / p. 266		Radisson Admiral Semmes Hotel	3	$189	270
3 / p. 266		Red Roof Inn North	2	$50-$70	270
4 / p. 266		Drury Inn-Mobile	2	$70-$130	268
5 / p. 266		Regency Inn	3	Failed to provide	270
6 / p. 266	AAA	**Best Western Ashbury Hotel & Suites** - see color ad p 268	3	$70-$110 SAVE	268
7 / p. 266		Mobile Marriott	3	$140-$229	270
8 / p. 266		La Quinta Inn Mobile - see color ad p 386	2	$88-$105	269
9 / p. 266	AAA	**Family Inns of America**	1	$45-$99 SAVE	269
10 / p. 266		Westmonte Inn	2	$69	271
11 / p. 266		Fairfield Inn by Marriott	3	Failed to provide	269
12 / p. 266		Residence Inn by Marriott Mobile	3	Failed to provide	270
13 / p. 266		Courtyard by Marriott	3	$89-$134	268
14 / p. 266		TownePlace Suites by Marriott	3	$108-$149	270
15 / p. 266	AAA	**Olsson Motel**	1	$45-$80 SAVE	270
16 / p. 266		Holiday Inn-Bellingrath Gardens	3	Failed to provide	269
17 / p. 266		Comfort Inn	2	$69-$159	268
18 / p. 266		Hampton Inn I-10 West/Bellingrath Gardens - see color ad p 269	2	$104-$129	269
19 / p. 266		Motel 6 #608	1	$52-$68	270
		MOBILE - Restaurants			
1 / p. 266		Dreamland Bar-B-Que	1	$6-$17	271
2 / p. 266		Riverview Cafe & Grill	2	$18-$25	272
3 / p. 266		Spot of Tea	2	$10-$13(L)	272
4 / p. 266	AAA	**The Pillars**	3	$18-$36	272
5 / p. 266		Bilotti's Italian Cafe	2	$8-$22	271
6 / p. 266		Ruth's Chris Steak House	3	$18-$30	272
8 / p. 266		Delhi Palace	2	$7-$15	271
9 / p. 266		Bistro 65	3	$12-$34	271
10 / p. 266		Wings Sports Grille	2	$7-$18	272
11 / p. 266		Dick Russell's	1	$5-$21	271
		SARALAND - Lodgings			
22 / p. 266		Holiday Inn Express	3	$89-$125	289
		CHICKASAW - Lodgings			
25 / p. 266		America's Best Inn	2	Failed to provide	243

MOBILE pop. 198,915 (See map and index starting on p. 266)

WHERE TO STAY

AMERICAS BEST VALUE INN & SUITES Book at AAA.com Phone: (251)344-2121 1

Motel

All Year 1P: $60-$100

Location: I-65, exit 4, just w on Dauphin St, then 0.5 mi s. 162 W I-65 Service Rd 36608. Fax: 251/344-5855. **Facility:** 53 one-bedroom standard units, some with whirlpools. 2 stories (no elevator), exterior corridors. *Bath:* combo or shower only. **Parking:** on-site. **Terms:** check-in 4 pm, package plans, small pets only ($10 extra charge). **Pool(s):** small outdoor. **Guest Services:** valet laundry. **Business Services:** meeting rooms. **Cards:** AX, DC, DS, MC, VI.

SOME UNITS FEE

THE BATTLE HOUSE A RENAISSANCE HOTEL Phone: 251/438-4000

fyi Large-scale Hotel

Property failed to provide current rates

Too new to rate. **Location:** I-10 E, exit 26B (Water St), left on Government St, then right. 26 N Royal St 36602 (64 S Water St). Fax: 251/415-0123. **Amenities:** 238 units, coffeemakers, pool. ***(See color ad p 200)***

BEST WESTERN ASHBURY HOTEL & SUITES Book great rates at AAA.com Phone: (251)344-8030 6

AAA SAVE Small-scale Hotel

All Year 1P: $70-$110 2P: $70-$110 XP: $5 F12

Location: I-65, exit 3, just w on Airport Blvd, then just n on service road. 600 S Beltline Hwy 36608. Fax: 251/344-8055. **Facility:** 194 units. 166 one- and 28 two-bedroom standard units. 2-4 stories, interior/exterior corridors. **Parking:** on-site. **Amenities:** voice mail, irons, hair dryers. *Some:* high-speed Internet. **Pool(s):** outdoor, heated indoor, wading. **Leisure Activities:** lighted tennis court, exercise room. **Guest Services:** valet and coin laundry, airport transportation-Mobile Airport, area transportation-within 1.5 mi. **Business Services:** conference facilities, PC. **Cards:** AX, CB, DC, DS, JC, MC, VI. *(See color ad below)*

SOME UNITS

COMFORT INN Book great rates at AAA.com Phone: (251)666-6604 17

Motel

All Year 1P: $69-$149 2P: $69-$159 XP: $10 F18

Location: I-10, exit 15B, just e on US 90, then just n. 5650 Tillman's Corner Pkwy 36619. Fax: 251/666-0710. **Facility:** 58 one-bedroom standard units, some with whirlpools. 2 stories (no elevator), exterior corridors. *Bath:* combo or shower only. **Parking:** on-site. **Terms:** [CP] meal plan available. **Amenities:** high-speed Internet, irons, hair dryers. **Pool(s):** outdoor. **Guest Services:** coin laundry. **Business Services:** PC. **Cards:** AX, CB, DC, DS, JC, MC, VI.

SOME UNITS

COURTYARD BY MARRIOTT Book great rates at AAA.com Phone: (251)344-5200 13

Small-scale Hotel

All Year 1P: $89-$134

Location: I-65, exit 3 (Airport Blvd), just w, then 0.4 mi s on service road. 1000 W I-65 Service Rd S 36609. Fax: 251/341-0300. **Facility:** 78 units. 75 one-bedroom standard units, some with whirlpools. 3 one-bedroom suites ($114-$154) with kitchens. 3 stories, interior corridors. *Bath:* combo or shower only. **Parking:** on-site. **Amenities:** dual phone lines, voice mail, irons, hair dryers. **Pool(s):** small heated indoor. **Leisure Activities:** whirlpool, exercise room. **Guest Services:** valet and coin laundry. **Business Services:** meeting rooms, PC. **Cards:** AX, CB, DC, DS, JC, MC, VI.

SOME UNITS

DRURY INN-MOBILE Book at AAA.com Phone: (251)344-7700 4

Small-scale Hotel

All Year [BP] 1P: $70-$120 2P: $80-$130 XP: $10 F18

Location: I-65, exit 3 (Airport Blvd), just w, then just s on service road. 824 W I-65 Service Rd S 36609. Fax: 251/344-7700. **Facility:** 110 one-bedroom standard units. 4 stories, interior corridors. **Parking:** on-site. **Terms:** small pets only. **Amenities:** high-speed Internet, dual phone lines, voice mail, irons, hair dryers. **Pool(s):** outdoor. **Leisure Activities:** limited exercise equipment. **Guest Services:** complimentary evening beverages: Mon-Thurs, valet and coin laundry. **Business Services:** meeting rooms. **Cards:** AX, CB, DC, DS, MC, VI.

SOME UNITS

(See map and index starting on p. 266)

FAIRFIELD INN BY MARRIOTT *Book great rates at AAA.com* **Phone:** 251/316-0029 **11**

Small-scale Hotel

Property failed to provide current rates

Location: I-65, exit 3 (Airport Blvd), just w, then 0.4 mi s. 950A W I-65 Service Rd S 36609. Fax: 251/316-0974. **Facility:** 80 one-bedroom standard units. 3 stories, interior corridors. *Bath:* combo or shower only. **Parking:** on-site. **Amenities:** irons, hair dryers. **Pool(s):** heated indoor. **Leisure Activities:** whirlpool, exercise room. **Guest Services:** valet and coin laundry. **Business Services:** PC.

SOME UNITS

FAMILY INNS OF AMERICA *Book great rates at AAA.com* **Phone:** (251)344-5500 **9**

AAA SAVE

Motel

All Year	1P: $45-$85	2P: $47-$99	XP: $5	F18

Location: I-65, exit 3 (Airport Blvd), just w, then just s. 900 W I-65 Service Rd S 36609. Fax: 251/342-4744. **Facility:** 83 one-bedroom standard units. 2 stories (no elevator), exterior corridors. **Parking:** on-site. **Terms:** pets ($50 deposit). **Pool(s):** outdoor. **Cards:** AX, DC, DS, MC, VI. **Free Special Amenities: continental breakfast and local telephone calls.**

SOME UNITS

FEE

HAMPTON INN I-10 WEST/BELLINGRATH GARDENS *Book great rates at AAA.com* **Phone:** 251/660-9202 **18**

Small-scale Hotel

All Year	1P: $104-$119	2P: $114-$129

Location: I-10, exit 15B, just e on US 90, then just n. 5478 Inn Rd 36619. Fax: 251/660-1724. **Facility:** 80 one-bedroom standard units. 3 stories, interior corridors. *Bath:* combo or shower only. **Parking:** on-site. **Amenities:** high-speed Internet, voice mail, irons, hair dryers. *Some:* DVD players. **Pool(s):** outdoor. **Leisure Activities:** exercise room. **Guest Services:** valet and coin laundry. **Business Services:** meeting rooms, PC. **Cards:** AX, CB, DC, DS, MC, VI. ***(See color ad below)***

SOME UNITS

ASK

HOLIDAY INN-BELLINGRATH GARDENS *Book at AAA.com* **Phone:** 251/666-5600 **16**

Small-scale Hotel

Property failed to provide current rates

Location: I-10, exit 15B, just e on US 90, then just s on Coca Cola Rd. 5465 Hwy 90 W 36619. Fax: 251/666-2773. **Facility:** 159 one-bedroom standard units. 5 stories, interior corridors. *Bath:* combo or shower only. **Parking:** on-site. **Terms:** small pets only ($25 deposit). **Amenities:** voice mail, irons, hair dryers. **Pool(s):** outdoor, wading. **Leisure Activities:** whirlpool, limited exercise equipment. **Guest Services:** complimentary evening beverages, valet and coin laundry. **Business Services:** meeting rooms, business center.

SOME UNITS

FEE

LA QUINTA INN MOBILE *Book great rates at AAA.com* **Phone:** (251)343-4051 **8**

Motel

All Year [ECP]	1P: $88-$98	2P: $95-$105	XP: $7	F18

Location: I-65, exit 3 (Airport Blvd), just w, then just s. 816 W I-65 Service Rd S 36609. Fax: 251/343-2897. **Facility:** 122 units. 120 one-bedroom standard units. 2 one-bedroom suites. 2 stories (no elevator), interior/exterior corridors. **Parking:** on-site. **Terms:** small pets only. **Amenities:** video games (fee), voice mail, irons, hair dryers. **Pool(s):** outdoor. **Guest Services:** valet and coin laundry. **Cards:** AX, CB, DC, DS, MC, VI. ***(See color ad p 386)***

SOME UNITS

ASK

(See map and index starting on p. 266)

MOBILE MARRIOTT Book great rates at AAA.com Phone: (251)476-6400 7

Large-scale Hotel

All Year 1P: $140-$229

Location: I-65, exit 3, 0.5 mi e. 3101 Airport Blvd 36606. Fax: 251/476-9050. **Facility:** Smoke free premises. 251 units. 250 one-bedroom standard units. 1 one-bedroom suite ($225-$425). 20 stories, interior corridors. *Bath:* combo or shower only. **Parking:** on-site. **Terms:** [AP], [BP], [CP] & [ECP] meal plans available. **Amenities:** voice mail, safes, irons, hair dryers. *Fee:* video games, high-speed Internet. **Dining:** Bistro 65, see separate listing. **Pool(s):** outdoor. **Leisure Activities:** exercise room. **Guest Services:** gift shop, valet and coin laundry. **Business Services:** conference facilities, business center. **Cards:** AX, DS, MC, VI.

MOTEL 6 #608 Book at AAA.com Phone: 251/660-1483 19

Motel

5/25-11/30	1P: $52-$62	2P: $58-$68	XP: $3	F17
12/1-5/24	1P: $49-$59	2P: $55-$65	XP: $3	F17

Location: I-10, exit 15B, just e on US 90, then just n. 5488 Inn Rd 36619. Fax: 251/660-7832. **Facility:** 98 one-bedroom standard units. 3 stories, exterior corridors. *Bath:* combo or shower only. **Parking:** on-site. **Terms:** small pets only. **Pool(s):** outdoor. **Guest Services:** coin laundry. **Cards:** AX, CB, DC, DS, MC, VI.

SOME UNITS

OLSSON MOTEL Phone: 251/661-5331 15

AAA SAVE

Motel

All Year	1P: $45-$55	2P: $65-$80	XP: $10	F10

Location: I-65, exit 1, 2 mi w on US 90. 4137 Government Blvd 36693. Fax: 251/666-6410. **Facility:** 25 one-bedroom standard units. 1 story, exterior corridors. **Parking:** on-site. **Terms:** 15 day cancellation notice-fee imposed, weekly rates available, pets (small dogs only, $5 extra charge). **Guest Services:** valet laundry. **Cards:** AX, DS, MC, VI.

SOME UNITS

FEE

RADISSON ADMIRAL SEMMES HOTEL Book at AAA.com Phone: (251)432-8000 2

Classic Large-scale Hotel

2/2-2/21	1P: $189	2P: $189	XP: $10	F18
12/1-2/1 & 2/22-11/30	1P: $179	2P: $179	XP: $10	F18

Location: I-10, exit 26B, just w of Water St; downtown. Located in the historic district. 251 Government St 36602. Fax: 251/405-5942. **Facility:** Dating from 1940, this historic downtown hotel offers large rooms. 170 units. 167 one-bedroom standard units. 3 one-bedroom suites. 12 stories, interior corridors. **Parking:** on-site (fee). **Terms:** [AP], [BP] & [CP] meal plans available, package plans. **Amenities:** voice mail, irons, hair dryers. *Fee:* video games, high-speed Internet. *Some:* fax. **Pool(s):** outdoor. **Guest Services:** gift shop, complimentary and valet laundry, area transportation. **Business Services:** conference facilities, business center. **Cards:** AX, CB, DC, DS, JC, MC, VI.

SOME UNITS

ASK

RED ROOF INN NORTH Book at AAA.com Phone: (251)476-2004 3

Motel

12/1-12/31	1P: $50-$65	2P: $55-$70	XP: $5	F18
1/1-11/30	1P: $49-$59	2P: $54-$64	XP: $5	F18

Location: I-65, exit 4, just e on Dauphin St, just s on Springdale Blvd, then just w. 33 I-65 Service Rd E 36606. Fax: 251/476-2054. **Facility:** 108 one-bedroom standard units. 2 stories (no elevator), exterior corridors. *Bath:* combo or shower only. **Parking:** on-site. **Terms:** small pets only. **Amenities:** video games (fee), voice mail. **Cards:** AX, CB, DC, DS, MC, VI.

SOME UNITS

REGENCY INN Phone: 251/343-9345 5

Small-scale Hotel

Property failed to provide current rates

Location: I-65, exit 4, just w on Dauphin St, then 0.5 mi s. 180 W I-65 Service Rd S 36608. Fax: 251/342-5366. **Facility:** 99 one-bedroom standard units, some with whirlpools. 3 stories, interior corridors. **Parking:** on-site. **Amenities:** irons, hair dryers. *Some:* high-speed Internet. **Pool(s):** outdoor. **Guest Services:** valet and coin laundry. **Business Services:** meeting rooms.

SOME UNITS

RESIDENCE INN BY MARRIOTT MOBILE Book great rates at AAA.com Phone: 251/304-0570 12

Small-scale Hotel

Property failed to provide current rates

Location: I-65, exit 3 (Airport Blvd), just w, then 0.4 mi s. 950 W I-65 Service Rd S 36609. Fax: 251/304-0580. **Facility:** 66 units. 18 one-bedroom standard units with efficiencies. 36 one- and 12 two-bedroom suites, some with efficiencies or kitchens. 3 stories, interior corridors. *Bath:* combo or shower only. **Parking:** on-site. **Terms:** check-in 4 pm, pets ($75 fee). **Amenities:** voice mail, irons, hair dryers. **Pool(s):** small heated indoor. **Leisure Activities:** whirlpool, exercise room, sports court. **Guest Services:** complimentary evening beverages: Mon-Thurs, valet and coin laundry. **Business Services:** meeting rooms, PC.

SOME UNITS

FEE

TOWNEPLACE SUITES BY MARRIOTT Book great rates at AAA.com Phone: (251)345-9588 14

Small-scale Hotel

1/1-11/30	1P: $108-$149
12/1-12/31	1P: $98-$129

Location: I-65, exit 3 (Airport Blvd), 0.5 mi w, then 0.5 mi s. Located in a commercial area. 1075 Montlimar Dr 36609. Fax: 251/345-9589. **Facility:** 95 units. 69 one-bedroom standard units with kitchens. 4 one- and 22 two-bedroom suites with kitchens. 3 stories, interior corridors. *Bath:* combo or shower only. **Parking:** on-site. **Terms:** check-in 4 pm, pets ($75 fee). **Amenities:** voice mail, irons, hair dryers. **Pool(s):** small outdoor. **Leisure Activities:** exercise room. **Guest Services:** valet and coin laundry, wireless Internet. **Cards:** AX, CB, DC, DS, JC, MC, VI.

SOME UNITS

ASK

FEE

(See map and index starting on p. 266)

WESTMONTE INN Book at AAA.com Phone: (251)344-4942 10

Motel

All Year 1P: $69 2P: $69 XP: $5 F12

Location: I-65, exit 3 (Airport Blvd), just w, then just s. 930 W I-65 Service Rd S 36609 (PO Box 16988, 36616). Fax: 251/341-4520. **Facility:** 118 one-bedroom standard units. 2 stories (no elevator), exterior corridors. **Parking:** on-site. **Amenities:** voice mail, irons, hair dryers. **Pool(s):** outdoor. **Guest Services:** valet laundry. **Business Services:** meeting rooms. **Cards:** AX, DS, MC, VI.

SOME UNITS

WHERE TO DINE

THE AMERICAN CAFE **Lunch:** $7-$11 **Dinner:** $7-$15 **Phone:** 251/343-2524

American

Location: I-65, exit 3 (Airport Blvd), just w; in Yester Oaks Shopping Center. 3662-A Airport Blvd 36608. **Hours:** 11 am-10 pm, Fri & Sat-11 pm. Closed: 11/22, 12/25. **Features:** You'll enjoy this popular and casual restaurant with a sports bar atmosphere. The menu includes steak, seafood and pasta. Casual dress; cocktails. **Parking:** on-site. **Cards:** AX, CB, DC, DS, MC, VI.

BARNHILL'S BUFFET **Lunch:** $5-$9 **Dinner:** $7-$10 **Phone:** 251/380-0356

American

Location: Jct University Blvd. 4628 Airport Blvd 36608. **Hours:** 10:45 am-8:45 pm, Fri-9 pm, Sat 7 am-9 pm, Sun 7 am-8:45 pm. Closed: 12/25. **Features:** Casual dress. **Parking:** on-site. **Cards:** AX, DS, MC, VI.

BILOTTI'S ITALIAN CAFE **Lunch:** $6-$12 **Dinner:** $8-$22 **Phone:** 251/476-6777 5

Italian

Location: I-65, exit 3 (Airport Blvd), 3 mi e. 1850 Airport Blvd 36606. **Hours:** 11 am-10 pm, Sat from 5 pm. Closed major holidays; also Sun. **Reservations:** accepted, suggested Fri & Sat. **Features:** Traditional dishes featuring pasta, chicken and veal, as well as Angus steaks, are headliners at the bistro-style restaurant. Pizza, salads and sandwiches round out the menu. Casual dress; cocktails. **Parking:** on-site. **Cards:** AX, DC, DS, MC, VI.

BISTRO 65 **Lunch:** $7-$10 **Dinner:** $12-$34 **Phone:** 251/476-6400 9

American

Location: I-65, exit 3, 0.5 mi e; in Mobile Marriott. 3101 Airport Blvd 36606. **Hours:** 6:30 am-2 & 5-10 pm. **Reservations:** accepted. **Features:** Steaks, chicken, seafood and pasta offerings are presented in an upscale manner. An enhanced ambience characterizes the dining room. Guests also can choose from a selection of lighter fare. Dressy casual; cocktails. **Parking:** on-site. **Cards:** AX, DC, DS, MC, VI.

DELHI PALACE **Lunch:** $7-$15 **Dinner:** $7-$15 **Phone:** 251/341-6171 8

Indian

Location: I-65, exit 3 (Airport Blvd), just w; in Yester Oaks Shopping Center. 3674 Airport Blvd 36608. **Hours:** 11 am-2:30 & 5-10 pm. Closed: 11/22, 12/25. **Features:** Simple, bright surroundings create an inviting mood at this restaurant, which serves generous portions of Indian fare from various regions of the subcontinent. A traditional tandoor oven is used to cook many of the dishes. Casual dress; cocktails. **Parking:** on-site. **Cards:** AX, DS, MC, VI.

DICK RUSSELL'S **Lunch:** $5-$21 **Dinner:** $5-$21 **Phone:** 251/661-6090 11

Barbecue

Location: I-10, exit 17, 0.4 mi n on SR 193, then just w. 5360 Hwy 90 W 36619. **Hours:** 6 am-9 pm, Fri & Sat-10 pm. Closed: 11/22, 12/24, 12/25 & Easter. **Features:** Offering good home-style food, the restaurant is a popular stop along the I-10 corridor. Casual dress; beer & wine only. **Parking:** on-site. **Cards:** AX, DC, DS, MC, VI.

DREAMLAND BAR-B-QUE **Lunch:** $6-$17 **Dinner:** $6-$17 **Phone:** 251/479-9898 1

Barbecue

Location: I-65, exit 5A (Springhill Ave), just e to service road, then just s. 3314 Old Shell Rd 36607. **Hours:** 10 am-10 pm, Sun 11 am-9 pm. Closed: 11/22, 12/25. **Features:** "Ain't nothing like 'em nowhere" is the mantra at this barbecue cafe. The original location, just outside of Tuscaloosa, has been an Alabama tradition for almost fifty years. Luckily for Mobile, the tradition has spread. The menu is small, but that's okay because everybody comes for one thing: the ribs. A few other BBQ items are available, all served with sliced white bread and a kicking sauce. Friendly southern hospitality and a casual backdrop help make this a favorite among the locals. Casual dress; beer only. **Parking:** on-site. **Cards:** AX, DC, DS, MC, VI.

LOGAN'S ROADHOUSE **Lunch:** $5-$18 **Dinner:** $9-$20 **Phone:** 251/473-2920

Steak House

Location: I-65, exit 3 (Airport Blvd), just e. 3250 Airport Blvd 36606. **Hours:** 11 am-10 pm, Fri & Sat-11 pm. Closed: 11/22, 12/25. **Features:** Steaks, ribs, chicken, steaks and sandwiches are served in the restaurant, which carries out a contemporary roadhouse theme. Casual dress; cocktails. **Parking:** on-site. **Cards:** AX, DC, DS, MC, VI.

LONGHORN STEAKHOUSE **Lunch:** $6-$13 **Dinner:** $10-$20 **Phone:** 251/316-3880

Steak House

Location: I-65, exit 3 (Airport Blvd), 3.5 mi w. 6201 Airport Blvd 36608. **Hours:** 11 am-10 pm, Fri & Sat-11 pm. Closed: 11/22, 12/25. **Features:** A nicely varied menu lists selections of steak, prime rib, chicken, ribs and seafood. The relaxed atmosphere has a decidedly Western feel. Casual dress; cocktails. **Parking:** on-site. **Cards:** AX, DC, DS, MC, VI.

(See map and index starting on p. 266)

O'CHARLEY'S Lunch: $7-$16 Dinner: $10-$16 Phone: 251/344-0200

American

Location: I-65, exit 3 (Airport Blvd), just w. 3649 Airport Blvd 36609. **Hours:** 11 am-midnight, Fri & Sat-1 am, Sun 10:30 am-10 pm. Closed: 11/22, 12/25. **Features:** Guests can sit indoors or out to sample steak, ribs, seafood, chicken and pasta dishes. Soups, salads and sandwiches are among selections of lighter fare. Casual dress; cocktails. **Parking:** on-site. **Cards:** AX, DC, DS, MC, VI.

ORIGINAL OYSTER HOUSE Lunch: $8-$17 Dinner: $13-$18 Phone: 251/626-2188

Seafood

Location: I-10, exit 30, 2.5 mi w. 3733 Battleship Pkwy 36527. **Hours:** 11 am-10 pm, Fri & Sat-11 pm. Closed: 11/22, 12/25 & Easter. **Reservations:** accepted, Sun-Thurs. **Features:** This family oriented restaurant is popular with locals and visitors alike, and it's easy to see why: fresh seafood served in generous portions by the friendliest servers you can find. The salad bar lets you get all the greens you need before you fill up on delicious items like parmesan baked shrimp, blackened fish or your own seafood platter, created from a variety of choices. Casual dress; cocktails. **Parking:** on-site. **Cards:** AX, DC, DS, MC, VI.

THE PILLARS Lunch: $8-$20 Dinner: $18-$36 Phone: 251/471-3411 (4)

American

Location: I-10, exit 26B, 2.5 mi w of Water St; downtown. 1757 Government St 36604. **Hours:** 11 am-3 & 5-10 pm, Sat from 5 pm. Closed: 1/1, 7/4, 12/25; also Sun. **Reservations:** suggested. **Features:** This elegant, intimate dining venue is set in a restored 1898 mansion. Specialties include Beef Wellington, filet mignon, rack of lamb and fresh seafood selections from the Gulf of Mexico. Expect to be impressed by the service. Dressy casual; cocktails. **Parking:** on-site. **Cards:** AX, CB, DC, DS, MC, VI.

RIVERVIEW CAFE & GRILL Lunch: $8-$12 Dinner: $18-$25 Phone: 251/438-4000 (2)

Continental

Location: Downtown; in The Riverview Plaza Hotel. 64 S Water St 36602. **Hours:** 6:30-10:30 am, 11:30-2 & 5:30-11 pm, Fri & Sat-midnight. **Reservations:** suggested. **Features:** Located across from the Convention Center, Riverview Cafe & Grill specializes in classic Gulf Coast cuisine and the inviting decor and bay view offer you a casual, relaxed atmosphere. Casual dress; cocktails. **Parking:** on-site (fee) and valet. **Cards:** AX, CB, DC, DS, MC, VI.

RUTH'S CHRIS STEAK HOUSE Dinner: $18-$30 Phone: 251/476-0516 (6)

Steak House

Location: I-65, exit 3, 2.1 mi e. 2058 Airport Blvd 36606. **Hours:** 5 pm-10 pm. Closed: 1/1, 11/22, 12/25. **Reservations:** suggested. **Features:** Diners looking for a good steak in a classy setting will find it at this classic restaurant. The steakhouse not only serves up some of the finest meat but also offers a history lesson via black and white pictures of famous Mobileans throughout the club room and hallways. The dimly lit dining rooms evoke a romantic mood. Dressy casual; cocktails. **Parking:** on-site. **Cards:** AX, DC, DS, MC, VI.

SONNY'S REAL PIT BAR-B-Q Lunch: $6-$8 Dinner: $8-$13 Phone: 251/634-0999

Barbecue

Location: I-65, exit 3, 6.1 mi w on Airport Blvd, then 0.6 mi s. 770 Schillinger Rd S 36695. **Hours:** 11 am-9 pm, Fri & Sat 10 pm. Closed: 11/22, 12/25. **Features:** House specialties include barbecue ribs, pork and chicken grilled over an open pit and fresh, homemade pie. Rustic and comfortable, the atmosphere is perfect for family meals.The salad bar is always a popular choice also. Casual dress; beer only. **Parking:** on-site. **Cards:** AX, DS, MC, VI.

SONNY'S REAL PIT BAR-B-Q Lunch: $6-$8 Dinner: $8-$13 Phone: 251/602-5711

Barbecue

Location: I-10, exit 17 westbound, just w, then just s; exit 15 eastbound, 0.8 mi n on US 90, then just ne. 5428 Halls Mills Rd 36619. **Hours:** 11 am-9 pm, Fri & Sat 10 pm. Closed: 11/22, 12/25. **Features:** House specialties include barbecue ribs, pork and chicken grilled over an open pit and fresh, homemade pie. Rustic and comfortable, the atmosphere is perfect for family meals.The salad bar is always a popular choice also. Casual dress; beer only. **Parking:** on-site. **Cards:** AX, DS, MC, VI.

SPOT OF TEA Lunch: $10-$13 Phone: 251/433-9009 (3)

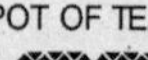

Continental

Location: Between Jackson and Claiborne sts; downtown in historic district. 310 Dauphin St 36602. **Hours:** 7 am-2 pm. Closed major holidays. **Reservations:** accepted. **Features:** As the name suggests, this popular breakfast and lunch spot is an ideal place for a spot of tea, particularly the signature strawberry iced tea. A Victorian influence is evident in the dining room, where patrons savor an excellent selection of omelets and sandwiches provided by swift servers. Casual dress. **Parking:** on-site (fee) and street. **Cards:** AX, DC, DS, MC, VI.

TIJUANA FLATS Lunch: $6-$9 Dinner: $6-$9 Phone: 251/479-0022

Tex-Mex

Location: I-65, exit 3A, 2.5 mi e on Airport Blvd, then just 0.6 mi ne; I-10, exit 23, 2.5 mi n on Michigan Ave, then just w. 1500 Government St, Suite 1 36604. **Hours:** 11 am-10 pm, Fri & Sat-10:30 pm, Sun-9 pm. Closed major holidays. **Features:** The quick-serve Tex-Mex eatery sets up a distinctive "hot sauce bar" to accompany its burritos, chimichangas, tacos and enchiladas. Guests can expect a line out the door at lunch. Casual dress; beer & wine only. **Parking:** on-site. **Cards:** MC, VI.

WINGS SPORTS GRILLE Lunch: $5-$18 Dinner: $7-$18 Phone: 251/344-2131 (10)

American

Location: I-65, exit 3 (Airport Blvd), 0.5 mi w. 3673 Airport Blvd 36608. **Hours:** 11 am-10 pm, Fri & Sat-11 pm. Closed: 7/4, 11/22, 12/25. **Features:** Steaks, baby back ribs, chicken and seafood complement the signature wings, which are served with a bountiful selection of sauces. Also on the upscale sports-themed restaurant's menu are salads, sandwiches and burgers. Casual dress; cocktails. **Parking:** on-site. **Cards:** AX, DC, DS, MC, VI.

MONROEVILLE pop. 6,862

WHERE TO STAY

AMERICAS BEST VALUE INN Book great rates at AAA.com **Phone:** (251)743-3154

AAA SAVE
Motel

All Year 1P: $45-$85 2P: $50-$95 XP: $10 F12

Location: On SR 21, just s of jct US 84. 50 Hwy 21 36460 (50 Hwy 21 S). Fax: 251/575-7876. **Facility:** 39 one-bedroom standard units. 2 stories (no elevator), exterior corridors. **Parking:** on-site. **Terms:** cancellation fee imposed, [CP] meal plan available, pets ($10 fee). **Amenities:** hair dryers. **Guest Services:** wireless Internet. **Cards:** AX, CB, DC, DS, JC, MC, VI. **Free Special Amenities: continental breakfast and high-speed Internet.**

SOME UNITS

FEE

BEST WESTERN OF MONROEVILLE Book great rates at AAA.com **Phone:** 251/575-9999

Motel

All Year 1P: $49-$99 2P: $52-$99 XP: $3 F16

Location: On SR 21, 0.5 mi n of jct US 84. 4419 S Alabama Ave 36460. Fax: 251/575-9117. **Facility:** 41 one-bedroom standard units, some with whirlpools. 2 stories (no elevator), exterior corridors. **Parking:** on-site. **Terms:** [CP] meal plan available, pets ($5 extra charge). **Amenities:** high-speed Internet, irons, hair dryers. **Pool(s):** outdoor. **Leisure Activities:** exercise room. **Cards:** AX, DC, DS, JC, MC, VI.

SOME UNITS

ASK FEE

DAYS INN OF MONROEVILLE Book great rates at AAA.com **Phone:** 251/743-3297

Motel

Property failed to provide current rates

Location: On SR 21, 0.5 mi n of jct US 84. 4389 S Alabama Ave 36460. Fax: 251/743-2920. **Facility:** 62 one-bedroom standard units, some with whirlpools. 2 stories (no elevator), exterior corridors. **Parking:** on-site. **Terms:** small pets only ($5 extra charge). **Amenities:** high-speed Internet, irons, hair dryers. **Pool(s):** outdoor. **Leisure Activities:** whirlpool. **Guest Services:** valet laundry. **Business Services:** meeting rooms.

SOME UNITS

FEE

HOLIDAY INN EXPRESS Book great rates at AAA.com **Phone:** (251)743-3333

AAA SAVE
Small-scale Hotel

All Year 1P: $65-$145 2P: $75-$185 XP: $15 F12

Location: On SR 21, just s of jct US 84. 120 Hwy 21 S 36460. Fax: 251/575-5916. **Facility:** 41 one-bedroom standard units, some with whirlpools. 2 stories (no elevator), interior corridors. **Parking:** on-site. **Terms:** cancellation fee imposed, [AP] meal plan available, pets ($10 extra charge). **Amenities:** high-speed Internet, dual phone lines, voice mail, irons, hair dryers. *Some:* DVD players. **Pool(s):** small outdoor. **Leisure Activities:** exercise room. **Guest Services:** valet laundry, wireless Internet. **Business Services:** meeting rooms, PC. **Cards:** AX, CB, DC, DS, JC, MC, VI. **Free Special Amenities: expanded continental breakfast and newspaper.**

SOME UNITS

VCR FEE

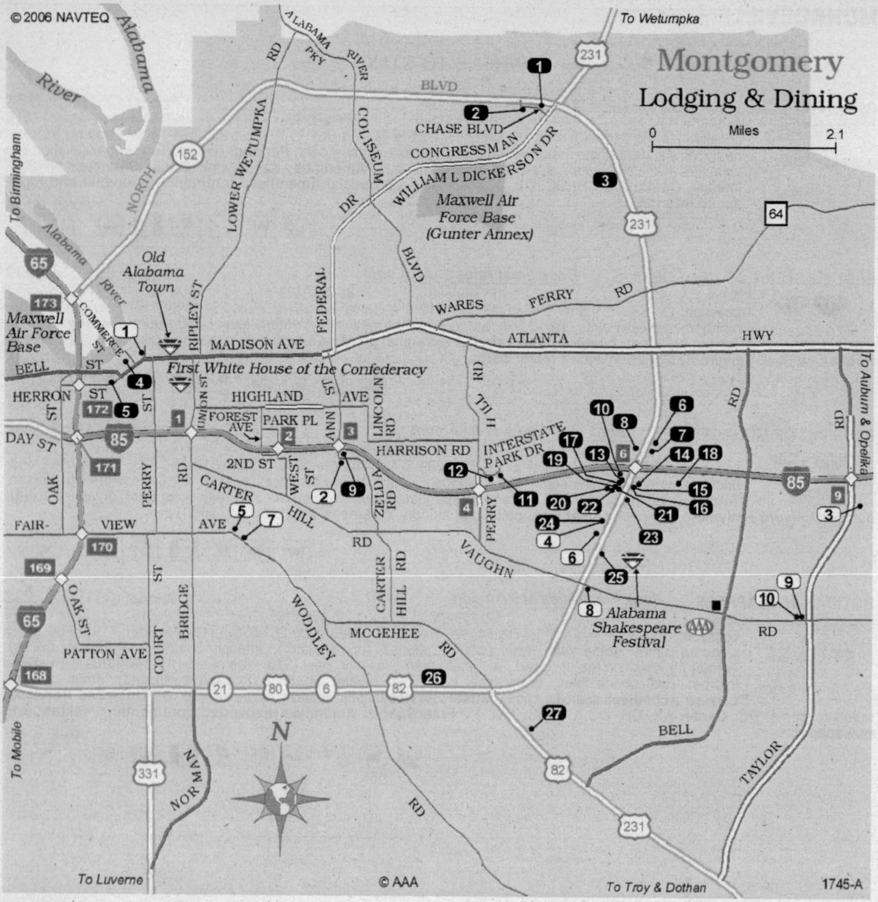

Montgomery Lodging & Dining

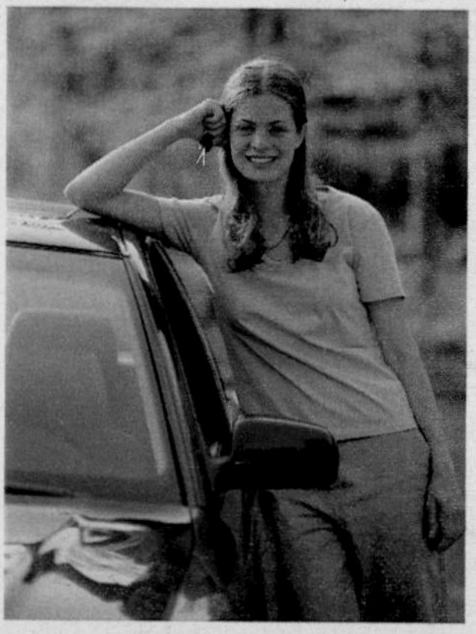

© 2006 NAVTEQ

© AAA

1745-A

Montgomery

This index helps you "spot" where approved accommodations and restaurants are located on the corresponding detailed maps. Lodging rate ranges are for comparison only and show the property's high season; rates are per night, unless only weekly (W) rates are available. Restaurant rate range is for dinner, unless only lunch (L) is served. Turn to the listing page for more detailed rate information and consult display ads for special promotions.

Spotter/Map Page Number	OA	**MONTGOMERY** - Lodgings	Diamond Rating	Rate Range High Season	Listing Page
1 / p. 274	AAA	**Comfort Inn-Gunter**	♦♦	$64-$84 SAVE	276
2 / p. 274		Days Inn Suites-Montgomery	♦♦	$70-$75	276
3 / p. 274		Holiday Inn-East	♦♦♦	$65-$79	278
4 / p. 274	AAA	**Embassy Suites Montgomery Conference Center** - see color ad p 277	♦♦♦	$99-$229 SAVE	277
5 / p. 274		Capitol Inn	♦♦	$54-$64	276
6 / p. 274		Motel 6 #149	♦	$45-$61	279
7 / p. 274		Best Western Monticello Inn	♦♦	$62	276
8 / p. 274		Drury Inn & Suites-Montgomery	♦♦♦	$70-$170	277
9 / p. 274	AAA	**Days Inn Midtown**	♦♦	$59-$64 SAVE	276
10 / p. 274		SpringHill Suites by Marriott	♦♦♦	$93	279
11 / p. 274		Homewood Suites by Hilton	♦♦♦	Failed to provide	279
12 / p. 274		Hilton Garden Inn Montgomery East	♦♦♦	$79-$149	278
13 / p. 274		La Quinta Inn Montgomery - see color ad p 386	♦♦♦	$78-$95	279
14 / p. 274		Fairfield Inn by Marriott	♦♦	$70-$99	277
15 / p. 274	AAA	**Courtyard by Marriott**	♦♦♦	$89-$169 SAVE	276
16 / p. 274		La Quinta Inn & Suites Montgomery - see color ad p 386	♦♦♦	$74-$94	279
17 / p. 274		Country Inn & Suites	♦♦♦	$89-$159	276
18 / p. 274	AAA	**Residence Inn by Marriott**	♦♦♦	$169-$179 SAVE	279
19 / p. 274		America's Best Inns	♦♦	Failed to provide	276
20 / p. 274		StudioPLUS	♦♦	Failed to provide	280
21 / p. 274		Quality Inn	♦♦	$53-$77	279
22 / p. 274		TownePlace Suites by Marriott	♦♦♦	$119	280
23 / p. 274		Hampton Inn	♦♦	$75-$89	277
24 / p. 274		Wingate Inn	♦♦♦	$75-$139	280
25 / p. 274		Extended StayAmerica Montgomery-Eastern Blvd	♦♦	$49-$69	277
26 / p. 274		Quality Inn & Suites - Governors House & Convention Center	♦♦	$58	279
27 / p. 274		Econo Lodge	♦♦	$50-$70	277
		MONTGOMERY - Restaurants			
1 / p. 274		Montgomery Brewing Company	♦♦	$7-$22	281
2 / p. 274		Country's Barbeque	♦	$5-$15	280
3 / p. 274		La Jolla	♦♦♦	$21-$30	281
4 / p. 274		Up the Creek Fish Camp & Grill	♦♦	$7-$19	281
5 / p. 274		El Rey Burrito Lounge	♦♦	$7-$15	280
6 / p. 274		Wings Sports Grille	♦♦	$6-$14	281
7 / p. 274		Jubilee Seafood	♦♦	$14-$22	280
8 / p. 274		Gator's Restaurant	♦♦	$8-$18	280
9 / p. 274		Sinclair's East	♦♦	$8-$20	281
10 / p. 274		Serrano-Fusion Cuisine	♦♦♦	$12-$28	281

MONTGOMERY pop. 201,568 (See map and index starting on p. 274)

WHERE TO STAY

AMERICA'S BEST INNS Book at AAA.com Phone: 334/270-9199 19

Small-scale Hotel

Property failed to provide current rates

Location: I-85, exit 6, just s on Eastern Blvd, then just w. 5135 Carmichael Rd 36106. Fax: 334/270-9199. **Facility:** 76 units. 66 one-bedroom standard units, some with whirlpools. 10 one-bedroom suites with whirlpools. 3 stories, interior corridors. *Bath:* combo or shower only. **Parking:** on-site. **Amenities:** irons, hair dryers. **Pool(s):** small heated indoor. **Leisure Activities:** whirlpool, exercise room. **Guest Services:** coin laundry, wireless Internet. **Business Services:** fax.

SOME UNITS

BEST WESTERN MONTICELLO INN Book great rates at AAA.com Phone: (334)277-4442 7

Motel

All Year 1P: $62 2P: $62 XP: $5 F17

Location: I-85, exit 6, just n on Eastern Blvd, then just e. 5837 Monticello Dr 36117. Fax: 334/277-9669. **Facility:** 49 one-bedroom standard units. 2 stories (no elevator), exterior corridors. **Parking:** on-site. **Terms:** package plans, small pets only ($10 extra charge). **Amenities:** irons, hair dryers. *Some:* high-speed Internet. **Pool(s):** outdoor. **Guest Services:** wireless Internet. **Business Services:** fax (fee). **Cards:** AX, DS, MC, VI.

SOME UNITS

FEE

CAPITOL INN Phone: (334)265-3844 5

Motel

All Year 1P: $54 2P: $64 XP: $10 F

Location: I-65, exit 172, just e on Heron St; in historic downtown. 205 N Goldwaite St 36104. Fax: 334/265-3844. **Facility:** 91 units. 90 one-bedroom standard units. 1 one-bedroom suite ($175-$185). 2 stories (no elevator), exterior corridors. **Parking:** on-site. **Terms:** office hours 6 am-11 am, cancellation fee imposed. **Amenities:** voice mail, irons, hair dryers. **Pool(s):** outdoor. **Guest Services:** wireless Internet. **Business Services:** meeting rooms. **Cards:** AX, CB, DC, DS, MC, VI.

SOME UNITS

COMFORT INN-GUNTER Book great rates at AAA.com Phone: (334)270-0099 1

AAA SAVE

Small-scale Hotel

All Year 1P: $64-$74 2P: $74-$84 XP: $5 F16

Location: I-85, exit 6, 4.2 mi n on US 231 to Wetumpka exit, then just w. 4480 N Chase Blvd 36110. Fax: 334/270-1124. **Facility:** 58 one-bedroom standard units, some with whirlpools. 2 stories (no elevator), interior corridors. *Bath:* combo or shower only. **Parking:** on-site. **Amenities:** voice mail, irons, hair dryers. **Pool(s):** small outdoor. **Guest Services:** wireless Internet. **Business Services:** meeting rooms. **Cards:** AX, CB, DC, DS, MC, VI. **Free Special Amenities: continental breakfast and high-speed Internet.**

SOME UNITS

COUNTRY INN & SUITES Book at AAA.com Phone: (334)270-3223 17

Small-scale Hotel

All Year [ECP] 1P: $89-$159 2P: $89-$159

Location: I-85, exit 6, just s on Eastern Blvd, then just w. 5155 Carmichael Rd 36106. Fax: 334/270-1423. **Facility:** 108 units. 65 one-bedroom standard units. 43 one-bedroom suites, some with whirlpools. 3 stories, interior corridors. *Bath:* combo or shower only. **Parking:** on-site. **Terms:** cancellation fee imposed, package plans. **Amenities:** voice mail, irons, hair dryers. **Pool(s):** heated indoor. **Leisure Activities:** whirlpool, exercise room. **Guest Services:** coin laundry, wireless Internet. **Business Services:** meeting rooms, business center. **Cards:** AX, DC, DS, MC, VI.

SOME UNITS

COURTYARD BY MARRIOTT Book great rates at AAA.com Phone: (334)272-5533 15

AAA SAVE

Small-scale Hotel

All Year 1P: $89-$169 2P: $89-$169

Location: I-85, exit 6, just s on Eastern Blvd, then just e. 5555 Carmichael Rd 36117. Fax: 334/279-0853. **Facility:** 146 units. 134 one-bedroom standard units. 12 one-bedroom suites ($119-$199). 3 stories, interior corridors. *Bath:* combo or shower only. **Parking:** on-site. **Terms:** cancellation fee imposed, [BP] meal plan available, package plans. **Amenities:** high-speed Internet, dual phone lines, voice mail, irons, hair dryers. **Dining:** 6 am-10 & 5-10 pm, Sat & Sun 7 am-11 & 5-10 pm, cocktails. **Pool(s):** heated outdoor. **Leisure Activities:** whirlpool, exercise room. **Guest Services:** sundries, valet and coin laundry, wireless Internet. **Business Services:** meeting rooms, business center. **Cards:** AX, CB, DC, DS, JC, MC, VI. **Free Special Amenities: high-speed Internet.**

SOME UNITS

DAYS INN MIDTOWN Book great rates at AAA.com Phone: (334)269-9611 9

AAA SAVE

Motel

All Year 1P: $59-$64 2P: $59-$64 XP: $5 F16

Location: I-85, exit 3, just s on Ann St. 2625 Zelda Rd 36107. Fax: 334/262-7393. **Facility:** 130 one-bedroom standard units. 2 stories (no elevator), exterior corridors. **Parking:** on-site. **Terms:** package plans, pets ($5 extra charge). **Amenities:** hair dryers. **Pool(s):** outdoor. **Leisure Activities:** barbecue grills & picnic tables. **Guest Services:** coin laundry, wireless Internet. **Business Services:** meeting rooms, PC. **Cards:** AX, CB, DC, DS, JC, MC, VI. **Free Special Amenities: local telephone calls and high-speed Internet.**

SOME UNITS

FEE

DAYS INN SUITES-MONTGOMERY Book great rates at AAA.com Phone: (334)396-3060 2

Small-scale Hotel

All Year 1P: $70-$75 2P: $70-$75 XP: $10 F

Location: I-85, exit 6, 4.2 mi n on US 231 to Wetumpka exit, then just w. 4470 N Chase Blvd 36110. Fax: 334/396-2942. **Facility:** 39 one-bedroom standard units, some with whirlpools. 2 stories (no elevator), interior corridors. **Parking:** on-site. **Amenities:** high-speed Internet, irons, hair dryers. **Pool(s):** small outdoor. **Guest Services:** coin laundry. **Cards:** AX, DS, MC, VI.

SOME UNITS

(See map and index starting on p. 274)

DRURY INN & SUITES-MONTGOMERY Book at AAA.com Phone: (334)273-1101 8

Small-scale Hotel

All Year [BP] 1P: $70-$160 2P: $80-$170 XP: $10 F18

Location: I-85, exit 6, just n. 1124 Eastern Blvd 36117-1942. Fax: 334/273-1101. **Facility:** 180 units. 152 one-bedroom standard units, some with whirlpools. 8 one- and 20 two-bedroom suites ($140-$160). 7 stories, interior corridors. *Bath:* combo or shower only. **Parking:** on-site. **Amenities:** dual phone lines, voice mail, irons, hair dryers. **Pool(s):** heated indoor/outdoor. **Leisure Activities:** whirlpool, exercise room. **Guest Services:** sundries, complimentary evening beverages, valet and coin laundry, wireless Internet. **Business Services:** meeting rooms, business center. **Cards:** AX, CB, DC, DS, MC, VI.

SOME UNITS

ASK / /

ECONO LODGE Book great rates at AAA.com Phone: (334)284-3400 27

Motel

All Year 1P: $50-$60 2P: $60-$70 XP: $5 F

Location: On US 82/231, 0.7 mi e of jct South and East blvds. 4135 Troy Hwy 36116. Fax: 334/284-3400. **Facility:** 45 one-bedroom standard units, some with whirlpools. 2 stories (no elevator), exterior corridors. **Parking:** on-site. **Terms:** cancellation fee imposed, [CP] meal plan available, small pets only ($10 extra charge, in 2nd floor smoking units). **Amenities:** *Some:* irons, hair dryers. **Pool(s):** small outdoor. **Business Services:** fax (fee). **Cards:** AX, DC, DS, MC, VI.

SOME UNITS

ASK / /

FEE

EMBASSY SUITES MONTGOMERY CONFERENCE CENTER Book great rates at AAA.com Phone: (334)269-5055 4

AAA SAVE

Large-scale Hotel

All Year [BP] 1P: $99-$229 2P: $99-$229 XP: $10 F18

Location: Between Motton and Commerce sts; in historic downtown. 300 Tallapoosa St 36104. Fax: 334/269-0360. **Facility:** 237 one-bedroom suites. 8 stories, interior corridors. *Bath:* combo or shower only. **Parking:** on-site. **Terms:** cancellation fee imposed, pets ($25 fee). **Amenities:** voice mail, irons, hair dryers. *Fee:* video games, high-speed Internet. **Dining:** 11 am-2 & 5-11 pm, cocktails. **Pool(s):** heated indoor. **Leisure Activities:** sauna, whirlpool, exercise room. *Fee:* game room. **Guest Services:** gift shop, complimentary evening beverages, valet and coin laundry. **Business Services:** meeting rooms, business center. **Cards:** AX, CB, DC, DS, JC, MC, VI. **Free Special Amenities: full breakfast and newspaper.** *(See color ad below)*

SOME UNITS

/ VCR /

FEE FEE

EXTENDED STAYAMERICA MONTGOMERY-EASTERN BLVD Book at AAA.com Phone: (334)279-1204 25

Motel

All Year 1P: $49-$64 2P: $54-$69 XP: $5 F17

Location: I-85, exit 6, 1.3 mi s on US 231. 2491 Eastern Blvd 36117. Fax: 334/279-1076. **Facility:** 120 one-bedroom standard units with efficiencies. 3 stories, exterior corridors. *Bath:* combo or shower only. **Parking:** on-site. **Terms:** office hours 7 am-11 pm, small pets only ($25 fee). **Amenities:** voice mail, irons. **Guest Services:** coin laundry, wireless Internet. **Cards:** AX, CB, DC, DS, MC, VI.

SOME UNITS

ASK / /

FEE

FAIRFIELD INN BY MARRIOTT Book great rates at AAA.com Phone: (334)270-0007 14

Small-scale Hotel

All Year [CP] 1P: $70-$99 2P: $70-$99

Location: I-85, exit 6, just s on Eastern Blvd, then just e. 5601 Carmichael Rd 36117. Fax: 334/270-0007. **Facility:** 133 one-bedroom standard units. 3 stories, interior/exterior corridors. **Parking:** on-site. **Terms:** 7 day cancellation notice. **Amenities:** high-speed Internet, irons, hair dryers. **Pool(s):** outdoor. **Guest Services:** valet laundry. **Cards:** AX, DC, DS, MC, VI.

SOME UNITS

ASK / /

HAMPTON INN Book great rates at AAA.com Phone: (334)277-2400 23

Motel

All Year 1P: $75-$86 2P: $82-$89

Location: I-85, exit 6, just s. 1401 Eastern Blvd 36117. Fax: 334/277-6546. **Facility:** 105 one-bedroom standard units. 2 stories (no elevator), exterior corridors. **Parking:** on-site. **Amenities:** voice mail, irons, hair dryers. **Pool(s):** small outdoor. **Guest Services:** valet laundry, wireless Internet. **Business Services:** meeting rooms, PC. **Cards:** AX, CB, DC, DS, MC, VI.

SOME UNITS

ASK / /

(See map and index starting on p. 274)

HAMPTON INN & SUITES MONTGOMERY EASTCHASE Book great rates at AAA.com — Phone: (334)277-1818

Small-scale Hotel

All Year [BP] 1P: $115-$139 2P: $120-$144

Location: I-85, exit 9 (Taylor Rd), just s, then 0.9 mi e; in The Shoppes of EastChase. 7651 EastChase Pkwy 36117. Fax: 334/277-1560. **Facility:** 102 units. 89 one-bedroom standard units. 13 one-bedroom suites ($133-$150). 4 stories, interior corridors. *Bath:* combo or shower only. **Parking:** on-site. **Amenities:** video library, DVD players, high-speed Internet, voice mail, irons, hair dryers. **Pool(s):** heated outdoor. **Leisure Activities:** putting green, exercise room. **Guest Services:** sundries, valet laundry, wireless Internet. **Business Services:** meeting rooms, business center. **Cards:** AX, DC, DS, MC, VI.

SOME UNITS

HILTON GARDEN INN MONTGOMERY EAST Book great rates at AAA.com — Phone: 334/272-2225 12

Small-scale Hotel

All Year 1P: $79-$149 2P: $79-$149

Location: I-85, exit 4, just n on Perry Hill, then just e. 1600 Interstate Park Dr 36109. Fax: 334/277-4559. **Facility:** 97 one-bedroom standard units. 4 stories, interior corridors. *Bath:* combo or shower only. **Parking:** on-site. **Amenities:** high-speed Internet, dual phone lines, voice mail, irons, hair dryers. **Pool(s):** outdoor. **Leisure Activities:** whirlpool, exercise room. **Guest Services:** sundries, valet and coin laundry. **Business Services:** meeting rooms, business center. **Cards:** AX, DC, DS, MC, VI.

SOME UNITS

HOLIDAY INN-EAST Book at AAA.com — Phone: (334)272-0370 3

Small-scale Hotel

All Year 1P: $65-$79

Location: I-85, exit 6, just n. 1185 Eastern Bypass 36117. Fax: 334/270-0339. **Facility:** 210 one-bedroom standard units. 2 stories (no elevator), interior/exterior corridors. *Bath:* combo or shower only. **Parking:** on-site. **Terms:** check-in 4 pm, cancellation fee imposed, [CP] & [MAP] meal plans available, package plans, small pets only ($25 fee, in designated units). **Amenities:** video games (fee), voice mail, irons, hair dryers. **Pool(s):** heated indoor. **Leisure Activities:** sauna, whirlpool, exercise room. *Fee:* game room. **Guest Services:** valet and coin laundry, wireless Internet. **Business Services:** meeting rooms, business center. **Cards:** AX, CB, DC, DS, JC, MC, VI.

SOME UNITS

FEE

HOLIDAY INN EXPRESS Book great rates at AAA.com — Phone: (334)271-5516

SAVE

Small-scale Hotel

All Year 1P: $95 2P: $95

Location: I-85, exit 11, just s. 9250 Boyd Cooper Pkwy 36117. Fax: 334/271-5517. **Facility:** 106 one-bedroom standard units. 4 stories, interior corridors. *Bath:* combo or shower only. **Parking:** on-site. **Amenities:** high-speed Internet, dual phone lines, voice mail, irons, hair dryers. **Pool(s):** heated indoor. **Leisure Activities:** whirlpool, exercise room. **Guest Services:** valet and coin laundry, wireless Internet. **Business Services:** meeting rooms, business center. **Cards:** AX, CB, DC, DS, JC, MC, VI. **Free Special Amenities:** **expanded continental breakfast and high-speed Internet.** *(See color ad below)*

SOME UNITS

(See map and index starting on p. 274)

HOMEWOOD SUITES BY HILTON Book at AAA.com Phone: 334/272-3010 11

Property failed to provide current rates

Large-scale Hotel

Location: I-85, exit 4, just n on Penny Mill, then just e. 1800 Interstate Park Dr 36109. Fax: 334/272-5020. **Facility:** 91 units. 36 one-bedroom standard units with efficiencies. 52 one- and 3 two-bedroom suites, some with efficiencies. 4 stories, interior corridors. *Bath:* combo or shower only. **Parking:** on-site. **Amenities:** DVD players, high-speed Internet, voice mail, irons, hair dryers. **Pool(s):** outdoor. **Leisure Activities:** exercise room, sports court. **Guest Services:** sundries, complimentary evening beverages: Mon-Thurs. **Business Services:** meeting rooms, business center.

SOME UNITS

LA QUINTA INN & SUITES MONTGOMERY Book great rates at AAA.com Phone: (334)277-6000 16

Small-scale Hotel

All Year	1P: $74-$94	2P: $74-$94	XP: $6	F18

Location: I-85, exit 6, just s on Eastern Blvd, then just w. 5225 Carmichael Rd 36106. Fax: 334/279-8207. **Facility:** 99 units. 96 one-bedroom standard units. 3 one-bedroom suites, some with kitchens (no utensils). 3 stories, interior corridors. **Parking:** on-site. **Terms:** [ECP] meal plan available. **Amenities:** video games (fee), voice mail, irons, hair dryers. **Pool(s):** outdoor. **Guest Services:** valet and coin laundry, wireless Internet. **Cards:** AX, CB, DC, DS, MC, VI. ***(See color ad p 386)***

SOME UNITS

FEE

LA QUINTA INN MONTGOMERY Book great rates at AAA.com Phone: (334)271-1620 13

Motel

All Year [ECP]	1P: $78-$88	2P: $85-$95	XP: $7	F18

Location: I-85, exit 6, just s. 1280 East Blvd 36117-2231. Fax: 334/244-7919. **Facility:** 130 units. 128 one-bedroom standard units. 2 one-bedroom suites. 2 stories (no elevator), exterior corridors. **Parking:** on-site. **Terms:** small pets only. **Amenities:** video games (fee), voice mail, irons, hair dryers. **Pool(s):** outdoor. **Guest Services:** valet laundry, wireless Internet. **Cards:** AX, CB, DC, DS, MC, VI. ***(See color ad p 386)***

SOME UNITS

MOTEL 6 #149 Book at AAA.com Phone: 334/277-6748 6

Motel

5/25-11/30	1P: $45-$55	2P: $51-$61	XP: $3	F17
12/1-5/24	1P: $39-$49	2P: $45-$55	XP: $3	F17

Location: I-85, exit 6, just n. 1051 Eastern Blvd 36117. Fax: 334/277-9156. **Facility:** 102 one-bedroom standard units. 2 stories (no elevator), exterior corridors. *Bath:* combo or shower only. **Parking:** on-site. **Terms:** small pets only. **Pool(s):** outdoor. **Guest Services:** coin laundry. **Business Services:** fax (fee). **Cards:** AX, CB, DC, DS, MC, VI.

SOME UNITS

QUALITY INN Book great rates at AAA.com Phone: (334)277-1919 21

Motel

All Year	1P: $53-$75	2P: $55-$77

Location: I-85, exit 6, just s on Eastern Blvd, then just w. 5175 Carmichael Rd 36106. Fax: 334/279-6624. **Facility:** 108 one-bedroom standard units. 2 stories (no elevator), exterior corridors. **Parking:** on-site. **Terms:** [ECP] meal plan available. **Amenities:** voice mail, irons, hair dryers. **Pool(s):** outdoor. **Leisure Activities:** exercise room. **Guest Services:** valet and coin laundry, wireless Internet. **Business Services:** meeting rooms. **Cards:** AX, DC, DS, MC, VI.

SOME UNITS

QUALITY INN & SUITES - GOVERNORS HOUSE & CONVENTION CENTER Book great rates at AAA.com Phone: (344)288-2800 26

Small-scale Hotel

All Year	1P: $58	2P: $58	XP: $10	F17

Location: I-85, exit 6, 3.7 mi s on East Blvd. 2705 E South Blvd 36116. Fax: 334/284-3609. **Facility:** 174 units. 168 one-bedroom standard units, some with whirlpools. 6 one-bedroom suites ($90), some with kitchens (no utensils) and/or whirlpools. 2 stories (no elevator), exterior corridors. **Parking:** on-site. **Terms:** 3 day cancellation notice, package plans. **Amenities:** voice mail, irons, hair dryers. *Some:* DVD players. **Pool(s):** outdoor. **Leisure Activities:** exercise room. **Guest Services:** wireless Internet. **Business Services:** conference facilities, business center. **Cards:** AX, DC, DS, MC, VI.

SOME UNITS

RESIDENCE INN BY MARRIOTT Book great rates at AAA.com Phone: (334)270-3300 18

AAA SAVE

Small-scale Hotel

All Year [BP]	1P: $169-$179

Location: I-85, exit 6, just s on Eastern Blvd, then just e. 1200 Hilmar Ct 36117. Fax: 334/260-0907. **Facility:** 94 units. 66 one-bedroom standard units with kitchens. 4 one- and 24 two-bedroom suites with kitchens. 2 stories (no elevator), interior/exterior corridors. *Bath:* combo or shower only. **Parking:** on-site. **Terms:** cancellation fee imposed, pets ($75 fee). **Amenities:** high-speed Internet, voice mail, irons, hair dryers. **Pool(s):** outdoor. **Leisure Activities:** whirlpool, exercise room, sports court. **Guest Services:** sundries, complimentary evening beverages: Mon-Thurs, valet and coin laundry. **Business Services:** meeting rooms, PC. **Cards:** AX, DC, DS, JC, MC, VI. **Free Special Amenities: full breakfast and high-speed Internet.**

SOME UNITS

FEE

SPRINGHILL SUITES BY MARRIOTT Book great rates at AAA.com Phone: (334)409-9999 10

Small-scale Hotel

All Year	1P: $93

Location: I-85, exit 6, just s on Eastern Blvd, then just w on Carmichael Rd. 1201 Townplace Dr 36106. Fax: 334/409-0061. **Facility:** 79 one-bedroom standard units. 3 stories, interior corridors. *Bath:* combo or shower only. **Parking:** on-site. **Terms:** cancellation fee imposed, 13% service charge. **Amenities:** voice mail, irons, hair dryers. **Pool(s):** small heated indoor. **Leisure Activities:** whirlpool, exercise room. **Guest Services:** sundries, valet and coin laundry, wireless Internet. **Business Services:** meeting rooms, business center. **Cards:** AX, CB, DC, DS, MC, VI.

SOME UNITS

(See map and index starting on p. 274)

STUDIOPLUS Book at AAA.com Phone: 334/273-0075 20

Small-scale Hotel

Property failed to provide current rates

Location: I-85, exit 6, 0.5 mi s on US 231. 5115 Carmichael Rd 36106. Fax: 334/273-1092. **Facility:** 72 one-bedroom standard units with kitchens. 3 stories (no elevator), interior corridors. *Bath:* combo or shower only. **Parking:** on-site. **Terms:** office hours 7 am-11 pm, pets ($25 fee). **Amenities:** voice mail, irons. **Pool(s):** small outdoor. **Guest Services:** wireless Internet.

SOME UNITS

FEE

TOWNEPLACE SUITES BY MARRIOTT Book great rates at AAA.com Phone: 334/396-5505 22

Small-scale Hotel

All Year 1P: $119

Location: I-85, exit 6, just s on Eastern Blvd, then just w on Carmichael Rd. 5047 Townplace Dr 36106. Fax: 334/396-5504. **Facility:** 95 units. 69 one-bedroom standard units with kitchens. 4 one- and 22 two-bedroom suites ($129-$139), some with kitchens. 3 stories, interior corridors. *Bath:* combo or shower only. **Parking:** on-site. **Terms:** small pets only ($75 fee). **Amenities:** dual phone lines, voice mail, irons, hair dryers. **Pool(s):** small outdoor. **Leisure Activities:** exercise room. **Guest Services:** valet and coin laundry, wireless Internet. **Business Services:** fax (fee). **Cards:** AX, CB, DC, DS, JC, MC, VI.

SOME UNITS

ASK FEE

WINGATE INN Book at AAA.com Phone: (334)244-7880 24

Small-scale Hotel

All Year 1P: $75-$139 2P: $75-$139 XP: $8 F

Location: I-85, exit 6, 0.7 mi s. Located next to Lowe's. 2060 Eastern Blvd 36117. Fax: 334/244-4155. **Facility:** 84 one-bedroom standard units, some with whirlpools. 3 stories, interior corridors. *Bath:* combo or shower only. **Parking:** on-site. **Amenities:** video games (fee), high-speed Internet, voice mail, safes, irons, hair dryers. **Pool(s):** outdoor. **Leisure Activities:** whirlpool, exercise room. **Guest Services:** valet and coin laundry, wireless Internet. **Business Services:** meeting rooms, business center. **Cards:** AX, CB, DC, DS, MC, VI.

SOME UNITS

ASK

WHERE TO DINE

ATLANTA BREAD COMPANY **Lunch:** $4-$6 **Dinner:** $4-$6 **Phone:** 334/271-1170

Bakery/Desserts

Location: I-85, exit 9, 1.7 mi s on Taylor Rd; in Festival Plaza. 7921 Vaughn Rd 36116. **Hours:** 6:30 am-8:30 pm, Fri & Sat-9:30 pm, Sun 7 am-8 pm. Closed: 11/22, 12/25. **Features:** Offering a wide variety of soups and made-to-order sandwiches, the eatery is a good bet for tasty food in a quiet, relaxing atmosphere. Casual dress. **Parking:** on-site. **Cards:** AX, MC, VI.

BARNHILL'S BUFFET **Lunch:** $5-$9 **Dinner:** $7-$10 **Phone:** 334/284-9446

American

Location: Jct US 231, 0.5 mi w on US 80; in Governor's Square. 2875 E South Blvd 36116. **Hours:** 10:45 am-8:45 pm, Fri-9 pm, Sat 7 am-9 pm, Sun 7 am-8:45 pm. Closed: 12/25. **Features:** Casual dress. **Parking:** on-site. **Cards:** AX, DS, MC, VI.

COUNTRY'S BARBEQUE **Lunch:** $5-$15 **Dinner:** $5-$15 **Phone:** 334/262-6211 2

Barbecue

Location: I-85, exit 3, just e. 2610 Zelda Rd 36106. **Hours:** 11 am-9 pm, Fri & Sat-10 pm. Closed major holidays. **Features:** Pullled pork, beef ribs, chicken, brunswick stew and barbeque cole slaw are some of the dishes that will give you an example of the tasty treats offered at this eatery. Casual dress; beer only. **Parking:** on-site. **Cards:** AX, MC, VI.

EL REY BURRITO LOUNGE **Dinner:** $7-$15 **Phone:** 834/832-9688 5

Mexican

Location: I-85, exit 1, 1.1 mi s, then 1 mi e; between Boultier St and Cloverdale Rd. 1031 E Fairview Ave 36106. **Hours:** 4 pm-10 pm, Sat-11 pm. Closed major holidays; also Sun. **Features:** The cool and mellow atmosphere enhances this delicious dinning expierence; overstuffed burritos, freshly made guacamole and a delicious array of salsas make this one hot spot. Casual dress; cocktails. **Parking:** street. **Cards:** MC, VI.

FOX AND HOUND PUB & GRILLE **Lunch:** $6-$18 **Dinner:** $6-$18 **Phone:** 334/260-0092

American

Location: I-85, exit 6, 1.5 mi n on US 231. 163 Eastern Blvd, Suite 14-17 36117. **Hours:** 11 am-2 am. Closed: 12/25. **Features:** Casual dress; cocktails. **Parking:** on-site. **Cards:** AX, DS, MC, VI.

GATOR'S RESTAURANT **Lunch:** $5-$10 **Dinner:** $8-$18 **Phone:** 334/274-0330 8

Cajun

Location: I-85, exit 6, 1.7 mi s on Eastern Blvd, then just e; in Vaughn Plaza. 5040 Vaughn Rd 36116. **Hours:** 11 am-9 pm, Wed-Fri to 10 pm, Sat 4 pm-10 pm, Sun 11 am-2 pm. Closed: 1/1, 11/22, 12/25. **Features:** This is a fun, funky place to eat Cajun and Caribbean-influenced cuisine. Daily specials are offered, with everything freshly cooked and made-to-order. A bright, cartoon-style decor, and a mix of blues, jazz and Cajun music make for a lively atmosphere. Casual dress; cocktails. **Parking:** on-site. **Cards:** AX, DS, MC, VI.

JUBILEE SEAFOOD **Dinner:** $14-$22 **Phone:** 334/262-6224 7

Seafood

Location: Jct Woodley Rd and Fairview Ave; in Historic Old Cloverdale. 1057 Woodley Rd 36106. **Hours:** 5 pm-10 pm. Closed major holidays; also Sun & Mon. **Features:** Enjoy what many rave is the best and freshest seafood this side of the gulf. You can begin with a succulent West Indies salad, then sample any number of daily fish specials and finally delve into a mouth-watering slice of key lime pie. Casual dress; cocktails. **Parking:** on-site. **Cards:** AX, MC, VI.

(See map and index starting on p. 274)

LA JOLLA **Lunch:** $12-$21 **Dinner:** $21-$30 **Phone:** 334/356-2600 (3)

American

Location: I-85, exit 4, just s; in Eastchase Shoppes. 6854 Eastchase Pkwy 36117. **Hours:** 11 am-2 & 5:30-10 pm, Sat from 5:30 pm. Closed: Sun. **Reservations:** accepted. **Features:** Smart and hip, the restaurant sits amid the best shops in town. Distinctive modern dishes are presented attractively. Dressy casual; cocktails. **Parking:** street. **Cards:** AX, DS, MC, VI.

MONTGOMERY BREWING COMPANY **Lunch:** $6-$9 **Dinner:** $7-$22 **Phone:** 334/834-2739 (1)

American

Location: Corner of N Court; in historic downtown. 12 W Jefferson St 36104. **Hours:** 11 am-9 pm, Fri-10 pm, Sat 4:30 pm-10 pm. Closed major holidays; also Sun. **Reservations:** accepted, except Fri & Sat night. **Features:** This charming brewpub quartered in an old converted railroad warehouse brews and bottles their own beer right on the premises. Their best-selling entree is the parmesan-crusted trout, and the sauteed crab claws make an excellent appetizer. Casual dress; cocktails. **Parking:** on-site. **Cards:** AX, DC, DS, MC, VI.

ROADHOUSE GRILL **Lunch:** $6-$9 **Dinner:** $8-$17 **Phone:** 334/396-4525

Steak House

Location: I-85, exit 6, 0.9 mi s. 2430 Eastern Blvd 36106. **Hours:** 11 am-10 pm, Fri & Sat-11 pm. Closed: 11/22, 12/25. **Reservations:** accepted. **Features:** Jumbo steaks cooked on the grill and a rustic country look make for pleasant, informal dining experience. Particularly special here is dessert; try the messy sundae, a perfect finish to a fine meal. Casual dress; cocktails. **Parking:** on-site. **Cards:** AX, DC, DS, MC, VI.

SERRANO-FUSION CUISINE **Dinner:** $12-$28 **Phone:** 334/244-6160 (10)

Southern

Location: I-85, exit 9, 1.7 mi s on Taylor Rd, then just w; in Halcyon Village Plaza. 7839 Vaughn Rd 36116. **Hours:** 5 pm-10 pm. Closed: 11/22, 12/24, 12/25; also Sun & Mon. **Reservations:** accepted. **Features:** The chef successfully fuses traditional Southern cooking with Asian ingredients; the dishes here are creative and include such things as pan-seared Long Island muscovy duck breast with red chile pear sauce, bourbon brown sugar asian pear and relish potato blue cheese cake. Her creations make use of exotic meats and fish like skate and elk tenderloin. There's a definite upscale bistro-like feel to the place but it is comfortable and service is efficient and accomplished. Casual dress; cocktails. **Parking:** on-site. **Cards:** AX, DS, MC, VI.

SINCLAIR'S EAST **Lunch:** $8-$20 **Dinner:** $8-$20 **Phone:** 334/271-7654 (9)

American

Location: I-85, exit 9, 1.7 mi s on Taylor Rd, then just w; in Halcyon Village Plaza. 7847 Vaughn Rd 36116. **Hours:** 11 am-10 pm, Fri & Sat-11 pm. Closed: 7/4, 11/22, 12/24, 12/25. **Features:** Patrons can enjoy great food while stepping into the past. Pictures of Hollywood stars, such as Clark Gable, James Dean, Marilyn Monroe and Greta Garbo, line the walls of the retro-style diner. Casual dress; cocktails. **Parking:** on-site. **Cards:** AX, DS, MC, VI.

SMOKEY BONES BARBEQUE & GRILL **Lunch:** $5-$13 **Dinner:** $9-$21 **Phone:** 334/270-1004

Barbecue

Location: I-85, exit 6, 0.9 mi s. 2465 Eastern Blvd 36117. **Hours:** 11 am-10 pm, Fri & Sat-11 pm. Closed: 11/22, 12/25. **Features:** More than 15 televisions surround the energetic sports bar, where patrons can savor mouthwatering barbecue. Service is friendly in the upbeat setting. Casual dress; cocktails. **Parking:** on-site. **Cards:** AX, DS, MC, VI.

UP THE CREEK FISH CAMP & GRILL **Lunch:** $4-$19 **Dinner:** $7-$19 **Phone:** 334/279-2077 (4)

Seafood

Location: I-85, exit 6, 0.7 mi s. 2070 Eastern Blvd 36116. **Hours:** 11 am-11 pm, Fri & Sat-midnight, Sun 10:30 am-10 pm. Closed major holidays. **Features:** Done in the style of a fishing hut, the restaurant prepares a wide variety of seafood, steak and pasta dishes. The entire family can enjoy good food and casual fun. Casual dress; cocktails. **Parking:** on-site. **Cards:** AX, DS, MC, VI.

WINGS SPORTS GRILLE **Lunch:** $6-$14 **Dinner:** $6-$14 **Phone:** 334/271-1831 (6)

American

Location: I-85, exit 6, 0.8 mi s; in Colonial Promenade. 2232 Eastern Blvd 36117. **Hours:** 11 am-10 pm, Fri & Sat-11 pm. Closed major holidays; also 12/24. **Features:** Every member of the family can enjoy hearty portions, good food and fun. The friendly staff makes guests feel right at home, and the multitude of games helps keep everyone entertained. Casual dress; cocktails. **Parking:** on-site. **Cards:** AX, DS, MC, VI.

MOODY *—See Birmingham p. 237.*

MOULTON pop. 3,260

WHERE TO STAY

DAYS INN *Book great rates at AAA.com* **Phone:** (256)974-1214

Motel

All Year 1P: $50 2P: $55 XP: $5 F

Location: 0.4 mi nw of jct SR 24. 12701 SR 157 35650. Fax: 256/974-1582. **Facility:** 25 one-bedroom standard units, some with whirlpools. 1 story, exterior corridors. **Parking:** on-site. **Terms:** [CP] meal plan available, package plans. **Amenities:** high-speed Internet, hair dryers. *Some:* irons. **Pool(s):** outdoor. **Business Services:** meeting rooms. **Cards:** AX, CB, DC, DS, JC, MC, VI.

SOME UNITS

MOUNTAIN BROOK *—See Birmingham p. 238.*

MUNFORD pop. 2,446

WHERE TO STAY

THE CEDARS PLANTATION BED AND BREAKFAST **Phone:** (256)761-9090

Bed & Breakfast

All Year [BP] 1P: $85-$125 2P: $85-$125 XP: $15

Location: I-20, exit 185 (SR 21), 9.2 mi s, then 2.7 mi s on CR 107 to "T" intersection. 590 Cheaha Rd 36268. Fax: 256/761-9090. **Facility:** Built in 1834, this plantation house with balconies, 15-foot ceilings and a Civil War library is near Talladega Speedway, Mount Cheaha and Anniston. Designated smoking area. 4 units. 3 one-bedroom standard units. 1 two-bedroom suite. 2 stories (no elevator), interior/exterior corridors. *Bath:* combo or shower only. **Parking:** on-site. **Terms:** age restrictions may apply, 3 day cancellation notice-fee imposed, package plans, no pets allowed (owner's pet on premises). **Amenities:** *Some:* irons. **Pool(s):** outdoor. **Leisure Activities:** whirlpool, lighted tennis court, hiking trails.

SOME UNITS

NORTHPORT pop. 19,435

WHERE TO STAY

BEST WESTERN CATALINA INN *Book great rates at AAA.com* **Phone:** (205)339-5200

Motel

All Year 1P: $65-$130 2P: $70-$140 XP: $5 F14

Location: On US 82, just nw of jct US 43/SR 69. 2015 McFarland Blvd 35476. Fax: 205/330-1335. **Facility:** 37 one-bedroom standard units. 1 story, exterior corridors. **Parking:** on-site. **Amenities:** high-speed Internet, irons, hair dryers. **Pool(s):** outdoor. **Business Services:** fax (fee). **Cards:** AX, DC, DS, MC, VI. **Free Special Amenities: continental breakfast and high-speed Internet.**

SOME UNITS

ECONO LODGE INN & SUITES *Book great rates at AAA.com* **Phone:** (205)330-0345

Small-scale Hotel

All Year 1P: $55-$145 2P: $60-$160 XP: $5 F18

Location: On US 82, just nw of jct US 43/SR 69. 1930 McFarland Blvd 35476. Fax: 205/330-0345. **Facility:** 42 one-bedroom standard units, some with whirlpools. 2 stories (no elevator), exterior corridors. **Parking:** on-site. **Terms:** cancellation fee imposed. **Amenities:** hair dryers. *Some:* irons. **Pool(s):** outdoor. **Business Services:** fax (fee). **Cards:** AX, CB, DC, DS, MC, VI.

SOME UNITS

WHERE TO DINE

CITY CAFE **Lunch:** $2-$10 **Phone:** 205/758-9171

Southern

Location: US 69 N, just w to Robert Cardinal Airport Rd, just s; in historic downtown. 408 Main Ave 35476. **Hours:** 4 am-3:30 pm. Closed major holidays; also Sat & Sun. **Features:** Guests can retreat to the good old days at the cafe, where customers are treated like family but the dishes are better than Mom's. Casual dress. **Parking:** street.

THE GLOBE **Lunch:** $7-$17 **Dinner:** $11-$17 **Phone:** 205/391-0949

International

Location: In historic downtown. 430 Main Ave 35476. **Hours:** 11 am-3 & 5-10 pm. Closed major holidays; also Sun & Mon. **Reservations:** accepted. **Features:** In the quaint and historic downtown district, the restaurant presents a creative and international menu. The setting is intimate and romantic. Casual dress; beer & wine only. **Parking:** street. **Cards:** AX, MC, VI.

NORTHPORT DINER **Lunch:** $3-$6 **Dinner:** $3-$6 **Phone:** 205/333-7190

American

Location: On US 82, 0.8 mi e of jct US 43/SR 69; in Northbrook Plaza. 450 McFarland Blvd 35476. **Hours:** 10:30 am-9 pm. Closed major holidays. **Features:** A casual and fun atmosphere with retro elements greets diners here. Reminiscent of the 1950s, complete with a checkerboard floor, chrome-trimmed vinyl booths, old Hollywood posters and homestyle comfort food, this diner will take you back to the "Happy Days.". Casual dress. **Parking:** on-site. **Cards:** MC, VI.

ONEONTA —*See Birmingham p. 238.*

OPELIKA pop. 23,498

WHERE TO STAY

AUBURN OPELIKA MARRIOTT AT GRAND NATIONAL *Book great rates at AAA.com* **Phone:** (334)741-9292

Small-scale Hotel

All Year 1P: $89-$209 2P: $89-$209 XP: $10 F16

Location: I-85, exit 58, 4.1 mi n on US 280, then 2.5 mi e on CR 97 (Grand National Pkwy). 3700 Sunbelt Pkwy 36801. Fax: 334/741-9733. **Facility:** 129 units. 125 one-bedroom standard units. 4 one-bedroom suites ($109-$350). 4 stories, interior corridors. *Bath:* combo or shower only. **Parking:** on-site. **Terms:** check-in 4 pm, cancellation fee imposed, package plans. **Amenities:** dual phone lines, voice mail, irons, hair dryers. *Fee:* video games, high-speed Internet. **Pool(s):** outdoor, heated indoor. **Leisure Activities:** saunas, whirlpool, golf-54 holes, exercise room, volleyball, game room. *Fee:* massage. **Guest Services:** gift shop, valet laundry, area transportation. **Business Services:** conference facilities, business center. **Cards:** CB, DC, DS, JC, MC, VI. ***(See color ad p 200)***

SOME UNITS

COMFORT INN *Book great rates at AAA.com* **Phone:** (334)741-9977

Small-scale Hotel

8/24-11/30	1P: $70-$199	2P: $74-$225	XP: $8	F
12/1-8/23	1P: $70-$129	2P: $74-$139	XP: $8	F

Location: I-85, exit 62, just w to Foxrun Pkwy, then just n. 811 Foxrun Pkwy 36801. Fax: 334/741-9901. **Facility:** 59 units. 57 one-bedroom standard units. 2 one-bedroom suites ($99-$249). 3 stories, interior corridors. **Parking:** on-site. **Amenities:** voice mail, irons, hair dryers. **Pool(s):** small outdoor. **Leisure Activities:** limited exercise equipment. **Guest Services:** valet laundry, wireless Internet. **Business Services:** business center. **Cards:** AX, CB, DC, DS, JC, MC, VI.

SOME UNITS

ASK / /

DAYS INN OPELIKA *Book great rates at AAA.com* **Phone:** (334)749-5080

Motel

All Year	1P: $63-$65	2P: $68-$70	XP: $5	F12

Location: I-85, exit 62, just e on US 280. 1014 Anand Ave 36804. Fax: 334/749-4701. **Facility:** 44 units. 43 one-bedroom standard units. 1 one-bedroom suite with whirlpool. 2 stories (no elevator), exterior corridors. **Parking:** on-site. **Terms:** 14 day cancellation notice, pets ($20 fee). **Amenities:** hair dryers. *Some:* irons. **Pool(s):** heated indoor. **Guest Services:** wireless Internet. **Cards:** AX, DS, MC, VI.

SOME UNITS

ASK FEE / /

HOLIDAY INN *Book at AAA.com* **Phone:** (334)745-6331

Small-scale Hotel

All Year	1P: $65-$69	2P: $65-$69

Location: I-85, exit 62, just e. 1102 Columbus Pkwy 36801 (PO Box 391). Fax: 334/749-3933. **Facility:** 119 one-bedroom standard units. 2 stories (no elevator), exterior corridors. *Bath:* combo or shower only. **Parking:** on-site. **Amenities:** voice mail, irons, hair dryers. **Pool(s):** outdoor. **Leisure Activities:** exercise room. **Guest Services:** valet laundry. **Business Services:** meeting rooms. **Cards:** AX, CB, DC, DS, JC, MC, VI.

SOME UNITS

ASK / /

RAMADA LIMITED **Phone:** 334/745-6293

Small-scale Hotel

Property failed to provide current rates

Location: I-85, exit 58, 1.4 mi w on US 280, then just n on 2nd Ave. 205 N 21st St 36801. Fax: 334/745-7695. **Facility:** 56 one-bedroom standard units, some with efficiencies (no utensils). 2 stories (no elevator), interior corridors. **Parking:** on-site. **Amenities:** voice mail, irons, hair dryers. **Pool(s):** outdoor. **Leisure Activities:** whirlpool. **Guest Services:** valet and coin laundry, wireless Internet. **Business Services:** meeting rooms, PC.

SOME UNITS

/ /

WHERE TO DINE

COCK OF THE WALK **Dinner:** $10-$15 **Phone:** 334/705-0004

Seafood

Location: I-85, exit 58, just w to Frederick Rd, then 0.3 mi n. 1702 Frederick Rd 36801. **Hours:** 5 pm-9 pm, Fri & Sat 4 pm-9:30 pm. Closed major holidays; also Sun. **Features:** Fried catfish fillets are the house specialty at the distinctive eatery, which is built around a river keelboat theme and set in the midst of a pleasant wooded site. The menu centers on such dishes as oysters, shrimp, chicken, crab claws and fried dill pickles. Casual dress; beer & wine only. **Parking:** on-site. **Cards:** AX, DC, DS, MC, VI.

DURANGO MEXICAN RESTAURANT **Lunch:** $6-$10 **Dinner:** $7-$12 **Phone:** 334/742-0149

Mexican

Location: I-85, exit 62, just e. 1107 Columbus Pkwy 36801. **Hours:** 11 am-10 pm. Closed major holidays; also Sun. **Features:** Great drink specials pair with plates of Mexican favorites at the lively restaurant. Casual dress; cocktails. **Parking:** on-site. **Cards:** MC, VI.

OPP pop. 6,607

WHERE TO STAY

EXECUTIVE INN **Phone:** 334/493-6399

Motel

All Year	1P: $60-$79	2P: $60-$79

Location: On US 331, 0.9 mi s of jct US 84, through town center. 812 Florala Hwy 331 S 36467 (PO Box 988). Fax: 334/493-7897. **Facility:** 42 units. 40 one-bedroom standard units. 2 one-bedroom suites. 2 stories (no elevator), exterior corridors. **Parking:** on-site. **Pool(s):** small outdoor. **Guest Services:** wireless Internet. **Business Services:** meeting rooms. **Cards:** AX, CB, DC, DS, MC, VI.

SOME UNITS

ASK / /

ORANGE BEACH pop. 3,784

WHERE TO STAY

ISLAND HOUSE HOTEL **Phone:** (251)981-6100

Small-scale Hotel

5/15-8/15	1P: $165-$299	2P: $165-$299
3/1-5/14	1P: $125-$265	2P: $125-$265
8/16-11/30	1P: $116-$265	2P: $116-$265
12/1-2/28	1P: $74-$221	2P: $74-$221

Location: Oceanfront. On SR 182, 7.3 mi e of jct SR 59. 26650 Perdido Beach Blvd 36561. Fax: 251/981-6543. **Facility:** 161 units. 152 one-bedroom standard units. 9 one-bedroom suites with whirlpools. 10 stories, interior corridors. *Bath:* combo or shower only. **Parking:** on-site. **Terms:** 3 day cancellation notice. **Amenities:** voice mail, safes, irons, hair dryers. *Some:* DVD players. **Pool(s):** heated outdoor, wading. **Leisure Activities:** *Fee:* game room. **Guest Services:** coin laundry. **Business Services:** meeting rooms. **Cards:** AX, DS, MC, VI. ***(See color ad p 284)***

SOME UNITS

ASK / VCR /

PERDIDO BEACH RESORT   Book at AAA.com   **Phone:** 251/981-9811

Property failed to provide current rates

Resort
Large-scale Hotel

Location: Oceanfront. On SR 182, 7.8 mi e of jct SR 59. 27200 Perdido Beach Blvd 36561. Fax: 251/981-5672. **Facility:** The beach is steps away and a view of the water comes with every room at this resort which fronts on the Gulf. 347 units. 334 one-bedroom standard units. 13 one-bedroom suites. 8 stories, interior corridors. **Parking:** on-site and valet. **Terms:** check-in 4 pm. **Amenities:** voice mail, safes, irons, hair dryers. **Dining:** Voyagers Restaurant, see separate listing. **Pool(s):** heated indoor/outdoor, wading. **Leisure Activities:** whirlpools, fishing, 4 lighted tennis courts, exercise room, volleyball. *Fee:* paddleboats, sailboats, game room. **Guest Services:** gift shop, valet laundry. **Business Services:** conference facilities, administrative services.

SOME UNITS

   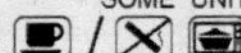

PHOENIX ON THE BAY I   **Phone:** 251/980-5700

Property failed to provide current rates

Resort
Condominium

Location: Foley Beach Expwy; to SR 180 (Canal Rd) 4.6 mi e. 27580 Canal Rd 36561. Fax: 251/980-1425. **Facility:** Smoke free premises. 163 units. 1 one-, 81 two- and 81 three-bedroom suites with kitchens and whirlpools. 5 stories, exterior corridors. **Parking:** on-site. **Amenities:** DVD players, voice mail, irons. *Some:* high-speed Internet. **Pool(s):** outdoor, heated outdoor, heated indoor, wading. **Leisure Activities:** saunas, whirlpools, waterslide, boat dock, fishing, putting green, exercise room. **Business Services:** meeting rooms.

(See color ad below)

WHERE TO DINE

CAFE GRAZIE **Lunch:** $9-$16 **Dinner:** $8-$22 **Phone:** 251/981-7278

Italian

Location: On SR 182, 7.8 mi e of jct SR 59; at San Roc Cay Marina. 27267 Perdido Beach Blvd, Suite 302 36561. **Hours:** 4 pm-9 pm, Fri & Sat-10 pm; also 11 am-3 pm 6/1-9/5. Closed: 11/22, 12/25. **Features:** You will "thank" this eatery for offering a nice change of pace from this seafood-loaded coastal area. From the antipasta to the house specialties, you will be pleased with offerings such as toasted ravioli, margherita pizza, linguini with clams and grouper picatta. The menu has great variety and the whimsical decor provides a casual but inviting experience. Casual dress; cocktails. **Parking:** on-site. **Cards:** AX, DC, DS, MC, VI.

VOYAGERS RESTAURANT **Dinner:** $19-$34 **Phone:** 251/981-9811

Steak & Seafood

Location: On SR 182, 7.8 mi e of jct SR 59; in Perdido Beach Resort. 27200 Perdido Beach Blvd 36561. **Hours:** 5 pm-10 pm. Closed: 12/25. **Reservations:** suggested. **Features:** This wonderful restaurant offers an elegant dining room that overlooks the Gulf of Mexico. Featuring "Light Gulf Coast Creole" cuisine. Highly recommended are the oysters Rockefeller, turtle soup and rack of lamb. Casual resort attire. Dressy casual; cocktails. **Parking:** on-site and valet. **Cards:** AX, DC, DS, MC, VI.

OXFORD pop. 14,592

WHERE TO STAY

COMFORT INN *Book great rates at AAA.com* **Phone:** 256/831-0860

Motel

Property failed to provide current rates

Location: I-20, exit 185, just s. 138 Elm St 36203. Fax: 256/831-7850. **Facility:** 62 one-bedroom standard units, some with whirlpools. 2 stories (no elevator), exterior corridors. *Bath:* combo or shower only. **Parking:** on-site. **Amenities:** irons, hair dryers. *Some:* high-speed Internet. **Pool(s):** small outdoor. **Guest Services:** valet and coin laundry, wireless Internet. **Business Services:** fax (fee).

SOME UNITS

COMFORT SUITES **Phone:** 256/835-8873

fyi

Small-scale Hotel

All Year [ECP] 1P: $99-$109 2P: $110-$120 XP: $10 F18

Too new to rate. **Location:** I-20, exit 188. 125 Davis Loop Rd 36203. Fax: 256/835-6997. **Amenities:** 63 units, coffeemakers, microwaves, refrigerators, pool. **Terms:** cancellation fee imposed. **Cards:** AX, DC, DS, MC, VI.

ECONO LODGE OXFORD *Book great rates at AAA.com* **Phone:** (256)831-9480

AAA SAVE

Motel

All Year [CP] 1P: $43-$175 2P: $48-$180 XP: $5 F18

Location: I-20, exit 185, just s. 25 Elm St 36203. Fax: 256/831-1970. **Facility:** 47 one-bedroom standard units. 1 story, exterior corridors. *Bath:* combo or shower only. **Parking:** on-site. **Terms:** pets ($10 fee). **Amenities:** hair dryers. *Some:* DVD players (fee), irons. **Pool(s):** small outdoor. **Guest Services:** wireless Internet. **Business Services:** fax (fee). **Cards:** AX, CB, DC, DS, MC, VI. **Free Special Amenities: continental breakfast and high-speed Internet.**

SOME UNITS

FEE FEE

HAMPTON INN & SUITES *Book great rates at AAA.com* **Phone:** (256)831-8958

AAA SAVE

Small-scale Hotel

All Year 1P: $79-$114 2P: $79-$114 XP: $5 F18

Location: I-20, exit 188, just n, then w. 210 Colonial Dr 36203. Fax: 256/831-9573. **Facility:** 101 one-bedroom standard units, some with whirlpools. 4 stories, interior corridors. *Bath:* combo or shower only. **Parking:** on-site. **Terms:** cancellation fee imposed. **Amenities:** high-speed Internet, voice mail, irons, hair dryers. **Pool(s):** small indoor. **Leisure Activities:** whirlpool, limited exercise equipment. **Guest Services:** sundries, complimentary evening beverages: Tues, valet and coin laundry, wireless Internet. **Business Services:** meeting rooms, business center. **Cards:** AX, CB, DC, DS, JC, MC, VI. **Free Special Amenities: expanded continental breakfast and high-speed Internet.**

SOME UNITS

HOLIDAY INN EXPRESS ANNISTON/OXFORD *Book great rates at AAA.com* **Phone:** (256)835-8768

AAA SAVE

Small-scale Hotel

All Year 1P: $89-$109 2P: $89-$119 XP: $10 F18

Location: I-20, exit 188, just n, then w. 160 Colonial Dr 36203. Fax: 256/835-3749. **Facility:** 80 one-bedroom standard units, some with whirlpools. 3 stories, interior corridors. *Bath:* combo or shower only. **Parking:** on-site. **Terms:** cancellation fee imposed. **Amenities:** video games (fee), high-speed Internet, dual phone lines, voice mail, irons, hair dryers. **Pool(s):** heated indoor. **Leisure Activities:** whirlpool, limited exercise equipment. **Guest Services:** complimentary evening beverages: Tues, valet and coin laundry, wireless Internet. **Business Services:** meeting rooms, business center. **Cards:** AX, CB, DC, DS, JC, MC, VI. **Free Special Amenities: expanded continental breakfast and high-speed Internet.**

SOME UNITS

JAMESON INN OXFORD *Book at AAA.com* **Phone:** (256)835-2170

Motel

All Year [ECP] 1P: $54-$120

Location: I-20, exit 188, just n, then w. 161 Colonial Dr 36203. Fax: 256/835-2133. **Facility:** 62 one-bedroom standard units, some with whirlpools. 2 stories (no elevator), exterior corridors. *Bath:* combo or shower only. **Parking:** on-site. **Terms:** cancellation fee imposed, small pets only ($10 fee). **Amenities:** irons, hair dryers. **Pool(s):** small outdoor. **Leisure Activities:** exercise room. **Guest Services:** wireless Internet. **Business Services:** PC, fax (fee). **Cards:** AX, DC, DS, MC, VI.

SOME UNITS

ASK

FEE

MOTEL 6 #542 Book at AAA.com Phone: 256/831-5463

Motel

4/20-11/30	1P: $37-$47	2P: $43-$53	XP: $3	F17
12/1-4/19	1P: $34-$44	2P: $40-$50	XP: $3	F17

Location: I-20, exit 185, just s. 202 Grace St 36203. Fax: 256/831-5628. **Facility:** 115 one-bedroom standard units. 2 stories (no elevator), exterior corridors. *Bath:* combo or shower only. **Parking:** on-site. **Terms:** small pets only. **Pool(s):** small outdoor. **Business Services:** fax (fee). **Cards:** AX, CB, DC, DS, MC, VI.

SOME UNITS

FEE FEE

QUALITY INN Book at AAA.com Phone: (256)831-3410

Small-scale Hotel

4/1-7/31 & 10/1-11/30	1P: $69-$199	2P: $69-$199
12/1-3/31	1P: $49-$199	2P: $49-$199
8/1-9/30	1P: $69-$89	2P: $69-$89

Location: I-20, exit 185, just n. US 78 & SR 21 36203 (PO Box 3308). Fax: 256/831-9560. **Facility:** 190 units. 186 one-bedroom standard units, some with whirlpools. 4 one-bedroom suites ($89-$199). 2 stories (no elevator), exterior corridors. **Parking:** on-site. **Terms:** [CP] meal plan available, pets ($10 fee). **Amenities:** video games (fee), irons, hair dryers. **Pool(s):** outdoor. **Leisure Activities:** whirlpool. **Guest Services:** valet and coin laundry. **Business Services:** meeting rooms, PC, fax (fee). **Cards:** AX, CB, DC, DS, MC, VI.

SOME UNITS

FEE

SLEEP INN Book great rates at AAA.com Phone: (256)831-2191

Small-scale Hotel

All Year	1P: $60-$250	2P: $68-$250	XP: $7	F17

Location: I-20, exit 188, just n, then w. 88 Colonial Dr 36203. Fax: 256/831-1415. **Facility:** 61 one-bedroom standard units, some with whirlpools. 3 stories, interior corridors. *Bath:* combo or shower only. **Parking:** on-site. **Terms:** [ECP] meal plan available, package plans. **Amenities:** high-speed Internet, voice mail, irons, hair dryers. **Pool(s):** small outdoor. **Leisure Activities:** exercise room. **Guest Services:** valet and coin laundry. **Business Services:** business center. **Cards:** AX, DS, MC, VI.

SOME UNITS

ASK

WINGATE INN Book at AAA.com Phone: (256)831-1921

Small-scale Hotel

All Year	1P: $74-$105	2P: $79-$109	XP: $5	F15

Location: I-20, exit 188, just n, then w. 143 Colonial Dr 36203. Fax: 256/831-1952. **Facility:** 81 one-bedroom standard units. 4 stories, interior corridors. *Bath:* combo or shower only. **Parking:** on-site. **Terms:** [ECP] meal plan available. **Amenities:** video games (fee), high-speed Internet, dual phone lines, voice mail, safes, irons, hair dryers. **Pool(s):** outdoor. **Leisure Activities:** whirlpool, exercise room. **Guest Services:** complimentary evening beverages: Mon-Wed, valet and coin laundry, wireless Internet. **Business Services:** meeting rooms, business center. **Cards:** AX, DC, DS, MC, VI.

SOME UNITS

ASK

WHERE TO DINE

EL POBLANO **Lunch:** $5-$12 **Dinner:** $7-$12 **Phone:** 256/835-2277

Mexican

Location: I-20, exit 185, just s, then e. 230 Spring Branch Rd 36203. **Hours:** 11 am-9:30 pm, Fri & Sat-10:30 pm. Closed major holidays. **Reservations:** accepted. **Features:** Monster margaritas wash down the fun and upbeat restaurant's traditional Mexican food. Diners can kick back in the large bar. Casual dress; cocktails. **Parking:** on-site. **Cards:** AX, DC, DS, MC, VI.

SONNY'S REAL PIT BAR-B-Q **Lunch:** $6-$8 **Dinner:** $8-$13 **Phone:** 256/831-7933

Barbecue

Location: I-20, exit 188, 0.4 mi n on Golden Springs Rd, just w on Jimmy Hinton Dr, then just n. 219 Colonial Dr 36203. **Hours:** 11 am-9:30 pm, Fri & Sat 10 pm. Closed major holidays. **Features:** House specialties include barbecue ribs, pork and chicken grilled over an open pit and fresh, homemade pie. Rustic and comfortable, the atmosphere is perfect for family meals.The salad bar is always a popular choice also. Casual dress; beer only. **Parking:** on-site. **Cards:** AX, DS, MC, VI.

OZARK pop. 15,119

WHERE TO STAY

ALL AMERICAN OZARK INN **Phone:** 334/774-5166

SAVE

Motel

All Year [ECP]	1P: $55-$65	XP: $5	F

Location: 1 mi s of jct SR 249. Located in a quiet area. 2064 Hwy 231 S 36360 (PO Box 1396, 36361). Fax: 334/774-2392. **Facility:** 62 one-bedroom standard units. 1-2 stories (no elevator), exterior corridors. **Parking:** on-site. **Terms:** weekly rates available, small pets only. **Amenities:** voice mail. **Pool(s):** outdoor. **Business Services:** meeting rooms. **Cards:** AX, DS, MC, VI. **Free Special Amenities: expanded continental breakfast and local telephone calls.**

SOME UNITS

FEE FEE

JAMESON INN Book at AAA.com Phone: (334)774-0233

Motel

All Year [ECP]	1P: $54-$120

Location: 0.3 mi s of jct SR 249. 1360 S US Hwy 231 36360. Fax: 334/445-1900. **Facility:** 40 one-bedroom standard units, some with whirlpools. 2 stories (no elevator), exterior corridors. **Parking:** on-site. **Terms:** cancellation fee imposed, small pets only ($10 fee). **Amenities:** irons, hair dryers. **Pool(s):** outdoor. **Leisure Activities:** exercise room. **Guest Services:** valet laundry, wireless Internet. **Business Services:** PC. **Cards:** AX, DC, DS, MC, VI.

SOME UNITS

ASK

FEE

QUALITY INN & SUITES-OZARK/FT RUCKER *Book great rates at AAA.com* **Phone:** (334)774-7300

AAA SAVE — Small-scale Hotel

All Year [ECP] 1P: $70 2P: $70 XP: $5 F18

Location: Just n of jct SR 249. 858 US 231 S 36360. Fax: 334/774-1249. **Facility:** 84 units. 70 one-bedroom standard units. 14 one-bedroom suites ($130) with kitchens. 2 stories (no elevator), exterior corridors. **Parking:** on-site. **Terms:** pets ($25 fee). **Amenities:** voice mail, irons, hair dryers. **Dining:** 10 am-11 pm, cocktails. **Pool(s):** outdoor. **Leisure Activities:** picnic area with charcoal grill, exercise room. **Guest Services:** coin laundry, wireless Internet. **Business Services:** meeting rooms, fax (fee). **Cards:** AX, DC, DS, MC, VI. **Free Special Amenities: expanded continental breakfast and high-speed Internet.**

SOME UNITS

FEE

PELHAM —*See Birmingham p. 239.*

PELL CITY —*See Birmingham p. 240.*

PHENIX CITY pop. 28,265

WHERE TO STAY

DAYS INN OF PHENIX CITY *Book great rates at AAA.com* **Phone:** (334)298-1005

AAA SAVE — Small-scale Hotel

4/1-11/30 1P: $69-$110 2P: $75-$110 XP: $7 F13
12/1-3/31 1P: $59-$110 2P: $65-$110 XP: $7 F13

Location: Just s of US 280 and 431. 600 Martin Luther King Jr Pkwy 36869. Fax: 334/298-0155. **Facility:** 64 one-bedroom standard units. 2 stories (no elevator), interior corridors. **Parking:** on-site. **Terms:** [ECP] meal plan available. **Amenities:** safes (fee), irons, hair dryers. **Pool(s):** outdoor. **Guest Services:** coin laundry, wireless Internet. **Business Services:** meeting rooms, business center. **Cards:** AX, CB, DC, DS, JC, MC, VI. **Free Special Amenities: expanded continental breakfast and local telephone calls.**

SOME UNITS

HOLIDAY INN EXPRESS *Book great rates at AAA.com* **Phone:** (334)298-9321

AAA SAVE — Small-scale Hotel

All Year 1P: $70-$125

Location: On US 280/431 Bypass. 1700 E US 280 Bypass 36867. Fax: 334/297-3958. **Facility:** 119 one-bedroom standard units. 2-3 stories (no elevator), exterior corridors. **Parking:** on-site. **Terms:** cancellation fee imposed. **Amenities:** dual phone lines, voice mail, irons, hair dryers. **Pool(s):** outdoor. **Leisure Activities:** exercise room. **Guest Services:** valet laundry, wireless Internet. **Business Services:** meeting rooms. **Cards:** AX, CB, DC, DS, JC, MC, VI. **Free Special Amenities: continental breakfast and high-speed Internet.**

SOME UNITS

WHERE TO DINE

MIKE & ED'S BAR-B-Q **Lunch:** $3-$11 **Dinner:** $3-$11 **Phone:** 334/297-1012

Barbecue

Location: 0.5 mi n of jct US 280. 2001 Crawford Rd 36867. **Hours:** 10:30 am-8 pm, Fri & Sat- 9 pm. Closed: 1/1, 11/22, 12/25; also Sun. **Features:** The meat plate, cool cole slaw, baked beans, brunswick stew and some tempting desserts are some examples of the tasty treats at this no-frills barbecue house. Casual dress. **Parking:** on-site. **Cards:** AX, MC, VI.

POINT CLEAR pop. 1,876

WHERE TO STAY

THE GRAND HOTEL MARRIOTT RESORT, GOLF CLUB & SPA *Book great rates at AAA.com* **Phone:** (251)928-9201

AAA SAVE — Resort Large-scale Hotel

All Year 1P: $250-$300 2P: $250-$300

Location: US Scenic 98, 1.2 mi n of jct CR 32. One Grand Blvd 36564 (PO Box 639, 36564-0639). Fax: 251/928-1149. **Facility:** Located on Mobile Bay, you'll be enchanted by the public areas which reflect a bygone era of elegance and are sprinkled with historical mementos. 405 units. 380 one-bedroom standard units. 25 one-bedroom suites, some with whirlpools. 2-4 stories, interior corridors. *Bath:* combo or shower only. **Parking:** on-site and valet. **Terms:** check-in 4 pm, 5 day cancellation notice-fee imposed, 14% service charge. **Amenities:** voice mail, irons, hair dryers. *Fee:* video games, high-speed Internet. **Dining:** 4 restaurants, 6:30 am-10 pm, cocktails, entertainment. **Pool(s):** outdoor, heated outdoor, heated indoor. **Leisure Activities:** saunas, whirlpools, steamrooms, waterslide, rental paddleboats, rental sailboats, fishing, recreation programs, croquet, rental bicycles, playground, spa, horseshoes, volleyball, game room. *Fee:* marina, kayaks, personal watercraft, golf-36 holes, 8 tennis courts (4 lighted). **Guest Services:** gift shop, valet laundry, airport transportation (fee)-Mobile & Pensacola airports, area transportation-Fairhope, beauty salon. **Business Services:** conference facilities, business center. **Cards:** AX, CB, DC, DS, JC, MC, VI. *(See color ad p 200)*

SOME UNITS

FEE FEE

PRATTVILLE pop. 24,303

WHERE TO STAY

DAYS INN & SUITES *Book great rates at AAA.com* **Phone:** (334)285-5312

Small-scale Hotel

All Year [ECP] 1P: $65-$85 2P: $65-$85 XP: $5 F17

Location: I-65, exit 179, 0.8 mi w. 600 Old Farm Ln S 36066. Fax: 334/290-0277. **Facility:** 52 one-bedroom standard units, some with whirlpools. 3 stories, interior corridors. **Parking:** on-site. **Amenities:** high-speed Internet, irons, hair dryers. **Pool(s):** small outdoor. **Guest Services:** coin laundry. **Business Services:** business center. **Cards:** AX, CB, DC, DS, JC, MC, VI.

SOME UNITS

ASK

HAMPTON INN *Book great rates at AAA.com* **Phone:** (334)285-6767

Small-scale Hotel

All Year [ECP] 1P: $65-$105 2P: $72-$112 XP: $7 F

Location: I-65, exit 179, just nw. 2585 Cobb Hill Pl 36066. Fax: 334/285-0932. **Facility:** 112 one-bedroom standard units. 2-3 stories, interior/exterior corridors. *Bath:* combo or shower only. **Parking:** on-site. **Amenities:** high-speed Internet, voice mail, irons, hair dryers. **Pool(s):** outdoor. **Guest Services:** valet laundry, wireless Internet. **Business Services:** fax (fee). **Cards:** AX, CB, DC, DS, MC, VI.

SOME UNITS

ASK / /

HOLIDAY INN-PRATTVILLE *Book at AAA.com* **Phone:** (334)285-3420

Small-scale Hotel

All Year 1P: $69-$81 2P: $69-$81 XP: $5 F19

Location: I-65, exit 179, just sw. 2598 Cobbs Ford Rd 36066. Fax: 334/285-0007. **Facility:** 129 one-bedroom standard units. 2 stories (no elevator), exterior corridors. **Parking:** on-site. **Amenities:** high-speed Internet, voice mail, irons, hair dryers. **Pool(s):** outdoor, wading. **Leisure Activities:** exercise room. **Guest Services:** valet laundry, wireless Internet. **Business Services:** meeting rooms, fax (fee). **Cards:** CB, DC, DS, JC, MC, VI.

SOME UNITS

ASK / /

JAMESON INN *Book at AAA.com* **Phone:** (334)361-6463

Small-scale Hotel

All Year [ECP] 1P: $54-$120

Location: I-65, exit 179, 1 mi w. 104 Jameson Ct 36067. Fax: 334/361-1783. **Facility:** 60 one-bedroom standard units, some with whirlpools. 2 stories (no elevator), exterior corridors. **Parking:** on-site. **Terms:** cancellation fee imposed, small pets only ($10 fee). **Amenities:** high-speed Internet, irons, hair dryers. **Pool(s):** small outdoor. **Leisure Activities:** exercise room. **Business Services:** PC, fax (fee). **Cards:** AX, DC, DS, MC, VI.

SOME UNITS

ASK FEE / /

MARRIOTT MONTGOMERY PRATTVILLE HOTEL & CONFERENCE CENTER AT CAPITOL HILL *Book great rates at AAA.com* **Phone:** (334)290-1235

Small-scale Hotel

All Year 1P: $199-$209 2P: $209-$219 XP: $20 F18

Location: I-65, exit 179, 1.3 mi w on SR 6. 2500 Legends Cir 36066. Fax: 334/290-2222. **Facility:** 90 units. 85 one-bedroom standard units. 2 one-bedroom suites ($300-$6000) with whirlpools. 2 cabins and 1 cottage. 3 stories, interior corridors. *Bath:* combo or shower only. **Parking:** on-site. **Terms:** cancellation fee imposed, package plans. **Amenities:** dual phone lines, voice mail, irons, hair dryers. *Fee:* video games, high-speed Internet. **Pool(s):** outdoor. **Leisure Activities:** whirlpool, lighted tennis court, exercise room, horseshoes, volleyball. *Fee:* golf-54 holes. **Guest Services:** gift shop, valet laundry, area transportation. **Business Services:** conference facilities, business center. **Cards:** AX, CB, DC, DS, JC, MC, VI. ***(See color ad p 200)***

SOME UNITS

ASK FEE 24 / VCR FEE /

WHERE TO DINE

MEXICO TIPICO **Lunch:** $5-$10 **Dinner:** $7-$12 **Phone:** 334/365-8677

Mexican

Location: I-65, exit 179, 1.5 mi w; in Kmart Shopping Center. 1870 Main St 36066. **Hours:** 11 am-9 pm. **Features:** Convenient, quick and delicious Mexican food is served in a festive environment. Casual dress; cocktails. **Parking:** on-site. **Cards:** AX, DS, MC, VI.

PRICEVILLE pop. 1,631

WHERE TO STAY

COMFORT INN *Book great rates at AAA.com* **Phone:** (256)355-1037

AAA SAVE

Small-scale Hotel

3/1-10/31 1P: $69-$150 2P: $69-$150

12/1-2/28 & 11/1-11/30 1P: $59-$105 2P: $59-$105

Location: I-65, exit 334, just w. 3239 Point Mallard Pkwy 35601. Fax: 256/355-3087. **Facility:** 58 units. 56 one-bedroom standard units, some with kitchens and/or whirlpools. 2 one-bedroom suites ($100-$150). 3 stories, interior corridors. *Bath:* combo or shower only. **Parking:** on-site. **Terms:** pets ($10 extra charge). **Amenities:** high-speed Internet, voice mail, safes (fee), irons, hair dryers. **Pool(s):** small heated indoor. **Leisure Activities:** exercise room. **Guest Services:** coin laundry, wireless Internet. **Business Services:** meeting rooms, business center. **Cards:** AX, DS, MC, VI. **Free Special Amenities: expanded continental breakfast and high-speed Internet.**

SOME UNITS

FEE / /

DAYS INN *Book great rates at AAA.com* **Phone:** (256)355-3297

Small-scale Hotel

3/1-11/30 1P: $59-$99 2P: $59-$99 XP: $5 F12

12/1-2/28 1P: $49-$79 2P: $49-$79 XP: $5 F12

Location: I-65, exit 334, just e. 63 Marco Dr 35603. Fax: 256/340-1902. **Facility:** 52 one-bedroom standard units, some with whirlpools. 2 stories (no elevator), exterior corridors. *Bath:* combo or shower only. **Parking:** on-site. **Terms:** pets ($5 extra charge). **Amenities:** irons, hair dryers. **Pool(s):** outdoor. **Guest Services:** coin laundry, wireless Internet. **Business Services:** fax (fee). **Cards:** AX, DC, DS, MC, VI.

SOME UNITS

ASK FEE / /

SUPER 8 MOTEL DECATUR/PRICEVILLE *Book at AAA.com* **Phone:** (256)355-2525

Motel

All Year [ECP] 1P: $55-$80 2P: $55-$89 XP: $5 F12

Location: I-65, exit 334, just e. 70 Marco Dr 35603. Fax: 256/355-2526. **Facility:** 55 one-bedroom standard units. 2 stories (no elevator), exterior corridors. *Bath:* combo or shower only. **Parking:** on-site. **Pool(s):** small outdoor. **Guest Services:** coin laundry, wireless Internet. **Business Services:** fax (fee). **Cards:** AX, DC, DS, MC, VI.

SOME UNITS

ASK / /

RUSSELLVILLE pop. 8,971

WHERE TO STAY

RUSSELLVILLE HOTEL & SUITES Book great rates at AAA.com **Phone:** 256/332-1002

AAA SAVE

Small-scale Hotel

All Year 1P: $55-$89 2P: $55-$89 XP: $10 F19

Location: On US 43, 0.4 mi n of jct SR 24. 13770 Hwy 43 35653. Fax: 256/332-1026. **Facility:** 60 units. 58 one-bedroom standard units, some with whirlpools. 2 one-bedroom suites ($79-$89) with whirlpools. 3 stories, interior corridors. *Bath:* combo or shower only. **Parking:** on-site. **Terms:** cancellation fee imposed. **Amenities:** high-speed Internet, dual phone lines, voice mail, irons, hair dryers. **Pool(s):** small outdoor. **Leisure Activities:** exercise room. **Guest Services:** valet and coin laundry. **Business Services:** meeting rooms, fax (fee). **Cards:** AX, CB, DC, DS, MC, VI. **Free Special Amenities: continental breakfast and local telephone calls.**

SOME UNITS

SARALAND pop. 12,288 (See map and index starting on p. 266)

WHERE TO STAY

HOLIDAY INN EXPRESS Book at AAA.com **Phone:** 251/679-8880 22

Small-scale Hotel

All Year 1P: $89-$125 2P: $89-$125

Location: I-65, exit 13, just e on SR 158. 1111 Industrial Pkwy 36571. Fax: 251/706-0291. **Facility:** 59 one-bedroom standard units, some with whirlpools. 2 stories, interior corridors. *Bath:* combo or shower only. **Parking:** on-site. **Amenities:** high-speed Internet, voice mail, irons, hair dryers. **Pool(s):** outdoor. **Guest Services:** valet and coin laundry. **Business Services:** meeting rooms. **Cards:** AX, CB, DC, DS, JC, MC, VI.

SOME UNITS

SCOTTSBORO pop. 14,762

WHERE TO STAY

AMERICAS BEST VALUE INN & SUITES Book at AAA.com **Phone:** (256)259-4300

Small-scale Hotel

All Year 1P: $45-$55 2P: $49-$59 XP: $5 F

Location: On US 72, just s of jct SR 35. 46 Micah Way 35769. Fax: 256/259-0919. **Facility:** 50 units. 48 one- and 2 two-bedroom standard units, some with whirlpools. 2 stories (no elevator), exterior corridors. **Parking:** on-site. **Terms:** small pets only ($10 fee). **Amenities:** irons, hair dryers. **Pool(s):** small outdoor. **Guest Services:** coin laundry, wireless Internet. **Business Services:** meeting rooms, PC. **Cards:** AX, DS, MC, VI.

SOME UNITS

ASK FEE

COMFORT INN Book great rates at AAA.com **Phone:** (256)574-6740

AAA SAVE

Small-scale Hotel

All Year 1P: $60 2P: $60-$65 XP: $5 F18

Location: On US 72, 0.7 mi s of jct SR 35. 23518 John T Reid Pkwy 35768. Fax: 256/259-0750. **Facility:** 61 one-bedroom standard units, some with whirlpools. 2 stories (no elevator), exterior corridors. *Bath:* combo or shower only. **Parking:** on-site. **Amenities:** irons, hair dryers. **Pool(s):** small outdoor. **Guest Services:** wireless Internet. **Business Services:** meeting rooms, fax (fee). **Cards:** AX, DS, MC, VI. **Free Special Amenities: continental breakfast and high-speed Internet.**

SOME UNITS

JAMESON INN Book at AAA.com **Phone:** (256)574-6666

Small-scale Hotel

All Year [ECP] 1P: $54-$120

Location: On US 72, just s of jct SR 35. 208 Micah Way 35768. Fax: 256/574-6767. **Facility:** 60 one-bedroom standard units, some with whirlpools. 2 stories (no elevator), exterior corridors. *Bath:* combo or shower only. **Parking:** on-site. **Terms:** cancellation fee imposed, small pets only ($10 fee). **Amenities:** hair dryers. *Some:* irons. **Pool(s):** outdoor. **Leisure Activities:** exercise room. **Guest Services:** wireless Internet. **Business Services:** PC, fax (fee). **Cards:** AX, DC, DS, MC, VI.

SOME UNITS

ASK FEE

WHERE TO DINE

GENO'S PIZZA & GRILL **Lunch:** $5-$10 **Dinner:** $5-$10 **Phone:** 256/574-1533

Pizza

Location: On US 72, just s of jct SR 35. 102 Micah Way 35769. **Hours:** 11 am-9 pm, Sat-10 pm. Closed: Sun. **Features:** Anything goes at the family restaurant, where patrons can watch sports, chow down on pizza and play video games. Casual dress; cocktails. **Parking:** on-site. **Cards:** AX, DS, MC, VI.

TRIPLE R BBQ **Lunch:** $4-$14 **Dinner:** $4-$14 **Phone:** 256/574-1620

Barbecue

Location: 1.8 mi s on SR 35 from jct US 72. 2940 Veterans Dr 35768. **Hours:** 5 am-8 pm, Sun-3 pm. Closed: 11/22, 12/25. **Features:** Parts of the family-owned restaurant's dining area are assembled from a 175-year-old log cabin, and rustic antiques serve as fitting decor. Mouthwatering barbecue choices—chicken, ribs, pork and catfish—are pleasing in sandwiches or on filling platters. Casual dress. **Parking:** on-site. **Cards:** DS, MC, VI.

SELMA pop. 20,512

WHERE TO STAY

COMFORT INN *Book great rates at AAA.com* **Phone:** (334)875-5700

Small-scale Hotel

All Year 1P: $55-$60 2P: $60-$75 XP: $5 F18

Location: Jct SR 14 and US 80 Bypass. 1812 Hwy 14 E 36703. Fax: 334/874-7955. **Facility:** 51 one-bedroom standard units, some with efficiencies (no utensils). 2 stories (no elevator), interior corridors. **Parking:** on-site. **Terms:** [CP] meal plan available, small pets only ($10 extra charge). **Amenities:** irons, hair dryers. **Pool(s):** small outdoor. **Leisure Activities:** exercise room. **Guest Services:** wireless Internet. **Business Services:** fax (fee). **Cards:** AX, DC, DS, JC, MC, VI.

SOME UNITS

FEE

HAMPTON INN *Book great rates at AAA.com* **Phone:** (334)876-9995

Small-scale Hotel

All Year 1P: $99-$124 2P: $104-$129 XP: $5 F12

Location: On US 80, jct SR 14. 2200 Highland Ave 36701. Fax: 334/876-9993. **Facility:** 60 one-bedroom standard units, some with whirlpools. 3 stories, interior corridors. *Bath:* combo or shower only. **Parking:** on-site. **Terms:** [BP] meal plan available. **Amenities:** high-speed Internet, dual phone lines, voice mail, irons, hair dryers. **Pool(s):** heated indoor. **Leisure Activities:** whirlpool, exercise room. **Guest Services:** valet and coin laundry, wireless Internet. **Business Services:** meeting rooms, PC. **Cards:** AX, CB, DC, DS, JC, MC, VI.

SOME UNITS

JAMESON INN *Book at AAA.com* **Phone:** (334)874-8600

Motel

All Year [ECP] 1P: $54-$120

Location: On SR 22, just n of jct US 80. 2420 Broad St 36701. Fax: 334/874-2656. **Facility:** 62 one-bedroom standard units, some with whirlpools. 2 stories (no elevator), exterior corridors. **Parking:** on-site. **Terms:** cancellation fee imposed, small pets only ($10 fee). **Amenities:** hair dryers. **Pool(s):** outdoor. **Leisure Activities:** exercise room. **Guest Services:** wireless Internet. **Business Services:** PC. **Cards:** AX, DC, DS, MC, VI.

SOME UNITS

FEE

The following lodging was either not evaluated or did not meet AAA rating requirements but is listed for your information only.

ST. JAMES HOTEL **Phone:** 334/872-3234

fyi

Historic Small-scale Hotel

Did not meet all AAA rating requirements for locking devices in some guest rooms at time of last evaluation on 04/06/2006. **Location:** In historic downtown. 1200 Water St 36701. Facilities, services, and decor characterize a mid-range property.

WHERE TO DINE

MAJOR GRUMBLES **Lunch:** $7-$12 **Dinner:** $14-$19 **Phone:** 334/872-2006

American

Location: Corner of Water Ave; in historic downtown. 1 Grumbles Alley 36701. **Hours:** 11 am-9 pm, Fri & Sat-10 pm. Closed major holidays; also for dinner Mon. **Reservations:** accepted. **Features:** This riverside, converted downtown cotton warehouse is now a bar and grill offering salad, soup, overstuffed sandwiches and a good selection of hamburgers, steak and chicken. Casual dress; cocktails. **Parking:** on-site. **Cards:** AX, CB, DC, MC, VI.

TALLY-HO RESTAURANT **Dinner:** $12-$19 **Phone:** 334/872-1390

Steak & Seafood

Location: 0.5 mi n on Summerfield Rd from jct US 80, then just e. 507 Magnum Ave 36701. **Hours:** 5 pm-10 pm. Closed: 7/4, 11/22, 12/24, 12/25; also Sun. **Reservations:** suggested. **Features:** Established in 1942, Tally-Ho presents a unique log cabin setting and has an interesting collection of menus from World War II. They have an excellent seafood and steak selection, and are known for their homemade zucchini bread and chocolate cheesecake. Casual dress; cocktails. **Parking:** on-site. **Cards:** AX, DS, MC, VI.

THE TROUP HOUSE RESTAURANT **Lunch:** $4-$14 **Dinner:** $11-$24 **Phone:** 334/872-3234

American

Location: In historic downtown; in St. James Hotel. 1200 Water Ave 36701. **Hours:** 6:30-10 am, 11-2 & 6-9 pm, Fri & Sat 6 pm-10 pm. Closed: 12/25. **Reservations:** accepted. **Features:** The restaurant lets you step back 150 years to enjoy modern-day favorites. In the elegant dining room, painstakingly restored to reflect the period, true Southern hospitality comes into play. Tasty appetizers whet the palate for chicken, meat and seafood. Dressy casual; cocktails. **Parking:** on-site. **Cards:** AX, CB, DC, DS, MC, VI. **Historic**

SHEFFIELD pop. 9,652

WHERE TO STAY

HOLIDAY INN SHEFFIELD/FLORENCE *Book great rates at AAA.com* **Phone:** (256)381-4710

AAA SAVE

Small-scale Hotel

All Year 1P: $69-$119 2P: $69-$119

Location: 4 mi n on US 43 from jct US 72. 4900 Hatch Blvd 35660. Fax: 256/381-7313. **Facility:** 201 units. 199 one-bedroom standard units. 2 one-bedroom suites. 3 stories, interior/exterior corridors. **Parking:** on-site. **Terms:** 3 day cancellation notice-fee imposed, [BP] meal plan available. **Amenities:** high-speed Internet, voice mail, irons, hair dryers. **Dining:** 6 am-10 & 6-10 pm, Sun-2 pm, cocktails. **Pool(s):** outdoor. **Leisure Activities:** whirlpool. **Guest Services:** valet and coin laundry, area transportation-within 6 mi. **Business Services:** meeting rooms. **Cards:** AX, DC, DS, MC, VI.

SOME UNITS

FEE

SPANISH FORT pop. 5,423

WHERE TO DINE

FELIX'S FISH CAMP Lunch: $9-$12 Dinner: $14-$30 Phone: 251/626-6710

Seafood

Location: I-10, exit 30 westbound, 0.8 mi w; exit 27 eastbound, 2 mi e. 1530 Battleship Pkwy 36527. **Hours:** 11 am-10 pm. Closed: 1/1, 11/22, 12/25. **Reservations:** accepted. **Features:** Copious selections of fresh fish as well as some steak entrees are the oder of the day at this bayside restaurant. Casual dress; cocktails; entertainment. **Parking:** on-site. **Cards:** AX, DS, MC, VI.

STEVENSON pop. 1,770

WHERE TO STAY

BUDGET HOST INN *Book at AAA.com* **Phone:** (256)437-2215

Motel

All Year 1P: $45-$50 2P: $50-$55 XP: $5 F

Location: On US 72, just s of CR 85. 42973 US Hwy 72 35772. Fax: 256/437-2215. **Facility:** 30 one-bedroom standard units. 1 story, exterior corridors. **Parking:** on-site. **Terms:** 3 day cancellation notice, small pets only ($5 extra charge). **Amenities:** hair dryers. *Some:* high-speed Internet. **Guest Services:** wireless Internet. **Business Services:** fax (fee). **Cards:** AX, DS, MC, VI.

SOME UNITS

ASK FEE

SYLACAUGA pop. 12,616

WHERE TO STAY

JAMESON INN *Book at AAA.com* **Phone:** (256)245-4141

Small-scale Hotel

All Year [ECP] 1P: $54-$120

Location: Off US 280, just s. 89 Gene Stewart Blvd 35151. Fax: 256/245-4144. **Facility:** 62 one-bedroom standard units, some with whirlpools. 2 stories (no elevator), exterior corridors. *Bath:* combo or shower only. **Parking:** on-site. **Terms:** cancellation fee imposed, pets ($10 extra charge). **Amenities:** hair dryers. *Some:* irons. **Pool(s):** small outdoor. **Leisure Activities:** exercise room. **Guest Services:** wireless Internet. **Business Services:** PC, fax (fee). **Cards:** AX, DC, DS, MC, VI.

SOME UNITS

ASK FEE

THOMASVILLE pop. 4,649

WHERE TO STAY

HOLIDAY INN EXPRESS *Book at AAA.com* **Phone:** 334/636-2000

Small-scale Hotel

Property failed to provide current rates

Location: On US 43, 0.6 mi s of jct SR 5. 571 N Park Dr 36784. Fax: 334/636-2022. **Facility:** 50 one-bedroom standard units, some with whirlpools. 2 stories (no elevator), interior corridors. *Bath:* combo or shower only. **Parking:** on-site. **Amenities:** voice mail, irons, hair dryers. **Pool(s):** small outdoor. **Leisure Activities:** exercise room privileges. **Guest Services:** valet and coin laundry, wireless Internet. **Business Services:** meeting rooms, PC.

SOME UNITS

TROY pop. 13,935

WHERE TO STAY

COMFORT INN *Book great rates at AAA.com* **Phone:** (334)566-7799

AAA SAVE

Motel

All Year 1P: $49-$99 2P: $54-$104

Location: On US 231, 1.5 mi s of jct US 29. 811 Hwy 231 S 36081 (PO Box 486). Fax: 334/566-8039. **Facility:** 48 one-bedroom standard units. 2 stories (no elevator), exterior corridors. **Parking:** on-site. **Terms:** [ECP] meal plan available. **Amenities:** high-speed Internet, safes, irons, hair dryers. **Pool(s):** outdoor. **Guest Services:** complimentary laundry. **Cards:** AX, CB, DC, DS, JC, MC, VI. **Free Special Amenities: expanded continental breakfast and high-speed Internet.**

SOME UNITS

HAMPTON INN *Book great rates at AAA.com* **Phone:** (334)807-5900

Small-scale Hotel

5/1-11/30 [ECP]	1P: $84-$104	2P: $89-$109
12/1-4/30 [ECP]	1P: $84-$94	2P: $89-$99

Location: On US 231, 2 mi s of jct US 29. 103 Troy Plaza Loop 36081. Fax: 334/807-0000. **Facility:** 82 units. 79 one-bedroom standard units. 3 one-bedroom suites. 3 stories, interior corridors. *Bath:* combo or shower only. **Parking:** on-site. **Amenities:** high-speed Internet, voice mail, irons, hair dryers. **Pool(s):** outdoor. **Leisure Activities:** exercise room. **Guest Services:** valet laundry, wireless Internet. **Business Services:** meeting rooms. **Cards:** AX, CB, DC, DS, MC, VI.

SOME UNITS

ASK

HOLIDAY INN EXPRESS *Book at AAA.com* **Phone:** (334)670-0012

Motel

All Year [CP] 1P: $74 2P: $74

Location: On US 231, just n of jct US 29. Hwy 231 at US 29 36081 (PO Box 564). Fax: 334/670-0012. **Facility:** 58 one-bedroom standard units. 2 stories (no elevator), exterior corridors. **Parking:** on-site. **Amenities:** high-speed Internet, voice mail, irons, hair dryers. **Guest Services:** valet and coin laundry, wireless Internet. **Cards:** AX, DC, DS, JC, MC, VI.

SOME UNITS

ASK

HOLIDAY INN OF TROY *Book great rates at AAA.com* **Phone:** (334)566-1150

Small-scale Hotel

All Year [BP] 1P: $74-$99 2P: $74-$99 XP: $10 F17

Location: On US 231, just n of jct US 29. Hwy 231 at US 29 36081 (PO Box 564). Fax: 334/566-7666. **Facility:** 98 one-bedroom standard units. 2 stories (no elevator), exterior corridors. **Parking:** on-site. **Terms:** package plans, small pets only ($10 fee). **Amenities:** high-speed Internet, dual phone lines, voice mail, irons, hair dryers. **Dining:** 6 am-9:30 & 5-9 pm, Sun & Thurs also 11 am-2 pm, cocktails. **Pool(s):** small outdoor, wading. **Leisure Activities:** limited exercise equipment. **Guest Services:** valet and coin laundry, wireless Internet. **Business Services:** meeting rooms. **Cards:** AX, DC, DS, MC, VI. **Free Special Amenities: full breakfast and high-speed Internet.**

SOME UNITS

FEE

WHERE TO DINE

BARNHILL'S BUFFET **Lunch:** $5-$9 **Dinner:** $7-$10 **Phone:** 334/807-0004

American

Location: Jct US 29, 2 mi s. 1117 Hwy 231 Bypass 36081. **Hours:** 10:45 am-8:45 pm, Fri-9 pm, Sat 7 am-9 pm, Sun 7 am-8:45 pm. Closed: 12/25. **Features:** Casual dress. **Parking:** on-site. **Cards:** AX, DS, MC, VI.

BRITTANY'S **Lunch:** $6-$24 **Dinner:** $13-$25 **Phone:** 334/566-8800

American

Location: 2 mi s of jct US 29. 1208 US 231 36081. **Hours:** 11 am-9 pm, Fri & Sat-10 pm. Closed: 11/22, 12/25 & Easter; also Sun. **Reservations:** accepted. **Features:** This sports-themed eatery specializes in standards such as steaks, chicken and seafood. You can also warm up with an appetizer like spicy Buffalo wings. Casual dress; cocktails. **Parking:** on-site. **Cards:** AX, DS, MC, VI.

COUNTRY'S BARBEQUE **Lunch:** $6-$9 **Dinner:** $6-$9 **Phone:** 334/566-9940

Barbecue

Location: Jct US 231/167; in Southland Village. 100 Southland Village, US Hwy 231 36079. **Hours:** 11 am-9 pm, Fri & Sat-10 pm. Closed major holidays. **Features:** Pullled pork, beef ribs, chicken, brunswick stew and barbecue cole slaw are some of the dishes that will give you an example of the tasty treats offered at this eatery. Casual dress; beer only. **Parking:** on-site. **Cards:** AX, MC, VI.

JULIA'S RESTAURANT **Lunch:** $6-$16 **Dinner:** $6-$16 **Phone:** 334/566-5440

Southern

Location: 1.3 mi s of jct US 29. 809 US Hwy 231 S 36081. **Hours:** 6 am-8 pm, Sun-2 pm. Closed: 1/1, 7/4, 12/25. **Features:** Feast on the bountiful buffet of Southern favorites at lunch and come back to try something off the menu for dinner at this local favorite. Don't forget breakfast either, as they open at 5 am! Casual dress. **Parking:** on-site. **Cards:** AX, DC, DS, MC, VI.

TRUSSVILLE —*See Birmingham p. 241.*

TUSCALOOSA pop. 77,906

WHERE TO STAY

AMERICAS BEST VALUE INN *Book great rates at AAA.com* **Phone:** 205/556-7950

Small-scale Hotel

All Year [CP] 1P: $45-$100

Location: I-59/20, exit 73, just ne on US 82. 3501 McFarland Blvd 35405. Fax: 205/556-5119. **Facility:** 109 one-bedroom standard units. 2 stories (no elevator), exterior corridors. **Parking:** on-site. **Terms:** pets (in smoking units). **Amenities:** irons. *Some:* high-speed Internet. **Pool(s):** outdoor. **Business Services:** meeting rooms, fax (fee). **Cards:** AX, DC, DS, MC, VI. **Free Special Amenities: continental breakfast and high-speed Internet.**

SOME UNITS

BEST WESTERN PARK PLAZA MOTOR INN *Book great rates at AAA.com* **Phone:** (205)556-9690

AAA SAVE

Small-scale Hotel

All Year 1P: $71-$79

Location: I-59/20, exit 73, just ne on US 82. 3801 McFarland Blvd 35405. Fax: 205/561-0184. **Facility:** 118 one-bedroom standard units. 2 stories (no elevator), exterior corridors. *Bath:* combo or shower only. **Parking:** on-site. **Terms:** package plans. **Amenities:** high-speed Internet, voice mail, irons, hair dryers. **Pool(s):** outdoor. **Leisure Activities:** whirlpool, exercise room. **Guest Services:** valet laundry. **Business Services:** meeting rooms, PC, fax (fee). **Cards:** AX, DC, DS, MC, VI. **Free Special Amenities: expanded continental breakfast and high-speed Internet.** *(See color ad p 292)*

SOME UNITS

COMFORT INN *Book great rates at AAA.com* **Phone:** (205)556-3232

AAA SAVE

Small-scale Hotel

All Year 1P: $68-$81 2P: $68-$81 XP: $5 F18

Location: I-59/20, exit 76, just n. 4700 Doris Pate Dr 35405. Fax: 205/556-7797. **Facility:** 59 units. 55 one-bedroom standard units. 4 one-bedroom suites. 2 stories, interior corridors. *Bath:* combo or shower only. **Parking:** on-site. **Terms:** [ECP] meal plan available. **Amenities:** high-speed Internet, safes (fee), irons, hair dryers. **Pool(s):** outdoor. **Guest Services:** wireless Internet. **Cards:** AX, DC, DS, MC, VI. **Free Special Amenities: expanded continental breakfast and high-speed Internet.**

SOME UNITS

FEE

COUNTRY INN & SUITES *Book at AAA.com* **Phone:** (205)345-9999

Small-scale Hotel

2/1-11/30 1P: $89-$94 2P: $89-$94
12/1-1/31 1P: $86-$89 2P: $86-$89

Location: I-59/20, exit 73, 0.5 mi se on US 82. 4801 McFarland Blvd E 35405. Fax: 205/345-9940. **Facility:** 62 units. 52 one-bedroom standard units, some with whirlpools. 10 one-bedroom suites ($104-$139), some with whirlpools. 3 stories, interior corridors. *Bath:* combo or shower only. **Parking:** on-site. **Terms:** cancellation fee imposed, [ECP] meal plan available, package plans. **Amenities:** high-speed Internet, voice mail, irons, hair dryers. **Pool(s):** outdoor. **Leisure Activities:** exercise room. **Guest Services:** valet and coin laundry. **Business Services:** meeting rooms, business center. **Cards:** AX, CB, DC, DS, MC, VI.

SOME UNITS

ASK

DAYS INN SUITES OF TUSCALOOSA *Book great rates at AAA.com* **Phone:** 205/759-5000

Small-scale Hotel

8/1-11/30 1P: $60-$120 2P: $60-$120 XP: $10 F17
5/1-7/31 1P: $65-$80 2P: $65-$80 XP: $10 F17
12/1-4/30 1P: $60-$70 2P: $60-$70 XP: $10 F17

Location: I-59/20, exit 73, just e on US 82, then just n. 1201 Skyland Blvd 35405. Fax: 205/759-9864. **Facility:** 59 one-bedroom standard units. 2 stories (no elevator), exterior corridors. *Bath:* combo or shower only. **Parking:** on-site. **Amenities:** irons, hair dryers. **Pool(s):** small heated indoor. **Business Services:** fax. **Cards:** AX, DC, DS, MC, VI.

SOME UNITS

ASK

ECONO LODGE INN & SUITES *Book great rates at AAA.com* **Phone:** (205)345-1434

Small-scale Hotel

All Year 1P: $55-$135 2P: $65-$160 XP: $5 F12

Location: I-59/20, exit 73, 0.4 mi se on US 82. 4501 McFarland Blvd E 35405. Fax: 205/345-1434. **Facility:** 50 one-bedroom standard units. 2 stories (no elevator), exterior corridors. **Parking:** on-site. **Terms:** 2 night minimum stay - seasonal and/or weekends, [CP] meal plan available. **Amenities:** irons, hair dryers. **Pool(s):** outdoor. **Guest Services:** valet laundry. **Cards:** AX, CB, DC, DS, MC, VI.

SOME UNITS

ASK

FEE

FAIRFIELD INN BY MARRIOTT *Book great rates at AAA.com* **Phone:** 205/366-0900

Small-scale Hotel

All Year 1P: $76-$94

Location: I-59/20, exit 71A, just s on SR 69, just e on Skyland Blvd, then just n. 4101 Courtney Dr 35405. Fax: 205/366-0967. **Facility:** 63 one-bedroom standard units. 3 stories, interior corridors. *Bath:* combo or shower only. **Parking:** on-site. **Terms:** 10 day cancellation notice, [CP] meal plan available. **Amenities:** irons, hair dryers. **Pool(s):** small heated indoor. **Leisure Activities:** exercise room. **Guest Services:** valet laundry, wireless Internet. **Cards:** AX, CB, DC, DS, MC, VI.

SOME UNITS

ASK

FOUR POINTS BY SHERATON *Book great rates at AAA.com* **Phone:** 205/752-3200

Large-scale Hotel

Property failed to provide current rates

Location: I-59/20, exit 73, 2.6 mi w on US 82, exit University Blvd, just s on SR 215 and 1 mi n. Located on the University of Alabama campus. 320 Paul Bryant Dr 35401. Fax: 205/343-1139. **Facility:** 150 units. 147 one-bedroom standard units. 3 one-bedroom suites. 3 stories, interior corridors. *Bath:* combo or shower only. **Parking:** on-site. **Amenities:** video games (fee), voice mail, irons, hair dryers. **Pool(s):** outdoor. **Leisure Activities:** exercise room. **Guest Services:** valet laundry, area transportation, wireless Internet. **Business Services:** conference facilities, business center.

SOME UNITS

HAMPTON INN EAST TUSCALOOSA I-59/20 *Book great rates at AAA.com* **Phone:** (205)562-9000

Small-scale Hotel

All Year [BP] 1P: $68-$150 2P: $78-$150 XP: $10 F18

Location: I-59/20, exit 77, just nw. 6400 Interstate Dr 35453. Fax: 205/562-9859. **Facility:** 80 one-bedroom standard units. 3 stories, interior corridors. *Bath:* combo or shower only. **Parking:** on-site. **Amenities:** high-speed Internet, voice mail, irons, hair dryers. **Pool(s):** outdoor. **Guest Services:** valet and coin laundry. **Business Services:** meeting rooms, business center. **Cards:** AX, DC, DS, MC, VI.

SOME UNITS

HAMPTON INN-UNIVERSITY *Book great rates at AAA.com*

Small-scale Hotel

Phone: (205)553-9800

All Year [BP] 1P: $91-$195 2P: $101-$205 XP: $10 F18

Location: I-59/20, exit 73, 2.8 mi nw on US 82, exit Campus Dr. 600 Harper Lee Dr 35404. Fax: 205/553-0082. **Facility:** 102 one-bedroom standard units. 3 stories, interior corridors. *Bath:* combo or shower only. **Parking:** on-site. **Amenities:** voice mail, irons, hair dryers. **Pool(s):** outdoor. **Guest Services:** sundries, valet laundry, wireless Internet. **Business Services:** business center. **Cards:** AX, DC, DS, MC, VI.

SOME UNITS

HOLIDAY INN EXPRESS HOTEL AND SUITES UNIVERSITY *Book great rates at AAA.com*

AAA SAVE

Small-scale Hotel

Phone: 205/464-4000

1/9-11/30 1P: $119 2P: $129

12/1-1/8 1P: $104 2P: $114

Location: I-59/20, exit 73, 1.8 mi n on US 82 W, then just e. 1120 Veterans Memorial Pkwy 35404. Fax: 205/344-6654. **Facility:** 109 units. 107 one- and 2 two-bedroom standard units. 4 stories, interior corridors. *Bath:* combo or shower only. **Parking:** on-site. **Terms:** check-in 4 pm, cancellation fee imposed. **Amenities:** high-speed Internet, voice mail, irons, hair dryers. **Pool(s):** small outdoor. **Leisure Activities:** exercise room. **Guest Services:** complimentary evening beverages: seasonal, valet laundry. **Business Services:** meeting rooms, fax. **Cards:** AX, DC, DS, JC, MC, VI.

SOME UNITS

HOWARD JOHNSON *Book at AAA.com*

Small-scale Hotel

Phone: 205/469-1500

All Year 1P: $59-$169 2P: $64-$174 XP: $5 F17

Location: I-59/20, exit 79, just n. 4810 Skyland Blvd E 35405. Fax: 205/469-1505. **Facility:** 53 one-bedroom standard units, some with whirlpools. 2 stories (no elevator), interior corridors. *Bath:* combo or shower only. **Parking:** on-site. **Terms:** 3 day cancellation notice. **Amenities:** high-speed Internet, irons, hair dryers. **Guest Services:** coin laundry. **Business Services:** fax (fee). **Cards:** AX, CB, DC, DS, MC, VI.

SOME UNITS

ASK

JAMESON INN *Book at AAA.com*

Small-scale Hotel

Phone: (205)345-5018

All Year [ECP] 1P: $54-$120

Location: I-59/20, exit 71A, just s. 5021 Oscar Baxter Rd 35403. Fax: 205/345-5828. **Facility:** 62 one-bedroom standard units. 2 stories (no elevator), exterior corridors. *Bath:* combo or shower only. **Parking:** on-site. **Terms:** cancellation fee imposed, pets ($10 fee). **Amenities:** hair dryers. **Pool(s):** outdoor. **Leisure Activities:** exercise room. **Guest Services:** wireless Internet. **Business Services:** PC, fax (fee). **Cards:** AX, DC, DS, MC, VI.

SOME UNITS

ASK FEE

LA QUINTA INN TUSCALOOSA *Book great rates at AAA.com*

Motel

Phone: (205)349-3270

All Year [ECP] 1P: $74-$84 2P: $80-$90 XP: $6 F18

Location: I-59/20, exit 73, just sw on US 82. 4122 McFarland Blvd E 35403. Fax: 205/758-0440. **Facility:** 122 one-bedroom standard units. 2 stories (no elevator), exterior corridors. **Parking:** on-site. **Amenities:** video games (fee), voice mail, irons, hair dryers. **Pool(s):** outdoor. **Guest Services:** valet laundry. **Cards:** AX, CB, DC, DS, MC, VI. ***(See color ad p 386)***

SOME UNITS

ASK

MASTERS INN *Book great rates at AAA.com*

AAA SAVE

Motel

Phone: (205)556-2010

All Year 1P: $35-$39 2P: $35-$39 XP: $4 F18

Location: I-59/20, exit 73, just nw on US 82. 3600 McFarland Blvd 35405. Fax: 205/556-8522. **Facility:** 151 one-bedroom standard units. 2 stories (no elevator), exterior corridors. **Parking:** on-site. **Terms:** cancellation fee imposed, weekly rates available, [CP] meal plan available, pets ($6 fee). **Amenities:** *Some:* irons. **Pool(s):** outdoor. **Guest Services:** coin laundry. **Business Services:** fax (fee). **Cards:** AX, CB, DC, DS, MC, VI. **Free Special Amenities: continental breakfast and local telephone calls.**

SOME UNITS

FEE FEE FEE

MICROTEL INN *Book at AAA.com*

Small-scale Hotel

Phone: 205/556-1555

Property failed to provide current rates

Location: I-59/20, exit 77, just sw. 6331 Interstate Dr 35453. Fax: 205/556-9722. **Facility:** 61 one-bedroom standard units. 2 stories (no elevator), interior corridors. *Bath:* combo or shower only. **Parking:** on-site. **Amenities:** high-speed Internet. *Some:* irons, hair dryers. **Business Services:** fax.

SOME UNITS

MOTEL 6 #432 *Book at AAA.com*

Motel

Phone: 205/759-4942

4/21-11/30 1P: $42-$52 2P: $48-$58 XP: $3 F17

12/1-4/20 1P: $39-$49 2P: $45-$55 XP: $3 F17

Location: I-59/20, exit 73, just se on US 82. 4700 McFarland Blvd E 35405. Fax: 205/759-1093. **Facility:** 124 one-bedroom standard units. 2 stories (no elevator), exterior corridors. *Bath:* combo or shower only. **Parking:** on-site. **Terms:** small pets only. **Pool(s):** outdoor. **Guest Services:** coin laundry. **Cards:** AX, CB, DC, DS, MC, VI.

SOME UNITS

FEE FEE

SLEEP INN *Book great rates at AAA.com*

AAA SAVE

Small-scale Hotel

Phone: (205)556-5696

All Year 1P: $57-$62 2P: $84-$90 XP: $5 F10

Location: I-59/20, exit 76, 0.4 mi s. 4300 Skyland Blvd E 35405. Fax: 205/556-3205. **Facility:** 72 units. 52 one- and 20 two-bedroom standard units. 2 stories (no elevator), interior corridors. *Bath:* combo or shower only. **Parking:** on-site. **Terms:** [ECP] meal plan available. **Amenities:** video library (fee), voice mail, irons, hair dryers. **Pool(s):** outdoor. **Leisure Activities:** exercise room. **Guest Services:** coin laundry, wireless Internet. **Business Services:** meeting rooms, fax (fee). **Cards:** AX, CB, DC, DS, MC, VI. **Free Special Amenities: expanded continental breakfast and local telephone calls.**

SOME UNITS

VCR

SUPER 8 MOTEL Book at AAA.com Phone: (205)758-8878

Small-scale Hotel

9/1-11/30 [CP]	1P: $55-$125	2P: $65-$145	XP: $5	F12
12/1-8/31 [CP]	1P: $55-$85	2P: $65-$99	XP: $5	F12

Location: I-59/20, exit 73, just se on US 82. 4125 McFarland Blvd E 35405. Fax: 205/752-8331. **Facility:** 58 one-bedroom standard units. 3 stories (no elevator), interior corridors. **Parking:** on-site. **Amenities:** irons, hair dryers. **Cards:** AX, DC, DS, MC, VI.

SOME UNITS

ASK

WHERE TO DINE

BARNHILL'S BUFFET **Lunch:** $5-$9 **Dinner:** $7-$10 **Phone:** 205/759-5947

American

Location: Jct US 82, 0.5 mi w. 220 15th St 35401. **Hours:** 10:45 am-8:45 pm, Fri-9 pm, Sat 7 am-9 pm, Sun 7 am-8:45 pm. Closed: 12/25. **Features:** Casual dress. **Parking:** on-site. **Cards:** AX, DS, MC, VI.

CAFE VENICE **Lunch:** $5-$12 **Dinner:** $7-$18 **Phone:** 205/366-1209

Italian

Location: US 69 N to University Blvd, just e. 2321 University Blvd 35401. **Hours:** 10:30 am-1:30 & 5-10 pm, Sun-2 pm. Closed major holidays; also Mon. **Reservations:** accepted. **Features:** In the cute and busy downtown area, the relaxed restaurant specializes in pizza and pasta, including the lasagna for which it's known. Crowds pack the place on Wednesday night for half-price pizza and wine. Casual dress; cocktails. **Parking:** street. **Cards:** AX, DS, MC, VI.

CANCUN MEXICAN RESTAURANT **Lunch:** $4-$8 **Dinner:** $6-$13 **Phone:** 205/758-0875

Mexican

Location: I-59/20, exit 73, just n on US 82/McFarland Blvd. 2200 McFarland Blvd E 35404. **Hours:** 11 am-10 pm. Closed major holidays. **Features:** Typical, traditional Mexican dishes are served at this restaurant, which features a large deck and great margaritas and is popular with the students. Casual dress. **Parking:** on-site. **Cards:** MC, VI.

CHUCK'S CATFISH HOUSE **Lunch:** $5-$15 **Dinner:** $5-$15 **Phone:** 205/553-3377

Seafood

Location: I-59/20, exit 73, just e. 3520 McFarland Blvd E 35405. **Hours:** 10:30 am-9 pm, Sun-8 pm. Closed major holidays. **Features:** This place can't be missed for fried catfish, and countless fillets are served daily. To-go boxes are a common sight as full patrons leave the family restaurant. Casual dress. **Parking:** on-site. **Cards:** MC, VI.

CYPRESS INN **Lunch:** $7-$10 **Dinner:** $12-$20 **Phone:** 205/345-6963

Seafood

Location: I-59/20, exit 73, 4 mi w on US 82 to Rice Mine Rd, then 1.3 mi s. 501 Rice Mine Rd N 35406. **Hours:** 11 am-2 & 5:30-9:30 pm, Fri-10 pm, Sat 5 pm-10 pm, Sun 11 am-2 & 5:30-9 pm. Closed major holidays. **Features:** Overlooking Black Warrior River, this restaurant presents simply prepared dishes in a rustic setting. Their specialty is smoked chicken with white barbecue sauce, and a wide array of seafood choices. This is casual dining that will appeal to many tastes. Casual dress; cocktails. **Parking:** on-site. **Cards:** AX, DS, MC, VI.

DREAMLAND BAR-B-QUE **Lunch:** $5-$17 **Dinner:** $5-$17 **Phone:** 205/758-8135

Barbecue

Location: I-59/20, exit 73, 0.5 mi e on US 82, then 0.8 mi n on Jug Factory Rd, follow signs. 5535 15th Ave E 35405. **Hours:** 10 am-9 pm, Fri & Sat-10 pm, Sun 11 am-4 pm. Closed major holidays. **Features:** An Alabama staple for more than 50 years, the restaurant treats patrons to delicious plates of tender ribs covered in a finger-licking-good secret sauce that can be wiped up with soft white bread. Guests believe it when this place professes "ain't nothing like 'em nowhere". Casual dress; beer only. **Parking:** on-site. **Cards:** MC, VI.

PEPITO'S GRILL **Lunch:** $5-$8 **Dinner:** $5-$13 **Phone:** 205/391-4861

Mexican

Location: On US 82, 1.2 mi nw of Campus Dr exit. 1301 McFarland Blvd NE 35406. **Hours:** 11 am-10 pm, Fri & Sat-midnight, Sun-9:30 pm. Closed major holidays. **Features:** Diners can enjoy good Mexican food, authentic music and friendly service at the popular eatery. Casual dress; cocktails. **Parking:** on-site. **Cards:** AX, MC, VI.

WINGS SPORTS GRILLE **Lunch:** $6-$14 **Dinner:** $6-$14 **Phone:** 205/556-5658

American

Location: I-59/20, exit 73, 2.8 mi nw on US 82, exit Campus Dr. 500 Harper Lee Dr 35404. **Hours:** 11 am-10 pm, Fri & Sat-11 pm. Closed major holidays. **Features:** Enjoy hearty portions, good food and fun for the entire family. The friendly staff makes you feel right at home and the multitude of games helps keep everyone entertained. Casual dress. **Parking:** on-site. **Cards:** AX, DS, MC, VI.

TUSKEGEE pop. 11,846

WHERE TO STAY

KELLOGG HOTEL & CONFERENCE CENTER AT TUSKEGEE UNIVERSITY **Phone:** (334)727-3000

AAA SAVE

Small-scale Hotel

All Year 1P: $85

Location: I-85, exit 38, 3.3 mi s on SR 81, then 0.9 mi w on W Montgomey Ave to Lincoln Gates; in Tuskegee University Campus. Located next to the Carver Museum. One Booker T Washington Blvd 36088 (PO Box 1243). Fax: 334/727-5119. **Facility:** 106 units. 95 one-bedroom standard units. 9 one- and 2 two-bedroom suites ($150-$400). 4 stories, interior corridors. *Bath:* combo or shower only. **Parking:** on-site. **Terms:** 7 day cancellation notice, $1 service charge. **Amenities:** dual phone lines, voice mail, irons, hair dryers. *Some:* DVD players. **Dining:** 2 restaurants, 6:30 am-2 & 5-8 pm, Fri & Sat-9 pm, Sun-3 pm, cocktails. **Pool(s):** heated indoor. **Leisure Activities:** whirlpool, exercise room. **Guest Services:** gift shop, valet laundry, wireless Internet. **Business Services:** conference facilities, business center. **Cards:** AX, DS, MC, VI.

SOME UNITS

VCR

FEE FEE

VANCE pop. 500

WHERE TO STAY

BAYMONT INN & SUITES **Book at AAA.com**

Phone: (205)556-3606

Small-scale Hotel

All Year [ECP] 1P: $72-$100 2P: $72-$100 XP: $10 F15

Location: I-59/20, exit 89 southbound, just s; exit northbound, 0.8 mi n on Mercedes Dr, 0.3 mi w, then just s. 11170 Will Walker Rd/Daimler Benz Blvd 35490. Fax: 205/556-3607. **Facility:** 65 units. 59 one-bedroom standard units, some with efficiencies (utensils extra charge) and/or whirlpools. 6 one-bedroom suites with efficiencies (utensils extra charge). 3 stories, interior corridors. *Bath:* combo or shower only. **Parking:** on-site. **Terms:** 14 day cancellation notice-fee imposed, weekly rates available, small pets only ($25 extra charge). **Amenities:** voice mail, irons, hair dryers. **Leisure Activities:** exercise room. **Guest Services:** sundries, coin laundry, wireless Internet. **Business Services:** meeting rooms, fax (fee). **Cards:** AX, DC, DS, MC, VI.

ASK FEE VCR SOME UNITS

VESTAVIA HILLS —*See Birmingham p. 241.*

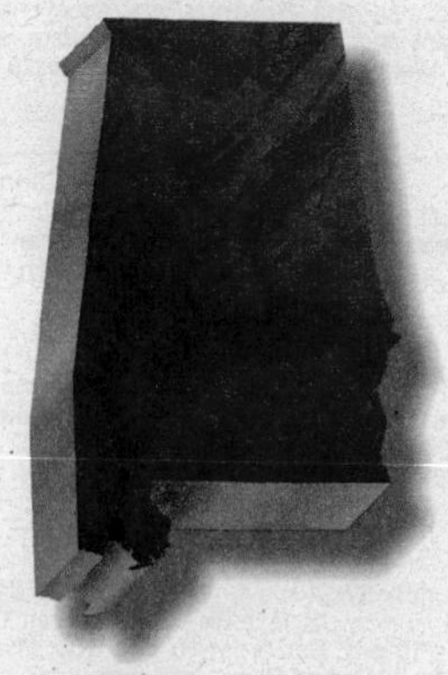

Louisiana

Oak Alley Plantation,
Vacherie

ALEXANDRIA pop. 46,342

WHERE TO STAY

BEST WESTERN INN & SUITES & CONFERENCE CENTER OF ALEXANDRIA *Book great rates at AAA.com* **Phone:** 318/445-5530

Small-scale Hotel

All Year [CP] 1P: $75-$95 2P: $75-$95 XP: $10 F12

Location: I-49, exit 86 (MacArthur Dr), 1.3 mi sw. 2720 W MacArthur Dr 71303. Fax: 318/445-8496. **Facility:** 192 units. 142 one-bedroom standard units, some with whirlpools. 50 one-bedroom suites ($95-$115), some with whirlpools. 2 stories, interior/exterior corridors. **Parking:** on-site. **Terms:** 3 day cancellation notice, pets ($10 extra charge, in designated units). **Amenities:** voice mail, irons, hair dryers. *Some:* high-speed Internet. **Pool(s):** outdoor, heated indoor, wading. **Leisure Activities:** whirlpools, exercise room. **Guest Services:** valet and coin laundry. **Business Services:** conference facilities, PC. **Cards:** AX, CB, DC, DS, MC, VI. **Free Special Amenities: expanded continental breakfast and high-speed Internet.** *(See color ad below)*

SOME UNITS

FEE

COMFORT INN *Book great rates at AAA.com* **Phone:** (318)484-9155

Small-scale Hotel

All Year 1P: $75-$80 2P: $80-$105 XP: $10 F18

Location: I-49, exit 86 (MacArthur), s at fork, exit 70, just n on SR 1. 2001 N Bolton Ave 71303. Fax: 318/484-9155. **Facility:** 68 one-bedroom standard units. 4 stories, interior corridors. *Bath:* combo or shower only. **Parking:** on-site. **Terms:** package plans. **Amenities:** high-speed Internet, irons, hair dryers. *Some:* dual phone lines. **Pool(s):** small outdoor. **Leisure Activities:** exercise room. **Guest Services:** valet laundry. **Business Services:** PC. **Cards:** AX, CB, DC, DS, JC, MC, VI.

SOME UNITS

LA QUINTA INN & SUITES ALEXANDRIA *Book great rates at AAA.com* **Phone:** (318)442-3700

Small-scale Hotel

All Year [ECP] 1P: $106-$116 2P: $116-$126 XP: $10 F18

Location: I-49, exit 90 (Air Base Rd), just w. 6116 W Calhoun Dr 71303. Fax: 318/442-0870. **Facility:** 117 units. 113 one-bedroom standard units. 4 one-bedroom suites. 4 stories, interior corridors. *Bath:* combo or shower only. **Parking:** on-site. **Terms:** small pets only. **Amenities:** video games (fee), high-speed Internet, voice mail, irons, hair dryers. *Some:* dual phone lines. **Pool(s):** outdoor. **Leisure Activities:** whirlpool, exercise room. **Guest Services:** valet and coin laundry. **Business Services:** meeting rooms. **Cards:** AX, CB, DC, DS, MC, VI.

SOME UNITS

RAMADA LIMITED *Book great rates at AAA.com* **Phone:** (318)448-1611

Small-scale Hotel

All Year 1P: $50-$93 2P: $55-$99 XP: $6 F17

Location: 0.4 mi s of jct SR 28 and US 71/165 (MacArthur Dr). 742 MacArthur Dr 71303. Fax: 318/473-2984. **Facility:** 119 units. 117 one-bedroom standard units. 2 one-bedroom suites, some with kitchens. 2 stories (no elevator), exterior corridors. **Parking:** on-site. **Terms:** pets ($20 fee). **Amenities:** high-speed Internet, voice mail, irons, hair dryers. **Pool(s):** outdoor, wading. **Guest Services:** coin laundry. **Business Services:** PC. **Cards:** AX, CB, DC, DS, MC, VI. **Free Special Amenities: expanded continental breakfast and high-speed Internet.**

SOME UNITS

FEE

SUPER 8 Book at AAA.com Phone: (318)619-9200

Motel

All Year 1P: $60-$70 2P: $70-$80 XP: $5 F5

Location: I-49, exit 90 (Air Base Rd), just w. 6017 Old Boyce Rd 71303. Fax: 318/619-9350. **Facility:** 61 one-bedroom standard units, some with whirlpools. 2 stories (no elevator), interior corridors. *Bath:* combo or shower only. **Parking:** on-site. **Terms:** [ECP] meal plan available. **Amenities:** high-speed Internet, irons, hair dryers. **Pool(s):** outdoor. **Leisure Activities:** exercise room. **Guest Services:** coin laundry. **Cards:** AX, DC, DS, MC, VI.

SOME UNITS

SUPER 8 MOTEL Book great rates at AAA.com **Phone:** (318)445-6541

SAVE

Motel

All Year [ECP] 1P: $51-$70 2P: $51-$70 XP: $6 F12

Location: I-49, exit 86 (MacArthur Dr), 2.4 mi sw. 700 MacArthur Dr 71303. Fax: 318/443-9411. **Facility:** 79 units. 78 one-bedroom standard units. 1 one-bedroom suite. 2 stories (no elevator), interior/exterior corridors. **Parking:** on-site. **Terms:** pets ($25 extra charge). **Amenities:** irons, hair dryers. *Some:* high-speed Internet. **Pool(s):** outdoor. **Leisure Activities:** picnic area with grills. **Guest Services:** coin laundry. **Business Services:** PC. **Cards:** AX, CB, DC, DS, MC, VI. **Free Special Amenities: expanded continental breakfast and local telephone calls.**

SOME UNITS

FEE

WHERE TO DINE

BISTRO ON THE BAYOU **Lunch:** $7-$17 **Dinner:** $19-$40 **Phone:** 318/445-7574

Regional American

Location: At England Airpark. 1321 Chappie James Ave 71303. **Hours:** 11:30 am-1:30 & 6-10 pm, Sat from 6 pm. Closed major holidays; also Sun & Mon. **Reservations:** suggested. **Features:** Looks can be deceiving. This understated jewel on the former England Air Force Base offers an elegant dining experience, superb service and American dishes prepared with an original Cajun flair. Dressy casual; cocktails. **Parking:** on-site. **Cards:** AX, MC, VI.

CAJUN LANDING **Lunch:** $5-$13 **Dinner:** $9-$24 **Phone:** 318/487-4912

Seafood

Location: I-49, exit 86 (MacArthur Dr), 1.3 mi sw. 2728 N MacArthur Dr 71303. **Hours:** 11 am-2 & 5-10 pm. Closed major holidays; also Sun. **Reservations:** accepted. **Features:** Featuring a highly recommended crawfish bisque, the locally popular restaurant also offers grilled red snapper, catfish, fried oysters and etoufee as well as chicken and steak items. Casual dress; cocktails. **Parking:** on-site. **Cards:** AX, DC, DS, MC, VI.

FIRE MOUNTAIN GRILL **Lunch:** $8 **Dinner:** $12 **Phone:** 318/445-8796

American

Location: I-49, exit 86 (MacArthur Dr), 2.9 mi sw. 3024 W MacArthur Dr 71303. **Hours:** 10:45 am-9:30 pm, Fri & Sat-10 pm. Closed: 12/24, 12/25. **Features:** This mega buffet also offers cooking stations where freshly prepared steaks, chicken, fish, pizzas and more are served. Casual dress. **Parking:** on-site. **Cards:** AX, CB, DC, DS, JC, MC, VI.

JOHNNY CARINO'S **Lunch:** $5-$8 **Dinner:** $7-$13 **Phone:** 318/767-5942

Italian

Location: On US 71; 1.2 mi s of Alexandria Mall and South Traffic Circle. 3213 S MacArthur Rd 71303. **Hours:** 11 am-10 pm, Fri & Sat-11 pm. Closed: 11/22, 12/25. **Features:** The popular restaurant serves country Italian dishes in a casual atmosphere. Casual dress; cocktails. **Parking:** on-site. **Cards:** AX, DS, MC, VI.

ORIENTAL WOK **Lunch:** $6-$12 **Dinner:** $8-$12 **Phone:** 318/448-8247

Chinese

Location: On SR 1; 0.4 mi s of jct US 71/165 (MacArthur Dr). 6 N Bolton Ave 71301. **Hours:** 11 am-9:30 pm, Fri & Sat-10 pm, Sun noon-9:30 pm. Closed major holidays. **Reservations:** accepted. **Features:** This place is the only area Chinese restaurant that does not offer a buffet—and for good reason. The food is so good that dishes would be depleted well before the buffet is taken down. Expect a wait during lunch hours. Casual dress. **Parking:** on-site. **Cards:** AX, MC, VI.

OUTLAW'S BAR-B-Q **Lunch:** $5-$10 **Dinner:** $5-$10 **Phone:** 318/443-8723

American

Location: I-49, exit 86 (MacArthur Dr), 2.6 mi sw. 818 MacArthur Dr 71301. **Hours:** 11 am-10 pm, Fri-11 pm. Closed: 11/22, 12/25. **Features:** Top quality beef, chicken, and pork are featured at Outlaw's. The food is nothing fancy, just good barbecue. Hamburgers and other sandwiches are also available if you don't happen to be in the mood for barbecue. Casual dress; beer only. **Parking:** on-site. **Cards:** AX, MC, VI.

AMITE pop. 4,110

WHERE TO STAY

COMFORT INN Book great rates at AAA.com **Phone:** 985/748-5550

Small-scale Hotel

All Year 1P: $70-$85 2P: $75-$90 XP: $5 F14

Location: I-55, exit 46, 0.3 mi e. 1117 W Oak St 70422. Fax: 985/748-4525. **Facility:** 61 units. 58 one- and 3 two-bedroom standard units. 3 stories, interior corridors. *Bath:* combo or shower only. **Parking:** on-site. **Amenities:** irons, hair dryers. **Pool(s):** outdoor. **Leisure Activities:** limited exercise equipment. **Guest Services:** coin laundry, wireless Internet. **Business Services:** meeting rooms, PC, fax (fee). **Cards:** AX, CB, DC, DS, JC, MC, VI.

SOME UNITS

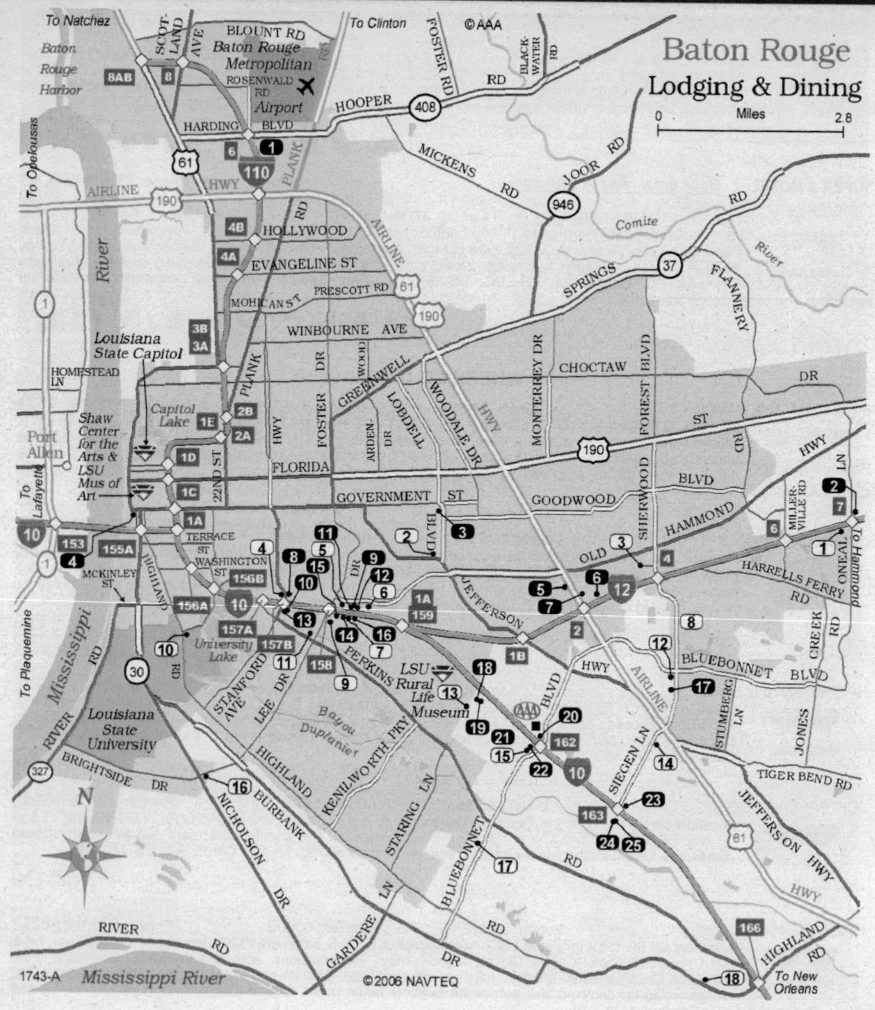

Baton Rouge

This index helps you "spot" where approved accommodations and restaurants are located on the corresponding detailed maps. Lodging rate ranges are for comparison only and show the property's high season; rates are per night, unless only weekly (W) rates are available. Restaurant rate range is for dinner, unless only lunch (L) is served. Turn to the listing page for more detailed rate information and consult display ads for special promotions.

Spotter/Map Page Number	OA	**BATON ROUGE - Lodgings**	Diamond Rating	Rate Range High Season	Listing Page
1 / above		Hilton Garden Inn Baton Rouge Airport - see color ad p 304	◆◆◆	Failed to provide	304
2 / above	AAA	**Comfort Suites**	◆◆◆	$70-$120 SAVE	303
3 / above	AAA	**Best Western Chateau Louisianne All-Suite Hotel**	◆◆◆	$79-$109 SAVE	302
4 / above	AAA	**Sheraton Baton Rouge Convention Center Hotel** - see color ad p 306	◆◆◆	$169-$199 SAVE	306
5 / above	AAA	**Holiday Inn-South**	◆◆◆	$84-$94 SAVE	304

Spotter/Map Page Number	OA	BATON ROUGE - Lodgings (continued)	Diamond Rating	Rate Range High Season	Listing Page
6 / p. 300	AAA	**Sleep Inn**	♦♦	$70 SAVE	306
7 / p. 300		Ramada I-12/Airline Highway	♦♦	$72-$100	305
8 / p. 300		La Quinta Inn Baton Rouge - see color ad p 386	♦♦	$85-$105	305
9 / p. 300	AAA	**Chase Suites by Woodfin**	♦♦♦	$134-$199 SAVE	303
10 / p. 300	AAA	**Courtyard by Marriott**	♦♦♦	$149 SAVE	303
11 / p. 300		Baton Rouge Marriott	♦♦♦	$189-$220	302
12 / p. 300	AAA	**Best Western Richmond Suites Hotel - Baton Rouge**	♦♦♦	$89-$199 SAVE	303
13 / p. 300		University Inn & Conference Center	fyi	Failed to provide	307
14 / p. 300	AAA	**Holiday Inn Select Executive Center Baton Rouge - see color ad p 305**	♦♦♦	$99-$129 SAVE	304
15 / p. 300		Hampton Inn College	♦♦♦	Failed to provide	304
16 / p. 300		Embassy Suites Baton Rouge	♦♦♦	$109-$209	303
17 / p. 300		Crestwood Suites Hotel	♦♦	$70-$130	303
18 / p. 300		Fairfield Inn by Marriott	♦♦♦	Failed to provide	304
19 / p. 300		SpringHill Suites by Marriott	♦♦♦	Failed to provide	306
20 / p. 300	AAA	**Quality Suites**	♦♦♦	$129-$179 SAVE	305
21 / p. 300		TownePlace Suites by Marriott	♦♦♦	$139-$199	307
22 / p. 300	AAA	**AmeriSuites (Baton Rouge/East)**	♦♦♦	$109-$143 SAVE	302
23 / p. 300		La Quinta Inn & Suites Baton Rouge - see color ad p 386	♦♦♦	$74-$94	305
24 / p. 300		Courtyard by Marriott-Siegen Lane	♦♦♦	Failed to provide	303
25 / p. 300		Residence Inn by Marriott-Baton Rouge	♦♦♦	$139-$179	305
		BATON ROUGE - Restaurants			
1 / p. 300		Las Palmas	♦♦	$7-$15	308
2 / p. 300		Da Jo Nell's	♦♦	$17-$36	308
3 / p. 300	AAA	**Maison Lacour**	♦♦♦	$18-$35	308
4 / p. 300		T J Ribs	♦♦	$6-$19	310
5 / p. 300		Sullivan's Steakhouse	♦♦♦	$18-$29	309
6 / p. 300		Albasha	♦♦	$8-$14	307
7 / p. 300		Ruth's Chris Steak House	♦♦♦	$17-$37	309
8 / p. 300		Capital City Grill	♦♦	$11-$19	308
9 / p. 300		Marina's Mexican Restaurant	♦♦	$7-$13	309
10 / p. 300		Serrano's Salsa Company	♦♦	$8-$22	309
11 / p. 300		Thai Kitchen	♦♦	$8-$14	309
12 / p. 300		Mestizo	♦	$6-$10	309
13 / p. 300		Copeland's of New Orleans	♦♦	$10-$20	308
14 / p. 300		Taqueria El Sol de Guerrero	♦	$3-$12	309
15 / p. 300		Ralph & Kacoo's	♦♦	$14-$25	309
16 / p. 300		Mike Andersons Seafood	♦♦	$10-$25	309
17 / p. 300	AAA	**Boutin's-A Cajun Music & Dining Experience**	♦♦	$9-$17	308
18 / p. 300		French Market Bistro	♦♦♦	$10-$22	308

BATON ROUGE pop. 227,818 (See map and index starting on p. 300)

WHERE TO STAY

AMERISUITES (BATON ROUGE/EAST) Book great rates at AAA.com **Phone:** (225)769-4400 22

AAA SAVE

Small-scale Hotel

All Year 1P: $109-$143 2P: $109-$143 XP: $10 F18

Location: I-10, exit 162. 6080 Bluebonnet Blvd 70809. Fax: 225/769-7444. **Facility:** 128 one-bedroom standard units. 6 stories, interior corridors. *Bath:* combo or shower only. **Parking:** on-site. **Terms:** cancellation fee imposed, small pets only ($10 extra charge). **Amenities:** voice mail, irons, hair dryers. **Pool(s):** outdoor. **Leisure Activities:** exercise room. **Guest Services:** valet and coin laundry, wireless Internet. **Business Services:** meeting rooms, fax (fee). **Cards:** AX, DS, MC, VI. **Free Special Amenities: expanded continental breakfast and high-speed Internet.**

SOME UNITS

FEE

BATON ROUGE MARRIOTT Book great rates at AAA.com **Phone:** (225)924-5000 11

Large-scale Hotel

All Year 1P: $189-$220 XP: $10 F18

Location: I-10, exit 158, 0.5 mi ne. 5500 Hilton Ave 70808. Fax: 225/925-1330. **Facility:** 300 units. 298 one-bedroom standard units. 1 one- and 1 three-bedroom suites ($300-$675). 21 stories, interior corridors. *Bath:* combo or shower only. **Parking:** on-site. **Terms:** cancellation fee imposed, package plans. **Amenities:** high-speed Internet (fee), dual phone lines, voice mail, irons, hair dryers. **Pool(s):** outdoor. **Leisure Activities:** whirlpool, exercise room. **Guest Services:** gift shop, valet laundry, wireless Internet. **Business Services:** conference facilities, business center. **Cards:** AX, CB, DC, DS, JC, MC, VI.

SOME UNITS

ASK VCR

FEE

BEST WESTERN CHATEAU LOUISIANNE ALL-SUITE HOTEL Book great rates at AAA.com **Phone:** (225)927-6700 3

AAA SAVE

Small-scale Hotel

All Year 1P: $79-$109 2P: $79-$109

Location: Jct I-10 and 110 N, 4.6 mi e on Florida Blvd, then 0.3 mi n. 710 N Lobdell Blvd 70806. Fax: 225/927-6709. **Facility:** 50 units. 45 one-bedroom standard units. 5 one-bedroom suites ($109-$139). 3 stories, interior corridors. **Parking:** on-site. **Terms:** package plans. **Amenities:** voice mail, irons, hair dryers. *Some:* high-speed Internet. **Pool(s):** outdoor. **Leisure Activities:** whirlpool, steamroom, exercise room. **Guest Services:** complimentary evening beverages: Mon-Fri, valet and coin laundry, wireless Internet. **Business Services:** meeting rooms, fax (fee). **Cards:** AX, CB, DC, DS, JC, MC, VI. **Free Special Amenities: continental breakfast and local telephone calls.**

SOME UNITS

(See map and index starting on p. 300)

BEST WESTERN RICHMOND SUITES HOTEL - BATON ROUGE Book great rates at AAA.com **Phone:** (225)924-6500 12

AAA SAVE Small-scale Hotel

All Year [BP] 1P: $89-$199 2P: $89-$199 XP: $10 F18

Location: I-10, exit 158, just ne. 5668 Hilton Ave 70808. Fax: 225/924-3074. **Facility:** 141 units. 70 one-bedroom standard units, some with whirlpools. 71 one-bedroom suites ($109-$199) with kitchens, some with whirlpools. 2 stories (no elevator), interior corridors. *Bath:* combo or shower only. **Parking:** on-site. **Amenities:** high-speed Internet, dual phone lines, voice mail, irons, hair dryers. *Some:* CD players. **Pool(s):** outdoor. **Leisure Activities:** whirlpool, exercise room, sports court. **Guest Services:** complimentary evening beverages: Mon-Sat, valet and coin laundry. **Business Services:** meeting rooms, business center. **Cards:** AX, CB, DC, DS, JC, MC, VI. **Free Special Amenities: full breakfast and high-speed Internet.**

SOME UNITS

CHASE SUITES BY WOODFIN Book great rates at AAA.com **Phone:** (225)927-5630 9

AAA SAVE Small-scale Hotel

All Year 1P: $134-$159 2P: $169-$199

Location: I-10, exit 158, just n on College Dr, then just e. 5522 Corporate Blvd 70808. Fax: 225/926-2317. **Facility:** 80 units. 60 one- and 20 two-bedroom suites ($134-$159) with kitchens, some with whirlpools. 2 stories (no elevator), exterior corridors. *Bath:* combo or shower only. **Parking:** on-site. **Terms:** [ECP] meal plan available, package plans, pets ($150 deposit, $5 extra charge). **Amenities:** high-speed Internet (fee), voice mail, irons, hair dryers. **Pool(s):** small outdoor. **Leisure Activities:** whirlpool, sports court. **Guest Services:** complimentary evening beverages, valet and coin laundry. **Business Services:** meeting rooms, business center. **Cards:** AX, DC, DS, MC, VI. **Free Special Amenities: expanded continental breakfast and newspaper.**

SOME UNITS

FEE VCR FEE

COMFORT SUITES Book great rates at AAA.com **Phone:** (225)273-3388 2

AAA SAVE Small-scale Hotel

All Year 1P: $70-$110 2P: $80-$120 XP: $5 F5

Location: I-12, exit 7. 1755 O'Neal Ln 70816. Fax: 225/273-7771. **Facility:** 63 one-bedroom standard units, some with whirlpools. 3 stories, interior corridors. *Bath:* combo or shower only. **Parking:** on-site. **Amenities:** high-speed Internet, dual phone lines, voice mail, irons, hair dryers. **Pool(s):** outdoor. **Leisure Activities:** exercise room. **Business Services:** meeting rooms, business center. **Cards:** AX, DC, DS, MC, VI. **Free Special Amenities: continental breakfast and local telephone calls.**

SOME UNITS

COURTYARD BY MARRIOTT Book great rates at AAA.com **Phone:** (225)924-6400 10

AAA SAVE Small-scale Hotel

All Year 1P: $149 2P: $149

Location: I-10, exit 157B, just s. 2421 S Acadian Thruway 70808. Fax: 225/923-3041. **Facility:** 149 units. 137 one-bedroom standard units. 12 one-bedroom suites ($199). 3 stories, interior corridors. *Bath:* combo or shower only. **Parking:** on-site. **Amenities:** high-speed Internet, voice mail, irons, hair dryers. **Dining:** 6-10 am, Sat & Sun 7-11 am. **Pool(s):** heated outdoor. **Leisure Activities:** whirlpool, exercise room. **Guest Services:** valet and coin laundry, wireless Internet. **Business Services:** meeting rooms, PC, fax (fee). **Cards:** AX, DC, DS, MC, VI. **Free Special Amenities: high-speed Internet.**

SOME UNITS

COURTYARD BY MARRIOTT-SIEGEN LANE Book great rates at AAA.com **Phone:** 225/293-7200 24

Small-scale Hotel

Property failed to provide current rates

Location: I-10, exit 163 westbound, just s on Siegen Ln to N Mall Dr, then just e; exit eastbound, 0.5 mi to S Mall Dr, just e to Andrea (at Lowe's), then just n. Located in Marketplace Center. 10307 N Mall Dr 70809. Fax: 225/293-0323. **Facility:** 121 units. 115 one-bedroom standard units, some with whirlpools. 6 one-bedroom suites. 3 stories, interior corridors. *Bath:* combo or shower only. **Parking:** on-site. **Amenities:** high-speed Internet, dual phone lines, voice mail, irons, hair dryers. **Pool(s):** indoor. **Leisure Activities:** whirlpool, exercise room. **Guest Services:** valet and coin laundry, wireless Internet. **Business Services:** meeting rooms, fax (fee).

SOME UNITS

CRESTWOOD SUITES HOTEL Book at AAA.com **Phone:** (225)291-5200 17

Small-scale Hotel

All Year 1P: $70-$130 2P: $70-$130

Location: I-12, exit 4, 1.7 mi s. 5222 S Sherwood Forest Blvd 70816. Fax: 225/291-5277. **Facility:** 137 units. 129 one-bedroom standard units with efficiencies. 8 one-bedroom suites with efficiencies. 3 stories, interior corridors. *Bath:* combo or shower only. **Parking:** on-site. **Terms:** weekly rates available, small pets only ($25 fee). **Amenities:** voice mail, irons. **Guest Services:** coin laundry, wireless Internet. **Business Services:** fax (fee). **Cards:** AX, CB, DC, DS, JC, MC, VI.

SOME UNITS

FEE

EMBASSY SUITES BATON ROUGE Book at AAA.com **Phone:** (225)924-6566 16

Large-scale Hotel

All Year 1P: $109-$209 2P: $109-$209 XP: $10 F18

Location: I-10, exit 158, just se on frontage road. 4914 Constitution Ave 70808. Fax: 225/923-3712. **Facility:** 223 one-bedroom suites. 8 stories, interior corridors. **Parking:** on-site. **Terms:** cancellation fee imposed. **Amenities:** video games (fee), high-speed Internet, dual phone lines, voice mail, irons, hair dryers. **Pool(s):** heated indoor. **Leisure Activities:** sauna, whirlpool, steamroom, putting green, exercise room. **Guest Services:** gift shop, complimentary evening beverages, valet and coin laundry, area transportation, wireless Internet. **Business Services:** conference facilities, business center. **Cards:** AX, DS, MC, VI.

SOME UNITS

(See map and index starting on p. 300)

FAIRFIELD INN BY MARRIOTT Book great rates at AAA.com Phone: 225/766-9493 18

Property failed to provide current rates

Small-scale Hotel **Location:** I-10, exit 160, 1 blk s to Essen Park Ave, then just e. 7959 Essen Park Ave 70809. Fax: 225/766-9175. **Facility:** 79 one-bedroom standard units. 3 stories, interior corridors. *Bath:* combo or shower only. **Parking:** on-site. **Amenities:** dual phone lines, voice mail, irons, hair dryers. **Pool(s):** small heated indoor. **Leisure Activities:** whirlpool, exercise room. **Guest Services:** valet laundry, wireless Internet. **Business Services:** business center.

SOME UNITS

HAMPTON INN COLLEGE Book great rates at AAA.com Phone: 225/926-9990 15

Property failed to provide current rates

Small-scale Hotel **Location:** I-10, exit 158, on eastbound service road. 4646 Constitution Ave 70808. Fax: 225/923-3007. **Facility:** 140 one-bedroom standard units. 8 stories, interior corridors. **Parking:** on-site. **Amenities:** voice mail, irons, hair dryers. **Pool(s):** outdoor. **Guest Services:** valet laundry, wireless Internet. **Business Services:** meeting rooms, business center.

SOME UNITS

VCR

FEE

HILTON GARDEN INN BATON ROUGE AIRPORT Book great rates at AAA.com Phone: 225/357-6177 1

Property failed to provide current rates

Small-scale Hotel **Location:** I-110, exit 6, just e. 3330 Harding Blvd 70807. Fax: 225/357-6175. **Facility:** 131 one-bedroom standard units. 5 stories, interior corridors. *Bath:* combo or shower only. **Parking:** on-site. **Amenities:** video games (fee), high-speed Internet, dual phone lines, voice mail, irons, hair dryers. **Pool(s):** outdoor. **Leisure Activities:** whirlpool, exercise room. **Guest Services:** sundries, valet and coin laundry, wireless Internet. **Business Services:** meeting rooms, business center. ***(See color ad below)***

SOME UNITS

HOLIDAY INN SELECT EXECUTIVE CENTER BATON ROUGE Book great rates at AAA.com Phone: (225)925-2244 14

AAA SAVE

Large-scale Hotel

All Year	1P: $99-$129	2P: $99-$129	XP: $10	F19

Location: I-10, exit 158, just se on frontage road. 4728 Constitution Ave 70808. Fax: 225/930-0140. **Facility:** 294 units. 288 one-bedroom standard units. 6 one-bedroom suites. 5 stories, interior corridors. *Bath:* combo or shower only. **Parking:** on-site. **Terms:** check-in 4 pm, cancellation fee imposed. **Amenities:** video games (fee), dual phone lines, voice mail, irons, hair dryers. **Dining:** 6 am-10 pm, cocktails. **Pool(s):** outdoor. **Leisure Activities:** *Fee:* massage. **Guest Services:** gift shop, valet laundry, airport transportation-Baton Rouge Metropolitan Airport, wireless Internet. **Business Services:** conference facilities, business center. **Cards:** AX, DC, DS, MC, VI. **Free Special Amenities: local telephone calls and high-speed Internet.** *(See color ad p 305)*

SOME UNITS

HOLIDAY INN-SOUTH Book great rates at AAA.com Phone: (225)924-7021 5

AAA SAVE

Large-scale Hotel

All Year	1P: $84-$94	2P: $84-$94	XP: $10	F18

Location: I-12, exit 2B, just n on US 61. 9940 Airline Hwy 70816. Fax: 225/924-7021. **Facility:** 333 units. 332 one-bedroom standard units. 1 one-bedroom suite. 2-6 stories, interior/exterior corridors. *Bath:* combo or shower only. **Parking:** on-site. **Terms:** cancellation fee imposed. **Amenities:** voice mail, irons, hair dryers. *Some:* dual phone lines. **Dining:** 6-10:30 am, 11-2 & 5-10 pm, Sun-9 pm, cocktails. **Pool(s):** outdoor, heated indoor/outdoor, wading. **Leisure Activities:** exercise room. **Guest Services:** valet and coin laundry, wireless Internet. **Business Services:** conference facilities, business center. **Cards:** AX, DC, DS, MC, VI. **Free Special Amenities: local telephone calls and high-speed Internet.**

SOME UNITS

(See map and index starting on p. 300)

LA QUINTA INN & SUITES BATON ROUGE Book great rates at AAA.com Phone: (225)291-6600 23

Small-scale Hotel

All Year [ECP] 1P: $74-$84 2P: $84-$94 XP: $10 F18

Location: I-10, exit 163 (Siegen Ln), just n, then just e. 10555 Rieger Rd 70809. Fax: 225/296-0474. **Facility:** 99 units. 96 one-bedroom standard units. 3 one-bedroom suites, some with efficiencies (no utensils). 3 stories, interior corridors. **Parking:** on-site. **Terms:** small pets only. **Amenities:** video games (fee), voice mail, irons, hair dryers. **Pool(s):** outdoor. **Leisure Activities:** exercise room. **Guest Services:** valet and coin laundry, wireless Internet. **Business Services:** fax (fee). **Cards:** AX, CB, DC, DS, MC, VI. *(See color ad p 386)*

SOME UNITS

LA QUINTA INN BATON ROUGE Book great rates at AAA.com Phone: (225)924-9600 8

Small-scale Hotel

All Year [ECP] 1P: $85-$95 2P: $95-$105 XP: $10 F18

Location: I-10, exit 157B. 2333 S Acadian Thruway 70808-2304. Fax: 225/924-2609. **Facility:** 142 units. 140 one-bedroom standard units. 2 one-bedroom suites. 2 stories (no elevator), exterior corridors. **Parking:** on-site. **Amenities:** video games (fee), voice mail, irons, hair dryers. **Pool(s):** outdoor. **Guest Services:** coin laundry, wireless Internet. **Business Services:** fax (fee). **Cards:** AX, CB, DC, DS, MC, VI. *(See color ad p 386)*

SOME UNITS

QUALITY SUITES Book great rates at AAA.com Phone: 225/293-1199 20

AAA SAVE

Small-scale Hotel

All Year [BP] 1P: $129-$179 2P: $129-$179 XP: $10 F17

Location: I-10, exit 162. 9138 Bluebonnet Blvd 70809. Fax: 225/296-5014. **Facility:** 120 one-bedroom suites, some with whirlpools. 3 stories, exterior corridors. **Parking:** on-site. **Terms:** cancellation fee imposed, package plans. **Amenities:** voice mail, irons, hair dryers. **Pool(s):** outdoor. **Leisure Activities:** picnic area with charcoal grills, exercise room. **Guest Services:** complimentary evening beverages: Mon-Sat, valet and coin laundry, wireless Internet. **Business Services:** meeting rooms, business center. **Cards:** AX, DS, MC, VI. **Free Special Amenities: full breakfast.**

SOME UNITS

RAMADA I-12/AIRLINE HIGHWAY Book at AAA.com Phone: 225/706-5500 7

Small-scale Hotel

All Year [BP] 1P: $72-$76 2P: $80-$100 XP: $4 F12

Location: I-12, exit 2B, just n on US 61. 10045 Gwenadele Ave 70816. Fax: 225/706-5520. **Facility:** 116 one-bedroom standard units. 2 stories (no elevator), exterior corridors. **Parking:** on-site. **Terms:** package plans, small pets only ($20 fee, $25 deposit). **Amenities:** voice mail, irons, hair dryers. **Pool(s):** outdoor. **Guest Services:** valet laundry, wireless Internet. **Business Services:** fax (fee). **Cards:** AX, CB, DC, DS, JC, MC, VI.

SOME UNITS

FEE

RESIDENCE INN BY MARRIOTT-BATON ROUGE Book great rates at AAA.com Phone: (225)293-8700 25

Small-scale Hotel

All Year 1P: $139-$179 2P: $139-$179

Location: I-10, exit 163 westbound, just s on Siegen Ln, then just e; exit eastbound, 0.5 mi to S Mall Dr, just e to Andrea (at Lowe's), then just n. Located inside Marketplace Center. 10333 N Mall Dr 70809. Fax: 225/293-9169. **Facility:** 108 units. 37 one-bedroom standard units with kitchens. 50 one- and 21 two-bedroom suites with kitchens. 3 stories, interior corridors. *Bath:* combo or shower only. **Parking:** on-site. **Terms:** cancellation fee imposed, weekly rates available, [BP] meal plan available, small pets only ($75 fee). **Amenities:** high-speed Internet, dual phone lines, voice mail, irons, hair dryers. **Pool(s):** outdoor. **Leisure Activities:** whirlpool, exercise room, sports court, basketball, volleyball. **Guest Services:** complimentary evening beverages: Mon-Thurs, valet and coin laundry, wireless Internet. **Business Services:** meeting rooms, fax (fee). **Cards:** AX, DC, DS, JC, MC, VI.

SOME UNITS

FEE

(See map and index starting on p. 300)

SHERATON BATON ROUGE CONVENTION CENTER HOTEL *Book great rates at AAA.com* **Phone:** (225)242-2600 **4**

Large-scale Hotel

All Year 1P: $169-$199 2P: $169-$199

Location: I-110, exit 1A (Government St), 0.8 mi w to St. James, then just s. 102 France St 70802. Fax: 225/242-2601. **Facility:** 300 units. 298 one-bedroom standard units. 2 one-bedroom suites. 10 stories, interior corridors. *Bath:* combo or shower only. **Parking:** on-site. **Terms:** cancellation fee imposed, package plans, small pets only. **Amenities:** video games (fee), high-speed Internet, dual phone lines, voice mail, irons, hair dryers. **Dining:** 3 restaurants, 6:30-11 am, 11:30-2 & 5:30-10 pm. **Pool(s):** heated outdoor. **Leisure Activities:** whirlpool, exercise room. **Guest Services:** valet and coin laundry, wireless Internet. **Business Services:** conference facilities, business center. **Cards:** AX, DC, DS, JC, MC, VI. **Free Special Amenities: high-speed Internet.**
(See color ad below)

SOME UNITS

SLEEP INN *Book great rates at AAA.com* **Phone:** (225)926-8488 **6**

Small-scale Hotel

All Year 1P: $70 2P: $70

Location: I-12, exit 2B. 10332 Plaza Americana Dr 70816. Fax: 225/926-7989. **Facility:** 101 one-bedroom standard units. 3 stories, interior corridors. *Bath:* shower or tub only. **Parking:** on-site. **Terms:** cancellation fee imposed. **Amenities:** video games (fee), high-speed Internet, voice mail, irons, hair dryers. **Pool(s):** outdoor. **Guest Services:** wireless Internet. **Business Services:** fax (fee). **Cards:** AX, CB, DC, DS, JC, MC, VI.

SOME UNITS

SPRINGHILL SUITES BY MARRIOTT *Book great rates at AAA.com* **Phone:** 225/766-5252 **19**

Small-scale Hotel

Property failed to provide current rates

Location: I-10, exit 160, 1 blk s to Essen Park Ave, then just w. 7979 Essen Park Ave 70809. Fax: 225/766-0797. **Facility:** 78 one-bedroom standard units. 3 stories, interior corridors. *Bath:* combo or shower only. **Parking:** on-site. **Amenities:** dual phone lines, voice mail, irons, hair dryers. *Some:* high-speed Internet. **Pool(s):** small heated indoor. **Leisure Activities:** whirlpool, exercise room. **Guest Services:** sundries, valet and coin laundry, wireless Internet. **Business Services:** meeting rooms, business center.

SOME UNITS

(See map and index starting on p. 300)

TOWNEPLACE SUITES BY MARRIOTT *Book great rates at AAA.com* **Phone:** 225/819-2112 **21**

1/1-11/30	1P: $139-$199	2P: $139-$199
12/1-12/31	1P: $129-$189	2P: $129-$189

Small-scale Hotel **Location:** I-10, exit 162 (Bluebonnet Blvd), just s to Picardy, just w to Summa Ave, then 0.5 mi nw. 8735 Summa Ave 70809. Fax: 225/819-2117. **Facility:** 90 units. 64 one-bedroom standard units with kitchens. 4 one- and 22 two-bedroom suites with kitchens. 3 stories, interior corridors. *Bath:* combo or shower only. **Parking:** on-site. **Terms:** small pets only ($75 fee). **Amenities:** dual phone lines, voice mail, irons, hair dryers. **Pool(s):** small heated indoor. **Leisure Activities:** whirlpool, exercise room. **Guest Services:** valet and coin laundry. **Business Services:** fax (fee). **Cards:** AX, CB, DC, DS, JC, MC, VI.

SOME UNITS

ASK FEE

UNIVERSITY INN & CONFERENCE CENTER **Phone:** 225/236-4000 **13**

fyi Property failed to provide current rates

Small-scale Hotel Under major renovation, scheduled to be completed September 2006. **Last rated:** ◆◆◆ **Location:** I-10, exit 157B, just n. 2445 S Acadian Thruway 70808. Fax: 225/925-0084. **Facility:** 145 one-bedroom standard units. 4 stories, interior corridors. *Bath:* combo or shower only. **Parking:** on-site. **Terms:** small pets only ($25 extra charge). **Amenities:** video games (fee), irons, hair dryers. *Some:* high-speed Internet. **Pool(s):** outdoor. **Leisure Activities:** limited exercise equipment. **Guest Services:** valet and coin laundry. **Business Services:** meeting rooms, business center.

SOME UNITS

FEE

WHERE TO DINE

ALBASHA **Lunch:** $6-$10 **Dinner:** $8-$14 **Phone:** 225/216-1444 **6**

Lebanese **Location:** I-10, exit 158 (College Dr), just n to Corporate, then just e; in Citiplace Shopping Center. 2561 Citiplace Ct, Suite 500 70808. **Hours:** 11 am-2:30 & 5-9:30 pm, Fri-10 pm, Sat 11:30 am-10 pm, Sun 11:30 am-8:30 pm. Closed: 11/22, 12/25. **Reservations:** accepted. **Features:** The cozy cafe serves items such as kebabs, shawarma, falafel and lamb shank, which wash down nicely with the refreshing Lebanese iced tea. Next to a movie theater, the location is fitting for a casual day out. Casual dress; cocktails. **Parking:** on-site. **Cards:** AX, DC, DS, MC, VI.

(See map and index starting on p. 300)

BOUTIN'S-A CAJUN MUSIC & DINING EXPERIENCE **Lunch:** $7-$10 **Dinner:** $9-$17 **Phone:** 225/819-9862 (17)

AAA Cajun

Location: I-10, exit 162, 1.5 mi s. 8322 Bluebonnet Blvd 70810. **Hours:** 11 am-2 & 5-10 pm, Sat 11 am-10 pm, Sun 11 am-9 pm. Closed: 11/22, 12/25 & Easter. **Reservations:** accepted. **Features:** With its laid-back atmosphere, the restaurant is a family favorite for authentic Cajun preparations of seafood, steak and chicken. For a true taste of Louisiana, try fried alligator served with jambalaya. For dessert, opt for homemade bread pudding. Casual dress; cocktails; entertainment. **Parking:** on-site. **Cards:** AX, DS, MC, VI.

CAPITAL CITY GRILL **Lunch:** $6-$15 **Dinner:** $11-$19 **Phone:** 225/291-2233 (8)

Regional American

Location: I-12, exit 4 (Sherwood Forest Blvd), 1 mi s. 3535 S Sherwood Forest Blvd 70816. **Hours:** 11 am-10 pm, Sun-9 pm. Closed: 11/22, 12/25. **Reservations:** accepted. **Features:** Excellent Creole and Cajun dishes are served in a lively atmosphere. The menu offers seafood, chicken, steak and some pasta selections brought to diners' tables in ample portions by efficient servers. A nice choice is coconut beer-battered shrimp. Casual dress; cocktails. **Parking:** on-site. **Cards:** AX, DC, DS, MC, VI.

COPELAND'S OF NEW ORLEANS **Lunch:** $5-$10 **Dinner:** $10-$20 **Phone:** 225/769-1800 (13)

Regional American

Location: I-10, exit 160 (Essen Ln), 0.5 mi w. 4957 Essen Ln 70809. **Hours:** 10 am-10 pm, Fri & Sat-11 pm. Closed: 12/25. **Reservations:** accepted. **Features:** The New Orleans neighborhood restaurant serves Louisiana Cajun cuisine in a lively Mardi Gras atmosphere. Meats, fish and chicken are grilled over cured hickory wood. Complementing menu offerings are made-from-scratch biscuits, tempting homemade ice cream, fresh vegetables and sauces made from drippings. Efficient servers deliver hearty helpings of regional food, such as grilled chicken breasts with fried sweet potatoes, fried oysters, barbecue shrimp and grilled and Cajun seafood. Casual dress; cocktails. **Parking:** on-site. **Cards:** AX, DC, DS, MC, VI.

DA JO NELL'S **Lunch:** $7-$27 **Dinner:** $17-$36 **Phone:** 225/924-7537 (2)

Steak & Seafood

Location: I-10, exit 158, 1.5 mi ne to Jefferson Hwy, then 1 mi s. 7327 Jefferson Hwy 70806. **Hours:** 11:30 am-2 & 5-10 pm, Sat from 5 pm, Sun 11 am-2 pm, Mon 11:30 am-2 pm. Closed: 1/1, 7/4, 12/25. **Reservations:** suggested. **Features:** Appointed in understatedly elegant decor, the small dining room sustains a quaint, romantic atmosphere. Freshly prepared entrees—such as steak Dauphine, oysters Bienville and roast rack of lamb—are served by the attentive, semi-formal wait staff. A good wine selection is offered. Casual dress; cocktails. **Parking:** on-site. **Cards:** AX, DS, MC, VI.

FOX AND HOUND PUB & GRILLE **Lunch:** $6-$18 **Dinner:** $6-$18 **Phone:** 225/926-1444

American

Location: I-10, exit 158, just n on College Dr, then just se. 5246 Corporate Rd 70808. **Hours:** 11 am-2 am. Closed: 12/25. **Features:** Casual dress; cocktails. **Parking:** on-site. **Cards:** AX, DS, MC, VI.

FRENCH MARKET BISTRO **Lunch:** $7-$17 **Dinner:** $10-$22 **Phone:** 225/753-3500 (18)

American

Location: I-10, exit 166, 0.9 mi sw; in Highland Place Shopping Center. 16645 Highland Rd 70810. **Hours:** 11:30 am-2 & 5:30-9 pm, Fri & Sat-10 pm, Mon-2 pm. Closed: 11/22, 12/25; also Sun. **Reservations:** accepted. **Features:** For dining in casual sophistication, the bistro is a fitting choice. Wood beams, brick walls and cozy dining rooms provide the perfect backdrop. Among delicious menu offerings are cedar-roasted salmon, lobster cannelloni, raspberry tuna and veal piccata. A bonus for out-of-towners is the opportunity to take in ever-changing displays of works by Louisiana artists. Casual dress; cocktails. **Parking:** on-site. **Cards:** AX, DC, DS, MC, VI.

LA MADELEINE FRENCH BAKERY & CAFE **Lunch:** $7-$13 **Dinner:** $7-$13 **Phone:** 225/767-7571

French

Location: Jct Bluebonnet and I-10; in Mall of Louisiana. 6401 Bluebonnet Blvd, Suite 1164 70836. **Hours:** 9 am-9 pm, Sun 11:30 am-6 pm. Closed: 11/22, 12/25 & Easter. **Features:** Casual dress; beer & wine only. **Parking:** on-site. **Cards:** AX, DS, MC, VI.

LA MADELEINE FRENCH BAKERY & CAFE **Lunch:** $7-$13 **Dinner:** $7-$13 **Phone:** 225/927-6072

French

Location: Jct Old Hammond and Jefferson hwys, just s. 7615 Jefferson Hwy 70809. **Hours:** 7 am-10 pm. Closed: 12/25. **Features:** Casual dress; beer & wine only. **Parking:** on-site. **Cards:** AX, DS, MC, VI.

LAS PALMAS **Lunch:** $6-$10 **Dinner:** $7-$15 **Phone:** 225/751-4330 (1)

Tex-Mex

Location: I-12, exit 7, just sw. 16060 Hattaras Ave 70816. **Hours:** 11 am-9:30 pm, Fri & Sat-10:30 pm. Closed: 11/22, 12/25. **Features:** Patrons can savor predictable but tasty Tex-Mex fare in a dining area marked by quaint mural-covered walls and a lively mood. The family restaurant offers discounts on children's meals on Tuesday nights. Casual dress; cocktails. **Parking:** on-site. **Cards:** AX, DS, MC, VI.

MAISON LACOUR **Lunch:** $9-$19 **Dinner:** $18-$35 **Phone:** 225/275-3755 (3)

AAA French

Location: I-12, exit 4 (Sherwood Forest Blvd), just w, just n to Harrells Ferry Rd, then 0.3 mi w. 11025 N Harrells Ferry Rd 70816. **Hours:** 11:30 am-2 & 5:30-8 pm, Fri & Sat-8:30 pm. Closed major holidays; also 12/26, 12/27, 1/2, 1/3 & Sun. **Reservations:** suggested. **Features:** Nestled in a cottage built in 1927, the French restaurant boasts five intimate dining rooms. Specialties, menu offers a wide range of seafood, veal, lamb, beef and game. Served in a comfortable French style. Light lunches and desserts also are available. Dressy casual; cocktails. **Parking:** on-site. **Cards:** AX, DS, MC, VI.

(See map and index starting on p. 300)

MARINA'S MEXICAN RESTAURANT **Lunch:** $7-$13 **Dinner:** $7-$13 **Phone:** 225/925-5005 (9)

Mexican

Location: I-10, exit 158, just s to Bennington St, then just e. 4608 A Bennington St 70808. **Hours:** 11 am-3 & 5-9:30 pm, Thurs-Sat to 10 pm. Closed major holidays; also Sun. **Reservations:** accepted. **Features:** In a small brick building set back off a busy road, the restaurant is owned by Marina, who prides herself on preparing everything by hand. On the menu are the usual suspects. Guests can count on friendly service. Casual dress; beer & wine only. **Parking:** on-site. **Cards:** AX, DC, DS, MC, VI.

MCALISTERS DELI **Lunch:** $5-$7 **Dinner:** $5-$7 **Phone:** 225/291-0122

Deli/Subs Sandwiches

Location: I-10, exit 163 (Siegen Ln), just n. 6808 Siegen Ln 70810. **Hours:** 10:30 am-10 pm. Closed major holidays. **Features:** The delicatessen might be called a crowd pleaser because it offers something for everyone. The extensive menu lists hot and cold sandwiches, salads, stuffed baked potatoes, soups and a kid-friendly selections. The staff will customize sandwiches for picky eaters. Try the signature club sandwich with the delicious sweet tea. Casual dress. **Parking:** on-site. **Cards:** AX, DS, MC, VI.

MESTIZO **Lunch:** $5-$8 **Dinner:** $6-$10 **Phone:** 225/293-6394 (12)

Mexican

Location: I-12, exit 4 (Sherwood Forest Blvd), 1.8 mi s. 4850 S Sherwood Forest Blvd 70816. **Hours:** 11 am-2 & 5-9 pm, Fri-10 pm, Sat 5 pm-10 pm. Closed major holidays; also Sun. **Reservations:** accepted. **Features:** This small restaurant offers an eclectic mix of south-of-the-border and Louisiana fare. Casual dress; cocktails. **Parking:** on-site. **Cards:** AX, MC, VI.

MIKE ANDERSONS SEAFOOD **Lunch:** $10-$20 **Dinner:** $10-$25 **Phone:** 225/766-7823 (16)

Seafood

Location: I-10, exit 158, 3 mi s; between Nicholson Dr and Highland Rd. 1031 W Lee Dr 70820. **Hours:** 11 am-2 & 5-9:30 pm, Fri & Sat 11 am-10:30 pm, Sun 11 am-9 pm. **Features:** Casual and family-friendly, the restaurant specializes in the flavorful cuisine of southern Louisiana. The house specialty is guitreau, a grilled fish fillet topped with crawfish, shrimp and mushrooms in a lightly seasoned, white wine butter sauce. Casual dress; cocktails. **Parking:** on-site. **Cards:** AX, DC, DS, MC, VI.

RALPH & KACOO'S **Lunch:** $7-$12 **Dinner:** $14-$25 **Phone:** 225/766-2113 (15)

Seafood

Location: I-10, exit 162, 0.3 mi s. 6110 Bluebonnet Blvd 70809. **Hours:** 11 am-9:30 pm, Fri & Sat-10:30 pm. Closed: 12/25. **Features:** The cuisine consists primarily of seafood with an emphasis on regional American, Cajun dishes. Some of the tasty selections include gumbo, bacon-wrapped shrimp stuffed with crab and bread pudding. Private dining rooms and a cigar bar are available. Casual dress; cocktails. **Parking:** on-site. **Cards:** AX, DC, DS, MC, VI.

RUTH'S CHRIS STEAK HOUSE **Lunch:** $10-$28 **Dinner:** $17-$37 **Phone:** 225/925-0163 (7)

Steak House

Location: I-10, exit 158, just e on E Frontage Rd. 4836 Constitution Ave 70808. **Hours:** 11:30 am-11:30 pm, Sat 4 pm-midnight. Closed: 1/1, 11/22; also Sun. **Reservations:** accepted. **Features:** Steaks are king at this popular restaurant, but don't overlook the pork, veal, or lamb chops as well as other delicious selections. Remember to save room for the homemade desserts. Casual dress; cocktails. **Parking:** on-site. **Cards:** AX, MC, VI.

SERRANO'S SALSA COMPANY **Lunch:** $6-$9 **Dinner:** $8-$22 **Phone:** 225/344-2354 (10)

Latino

Location: I-10, exit 156B (Dalrymple Dr), 1.2 mi sw, then just n. 3347 Highland Rd 70802. **Hours:** 11 am-11 pm, Sun-Tues to 10 pm. Closed major holidays. **Features:** At the front gates of Louisiana State University, the eatery features a mix of Latin American and Mexican plates. Offerings include empanadas, fajitas and Cuban steak. Its proximity to the campus makes this place a popular hangout for students and the young at heart. Casual dress; cocktails. **Parking:** on-site. **Cards:** AX, DS, MC, VI.

SULLIVAN'S STEAKHOUSE **Lunch:** $9-$24 **Dinner:** $18-$29 **Phone:** 225/925-1161 (5)

Steak House

Location: I-10, exit 158, just n on College Dr, then just se. 5252 Corporate Blvd 70808. **Hours:** 11 am-2 & 5:30-11 pm, Sat from 5:30 pm, Sun 5 pm-10 pm. Closed: 11/22, 12/25. **Reservations:** suggested. **Features:** The 1940's style steakhouse features an upscale dining room with luxurious mahogany paneling throughout and a boxing motif bolstered with period photos. White linen table covers accent the formal look. Fine beef is served here, as well as specialty seafood; a great martini selection is also offered. Dressy casual; cocktails. **Parking:** on-site. **Cards:** AX, MC, VI.

TAQUERIA EL SOL DE GUERRERO **Lunch:** $3-$12 **Dinner:** $3-$12 **Phone:** 225/293-0879 (14)

Mexican

Location: I-10, exit 163 (Siegen Ln), 0.7 mi n. 6031 Siegen Ln 70809. **Hours:** 8:30 am-9 pm, Sun-6 pm. Closed major holidays. **Features:** Born from a small Mexican grocery store, the restaurant makes no attempt to Americanize anything. A few TVs populate the otherwise sparsely decorated space, and Mexican music plays in the background. Casual dress. **Parking:** on-site. **Cards:** MC, VI.

THAI KITCHEN **Lunch:** $6-$12 **Dinner:** $8-$14 **Phone:** 225/346-1230 (11)

Thai

Location: I-10, exit 158 (College Dr), just s, then just w; in Southdowns Shopping Center. 4335 Perkins Rd 70808. **Hours:** 11 am-2 & 5-9:30 pm, Fri-10:30 pm, Sat 5 pm-10:30 pm. Closed major holidays; also Sun. **Reservations:** accepted. **Features:** A favorite among nearby Louisiana State University students, the family-run restaurant serves traditional cuisine in a casual environment. The kitchen prides itself on using the freshest ingredients, and all items are made when ordered. The lunch buffet is popular with the locals. Casual dress; cocktails. **Parking:** on-site. **Cards:** AX, DS, MC, VI.

(See map and index starting on p. 300)

T J RIBS Lunch: $6-$19 Dinner: $6-$19 **Phone:** 225/383-7427 (4)

American

Location: I-10, exit 157B. 2324 S Acadian Thruway 70808. **Hours:** 11 am-11 pm, Sun-10 pm. Closed: 11/22, 12/25. **Reservations:** accepted. **Features:** Close to the Louisiana State University campus, the restaurant projects a casual sports bar atmosphere and displays an extensive collection of Lousiana State University memorabilia, including items related to 1959 Heisman trophy winner Billy Cannon. The house specialty on a menu of savory barbecue choices is baby back ribs. Selections are served in large portions. Casual dress; cocktails. **Parking:** on-site. **Cards:** AX, DS, MC, VI.

BOSSIER CITY pop. 56,461 (See map and index starting on p. 420)—*See also SHREVEPORT.*

WHERE TO STAY

BEST WESTERN-AIRLINE MOTOR INN *Book great rates at AAA.com* **Phone:** (318)742-6000 15

Small-scale Hotel

All Year	1P: $75-$125	2P: $75-$125	XP: $10	F12

Location: I-20, exit 22 (Airline Dr), just n. 1984 Airline Dr 71112 (PO Box 72549, 71172). Fax: 318/742-4615. **Facility:** 120 one-bedroom standard units. 2 stories (no elevator), exterior corridors. **Parking:** on-site. **Terms:** [CP] meal plan available, package plans, small pets only ($10 extra charge). **Amenities:** high-speed Internet, voice mail, irons, hair dryers. **Pool(s):** small outdoor. **Guest Services:** valet laundry, area transportation. **Cards:** AX, DC, DS, MC, VI.

SOME UNITS

FEE

COMFORT INN *Book great rates at AAA.com* **Phone:** 318/221-2400 22

Small-scale Hotel

Property failed to provide current rates

Location: I-20, exit 20A (Hamilton Rd), just n, then just w. Located in a commercial area. 1100 Delhi St 71111. Fax: 318/221-2909. **Facility:** 77 one-bedroom standard units, some with whirlpools. 2 stories (no elevator), exterior corridors. *Bath:* combo or shower only. **Parking:** on-site. **Amenities:** high-speed Internet, irons, hair dryers. **Pool(s):** outdoor. **Business Services:** PC.

SOME UNITS

CROSSLAND STUDIOS SHREVEPORT-BOSSIER CITY *Book at AAA.com* **Phone:** 318/747-5800 14

Small-scale Hotel

Property failed to provide current rates

Location: I-20, exit 22, just s. 3070 E Texas St 71111. Fax: 318/747-5805. **Facility:** 117 one-bedroom standard units with efficiencies. 3 stories, exterior corridors. *Bath:* combo or shower only. **Parking:** on-site. **Terms:** office hours 7 am-11 pm, pets ($75 fee). **Amenities:** high-speed Internet (fee), voice mail. **Guest Services:** coin laundry.

FEE

ECONO LODGE INN & SUITES *Book great rates at AAA.com* **Phone:** (318)746-5050 13

Small-scale Hotel

All Year	1P: $49-$79	2P: $49-$79	XP: $5	F18

Location: I-20, exit 23 (Industrial Dr). Located in a commercial area. 4300 Industrial Dr 71112. Fax: 318/742-6154. **Facility:** 165 one-bedroom standard units, some with efficiencies (no utensils). 2 stories (no elevator), exterior corridors. **Parking:** on-site. **Terms:** [CP] meal plan available. **Amenities:** video games (fee), irons, hair dryers. **Pool(s):** outdoor, wading. **Leisure Activities:** whirlpools. **Guest Services:** valet and coin laundry. **Cards:** AX, CB, DC, DS, MC, VI.

SOME UNITS

HAMPTON INN *Book great rates at AAA.com* **Phone:** 318/752-1112 18

Small-scale Hotel

Property failed to provide current rates

Location: I-20, exit 21, 0.5 mi ne on service road. 1005 Gould Dr 71111. Fax: 318/752-1405. **Facility:** 123 one-bedroom standard units. 4 stories, interior corridors. *Bath:* combo or shower only. **Parking:** on-site. **Terms:** small pets only. **Amenities:** video games (fee), high-speed Internet, voice mail, irons, hair dryers. **Pool(s):** outdoor. **Leisure Activities:** exercise room. **Guest Services:** complimentary evening beverages: Tues-Thurs, valet laundry. **Business Services:** meeting rooms, PC.

SOME UNITS

HOLIDAY INN BOSSIER *Book at AAA.com* **Phone:** (318)742-9700 19

Small-scale Hotel

All Year	1P: $89-$99

Location: I-20, exit 21, just n. 2015 Old Minden Rd 71111. Fax: 318/747-4651. **Facility:** 212 units. 210 one-bedroom standard units. 2 one-bedroom suites ($150-$175). 2 stories, exterior corridors. *Bath:* combo or shower only. **Parking:** on-site. **Terms:** [AP] & [BP] meal plans available. **Amenities:** video games (fee), high-speed Internet, voice mail, irons, hair dryers. **Pool(s):** outdoor. **Leisure Activities:** saunas, whirlpool, exercise room, volleyball. **Guest Services:** gift shop, valet laundry, area transportation. **Business Services:** conference facilities. **Cards:** AX, CB, DC, DS, JC, MC, VI.

SOME UNITS

LA QUINTA INN BOSSIER CITY *Book great rates at AAA.com* **Phone:** (318)747-4400 21

Small-scale Hotel

5/27-9/6 [ECP]	1P: $78-$99	2P: $88-$109	XP: $10	F18
9/7-11/30 [ECP]	1P: $78-$88	2P: $88-$98	XP: $10	F18
12/1-5/26 [ECP]	1P: $72-$82	2P: $82-$92	XP: $10	F18

Location: I-20, exit 21, just n. 309 Preston Blvd 71111-4969. Fax: 318/747-1516. **Facility:** 130 one-bedroom standard units. 2 stories (no elevator), exterior corridors. **Parking:** on-site. **Terms:** small pets only. **Amenities:** video games (fee), high-speed Internet, voice mail, irons, hair dryers. **Pool(s):** outdoor. **Guest Services:** valet and coin laundry. **Cards:** AX, CB, DC, DS, MC, VI. ***(See color ad p 386)***

SOME UNITS

(See map and index starting on p. 420)

MICROTEL INN & SUITES Book at AAA.com Phone: (318)742-7882 17

Small-scale Hotel

All Year [ECP] 1P: $50-$70 2P: $59-$79 XP: $5 F16

Location: I-20, exit 22 (Airline Dr), just s, then just w. 2713 Village Ln 71112. Fax: 318/213-6316. **Facility:** 101 one-bedroom standard units. 4 stories, interior corridors. *Bath:* combo or shower only. **Parking:** on-site. **Terms:** small pets only ($25 fee). **Amenities:** high-speed Internet, voice mail, hair dryers. **Guest Services:** coin laundry. **Cards:** AX, CB, DC, DS, JC, MC, VI.

SOME UNITS

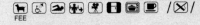

FEE

QUALITY INN & SUITES Book great rates at AAA.com Phone: (318)742-7890 16

Small-scale Hotel

All Year [ECP] 1P: $70-$80 2P: $79-$89 XP: $5 F16

Location: I-20, exit 22 (Airline Dr), just s, then just w. 2717 Village Ln 71112. Fax: 318/742-7891. **Facility:** 103 units. 99 one-bedroom standard units. 4 one-bedroom suites. 4 stories, interior corridors. *Bath:* combo or shower only. **Parking:** on-site. **Terms:** pets ($25 fee). **Amenities:** high-speed Internet, voice mail, irons, hair dryers. **Pool(s):** small outdoor. **Leisure Activities:** exercise room. **Guest Services:** complimentary evening beverages: Mon-Thurs, valet and coin laundry. **Business Services:** PC. **Cards:** AX, CB, DC, DS, JC, MC, VI.

SOME UNITS

FEE

RESIDENCE INN BY MARRIOTT-SHREVEPORT/BOSSIER CITY Book great rates at AAA.com Phone: 318/747-6220 20

Small-scale Hotel

All Year 1P: $129-$230 2P: $129-$230

Location: I-20, exit 21, just ne. 1001 Gould Dr 71111. Fax: 318/747-3424. **Facility:** 72 units. 54 one-bedroom standard units with kitchens. 18 two-bedroom suites ($129-$230) with kitchens. 2 stories (no elevator), exterior corridors. *Bath:* combo or shower only. **Parking:** on-site. **Terms:** cancellation fee imposed, pets ($75 extra charge). **Amenities:** high-speed Internet, voice mail, irons, hair dryers. **Pool(s):** outdoor. **Leisure Activities:** whirlpool, sports court. **Guest Services:** sundries, complimentary evening beverages: Mon-Thurs, valet and coin laundry. **Business Services:** meeting rooms, PC. **Cards:** AX, CB, DC, DS, JC, MC, VI. **Free Special Amenities: high-speed Internet.**

SOME UNITS

FEE

WHERE TO DINE

BARNHILL'S BUFFET **Lunch:** $5-$9 **Dinner:** $7-$10 **Phone:** 318/742-2552

American

Location: I-20, exit 23, 0.5 mi n, then just e on US 79. 4630 E Texas St 71111. **Hours:** 10:45 am-8:45 pm, Fri-9 pm, Sat 7 am-9 pm, Sun 7 am-8:45 pm. Closed: 12/25. **Features:** Casual dress. **Parking:** on-site. **Cards:** AX, DS, MC, VI.

FIRE MOUNTAIN GRILL **Lunch:** $8 **Dinner:** $12 **Phone:** 318/549-2133

American

Location: I-20, exit 22 (Airline Dr), 1.6 mi s. 2400 Airline Dr 71111. **Hours:** 10:45 am-9:30 pm, Fri & Sat-10 pm. Closed: 12/24, 12/25. **Features:** The mega buffett also offers cooking stations where freshly prepared steaks, chicken, fish, pizzas and more are served. Casual dress. **Parking:** on-site. **Cards:** AX, CB, DC, DS, JC, MC, VI.

JACK BINION'S STEAK HOUSE **Dinner:** $24-$54 **Phone:** 318/742-0711 20

Steak House

Location: I-20, exit 19B (Traffic St), just n. 711 Horseshoe Blvd 71111. **Hours:** 5:30 pm-10:30 pm, Fri & Sat-11:30 pm. **Reservations:** accepted. **Features:** Inside the Horseshoe Casino is this upscale steakhouse, which features a wall of windows that offers a great view of the city's evening lights. As the name suggests, steaks are the main attraction here, but many seafood choices are also available. Casual dress; cocktails. **Parking:** valet. **Cards:** AX, DS, MC, VI.

POSADO'S CAFE **Lunch:** $6-$9 **Dinner:** $9-$18 **Phone:** 318/747-6200 18

Mexican

Location: I-20, exit 20B (Benton Rd/SR 3) eastbound; exit 21 (Old Minden Rd) westbound; at the northwest corner of Benton and Old Minden rds. 1703 Old Minden Rd 71111. **Hours:** 11 am-10 pm, Fri & Sat-11 pm. Closed major holidays. **Features:** This restaurant offers authentic Tex-Mex cuisine, such as beef and chicken combination fajitas with tortilla soup and pico de gallo. The service is prompt and friendly, which seems to be the standard at Posado's: good food and good service, Tex-Mex style. Casual dress; cocktails. **Parking:** on-site. **Cards:** AX, DS, MC, VI.

RALPH & KACOO'S **Lunch:** $7-$11 **Dinner:** $13-$22 **Phone:** 318/747-6660 19

Seafood

Location: I-20, exit 20B (Benton Rd/SR 3) eastbound; exit 21 (Old Minden Rd) westbound, just w. 1700 Old Minden Rd 71111. **Hours:** 11 am-9 pm, Fri & Sat-10:30 pm. Closed major holidays. **Features:** Here the emphasis is on regional seafood dishes such as mesquite grilled catfish with cajun stuffed potato, coleslaw and hushpuppies. Also of note is a jazz brunch on Sunday, a small banquet room for private parties, and a gift shop perfect for browsing. Cocktails. **Parking:** on-site. **Cards:** AX, DC, DS, MC, VI.

BOYCE pop. 1,190

WHERE TO DINE

TUNK'S CYPRESS INN **Dinner:** $10-$32 **Phone:** 318/487-4014

Swiss

Location: 5 mi e of jct SR 121. 9507 Hwy 28 W 71409. **Hours:** 5 pm-10 pm. Closed major holidays; also Sun & Mon. **Features:** Set on the shores of rustic Kincaid Lake, this family dining establishment offers seafood, fresh water fish and Louisiana specialties. Try the Snapper Sandy — two snapper fillets topped with a rich cream sauce. An oyster bar is also featured. Casual dress; cocktails; entertainment. **Parking:** on-site. **Cards:** AX, CB, DC, DS, MC, VI.

BREAUX BRIDGE pop. 7,281

WHERE TO STAY

HOLIDAY INN EXPRESS OF BREAUX BRIDGE *Book at AAA.com* **Phone:** 337/667-8913

Small-scale Hotel

All Year 1P: $73 2P: $73 XP: $10 F18

Location: I-10, exit 115, just n. 2942 H Grand Point Hwy 70517. Fax: 337/667-8914. **Facility:** 58 one-bedroom standard units. 2 stories, interior corridors. *Bath:* combo or shower only. **Parking:** on-site. **Terms:** cancellation fee imposed, [ECP] meal plan available. **Amenities:** dual phone lines, voice mail, irons, hair dryers. **Pool(s):** heated outdoor. **Leisure Activities:** whirlpool. **Guest Services:** valet laundry, wireless Internet. **Business Services:** business center. **Cards:** AX, CB, DC, DS, MC, VI.

SOME UNITS

ASK / FEE /

MAISON DES AMIS **Phone:** (337)507-3399

AAA SAVE

Bed & Breakfast

All Year [BP] 1P: $90-$125 2P: $100-$125 XP: $25

Location: I-10, exit 109, 0.8 mi s, then just w. 111 Washington St 70517. **Facility:** 4 one-bedroom standard units. 1 story, exterior corridors. **Parking:** on-site. **Terms:** age restrictions may apply, 14 day cancellation notice-fee imposed, package plans. **Amenities:** hair dryers. **Guest Services:** complimentary laundry. **Cards:** AX, DS, MC, VI.

WHERE TO DINE

CAFE DES AMIS **Lunch:** $10-$20 **Dinner:** $15-$26 **Phone:** 337/332-5273

Cajun

Location: I-10, exit 109, 0.8 mi s, then just w. 140 E Bridge St 70517. **Hours:** 9 am-9 pm, Fri & Sat 7:30 am-9:30 pm, Sun 8 am-2:30 pm. Closed: 1/1, 7/4, 12/25; also Mon, Tues & Mardi Gras. **Reservations:** suggested. **Features:** In a converted general store in the epicenter of Cajun country, the cafe has been singled out by numerous publications. The menu centers on solid Cajun food, with selections such as gumbo, barbecue shrimp and crawfish pie. Loyalists rave about the popular Saturday zydeco breakfast, featuring live music, from 8:30 to 11:30 a.m. Casual dress; cocktails. **Parking:** street. **Cards:** AX, DS, MC, VI.

MULATE'S **Lunch:** $7-$18 **Dinner:** $7-$18 **Phone:** 337/332-4648

Regional Cajun

Location: I-10, exit 109 (Breaux Bridge), 1.8 mi se. 325 Mills Ave 70517. **Hours:** 11 am-10 pm. Closed: 11/22, 12/25; also for dinner 12/24. **Features:** Since 1980, Mulate's has been dedicated to preserving Cajun heritage. The lively restaurant features original Cajun cooking accompanied by Cajun music. Suggestions for dining include zydeco salad, seafood gumbo, fried alligator, shrimp and oyster en brochette and bread pudding. Service is casual and friendly. Casual dress; cocktails; entertainment. **Parking:** on-site. **Cards:** AX, DC, DS, MC, VI.

BURNSIDE

WHERE TO DINE

THE CABIN RESTAURANT *Menu on AAA.com* **Lunch:** $7-$25 **Dinner:** $7-$25 **Phone:** 225/473-3007

AAA

Cajun

Location: I-10, exit 182 (SR 44) westbound, 3.5 mi w; exit 179 (SR 22) eastbound, 3 mi w of jct SR 44 and 22. 5405 Hwy 44 70737. **Hours:** 11 am-9 pm, Fri & Sat-10 pm, Sun-6 pm, Mon-3 pm. Closed: 1/1, 11/22, 12/25. **Reservations:** accepted. **Features:** Although a little off the beaten path, the distinctive restaurant—built from slave cabins taken from nearby plantations—is worth the short drive from I-10. The menu focuses on Cajun and Creole cuisine, including such selections as blackened redfish with red beans and rice, preceded by delicious sweet cornbread. Casual dress; cocktails. **Parking:** on-site. **Cards:** AX, DS, MC, VI.

CHARENTON pop. 1,944

WHERE TO DINE

MR. LESTER'S STEAKHOUSE **Dinner:** $22-$44 **Phone:** 337/923-7408

Steak & Seafood

Location: US 90, exit SR 83, 1.4 mi e to SR 182, 0.6 mi n, then 2 mi e on Ralph Darden Memorial Pkwy, follow signs. 832 Martin Luther King Rd 70523. **Hours:** 6 pm-11 pm, Fri & Sat-11:30 pm. Closed: 11/22, 12/24, 12/25; also Mon & Tues. **Reservations:** suggested. **Features:** Located within Cypress Bayou Casino, Mr. Lester's serves an American menu featuring steak, seafood, homemade dessert and pastry in a quiet, relaxing atmosphere. The lemon tart pie is a good choice for dessert. An elegant cigar lounge is also available. Dressy casual; cocktails. **Parking:** valet. **Cards:** AX, DC, DS, MC, VI.

CONVENT

WHERE TO STAY

POCHE PLANTATION BED & BREAKFAST AND RV RESORT **Phone:** (225)562-7728

Bed & Breakfast

All Year [CP] 1P: $49-$149 2P: $59-$149 XP: $10 D15

Location: Jct SR 44 and 641; 10.1 mi s of Sunshine Bridge (SR 70), then 10.2 mi n. 6554 Louisiana Hwy 44 70723 (PO Box 201). Fax: 225/562-0550. **Facility:** Located on the Mississippi River and listed on the National Register of Historic Places. The "cottages" are built utilizing modern materials built to resemble the rest of the plantation buildings. Smoke free premises. 7 units. 6 one-bedroom standard units. 1 one-bedroom suite ($69-$89) with kitchen. 2 stories, interior/exterior corridors. **Parking:** on-site. **Terms:** 30 day cancellation notice-fee imposed, weekly rates available, [AP] & [BP] meal plans available, package plans. **Amenities:** *Some:* high-speed Internet. **Pool(s):** small heated outdoor. **Guest Services:** coin laundry. **Cards:** AX, DS, MC, VI.

ASK

COVINGTON —*See New Orleans p. 402.*

CROWLEY pop. 14,225

WHERE TO STAY

DAYS INN Book great rates at AAA.com Phone: 337/783-2378

Small-scale Hotel

Property failed to provide current rates

Location: I-10, exit 80. 9571 Egan Hwy 70526. Fax: 337/783-2378. **Facility:** 46 one-bedroom standard units. 2 stories (no elevator), exterior corridors. **Parking:** on-site. **Terms:** pets ($10 extra charge). **Amenities:** irons, hair dryers. **Pool(s):** outdoor. **Business Services:** fax (fee).

SOME UNITS

FEE

DENHAM SPRINGS pop. 8,757

WHERE TO STAY

BEST WESTERN DENHAM SPRINGS INN Book great rates at AAA.com Phone: 225/665-0222

SAVE

Motel

All Year 1P: $72 2P: $81-$85 XP: $10 F12

Location: I-12, exit 10, just n on SR 3002, then just w on SR 3003. 146 Rushing Rd 70726. Fax: 225/665-0274. **Facility:** 56 one-bedroom standard units. 2 stories (no elevator), exterior corridors. *Bath:* combo or shower only. **Parking:** on-site. **Amenities:** irons, hair dryers. **Pool(s):** outdoor. **Guest Services:** wireless Internet. **Business Services:** fax (fee). **Cards:** AX, CB, DC, DS, MC, VI. **Free Special Amenities: continental breakfast and local telephone calls.**

SOME UNITS

DERIDDER pop. 9,808

WHERE TO STAY

STAGECOACH INN Phone: 337/462-0022

SAVE

Small-scale Hotel

All Year 1P: $69 2P: $79 XP: $10 F18

Location: 2 mi on east side; between US 171. Located next to busy highway. 505 E 1st St 70634. Fax: 337/462-2104. **Facility:** 50 one-bedroom standard units. 2 stories (no elevator), exterior corridors. **Parking:** on-site. **Terms:** package plans, small pets only ($25 extra charge). **Amenities:** high-speed Internet, irons, hair dryers. **Pool(s):** outdoor. **Leisure Activities:** whirlpool, barbecue pits. **Guest Services:** valet and coin laundry, wireless Internet. **Business Services:** meeting rooms, fax (fee). **Cards:** AX, CB, DC, DS, MC, VI. **Free Special Amenities: expanded continental breakfast and local telephone calls.**

SOME UNITS

FEE

DONALDSONVILLE pop. 7,605

WHERE TO STAY

BEST WESTERN PLANTATION INN Book great rates at AAA.com Phone: (225)746-9050

SAVE

Small-scale Hotel

All Year 1P: $94 2P: $99 XP: $5 F

Location: 0.8 mi w of Sunshine Bridge. 2179 Hwy 70 70346. Fax: 225/746-1304. **Facility:** 60 one-bedroom standard units, some with whirlpools. 2 stories, interior corridors. *Bath:* combo or shower only. **Parking:** on-site. **Amenities:** high-speed Internet, voice mail, irons, hair dryers. *Some:* dual phone lines. **Pool(s):** outdoor. **Guest Services:** coin laundry, wireless Internet. **Business Services:** PC. **Cards:** AX, CB, DC, DS, MC, VI.

SOME UNITS

DUSON pop. 1,672

WHERE TO STAY

SUPER 8 MOTEL Book great rates at AAA.com Phone: (337)873-8883

SAVE

Small-scale Hotel

All Year 1P: $49-$150 2P: $55-$150 XP: $7 F12

Location: I-10, exit 92, just s. 3001 Daulat Dr 70529. Fax: 337/873-8823. **Facility:** 54 one-bedroom standard units, some with whirlpools. 3 stories, interior corridors. *Bath:* combo or shower only. **Parking:** on-site. **Terms:** [ECP] meal plan available. **Amenities:** video library (fee), irons, hair dryers. *Some:* high-speed Internet. **Pool(s):** small outdoor. **Leisure Activities:** limited exercise equipment. **Guest Services:** complimentary evening beverages: Wed, coin laundry, wireless Internet. **Business Services:** meeting rooms, fax (fee). **Cards:** AX, CB, DC, DS, JC, MC, VI. **Free Special Amenities: expanded continental breakfast and high-speed Internet.**

SOME UNITS

VCR

FEE

EUNICE pop. 11,499

WHERE TO STAY

DAYS INN & SUITES Book great rates at AAA.com Phone: 337/457-3040

Small-scale Hotel

Property failed to provide current rates

Location: Just e of jct SR 13 and US 190. 1251 E Laurel Ave 70535. Fax: 337/457-3050. **Facility:** 41 one-bedroom standard units, some with whirlpools. 2 stories (no elevator), interior corridors. **Parking:** on-site. **Amenities:** high-speed Internet, irons, hair dryers. **Guest Services:** valet laundry, wireless Internet. **Business Services:** fax (fee).

SOME UNITS

FRANKLIN pop. 8,354

WHERE TO STAY

BEST WESTERN FOREST MOTOR INN *Book great rates at AAA.com* **Phone:** (337)828-1810

Small-scale Hotel

All Year 1P: $89-$99 2P: $99-$109 XP: $10 F12

Location: SR 182, 0.3 mi e of jct SR 182 and 3211. 1909 W Main St, Hwy 182 W 70538 (PO Box 1069). Fax: 337/828-1810. **Facility:** 89 units. 85 one-bedroom standard units, some with whirlpools. 4 one-bedroom suites, some with kitchens and/or whirlpools. 1-2 stories (no elevator), exterior corridors. **Parking:** on-site. **Amenities:** high-speed Internet, voice mail, irons, hair dryers. *Some:* dual phone lines. **Pool(s):** outdoor. **Guest Services:** valet and coin laundry. **Business Services:** meeting rooms, fax (fee). **Cards:** AX, CB, DC, DS, JC, MC, VI.

SOME UNITS

GALLIANO pop. 7,356

WHERE TO STAY

DAYS INN *Book great rates at AAA.com* **Phone:** 985/475-7007

Small-scale Hotel

Property failed to provide current rates

Location: 3.7 mi s of jct SR 3162. 18434 Hwy 3235 70354 (PO Box 967). Fax: 985/475-7895. **Facility:** 49 one-bedroom standard units. 2 stories (no elevator), interior corridors. **Parking:** on-site. **Amenities:** high-speed Internet, voice mail, irons, hair dryers. **Pool(s):** small outdoor, wading. **Guest Services:** valet laundry, wireless Internet. **Business Services:** fax (fee).

SOME UNITS

GONZALES pop. 8,156

WHERE TO STAY

BEST WESTERN INN OF GONZALES *Book great rates at AAA.com* **Phone:** 225/647-2001

Small-scale Hotel

All Year 1P: $86

Location: I-10, exit 177, just e. 1918 W Hwy 30 70737. Fax: 225/647-7604. **Facility:** 47 units. 46 one-bedroom standard units. 1 two-bedroom suite with efficiency. 2 stories (no elevator), exterior corridors. *Bath:* combo or shower only. **Parking:** on-site. **Amenities:** high-speed Internet, irons, hair dryers. **Pool(s):** outdoor. **Guest Services:** coin laundry. **Business Services:** fax (fee). **Cards:** AX, DC, DS, MC, VI.

SOME UNITS

HOLIDAY INN *Book great rates at AAA.com* **Phone:** 225/647-8000

AAA SAVE

Small-scale Hotel

All Year 1P: $86-$90

Location: I-10, exit 177, 0.3 mi e. 1500 Hwy 30 70737 (PO Box 1210). Fax: 225/647-7741. **Facility:** 170 units. 169 one-bedroom standard units, some with whirlpools. 1 one-bedroom suite. 2 stories (no elevator), exterior corridors. *Bath:* combo or shower only. **Parking:** on-site. **Terms:** 2% service charge. **Amenities:** high-speed Internet, voice mail, irons, hair dryers. **Dining:** 6 am-2 & 5-10 pm, Fri 6 am-10 pm, Sat 7 am-10 pm, Sun 7 am-9 pm, cocktails. **Pool(s):** outdoor. **Leisure Activities:** exercise room. **Guest Services:** valet and coin laundry. **Business Services:** meeting rooms, fax (fee). **Cards:** AX, CB, DC, DS, MC, VI. **Free Special Amenities: local telephone calls and newspaper.**

SOME UNITS

GRAND COTEAU pop. 1,040

WHERE TO DINE

CATAHOULA'S, A RESTAURANT **Lunch:** $9-$15 **Dinner:** $13-$32 **Phone:** 337/662-2275

Regional American

Location: I-49, exit 11 (SR 93), 0.7 mi e on SR 93; jct SR 760-1 and 93. 234 Martin Luther King Dr 70541. **Hours:** 5 pm-9 pm, Fri & Sat-10 pm, Fri & Sun also 11 am-2 pm. Closed major holidays; also Mon. **Reservations:** suggested. **Features:** Housed in a renovated general store, the stylish restaurant offers fine gourmet dining where it's least expected. Among specialties of New Louisiana cooking are such entrees as raspberry duckling, crabmeat cheesecake and pecan-crusted shrimp. This place ably mingles city fare with small-town hospitality. Casual dress; cocktails. **Parking:** on-site. **Cards:** AX, DS, MC, VI.

GRAY pop. 4,958

WHERE TO STAY

BEST WESTERN HOUMA INN *Book great rates at AAA.com* **Phone:** (985)580-4300

AAA SAVE

Small-scale Hotel

All Year 1P: $89-$99 2P: $89-$99 XP: $10 F13

Location: US 90, exit SR 24, just n. 117 Linda Ann Ave 70359. Fax: 985/853-2777. **Facility:** 62 one-bedroom standard units, some with whirlpools. 3 stories, interior corridors. *Bath:* combo or shower only. **Parking:** on-site. **Terms:** cancellation fee imposed. **Amenities:** high-speed Internet, voice mail, irons, hair dryers. **Pool(s):** outdoor. **Guest Services:** valet and coin laundry, wireless Internet. **Business Services:** meeting rooms, business center. **Cards:** AX, DC, DS, MC, VI. **Free Special Amenities: local telephone calls and high-speed Internet.**

SOME UNITS

GRETNA —*See New Orleans p. 403.*

HAMMOND pop. 17,639

WHERE TO STAY

BEST WESTERN HAMMOND INN & SUITES *Book great rates at AAA.com* **Phone:** (985)419-2001

AAA SAVE

Small-scale Hotel

All Year [CP] 1P: $75-$95 2P: $80-$100 XP: $5 F17

Location: I-12, exit 40 (US 51), just ne. 107 Duo Dr 70403. Fax: 985/419-8001. **Facility:** 63 one-bedroom standard units, some with whirlpools. 2 stories (no elevator), exterior corridors. *Bath:* combo or shower only. **Parking:** on-site. **Terms:** pets ($10 extra charge). **Amenities:** high-speed Internet, voice mail, irons, hair dryers. **Pool(s):** outdoor. **Guest Services:** coin laundry, wireless Internet. **Business Services:** meeting rooms, fax (fee). **Cards:** AX, CB, DC, DS, JC, MC, VI. **Free Special Amenities: continental breakfast and high-speed Internet.**

SOME UNITS

FEE

COMFORT INN *Book great rates at AAA.com* **Phone:** 985/429-0120

Small-scale Hotel

Property failed to provide current rates

Location: I-55, exit 31, just e, then just s. 110 Westin Oak Dr 70403. Fax: 985/429-0015. **Facility:** 53 one-bedroom standard units, some with whirlpools. 3 stories, interior corridors. *Bath:* combo or shower only. **Parking:** on-site. **Amenities:** high-speed Internet, irons, hair dryers. **Pool(s):** heated outdoor. **Leisure Activities:** whirlpool, exercise room. **Guest Services:** coin laundry. **Business Services:** meeting rooms.

SOME UNITS

DAYS INN *Book great rates at AAA.com* **Phone:** (985)419-1000

AAA SAVE

Small-scale Hotel

All Year 1P: $75-$90 2P: $75-$90 XP: $5 F12

Location: I-12, exit 40 (US 51), just sw. 2150 SW Railroad Ave 70403. Fax: 985/419-1009. **Facility:** 62 one-bedroom standard units. 2 stories (no elevator), exterior corridors. *Bath:* combo or shower only. **Parking:** on-site. **Terms:** 15 day cancellation notice, [CP] meal plan available. **Amenities:** hair dryers. **Pool(s):** outdoor. **Guest Services:** wireless Internet. **Business Services:** fax (fee). **Cards:** AX, CB, DC, DS, JC, MC, VI. **Free Special Amenities: continental breakfast and high-speed Internet.**

SOME UNITS

HAMPTON INN *Book great rates at AAA.com* **Phone:** (985)419-2188

Small-scale Hotel

All Year [ECP] 1P: $109-$139 2P: $109-$139

Location: I-55, exit 31, exit 32 northbound; exit 31 southbound, just e, then just s. 401 Westin Oak St 70403. Fax: 985/419-0881. **Facility:** 81 one-bedroom standard units, some with whirlpools. 3 stories, interior corridors. *Bath:* combo or shower only. **Parking:** on-site. **Amenities:** high-speed Internet, voice mail, irons, hair dryers. **Pool(s):** small outdoor. **Leisure Activities:** exercise room. **Guest Services:** coin laundry, wireless Internet. **Business Services:** meeting rooms, business center. **Cards:** AX, DS, MC, VI.

SOME UNITS

ASK

LANDMARK HOTEL & CONFERENCE CENTER **Phone:** 985/345-0556

AAA SAVE

Small-scale Hotel

All Year [BP] 1P: $89-$99 2P: $89-$99

Location: I-55, exit 28 (US 51), 0.5 mi nw. 2000 S Morrison Blvd 70403. Fax: 985/345-0557. **Facility:** 173 one-bedroom standard units. 2 stories (no elevator), interior/exterior corridors. *Bath:* combo or shower only. **Parking:** on-site. **Amenities:** high-speed Internet, voice mail, irons, hair dryers. **Dining:** 6 am-10 & 6-9 pm, cocktails. **Pool(s):** outdoor, heated indoor, wading. **Leisure Activities:** whirlpool, limited exercise equipment. **Guest Services:** valet and coin laundry, wireless Internet. **Business Services:** conference facilities, business center. **Cards:** AX, CB, DC, DS, MC, VI. **Free Special Amenities: full breakfast and high-speed Internet.**

SOME UNITS

MICHABELLE-A LITTLE INN **Phone:** (985)419-0550

AAA SAVE

Historic Country Inn

All Year 1P: $75-$100 2P: $75-$100

Location: I-12, exit 40 (US 51), 0.8 mi n, just e on Old Covington Hwy, then n, follow signs. 1106 S Holly St 70403. Fax: 985/542-1746. **Facility:** This Northshore property is a plantation home built in 1908 offering richly appointed rooms in a main house plus large, themed cottage accommodations. Smoke free premises. 7 one-bedroom standard units, some with whirlpools. 1-2 stories (no elevator), interior/exterior corridors. **Parking:** on-site. **Terms:** 5 day cancellation notice, [BP] meal plan available, package plans, small pets only. **Dining:** Michabelle, see separate listing. **Guest Services:** wireless Internet. **Business Services:** meeting rooms, fax. **Cards:** DC, DS, MC, VI. **Free Special Amenities: full breakfast and local telephone calls.**

SOME UNITS

WHERE TO DINE

MICHABELLE **Dinner:** $15-$20 **Phone:** 985/419-0550

Regional French

Location: I-12, exit 40 (US 51), 0.8 mi n, just e on Old Covington Hwy, then n, follow signs; in Michabelle-A Little Inn. 1106 S Holly St 70403. **Hours:** 6 pm-10 pm. Closed: Mon. **Reservations:** suggested. **Features:** Tucked away in a residential part of town, the renovated 1908 Greek revival house is now a cozy inn, tastefully decorated and offering elegant dining with a truly French flair. The celebrated chef, a maitre cuisine of France, makes the dining experience personal. Casual dress; cocktails. **Parking:** on-site. **Cards:** AX, CB, DC, DS, MC, VI. **Historic**

TOPE LA! **Lunch:** $7-$18 **Dinner:** $10-$26 **Phone:** 985/542-7600

Regional American

Location: I-12, exit 40 (US 51), 1.9 mi n, just e on W Morris, then just n. 104 N Cate St 70401. **Hours:** 11 am-10 pm, Fri & Sat-11 pm. Closed: 1/1, 11/22, 12/25. **Reservations:** accepted. **Features:** "Tope la" means the joining of hands, which the restaurant does in bringing together French and Louisiana cuisine. Patrons can savor filet mignon or pecan-crusted tilapia. The service is friendly, and rich woods and brass accents lend to a casually sophisticated atmosphere. Dressy casual; cocktails. **Parking:** street. **Cards:** AX, DC, DS, MC, VI.

HARAHAN —See New Orleans p. 403.

HARVEY —See New Orleans p. 404.

HOUMA pop. 32,393

WHERE TO STAY

FAIRFIELD INN BY MARRIOTT *Book great rates at AAA.com* **Phone:** (985)580-1050

Small-scale Hotel

All Year 1P: $79-$109 2P: $79-$109

Location: Just n of jct S Hollywood Rd and Martin Luther King Blvd. 1530 Martin Luther King Blvd 70360. Fax: 985/580-1050. **Facility:** 79 one-bedroom standard units. 3 stories, interior corridors. *Bath:* combo or shower only. **Parking:** on-site. **Amenities:** irons, hair dryers. **Pool(s):** small heated indoor. **Leisure Activities:** whirlpool, exercise room. **Guest Services:** valet laundry, wireless Internet. **Business Services:** fax (fee). **Cards:** AX, CB, DC, DS, JC, MC, VI.

SOME UNITS

QUALITY INN-HOUMA *Book great rates at AAA.com* **Phone:** 985/868-5851

Small-scale Hotel

All Year [CP] 1P: $85 2P: $85

Location: Just w of jct SR 3040 (Tunnel Blvd) and Hollywood Rd. 210 S Hollywood Rd 70360. Fax: 985/879-1953. **Facility:** 200 units. 197 one-bedroom standard units. 3 one-bedroom suites ($153-$250). 2 stories (no elevator), interior/exterior corridors. **Parking:** on-site. **Terms:** cancellation fee imposed, [AP], [BP] & [ECP] meal plans available. **Amenities:** video games (fee), high-speed Internet, dual phone lines, voice mail, irons, hair dryers. **Pool(s):** heated indoor. **Leisure Activities:** whirlpool, exercise room. *Fee:* game room. **Guest Services:** valet laundry, wireless Internet. **Business Services:** meeting rooms, business center. **Cards:** AX, CB, DC, DS, JC, MC, VI.

SOME UNITS

RAMADA INN *Book at AAA.com* **Phone:** (985)879-4871

Small-scale Hotel

All Year 1P: $90-$129 2P: $90-$129 XP: $5 F18

Location: Just s of jct SR 3040 (Tunnel Blvd) and Hollywood Rd. 1400 W Tunnel Blvd 70360. Fax: 985/868-3607. **Facility:** 153 units. 150 one-bedroom standard units. 3 one-bedroom suites ($125-$225). 2 stories (no elevator), exterior corridors. **Parking:** on-site. **Terms:** 3 day cancellation notice-fee imposed. **Amenities:** high-speed Internet, voice mail, irons, hair dryers. **Pool(s):** outdoor. **Leisure Activities:** whirlpool. **Guest Services:** valet and coin laundry, wireless Internet. **Business Services:** meeting rooms, business center. **Cards:** AX, DC, DS, MC, VI.

SOME UNITS

WHERE TO DINE

CAFE MILANO **Lunch:** $8-$20 **Dinner:** $10-$35 **Phone:** 985/879-2426

Italian

Location: E on SR 24 (W Main), 1.6 mi to Belanger, just e; between Church and Grinage rds; downtown. 314 Belanger St 70360. **Hours:** 11 am-2 & 5:30-10 pm, Fri-10:30 pm, Sat 5:30 pm-10:30 pm, Sun 10:30 am-3 pm. Closed major holidays. **Reservations:** suggested. **Features:** Located in downtown Houma, Cafe Milano serves delicious Italian cuisine, such as pizza prepared in real wood-burning brick ovens. The staff provides very good, attentive service. Also, a new lounge has been added — perfect for after-dinner gatherings. Casual dress; cocktails. **Parking:** on-site. **Cards:** AX, DC, DS, MC, VI.

COPELAND'S **Lunch:** $7-$16 **Dinner:** $11-$26 **Phone:** 985/873-9600

Cajun

Location: Just n of jct S Hollywood Rd and Martin Luther King Blvd. 1534 Martin Luther King Jr Blvd 70360. **Hours:** 11 am-11 pm, Fri & Sat-midnight, Sun-10 pm. Closed: 12/25. **Features:** A New Orleans-born idea, the restaurant prepares such dishes as barbecue shrimp, red beans and rice, blackened fish, steaks, po' boys and, of course, some lagniappe. Accompanying most dishes is the signature melt-in-your-mouth biscuit. Casual dress; cocktails. **Parking:** on-site. **Cards:** AX, DC, DS, MC, VI.

DAVE'S CAJUN KITCHEN **Lunch:** $6-$17 **Dinner:** $6-$17 **Phone:** 985/868-3870

Cajun

Location: 1.4 mi n of jct SR 3040 (Tunnel Blvd) and 24 (W Main St). 6240 W Main St 70360. **Hours:** 11 am-9 pm. Closed: 1/1, 12/25; also Sun & Mardi Gras. **Reservations:** not accepted. **Features:** Cajun dishes, seafood and steak are the focus at the laid-back eatery, which offers a bayou atmosphere and is popular with both locals and tourists. Some specialties of the house include shrimp and crab corn soup, seafood-stuffed baked potato and crawfish etouffee. Casual dress; cocktails. **Parking:** on-site. **Cards:** AX, CB, DC, DS, MC, VI.

IOWA pop. 2,663

WHERE TO STAY

HOWARD JOHNSON EXPRESS INN *Book at AAA.com* **Phone:** 337/582-2440

Small-scale Hotel

Property failed to provide current rates

Location: I-10, exit 43, just n, then just e. 107 E Frontage Rd 70647. Fax: 337/582-2360. **Facility:** 41 one-bedroom standard units. 2 stories (no elevator), interior corridors. **Parking:** on-site. **Amenities:** voice mail, irons, hair dryers. **Business Services:** fax (fee).

SOME UNITS

JEANERETTE pop. 5,997

WHERE TO DINE

YELLOW BOWL RESTAURANT **Lunch:** $7-$19 **Dinner:** $8-$19 **Phone:** 337/276-5512

Cajun

Location: 1.9 mi e of jct US 90 and SR 318 on SR 318; 0.9 mi s of jct SR 318 and 182. 19466 Hwy 182 W 70544. **Hours:** 11 am-9:15 pm, Sat from 5:30 pm, Sun 11 am-2:30 pm. Closed major holidays; also Mon & Tues. **Features:** One of the oldest Cajun restaurants in Acadiana, the Yellow Bowl is considered the birthplace of fried crawfish. So for good food and good service, Cajun-style, stop in for a visit at the Yellow Bowl. Casual dress; cocktails. **Parking:** on-site. **Cards:** AX, DS, MC, VI.

JEAN LAFITTE —*See New Orleans p. 405.*

JENNINGS pop. 10,986

WHERE TO STAY

COMFORT INN *Book great rates at AAA.com* **Phone:** (337)824-8589

Small-scale Hotel

All Year [CP] 1P: $70-$100 2P: $70-$100 XP: $10 F19

Location: I-10, exit 64. 607 Holiday Dr 70546. Fax: 337/824-8595. **Facility:** 64 one-bedroom standard units. 2 stories (no elevator), exterior corridors. *Bath:* combo or shower only. **Parking:** on-site. **Terms:** 1-2 night minimum stay, no pets allowed (kennels available). **Amenities:** irons, hair dryers. **Pool(s):** outdoor. **Guest Services:** valet laundry. **Business Services:** fax (fee). **Cards:** AX, DC, DS, JC, MC, VI.

SOME UNITS

ASK

HOLIDAY INN JENNINGS *Book at AAA.com* **Phone:** 337/824-5280

Small-scale Hotel

Property failed to provide current rates

Location: I-10, exit 64. 603 Holiday Dr 70546. Fax: 337/824-7941. **Facility:** 127 one-bedroom standard units. 2 stories (no elevator), exterior corridors. *Bath:* combo or shower only. **Parking:** on-site. **Amenities:** high-speed Internet, dual phone lines, voice mail, irons, hair dryers. **Pool(s):** outdoor. **Leisure Activities:** exercise room. **Guest Services:** valet and coin laundry. **Business Services:** meeting rooms, fax (fee).

SOME UNITS

FEE

KENNER —*See New Orleans p. 405.*

KINDER pop. 2,148

WHERE TO STAY

BEST WESTERN INN AT COUSHATTA *Book great rates at AAA.com* **Phone:** (337)738-4800

AAA SAVE

Small-scale Hotel

All Year 1P: $79-$109 2P: $89-$119 XP: $10 F17

Location: 5 mi n of jct US 190/165. Located next to a casino. 12102 US Hwy 165 N 70648 (PO Box 337). Fax: 337/738-4899. **Facility:** 99 units. 93 one-bedroom standard units, some with whirlpools. 6 one-bedroom suites ($149-$199) with whirlpools. 3 stories, interior corridors. **Parking:** on-site. **Terms:** 7 day cancellation notice, [ECP] meal plan available, small pets only ($25 deposit). **Amenities:** high-speed Internet, irons, hair dryers. **Pool(s):** outdoor. **Guest Services:** area transportation-on casino property. **Business Services:** meeting rooms, PC, fax (fee). **Cards:** AX, CB, DC, DS, MC, VI. **Free Special Amenities: expanded continental breakfast and local telephone calls.**

SOME UNITS

FEE

COUSHATTA GRAND HOTEL **Phone:** 337/738-1327

Large-scale Hotel

All Year 1P: $109-$179 2P: $109-$179

Location: US 165, 4 mi n. 777 Coushatta Dr 70648 (PO Box 1510). Fax: 338/738-1330. **Facility:** One of several lodgings on Louisiana's largest gaming resort, this propery offers upscale and comfortable accommodations along with many luxury suites. 208 units. 172 one-bedroom standard units, some with whirlpools. 36 one-bedroom suites ($229-$449), some with whirlpools. 6 stories, interior corridors. *Bath:* combo or shower only. **Parking:** on-site and valet. **Terms:** check-in 4 pm, package plans. **Amenities:** video games (fee), voice mail, irons, hair dryers. *Some:* dual phone lines. **Pool(s):** heated indoor. **Leisure Activities:** whirlpool, exercise room. *Fee:* golf-18 holes. **Guest Services:** gift shop, valet and coin laundry. **Business Services:** meeting rooms, PC (fee). **Cards:** AX, DC, DS, MC, VI.

SOME UNITS

HOLIDAY INN EXPRESS HOTEL & SUITES *Book at AAA.com* **Phone:** 337/738-3381

Small-scale Hotel

Property failed to provide current rates

Location: 5.2 mi n of jct US 190/165, 5.1 mi on US 165. Located next to a casino. 11750 US Hwy 165 70648. Fax: 337/738-3381. **Facility:** 139 units. 137 one-bedroom standard units, some with whirlpools. 2 one-bedroom suites with whirlpools. 2 stories, interior/exterior corridors. *Bath:* combo or shower only. **Parking:** on-site. **Terms:** check-in 4 pm, small pets only. **Amenities:** video games (fee), voice mail, irons, hair dryers. **Pool(s):** outdoor. **Guest Services:** coin laundry, wireless Internet. **Business Services:** business center.

SOME UNITS

WHERE TO DINE

FAUSTO'S RESTAURANT **Lunch:** $4-$13 **Dinner:** $4-$13 **Phone:** 337/738-5676

Cajun

Location: Jct US 165 and SR 383. Hwy 165 & Hwy 383 70648. **Hours:** 10 am-9 pm, Fri & Sat-11 pm. Closed: 1/1, 11/22, 12/25. **Features:** With a colorful green exterior, painted murals and neon lighting, the restaurant is hard to miss. That's a good thing because the staff alone makes it worth the stop. Oh, and the food is good, too. Guests can expect simple fare along the lines of fried chicken, seafood platters, po' boys and hamburgers. Casual dress. **Parking:** on-site. **Cards:** AX, DC, DS, MC, VI.

LACOMBE —*See New Orleans p. 407.*

LAFAYETTE pop. 110,257

WHERE TO STAY

AMERICA'S BEST SUITES OF LAFAYETTE Book at AAA.com **Phone:** (337)235-1367

Small-scale Hotel

All Year [BP] 1P: $89-$139 2P: $99-$149 XP: $10 F18

Location: I-10, exit 103A, 1 mi w of jct E Kaliste Saloom Rd and US 90 (SW Evangeline Thruway). 125 E Kaliste Saloom Rd 70508. Fax: 337/235-2887. **Facility:** 97 one-bedroom suites, some with whirlpools. 3 stories, interior corridors. *Bath:* combo or shower only. **Parking:** on-site. **Terms:** small pets only. **Amenities:** voice mail, irons, hair dryers. **Pool(s):** heated indoor. **Leisure Activities:** whirlpool, exercise room. **Guest Services:** sundries, complimentary evening beverages, valet and coin laundry, wireless Internet. **Business Services:** meeting rooms, PC, fax (fee). **Cards:** AX, DC, DS, MC, VI.

SOME UNITS

BEST WESTERN HOTEL ACADIANA Book great rates at AAA.com **Phone:** (337)233-8120

Small-scale Hotel

All Year 1P: $79-$109

Location: SR 182, 1.5 mi s of US 90 (Evangeline Thruway). 1801 W Pinhook Rd 70508. Fax: 337/234-6963. **Facility:** 293 units. 290 one-bedroom standard units, some with whirlpools. 3 two-bedroom suites ($150-$280). 6 stories, interior corridors. *Bath:* combo or shower only. **Parking:** on-site. **Terms:** cancellation fee imposed, [BP] meal plan available, pets ($25 fee). **Amenities:** voice mail, irons, hair dryers. **Pool(s):** small outdoor. **Leisure Activities:** whirlpool, exercise room. **Guest Services:** valet and coin laundry, wireless Internet. **Business Services:** conference facilities, fax (fee). **Cards:** AX, DC, DS, MC, VI.

SOME UNITS

FEE

BEST WESTERN-LAFAYETTE Book great rates at AAA.com **Phone:** (337)289-9907

Small-scale Hotel

All Year [CP] 1P: $65-$115 2P: $75-$125 XP: $10 F18

Location: I-10, exit 101, just s. 126 Alcide Dominique 70506. Fax: 866/873-8273. **Facility:** 64 one-bedroom standard units. 4 stories, interior corridors. *Bath:* combo or shower only. **Parking:** on-site. **Amenities:** high-speed Internet, irons, hair dryers. **Pool(s):** outdoor. **Leisure Activities:** exercise room. **Guest Services:** sundries, coin laundry. **Business Services:** PC, fax (fee). **Cards:** AX, CB, DC, DS, MC, VI.

SOME UNITS

COMFORT INN LAFAYETTE *Book great rates at AAA.com* **Phone:** (337)232-9000

1/1-11/30	1P: $80-$96	2P: $85-$101	XP: $5	F12
12/1-12/31	1P: $79-$95	2P: $84-$100	XP: $5	F12

Small-scale Hotel **Location:** 3 mi s of I-10 at jct US 90 (Evangeline Thruway). 1421 SE Evangeline Thruway 70501. Fax: 337/233-8629. **Facility:** 200 one-bedroom standard units, some with whirlpools. 2 stories (no elevator), interior corridors. **Parking:** on-site. **Terms:** cancellation fee imposed, small pets only. **Amenities:** voice mail, irons, hair dryers. **Pool(s):** outdoor. **Leisure Activities:** exercise room. **Guest Services:** valet and coin laundry, wireless Internet. **Business Services:** meeting rooms, fax (fee). **Cards:** AX, DC, DS, MC, VI.

SOME UNITS

COMFORT SUITES *Book great rates at AAA.com* **Phone:** (337)291-6008

All Year [BP]	1P: $80-$100	2P: $90-$100	XP: $10	F17

SAVE Small-scale Hotel **Location:** I-10, exit 103A, just s of jct I-49. 2300 NE Evangeline Thruway 70501. Fax: 337/289-5681. **Facility:** 58 units. 57 one-bedroom standard units, some with whirlpools. 1 one-bedroom suite with whirlpool. 2 stories (no elevator), interior corridors. *Bath:* combo or shower only. **Parking:** on-site. **Terms:** cancellation fee imposed. **Amenities:** high-speed Internet, dual phone lines, voice mail, irons, hair dryers. **Pool(s):** heated indoor. **Guest Services:** valet laundry. **Business Services:** meeting rooms, PC, fax (fee). **Cards:** AX, CB, DC, DS, MC, VI. **Free Special Amenities: full breakfast and high-speed Internet.**

SOME UNITS

COURTYARD BY MARRIOTT LAFAYETTE *Book great rates at AAA.com* **Phone:** (337)232-5005

All Year	1P: $99-$139

SAVE Small-scale Hotel **Location:** 0.9 mi w of jct E Kaliste Saloom Rd and US 90 (SW Evangeline Thruway). 214 E Kaliste Saloom Rd 70508. Fax: 337/231-0049. **Facility:** 90 units. 87 one-bedroom standard units, some with whirlpools. 3 one-bedroom suites. 3 stories, interior corridors. *Bath:* combo or shower only. **Parking:** on-site. **Terms:** [BP] meal plan available. **Amenities:** voice mail, irons, hair dryers. **Dining:** 6-10 am, Sat & Sun 7-11 am. **Pool(s):** heated indoor. **Leisure Activities:** whirlpool, exercise room. **Guest Services:** valet and coin laundry, wireless Internet. **Business Services:** meeting rooms, fax (fee). **Cards:** AX, CB, DC, DS, JC, MC, VI.

SOME UNITS

DAYS INN-LAFAYETTE *Book great rates at AAA.com* **Phone:** 337/237-8880

All Year	1P: $65	2P: $65

Motel **Location:** I-10, exit 101. 1620 N University 70506. Fax: 337/235-1386. **Facility:** 121 one-bedroom standard units. 2 stories (no elevator), exterior corridors. **Parking:** on-site. **Terms:** cancellation fee imposed, [CP] meal plan available, small pets only ($10 fee). **Amenities:** hair dryers. *Some:* irons. **Pool(s):** outdoor. **Guest Services:** complimentary evening beverages: Wed, coin laundry, wireless Internet. **Business Services:** meeting rooms, fax (fee). **Cards:** AX, DC, DS, MC, VI.

SOME UNITS

FEE

DRURY INN & SUITES-LAFAYETTE *Book at AAA.com* **Phone:** (337)262-0202

All Year [BP]	1P: $75-$120	2P: $85-$130	XP: $10	F18

Small-scale Hotel **Location:** I-10, exit 101 (SR 182), just s on University Ave, then just w. 120 Alcide Dominique 70506. Fax: 337/262-0202. **Facility:** 102 units. 64 one-bedroom standard units. 38 one-bedroom suites ($100-$145). 5 stories, interior corridors. *Bath:* combo or shower only. **Parking:** on-site. **Amenities:** high-speed Internet, dual phone lines, voice mail, irons, hair dryers. **Pool(s):** outdoor. **Leisure Activities:** whirlpool, exercise room. **Guest Services:** sundries, complimentary evening beverages, valet and coin laundry. **Business Services:** meeting rooms, business center. **Cards:** AX, CB, DC, DS, MC, VI.

SOME UNITS

FAIRFIELD INN & SUITES-LAFAYETTE

fyi Small-scale Hotel

Property failed to provide current rates

Too new to rate, opening scheduled for September 2006. **Location:** I-10, exit SR 182, right on Pinhook Rd, cross Vermillion River. 1600-A W Pinhook Rd 70508. **Amenities:** 80 units, pool.

FAIRFIELD INN BY MARRIOTT Book great rates at AAA.com **Phone:** (337)235-9898

Small-scale Hotel

All Year 1P: $65-$99 2P: $65-$99

Location: I-10, exit 103A, just sw on US 167. 2225 NW Evangeline Thruway 70501. Fax: 337/235-9898. **Facility:** 80 one-bedroom standard units. 3 stories, interior corridors. *Bath:* combo or shower only. **Parking:** on-site. **Amenities:** irons, hair dryers. **Pool(s):** small heated indoor. **Leisure Activities:** whirlpool, exercise room. **Guest Services:** valet laundry, wireless Internet. **Business Services:** fax (fee). **Cards:** AX, CB, DC, DS, JC, MC, VI.

SOME UNITS

ASK / /

HAMPTON INN & SUITES-LAFAYETTE Book great rates at AAA.com **Phone:** (337)266-5858

Small-scale Hotel

All Year [ECP] 1P: $99-$119 2P: $99-$119 XP: $10 F19

Location: I-10, exit 103A, 3.1 mi s to Kaliste Saloom Rd, 0.7 mi w, then just s. 1910 S College 70508. Fax: 337/266-9618. **Facility:** 95 one-bedroom standard units, some with whirlpools. 4 stories, interior corridors. *Bath:* combo or shower only. **Parking:** on-site. **Amenities:** voice mail, irons, hair dryers. *Some:* high-speed Internet. **Pool(s):** heated outdoor. **Leisure Activities:** exercise room. **Guest Services:** sundries, complimentary evening beverages: Thurs, valet and coin laundry, wireless Internet. **Business Services:** meeting rooms, business center. **Cards:** AX, DC, DS, MC, VI. ***(See color ad below)***

SOME UNITS

ASK / /

HILTON LAFAYETTE Book great rates at AAA.com **Phone:** (337)235-6111

Large-scale Hotel

All Year 1P: $89-$319 2P: $99-$329 XP: $10 F18

Location: SR 182, 1.3 mi sw of US 90 (Evangeline Thruway). 1521 W Pinhook Rd 70503 (PO Box 52286, 70505). Fax: 337/237-6313. **Facility:** 327 units. 320 one-bedroom standard units, some with whirlpools. 5 one- and 2 two-bedroom suites. 15 stories, interior corridors. *Bath:* combo or shower only. **Parking:** on-site. **Terms:** check-in 4 pm, cancellation fee imposed, package plans. **Amenities:** video games (fee), voice mail, irons, hair dryers. **Pool(s):** outdoor. **Guest Services:** gift shop, valet and coin laundry, wireless Internet. **Business Services:** conference facilities, business center. **Cards:** AX, CB, DC, DS, JC, MC, VI.

SOME UNITS

ASK FEE / FEE /

HOLIDAY INN EXPRESS HOTEL & SUITES Book at AAA.com **Phone:** (337)981-0600

Small-scale Hotel

All Year 1P: $119-$250 2P: $119-$250 XP: $15 F

Location: I-10, exit 100, jct US 167 (Johnston St), 1 mi s. 3903 Ambassador Caffery Pkwy 70503. Fax: 337/981-2779. **Facility:** 84 one-bedroom standard units, some with whirlpools. 3 stories, interior corridors. *Bath:* combo or shower only. **Parking:** on-site. **Amenities:** voice mail, irons, hair dryers. *Some:* CD players. **Pool(s):** outdoor. **Leisure Activities:** exercise room. **Guest Services:** valet laundry, wireless Internet. **Business Services:** meeting rooms, business center. **Cards:** AX, CB, DC, DS, JC, MC, VI.

SOME UNITS

ASK / /

HOLIDAY INN LAFAYETTE-HOLIDOME Book great rates at AAA.com **Phone:** 337/233-6815

AAA SAVE

Small-scale Hotel

All Year 1P: $60-$179 2P: $70-$189 XP: $10 F18

Location: I-10, exit 103A, just s. 2032 NE Evangeline Thruway 70501. Fax: 337/235-1954. **Facility:** 243 units. 239 one-bedroom standard units. 3 one- and 1 two-bedroom suites ($159-$800). 2 stories (no elevator), interior/exterior corridors. *Bath:* combo or shower only. **Parking:** on-site. **Terms:** cancellation fee imposed, [AP] meal plan available, package plans, small pets only ($50 fee). **Amenities:** video games (fee), voice mail, irons, hair dryers. **Dining:** 6:30 am-1:30 & 5:30-9 pm, cocktails. **Pool(s):** heated indoor. **Leisure Activities:** sauna, whirlpool, 2 lighted tennis courts, picnic area, soccer field, playground, exercise room, basketball, volleyball. *Fee:* game room. **Guest Services:** valet and coin laundry, airport transportation-Lafayette Regional Airport, wireless Internet. **Business Services:** conference facilities, business center. **Cards:** AX, CB, DC, DS, JC, MC, VI. **Free Special Amenities: newspaper and high-speed Internet.** *(See color ad p 321)*

SOME UNITS

FEE / /

JAMESON INN OF LAFAYETTE Book at AAA.com **Phone:** (337)291-2916

Small-scale Hotel

All Year [ECP] 1P: $54-$120

Location: I-10, exit 103A, just s. 2200 NE Evangeline Thruway 70501. Fax: 337/291-2917. **Facility:** 79 units. 77 one-bedroom standard units. 2 one-bedroom suites. 3 stories, interior corridors. *Bath:* combo or shower only. **Parking:** on-site. **Terms:** cancellation fee imposed, pets ($10 extra charge). **Amenities:** voice mail, irons, hair dryers. **Pool(s):** outdoor. **Leisure Activities:** limited exercise equipment. **Guest Services:** wireless Internet. **Business Services:** meeting rooms, PC, fax (fee). **Cards:** AX, DC, DS, MC, VI.

SOME UNITS

ASK FEE / /

LA QUINTA INN & SUITES LAFAYETTE OIL CENTER *Book great rates at AAA.com* **Phone:** (337)291-1088

Small-scale Hotel

All Year	1P: $109-$129	2P: $109-$139	XP: $10	F18

Location: I-10, exit 101 (University Ave), 3.5 mi to SR 182 (Pinhook Rd), then 0.5 mi w. 1015 W Pinhook Rd 70503. Fax: 337/235-4703. **Facility:** 50 one-bedroom standard units. 3 stories, interior corridors. *Bath:* combo or shower only. **Parking:** on-site. **Terms:** [ECP] meal plan available, pets ($100 deposit). **Amenities:** voice mail, irons, hair dryers. **Pool(s):** outdoor. **Leisure Activities:** whirlpool, exercise room. **Guest Services:** valet and coin laundry, wireless Internet. **Business Services:** meeting rooms, business center. **Cards:** AX, CB, DC, DS, JC, MC, VI.

SOME UNITS

FEE

LA QUINTA INN LAFAYETTE (NORTH) *Book great rates at AAA.com* **Phone:** (337)233-5610

Small-scale Hotel

3/1-9/30 [ECP]	1P: $74-$85	2P: $85-$95	XP: $10	F18
10/1-11/30 [ECP]	1P: $74-$84	2P: $84-$94	XP: $10	F18
12/1-2/28 [ECP]	1P: $69-$79	2P: $79-$89	XP: $10	F18

Location: I-10, exit 103A, 0.3 mi s on US 167. 2100 NE Evangeline Thruway 70501. Fax: 337/235-2104. **Facility:** 140 units. 138 one-bedroom standard units. 2 one-bedroom suites. 2 stories (no elevator), exterior corridors. **Parking:** on-site. **Terms:** small pets only. **Amenities:** video games (fee), voice mail, irons, hair dryers. *Some:* high-speed Internet. **Pool(s):** outdoor. **Guest Services:** coin laundry, wireless Internet. **Business Services:** fax (fee). **Cards:** AX, CB, DC, DS, MC, VI.

SOME UNITS

MOTEL 6 #461 *Book at AAA.com* **Phone:** 337/233-2055

Motel

5/25-11/30	1P: $39-$49	2P: $45-$55	XP: $3	F17
12/1-5/24	1P: $35-$45	2P: $41-$51	XP: $3	F17

Location: I-49, exit 1B (Pont des Mouton Rd), just e, then just s on frontage road. 2724 NE Evangeline Thruway 70507. Fax: 337/269-9267. **Facility:** 101 one-bedroom standard units. 2 stories (no elevator), exterior corridors. **Parking:** on-site. **Terms:** small pets only. **Pool(s):** outdoor. **Guest Services:** coin laundry. **Cards:** AX, CB, DC, DS, MC, VI.

SOME UNITS

RAMADA INN *Book at AAA.com* **Phone:** (337)235-0858

Small-scale Hotel

All Year	1P: $59	2P: $64	XP: $5	F18

Location: I-10, exit 103A, 4.4 mi e on US 90 (Evangeline Thruway), then 1 mi s. 120 E Kaliste Saloom Rd 70508. Fax: 337/235-4586. **Facility:** 96 units. 95 one-bedroom standard units. 1 one-bedroom suite. 2 stories (no elevator), exterior corridors. **Parking:** on-site. **Terms:** pets ($10 fee). **Amenities:** voice mail, irons, hair dryers. **Pool(s):** outdoor. **Guest Services:** valet and coin laundry, wireless Internet. **Business Services:** meeting rooms, fax (fee). **Cards:** AX, CB, DC, DS, MC, VI.

SOME UNITS

FEE

TRAVELODGE LAFAYETTE CENTER *Book at AAA.com* **Phone:** (337)234-7402

Motel

All Year 1P: $49 2P: $49 XP: $5 F17

Location: I-10, exit 101 on SR 182 (Pinhook Rd), 1.1 mi sw of US 90 (Evangeline Thruway). 1101 W Pinhook Rd 70503. Fax: 337/234-7404. **Facility:** 61 one-bedroom standard units. 2 stories (no elevator), exterior corridors. *Bath:* combo or shower only. **Parking:** on-site. **Terms:** 7 day cancellation notice. **Pool(s):** outdoor. **Guest Services:** wireless Internet. **Business Services:** fax (fee). **Cards:** AX, DC, DS, MC, VI.

SOME UNITS

FEE

WHERE TO DINE

AZTECAS **Lunch:** $6-$9 **Dinner:** $6-$16 **Phone:** 337/769-1088

Mexican

Location: Jct US 167 (Johnston St); in Ambassador Row Shopping Center. 3535 Ambassador Caffery Pkwy 70503. **Hours:** 11 am-10 pm, Sun-9 pm. Closed: 11/22, 12/25. **Features:** Colorful murals depicting rural Mexican life lend to a picturesque setting for dining. On the menu are such items as blackened fish tacos, fajitas, enchiladas, chimichangas and combination platters. The extensive menu includes something for everyone. Casual dress; beer & wine only. **Parking:** on-site. **Cards:** AX, MC, VI.

BELLA FIGURA **Lunch:** $6-$30 **Dinner:** $8-$30 **Phone:** 337/237-5800

Italian

Location: 0.4 mi sw of jct Pinhook Rd. 340-C Kaliste Saloom Rd 70508. **Hours:** 11 am-2 & 5-10 pm, Fri-10:30 pm, Sat 5 pm-10:30 pm, Sun 5 pm-10 pm. Closed major holidays. **Reservations:** suggested, weekends. **Features:** Escape, if only for just an hour, to Old World Italy. A sophisticated setting offers the perfect backdrop for a memorable meal, such as sauteed veal piccata, lamb chops, shrimp Torino, pasta Sicilia and margherite pizza. Dressy casual; cocktails. **Parking:** on-site. **Cards:** AX, DC, DS, MC, VI.

BLAIR HOUSE RESTAURANT **Lunch:** $9-$14 **Dinner:** $14-$26 **Phone:** 337/234-0357

Steak & Seafood

Location: 0.5 mi e of US 90 (Evangeline Thruway) on Pinhook Rd to Surrey St, then just s. 1316 Surrey St 70501. **Hours:** 11 am-2 & 5-10 pm, Sat from 5 pm. Closed: 1/1, 12/25; also Sun. **Reservations:** accepted. **Features:** Locally popular since 1950 for its well-prepared steak and seafood entrees, the restaurant invites casual dining in a somewhat formal environment. Try snapper vermilion, a broiled fillet stuffed with crabmeat and topped with hollandaise. Casual dress; cocktails. **Parking:** on-site. **Cards:** AX, DC, DS, MC, VI.

BLUE DOG CAFE **Lunch:** $8-$18 **Dinner:** $13-$22 **Phone:** 337/237-0005

Cajun

Location: SR 182, 1.1 mi w of jct US 90 (Evangeline Thruway). 1211 W Pinhook Rd 70503. **Hours:** 11 am-2 & 5-9 pm, Thurs & Fri-10 pm, Sat 5 pm-10 pm; Sunday brunch 10:30 am-2 pm. **Reservations:** accepted. **Features:** Those familiar with "Blue Dog" art might be disappointed to hear that the art can't be bought here, as it's sold only in New Orleans and Carmel, Calif. However, the walls are covered with George Rodrigue's famous art. Representative of delicious Louisiana fare are award-winning crawfish etouffee and seafood gumbo, as well as crab cakes, blackened redfish and varied fried items. Casual dress; cocktails. **Parking:** on-site. **Cards:** AX, DC, DS, MC, VI.

CAFE VERMILIONVILLE **Lunch:** $8-$16 **Dinner:** $18-$32 **Phone:** 337/237-0100

AAA

Cajun

Location: SR 182, 1.5 mi sw of jct US 90 (Evangeline Thruway). 1304 W Pinhook Rd 70503. **Hours:** 11 am-2 & 5:30-10 pm, Sat from 5:30 pm. Closed major holidays; also Sun. **Reservations:** suggested. **Features:** Built in the early 1800s using the French-English architectural style, the lovely restaurant is listed on the National Register of Historic Places. Fine Cajun cuisine reflects a pronounced French influence. Menu items, such as succulent steak Louis, are suited primarily for adult tastes. Dressy casual; cocktails. **Parking:** on-site. **Cards:** AX, DC, DS, MC, VI. **Historic**

LAFAYETTE'S RESTAURANT **Lunch:** $7-$36 **Dinner:** $11-$36 **Phone:** 337/216-9024

Cajun

Location: 1.3 mi sw of jct Pinhook Rd. 1025 Kaliste Saloom Rd 70508. **Hours:** 11 am-10 pm, Fri & Sat-11 pm. **Features:** Lafayette's can be called a crowd pleaser due to its diverse menu featuring chicken, angus steaks, seafood and a variety of house favorites, all served for big appetites. Boiled crawfish and lobster are seasonal favorites. Casual dress; cocktails. **Parking:** on-site. **Cards:** AX, CB, DC, DS, MC, VI.

THE ORIGINAL DON'S SEAFOOD & STEAKHOUSE **Lunch:** $6-$11 **Dinner:** $8-$25 **Phone:** 337/235-3551

Seafood

Location: Just w of jct US 90 (Evangeline Thruway) and Johnston to Vermilion St, just n. 301 E Vermilion St 70501. **Hours:** 11 am-9:30 pm, Fri & Sat-10:30 pm. Closed: 12/25; also Mardi Gras. **Reservations:** accepted. **Features:** Operated by the same owners since 1936, the restaurant is near St. John Cathedral downtown. On the menu are authentic Cajun specialties ranging from broiled tilapia with crawfish etouffee to a seafood platter featuring frog legs and catfish. Friendly service contributes to this place's reputation as a local favorite. Casual dress; cocktails. **Parking:** on-site. **Cards:** AX, CB, DC, MC, VI.

PICANTE MEXICAN RESTAURANT **Lunch:** $7-$15 **Dinner:** $10-$27 **Phone:** 337/896-1200

Mexican

Location: I-49, exit 2 (Gloria Switch), on southbound frontage road. 3235 NW Evangeline Thrwy 70507. **Hours:** 11 am-10 pm, Fri & Sat-11 pm, Sun-9 pm. Closed: 12/24, 12/25; also Good Friday. **Reservations:** accepted. **Features:** A short drive up I-49 leads to this spot for good Mexican food. The fairly predictable menu leans more toward Tex-Mex, but the kitchen applies a more authentic taste to its dishes than most other local Mexican eateries. Casual dress; cocktails. **Parking:** on-site. **Cards:** AX, DC, DS, MC, VI.

POSADOS CAFE **Lunch:** $6-$10 **Dinner:** $8-$22 **Phone:** 337/988-0835

Mexican

Location: 0.6 mi se of jct US 167 and SR 3063 (Ambassador Caffery Pkwy). 3822 Ambassador Caffery Pkwy 70503. **Hours:** 11 am-10 pm, Fri & Sat-11 pm. Closed: 11/22, 12/25. **Features:** The restaurant's charming interior resembles a small Mexican village. Good Tex-Mex food and prompt, friendly service are key to its popularity. Although the menu centers on fajitas, nachos and enchiladas, it also includes a few steak options. Casual dress; cocktails. **Parking:** on-site. **Cards:** AX, DC, DS, MC, VI.

PREJEANS **Lunch:** $8-$10 **Dinner:** $15-$26 **Phone:** 337/896-3247

Regional Cajun

Location: I-49, exit 2 northbound, 0.8 mi n on east frontage road; 3 mi n of I-10. 3480 I-49 N 70507. **Hours:** 7 am-9:30 pm, Fri & Sat-10 pm. Closed major holidays. **Features:** Live Cajun music and dancing, combined with good regional food, makes for a fun, family-oriented atmosphere. Among offerings of Cajun cuisine are corn macque choux, crawfish and alligator specialties. Combine the food with friendly service for a total Cajun experience. Casual dress; cocktails; entertainment. **Parking:** on-site. **Cards:** AX, CB, DC, DS, MC, VI.

RANDOL'S CAJUN RESTAURANT **Dinner:** $11-$18 **Phone:** 337/981-7080

Cajun

Location: 2.5 mi sw on Pinhook Rd, then 2.8 mi w. 2320 Kaliste Saloom Rd 70508. **Hours:** 5 pm-10 pm, Fri & Sat-11 pm. Closed: 11/22, 12/24, 12/25 & Easter. **Features:** The family-oriented restaurant offers live Cajun music and dancing nightly. The upbeat, casual atmosphere is popular with locals and appeals to all tastes. Menu favorites include crawfish and shrimp etouffee, boiled crab and crawfish. Casual dress; cocktails; entertainment. **Parking:** on-site. **Cards:** MC, VI.

SHANGRI LA RESTAURANT HIBACHI GRILL & SUSHI BAR **Lunch:** $7-$16 **Dinner:** $7-$16 **Phone:** 337/988-4588

Chinese

Location: Between Ambassador Caffery Pkwy and Guilbeau Rd. 4702 Johnston St 70503. **Hours:** 11 am-9:30 pm, Fri-10:30 pm, Sat & Sun 3 pm-10:30 pm. Closed: 1/1, 11/22, 12/25. **Features:** The restaurant offers a large selection from the sushi bar, including sashimi choices of tuna, yellowtail or octopus. Chinese favorites, such as shrimp tempura or Mandarin chicken, tempt and satisfy a wide variety of tastes. Casual dress; cocktails. **Parking:** on-site. **Cards:** AX, DS, MC, VI.

TAMPICO'S **Lunch:** $7-$9 **Dinner:** $8-$16 **Phone:** 337/988-0102

Mexican

Location: Jct US 167 and SR 3063 (Ambassador Caffery Pkwy), 0.4 mi w on US 167. 5713 Johnston St 70503. **Hours:** 11 am-10 pm, Fri & Sat-11 pm, Sun-9 pm. Closed: 1/1, 11/22, 12/25. **Features:** This family owned and operated establishment across from Acadiana Mall features authentic Mexican cuisine. After browsing at the mall, stop by and enjoy the combination fajitas with beef, chicken and shrimp, chips and salsa, and sopapillas for desert. Casual dress; cocktails. **Parking:** on-site. **Cards:** AX, DS, MC, VI.

ZEUS CAFE **Lunch:** $6-$9 **Dinner:** $9-$16 **Phone:** 337/269-1434

Greek

Location: I-10, exit 103A (US 90), 3.5 mi s to Pinhook Rd, then 1.1 mi w. 1103 W Pinhook Rd 70503. **Hours:** 11 am-9 pm, Fri & Sat-10 pm, Sun 11:30 am-4 pm. Closed: 11/22, 12/25 & Easter. **Features:** Representative of the tasty Greek and Lebanese food are such dishes as tabbouleh, falafel, gyros, kebabs and shawarma. The simple dining room is enhanced by beaded lamps and traditional music. On weekends, this place is popular for belly dancing. Casual dress; cocktails. **Parking:** on-site. **Cards:** AX, DS, MC, VI.

LAFITTE —*See New Orleans p. 407.*

LAKE CHARLES pop. 71,757

WHERE TO STAY

BAYMONT INN & SUITES *Book at AAA.com* **Phone:** 337/310-7666

Property failed to provide current rates

Small-scale Hotel

Location: I-10, exit 33, just n. 1004 MLK Hwy (171 N) 70601. Fax: 337/310-0536. **Facility:** 51 one-bedroom standard units, some with whirlpools. 2 stories (no elevator), exterior corridors. **Parking:** on-site. **Amenities:** high-speed Internet, voice mail, irons, hair dryers.

SOME UNITS

BEST SUITES OF AMERICA *Book at AAA.com* **Phone:** 337/439-2444

Property failed to provide current rates

Small-scale Hotel

Location: I-10, exit 29 (business district/tourist bureau) eastbound; exit 30B (Ryan St business district) westbound, just s to Pine, then just w. 401 Lakeshore Dr 70601. Fax: 337/439-5740. **Facility:** 111 one-bedroom suites, some with whirlpools. 4 stories, interior corridors. *Bath:* combo or shower only. **Parking:** on-site. **Terms:** check-in 4 pm, small pets only. **Amenities:** high-speed Internet, voice mail, irons, hair dryers. **Pool(s):** heated indoor. **Leisure Activities:** whirlpool, exercise room. **Guest Services:** sundries, complimentary evening beverages: Mon-Sat, coin laundry, wireless Internet. **Business Services:** meeting rooms, PC, fax (fee).

SOME UNITS

BEST WESTERN RICHMOND SUITES HOTEL *Book great rates at AAA.com* **Phone:** (337)433-5213

All Year [BP]	1P: $89-$99	2P: $89-$99	XP: $10	F17

Small-scale Hotel

Location: I-10, exit 33, just n. 2600 Moeling St 70615. Fax: 337/439-4243. **Facility:** 140 units. 81 one-bedroom standard units. 59 one-bedroom suites, some with kitchens and/or whirlpools. 2 stories (no elevator), interior/exterior corridors. *Bath:* combo or shower only. **Parking:** on-site. **Terms:** cancellation fee imposed, package plans, pets ($75 fee). **Amenities:** video games (fee), high-speed Internet, dual phone lines, voice mail, irons, hair dryers. **Pool(s):** outdoor, wading. **Leisure Activities:** whirlpool, grills in pool area, exercise room, sports court. **Guest Services:** sundries, valet and coin laundry, airport transportation-Lake Charles Regional Airport, wireless Internet. **Business Services:** meeting rooms, business center. **Cards:** AX, CB, DC, DS, JC, MC, VI. **Free Special Amenities: full breakfast and high-speed Internet.**

SOME UNITS

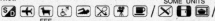

FEE

LA QUINTA INN LAKE CHARLES *Book great rates at AAA.com* **Phone:** (337)436-5998

Small-scale Hotel

All Year 1P: $70-$140 2P: $70-$140 XP: $5 F

Location: I-10, exit 33, 0.8 mi n. 1320 MLK Hwy 171 N 70601. Fax: 337/436-3493. **Facility:** 55 units. 53 one-bedroom standard units, some with whirlpools. 2 one-bedroom suites. 2 stories, interior corridors. *Bath:* combo or shower only. **Parking:** on-site. **Terms:** [CP] meal plan available, pets ($50 deposit). **Amenities:** high-speed Internet, voice mail, irons, hair dryers. **Pool(s):** outdoor. **Leisure Activities:** whirlpool, limited exercise equipment. **Guest Services:** valet and coin laundry. **Business Services:** meeting rooms, business center. **Cards:** AX, CB, DC, DS, JC, MC, VI. **Free Special Amenities: expanded continental breakfast and high-speed Internet.** *(See color ad p 386)*

SOME UNITS

FEE

SLEEP INN & SUITES *Book great rates at AAA.com* **Phone:** (337)480-0898

Small-scale Hotel

All Year 1P: $88 2P: $88

Location: I-210, exit 8 (Cameron), just s, then 0.5 mi e on E Prien Lake Rd. 3211 Venture Park Dr 70615. Fax: 337/480-1819. **Facility:** 67 one-bedroom standard units, some with whirlpools. 3 stories, interior corridors. *Bath:* combo or shower only. **Parking:** on-site. **Terms:** [CP] meal plan available. **Amenities:** high-speed Internet, dual phone lines, voice mail, irons, hair dryers. **Pool(s):** outdoor. **Guest Services:** valet and coin laundry, wireless Internet. **Business Services:** fax (fee). **Cards:** AX, CB, DC, DS, JC, MC, VI. **Free Special Amenities: continental breakfast and high-speed Internet.**

SOME UNITS

SUPER 8 MOTEL-LAKE CHARLES *Book great rates at AAA.com* **Phone:** (337)477-1606

Motel

All Year 1P: $69-$150 2P: $69-$150 XP: $5 F17

Location: I-210, exit 6B (Enterprise Blvd), just n, then just e. 1350 E Prien Lake Rd 70601. Fax: 337/477-9930. **Facility:** 59 one-bedroom standard units, some with whirlpools. 2 stories (no elevator), interior corridors. *Bath:* combo or shower only. **Parking:** on-site. **Terms:** 7 day cancellation notice, [CP] meal plan available. **Amenities:** high-speed Internet, irons, hair dryers. **Pool(s):** outdoor. **Guest Services:** valet and coin laundry, wireless Internet. **Business Services:** meeting rooms, fax (fee). **Cards:** AX, CB, DC, DS, JC, MC, VI. **Free Special Amenities: expanded continental breakfast and high-speed Internet.**

SOME UNITS

WHERE TO DINE

HONG KONG RESTAURANT **Lunch:** $7 **Dinner:** $9 **Phone:** 337/477-5126

Chinese

Location: I-210, exit 5 (Lake St), just n to Prien Lake Rd, then just e. 629 W Prien Lake Rd 70601. **Hours:** 11 am-9:30 pm, Fri & Sat-10:30 pm. Closed: 1/1, 11/22. **Features:** A popular Oriental restaurant featuring an extensive buffet with a variety of traditional Chinese dishes. Favorites include lomein, sweet-and-sour chicken and pork selections. Also, they offer a good choice of desserts and an adequate wine list. Casual dress; beer only. **Parking:** on-site. **Cards:** AX, DS, MC, VI.

LA TRUFFE SAUVAGE **Lunch:** $13-$18 **Dinner:** $27-$34 **Phone:** 337/439-8364

Regional American

Location: I-210, exit 5 (Lake St), 0.8 mi n, then just w. 815 Bayou Pines W 70601. **Hours:** 11 am-2 & 6-10 pm, Sat from 6 pm, Sunday brunch 11 am-2 pm. Closed: 1/1, 7/4, 12/25; also Mon. **Reservations:** accepted. **Features:** The often changing menu incorporates a distinctive blend of French, Italian, southwestern Louisiana and Mediterranean cuisine. Several seafood choices are offered alongside steak and pasta dishes. High ceilings and windows on two sides lend to the open feel of the interior. Appropriate dinner music sets the stage for a pleasant dining experience. Casual dress; cocktails. **Parking:** on-site. **Cards:** AX, CB, DC, DS, MC, VI.

OB'S BAR & GRILL **Lunch:** $5-$9 **Dinner:** $5-$9 **Phone:** 337/494-7336

American

Location: I-10, exit 30B (Ryan St) westbound, 1 mi s; exit 29 (downtown) eastbound, 0.6 mi se on Lakeshore Dr/Broad St to Ryan St, then 0.5 mi s. 1301 Ryan St 70601. **Hours:** 11 am-close. Closed: 11/22, 12/25; also Sun. **Features:** The focal point is the large center bar with inset TVs showing whatever sport is in season. The menu centers on basic bar food, including burgers, sandwiches, po' boys and pizza. Live entertainment is a regular feature. During the day, this is a casual hangout, but nightfall ushers in a more adult environment. Casual dress; cocktails. **Parking:** on-site. **Cards:** AX, DS, MC, VI.

PAT'S OF HENDERSON **Lunch:** $10-$11 **Dinner:** $6-$26 **Phone:** 337/439-6619

Cajun

Location: I-210, exit 10A (Legion St), on W Service Rd. 1500 Siebarth Dr 70615. **Hours:** 11 am-9 pm, Fri & Sat-10 pm. Closed: 1/1, 11/22, 12/24, 12/25; also Mon. **Reservations:** suggested. **Features:** This family-owned eatery specializes in Cajun cuisine, a savory selection of seafood, steak, chicken and pasta dishes. The blackened snapper is quite good, they have a delicious selection of desserts, and the wine list is adequate. Simple Cajun fare. Dressy casual; cocktails. **Parking:** on-site. **Cards:** AX, CB, DS, MC, VI.

PUJO STREET CAFE **Lunch:** $7-$19 **Dinner:** $14-$26 **Phone:** 337/439-2054

American

Location: I-10, exit 30B (Ryan St) westbound; exit 29 (downtown) eastbound, 0.7 mi se on Lakeshore/Broad St to Ryan St, then just s to Pujo St; in historic downtown. 901 Ryan St 70601. **Hours:** 11 am-9:30 pm, Fri-10 pm, Sat noon-10 pm. Closed major holidays; also Sun. **Features:** In historic downtown, the cafe treats patrons to a casual but classy dining experience. On the menu is an eclectic blend of Louisiana-inspired fare infused with French nuances and spiked with a Latino influence. Among choices are crab cakes, seafood linguine, pecan-crusted tilapia and filet mignon. For a topper, try delicious blackberry cobbler. Casual dress; cocktails. **Parking:** street. **Cards:** AX, DC, DS, MC, VI.

LA PLACE —*See New Orleans p. 407.*

LECOMPTE pop. 1,366

WHERE TO DINE

LEA'S LUNCHROOM **Lunch:** $7-$9 **Phone:** 318/776-5178

Southern

Location: I-49, exit 66, 2.7 mi e on SR 112, at jct US 71/167. 1810 Hwy 71 S 71346. **Hours:** 7 am-5 pm. Closed major holidays; also Mon. **Features:** Owned and operated by the same family since 1928, the restaurant serves Southern cooking at its best. Known for its homemade pies and dough-baked ham, this place has been featured on numerous TV programs and in magazines. With more than 65,000 pies baked annually, it is no wonder Lea's is called the "Pie Capital of Louisiana". Casual dress. **Parking:** on-site. **Cards:** MC, VI.

LIVONIA pop. 1,339

WHERE TO STAY

OAK TREE INN *Book at AAA.com* **Phone:** 225/637-2590

Small-scale Hotel

Property failed to provide current rates

Location: Jct SR 77 and US 190, 0.3 mi w. 7875 Airline Hwy 70755 (PO Box 188). Fax: 225/637-3672. **Facility:** Smoke free premises. 42 one-bedroom standard units. 2 stories (no elevator), exterior corridors. *Bath:* combo or shower only. **Parking:** on-site. **Terms:** small pets only. **Amenities:** *Some:* irons, hair dryers. **Guest Services:** coin laundry, wireless Internet. **Business Services:** PC, fax.

SOME UNITS

MANCHAC

WHERE TO DINE

MIDDENDORF'S RESTAURANT **Lunch:** $8-$16 **Dinner:** $8-$16 **Phone:** 985/386-6666

Seafood

Location: I-55, exit 15 (Manchac), just e, then just s. 30160 Hwy 51 70421. **Hours:** 10:45 am-9:30 pm, Sun-9 pm. Closed major holidays; also Mon. **Features:** Catfish is the star of this traditional Louisiana seafood menu which includes oyster stew, broiled and fried soft-shell crab, shrimp and bread pudding. It was established on Lake Maurepas in 1934. Boat docking is available. Casual dress; cocktails. **Parking:** on-site. **Cards:** MC, VI.

MANDEVILLE —*See New Orleans p. 408.*

MANY pop. 2,889

WHERE TO STAY

CYPRESS BEND GOLF RESORT & CONFERENCE CENTER *Book great rates at AAA.com* **Phone:** (318)590-1500

Resort Large-scale Hotel

All Year	1P: $99-$399	2P: $99-$399	XP: $10	F18

Location: 13 mi w on SR 6, 3 mi s on SR 191, 3 mi w on Cypress Bend Dr, then 1.5 mi w. Located in a rural lakefront area. 2000 Cypress Bend Pkwy 71449. Fax: 318/590-0550. **Facility:** This resort and conference center complete with an 18-hole golf course features a rural, wooded setting overlooking scenic Toledo Bend Lake. 94 units. 77 one-bedroom standard units. 17 one-bedroom suites with whirlpools, some with kitchens. 2-3 stories, interior corridors. *Bath:* combo or shower only. **Parking:** on-site. **Terms:** 7 day cancellation notice-fee imposed. **Amenities:** high-speed Internet, dual phone lines, voice mail, irons, hair dryers. *Some:* DVD players, CD players. **Dining:** 2 restaurants, 7 am-2 & 5-9 pm, Fri & Sat-10 pm, cocktails. **Pool(s):** heated indoor/outdoor. **Leisure Activities:** sauna, whirlpool, recreation programs in season, bicycles, hiking trails, playground, exercise room, spa. *Fee:* boat ramp, fishing, charter fishing, lake boat tours, golf-18 holes. **Guest Services:** gift shop, coin laundry, airport transportation (fee)-Shreveport Airport, area transportation-within 20 mi. **Business Services:** conference facilities, business center. **Cards:** AX, CB, DC, DS, JC, MC, VI. **Free Special Amenities: high-speed Internet.**

SOME UNITS

FEE

METAIRIE —*See New Orleans p. 408.*

MINDEN pop. 13,027

WHERE TO STAY

BEST WESTERN MINDEN INN *Book great rates at AAA.com* **Phone:** (318)377-1001

Small-scale Hotel

All Year [CP]	1P: $70-$80	2P: $70-$80	XP: $5	F15

Location: I-20, exit 47, just n. 1411 Sibley Rd 71055. Fax: 318/377-3221. **Facility:** 40 one-bedroom standard units, some with whirlpools. 2 stories (no elevator), exterior corridors. *Bath:* combo or shower only. **Parking:** on-site. **Terms:** pets ($10 fee). **Amenities:** high-speed Internet, irons, hair dryers. **Pool(s):** outdoor. **Leisure Activities:** exercise room. **Cards:** AX, CB, DC, DS, JC, MC, VI. **Free Special Amenities: continental breakfast and high-speed Internet.**

SOME UNITS

FEE

EXACTA INN **Phone:** (318)377-3200

Small-scale Hotel

All Year	1P: $49-$69	2P: $49-$69

Location: I-20, exit 47, just n. 1404 Sibley Rd 71055. Fax: 318/377-8152. **Facility:** 62 one-bedroom standard units, some with efficiencies (no utensils). 1 story, exterior corridors. **Parking:** on-site. **Amenities:** irons. **Dining:** 5:30 am-9 pm, Sun-2 pm. **Pool(s):** outdoor. **Guest Services:** coin laundry, airport transportation-Minden Airport. **Business Services:** meeting rooms. **Cards:** AX, CB, DC, DS, MC, VI. **Free Special Amenities: local telephone calls and high-speed Internet.**

SOME UNITS

HOLIDAY INN EXPRESS Book great rates at AAA.com Phone: 318/377-1111

SAVE

Small-scale Hotel

All Year 1P: $80-$139

Location: I-20, exit 47, just n. 1332 Sibley Rd 71055 (PO Box 1181, 71058). Fax: 318/377-4499. **Facility:** 60 one-bedroom standard units, some with whirlpools. 3 stories, interior corridors. *Bath:* combo or shower only. **Parking:** on-site. **Terms:** check-in 4 pm. **Amenities:** high-speed Internet, dual phone lines, voice mail, irons, hair dryers. **Pool(s):** outdoor. **Guest Services:** coin laundry. **Business Services:** meeting rooms, business center. **Cards:** AX, DC, DS, MC, VI. **Free Special Amenities: expanded continental breakfast and high-speed Internet.**

SOME UNITS

FEE

MONROE pop. 53,107—*See also WEST MONROE.*

WHERE TO STAY

COMFORT SUITES Book great rates at AAA.com Phone: 318/410-1005

Small-scale Hotel

Property failed to provide current rates

Location: I-20, exit 118A, just s. 1401 Martin Luther King Dr 71202. Fax: 318/410-0145. **Facility:** 72 one-bedroom standard units, some with whirlpools. 3 stories, interior corridors. *Bath:* combo or shower only. **Parking:** on-site. **Amenities:** high-speed Internet, dual phone lines, voice mail, irons, hair dryers. **Pool(s):** outdoor. **Leisure Activities:** whirlpool, exercise room. **Guest Services:** complimentary evening beverages: Mon-Thurs, valet and coin laundry. **Business Services:** meeting rooms, business center.

SOME UNITS

COURTYARD BY MARRIOTT Book great rates at AAA.com Phone: 318/388-0034

Small-scale Hotel

Property failed to provide current rates

Location: I-20, exit 120, just n of Pecanland Mall. 4915 Pecanland Mall Dr 71203. Fax: 318/388-1450. **Facility:** 90 units. 87 one-bedroom standard units, some with whirlpools. 3 one-bedroom suites. 3 stories, interior corridors. *Bath:* combo or shower only. **Parking:** on-site. **Amenities:** video games (fee), high-speed Internet, dual phone lines, voice mail, irons, hair dryers. **Pool(s):** heated indoor. **Leisure Activities:** whirlpool, exercise room. **Guest Services:** sundries, valet and coin laundry. **Business Services:** meeting rooms, business center.

SOME UNITS

HAMPTON INN Book great rates at AAA.com Phone: (318)361-9944

Small-scale Hotel

All Year 1P: $79-$94 2P: $86-$99

Location: I-20, exit 118A, just s. 1407 Martin Luther King Dr 71202. Fax: 318/322-1785. **Facility:** 69 one-bedroom standard units. 2 stories (no elevator), exterior corridors. *Bath:* combo or shower only. **Parking:** on-site. **Terms:** package plans. **Amenities:** video games (fee), high-speed Internet, voice mail, irons, hair dryers. **Pool(s):** outdoor. **Guest Services:** valet laundry. **Business Services:** PC, fax. **Cards:** AX, CB, DC, DS, JC, MC, VI.

SOME UNITS

ASK

HOLIDAY INN HOTEL & SUITES CONFERENCE CENTER Book at AAA.com Phone: (318)387-5100

Small-scale Hotel

All Year 1P: $69-$129 2P: $69-$129

Location: I-20, exit 118B, just ne on US 165 service road. Located in a commercial area/near train tracks. 1051 Hwy 165 Bypass 71203. Fax: 318/329-9126. **Facility:** 260 units. 209 one-bedroom standard units. 51 one-bedroom suites. 2 stories (no elevator), interior/exterior corridors. *Bath:* combo or shower only. **Parking:** on-site. **Terms:** pets ($20 fee). **Amenities:** video games (fee), high-speed Internet, voice mail, irons, hair dryers. *Some:* dual phone lines. **Pool(s):** outdoor, heated indoor, wading. **Leisure Activities:** whirlpool, game room. **Guest Services:** sundries, valet and coin laundry, area transportation. **Business Services:** conference facilities, business center. **Cards:** AX, CB, DC, DS, MC, VI.

SOME UNITS

FEE

LA QUINTA INN MONROE Book great rates at AAA.com Phone: (318)322-3900

Small-scale Hotel

3/1-11/30 [ECP]	1P: $74-$84	2P: $84-$94	XP: $10	F18
12/1-2/28 [ECP]	1P: $68-$78	2P: $78-$88	XP: $10	F18

Location: I-20, exit 118B, just ne on US 165 service road. Located in a commercial area and close to train tracks. 1035 Hwy 165 Bypass 71203-5542. Fax: 318/323-5537. **Facility:** 129 one-bedroom standard units. 2 stories (no elevator), exterior corridors. **Parking:** on-site. **Terms:** small pets only. **Amenities:** video games (fee), high-speed Internet, voice mail, irons, hair dryers. **Pool(s):** outdoor. **Guest Services:** valet and coin laundry. **Business Services:** meeting rooms. **Cards:** AX, CB, DC, DS, MC, VI. ***(See color ad p 386)***

SOME UNITS

ASK

RESIDENCE INN BY MARRIOTT Book great rates at AAA.com Phone: 318/387-0210

Small-scale Hotel

All Year 1P: $107-$123 2P: $107-$123

Location: I-20, exit 120, just n of Pecanland Mall. 4960 Millhaven Rd 71203. Fax: 318/387-0214. **Facility:** 66 units. 27 one-bedroom standard units, some with efficiencies or kitchens. 28 one- and 11 two-bedroom suites, some with efficiencies or kitchens. 3 stories, interior corridors. *Bath:* combo or shower only. **Parking:** on-site. **Terms:** cancellation fee imposed, weekly rates available, pets ($75 extra charge). **Amenities:** high-speed Internet, dual phone lines, voice mail, irons, hair dryers. **Pool(s):** heated outdoor. **Leisure Activities:** whirlpool, exercise room, sports court. **Guest Services:** sundries, complimentary evening beverages: Mon-Thurs, valet and coin laundry. **Business Services:** meeting rooms, business center. **Cards:** AX, CB, DC, DS, JC, MC, VI.

SOME UNITS

FEE

WHERE TO DINE

BARNHILL'S BUFFET **Lunch:** $5-$9 **Dinner:** $7-$10 **Phone:** 318/325-4886

American

Location: Jct US 165, 0.5 mi e on US 80; in Eastgate Shopping Center. 3110 Louisville Ave 71201. **Hours:** 10:45 am-8:45 pm, Fri-9 pm, Sat 7 am-9 pm, Sun 7 am-8:45 pm. Closed: 12/25. **Features:** Casual dress. **Parking:** on-site. **Cards:** AX, DS, MC, VI.

THE CHATEAU **Lunch:** $7-$11 **Dinner:** $9-$24 **Phone:** 318/325-0384

American

Location: On US 80/165 business route, 0.4 mi e of jct SR 840-6. 2007 Louisville Ave 71201. **Hours:** 11 am-10 pm, Fri & Sat-11 pm. Closed major holidays; also Sun. **Reservations:** accepted. **Features:** Guests can try a wide variety of Italian dishes in the cozy, family-owned restaurant. Casual dress; cocktails. **Parking:** on-site. **Cards:** AX, CB, DC, DS, JC, MC, VI.

COPELAND'S FAMOUS NEW ORLEANS RESTAURANT AND BAR **Lunch:** $8-$10 **Dinner:** $8-$20 **Phone:** 318/324-1212

Regional American

Location: I-20, exit 120, just sw of Pecanland Mall. 385 Pecanland Mall Rd 71203. **Hours:** 11 am-10 pm, Fri & Sat-11 pm, Sun 10 am-10 pm. **Reservations:** accepted. **Features:** While the restaurant's most popular dish is eggplant pirouge, other originals are also offered including catfish Acadiana, veal Copeland, crab cakes and shrimp Alfredo; many desserts "for two" are available. Casual dress; cocktails. **Parking:** on-site. **Cards:** AX, CB, DC, DS, JC, MC, VI.

CYPRESS INN RESTAURANT **Lunch:** $6-$22 **Dinner:** $7-$22 **Phone:** 318/345-0202

Seafood

Location: 2.3 mi e of jct US 165. 7805 Desiard St (Hwy 80) 71203. **Hours:** 11 am-9:30 pm, Fri & Sat-10:30 pm. Closed major holidays. **Features:** This casual restaurant overlooking a scenic bayou offers many fresh seafood favorites. The menu also features chicken and steak selections all cooked with a Cajun flair. The restaurant's view is wonderful even at night as spotlights illuminate the bayou. Casual dress; cocktails. **Parking:** on-site. **Cards:** AX, DS, MC, VI.

GRANDY'S **Lunch:** $6-$9 **Dinner:** $6-$9 **Phone:** 318/325-2078

American

Location: Just w of jct US 165 and 80. 2813 Louisville Ave 71201. **Hours:** 6 am-9:30 pm, Sun-9 pm. Closed: 11/22. **Features:** Casual dress. **Parking:** on-site. **Cards:** AX, DS, MC, VI.

THE PICKLE BARREL **Lunch:** $5-$9 **Dinner:** $5-$17 **Phone:** 318/325-5996

American

Location: Jct Louisville Ave, 0.8 mi n on N 18th St, then just e on Avenue of America; in Avenue Plaza. 1827 Avenue of America 71201. **Hours:** 10 am-8 pm. Closed major holidays; also Sun. **Features:** Offering a casual atmosphere, friendly service and reasonable prices, the favorite eatery serves a nice selection of freshly made sandwiches and more than 50 varieties of beer. Casual dress; beer only. **Parking:** on-site. **Cards:** AX, MC, VI.

PODNUH'S BAR-B-QUE **Lunch:** $4-$8 **Dinner:** $5-$11 **Phone:** 318/325-8747

Barbecue

Location: I-20, exit 118A, just s. 1510 US 165 S 71202. **Hours:** 10:30 am-9 pm. Closed major holidays. **Features:** A favorite of the local crowd, the restaurant serves large and tasty portions at inexpensive prices. Casual dress. **Parking:** on-site. **Cards:** AX, DS, MC, VI.

R. J. GATOR'S FLORIDA SEA GRILL & BAR **Lunch:** $7-$20 **Dinner:** $7-$20 **Phone:** 318/342-8776

Regional American

Location: I-20, exit 120; across from Pecanland Mall. 1119 Garrett Rd 71203. **Hours:** 11 am-11 pm, Fri & Sat-midnight, Sun-10 pm. Closed: 12/25. **Features:** The laid-back eatery is famous for its Key West atmosphere as well as for BBQ chicken, ribs, fresh seafood and tropical drinks. Casual dress; cocktails. **Parking:** on-site. **Cards:** AX, DS, MC, VI.

WAREHOUSE NO. 1 RESTAURANT **Lunch:** $8-$15 **Dinner:** $8-$30 **Phone:** 318/322-1340

Steak & Seafood

Location: I-20, exit 117A (Hall St) eastbound; exit 117C (Civic Center Blvd) westbound, 0.8 mi nw of Civic Center Complex, just w at Ouachita River. One Olive St 71201. **Hours:** 11 am-2 & 5-close, Sat from 5 pm. Closed major holidays; also Sun & Mon. **Reservations:** accepted. **Features:** A restored warehouse is the distinctive setting for this riverfront eatery. Focusing mainly on seafood, the cuisine reflects the Cajun tastes of the region. An example is catfish excelsior: baked catfish with a light topping of sauteed vegetables and shrimp. Also offered are chicken, steak and pasta preparations. A deck overlooking the Ouachita River allows for outdoor dining. Casual dress; cocktails. **Parking:** on-site and valet. **Cards:** AX, CB, DC, DS, JC, MC, VI. **Historic**

MORGAN CITY pop. 12,703

WHERE TO STAY

BEST WESTERN MORGAN CITY *Book great rates at AAA.com* **Phone:** (985)385-9175

Small-scale Hotel

All Year 1P: $92-$129 2P: $92-$129 XP: $5 F

Location: US 90 eastbound, exit Morgan City/SR 70; westbound, exit Brashear Ave, just n of jct US 90 and SR 70. 1011 Brashear Ave 70380-1927. Fax: 985/385-9177. **Facility:** 61 one-bedroom standard units, some with whirlpools. 2 stories (no elevator), exterior corridors. *Bath:* combo or shower only. **Parking:** on-site. **Terms:** [ECP] meal plan available. **Amenities:** high-speed Internet, voice mail, irons, hair dryers. *Some:* dual phone lines. **Pool(s):** outdoor. **Guest Services:** coin laundry, wireless Internet. **Business Services:** meeting rooms, fax (fee). **Cards:** AX, DC, DS, JC, MC, VI. **Free Special Amenities: continental breakfast and local telephone calls.**

SOME UNITS

HOLIDAY INN-MORGAN CITY *Book at AAA.com* **Phone:** (985)385-2200

Small-scale Hotel

All Year 1P: $99-$209 2P: $109-$209 XP: $10 F12

Location: 1.5 mi s of jct US 90 and SR 70. 520 Roderick St 70380. Fax: 985/384-3810. **Facility:** 221 units. 218 one-bedroom standard units. 3 one-bedroom suites ($199-$299) with whirlpools. 2 stories (no elevator), exterior corridors. *Bath:* combo or shower only. **Parking:** on-site. **Terms:** [BP] meal plan available, package plans, pets ($50 fee). **Amenities:** video games (fee), voice mail, irons, hair dryers. **Pool(s):** outdoor. **Guest Services:** valet and coin laundry, wireless Internet. **Business Services:** meeting rooms, fax (fee). **Cards:** AX, CB, DC, DS, JC, MC, VI.

SOME UNITS

ASK FEE

WHERE TO DINE

MANNY'S FAMILY RESTAURANT **Lunch:** $5-$17 **Dinner:** $5-$17 **Phone:** 985/384-2359

American

Location: 0.6 mi s of jct US 90 and SR 70. 7027 Hwy 90 E 70380. **Hours:** 6 am-8:30 pm, Sun 7 am-2 pm. Closed: 1/1, 11/22, 12/25. **Features:** Family owned and operated, this is a good choice for simple family dining. Homegrown vegetables are featured daily, and all dishes are prepared with fresh ingredients only. This is basic, home-style cooking at its best, fresh and flavorful. Casual dress. **Parking:** on-site. **Cards:** AX, DC, DS, MC, VI.

NATCHITOCHES pop. 17,865

WHERE TO STAY

CHURCH STREET INN **Phone:** (318)238-8888

Small-scale Hotel

12/1-1/1	1P: $125-$155	2P: $125-$155	XP: $5
1/2-11/30	1P: $89-$155	2P: $89-$155	XP: $5

Location: At Church and Front sts; in historic downtown. 120 Church St 71457. Fax: 318/238-8890. **Facility:** Smoke free premises. 20 one-bedroom standard units, some with whirlpools. 2 stories, interior corridors. **Parking:** on-site. **Terms:** age restrictions may apply, 7 day cancellation notice-fee imposed, [ECP] meal plan available. **Amenities:** high-speed Internet, voice mail, safes, irons, hair dryers. **Guest Services:** valet laundry. **Business Services:** meeting rooms. **Cards:** AX, DC, DS, MC, VI.

COMFORT INN **Phone:** (318)352-7500

AAA SAVE

Small-scale Hotel

12/1-12/3	1P: $139	2P: $139
12/4-12/31	1P: $79	2P: $79
1/1-11/30	1P: $69	2P: $69

Location: I-49, exit 138, just w. 5362 University Pkwy 71457. Fax: 318/352-7500. **Facility:** 59 one-bedroom standard units. 2 stories (no elevator), exterior corridors. *Bath:* combo or shower only. **Parking:** on-site. **Terms:** [CP] meal plan available. **Amenities:** high-speed Internet, irons, hair dryers. **Pool(s):** outdoor. **Guest Services:** valet laundry. **Cards:** AX, CB, DC, DS, JC, MC, VI.

SOME UNITS

FLEUR DE LIS BED & BREAKFAST **Phone:** (318)352-6621

AAA SAVE

Bed & Breakfast

All Year	1P: $80-$135	2P: $90-$150	XP: $10	F6

Location: Between rue Poet and Amulet. Located in a historic district. 336 2nd St 71457. **Facility:** 5 one-bedroom standard units. 2 stories (no elevator), interior corridors. *Bath:* combo or shower only. **Parking:** on-site. **Terms:** age restrictions may apply, 7 day cancellation notice-fee imposed, no pets allowed (owner's pet on premises). **Cards:** AX, CB, DC, DS, JC, MC, VI.

HAMPTON INN *Book great rates at AAA.com* **Phone:** 318/354-0010

Small-scale Hotel

Property failed to provide current rates

Location: I-49, exit 138, just w. 5300 University Pkwy 71457. Fax: 318/354-7771. **Facility:** 74 one-bedroom standard units, some with whirlpools. 3 stories, interior corridors. *Bath:* combo or shower only. **Parking:** on-site. **Amenities:** video games (fee), high-speed Internet, voice mail, irons, hair dryers. **Pool(s):** outdoor. **Leisure Activities:** exercise room. **Guest Services:** complimentary evening beverages: Mon-Thurs, valet and coin laundry. **Business Services:** meeting rooms, PC.

SOME UNITS

HOLIDAY INN EXPRESS *Book great rates at AAA.com* **Phone:** (318)354-9911

AAA SAVE

Small-scale Hotel

All Year	1P: $70-$200	2P: $70-$200

Location: I-49, exit 138, just e. 5131 University Pkwy 71457. Fax: 318/354-9333. **Facility:** 64 one-bedroom standard units. 2 stories (no elevator), interior corridors. *Bath:* combo or shower only. **Parking:** on-site. **Terms:** [CP] meal plan available. **Amenities:** high-speed Internet, dual phone lines, voice mail, irons, hair dryers. **Pool(s):** outdoor. **Leisure Activities:** exercise room. **Guest Services:** complimentary evening beverages: Mon-Thurs, valet and coin laundry. **Business Services:** meeting rooms, business center. **Cards:** AX, CB, DC, DS, JC, MC, VI. **Free Special Amenities: newspaper and high-speed Internet.**

SOME UNITS

WHERE TO DINE

JUST FRIENDS RESTAURANT **Lunch:** $6-$8 **Phone:** 318/352-3836

American

Location: Between Church St and rue Lafayette; adjacent to Cane River Lake. 750 Front St 71457. **Hours:** 11 am-3 pm. Closed major holidays; also Sun & Mon. **Features:** Popular among tourists, Just Friends specializes in sandwiches, homemade soups and desserts. They recently expanded to add more seating as well as a carry-out counter that is perfect for vacationers on the go. Casual dress. **Parking:** street. **Cards:** MC, VI.

THE LANDING RESTAURANT & BAR **Lunch:** $7-$20 **Dinner:** $7-$20 **Phone:** 318/352-1579

American

Location: Between Touline and Trudeau sts; on Cane River Lake; in historic district. 530 Front St 71457. **Hours:** 11 am-10 pm, Sun-9 pm. Closed major holidays; also Mon. **Reservations:** accepted. **Features:** Situated on a lovely, brick-paved street, this restaurant features a Cajun/Creole menu with a variety of steak, chicken, seafood and pasta dishes available. Enjoy eggplant lafourche, blackened alligator or red dirt shrimp. Casual dress; cocktails. **Parking:** on-site. **Cards:** AX, MC, VI. **Historic**

LASYONE'S MEAT PIE KITCHEN & RESTAURANT **Lunch:** $4-$9 **Phone:** 318/352-3353

Cajun

Location: 0.7 mi n of jct SR 6; in historic downtown district. 622 Second St 71457. **Hours:** 7 am-4 pm. Closed major holidays; also Sun. **Features:** Guests can't say much more than "simple but delicious" to describe the restaurant, which has been family-owned for decades. Patrons can look forward to friendly service with a smile. This place is a must stop, and the meat pies are unbelievable. Casual dress. **Parking:** street. **Cards:** AX, MC, VI.

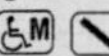

MARINER'S RESTAURANT **Lunch:** $16 **Dinner:** $14-$30 **Phone:** 318/357-1220

Regional Steak & Seafood

Location: I-49, exit 138, 3.5 mi e, then 1 mi n on SR 1; on Sibley Lake. 5948 Hwy 1 Bypass 71457. **Hours:** 4:30 pm-10 pm, Sun 11 am-9 pm. Closed major holidays. **Reservations:** suggested, weekends. **Features:** A favorite with local residents, this seafood and steakhouse overlooks picturesque Sibley Lake, and features good Cajun and Creole cooking. A plentiful salad bar, good dessert selection, and prompt, attentive service are this restaurant's highlights. Casual dress; cocktails. **Parking:** on-site. **Cards:** AX, DS, MC, VI.

MERCI BEAUCOUP **Lunch:** $5-$15 **Dinner:** $5-$15 **Phone:** 318/352-6634

Regional American

Location: Just e of Cane River Lake (Front St); downtown; in historic district. 127 Church St 71457. **Hours:** 10 am-5 pm; to 8 pm 12/1-12/31. Closed major holidays. **Features:** Here the emphasis is on Cajun and Creole cuisine, with a variety of dishes including seafood, steak, chicken and pasta. The service is good, and the wine list is adequate. A gift shop attached to the restaurant provides a little after-dinner browsing. Courtyard dining and a gourmet coffee bar are offered here. Casual dress; cocktails. **Parking:** on-site. **Cards:** AX, DS, MC, VI.

NEW IBERIA pop. 32,623

WHERE TO STAY

BEST WESTERN INN & SUITES *Book great rates at AAA.com* **Phone:** (337)364-3030

SAVE

Small-scale Hotel

All Year [ECP] 1P: $70-$84 2P: $70-$84 XP: $10 F17

Location: 0.3 mi e of jct US 90. 2714 Hwy 14 70560. Fax: 337/367-5311. **Facility:** 151 one-bedroom standard units, some with whirlpools. 2 stories (no elevator), interior/exterior corridors. **Parking:** on-site. **Terms:** 3 day cancellation notice, weekly rates available, package plans, small pets only ($50 deposit). **Amenities:** high-speed Internet, voice mail, irons, hair dryers. **Dining:** 11 am-10 pm, Fri & Sat-11 pm, cocktails. **Pool(s):** outdoor, wading. **Leisure Activities:** exercise room. **Guest Services:** valet and coin laundry, wireless Internet. **Business Services:** meeting rooms, PC, fax (fee). **Cards:** AX, DC, DS, MC, VI. **Free Special Amenities: high-speed Internet.** *(See color ad p 298)*

SOME UNITS

FEE

COMFORT SUITES *Book great rates at AAA.com* **Phone:** (337)367-0855

SAVE

Small-scale Hotel

All Year 1P: $93-$220 XP: $10 F17

Location: Just e of jct US 90 and SR 14. 2817 Hwy 14 70560. Fax: 337/367-0845. **Facility:** 78 units. 75 one-bedroom standard units, some with whirlpools. 3 one-bedroom suites with whirlpools. 3 stories, interior corridors. *Bath:* combo or shower only. **Parking:** on-site. **Terms:** cancellation fee imposed, [CP] meal plan available. **Amenities:** high-speed Internet, dual phone lines, voice mail, irons, hair dryers. **Pool(s):** small heated indoor. **Leisure Activities:** whirlpool, exercise room. **Guest Services:** valet and coin laundry. **Business Services:** meeting rooms, fax (fee). **Cards:** AX, DC, DS, MC, VI. **Free Special Amenities: early check-in/late check-out and high-speed Internet.**

SOME UNITS

DAYS INN & SUITES **Phone:** (337)560-9500

SAVE

Small-scale Hotel

All Year 1P: $73-$93 2P: $73-$93 XP: $10 F16

Location: US 90, exit SR 14, just e. 611 Queen City Dr 70560. Fax: 337/560-5611. **Facility:** 59 one-bedroom standard units, some with whirlpools. 2 stories (no elevator), interior corridors. **Parking:** on-site. **Amenities:** high-speed Internet, voice mail, irons, hair dryers. **Pool(s):** heated outdoor. **Leisure Activities:** exercise room. **Guest Services:** valet laundry. **Business Services:** business center. **Cards:** AX, DC, DS, MC, VI. **Free Special Amenities: expanded continental breakfast and high-speed Internet.**

SOME UNITS

HOLIDAY INN NEW IBERIA-AVERY ISLAND *Book at AAA.com* **Phone:** (337)367-1201

Small-scale Hotel

All Year 1P: $89-$99

Location: SR 14, just e of jct US 90. 2915 Hwy 14 70560. Fax: 337/367-7877. **Facility:** 176 units. 174 one-bedroom standard units. 2 one-bedroom suites, some with whirlpools. 2 stories (no elevator), exterior corridors. **Parking:** on-site. **Terms:** small pets only ($100 deposit). **Amenities:** voice mail, irons, hair dryers. *Some:* video games (fee). **Pool(s):** outdoor. **Leisure Activities:** exercise room. **Guest Services:** valet and coin laundry, wireless Internet. **Business Services:** meeting rooms, fax (fee). **Cards:** AX, CB, DC, DS, JC, MC, VI.

SOME UNITS

ASK

FEE

LE ROSIER COUNTRY INN BED & BREAKFAST **Phone:** 337/367-5306

Country Inn

Property failed to provide current rates

Location: US 90, 3 mi e on SR 14, just w on SR 182. 314 E Main St 70560. Fax: 337/367-1009. **Facility:** Verandas overlook a walled rose garden at this home dating from 1870; all rooms feature large, bright bathrooms. Smoke free premises. 6 one-bedroom standard units, some with whirlpools. 2 stories (no elevator), exterior corridors. **Parking:** on-site. **Amenities:** high-speed Internet, hair dryers. *Some:* DVD players, irons.

SOME UNITS

VCR

WHERE TO DINE

The following restaurant has not been evaluated by AAA but is listed for your information only.

CLEMENTINE **Phone:** 337/560-1007

fyi

Not evaluated. **Location:** Center. 113 E Main St 70560. **Features:** Named after Louisiana artist Clementine Hunter, the restaurant in the historic downtown area pays homage with one of her paintings at the bar. On the menu are such dishes as seafood gumbo, blackened redfish, stuffed red snapper and filet mignon.

Destination New Orleans

pop. 484,674

© F. Gordon Robertstock

Historic streetcars, New Orleans. See the sights while traveling in style on New Orleans' wooden-seated, clanging streetcars dating back to the 1920s.

Whether you're enjoying the nightlife or touring historic sites, sooner or later you will have to eat. With so many restaurants to choose from, New Orleans has just three types of dining experiences: fine, finer and finest.

Brunch among tropical flora in a secluded Spanish courtyard; mosey into a gumbo shop for the soup *du jour;* reserve a table at Commander's Palace, one of the city's many venerables; or take a "dressed" po-boy to the park.

Carl Purcell / © New Orleans Metropolitan CVB

French Quarter architecture, New Orleans. Creole cottages, American townhouses and buildings of French and Spanish influence characterize the architecture of the city's oldest section.

See Vicinity map page 336

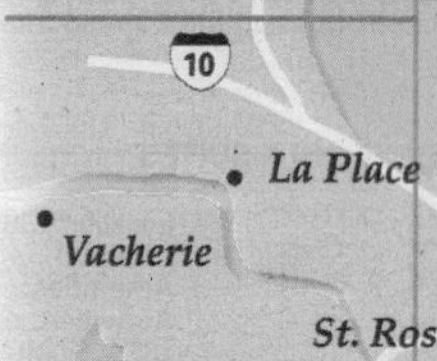

Places included in this AAA Destination City:

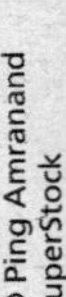

Audubon Aquarium of the Americas, New Orleans.
On the banks of the Mississippi River you can visit a Caribbean reef, an Amazon rainforest and the Gulf of Mexico, all under one roof. (See listing page 127)

12
Covington
Mandeville
59
MISS.
LA.
Lacombe
Slidell
10
New Orleans
Metairie
Kenner
Harahan
Gretna
Westwego
Harvey
Jean Lafitte
Lafitte

See Downtown map page 336

Louisiana Office of Tourism

French Market, New Orleans.
Blend in with the locals at the French Market's restaurants, coffee stands, boutiques, farmer's market and flea market, all found in the legendary French Quarter. (See listing page 120)

Louisiana Office of Tourism

Po-boy, New Orleans.
Fresh, crispy French bread and fillings such as fried fish or sliced roast beef combine for a tasty treat, New Orleans-style.

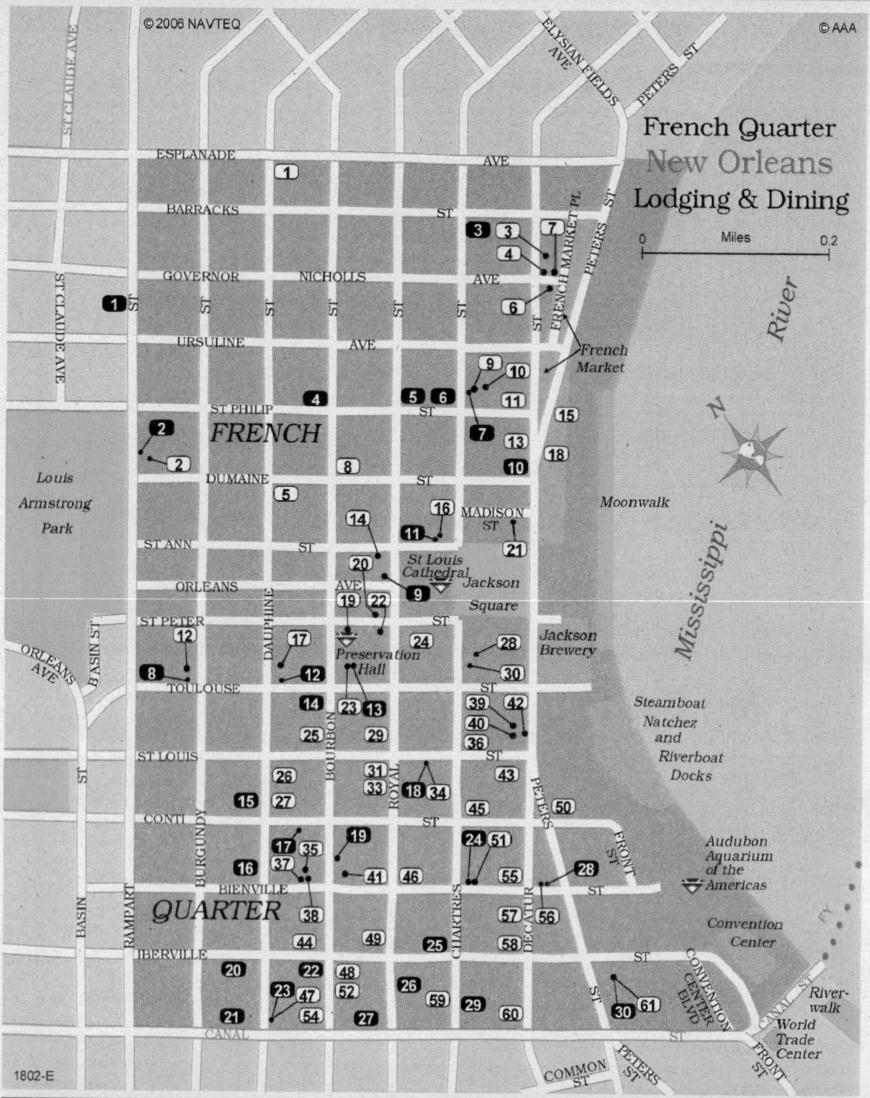

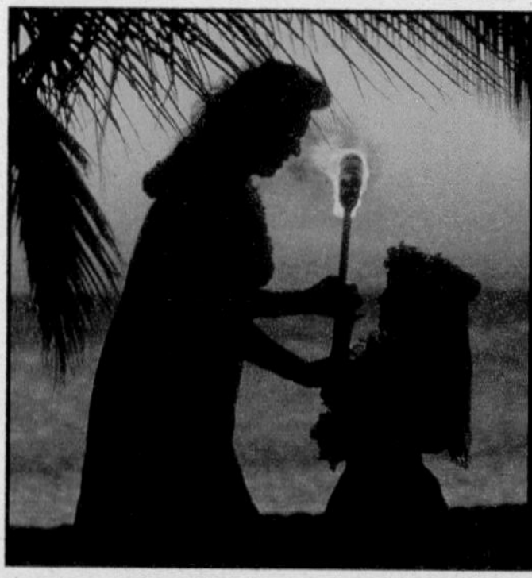

French Quarter New Orleans Lodging & Dining

© 2006 NAVTEQ

© AAA

Miles 0 0.2

1802-E

French Quarter New Orleans

This index helps you "spot" where approved accommodations and restaurants are located on the corresponding detailed maps. Lodging rate ranges are for comparison only and show the property's high season; rates are per night, unless only weekly (W) rates are available. Restaurant rate range is for dinner, unless only lunch (L) is served. Turn to the listing page for more detailed rate information and consult display ads for special promotions.

Spotter/Map Page Number	OA	**FRENCH QUARTER** - Lodgings	Diamond Rating	Rate Range High Season	Listing Page
1 / p. 332		French Quarter Suites Hotel - see color ad p 357	◆◆	$59-$299	354
2 / p. 332	AAA	**Best Western French Quarter Landmark Hotel**	◆◆◆	$89-$359 SAVE	349
3 / p. 332	AAA	**Le Richelieu in the French Quarter** - see color ad p 363	◆◆◆	$85-$185 SAVE	362
4 / p. 332		LaFitte Guest House	◆◆◆	$100-$229	362
5 / p. 332	AAA	**Hotel Royal** - see color ad p 359	◆◆	$95-$350 SAVE	359
6 / p. 332	AAA	**The Chateau Hotel** - see color ad p 353	◆◆	$69-$169 SAVE	353
7 / p. 332	AAA	**Hotel Provincial** - see color ad p 359	◆◆◆	$99-$269 SAVE	357
8 / p. 332	AAA	**Maison Dupuy Hotel** - see color ad p 364	◆◆◆	$79-$249 SAVE	362
9 / p. 332	AAA	**Bourbon Orleans, A Wyndham Historic Hotel**	◆◆◆	$143-$176 SAVE	349
10 / p. 332		Rue Dumaine Guesthouse	◆◆◆	$195-$425	367
11 / p. 332	AAA	**Place D'Armes Hotel** - see color ad p 344	◆◆◆	$69-$259 SAVE	364
12 / p. 332	AAA	**Hotel St. Marie** - see color ad p 344	◆◆◆	$69-$259 SAVE	360
13 / p. 332		Hotel Maison de Ville	◆◆◆	$249-$699	357
14 / p. 332	AAA	**The Inn On Bourbon Ramada Plaza Hotel** - see color ad p 361	◆◆◆	$89-$349 SAVE	360
15 / p. 332	AAA	**Dauphine Orleans Hotel** - see color ad p 355	◆◆◆	$109-$199 SAVE	354
16 / p. 332	AAA	**Chateau Le Moyne French Quarter, a Holiday Inn Hotel** - see color ad p 358	◆◆◆	$89-$299 SAVE	354
17 / p. 332	AAA	**Prince Conti Hotel** - see color ad p 344	◆◆◆	$69-$239 SAVE	364
18 / p. 332	AAA	**Omni Royal Orleans Hotel** - see color ad p 366	◆◆◆◆	$169-$320 SAVE	364
19 / p. 332	AAA	**Royal Sonesta Hotel New Orleans** - see color ad p 367	◆◆◆◆	$199-$329 SAVE	367
20 / p. 332	AAA	**The Maison Orleans-Ritz Carlton**	◆◆◆◆	$209-$419 SAVE	362
21 / p. 332	AAA	**The Iberville Suites** - see color ad p 360	◆◆◆◆	$99-$268 SAVE	360
22 / p. 332	AAA	**Chateau Sonesta Hotel** - see color ad p 354	◆◆◆	$99-$249 SAVE	354
23 / p. 332	AAA	**The Ritz-Carlton New Orleans** - see color ad p 360	◆◆◆◆	$419-$459 SAVE	366
24 / p. 332	AAA	**W French Quarter** - see color ad p 392	◆◆◆	$179-$369 SAVE	368
25 / p. 332	AAA	**Hotel Monteleone** - see color ad p 358	◆◆◆◆	$165-$250 SAVE	357
26 / p. 332	AAA	**Holiday Inn French Quarter** - see color ad p 358	◆◆◆	$89-$299 SAVE	354
27 / p. 332	AAA	**Astor Crowne Plaza Hotel New Orleans**	◆◆◆◆	$159-$269 SAVE	348
28 / p. 332	AAA	**The Bienville House Hotel** - see color ad p 349	◆◆◆	$129-$325 SAVE	349
29 / p. 332	AAA	**New Orleans Marriott** - see color ad p 365	◆◆◆	$139-$329 SAVE	362
30 / p. 332	AAA	**Wyndham New Orleans at Canal Place**	◆◆◆◆	$149-$179 SAVE	369
		FRENCH QUARTER - Restaurants			
1 / p. 332		Port of Call	◆	$6-$22	375
2 / p. 332		Peristyle	◆◆◆	$24-$28	375

Spotter/Map Page Number	OA	FRENCH QUARTER - Restaurants (continued)	Diamond Rating	Rate Range High Season	Listing Page
3 / p. 332		Louisiana Pizza Kitchen	◆◆	$7-$15	373
4 / p. 332		The Palm Court Jazz Cafe	◆◆	$15-$25	374
5 / p. 332		Quarter Scene	◆	$12-$25	375
6 / p. 332	AAA	**Jimmy Buffett's Margaritaville**	◆◆	$5-$17	373
7 / p. 332		Fiorella's	◆	$6-$20	372
8 / p. 332		Clover Grill	◆	$3-$7	371
9 / p. 332		Stella!	◆◆◆	$20-$36	376
10 / p. 332		Irene's Cuisine	◆◆◆	$15-$20	373
11 / p. 332		Cafe Sbisa	◆◆◆	$18-$32	371
12 / p. 332		Dominique's - see color ad p 364	◆◆◆	$22-$34	372
13 / p. 332		Central Grocery Company LLC	◆	$6-$12(L)	371
14 / p. 332		Pere Antoine Restaurant	◆◆	$11-$20	375
15 / p. 332		Cafe GumbOlaya	◆	$7-$13(L)	371
16 / p. 332	AAA	**Muriel's Jackson Square** - **see color ad p 374**	◆◆◆	$13-$25	373
17 / p. 332		Hillery's On Toulouse	◆◆◆	$16-$28	372
18 / p. 332		Bella Luna	◆◆◆	$18-$26	370
19 / p. 332		Embers "Original" Bourbon House	◆◆	$15-$33	372
20 / p. 332	AAA	**The Court of Two Sisters** - **see color ad p 371, p 137**	◆◆	$24-$28	371
21 / p. 332		Tujague's	◆◆	$32-$38	376
22 / p. 332		Old Coffee Pot	◆◆	$14-$22	374
23 / p. 332		The Bistro	◆◆◆	$19-$35	370
24 / p. 332	AAA	**Gumbo Shop**	◆	$8-$20	372
25 / p. 332		Petunias, A Restaurant	◆◆	$6-$17(L)	375
26 / p. 332		Bayona - see color ad p 355	◆◆◆	$16-$28	370
27 / p. 332		Broussard's	◆◆◆	$21-$35	371
28 / p. 332		The Alpine Restaurant	◆◆	$13-$24	370
29 / p. 332		Antoine's	◆◆◆	$23-$47	370
30 / p. 332		Ralph & Kacoo's	◆◆	$13-$27	375
31 / p. 332		Brennan's Restaurant	◆◆◆	$30-$40	371
33 / p. 332		Tortorici's	◆◆	$21-$30	376
34 / p. 332		The Rib Room-Rotisserie Extraordinaire	◆◆◆	$26-$39	375
35 / p. 332		Arnaud's	◆◆◆	$25-$38	370
36 / p. 332		Napoleon House Bar & Cafe	◆	$12-$25	373
37 / p. 332		GW Fins	◆◆◆	$21-$28	372
38 / p. 332		Remoulade	◆	$7-$20	375
39 / p. 332		Ristorante Carmelo	◆◆	$10-$30	375
40 / p. 332	AAA	**Crescent City Brewhouse**	◆◆	$8-$25	372
41 / p. 332	AAA	**Begue's** - **see color ad p 367**	◆◆◆◆	$22-$40	370
42 / p. 332		Johnny's Po-Boys	◆	$5-$10(L)	373

Spotter/Map Page Number	OA	FRENCH QUARTER - Restaurants (continued)	Diamond Rating	Rate Range High Season	Listing Page
43 / p. 332		Nola	◆◆◆	$24-$36	374
44 / p. 332		Galatoire's Restaurant	◆◆	$8-$30	372
45 / p. 332		K-Paul's Louisiana Kitchen	◆◆◆	$26-$38	373
46 / p. 332	AAA	**The Pelican Club Restaurant**	◆◆◆	$20-$30	374
47 / p. 332	AAA	**Victor's Grill**	◆◆◆	$18-$32	376
48 / p. 332		Dickie Brennan's Steakhouse	◆◆◆	$20-$36	372
49 / p. 332		Mr. B's Bistro	◆◆◆	$16-$26	373
50 / p. 332		Hard Rock Cafe-New Orleans	◆◆	$8-$20	372
51 / p. 332		Bacco	◆◆◆	$18-$30	370
52 / p. 332		Bourbon House Restaurant	◆◆◆	$16-$32	370
54 / p. 332	AAA	**Red Fish Grill**	◆◆◆	$20-$30	375
55 / p. 332		Asian Cajun Bistro	◆◆	$8-$26	370
56 / p. 332	AAA	**Olivier's Creole Restaurant**	◆◆	$15-$20	374
57 / p. 332		Sekisui Samurai	◆◆	$15-$25	376
58 / p. 332		House of Blues	◆◆	$8-$25	373
59 / p. 332		Palace Cafe	◆◆◆	$18-$29	374
60 / p. 332		Cafe Giovanni	◆◆◆	$19-$33	371
61 / p. 332		River 127	◆◆◆	$21-$33	375

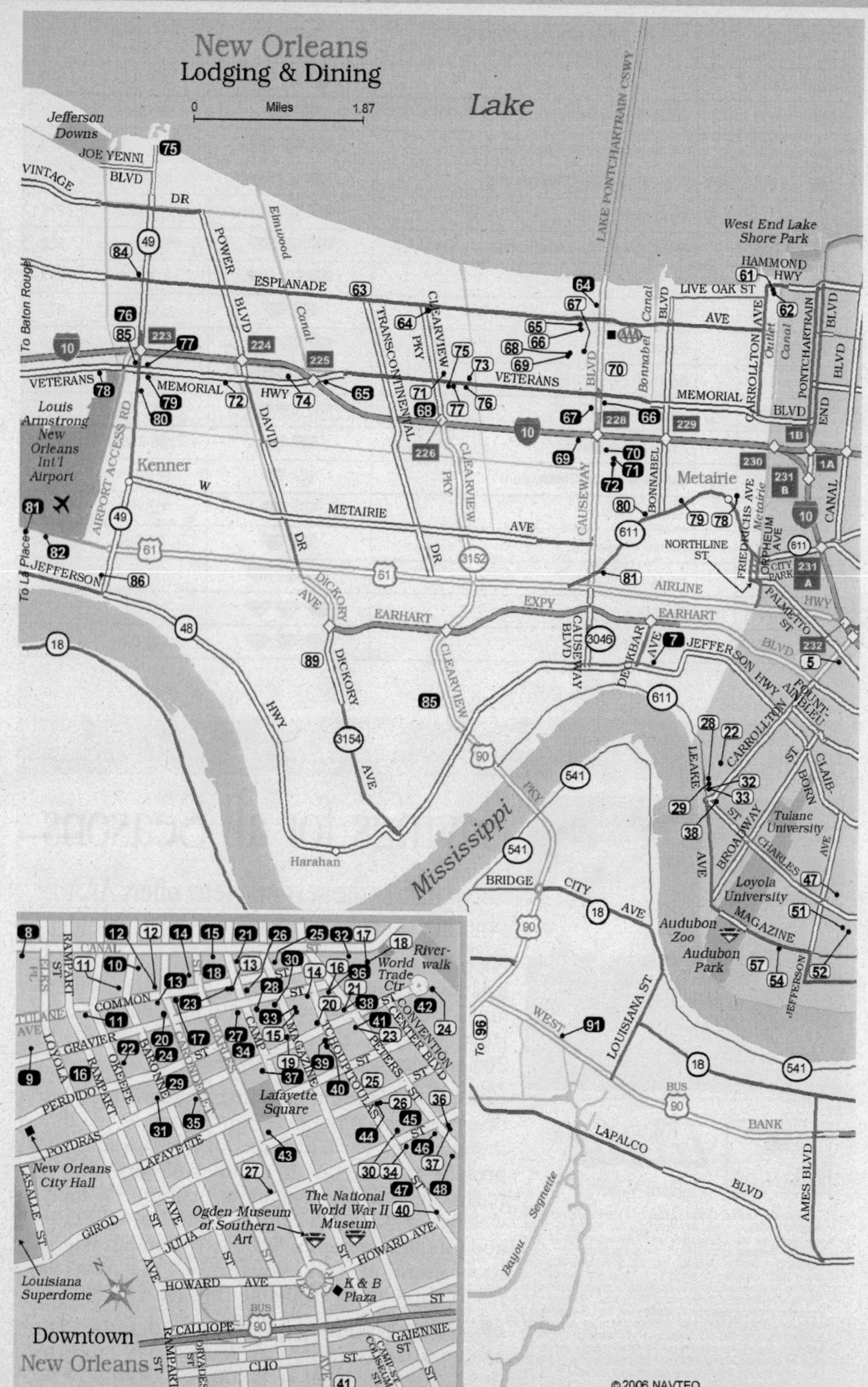
New Orleans
Lodging & Dining
0 Miles 1.87
Lake
Jefferson Downs
West End Lake Shore Park
Louis Armstrong New Orleans Int'l Airport
Kenner
Metairie
Harahan
Mississippi
Tulane University
Loyola University
Audubon Zoo
Audubon Park
Downtown New Orleans
Lafayette Square
New Orleans City Hall
Louisiana Superdome
Ogden Museum of Southern Art
The National World War II Museum
K & B Plaza
World Trade Ctr
Riverwalk
©2006 NAVTEQ

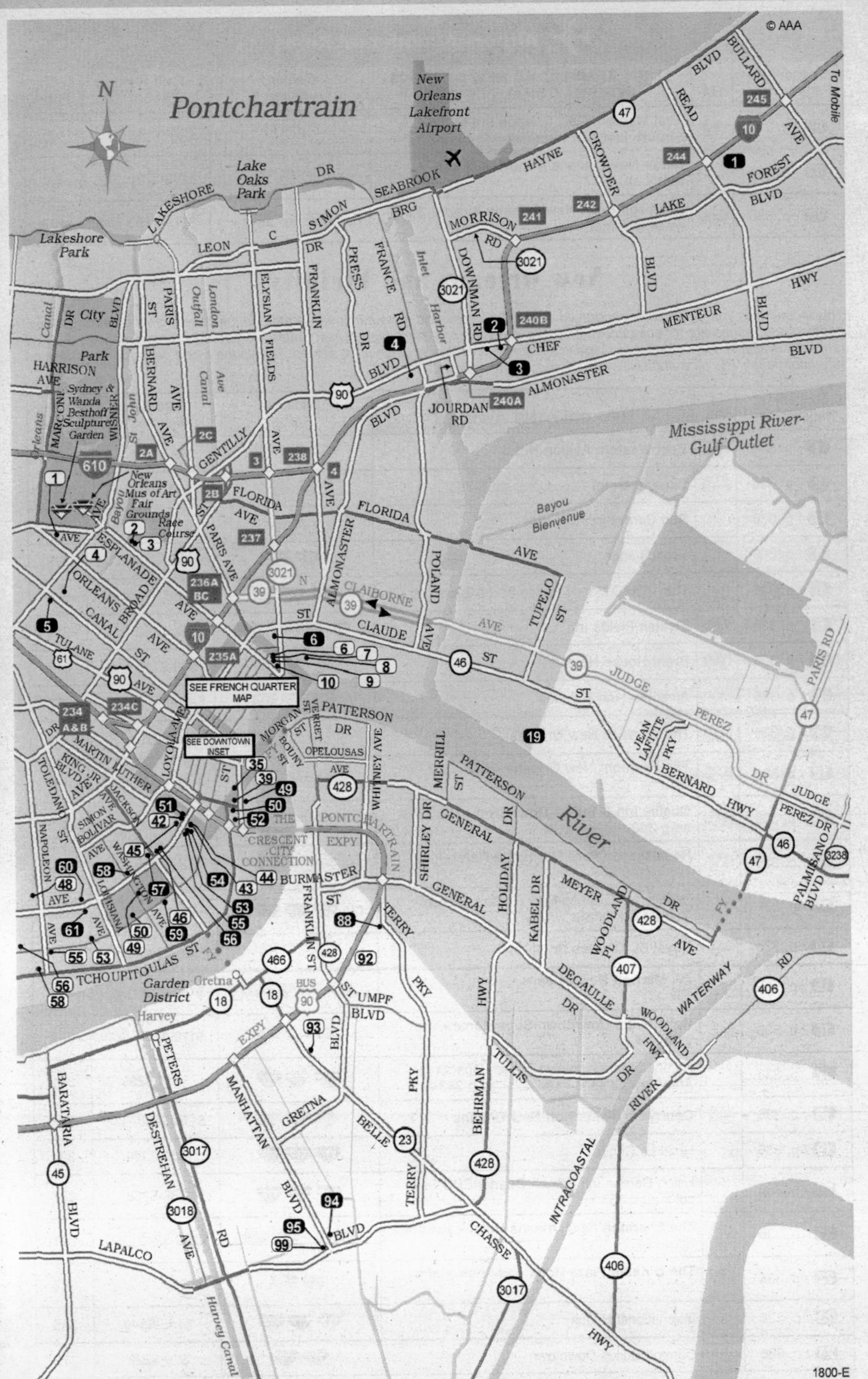
© AAA
Pontchartrain
New Orleans Lakefront Airport
Lake Oaks Park
Lakeshore Park
City Park
Sydney & Wanda Besthoff Sculpture Garden
New Orleans Mus of Art
Fair Grounds Race Course
SEE FRENCH QUARTER MAP
SEE DOWNTOWN INSET
Mississippi River-Gulf Outlet
Bayou Bienvenue
River
CRESCENT CITY CONNECTION
Garden District
Gretna
Harvey
Harvey Canal
To Mobile
1800-E

Airport Accommodations

Spotter/Map Page Number	OA	LOUIS ARMSTRONG NEW ORLEANS INTERNATIONAL AIRPORT	Diamond Rating	Rate Range High Season	Listing Page
81 / p. 336	AAA	**Best Western New Orleans Inn at the Airport, just s of terminal**	◆◆	$59-$139 SAVE	405
82 / p. 336	AAA	**Hilton New Orleans Airport, just s of terminal**	◆◆◆	$109-$229 SAVE	406
77 / p. 336	AAA	**Radisson Hotel New Orleans Airport, 3 mi ne of terminal**	◆◆◆	$119-$199 SAVE	407

New Orleans and Vicinity

This index helps you "spot" where approved accommodations and restaurants are located on the corresponding detailed maps. Lodging rate ranges are for comparison only and show the property's high season; rates are per night, unless only weekly (W) rates are available. Restaurant rate range is for dinner, unless only lunch (L) is served. Turn to the listing page for more detailed rate information and consult display ads for special promotions.

Spotter/Map Page Number	OA	NEW ORLEANS - Lodgings	Diamond Rating	Rate Range High Season	Listing Page
1 / p. 336	AAA	**Best Western Avalon Hotel**	◆◆◆	$49-$189 SAVE	377
2 / p. 336	AAA	**Super 8 Motel** - see color ad p 393	◆◆	$65-$99 SAVE	391
3 / p. 336	AAA	**Red Carpet Inn & Suites**	◆◆	$54-$59 SAVE	390
4 / p. 336		Econo Lodge	◆◆	Failed to provide	379
5 / p. 336		The 1896 O'Malley House Bed & Breakfast	◆◆◆	Failed to provide	376
6 / p. 336	AAA	**Elysian Fields Inn**	◆◆◆◆	$99-$250 SAVE	379
7 / p. 336	AAA	**Brent House Hotel**	◆◆◆	$99-$119 SAVE	377
8 / p. 336		AmeriHost Inn & Suites	◆◆◆	Failed to provide	377
9 / p. 336	AAA	**The Warwick New Orleans**	fyi	$59-$229 SAVE	391
10 / p. 336	AAA	**The Fairmont New Orleans** - see color ad p 380	◆◆◆◆	$139-$319 SAVE	380
11 / p. 336	AAA	**Quality Inn & Suites Downtown** - see color ad p 388	◆◆◆	$89-$169 SAVE	388
12 / p. 336	AAA	**Renaissance Pere Marquette Hotel** - see color ad p 368	◆◆◆◆	$209-$335 SAVE	390
13 / p. 336		Holiday Inn Express-New Orleans French Quarter Downtown	◆◆◆	Failed to provide	382
14 / p. 336	AAA	**Royal St. Charles Hotel** - see color ad p 369	◆◆◆	$89-$209 SAVE	391
15 / p. 336	AAA	**JW Marriott New Orleans** - see color ad p 362	◆◆◆◆	$151-$246 SAVE	385
16 / p. 336	AAA	**Holiday Inn Downtown-Superdome** - see color ad p 382	◆◆◆	$119-$264 SAVE	382
17 / p. 336		Hampton Inn Downtown-French Quarter Area/New Orleans - see color ad p 383	◆◆◆	$119-$239	381
18 / p. 336	AAA	**Courtyard by Marriott-New Orleans**	◆◆◆	$116-$188 SAVE	378
19 / p. 336		Hotel Le Cirque	◆◆◆	$59-$299	384
20 / p. 336		Hilton Garden Inn French Quarter/CBD - see color ad p 383	◆◆◆	$89-$259	382
21 / p. 336	AAA	**The Sheraton New Orleans Hotel** - see color ad p 392	◆◆◆◆	$199-$249 SAVE	391
22 / p. 336	AAA	**The O'Keefe Plaza Hotel** - see color ad p 387	◆◆	$99-$109 SAVE	387
23 / p. 336		International House	◆◆◆	$139-$549	385
24 / p. 336		Comfort Suites Downtown	◆◆	$79-$229	378

Spotter/Map Page Number	OA	**NEW ORLEANS** - Lodgings (continued)	Diamond Rating	Rate Range High Season	Listing Page
25 / p. 336	AAA	**Best Western St. Christopher Hotel** - see color ad p 377	◆◆◆	$99-$269 SAVE	377
26 / p. 336		Omni Royal Crescent Hotel	◆◆◆	Failed to provide	387
27 / p. 336		La Quinta Inn & Suites New Orleans - Downtown Flagship - see color ad p 386	◆◆◆	$109-$189	385
28 / p. 336	AAA	**Queen & Crescent Hotel** - see color ad p 367	◆◆◆	$89-$209 SAVE	390
29 / p. 336	AAA	**Le Pavillon**	◆◆◆◆	$99-$545 SAVE	385
30 / p. 336		Country Inn & Suites by Carlson New Orleans - see color ad p 378	◆◆◆	$79-$199	378
31 / p. 336		Homewood Suites by Hilton - see color ad p 383	◆◆◆	$159-$229	384
32 / p. 336		Doubletree Hotel - see color ad p 383	◆◆◆	$109-$289	379
33 / p. 336		St. James Hotel	◆◆◆	Failed to provide	391
34 / p. 336	AAA	**InterContinental New Orleans** - see color ad p 384	◆◆◆◆	$179-$399 SAVE	385
35 / p. 336		Drury Inn & Suites-New Orleans	◆◆◆	$95-$195	379
36 / p. 336	AAA	**Windsor Court Hotel** - see color ad p 395	◆◆◆◆	$200-$455 SAVE	395
37 / p. 336		The Whitney-A Wyndham Historic Hotel	◆◆◆	$119-$269	393
38 / p. 336	AAA	**W New Orleans** - see color ad p 392	◆◆◆◆	$169-$369 SAVE	395
39 / p. 336	AAA	**Staybridge Suites by Holiday Inn** - see color ad p 358	◆◆◆	$159-$229 SAVE	391
40 / p. 336	AAA	**Ambassador Hotel** - see color ad p 350	◆◆◆	$59-$279 SAVE	376
41 / p. 336		Loews New Orleans Hotel	◆◆◆◆	Failed to provide	387
42 / p. 336	AAA	**Hilton New Orleans Riverside** - see color ad p 383	◆◆◆	$99-$419 SAVE	382
43 / p. 336		The Lafayette Hotel	◆◆◆	Failed to provide	385
44 / p. 336	AAA	**Renaissance Arts Hotel New Orleans** - see color ad p 368	◆◆◆◆	$209-$325 SAVE	390
45 / p. 336	AAA	**Embassy Suites Hotel New Orleans Convention Center** - see color ad p 383	◆◆◆	$109-$334 SAVE	379
46 / p. 336	AAA	**Courtyard by Marriott-New Orleans Convention Center**	◆◆◆	$219-$239 SAVE	379
47 / p. 336	AAA	**Residence Inn by Marriott**	◆◆◆	$199-$239 SAVE	390
48 / p. 336	AAA	**SpringHill Suites by Marriott Convention Center**	◆◆◆	$59-$259 SAVE	391
49 / p. 336	AAA	**Holiday Inn Select-Convention Center**	◆◆◆	$149-$209 SAVE	384
50 / p. 336		Hilton Garden Inn-Convention Center - see color ad p 383	◆◆◆	$89-$259	381
51 / p. 336	AAA	**Maison St. Charles Quality Inn & Suites**	◆◆◆	$92-$268 SAVE	387
52 / p. 336		Hampton Inn & Suites-Convention Center - see color ad p 383	◆◆◆	$129-$259	381
53 / p. 336	AAA	**The Prytania Park Hotel** - see color ad p 388	◆◆	$75-$295 SAVE	388
54 / p. 336		Fairchild House Bed & Breakfast	◆◆	$75-$145	379
55 / p. 336	AAA	**Queen Anne Hotel** - see color ad p 388	◆◆◆	$90-$300 SAVE	390
56 / p. 336		Clarion Grand Boutique Hotel	fyi	Failed to provide	378
57 / p. 336	AAA	**Garden District Hotel Clarion Collection** - see color ad p 381	◆◆◆	$89-$209 SAVE	380

Spotter/Map Page Number	OA	**NEW ORLEANS** - Lodgings (continued)	Diamond Rating	Rate Range High Season	Listing Page
58 / p. 336		Grand Victorian Bed & Breakfast	◆◆◆	$125-$300	380
59 / p. 336	AAA	**Garden District Bed & Breakfast**	◆◆	$80-$110 SAVE	380
60 / p. 336	AAA	**Best Western St. Charles Inn**	◆◆◆	$119 SAVE	377
61 / p. 336		Hampton Inn Garden District - see color ad p 383	◆◆◆	$119-$209	381
		NEW ORLEANS - Restaurants			
1 / p. 336		Ralph's on the Park	◆◆◆	$17-$29	400
2 / p. 336		Gabrielle Restaurant	◆◆	$14-$32	398
3 / p. 336		Cafe Degas	◆◆◆	$16-$22	396
4 / p. 336		Christian's Restaurant	◆◆◆	$20-$31	396
5 / p. 336		Five Happiness	◆◆	$9-$16	397
6 / p. 336		The Marigny Brasserie	◆◆◆	$16-$26	399
7 / p. 336		Snug Harbor Jazz Bistro	◆◆	$10-$25	400
8 / p. 336		Feelings Cafe	◆◆◆	$15-$24	397
9 / p. 336		The Praline Connection Restaurant	◆	$12-$19	400
10 / p. 336		Mona's Cafe on Frenchmen	◆	$8-$13	399
11 / p. 336		Sazerac	◆◆◆	$16-$34	400
12 / p. 336		Rene Bistrot	◆◆◆	$15-$24	400
13 / p. 336		Lemon Grass Restaurant	◆◆◆	$12-$22	399
14 / p. 336		Restaurant August	◆◆◆◆	$20-$35	400
15 / p. 336		Restaurant Cuvee	◆◆◆	$22-$30	400
16 / p. 336	AAA	**New Orleans Grill**	◆◆◆◆	$25-$45	399
17 / p. 336		The Besh Steakhouse at Harrah's	◆◆◆	$30-$48	396
18 / p. 336		The Buffet at Harrah's	◆	$19-$28	396
19 / p. 336		Bon Ton Cafe	◆◆	$25-$39	396
20 / p. 336		Mother's	◆	$7-$21	399
21 / p. 336		Zoe Restaurant and Bar	◆◆◆	$14-$28	401
22 / p. 336	AAA	**Jacques-Imo's Cafe**	◆◆	$11-$20	398
23 / p. 336		Cafe Adelaide	◆◆◆	$16-$36	396
24 / p. 336		Kabby's On The River	◆◆◆	$10-$20(L)	398
25 / p. 336		Vic's Kangaroo Cafe	◆	$5-$11	401
26 / p. 336		La Cote Brasserie	◆◆◆	$17-$30	398
27 / p. 336		Herbsaint	◆◆◆	$22-$26	398
28 / p. 336		Dante's Kitchen	◆◆	$18-$26	397
29 / p. 336		Brigtsen's	◆◆◆	$19-$32	396
30 / p. 336	AAA	**Tommy's Cuisine**	◆◆◆	$18-$30	401
32 / p. 336		Sara's Restaurant	◆◆◆	$13-$19	400
33 / p. 336		Cafe Volage	◆◆	$17-$24	396

Spotter/Map Page Number	OA	NEW ORLEANS - Restaurants (continued)	Diamond Rating	Rate Range High Season	Listing Page
34 / p. 336		Emeril's	◆◆◆	$24-$39	397
35 / p. 336		Mulate's	◆◆	$14-$22	399
36 / p. 336		Rio Mar	◆◆	$16-$22	400
37 / p. 336		Rock-n-Sake Bar & Sushi	◆◆	$10-$22	400
38 / p. 336		O'Henry's Food and Spirits	◆◆	$6-$15	399
39 / p. 336		Wolfe's in the Warehouse	◆◆◆	$21-$34	401
40 / p. 336		Ugly Dog Saloon & BBQ	◆	$6-$15	401
41 / p. 336		Emeril's Delmonico Restaurant & Bar	◆◆◆◆	$21-$38	397
42 / p. 336		Miyako Japanese Seafood & Steakhouse	◆◆	$9-$35	399
43 / p. 336		Coyoacan	◆◆◆	$16-$38	397
44 / p. 336		Taqueros	◆◆	$14-$32	401
45 / p. 336		Voo Doo BBQ	◆	$5-$15	401
46 / p. 336		Mr. John's Steakhouse	◆◆◆	$17-$39	399
47 / p. 336		Gautreau's Restaurant	◆◆◆	$19-$32	398
48 / p. 336		Pascal's Manale Restaurant	◆◆	$12-$26	399
49 / p. 336		Commander's Palace	◆◆◆◆	$35-$40	397
50 / p. 336		Joey K's	◆	$6-$13	398
51 / p. 336		La Crepe Nanou	◆◆	$9-$18	398
52 / p. 336		Upperline Restaurant	◆◆◆	$20-$26	401
53 / p. 336		Lilette Restaurant	◆◆◆	$20-$26	399
54 / p. 336		Taqueria Corona	◆	$2-$8	401
55 / p. 336		Casamento's Restaurant	◆	$5-$13	396
56 / p. 336		Le Bon Temps Roule	◆	$5-$8	398
57 / p. 336		Clancy's	◆◆◆	$18-$28	397
58 / p. 336		Dick and Jenny's	◆◆	$13-$20	397
		METAIRIE - Lodgings			
64 / p. 336		New Orleans Marriott Metairie at Lakeway	fyi	$209-$269	410
65 / p. 336		La Quinta Inn New Orleans (Veterans) - see color ad p 386	◆◆	$99-$149	409
66 / p. 336	AAA	**Ramada Limited Causeway** - see color ad p 361	◆◆◆	$109-$149 SAVE	410
67 / p. 336		Hampton Inn Metairie - see color ad p 383	◆◆◆	$109-$169	409
68 / p. 336	AAA	**Sleep Inn & Suites**	◆◆	$99-$199 SAVE	410
69 / p. 336	AAA	**Days Hotel New Orleans-Metairie** - see color ad p 409	◆◆◆	$49-$229 SAVE	408
70 / p. 336		La Quinta Inn New Orleans (Causeway) - see color ad p 386	◆◆	$99-$149	409
71 / p. 336	AAA	**Residence Inn by Marriott-Metairie**	◆◆◆	$149-$299 SAVE	410
72 / p. 336		Metairie Hotel	◆◆◆	Failed to provide	409

Spotter/Map Page Number	OA	**METAIRIE** - Restaurants	Diamond Rating	Rate Range High Season	Listing Page
61 / p. 336		R & O's Pizza Place Restaurant	2 diamonds	$7-$20	411
62 / p. 336	AAA	**Deanie's Seafood**	2 diamonds	$12-$40	411
63 / p. 336		Vincent's Italian Cuisine	2 diamonds	$15-$20	412
64 / p. 336		Caffe Caffe	1 diamond	$5-$9	411
65 / p. 336		Taqueria Corona	1 diamond	$5-$13	412
66 / p. 336		Riccobono's Peppermill	2 diamonds	$10-$18	411
67 / p. 336		Impastato's Restaurant	2 diamonds	$12-$26	411
68 / p. 336		Drago's	2 diamonds	$13-$31	411
69 / p. 336		Salvatore Ristorante	2 diamonds	$16-$28	412
70 / p. 336	AAA	**Andrea's**	3 diamonds	$14-$28	410
71 / p. 336		Copeland's Cheesecake Bistro	2 diamonds	$10-$26	411
72 / p. 336		Casa Garcia	2 diamonds	$10-$15	411
73 / p. 336		Corky's Bar-B-Q	1 diamond	$7-$20	411
74 / p. 336		Siamese Restaurant	2 diamonds	$9-$20	412
75 / p. 336		Zea Rotisserie & Brewery	2 diamonds	$10-$23	412
76 / p. 336		Sal and Sam's	2 diamonds	$12-$30	412
77 / p. 336		Serranos Salsa Company	2 diamonds	$8-$15	412
78 / p. 336		Sun Ray Grill	2 diamonds	$10-$22	412
79 / p. 336		Byblos	2 diamonds	$10-$20	410
80 / p. 336		Vega Tapas Cafe	3 diamonds	$6-$11	412
81 / p. 336		Barreca's	2 diamonds	$12-$24	410
		KENNER - Lodgings			
75 / p. 336		Hilton Garden Inn New Orleans Airport - see color ad p 383	3 diamonds	$169-$189	405
76 / p. 336		Fairfield Inn New Orleans Airport	3 diamonds	Failed to provide	405
77 / p. 336	AAA	**Radisson Hotel New Orleans Airport** - see color ad p 406	3 diamonds	$119-$199 SAVE	407
78 / p. 336		Hotel Airport	3 diamonds	Failed to provide	406
79 / p. 336	AAA	**Comfort Suites New Orleans Airport Kenner** - see color ad p 405	3 diamonds	$79-$199 SAVE	405
80 / p. 336		La Quinta Inn New Orleans (Airport) - see color ad p 386	3 diamonds	$99-$149	406
81 / p. 336	AAA	**Best Western New Orleans Inn at the Airport**	2 diamonds	$59-$139 SAVE	405
82 / p. 336	AAA	**Hilton New Orleans Airport** - see color ad p 383	3 diamonds	$109-$229 SAVE	406
		KENNER - Restaurants			
84 / p. 336		Smitty's Seafood Restaurant & Oyster Bar	1 diamond	$6-$17	407
85 / p. 336		The Brick Oven	2 diamonds	$10-$26	407
86 / p. 336		Le Parvenu	3 diamonds	$14-$31	407
		HARAHAN - Lodgings			
85 / p. 336		Hampton Inn & Suites Elmwood Hotel - see color ad p 383	3 diamonds	$159-$209	403

Spotter/Map Page Number	OA	HARAHAN - Restaurant	Diamond Rating	Rate Range High Season	Listing Page
89 / p. 336		Taqueria Corona		$5-$14	404
		GRETNA - Lodgings			
88 / p. 336		La Quinta Inn New Orleans (West Bank) - see color ad p 386		$99-$149	403
		GRETNA - Restaurants			
92 / p. 336		Kim Son		$6-$18	403
93 / p. 336		Tan Dinh		$5-$8	403
		WESTWEGO - Lodgings			
91 / p. 336		Best Western Bayou Inn		$129-$189	415
		HARVEY - Lodgings			
94 / p. 336		Holiday Inn Express		$99-$109	404
95 / p. 336	AAA	**Best Western Westbank**		$79-$169 SAVE	404
		HARVEY - Restaurant			
99 / p. 336		Copeland's of New Orleans		$8-$22	404
		ST. JOSEPH - Restaurant			
96 / p. 336		Mosca's		$6-$28	419

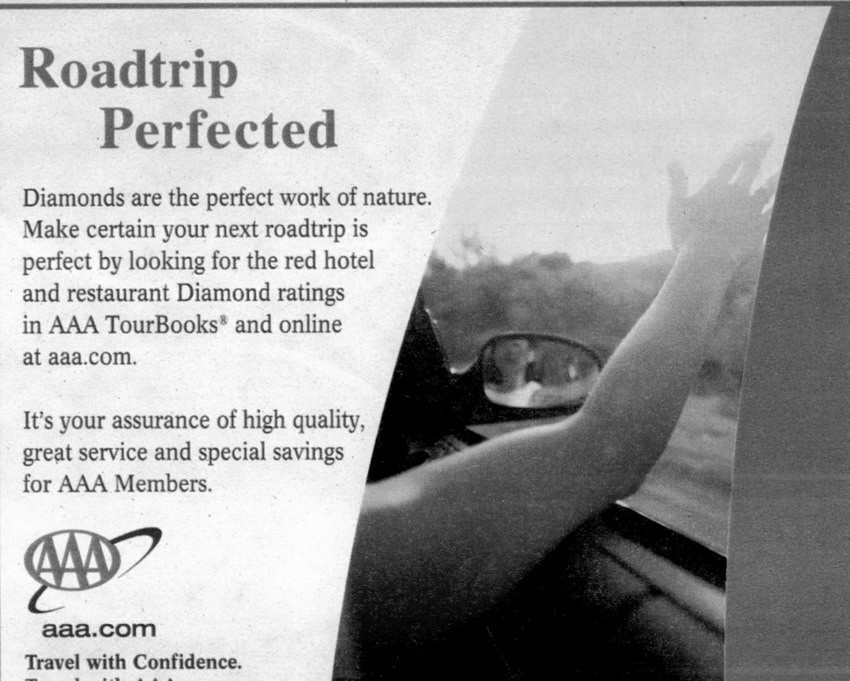

FRENCH QUARTER (See map and index starting on p. 332)

WHERE TO STAY

ASTOR CROWNE PLAZA HOTEL NEW ORLEANS *Book great rates at AAA.com* **Phone:** (504)962-0500 27

AAA SAVE

1/12-5/25 & 9/1-11/30	1P: $159-$249	2P: $169-$269	XP: $20	F18
12/1-1/11 & 5/26-8/31	1P: $99-$149	2P: $109-$159	XP: $20	F18

Large-scale Hotel

Location: Between Bourbon and Royal sts. 739 Canal St at Bourbon 70130. Fax: 504/962-0501. **Facility:** A new addition to the downtown luxury hotel scene, this fine, upscale hotel sits at the edge of the French Quarter. 707 units. 677 one-bedroom standard units. 28 one- and 2 two-bedroom suites ($395-$795). 14 stories, interior corridors. **Parking:** valet. **Terms:** check-in 4 pm, 3 day cancellation notice-fee imposed, [AP] meal plan available. **Amenities:** CD players, dual phone lines, voice mail, irons, hair dryers. *Fee:* video games, high-speed Internet, safes. **Dining:** Bourbon House Restaurant, see separate listing. **Pool(s):** small outdoor. **Leisure Activities:** whirlpool, exercise room. **Guest Services:** gift shop, valet laundry. **Business Services:** meeting rooms, business center. **Cards:** AX, DC, DS, MC, VI.

SOME UNITS

FEE

(See map and index starting on p. 332)

BEST WESTERN FRENCH QUARTER LANDMARK HOTEL *Book great rates at AAA.com* **Phone:** (504)524-3333 **2**

Small-scale Hotel

All Year 1P: $89-$339 2P: $99-$359 XP: $10 F17

Location: Between Dumaine and St. Philip sts. 920 N Rampart St 70116. Fax: 504/523-5431. **Facility:** 102 one-bedroom standard units, some with whirlpools. 3 stories, interior/exterior corridors. **Parking:** on-site (fee). **Terms:** check-in 4 pm, 2 night minimum stay - seasonal and/or weekends, 7 day cancellation notice, [AP] meal plan available. **Amenities:** voice mail, safes (fee), irons, hair dryers. *Some:* high-speed Internet. **Dining:** 7 am-11. **Pool(s):** outdoor. **Guest Services:** valet and coin laundry, area transportation-within French Quarter, wireless Internet. **Business Services:** fax (fee). **Cards:** AX, CB, DC, DS, MC, VI. **Free Special Amenities: local telephone calls and newspaper.**

SOME UNITS

THE BIENVILLE HOUSE HOTEL *Book great rates at AAA.com* **Phone:** (504)529-2345 **28**

Small-scale Hotel

1/1-5/31 & 9/1-11/30	1P: $129-$325	2P: $129-$325	XP: $25	F17
12/1-12/31	1P: $89-$225	2P: $89-$225	XP: $25	F17
6/1-8/31	1P: $89-$189	2P: $89-$189	XP: $25	F17

Location: Between Conti and Bienville sts. 320 Decatur St 70130. Fax: 504/525-6079. **Facility:** 83 units. 80 one-bedroom standard units, some with whirlpools. 3 one-bedroom suites. 4 stories, interior/exterior corridors. *Bath:* combo or shower only. **Parking:** valet. **Terms:** 3 day cancellation notice-fee imposed, package plans. **Amenities:** video games (fee), voice mail, irons, hair dryers. **Dining:** 8 am-noon, Wed-Sun 8 am-noon & 5-10 pm; closed Tues, cocktails. **Pool(s):** outdoor. **Guest Services:** valet laundry. **Business Services:** meeting rooms. **Cards:** AX, CB, DC, DS, JC, MC, VI. **Free Special Amenities: newspaper.** *(See color ad below)*

SOME UNITS

BOURBON ORLEANS, A WYNDHAM HISTORIC HOTEL *Book great rates at AAA.com* **Phone:** (504)523-2222 **9**

Small-scale Hotel

12/1-5/28 & 8/30-11/30	1P: $143-$176
5/29-8/29	1P: $105-$119

Location: Between Bourbon and Royal sts. 717 Orleans St 70116. Fax: 504/571-4166. **Facility:** 218 units. 188 one-bedroom standard units. 30 one-bedroom suites. 7 stories, interior corridors. *Bath:* combo or shower only. **Parking:** valet. **Terms:** 3 day cancellation notice-fee imposed, [AP], [BP], [CP], [ECP] & [MAP] meal plans available, package plans. **Amenities:** dual phone lines, voice mail, safes, honor bars, irons, hair dryers. *Fee:* video games, high-speed Internet. *Some:* CD players. **Dining:** 6:30 am-2 & 5-10 pm. **Pool(s):** outdoor. **Leisure Activities:** exercise room. **Guest Services:** valet laundry, wireless Internet. **Business Services:** meeting rooms, business center. **Cards:** AX, CB, DC, DS, MC, VI.

SOME UNITS

FEE

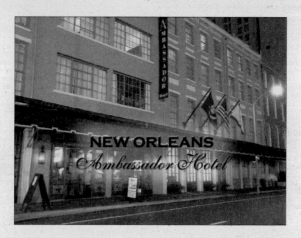

(See map and index starting on p. 332)

THE CHATEAU HOTEL *Book great rates at AAA.com* **Phone:** (504)524-9636 6

AAA SAVE

Small-scale Hotel

All Year [CP]	1P: $69-$109	2P: $79-$169	XP: $15	F

Location: At St. Philip and Chartres sts. 1001 Chartres St 70116. Fax: 504/525-2989. **Facility:** 48 units. 46 one-bedroom standard units. 1 one- and 1 two-bedroom suites. 2 stories (no elevator), interior/exterior corridors. *Bath:* combo or shower only. **Parking:** valet. **Terms:** 2 night minimum stay - weekends, 3 day cancellation notice. **Amenities:** irons, hair dryers. **Pool(s):** small outdoor. **Cards:** AX, CB, DC, DS, MC, VI. **Free Special Amenities: continental breakfast and newspaper.** *(See color ad below)*

SOME UNITS

(See map and index starting on p. 332)

CHATEAU LE MOYNE FRENCH QUARTER, A HOLIDAY INN HOTEL Book great rates at AAA.com

Phone: (504)581-1303 16

Small-scale Hotel

All Year 1P: $89-$299 2P: $89-$299 XP: $20 F18

Location: Between Conti and Bienville sts. 301 Dauphine St 70112. Fax: 504/523-5709. **Facility:** 171 units. 160 one-bedroom standard units. 11 one-bedroom suites, some with whirlpools. 5 stories, interior corridors. *Bath:* combo or shower only. **Parking:** valet. **Terms:** check-in 4 pm, cancellation fee imposed, package plans. **Amenities:** video games (fee), voice mail, irons, hair dryers. **Dining:** 6:30-10:30 am. **Pool(s):** heated outdoor. **Guest Services:** valet laundry, wireless Internet. **Business Services:** meeting rooms. **Cards:** AX, CB, DC, DS, JC, MC, VI. **Free Special Amenities: newspaper and high-speed Internet.** *(See color ad p 358)*

SOME UNITS

CHATEAU SONESTA HOTEL Book great rates at AAA.com

Phone: 504/586-0800 22

Large-scale Hotel

All Year 1P: $99-$249 2P: $99-$249 XP: $40 F

Location: Between Dauphine and Bourbon sts. 800 Iberville St 70112. Fax: 504/586-1987. **Facility:** 251 units. 240 one-bedroom standard units. 8 one- and 3 two-bedroom suites ($195-$750). 4 stories, interior corridors. **Parking:** on-site (fee) and valet. **Terms:** 3 day cancellation notice, [AP] meal plan available, package plans, pets ($75 fee). **Amenities:** CD players, voice mail, safes, honor bars, irons, hair dryers. *Fee:* video games, high-speed Internet. *Some:* dual phone lines. **Dining:** 2 restaurants, 6 am-11 & noon-midnight, cocktails. **Pool(s):** heated outdoor. **Leisure Activities:** exercise room. **Guest Services:** gift shop, valet laundry. **Business Services:** conference facilities, business center. **Cards:** AX, CB, DC, DS, JC, MC, VI. **Free Special Amenities: newspaper and early check-in/late check-out.** *(See color ad below)*

SOME UNITS

FEE

DAUPHINE ORLEANS HOTEL Book great rates at AAA.com

Phone: (504)586-1800 15

Small-scale Hotel

All Year 1P: $109-$199 2P: $109-$199 XP: $20 F

Location: I-10, exit 235A (Orleans Ave/Vieux Carre), proceed on Basin St, 0.8 mi to Toulouse St, turn left 3 blks to Dauphine St, then right 2 blks, jct Conti St. 415 Dauphine St 70112. Fax: 504/586-1409. **Facility:** 111 units. 107 one-bedroom standard units, some with whirlpools. 4 one-bedroom suites ($199-$249). 1-4 stories, interior/exterior corridors. *Bath:* combo or shower only. **Parking:** valet. **Terms:** package plans. **Amenities:** video games (fee), dual phone lines, voice mail, safes, irons, hair dryers. **Pool(s):** outdoor. **Leisure Activities:** whirlpool, exercise room. **Guest Services:** valet laundry. **Business Services:** meeting rooms, PC, fax (fee). **Cards:** AX, CB, DC, DS, MC, VI. **Free Special Amenities: expanded continental breakfast and newspaper.** *(See color ad p 355)*

SOME UNITS

FRENCH QUARTER SUITES HOTEL Book great rates at AAA.com

Phone: (504)524-7725 1

Small-scale Hotel

All Year 1P: $59-$299 2P: $59-$299 XP: $15 F3

Location: Between Ursuline and Governor Nicholls. 1119 N Rampart St 70116. Fax: 504/522-9716. **Facility:** 18 units. 2 one-bedroom standard units. 8 one- and 8 two-bedroom suites, some with kitchens. 3 stories, exterior corridors. **Parking:** on-site (fee). **Terms:** 2 night minimum stay - weekends, 7 day cancellation notice-fee imposed, [CP] meal plan available, package plans, pets ($15 extra charge). **Amenities:** safes, irons, hair dryers. **Pool(s):** small outdoor. **Guest Services:** complimentary and valet laundry. **Cards:** AX, DS, MC, VI. ***(See color ad p 357)***

SOME UNITS

ASK

FEE

HOLIDAY INN FRENCH QUARTER Book great rates at AAA.com

Phone: (504)529-7211 26

Small-scale Hotel

All Year 1P: $89-$299 2P: $89-$299

Location: Between Iberville and Canal sts. 124 Royal St 70130. Fax: 504/566-1127. **Facility:** 374 one-bedroom standard units. 20 stories, interior corridors. *Bath:* combo or shower only. **Parking:** on-site (fee). **Terms:** check-in 4 pm, cancellation fee imposed, package plans, small pets only ($25 fee, $125 deposit). **Amenities:** video games (fee), voice mail, irons, hair dryers. **Dining:** 6:30 am-midnight, cocktails. **Pool(s):** heated indoor. **Leisure Activities:** exercise room. **Guest Services:** valet and coin laundry, wireless Internet. **Business Services:** fax (fee). **Cards:** AX, CB, DC, DS, JC, MC, VI. **Free Special Amenities: newspaper and room upgrade (subject to availability with advance reservations).** *(See color ad p 358)*

SOME UNITS

FEE FEE FEE

(See map and index starting on p. 332)

HOTEL MAISON DE VILLE *Book at AAA.com* Phone: (504)561-5858 **13**

Historic Small-scale Hotel

12/1-5/31 & 9/1-11/30	1P: $249-$699	2P: $249-$699
6/1-8/31	1P: $139-$499	2P: $139-$499

Location: Jct Toulouse and Bourbon sts, just s. 727 rue Toulouse 70130. Fax: 504/528-9939. **Facility:** The 1783 hotel has an idyllic courtyard and charming cottages with antiques; celebrities have stayed here and dined in the property's fine restaurant. Smoke free premises. 23 units. 14 one-bedroom standard units. 2 one-bedroom suites. 7 cottages ($499-$699), some with whirlpools. 1-3 stories (no elevator), interior/exterior corridors. *Bath:* combo or shower only. **Parking:** valet. **Terms:** 2-3 night minimum stay - weekends, age restrictions may apply, 3 day cancellation notice, [CP] meal plan available, $5 service charge. **Amenities:** video library, dual phone lines, voice mail, honor bars, irons, hair dryers. *Some:* CD players. **Dining:** The Bistro, see separate listing. **Pool(s):** outdoor. **Guest Services:** complimentary evening beverages, valet laundry, wireless Internet. **Business Services:** PC. **Cards:** AX, CB, DC, DS, JC, MC, VI.

SOME UNITS

HOTEL MONTELEONE *Book great rates at AAA.com* Phone: (504)523-3341 **25**

Historic Large-scale Hotel

1/16-5/30 & 9/16-11/30	1P: $165-$225	2P: $185-$250	XP: $25	F18
5/31-9/15	1P: $125-$150	2P: $135-$195	XP: $25	F18
12/1-1/15	1P: $150-$175	2P: $160-$185	XP: $25	F18

Location: Between Iberville and Bienville sts. 214 Royal St 70130. Fax: 504/528-1019. **Facility:** The historic hotel, owned by the same family for generations, offers spacious, richly appointed rooms, a distinctive lobby and a revolving lounge. 570 units. 515 one-bedroom standard units. 55 one-bedroom suites ($295-$2000) with whirlpools. 17 stories, interior corridors. *Bath:* combo or shower only. **Parking:** valet. **Terms:** 2 night minimum stay - weekends, 3 day cancellation notice-fee imposed. **Amenities:** dual phone lines, voice mail, safes, honor bars, irons, hair dryers. *Fee:* video games, high-speed Internet. *Some:* CD players. **Dining:** 3 restaurants, 6:30 am-11 pm, cocktails, entertainment. **Pool(s):** heated outdoor. **Leisure Activities:** exercise room, spa. **Guest Services:** gift shop, valet laundry, barber shop, wireless Internet. **Business Services:** conference facilities, business center. **Cards:** AX, DC, DS, MC, VI. **Free Special Amenities: local telephone calls and preferred room (subject to availability with advance reservations).**

(See color ad p 358)

SOME UNITS

HOTEL PROVINCIAL *Book great rates at AAA.com* Phone: (504)581-4995 **7**

Small-scale Hotel

2/1-5/31 & 9/1-11/30	1P: $99-$269	2P: $99-$269	XP: $20	F17
12/1-1/31 & 6/1-8/31	1P: $89-$209	2P: $89-$209	XP: $20	F17

Location: Between Ursuline Ave and St. Philip St. 1024 rue Chartres St 70116. Fax: 504/581-1018. **Facility:** 93 units. 90 one-bedroom standard units. 3 one-bedroom suites. 2-4 stories, interior/exterior corridors. *Bath:* combo or shower only. **Parking:** valet. **Terms:** 2 night minimum stay - weekends, 3 day cancellation notice-fee imposed. **Amenities:** voice mail, irons, hair dryers. **Dining:** 2 restaurants, 7 am-10 pm, cocktails. **Pool(s):** 2 outdoor. **Guest Services:** valet laundry. **Business Services:** meeting rooms, fax (fee). **Cards:** AX, CB, DC, DS, MC, VI. **Free Special Amenities: newspaper and room upgrade (subject to availability with advance reservations).**

(See color ad p 359)

SOME UNITS

(See map and index starting on p. 332)

HOTEL ROYAL Book great rates at AAA.com **Phone:** (504)524-3900 **5**

AAA SAVE

Small-scale Hotel

12/1-5/31 & 8/16-11/30 [CP]	1P: $95-$350	2P: $95-$350	XP: $25	F12
6/1-8/15 [CP]	1P: $79-$300	2P: $79-$300	XP: $25	F12

Location: Between Ursuline Ave and St. Philip St. 1006 Royal St 70116. Fax: 504/558-0566. **Facility:** 39 units. 32 one- and 7 two-bedroom standard units, some with whirlpools. 4 stories (no elevator), interior/exterior corridors. *Bath:* combo or shower only. **Parking:** on-site (fee). **Terms:** 30 day cancellation notice-fee imposed. **Amenities:** high-speed Internet, voice mail, irons, hair dryers. *Some:* CD players. **Business Services:** fax. **Cards:** AX, DS, MC, VI. **Free Special Amenities: continental breakfast and high-speed Internet.**

(See color ad below)

SOME UNITS

(See map and index starting on p. 332)

HOTEL ST. MARIE *Book great rates at AAA.com* **Phone:** (504)561-8951 **12**

AAA SAVE — Small-scale Hotel

All Year 1P: $69-$259 2P: $69-$259

Location: Between Dauphine and Bourbon sts. 827 Toulouse St 70112 (830 Conti St, NEW ORLEANS). Fax: 504/571-2802. **Facility:** 103 one-bedroom standard units. 5 stories, interior corridors. **Parking:** valet. **Terms:** check-in 4 pm, 2 night minimum stay - weekends, 3 day cancellation notice-fee imposed, package plans. **Amenities:** voice mail, irons, hair dryers. *Some:* high-speed Internet (fee). **Dining:** 7 am-10 pm, cocktails, also, Hillery's On Toulouse, see separate listing. **Pool(s):** outdoor. **Guest Services:** valet laundry, wireless Internet. **Business Services:** meeting rooms, fax (fee). **Cards:** AX, CB, DC, DS, MC, VI. **Free Special Amenities: newspaper and preferred room (subject to availability with advance reservations).** *(See color ad p 344)*

SOME UNITS

THE IBERVILLE SUITES *Book great rates at AAA.com* **Phone:** (504)523-2400 **21**

AAA SAVE — Historic Small-scale Hotel

All Year 1P: $99-$268 XP: $25 F17

Location: Between Burgundy and Dauphine sts. 910 Iberville St 70112. Fax: 504/524-7233. **Facility:** This boutique hotel is housed in the historic Maison Blanche Building, a structure rooted in the 1800s; personalized service is a property standard. 230 units. 15 one-bedroom standard units. 215 one-bedroom suites. 7 stories, interior corridors. *Bath:* combo or shower only. **Parking:** valet. **Terms:** 3 day cancellation notice-fee imposed, $1 service charge, small pets only ($100 fee). **Amenities:** CD players, dual phone lines, voice mail, safes, irons, hair dryers. *Fee:* video games, high-speed Internet. **Guest Services:** gift shop, valet laundry, wireless Internet. **Business Services:** meeting rooms, business center. **Cards:** AX, CB, DC, DS, MC, VI. **Free Special Amenities: continental breakfast.** *(See color ad below)*

SOME UNITS

FEE FEE

THE INN ON BOURBON RAMADA PLAZA HOTEL *Book great rates at AAA.com* **Phone:** (504)524-7611 **14**

AAA SAVE — Small-scale Hotel

All Year 1P: $89-$349 2P: $89-$349 XP: $35 F17

Location: Between Toulouse and St. Louis sts. 541 Bourbon St 70130. Fax: 504/568-9427. **Facility:** 186 one-bedroom standard units. 5 stories, interior corridors. *Bath:* combo or shower only. **Parking:** valet. **Terms:** check-in 4 pm, [BP] meal plan available, package plans. **Amenities:** voice mail, safes (fee), honor bars, irons, hair dryers. **Dining:** 6:30-11 am, Sat & Sun-noon. **Pool(s):** outdoor. **Leisure Activities:** exercise room. **Guest Services:** gift shop, valet laundry, wireless Internet. **Business Services:** meeting rooms, business center. **Cards:** AX, DC, DS, JC, MC, VI. **Free Special Amenities: full breakfast and high-speed Internet.** *(See color ad p 361)*

SOME UNITS

(See map and index starting on p. 332)

LAFITTE GUEST HOUSE Phone: 504/581-2678 4

Bed & Breakfast

All Year 1P: $100-$229

Location: Between Ursuline Ave and St. Philip St. 1003 Bourbon St 70116. Fax: 504/581-2677. **Facility:** A small Victorian parlor adds character to this property; an impressive staircase leads guests to antique-filled rooms, some with large balconies. Smoke free premises. 14 one-bedroom standard units. 4 stories, interior/exterior corridors. *Bath:* combo or shower only. **Parking:** on-site (fee). **Terms:** 7 day cancellation notice, [CP] meal plan available. **Amenities:** high-speed Internet. *Some:* irons, hair dryers. **Guest Services:** wireless Internet. **Cards:** AX, MC, VI.

SOME UNITS

LE RICHELIEU IN THE FRENCH QUARTER Book great rates at AAA.com Phone: (504)529-2492 3

Historic Small-scale Hotel

All Year 1P: $85-$170 2P: $95-$185 XP: $15

Location: Between Governor Nicholls and Barracks. 1234 Chartres St 70116. Fax: 504/524-8179. **Facility:** The serene Le Richelieu offers a lovely courtyard; a notable amenity for the French Quarter, is available. 86 units. 70 one-bedroom standard units. 10 one-, 5 two- and 1 three-bedroom suites ($180-$555). 4 stories, interior corridors. *Bath:* combo or shower only. **Parking:** on-site. **Terms:** 2 night minimum stay - weekends, package plans - seasonal. **Amenities:** voice mail, irons, hair dryers. *Some:* DVD players. **Dining:** 7 am-9 pm, cocktails. **Pool(s):** outdoor. **Guest Services:** valet laundry, wireless Internet. **Business Services:** fax (fee). **Cards:** AX, DC, DS, MC, VI. **Free Special Amenities: local telephone calls.** *(See color ad p 363)*

SOME UNITS

MAISON DUPUY HOTEL Book great rates at AAA.com Phone: (504)586-8000 8

Small-scale Hotel

1/1-11/30	1P: $79-$249	2P: $79-$249	XP: $20	F17
12/1-12/31	1P: $79-$209	2P: $79-$209	XP: $20	F17

Location: Between Burgundy and Rampart sts. 1001 Toulouse St 70112. Fax: 504/566-7450. **Facility:** 200 units. 189 one-bedroom standard units. 11 one-bedroom suites, some with whirlpools. 5 stories, interior corridors. *Bath:* combo or shower only. **Parking:** valet. **Terms:** check-in 4 pm, 3 day cancellation notice-fee imposed, [BP] & [CP] meal plans available. **Amenities:** video games (fee), voice mail, safes, honor bars, irons, hair dryers. **Dining:** 7 am-11 pm, cocktails, also, Dominique's, see separate listing. **Pool(s):** heated outdoor, saltwater. **Leisure Activities:** sauna, whirlpool, exercise room. *Fee:* massage. **Guest Services:** valet laundry, wireless Internet. **Business Services:** meeting rooms, business center. **Cards:** AX, DS, MC, VI. *(See color ad p 364)*

SOME UNITS

THE MAISON ORLEANS-RITZ CARLTON Book great rates at AAA.com Phone: (504)670-2900 20

Small-scale Hotel

1/1-11/30 1P: $209-$419 XP: $25 F18

Location: Between Burgundy and Dauphine sts. 904 Iberville St 70112. Fax: 504/670-2910. **Facility:** Highly personalized service is the hallmark of this boutique hotel. The staff will impress you and the room amenities may just entice you to stay in. 75 units. 74 one-bedroom standard units. 1 one-bedroom suite ($369-$569). 6 stories, interior corridors. *Bath:* combo or shower only. **Parking:** valet. **Terms:** open 1/1-11/30, cancellation fee imposed, package plans, 13% service charge, pets ($100 fee). **Amenities:** video library, DVD players, CD players, dual phone lines, voice mail, safes, irons, hair dryers. *Fee:* video games, high-speed Internet. **Dining:** 6:30 am-11 & 6-10:30 pm, Sun & Mon-11 am, entertainment. **Pool(s):** small heated indoor. **Leisure Activities:** whirlpool, spa. **Guest Services:** complimentary evening beverages, valet laundry, wireless Internet. **Business Services:** administrative services. **Cards:** AX, DC, DS, MC, VI. **Free Special Amenities: expanded continental breakfast and newspaper.**

FEE

NEW ORLEANS MARRIOTT Book great rates at AAA.com Phone: (504)581-1000 29

Large-scale Hotel

All Year 1P: $139-$329 2P: $139-$329

Location: Corner of Canal and Chartres sts. 555 Canal St 70130. Fax: 504/523-6755. **Facility:** 1290 units. 1287 one-bedroom standard units. 3 one-bedroom suites. 41 stories, interior corridors. *Bath:* combo or shower only. **Parking:** valet. **Terms:** cancellation fee imposed, package plans, $3 service charge. **Amenities:** high-speed Internet (fee), dual phone lines, voice mail, irons, hair dryers. *Some:* CD players. **Dining:** 2 restaurants, 6:30 am-11 pm, Fri & Sat-midnight, cocktails, entertainment. **Pool(s):** heated outdoor, wading. **Leisure Activities:** saunas, exercise room. **Guest Services:** gift shop, valet and coin laundry. **Business Services:** conference facilities, business center. **Cards:** AX, CB, DC, DS, JC, MC, VI. *(See color ad p 365)*

SOME UNITS

(See map and index starting on p. 332)

OMNI ROYAL ORLEANS HOTEL *Book great rates at AAA.com* **Phone:** (504)529-5333 **18**

AAA SAVE

1/12-5/26 & 8/31-11/30	1P: $169-$299	2P: $179-$320	XP: $20	F18
12/1-1/11 & 5/27-8/30	1P: $119-$169	2P: $129-$179	XP: $20	F18

Large-scale Hotel

Location: At Royal and St. Louis sts. 621 St. Louis St 70140. Fax: 504/529-7089. **Facility:** A notable feature here is the observation deck offering a bird's-eye view of the city; rooms feature rich wood furniture and marble bathroom floors. 346 units. 330 one-bedroom standard units, some with whirlpools. 16 one-bedroom suites ($495-$899), some with whirlpools. 7 stories, interior corridors. *Bath:* combo or shower only. **Parking:** valet. **Terms:** check-in 4 pm, 3 day cancellation notice-fee imposed, [AP] meal plan available, package plans, small pets only ($50 fee). **Amenities:** video games (fee), dual phone lines, voice mail, safes, honor bars, irons, hair dryers. *Some:* CD players. **Dining:** The Rib Room-Rotisserie Extraordinaire, see separate listing, entertainment. **Pool(s):** heated outdoor. **Leisure Activities:** exercise room. **Guest Services:** gift shop, valet laundry, wireless Internet. **Business Services:** conference facilities, business center. **Cards:** AX, DC, DS, JC, MC, VI. **Free Special Amenities: newspaper.** *(See color ad p 366)*

SOME UNITS

FEE FEE

PLACE D'ARMES HOTEL *Book great rates at AAA.com* **Phone:** (504)524-4531 **11**

AAA SAVE

All Year	1P: $69-$259	2P: $69-$259	XP: $20	F12

Small-scale Hotel

Location: Between Royal and Chartres sts. On Jackson Square. 625 St Ann St 70116 (830 Conti St, NEW ORLEANS, 70112). Fax: 504/571-2803. **Facility:** 86 units. 84 one-bedroom standard units. 2 one-bedroom suites. 2-5 stories, interior/exterior corridors. *Bath:* combo or shower only. **Parking:** valet. **Terms:** check-in 4 pm, 2 night minimum stay - weekends, 3 day cancellation notice-fee imposed, package plans. **Amenities:** voice mail, irons, hair dryers. *Some:* high-speed Internet (fee). **Pool(s):** small outdoor. **Guest Services:** valet laundry, wireless Internet. **Business Services:** fax (fee). **Cards:** AX, CB, DC, DS, MC, VI. **Free Special Amenities: newspaper and preferred room (subject to availability with advance reservations).** *(See color ad p 344)*

FEE

PRINCE CONTI HOTEL *Book great rates at AAA.com* **Phone:** (504)529-4172 **17**

AAA SAVE

All Year	1P: $69-$239	2P: $69-$239	XP: $20	F12

Small-scale Hotel

Location: Between Dauphine and Bourbon sts. 830 Conti St 70112. Fax: 504/636-1046. **Facility:** 76 units. 73 one-bedroom standard units, some with whirlpools. 3 one-bedroom suites. 3 stories, interior/exterior corridors. **Parking:** valet. **Terms:** check-in 4 pm, 2 night minimum stay - weekends, 3 day cancellation notice-fee imposed, package plans. **Amenities:** voice mail, irons, hair dryers. *Some:* high-speed Internet (fee). **Dining:** 2 restaurants, 7 am-11 & 4-close, cocktails. **Guest Services:** valet laundry, wireless Internet. **Business Services:** meeting rooms, fax (fee). **Cards:** AX, CB, DC, DS, MC, VI. **Free Special Amenities: newspaper and preferred room (subject to availability with advance reservations).** *(See color ad p 344)*

SOME UNITS

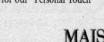

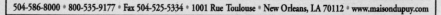

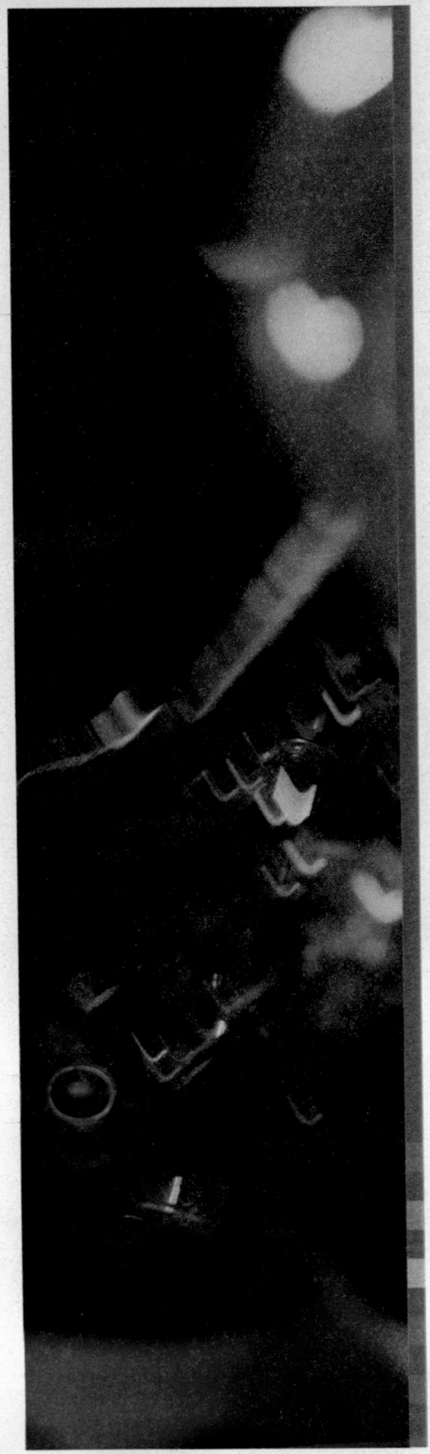

(See map and index starting on p. 332)

THE RITZ-CARLTON NEW ORLEANS Book great rates at AAA.com **Phone:** (504)524-1331 23

All Year 1P: $419-$459 XP: $25 F17

Large-scale Hotel

Location: Between Dauphine and Burgundy sts. 921 Canal St 70112. Fax: 504/524-7675. **Facility:** Created from the turn-of-the-century architectural beauty that was the Maison Blanche Department Store, the property offers extensive facilities. 452 units. 415 one-bedroom standard units. 37 one-bedroom suites, some with whirlpools. 12 stories, interior corridors. *Bath:* combo or shower only. **Parking:** valet. **Terms:** 3 day cancellation notice-fee imposed, package plans, $2 service charge, pets ($100 fee). **Amenities:** CD players, dual phone lines, voice mail, safes, honor bars, irons, hair dryers. *Fee:* video games, high-speed Internet. **Dining:** 2 restaurants, 6:30 am-2 am, cocktails, also, Victor's Grill, see separate listing, entertainment. **Pool(s):** small heated indoor. **Leisure Activities:** spa. **Guest Services:** gift shop, valet laundry, wireless Internet. **Business Services:** conference facilities, business center. **Cards:** AX, CB, DC, DS, MC, VI. *(See color ad p 360)*

SOME UNITS

FEE FEE

(See map and index starting on p. 332)

ROYAL SONESTA HOTEL NEW ORLEANS *Book great rates at AAA.com* **Phone:** (504)586-0300 **19**

AAA SAVE

1/21-6/18 & 9/16-11/30	1P: $199-$329	2P: $199-$329	XP: $40	F16
12/1-1/20	1P: $159-$289	2P: $159-$289	XP: $40	F16
6/19-9/15	1P: $109-$269	2P: $109-$269	XP: $40	F16

Large-scale Hotel

Location: Garage entrance on Conti or Bienville sts. 300 Bourbon St 70130. Fax: 504/586-0335. **Facility:** The lobby, public areas and guest rooms in this service-oriented hotel are attractively furnished; cozy guest rooms feature upscale amenities. 483 units. 467 one-bedroom standard units, some with whirlpools. 16 one-bedroom suites ($350-$1200), some with whirlpools. 5-7 stories, interior corridors. *Bath:* combo or shower only. **Parking:** on-site (fee) and valet. **Terms:** 3 day cancellation notice, package plans, small pets only ($50 fee). **Amenities:** CD players, voice mail, safes, honor bars, irons, hair dryers. *Fee:* video games, high-speed Internet. *Some:* dual phone lines. **Dining:** 2 restaurants, 6:30 am-midnight, cocktails, also, Begue's, see separate listing, entertainment. **Pool(s):** heated outdoor. **Leisure Activities:** exercise room. **Guest Services:** gift shop, valet laundry, wireless Internet. **Business Services:** conference facilities, business center. **Cards:** AX, CB, DC, DS, JC, MC, VI. **Free Special Amenities: newspaper.** *(See color ad below)*

SOME UNITS

FEE FEE FEE FEE

RUE DUMAINE GUESTHOUSE **Phone:** (504)522-1158 **10**

All Year	1P: $195-$240	2P: $195-$425

Bed & Breakfast

Location: Between Decatur and Chartres. 517 Rue Dumaine 70116. Fax: 504/309-3517. **Facility:** 12 units. 2 one-bedroom standard units. 6 one- and 4 two-bedroom suites ($425-$750). 3-4 stories, interior/exterior corridors. *Bath:* combo or shower only. **Parking:** street. **Terms:** office hours 9 am-6 pm, 3 day cancellation notice, package plans. **Amenities:** high-speed Internet, voice mail, irons, hair dryers. **Pool(s):** small outdoor. **Leisure Activities:** whirlpool. **Guest Services:** complimentary evening beverages, valet laundry, wireless Internet. **Business Services:** administrative services. **Cards:** AX, DS, MC, VI.

SOME UNITS

ASK

FEE

(See map and index starting on p. 332)

W FRENCH QUARTER Book great rates at AAA.com **Phone:** (504)581-1200 24

AAA SAVE

12/1-5/31 & 9/2-11/30	1P: $179-$369	2P: $179-$369	XP: $20	F18
6/1-9/1	1P: $139-$369	2P: $139-$369	XP: $20	F18

Small-scale Hotel

Location: Between Conti and Bienville sts. 316 rue Chartres St 70130. Fax: 504/523-2910. **Facility:** 98 units. 96 one-bedroom standard units, some with whirlpools. 2 one-bedroom suites with whirlpools. 5 stories, interior corridors. *Bath:* combo or shower only. **Parking:** valet. **Terms:** 3 day cancellation notice-fee imposed, pets ($100 fee, $25 extra charge). **Amenities:** video library, DVD players, CD players, high-speed Internet (fee), dual phone lines, voice mail, safes, honor bars, irons, hair dryers. *Some:* video games (fee). **Dining:** Bacco, see separate listing. **Pool(s):** small heated outdoor. **Guest Services:** valet laundry. **Business Services:** meeting rooms, business center. **Cards:** AX, CB, DC, DS, JC, MC, VI. *(See color ad p 391)*

SOME UNITS

FEE

(See map and index starting on p. 332)

WYNDHAM NEW ORLEANS AT CANAL PLACE Book great rates at AAA.com **Phone:** (504)566-7006 30

12/1-6/9 & 10/5-11/30	1P: $149-$179	2P: $149-$179	XP: $25	F17
6/10-10/4	1P: $119-$139	2P: $119-$139	XP: $25	F17

Large-scale Hotel

Location: At Canal Place, near Mississippi River. Located adjacent to Canal Place Mall. 100 rue Iberville 70130. Fax: 504/553-5120. **Facility:** This hotel's lobby offers sweeping views of the Mississippi River and French Quarter; upscale shopping is steps away at The Shops at Canal Place. 438 units. 395 one-bedroom standard units. 43 one-bedroom suites, some with whirlpools. 29 stories, interior corridors. *Bath:* combo or shower only. **Parking:** on-site (fee) and valet. **Terms:** 3 day cancellation notice-fee imposed. **Amenities:** dual phone lines, voice mail, safes, honor bars, irons, hair dryers. *Fee:* video games, high-speed Internet. *Some:* CD players. **Dining:** River 127, see separate listing. **Pool(s):** heated outdoor. **Leisure Activities:** exercise room, spa. **Guest Services:** valet laundry. **Business Services:** conference facilities, business center. **Cards:** AX, DC, DS, MC, VI.

SOME UNITS

FEE

(See map and index starting on p. 332)

WHERE TO DINE

THE ALPINE RESTAURANT Lunch: $7-$15 Dinner: $13-$24 Phone: 504/523-3005 (28)

Cajun

Location: Corner of Toulouse St. 620 rue Chartres 70130. **Hours:** 11 am-4 & 5-10 pm, Fri & Sat 9 am-11 pm, Sun 9 am-10 pm. **Reservations:** suggested. **Features:** The restaurant is a real crowd-pleaser due in part to its varied menu of both Cajun and American classics. The dining room, with its mix of French Quarter vintage and Mediterranean embellishments, provides a fresh backdrop that serves as a respite from the bustling historic area. Casual dress; cocktails. **Parking:** street. **Cards:** AX, CB, DC, DS, MC, VI.

ANTOINE'S **Lunch:** $8-$23 **Dinner:** $23-$47 **Phone:** 504/581-4422 (29)

French

Location: Between Bourbon and Royal sts. 713 St. Louis St 70130. **Hours:** 11:30 am-2 & 5:30-9:30 pm. Closed major holidays; also Sun & Mardi Gras. **Reservations:** suggested. **Features:** A New Orleans landmark, the French Quarter restaurant has been in continuous operation since 1840. Diners savor French-Creole cuisine in a distinctive and stylishly decorated dining room. Dressy casual; cocktails. **Parking:** street. **Cards:** AX, CB, DC, DS, MC, VI.

ARNAUD'S **Lunch:** $12-$30 **Dinner:** $25-$38 **Phone:** 504/523-5433 (35)

Creole

Location: Between Bourbon and Dauphine sts. 813 Bienville St 70112. **Hours:** 11:30 am-2:30 & 6-10 pm, Fri-10:30 pm, Sat from 6 pm, Sun 10 am-2:30 & 6-10 pm. Closed major holidays; also Mardi Gras. **Reservations:** suggested. **Features:** Served in an elegant and historic atmosphere, the cuisine caters to both creative and classic French-Creole tastes. Attentive servers bring such signature dishes as shrimp Arnaud and souffle potatoes. After dinner, browse Arnaud's Mardi Gras museum, a revered New Orleans institution that can be loud. Dressy casual; cocktails. **Parking:** street. **Cards:** AX, DC, DS, MC, VI.

ASIAN CAJUN BISTRO **Lunch:** $8-$21 **Dinner:** $8-$26 **Phone:** 504/522-4964 (55)

Asian

Location: Northeast corner of Bienville and Decatur sts. 301 Decatur St 70130. **Hours:** 11 am-3 & 5-11 pm. Closed: 11/22, 12/25. **Reservations:** suggested. **Features:** Near shopping and many attractions in the French Quarter, the restaurant specializes in seafood and prepares several types of dishes, including Cajun, Sicilian, Vietnamese, Cantonese and Italian. Live piano music enhances the dining setting. Casual dress; cocktails. **Parking:** street. **Cards:** AX, DC, DS, MC, VI.

BACCO **Lunch:** $10-$16 **Dinner:** $18-$30 **Phone:** 504/522-2426 (51)

Italian

Location: Between Conti and Bienville sts; in W French Quarter. 310 Chartres St 70130. **Hours:** 11:30 am-2:30 & 6-10 pm. Closed: 12/24, 12/25; also Mardi Gras. **Reservations:** suggested. **Features:** Venetian silk chandeliers, baroque ceiling paintings and hand-blown Venetian glass enhance the beautiful, serene decor. The menu offers Creole-Italian cuisine such as foie gras pizza, seasonal crawfish ravioli, and black truffle fettuccine. Casual dress; cocktails. **Parking:** valet. **Cards:** AX, CB, DC, DS, MC, VI.

BAYONA **Lunch:** $9-$14 **Dinner:** $16-$28 **Phone:** 504/525-4455 (26)

Mediterranean

Location: Between Conti and St. Louis sts. 430 Dauphine St 70112. **Hours:** 11:30 am-2 & 6-10 pm, Fri-11 pm, Sat 6 pm-11 pm. Closed: 7/4, 12/25; also Sun, Mon & Mardi Gras. **Reservations:** suggested. **Features:** The setting is a 200-year-old Creole cottage with a patio, banana trees, magnolias and crepe myrtles. Imaginative "global eclectic" dishes, many featuring seafood, include such elegant specialties as grilled duck breast with pepper jelly glaze. Dressy casual; cocktails. **Parking:** street. **Cards:** AX, DC, DS, MC, VI.
(See color ad p 355)

BEGUE'S **Lunch:** $11-$19 **Dinner:** $22-$40 **Phone:** 504/553-2278 (41)

AAA

French

Location: Garage entrance on Conti or Bienville sts; in Royal Sonesta Hotel New Orleans. 300 Bourbon St 70130. **Hours:** 6:30 am-2 & 6-10 pm. **Reservations:** suggested. **Features:** Patrons can savor Creole-French cuisine in a bright, comfortable atmosphere. Recommended are fillet of tilapia with beurre blanc sauce and turtle soup. The wait staff provides attentive, friendly service, making an experience here pleasant overall. Dressy casual; cocktails. **Parking:** on-site. **Cards:** AX, CB, DC, DS, JC, MC, VI. *(See color ad p 367)*

BELLA LUNA **Dinner:** $18-$26 **Phone:** 504/529-1583 (18)

Nouvelle Continental

Location: In French Market area. 914 N Peters 70116. **Hours:** 6 pm-10:30 pm, Sun-9:30 pm. Closed: 11/22, 12/25; also Mardi Gras. **Reservations:** suggested. **Features:** Elegant and fashionable, Bella Luna offers a fine view of the Mississippi River that is particularly lovely at night. A creative, eclectic Continental menu displays local influences and variety of cooking styles, as seen in the house-cured pork chop in a New Orleans-style pecan crust. Dressy casual; cocktails. **Parking:** valet. **Cards:** AX, CB, DC, DS, MC, VI.

THE BISTRO **Lunch:** $10-$15 **Dinner:** $19-$35 **Phone:** 504/528-9206 (23)

Continental

Location: Jct Toulouse and Bourbon sts; just s, in Hotel Maison De Ville. 733 Toulouse St 70130. **Hours:** 11:30 am-2 & 6-10 pm, Sun from 6 pm. Closed: 12/24 & Mardi Gras. **Reservations:** suggested. **Features:** The intimate, Parisian bistro setting is perfect for a romantic night out. Crawfish remoulade and ravioli stuffed with duck are among the menu selections, as are seasonal wild game dishes. Outdoor dining is available in the courtyard. Dressy casual; cocktails. **Parking:** street. **Cards:** AX, CB, DC, DS, MC, VI.

BOURBON HOUSE RESTAURANT **Lunch:** $8-$24 **Dinner:** $16-$32 **Phone:** 504/522-0111 (52)

Regional American

Location: Between Bourbon and Royal sts; in Astor Crowne Plaza Hotel New Orleans. 144 Bourbon St 70130. **Hours:** 11:30 am-9 pm, Fri & Sat-10 pm. Closed: Mardi Gras. **Reservations:** accepted. **Features:** The emphasis is on the plentiful yield of the nearby gulf. Fresh shrimp and seafood are prepared New Orleans-style and served in an upscale, wood-paneled dining room. Service is smoothly professional and timely. Dressy casual; cocktails. **Parking:** street. **Cards:** AX, CB, DC, DS, MC, VI.

(See map and index starting on p. 332)

BRENNAN'S RESTAURANT Lunch: $16-$36 Dinner: $30-$40 Phone: 504/525-9711 (31)

Creole

Location: Between Conti and St. Louis sts. 417 Royal St 70130. **Hours:** 8 am-2:30 & 6-10 pm. Closed: 12/25; also for dinner 12/24. **Reservations:** suggested. **Features:** A formally attired wait staff serves French-Creole delights such as trout Nancy, sauteed and topped with lump crabmeat, capers and lemon-butter sauce. Also renowned for breakfast, this place offers a nice selection of omelets. Jackets are requested at night. Dressy casual; cocktails. **Parking:** street. **Cards:** AX, CB, DC, DS, MC, VI.

BROUSSARD'S Dinner: $21-$35 Phone: 504/581-3866 (27)

Creole

Location: Just off Bourbon St. 819 Conti St 70112. **Hours:** 5:30 pm-10 pm. Closed: 12/25; also Mardi Gras. **Reservations:** suggested. **Features:** A sophisticated ambience envelops diners who slip away for elegant contemporary Creole cuisine. Since 1920, this place has offered an experience in fine dining in either the tastefully decorated dining rooms or the attractively landscaped courtyard. Among entrees is bouillabaisse. Chef Gunter Preuss also serves as co-owner and operator. Dressy casual; cocktails. **Parking:** street. **Cards:** AX, MC, VI.

CAFE GIOVANNI Dinner: $19-$33 Phone: 504/529-2154 (60)

Italian

Location: Between Iberville and Canal sts. 117 Decatur St 70130. **Hours:** 5:30 pm-10 pm, Sat-11 pm. Closed major holidays; also Sun, Mon & Mardi Gras. **Reservations:** accepted. **Features:** Lavish, colorful dishes expand on basic themes, with complex butter, tomato and cream sauces. Exposed brick and concrete floors lend to the liveliness of the dining room. The atmosphere is enhanced by professional opera singers who entertain Wednesday through Sunday night. The hopping bar is a great place to start the evening. Casual dress; cocktails. **Parking:** on-site (fee). **Cards:** AX, DC, MC, VI.

CAFE GUMBOLAYA Lunch: $7-$13 Phone: 504/523-7418 (15)

Cajun

Location: Jct Decatur and St. Philips; at French Market. 1000 N Peters St 70116. **Hours:** 8 am-4 pm; summer hours may vary. Closed: 12/25, 12/26; also 12/24 for dinner. **Reservations:** accepted. **Features:** Before or after browsing through the marketplace, diners often stop in the pleasant eatery. Among choices are all-day breakfast items, hearty gumbo and po' boy specialties. The light and rich bread pudding is not to be missed. Casual dress; cocktails. **Parking:** street. **Cards:** AX, DC, DS, MC, VI.

CAFE SBISA Lunch: $11-$16 Dinner: $18-$32 Phone: 504/522-5565 (11)

Creole

Location: Corner of Decatur and St. Phillips sts. 1011 Decatur St 70116. **Hours:** 5:30 pm-10:30 pm, Fri & Sat-11 pm, Sun also 10 am-3 pm; Sunday brunch. Closed: Call for days. **Reservations:** suggested. **Features:** A French Quarter tradition since 1899, the cafe serves Creole cuisine in an elegant, intimate atmosphere. Guests can enjoy a romantic dinner on the balcony overlooking the historic French Market. Don't miss pan-seared grouper topped with shrimp, crawfish and crab. Casual dress; cocktails. **Parking:** on-site. **Cards:** AX, CB, DC, DS, MC, VI.

CENTRAL GROCERY COMPANY LLC Lunch: $6-$12 Phone: 504/523-1620 (13)

Italian

Location: Jct Decatur and St. Ann sts, just e. 923 Decatur St 70116. **Hours:** 8:30 am-5:30 pm, Sun from 9 am. Closed major holidays; also Mardi Gras & Mother's & Father's Day. **Reservations:** not accepted. **Features:** The original home of the Italian muffuletta sandwich treats patrons to quick service and tasty food, particularly the great side portion of olive salad. Some seating is available inside the fascinating ethnic grocery store. Casual dress. **Parking:** street. **Cards:** DS, MC, VI.

CLOVER GRILL Lunch: $3-$7 Dinner: $3-$7 Phone: 504/598-1010 (8)

American

Location: Corner of Dumaine St. 900 Bourbon St 70116. **Hours:** 24 hours. **Features:** Guests step back into the '50s at the retro diner. With swiveling red and chrome stools, pink tiles, a jukebox and a checkerboard floor, the grill is a treat. Mammoth portions of delicious, no-frills comfort food are priced reasonably. Casual dress. **Parking:** street. **Cards:** AX, MC, VI.

THE COURT OF TWO SISTERS *Menu on AAA.com* Lunch: $25 Dinner: $24-$28 Phone: 504/522-7261 (20)

AAA

Creole

Location: Between St. Peter and Toulouse sts. 613 Royal St 70130. **Hours:** 9 am-3 & 5:30-9 pm. Closed: 12/25. **Reservations:** required. **Features:** In the French Quarter, the large historical dining courtyard has a daily jazz brunch buffet until 3 pm. Traditional French-Creole cuisine—such as shrimp etouffee, oysters Bienville and courtyard bread pudding with whiskey sauce—is the specialty. Dinner guests appreciate the enchanting, lighted trees in the courtyard. Casual dress; cocktails; entertainment. **Parking:** street. **Cards:** AX, CB, DC, DS, MC, VI. *(See color ad below & p 137)*

(See map and index starting on p. 332)

CRESCENT CITY BREWHOUSE Menu on AAA.com **Lunch:** $8-$25 **Dinner:** $8-$25 **Phone:** 504/522-0571 (40)

Regional Southern

Location: Between St. Louis and Toulouse sts. 527 Decatur St 70130. **Hours:** 4 pm-10 pm, Sat & Sun noon-10 pm. Closed: 11/22, 12/25. **Reservations:** accepted. **Features:** In the French Quarter across from the Mississippi River, the brewhouse accents its festive atmosphere with nightly live music. Interesting preparations fuse New World and Cajun influences and are well complemented by handcrafted lagers. Casual dress; cocktails; entertainment. **Parking:** street. **Cards:** AX, DS, MC, VI.

DICKIE BRENNAN'S STEAKHOUSE **Lunch:** $16 **Dinner:** $20-$36 **Phone:** 504/522-2467 (48)

Steak House

Location: Between Bourbon and Royal sts. 716 Iberville St 70130. **Hours:** 5:30 pm-10 pm, Fri from 5 pm. Closed: 9/3, 12/24, 12/25; also Mon, Tues & Mardi Gras. **Reservations:** suggested. **Features:** Featuring USDA prime beef with the flavor of New Orleans. All meats are seasoned with a Creole butter and presented with signature sauces. A tempting menu awaits those who crave the meats and local seafoods. The atmosphere is club like with rich woods, lighting with a golden glow, and wonderful service that compliments the entire experience. Dressy casual; cocktails. **Parking:** on-site. **Cards:** AX, DC, DS, MC, VI.

DOMINIQUE'S **Dinner:** $22-$34 **Phone:** 504/586-8000 (12)

Continental

Location: Between Burgundy and Rampart sts; in Maison Dupuy Hotel. 1001 Toulouse St 70112. **Hours:** 6 pm-10 pm; Sunday brunch 11 am-2 pm. **Reservations:** suggested. **Features:** Nationally recognized for its contemporary, Asian-influenced French cuisine, Dominique's presents unique and creative dishes served in an elegant atmosphere. Try cappamisu, a tiramisu made with cappuccino and chocolate sauce, covered with sugar ribbons. Dressy casual; cocktails. **Parking:** valet. **Cards:** AX, CB, DC, DS, MC, VI. ***(See color ad p 364)***

EMBERS "ORIGINAL" BOURBON HOUSE **Lunch:** $10-$27 **Dinner:** $15-$33 **Phone:** 504/523-1485 (19)

Steak House

Location: Corner of S Peters St. 700 Bourbon St 70116. **Hours:** 5 pm-close, Sat & Sun also 11 am-2 pm. **Reservations:** suggested. **Features:** Patrons can unwind on the largest balcony on Bourbon Street at the warm, cozy steakhouse. Service is friendly, the food is good, and the atmosphere is rocking. A Mardi Gras atmosphere prevails all year long. Casual dress; cocktails. **Parking:** street. **Cards:** AX, CB, DC, DS, JC, MC, VI.

FIORELLA'S **Lunch:** $6-$20 **Dinner:** $6-$20 **Phone:** 504/528-9566 (7)

Regional American

Location: Between French Market and Decatur sts; on the edge of the French Market; in the Vieux Carre; enter on either Governor Nicholls St or French Market Pl. 45 French Market Pl 70116. **Hours:** 10:30 am-2 am, Sat & Sun from 7 am. Closed: 11/22, 12/25. **Features:** The basic neighborhood restaurant serves the regional classic—a fried shrimp or oyster po' boy—as well as such favorites as red beans with rice, grilled pork chops, fried chicken and meat loaf. Italian dishes also are offered. After eating, patrons can stroll over to the French Market to shop. Casual dress; cocktails. **Parking:** street. **Cards:** AX, DS, MC, VI.

GALATOIRE'S RESTAURANT **Lunch:** $8-$30 **Dinner:** $8-$30 **Phone:** 504/525-2021 (44)

French

Location: Between Iberville and Bienville sts. 209 Bourbon St 70130. **Hours:** 11:30 am-9 pm, Sun from noon. Closed major holidays; also Mon. **Reservations:** accepted. **Features:** French-Creole cuisine is outlined on a varied, all-day menu. Fresh seafood is the focus of quality preparations, including richly satisfying oysters Rockefeller or crab Yvonne. One dining room with closely spaced tables is bustling though pleasant. Mid-afternoon often is the best time to visit, as reservations are not accepted and demand for seating is high. Semi-formal attire; cocktails. **Parking:** street. **Cards:** AX, DC, DS, MC, VI.

GUMBO SHOP **Lunch:** $8-$20 **Dinner:** $8-$20 **Phone:** 504/525-1486 (24)

Regional Creole

Location: Behind Jackson Square. 630 St. Peter St 70116. **Hours:** 11 am-11 pm. Closed: 12/25. **Features:** The small, busy Cajun/Creole eatery offers several gumbo choices, crawfish etouffee, grilled or blackened fish and jambalaya. Built in 1795, the brick building houses an intimate dining area set off by hand-painted murals and a charming courtyard. Those seeking privacy should go elsewhere, as seating tends to be very crowded. Casual dress; cocktails. **Parking:** street. **Cards:** AX, DC, DS, MC, VI.

GW FINS **Dinner:** $21-$28 **Phone:** 504/581-3467 (37)

Seafood

Location: Between Bourbon and Dauphine sts. 808 Bienville St 70112. **Hours:** 5 pm-11 pm. Closed major holidays; also Mardi Gras. **Reservations:** suggested. **Features:** Tucked into the heart of the French Quarter, the eatery specializes in the freshest of seafood, both local and imported from around the world. Tables are well spaced for comfort, and the service aims to best the famous eateries from the Quarter. Dressy casual; cocktails. **Parking:** street. **Cards:** AX, CB, DC, DS, JC, MC, VI.

HARD ROCK CAFE-NEW ORLEANS **Lunch:** $8-$20 **Dinner:** $8-$20 **Phone:** 504/529-5617 (50)

American

Location: Jct Canal and N Peters sts, just e. 418 N Peters St 70130. **Hours:** 11 am-11 pm, Fri & Sat-midnight. Closed: 11/22, 12/25. **Features:** Housed in the shell of an old Jax Brewery, this Hard Rock fits right in to the French Quarter, balcony and all. Try out the drink for which this city is known—the Hurricane—or partake of the crowd-pleasing menu. Parking is very accessible and shopping and sights are within walking distance. Casual dress; cocktails. **Parking:** on-site (fee). **Cards:** AX, DC, DS, MC, VI.

HILLERY'S ON TOULOUSE **Lunch:** $5-$12 **Dinner:** $16-$28 **Phone:** 504/571-2888 (17)

Cajun

Location: Between Dauphine and Bourbon sts; in Hotel St. Marie. 827 1/2 Toulouse St 70112. **Hours:** 7 am-10 pm. **Reservations:** accepted. **Features:** Patrons can enjoy breakfast and lunch in a bistro setting or dinner in a formal room. The dinner menu lists choices of fresh daily seafood, duck, liver, beef tenderloin and center-cut pork chops. Casual dress; cocktails. **Parking:** street. **Cards:** AX, DC, DS, MC, VI.

(See map and index starting on p. 332)

HOUSE OF BLUES **Lunch:** $8-$25 **Dinner:** $8-$25 **Phone:** 504/310-4999 (58)

American

Location: Between Iberville & Bienville. 225 Decatur St 70130. **Hours:** 11:30 am-2 pm, Wed-Fri to 10 pm, Sat 4 pm-10 pm. Closed: 11/22, 12/25; also Sun & Mon. **Reservations:** accepted. **Features:** A famous venue for music, this place brings in local and national artists weekly. It also functions as a restaurant where hungry patrons can get sandwiches, salads and more substantial entrees, including baby back ribs, country-fried steak and jambalaya. Casual dress; cocktails. **Parking:** street. **Cards:** AX, DS, MC, VI.

IRENE'S CUISINE **Dinner:** $15-$20 **Phone:** 504/529-8811 (10)

Italian

Location: Between Decatur and Chartres sts. 539 St. Philip St 70116. **Hours:** 5:30 pm-10 pm. Closed major holidays; also Sun & Mardi Gras. **Features:** This charming Italian-Creole eatery, which has walls lined with pictures of famous and not-so-famous customers, can be found on an obscure corner in the French Quarter. A specialty is an Italian-style baked Alaska, engulfed in a blue flame of ignited grappa liqueur. There may be a wait as this restaurant is quite popular. Casual dress; cocktails. **Parking:** street. **Cards:** AX, MC, VI.

JIMMY BUFFETT'S MARGARITAVILLE Menu on AAA.com **Lunch:** $5-$17 **Dinner:** $5-$17 **Phone:** 504/592-2565 (6)

AAA

Caribbean

Location: In the French Market. 1104 Decatur St 70116. **Hours:** 11 am-10:30 pm. **Features:** Diners sip margaritas and nosh on cheeseburgers (in Paradise) and other Gulf Coast and Caribbean cooking at the lighthearted getaway. Those who enjoy good music while quaffing tasty drinks can hang out in the bar. Casual dress; cocktails; entertainment. **Parking:** street. **Cards:** AX, DC, DS, MC, VI.

JOHNNY'S PO-BOYS **Lunch:** $5-$10 **Phone:** 504/524-8129 (42)

Creole

Location: Between Chartres and Decatur sts. 511 St. Louis St 70130. **Hours:** 8 am-4:30 pm, Sat & Sun 9 am-4 pm. Closed: 11/22, 12/25 & Easter. **Features:** Diners will find a cornucopia of po'boy sandwiches, put together in the time-honored New Orleans tradition. Classic fillings include lean boiled ham, well-done roast beef in a garlicky gravy, crispy fried oysters or shrimp, and a wide variety of others. Casual dress; beer only. **Parking:** street.

K-PAUL'S LOUISIANA KITCHEN **Lunch:** $8-$15 **Dinner:** $26-$38 **Phone:** 504/524-7394 (45)

Cajun

Location: Between Conti and St. Louis sts. 416 Chartres St 70130. **Hours:** 11:30 am-2:30 & 5:30-10 pm, Tues-Thurs from 5:30 pm. Closed major holidays; also Sun & Mardi Gras. **Reservations:** accepted. **Features:** Considered to be ground zero for contemporary Cajun cooking, the restaurant is a mecca for tourists, due in part to its friendly staff and unpretentious atmosphere. The menu lists some vegetarian dishes. Casual dress; cocktails. **Parking:** street. **Cards:** AX, DC, DS, MC, VI.

LA MADELEINE FRENCH BAKERY & CAFE **Lunch:** $7-$13 **Dinner:** $7-$13 **Phone:** 504/568-0073

French

Location: Jct Decatur and Saint Ann sts, just nw. 547 Saint Ann St 70116. **Hours:** 6:30 am-10 pm. Closed: 12/25. **Features:** Casual dress; beer & wine only. **Parking:** street. **Cards:** AX, DS, MC, VI.

LOUISIANA PIZZA KITCHEN **Lunch:** $7-$15 **Dinner:** $7-$15 **Phone:** 504/522-9500 (3)

Regional Pizza

Location: Corner of French Market Pl and Barracks St; in French Market District. 95 French Market Pl 70116. **Hours:** 11 am-10 pm, Fri & Sat-11 pm. Closed: 11/22. **Reservations:** not accepted. **Features:** Facing the French Market Place, the casual restaurant serves brick-oven pizzas, wraps and salads using specialty ingredients. The turn-of-the-20th-century building is adorned with local art. Casual dress; cocktails. **Parking:** street. **Cards:** AX, DC, DS, MC, VI.

MR. B'S BISTRO **Lunch:** $12-$17 **Dinner:** $16-$26 **Phone:** 504/523-2078 (49)

Creole

Location: Between Iberville and Bienville sts. 201 Royal St 70130. **Hours:** 11:30 am-3 & 5:30-10 pm, Sun from 10:30 am. Closed: 12/24, 12/25; also Mardi Gras. **Reservations:** suggested. **Features:** Traditional and regional Creole cuisine is served in a clubby, relaxed setting. Courteous servers attend to guests' needs in a professional manner. On the menu are preparations of seafood, steak, poultry and game. Nightly piano music adds to the atmosphere. Dressy casual; cocktails. **Parking:** on-site. **Cards:** AX, CB, DC, DS, MC, VI.

MURIEL'S JACKSON SQUARE **Lunch:** $9-$14 **Dinner:** $13-$25 **Phone:** 504/568-1885 (16)

AAA

Creole

Location: On Jackson Square. 801 Chartres St 70116. **Hours:** 11:30 am-2:30 & 5:30-10 pm, Fri & Sat-11 pm. Closed: 7/4, 12/24, 12/25; also Mardi Gras. **Reservations:** suggested, weekends. **Features:** In the heart of New Orleans, the eatery exudes class and elegance without pretense. Fine contemporary Creole selections—such as wood-grilled barbecue shrimp, soft-shell crabs and herb-crusted rack of lamb—are just a sampling of the menu offerings. The lunch bistro menu lists some lighter fare, such as po' boys. All dishes are done to perfection, but just as memorable as the food is the gracious staff's hospitality. Dressy casual; cocktails. **Parking:** on-site. **Cards:** AX, DC, DS, MC, VI. *(See color ad p 374)*

NAPOLEON HOUSE BAR & CAFE **Lunch:** $5-$10 **Dinner:** $12-$25 **Phone:** 504/524-9752 (36)

Regional American

Location: Corner of Chartres and St. Louis sts. 500 Chartres St 70130. **Hours:** 11 am-midnight, Fri & Sat-1 am, Sun & Mon-6 pm. Closed major holidays; also 12/24. **Features:** Only two blocks from Jackson Square, the Old World, European-style cafe offers a limited menu and specializes in muffuletta sandwiches as well as seafood gumbo and Creole jambalaya. Courtyard dining available. Casual dress; cocktails. **Parking:** street. **Cards:** AX, DC, DS, MC, VI.

(See map and index starting on p. 332)

NOLA Lunch: $11-$18 Dinner: $24-$36 Phone: 504/522-6652 43

Creole

Location: Between Decatur and Chartres sts. 534 St. Louis St 70130. **Hours:** 6 pm-10:00 pm, Sat 11:30 am-2 pm. Closed: 11/22, 12/24, 12/25; also Mon & Tues & Mardi Gras. **Reservations:** suggested. **Features:** A doting wait staff complements the innovative, upscale cuisine prepared in this busy, casual restaurant. Cajun and Creole influences dominate intriguing, colorfully presented creations. Carefully selected fresh herbs and spices blend to create savory cedar plank roasted fish, wood-burning oven pizzas and hickory- and pan-roasted selections. Dishes are prepared a la minute for the freshest possible flavor. Dressy casual; cocktails. **Parking:** on-site. **Cards:** AX, DC, DS, MC, VI.

OLD COFFEE POT Lunch: $5-$15 Dinner: $14-$22 Phone: 504/524-3500 22

Creole

Location: Between Royal and Bourbon sts. 714 St. Peter St 70130. **Hours:** 9 am-9 pm, Mon-3 pm. **Features:** A friendly and dependable stop, the eatery is known for its legendary New Orleans specialties, including grillades and grits and tasty calas (Creole rice cakes topped with powdered sugar). Have an order of fluffy pancakes or an overflowing omelet for breakfast. For something more substantial, try yummy catfish and jambalaya. Casual dress; cocktails. **Parking:** street. **Cards:** AX, MC, VI.

OLIVIER'S CREOLE RESTAURANT Lunch: $8-$13 Dinner: $15-$20 Phone: 504/525-7734 56

Creole

Location: Between Iberville and Bienville; center. 204 Decatur St 70130. **Hours:** 11 am-3 & 5-10 pm. Closed: Wed. **Reservations:** suggested. **Features:** Three generations of Oliviers have brought their family recipes and gracious service to the French Quarter. In a casually elegant setting, patrons may choose from dishes such as etouffee, Creole rabbit and beef bourguignonne. Among classic desserts is peach cobbler. Casual dress; cocktails. **Parking:** street. **Cards:** AX, DC, DS, MC, VI.

PALACE CAFE Lunch: $13-$17 Dinner: $18-$29 Phone: 504/523-1661 59

Creole

Location: Between Royal and Chartres sts; on edge of the French Quarter. 605 Canal St 70130. **Hours:** 11:30 am-2:30 & 5:30-9 pm, Sat & Sun from 10:30 am. Closed: 12/24, 12/25; also Mon & Mardi Gras. **Reservations:** accepted. **Features:** The upscale cafe offers a tempting array of contemporary Cajun and Creole dishes. Brunch is offered on Saturday and Sunday with live jazz music. Choices on the standard menu, also available at lunch, range from seafood and filet mignon to catfish and rabbit. Casual dress; cocktails. **Parking:** on-site. **Cards:** AX, CB, MC, VI.

THE PALM COURT JAZZ CAFE Dinner: $15-$25 Phone: 504/525-0200 4

Creole

Location: Between Barracks St and Governor Nicholls Ave. 1204 Decatur St 70116. **Hours:** 7 pm-11 pm. Closed major holidays; also Mon & Tues. **Reservations:** suggested. **Features:** Walls are lined with famous jazz musicians' photos and albums. The jazz band begins at 8 pm and plays into the night. Get ready to sit back and enjoy good music and entertainment at this loud and fun cafe. Casual dress; cocktails; entertainment. **Parking:** street. **Cards:** AX, DC, DS, MC, VI.

THE PELICAN CLUB RESTAURANT Dinner: $20-$30 Phone: 504/523-1504 46

Creole

Location: At Exchange Alley. 615 Bienville St 70130. **Hours:** 5:30 pm-10 pm. Closed major holidays; also Sun, Mon & Mardi Gras Day. **Reservations:** suggested. **Features:** This restaurant offers contemporary, regional American cuisine. Its stylish ambience is accented by original artworks. The menu includes seafood and steak, as well as Regional dishes such as Cajun jambalaya. Validated parking is available. Dressy casual; cocktails. **Parking:** on-site. **Cards:** AX, DC, DS, MC, VI.

(See map and index starting on p. 332)

PERE ANTOINE RESTAURANT **Lunch:** $11-$20 **Dinner:** $11-$20 **Phone:** 504/581-4478 (14)

Creole

Location: Northwest corner of St. Ann and Royal sts. 741 Royal St 70116. **Hours:** 9 am-midnight, Sat & Sun from 8 am. Closed: 11/22, 12/25. **Features:** In the heart of the famous French Quarter, the restaurant presents a menu of Creole cuisine, including favorite dishes with pork, crayfish and other seafood. The dining room feels airy and open, as large French doors open to the sidewalk and let the French Quarter atmosphere in. A small patio in the back pleases patrons who prefer to be outside. A casino is next door. Casual dress; cocktails. **Parking:** street. **Cards:** AX, MC, VI.

PERISTYLE **Lunch:** $24 **Dinner:** $24-$28 **Phone:** 504/593-9535 (2)

French

Location: Jct Rampart St. 1041 rue Dumaine 70116. **Hours:** 6 pm-9:30 pm, also Fri 11:30 am-1:30 pm. Closed major holidays; also Sun, Mon & Mardi Gras. **Reservations:** suggested. **Features:** Small restaurant located in the French Quarter with contemporary Louisiana-New American cuisine. Lunch offers a limited prefix menu. Dressy casual; cocktails. **Parking:** valet. **Cards:** AX, DC, DS, MC, VI.

PETUNIAS, A RESTAURANT **Lunch:** $6-$17 **Phone:** 504/522-6440 (25)

Creole

Location: Between Bourbon and Dauphine sts. 817 St. Louis St 70112. **Hours:** 8 am-3 pm. Closed: 12/22-12/28 & Mardi Gras. **Reservations:** suggested, for dinner weekends. **Features:** The intriguing menu is lined with a tempting selection of crepes filled with fresh ingredients, including the outstanding St. Francis crepe with shrimp, Louisiana crabmeat, onions, bell peppers and cheese sauce. The delicious peanut butter pie is among choices that quell a sweet tooth. Casual dress; cocktails. **Parking:** street. **Cards:** AX, CB, DC, DS, MC, VI.

PORT OF CALL **Lunch:** $6-$22 **Dinner:** $6-$22 **Phone:** 504/523-0120 (1)

American

Location: Jct Esplanade and Dauphine sts, just s. 838 Esplanade St 70116. **Hours:** 11 am-1 am, Fri & Sat-2 am. Closed: 11/22, 12/25. **Features:** A nautical theme dominates the neighborhood eatery, which prepares steaks, half-pound cooked-to-order burgers and pizzas. Casual dress; cocktails. **Parking:** street. **Cards:** AX, MC, VI.

QUARTER SCENE **Lunch:** $8-$20 **Dinner:** $12-$25 **Phone:** 504/522-6533 (5)

Regional American

Location: Between Dauphine and Burgundy sts. 900 rue Dumaine 70116. **Hours:** 8 am-10 pm. Closed: 12/25. **Features:** In the heart of the Quarter, the casual, unassuming spot is a longtime local favorite. Patrons are rejuvenated with freshly prepared New Orleans favorites, including po' boys, gumbo and salads. Casual dress; beer & wine only. **Parking:** street. **Cards:** AX, DC, DS, MC, VI.

RALPH & KACOO'S **Lunch:** $13-$27 **Dinner:** $13-$27 **Phone:** 504/522-5226 (30)

Seafood

Location: Between Decatur and Chartres sts. 519 Toulouse St 70130. **Hours:** 4 pm-10 pm, Fri-11 pm, Sat noon-11 pm, Sun noon-10 pm. Closed: 11/22, 12/25. **Features:** In the French Quarter, the popular chain restaurant serves Cajun and Creole seafood dishes, such as mesquite-grilled shrimp and deep-fried, blackened and grilled specials, in a comfortable, casual atmosphere. Portion sizes are ample. Purchased by the current owners in 1984, the 1820 building originated as the Star of David house and also did time as a brewery and storage facility. Casual dress; cocktails. **Parking:** on-site (fee) and street. **Cards:** AX, DC, DS, MC, VI.

RED FISH GRILL **Lunch:** $15-$22 **Dinner:** $20-$30 **Phone:** 504/598-1200 (54)

Seafood

Location: Between Canal and Iberville sts. 115 Bourbon St 70130. **Hours:** 11 am-3 & 5-10 pm. Closed: 12/24, 12/25; also Mardi Gras. **Reservations:** suggested. **Features:** Just off Canal Street in the famous French Quarter, the grill benefits from a convenient location. The menu lists a variety of seafood dishes, with its namesake "red fish" as the featured entree. The atmosphere is boisterous and lively. Casual dress; cocktails. **Parking:** street. **Cards:** AX, DC, DS, MC, VI.

REMOULADE **Lunch:** $7-$20 **Dinner:** $7-$20 **Phone:** 504/523-0377 (38)

Regional American

Location: Between Conti and Bienville sts. 309 Bourbon St 70130. **Hours:** 11:30 am-midnight. Closed: 12/25. **Features:** Located in what was once a jazz club, the atmosphere is set off by dark wood paneling, brass sconces and a "drugstore" tile floor. Po'boy sandwiches of fried catfish, shrimp or oysters, boiled shrimp in remoulade sauce and a raw oyster bar are featured. Casual dress; cocktails. **Parking:** street. **Cards:** AX, CB, DC, DS, MC, VI.

THE RIB ROOM-ROTISSERIE EXTRAORDINAIRE **Lunch:** $13-$22 **Dinner:** $26-$39 **Phone:** 504/529-7046 (34)

Creole

Location: At Royal and St. Louis sts; in Omni Royal Orleans Hotel. 621 St. Louis St 70140. **Hours:** 6:30-10:30 am, 11:30-2 & 6-10 pm. **Reservations:** suggested. **Features:** The restaurant specializes in rotisserie-roasted prime rib of beef. Flavorful, regional American cuisine also includes charbroiled yellowfin tuna fillet, home-fried potatoes, gumbo and such desserts as creme brulee. Dressy casual; cocktails. **Parking:** valet. **Cards:** AX, CB, DC, DS, JC, MC, VI.

RISTORANTE CARMELO **Lunch:** $8-$11 **Dinner:** $10-$30 **Phone:** 504/586-1414 (39)

Italian

Location: Corner of Decatur and Toulouse sts. 541 Decatur St 70130. **Hours:** noon-3 & 6-11 pm. **Reservations:** suggested. **Features:** In the heart of the French Quarter, the eatery presents a menu of traditional cuisine. Homemade tiramisu is a fitting topper to a tasty preparation of veal or pasta. Seating on the second floor affords better views. Dressy casual; cocktails. **Parking:** street. **Cards:** AX, DC, DS, MC, VI.

RIVER 127 **Lunch:** $15-$26 **Dinner:** $21-$33 **Phone:** 504/553-5082 (61)

Creole

Location: At Canal Place, near Mississippi River; in Wyndham New Orleans at Canal Place. 100 rue Iberville 70130. **Hours:** 6:00 am-2 & 6-10 pm. **Reservations:** suggested. **Features:** Few places can provide the stunning Mississippi River views that can be enjoyed through the windows of this 11th-floor restaurant in the Wyndham Canal Place Hotel. Patrons can peruse a carefully mixed menu in a lovely space that breathes casual elegance. Casual dress; cocktails. **Parking:** on-site (fee). **Cards:** AX, DC, DS, MC, VI.

(See map and index starting on p. 332)

SEKISUI SAMURAI **Lunch:** $10-$20 **Dinner:** $15-$25 **Phone:** 504/525-9595 (57)

Sushi

Location: Between Iberville and Bienville sts. 239 Decatur St 70130. **Hours:** 11:30 am-3 & 5-10 pm, Fri & Sat-10:30 pm. Closed: 11/22, 12/25. **Reservations:** accepted. **Features:** The long, narrow dining room is tucked into a tight row of storefronts on a busy street. The theater kitchen in the rear allows the chef to show prowess in assembling assorted platters. This place is worth the search. Casual dress; cocktails. **Parking:** street. **Cards:** AX, CB, DC, DS, MC, VI.

STELLA! **Dinner:** $20-$36 **Phone:** 504/587-0091 (9)

Regional American

Location: Between St. Philip and Ursulines sts. 1032 Chartres St 70116. **Hours:** 5:30 pm-10 pm, Fri & Sat-10:30 pm. Closed: 12/25; also Tues & Wed. **Reservations:** suggested. **Features:** A superb staff keeps busy in the elegant, upscale, cozy dining room, which was renovated in 2006 and nurtures an Old World feel. Skillful creations of New American cuisine are made from the finest quality ingredients. The refined atmosphere helps make this a "must visit" spot. Dressy casual; cocktails. **Parking:** valet. **Cards:** AX, DC, DS, MC, VI.

TORTORICI'S **Lunch:** $11-$20 **Dinner:** $21-$30 **Phone:** 504/522-4295 (33)

Italian

Location: Corner of Royal and St. Louis sts. 441 Royal St 70130. **Hours:** 5 pm-close, Sat & Sun from 11 am. **Reservations:** suggested. **Features:** Established in the French Quarter in 1900, this Italian-Creole eatery has been maintained by four generations of Tortorici's. The Tournedo Rossini filet, steak pizzola, and tiramisu are served in a cozy, brick dining room while live piano music plays. Casual dress; cocktails; entertainment. **Parking:** street. **Cards:** AX, DC, DS, MC, VI.

TUJAGUE'S **Lunch:** $10-$16 **Dinner:** $32-$38 **Phone:** 504/525-8676 (21)

Creole

Location: Between St. Ann and Dumaine sts. 823 Decatur St 70116. **Hours:** 11 am-3 & 5-10 pm. **Reservations:** accepted. **Features:** The city's second oldest restaurant (est. 1856), it presents six-course meals in traditional Creole style. A lunch menu is available, a highlight of which is Creole jambalaya, a mix of chicken, sausage and shrimp in tomato sauce served over rice. Casual dress; cocktails. **Parking:** street. **Cards:** AX, CB, DC, DS, JC, MC, VI.

VICTOR'S GRILL **Dinner:** $18-$32 **Phone:** 504/524-1331 (47)

AAA

Steak & Seafood

Location: Between Dauphine and Burgundy sts; in The Ritz-Carlton New Orleans. 921 Canal St 70112. **Hours:** 6:30 am-11 & 6-10:30 pm, Sun & Mon-11 am. **Reservations:** suggested. **Features:** Victors has undergone a revamping that has left it with a more casual air and focused menu, but still delivers a memorable dining experience. Dressy casual; cocktails. **Parking:** valet. **Cards:** AX, CB, DC, DS, JC, MC, VI.

The following restaurants have not been evaluated by AAA but are listed for your information only.

CAFE DU MONDE **Phone:** 504/581-2914

fyi

Not evaluated. **Location:** Center. 800 Decatur St 70116. **Features:** In business for nearly 150 years, a visit to New Orleans would not be complete with out a visit to Cafe Du Monde. Beignets and coffee are the only items served here, and getting a table can be a bit of a competition. However, its open air environment across from Jackson Square makes this one of the best spots to take a break in the French Quarter.

CAFE PONTALBA **Phone:** 504/522-1180

fyi

Not evaluated. **Location:** 546 St. Peter St 70130. **Features:** The cafe sits in the heart of the French Quarter: Jackson Square. Just about every table allows for good people-watching. The menu revolves around simply prepared New Orleans fare.

PIERRE MASPERO'S RESTAURANT **Phone:** 504/524-8990

fyi

Not evaluated. **Location:** Southeast corner of Chartres and St. Louis sts. 440 Chartres St 70130. **Features:** One of the area's oldest buildings, the former coffeehouse is where the LaFitte brothers met Andrew Jackson. Now, visitors will find Cajun food served in a friendly atmosphere.

NEW ORLEANS pop. 484,674 (See map and index starting on p. 336)

WHERE TO STAY

THE 1896 O'MALLEY HOUSE BED & BREAKFAST **Phone:** 504/488-5896 (5)

Property failed to provide current rates

Historic Bed & Breakfast

Location: Just s of Canal St. Located in Mid-City New Orleans. 120 S Pierce St 70119. Fax: 504/483-7898. **Facility:** Rooms in this 1896 Colonial Revival home are nicely appointed but not frilly and are characterized by hardwood floors and modern, stylish baths. Smoke free premises. 8 one-bedroom standard units, some with whirlpools. 3 stories (no elevator), interior corridors. **Parking:** street. **Terms:** no pets allowed (owner's pet on premises). **Amenities:** voice mail, hair dryers. **Leisure Activities:** *Fee:* massage. **Guest Services:** complimentary evening beverages, complimentary laundry, wireless Internet. **Business Services:** PC, fax (fee).

AMBASSADOR HOTEL *Book great rates at AAA.com* **Phone:** (504)527-5271 (40)

AAA SAVE

Small-scale Hotel

All Year	1P: $59-$279	2P: $59-$279	XP: $15	F12

Location: Between Poydras and Lafayette; downtown. 535 Tchoupitoulas St 70130. Fax: 504/599-2107. **Facility:** 165 one-bedroom standard units. 4 stories, interior corridors. *Bath:* combo or shower only. **Parking:** valet. **Terms:** check-in 4 pm, 3 day cancellation notice-fee imposed, $5 service charge. **Amenities:** video games (fee), voice mail, safes, irons, hair dryers. *Some:* high-speed Internet. **Dining:** 8 am-11 pm, cocktails. **Leisure Activities:** exercise room. **Guest Services:** valet laundry, wireless Internet. **Business Services:** meeting rooms, PC, fax (fee). **Cards:** AX, CB, DC, DS, MC, VI. **Free Special Amenities: early check-in/late check-out and room upgrade (subject to availability with advance reservations).** *(See color ad p 350)*

SOME UNITS

(See map and index starting on p. 336)

AMERIHOST INN & SUITES Book at AAA.com Phone: 504/299-9900 8

Property failed to provide current rates

Small-scale Hotel

Location: Jct Saratoga St; downtown. 1300 Canal St 70112. Fax: 504/299-1737. **Facility:** 159 units. 111 one-bedroom standard units, some with efficiencies (no utensils) and/or whirlpools. 48 one-bedroom suites. 16 stories, interior corridors. *Bath:* combo or shower only. **Parking:** on-site (fee). **Amenities:** high-speed Internet, dual phone lines, voice mail, irons, hair dryers. **Leisure Activities:** exercise room. **Guest Services:** valet laundry. **Business Services:** meeting rooms, business center.

SOME UNITS

BEST WESTERN AVALON HOTEL Book great rates at AAA.com Phone: (504)378-7000 1

Small-scale Hotel

All Year	1P: $49-$189	2P: $49-$189	XP: $10	F18

Location: I-10, exit 244 (Read Rd), just e. 10100 I-10 Service Rd 70127 (830 Conti St, 70112). Fax: 504/378-7800. **Facility:** 174 units. 167 one-bedroom standard units. 7 one-bedroom suites. 8 stories, interior corridors. *Bath:* combo or shower only. **Parking:** on-site. **Terms:** check-in 4 pm, 2 night minimum stay - weekends, 3 day cancellation notice-fee imposed. **Amenities:** high-speed Internet, dual phone lines, voice mail, irons, hair dryers. **Dining:** 6 am-2 pm, Thurs-Sat also 6 pm-10 pm, Sun 11 am-2 pm. **Pool(s):** outdoor. **Guest Services:** valet laundry. **Business Services:** meeting rooms, fax (fee). **Cards:** AX, CB, DC, DS, MC, VI. **Free Special Amenities: local telephone calls and newspaper.**

SOME UNITS

BEST WESTERN ST. CHARLES INN Book great rates at AAA.com Phone: (504)899-8888 60

Small-scale Hotel

All Year	1P: $119	2P: $119	XP: $20	F11

Location: I-10, exit US90 (Pontchatrain Expy), just n to Caronelet St, then just s onto Howard Ave; exit St. Charles Ave, 1.8 mi s. 3636 St. Charles Ave 70115. Fax: 504/899-8892. **Facility:** 40 one-bedroom standard units. 3 stories, interior corridors. **Parking:** on-site. **Terms:** 3 day cancellation notice, package plans. **Amenities:** voice mail, irons, hair dryers. *Some:* high-speed Internet. **Leisure Activities:** exercise room. **Guest Services:** wireless Internet. **Business Services:** meeting rooms, business center. **Cards:** AX, DC, DS, MC, VI. **Free Special Amenities: continental breakfast and high-speed Internet.**

SOME UNITS

BEST WESTERN ST. CHRISTOPHER HOTEL Book great rates at AAA.com Phone: (504)648-0444 25

Small-scale Hotel

12/1-5/31 & 10/1-11/30	1P: $99-$259	2P: $99-$269	XP: $10	F18
6/1-9/30	1P: $79-$259	2P: $79-$269	XP: $10	F18

Location: Between Canal and Common sts. 114 Magazine St 70130. Fax: 504/648-0445. **Facility:** 108 one-bedroom standard units, some with whirlpools. 10 stories, interior corridors. *Bath:* combo or shower only. **Parking:** valet. **Terms:** 2 night minimum stay - seasonal, 3 day cancellation notice-fee imposed, pets (small dogs only, $50 fee). **Amenities:** high-speed Internet, voice mail, safes, irons, hair dryers. **Guest Services:** valet laundry, wireless Internet. **Business Services:** meeting rooms, fax (fee). **Cards:** AX, DC, DS, MC, VI. **Free Special Amenities: expanded continental breakfast and high-speed Internet.** *(See color ad below)*

SOME UNITS

FEE

BRENT HOUSE HOTEL Book great rates at AAA.com Phone: (504)835-5411 7

Small-scale Hotel

All Year	1P: $99-$119	2P: $99-$119	XP: $20	F12

Location: On US 90 (Jefferson Hwy). Located adjacent to Ochsner Hospital. 1512 Jefferson Hwy 70121. Fax: 504/842-4160. **Facility:** 143 units. 139 one-bedroom standard units. 4 one-bedroom suites ($269). 6 stories, interior corridors. **Parking:** on-site (fee). **Terms:** check-in 4 pm. **Amenities:** video games (fee), voice mail, irons, hair dryers. *Some:* dual phone lines. **Dining:** 2 restaurants, 6 am-8:30 pm. **Pool(s):** heated outdoor. **Leisure Activities:** whirlpool. *Fee:* exercise room. **Guest Services:** gift shop, valet and coin laundry, wireless Internet. **Business Services:** conference facilities. **Cards:** AX, CB, DC, DS, JC, MC, VI. **Free Special Amenities: early check-in/late check-out and room upgrade (subject to availability with advance reservations).**

SOME UNITS

(See map and index starting on p. 336)

CLARION GRAND BOUTIQUE HOTEL Phone: 504/558-9966 56

fyi

Small-scale Hotel

Property failed to provide current rates

Under major renovation, scheduled to be completed December 2006. **Last rated:** ◆◆◆ **Location:** Corner of St. Andrew and St. Charles aves. Located in the Garden District. 2001 St. Charles Ave 70130. Fax: 504/571-6464. **Facility:** 44 one-bedroom standard units, some with whirlpools. 3 stories, interior corridors. **Parking:** on-site (fee). **Amenities:** voice mail, irons, hair dryers. *Fee:* video games, safes. **Guest Services:** valet laundry. **Business Services:** meeting rooms.

SOME UNITS

FEE

COMFORT SUITES DOWNTOWN *Book great rates at AAA.com* Phone: (504)524-1140 24

◆◆

Small-scale Hotel

12/1-4/30 & 9/1-11/30	1P: $79-$229	2P: $79-$229	XP: $10	F17
5/1-8/31	1P: $69-$179	2P: $69-$179	XP: $10	F17

Location: At Perdido St. 346 Baronne St 70112. Fax: 504/523-4444. **Facility:** 103 one-bedroom standard units, some with whirlpools. 7 stories, interior corridors. *Bath:* combo or shower only. **Parking:** valet. **Terms:** 3 day cancellation notice-fee imposed. **Amenities:** dual phone lines, voice mail, irons, hair dryers. *Fee:* video games, safes. **Leisure Activities:** whirlpool, exercise room. **Guest Services:** gift shop, valet and coin laundry, wireless Internet. **Business Services:** business center. **Cards:** AX, CB, DC, DS, JC, MC, VI.

SOME UNITS

ASK

COUNTRY INN & SUITES BY CARLSON NEW ORLEANS *Book great rates at AAA.com* Phone: (504)324-5400 30

◆◆◆

Small-scale Hotel

All Year	1P: $79-$199	2P: $79-$199	XP: $10	F18

Location: Between Natchez and Gravier. 315 Magazine St 70130. Fax: 504/324-5439. **Facility:** 155 units. 114 one-bedroom standard units. 41 one-bedroom suites ($99-$229). 5 stories, interior corridors. *Bath:* combo or shower only. **Parking:** valet. **Terms:** [ECP] meal plan available, package plans. **Amenities:** high-speed Internet, voice mail, safes, irons, hair dryers. **Pool(s):** small outdoor. **Leisure Activities:** exercise room. **Guest Services:** sundries, valet and coin laundry, wireless Internet. **Business Services:** meeting rooms, fax (fee). **Cards:** AX, CB, DC, DS, JC, MC, VI. ***(See color ad below)***

SOME UNITS

ASK

COURTYARD BY MARRIOTT-NEW ORLEANS *Book great rates at AAA.com* Phone: (504)581-9005 18

AAA SAVE

◆◆◆

Small-scale Hotel

All Year	1P: $116-$188	2P: $116-$188	XP: $20	F17

Location: Between Common and Canal sts; downtown. 124 St. Charles Ave 70130. Fax: 504/581-6264. **Facility:** 140 one-bedroom standard units. 6 stories, interior corridors. *Bath:* combo or shower only. **Parking:** valet. **Terms:** 3 day cancellation notice-fee imposed. **Amenities:** high-speed Internet, dual phone lines, voice mail, irons, hair dryers. **Dining:** 6:30-10:30 am, Sat & Sun 7 am-noon. **Leisure Activities:** whirlpool, exercise room. **Guest Services:** valet and coin laundry. **Business Services:** meeting rooms, business center. **Cards:** AX, DC, DS, MC, VI. **Free Special Amenities: high-speed Internet.**

SOME UNITS

(See map and index starting on p. 336)

COURTYARD BY MARRIOTT-NEW ORLEANS CONVENTION CENTER *Book great rates at AAA.com* **Phone:** (504)598-9898 46

Small-scale Hotel

All Year 1P: $219 2P: $239

Location: Corner of Julia and S Peters sts; downtown. 300 Julia St 70130. Fax: 504/598-9897. **Facility:** 202 units. 197 one-bedroom standard units, some with whirlpools. 5 one-bedroom suites. 5 stories, interior corridors. *Bath:* combo or shower only. **Parking:** on-site (fee). **Terms:** cancellation fee imposed. **Amenities:** high-speed Internet, voice mail, irons, hair dryers. **Dining:** 6-10 am. **Pool(s):** heated outdoor. **Leisure Activities:** whirlpool, exercise room. **Guest Services:** sundries, valet and coin laundry, wireless Internet. **Business Services:** meeting rooms, fax (fee). **Cards:** AX, CB, DC, DS, JC, MC, VI. **Free Special Amenities: high-speed Internet.**

SOME UNITS

DOUBLETREE HOTEL *Book great rates at AAA.com* **Phone:** (504)581-1300 32

Large-scale Hotel

All Year 1P: $109-$269 2P: $129-$289 XP: $20 F16

Location: Corner of Canal and Tchoupitoulas sts. 300 Canal St 70130. Fax: 504/522-4100. **Facility:** 363 units. 355 one-bedroom standard units. 8 one-bedroom suites, some with whirlpools. 17 stories, interior corridors. **Parking:** valet. **Terms:** 3 day cancellation notice, [AP] meal plan available. **Amenities:** voice mail, irons, hair dryers. *Fee:* video games, high-speed Internet. *Some:* dual phone lines. **Pool(s):** outdoor. **Leisure Activities:** exercise room. **Guest Services:** valet laundry. **Business Services:** conference facilities, business center. **Cards:** AX, DS, MC, VI.

(See color ad p 383)

SOME UNITS

FEE

DRURY INN & SUITES-NEW ORLEANS *Book at AAA.com* **Phone:** (504)529-7800 35

Small-scale Hotel

All Year [BP] 1P: $95-$185 2P: $105-$195 XP: $10 F18

Location: Between Baronne and Carondelet sts. 820 Poydras St 70112. Fax: 504/581-3328. **Facility:** 156 units. 130 one-bedroom standard units, some with whirlpools. 26 one-bedroom suites ($125-$225), some with whirlpools. 10 stories, interior corridors. *Bath:* combo or shower only. **Parking:** on-site (fee). **Terms:** small pets only. **Amenities:** high-speed Internet, dual phone lines, voice mail, irons, hair dryers. **Pool(s):** heated outdoor. **Leisure Activities:** whirlpool, exercise room. **Guest Services:** complimentary evening beverages, valet and coin laundry, wireless Internet. **Business Services:** meeting rooms, business center. **Cards:** AX, CB, DC, DS, MC, VI.

SOME UNITS

ECONO LODGE *Book great rates at AAA.com* **Phone:** 504/940-5550 4

Motel

Property failed to provide current rates

Location: I-10, exit 239 (Louisa St) westbound, go left at fork, just n, then just e; exit 239B (Louisa St N) eastbound, just n, then just e. 4940 Chef Menteur Hwy 70126. Fax: 504/945-5542. **Facility:** 59 one-bedroom standard units. 2 stories (no elevator), exterior corridors. *Bath:* combo or shower only. **Parking:** on-site. **Amenities:** voice mail, irons, hair dryers. **Guest Services:** wireless Internet. **Business Services:** fax (fee).

SOME UNITS

ELYSIAN FIELDS INN **Phone:** (504)948-9420 6

Historic Bed & Breakfast

All Year [ECP] 1P: $99-$250 2P: $99-$250 XP: $25 F

Location: I-610, exit 3 (Elysian Fields), 1.2 mi s. 930 Elysian Fields Ave 70117. Fax: 504/948-0053. **Facility:** This Greek Revival home has been transformed into a luxurious 21st Century property, yet it retains that grand inn appeal. Smoke free premises. 8 units. 7 one-bedroom standard units, some with whirlpools. 1 one-bedroom suite with whirlpool. 2 stories, interior corridors. *Bath:* combo or shower only. **Parking:** on-site. **Terms:** 2 night minimum stay - weekends, 15 day cancellation notice, pets ($10 extra charge). **Amenities:** video library, DVD players, CD players, hair dryers. *Some:* irons. **Business Services:** PC, fax. **Cards:** AX, DS, MC, VI. **Free Special Amenities: expanded continental breakfast and high-speed Internet.**

VCR

FEE

EMBASSY SUITES HOTEL NEW ORLEANS CONVENTION CENTER *Book great rates at AAA.com* **Phone:** (504)525-1993 45

Large-scale Hotel

1/22-5/6 & 10/1-11/30 [BP]	1P: $109-$309	2P: $134-$334	XP: $25	F18
12/1-1/21 & 5/7-9/30 [BP]	1P: $109-$229	2P: $134-$254	XP: $25	F18

Location: Corner of Julia and S Peters sts; downtown. 315 Julia St 70130. Fax: 504/525-3437. **Facility:** 372 units. 25 one-bedroom standard units. 345 one- and 2 two-bedroom suites, some with whirlpools. 9-16 stories, interior/exterior corridors. *Bath:* combo or shower only. **Parking:** valet. **Terms:** 3 day cancellation notice-fee imposed, $2 service charge. **Amenities:** video games (fee), dual phone lines, voice mail, irons, hair dryers. *Some:* high-speed Internet (fee). **Dining:** 11 am-2 & 5-10 pm, cocktails. **Pool(s):** lap. **Leisure Activities:** whirlpool, exercise room. **Guest Services:** gift shop, complimentary evening beverages, valet laundry, wireless Internet. **Business Services:** meeting rooms, PC. **Cards:** AX, DC, DS, MC, VI. **Free Special Amenities: full breakfast and local telephone calls.**

(See color ad p 383)

SOME UNITS

FAIRCHILD HOUSE BED & BREAKFAST *Book at AAA.com* **Phone:** (504)524-0154 54

Historic Bed & Breakfast

12/27-5/28 & 8/31-11/30 [ECP]	1P: $75-$145	2P: $75-$145	XP: $15	F12
12/1-12/26 & 5/29-8/30 [ECP]	1P: $55-$105	2P: $65-$115	XP: $10	F12

Location: Just w of jct St. Charles Ave and Calliope to Melpomene, just s to Prytania St, then just w. Located in the lower Garden District. 1518 Prytania St 70130. Fax: 504/568-0063. **Facility:** This restored 1841, Greek Revival home offers individually decorated guest rooms of various sizes. Smoke free premises. 19 units. 16 one-bedroom standard units. 3 one-bedroom suites ($105-$145). 2 stories (no elevator), interior/exterior corridors. *Bath:* combo, shower or tub only. **Parking:** on-site. **Terms:** 2 night minimum stay - weekends, 5 day cancellation notice. **Amenities:** voice mail. **Business Services:** fax (fee). **Cards:** AX, MC, VI.

SOME UNITS

(See map and index starting on p. 336)

THE FAIRMONT NEW ORLEANS *Book great rates at AAA.com* **Phone:** (504)529-7111 **10**

Large-scale Hotel

All Year 1P: $139-$319 2P: $139-$319 XP: $30

Location: Between Canal and University sts; entrance on University St; downtown. 123 Baronne St 70112. Fax: 504/529-4775. **Facility:** Completely renovated in 2006, the historic hotel is located just west of the French Quarter and is the site of the famous Sazarac Bar. 701 units. 616 one-bedroom standard units. 85 one-bedroom suites ($244-$574), some with whirlpools. 12 stories, interior corridors. *Bath:* combo or shower only. **Parking:** on-site (fee) and valet. **Terms:** check-in 4 pm, cancellation fee imposed, package plans, small pets only ($25 extra charge). **Amenities:** video games (fee), dual phone lines, voice mail, irons, hair dryers. **Dining:** Sazerac, see separate listing. **Pool(s):** heated outdoor. **Leisure Activities:** 2 lighted tennis courts, exercise room. *Fee:* massage. **Guest Services:** gift shop, valet laundry, wireless Internet. **Business Services:** conference facilities, business center. **Cards:** AX, CB, DC, DS, JC, MC, VI. *(See color ad below)*

SOME UNITS

FEE FEE

GARDEN DISTRICT BED & BREAKFAST **Phone:** 504/895-4302 **59**

Historic Bed & Breakfast

All Year [ECP] 1P: $80-$110 2P: $80-$110 XP: $10 F12

Location: Between 1st and 2nd sts. Located in the Garden District. 2418 Magazine St 70130. Fax: 504/895-4306. **Facility:** This 1870 B&B has 12-foot ceilings, Southern pine-plank floors and 18 fireplaces. Smoke free premises. 4 one-bedroom standard units. 2 stories (no elevator), interior/exterior corridors. *Bath:* combo or shower only. **Parking:** street. **Terms:** age restrictions may apply, 15 day cancellation notice-fee imposed, weekly rates available. **Cards:** AX, DS, MC, VI. **Free Special Amenities: expanded continental breakfast and room upgrade (subject to availability with advance reservations).**

SOME UNITS

GARDEN DISTRICT HOTEL CLARION COLLECTION *Book great rates at AAA.com* **Phone:** (504)566-1200 **57**

Small-scale Hotel

12/1-5/31 & 10/1-11/30 1P: $89-$199 2P: $99-$209 XP: $10 F17

6/1-9/30 1P: $79-$199 2P: $89-$209 XP: $10 F17

Location: 1 mi w of US 90; at corner of Jackson Ave. 2203 St. Charles Ave 70130. Fax: 504/581-1352. **Facility:** 132 units. 124 one-bedroom standard units. 8 one-bedroom suites. 9 stories, interior corridors. *Bath:* combo or shower only. **Parking:** valet. **Terms:** 2-3 night minimum stay - seasonal and/or weekends, cancellation fee imposed. **Amenities:** voice mail, honor bars, irons, hair dryers. *Fee:* video games, safes. **Dining:** 6 pm-10 pm, cocktails. **Leisure Activities:** whirlpool, exercise room. **Guest Services:** wireless Internet. **Business Services:** meeting rooms, business center. **Cards:** AX, DC, DS, MC, VI. **Free Special Amenities: local telephone calls and high-speed Internet.** *(See color ad p 381)*

SOME UNITS

FEE FEE

GRAND VICTORIAN BED & BREAKFAST **Phone:** (504)895-1104 **58**

Historic Bed & Breakfast

All Year 1P: $125-$300 2P: $125-$300 XP: $25 F

Location: I-10, exit US 90/Pontchatrain, just n to Carondelet St, then just s to Howard Ave Expwy; exit St Charles Ave, 1.1 mi s. 2727 St. Charles Ave 70130. Fax: 504/896-8688. **Facility:** Smoke free premises. 8 one-bedroom standard units, some with whirlpools. 3 stories (no elevator), interior corridors. **Parking:** street. **Terms:** 2-3 night minimum stay - seasonal and/or weekends, age restrictions may apply, 10 day cancellation notice-fee imposed, package plans. **Amenities:** voice mail, irons, hair dryers. **Guest Services:** wireless Internet. **Business Services:** fax. **Cards:** AX, DS, MC, VI.

ASK

(See map and index starting on p. 336)

HAMPTON INN & SUITES-CONVENTION CENTER Book great rates at AAA.com Phone: (504)566-9990 52

Small-scale Hotel

1/1-5/31 & 9/1-11/30 [BP]	1P: $129-$259	2P: $129-$259
12/1-12/31 & 6/1-8/31 [BP]	1P: $79-$189	2P: $79-$189

Location: Between Calliope St and John Chase Blvd; 0.5 mi s of jct Convention Center Blvd and Poydras St; center. Located across from the convention center. 1201 Convention Center Blvd 70130. Fax: 504/566-9997. **Facility:** 288 units. 252 one-bedroom standard units, some with efficiencies. 36 one-bedroom suites ($129-$299) with efficiencies, some with whirlpools. 5-8 stories, interior corridors. *Bath:* combo or shower only. **Parking:** on-site (fee). **Terms:** 3 day cancellation notice-fee imposed. **Amenities:** dual phone lines, voice mail, irons, hair dryers. **Pool(s):** outdoor. **Leisure Activities:** exercise room. **Guest Services:** sundries, valet and coin laundry, wireless Internet. **Business Services:** conference facilities, business center. **Cards:** AX, DC, DS, MC, VI. ***(See color ad p 383)***

SOME UNITS

ASK / VCR /

HAMPTON INN DOWNTOWN-FRENCH QUARTER AREA/NEW ORLEANS Book great rates at AAA.com Phone: (504)529-9990 17

Small-scale Hotel

1/1-5/31 & 10/1-11/30	1P: $119-$229	2P: $129-$239
12/1-12/31	1P: $99-$229	2P: $109-$239
6/1-9/30	1P: $99-$199	2P: $109-$209

Location: Jct Carondelet and Gravier sts; downtown. 226 Carondelet St 70130. Fax: 504/529-9996. **Facility:** 187 units. 185 one-bedroom standard units, some with whirlpools. 2 one-bedroom suites with whirlpools. 14 stories, interior corridors. *Bath:* combo or shower only. **Parking:** valet. **Terms:** 3 day cancellation notice-fee imposed, [BP] meal plan available. **Amenities:** high-speed Internet, voice mail, irons, hair dryers. *Some:* CD players. **Leisure Activities:** exercise room. **Guest Services:** complimentary evening beverages: Mon-Thurs, valet laundry. **Business Services:** meeting rooms, fax (fee). **Cards:** AX, DC, DS, MC, VI. ***(See color ad p 383)***

SOME UNITS

ASK / /

HAMPTON INN GARDEN DISTRICT Book great rates at AAA.com Phone: (504)899-9990 61

Small-scale Hotel

All Year	1P: $119-$209	2P: $119-$209

Location: Between Louisiana and Napoleon sts. 3626 St. Charles Ave 70115. Fax: 504/899-9908. **Facility:** 100 one-bedroom standard units, some with whirlpools. 6 stories, interior corridors. *Bath:* combo or shower only. **Parking:** on-site. **Terms:** 3 day cancellation notice-fee imposed. **Amenities:** voice mail, irons, hair dryers. **Pool(s):** lap. **Guest Services:** valet laundry, wireless Internet. **Business Services:** meeting rooms, business center. **Cards:** AX, DS, MC, VI. ***(See color ad p 383)***

SOME UNITS

ASK / /

FEE

HILTON GARDEN INN-CONVENTION CENTER Book great rates at AAA.com Phone: (504)525-0044 50

Small-scale Hotel

All Year	1P: $89-$239	2P: $109-$259	XP: $20	F18

Location: Between John Chase Blvd and St. Joseph's St. 1001 S Peters St 70130. Fax: 504/525-0035. **Facility:** 284 units. 282 one-bedroom standard units. 2 one-bedroom suites. 6 stories, interior corridors. *Bath:* combo or shower only. **Parking:** valet. **Terms:** 2 night minimum stay - seasonal, 3 day cancellation notice-fee imposed, [AP] & [BP] meal plans available. **Amenities:** video games (fee), high-speed Internet, dual phone lines, voice mail, irons, hair dryers. **Pool(s):** small heated outdoor. **Leisure Activities:** whirlpool, exercise room. **Guest Services:** sundries, valet and coin laundry, wireless Internet. **Business Services:** meeting rooms, business center. **Cards:** AX, CB, DC, DS, JC, MC, VI. ***(See color ad p 383)***

SOME UNITS

/ /

(See map and index starting on p. 336)

HILTON GARDEN INN FRENCH QUARTER/CBD *Book great rates at AAA.com* **Phone:** (504)324-6000 20

Small-scale Hotel

	1P	2P	XP	
All Year	1P: $89-$239	2P: $109-$259	XP: $20	F18

Location: Between Baronne and Carondelet sts. 821 Gravier St 70112. Fax: 504/324-6307. **Facility:** 155 units. 142 one-bedroom standard units. 13 one-bedroom suites. 18 stories, interior corridors. *Bath:* combo or shower only. **Parking:** valet. **Terms:** 2 night minimum stay - seasonal, 3 day cancellation notice-fee imposed. **Amenities:** video games (fee), high-speed Internet, dual phone lines, voice mail, irons, hair dryers. **Pool(s):** heated outdoor. **Leisure Activities:** exercise room. **Guest Services:** sundries, valet and coin laundry. **Business Services:** meeting rooms, business center. **Cards:** AX, CB, DC, DS, JC, MC, VI. ***(See color ad p 383)***

SOME UNITS

HILTON NEW ORLEANS RIVERSIDE *Book great rates at AAA.com* **Phone:** (504)561-0500 42

Large-scale Hotel

	1P	2P	XP	
All Year	1P: $99-$389	2P: $129-$419	XP: $30	F18

Location: At the Mississippi River. 2 Poydras St 70140. Fax: 504/568-1721. **Facility:** 1616 one-bedroom standard units. 5-29 stories, interior corridors. *Bath:* combo or shower only. **Parking:** on-site (fee) and valet. **Terms:** 3 day cancellation notice, [AP] & [CP] meal plans available. **Amenities:** video games (fee), dual phone lines, voice mail, honor bars, irons, hair dryers. *Some:* fax. **Dining:** 2 restaurants, 6 am-midnight, cocktails, also, Kabby's On The River, see separate listing. **Pool(s):** 2 heated outdoor. **Leisure Activities:** saunas, whirlpools, squash. *Fee:* golf studio, 12 indoor tennis courts, racquetball courts, aerobics & instruction, massage. **Guest Services:** gift shop, valet laundry. **Business Services:** conference facilities, business center. **Cards:** AX, CB, DC, DS, JC, MC, VI. **Free Special Amenities: newspaper.** *(See color ad p 383)*

SOME UNITS

FEE FEE

HOLIDAY INN DOWNTOWN-SUPERDOME *Book great rates at AAA.com* **Phone:** (504)581-1600 16

Large-scale Hotel

	1P	2P	XP	
12/31-5/15 & 9/16-11/30	1P: $119-$249	2P: $134-$264	XP: $15	F19
12/1-12/30	1P: $99-$129	2P: $114-$144	XP: $15	F19
5/16-9/15	1P: $89-$129	2P: $104-$144	XP: $15	F19

Location: Between Perdido and Gravier sts; center. 330 Loyola Ave 70112. Fax: 504/586-0833. **Facility:** 296 units. 293 one-bedroom standard units. 3 one-bedroom suites. 18 stories, interior corridors. **Parking:** on-site (fee). **Terms:** 3 day cancellation notice-fee imposed, package plans. **Amenities:** video games (fee), voice mail, safes, irons, hair dryers. **Dining:** 6:30 am-2 & 5-10 pm, cocktails. **Pool(s):** heated outdoor. **Leisure Activities:** exercise room. **Guest Services:** valet laundry, area transportation-area attractions within 4 mi, wireless Internet. **Business Services:** meeting rooms. *Fee:* PC, fax. **Cards:** AX, CB, DC, DS, JC, MC, VI. **Free Special Amenities: newspaper and high-speed Internet.** *(See color ad below)*

SOME UNITS

FEE FEE

HOLIDAY INN EXPRESS-NEW ORLEANS FRENCH QUARTER DOWNTOWN *Book at AAA.com* **Phone:** 504/962-0800 13

Small-scale Hotel

Property failed to provide current rates

Location: Between Common and Gravier sts. 221 Carondelet St 70130. Fax: 504/962-0801. **Facility:** 223 one-bedroom standard units. 5 stories, interior corridors. *Bath:* combo or shower only. **Parking:** valet. **Terms:** check-in 4 pm, pets ($200 fee). **Amenities:** video games (fee), high-speed Internet, dual phone lines, voice mail, irons, hair dryers. **Pool(s):** small heated outdoor. **Guest Services:** valet laundry, wireless Internet. **Business Services:** meeting rooms, PC, fax (fee).

SOME UNITS

FEE FEE FEE FEE

(See map and index starting on p. 336)

HOLIDAY INN SELECT-CONVENTION CENTER *Book great rates at AAA.com* **Phone:** (504)524-1881 49

Small-scale Hotel

9/1-11/30	1P: $149-$209	2P: $149-$209	XP: $10	F19
12/1-5/31	1P: $129-$179	2P: $129-$179	XP: $10	F19
6/1-8/31	1P: $89-$129	2P: $89-$129	XP: $10	F19

Location: Between N Diamond and St. Joseph's sts. Located opposite the convention center. 881 Convention Center Blvd 70130. Fax: 504/528-1005. **Facility:** 170 one-bedroom standard units. 8 stories, interior corridors. *Bath:* combo or shower only. **Parking:** valet. **Terms:** 3 day cancellation notice-fee imposed, [AP], [BP] & [CP] meal plans available, package plans. **Amenities:** high-speed Internet, dual phone lines, voice mail, safes, irons, hair dryers. *Some:* CD players. **Dining:** 6:30-11 am, 11:30-2 & 5:30-9 pm, cocktails. **Leisure Activities:** exercise room. **Guest Services:** valet and coin laundry. **Business Services:** meeting rooms, business center. **Cards:** AX, DS, MC, VI. **Free Special Amenities: newspaper and room upgrade (subject to availability with advance reservations).**

SOME UNITS

HOMEWOOD SUITES BY HILTON *Book great rates at AAA.com* **Phone:** 504/581-5599 31

Small-scale Hotel

12/1-5/31 & 9/16-11/30 [ECP]	1P: $159-$229	2P: $159-$229	XP: $30	F18
6/1-9/15 [ECP]	1P: $109-$199	2P: $109-$199	XP: $30	F18

Location: Between O'Keefe Ave and Baronne St; downtown. 901 Poydras St 70112. Fax: 504/581-9133. **Facility:** 166 units. 136 one- and 30 two-bedroom suites with efficiencies. 12 stories, interior corridors. *Bath:* combo or shower only. **Parking:** on-site (fee). **Terms:** cancellation fee imposed. **Amenities:** video games (fee), high-speed Internet, dual phone lines, voice mail, irons, hair dryers. **Pool(s):** heated indoor. **Leisure Activities:** whirlpool, limited exercise equipment. **Guest Services:** sundries, complimentary evening beverages: Mon-Thurs, valet and coin laundry. **Business Services:** meeting rooms, business center. **Cards:** AX, CB, DC, DS, MC, VI. ***(See color ad p 383)***

SOME UNITS

HOTEL LE CIRQUE **Phone:** (504)962-0900 19

Small-scale Hotel

All Year	1P: $59-$289	2P: $69-$299

Location: Just e of US 90 business, exit St. Charles Ave; on southeast block of circle. 2 Lee Cir 70130. Fax: 504/962-0901. **Facility:** 137 one-bedroom standard units. 10 stories, interior corridors. *Bath:* combo or shower only. **Parking:** valet. **Terms:** check-in 4 pm, 3 day cancellation notice. **Amenities:** voice mail, irons, hair dryers. *Fee:* video games, safes. **Guest Services:** valet laundry, wireless Internet. **Business Services:** meeting rooms, fax (fee). **Cards:** AX, DC, DS, JC, MC, VI.

SOME UNITS

(See map and index starting on p. 336)

INTERCONTINENTAL NEW ORLEANS Book great rates at AAA.com **Phone:** (504)525-5566 34

SAVE Large-scale Hotel

12/29-5/31	1P: $179-$399	2P: $179-$399	XP: $30	F17
6/1-11/30	1P: $129-$399	2P: $129-$399	XP: $30	F17
12/1-12/28	1P: $99-$109	2P: $99-$109	XP: $30	F17

Location: Between Perdido and Poydras sts. 444 St. Charles Ave 70130. Fax: 504/523-7310. **Facility:** This hotel on the St. Charles streetcar line features richly appointed rooms with large baths. 479 units. 459 one-bedroom standard units. 19 one- and 1 two-bedroom suites ($259-$2500), some with whirlpools. 15 stories, interior corridors. *Bath:* combo or shower only. **Parking:** on-site (fee). **Terms:** check-in 4 pm, cancellation fee imposed. **Amenities:** dual phone lines, voice mail, safes, honor bars, irons, hair dryers. *Fee:* video games, high-speed Internet. *Some:* CD players. **Dining:** 2 restaurants, 6:30 am-2 & 5-midnight, cocktails. **Pool(s):** heated outdoor. **Leisure Activities:** exercise room. **Guest Services:** gift shop, valet laundry, wireless Internet. **Business Services:** conference facilities, business center. **Cards:** AX, DC, DS, MC, VI. *(See color ad p 384)*

SOME UNITS / FEE FEE

INTERNATIONAL HOUSE Book at AAA.com **Phone:** (504)553-9550 23

Historic Small-scale Hotel

All Year	1P: $139-$549	2P: $139-$549

Location: Corner of Gravier and Camp sts; downtown. Two blocks from French Quarter. 221 Camp St 70130. Fax: 504/553-9560. **Facility:** Some rooms feature exterior landscaped terraces with panaromic views of the Mississippi River and downtown. 119 units. 116 one-bedroom standard units. 3 one-bedroom suites. 12 stories, interior corridors. *Bath:* combo or shower only. **Parking:** on-site (fee) and valet. **Terms:** check-in 4 pm, 3 day cancellation notice-fee imposed. **Amenities:** CD players, dual phone lines, voice mail, irons, hair dryers. *Some:* DVD players. **Dining:** Lemon Grass Restaurant, see separate listing. **Guest Services:** valet laundry, wireless Internet. **Business Services:** conference facilities, PC, fax (fee). **Cards:** AX, DS, MC, VI.

SOME UNITS ASK / VCR / FEE

JW MARRIOTT NEW ORLEANS Book great rates at AAA.com **Phone:** (504)525-6500 15

SAVE Large-scale Hotel

All Year	1P: $151-$246	2P: $151-$246

Location: Registration and parking on Common St. 614 Canal St 70130. Fax: 504/525-8068. **Facility:** Pleasant views of downtown or the French Quarter enhance most of the guest rooms at this large, busy hotel with contemporary appointments. 494 units. 487 one-bedroom standard units. 4 one- and 3 two-bedroom suites, some with whirlpools. 30 stories, interior corridors. *Bath:* combo or shower only. **Parking:** valet. **Terms:** cancellation fee imposed. **Amenities:** CD players, dual phone lines, voice mail, safes, honor bars, irons, hair dryers. *Fee:* video games, high-speed Internet. *Some:* fax. **Dining:** 6:30-10 am, 11-2 & 5:30-10 pm, cocktails. **Pool(s):** small heated outdoor. **Leisure Activities:** exercise room. *Fee:* massage. **Guest Services:** gift shop, valet laundry, wireless Internet. **Business Services:** conference facilities, business center. **Cards:** AX, CB, DC, DS, JC, MC, VI. **Free Special Amenities: newspaper.** *(See color ad p 362)*

SOME UNITS / VCR /

THE LAFAYETTE HOTEL Book great rates at AAA.com **Phone:** 504/524-4441 43

Small-scale Hotel

Property failed to provide current rates

Location: At S Maestri; between Girod and Poydras sts. Located on Lafayette Square. 600 St. Charles Ave 70130. Fax: 504/523-7327. **Facility:** 44 units. 24 one-bedroom standard units, some with whirlpools. 20 one-bedroom suites. 5 stories, interior corridors. **Parking:** valet. **Terms:** check-in 4 pm. **Amenities:** dual phone lines, voice mail, safes (fee), honor bars, irons, hair dryers. **Guest Services:** valet laundry, wireless Internet. **Business Services:** fax (fee).

SOME UNITS / VCR / FEE FEE

LA QUINTA INN & SUITES NEW ORLEANS - DOWNTOWN FLAGSHIP Book great rates at AAA.com **Phone:** (504)598-9977 27

Small-scale Hotel

6/1-11/30 [ECP]	1P: $109-$179	2P: $129-$189	XP: $10	F18
12/1-5/31 [ECP]	1P: $99-$169	2P: $109-$189	XP: $10	F18

Location: Corner of Gravier and Camp sts; downtown. 301 W Camp St 70130. Fax: 504/598-9978. **Facility:** 166 units. 150 one-bedroom standard units. 16 one-bedroom suites. 14 stories, interior corridors. *Bath:* combo or shower only. **Parking:** valet. **Terms:** small pets only. **Amenities:** video games (fee), high-speed Internet, voice mail, irons, hair dryers. *Some:* CD players, dual phone lines. **Pool(s):** small heated outdoor. **Leisure Activities:** whirlpool, exercise room. **Guest Services:** valet and coin laundry. **Business Services:** business center. **Cards:** AX, CB, DC, DS, MC, VI. ***(See color ad p 386)***

SOME UNITS ASK / /

LE PAVILLON Book great rates at AAA.com **Phone:** (504)581-3111 29

SAVE Large-scale Hotel

All Year	1P: $99-$525	2P: $109-$545	XP: $20	F17

Location: At Baronne St; downtown. 833 Poydras St 70112. Fax: 504/620-4130. **Facility:** The hotel features Old World elegance in both public areas and guest rooms and is convenient to the Superdome. 226 units. 219 one-bedroom standard units, some with whirlpools. 1 one- and 6 two-bedroom suites ($895-$1695). 10 stories, interior corridors. *Bath:* combo or shower only. **Parking:** valet. **Terms:** 3 day cancellation notice-fee imposed. **Amenities:** high-speed Internet, dual phone lines, voice mail, safes, honor bars, irons, hair dryers. *Some:* CD players, fax. **Dining:** 6:30 am-2:30 & 6-10 pm, cocktails, entertainment. **Pool(s):** small heated outdoor. **Leisure Activities:** whirlpool, exercise room. **Guest Services:** valet laundry, wireless Internet. **Business Services:** meeting rooms, PC, fax (fee). **Cards:** AX, CB, DC, DS, MC, VI. **Free Special Amenities: newspaper and room upgrade (subject to availability with advance reservations).**

SOME UNITS / /

(See map and index starting on p. 336)

LOEWS NEW ORLEANS HOTEL Book great rates at AAA.com Phone: 504/595-3300 41

Property failed to provide current rates

Large-scale Hotel

Location: Corner of S Peters St; downtown. 300 Poydras St 70130. Fax: 504/595-3310. **Facility:** Notable for its modern rooms and detail-oriented staff, the property offers some suites with river views. 285 units. 273 one-bedroom standard units. 12 one-bedroom suites with whirlpools. 21 stories, interior corridors. *Bath:* combo or shower only. **Parking:** valet. **Terms:** check-in 4 pm. **Amenities:** CD players, dual phone lines, voice mail, safes, honor bars, irons, hair dryers. *Fee:* video games, high-speed Internet. **Dining:** Cafe Adelaide, see separate listing. **Pool(s):** lap. **Leisure Activities:** sauna, whirlpool, exercise room. *Fee:* massage. **Guest Services:** gift shop, valet laundry. **Business Services:** conference facilities, business center.

SOME UNITS

MAISON ST. CHARLES QUALITY INN & SUITES Book great rates at AAA.com **Phone:** (504)522-0187 51

AAA SAVE

2/1-5/31 & 10/1-11/30	1P: $92-$268
12/1-1/31	1P: $79-$189
6/1-9/30	1P: $79-$160

Small-scale Hotel

Location: I-90 business, exit St. Charles Ave, just w; between Thalia and Erato sts. 1319 St. Charles Ave 70130. Fax: 504/529-4379. **Facility:** 130 units. 117 one-bedroom standard units. 11 one- and 2 two-bedroom suites ($131-$437), some with whirlpools. 2-3 stories, exterior corridors. *Bath:* combo or shower only. **Parking:** valet. **Terms:** 2 night minimum stay - seasonal and/or weekends, small pets only ($50 deposit, with prior approval). **Amenities:** voice mail, safes, irons, hair dryers. **Dining:** 6:30 am-10:30 pm. **Pool(s):** outdoor. **Leisure Activities:** whirlpool, billiards. **Guest Services:** valet laundry, wireless Internet. **Business Services:** meeting rooms, fax (fee). **Cards:** AX, CB, DC, DS, JC, MC, VI. **Free Special Amenities: local telephone calls and high-speed Internet.**

SOME UNITS

FEE

NEW ORLEANS MARRIOTT AT THE CONVENTION CENTER **Phone:** 504/613-2888

fyi

9/16-11/30	1P: $269
12/1-4/30	1P: $197
5/1-9/15	1P: $125

Large-scale Hotel

Too new to rate, opening scheduled for July 2006. **Location:** I-10 E, exit Poydras St, 1 mi e, then right. 859 Convention Center Blvd 70130. Fax: 504/613-2860. **Amenities:** 331 units, restaurant, coffeemakers, pool. **Terms:** cancellation fee imposed. **Cards:** AX, DC, DS, MC, VI.

THE O'KEEFE PLAZA HOTEL **Phone:** (504)524-5400 22

AAA SAVE

All Year	1P: $99-$109	2P: $99-$109	XP: $10	F18

Small-scale Hotel

Location: Between Perdido and Union sts. 334 O'Keefe Ave 70112. Fax: 504/524-5450. **Facility:** 129 one-bedroom standard units. 6 stories, interior corridors. *Bath:* combo or shower only. **Parking:** on-site (fee). **Terms:** weekly rates available. **Amenities:** voice mail, safes (fee), irons, hair dryers. **Pool(s):** small outdoor. **Leisure Activities:** limited exercise equipment. **Guest Services:** gift shop, coin laundry, wireless Internet. **Business Services:** meeting rooms, business center. **Cards:** AX, CB, DC, DS, MC, VI. **Free Special Amenities: expanded continental breakfast and local telephone calls.** *(See color ad below)*

SOME UNITS

OMNI ROYAL CRESCENT HOTEL Book at AAA.com **Phone:** 504/527-0006 26

Property failed to provide current rates

Small-scale Hotel

Location: 0.3 mi w of Canal St; downtown. 535 Gravier St 70130. Fax: 504/571-7575. **Facility:** 98 units. 91 one-bedroom standard units, some with whirlpools. 7 one-bedroom suites, some with whirlpools. 8 stories, interior corridors. *Bath:* combo or shower only. **Parking:** valet. **Terms:** small pets only ($50 fee). **Amenities:** video games (fee), dual phone lines, voice mail, honor bars, irons, hair dryers. *Some:* CD players. **Leisure Activities:** saunas, whirlpool, exercise room. *Fee:* massage. **Guest Services:** valet laundry. **Business Services:** meeting rooms. *Fee:* PC, fax.

SOME UNITS

FEE FEE

(See map and index starting on p. 336)

THE PRYTANIA PARK HOTEL **Phone:** (504)524-0427 53

Small-scale Hotel

All Year 1P: $75-$295 2P: $85-$295 XP: $10 F13

Location: Between Prytania St and St. Charles Ave on Terpsichore St. 1525 Prytania St 70130. Fax: 504/522-2977. **Facility:** Smoke free premises. 62 units. 36 one- and 26 two-bedroom standard units. 2 stories (no elevator), interior/exterior corridors. *Bath:* combo or shower only. **Parking:** on-site. **Terms:** cancellation fee imposed, [CP] meal plan available. **Amenities:** voice mail, hair dryers. *Some:* irons. **Guest Services:** valet laundry, wireless Internet. **Cards:** AX, CB, DC, DS, JC, MC, VI. **Free Special Amenities: continental breakfast and early check-in/late check-out.** *(See color ad below)*

SOME UNITS

QUALITY INN & SUITES DOWNTOWN Book great rates at AAA.com **Phone:** (504)525-6800 11

Small-scale Hotel

All Year [CP] 1P: $89-$129 2P: $89-$169 XP: $10 F17

Location: I-10, exit 234B (Poydras St) eastbound, 0.5 mi s, just e; exit 235B (Canal St) westbound, 0.6 mi s on Canal St, just w on Baronne St, just n on Union St, then just e. 210 O'Keefe Ave 70112 (PO Box 56271, 70156). Fax: 504/525-6808. **Facility:** 100 units. 58 one- and 16 two-bedroom standard units. 26 one-bedroom suites ($119-$189). 10 stories, interior corridors. *Bath:* combo or shower only. **Parking:** on-site (fee). **Amenities:** high-speed Internet, dual phone lines, voice mail, safes, irons, hair dryers. **Guest Services:** valet and coin laundry, wireless Internet. **Business Services:** meeting rooms, business center. **Cards:** AX, CB, DC, DS, MC, VI. **Free Special Amenities: continental breakfast and high-speed Internet.** *(See color ad below)*

SOME UNITS

(See map and index starting on p. 336)

QUEEN & CRESCENT HOTEL *Book great rates at AAA.com* **Phone:** (504)587-9700 28

AAA SAVE

Small-scale Hotel

12/1-5/31 & 10/1-11/30	1P: $89-$199	2P: $99-$209	XP: $10	F17
6/1-9/30	1P: $79-$199	2P: $89-$209	XP: $10	F17

Location: Just n of World Trade Center; downtown. 344 Camp St 70130 (610 S Peters St, Suite 201). Fax: 504/587-9701. **Facility:** 196 one-bedroom standard units. 8-12 stories, interior corridors. *Bath:* combo or shower only. **Parking:** on-site (fee) and valet. **Terms:** check-in 4 pm, 2-3 night minimum stay - seasonal and/or weekends, cancellation fee imposed. **Amenities:** voice mail, safes, honor bars, irons, hair dryers. **Leisure Activities:** exercise room. **Guest Services:** valet laundry, wireless Internet. **Business Services:** meeting rooms. *Fee:* PC, fax. **Cards:** AX, DC, DS, MC, VI. **Free Special Amenities: local telephone calls and high-speed Internet.**
(See color ad p 367)

SOME UNITS

QUEEN ANNE HOTEL **Phone:** (504)524-0427 55

AAA SAVE

Historic Small-scale Hotel

All Year	1P: $90-$300	2P: $90-$300	XP: $10	F12

Location: Between Prytania St and St. Charles Ave on Terpsichore St. Located in the Garden District. 1625 Prytania St 70130. Fax: 504/522-2977. **Facility:** Built in 1890, this 6,500-square-foot building is a restored Victorian mansion. Smoke free premises. 12 one-bedroom standard units. 3 stories (no elevator), interior corridors. *Bath:* combo or shower only. **Parking:** on-site. **Terms:** off-site registration, [CP] meal plan available. **Amenities:** voice mail, safes (fee), irons, hair dryers. **Guest Services:** valet laundry. **Cards:** AX, CB, DC, DS, JC, MC, VI. **Free Special Amenities: continental breakfast and early check-in/late check-out.**
(See color ad p 388)

SOME UNITS

VCR

RED CARPET INN & SUITES *Book great rates at AAA.com* **Phone:** (504)243-0433 3

AAA SAVE

Motel

All Year	1P: $54	2P: $59	XP: $10	F8

Location: I-10, exit 240B westbound, just w; exit 240A (Downman Rd) eastbound, just e. 6050 Chef Menteur Hwy 70126. Fax: 504/243-0085. **Facility:** 23 one-bedroom standard units, some with whirlpools. 2 stories (no elevator), exterior corridors. *Bath:* combo or shower only. **Parking:** on-site. **Terms:** 3 day cancellation notice-fee imposed, [ECP] meal plan available, package plans. **Amenities:** voice mail, irons, hair dryers. **Pool(s):** outdoor, wading. **Guest Services:** coin laundry, wireless Internet. **Business Services:** meeting rooms, fax (fee). **Cards:** AX, DS, MC, VI. **Free Special Amenities: continental breakfast and local telephone calls.**

SOME UNITS

RENAISSANCE ARTS HOTEL NEW ORLEANS *Book great rates at AAA.com* **Phone:** (504)613-2330 44

AAA SAVE

Large-scale Hotel

12/1-5/25 & 9/8-11/30	1P: $209-$325	2P: $209-$325
5/26-9/7	1P: $109-$295	2P: $109-$295

Location: Corner Girod St; in Warehouse District. 700 Tchoupitoulas St 70130. Fax: 504/613-2331. **Facility:** Blocks from the Ogden Museum of Southern Art in the warehouse district, this remarkable hotel houses artwork from both local and well-known artists. 217 units. 212 one-bedroom standard units. 5 one-bedroom suites. 5 stories, interior corridors. *Bath:* combo or shower only. **Parking:** valet. **Terms:** package plans. **Amenities:** CD players, high-speed Internet (fee), dual phone lines, voice mail, safes, honor bars, irons, hair dryers. **Dining:** La Cote Brasserie, see separate listing. **Pool(s):** heated outdoor. **Leisure Activities:** whirlpool, steamrooms, exercise room. **Guest Services:** sundries, valet laundry. **Business Services:** conference facilities, business center. **Cards:** AX, CB, DC, DS, JC, MC, VI. **Free Special Amenities: newspaper and early check-in/late check-out.** *(See color ad p 368)*

SOME UNITS

RENAISSANCE PERE MARQUETTE HOTEL *Book great rates at AAA.com* **Phone:** (504)525-1111 12

AAA SAVE

Large-scale Hotel

12/1-5/25 & 9/8-11/30	1P: $209-$335	2P: $209-$335
5/26-9/7	1P: $109-$295	2P: $109-$295

Location: Corner of Common and Baronne sts; downtown. 817 Common St 70112. Fax: 504/525-0688. **Facility:** A highly contemporary interior provides all the desired amenities within a transformed 1920s building; bright colors and local art accent the rooms. 280 one-bedroom standard units. 18 stories, interior corridors. *Bath:* combo or shower only. **Parking:** valet. **Terms:** package plans. **Amenities:** CD players, dual phone lines, voice mail, safes, honor bars, irons, hair dryers. *Fee:* video games, high-speed Internet. **Dining:** Rene Bistrot, see separate listing. **Pool(s):** small heated outdoor. **Leisure Activities:** exercise room. **Guest Services:** sundries, valet laundry, wireless Internet. **Business Services:** conference facilities, business center. **Cards:** AX, CB, DC, DS, JC, MC, VI. **Free Special Amenities: newspaper and early check-in/late check-out.** *(See color ad p 368)*

SOME UNITS

RESIDENCE INN BY MARRIOTT *Book great rates at AAA.com* **Phone:** (504)522-1300 47

AAA SAVE

Small-scale Hotel

All Year	1P: $199	2P: $239

Location: Jct Tchoupitoulas St. Located in the Warehouse District. 345 St. Joseph's St 70130. Fax: 504/522-6060. **Facility:** 231 units. 63 one-bedroom standard units with efficiencies. 119 one- and 49 two-bedroom suites with kitchens. 3-4 stories, interior corridors. *Bath:* combo or shower only. **Parking:** on-site (fee). **Terms:** cancellation fee imposed, pets ($75 fee, $7.50 extra charge). **Amenities:** video games (fee), high-speed Internet, voice mail, irons, hair dryers. **Pool(s):** heated outdoor. **Leisure Activities:** whirlpool, barbecue grill, picnic area, exercise room, sports court. **Guest Services:** sundries, complimentary evening beverages: Mon-Thurs, valet and coin laundry. **Business Services:** meeting rooms, fax (fee). **Cards:** AX, CB, DC, DS, JC, MC, VI. **Free Special Amenities: high-speed Internet.**

SOME UNITS

FEE

If New Orleans is the city, a Starwood hotel is the destination.

From $109* per night, per room

Located on Canal Street, bordering the French Quarter and steps from the Mississippi River and Harrah's Casino, we offer 1,110 new guest rooms and suites featuring the Sheraton Sweet Sleeper Bed.™ Hotel amenities include fitness center, pool, onsite Starbucks® Coffee Store and casual dining at Roux Bistro Restaurant.

From $149* per night, per room

Located in the heart of the French Quarter, savvy travelers will enjoy our 98 luxurious guest rooms with high-speed Internet access, outdoor heated pool, romantic dining at Bacco Restaurant, and 24-hour Whatever/Whenever unconditionally dedicated service.

From $139* per night, per room

Located on Poydras Street, discerning guests will indulge in our 423 guest rooms with river or city views featuring the luxurious W signature bed and 24-hour Whatever/Whenever service. Experience modern dining at Zoë Restaurant or play at the newest hot spot, the Whiskey Blue Bar.

To make reservations or to learn about AAA special rates and member benefits call **866 782 7737**

starwood.com/AAA

STARWOOD PREFERRED GUEST®

Basic room rates do not include additional state or local taxes. Rates are per room, per night, based on single/double occupancy and availability. Additional restrictions and black-out dates may apply. Offer not applicable to groups or with other special offers. Please mention promotion code AAA when making your reservation. Valid through 11/30/07 based on availability. Call 888-627-7033 for specific details. Not responsible for omissions or typographical errors. Void where prohibited by law.

(See map and index starting on p. 336)

ROYAL ST. CHARLES HOTEL *Book great rates at AAA.com* **Phone:** (504)587-3700 **14**

AAA SAVE

12/1-5/31 & 10/1-11/30	1P: $89-$199	2P: $99-$209	XP: $10	F17
6/1-9/30	1P: $79-$199	2P: $89-$209	XP: $10	F17

Small-scale Hotel **Location:** Corner of Common St; downtown. 135 St. Charles Ave 70130 (610 S Peters St, Suite 201). Fax: 504/587-3701. **Facility:** 143 units. 135 one-bedroom standard units. 8 one-bedroom suites. 10 stories, interior corridors. *Bath:* combo or shower only. **Parking:** valet. **Terms:** check-in 4 pm, 2-3 night minimum stay - seasonal and/or weekends, cancellation fee imposed. **Amenities:** dual phone lines, voice mail, irons, hair dryers. *Fee:* video games, safes. *Some:* CD players. **Leisure Activities:** exercise room. **Guest Services:** valet laundry, wireless Internet. **Business Services:** meeting rooms, business center. **Cards:** AX, DC, DS, MC, VI. **Free Special Amenities: local telephone calls and high-speed Internet.** *(See color ad p 369)*

SOME UNITS

ST. JAMES HOTEL *Book at AAA.com* **Phone:** 504/304-4000 **33**

Property failed to provide current rates

Historic Small-scale Hotel **Location:** Jct Magazine and Natchez sts; downtown. 330 Magazine St 70130 (317 Magazine St). Fax: 504/304-4444. **Facility:** This 1857 New Orleans landmark was renovated in French Indies style with 21st-century conveniences; guest rooms are cozy and comfortable. 86 units. 80 one-bedroom standard units. 6 one-bedroom suites. 4 stories, interior corridors. *Bath:* combo or shower only. **Parking:** valet. **Terms:** check-in 4 pm, small pets only ($50 fee). **Amenities:** video games (fee), CD players, voice mail, safes, honor bars, irons, hair dryers. **Dining:** Restaurant Cuvee, see separate listing. **Guest Services:** valet laundry, wireless Internet. **Business Services:** fax (fee).

SOME UNITS

FEE FEE

THE SHERATON NEW ORLEANS HOTEL *Book great rates at AAA.com* **Phone:** (504)525-2500 **21**

AAA SAVE

12/1-6/13 & 9/6-11/30	1P: $199-$249	2P: $199-$249	XP: $25	F18
6/14-9/5	1P: $109-$149	2P: $109-$149	XP: $25	F18

Large-scale Hotel **Location:** Between Camp and Magazine sts. Located on the edge of the French Quarter. 500 Canal St 70130. Fax: 504/595-5552. **Facility:** Complete with warm earth tones and a comfortable leather armchair, this hotel's rooms are residential in style. 1110 units. 1057 one-bedroom standard units. 46 one- and 7 two-bedroom suites ($750-$1500). 49 stories, interior corridors. *Bath:* combo or shower only. **Parking:** valet. **Terms:** 3 day cancellation notice-fee imposed, pets (dogs only). **Amenities:** dual phone lines, voice mail, safes, irons, hair dryers. *Fee:* video games, high-speed Internet. *Some:* CD players, fax, honor bars. **Dining:** 2 restaurants, 6 am-2 & 5:30-10 pm, cocktails. **Pool(s):** heated outdoor. **Leisure Activities:** saunas, whirlpool, steamrooms. *Fee:* massage. **Guest Services:** gift shop, valet laundry, wireless Internet. **Business Services:** conference facilities, business center. **Cards:** AX, DC, DS, MC, VI. *(See color ad p 391)*

SOME UNITS

FEE

SPRINGHILL SUITES BY MARRIOTT CONVENTION CENTER *Book great rates at AAA.com* **Phone:** (504)522-3100 **48**

AAA SAVE

All Year	1P: $59-$259	2P: $59-$259

Small-scale Hotel **Location:** Between Tchoupitoulas and S Peters sts. 301 St. Joseph St 70130. Fax: 504/522-3101. **Facility:** 208 units. 204 one-bedroom standard units. 4 one-bedroom suites. 4 stories, interior corridors. *Bath:* combo or shower only. **Parking:** on-site (fee). **Terms:** package plans. **Amenities:** video games (fee), high-speed Internet, dual phone lines, voice mail, irons, hair dryers. **Pool(s):** heated outdoor. **Leisure Activities:** whirlpool, exercise room. **Guest Services:** sundries, valet and coin laundry, wireless Internet. **Business Services:** meeting rooms, business center. **Cards:** AX, DC, DS, MC, VI. **Free Special Amenities: high-speed Internet.**

SOME UNITS

STAYBRIDGE SUITES BY HOLIDAY INN *Book great rates at AAA.com* **Phone:** (504)571-1818 **39**

AAA SAVE

12/1-5/31 & 9/1-11/30	1P: $159-$229	2P: $159-$229
6/1-8/31	1P: $99-$159	2P: $99-$159

Small-scale Hotel **Location:** Corner of Poydras St; downtown. 501 Tchoupitoulas St 70130. Fax: 504/571-1811. **Facility:** 182 units. 138 one-bedroom standard units with efficiencies. 29 one- and 15 two-bedroom suites with efficiencies. 17 stories, interior corridors. *Bath:* some combo or shower only. **Parking:** valet. **Terms:** check-in 4 pm, 30 day cancellation notice-fee imposed, 13% service charge. **Amenities:** high-speed Internet, dual phone lines, voice mail, irons, hair dryers. **Pool(s):** lap. **Leisure Activities:** exercise room. **Guest Services:** gift shop, complimentary evening beverages: Tues-Thurs, complimentary and valet laundry. **Business Services:** meeting rooms, business center. **Cards:** AX, CB, DC, DS, JC, MC, VI. **Free Special Amenities: full breakfast and high-speed Internet.** *(See color ad p 358)*

SOME UNITS

SUPER 8 MOTEL *Book great rates at AAA.com* **Phone:** (504)241-5650 **2**

AAA SAVE

All Year [CP]	1P: $65-$89	2P: $75-$99	XP: $7	F17

Small-scale Hotel **Location:** I-10, exit 240A (US 90) eastbound; exit 240B westbound. 6322 Chef Menteur Hwy 70126. Fax: 504/241-2178. **Facility:** 104 one-bedroom standard units. 3 stories, interior/exterior corridors. **Parking:** on-site. **Amenities:** *Some:* safes. **Pool(s):** outdoor. **Guest Services:** coin laundry. **Business Services:** fax (fee). **Cards:** AX, DS, MC, VI. **Free Special Amenities: continental breakfast and newspaper.** *(See color ad p 393)*

SOME UNITS

THE WARWICK NEW ORLEANS **Phone:** (504)586-0100 **9**

AAA SAVE fyi

All Year	1P: $59-$229	2P: $59-$229	XP: $20	F17

Small-scale Hotel Under major renovation, scheduled to be completed April 2007. **Last rated:** **Location:** Between Lasalle St and Loyola Ave. 1315 Gravier St 70112. Fax: 504/524-0825. **Facility:** 155 units. 133 one-bedroom standard units. 22 one-bedroom suites. 12 stories, interior corridors. *Bath:* combo or shower only. **Parking:** no self-parking. **Terms:** 3 day cancellation notice-fee imposed. **Amenities:** dual phone lines, voice mail, irons, hair dryers. **Pool(s):** outdoor. **Guest Services:** valet laundry. **Cards:** AX, DC, DS, MC, VI. **Free Special Amenities: local telephone calls and preferred room (subject to availability with advance reservations).**

SOME UNITS

(See map and index starting on p. 336)

THE WHITNEY-A WYNDHAM HISTORIC HOTEL Book at AAA.com Phone: (504)581-4222 37

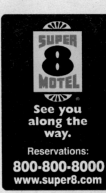

Small-scale Hotel	Dates	1P	2P	XP	
	9/7-11/30	1P: $119-$259	2P: $129-$269	XP: $10	F18
	2/8-5/28	1P: $115-$249	2P: $125-$259	XP: $10	F18
	5/29-9/6	1P: $89-$229	2P: $99-$239	XP: $10	F18
	12/1-2/7	1P: $85-$225	2P: $95-$235	XP: $10	F18

Location: Between St. Charles Ave and Camp St; downtown. 610 Poydras St 70130. Fax: 504/207-0100. **Facility:** 93 units. 70 one-bedroom standard units. 23 one-bedroom suites ($129-$315). 7 stories, interior corridors. *Bath:* combo or shower only. **Parking:** valet. **Terms:** package plans. **Amenities:** high-speed Internet (fee), dual phone lines, voice mail, irons, hair dryers. *Some:* CD players. **Leisure Activities:** exercise room. **Guest Services:** valet laundry. **Business Services:** meeting rooms, fax (fee). **Cards:** AX, DC, DS, MC, VI.

SOME UNITS
ASK / FEE

(See map and index starting on p. 336)

WINDSOR COURT HOTEL Book great rates at AAA.com **Phone:** (504)523-6000 36

AAA SAVE All Year 1P: $200-$455 2P: $200-$455 XP: $50 F17

Large-scale Hotel

Location: Between Magazine and Tchoupitoulas sts. 300 Gravier St 70130. Fax: 504/596-4513. **Facility:** The hotel has a refined atmosphere characterized by 18th-century paintings, English-style furniture and formal offerings such as afternoon tea. 324 units. 58 one-bedroom standard units. 266 one-bedroom suites with kitchens. 23 stories, interior corridors. **Parking:** valet. **Terms:** cancellation fee imposed, package plans, pets ($150 fee). **Amenities:** video library, high-speed Internet, dual phone lines, voice mail, safes, honor bars, irons, hair dryers. *Some:* fax. **Dining:** New Orleans Grill, see separate listing, entertainment. **Pool(s):** heated outdoor. **Leisure Activities:** saunas, whirlpool, steamroom, exercise room. *Fee:* massage. **Guest Services:** gift shop, valet laundry. **Business Services:** conference facilities, business center. **Cards:** AX, CB, DC, DS, JC, MC, VI. **Free Special Amenities: newspaper and high-speed Internet.** Affiliated with A Preferred Hotel. *(See color ad below)*

SOME UNITS

FEE

W NEW ORLEANS Book great rates at AAA.com **Phone:** (504)525-9444 38

AAA SAVE

12/1-5/31 & 9/2-11/30	1P: $169-$369	2P: $169-$369	XP: $75	F18
6/1-9/1	1P: $139-$369	2P: $139-$369	XP: $75	F18

Large-scale Hotel

Location: Close to Riverfront area/convention center; jct Poydras and S Peters sts; downtown. Located next to Harrah's Casino. 333 Poydras St 70130. Fax: 504/581-7179. **Facility:** Featuring ultra-contemporary style, trendy gathering places and even individual hot-tamale candy machines, this distinctive hotel has a hip ambience. 423 units. 400 one-bedroom standard units, some with whirlpools. 23 one-bedroom suites, some with whirlpools. 23 stories, interior corridors. *Bath:* combo or shower only. **Parking:** valet. **Terms:** 3 day cancellation notice-fee imposed, pets ($100 extra charge). **Amenities:** video library, DVD players, CD players, high-speed Internet (fee), dual phone lines, voice mail, safes, honor bars, irons, hair dryers. *Some:* fax. **Dining:** 6 am-close, cocktails, also, Zoe Restaurant and Bar, see separate listing. **Pool(s):** small outdoor. **Leisure Activities:** exercise room. *Fee:* massage. **Guest Services:** valet laundry. **Business Services:** conference facilities, business center. **Cards:** AX, CB, DC, DS, JC, MC, VI. *(See color ad p 391)*

SOME UNITS

FEE

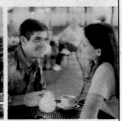

(See map and index starting on p. 336)

The following lodging was either not evaluated or did not meet AAA rating requirements but is listed for your information only.

HOTEL STORYVILLE **Phone:** 504/948-4800

fyi

Not evaluated. **Location:** I-10, exit 236A, just s; between Marais and Tremme sts. 1261 Esplanade Ave 70116. Facilities, services, and decor characterize a basic property.

WHERE TO DINE

THE BESH STEAKHOUSE AT HARRAH'S **Dinner:** $30-$48 **Phone:** 504/533-6111 (17)

Steak House

Location: Jct S Peters and Canal sts; in Harrah's New Orleans Casino. 8 Canal St 70130. **Hours:** 5 pm-11 pm. Closed: Tues & Wed. **Reservations:** accepted. **Features:** This fine-dining restaurant offers semiformal service and outstanding steaks. Guests can enjoy the sights and sounds of the casino while they dine. Dressy casual; cocktails. **Parking:** valet. **Cards:** AX, CB, DC, DS, MC, VI.

BON TON CAFE **Lunch:** $12-$21 **Dinner:** $25-$39 **Phone:** 504/524-3386 (19)

Cajun

Location: Between Gravier and Poydras sts. 401 Magazine St 70130. **Hours:** 11 am-2 & 5-9:30 pm. Closed major holidays; also Sat & Sun. **Reservations:** suggested, evenings. **Features:** Conveniently located near the Riverwalk Mall & Casino, Bon Ton Cafe dishes up good Cajun cooking that features such savory choices as grilled redfish with dirty rice and steamed vegetables. This is a popular lunch spot in the downtown area. Dressy casual; cocktails. **Parking:** street. **Cards:** AX, DC, MC, VI.

BRIGTSEN'S **Dinner:** $19-$32 **Phone:** 504/861-7610 (29)

Creole

Location: Jct Carrollton and St. Charles aves; in Riverbend area. 723 Dante St 70118. **Hours:** 5:30 pm-10 pm. Closed major holidays; also Sun, Mon, Mardi Gras & Ash Wednesday. **Reservations:** suggested. **Features:** Family-fun Cajun restaurant with wonderful food/consistently rated highly by locals. Located in the Riverbend in a quaint house. It can be quite crowded. Dressy casual; cocktails. **Parking:** street. **Cards:** AX, DC, DS, MC, VI.

THE BUFFET AT HARRAH'S **Lunch:** $12 **Dinner:** $19-$28 **Phone:** 504/533-6000 (18)

American

Location: Jct Canal and S Peters sts. 8 Canal St 70130. **Hours:** 6-9:45 am, 11-2:45 & 4-4:45 am; Sun 6-8:45 am, 10-3 & 4-4:45 am. **Features:** Take a break from the slots and hit this large buffet. Numerous types of foods are available including a pizza plus station with pasta, calzones and pizza; Louisiana Classics station with items like jambalaya, red beans and rice, and a large dessert station to satisfy any sweet tooth, even those who want sugar free. American Bounty has southern favorites like corn on the cob, fried chicken and biscuits and gravy and don't miss the Pacific Rim where guests can enjoy food with Asian influences. Casual dress. **Parking:** valet. **Cards:** AX, DS, MC, VI.

CAFE ADELAIDE **Lunch:** $11-$22 **Dinner:** $16-$36 **Phone:** 504/595-3305 (23)

Creole

Location: Corner of S Peters St; downtown; in Loews New Orleans Hotel. 300 Poydras 70130. **Hours:** 7-10:30 am, 11:30-2:30 & 6-10 pm; Saturday & Sunday brunch 11 am-2 pm. **Reservations:** accepted. **Features:** Named after the sister of the Brennan family matriarch, Cafe Adelaide strives to reflect a playful yet sophisticated attitude. Delicious Creole creations can be enjoyed in a West Indies-inspired dining room. Casual dress; cocktails. **Parking:** valet. **Cards:** AX, CB, DC, DS, MC, VI.

CAFE DEGAS **Lunch:** $9-$12 **Dinner:** $16-$22 **Phone:** 504/945-5635 (3)

French

Location: Jct Carrollton and Esplanade aves, just se. 3127 Esplanade Ave 70119. **Hours:** 11:30 am-2:30 & 6-10 pm, Fri & Sat-10:30 pm, Sun-10:30 am-3 & 6-9 pm. Closed: 7/4, 11/22, 12/25; also Mon, Tues & Mardi Gras. **Reservations:** suggested. **Features:** The French restaurant incorporates all the niceties: wine, bread, delicious pates and salads, and finely prepared entrees of beef, fish and poultry. The staff is friendly, competent and knowledgeable. Dressy casual; cocktails. **Parking:** street. **Cards:** AX, DC, DS, MC, VI.

CAFE VOLAGE **Lunch:** $8-$13 **Dinner:** $17-$24 **Phone:** 504/861-4227 (33)

Italian

Location: Jct St. Charles St, just n on Carrollton Ave, just w on Maple Ave, then just s. 720 Dublin St 70118. **Hours:** 11 am-2:30 & 4-9:30 pm, Fri & Sat-10 pm, Sun 11 am-2:30 & 3-8 pm; Sunday brunch. Closed: Mardi Gras. **Reservations:** accepted. **Features:** In a neighborhood filled with antebellum homes, the cottage eatery has friendly owners and staff who greet guests with a warm welcome and offer attentive service. Such menu offerings as shrimp in Creole sauce reflect local influences, while other choices, including veal Marsala, are simply classic. Casual dress; cocktails. **Parking:** street. **Cards:** AX, DS, MC, VI.

CASAMENTO'S RESTAURANT **Lunch:** $3-$11 **Dinner:** $5-$13 **Phone:** 504/895-9761 (55)

Seafood

Location: Jct Napoleon Ave and Magazine St; uptown. 4330 Magazine St 70115. **Hours:** Open 12/1-6/1 & 9/1-11/30; 11:30 am-1:30 & 5:30-9 pm. Closed major holidays; also Mon. **Reservations:** not accepted. **Features:** The small, casual seafood house has been in the same family since 1919. A long marble oyster bar and '50s-style ceramic tiles on the walls and floor create a nostalgic feel. House specialties include raw oysters, oyster loaf sandwich and seafood gumbo. Items are served simply, and everything, including the delicious homemade fries, is cooked when ordered. Casual dress; beer only. **Parking:** street.

CHRISTIAN'S RESTAURANT **Lunch:** $15-$23 **Dinner:** $20-$31 **Phone:** 504/482-4924 (4)

Creole

Location: I-10, exit 232, 0.8 mi n, just e. 3835 Iberville St Mid City 70119. **Hours:** 11:30 am-2 & 5:30-9:30 pm, Sat from 5:30 pm. Closed: 1/1, 7/4, 12/25; also Sun, Mon & Mardi Gras. **Reservations:** suggested. **Features:** Upscale casual atmosphere uniquely located in a restored church. Featuring French-Creole cuisine, the menu includes seafood, duck, veal, filet mignon, and sweetbreads. A formally attired staff will attend to your needs in a polite, pleasant fashion. Dressy casual; cocktails. **Parking:** on-site. **Cards:** AX, DC, DS, MC, VI. **Historic**

(See map and index starting on p. 336)

CLANCY'S **Lunch:** $11-$14 **Dinner:** $18-$28 **Phone:** 504/895-1111 (57)

Creole

Location: Jct of Webster and Annunciation sts; uptown. 6100 Annunciation St 70118. **Hours:** 11:30 am-2 & 5:30-10:30 pm, Fri-11 pm, Sat 5:30 pm-11 pm. Closed major holidays; also Sun & for lunch Mon. **Reservations:** suggested. **Features:** The modestly decorated bistro presents imaginative treatments of local favorites. Among the friendly restaurant's distinctive seasonally changing creations, which focus on regional ingredients and local seafood, are smoked soft-shell crab in meuniere sauce, fried oysters topped with melted brie and chicken with salsa. The signature ice box lemon pie merits consideration. Casual dress; cocktails. **Parking:** street. **Cards:** AX, DC, DS, MC, VI.

COMMANDER'S PALACE **Lunch:** $15-$17 **Dinner:** $35-$40 **Phone:** 504/899-8221 (49)

Creole

Location: Just s of jct St. Charles and Washington aves; in the Garden District. 1403 Washington Ave 70130. **Hours:** 11:30 am-1:30 & 6-10 pm, Sat 11:30 am-12:30 & 6-9:30 pm, Sun 10:30 am-1:30 & 6-10 pm; Sunday brunch. Closed: 12/25; also Mardi Gras. **Reservations:** required. **Features:** This sophisticated spot is the place for haute Creole cuisine. The menu offers American and Creole preparations of seafood, veal and filet mignon as well as such decadent desserts as bread pudding souffle. The wait staff is polished and professional. Jazz brunches are the attraction Saturday and Sunday. Gentlemen's jackets are required evenings and for Sunday brunch. Dressy casual; cocktails. **Parking:** valet. **Cards:** AX, CB, DC, DS, MC, VI.

COYOACAN **Dinner:** $16-$38 **Phone:** 504/525-9996 (43)

Mexican

Location: US 90 business route, exit St. Charles Ave, just sw. 1432 St. Charles Ave 70130. **Hours:** 6 pm-10 pm. Closed major holidays; also Sun. **Reservations:** suggested. **Features:** What is arguably the city's most authentic Mexican restaurant, Coyoacan offers upscale dining in a casually sophisticated environment. Dishes derived from Mexico City cuisine have nothing to do with what is commonly called Mexican food on this side of the border. Tequila carts let diners sample an appetite-whetting aperitif. Dressy casual; cocktails. **Parking:** on-site. **Cards:** AX, DS, MC, VI.

DANTE'S KITCHEN **Lunch:** $9-$15 **Dinner:** $18-$26 **Phone:** 504/861-3121 (28)

Creole

Location: Jct Leake and Dante sts, just n; in the Garden District. 736 Dante St 70118. **Hours:** 11:30 am-2 & 5:30-9:30 pm, Sat & Sun from 11 am. Closed: 11/22, 12/25; also Tues, Wed & day after Mardi Gras. **Features:** The menu focuses on Louisiana comfort food: dishes of seafood, duck, pork, beef and other specialty items. Guests can choose from indoor or patio seating. Casual dress; cocktails. **Parking:** street. **Cards:** AX, MC, VI.

DICK AND JENNY'S **Dinner:** $13-$20 **Phone:** 504/894-9880 (58)

Creole

Location: Just w of Napoleon; uptown. 4501 Tchoupitoulas St 70115. **Hours:** 5:30 pm-10 pm, Fri & Sat-10:30 pm. Closed major holidays; also Sun, Mon, Mardi Gras & Ash Wednesday. **Features:** Although the eatery is off the beaten path, the diversion comes highly recommended. Guests should know that a well-timed visit is important, as this place doesn't accept reservations and isn't hurting for business. The New Orleans favorite's popularity is no surprise because it prepares delicious local fare and serves it in a whimsical environment. Casual dress; cocktails. **Parking:** street. **Cards:** AX, DS, MC, VI.

EMERIL'S **Lunch:** $18-$23 **Dinner:** $24-$39 **Phone:** 504/528-9393 (34)

Creole

Location: Corner of Tchoupitoulas and Julia sts. 800 Tchoupitoulas St 70130. **Hours:** 6 pm-10 pm, Fri 11:30 am-2 & 6-11 pm. Closed: 11/22; also Mardi Gras. **Reservations:** suggested. **Features:** An exquisite dining experience. Creative cuisine is served in a contemporary atmosphere by a very gracious wait staff. Highlights include oven-roasted quail and seared yellowfin tuna. An outstanding wine list features American wines. Jackets preferred. Dressy casual; cocktails. **Parking:** valet and street. **Cards:** AX, CB, DC, DS, MC, VI.

EMERIL'S DELMONICO RESTAURANT & BAR **Lunch:** $16-$26 **Dinner:** $21-$38 **Phone:** 504/525-4937 (41)

Provincial Creole

Location: 0.5 mi w of US 90; in the Garden District. 1300 St. Charles Ave 70130. **Hours:** 11:30 am-2 & 6-10 pm, Fri-11 pm, Sat 6 pm-11 pm, Sun 10:30 am-2 & 6-10 pm. Closed: 11/22, 12/24-12/26; also Mardi Gras. **Reservations:** suggested. **Features:** This Garden District eatery sits at the top of the celebrity chefs dynasty in New Orleans. It offers a truly memorable dining experience and one-of-a-kind dishes. Although the service is highly refined, the attentive staff is void of any pretentiousness. Dressy casual; cocktails. **Parking:** valet. **Cards:** AX, CB, DC, DS, MC, VI. **Classic Historic**

FEELINGS CAFE **Dinner:** $15-$24 **Phone:** 504/945-2222 (8)

Creole

Location: Just se of jct Elysian Fields; east end of town. 2600 Chartres St 70117. **Hours:** 6 pm-10 pm, Fri & Sat-11 pm, Sun 11 am-2 & 6-10 pm. Closed: 11/22, 12/25; also Mon-Wed & Mardi Gras Day. **Reservations:** suggested. **Features:** Sections of an immaculately preserved 1790s plantation serve as the romantic setting for French-inspired Creole cuisine. Guests can dine on the balcony or relax in the indoor courtyard while enjoying live piano entertainment. Be sure to save room for the amazing peanut butter pie. Dressy casual; cocktails. **Parking:** street. **Cards:** AX, DC, DS, MC, VI.

FIVE HAPPINESS **Lunch:** $7-$9 **Dinner:** $9-$16 **Phone:** 504/488-6468 (5)

Chinese

Location: I-10, exit 232 (Carrollton Ave), 0.4 mi s. 3605 S Carrollton Ave 70118. **Hours:** 11 am-10:30 pm, Fri & Sat-11:30 pm, Sun 11:30 am-10:30 pm. Closed: 11/22. **Features:** Everything, from several varieties of stuffed dumplings to honey banana, is fresh and competently executed. Although the restaurant is often very busy, the staff is efficient enough to handle the most bustling crowd, and the food is worth any wait. Casual dress; cocktails. **Parking:** on-site. **Cards:** AX, DC, DS, MC, VI.

FOX AND HOUND PUB & GRILLE **Lunch:** $6-$18 **Dinner:** $6-$18 **Phone:** 504/731-6000

American

Location: I-10, exit 226 (Clearview Pkwy S), 0.5 mi s. 1200 S Clearview Pkwy 70123. **Hours:** 11 am-2 am. Closed: 12/25. **Features:** Casual dress; cocktails. **Parking:** on-site. **Cards:** AX, DS, MC, VI.

(See map and index starting on p. 336)

GABRIELLE RESTAURANT Dinner: $14-$32 Phone: 504/948-6233 (2)

Creole

Location: I-10, exit Esplanade Ave, 1.4 mi w. 3201 Esplanade Ave 70119. **Hours:** 5:30 pm-10 pm, Fri also 11:30 am-2 pm. Closed major holidays; also Sun & Mon. **Reservations:** suggested. **Features:** Sophisticated, imaginative Creole food served in a small, romantic bistro atmosphere. Specialties include slow-roasted duck, seasonal crawfish enchiladas, and desserts like strawberry cheesecake. Located in the historic Fauborg St. John district. Dressy casual; cocktails. **Parking:** on-site. **Cards:** AX, CB, DC, DS, MC, VI.

GAUTREAU'S RESTAURANT Dinner: $19-$32 Phone: 504/899-7397 (47)

French

Location: US 90 to St. Charles Ave, 2.5 mi w, then just n. 1728 Soniat St 70115. **Hours:** 6 pm-10 pm. Closed: 1/1, 12/25; also Sun & Mardi Gras. **Reservations:** suggested. **Features:** Occupying a 1911 apothecary/pharmacy, the intimate dining room is suggestive of a French bistro. The setting is fitting for eclectic regional meals of seasonal seafood. Servers are knowledgeable and friendly. Dressy casual; cocktails. **Parking:** street. **Cards:** AX, DS, MC, VI.

HERBSAINT Lunch: $10-$14 Dinner: $22-$26 Phone: 504/524-4114 (27)

French

Location: At Girod St; downtown. 701 St. Charles Ave 70130. **Hours:** 11:30 am-2 & 5:30-10:30 pm, Sat 5:30 pm-11 pm. Closed major holidays; also Sun. **Reservations:** suggested. **Features:** Located along the famous streetcar line, Herbsaint offers delicious dining and excellent people watching opportunities. The ever changing menu features a new american french cuisine with a focus on high quality ingredients. Dressy casual; cocktails. **Parking:** street. **Cards:** DC, DS, MC, VI.

JACQUES-IMO'S CAFE Dinner: $11-$20 Phone: 504/861-0886 (22)

AAA

Creole

Location: Just s of S Carrollton Ave; in Riverbend area. 8324 Oak St 70118. **Hours:** 5:30 pm-10 pm, Fri & Sat-10:30 pm. Closed major holidays; also Sun. **Features:** The food is outstanding and the service friendly at this nice spot. However, those who don't get here early may have to wait because the tight dining rooms fill fast. Diners' eyes wander along the colorful hippie-eclectic walls. Food on the varied menu is best described as comfort Creole. Fried chicken and sweet cornbread leave patrons wanting more. Casual dress; cocktails. **Parking:** street. **Cards:** AX, CB, DC, DS, MC, VI.

JOEY K'S Lunch: $5-$10 Dinner: $6-$13 Phone: 504/891-0997 (50)

Regional American

Location: Jct 7th St; in the Garden District. 3001 Magazine St 70115. **Hours:** 11 am-close, Sat from 8 am. Closed major holidays; also Sun. **Features:** In the Garden District, the neighborhood establishment is popular with area residents and weekend tourists perusing Magazine Street antique shops. Home-style cooking is the theme on a menu of soup, sandwiches, salads and local favorites, such as the all-you-can-eat catfish and 18-ounce schooners. Daily specials round out the menu. Casual dress; cocktails. **Parking:** street. **Cards:** AX, DC, DS, MC, VI.

KABBY'S ON THE RIVER Lunch: $10-$20 Phone: 504/584-3880 (24)

American

Location: At the Mississippi River; in Hilton New Orleans Riverside. 2 Poydras St 70140. **Hours:** 10 am-2:30 pm, Sun 10 am-2:30 pm. Closed: 12/25; also Mon. **Reservations:** accepted. **Features:** Located in the Hilton New Orleans Riverside, Kabby's features large portions of American cuisine with a nice view of the Mississippi River. In the mood for a regional dish? Try the Catfish Barataria — fried catfish smothered in a crabmeat cream sauce. Casual dress; cocktails. **Parking:** valet. **Cards:** AX, CB, DC, DS, MC, VI.

LA COTE BRASSERIE Lunch: $11-$23 Dinner: $17-$30 Phone: 504/613-2350 (26)

Creole

Location: Corner Girod St; in Warehouse District; in Renaissance Arts Hotel New Orleans. 700 Tchoupitoulas St 70130. **Hours:** 6:30-11 am, 11:30-2:30 & 5:30-10:30 pm, Fri & Sat-11 pm. **Reservations:** suggested. **Features:** The elegant brasserie prepares contemporary coastal cuisine. Seared foie gras is a must. Because of the many delicious entree choices, guests enjoy sharing with their dinner partners for a taste variety. Dressy casual; cocktails. **Parking:** valet and street. **Cards:** AX, CB, DC, DS, MC, VI.

LA CREPE NANOU Dinner: $9-$18 Phone: 504/899-2670 (51)

French

Location: Just n of Prytania and Robert sts. 1410 Robert St 70115. **Hours:** 6 pm-10:30 pm, Fri & Sat-11 pm. Closed major holidays; also Mardi Gras. **Features:** A charming little uptown bistro with an artsy, Parisian atmosphere and small, intimate dining areas, it features all manner of crepes as well as dinner entrees. Savor steamed mussels in garlic, cream and white wine, then revel in a decadent dessert crepe. Casual dress; cocktails. **Parking:** on-site. **Cards:** AX, DC, MC, VI.

LA MADELEINE FRENCH BAKERY & CAFE Lunch: $7-$13 Dinner: $7-$13 Phone: 504/861-8662

French

Location: Jct S Carrollton and St Charles aves. 601 S Carrollton Ave 70118. **Hours:** 6:30 am-10 pm. Closed: 12/25. **Features:** Casual dress; beer & wine only. **Parking:** on-site. **Cards:** AX, DS, MC, VI.

LA MADELEINE FRENCH BAKERY & CAFE Lunch: $7-$13 Dinner: $7-$13 Phone: 504/410-8500

French

Location: Jct St Charles Ave and Thalia St, just ne. 1327 St Charles Ave 70130. **Hours:** 6:30 am-10 pm. Closed: 12/25. **Features:** Casual dress; beer & wine only. **Parking:** on-site. **Cards:** AX, DS, MC, VI.

LE BON TEMPS ROULE Lunch: $5-$8 Dinner: $5-$8 Phone: 504/897-3448 (56)

Creole

Location: Jct Bordeaux and Magazine sts, just w. 4801 Magazine St 70115. **Hours:** 11 am-3 am, Fri & Sat 24 hours. **Features:** The friendly neighborhood lounge serves good food and is a great spot to spend an afternoon shooting pool. There are two tables and plenty of folks to help visitors sharpen up their game. Casual dress; cocktails. **Parking:** street. **Cards:** AX, DS, MC, VI.

(See map and index starting on p. 336)

LEMON GRASS RESTAURANT **Lunch:** $7-$16 **Dinner:** $12-$22 **Phone:** 504/523-1200 (13)

Vietnamese

Location: Corner of Gravier and Camp sts; downtown; in International House. 217 Camp St 70130. **Hours:** 11 am-2 pm, Thurs & Fri also 6 pm-10 pm, Sat & Sun 6 pm-10 pm. Closed major holidays; also 12/21-12/27 & Mardi Gras. **Reservations:** suggested. **Features:** Upscale bistro-style decor sets the mood in this modern Vietnamese restaurant. Popular, colorfully presented dishes—such as a crispy noodle "basket" filled with cinnamon chicken and vegetables—are prepared with a local flair. Dressy casual; cocktails. **Parking:** street. **Cards:** AX, DC, MC, VI.

LILETTE RESTAURANT **Lunch:** $9-$20 **Dinner:** $20-$26 **Phone:** 504/895-1636 (53)

French

Location: Between Antoine and Amelia sts. 3637 Magazine St 70115. **Hours:** 11:30 am-2 & 5:30-10 pm, Fri & Sat-11 pm. Closed: 12/25; also Sun & Mon. **Reservations:** suggested. **Features:** In the Garden District, the restaurant would be an ideal place for lunch or dinner after browsing the galleries and antique shops. Artfully presented Creole-influenced dishes reflect interesting flavor combinations. Examples include eggplant crisps with skordalia and oven-dried tomatoes, and pan-roasted cod with chanterelles and sunchoke puree. Casual dress; cocktails. **Parking:** street. **Cards:** AX, DC, DS, MC, VI.

THE MARIGNY BRASSERIE **Lunch:** $7-$11 **Dinner:** $16-$26 **Phone:** 504/945-4472 (6)

American

Location: Jct Royal St. 640 Frenchmen St 70116. **Hours:** 11:30 am-2:30 & 5:30-10 pm, Sat & Sun 10:30 am-3 & 5:30-10 pm. Closed: 11/22, 12/25. **Reservations:** suggested. **Features:** For a memorable meal, diners might want to hop over from the French Quarter to Frenchmen Street. Across from Washington Square is the brasserie, which nurtures a stylish but casual atmosphere and prepares such creative dishes as mole-braised free-range chicken, seafood paella, mushroom-crusted salmon and duck and andouille spring rolls. Entertainers perform once a week in the cozy lounge; call ahead for details. Dressy casual; cocktails. **Parking:** street. **Cards:** AX, DS, MC, VI.

MR. JOHN'S STEAKHOUSE **Lunch:** $9-$15 **Dinner:** $17-$39 **Phone:** 504/679-7697 (46)

Steak House

Location: Between Jackson Ave and Josephine St. 2111 St. Charles St 70130. **Hours:** 7:30 am-2:30 & 5:30-10 pm, Sat 8:30 am-2 & 5:30-10 pm. Closed: 12/25; also Sun & for dinner Mon. **Reservations:** suggested. **Features:** The steakhouse's sirloin strip is promoted as one the "best sizzling dishes" in town. Executive chef Dwight Sherman was trained by celebrity chef Emeril Lagasse. A distinctive feature of this place is the "wine club," which meets here every Monday to taste and rate vintage wines. Needless to say, the wine selection is good. This is one of the few restaurants in New Orleans that offers sidewalk seating when the weather permits. Casual dress; cocktails. **Parking:** valet and street. **Cards:** AX, DC, DS, MC, VI.

MIYAKO JAPANESE SEAFOOD & STEAKHOUSE **Lunch:** $6-$10 **Dinner:** $9-$35 **Phone:** 504/410-9997 (42)

Japanese

Location: Between Thalia and Erato sts. 1403 St. Charles Ave 70130. **Hours:** 11 am-2:30 & 5-10:30 pm, Sat 11 am-11 pm, Sun noon-10:30 pm. Closed: 7/4; also Mardi Gras Day. **Reservations:** accepted. **Features:** Enjoy delicious hibachi, sushi and other Japanese cuisine in an intimate atmosphere. Casual dress; cocktails. **Parking:** on-site. **Cards:** AX, DS, MC, VI.

MONA'S CAFE ON FRENCHMEN **Lunch:** $4-$8 **Dinner:** $8-$13 **Phone:** 504/949-4115 (10)

Mediterranean

Location: Between Decatur and Chartres sts. 504 Frenchmen St 70116. **Hours:** 11 am-10 pm, Fri & Sat-11 pm. Closed: 11/22, 12/25. **Reservations:** accepted. **Features:** On the casual eatery's menu are thick, homemade soups, crispy salads and a selection of classic Middle Eastern dishes, such as chicken kebabs, stuffed grape leaves and fried kibbeh. The adjacent delicatessen offers packaged products for those who wish to try a special dish at home. Casual dress. **Parking:** street. **Cards:** AX, DS, MC, VI.

MOTHER'S **Lunch:** $7-$21 **Dinner:** $7-$21 **Phone:** 504/523-9656 (20)

Regional American

Location: 401 Poydras St 70130. **Hours:** 6:30 am-10 pm, Sun from 7 am. Closed: 11/22, 12/25 & Easter; also Mother's Day. **Features:** A well-known sandwich shop famous for its great po'boys, red beans and rice and best ham biscuits and cracklin. Expect long lines and higher prices. One of New Orlean's best home-style restaurants. Casual dress; cocktails. **Parking:** on-site (fee). **Cards:** AX, MC, VI.

MULATE'S **Lunch:** $10-$13 **Dinner:** $14-$22 **Phone:** 504/522-1492 (35)

Cajun

Location: From jct of Poydras and Convention Center Blvd, 0.5 mi sw. 201 Julia St 70130. **Hours:** 11 am-10 pm, Fri & Sat-11 pm. **Reservations:** not accepted. **Features:** The restaurant serves traditional Cajun cuisine in a friendly, relaxed environment. Talented Cajun bands perform nightly, making this restaurant a local favorite. Casual dress; cocktails; entertainment. **Parking:** street. **Cards:** AX, DC, DS, MC, VI.

NEW ORLEANS GRILL **Lunch:** $15-$21 **Dinner:** $25-$45 **Phone:** 504/523-6000 (16)

AAA

Continental

Location: Between Magazine and Tchoupitoulas sts; in Windsor Court Hotel. 300 Gravier St 70130. **Hours:** 7-10:30 am, 11:30-2 & 6-10 pm. **Reservations:** suggested. **Features:** Creatively blended ingredients from different cuisine styles, set off by beautiful and artistic presentations, contribute to an exquisite meal of seasonal fare. Jackets are required. Semi-formal attire; cocktails; entertainment. **Parking:** valet. **Cards:** AX, CB, DC, DS, MC, VI.

O'HENRY'S FOOD AND SPIRITS **Lunch:** $6-$8 **Dinner:** $6-$15 **Phone:** 504/866-9741 (38)

American

Location: Corner of S Carrollton Ave and Hampson St. 634 S Carrollton Ave 70118. **Hours:** 11 am-midnight, Fri & Sat-2 am. **Features:** Patrons can savor tasty and affordable food in a casual atmosphere. The O'Henry burger, topped with pastrami and melted Swiss, is a classic. The health-conscious might opt for a turkey or veggie burger. Casual dress; cocktails. **Parking:** on-site. **Cards:** AX, DS, MC, VI.

PASCAL'S MANALE RESTAURANT **Lunch:** $7-$14 **Dinner:** $12-$26 **Phone:** 504/895-4877 (48)

Italian

Location: Just n of jct St. Charles Ave. 1838 Napoleon Ave 70115. **Hours:** 11:30 am-10 pm, Sat from 4 pm, Sun 4 pm-9 pm. Closed major holidays; also 12/24 & Sun 5/29-9/4. **Reservations:** suggested. **Features:** A New Orleans landmark since 1913, the restaurant is home of the original barbecue shrimp. The tasty crustaceans aren't the only laudable choice, as the competitively priced Italian dishes are legendary. Dressy casual; cocktails. **Parking:** on-site. **Cards:** AX, DC, DS, MC, VI.

(See map and index starting on p. 336)

THE PRALINE CONNECTION RESTAURANT **Lunch:** $7-$13 **Dinner:** $12-$19 **Phone:** 504/943-3934 (9)

Soul Food

Location: Jct Chartres St. 542 Frenchmen St 70116. **Hours:** 11 am-10 pm. Closed: 12/25. **Features:** Home-style foods make mouths water in anticipation. Fried chicken—with a choice of greens, lima beans, red beans or crowder peas—is a favorite among locals. Casual dress; cocktails. **Parking:** street. **Cards:** AX, DS, MC, VI.

RALPH'S ON THE PARK **Lunch:** $9-$18 **Dinner:** $17-$29 **Phone:** 504/488-1000 (1)

Creole

Location: Across from City Park. 900 City Park Ave 70119. **Hours:** 11:30 am-2:30 & 5:30-9:30 pm, Fri & Sat-10 pm. Closed: 12/24, 12/25; also Mardi Gras Day. **Reservations:** suggested. **Features:** With views of City Park, this elegant but understated dining room offers dishes using in-season, freshly picked ingredients under the direction of a gifted chef; the Creole menu varies seasonally and a vegetarian menu is available. Lunch includes less ambitious fare such as sandwiches, but your meal is always served by a skilled and well versed staff. Dressy casual; cocktails. **Parking:** valet. **Cards:** AX, MC, VI.

RENE BISTROT **Lunch:** $7-$18 **Dinner:** $15-$24 **Phone:** 504/412-2580 (12)

French

Location: Corner of Common and Baronne sts; downtown; in Renaissance Pere Marquette Hotel. 817 Common St 70130. **Hours:** 6:30-11 am, 11:30-2:30 & 6-10 pm, Fri & Sat-11 pm. **Reservations:** suggested. **Features:** Examples of creative fare on the contemporary French menu are sage-roasted pork loin and grilled salmon. A cozy atmosphere, open kitchen and attentive service add up to a pleasant dining experience. The extensive wine list includes many imported selections. Casual dress; cocktails. **Parking:** valet. **Cards:** AX, CB, DC, DS, MC, VI.

RESTAURANT AUGUST **Lunch:** $20-$22 **Dinner:** $20-$35 **Phone:** 504/299-9777 (14)

French

Location: Between Canal and Poydras sts. 301 Tchoupitoulas St 70130. **Hours:** 11 am-2 & 5:30-10 pm, Sat from 5:30 pm. Closed: 11/22, 12/25; also Sun & Mardi Gras. **Reservations:** required. **Features:** In a 19th-century building restored to its original grandeur, the restaurant provides a fine-dining experience in the Historic District, just blocks from the French Quarter. Contemporary French cuisine is created around ingredients indigenous to Louisiana. Dressy casual; cocktails. **Parking:** street. **Cards:** AX, MC, VI.

RESTAURANT CUVEE **Lunch:** $12-$15 **Dinner:** $22-$30 **Phone:** 504/587-9001 (15)

Creole

Location: Jct of Canal and Magazine sts, just sw. 322 Magazine St 70130. **Hours:** 5:30 pm-11 pm, Fri also 11:30 am-2 pm. Closed major holidays; also Sun & Mardi Gras. **Reservations:** suggested. **Features:** Kobe beef is an experience at this upscale stop for fine dining. Hallmarks of the restaurant include an eclectic menu, personalized service and a staff that is eager to please. Dressy casual; cocktails. **Parking:** on-site (fee) and valet. **Cards:** AX, DC, MC, VI.

RIO MAR **Lunch:** $4-$8 **Dinner:** $16-$22 **Phone:** 504/525-3474 (36)

Seafood

Location: Corner of Julia St; in the Warehouse District. 800 S Peters St 70130. **Hours:** 11:30 am-2 & 6-10 pm, Fri-10 pm, Sat 6 pm-10 pm. Closed major holidays; also Sun & Mardi Gras. **Reservations:** suggested. **Features:** Rio Mar, which translates to "river sea" in Spanish, focuses its menu on sea fare. The chef of the small restaurant applies a distinctive ethnic twist to both finfish and shellfish. While lunch is casual, dinner is a white-linen experience. Casual dress; cocktails. **Parking:** street. **Cards:** AX, DC, DS, MC, VI.

ROCK-N-SAKE BAR & SUSHI **Lunch:** $10-$16 **Dinner:** $10-$22 **Phone:** 504/581-7253 (37)

Japanese

Location: Jct Julia and Fulton sts, just s. 823 Fulton St 70130. **Hours:** 11:30 am-2:30 & 5:30-10 pm, Fri-midnight, Sat 5:30 pm-midnight, Sun 6 pm-10 pm. Closed major holidays; also Mardi Gras. **Reservations:** not accepted. **Features:** Artfully prepared sushi is the house specialty. Also featured are other tasty Japanese specialties, such as teriyaki chicken and tempura shrimp. Rock is always the background music of choice, and the selection of sake is magnificent. Casual dress; cocktails. **Parking:** street. **Cards:** AX, DC, DS, MC, VI.

SARA'S RESTAURANT **Lunch:** $7-$12 **Dinner:** $13-$19 **Phone:** 504/861-0565 (32)

Creole

Location: Between Hamson and Maple sts. 724 Dublin St 70118. **Hours:** 11:30 am-2:30 & 5:30-10:30 pm. Closed: Sun & Mon. **Reservations:** suggested. **Features:** In a quaint cottage house in the historic Carrollton Riverbend, the restaurant presents a menu of dishes that couple Asian flavors with Western preparation techniques. Diners often return here to try the results, such as green curried eggplant and grilled Muscovy duck breast. Dressy casual; cocktails. **Parking:** street. **Cards:** AX, CB, DC, DS, JC, MC, VI.

SAZERAC **Lunch:** $10-$18 **Dinner:** $16-$34 **Phone:** 504/529-4733 (11)

Creole

Location: Between Canal and University sts; entrance on University St; downtown; in The Fairmont New Orleans. 123 Baronne St 70112. **Hours:** 6 am-2 & 5:30-10 pm. **Reservations:** accepted. **Features:** Guests can unwind in an upscale setting and nosh on varied appetizers before savoring a lamb, veal or pork chop, seafood or filet mignon entree or an interesting Creole creation. Dressy casual; cocktails. **Parking:** on-site (fee) and valet. **Cards:** AX, CB, DC, DS, JC, MC, VI.

SNUG HARBOR JAZZ BISTRO **Dinner:** $10-$25 **Phone:** 504/949-0696 (7)

American

Location: Just n of jct Esplanade Ave and Frenchmen St; between Chartres and Royal sts. 626 Frenchmen St 70116. **Hours:** 5 pm-11 pm, Fri & Sat-midnight. Closed: 11/22, 12/24, 12/25; also Mardi Gras. **Reservations:** required. **Features:** The restaurant is small but offers a bar on one side and a cozy jazz auditorium in back. Two performances of jazz music are scheduled in the evenings for a fee. The food is predominantly American, with some dishes offering a Cajun flair. Casual dress; cocktails; entertainment. **Parking:** street. **Cards:** AX, MC, VI.

(See map and index starting on p. 336)

TAQUERIA CORONA Lunch: $2-$8 Dinner: $2-$8 Phone: 504/897-3974 (54)

Mexican

Location: 0.6 mi s of jct St. Charles and Nashville aves, just w. 5932 Magazine St 70115. **Hours:** 11:30 am-2 & 5-9:30 pm, Fri & Sat-10 pm. Closed: 11/22 & Easter; also 12/24 & 12/31. **Features:** In the Garden District, the homey, Mexican-style grill has a limited entree menu but good food. Here you will find such traditional favorites as tacos and burritos, as well as such selections as shrimp flauta topped with guacamole and sour cream. Casual dress; beer & wine only. **Parking:** street. **Cards:** AX, DS, MC, VI.

TAQUEROS Lunch: $10-$18 Dinner: $14-$32 Phone: 504/525-9996 (44)

Mexican

Location: US 90 business route, exit St. Charles Ave, just sw. 1432 St. Charles Ave 70130. **Hours:** 11:30 am-2 & 6-10 pm. Closed major holidays; also Sun. **Features:** Taking its inspiration from a Mexico City taqueria, the eatery serves tacos, Mexican sandwiches and a handful of entree plates. Among favorites are the classic enfrijoladas: pan-fried corn tortillas dipped in black bean sauce and topped with chicken, cheese and cream. Keep in mind this is authentic Mexican cuisine; don't expect to find cheesy entrees or combination plates. Casual dress; cocktails. **Parking:** on-site. **Cards:** AX, DS, MC, VI.

TOMMY'S CUISINE Dinner: $18-$30 Phone: 504/581-1103 (30)

AAA

Regional French

Location: Between Julia and Notre Dame sts. 746 Tchoupitoulas St 70130. **Hours:** 5:30 pm-10 pm, Fri & Sat-11 pm, Sun-10:30 pm. Closed: 1/1, 11/22, 12/25; also Mardi Gras. **Reservations:** accepted. **Features:** On the bistro's menu are classic Italian fare and French-influenced Creole dishes, such as soft-shell crab with linguine in crawfish sauce. Attentive service in the intimate dining room makes an evening memorable. Dressy casual; cocktails. **Parking:** street. **Cards:** AX, CB, DC, DS, MC, VI.

UGLY DOG SALOON & BBQ Lunch: $6-$15 Dinner: $6-$15 Phone: 504/569-8459 (40)

Regional American

Location: Corner of Tchoupitoulas St. 401 Andrew Higgins Blvd 70130. **Hours:** 11 am-10 pm, Fri & Sat-11 pm. Closed: 11/22, 12/25; also Sun. **Reservations:** not accepted. **Features:** A selection of barbecue and other sandwiches can be accompanied by a favorite beverage. Sporting events are shown on TV, and pool tables offer a diversion. Casual dress; cocktails. **Parking:** on-site and street. **Cards:** AX, DS, MC, VI.

UPPERLINE RESTAURANT Dinner: $20-$26 Phone: 504/891-9822 (52)

Creole

Location: US 90 business route, exit St. Charles Ave, 2.4 mi w, then just s. 1413 Upperline St 70115. **Hours:** 5:30 pm-9:30 pm, Fri & Sat-10 pm. Closed: 12/25; also Mon, Tues & Mardi Gras. **Reservations:** accepted. **Features:** Local artwork adorns the walls of this establishment where delicious Creole cuisine is featured. The menu includes seafood, steaks, veal and regional specialties. You will receive a pleasant greeting and attentive, polite service. Semi-formal attire; cocktails. **Parking:** on-site. **Cards:** AX, CB, DC, MC, VI.

VIC'S KANGAROO CAFE Lunch: $5-$11 Dinner: $5-$11 Phone: 504/524-4329 (25)

Australian

Location: Jct Poydras and Tchoupitoulas sts, 2 blks w. 636 Tchoupitoulas St 70130. **Hours:** 11 am-3 am, Sat & Sun from 3 pm. **Reservations:** not accepted. **Features:** A little slice of Australia resides at the friendly neighborhood pub. The food is good, and the party goes on until late at night. The bar scene is lively. Casual dress. **Parking:** street. **Cards:** AX, CB, DC, DS, MC, VI.

VOO DOO BBQ Lunch: $5-$15 Dinner: $5-$15 Phone: 504/522-4647 (45)

Barbecue

Location: Between Melpomene Ave and Terpsichore St. 1501 St. Charles Ave 70130. **Hours:** 11 am-10:30 pm, Fri & Sat-11:30 pm. Closed: 11/22, 12/25. **Features:** Pecan and oak woods give a distinctive "smoked" flavor to the meats served. Sides such as rattlesnake beans and corn pudding as well as homemade desserts are favorites here. Self-service lends to the relaxed atmosphere. Casual dress; cocktails. **Parking:** street. **Cards:** AX, DS, MC, VI.

WOLFE'S IN THE WAREHOUSE Lunch: $12-$21 Dinner: $21-$34 Phone: 504/613-2882 (39)

Regional Creole

Location: I-10 E, exit Poydras St, 1 mi e, then right; in New Orleans Marriott at the Convention Center. 859 Convention Center Blvd 70130. **Hours:** 6:30-10:30 am & 11:30-2 & 5:30-10 pm. **Reservations:** suggested. **Features:** The seasonal menu of contemporary New Orleans cuisine might list such dishes as Steen's cane syrup-glazed pork chop, pan crispy red trout and grilled filet mignon. Modern decor punctuates the sophisticated spot. Casual dress; cocktails. **Parking:** valet. **Cards:** AX, CB, DC, DS, MC, VI.

ZOE RESTAURANT AND BAR Lunch: $10-$19 Dinner: $14-$28 Phone: 504/207-5018 (21)

Regional American

Location: Close to Riverfront area/convention center; jct Poydras and S Peters sts; downtown; in W New Orleans. 333 Poydras St 70130. **Hours:** 6-11 am, 11:30-2:30 & 6-10 pm. **Reservations:** suggested. **Features:** Diners can relax in contemporary candlelit elegance. A doting, professional staff delivers contemporary French cuisine with Continental influences, such as the signature lobster shepherd's pie, juicy filet mignon or fresh sea bass. A playful pink poodle dessert teases and is delightful. Casual dress; cocktails. **Parking:** valet. **Cards:** AX, CB, DC, DS, JC, MC, VI.

The following restaurants have not been evaluated by AAA but are listed for your information only.

PARASOL'S Phone: 504/899-2054

fyi

Not evaluated. **Location:** Between 2nd and 3rd sts. 2533 Constance St 70130. **Features:** Diners shouldn't let the unassuming exterior keep them from the great fried shrimp plates and hearty beef, ham and turkey po' boy sandwiches.

UGLESICH'S Phone: 504/523-8571

fyi

Not evaluated. **Location:** 1238 Baronne St 70113. **Features:** Although located in a downscale neighborhood, this lunch only Cajun-Creole seafood restaurant is touted as having the best fried seafood, great shrimp po'boys and perfect oysters.

The New Orleans Vicinity

COVINGTON pop. 8,483

WHERE TO STAY

BEST WESTERN NORTHPARK INN *Book great rates at AAA.com* **Phone:** (985)892-2681

Small-scale Hotel

All Year [ECP] 1P: $69-$299 2P: $69-$299 XP: $10 F17

Location: I-12, exit 63B, just n. 625 N Hwy 190 70433. Fax: 985/893-0115. **Facility:** 74 one-bedroom standard units, some with kitchens. 2 stories (no elevator), interior/exterior corridors. **Parking:** on-site. **Amenities:** high-speed Internet, irons, hair dryers. **Pool(s):** outdoor. **Guest Services:** valet and coin laundry, wireless Internet. **Business Services:** meeting rooms, PC, fax (fee). **Cards:** AX, CB, DC, DS, MC, VI. **Free Special Amenities: continental breakfast and high-speed Internet.**

SOME UNITS

COMFORT INN & SUITES *Book great rates at AAA.com* **Phone:** (985)809-1234

Small-scale Hotel

All Year [ECP] 1P: $79-$149 2P: $79-$149 XP: $10 F17

Location: I-12, exit 63B, 0.5 mi n, then just e. 30 Louis Prima Dr 70433. Fax: 985/809-0466. **Facility:** 75 one-bedroom standard units, some with whirlpools. 3 stories, interior corridors. *Bath:* combo or shower only. **Parking:** on-site. **Terms:** 7 day cancellation notice. **Amenities:** dual phone lines, voice mail, irons, hair dryers. **Pool(s):** small outdoor. **Leisure Activities:** exercise room. **Guest Services:** valet and coin laundry, wireless Internet. **Business Services:** meeting rooms, business center. **Cards:** AX, CB, DC, DS, MC, VI.

SOME UNITS

ASK

COURTYARD BY MARRIOTT *Book great rates at AAA.com* **Phone:** (985)871-0244

Small-scale Hotel

All Year 1P: $119-$209

Location: I-12, exit 63B, 0.5 mi n, then just w. 101 N Park Blvd 70433. Fax: 985/867-9938. **Facility:** 141 units. 135 one-bedroom standard units, some with whirlpools. 6 one-bedroom suites. 3-4 stories, interior corridors. *Bath:* combo or shower only. **Parking:** on-site. **Terms:** [AP], [BP] & [CP] meal plans available, package plans. **Amenities:** high-speed Internet, dual phone lines, voice mail, irons, hair dryers. **Dining:** 6-10 am, Sat & Sun 7 am-noon. **Pool(s):** heated indoor. **Leisure Activities:** whirlpool, exercise room. **Guest Services:** sundries, valet and coin laundry, wireless Internet. **Business Services:** meeting rooms, business center. **Cards:** AX, DC, DS, JC, MC, VI. **Free Special Amenities: high-speed Internet.**

SOME UNITS

HAMPTON INN-COVINGTON/MANDEVILLE *Book great rates at AAA.com* **Phone:** 985/809-0019

Small-scale Hotel

Property failed to provide current rates

Location: I-12, exit 63B, just n, then just e on service road. 68700 Hwy 190 Service Rd 70433 (PO Box 1628, MANDEVILLE, 70470). Fax: 985/809-0211. **Facility:** 72 one-bedroom standard units, some with whirlpools. 3 stories, interior corridors. *Bath:* combo or shower only. **Parking:** on-site. **Amenities:** dual phone lines, voice mail, irons, hair dryers. **Pool(s):** outdoor. **Leisure Activities:** exercise room. **Guest Services:** valet laundry, wireless Internet. **Business Services:** meeting rooms, fax (fee).

SOME UNITS

HOLIDAY INN & SUITES COVINGTON NORTHSHORE *Book at AAA.com* **Phone:** (985)893-3580

Small-scale Hotel

All Year 1P: $109-$199 2P: $109-$199 XP: $10 F18

Location: I-12, exit 63B, just n. 501 N Hwy 190 70433. Fax: 985/893-4807. **Facility:** 155 units. 131 one-bedroom standard units. 20 one- and 4 two-bedroom suites with efficiencies. 2 stories (no elevator), interior/exterior corridors. **Parking:** on-site. **Terms:** check-in 4 pm, 5 day cancellation notice-fee imposed, pets ($50 fee). **Amenities:** video games (fee), high-speed Internet, dual phone lines, voice mail, irons, hair dryers. **Pool(s):** heated indoor/outdoor. **Leisure Activities:** whirlpools, exercise room, sports court. **Guest Services:** valet and coin laundry, wireless Internet. **Business Services:** meeting rooms, fax (fee). **Cards:** AX, DC, DS, MC, VI.

SOME UNITS

ASK FEE

SUPER 8 MOTEL *Book great rates at AAA.com* **Phone:** (985)892-4470

Motel

All Year [ECP] 1P: $99-$125 2P: $99-$135 XP: $10 F17

Location: I-12, exit 63B (US 190), just nw. Located behind the Waffle House. 120 Holiday Blvd 70433. Fax: 985/892-0370. **Facility:** 61 one-bedroom standard units, some with whirlpools. 2 stories (no elevator), exterior corridors. *Bath:* combo or shower only. **Parking:** on-site. **Amenities:** hair dryers. *Some:* irons. **Pool(s):** outdoor. **Guest Services:** wireless Internet. **Business Services:** fax (fee). **Cards:** AX, CB, DC, DS, JC, MC, VI. **Free Special Amenities: continental breakfast and high-speed Internet.**

SOME UNITS

WHERE TO DINE

ACME OYSTER HOUSE **Lunch:** $7-$15 **Dinner:** $7-$15 **Phone:** 985/898-0667

Seafood

Location: I-12, exit 63B (US 190), 3 mi n, then 0.5 mi w at jct SR 21; in historic Covington. 519 E Boston St 70433. **Hours:** 11 am-10 pm. Closed: 11/22, 12/25. **Features:** Although the original is still in the Big Easy, the New Orleans institution also has a home on the North Shore. The restaurant's oyster tradition goes back to 1910, but patrons also can sample po' boys, gumbo, jambalaya and fried catfish. Casual dress; cocktails. **Parking:** on-site. **Cards:** AX, DC, DS, MC, VI.

THE DAKOTA RESTAURANT **Lunch:** $12-$30 **Dinner:** $21-$41 **Phone:** 985/892-3712

American

Location: I-12, exit 63B, 0.5 mi n. 629 N Hwy 190 70433. **Hours:** 5:30 pm-9:30 pm, Thurs 11:30 am-2:15 & 5:30-9:30 pm, Fri 11:30 am-2:15 & 5:30-10:30 pm, Sat 5:30-10:30 pm. Closed: 12/25; also Sun & Mardi Gras. **Reservations:** suggested. **Features:** Folks don't have to head to New Orleans for a great dining experience. Sophisticated, contemporary cuisine reflects a Louisiana flair. The attentive, friendly staff serves delicious seasonal offerings, such as stuffed shrimp, Creole catfish and bacon oysters. Its sister restaurant—Cuvee in New Orleans—confirms a strong pedigree. Dressy casual; cocktails. **Parking:** on-site. **Cards:** AX, CB, DC, MC, VI.

GRETNA pop. 17,423 (See map and index starting on p. 336)

WHERE TO STAY

LA QUINTA INN NEW ORLEANS (WEST BANK) *Book great rates at AAA.com* **Phone:** (504)368-5600 88

Small-scale Hotel

All Year [ECP] 1P: $99-$139 2P: $109-$149 XP: $10 F18

Location: S US 90 business route, exit 9A (Terry Pkwy); N US 90 (Westbank Expwy), exit 9 (Terry Pkwy/General DeGaulle). 50 Terry Pkwy 70056-2564. Fax: 504/362-7430. **Facility:** 154 one-bedroom standard units. 2-3 stories, exterior corridors. *Bath:* combo or shower only. **Parking:** on-site. **Terms:** small pets only. **Amenities:** video games (fee), voice mail, irons, hair dryers. **Pool(s):** outdoor. **Guest Services:** valet and coin laundry, wireless Internet. **Business Services:** fax (fee). **Cards:** AX, CB, DC, DS, MC, VI. ***(See color ad p 386)***

SOME UNITS

ASK

WHERE TO DINE

KIM SON **Lunch:** $6-$8 **Dinner:** $6-$18 **Phone:** 504/366-2489 92

Asian

Location: US 90 business route, exit 9A (Terry Pkwy) westbound, 0.5 mi s on Frontage Rd, then just e; exit 8 (Stumpf Rd) eastbound, 0.6 mi n on Service Rd, then just e. 349 Whitney Ave 70053. **Hours:** 11 am-2:45 & 5-9 pm. Closed major holidays; also Sun & Mardi Gras. **Features:** Exotic spice combinations and fresh greens augment the deftly cooked meat and seafood of a large Vietnamese-Chinese menu. Vietnamese hot-and-sour soup and salt-baked shrimp are recommended. Accommodations include two large dining rooms. Casual dress; cocktails. **Parking:** on-site. **Cards:** AX, MC, VI.

TAN DINH **Lunch:** $5-$8 **Dinner:** $5-$8 **Phone:** 504/361-8008 93

Vietnamese

Location: US 90 business route, exit 7 (Lafayette), just s. 1705 Lafayette St 70053. **Hours:** 9:30 am-9 pm, Sat from 9 am, Sun 9 am-8 pm. Closed: Tues, Chinese New Year. **Features:** Despite a simple setting and basic food, the eatery has garnered national recognition. Extensive menu offerings including classic vermicelli bowls, in addition to tapioca drinks and desserts that appeal to the adventurous. Casual dress; beer only. **Parking:** on-site.

HARAHAN pop. 9,885 (See map and index starting on p. 336)

WHERE TO STAY

HAMPTON INN & SUITES ELMWOOD HOTEL *Book great rates at AAA.com* **Phone:** 504/733-5646 85

Small-scale Hotel

All Year 1P: $159-$209 2P: $159-$209

Location: I-10, exit 226 (Clearview Pkwy S), 3 mi s to Mounes St, then just w. 5150 Mounes St 70123. Fax: 504/733-5609. **Facility:** 128 one-bedroom standard units, some with efficiencies and/or whirlpools. 3 stories, interior corridors. *Bath:* combo or shower only. **Parking:** on-site. **Amenities:** voice mail, irons, hair dryers. **Pool(s):** outdoor. **Guest Services:** sundries, complimentary evening beverages: Wed, valet and coin laundry, wireless Internet. **Business Services:** meeting rooms, business center. **Cards:** AX, DC, DS, MC, VI. ***(See color ad p 383)***

SOME UNITS

ASK VCR

WHERE TO DINE

LA MADELEINE FRENCH BAKERY & CAFE **Lunch:** $7-$13 **Dinner:** $7-$13 **Phone:** 504/818-2450

French

Location: Jct Citrus and Elmwood Park blvds. 5171 Citrus Blvd, Suite 2000 70123. **Hours:** 6:30 am-10 pm. Closed: 12/25. **Features:** Casual dress; beer & wine only. **Parking:** on-site. **Cards:** AX, DS, MC, VI.

(See map and index starting on p. 336)

TAQUERIA CORONA **Lunch:** $5-$14 **Dinner:** $5-$14 **Phone:** 504/738-6722 (89)

Mexican

Location: Between Citrus and Dock. 1827 Hickory Ave 70123. **Hours:** 11:30 am-2 & 5-9:30 pm, Sat & Sun from 5 pm. Closed: 11/22, 12/25. **Features:** Located in a nondescript strip mall, this branch of a popular local chain serves yummy tacos, chunky tomato salsa and Mexican pizza while Spanish music plays in the background. Beer & wine only. **Parking:** on-site. **Cards:** AX, DS, MC, VI.

HARVEY pop. 22,226 (See map and index starting on p. 336)

WHERE TO STAY

BEST WESTERN WESTBANK *Book great rates at AAA.com* **Phone:** (504)366-5369 (95)

AAA SAVE

Small-scale Hotel

All Year [ECP]	1P: $79-$169	2P: $79-$169	XP: $10	F12

Location: US 90 business route, exit 6 (Manhattan Blvd), 2.3 mi s, then just w. 1700 Lapalco Blvd 70058. Fax: 504/262-0949. **Facility:** 139 one-bedroom standard units. 3 stories, exterior corridors. **Parking:** on-site. **Terms:** 30 day cancellation notice. **Amenities:** high-speed Internet, voice mail, irons, hair dryers. **Dining:** Copeland's of New Orleans, see separate listing. **Pool(s):** outdoor. **Leisure Activities:** whirlpool, exercise room. **Guest Services:** gift shop, valet and coin laundry. **Business Services:** meeting rooms, business center. **Cards:** AX, CB, DC, DS, MC, VI. **Free Special Amenities: expanded continental breakfast and high-speed Internet.**

SOME UNITS

HOLIDAY INN EXPRESS *Book at AAA.com* **Phone:** 504/366-5055 (94)

Small-scale Hotel

12/1-2/28	1P: $99-$109	2P: $99-$109	XP: $5	F
3/1-5/31 & 10/1-11/30	1P: $99	2P: $99	XP: $5	F
6/1-9/30	1P: $89	2P: $89	XP: $5	F

Location: US 90, exit 6 (Manhattan Blvd), 2 mi s. 2433 Manhattan Blvd 70058. Fax: 504/366-5018. **Facility:** 62 one-bedroom standard units. 3 stories, interior corridors. *Bath:* combo or shower only. **Parking:** on-site. **Terms:** cancellation fee imposed. **Amenities:** high-speed Internet, dual phone lines, voice mail, irons, hair dryers. **Pool(s):** heated outdoor. **Leisure Activities:** exercise room. **Guest Services:** valet and coin laundry. **Business Services:** meeting rooms, business center. **Cards:** AX, CB, DC, DS, MC, VI.

SOME UNITS

ASK

WHERE TO DINE

COPELAND'S OF NEW ORLEANS **Lunch:** $8-$14 **Dinner:** $8-$22 **Phone:** 504/364-1575 (99)

Regional American

Location: US 90 business route, exit 6 (Manhattan Blvd), 2.3 mi s, then just w; in Best Western Westbank. 1700 Lapalco Blvd 70058. **Hours:** 11 am-10 pm, Fri & Sat-11 pm. Closed: 12/25. **Features:** Cajun-American cuisine is the focus at the warm, cozy family restaurant. Ricochet catfish, pasta LuAn and grilled fish Copeland are a few house specialties. An art deco design, split-level dining areas and a full bar create an attractive setting. Casual dress; cocktails. **Parking:** on-site. **Cards:** AX, CB, DC, DS, MC, VI.

JEAN LAFITTE pop. 2,137

WHERE TO DINE

RESTAURANT DES FAMILLES **Lunch:** $7-$23 **Dinner:** $9-$23 **Phone:** 504/689-7834

Regional American

Location: Corner of SR 3134 (Lafitte-LaRose Hwy) and 45 (Barataria Blvd). 7163 Barataria Blvd 70072. **Hours:** noon-8 pm, Fri & Sat-9 pm, Sun 11:30 am-3 pm. Closed: 1/1, 7/4, 12/25; also Mon, Tues & Mardi Gras. **Reservations:** suggested. **Features:** Moss-draped trees shade the raised cottage with its inviting wraparound porch and picture window that affords a view of the bayou. Cajun and Creole offerings like oysters lafitte, soft-shell crab Foster and turtle or oyster-artichoke soup are the focus. Casual dress; cocktails. **Parking:** on-site. **Cards:** AX, DS, MC, VI.

KENNER pop. 70,517 (See map and index starting on p. 336)

WHERE TO STAY

BEST WESTERN NEW ORLEANS INN AT THE AIRPORT *Book great rates at AAA.com* **Phone:** 504/464-1644 81

SAVE

Small-scale Hotel

All Year 1P: $59-$139 2P: $59-$139 XP: $10 F17

Location: US 61, 0.6 mi w from jct SR 49. 1021 Airline Dr 70062. Fax: 504/469-1193. **Facility:** 166 units. 164 one-bedroom standard units. 2 one-bedroom suites. 4 stories, exterior corridors. **Parking:** on-site. **Terms:** 3 day cancellation notice-fee imposed, package plans. **Amenities:** voice mail, irons, hair dryers. **Dining:** 24 hours, cocktails. **Pool(s):** outdoor. **Leisure Activities:** exercise room. **Guest Services:** valet and coin laundry, wireless Internet. **Business Services:** meeting rooms, fax (fee). **Cards:** DC, DS, MC, VI. **Free Special Amenities: local telephone calls and newspaper.**

SOME UNITS

COMFORT SUITES NEW ORLEANS AIRPORT KENNER *Book great rates at AAA.com* **Phone:** (504)466-6066 79

SAVE

Small-scale Hotel

All Year 1P: $79-$189 2P: $89-$199 XP: $10 F

Location: I-10, exit 223A (Williams Blvd), just s, just e on Veterans, then just s. 2710 Idaho Ave 70062. Fax: 504/466-8282. **Facility:** 95 units. 90 one-bedroom standard units, some with whirlpools. 5 two-bedroom suites ($99-$209), some with whirlpools. 5 stories, interior corridors. *Bath:* combo or shower only. **Parking:** on-site. **Terms:** cancellation fee imposed. **Amenities:** high-speed Internet, dual phone lines, voice mail, safes, irons, hair dryers. **Pool(s):** indoor/outdoor. **Leisure Activities:** whirlpool, exercise room. **Guest Services:** sundries, coin laundry, area transportation-within 3 mi, wireless Internet. **Business Services:** meeting rooms, business center. **Cards:** AX, CB, DC, DS, JC, MC, VI. **Free Special Amenities: expanded continental breakfast and high-speed Internet.** *(See color ad below)*

SOME UNITS

FAIRFIELD INN NEW ORLEANS AIRPORT *Book great rates at AAA.com* **Phone:** 504/443-9800 76

Small-scale Hotel

Property failed to provide current rates

Location: I-10, exit 223A (Williams Blvd), just n to 32nd St, then just w. 1801 32nd St 70065. Fax: 504/443-0700. **Facility:** 106 one-bedroom standard units, some with whirlpools. 3 stories, interior corridors. *Bath:* combo or shower only. **Parking:** on-site. **Amenities:** high-speed Internet, irons, hair dryers. **Pool(s):** small outdoor. **Leisure Activities:** whirlpool, exercise room. **Guest Services:** valet laundry. **Business Services:** meeting rooms, fax.

SOME UNITS

HILTON GARDEN INN NEW ORLEANS AIRPORT *Book great rates at AAA.com* **Phone:** (504)712-0504 75

Small-scale Hotel

All Year 1P: $169-$189 2P: $169-$189 XP: $10 F18

Location: I-10, exit 223A (Williams Blvd), 1.9 mi n. 4535 Williams Blvd 70065. Fax: 504/712-0109. **Facility:** 122 units. 121 one-bedroom standard units. 1 one-bedroom suite. 3 stories, interior corridors. *Bath:* combo or shower only. **Parking:** on-site. **Terms:** cancellation fee imposed. **Amenities:** video games (fee), high-speed Internet, dual phone lines, voice mail, irons, hair dryers. **Pool(s):** heated outdoor. **Leisure Activities:** whirlpool, exercise room. **Guest Services:** sundries, valet and coin laundry, wireless Internet. **Business Services:** meeting rooms, business center. **Cards:** AX, CB, DC, DS, MC, VI. *(See color ad p 383)*

SOME UNITS

(See map and index starting on p. 336)

HILTON NEW ORLEANS AIRPORT Book great rates at AAA.com **Phone:** (504)469-5000 82

SAVE Large-scale Hotel

All Year 1P: $109-$209 2P: $129-$229 XP: $20 F18

Location: I-10, exit 223A (Williams Blvd), 2 mi s, then 0.8 mi w. 901 Airline Dr 70062. Fax: 504/465-1101. **Facility:** 317 units. 315 one-bedroom standard units. 2 one-bedroom suites. 6 stories, interior corridors. *Bath:* combo or shower only. **Parking:** on-site. **Terms:** 3 day cancellation notice-fee imposed, package plans. **Amenities:** video games (fee), high-speed Internet, dual phone lines, voice mail, irons, hair dryers. **Dining:** 6 am-2 & 5-10:30 pm, cocktails. **Pool(s):** outdoor. **Leisure Activities:** whirlpool, exercise room. **Guest Services:** gift shop, valet laundry, wireless Internet. **Business Services:** conference facilities, business center. **Cards:** AX, CB, DC, DS, JC, MC, VI. *(See color ad p 383)*

SOME UNITS / FEE

HOTEL AIRPORT Book at AAA.com **Phone:** 504/305-1501 78

Small-scale Hotel

Property failed to provide current rates

Location: I-10, exit 223A (Williams Blvd), just s, then 0.4 mi w. 1501 Veterans Memorial Blvd 70062. Fax: 504/305-1500. **Facility:** 102 units. 101 one-bedroom standard units. 1 one-bedroom suite. 6 stories, interior corridors. *Bath:* combo or shower only. **Parking:** on-site. **Amenities:** video games (fee), dual phone lines, voice mail, safes, irons, hair dryers. **Leisure Activities:** whirlpool, exercise room. **Guest Services:** complimentary laundry, wireless Internet. **Business Services:** meeting rooms, business center.

SOME UNITS

LA QUINTA INN NEW ORLEANS (AIRPORT) Book great rates at AAA.com **Phone:** (504)466-1401 80

Small-scale Hotel

All Year [ECP] 1P: $99-$139 2P: $109-$149 XP: $10 F18

Location: I-10, exit 223A (Williams Blvd), 0.3 mi s. 2610 Williams Blvd 70062. Fax: 504/466-0319. **Facility:** 195 units. 188 one-bedroom standard units. 7 one-bedroom suites. 5 stories, interior corridors. **Parking:** on-site. **Terms:** small pets only. **Amenities:** video games (fee), high-speed Internet, voice mail. **Pool(s):** outdoor. **Leisure Activities:** exercise room. **Guest Services:** coin laundry, wireless Internet. **Business Services:** meeting rooms, business center. **Cards:** AX, CB, DC, DS, MC, VI. ***(See color ad p 386)***

ASK SOME UNITS

MOTEL 6 **Phone:** (504)466-9666

Small-scale Hotel

All Year 1P: $70-$150 2P: $70-$150 XP: $5 F

Location: I-10, exit 221, just s. 2830 Loyola Dr 70062. Fax: 504/464-3801. **Facility:** 120 one-bedroom standard units. 6 stories, interior corridors. *Bath:* combo or shower only. **Parking:** on-site. **Terms:** weekly rates available. **Amenities:** voice mail. *Some:* irons, hair dryers. **Leisure Activities:** exercise room. **Guest Services:** coin laundry. **Business Services:** meeting rooms, fax (fee). **Cards:** AX, DS, MC, VI.

ASK SOME UNITS / FEE FEE

(See map and index starting on p. 336)

RADISSON HOTEL NEW ORLEANS AIRPORT Book great rates at AAA.com **Phone:** (504)467-3111 77

1/14-5/12	1P: $119-$199	2P: $119-$199	XP: $10	F14
12/1-1/13 & 9/16-11/30	1P: $99-$199	2P: $99-$199	XP: $10	F14
5/13-9/15	1P: $99-$179	2P: $99-$179	XP: $10	F14

Large-scale Hotel

Location: I-10, exit 223A (Williams Blvd), just s, then just e. 2150 Veterans Blvd 70062. Fax: 504/469-4634. **Facility:** 244 units. 243 one-bedroom standard units. 1 one-bedroom suite. 8 stories, interior corridors. *Bath:* combo or shower only. **Parking:** on-site. **Terms:** [CP] meal plan available. **Amenities:** dual phone lines, voice mail, irons, hair dryers. **Dining:** 6 am-2 & 5-10 pm. **Pool(s):** outdoor. **Leisure Activities:** exercise room. **Guest Services:** sundries, valet laundry, wireless Internet. **Business Services:** meeting rooms, PC. **Cards:** AX, CB, DC, DS, JC, MC, VI. **Free Special Amenities: room upgrade (subject to availability with advance reservations) and high-speed Internet.**

(See color ad p 406)

SOME UNITS

WHERE TO DINE

THE BRICK OVEN **Lunch:** $10-$26 **Dinner:** $10-$26 **Phone:** 504/466-2097 85

Italian

Location: I-10, exit 223A (Williams Blvd), just s; at Veterans Memorial Blvd. 2805 Williams Blvd 70062. **Hours:** 11 am-10 pm. Closed: 11/22, 12/25. **Features:** A statue of liberty stands outside, but the large brick oven is the popular eatery's central focus. The menu lists traditional pasta and veal dishes, as well as several chicken items and some of the best pizza in town. Casual dress; cocktails. **Parking:** on-site. **Cards:** AX, DC, MC, VI.

CHEVY'S FRESH MEX **Lunch:** $7-$9 **Dinner:** $7-$15 **Phone:** 504/469-5657

Tex-Mex

Location: I-10, exit 223A (Williams Blvd), 0.5 mi n, then 0.5 mi w. 1325 W Esplanade Ave 70065. **Hours:** 11 am-10 pm, Fri & Sat-11 pm. Closed: 11/22, 12/25. **Reservations:** accepted. **Features:** The restaurant takes pride in offering only the freshest ingredients for its Tex-Mex fare. This spot is known for its fajitas and karaoke Thursdays. Casual dress; cocktails. **Parking:** on-site. **Cards:** AX, DC, DS, MC, VI.

LE PARVENU **Dinner:** $14-$31 **Phone:** 504/471-0534 86

Creole

Location: I-10, exit 223A (Williams Blvd), 4 mi s. 509 Williams Blvd 70062. **Hours:** 5 pm-close. Closed: 1/1, 7/4, 12/25; also Sun. **Reservations:** suggested. **Features:** The owner/chef cites fresh local seafood as key to the innovative Creole cuisine prepared at the newly renovated house. Specialties on a rotating menu may include mirliton shrimp and crabmeat bisque with creme fraiche or paneed veal with fresh European tomato sauce and capers. Service is efficient and casual. Dressy casual; cocktails. **Parking:** on-site. **Cards:** AX, DC, DS, MC, VI.

SMITTY'S SEAFOOD RESTAURANT & OYSTER BAR **Lunch:** $6-$17 **Dinner:** $6-$17 **Phone:** 504/468-1647 84

Seafood

Location: Just w of jct Williams Blvd and W Esplanade Ave. 2000 W Esplanade Ave 70065. **Hours:** 11 am-10 pm, Fri & Sat-11 pm, Sun noon-9 pm. **Features:** Freshness and skillful seasoning distinguish the locally familiar seafood menu. Boiled shellfish and broiled fish are the standouts with a few home-style dishes, and some steak and chicken entrees. Servers are pleasant, and the atmosphere is very casual. Casual dress; cocktails. **Parking:** on-site. **Cards:** AX, DS, MC, VI.

LACOMBE pop. 7,518

WHERE TO DINE

SAL 'N' JUDY'S **Dinner:** $12-$20 **Phone:** 985/882-9443

Italian

Location: I-12, exit 74, 3 mi s to US 190, then 0.8 mi w. US 190 at N 14th St 70445. **Hours:** 5 pm-10 pm, Sun noon-7 pm. Closed: 11/22, 12/25 & Easter; also Mon, Tues & Super Bowl Sun. **Reservations:** required. **Features:** Merges the traditions of Sicily's rich and vigorous country cooking with those of exotic New Orleans Creole. Framed posters and old photos cast the dining rooms in a homey, casual mood. Feast on crab claws, veal pane, scampi and brucioloni specialties. Casual dress. **Parking:** on-site. **Cards:** AX, DS, MC, VI.

LAFITTE pop. 1,576

WHERE TO DINE

VOLEO'S **Lunch:** $4-$12 **Dinner:** $8-$23 **Phone:** 504/689-2482

Regional American

Location: 1 mi s of Goose Bayour Bridge. 5134 Nunez St 70067. **Hours:** 11 am-9 pm. Closed major holidays; also Sun & Tues. **Features:** Fresh seafood and a talent for seasoning elevate a menu of fried items and home-style, coastal Louisiana dishes to real distinction. Also, German favorites like wiener schnitzel are available. Your food will be cooked to order, so there may be a wait. Casual dress; beer & wine only. **Parking:** on-site. **Cards:** AX, CB, DC, DS, MC, VI.

LA PLACE pop. 27,684

WHERE TO STAY

BEST WESTERN LA PLACE INN Book great rates at AAA.com **Phone:** (985)651-4000

All Year	1P: $69-$109	2P: $69-$109	XP: $10	F12

Small-scale Hotel

Location: I-10, exit 209, just s. 4289 Main St 70068. Fax: 985/651-8666. **Facility:** 77 one-bedroom standard units, some with whirlpools. 2 stories (no elevator), exterior corridors. **Parking:** on-site. **Terms:** small pets only ($25 extra charge). **Amenities:** high-speed Internet, voice mail, irons, hair dryers. **Pool(s):** outdoor. **Leisure Activities:** limited exercise equipment. **Guest Services:** valet and coin laundry, wireless Internet. **Business Services:** meeting rooms, business center. **Cards:** AX, CB, DC, DS, MC, VI.

SOME UNITS

FEE

DAYS INN-LA PLACE *Book great rates at AAA.com* **Phone:** (985)652-1223

Small-scale Hotel

All Year 1P: $90-$150 XP: $15 F12

Location: I-10, exit 209, just s. 3912 Hwy 51 70068. Fax: 985/652-9993. **Facility:** 53 one-bedroom standard units, some with whirlpools. 3 stories, interior corridors. *Bath:* combo or shower only. **Parking:** on-site. **Terms:** 3 day cancellation notice-fee imposed, [ECP] meal plan available. **Amenities:** dual phone lines, safes, hair dryers. **Pool(s):** outdoor. **Guest Services:** valet laundry, wireless Internet. **Business Services:** fax (fee). **Cards:** AX, DC, DS, MC, VI. **Free Special Amenities: expanded continental breakfast and high-speed Internet.**

SOME UNITS

HAMPTON INN *Book great rates at AAA.com* **Phone:** 985/652-5002

Small-scale Hotel

All Year [CP] 1P: $109-$129 2P: $109-$129 XP: $10 F12

Location: I-10, exit 209, just s. 4288 Hwy 51 70068. Fax: 985/651-3009. **Facility:** 80 one-bedroom standard units, some with whirlpools. 3 stories, interior corridors. *Bath:* combo or shower only. **Parking:** on-site. **Terms:** cancellation fee imposed. **Amenities:** video games (fee), high-speed Internet, dual phone lines, voice mail, irons, hair dryers. **Pool(s):** outdoor. **Leisure Activities:** exercise room. **Guest Services:** valet and coin laundry, wireless Internet. **Business Services:** meeting rooms, business center. **Cards:** AX, DS, MC, VI. **Free Special Amenities: expanded continental breakfast and high-speed Internet.**

SOME UNITS

QUALITY INN-LA PLACE *Book great rates at AAA.com* **Phone:** (985)652-5544

Small-scale Hotel

All Year [BP] 1P: $72-$94 2P: $77-$99 XP: $5 F

Location: I-10, exit 209, 0.5 mi s. 3900 Hwy 51 70068 (PO Drawer 460, 70069). Fax: 985/652-8209. **Facility:** 100 one-bedroom standard units. 2 stories (no elevator), exterior corridors. *Bath:* combo or shower only. **Parking:** on-site. **Terms:** small pets only ($125 fee). **Amenities:** voice mail, irons, hair dryers. **Pool(s):** outdoor. **Leisure Activities:** limited exercise equipment. **Guest Services:** valet and coin laundry, wireless Internet. **Business Services:** meeting rooms, fax (fee). **Cards:** AX, CB, DC, DS, JC, MC, VI.

SOME UNITS

ASK FEE

MANDEVILLE pop. 10,489

WHERE TO DINE

THE BROKEN EGG CAFE **Lunch:** $7-$13 **Phone:** 985/624-3388

American

Location: I-12, exit 63A, 3.9 mi s, exit Monroe St, 1.9 mi e, then just s. 200 Gerard St 70448. **Hours:** 7:30 am-2 pm. Closed: 11/22, 12/25; also Mardi Gras. **Features:** Voted as offering the best breakfast on the north shore, the charming eatery occupies a 1920s home just a block from Lake Pontchartrain. Among more than 30 variations of eggs are such choices as Southwest scrambled, Italiano omelet and veggie Benedict. Gourmet pancakes, waffles and cinnamon rolls are tasty breakfast accompaniments, while sandwiches and burgers round out the lunch choices. Late risers will appreciate being able to eat breakfast until closing. Casual dress; beer & wine only. **Parking:** on-site. **Cards:** AX, DC, DS, MC, VI.

FAZZIO'S **Lunch:** $6-$10 **Dinner:** $8-$20 **Phone:** 985/624-9704

Regional Italian

Location: Just e on S Frontage Rd. 1841 N Causeway Blvd 70471. **Hours:** 11 am-9 pm, Fri & Sat-10 pm. Closed: 1/1, 11/22; also Sun & Mardi Gras. **Features:** The restaurant presents an unusual combination: Sicilian cooking with Creole accents. Pasta, tomato sauces and seafood abound. Friendly, efficient service enhances any meal. Casual dress; cocktails. **Parking:** on-site. **Cards:** AX, DC, DS, MC, VI.

LA MADELEINE FRENCH BAKERY & CAFE **Lunch:** $7-$13 **Dinner:** $8-$13 **Phone:** 985/626-7004

French

Location: Jct US 190 and SR 22, 0.5 mi se. 3434 Hwy 190 70471. **Hours:** 7 am-9 pm, Fri & Sat-10 pm. Closed: 12/25. **Features:** Casual dress; beer & wine only. **Parking:** on-site. **Cards:** AX, DS, MC, VI.

TREY YUEN CUISINE OF CHINA **Lunch:** $6-$7 **Dinner:** $7-$15 **Phone:** 985/626-4476

Chinese

Location: 0.5 mi n of Lake Ponchartrain Cswy, on west side of causeway approach, northwest side; jct I-12 and US 190, exit 63A, 3.5 mi s, then exit Monroe St. 600 N Causeway Approach 70448. **Hours:** 11:30 am-2 & 5-9 pm, Fri-10 pm, Sat 5 pm-10 pm, Sun 11:30 am-9:30 pm. Closed: 12/24, Mon & Mardi Gras. **Reservations:** suggested. **Features:** Trey Yuen features Cantonese, Hunan and Szechuan cuisine. The attractive decor consists of Chinese antiques and architectural details, a fish pond and gardens. Menu highlights include crawfish with spicy lobster sauce and lotus banana. Casual dress; cocktails. **Parking:** on-site. **Cards:** AX, CB, DC, DS, MC, VI.

METAIRIE pop. 146,136 (See map and index starting on p. 336)

WHERE TO STAY

DAYS HOTEL NEW ORLEANS-METAIRIE *Book great rates at AAA.com* **Phone:** (504)833-8201 69

Small-scale Hotel

All Year 1P: $49-$229 2P: $49-$229 XP: $10 F17

Location: I-10, exit 228 (Causeway Blvd), just sw via Frontage Rd. 3400 I-10 S Service Rd W 70001. Fax: 504/838-6829. **Facility:** 193 one-bedroom standard units. 4 stories, interior corridors. *Bath:* combo or shower only. **Parking:** on-site. **Terms:** check-in 4 pm, cancellation fee imposed, [AP], [BP], [CP], [ECP] & [MAP] meal plans available, package plans. **Amenities:** voice mail, irons, hair dryers. **Pool(s):** outdoor. **Leisure Activities:** whirlpool, limited exercise equipment. **Guest Services:** valet and coin laundry, wireless Internet. **Business Services:** meeting rooms, fax (fee). **Cards:** AX, DC, DS, MC, VI. **Free Special Amenities: newspaper and early check-in/late check-out.** *(See color ad p 409)*

SOME UNITS

(See map and index starting on p. 336)

HAMPTON INN METAIRIE Book great rates at AAA.com Phone: (504)831-7676 67

Small-scale Hotel

All Year [ECP] 1P: $109-$169 2P: $109-$169

Location: I-10, exit 228 (Causeway Blvd), just n. 2730 N Causeway Blvd at Veterans 70002. Fax: 504/831-7478. **Facility:** 111 one-bedroom standard units. 5 stories, interior corridors. *Bath:* combo or shower only. **Parking:** on-site. **Terms:** cancellation fee imposed. **Amenities:** video games (fee), high-speed Internet, dual phone lines, voice mail, irons, hair dryers. **Pool(s):** outdoor. **Leisure Activities:** exercise room. **Guest Services:** valet and coin laundry, area transportation, wireless Internet. **Business Services:** meeting rooms, business center. **Cards:** AX, DC, DS, MC, VI. *(See color ad p 383)*

SOME UNITS

LA QUINTA INN NEW ORLEANS (CAUSEWAY) Book great rates at AAA.com Phone: (504)835-8511 70

Small-scale Hotel

All Year [ECP] 1P: $99-$139 2P: $109-$149 XP: $10 F18

Location: I-10, exit 228 (Causeway Blvd), just s. 3100 I-10 Service Rd 70001-2091. Fax: 504/837-3383. **Facility:** 101 one-bedroom standard units. 2 stories (no elevator), exterior corridors. **Parking:** on-site. **Terms:** small pets only. **Amenities:** video games (fee), voice mail, irons, hair dryers. **Pool(s):** outdoor. **Guest Services:** valet and coin laundry, wireless Internet. **Business Services:** fax (fee). **Cards:** AX, CB, DC, DS, MC, VI. *(See color ad p 386)*

SOME UNITS

LA QUINTA INN NEW ORLEANS (VETERANS) Book great rates at AAA.com Phone: (504)456-0003 65

Small-scale Hotel

All Year [ECP] 1P: $99-$139 2P: $109-$149 XP: $10 F18

Location: I-10, exit 225, just n. 5900 Veterans Memorial Blvd 70003-1738. Fax: 504/885-0863. **Facility:** 153 units. 150 one-bedroom standard units. 3 one-bedroom suites. 3 stories, exterior corridors. *Bath:* combo or shower only. **Parking:** on-site. **Terms:** small pets only. **Amenities:** video games (fee), voice mail, irons, hair dryers. **Pool(s):** outdoor. **Guest Services:** coin laundry, wireless Internet. **Business Services:** fax (fee). **Cards:** AX, CB, DC, DS, MC, VI. *(See color ad p 386)*

SOME UNITS

METAIRIE HOTEL Book at AAA.com Phone: 504/837-6707 72

Small-scale Hotel

Property failed to provide current rates

Location: I-10, exit 228 (Causeway Blvd), just s to 36th St, just e, then just n. 4 Galleria Blvd 70001. Fax: 504/837-6906. **Facility:** 182 one-bedroom standard units, some with whirlpools. 7 stories, interior corridors. *Bath:* combo or shower only. **Parking:** on-site. **Amenities:** video games (fee), high-speed Internet, dual phone lines, voice mail, irons, hair dryers. *Some:* CD players. **Pool(s):** lap. **Leisure Activities:** exercise room. **Guest Services:** valet laundry. **Business Services:** conference facilities, PC.

SOME UNITS

(See map and index starting on p. 336)

NEW ORLEANS MARRIOTT METAIRIE AT LAKEWAY **Phone:** (504)836-5253 64

fyi 2/1-6/30 & 9/16-11/30 1P: $209-$249 2P: $229-$269 XP: $20 F18
12/1-1/31 & 7/1-9/15 1P: $129-$179 2P: $149-$199 XP: $20 F18

Large-scale Hotel Under major renovation, scheduled to be completed October 2006. **Last rated:** ◆◆◆ **Location:** I-10, exit 228 (Causeway Blvd), 2 mi n; entrance on Lakeside Dr. 3838 N Causeway Blvd 70002. Fax: 504/846-4562. **Facility:** 210 one-bedroom standard units. 16 stories, interior corridors. *Bath:* combo or shower only. **Parking:** on-site (fee) and valet. **Terms:** 3 day cancellation notice-fee imposed. **Amenities:** high-speed Internet (fee), voice mail, irons, hair dryers. **Pool(s):** heated indoor. **Leisure Activities:** whirlpool, jogging. *Fee:* massage. **Guest Services:** gift shop, valet laundry, area transportation. **Business Services:** conference facilities, fax (fee). **Cards:** AX, CB, DC, DS, MC, VI. Affiliated with Marriott Hotels, Resorts and Suites.

SOME UNITS

FEE

RAMADA LIMITED CAUSEWAY *Book great rates at AAA.com* **Phone:** (504)835-4141 66

All Year [CP] 1P: $109-$149 2P: $109-$149 XP: $10 F17

Small-scale Hotel **Location:** I-10, exit 228 (Causeway Blvd), just ne. 2713 N Causeway Blvd 70002. Fax: 504/833-6942. **Facility:** 138 one-bedroom standard units. 3 stories, interior/exterior corridors. *Bath:* combo or shower only. **Parking:** on-site. **Amenities:** video games (fee), voice mail, safes, irons, hair dryers. **Pool(s):** small outdoor. **Leisure Activities:** exercise room. **Guest Services:** valet laundry, area transportation-French Quarter, wireless Internet. **Business Services:** meeting rooms, business center. **Cards:** AX, DC, DS, JC, MC, VI. **Free Special Amenities: continental breakfast and high-speed Internet.** *(See color ad p 361)*

SOME UNITS

RESIDENCE INN BY MARRIOTT-METAIRIE *Book great rates at AAA.com* **Phone:** (504)832-0888 71

All Year 1P: $149-$299

Small-scale Hotel **Location:** I-10, exit 228 (Causeway Blvd), just se to 36th St, then just e. 3 Galleria Blvd 70001. Fax: 504/832-4916. **Facility:** 120 units. 48 one-bedroom standard units, some with efficiencies or kitchens. 48 one- and 24 two-bedroom suites, some with efficiencies or kitchens. 3 stories, interior corridors. *Bath:* combo or shower only. **Parking:** on-site. **Terms:** check-in 4 pm, 3 day cancellation notice-fee imposed, pets ($75 fee). **Amenities:** high-speed Internet, voice mail, irons, hair dryers. **Pool(s):** heated outdoor. **Leisure Activities:** whirlpool, barbecue grill, exercise room, sports court, basketball. **Guest Services:** complimentary evening beverages: Mon-Thurs, valet and coin laundry, wireless Internet. **Business Services:** meeting rooms. **Cards:** AX, CB, DC, DS, JC, MC, VI. **Free Special Amenities: high-speed Internet.**

SOME UNITS

FEE

SLEEP INN & SUITES *Book great rates at AAA.com* **Phone:** (504)887-5337 68

All Year 1P: $99-$199 2P: $99-$199 XP: $10 F18

Small-scale Hotel **Location:** I-10, exit 226 (Clearview Blvd), just n, then just w on frontage road. 4601 N I-10 Service Rd 70006. Fax: 504/883-5895. **Facility:** 70 one-bedroom standard units, some with whirlpools. 5 stories, interior corridors. *Bath:* combo or shower only. **Parking:** on-site. **Terms:** 3 day cancellation notice. **Amenities:** high-speed Internet, dual phone lines, voice mail, safes (fee), irons, hair dryers. **Leisure Activities:** exercise room. **Guest Services:** valet and coin laundry, wireless Internet. **Business Services:** business center. **Cards:** AX, CB, DC, DS, JC, MC, VI. **Free Special Amenities: continental breakfast and high-speed Internet.**

SOME UNITS

WHERE TO DINE

ANDREA'S **Lunch:** $11-$15 **Dinner:** $14-$28 **Phone:** 504/834-8583 70

Northern Italian **Location:** I-10, exit 228 (Causeway Blvd), 1.2 mi n. 3100 19th St 70002. **Hours:** 11:30 am-10 pm, Fri-11 pm, Sat 5 pm-11 pm, Sun 11 am-9 pm. Closed: 9/3; also for lunch Mardi Gras. **Reservations:** suggested. **Features:** Andrea's serves traditional Italian cuisine in a casual, but upscale atmosphere. The owner/chef is usually on the premises to greet guests at their tables. All desserts are homemade, and fresh seafood is available daily. Private parties are welcome. Dressy casual; cocktails. **Parking:** on-site. **Cards:** AX, CB, DC, DS, MC, VI.

BARRECA'S **Lunch:** $9-$15 **Dinner:** $12-$24 **Phone:** 504/831-4546 81

Regional American **Location:** Just e of jct Causeway Blvd and Metairie Rd. 3100 Metairie Rd 70001. **Hours:** 11 am-9 pm, Fri-10 pm, Sat 3 pm-10 pm, Sun 11 am-8 pm. Closed: Mon & Mardi Gras. **Reservations:** suggested, weekends. **Features:** Family-owned and operated for three generations, Barreca's features regional favorites using seafood from local waters. Theirs is a very good menu with seafood, chicken and beef choices represented. A variety of veal and pasta dishes are also available. Dressy casual; cocktails. **Parking:** valet. **Cards:** AX, CB, DC, DS, MC, VI.

BRAVO ITALIAN KITCHEN **Lunch:** $9-$21 **Dinner:** $9-$21 **Phone:** 504/828-8828

Italian **Location:** I-10, exit 228 (Causeway Blvd), just n to Veterans Memorial Blvd, then just w; at Lakeside Mall. 3413 Veterans Memorial Blvd 70002. **Hours:** 11 am-9 pm, Fri & Sat-10 pm. Closed: 11/22, 12/25; also Mardi Gras. **Reservations:** accepted. **Features:** Occupying a table is like sitting in the midst of Roman ruins. On a menu of Old World specialties are wood-fired pizzas and flatbreads, pasta dishes, wood-grilled specialties, seafood and steaks. This location is especially popular at dinnertime and on the weekends. Casual dress; cocktails. **Parking:** on-site. **Cards:** AX, DS, MC, VI.

BYBLOS **Lunch:** $7-$12 **Dinner:** $10-$20 **Phone:** 504/834-9773 79

Lebanese **Location:** I-10, exit 229 (Bonnabel Blvd), 0.8 mi s to Metairie Rd, then just e. 1501 Metairie Rd 70005. **Hours:** 11 am-9 pm, Fri-10 pm, Sat noon-10 pm, Sun noon-8 pm. Closed: 1/1, 11/22, 12/24, 12/25; also Mardi Gras. **Features:** Authentic combinations of Middle Eastern cooking are admirably seasoned. Among selections of Lebanese fare are hummus, baba ghanoush (pureed eggplant with lemon and garlic) and moussaka. The interior replicates an old village in Lebanon. Casual dress; cocktails. **Parking:** on-site. **Cards:** AX, DC, DS, MC, VI.

(See map and index starting on p. 336)

CAFFE CAFFE **Lunch:** $5-$9 **Dinner:** $5-$9 **Phone:** 504/885-4845 (64)

American

Location: I-10, exit 226 (Clearview Pkwy), 0.5 mi n. 4301 Clearview Pkwy 70006. **Hours:** 7 am-8 pm, Sat & Sun 8 am-3 pm. Closed major holidays; also Mardi Gras. **Features:** Midday jumps with ladies who lunch, families and anyone else who appreciates the small coffee shop's wholesome offerings. Signature sandwiches and salads make up the menu, and the dessert case that greets at the entry is designed to tempt. Once the kitchen closes, patrons still can sip on an espresso or indulge their sweet tooth. Casual dress. **Parking:** on-site. **Cards:** AX, DS, MC, VI.

CASA GARCIA **Lunch:** $7-$10 **Dinner:** $10-$15 **Phone:** 504/464-0354 (72)

Mexican

Location: 1 mi w of jct I-10 and Veterans Memorial Blvd. 8814 Veterans Memorial Blvd 70003. **Hours:** 11 am-10 pm, Fri & Sat-11 pm. Closed: 1/1, 11/22, 12/25. **Features:** Family owned and operated, the neighborhood eatery presents a menu of tasty Mexican cuisine. The atmosphere evokes the feel of a hacienda, with a fountain and courtyard. On the traditional menu are enchiladas, tacos and nachos. Casual dress; cocktails. **Parking:** on-site. **Cards:** AX, CB, DC, DS, MC, VI.

COPELAND'S CHEESECAKE BISTRO **Lunch:** $8-$14 **Dinner:** $10-$26 **Phone:** 504/454-7620 (71)

American

Location: I-10, exit 226 (Clearview Pkwy), just n to Veterans Memorial Blvd, then just e; across from Clearview Mall. 4517 Veterans Memorial Blvd 70006. **Hours:** 11 am-10:30 pm, Fri & Sat-midnight, Sun 10 am-10:30 pm. Closed: 11/22, 12/25. **Features:** Although the similarities to that "other" cheesecake restaurant are apparent, rest assured that the bistro's menu is not as daunting and just as good. Pasta dishes, sandwiches, pizza, steak, seafood and home-style meals round out the menu. Leave room for one of the many selections of cheesecake or stop by the dessert case and take something home. Casual dress; cocktails. **Parking:** valet. **Cards:** AX, DC, DS, MC, VI.

CORKY'S BAR-B-Q **Lunch:** $6-$10 **Dinner:** $7-$20 **Phone:** 504/887-5000 (73)

American

Location: I-10, exit 228 (Causeway Blvd), 1.5 mi w. 4243 Veterans Memorial Blvd 70006. **Hours:** 11 am-9:30 pm, Fri & Sat-10:30 pm. Closed: 11/22, 12/25. **Features:** The Memphis transplant features strictly American food. Dishes are prepared with super-lean, top-quality cuts of meat, including beef, chicken and turkey. Popular choices are both wet and dry ribs and pulled-pork sandwiches. Old-fashioned barbecue is nothing fancy, but it's good. Casual dress; beer & wine only. **Parking:** on-site. **Cards:** AX, CB, DC, DS, MC, VI.

DEANIE'S SEAFOOD **Lunch:** $7-$14 **Dinner:** $12-$40 **Phone:** 504/831-4141 (62)

Seafood

Location: Veterans Memorial Blvd, 1.5 mi n. 1713 Lake Ave 70005. **Hours:** 11 am-10 pm, Fri & Sat-11 pm. Closed: 7/4, 11/22, 12/25. **Features:** Popular locally for heaping portions of fresh fried seafood, this bustling, family-oriented restaurant also has a market for fresh and boiled carry-out seafood. For something unique, try the boiled, spicy potatoes brought to each table as an appetizer. Casual dress; cocktails. **Parking:** on-site. **Cards:** AX, MC, VI.

DRAGO'S **Lunch:** $7-$23 **Dinner:** $13-$31 **Phone:** 504/888-9254 (68)

Seafood

Location: I-10, exit 228 (Causeway Blvd), just n to Veterans Memorial Blvd, just w to N Arnoult Rd, then just n. 3232 N Arnoult Rd 70002. **Hours:** 11 am-9 pm, Fri & Sat-10 pm. Closed major holidays; also Sun. **Features:** In a busy retail area, the restaurant is a local favorite for oysters and seafood. Fried items factor heavily on the lunch menu, which also lists daily specials that shouldn't be overlooked. Although live Maine lobster takes center stage for dinner, other dishes—including blackened duck breast, seafood pasta and cheese-crusted chicken breast—also are worth a try. Casual dress; cocktails. **Parking:** on-site. **Cards:** AX, DC, DS, MC, VI.

IMPASTATO'S RESTAURANT **Dinner:** $12-$26 **Phone:** 504/455-1545 (67)

Italian

Location: 0.5 mi n of jct Veterans Memorial Blvd and Severn Ave, just e. 3400 16th St 70002. **Hours:** 5 pm-10 pm, Fri & Sat-11 pm. Closed: 11/22, 12/25; also Sun & Mon. **Reservations:** suggested. **Features:** The restaurant serves a good variety of traditional veal, seafood and pasta specialties. The environment is moderately formal. A piano bar enhances the atmosphere weeknights from 7 p.m. to 11 p.m. and weekends from 8 p.m. Casual dress; cocktails; entertainment. **Parking:** on-site. **Cards:** AX, DC, DS, MC, VI.

LA MADELEINE FRENCH BAKERY & CAFE **Lunch:** $7-$13 **Dinner:** $7-$13 **Phone:** 504/456-1624

French

Location: Jct Severn and 17th; in Lakeside Shopping Center. 3300 Severn, Suite 201 70002. **Hours:** 7 am-10 pm. Closed: 12/25. **Features:** Casual dress; beer & wine only. **Parking:** on-site. **Cards:** AX, DS, MC, VI.

R & O'S PIZZA PLACE RESTAURANT **Lunch:** $5-$8 **Dinner:** $7-$20 **Phone:** 504/831-1248 (61)

Seafood

Location: Lake Ave and Metairie Hammond Hwy, just w; on Lake Pontchartrain. 216 Old Hammond Hwy 70005. **Hours:** 11 am-10 pm, Fri & Sat-11 pm. Closed major holidays; also Tues & Mardi Gras. **Reservations:** not accepted. **Features:** Seafood, Italian dishes, pizza and sandwiches are specialties of the restaurant, which sits on the banks of Lake Pontchartrain. Casual dress; cocktails. **Parking:** on-site. **Cards:** AX, DS, MC, VI.

RICCOBONO'S PEPPERMILL **Lunch:** $7-$11 **Dinner:** $10-$18 **Phone:** 504/455-2266 (66)

Italian

Location: 0.7 mi n of jct Veterans Memorial Blvd. 3524 Severn Ave 70002. **Hours:** 7 am-9:30 pm, Fri & Sat-10 pm, Mon-3 pm. Closed: 11/22, 12/25; also Mardi Gras. **Reservations:** accepted. **Features:** Italian cuisine is served in a comfortable, casual atmosphere. Menu includes dishes like crabmeat Angelique and oysters Riccobono. A champagne brunch is offered on Sundays serving upscale breakfast specialties. Lunch and dinner specials daily. Casual dress; cocktails. **Parking:** on-site. **Cards:** AX, DC, MC, VI.

(See map and index starting on p. 336)

SAL AND SAM'S **Lunch:** $12-$30 **Dinner:** $12-$30 **Phone:** 504/885-5566 (76)

Italian

Location: I-10, exit 228 (Causeway Blvd), 1.5 mi w. 4300 Veterans Memorial Blvd 70006. **Hours:** 11 am-11 pm, Fri-midnight, Sat 5 pm-midnight, Sun 5 pm-11 pm. **Reservations:** accepted. **Features:** Family owned for over 20 years, this proves to be a pleasant dining experience. The all-day menu offers soups, hot and cold appetizers, salads, pasta, and entrees that include seafood, chicken, quail, steak and veal. Servers are courteous and prompt. Casual dress; cocktails. **Parking:** on-site. **Cards:** AX, CB, DC, DS, MC, VI.

SALVATORE RISTORANTE **Lunch:** $9-$18 **Dinner:** $16-$28 **Phone:** 504/455-2433 (69)

Italian

Location: 0.5 mi n of jct Veterans Memorial Blvd and Arnoult Rd. 3226 N Arnoult Rd 70002. **Hours:** 11 am-10 pm, Sun 9 am-9 pm. Closed: 7/4; also Mardi Gras. **Reservations:** suggested, weekends. **Features:** On the menu are many satisfying Italian specialties, including some fresh game items. Veal parmigiana and spaghetti with tomato sauce are particularly good. Nightly piano performances evoke an elegant, club-like atmosphere. Dressy casual; cocktails. **Parking:** valet and street. **Cards:** AX, CB, DC, DS, MC, VI.

SERRANOS SALSA COMPANY **Lunch:** $8-$10 **Dinner:** $8-$15 **Phone:** 504/780-2354 (77)

Latino

Location: I-10, exit 226, just n on Clearview Pkwy; in Clearview Mall. 4436 Veterans Memorial Blvd 70006. **Hours:** 11 am-10 pm, Wed-Sat to 11 pm. Closed major holidays. **Features:** Diners who have had their fill of Cajun and Creole food should take a look at this eatery, which features a mix of Latin American and Mexican plates. Offerings include empanadas, fajitas and Cuban steak. The Clearview Mall location makes this place convenient for a break from afternoon shopping. Casual dress; cocktails. **Parking:** on-site. **Cards:** AX, DS, MC, VI.

SIAMESE RESTAURANT **Lunch:** $6-$10 **Dinner:** $9-$20 **Phone:** 504/454-8752 (74)

Thai

Location: I-10, exit 225 (Veterans), just sw on Veterans. 6601 Veterans Memorial Blvd, Suite 29 70003. **Hours:** 11 am-9 pm, Sat & Sun from noon. Closed major holidays. **Features:** The restaurant serves nearly 80 selections of simply prepared, traditional fare. A peaceful mood prevails in the modest, but true-to-its-theme, dining room. Casual dress; cocktails. **Parking:** on-site. **Cards:** AX, DC, DS, MC, VI.

SUN RAY GRILL **Lunch:** $6-$22 **Dinner:** $10-$22 **Phone:** 504/837-0055 (78)

International

Location: I-10, exit 229 (Bonnabel Pl), 0.7 mi s to Metairie Rd, 0.9 mi e to Focis St, then just n to Pink St. 619 Pink St 70005. **Hours:** 11 am-9 pm, Fri & Sat-10 pm. Closed major holidays; also Mardi Gras. **Features:** The restaurant is a good choice for parties in which not every member can agree on where to eat. An amalgamation of global cuisines, the menu lists everything from quesadillas, burgers and pasta to fish, salads, filet mignon and pork chops. Casual dress; cocktails. **Parking:** on-site. **Cards:** AX, DC, DS, MC, VI.

TAQUERIA CORONA **Lunch:** $5-$13 **Dinner:** $5-$13 **Phone:** 504/885-5088 (65)

Mexican

Location: I-10, exit 228 (Causeway Blvd), 1 mi n to W Esplanade Ave, just w, then just s; in Esplanade Plaza Shopping Center. 3535 Severn Ave 70002. **Hours:** 11:30 am-2 & 5-9:30 pm, Fri & Sat 11:30 am-10 pm. Closed major holidays. **Features:** Tucked in a small shopping center, the small eatery serves tacos and burritos with a fillings including chorizo, shrimp and fish. For those who want to try something a little different, Mexican pizzas are good bets. Casual dress; cocktails. **Parking:** on-site. **Cards:** AX, DC, DS, MC, VI.

VEGA TAPAS CAFE **Dinner:** $6-$11 **Phone:** 504/836-2007 (80)

Spanish

Location: I-10, exit 228 (Causeway Blvd), 1.3 mi s to Matairie Rd exit, then 0.9 mi e. 2051 Metairie Rd 70005. **Hours:** 5:30 pm-close. Closed major holidays; also Mardi Gras. **Reservations:** accepted. **Features:** Visitors and locals alike can be grateful for this gem. Tapas, which means "little plates" in Spanish, can be devoured in many exquisite little servings. Among choices are sweet potato gnocchi, Moorish pork, paella, rare pepper steak and apple and brie salad. The more friends that come along, the more plates that can be sampled. Leave room for the signature creme brulee, which changes daily. Dressy casual; cocktails. **Parking:** street. **Cards:** AX, CB, DC, DS, JC, MC, VI.

VINCENT'S ITALIAN CUISINE **Lunch:** $12-$16 **Dinner:** $15-$20 **Phone:** 504/885-2984 (63)

Italian

Location: Just w of jct W Esplanade Ave and Transcontinental Dr to Chastant St, then just n. 4411 Chastant St 70006. **Hours:** 11:30 am-2 & 5-10 pm, Sat from 5 pm. Closed major holidays; also Sun, for lunch Mon & Mardi Gras. **Reservations:** accepted. **Features:** Traditional Italian dishes and regional fare combine on the restaurant's menu. Friendly service is the norm in the close, casual atmosphere. Casual dress; cocktails. **Parking:** on-site. **Cards:** AX, DC, DS, MC, VI.

ZEA ROTISSERIE & BREWERY **Lunch:** $8-$12 **Dinner:** $10-$23 **Phone:** 504/780-9090 (75)

American

Location: I-10, exit 226 (Clearview Pkwy), just n; in Clearview Mall. 4450 Veterans Memorial Blvd 70006. **Hours:** 11 am-9 pm, Fri & Sat-10 pm. Closed: 11/22, 12/25; also Mardi Gras. **Features:** Popular with Metairie residents, the restaurant can all but guarantee patrons a wait for dinner. Although simple rotisserie chicken is among the choices, the menu blends varied cuisines, such as Asian and Latino. Sample items include duck empanadas, arroz con pollo, Thai ribs, buttermilk-battered shrimp and a multitude of chicken dishes. Equally worthy of consideration are the house-brewed beers and custom-made sodas. Casual dress; cocktails. **Parking:** on-site. **Cards:** AX, DC, DS, MC, VI.

ST. ROSE pop. 6,540

WHERE TO STAY

RAMADA INN & SUITES NEW ORLEANS AIRPORT *Book at AAA.com* **Phone:** (504)466-1355

Small-scale Hotel

All Year 1P: $189-$399 XP: $10 F17

Location: I-310, exit 2, 1.5 mi e. 110 James Dr 70087. Fax: 504/466-1378. **Facility:** 130 units. 126 one-bedroom standard units, some with whirlpools. 4 one-bedroom suites. 3 stories, interior corridors. *Bath:* combo or shower only. **Parking:** on-site. **Amenities:** high-speed Internet, dual phone lines, voice mail, irons, hair dryers. **Dining:** VooDoo BBQ & Grill, see separate listing. **Pool(s):** outdoor. **Leisure Activities:** exercise room. **Guest Services:** valet and coin laundry, wireless Internet. **Business Services:** meeting rooms, business center. **Cards:** AX, CB, DC, DS, JC, MC, VI.

SOME UNITS

ASK

WHERE TO DINE

VOODOO BBQ & GRILL **Lunch:** $6-$15 **Dinner:** $6-$15 **Phone:** 504/464-1880

Barbecue

Location: I-310, exit 2, 1.5 mi e; in Ramada Inn & Suites New Orleans Airport. 100 James Dr E 70087. **Hours:** 11 am-10 pm, Fri & Sat-11 pm. Closed: 11/22, 12/25. **Features:** Locals know VooDoo as the place to get barbecue, but this location west of New Orleans enhances the experience with an expanded menu and a more refined atmosphere. Casual dress; cocktails. **Parking:** on-site. **Cards:** AX, DS, MC, VI.

SLIDELL pop. 25,695

WHERE TO STAY

BEST WESTERN SLIDELL INN *Book great rates at AAA.com* **Phone:** (985)781-5655

Small-scale Hotel

All Year 1P: $90-$199 2P: $90-$199

Location: I-10, exit 266 (Gause Blvd), just n, just w on Linberg, then just s. 120 Taos St 70458. Fax: 985/781-0077. **Facility:** 63 one-bedroom standard units. 3 stories, interior corridors. *Bath:* combo or shower only. **Parking:** on-site. **Terms:** [CP] meal plan available, package plans. **Amenities:** high-speed Internet, dual phone lines, voice mail, irons, hair dryers. **Pool(s):** outdoor. **Leisure Activities:** exercise room. **Guest Services:** valet, and coin laundry, wireless Internet. **Business Services:** business center. **Cards:** AX, DC, DS, MC, VI. **Free Special Amenities: continental breakfast and high-speed Internet.**

SOME UNITS

EXECUTIVE INN **Phone:** 985/641-4147

Small-scale Hotel

Property failed to provide current rates

Location: I-10, exit 263, just nw on SR 433. 2010 Old Spanish Tr 70458. Fax: 985/847-1220. **Facility:** 62 one-bedroom standard units, some with whirlpools. 2 stories (no elevator), exterior corridors. *Bath:* combo or shower only. **Parking:** on-site. **Amenities:** irons, hair dryers. **Pool(s):** outdoor. **Guest Services:** coin laundry, wireless Internet. **Business Services:** fax.

SOME UNITS

FEE

HAMPTON INN *Book great rates at AAA.com* **Phone:** (985)726-9777

Small-scale Hotel

All Year 1P: $119-$124 2P: $124-$135

Location: I-10, exit 263. 56460 Frank Pichon Rd 70458. Fax: 985/726-0141. **Facility:** 82 units. 80 one-bedroom standard units, some with whirlpools. 2 one-bedroom suites. 3 stories, interior corridors. *Bath:* combo or shower only. **Parking:** on-site. **Terms:** [ECP] meal plan available. **Amenities:** voice mail, irons, hair dryers. *Some:* high-speed Internet. **Pool(s):** outdoor. **Leisure Activities:** exercise room. **Guest Services:** valet and coin laundry, wireless Internet. **Business Services:** meeting rooms, fax (fee). **Cards:** AX, DS, JC, MC, VI.

SOME UNITS

FEE

HOLIDAY INN HOTEL & SUITES **Phone:** 985/639-0890

Property failed to provide current rates

Small-scale Hotel **Location:** I-10, exit 263. 372 Voter's Rd 70461. Fax: 985/639-0896. **Facility:** 91 units. 61 one-bedroom standard units, some with whirlpools. 30 one-bedroom suites. 3 stories, interior corridors. *Bath:* combo or shower only. **Parking:** on-site. **Amenities:** video games (fee), dual phone lines, voice mail, irons, hair dryers. *Some:* CD players. **Pool(s):** heated indoor. **Leisure Activities:** whirlpool, exercise room. **Guest Services:** sundries, valet and coin laundry, wireless Internet. **Business Services:** meeting rooms, business center.

SOME UNITS

LA QUINTA INN NEW ORLEANS/SLIDELL *Book great rates at AAA.com* **Phone:** (985)643-9770

All Year [ECP]	1P: $67-$77	2P: $77-$87	XP: $10	F18

Small-scale Hotel **Location:** I-10, exit 266 (Gause Blvd), just se. 794 E I-10 Service Rd 70461. Fax: 985/641-4476. **Facility:** 172 one-bedroom standard units. 2 stories (no elevator), exterior corridors. *Bath:* combo or shower only. **Parking:** on-site. **Amenities:** video games (fee), voice mail, irons, hair dryers. **Pool(s):** outdoor, wading. **Leisure Activities:** exercise room. **Guest Services:** coin laundry, wireless Internet. **Business Services:** meeting rooms, fax (fee). **Cards:** AX, CB, DC, DS, MC, VI. ***(See color ad p 386)***

SOME UNITS

ASK

FEE

SLEEP INN *Book great rates at AAA.com* **Phone:** (985)641-2143

All Year	1P: $89-$199	2P: $89-$199	XP: $6	F12

Small-scale Hotel **Location:** I-10, exit 261, just n. 142 Oak Ct 70458. Fax: 985/781-6856. **Facility:** 80 units. 79 one-bedroom standard units. 1 one-bedroom suite. 3 stories, interior corridors. *Bath:* combo or shower only. **Parking:** on-site. **Terms:** [CP] meal plan available. **Amenities:** *Some:* dual phone lines. **Pool(s):** outdoor. **Guest Services:** coin laundry, wireless Internet. **Business Services:** fax (fee). **Cards:** AX, DC, DS, JC, MC, VI.

SOME UNITS

ASK

WHERE TO DINE

ASSUNTA'S **Dinner:** $9-$18 **Phone:** 985/649-9768

Italian **Location:** I-12, exit 80, 0.7 mi s, then 1.6 mi w on US 190. 2631 Hwy 190 W 70458. **Hours:** 5 pm-10 pm, Sun 4 pm-9 pm. Closed major holidays; also Mon. **Features:** The home-style menu combines fresh, quality local ingredients with southern Italian sauces and seasonings. Housed in a raised cottage set back from the highway, the unusual decor includes a turn-of-the-century Greek Orthodox altar behind the bar. Casual dress; cocktails. **Parking:** on-site. **Cards:** AX, DS, MC, VI.

COPELAND'S **Lunch:** $6-$10 **Dinner:** $11-$26 **Phone:** 985/643-0001

Cajun **Location:** I-10, exit 266 (Gause Blvd), 0.5 mi n. 1337 Gause Blvd 70458. **Hours:** 11 am-11 pm, Fri & Sat-midnight, Sun 10 am-10 pm. Closed: 12/25. **Features:** A New Orleans-born idea, the restaurant prepares such dishes as barbecue shrimp, red beans and rice, blackened fish, steaks, po' boys and, of course, some lagniappe. Accompanying most dishes is the signature melt-in-your-mouth biscuit. Casual dress; cocktails. **Parking:** on-site. **Cards:** AX, DC, DS, MC, VI.

PHIL'S MARINA CAFE OAK HARBOR **Lunch:** $6-$13 **Dinner:** $6-$13 **Phone:** 985/641-0464

Seafood **Location:** I-10, exit 261, just w on Landmark Dr, then 0.5 mi sw. 1194 Harbor Dr 70458. **Hours:** 11 am-9 pm. Closed: Mon. **Features:** On the marina, the laid-back restaurant is a good place to catch a meal or snack on a nice warm day. Outlined on the menu is an array of soup, salad, sandwiches and seafood specialties. Casual dress; cocktails. **Parking:** on-site. **Cards:** AX, DS, MC, VI.

YOUNG'S **Dinner:** $14-$28 **Phone:** 985/643-9331

Steak & Seafood **Location:** I-10, exit 266 (Gause Blvd), 1.3 mi w, then 0.8 mi n. 850 S Robert Blvd 70458. **Hours:** 5 pm-10 pm, Fri & Sat-11 pm. Closed: 1/1, 11/22, 12/25; also Sun & Mon. **Features:** Imagine entering a clandestine building, no signs or markings to indicate what sort of mystery into which you are about to step. Then, once inside, you are treated to a delicious array of char-grilled steaks and seafood. Some mysteries are worth solving. Casual dress; cocktails. **Parking:** on-site. **Cards:** MC, VI.

VACHERIE

WHERE TO STAY

OAK ALLEY PLANTATION RESTAURANT & INN **Phone:** (225)265-2151

AAA SAVE

All Year [BP]	1P: $115-$165	2P: $115-$165	XP: $20	F12

Bed & Breakfast **Location:** I-10, exit 194, 5 mi s on SR 641 to Veterans Memorial Bridge, then 7 mi w. 3645 Hwy 18 70090. Fax: 225/265-7035. **Facility:** Southern hospitality shines at these cottages offering full accommodations in the shadow of a restored plantation homestead. Smoke free premises. 6 units. 2 one-bedroom standard units. 4 cottages ($115-$165), some with whirlpools. 1 story, exterior corridors. *Bath:* combo or shower only. **Parking:** on-site. **Terms:** 7 day cancellation notice-fee imposed. **Amenities:** irons, hair dryers. **Dining:** restaurant, see separate listing. **Guest Services:** gift shop. **Cards:** AX, DS, MC, VI. **Free Special Amenities: full breakfast.**

SOME UNITS

WHERE TO DINE

OAK ALLEY PLANTATION RESTAURANT **Lunch:** $8-$13 **Phone:** 225/265-2487

Regional American **Location:** I-10, exit 194, 5 mi s on SR 641 to Verterans Memorial Bridge, then 7 mi w. 3645 Hwy 18 70090. **Hours:** 8:30 am-3 pm. Closed: 1/1, 11/22, 12/25; also Mardi Gras. **Reservations:** not accepted. **Features:** One of the most popular historic plantations in the South, well worth the scenery; Cajun cuisine. Casual dress; cocktails. **Parking:** on-site. **Cards:** AX, DS, MC, VI.

WESTWEGO pop. 10,763 (See map and index starting on p. 336)

WHERE TO STAY

BEST WESTERN BAYOU INN *Book great rates at AAA.com* **Phone:** (504)304-7980 **91**

Small-scale Hotel

All Year 1P: $129-$189 2P: $129-$189 XP: $10 F12

Location: Between US 90 and Louisiana St. 9008 Westbank Expwy 70094. Fax: 504/304-7987. **Facility:** 67 one-bedroom standard units, some with whirlpools. 2 stories, interior corridors. **Parking:** on-site. **Terms:** check-in 4 pm, cancellation fee imposed. **Amenities:** high-speed Internet, voice mail, irons, hair dryers. **Pool(s):** outdoor. **Leisure Activities:** limited exercise equipment. **Guest Services:** valet and coin laundry. **Business Services:** business center. **Cards:** AX, CB, DC, DS, MC, VI.

SOME UNITS

© Brett Shoaf / Artistic Visuals

This ends listings for the New Orleans Vicinity.
The following page resumes the alphabetical listings of cities in Louisiana.

NEW ROADS pop. 4,966

WHERE TO STAY

SUNRISE ON THE RIVER **Phone:** 225/638-3642

Property failed to provide current rates

Bed & Breakfast **Location:** 14.1 mi n of jct US 190 and SR 1. 1825 False River Dr (LA SH 1) 70760. Fax: 225/638-3642. **Facility:** This newer property with spacious grounds fronting the False River is in a good area for bird watching. Smoke free premises. 3 one-bedroom standard units, some with whirlpools. 2 stories (no elevator), interior corridors. **Parking:** on-site. **Terms:** age restrictions may apply. **Amenities:** hair dryers. **Leisure Activities:** boat dock, fishing. **Guest Services:** wireless Internet. **Business Services:** fax (fee).

WHERE TO DINE

SATTERFIELD'S RIVERWALK RESTAURANT **Lunch:** $6-$22 **Dinner:** $11-$22 **Phone:** 225/638-5027

Regional American **Location:** Just e of jct SR 1 and 413; in historic district. 108 E Main St 70760. **Hours:** 11 am-8 pm, Fri & Sat-10 pm. Closed: 1/1, 11/22, 12/25. **Features:** Listed on the National Register of Historical Places, Satterfield's is uniquely located in the first permanent automobile dealership in Pointe Coupee Parish. Enjoy scenic views of the False River as you sample delicious regional dishes like crawfish pie. Casual dress; cocktails. **Parking:** on-site. **Cards:** AX, CB, DC, DS, MC, VI.

OPELOUSAS pop. 22,860

WHERE TO STAY

DAYS INN & SUITES *Book great rates at AAA.com* **Phone:** 337/407-0004

Property failed to provide current rates

Small-scale Hotel **Location:** I-49, exit 18 (Creswell Ln). 5761 I-49 S Service Rd 70570. Fax: 337/407-9885. **Facility:** 58 one-bedroom standard units, some with whirlpools. 2 stories (no elevator), exterior corridors. *Bath:* combo or shower only. **Parking:** on-site. **Terms:** pets ($20 fee). **Amenities:** irons, hair dryers. *Some:* dual phone lines. **Pool(s):** outdoor. **Leisure Activities:** exercise room. **Guest Services:** coin laundry, wireless Internet. **Business Services:** meeting rooms, fax (fee).

SOME UNITS

FEE

PINEVILLE pop. 13,829

WHERE TO STAY

SLEEP INN & SUITES *Book great rates at AAA.com* **Phone:** 318/640-8505

All Year 1P: $79-$200

Small-scale Hotel **Location:** On US 165; 0.4 mi ne of jct US 167. 3411 Monroe Hwy 71360. Fax: 318/640-3405. **Facility:** 68 units. 66 one-bedroom standard units, some with whirlpools. 2 one-bedroom suites. 3 stories, interior corridors. *Bath:* combo or shower only. **Parking:** on-site. **Terms:** cancellation fee imposed, [CP] meal plan available. **Amenities:** high-speed Internet, voice mail, irons, hair dryers. **Pool(s):** small heated indoor. **Leisure Activities:** whirlpool, exercise room. **Guest Services:** valet and coin laundry. **Business Services:** meeting rooms, business center. **Cards:** AX, DC, DS, MC, VI. **Free Special Amenities: continental breakfast and high-speed Internet.**

SOME UNITS

PONCHATOULA pop. 5,180

WHERE TO STAY

MICROTEL INN & SUITES *Book at AAA.com* **Phone:** 985/370-7378

Property failed to provide current rates

Small-scale Hotel **Location:** I-55, exit 26, just e on SR 22. 727 W Pine St 70454. Fax: 985/370-7379. **Facility:** 52 one-bedroom standard units. 2 stories, interior corridors. *Bath:* combo or shower only. **Parking:** on-site. **Amenities:** high-speed Internet, voice mail, hair dryers. **Pool(s):** outdoor. **Leisure Activities:** exercise room. **Guest Services:** coin laundry. **Business Services:** meeting rooms, fax (fee).

SOME UNITS

WHERE TO DINE

C'EST BON **Lunch:** $7-$13 **Dinner:** $8-$22 **Phone:** 985/386-4077

Creole **Location:** I-55, exit 26, 0.6 mi e on SR 22, then just s. 131 SW Railroad Ave 70454. **Hours:** 11 am-9 pm, Fri & Sat-10 pm. Closed: 11/22, 12/25 & Easter; also Mother's Day. **Features:** High ceilings, hardwood floors and a rich wood interior provide a fine backdrop for dining in the charming restaurant. On the menu are such items as chargrilled tuna, bourbon pecan chicken and pork tenderloin. Casual dress; cocktails. **Parking:** street. **Cards:** AX, DS, MC, VI.

PORT ALLEN pop. 5,278

WHERE TO STAY

BEST WESTERN MAGNOLIA MANOR *Book great rates at AAA.com* **Phone:** (225)344-3638

All Year [CP] 1P: $60-$75 2P: $60-$75 XP: $5

Small-scale Hotel **Location:** I-10, exit 151, just n. Located in a light commercial area. 234 Lobdell Hwy 70767. Fax: 225/387-3866. **Facility:** 100 one-bedroom standard units, some with whirlpools. 2 stories, interior corridors. **Parking:** on-site. **Terms:** cancellation fee imposed, small pets only ($10 extra charge). **Amenities:** irons, hair dryers. **Pool(s):** outdoor. **Guest Services:** coin laundry, wireless Internet. **Business Services:** fax (fee). **Cards:** AX, DS, MC, VI. **Free Special Amenities: continental breakfast and local telephone calls.**

SOME UNITS

FEE

COMFORT SUITES Book great rates at AAA.com **Phone:** (225)343-4300

AAA SAVE

Small-scale Hotel

All Year [BP] 1P: $65-$159 2P: $70-$169 XP: $5 F

Location: I-10, exit 151, on northeast corner. 2880 N Westport Dr 70767. Fax: 225/343-4375. **Facility:** 65 one-bedroom standard units, some with whirlpools. 3 stories, interior corridors. *Bath:* combo or shower only. **Parking:** on-site. **Amenities:** voice mail, irons, hair dryers. *Some:* high-speed Internet. **Pool(s):** small outdoor. **Leisure Activities:** exercise room. **Guest Services:** valet and coin laundry, wireless Internet. **Business Services:** business center. **Cards:** AX, CB, DC, DS, JC, MC, VI. **Free Special Amenities: full breakfast and high-speed Internet.**

SOME UNITS

HOLIDAY INN EXPRESS I-10 & LA 415 Book at AAA.com **Phone:** 225/343-4821

Small-scale Hotel

All Year 1P: $79-$129 2P: $79-$129 XP: $5 F12

Location: I-10, exit 151, just on SR 415. 131 Lobdell Hwy 70767. Fax: 225/343-4821. **Facility:** 140 one-bedroom standard units. 4 stories, exterior corridors. *Bath:* combo or shower only. **Parking:** on-site. **Terms:** cancellation fee imposed, [CP] meal plan available. **Amenities:** voice mail, irons, hair dryers. **Pool(s):** outdoor. **Guest Services:** valet and coin laundry, wireless Internet. **Business Services:** meeting rooms, fax (fee). **Cards:** AX, CB, DC, DS, JC, MC, VI.

SOME UNITS

MOTEL 6 BATON ROUGE-PORT ALLEN #406 Book at AAA.com **Phone:** 225/343-5945

Motel

All Year 1P: $45-$55 2P: $51-$61 XP: $3 F17

Location: I-10, exit 151, just s. 2800 I-10 Frontage Rd 70767. Fax: 225/389-5803. **Facility:** 124 one-bedroom standard units, some with efficiencies. 2 stories, exterior corridors. *Bath:* combo or shower only. **Parking:** on-site. **Terms:** small pets only. **Pool(s):** outdoor. **Business Services:** fax (fee). **Cards:** AX, CB, DC, DS, MC, VI.

SOME UNITS

RAYNE pop. 8,552

WHERE TO DINE

CHEF ROY'S FROG CITY CAFE **Lunch:** $5-$22 **Dinner:** $9-$22 **Phone:** 337/334-7913

Cajun

Location: I-10, exit 87, just n. 1131 Church Point Hwy 70578. **Hours:** 11 am-9:30 pm, Fri & Sat-10 pm, Sun-2 pm. Closed major holidays. **Reservations:** accepted. **Features:** For drivers passing through western Louisiana, a stop at the cafe makes good sense. Right off the interstate, this spot provides a wholesome alternative to the plethora of fast food stops. On the lengthy menu are choices to please almost anyone, ranging from shrimp, crawfish and catfish to steak and chicken. Desserts are homemade and servers are friendly and eager to please. Casual dress; cocktails. **Parking:** on-site. **Cards:** AX, DC, DS, MC, VI.

RAYVILLE pop. 4,234

WHERE TO STAY

DAYS INN Book great rates at AAA.com **Phone:** 318/728-4500

Motel

All Year [BP] 1P: $60-$70 2P: $60-$70 XP: $5 F4

Location: I-20, exit 138, just n. Located in a commercial area. 125 Maxwell Dr 71269. Fax: 318/728-4591. **Facility:** 36 one-bedroom standard units. 2 stories (no elevator), exterior corridors. **Parking:** on-site. **Terms:** small pets only ($10 extra charge). **Amenities:** irons, hair dryers. **Pool(s):** outdoor. **Cards:** AX, DS, MC, VI.

SOME UNITS

ASK FEE

RUSTON pop. 20,546

WHERE TO STAY

BUDGET LODGE **Phone:** (318)255-0354

Small-scale Hotel

All Year 1P: $55-$75 2P: $55-$75 XP: $10 F12

Location: I-20, exit 85, just n on US 167, then just e on N Service Rd. Located in a commercial area. 1301 Goodwin Rd 71270. Fax: 318/255-0354. **Facility:** 81 one-bedroom standard units. 1-2 stories (no elevator), exterior corridors. **Parking:** on-site. **Terms:** 3 day cancellation notice, pets ($10 fee). **Amenities:** irons. *Some:* hair dryers. **Guest Services:** coin laundry. **Cards:** AX, CB, DC, DS, JC, MC, VI.

SOME UNITS

ASK FEE

COMFORT INN OF RUSTON Book great rates at AAA.com **Phone:** (318)242-0070

Small-scale Hotel

All Year 1P: $75-$100 2P: $80-$100 XP: $5 F18

Location: I-20, exit 86, 0.4 mi ne. 1951 N Service Rd E 71270. Fax: 318/242-0080. **Facility:** 57 one-bedroom standard units. 2 stories (no elevator), interior corridors. *Bath:* combo or shower only. **Parking:** on-site. **Amenities:** high-speed Internet, voice mail, irons, hair dryers. **Pool(s):** outdoor. **Guest Services:** valet laundry. **Business Services:** meeting rooms. **Cards:** AX, DC, DS, MC, VI.

SOME UNITS

ASK

DAYS INN Book great rates at AAA.com **Phone:** (318)251-2360

AAA SAVE

Small-scale Hotel

12/1-12/31 & 5/1-11/30	1P: $60-$100	2P: $65-$100	XP: $5	F17
1/1-4/30	1P: $60-$75	2P: $60-$75	XP: $5	F17

Location: I-20, exit 86, just ne. 1801 N Service Rd E 71270. Fax: 318/251-2360. **Facility:** 61 units. 60 one-bedroom standard units. 1 two-bedroom suite with kitchen (no utensils). 2 stories (no elevator), exterior corridors. *Bath:* combo or shower only. **Parking:** on-site. **Terms:** package plans. **Amenities:** irons, hair dryers. **Pool(s):** outdoor. **Cards:** AX, DC, DS, MC, VI.

SOME UNITS

HOLIDAY INN EXPRESS HOTEL & SUITES Book at AAA.com Phone: 318/513-9777

Property failed to provide current rates

Small-scale Hotel

Location: I-20, exit 86, just se. 1825 Roberta Ave 71270 (PO Box 1189). Fax: 318/513-2558. **Facility:** 82 units. 81 one-bedroom standard units, some with whirlpools. 1 one-bedroom suite. 3 stories, interior corridors. *Bath:* combo or shower only. **Parking:** on-site. **Amenities:** video library, video games (fee), high-speed Internet, dual phone lines, voice mail, irons, hair dryers. **Pool(s):** outdoor. **Leisure Activities:** exercise room. **Guest Services:** valet laundry. **Business Services:** meeting rooms, business center.

SOME UNITS

RAMADA INN Phone: 318/255-5901

Property failed to provide current rates

Small-scale Hotel

Location: I-20, exit 85, just ne. Located in a commercial area. 401 N Service Rd 71270. Fax: 318/255-3729. **Facility:** 140 units. 137 one-bedroom standard units. 3 one-bedroom suites. 1 story, exterior corridors. **Parking:** on-site. **Terms:** pets ($10 fee). **Amenities:** high-speed Internet, voice mail, irons, hair dryers. **Pool(s):** 2 outdoor, wading. **Leisure Activities:** playground, exercise room. **Guest Services:** valet and coin laundry. **Business Services:** conference facilities, business center.

SOME UNITS

FEE

WHERE TO DINE

LOG CABIN MESQUITE GRILL **Lunch:** $6-$12 **Dinner:** $10-$23 **Phone:** 318/255-8023

Tex-Mex

Location: I-20, exit 86, 0.3 mi ne. 1906 Farmerville Hwy 71270. **Hours:** 11 am-2 & 4:30-9 pm, Sat 11 am-10 pm. Closed: 1/1, 11/22, 12/25; also Sun. **Reservations:** accepted. **Features:** In addition to fajitas and enchiladas, the modern restaurant serves mesquite-grilled rib-eye steaks, ribs, burgers and seafood. Casual dress; cocktails. **Parking:** on-site. **Cards:** AX, DS, MC, VI.

PEKING RESTAURANT **Lunch:** $4-$9 **Dinner:** $6-$10 **Phone:** 318/251-9988

Chinese

Location: I-20, exit 85. 1300 N Vienna St 71270. **Hours:** 11 am-2:30 & 5-9:30 pm, Fri-10 pm, Sat 11 am-3 & 4-10 pm, Sun 11 am-9:30 pm. Closed major holidays. **Features:** Nothing fancy, but it features an extensive buffet for lunch and dinner stocked with a variety of traditional Chinese offerings. Lo mein, sweet-and-sour chicken, and fried rice are among the many favorites sure to please those who enjoy Chinese cuisine. Casual dress. **Parking:** on-site. **Cards:** AX, DS, MC, VI.

PONCHATOULAS **Lunch:** $6-$13 **Dinner:** $7-$13 **Phone:** 318/254-5200

Cajun

Location: I-20, exit 85, 0.9 mi s on US 167, on northeast side. 109 E Park Ave 71270. **Hours:** 11 am-9 pm, Fri & Sat-9:30 pm. Closed major holidays; also Sun. **Features:** The well-known downtown eatery prepares Cajun fare in a casual, homey setting. Don't pass up the crawfish etouffee or the shrimp po' boy. Casual dress; cocktails. **Parking:** street. **Cards:** AX, MC, VI.

RABB'S STEAKHOUSE & SPIRITS **Lunch:** $7-$12 **Dinner:** $15-$30 **Phone:** 318/255-1008

Steak House

Location: I-20; between exits 83 and 84, on the south service road. 2647 S Service Rd W 71273. **Hours:** 10 am-2 & 5-10 pm, Sat from 5 pm. Closed: 11/22, 12/25; also Sun. **Reservations:** accepted. **Features:** The popular restaurant is known for its delicious Angus beef steaks and hamburgers cooked on an open grill in the dining room. Live concerts and entertainment are held in season. Casual dress; cocktails. **Parking:** on-site. **Cards:** AX, DS, MC, VI.

SWEET PEA'S SOUL FOOD RESTAURANT **Lunch:** $7-$8 **Phone:** 318/251-2805

Soul Food

Location: I-20, exit 85, 1.1 mi s on US 167 to California Ave, just w, then just n. 500 S Monroe St 71270. **Hours:** 11 am-1:30 pm, Sun-2:30 pm. Closed major holidays. **Features:** The popular lunch spot offers an outstanding buffet and friendly service. Patrons can savor soul food at its best. Casual dress. **Parking:** on-site. **Cards:** AX, CB, DC, DS, JC, MC, VI.

ST. FRANCISVILLE pop. 1,712

WHERE TO STAY

BEST WESTERN ST. FRANCIS HOTEL ON THE LAKE Book great rates at AAA.com **Phone:** (225)635-3821

Small-scale Hotel

All Year [CP] 1P: $75-$85 2P: $80-$90 XP: $5 F17

Location: Just s of jct US 61 and SR 10. US Hwy 61 At Louisiana Hwy 10 70775 (PO Box 440). Fax: 225/635-4749. **Facility:** 99 units. 95 one-bedroom standard units. 4 one-bedroom suites. 2 stories (no elevator), exterior corridors. *Bath:* combo or shower only. **Parking:** on-site. **Amenities:** voice mail, irons, hair dryers. **Pool(s):** outdoor. **Guest Services:** coin laundry, wireless Internet. **Business Services:** meeting rooms, fax (fee). **Cards:** AX, DC, DS, MC, VI.

SOME UNITS

FEE FEE

LAKE ROSEMOUND INN BED & BREAKFAST **Phone:** 225/635-3176

Bed & Breakfast

All Year 1P: $80-$135 2P: $80-$135 XP: $10 F12

Location: 13 mi n on SR 61, then 3 mi w using Rosemound Loop, Sligo Rd, Lake Rosemound Rd and Lindsey Ln, follow signs. 10473 Lindsey Ln 70775. Fax: 225/635-2224. **Facility:** Smoke free premises. 4 one-bedroom standard units, some with whirlpools. 2 stories, interior/exterior corridors. **Parking:** on-site. **Terms:** 3 day cancellation notice. **Leisure Activities:** beach access, canoeing, paddleboats, fishing. **Business Services:** meeting rooms. **Cards:** AX, DS, MC, VI.

WHERE TO DINE

THE OXBOW CARRIAGE HOUSE RESTAURANT **Lunch:** $6-$13 **Dinner:** $12-$25 **Phone:** 225/635-6276

Regional American

Location: Jct US 61 and SR 10, 1 mi n; on the Myrtles Plantation. 7747 Hwy 61 70775. **Hours:** 11:30 am-1:30 & 5-9 pm, Sun-1:30 pm. Closed: 1/1, 12/24, 12/25; also Mon. **Features:** A full menu of offerings including seafood, pasta dishes, steaks, pork, and creole creations await the diner in this upscale restaurant located on a historic plantation. Casual dress; cocktails. **Parking:** on-site. **Cards:** AX, MC, VI.

ST. JOSEPH pop. 1,340 (See map and index starting on p. 336)

WHERE TO DINE

MOSCA'S **Dinner:** $6-$28 **Phone:** 504/436-9942 (96)

South Italian

Location: Jct US 90 and Huey Long Bridge, 4.5 mi w. 4137 US 90 W 70094. **Hours:** 5:30 pm-9:30 pm. Closed: Sun, Mon & 12/21-12/29. **Reservations:** accepted. **Features:** Traditional Southern Italian dishes and chicken entrees, as well as seasonal specials, await the diner in the family-run restaurant. Casual dress; cocktails. **Parking:** on-site.

ST. ROSE —*See New Orleans p. 412.*

SCOTT pop. 7,870

WHERE TO STAY

HAMPTON INN LAFAYETTE *Book great rates at AAA.com* **Phone:** 337/236-6161

Small-scale Hotel

Property failed to provide current rates

Location: I-10, exit 100, just s. 2144 W Willow St 70583. Fax: 337/236-8768. **Facility:** 79 one-bedroom standard units. 3 stories, interior corridors. *Bath:* combo or shower only. **Parking:** on-site. **Amenities:** voice mail, irons, hair dryers. **Pool(s):** outdoor. **Guest Services:** valet laundry, wireless Internet. **Business Services:** meeting rooms, business center.

SOME UNITS

HOWARD JOHNSON *Book at AAA.com* **Phone:** 337/593-0849

Small-scale Hotel

Property failed to provide current rates

Location: I-10, exit 97. 103 Harold Gauthe Dr 70583. Fax: 337/593-0965. **Facility:** 49 one-bedroom standard units. 2 stories (no elevator), interior corridors. **Parking:** on-site. **Terms:** small pets only ($25 deposit). **Amenities:** high-speed Internet, voice mail, irons, hair dryers. **Pool(s):** outdoor. **Business Services:** fax (fee).

SOME UNITS

FEE

SLEEP INN OF LAFAYETTE *Book great rates at AAA.com* **Phone:** (337)264-0408

AAA SAVE

Small-scale Hotel

All Year	1P: $74-$94	2P: $74-$94	XP: $10	F17

Location: I-10, exit 100, just s, then e. 2140 W Willow St 70583. Fax: 337/264-0356. **Facility:** 83 one-bedroom standard units, some with whirlpools. 3 stories, interior corridors. *Bath:* combo or shower only. **Parking:** on-site. **Amenities:** voice mail, irons, hair dryers. **Pool(s):** outdoor. **Guest Services:** valet laundry, wireless Internet. **Business Services:** fax (fee). **Cards:** AX, DC, DS, MC, VI.

SOME UNITS

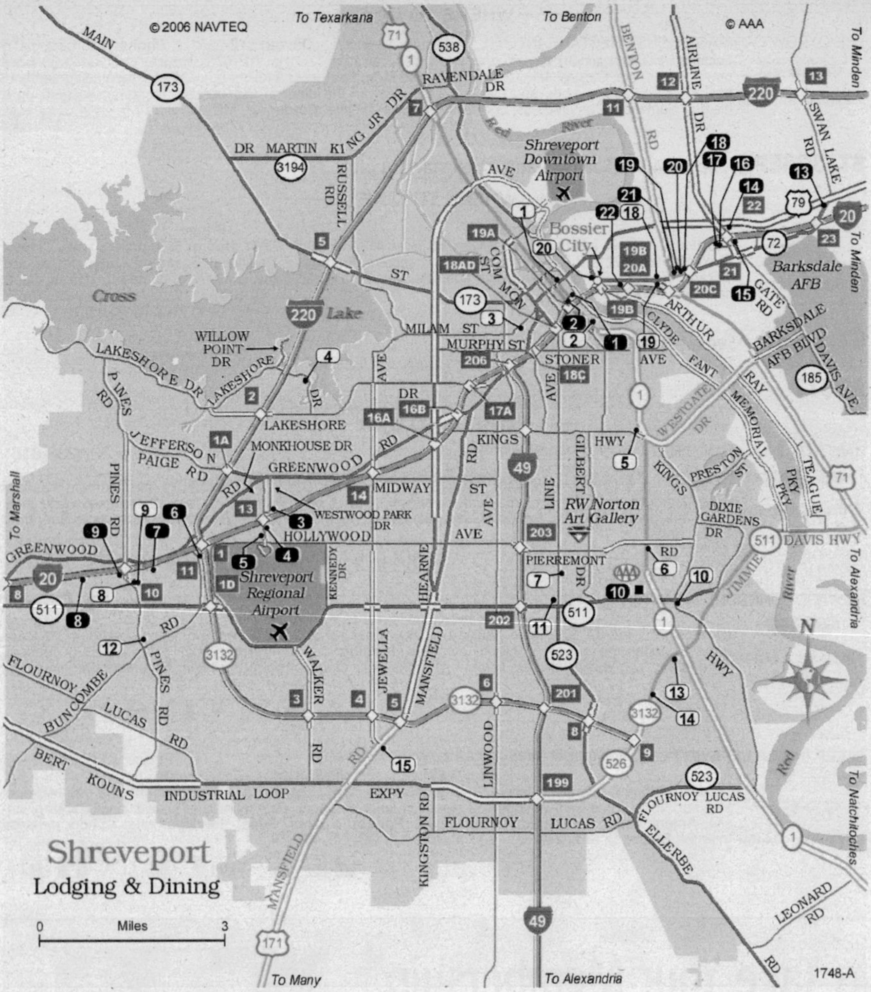
Shreveport
Lodging & Dining
© 2006 NAVTEQ
© AAA
To Texarkana
To Benton
To Minden
To Marshall
To Alexandria
To Natchitoches
To Many
Shreveport Downtown Airport
Shreveport Regional Airport
Bossier City
Barksdale AFB
Cross Lake
RW Norton Art Gallery
Red River
Miles
0
3
1748-A

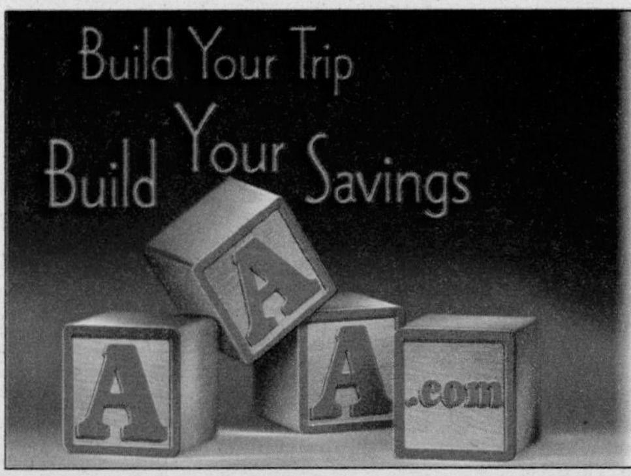
Build Your Trip
Build Your Savings
.com

Airport Accommodations

Spotter/Map Page Number	OA	**SHREVEPORT REGIONAL**	Diamond Rating	Rate Range High Season	Listing Page
4 / p. 420	AAA	**Best Western Richmond Suites Hotel, 0.5 mi n of entrance**	♦♦♦	$89-$99 SAVE	423
3 / p. 420		Holiday Inn Express-Shreveport Airport, 1 mi n of entrance	♦♦♦	Failed to provide	424

Shreveport

This index helps you "spot" where approved accommodations and restaurants are located on the corresponding detailed maps. Lodging rate ranges are for comparison only and show the property's high season; rates are per night, unless only weekly (W) rates are available. Restaurant rate range is for dinner, unless only lunch (L) is served. Turn to the listing page for more detailed rate information and consult display ads for special promotions.

Spotter/Map Page Number	OA	**SHREVEPORT** - Lodgings	Diamond Rating	Rate Range High Season	Listing Page
1 / p. 420		Holiday Inn Downtown	♦♦♦	Failed to provide	424
2 / p. 420	AAA	**Best Western Chateau Suite Hotel**	♦♦♦	$94-$154 SAVE	423
3 / p. 420		Holiday Inn Express-Shreveport Airport	♦♦♦	Failed to provide	424
4 / p. 420	AAA	**Best Western Richmond Suites Hotel**	♦♦♦	$89-$99 SAVE	423
5 / p. 420		Hampton Inn-Airport	♦♦♦	$74-$149	424
6 / p. 420		Holiday Inn Financial Plaza	♦♦♦	$90-$105	424
7 / p. 420		Courtyard by Marriott Shreveport	♦♦♦	$102-$119	424
8 / p. 420		La Quinta Inn & Suites Shreveport - see color ad p 386	♦♦♦	$105-$125	424
9 / p. 420		Fairfield Inn by Marriot	♦♦	Failed to provide	424
10 / p. 420	AAA	**Clarion Hotel Shreveport**	♦♦♦	$109-$139 SAVE	423
		SHREVEPORT - Restaurants			
1 / p. 420		The Blind Tiger	♦♦	$7-$18	425
2 / p. 420		Ernest's Orleans Restaurant	♦♦♦	$13-$35	425
3 / p. 420		Pete Harris' Cafe	♦	$6-$28	425
4 / p. 420		Smith's Cross Lake Inn	♦♦	$10-$26	426
5 / p. 420	AAA	**Don's Seafood & Steak-House**	♦♦	$9-$25	425
6 / p. 420		Kon Tiki	♦♦	$14-$40	425
7 / p. 420		Bistro 6301	♦♦	$15-$25	425
8 / p. 420		Savoie's Steak & Seafood	♦♦	$11-$24	426
9 / p. 420		Nicky's Mexican Restaurant and Bar	♦♦	$8-$16	425
10 / p. 420		Savoie's The Cajun Restaurant	♦♦	$11-$24	426
11 / p. 420		Superior's Steakhouse	♦♦♦	$22-$45	426
12 / p. 420		Crescent Landing Catfish Restaurant	♦	$6-$17	425
13 / p. 420		Copeland's Famous New Orleans Restaurant & Bar	♦♦♦	$10-$20	425
14 / p. 420		Posado's Cafe	♦♦	$9-$18	426
15 / p. 420		Podnuh's Bar-B-Q	♦	$4-$12	425
		BOSSIER CITY - Lodgings			
13 / p. 420		Econo Lodge Inn & Suites	♦♦	$49-$79	310

Spotter/Map Page Number	OA	**BOSSIER CITY** - Lodgings (continued)	Diamond Rating	Rate Range High Season	Listing Page
14 / p. 420		Crossland Studios Shreveport-Bossier City	◆	Failed to provide	310
15 / p. 420		Best Western-Airline Motor Inn	◆◆	$75-$125	310
16 / p. 420		Quality Inn & Suites	◆◆◆	$70-$89	311
17 / p. 420		Microtel Inn & Suites	◆◆	$50-$79	311
18 / p. 420		Hampton Inn	◆◆◆	Failed to provide	310
19 / p. 420		Holiday Inn Bossier	◆◆	$89-$99	310
20 / p. 420	AAA	**Residence Inn by Marriott-Shreveport/Bossier City**	◆◆◆	$129-$230 SAVE	311
21 / p. 420		La Quinta Inn Bossier City	◆◆	$78-$109	310
22 / p. 420		Comfort Inn	◆◆	Failed to provide	310
		BOSSIER CITY - Restaurants			
18 / p. 420		Posado's Cafe	◆◆	$9-$18	311
19 / p. 420		Ralph & Kacoo's	◆◆	$13-$22	311
20 / p. 420		Jack Binion's Steak House	◆◆◆	$24-$54	311

SHREVEPORT pop. 200,145 (See map and index starting on p. 420)—*See also BOSSIER CITY.*

WHERE TO STAY

BEST WESTERN CHATEAU SUITE HOTEL *Book great rates at AAA.com* **Phone:** (318)222-7620 **2**

Small-scale Hotel

All Year [BP] 1P: $94-$154 2P: $94-$154 XP: $10 F18

Location: I-20, exit 19A (Spring St), just nw. 201 Lake St 71101. Fax: 318/424-2014. **Facility:** 101 units. 49 one-bedroom standard units. 52 one-bedroom suites ($104-$154), some with efficiencies, kitchens and/or whirlpools. 2-5 stories, interior corridors. *Bath:* combo or shower only. **Parking:** on-site. **Terms:** 21 day cancellation notice, package plans. **Amenities:** video games (fee), voice mail, honor bars, irons, hair dryers. *Some:* high-speed Internet, safes. **Pool(s):** outdoor. **Leisure Activities:** exercise room. **Guest Services:** complimentary evening beverages: Mon-Sat, valet and coin laundry, area transportation-within 2 mi. **Business Services:** meeting rooms, business center. **Cards:** AX, DC, DS, MC, VI. **Free Special Amenities: full breakfast and local telephone calls.**

SOME UNITS

BEST WESTERN RICHMOND SUITES HOTEL *Book great rates at AAA.com* **Phone:** (318)635-6431 **4**

Small-scale Hotel

All Year 1P: $89-$99 2P: $89-$99 XP: $10 F18

Location: I-20, exit 13 (Monkhouse Rd), just s. 5101 Monkhouse Dr 71109. Fax: 318/635-6040. **Facility:** 120 units. 63 one-bedroom standard units. 57 one-bedroom suites ($109-$149), some with kitchens and/or whirlpools. 2 stories (no elevator), interior corridors. *Bath:* combo or shower only. **Parking:** on-site. **Terms:** 21 day cancellation notice, [BP] meal plan available, package plans, pets ($75 fee). **Amenities:** video games (fee), high-speed Internet, voice mail, irons, hair dryers. **Pool(s):** outdoor, wading. **Leisure Activities:** sauna, whirlpool, poolside gas grills, exercise room, sports court. **Guest Services:** sundries, complimentary evening beverages, valet and coin laundry. **Business Services:** meeting rooms, business center. **Cards:** AX, CB, DC, DS, MC, VI. **Free Special Amenities: full breakfast and high-speed Internet.**

SOME UNITS

FEE

CLARION HOTEL SHREVEPORT *Book great rates at AAA.com* **Phone:** (318)797-9900 **10**

Large-scale Hotel

All Year 1P: $109 2P: $139 XP: $20 F18

Location: I-20, exit 19A (SR 1 S), 6 mi s to E 70th St, then 0.4 mi w. 1419 E 70th St 71105. Fax: 318/798-2923. **Facility:** 231 units. 228 one-bedroom standard units. 3 one-bedroom suites. 6 stories, interior corridors. **Parking:** on-site. **Terms:** small pets only (with prior approval). **Amenities:** high-speed Internet, voice mail, irons, hair dryers. **Dining:** 6:30 am-2 & 5-10 pm, cocktails. **Pool(s):** outdoor. **Leisure Activities:** exercise room. **Guest Services:** gift shop, valet laundry. **Business Services:** conference facilities, business center. **Cards:** AX, CB, DC, DS, JC, MC, VI. **Free Special Amenities: continental breakfast and local telephone calls.**

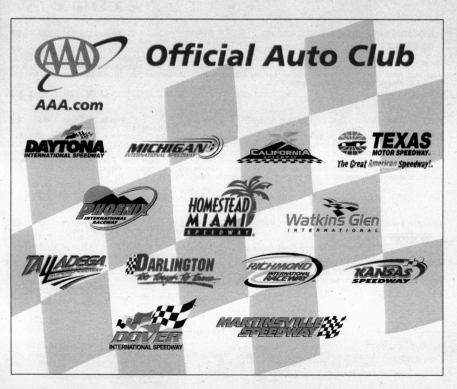

SOME UNITS

(See map and index starting on p. 420)

COURTYARD BY MARRIOTT SHREVEPORT Book great rates at AAA.com Phone: (318)686-0880 7

Small-scale Hotel

All Year 1P: $102-$119

Location: I-20, exit 10, 0.5 mi e on frontage road. 6001 Financial Plaza 71129. Fax: 318/686-0545. **Facility:** 90 units. 87 one-bedroom standard units, some with whirlpools. 3 one-bedroom suites. 3 stories, interior corridors. *Bath:* combo or shower only. **Parking:** on-site. **Terms:** [BP] meal plan available. **Amenities:** video games (fee), high-speed Internet, dual phone lines, voice mail, irons, hair dryers. **Pool(s):** small heated indoor. **Leisure Activities:** whirlpool, exercise room. **Guest Services:** sundries, valet and coin laundry. **Business Services:** meeting rooms, business center. **Cards:** AX, DC, DS, JC, MC, VI.

SOME UNITS

FAIRFIELD INN BY MARRIOT Book great rates at AAA.com Phone: 318/686-0102 9

Small-scale Hotel

Property failed to provide current rates

Location: I-20, exit 10 (Pines Rd), 0.4 mi sw. 6245 Westport Ave 71129. Fax: 318/686-8791. **Facility:** 105 one-bedroom standard units. 3 stories, interior corridors. *Bath:* combo or shower only. **Parking:** on-site. **Amenities:** video games (fee), high-speed Internet, irons, hair dryers. **Pool(s):** outdoor. **Leisure Activities:** exercise room. **Guest Services:** valet laundry. **Business Services:** meeting rooms.

SOME UNITS

HAMPTON INN-AIRPORT Book great rates at AAA.com Phone: (318)636-4447 5

Small-scale Hotel

All Year 1P: $74-$149 2P: $74-$149 XP: $5

Location: I-20, exit 13, 0.4 mi s. 5226 Monkhouse Dr 71109. Fax: 318/636-4407. **Facility:** 79 units. 73 one-bedroom standard units, some with whirlpools. 6 one-bedroom suites with whirlpools. 4 stories, interior corridors. *Bath:* combo or shower only. **Parking:** on-site. **Terms:** cancellation fee imposed, [ECP] meal plan available. **Amenities:** video games (fee), high-speed Internet, voice mail, irons, hair dryers. *Some:* DVD players, CD players. **Pool(s):** small outdoor. **Leisure Activities:** exercise room. **Guest Services:** complimentary evening beverages: Mon-Thurs, valet and coin laundry. **Business Services:** meeting rooms, business center. **Cards:** AX, DC, DS, JC, MC, VI.

SOME UNITS

HOLIDAY INN DOWNTOWN Book at AAA.com Phone: 318/222-7717 1

Large-scale Hotel

Property failed to provide current rates

Location: I-20, exit 19A (Spring St), just n. 102 Lake St 71101. Fax: 318/221-5951. **Facility:** 188 one-bedroom standard units, some with whirlpools. 6 stories, interior corridors. **Parking:** on-site. **Terms:** pets ($25 fee). **Amenities:** video games (fee), high-speed Internet, dual phone lines, voice mail, irons, hair dryers. **Pool(s):** small outdoor. **Leisure Activities:** exercise room. **Guest Services:** valet laundry, area transportation. **Business Services:** conference facilities, business center.

SOME UNITS

FEE

HOLIDAY INN EXPRESS-SHREVEPORT AIRPORT Book at AAA.com Phone: 318/631-2000 3

Small-scale Hotel

Property failed to provide current rates

Location: I-20, exit 13 (Monkhouse Dr), just ne. 5101 Westwood Park Dr 71109. Fax: 318/631-2800. **Facility:** 115 one-bedroom standard units, some with efficiencies. 2 stories (no elevator), interior corridors. *Bath:* combo or shower only. **Parking:** on-site. **Amenities:** video games (fee), high-speed Internet, dual phone lines, voice mail, irons, hair dryers. **Pool(s):** outdoor. **Leisure Activities:** whirlpool, exercise room. **Guest Services:** valet and coin laundry. **Business Services:** meeting rooms.

SOME UNITS

HOLIDAY INN FINANCIAL PLAZA Book at AAA.com Phone: (318)688-3000 6

Large-scale Hotel

All Year 1P: $90-$105 2P: $90-$105 XP: $10 F12

Location: I-20, exit 10 (Pines Rd), 1 mi e on frontage road. 5555 Financial Plaza 71129. Fax: 318/687-4462. **Facility:** 225 units. 204 one-bedroom standard units. 17 one- and 4 two-bedroom suites ($140-$170) with kitchens. 2-6 stories, interior corridors. **Parking:** on-site. **Terms:** [CP] meal plan available, package plans, pets ($25 fee). **Amenities:** video games (fee), high-speed Internet, voice mail, irons, hair dryers. **Pool(s):** heated indoor/outdoor, wading. **Leisure Activities:** sauna, whirlpools, exercise room, sports court. **Guest Services:** valet and coin laundry. **Business Services:** conference facilities, business center. **Cards:** AX, CB, DC, DS, JC, MC, VI.

SOME UNITS

FEE

LA QUINTA INN & SUITES SHREVEPORT Book great rates at AAA.com Phone: (318)671-1100 8

Small-scale Hotel

3/1-11/30 [ECP] 1P: $105-$115 2P: $115-$125 XP: $10 F18
12/1-2/28 [ECP] 1P: $95-$105 2P: $105-$115 XP: $10 F18

Location: I-20, exit 10 (Pines Rd), 0.5 mi e on frontage road. 6700 Financial Cir 71129. Fax: 318/671-1600. **Facility:** 117 units. 113 one-bedroom standard units. 4 one-bedroom suites. 4 stories, interior corridors. *Bath:* combo or shower only. **Parking:** on-site. **Terms:** small pets only. **Amenities:** video games (fee), high-speed Internet, voice mail, irons, hair dryers. **Pool(s):** heated outdoor. **Leisure Activities:** whirlpool, exercise room. **Guest Services:** valet and coin laundry. **Business Services:** meeting rooms, business center. **Cards:** AX, CB, DC, DS, MC, VI. ***(See color ad p 386)***

SOME UNITS

WHERE TO DINE

BARNHILL'S BUFFET **Lunch:** $5-$9 **Dinner:** $7-$10 **Phone:** 318/687-6161

American

Location: Jct SR 3132 Loop, exit 5 (US 171/Mansfield Rd) westbound; exit 4 (Jewalla) eastbound, 1.5 mi s. 9176 Mansfield Rd 71118. **Hours:** 10:45 am-8:45 pm, Fri-9 pm, Sat 7 am-9 pm, Sun 7 am-8:45 pm. **Features:** Casual dress. **Parking:** on-site. **Cards:** AX, DS, MC, VI.

(See map and index starting on p. 420)

BISTRO 6301 **Dinner:** $15-$25 **Phone:** 318/865-6301 (7)

Steak & Seafood

Location: I-49, exit 203, 0.6 mi e on Pierremont, then 0.4 mi s. 6301 Line Ave 71106. **Hours:** 5 pm-10 pm, Fri & Sat-11 pm. Closed major holidays; also Sun & Mon. **Reservations:** suggested. **Features:** Experience fine cuisine and award winning wines at Bistro 6301. This restaurant caters to a slightly upscale crowd, serving contemporary global cuisine featuring filet and duck. Dressy casual; cocktails. **Parking:** on-site. **Cards:** AX, DC, DS, MC, VI.

THE BLIND TIGER **Lunch:** $7-$11 **Dinner:** $7-$18 **Phone:** 318/226-8747 (1)

Regional American

Location: Corner of Texas and Spring sts; downtown. 120 Texas St 71101. **Hours:** 11 am-10 pm, Fri & Sat-11 pm, Sun noon-9 pm. Closed major holidays. **Features:** A happening spot in the heart of downtown, the restaurant lures patrons with good food, good fun, good music and good drinks—all with a Southern touch. Prepare to wait for a table. Casual dress; cocktails. **Parking:** street. **Cards:** AX, DC, DS, MC, VI.

COPELAND'S FAMOUS NEW ORLEANS RESTAURANT & BAR **Lunch:** $8-$10 **Dinner:** $10-$20 **Phone:** 318/797-0143 (13)

Regional American

Location: 5.9 mi s to 70th St (SR 511), just sw. 1665 E Industrial Loop 71106. **Hours:** 11 am-10 pm, Fri & Sat-11 pm, Sun 10 am-10 pm. **Reservations:** accepted. **Features:** While the restaurant's most popular dish is eggplant pirouge, other originals are also offered including catfish Acadiana, veal Copeland, crab cakes and shrimp Alfredo; many desserts "for two" are available. Casual dress; cocktails. **Parking:** on-site. **Cards:** AX, CB, DC, DS, JC, MC, VI.

CRESCENT LANDING CATFISH RESTAURANT **Lunch:** $5-$11 **Dinner:** $6-$17 **Phone:** 318/686-4562 (12)

American

Location: I-20, exit 10 (Pines Rd), 1.2 mi s. 7601 Pines Rd 71129. **Hours:** 11 am-10 pm. Closed: 1/1, 11/22, 12/25. **Features:** Popular with locals, the casual restaurant serves such favorites as bean soup with jalapeno hushpuppies and, of course, fried catfish. Casual dress; beer only. **Parking:** on-site. **Cards:** AX, DC, DS, MC, VI.

DON'S SEAFOOD & STEAK-HOUSE **Lunch:** $8-$13 **Dinner:** $9-$25 **Phone:** 318/865-4291 (5)

AAA

Seafood

Location: I-49, exit 205 (Kings Hwy), 0.9 mi e. 3100 Highland Ave 71104. **Hours:** 11 am-9 pm, Fri & Sat-10 pm. Closed major holidays. **Reservations:** suggested. **Features:** Offering some Cajun dishes, this restaurant is a comfortable, family-friendly place for good seafood and steak. Some menu highlights include blackened red snapper, gumbo and bread pudding. An open interior and good service keep the atmosphere pleasant. Casual dress; cocktails. **Parking:** on-site. **Cards:** AX, CB, DC, DS, JC, MC, VI.

ERNEST'S ORLEANS RESTAURANT **Dinner:** $13-$35 **Phone:** 318/226-1325 (2)

Regional Steak & Seafood

Location: I-20, exit 19A (Market St), just s on SR 1 S; at top of the hill. 1601 Spring St S 71101. **Hours:** 4:30 pm-10:30 pm. Closed: Sun & Mon. **Reservations:** suggested. **Features:** This fine-dining restaurant is a pleasant surprise in the area. Upscale features include valet parking, a professional staff and an elegant setting. House favorites are snapper Orleans, marinated crab claws and any one of numerous flaming desserts. Dressy casual; cocktails; entertainment. **Parking:** on-site and valet. **Cards:** AX, CB, DC, DS, JC, MC, VI.

KON TIKI **Lunch:** $8-$15 **Dinner:** $14-$40 **Phone:** 318/869-2316 (6)

Polynesian

Location: On SR 1, 0.5 mi n of SR 511. 5815 Youree Dr 71105. **Hours:** 11 am-2:30 & 5-9:30 pm, Sat 5 pm-10:30 pm. Closed major holidays; also Sun. **Reservations:** accepted. **Features:** This terrific Polynesian eatery, which also offers American dishes, may be considered pricey but it is well worth it considering the quality of ingredients and thoughtful preparation. A perfect spot for a night on the town, special occasion, business meeting, or to simply impress. The Polynesian decor perfectly completes the experience. Dressy casual; cocktails. **Parking:** on-site. **Cards:** AX, DS, MC, VI.

MR. GATTI'S **Lunch:** $6-$12 **Dinner:** $8-$15 **Phone:** 318/797-2222

Pizza

Location: I-49, exit 199, 0.4 mi ne, then just nw. 7805 Youree Dr 71105. **Hours:** 11 am-9 pm. Closed major holidays. **Reservations:** not accepted. **Features:** Diners find great value for the dollar at this casual eatery. The extensive salad and pizza bar includes a variety of dessert pizzas. Casual dress. **Parking:** on-site. **Cards:** AX, DS, MC, VI.

NICKY'S MEXICAN RESTAURANT AND BAR **Lunch:** $6-$8 **Dinner:** $8-$16 **Phone:** 318/671-0811 (9)

Mexican

Location: I-20, exit 10 (Pines Rd), just sw. 6721 Klug Pines Rd 71129. **Hours:** 11 am-10 pm. Closed major holidays. **Features:** Since 1979 the restaurant has been serving up a very good selection of large and delicious portions in a casual atmosphere. Casual dress; cocktails. **Parking:** on-site. **Cards:** AX, CB, DC, DS, JC, MC, VI.

PETE HARRIS' CAFE **Lunch:** $6-$28 **Dinner:** $6-$28 **Phone:** 318/425-4277 (3)

Soul Food

Location: Corner of Milam and Hope sts; downtown. 1355 Milam St 71101. **Hours:** 8 am-midnight, Thurs-Sat to 2 am. Closed major holidays. **Features:** Representative of soul food at its best are such favorites as beef tips, shrimp with bell peppers, smothered pork chops and yummy homemade pecan pie. Casual dress; cocktails. **Parking:** on-site. **Cards:** AX, DS, MC, VI.

PODNUH'S BAR-B-Q **Lunch:** $4-$12 **Dinner:** $4-$12 **Phone:** 318/688-0818 (15)

Barbecue

Location: SR 3132 loop westbound, exit 5 (US 17/Mansfield Rd); eastbound exit 4 (Jewella); jct Mansfield Rd and SR 3132. 9030 Mansfield Rd 71118. **Hours:** 10 am-8 pm, Fri & Sat-9 pm. Closed major holidays. **Reservations:** accepted. **Features:** A favorite of the local crowd, the restaurant serves large and tasty portions at inexpensive prices. Casual dress. **Parking:** on-site. **Cards:** AX, CB, DC, DS, JC, MC, VI.

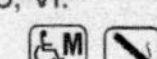

(See map and index starting on p. 420)

POSADO'S CAFE **Lunch:** $6-$10 **Dinner:** $9-$18 **Phone:** 318/524-2000 (14)

Mexican

Location: 0.8 mi w of jct SR 1 (Youree Dr) and W SR 3132 (Industrial Loop Expwy). 1355 E Bert Kouns Industrial Loop 71105. **Hours:** 11 am-10 pm, Fri & Sat-11 pm. **Features:** Posado's Cafe features delicious Mexican dishes served in large portions. Selections include beef fajitas, beef tacos, cheese enchiladas and more. Posado's also boasts a unique decor — the upstairs area is designed to look like a small Mexican village. Casual dress; cocktails. **Parking:** on-site. **Cards:** AX, DS, MC, VI.

SAVOIE'S STEAK & SEAFOOD **Lunch:** $8-$11 **Dinner:** $11-$24 **Phone:** 318/686-2811 (8)

Regional American

Location: I-20, exit 10 (Pines Rd), just e; in Kroger Shopping Center. 6715 Pines Rd, Suite 108 71129. **Hours:** 11 am-10 pm, Fri & Sat-10:30 pm, Sun-9 pm. Closed: 11/22, 12/25. **Reservations:** accepted. **Features:** Don't judge a book by its cover; once inside you will enjoy both the restaurant's atmosphere and its tasty menu selections. Casual dress; cocktails. **Parking:** on-site. **Cards:** AX, DS, MC, VI.

SAVOIE'S THE CAJUN RESTAURANT **Lunch:** $8-$11 **Dinner:** $11-$24 **Phone:** 318/797-3010 (10)

Regional American

Location: I-20, exit 19A (SR 1 South), 5 mi s, then 1.2 mi e on SR 511 (70th St). 2400 E 70th St 71105. **Hours:** 11 am-10 pm, Fri & Sat-10:30 pm, Sun-9 pm. Closed: 11/22, 12/25. **Reservations:** accepted. **Features:** Nothing fancy, but for those looking for excellent, authentic Cajun cuisine served in hearty portions, Savoie's is a good choice. The atmosphere is casual with an outdoor motif, and the service is good. Simply tasty food served in a rustic setting. Casual dress; cocktails. **Parking:** on-site. **Cards:** AX, DS, MC, VI.

SMITH'S CROSS LAKE INN **Dinner:** $10-$26 **Phone:** 318/631-0919 (4)

American

Location: I-220, exit 2 (Lakeshore Dr), 0.7 mi e, then 0.5 mi nw. 5301 S Lakeshore Dr 71109. **Hours:** 5 pm-10 pm. Closed major holidays; also Sun. **Reservations:** accepted. **Features:** Overlooking beautiful Lake Caddo, the popular restaurant employs professional servers and makes delicious food. Cocktails. **Parking:** on-site. **Cards:** AX, DC, DS, MC, VI.

SUPERIOR'S STEAKHOUSE **Dinner:** $22-$45 **Phone:** 318/219-7692 (11)

Steak House

Location: At Line Ave. 855 Pierremont St 71106. **Hours:** 5:30 pm-10 pm. Closed major holidays. **Reservations:** accepted. **Features:** Dressy casual; cocktails. **Parking:** on-site and valet. **Cards:** AX, MC, VI.

SLIDELL —*See New Orleans p. 413.*

SPRINGFIELD pop. 395

WHERE TO STAY

THE VILLAS AT CARTER PLANTATION *Book at AAA.com* **Phone:** (225)294-7555

Small-scale Hotel

All Year 1P: $99-$220 2P: $99-$220

Location: I-12, exit 32, 2.7 mi s on SR 43, 1.1 mi e on SR 42, 1.5 mi s on Carter Cemetery Rd. 23475 Carter Trace 70462. Fax: 225/294-7505. **Facility:** 54 units. 45 one-bedroom standard units. 9 one-bedroom suites, some with kitchens. 2 stories, exterior corridors. *Bath:* combo or shower only. **Parking:** on-site. **Terms:** cancellation fee imposed, package plans, small pets only ($125 fee). **Amenities:** DVD players, high-speed Internet, voice mail, irons, hair dryers. **Pool(s):** outdoor. **Leisure Activities:** *Fee:* golf-18 holes, massage. **Guest Services:** complimentary evening beverages: Mon-Thurs, valet laundry. **Business Services:** meeting rooms, business center. **Cards:** AX, DC, DS, MC, VI.

ASK FEE SOME UNITS

SULPHUR pop. 20,512

WHERE TO STAY

BEST WESTERN EXECUTIVE HOTEL & SUITES *Book great rates at AAA.com* **Phone:** (337)625-9000

AAA SAVE

Small-scale Hotel

All Year [CP] 1P: $99-$129 2P: $99-$129

Location: I-10, exit 23, just s. 1200 Pintail St 70665. Fax: 337/625-9700. **Facility:** 67 units. 57 one-bedroom standard units. 10 one-bedroom suites ($139-$159). 3 stories, interior corridors. *Bath:* combo or shower only. **Parking:** on-site. **Terms:** check-in 4 pm. **Amenities:** high-speed Internet, voice mail, irons, hair dryers. **Pool(s):** outdoor. **Leisure Activities:** exercise room. **Guest Services:** complimentary and valet laundry. **Business Services:** meeting rooms, business center. **Cards:** AX, CB, DC, DS, MC, VI. **Free Special Amenities: continental breakfast and high-speed Internet.**

SOME UNITS

COMFORT SUITES **Phone:** (337)626-7000

AAA SAVE

fyi

Small-scale Hotel

All Year 1P: $88 2P: $88

Under major renovation, scheduled to be completed November 2006. **Last rated:** (3 diamonds) **Location:** I-10, exit 23. 320 S Cities Service Hwy 70663. Fax: 337/626-7013. **Facility:** 80 units. 77 one-bedroom standard units, some with whirlpools. 3 one-bedroom suites, some with whirlpools. 3 stories, interior corridors. *Bath:* combo or shower only. **Parking:** on-site. **Terms:** [CP] meal plan available. **Amenities:** high-speed Internet, voice mail, irons, hair dryers. **Pool(s):** outdoor. **Leisure Activities:** exercise room. **Guest Services:** coin laundry. **Business Services:** meeting rooms, fax (fee). **Cards:** AX, CB, DC, DS, JC, MC, VI. **Free Special Amenities: continental breakfast and high-speed Internet.**

SOME UNITS

FAIRFIELD INN BY MARRIOTT LAKE CHARLES/SULPHUR *Book great rates at AAA.com* **Phone:** (337)528-2629

Small-scale Hotel

All Year 1P: $75-$95 2P: $75-$95

Location: I-10, exit 20 (SR 27), just s. Located in a commercial area. 2615 Ruth St 70665. Fax: 337/528-2629. **Facility:** 79 one-bedroom standard units. 3 stories, interior corridors. *Bath:* combo or shower only. **Parking:** on-site. **Amenities:** irons, hair dryers. **Pool(s):** small heated indoor. **Leisure Activities:** whirlpool, exercise room. **Guest Services:** valet laundry, wireless Internet. **Business Services:** fax. **Cards:** AX, CB, DC, DS, JC, MC, VI.

SOME UNITS

HOLIDAY INN EXPRESS HOTEL & SUITES *Book great rates at AAA.com* **Phone:** (337)625-2500

Small-scale Hotel

All Year [CP] 1P: $119-$139 2P: $119-$139

Location: I-10, exit 23. 102 Mallard St 70665. Fax: 337/625-1500. **Facility:** 84 units. 69 one-bedroom standard units. 15 one-bedroom suites ($149-$169). 3 stories, interior corridors. *Bath:* combo or shower only. **Parking:** on-site. **Terms:** check-in 4 pm. **Amenities:** voice mail, irons, hair dryers. *Some:* dual phone lines. **Pool(s):** indoor. **Leisure Activities:** whirlpool, exercise room. **Guest Services:** complimentary and valet laundry, wireless Internet. **Business Services:** meeting rooms, business center. **Cards:** AX, DC, DS, JC, MC, VI. **Free Special Amenities: expanded continental breakfast and high-speed Internet.**

SOME UNITS

MICROTEL INN *Book great rates at AAA.com* **Phone:** (337)527-1000

Small-scale Hotel

All Year 1P: $59-$100 2P: $69-$100 XP: $5 F18

Location: I-10, exit 20 (SR 27), just s. 2619 S Ruth St 70665. Fax: 337/527-4400. **Facility:** 99 one-bedroom standard units. 3 stories, interior corridors. *Bath:* combo or shower only. **Parking:** on-site. **Terms:** check-in 4 pm. **Amenities:** safes (fee). **Guest Services:** wireless Internet. **Business Services:** meeting rooms, fax (fee). **Cards:** DC, DS, MC, VI. **Free Special Amenities: continental breakfast and high-speed Internet.**

SOME UNITS

WINGATE INN *Book at AAA.com* **Phone:** 337/527-5151

Small-scale Hotel

Property failed to provide current rates

Location: I-10, exit 20 (SR 27), just s, then just w. Located in a commercial area. 300 Arena Rd 70665. Fax: 337/527-1414. **Facility:** 82 one-bedroom standard units, some with kitchens (no utensils) and/or whirlpools. 3 stories, interior corridors. *Bath:* combo or shower only. **Parking:** on-site. **Terms:** pets ($20 extra charge). **Amenities:** video games (fee), high-speed Internet, dual phone lines, voice mail, irons, hair dryers. **Pool(s):** outdoor. **Leisure Activities:** whirlpool, exercise room. **Guest Services:** valet and coin laundry. **Business Services:** meeting rooms, business center.

SOME UNITS

FEE

WHERE TO DINE

THE BOILING POINT **Lunch:** $5-$15 **Dinner:** $5-$15 **Phone:** 337/625-9282

Cajun

Location: I-10, exit 21, just s. 1730 S Beglis 70663. **Hours:** 7 am-8 pm, Thurs-Sat to 10 pm. Closed major holidays; also Sun. **Features:** Remarkably friendly staff members are happy to make suggestions for out-of-towners. Although the restaurant has just about anything Cajun, the servers are most prone to recommend the homemade boudin. During the week, a lunch buffet lays out home-cooked American choices, while on Friday and Saturday nights, the buffet centers on seafood. Casual dress; beer & wine only. **Parking:** on-site. **Cards:** AX, DS, MC, VI.

THIBODAUX pop. 14,431

WHERE TO STAY

RAMADA INN *Book at AAA.com* **Phone:** (985)446-0561

Small-scale Hotel

2/1-3/1	1P: $85-$105	2P: $95-$125	XP: $25	F18
3/2-11/30	1P: $75-$95	2P: $85-$115	XP: $15	F18
12/1-1/31	1P: $65-$95	2P: $75-$105	XP: $15	F18

Location: SR 1, just e of jct SR 20. 400 E 1st St 70301. Fax: 985/446-0559. **Facility:** 106 units. 104 one-bedroom standard units. 2 one-bedroom suites. 2 stories (no elevator), exterior corridors. *Bath:* combo or shower only. **Parking:** on-site. **Terms:** check-in 4 pm, 3 day cancellation notice-fee imposed. **Amenities:** irons, hair dryers. **Pool(s):** outdoor. **Leisure Activities:** 2 lighted tennis courts. **Guest Services:** valet laundry, wireless Internet. **Business Services:** meeting rooms, fax (fee). **Cards:** AX, CB, DC, DS, MC, VI.

SOME UNITS

WHERE TO DINE

THE DEMITASSE COFFEE & TEA HOUSE CAFE **Lunch:** $6-$7 **Dinner:** $6-$7 **Phone:** 985/449-0933

American

Location: Center. 424 St. Mary St 70301. **Hours:** 6 am-10 pm, Sat from 6:30 am, Sun 8 am-8 pm. Closed major holidays; also Mardi Gras. **Features:** The antique store that provides the background for this restaurant creates a gentle place to enjoy a casual lunch. The menu is short and sweet, comprised of panini sandwiches, soups and a great selections of coffees and other hot beverages. A scoop of ice cream makes a perfect closer. Casual dress. **Parking:** on-site. **Cards:** AX, DC, DS, MC, VI.

FLANAGAN'S CREATIVE FOOD & DRINK **Lunch:** $7-$9 **Dinner:** $13-$27 **Phone:** 985/447-7771

American

Location: SR 1 to Audubon Dr, 0.8 mi s. 1111 Audubon Dr 70301. **Hours:** 11 am-10 pm, Fri & Sat-11 pm, Sun 10 am-2 & 4-9 pm. Closed major holidays; also Mardi Gras. **Reservations:** suggested. **Features:** This is an upscale American grill with Cajun flair. Recommended are the blackened chicken with pecan cream sauce, grilled vegetables, Cajun rice and pecan pie. A friendly atmosphere, ample portions and a wide variety of menu choices are all noteworthy. Casual dress; cocktails. **Parking:** on-site. **Cards:** AX, DC, MC, VI.

VACHERIE —*See New Orleans p. 414.*

WESTLAKE pop. 4,668

WHERE TO STAY

ISLE OF CAPRI CASINO/TOWER HOTEL **Phone:** 337/430-2121

Property failed to provide current rates

Large-scale Hotel

Location: I-10, exit 27, on eastbound frontage road. 100 Westlake Ave 70669. Fax: 337/433-2505. **Facility:** 252 units. 222 one-bedroom standard units with whirlpools. 30 one-bedroom suites with whirlpools. 10 stories, interior corridors. **Parking:** on-site. **Terms:** check-in 4 pm. **Amenities:** video games (fee), voice mail, safes, irons, hair dryers. **Pool(s):** heated outdoor. **Leisure Activities:** saunas, whirlpool, exercise room. *Fee:* massage, game room. **Guest Services:** gift shop, valet laundry, area transportation, wireless Internet. **Business Services:** conference facilities, fax (fee).

SOME UNITS

ISLE OF CAPRIS CASINO/INN AT THE ISLE **Phone:** 337/430-0712

Property failed to provide current rates

Large-scale Hotel

Location: I-10, exit 27, on eastbound frontage road. 100 Westlake Ave 70669. Fax: 337/430-0124. **Facility:** 241 one-bedroom standard units. 6 stories, interior corridors. **Parking:** on-site. **Terms:** check-in 4 pm. **Amenities:** video games (fee), voice mail, safes, irons, hair dryers. **Guest Services:** area transportation, wireless Internet. **Business Services:** conference facilities, fax (fee).

SOME UNITS

WEST MONROE pop. 13,250—*See also MONROE.*

WHERE TO STAY

JAMESON INN *Book at AAA.com* **Phone:** (318)361-0750

Small-scale Hotel

All Year [ECP] 1P: $54-$120

Location: I-20, exit 114 (Thomas Rd), just s to Constitution Dr, then just w. 213 Constitution Dr 71292. Fax: 318/361-0751. **Facility:** 67 units. 65 one-bedroom standard units. 2 one-bedroom suites. 3 stories, interior corridors. *Bath:* combo or shower only. **Parking:** on-site. **Terms:** cancellation fee imposed, pets ($10 fee). **Amenities:** high-speed Internet, voice mail, irons, hair dryers. **Pool(s):** small outdoor. **Leisure Activities:** exercise room. **Guest Services:** valet laundry. **Business Services:** PC. **Cards:** AX, DC, DS, MC, VI.

SOME UNITS

FEE

QUALITY INN & SUITES-WEST MONROE *Book great rates at AAA.com* **Phone:** (318)387-2711

Small-scale Hotel

5/26-8/18 [CP]	1P: $84-$104	2P: $84-$104	XP: $5	F18
1/1-5/25 & 8/19-11/30 [CP]	1P: $79-$99	2P: $79-$99	XP: $5	F18
12/1-12/31 [CP]	1P: $72-$99	2P: $72-$99	XP: $5	F18

Location: I-20, exit 114 (Thomas Rd), just s to Constitution Dr, then 0.6 mi w. Located in a commercial area. 503 Constitution Dr 71292. Fax: 318/324-1143. **Facility:** 77 units. 75 one-bedroom standard units. 2 one-bedroom suites ($104-$119). 3 stories, interior corridors. *Bath:* combo or shower only. **Parking:** on-site. **Terms:** pets ($25 fee). **Amenities:** video games (fee), high-speed Internet, voice mail, irons, hair dryers. *Some:* dual phone lines. **Pool(s):** small outdoor. **Leisure Activities:** exercise room. **Guest Services:** valet and coin laundry. **Cards:** AX, CB, DC, DS, JC, MC, VI.

SOME UNITS

FEE

RED ROOF INN *Book at AAA.com* **Phone:** (318)388-2420

Motel

All Year	1P: $46-$55	2P: $50-$59	XP: $4	F18

Location: I-20, exit 114 (Thomas Rd), just s. Located in a commercial area. 102 Constitution Dr 71292. Fax: 318/388-2499. **Facility:** 97 one-bedroom standard units. 3 stories, exterior corridors. *Bath:* combo or shower only. **Parking:** on-site. **Terms:** small pets only. **Amenities:** video games (fee), voice mail. **Cards:** AX, CB, DC, DS, MC, VI.

SUPER 8 MOTEL *Book at AAA.com* **Phone:** (318)325-6361

Motel

All Year	1P: $50	2P: $56	XP: $6	F17

Location: I-20, exit 114 (Thomas Rd), 0.3 mi ne. Located in a commercial area. 1101 Glenwood Dr 71291. Fax: 318/324-0534. **Facility:** 97 one-bedroom standard units. 2 stories (no elevator), exterior corridors. **Parking:** on-site. **Pool(s):** outdoor. **Cards:** AX, CB, DC, DS, MC, VI.

SOME UNITS

WHERE TO DINE

BBQ WEST **Lunch:** $4-$8 **Dinner:** $4-$8 **Phone:** 318/396-7455

Barbecue

Location: I-20, exit 114 (Thomas Rd), 0.7 mi n to US 80, then 1.6 mi w; in Key West Plaza. 4900 Cypress St, Suite 9 71291. **Hours:** 10 am-9 pm, Sun-2 pm. Closed major holidays. **Features:** The good, no-frills barbecue joint offers hearty portions and a casual atmosphere. Don't leave without trying the scrumptious cobbler. Casual dress. **Parking:** on-site. **Cards:** AX, MC, VI.

GRANDY'S **Lunch:** $6-$9 **Dinner:** $6-$9 **Phone:** 318/323-8391

American

Location: Just w of jct SR 143 and US 80. 105 Thomas Rd 71291. **Hours:** 6 am-9:30 pm, Sun-9 pm. Closed: 11/22, 12/25. **Features:** Casual dress. **Parking:** on-site. **Cards:** AX, DS, MC, VI.

LA BELLA VITA ITALIAN GRILL **Lunch:** $7-$9 **Dinner:** $8-$17 **Phone:** 318/998-6900

Italian

Location: I-20, exit 114, just s to Constitution Dr, then 0.7 mi w. 407 Constitution Dr 71292. **Hours:** 11 am-9 pm, Fri & Sat-10 pm. Closed major holidays. **Reservations:** accepted. **Features:** Upon entering this must-stop restaurant guests will hear the busy kitchen and, most importantly, the hum of happy diners. The menu has so many options it's tough to choose; the Italian meatloaf is moist and flavorful and the veal picatta is rich with a lemon and caper sauce, and the selections go on from there. Preparations are from scratch, including their memorable desserts. Casual dress; cocktails. **Parking:** on-site. **Cards:** DS, MC, VI.

LOUISIANA SECRETS **Lunch:** $5-$7 **Phone:** 318/323-8117

American

Location: Downtown Antique Alley. 311 Natchitoches St 71291. **Hours:** 9 am-3 pm. Closed major holidays; also Sun. **Features:** Take a break from antique shopping and enjoy the soups, sandwiches, salads and desserts here — it's better than Mom's. Casual dress. **Parking:** street. **Cards:** MC, VI.

PEKING CHINESE RESTAURANT **Lunch:** $5-$7 **Dinner:** $10-$12 **Phone:** 318/329-8003

Chinese

Location: I-20, exit 114 (Thomas Rd), just s. 412 Thomas Rd 71292. **Hours:** 11 am-2:30 & 5-9:30 pm, Fri 5 pm-10 pm, Sat 11 am-3 & 4-10 pm, Sun 11 am-9:30 pm. Closed major holidays. **Reservations:** accepted. **Features:** This Chinese restaurant features a large buffet at lunch and dinner, stocked with a good variety of traditional offerings including chicken, beef, seafood, noodle and rice dishes. Help yourself and sample as many of the different tastes as you like. Casual dress; beer only. **Parking:** on-site. **Cards:** AX, DS, MC, VI.

PODNUH'S BAR-B-Q **Lunch:** $5-$12 **Dinner:** $5-$12 **Phone:** 318/388-0559

Barbecue

Location: I-20, exit 114 (Thomas Rd), 0.7 mi n; jct Thomas Rd and Cypress St. 810 Splane Rd 71291. **Hours:** 10:30 am-9 pm. Closed major holidays. **Features:** A favorite among the local crowd, the restaurant serves large and tasty portions at inexpensive prices. Casual dress. **Parking:** on-site. **Cards:** AX, DS, MC, VI.

TOKYO JAPANESE STEAKHOUSE, SEAFOOD & SUSHI BAR **Dinner:** $13-$32 **Phone:** 318/397-7588

Japanese

Location: I-20, exit 114 (Thomas Rd), 0.7 mi n to US 80, then just w; in Sunshine Heights Plaza. 3426 Cypress St 71291. **Hours:** 5 pm-10 pm, Fri & Sat-11 pm. Closed major holidays; also Sun. **Reservations:** accepted. **Features:** Cooks perform for diners while preparing food tableside at the popular Japanese eatery. Casual dress; cocktails. **Parking:** on-site. **Cards:** AX, MC, VI.

WESTWEGO

—See New Orleans p. 415.

WHITE CASTLE pop. 1,946

WHERE TO STAY

NOTTOWAY PLANTATION RESTAURANT & INN **Phone:** (225)545-2730

Historic Country Inn

All Year 1P: $130-$230 2P: $160-$230 XP: $30 F

Location: 2 mi n of jct SR 1 and 9. 30970 Hwy 405 70788 (PO Box 160). Fax: 225/545-8632. **Facility:** This riverfront inn offers rooms of various sizes within the antebellum plantation house, a guest house and an overseer's cabin. Smoke free premises. 15 units. 12 one-bedroom standard units, some with whirlpools. 3 one-bedroom suites, some with whirlpools. 3 stories (no elevator), interior/exterior corridors. *Bath:* combo or shower only. **Parking:** on-site. **Terms:** 3 day cancellation notice. **Amenities:** voice mail, irons, hair dryers. **Pool(s):** outdoor. **Guest Services:** gift shop. **Business Services:** meeting rooms. **Cards:** AX, DS, MC, VI.

ZACHARY pop. 11,275

WHERE TO STAY

BEST WESTERN ZACHARY INN Book great rates at AAA.com **Phone:** (225)658-2550

AAA SAVE

Small-scale Hotel

All Year 1P: $68 2P: $68 XP: $7 F16

Location: Just s of jct SR 64. 4030 Hwy 19 70791. Fax: 225/658-2570. **Facility:** 58 one-bedroom standard units, some with whirlpools. 2 stories, interior corridors. **Parking:** on-site. **Terms:** [BP] meal plan available, pets ($50 fee). **Amenities:** high-speed Internet, irons, hair dryers. **Pool(s):** outdoor. **Leisure Activities:** limited exercise equipment. **Guest Services:** coin laundry, wireless Internet. **Business Services:** meeting rooms, business center. **Cards:** AX, DC, DS, MC, VI. **Free Special Amenities: expanded continental breakfast and high-speed Internet.**

SOME UNITS

FEE

Vicksburg
© Andre Jenny
Alamy

ABERDEEN pop. 6,415

WHERE TO STAY

BEST WESTERN ABERDEEN INN *Book great rates at AAA.com* **Phone:** 662/369-4343

Motel

All Year 1P: $67-$70 2P: $72-$80 XP: $10 F7

Location: On US 45, just n of jct SR 25 and Tenn-Tom Bridge. Located in a rural area. 801 E Commerce St 39730. Fax: 662/369-9222. **Facility:** 63 one-bedroom standard units. 1 story, exterior corridors. **Parking:** on-site, winter plug-ins. **Terms:** 2 night minimum stay - seasonal, [BP] meal plan available, small pets only. **Amenities:** irons, hair dryers. **Dining:** 6 am-9 pm. **Pool(s):** outdoor. **Guest Services:** valet and coin laundry, wireless Internet. **Business Services:** meeting rooms. **Cards:** AX, DS, MC, VI. **Free Special Amenities: full breakfast and high-speed Internet.**

SOME UNITS

BATESVILLE pop. 7,113

WHERE TO STAY

AMERIHOST INN-BATESVILLE *Book at AAA.com* **Phone:** 662/563-6592

Small-scale Hotel

Property failed to provide current rates

Location: I-55, exit 243B, just nw on frontage road. 221 Lakewood Dr 38606. Fax: 662/561-1787. **Facility:** 60 one-bedroom standard units, some with whirlpools. 2 stories (no elevator), interior corridors. *Bath:* combo or shower only. **Parking:** on-site. **Amenities:** high-speed Internet, safes (fee), irons, hair dryers. **Pool(s):** heated indoor. **Leisure Activities:** sauna, whirlpool, limited exercise equipment. **Guest Services:** valet laundry. **Business Services:** meeting rooms.

SOME UNITS

COMFORT INN *Book great rates at AAA.com* **Phone:** (662)563-1188

Small-scale Hotel

5/1-11/30	1P: $65-$120	2P: $65-$120	XP: $5	F
12/1-4/30	1P: $58-$75	2P: $58-$75	XP: $5	F

Location: I-55, exit 243B, just ne on frontage road. 290 Power Dr 38606. Fax: 662/563-9865. **Facility:** 50 one-bedroom standard units. 2 stories (no elevator), exterior corridors. **Parking:** on-site. **Terms:** small pets only ($5 extra charge). **Amenities:** irons, hair dryers. **Pool(s):** outdoor. **Guest Services:** wireless Internet. **Cards:** AX, CB, DC, DS, JC, MC, VI.

SOME UNITS

FEE

BAY ST. LOUIS pop. 8,209

WHERE TO STAY

CASINO MAGIC INN **Phone:** 228/467-9257

Large-scale Hotel

Property failed to provide current rates

Location: US 90, 0.6 mi n on Meadow Rd, then e, follow signs. 711 Casino Magic Dr 39520. Fax: 228/469-2689. **Facility:** 201 units. 198 one-bedroom standard units. 3 two-bedroom suites. 4 stories, interior corridors. *Bath:* combo or shower only. **Parking:** on-site. **Terms:** pets ($50 fee). **Amenities:** video games (fee), voice mail, hair dryers. **Pool(s):** heated outdoor. **Leisure Activities:** whirlpool, spa. *Fee:* marina, golf-18 holes, game room. **Guest Services:** valet and coin laundry. **Business Services:** meeting rooms.

SOME UNITS

FEE FEE

HOLLYWOOD CASINO AND GOLF RESORT *Book at AAA.com* **Phone:** (228)467-9257

Classic Large-scale Hotel

5/31-9/3	1P: $99-$209	2P: $99-$209	XP: $15	F18
12/1-12/31	1P: $99-$199	2P: $99-$199	XP: $15	F18
1/1-5/30 & 9/4-11/30	1P: $89-$199	2P: $89-$199	XP: $15	F18

Location: US 90, 0.6 mi n on Meadow Rd, then e, follow signs. 711 Hollywood Blvd 39520. Fax: 228/469-2689. **Facility:** The property features over 1,200 of the latest reel slots and video poker machines and a variety of table games; a non-smoking section is available. 291 one-bedroom standard units, some with whirlpools. 14 stories, interior corridors. **Parking:** on-site and valet. **Terms:** cancellation fee imposed, package plans. **Amenities:** video games (fee), voice mail, irons, hair dryers. *Some:* safes. **Pool(s):** heated outdoor. **Leisure Activities:** whirlpool, spa. *Fee:* marina, golf-18 holes, game room. **Guest Services:** gift shop, valet laundry, area transportation. **Business Services:** conference facilities. **Cards:** AX, DC, DS, MC, VI.

SOME UNITS

FEE

WHERE TO DINE

The following restaurant has not been evaluated by AAA but is listed for your information only.

THE SYCAMORE HOUSE **Phone:** 228/469-0107

fyi

Not evaluated. **Location:** Just nw of SR 90; center. 210 Main St 39520. **Features:** The restaurant provides an upscale dining experience and offers Creole and Southern cuisine. It is located in a cottage which is on the National Register of Historic Places. Dine in one of the dining rooms, on the screened porch or on the patio.

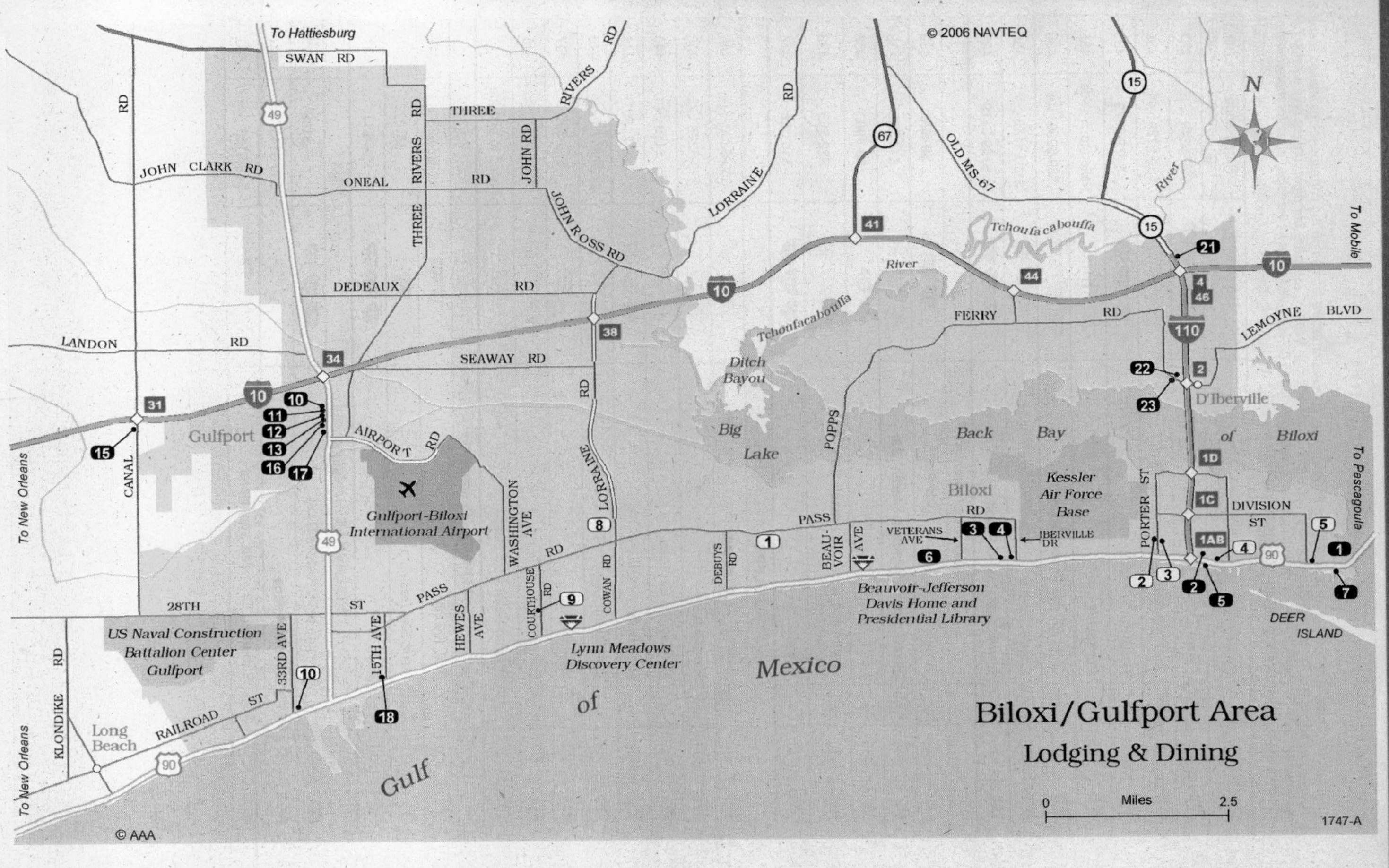
Biloxi/Gulfport Area
Lodging & Dining
0
Miles
2.5
1747-A
© 2006 NAVTEQ
© AAA
To Hattiesburg
To Mobile
To Pascagoula
To New Orleans
To New Orleans
Gulf
of
Mexico
Back Bay of Biloxi
Big Lake
Ditch Bayou
Tchoufacabouffa River
Tchoufacabouffa
River
Kessler Air Force Base
Beauvoir-Jefferson Davis Home and Presidential Library
Lynn Meadows Discovery Center
Gulfport-Biloxi International Airport
US Naval Construction Battalion Center Gulfport
D'Iberville
Biloxi
Gulfport
Long Beach
DEER ISLAND
SWAN RD
THREE RIVERS RD
JOHN RD
RIVERS RD
JOHN CLARK RD
ONEAL RD
JOHN ROSS RD
LORRAINE RD
OLD MS-67
DEDEAUX RD
LANDON RD
SEAWAY RD
FERRY RD
LEMOYNE BLVD
AIRPORT RD
CANAL RD
POPPS
PASS RD
WASHINGTON AVE
COURTHOUSE RD
COWAN RD
HEWES AVE
DEBUYS RD
BEAU-VOIR AVE
VETERANS AVE
IBERVILLE DR
PORTER ST
DIVISION ST
28TH ST
15TH AVE
33RD AVE
RAILROAD ST
KLONDIKE RD

Biloxi/Gulfport Area

This index helps you "spot" where approved accommodations and restaurants are located on the corresponding detailed maps. Lodging rate ranges are for comparison only and show the property's high season; rates are per night, unless only weekly (W) rates are available. Restaurant rate range is for dinner, unless only lunch (L) is served. Turn to the listing page for more detailed rate information and consult display ads for special promotions.

Spotter/Map Page Number	OA	**BILOXI** - Lodgings	Diamond Rating	Rate Range High Season	Listing Page
1 / p. 433	AAA	**Palace Casino Resort Hotel**	◆◆◆◆	$99-$249 SAVE	437
2 / p. 433	AAA	**Best Western Oak Manor Motel**	◆◆◆	$59-$229 SAVE	435
3 / p. 433		Holiday Inn-Biloxi Beach	◆◆◆	$129-$179	435
4 / p. 433		Comfort Inn	fyi	Failed to provide	435
5 / p. 433	AAA	**Beau Rivage Resort & Casino**	◆◆◆◆	$89-$299 SAVE	435
6 / p. 433	AAA	**Edgewater Inn**	◆◆◆	$110-$139 SAVE	435
7 / p. 433		Isle of Capri Casino Resort	◆◆◆	$159-$179	437
		BILOXI - Restaurants			
1 / p. 433		Sakura Restaurant and Sushi Bar	◆◆	$9-$20	439
2 / p. 433	AAA	**Jazzeppi's Ristorante & Martini Bar**	◆◆◆	$14-$25	438
3 / p. 433		Burger-Burger	◆	$3-$9(L)	438
4 / p. 433	AAA	**Mary Mahoney's Old French House Restaurant**	◆◆◆	$22-$35	438
5 / p. 433		Chopstix	◆◆◆	$16-$26	438
		GULFPORT - Lodgings			
10 / p. 433	AAA	**Best Western Seaway Inn**	◆◆◆	$50-$200 SAVE	446
11 / p. 433	AAA	**Hampton Inn**	◆◆◆	$99-$209 SAVE	446
12 / p. 433	AAA	**Holiday Inn Express**	◆◆◆	$89-$139 SAVE	447
13 / p. 433		Holiday Inn Airport	◆◆◆	$99-$150	446
15 / p. 433	AAA	**Crystal Inn** - see color ad p 435	◆◆◆	$129-$179 SAVE	446
16 / p. 433		Motel 6 #416	◆	$79-$95	447
17 / p. 433	AAA	**Comfort Inn**	◆◆◆	$59-$189 SAVE	446
18 / p. 433		Gulfport Beachfront Hotel	fyi	Failed to provide	446
		GULFPORT - Restaurants			
8 / p. 433		Blow Fly Inn	◆◆	$6-$25	447
9 / p. 433		China Star Restaurant	◆	$8	447
10 / p. 433		Vrazel's	◆◆◆	$14-$30	447
		D'IBERVILLE - Lodgings			
21 / p. 433		Wingate Inn D'Iberville/Biloxi	◆◆◆	$99-$139	443
22 / p. 433	AAA	**Comfort Lodge**	◆◆	$69-$140 SAVE	443
23 / p. 433	AAA	**Suburban Extended Stay Hotel**	◆◆	$69-$159 SAVE	443

BILOXI pop. 50,644 (See map and index starting on p. 433)

WHERE TO STAY

BEAU RIVAGE RESORT & CASINO *Book great rates at AAA.com* **Phone:** (228)386-7111 5

AAA SAVE — Large-scale Hotel

All Year 1P: $89-$299 2P: $89-$299 XP: $20 F21

Location: Oceanfront. I-10, exit 1A (US 90), just e. 875 Beach Blvd 39530. Fax: 228/386-7414. **Facility:** These elegantly appointed accommodations, which include 95 luxury suites, offer Gulf Coast or garden views. 1740 units. 1645 one-bedroom standard units. 68 one- and 27 two-bedroom suites with whirlpools. 29 stories, interior corridors. **Parking:** on-site and valet. **Amenities:** dual phone lines, voice mail, safes, irons, hair dryers. *Some:* DVD players, CD players, high-speed Internet. **Dining:** 12 restaurants, 24 hours, cocktails, nightclub, entertainment. **Pool(s):** outdoor. **Leisure Activities:** sauna, whirlpool, steamroom, rental boats, spa. *Fee:* marina, fishing, game room. **Guest Services:** gift shop, valet laundry, area transportation-casinos & hotels. **Business Services:** conference facilities, business center. **Cards:** AX, CB, DC, DS, MC, VI.

SOME UNITS — FEE — FEE — VCR

BEST WESTERN OAK MANOR MOTEL *Book great rates at AAA.com* **Phone:** (228)435-4331 2

AAA SAVE — Small-scale Hotel

All Year [ECP] 1P: $59-$229 2P: $59-$229 XP: $10 F18

Location: I-110, exit 1A (US 90), just e. 886 Beach Blvd 39530-4136. Fax: 228/374-7631. **Facility:** 116 one-bedroom standard units, some with whirlpools. 3 stories, interior corridors. *Bath:* combo or shower only. **Parking:** on-site. **Amenities:** high-speed Internet, dual phone lines, voice mail, safes (fee), irons, hair dryers. **Pool(s):** outdoor, wading. **Guest Services:** area transportation-casinos. **Cards:** AX, CB, DC, DS, MC, VI. **Free Special Amenities: early check-in/late check-out and room upgrade (subject to availability with advance reservations).**

SOME UNITS

COMFORT INN **Phone:** 228/432-1993 4

fyi — Small-scale Hotel

Property failed to provide current rates

Under major renovation, scheduled to be completed January 2007. **Last rated:** ◆◆◆ **Location:** I-110, exit 1B, 2.5 mi w on US 90. 1648 Beach Blvd 39531. Fax: 228/432-2297. **Facility:** 68 one-bedroom standard units, some with whirlpools. 2 stories (no elevator), interior corridors. *Bath:* combo or shower only. **Parking:** on-site. **Amenities:** irons, hair dryers. **Pool(s):** small outdoor. **Leisure Activities:** whirlpool. **Guest Services:** area transportation.

SOME UNITS

EDGEWATER INN *Book great rates at AAA.com* **Phone:** (228)388-1100 6

AAA SAVE — Small-scale Hotel

All Year 1P: $110-$139 2P: $110-$139 XP: $10 F13

Location: I-110, exit 1B, 3.4 mi w on US 90. 1936 Beach Blvd 39531. Fax: 228/385-2406. **Facility:** 65 units. 48 one-bedroom standard units. 12 one-bedroom suites ($218-$395), some with whirlpools. 5 cottages ($350-$395) with whirlpools. 1-3 stories (no elevator), exterior corridors. *Bath:* combo or shower only. **Parking:** on-site. **Terms:** weekly rates available, package plans. **Amenities:** safes (fee), irons, hair dryers. *Some:* dual phone lines. **Pool(s):** outdoor, small heated indoor. **Leisure Activities:** sauna, whirlpool. **Guest Services:** area transportation-casinos. **Cards:** AX, CB, DC, DS, MC, VI. **Free Special Amenities: early check-in/late check-out and high-speed Internet.**

SOME UNITS — VCR — FEE

FATHER RYAN HOUSE BED & BREAKFAST INN **Phone:** 228/435-1189

fyi — Bed & Breakfast

Under construction, scheduled to open April 2007. **Location:** I-110, exit 1B, 0.8 mi w on US 90. 1196 Beach Blvd 39530. Fax: 228/436-3063. **Planned Amenities:** 15 units, pets, coffeemakers, microwaves, refrigerators, pool.

HOLIDAY INN-BILOXI BEACH *Book at AAA.com* **Phone:** 228/436-0201 3

Small-scale Hotel

All Year 1P: $129-$169 2P: $139-$179 XP: $10 F17

Location: I-110, exit 1B, 2.7 mi w on US 90. 1686 Beach Blvd 39531. Fax: 228/436-9670. **Facility:** 99 one-bedroom standard units. 4 stories, interior corridors. *Bath:* combo or shower only. **Parking:** on-site. **Terms:** [BP] meal plan available. **Amenities:** high-speed Internet, dual phone lines, voice mail, irons, hair dryers. **Pool(s):** outdoor. **Leisure Activities:** exercise room. **Guest Services:** coin laundry, area transportation. **Business Services:** meeting rooms. **Cards:** AX, CB, DC, DS, MC, VI.

SOME UNITS

(See map and index starting on p. 433)

ISLE OF CAPRI CASINO RESORT Book at AAA.com Phone: (228)435-5400 7

Large-scale Hotel All Year 1P: $159-$179 2P: $159-$179

Location: I-110, exit 1A (US 90), 1.8 mi e. 151 Beach Blvd 39530. Fax: 228/436-7834. **Facility:** 741 units. 737 one-bedroom standard units. 4 one-bedroom suites ($199-$229). 12 stories, interior corridors. *Bath:* combo or shower only. **Parking:** on-site. **Terms:** check-in 4 pm. **Amenities:** video games (fee), voice mail, safes, irons, hair dryers. *Some:* honor bars. **Pool(s):** heated outdoor. **Leisure Activities:** sauna, whirlpool, exercise room. *Fee:* massage, game room. **Guest Services:** gift shop, valet laundry, area transportation. **Business Services:** conference facilities. **Cards:** AX, CB, DC, DS, MC, VI.

SOME UNITS

PALACE CASINO RESORT HOTEL Phone: (228)432-8888 1

Large-scale Hotel All Year 1P: $99-$249 2P: $99-$249 XP: $10 F12

Location: I-110, exit 1A (US 90), 2.1 mi e, then 0.4 mi n on Myrtle St. 158 E Howard Ave 39530 (PO Box 309, 39533). Fax: 228/386-2300. **Facility:** Bask in the luxury of his stunning Roman themed casino hotel, which offers stylishly appointed guest rooms, inviting lounges and impeccable service. 236 units. 223 one-bedroom standard units, some with whirlpools. 13 one-bedroom suites. 11 stories, interior corridors. *Bath:* combo or shower only. **Parking:** on-site and valet. **Terms:** check-in 4 pm, cancellation fee imposed. **Amenities:** dual phone lines, voice mail, safes, irons, hair dryers. *Fee:* video games, high-speed Internet. *Some:* honor bars. **Dining:** 5 restaurants, 24 hours, cocktails. **Pool(s):** outdoor. **Leisure Activities:** whirlpool, pool cabana, spa, volleyball. *Fee:* marina. **Guest Services:** gift shop, valet laundry, area transportation. **Business Services:** conference facilities, business center. **Cards:** AX, DC, DS, MC, VI. **Free Special Amenities: local telephone calls and high-speed Internet.**

SOME UNITS

(See map and index starting on p. 433)

The following lodging was either not evaluated or did not meet AAA rating requirements but is listed for your information only.

HAMPTON INN BILOXI Phone: 228/435-9010

fyi Not evaluated. **Location:** I-110, exit 1A, 0.9 mi w on SR 90. 1138 Beach Blvd 39530. Facilities, services, and decor characterize a mid-range property. ***(See color ad p 437)***

WHERE TO DINE

BURGER-BURGER Lunch: $3-$9 Phone: 228/432-5183 (3)

American

Location: I-110, exit 1A (US 90), 0.4 mi n on Porter Ave from Lighthouse. 1039 Howard Ave 39530. **Hours:** 7 am-10 & 11-3 pm. Closed: Sat & Sun. **Reservations:** not accepted. **Features:** Absent from the Gulf Coast for more than 20 years, Burger-Burger is back with a vengeance. Not to be missed is the specialty: a mouthwatering, hand-pressed hamburger po' boy on French bread with mustard, onions and chili. Casual dress. **Parking:** on-site. **Cards:** AX, DS, MC, VI.

CHOPSTIX **Dinner:** $16-$26 **Phone:** 228/386-1940 (5)

Chinese

Location: I-110, exit 1A (US 90), 1.6 mi e; in Grand Casino Biloxi Hotel. 265 Beach Blvd 39530. **Hours:** 5 pm-10 pm, Fri & Sat-11 pm. Closed: 12/25; also Mon & Tues. **Reservations:** suggested. **Features:** The fine-dining establishment's Asian dishes reflect French, Mediterranean and Continental influences. This place is in Grand Casino. Dressy casual; cocktails. **Parking:** on-site. **Cards:** AX, DC, DS, MC, VI.

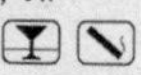

JAZZEPPI'S RISTORANTE & MARTINI BAR **Dinner:** $14-$25 **Phone:** 228/374-9660 (2)

Italian

Location: I-110, exit 1A (US 90), just n of lighthouse; s of railway tracks. 195 Porter Ave 39530. **Hours:** 5 pm-11 pm, Fri & Sat-midnight. Closed: 11/22, 12/25 & Easter; also Sun. **Reservations:** suggested. **Features:** Italian-style food with a new twist. The fine-dining atmosphere is enhanced by light jazz in the background, reminiscent of old supper clubs. A professional wait staff serves a good selection of seafood, steak, chicken, veal and pasta in hearty portions. Dressy casual; cocktails. **Parking:** on-site. **Cards:** AX, DS, MC, VI.

MARY MAHONEY'S OLD FRENCH HOUSE RESTAURANT **Lunch:** $10-$15 **Dinner:** $22-$35 **Phone:** 228/374-0163 (4)

Seafood

Location: I-110, exit 1A (US 90), just n. 116 rue Magnolia 39530. **Hours:** 11 am-10 pm. Closed major holidays; also Sun, except Mother's Day. **Reservations:** accepted. **Features:** Located in one of the oldest homes in America, built circa 1737, this one of a kind restaurant offers casual dining with a varied menu. Try the flavorful breaded veal with cheese and lump crab, then finish your meal with a yummy bread pudding with raisins. Casual dress; cocktails. **Parking:** on-site. **Cards:** AX, CB, DC, DS, MC, VI. **Historic**

(See map and index starting on p. 433)

SAKURA RESTAURANT AND SUSHI BAR **Lunch:** $5-$20 **Dinner:** $9-$20 **Phone:** 228/385-8515 (1)

Japanese

Location: Jct US 90, 0.8 mi n on Eisenhower Dr. 2667 Pass Rd 39531. **Hours:** 11 am-2:30 & 5-10 pm, Fri-11 pm, Sat noon-3 & 5-11 pm, Sun 4 pm-9 pm. Closed: 11/22; also 11/18-11/21. **Reservations:** suggested. **Features:** The extensive menu features sushi and a variety of traditional Japanese dishes including kushiyaki, itame and katsu. The more familiar teriyaki and tempura are also on the menu. Casual dress; cocktails. **Parking:** on-site. **Cards:** AX, DS, MC, VI.

BOONEVILLE pop. 8,625

WHERE TO STAY

SUPER 8 MOTEL *Book at AAA.com* **Phone:** (662)720-1688

Small-scale Hotel

All Year 1P: $55-$65 2P: $55-$65

Location: Jct US 45 and SR 4/30, 1.7 mi e to SR 145, then 0.5 mi s. 110 Hospitality Ave 38829. Fax: 662/720-3188. **Facility:** 40 one-bedroom standard units, some with whirlpools. 2 stories (no elevator), interior corridors. *Bath:* combo or shower only. **Parking:** on-site. **Terms:** package plans, pets ($5 extra charge, with prior approval). **Amenities:** irons, hair dryers. **Pool(s):** small outdoor. **Leisure Activities:** limited exercise equipment. **Guest Services:** wireless Internet. **Business Services:** meeting rooms. **Cards:** AX, CB, DC, DS, JC, MC, VI.

SOME UNITS

ASK FEE

BRANDON pop. 16,436

WHERE TO STAY

MICROTEL INN & SUITES **Phone:** 601/591-5858

Small-scale Hotel

All Year [CP] 1P: $40 2P: $50 XP: $5 D5

Location: I-20, exit 56, just n. 1130 Oak St 39042. Fax: 601/591-5859. **Facility:** 56 one-bedroom standard units. 3 stories, interior corridors. *Bath:* combo or shower only. **Parking:** on-site. **Terms:** check-in 4 pm. **Amenities:** hair dryers. **Leisure Activities:** exercise room. **Guest Services:** coin laundry, wireless Internet. **Business Services:** meeting rooms, fax. **Cards:** AX, CB, DC, DS, JC, MC, VI.

SOME UNITS

ASK

WHERE TO DINE

CINDY'S FISH HOUSE **Lunch:** $6-$13 **Dinner:** $6-$13 **Phone:** 601/829-1332

Regional American

Location: I-20, exit 56 (US 80), 0.5 mi s, then 7 mi ne. 2119 Hwy 471 39047. **Hours:** 11 am-8:30 pm, Sun-2 pm. Closed major holidays; also Mon. **Features:** The restaurant's name says it all. Here, diners find a modest establishment offering tried-and-true meals such as fried catfish with hush puppies and cole slaw. Desserts, such as homemade vanilla ice cream, are simple but good. This place is popular with the locals. Casual dress; beer only. **Parking:** on-site. **Cards:** DS, MC, VI.

SONNY'S REAL PIT BAR-B-Q **Lunch:** $4-$9 **Dinner:** $4-$9 **Phone:** 601/825-7675

Barbecue

Location: I-20, exit 56 (US 80), 0.6 mi ne. 1374 W Government St 39042. **Hours:** 11 am-9 pm. Closed major holidays. **Features:** House specialties include barbecue ribs, pork and chicken grilled over an open pit and fresh, homemade pie. Rustic and comfortable, the atmosphere is perfect for family meals.The salad bar is always a popular choice also. Casual dress. **Parking:** on-site. **Cards:** MC, VI.

BROOKHAVEN pop. 9,861

WHERE TO STAY

BUDGET INN **Phone:** 601/835-1053

Motel

Property failed to provide current rates

Location: I-55, exit 40, 0.3 mi e, then just ne. Located in a commercial area. 749 Magee Dr 39601. Fax: 601/835-4406. **Facility:** 63 units. 62 one-bedroom standard units. 1 one-bedroom suite. 1 story, exterior corridors. **Parking:** on-site. **Amenities:** irons, hair dryers. **Pool(s):** small outdoor. **Guest Services:** valet and coin laundry.

SOME UNITS

VCR

COMFORT INN *Book great rates at AAA.com* **Phone:** 601/835-0055

Small-scale Hotel

All Year 1P: $78-$90 XP: $7 F18

Location: I-55, exit 40, just ne. Located in a commercial area. 745 Magee Dr 39601. Fax: 601/823-6524. **Facility:** 49 units. 48 one-bedroom standard units, some with whirlpools. 1 two-bedroom suite ($100-$185) with whirlpool. 2 stories (no elevator), exterior corridors. *Bath:* combo or shower only. **Parking:** on-site. **Terms:** [ECP] meal plan available. **Amenities:** high-speed Internet, irons, hair dryers. **Pool(s):** outdoor. **Leisure Activities:** exercise room. **Guest Services:** valet and coin laundry, wireless Internet. **Business Services:** fax (fee). **Cards:** AX, CB, DC, DS, JC, MC, VI.

SOME UNITS

ASK

HAMPTON INN BROOKHAVEN *Book great rates at AAA.com* **Phone:** 601/823-3800

Small-scale Hotel

All Year 1P: $89 2P: $89 XP: $10 F18

Location: I-55, exit 40, just e. 1213 Hampton Dr 39601. Fax: 601/823-3833. **Facility:** 67 one-bedroom standard units. 3 stories, interior corridors. *Bath:* combo or shower only. **Parking:** on-site. **Terms:** cancellation fee imposed, [BP] meal plan available. **Amenities:** voice mail, irons, hair dryers. **Pool(s):** outdoor. **Guest Services:** valet laundry, wireless Internet. **Business Services:** meeting rooms, fax (fee). **Cards:** AX, DS, MC, VI.

SOME UNITS

ASK

WHERE TO DINE

COUNTRY FISHERMAN
Seafood

Lunch: $7-$8 **Dinner:** $7-$16 **Phone:** 601/833-2060

Location: I-55, exit 40, 1 mi e, then just n on US 51; in Lincoln Plaza. 204 Hwy 51 N 39601. **Hours:** 11 am-2 & 5-9 pm, Fri-9:30 pm, Sat 5 pm-9:30 pm, Sun 11 am-3 pm. Closed major holidays; also 11/25, 12/24 & 12/26. **Reservations:** accepted. **Features:** The popular family buffet presents a menu of good seafood and Southern foods. Don't miss the catfish fillets. Casual dress. **Parking:** on-site. **Cards:** AX, DS, MC, VI.

CANTON pop. 12,911

WHERE TO STAY

BEST WESTERN-CANTON INN *Book great rates at AAA.com*
Small-scale Hotel

Phone: 601/859-8600

All Year 1P: $55-$65 2P: $60-$70 XP: $10 D16

Location: I-55, exit 119, just se. 137 Soldiers Colony Rd 39046. Fax: 601/859-4455. **Facility:** 48 one-bedroom standard units, some with whirlpools. 2 stories (no elevator), interior corridors. **Parking:** on-site. **Terms:** 7 day cancellation notice-fee imposed, [BP] meal plan available, small pets only ($7 extra charge). **Amenities:** high-speed Internet, irons, hair dryers. **Pool(s):** small outdoor. **Guest Services:** coin laundry, wireless Internet. **Business Services:** fax. **Cards:** AX, CB, DC, DS, MC, VI. **Free Special Amenities: full breakfast and high-speed Internet.**

SOME UNITS
FEE

COMFORT INN *Book great rates at AAA.com*
Small-scale Hotel

Phone: (601)859-7575

6/1-8/31 1P: $75-$85 2P: $75-$85
12/1-5/31 & 9/1-11/30 1P: $69-$79 2P: $69-$79

Location: I-55, exit 119, just se. 145 Soldier Colony Rd 39046. Fax: 601/859-6411. **Facility:** 64 one-bedroom standard units. 2 stories (no elevator), interior corridors. *Bath:* combo or shower only. **Parking:** on-site. **Terms:** pets ($50 deposit). **Amenities:** high-speed Internet, irons, hair dryers. **Pool(s):** small outdoor. **Leisure Activities:** exercise room. **Guest Services:** coin laundry, wireless Internet. **Business Services:** meeting rooms, fax. **Cards:** AX, DC, DS, MC, VI. **Free Special Amenities: expanded continental breakfast and high-speed Internet.**

SOME UNITS
FEE

DAYS INN *Book great rates at AAA.com*
Small-scale Hotel

Phone: 601/859-0760

All Year 1P: $53-$70 2P: $53-$70 XP: $5 F12

Location: I-55, exit 119, just ne. 123 Sidney Runnels Dr 39046. Fax: 601/859-0760. **Facility:** 32 one-bedroom standard units, some with whirlpools. 2 stories (no elevator), exterior corridors. **Parking:** on-site. **Terms:** office hours 6 am-8:30 pm. **Amenities:** hair dryers. **Guest Services:** wireless Internet. **Cards:** AX, DC, DS, MC, VI.

SOME UNITS
ASK

ECONO LODGE *Book great rates at AAA.com*
Small-scale Hotel

Phone: (601)859-2643

7/1-8/31 1P: $65-$70 2P: $70-$75 XP: $7 F16
5/1-6/30 & 9/1-11/30 1P: $60-$65 2P: $65-$70 XP: $7 F16
12/1-4/30 1P: $55-$60 2P: $65-$70 XP: $7 F16

Location: I-55, exit 119, just se. 119 Soldier Colony Rd 39046. Fax: 601/859-2643. **Facility:** 40 one-bedroom standard units. 2 stories (no elevator), exterior corridors. **Parking:** on-site. **Terms:** [AP], [BP], [CP], [ECP] & [MAP] meal plans available. **Amenities:** hair dryers. **Pool(s):** small outdoor. **Cards:** AX, DC, DS, MC, VI.

SOME UNITS
ASK

WHERE TO DINE

CHRISTINE'S BACK PORCH
American

Lunch: $8-$9 **Phone:** 601/855-2484

Location: Just s of Peace St; center. 123 Depot Dr 39046. **Hours:** 6:30 am-9 & 11-2:30 pm, Sat 8 am-10 & 11-2 pm. Closed: 11/22, 12/25; also Sun. **Features:** The early 1900s cottage is home to good Southern cooking: eggs, grits and meat for breakfast and two daily changing prix fixe lunch entrees that include bread, salad and dessert. Fried catfish on Fridays, baked chicken and meatloaf are popular with the locals. Casual dress. **Parking:** on-site. **Cards:** MC, VI.

EL SOMBRERO
Mexican

Lunch: $6-$10 **Dinner:** $7-$15 **Phone:** 601/855-2020

Location: I-55, exit 119, just se. 111 Soldier Colony Dr 39046. **Hours:** 11 am-9:30 pm, Fri-Sun to 10 pm. Closed major holidays. **Features:** Enjoy traditional authentic meals served by a quick and friendly staff; easy access to the restaurant makes it even more appealing. Casual dress; cocktails. **Parking:** on-site. **Cards:** AX, DS, MC, VI.

CARTHAGE pop. 4,637

WHERE TO STAY

ECONOMY INN *Book at AAA.com*
Small-scale Hotel

Phone: 601/267-7900

All Year 2P: $60

Location: Jct SR 25/35 on Frontage Rd. 211 Hwy 25 N 39051. Fax: 601/267-8083. **Facility:** 26 one-bedroom standard units. 1 story, exterior corridors. **Parking:** on-site. **Terms:** 4 day cancellation notice. **Amenities:** hair dryers. **Pool(s):** outdoor. **Guest Services:** wireless Internet. **Business Services:** fax. **Cards:** AX, DC, DS, MC, VI.

SOME UNITS
ASK

CLARKSDALE pop. 20,645

WHERE TO STAY

BEST WESTERN EXECUTIVE INN *Book great rates at AAA.com* **Phone:** (662)627-9292

Small-scale Hotel

All Year 1P: $69-$72 2P: $69-$72 XP: $5 F12

Location: 1 mi s of jct US 49 and SR 161. Located adjacent to shopping mall. 710 S State St 38614. Fax: 662/624-4763. **Facility:** 93 units. 92 one-bedroom standard units. 1 one-bedroom suite ($79-$84). 2 stories (no elevator), interior/exterior corridors. **Parking:** on-site. **Terms:** 7 day cancellation notice, small pets only ($5 extra charge). **Amenities:** video games (fee), voice mail, irons, hair dryers. *Some:* high-speed Internet. **Pool(s):** heated indoor/outdoor. **Leisure Activities:** limited exercise equipment, basketball. **Guest Services:** valet and coin laundry, wireless Internet. **Business Services:** meeting rooms. **Cards:** AX, DC, DS, MC, VI. **Free Special Amenities: continental breakfast and local telephone calls.**

SOME UNITS FEE

COMFORT INN OF CLARKSDALE *Book great rates at AAA.com* **Phone:** (662)627-5122

Small-scale Hotel

All Year [ECP] 1P: $69-$99 2P: $69-$99 XP: $5 F18

Location: 1.2 mi s of jct US 49 and SR 161. 818 S State St 38614. Fax: 662/627-1668. **Facility:** 74 units. 72 one-bedroom standard units. 2 one-bedroom suites. 2 stories (no elevator), interior corridors. **Parking:** on-site. **Amenities:** dual phone lines, voice mail, irons, hair dryers. **Pool(s):** outdoor. **Leisure Activities:** exercise room. **Guest Services:** valet and coin laundry, wireless Internet. **Cards:** AX, CB, DC, DS, MC, VI.

SOME UNITS

ECONO LODGE **Phone:** (662)621-1110

Motel

4/1-10/15 1P: $55-$66 2P: $66-$76 XP: $5 F18
12/1-3/31 & 10/16-11/30 1P: $46-$56 2P: $55-$66 XP: $5 F18

Location. 0.5 mi s of jct US 49 amd SR 161. 350 S State St 38614. Fax: 662/621-9838. **Facility:** 50 one-bedroom standard units, some with whirlpools. 2 stories (no elevator), exterior corridors. **Parking:** on-site. **Terms:** [CP] meal plan available, pets ($10 extra charge). **Amenities:** hair dryers. **Cards:** AX, DC, DS, MC, VI. **Free Special Amenities: continental breakfast and local telephone calls.**

SOME UNITS FEE

WHERE TO DINE

MADIDI **Dinner:** $18-$34 **Phone:** 662/627-7770

Nouvelle Southern

Location: Corner of Delta Ave and W Second; downtown. 164 Delta Ave 38614. **Hours:** 5 pm-9 pm. Closed major holidays; also Sun & Mon. **Reservations:** suggested, weekends. **Features:** Co-owned by actor Morgan Freeman, Madidi is an unexpected find in the heart of the Delta. In a historic building that once was a grocery store, the intimate restaurant offers diners distinctive cuisine prepared with French technique and Southern flair. The charming spot is a must on the itinerary of any visitor or passer-through. Dressy casual; cocktails. **Parking:** street. **Cards:** AX, DS, MC, VI.

CLEVELAND pop. 13,841

WHERE TO STAY

COMFORT INN OF CLEVELAND *Book great rates at AAA.com* **Phone:** (662)843-4060

Motel

All Year [ECP] 1P: $49-$89 2P: $49-$89 XP: $5 F18

Location: On US 61, 1 mi n of jct US 61 and SR 8. 721 N Davis Ave 38732. Fax: 662/843-4060. **Facility:** 80 one-bedroom standard units. 2 stories (no elevator), exterior corridors. *Bath:* combo or shower only. **Parking:** on-site. **Terms:** small pets only ($50 deposit). **Amenities:** irons, hair dryers. **Pool(s):** outdoor. **Guest Services:** coin laundry, wireless Internet. **Cards:** AX, DC, DS, MC, VI.

SOME UNITS FEE

HAMPTON INN OF CLEVELAND *Book great rates at AAA.com* **Phone:** (662)846-1525

Small-scale Hotel

All Year [BP] 1P: $89-$109 2P: $89-$109 XP: $5 F18

Location: 1 mi n of jct US 61 and SR 8. 807 N Davis Ave 38732. Fax: 662/846-1528. **Facility:** 57 units. 56 one-bedroom standard units. 1 one-bedroom suite ($99). 3 stories, interior corridors. *Bath:* combo or shower only. **Parking:** on-site. **Amenities:** voice mail, irons, hair dryers. **Pool(s):** small outdoor. **Guest Services:** valet laundry, wireless Internet. **Cards:** AX, CB, DC, DS, MC, VI.

SOME UNITS FEE

WHERE TO DINE

K.C.'S **Lunch:** $10-$18 **Dinner:** $18-$30 **Phone:** 662/843-5301

American

Location: At First St; just n of jct SR 8. 400 Hwy 61 N 38732. **Hours:** 11 am-1:30 & 5:30-10 pm. Closed major holidays; also Sun. **Reservations:** suggested. **Features:** Many are surprised to find such exquisite dining in the small town of Cleveland, but K.C.'s is just that. Truly a "destination" restaurant, it lures folks to travel more than 200 miles—and justifiably so—to enjoy the dazzling creations of Chef Wally, who prepares American food with Southern, Asian and even French influences. His creations are imaginative and bold, and he was even commissioned to cook for the King of Spain. Dressy casual; cocktails. **Parking:** on-site. **Cards:** AX, MC, VI.

CLINTON pop. 23,347 (See map and index starting on p. 451)

WHERE TO STAY

DAYS INN *Book great rates at AAA.com* **Phone:** 601/925-5065 38

Motel

Property failed to provide current rates

Location: I-20, exit 36, just nw. 482 Springridge Rd 39056. Fax: 601/924-6028. **Facility:** 40 one-bedroom standard units, some with whirlpools. 2 stories (no elevator), exterior corridors. **Parking:** on-site. **Amenities:** hair dryers. **Guest Services:** wireless Internet.

SOME UNITS

WHERE TO DINE

ARCHESTRATUS GRILL **Lunch:** $7-$13 **Dinner:** $13-$27 **Phone:** 601/926-4422 34

Seafood

Location: I-20, exit 36, 0.4 mi s; in Springridge Village Shopping Center. 507 Springridge Rd 39056. **Hours:** 11 am-10 pm, Sunday brunch 10:30 am-4 pm. Closed major holidays. **Reservations:** accepted. **Features:** This bustling and popular dining room serves an extensive menu of steaks, seafood and pasta with a Cajun flair. Casual dress; cocktails. **Parking:** on-site. **Cards:** AX, DS, MC, VI.

COLLINS pop. 2,683

WHERE TO STAY

The following lodging was either not evaluated or did not meet AAA rating requirements but is listed for your information only.

BEST WESTERN COLLINS INN & SUITES **Phone:** 601/765-0800

fyi

Small-scale Hotel

Did not meet all AAA rating requirements for some property operations at time of last evaluation on 12/29/2004. **Location:** On US 49. Located in a rural area. 8 Grandview Dr 39428. Facilities, services, and decor characterize a mid-range property.

COLUMBIA pop. 6,603

WHERE TO STAY

COMFORT INN *Book great rates at AAA.com* **Phone:** (601)731-9955

Small-scale Hotel

All Year [CP]	1P: $84-$114	2P: $89-$119	XP: $5	F18

Location: Just e of jct US 98 Bypass and SR 13. Located across from a shopping center. 820 Hwy 98 Bypass 39429. Fax: 601/731-9955. **Facility:** 56 units. 55 one-bedroom standard units, some with whirlpools. 1 two-bedroom suite with kitchen. 2 stories (no elevator), interior corridors. *Bath:* combo or shower only. **Parking:** on-site. **Terms:** cancellation fee imposed, small pets only. **Amenities:** irons, hair dryers. **Pool(s):** small heated indoor. **Business Services:** meeting rooms, fax (fee). **Cards:** AX, DC, DS, MC, VI.

SOME UNITS

COLUMBUS pop. 25,944

WHERE TO STAY

COMFORT INN *Book great rates at AAA.com* **Phone:** (662)329-2422

Small-scale Hotel

All Year [CP]	1P: $70-$90	2P: $75-$95	XP: $5	F18

Location: Jct US 82 Bypass and 45 N. 1210 US Hwy 45 N 39705. Fax: 662/327-0311. **Facility:** 106 one-bedroom standard units. 2 stories (no elevator), exterior corridors. **Parking:** on-site. **Terms:** cancellation fee imposed. **Amenities:** irons, hair dryers. **Guest Services:** valet laundry, wireless Internet. **Business Services:** meeting rooms, PC. **Cards:** AX, CB, DC, DS, JC, MC, VI.

SOME UNITS

MASTER HOSTS INNS & SUITES *Book at AAA.com* **Phone:** (662)328-5202

Small-scale Hotel

6/1-10/1	1P: $55-$60	2P: $60-$65
12/1-5/31 & 10/2-11/30	1P: $45-$55	2P: $50-$60

Location: US 82, exit US 45 N, just s. 506 Hwy 45 N 39701. Fax: 662/327-6397. **Facility:** 98 one-bedroom standard units. 2 stories (no elevator), exterior corridors. **Parking:** on-site. **Terms:** weekly rates available, [CP] meal plan available, small pets only ($5 extra charge). **Amenities:** irons, hair dryers. **Pool(s):** outdoor. **Guest Services:** valet laundry, wireless Internet. **Business Services:** meeting rooms. **Cards:** AX, DC, DS, MC, VI.

SOME UNITS

FEE

WINGATE INN *Book at AAA.com* **Phone:** 662/327-9999

Small-scale Hotel

Property failed to provide current rates

Location: US 82, exit Military Rd, just s. 129 Brickerton St 39701. Fax: 662/329-1984. **Facility:** 80 one-bedroom standard units. 3 stories, interior corridors. *Bath:* combo or shower only. **Parking:** on-site. **Amenities:** video games (fee), high-speed Internet, dual phone lines, voice mail, safes, irons, hair dryers. **Pool(s):** small heated indoor. **Leisure Activities:** whirlpool, exercise room. **Guest Services:** complimentary evening beverages: Mon-Thurs, valet and coin laundry, wireless Internet. **Business Services:** meeting rooms, business center.

SOME UNITS

WHERE TO DINE

BARNHILL'S BUFFET **Lunch:** $5-$9 **Dinner:** $7-$10 **Phone:** 662/328-4313

American

Location: Jct US 82, just e. 625 18th Ave N 39701. **Hours:** 10:45 am-8:45 pm, Fri-9 pm, Sat 7 am-9 pm, Sun 7 am-8:45 pm. Closed: 12/25. **Features:** Casual dress. **Parking:** on-site. **Cards:** AX, DS, MC, VI.

GRILL AT JACKSON SQUARE **Lunch:** $6-$11 **Dinner:** $6-$14 **Phone:** 662/328-8656

American

Location: On US 45, 0.9 mi n of jct US 82; in Jackson Square. 1927 Hwy 45 N 39705. **Hours:** 11 am-11 pm, Fri & Sat-midnight, Sun-10 pm. Closed: 7/4, 12/24, 12/25. **Reservations:** accepted. **Features:** Casual and comfortable best describe the popular eatery. Offering such favorites as steak, Italian sausage pasta and fried portobello mushrooms, this place is sure to please. Casual dress; cocktails. **Parking:** on-site. **Cards:** AX, DS, MC, VI.

HARVEY'S **Lunch:** $6-$16 **Dinner:** $6-$21 **Phone:** 662/327-1639

American

Location: West end of town. 200 Main St 39701. **Hours:** 11 am-9:30 pm, Fri & Sat-10 pm. Closed: 7/4, 12/24, 12/25; also Sun. **Reservations:** suggested. **Features:** Beef, chicken, pasta, burgers and sandwiches are featured in this casual, family dining experience. Because of the restaurant's popularity, there may be a wait, but the comfortable seating, prompt, polite service, and good food make any wait worthwhile. Dressy casual; cocktails. **Parking:** on-site. **Cards:** AX, DS, MC, VI.

SWEET PEPPERS DELI **Lunch:** $6-$10 **Dinner:** $6-$10 **Phone:** 662/328-6889

Deli/Subs Sandwiches

Location: On US 45, 0.9 mi n of jct US 82; in Jackson Square. 2015 Hwy 45 N 39705. **Hours:** 11 am-10 pm. Closed: 7/4, 12/25; also for dinner 12/24. **Reservations:** not accepted. **Features:** The new and popular loft-style delicatessen serves a wide variety of sandwiches and wraps. Casual dress. **Parking:** on-site. **Cards:** AX, DS, MC, VI.

CORINTH pop. 14,054

WHERE TO STAY

COMFORT INN *Book great rates at AAA.com* **Phone:** 662/287-4421

Property failed to provide current rates

Small-scale Hotel

Location: Jct US 72 and 45, just e. 2101 Hwy 72 W 38834 (PO Box 1557). Fax: 662/286-9535. **Facility:** 98 units. 92 one-bedroom standard units. 6 one-bedroom suites, some with kitchens (no utensils) and/or whirlpools. 2 stories (no elevator), exterior corridors. **Parking:** on-site. **Terms:** pets ($25 deposit). **Amenities:** *Some:* irons, hair dryers. **Pool(s):** small outdoor. **Leisure Activities:** limited exercise equipment. **Guest Services:** valet and coin laundry, wireless Internet. **Business Services:** meeting rooms.

SOME UNITS

FEE

THE GENERALS' QUARTERS BED AND BREAKFAST INN *Book great rates at AAA.com* **Phone:** 662/286-3325

All Year [BP] 1P: $100-$150 2P: $100-$150 XP: $35 D10

Historic Bed & Breakfast

Location: Jct US 45, 2 mi e on US 72, 1.2 mi n on Cass St, then 0.4 mi w on Linden St. Located in the historic district. 924 Fillmore St 38834. Fax: 662/287-8188. **Facility:** You'll enjoy a scrumptious breakfast and good company at this restored Victorian property, originally built as a church in 1870. Smoke free premises. 9 units. 7 one- and 1 two-bedroom standard units. 1 one-bedroom suite. 2 stories (no elevator), interior corridors. *Bath:* combo or shower only. **Parking:** on-site. **Terms:** 3 day cancellation notice-fee imposed. **Amenities:** video library, hair dryers. **Leisure Activities:** hot tub. **Guest Services:** gift shop, valet laundry. **Business Services:** meeting rooms, PC, fax. **Cards:** AX, DS, MC, VI. **Free Special Amenities: full breakfast and local telephone calls.**

D'IBERVILLE pop. 7,608 (See map and index starting on p. 433)

WHERE TO STAY

COMFORT LODGE *Book great rates at AAA.com* **Phone:** (228)396-2110 22

All Year 1P: $69-$140 2P: $69-$140 XP: $10 F12

Small-scale Hotel

Location: I-110, exit 2, just nw. 10226 Rodriguez St 39540. Fax: 228/396-5345. **Facility:** 47 one-bedroom standard units. 2 stories (no elevator), exterior corridors. **Parking:** on-site. **Terms:** [CP] meal plan available. **Amenities:** high-speed Internet, voice mail, irons, hair dryers. **Pool(s):** outdoor. **Leisure Activities:** whirlpool. **Guest Services:** coin laundry, area transportation-casino. **Cards:** AX, DC, DS, MC, VI.

SOME UNITS

SUBURBAN EXTENDED STAY HOTEL *Book great rates at AAA.com* **Phone:** (228)396-5780 23

All Year 1P: $69-$119 2P: $79-$159 XP: $10 F18

Motel

Location: I-110, exit 2, just sw. 10221 Rodriguez St 39540. Fax: 228/396-5782. **Facility:** 132 one-bedroom standard units with efficiencies. 3 stories, exterior corridors. *Bath:* combo or shower only. **Parking:** on-site. **Amenities:** high-speed Internet, voice mail, irons, hair dryers. **Guest Services:** valet and coin laundry. **Cards:** AX, DS, MC, VI.

SOME UNITS

WINGATE INN D'IBERVILLE/BILOXI *Book at AAA.com* **Phone:** (228)396-0036 21

All Year 1P: $99-$139 2P: $99-$139

Small-scale Hotel

Location: I-10, exit 46B, just ne. Located in a quiet area. 12009 Indian River Rd 39540. Fax: 228/396-0073. **Facility:** 101 one-bedroom standard units, some with whirlpools. 4 stories, interior corridors. *Bath:* combo or shower only. **Parking:** on-site. **Terms:** pets ($10 extra charge). **Amenities:** video games (fee), high-speed Internet, dual phone lines, voice mail, safes, irons, hair dryers. **Pool(s):** small outdoor. **Leisure Activities:** whirlpool, exercise room. **Guest Services:** valet and coin laundry, area transportation. **Business Services:** meeting rooms, business center. **Cards:** AX, CB, DC, DS, MC, VI.

SOME UNITS

FEE

ESCATAWPA pop. 3,566

WHERE TO DINE

TUGUS FAMILY RESTAURANT Lunch: $4-$8 Dinner: $5-$15 Phone: 228/474-9910

American

Location: I-10, exit 68, just n. 6909 Hwy 613 39552. **Hours:** 11 am-2 & 5-9 pm, Mon, Tues & Sat from 5 pm. Closed major holidays; also Sun. **Features:** The family-owned restaurant presents a menu of home-style meals. A friendly touch punctuates the service. Casual dress. **Parking:** on-site. **Cards:** MC, VI.

FLOWOOD pop. 4,750 (See map and index starting on p. 451)

WHERE TO STAY

COUNTRY INN & SUITES BY CARLSON *Book at AAA.com* Phone: 601/939-2676 35

Property failed to provide current rates

Small-scale Hotel

Location: I-55, exit 98B/C (Lakeland Dr E), 3 mi e, then just s. 1004 Treetops Blvd 39232. Fax: 601/939-7029. **Facility:** 53 units. 41 one-bedroom standard units, some with whirlpools. 12 one-bedroom suites. 3 stories, interior corridors. *Bath:* combo or shower only. **Parking:** on-site. **Amenities:** high-speed Internet, voice mail, irons, hair dryers. **Pool(s):** small heated indoor. **Leisure Activities:** whirlpool, limited exercise equipment. **Guest Services:** coin laundry. **Business Services:** meeting rooms, business center.

SOME UNITS

FOREST pop. 5,987

WHERE TO STAY

AMERICAS BEST VALUE INN Phone: 601/469-2640

SAVE

Small-scale Hotel

All Year [BP] 1P: $54-$59 2P: $59 XP: $6 F12

Location: I-20, exit 88, just n. 1846 Hwy 35 S 39074 (PO Box 402). Fax: 601/469-3077. **Facility:** 79 one-bedroom standard units. 1 story, exterior corridors. **Parking:** on-site. **Amenities:** high-speed Internet, voice mail, irons, hair dryers. **Dining:** 6-10 am. **Pool(s):** small outdoor. **Guest Services:** valet and coin laundry. **Business Services:** meeting rooms, fax (fee). **Cards:** AX, DC, DS, MC, VI. **Free Special Amenities: full breakfast and high-speed Internet.**

SOME UNITS

COMFORT INN *Book great rates at AAA.com* Phone: 601/469-2100

SAVE

Small-scale Hotel

All Year 1P: $65-$75 2P: $65-$75 XP: $5 F15

Location: I-20, exit 88, just n. 1250 Hwy 35 S 39074. Fax: 601/469-5028. **Facility:** 51 one-bedroom standard units. 2 stories (no elevator), exterior corridors. **Parking:** on-site. **Terms:** pets ($12 extra charge). **Amenities:** high-speed Internet, irons, hair dryers. **Pool(s):** small outdoor. **Guest Services:** wireless Internet. **Cards:** AX, DC, DS, MC, VI. **Free Special Amenities: continental breakfast and local telephone calls.**

SOME UNITS

FEE

DAYS INN *Book great rates at AAA.com* Phone: 601/469-2500

Small-scale Hotel

All Year [CP] 1P: $50-$75 2P: $55-$80

Location: I-20, exit 88, just n. 1280 Hwy 35 S 39074. Fax: 601/469-1465. **Facility:** 38 one-bedroom standard units. 2 stories (no elevator), exterior corridors. **Parking:** on-site. **Amenities:** irons, hair dryers. **Pool(s):** small outdoor. **Leisure Activities:** exercise room. **Guest Services:** wireless Internet. **Cards:** AX, DC, DS, MC, VI.

SOME UNITS

ASK VCR

HOLIDAY INN EXPRESS HOTEL & SUITES *Book at AAA.com* Phone: 601/469-8288

Small-scale Hotel

5/1-9/8	1P: $90-$100	2P: $90-$100	XP: $5	F18
12/1-4/30 & 9/9-11/30	1P: $80-$90	2P: $80-$90	XP: $5	F18

Location: I-20, exit 88, just n. 1275 Hwy 35 S 39074. Fax: 601/469-5454. **Facility:** 62 one-bedroom standard units, some with whirlpools. 3 stories, interior corridors. *Bath:* combo or shower only. **Parking:** on-site. **Amenities:** high-speed Internet, dual phone lines, voice mail, irons, hair dryers. **Pool(s):** small outdoor. **Leisure Activities:** limited exercise equipment. **Guest Services:** valet and coin laundry. **Business Services:** meeting rooms, business center. **Cards:** AX, DC, DS, MC, VI.

SOME UNITS

WHERE TO DINE

PENN'S SANTA FE STEAKHOUSE Lunch: $4-$13 Dinner: $6-$13 Phone: 601/469-2536

American

Location: I-20, exit 88, just s; behind service station. 1550 Hwy 35 S 39074. **Hours:** 11 am-9 pm. Closed major holidays; also Sun. **Features:** Patrons rely on the popular spot for good food, large portions and reasonable prices. Casual dress. **Parking:** on-site. **Cards:** AX, DS, MC, VI.

GREENVILLE pop. 41,633

WHERE TO STAY

COMFORT INN OF GREENVILLE *Book great rates at AAA.com* Phone: (662)378-4976

Small-scale Hotel

All Year 1P: $59-$129 2P: $59-$129 XP: $5 F18

Location: 3 mi e of center. 3080 US 82 E 38702. Fax: 662/378-4980. **Facility:** 77 one-bedroom standard units. 2 stories (no elevator), exterior corridors. *Bath:* combo or shower only. **Parking:** on-site. **Terms:** small pets only ($50 fee). **Amenities:** irons, hair dryers. *Some:* high-speed Internet. **Pool(s):** outdoor. **Guest Services:** valet and coin laundry, wireless Internet. **Cards:** AX, CB, DC, DS, MC, VI.

SOME UNITS

ASK  

FEE

DAYS INN *Book great rates at AAA.com* **Phone:** 662/334-1818

Small-scale Hotel

All Year 1P: $59-$67 2P: $67-$75 XP: $8 F18

Location: 3 mi e on US 82. 2701 Hwy 82 E 38703. Fax: 662/332-1761. **Facility:** 120 one-bedroom standard units. 2 stories (no elevator), exterior corridors. **Parking:** on-site. **Terms:** 7 day cancellation notice, weekly rates available. **Amenities:** voice mail, irons, hair dryers. **Pool(s):** outdoor. **Leisure Activities:** limited exercise equipment, basketball. **Guest Services:** valet and coin laundry, wireless Internet. **Business Services:** meeting rooms. **Cards:** AX, CB, DC, DS, MC, VI.

SOME UNITS

ASK / /

GREENWOOD pop. 18,425

WHERE TO STAY

THE ALLUVIAN HOTEL **Phone:** 662/453-2114

Small-scale Hotel

All Year [BP] 1P: $175-$310

Location: Just w of Main St; downtown. 318 Howard St 38930. Fax: 662/453-2118. **Facility:** Southern hospitality pours out of the exceptional staff at this upscale boutique hotel in the heart of the Mississippi Delta. Luxurious accommodations include a full service spa, New Orleans-style courtyard and fine dining. Visit the Viking cooking school across the street and stroll through downtown's antique and gift shops. 50 units. 49 one-bedroom standard units, some with whirlpools. 1 one-bedroom suite with whirlpool. 4 stories, interior corridors. *Bath:* combo or shower only. **Parking:** on-site. **Terms:** cancellation fee imposed, package plans. **Amenities:** CD players, high-speed Internet, voice mail, safes, honor bars, irons, hair dryers. **Leisure Activities:** exercise room, spa. **Guest Services:** area transportation. **Business Services:** meeting rooms, business center. **Cards:** AX, DS, MC, VI.

SOME UNITS

ASK / /

BEST WESTERN-GREENWOOD *Book great rates at AAA.com* **Phone:** (662)455-5777

AAA SAVE

Small-scale Hotel

All Year 1P: $74-$85 2P: $74-$85 XP: $10 F12

Location: 1 mi w of Main St. 635 Hwy 82 W 38930. Fax: 662/455-4239. **Facility:** 100 one-bedroom standard units. 2 stories (no elevator), interior/exterior corridors. *Bath:* combo or shower only. **Parking:** on-site. **Terms:** 4 day cancellation notice. **Amenities:** video games (fee), high-speed Internet, voice mail, irons, hair dryers. **Pool(s):** heated indoor/outdoor, wading. **Leisure Activities:** racquetball court, exercise room, basketball. **Guest Services:** coin laundry, wireless Internet. **Business Services:** meeting rooms. **Cards:** AX, CB, DC, DS, MC, VI. **Free Special Amenities: continental breakfast and newspaper.**

SOME UNITS

/ /

ECONO LODGE INN & SUITES *Book great rates at AAA.com* **Phone:** (662)453-5974

Small-scale Hotel

All Year [ECP] 1P: $49-$79 2P: $49-$79 XP: $5 F18

Location: 0.4 mi w of Main St. 401 Hwy 82 W 38930. Fax: 662/455-6401. **Facility:** 60 one-bedroom standard units. 2 stories (no elevator), exterior corridors. **Parking:** on-site. **Terms:** small pets only. **Amenities:** irons, hair dryers. **Pool(s):** outdoor. **Guest Services:** wireless Internet. **Cards:** AX, CB, DC, DS, MC, VI.

SOME UNITS

ASK / VCR /

GRENADA pop. 14,879

WHERE TO STAY

AMERICAS BEST VALUE INN *Book at AAA.com* **Phone:** 662/226-7816

Small-scale Hotel

Property failed to provide current rates

Location: I-55, exit 206, just ne on frontage road. 1750 Sunset Dr 38901. Fax: 662/226-5623. **Facility:** 57 one-bedroom standard units. 2 stories (no elevator), exterior corridors. **Parking:** on-site, winter plug-ins. **Terms:** small pets only ($5 fee). **Amenities:** irons, hair dryers. **Pool(s):** small outdoor. **Leisure Activities:** playground, basketball. **Guest Services:** valet laundry, wireless Internet. **Business Services:** meeting rooms, PC.

SOME UNITS

FEE / /

COMFORT INN *Book great rates at AAA.com* **Phone:** (662)226-1683

Small-scale Hotel

All Year 1P: $70-$125 2P: $75-$125 XP: $5 F18

Location: I-55, exit 206, just e on SR 8. 1552 Sunset Dr 38901. Fax: 662/226-9484. **Facility:** 64 one-bedroom standard units. 2 stories (no elevator), exterior corridors. **Parking:** on-site. **Terms:** [ECP] meal plan available. **Amenities:** high-speed Internet, irons, hair dryers. **Pool(s):** outdoor. **Leisure Activities:** whirlpool. **Guest Services:** valet laundry. **Cards:** AX, CB, DC, DS, JC, MC, VI.

SOME UNITS

ASK / /

COUNTRY INN & SUITES BY CARLSON *Book at AAA.com* **Phone:** (662)227-8444

Small-scale Hotel

3/15-10/31 [ECP] 1P: $73-$95 2P: $78-$100 XP: $10 F18

12/1-3/14 & 11/1-11/30 [ECP] 1P: $68-$90 2P: $73-$95 XP: $10 F18

Location: I-55, exit 206, just sw. 255 SW Frontage Rd 38901. Fax: 662/229-0392. **Facility:** 76 units. 45 one-bedroom standard units, some with whirlpools. 31 one-bedroom suites, some with kitchens. 3 stories, interior corridors. **Parking:** on-site. **Terms:** 2 night minimum stay - seasonal and/or weekends, cancellation fee imposed, package plans, pets ($25 fee, with prior approval). **Amenities:** voice mail, irons, hair dryers. **Pool(s):** heated indoor. **Leisure Activities:** exercise room. **Guest Services:** valet and coin laundry, wireless Internet. **Business Services:** meeting rooms. **Cards:** AX, CB, DC, DS, MC, VI.

SOME UNITS

ASK FEE / /

WHERE TO DINE

JAKE & RIP'S — Regional American — **Lunch:** $7-$16 **Dinner:** $7-$16 **Phone:** 662/227-9955

Location: I-55, exit 206, 0.5 mi e on SR 8. 1525 Sunset Dr 38902. **Hours:** 11 am-10 pm, Fri & Sat-11 pm. Closed major holidays. **Features:** Barbecue, steak and catfish are featured at this popular restaurant. Service is attentive and courteous, though there may be some slight delays in getting your meal. If decent food and good value are what you are looking for, this is the place for you. Casual dress; cocktails. **Parking:** on-site. **Cards:** AX, DS, MC, VI.

LA CABANA MEXICAN CANTINA & GRILL — Mexican — **Lunch:** $3-$6 **Dinner:** $5-$22 **Phone:** 662/229-0056

Location: I-55, exit 206, 1.4 mi e on SR 8. 1248 Sunset Dr 38901. **Hours:** 11 am-10 pm, Fri & Sat-11 pm. Closed: 7/4, 11/22, 12/25. **Reservations:** suggested. **Features:** Flavorful Southwestern and Mexican cooking and a festively rustic atmosphere excite the senses at the comfortable, family-favorite eatery. On the menu are traditional favorites, such as tacos and burritos, as well as more inventive selections, including mushroom quesadillas and chicken flautas. Casual dress; cocktails. **Parking:** on-site. **Cards:** AX, DS, MC, VI.

GULFPORT pop. 71,127 (See map and index starting on p. 433)

WHERE TO STAY

BEST WESTERN SEAWAY INN — *Book great rates at AAA.com* — **Phone:** (228)864-0050 — 10

Small-scale Hotel. All Year [ECP] 1P: $50-$200 2P: $50-$200

Location: I-10, exit 34A, just sw. 9475 Hwy 49 39503. Fax: 228/864-0739. **Facility:** 180 one-bedroom standard units, some with whirlpools. 2 stories, exterior corridors. *Bath:* combo or shower only. **Parking:** on-site. **Terms:** small pets only ($10 extra charge). **Amenities:** voice mail, irons, hair dryers. *Some:* high-speed Internet. **Pool(s):** outdoor, wading. **Leisure Activities:** whirlpool, barbecue grills. **Guest Services:** valet and coin laundry, area transportation-casino. **Business Services:** fax (fee). **Cards:** AX, DC, DS, MC, VI. **Free Special Amenities: expanded continental breakfast and newspaper.**

SOME UNITS / FEE

COMFORT INN — *Book great rates at AAA.com* — **Phone:** (228)863-5500 — 17

Small-scale Hotel. All Year 1P: $59-$189 2P: $59-$189 XP: $10 F12

Location: I-10, exit 34A, just sw. 9343 Hwy 49 39503. Fax: 228/863-7341. **Facility:** 68 one-bedroom standard units, some with whirlpools. 2 stories (no elevator), exterior corridors. *Bath:* combo or shower only. **Parking:** on-site. **Amenities:** high-speed Internet, irons, hair dryers. **Pool(s):** small outdoor. **Guest Services:** valet and coin laundry, area transportation-casino. **Cards:** AX, CB, DC, DS, MC, VI. **Free Special Amenities: continental breakfast and high-speed Internet.**

SOME UNITS

CRYSTAL INN — *Book great rates at AAA.com* — **Phone:** (228)822-9600 — 15

Small-scale Hotel. All Year [BP] 1P: $129-$179 2P: $129-$179 XP: $10 F18

Location: I-10, exit 31, just s. 9379 Canal Rd 39503. Fax: 228/822-0666. **Facility:** 110 units. 107 one-bedroom standard units, some with whirlpools. 3 one-bedroom suites. 3 stories, interior corridors. *Bath:* combo or shower only. **Parking:** on-site. **Terms:** package plans, small pets only ($10 extra charge). **Amenities:** video library (fee), voice mail, irons, hair dryers. **Pool(s):** small heated indoor. **Leisure Activities:** whirlpool, sun deck, exercise room. **Guest Services:** sundries, valet and coin laundry, area transportation-casino. **Business Services:** meeting rooms. **Cards:** AX, DC, DS, MC, VI. **Free Special Amenities: full breakfast and high-speed Internet.** *(See color ad p 435)*

SOME UNITS / FEE

GULFPORT BEACHFRONT HOTEL — **Phone:** 228/864-4310 — 18

Small-scale Hotel. fyi. Property failed to provide current rates

Under major renovation, scheduled to be completed February 2006. **Last rated:** ♦♦♦ **Location:** US 90, 0.8 mi e of jct US 49. 1600 E Beach Blvd 39501. Fax: 228/865-0525. **Facility:** 148 one-bedroom standard units, some with whirlpools. 2-5 stories, interior/exterior corridors. *Bath:* combo or shower only. **Parking:** on-site. **Terms:** small pets only ($100 fee). **Amenities:** voice mail, irons, hair dryers. **Pool(s):** outdoor, wading. **Leisure Activities:** exercise room. **Guest Services:** valet and coin laundry, area transportation. **Business Services:** meeting rooms, business center.

SOME UNITS / FEE

HAMPTON INN — *Book great rates at AAA.com* — **Phone:** (228)868-3300 — 11

Small-scale Hotel. All Year [BP] 1P: $99-$199 2P: $109-$209 XP: $10 F17

Location: I-10, exit 34A, just sw. 9445 Hwy 49 39503. Fax: 228/864-3347. **Facility:** 155 one-bedroom standard units, some with whirlpools. 3 stories, exterior corridors. *Bath:* combo or shower only. **Parking:** on-site. **Amenities:** voice mail, irons, hair dryers. **Pool(s):** outdoor, wading. **Guest Services:** coin laundry, area transportation-casino. **Business Services:** meeting rooms. **Cards:** AX, DC, DS, MC, VI.

SOME UNITS

HOLIDAY INN AIRPORT — *Book at AAA.com* — **Phone:** (228)868-8200 — 13

Small-scale Hotel. All Year 1P: $99 2P: $150 XP: $10 F17

Location: I-10, exit 34A, 0.6 mi s. 9415 Hwy 49 39503. Fax: 228/865-9164. **Facility:** 152 units. 150 one-bedroom standard units. 1 one- and 1 two-bedroom suites. 2 stories (no elevator), exterior corridors. *Bath:* combo or shower only. **Parking:** on-site. **Terms:** package plans, small pets only ($35 fee). **Amenities:** dual phone lines, voice mail, irons, hair dryers. **Pool(s):** heated outdoor, wading. **Leisure Activities:** exercise room. **Guest Services:** valet and coin laundry. **Business Services:** meeting rooms, business center. **Cards:** AX, DC, DS, MC, VI.

SOME UNITS

(See map and index starting on p. 433)

HOLIDAY INN EXPRESS Book great rates at AAA.com Phone: (228)864-7222 12

Small-scale Hotel

All Year 1P: $89-$139 2P: $89-$139 XP: $5 F

Location: I-10, exit 34A, 0.6 mi s. 9435 Hwy 49 39503. Fax: 228/864-7454. **Facility:** 112 one-bedroom standard units, some with whirlpools. 2 stories (no elevator), exterior corridors. *Bath:* combo or shower only. **Parking:** on-site. **Terms:** [ECP] meal plan available, small pets only ($35 fee). **Amenities:** high-speed Internet, voice mail, irons, hair dryers. **Guest Services:** complimentary evening beverages, valet and coin laundry. **Business Services:** meeting rooms. **Cards:** AX, DC, DS, MC, VI. **Free Special Amenities: expanded continental breakfast and high-speed Internet.**

SOME UNITS

FEE

MOTEL 6 #416 Book at AAA.com Phone: 228/863-1890 16

Motel

12/1-5/24 1P: $79-$89 2P: $85-$95 XP: $3 F17

5/25-11/30 1P: $59-$69 2P: $65-$75 XP: $3 F17

Location: I-10, exit 34A, just s. 9355 US Hwy 49 39503. Fax: 228/868-2445. **Facility:** 98 one-bedroom standard units. 2 stories (no elevator), exterior corridors. *Bath:* combo or shower only. **Parking:** on-site. **Pool(s):** outdoor. **Guest Services:** coin laundry. **Cards:** AX, CB, DC, DS, MC, VI.

SOME UNITS

WHERE TO DINE

BARNHILL'S BUFFET **Lunch:** $5-$9 **Dinner:** $7-$10 **Phone:** 228/539-5886

American

Location: Jct 5th St, just n. 11487 Hwy 49 N 39503. **Hours:** 10:45 am-8:45 pm, Fri-9 pm, Sat 7 am-9 pm, Sun 7 am-8:45 pm. Closed: 12/25. **Features:** Casual dress. **Parking:** on-site. **Cards:** AX, DS, MC, VI.

BLOW FLY INN **Lunch:** $6-$25 **Dinner:** $6-$25 **Phone:** 228/896-9812 8

American

Location: I-10, exit 38 (Lorraine-Cowan), 3 mi s to W Pine St, then 0.3 mi w, follow signs. 1201 Washington Ave 39501. **Hours:** 11 am-9 pm, Fri & Sat-10 pm. Closed: 11/22, 12/24, 12/25 & Easter. **Reservations:** suggested. **Features:** For more than 30 years, the inn has served traditional fare, such as steak and seafood, in a nontraditional manner. As a testament to its sense of humor, the staff has a custom of garnishing each plate with a plastic fly. Whether dining on the dock or along the wall of windows, guests enjoy fantastic views and good food. Casual dress; beer only. **Parking:** on-site. **Cards:** AX, DS, MC, VI.

CHINA STAR RESTAURANT **Lunch:** $6 **Dinner:** $8 **Phone:** 228/897-1111 9

Chinese

Location: Just nw of US 90. 353 Courthouse Rd 39507. **Hours:** 11 am-4 & 4:30-9 pm, Fri & Sat-10 pm, Sun 11:30 am-4 & 4:30-9 pm. Closed: 11/22, 12/25. **Reservations:** accepted. **Features:** The restaurant gives diners a pleasant alternative to fried seafood but still uses the local catch in interesting Szechuan and Mandarin preparations. The comfortable setting, just north of the beach, is decorated modestly. The buffet affords an ample selection of choices. Casual dress; beer only. **Parking:** on-site. **Cards:** AX, DS, MC, VI.

VRAZEL'S **Lunch:** $9-$24 **Dinner:** $14-$30 **Phone:** 228/863-2229 10

Regional American

Location: On US 90, just w of jct US 49; opposite Grand Casino. 3206 W Beach Blvd 39501. **Hours:** 11 am-2 & 5-10 pm. Closed: 1/1, 12/24, 12/25; also Sun. **Reservations:** suggested. **Features:** Vrazel's presents fine dining with all the trimmings — white tablecloths, candles, fresh-cut flowers. The upscale cuisine includes many gourmet-style dishes such as seafood a la Vrazel, a delicious combination of fresh shrimp, scallops and crabmeat. Dressy casual; cocktails. **Parking:** on-site. **Cards:** AX, DC, DS, MC, VI.

HATTIESBURG pop. 44,779

WHERE TO STAY

BAYMONT INN & SUITES-HATTIESBURG Book at AAA.com **Phone:** (601)264-8380

Small-scale Hotel

2/1-10/31 1P: $98-$115 2P: $98-$115

12/1-1/31 & 11/1-11/30 1P: $90-$96 2P: $90-$96

Location: I-59, exit 65, just nw. 123 Plaza Dr 39402. Fax: 601/264-8381. **Facility:** 92 units. 88 one-bedroom standard units. 4 one-bedroom suites ($99-$115). 4 stories, interior corridors. *Bath:* combo or shower only. **Parking:** on-site. **Terms:** cancellation fee imposed, [ECP] meal plan available, package plans. **Amenities:** video games (fee), high-speed Internet, voice mail, irons, hair dryers. **Pool(s):** outdoor. **Leisure Activities:** limited exercise equipment. **Guest Services:** valet and coin laundry. **Business Services:** meeting rooms, fax. **Cards:** AX, DS, MC, VI.

SOME UNITS

ASK

COMFORT INN UNIVERSITY-THE LODGE Book great rates at AAA.com **Phone:** (601)264-1881

Small-scale Hotel

All Year [CP] 1P: $89-$129 2P: $99-$139 XP: $10 F18

Location: I-59, exit 67A, just s. 6541 US Hwy 49 39401. Fax: 601/268-3226. **Facility:** 160 one-bedroom standard units. 2 stories (no elevator), interior/exterior corridors. **Parking:** on-site. **Terms:** cancellation fee imposed, small pets only ($25 fee). **Amenities:** high-speed Internet, voice mail, irons, hair dryers. **Pool(s):** outdoor. **Guest Services:** complimentary evening beverages, coin laundry. **Cards:** AX, DC, DS, MC, VI.

SOME UNITS

ASK

FEE

COMFORT SUITES Book great rates at AAA.com **Phone:** (601)261-5555

Small-scale Hotel

All Year [CP] 1P: $109-$145 2P: $119-$155 XP: $10 F18

Location: I-59, exit 65, just nw. 122 Plaza Dr 39402. Fax: 601/261-5555. **Facility:** 67 units. 64 one-bedroom standard units, some with whirlpools. 3 one-bedroom suites with whirlpools. 3 stories, interior corridors. *Bath:* combo or shower only. **Parking:** on-site. **Terms:** cancellation fee imposed. **Amenities:** high-speed Internet, irons, hair dryers. **Pool(s):** small heated indoor. **Leisure Activities:** exercise room. **Guest Services:** valet and coin laundry, wireless Internet. **Business Services:** meeting rooms, business center. **Cards:** AX, DC, DS, MC, VI.

SOME UNITS

ASK VCR

DAYS INN - HATTIESBURG Book great rates at AAA.com Phone: 601/268-1157

Small-scale Hotel

Property failed to provide current rates

Location: I-59, exit 65A southbound; exit 65B northbound, just e. Located in commercial area. 111 Thornhill Dr 39402. Fax: 601/268-1992. **Facility:** 58 one-bedroom standard units. 2 stories (no elevator), interior corridors. *Bath:* combo or shower only. **Parking:** on-site. **Amenities:** irons, hair dryers. *Some:* high-speed Internet. **Leisure Activities:** exercise room. **Guest Services:** coin laundry. **Business Services:** meeting rooms, fax (fee).

SOME UNITS

FAIRFIELD INN HATTIESBURG Book great rates at AAA.com Phone: (601)296-7777

Small-scale Hotel

All Year 1P: $79-$109 2P: $79-$109

Location: I-59, exit 65, 0.5 mi e, then n. 173 Thornhill Rd 39402. Fax: 601/296-7777. **Facility:** 79 one-bedroom standard units. 3 stories, interior corridors. *Bath:* combo or shower only. **Parking:** on-site. **Amenities:** irons, hair dryers. **Pool(s):** heated indoor. **Leisure Activities:** whirlpool, exercise room. **Guest Services:** valet laundry. **Business Services:** PC. **Cards:** AX, CB, DC, DS, JC, MC, VI.

SOME UNITS

HAMPTON INN OF HATTIESBURG Book great rates at AAA.com Phone: 601/264-8080

Small-scale Hotel

Property failed to provide current rates

Location: I-59, exit 65, just nw. 4301 Hardy St 39402. Fax: 601/268-9916. **Facility:** 154 one-bedroom standard units, some with whirlpools. 2 stories (no elevator), interior/exterior corridors. *Bath:* combo or shower only. **Parking:** on-site. **Terms:** small pets only. **Amenities:** video games (fee), voice mail, irons, hair dryers. **Pool(s):** outdoor. **Guest Services:** complimentary evening beverages: Mon-Thurs, valet laundry. **Business Services:** meeting rooms.

SOME UNITS

HOLIDAY INN HOTEL & SUITES Book at AAA.com Phone: (601)296-0302

Small-scale Hotel

All Year 1P: $104-$159 2P: $104-$159 XP: $10 F18

Location: I-59, exit 67B, just n to Classic Dr, then just sw. 10 Gateway Dr 39402. Fax: 601/296-0343. **Facility:** 96 one-bedroom standard units, some with efficiencies and/or whirlpools. 5 stories, interior corridors. *Bath:* combo or shower only. **Parking:** on-site. **Terms:** cancellation fee imposed. **Amenities:** high-speed Internet, dual phone lines, voice mail, irons, hair dryers. **Pool(s):** small outdoor, small heated indoor. **Leisure Activities:** putting green, exercise room, sports court. **Guest Services:** complimentary evening beverages: Mon-Thurs, coin laundry. **Business Services:** meeting rooms. **Cards:** AX, DC, DS, MC, VI.

SOME UNITS

INN ON THE HILL AT CONVENTION CENTER Book great rates at AAA.com Phone: (601)599-2001

AAA SAVE

Small-scale Hotel

All Year 1P: $81-$90 2P: $81-$90 XP: $6 F18

Location: I-59, exit 67A, just se. Located in a commercial area. 6595 Hwy 49 N 39401. Fax: 601/599-2002. **Facility:** 119 units. 118 one-bedroom standard units. 1 one-bedroom suite ($135-$150). 2 stories (no elevator), exterior corridors. **Parking:** on-site. **Terms:** [BP] meal plan available, small pets only ($25 fee). **Amenities:** irons, hair dryers. **Dining:** 6-9:30 am, 11-2 & 5-9 pm, cocktails. **Pool(s):** outdoor. **Guest Services:** valet and coin laundry. **Business Services:** meeting rooms, fax (fee). **Cards:** AX, DC, DS, MC, VI. **Free Special Amenities: full breakfast and high-speed Internet.**

SOME UNITS

FEE

MOTEL 6 #0235 Book at AAA.com Phone: 601/544-6096

Motel

5/25-11/30	1P: $46-$56	2P: $52-$62	XP: $6	F17
12/1-5/24	1P: $39-$49	2P: $45-$55	XP: $3	F17

Location: I-59, exit 67A, 0.5 mi e. 6508 US Hwy 49 N 39401. Fax: 601/582-7743. **Facility:** 117 one-bedroom standard units. 2 stories (no elevator), exterior corridors. *Bath:* combo or shower only. **Parking:** on-site. **Terms:** small pets only. **Pool(s):** outdoor. **Guest Services:** coin laundry. **Cards:** AX, CB, DC, DS, MC, VI.

SOME UNITS

QUALITY INN & SUITES Phone: 601/296-0565

fyi

Small-scale Hotel

Under construction, scheduled to open May 2007. **Location:** I-59, exit 67A, 5 mi s. 6511 US Hwy 49 N 39401. Fax: 601/296-0596. **Planned Amenities:** coffeemakers, microwaves, refrigerators.

SUPER 8 MOTEL-HATTIESBURG Book great rates at AAA.com Phone: (601)264-2885

AAA SAVE

Motel

All Year 1P: $55-$90 2P: $55-$90 XP: $10 F12

Location: I-59, exit 67A, 0.5 mi se. 6529 Hwy 49 N 39401. Fax: 601/264-2885. **Facility:** 42 one-bedroom standard units. 2 stories (no elevator), exterior corridors. *Bath:* combo or shower only. **Parking:** on-site. **Terms:** [CP] meal plan available, package plans. **Guest Services:** coin laundry. **Cards:** AX, DC, DS, MC, VI. **Free Special Amenities: continental breakfast and high-speed Internet.**

SOME UNITS

UNIVERSITY INN Phone: 601/268-2850

Small-scale Hotel

All Year 1P: $84 2P: $89

Location: I-59, exit 67A, just se. 6563 Hwy 49 N 39401. Fax: 601/268-2823. **Facility:** 128 one-bedroom standard units. 2 stories (no elevator), interior corridors. **Parking:** on-site. **Terms:** small pets only ($25 fee). **Amenities:** irons, hair dryers. **Pool(s):** small outdoor. **Leisure Activities:** exercise room. **Guest Services:** valet laundry. **Business Services:** conference facilities. **Cards:** AX, DC, DS, MC, VI.

SOME UNITS

FEE

WESTERN MOTEL **Phone:** 601/264-0010

Motel

All Year 1P: $50-$90 2P: $60-$100 XP: $10 D17

Location: I-59, exit 65, 0.6 mi e. 3501 Hardy St 39402. Fax: 601/264-0010. **Facility:** 45 one-bedroom standard units. 2 stories (no elevator), exterior corridors. **Parking:** on-site. **Business Services:** fax (fee). **Cards:** AX, CB, DC, DS, JC, MC, VI. **Free Special Amenities: continental breakfast and high-speed Internet.**

SOME UNITS

WHERE TO DINE

BARNHILL'S BUFFET **Lunch:** $5-$9 **Dinner:** $7-$10 **Phone:** 601/264-1644

American

Location: I-59, exit 65, 0.9 mi e on SR 198. 3317 Hardy St 39401. **Hours:** 10:45 am-8:45 pm, Fri-9 pm, Sat 7 am-9 pm, Sun 7 am-8:45 pm. Closed: 12/25. **Features:** Casual dress. **Parking:** on-site. **Cards:** AX, DS, MC, VI.

COPELAND'S **Lunch:** $7-$20 **Dinner:** $7-$20 **Phone:** 601/296-9300

Cajun

Location: I-55, exit 65, 0.4 mi w on US 98. 4591 Hardy St 39402. **Hours:** 11 am-11 pm, Fri & Sat-midnight. Closed major holidays. **Reservations:** accepted. **Features:** The New Orleans-style restaurant serves Louisiana Cajun cuisine in a lively Mardi Gras atmosphere. Meats, fish and chicken are grilled over cured hickory wood. Complementing menu offerings are made-from-scratch biscuits, tempting homemade ice cream, fresh vegetables and sauces made from drippings. Efficient servers deliver hearty helpings of regional food, such as grilled chicken breasts with fried sweet potatoes, fried oysters, barbecue shrimp and grilled and Cajun seafood. Casual dress; cocktails. **Parking:** on-site. **Cards:** AX, DC, DS, MC, VI.

CRESCENT CITY GRILL **Lunch:** $7-$17 **Dinner:** $7-$17 **Phone:** 601/264-0657

Cajun

Location: I-59, exit 65, 0.4 mi e. 3804 Hardy St 39404. **Hours:** 11 am-10 pm, Fri & Sat-11 pm. Closed major holidays. **Features:** In a bustling commercial area, the restaurant presents a Cajun/Creole menu that emphasizes seafood. Casual dress; cocktails. **Parking:** on-site. **Cards:** AX, DS, MC, VI.

PANINO'S **Lunch:** $7-$12 **Dinner:** $7-$20 **Phone:** 601/264-0605

Italian

Location: I-59, exit 65, 0.5 mi e. 3801 Hardy St 39406. **Hours:** 11 am-10 pm. Closed major holidays; also Sun. **Reservations:** accepted. **Features:** Rich desserts and varied Italian dishes make the restaurant a favorite with both college students and locals. Brick-oven pizzas are made in front of guests, and pianists entertain in the evenings. Casual dress; cocktails. **Parking:** on-site. **Cards:** AX, MC, VI.

PURPLE PARROT CAFE' **Lunch:** $8-$16 **Dinner:** $16-$29 **Phone:** 601/264-0656

Cajun

Location: I-59, exit 65, 0.4 mi e. 3810 Hardy St 39402. **Hours:** 11 am-2 & 6-10 pm, Fri-11 pm, Sat 6 pm-11 pm, Sun 11 am-2 pm. Closed major holidays. **Reservations:** suggested. **Features:** A Southern Mississippi flair punctuates tempting selections of Creole and Cajun cuisine. A cozy, upscale atmosphere makes this a perfect place for a night on the town. Dressy casual; cocktails. **Parking:** on-site. **Cards:** AX, DS, MC, VI.

HERNANDO pop. 6,812

WHERE TO STAY

SASSAFRAS INN BED & BREAKFAST **Phone:** 662/429-5864

Property failed to provide current rates

Bed & Breakfast

Location: Jct SR 304 W, 1.8 mi n. Located in a rural area. 785 Hwy 51 S 38632. Fax: 662/429-5864. **Facility:** On the outskirts of town, the inn is a comfortable guest house with a pleasant owner and many modern conveniences. Smoke free premises. 4 units. 3 one-bedroom standard units. 1 cottage with whirlpool. 1-2 stories (no elevator), interior/exterior corridors. *Bath:* combo or shower only. **Parking:** on-site. **Terms:** age restrictions may apply. **Amenities:** video library, DVD players, irons, hair dryers. **Pool(s):** heated indoor. **Leisure Activities:** whirlpool. **Guest Services:** wireless Internet. **Business Services:** fax.

SOME UNITS

VCR

HOLLY SPRINGS pop. 7,957

WHERE TO STAY

HAMPTON INN *Book great rates at AAA.com* **Phone:** 662/252-5444

Property failed to provide current rates

Small-scale Hotel

Location: US 78, exit 30, just sw. 100 Brooks Rd 38635. Fax: 662/252-2888. **Facility:** 52 one-bedroom standard units. 2 stories, interior corridors. *Bath:* combo or shower only. **Parking:** on-site. **Terms:** pets ($10 extra charge). **Amenities:** video games (fee), high-speed Internet, voice mail, irons, hair dryers. **Pool(s):** small outdoor.

SOME UNITS

FEE

HORN LAKE pop. 14,099

WHERE TO STAY

DAYS INN *Book great rates at AAA.com* **Phone:** (662)349-3493

Small-scale Hotel

All Year 1P: $72-$89 2P: $72-$89 XP: $7 D17

Location: I-55, exit 289, just nw. 801 Desoto Cove 38637. Fax: 662/349-6653. **Facility:** 49 one-bedroom standard units, some with whirlpools. 3 stories, interior corridors. *Bath:* combo or shower only. **Parking:** on-site. **Terms:** [ECP] meal plan available, pets ($10 fee). **Amenities:** high-speed Internet, voice mail, irons, hair dryers. **Pool(s):** small outdoor. **Leisure Activities:** exercise room. **Guest Services:** coin laundry. **Business Services:** business center. **Cards:** AX, DC, DS, MC, VI. **Free Special Amenities: expanded continental breakfast and high-speed Internet.**

SOME UNITS

FEE

DRURY INN & SUITES-MEMPHIS SOUTH *Book at AAA.com* **Phone:** (662)349-6622

Small-scale Hotel

All Year [BP] 1P: $85-$120 2P: $95-$130 XP: $10 F18

Location: I-55, exit 289, just sw. 735 Goodman Rd W 38637. Fax: 662/349-6622. **Facility:** 159 units. 124 one-bedroom standard units. 35 one-bedroom suites ($130-$160). 6 stories, interior corridors. *Bath:* combo or shower only. **Parking:** on-site. **Amenities:** high-speed Internet, dual phone lines, voice mail, irons, hair dryers. **Pool(s):** heated indoor/outdoor. **Leisure Activities:** whirlpool, limited exercise equipment. **Guest Services:** complimentary evening beverages, valet and coin laundry, wireless Internet. **Business Services:** meeting rooms, PC. **Cards:** AX, CB, DC, DS, MC, VI.

SOME UNITS

ASK

MOTEL 6 *Book at AAA.com* **Phone:** 662/349-4439

Small-scale Hotel

3/1-11/30 1P: $44-$59 2P: $55-$65 XP: $6 F
12/1-2/28 1P: $40-$59 2P: $55-$65 XP: $3 F

Location: I-55, exit 289, just se. 701 Southwest Dr 38637. Fax: 662/349-4426. **Facility:** 57 one-bedroom standard units. 3 stories, interior corridors. *Bath:* combo or shower only. **Parking:** on-site. **Terms:** cancellation fee imposed, small pets only. **Amenities:** high-speed Internet. **Pool(s):** outdoor. **Guest Services:** coin laundry. **Cards:** AX, DC, DS, MC, VI.

SOME UNITS

SLEEP INN *Book great rates at AAA.com* **Phone:** (662)349-2773

Small-scale Hotel

All Year 1P: $82-$87 2P: $90-$95

Location: I-55, exit 289, just nw. 708 Desoto Cove 38637. Fax: 662/349-3744. **Facility:** 79 one-bedroom standard units. 2 stories, interior corridors. *Bath:* combo or shower only. **Parking:** on-site. **Terms:** [ECP] meal plan available. **Amenities:** high-speed Internet, voice mail, irons, hair dryers. **Pool(s):** small outdoor. **Leisure Activities:** exercise room. **Guest Services:** coin laundry, wireless Internet. **Business Services:** business center. **Cards:** AX, CB, DC, DS, MC, VI.

SOME UNITS

ASK

WHERE TO DINE

EL CHARRO **Lunch:** $4-$6 **Dinner:** $6-$11 **Phone:** 662/280-2610

Mexican

Location: I-55, exit 289, 1.1 mi w. 1651 Goodman Rd W 38637. **Hours:** 11 am-10 pm, Fri & Sat-10:30 pm. Closed major holidays. **Features:** The cozy Mexican restaurant has a standard menu, but the food is consistently good. Among traditional favorites are tacos and burritos. Casual dress; cocktails. **Parking:** on-site. **Cards:** AX, MC, VI.

INDIANOLA pop. 12,066

WHERE TO STAY

BEST WESTERN BLUES TRAVELER INN *Book great rates at AAA.com* **Phone:** (662)887-6611

Small-scale Hotel

All Year 1P: $55-$159 2P: $55-$179 XP: $6 F12

Location: Just w of jct US 49 W. 910 Hwy 82 E 38751. Fax: 662/887-1317. **Facility:** 49 one-bedroom standard units, some with whirlpools. 2 stories (no elevator), exterior corridors. **Parking:** on-site. **Terms:** [CP] meal plan available. **Amenities:** voice mail, irons, hair dryers. *Some:* high-speed Internet. **Pool(s):** outdoor. **Guest Services:** coin laundry, wireless Internet. **Business Services:** meeting rooms, PC. **Cards:** AX, CB, DC, DS, JC, MC, VI. **Free Special Amenities: early check-in/late check-out and preferred room (subject to availability with advance reservations).**

SOME UNITS

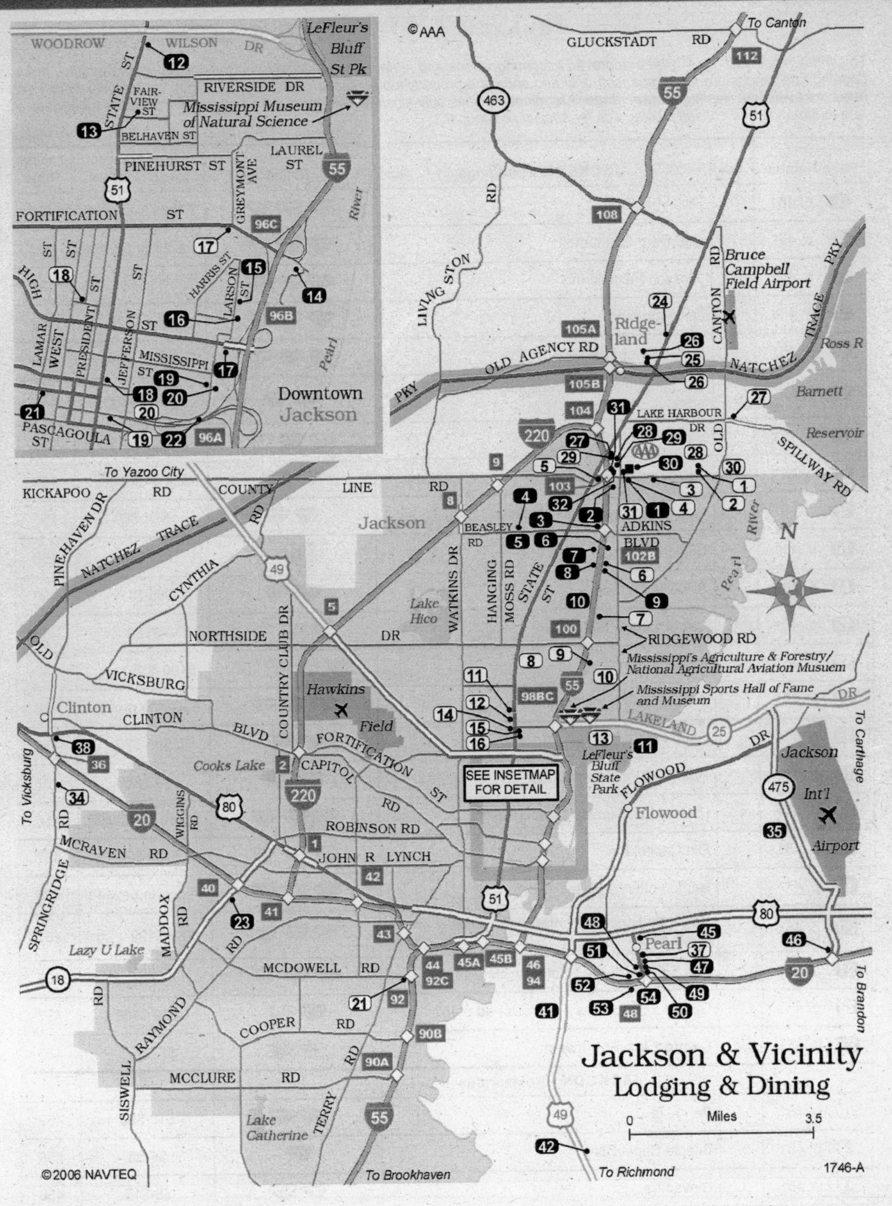

Jackson & Vicinity
Lodging & Dining
©AAA
©2006 NAVTEQ
1746-A
Miles
0
3.5
N
SEE INSETMAP FOR DETAIL
Downtown Jackson
LeFleur's Bluff St Pk
Mississippi Museum of Natural Science
WOODROW
WILSON DR
RIVERSIDE DR
FAIR-VIEW ST
BELHAVEN ST
STATE ST
PINEHURST ST
LAUREL ST
GREYMONT AVE
FORTIFICATION ST
HARRIS ST
LARSON ST
HIGH ST
LAMAR ST
WEST ST
PRESIDENT ST
JEFFERSON ST
MISSISSIPPI ST
PASCAGOULA ST
Pearl River
To Canton
GLUCKSTADT RD
LIVINGSTON RD
Bruce Campbell Field Airport
CANTON RD
Ridgeland
OLD AGENCY RD
NATCHEZ TRACE PKY
Ross R Barnett Reservoir
LAKE HARBOUR DR
OLD CANTON RD
SPILLWAY RD
To Yazoo City
KICKAPOO RD
COUNTY LINE RD
PINEHAVEN DR
CYNTHIA RD
Jackson
BEASLEY RD
ADKINS BLVD
WATKINS DR
HANGING MOSS RD
STATE ST
Lake Hico
NORTHSIDE DR
OLD VICKSBURG
COUNTRY CLUB DR
RIDGEWOOD RD
Mississippi's Agriculture & Forestry/ National Agricultural Aviation Musuem
Mississippi Sports Hall of Fame and Museum
LAKELAND DR
Hawkins Field
Clinton
CLINTON BLVD
Cooks Lake
CAPITOL ST
FORTIFICATION ST
ROBINSON RD
JOHN R LYNCH
LeFleur's Bluff State Park
FLOWOOD DR
Flowood
Jackson Int'l Airport
To Carthage
To Vicksburg
SPRINGRIDGE RD
MCRAVEN RD
WIGGINS RD
MADDOX RD
Lazy U Lake
MCDOWELL RD
Pearl
To Brandon
RAYMOND RD
SISWELL RD
COOPER RD
MCCLURE RD
TERRY RD
Lake Catherine
To Brookhaven
To Richmond

Jackson & Vicinity

This index helps you "spot" where approved accommodations and restaurants are located on the corresponding detailed maps. Lodging rate ranges are for comparison only and show the property's high season; rates are per night, unless only weekly (W) rates are available. Restaurant rate range is for dinner, unless only lunch (L) is served. Turn to the listing page for more detailed rate information and consult display ads for special promotions.

Spotter/Map Page Number	OA	**JACKSON** - Lodgings	Diamond Rating	Rate Range High Season	Listing Page
1 / p. 451		Hilton Jackson	♦♦♦	Failed to provide	456
2 / p. 451		Courtyard By Marriott	♦♦♦	Failed to provide	455
3 / p. 451		Jackson Fairfield Inn	♦♦♦	$65-$95	456
4 / p. 451		Jameson Inn	♦♦♦	$54-$120	456
5 / p. 451		Best Western Jackson North	♦♦♦	Failed to provide	455
6 / p. 451		La Quinta Inn Jackson (North) - see color ad p 386	♦♦	$64-$80	457
7 / p. 451		Hampton Inn North	♦♦♦	$85-$113	456
8 / p. 451	AAA	**Jackson Inn & Suites**	♦♦	$74-$100 SAVE	456
9 / p. 451		Extended StayAmerica Jackson-North	♦♦	$54-$69	455
10 / p. 451		Clarion Hotel	fyi	$79-$119	455
11 / p. 451		Sleep Inn Airport	♦♦	$85-$112	458
12 / p. 451	AAA	**Cabot Lodge Millsaps**	♦♦♦	$79-$129 SAVE	455
13 / p. 451	AAA	**Fairview Inn**	♦♦♦♦	$100-$350 SAVE	456
14 / p. 451		Residence Inn by Marriott	♦♦♦	Failed to provide	458
15 / p. 451		Days Inn Coliseum	♦♦	$55-$75	455
16 / p. 451		Red Roof Inn Fairgrounds	♦♦	$42-$63	457
17 / p. 451		Holiday Inn Express Hotel & Suites	♦♦♦	Failed to provide	456
18 / p. 451		Old Capitol Inn	♦♦♦	$135-$225	457
19 / p. 451		Hampton Inn & Suites	♦♦♦	Failed to provide	456
20 / p. 451	AAA	**Regency Hotel & Conference Center** - see color ad p 457	♦♦♦	$89-$129 SAVE	457
21 / p. 451		The Edison Walthall Hotel	♦♦♦	$99	455
22 / p. 451		Quality Inn & Suites - see color ad p 457	♦♦	$80-$109	457
23 / p. 451	AAA	**Comfort Inn Southwest**	♦♦	$69 SAVE	455
		JACKSON - Restaurants			
1 / p. 451		Pan-Asia	♦♦	$10-$23	459
2 / p. 451		Beagle Bagel Cafe	♦	$6-$8	458
3 / p. 451		Giovanni's	♦♦	$8-$17	458
4 / p. 451		Huntington's Grille	♦♦♦	$18-$44	459
5 / p. 451		Nagoya Japanese Cuisine & Sushi Bar	♦♦	$10-$19	459
6 / p. 451	AAA	**Steam Room Grille**	♦♦♦	$15-$30	459
7 / p. 451		Old Venice Pizza Co	♦♦	$7-$16	459
8 / p. 451		Mikhail's Northgate	♦	$7-$10(L)	459
9 / p. 451		Bravo!	♦♦♦	$14-$30	458

Spotter/Map Page Number	OA	JACKSON - Restaurants (continued)	Diamond Rating	Rate Range High Season	Listing Page
10 / p. 451		Char	◆◆◆	$8-$30	458
11 / p. 451		Broad Street Baking Company & Cafe	◆	$5-$10	458
12 / p. 451		Walker's Drive-In	◆◆◆	$21-$29	460
13 / p. 451		Nick's	◆◆◆	$19-$34	459
14 / p. 451		Que Sera'Sera'	◆◆	$6-$25	459
15 / p. 451		El Ranchero Mexican Restaurant	◆	$7-$10	458
16 / p. 451		Schimmel's	◆◆◆	$7-$16(L)	459
17 / p. 451		La Cazuela Mexican Restaurant	◆◆	$7-$12	459
18 / p. 451		Two Sisters' Kitchen	◆	$9-$14(L)	459
19 / p. 451		Hal & Mal's Restaurant and Brewery	◆	$8-$24	458
20 / p. 451		Dennery's	◆◆◆	$18-$35	458
21 / p. 451		Thai House Restaurant	◆◆	$8-$15	459
		RIDGELAND - Lodgings			
26 / p. 451	AAA	**Days Inn And Suites Ridgeland/Madison**	◆◆	$68-$109 SAVE	475
27 / p. 451		Red Roof Inn Ridgeland	◆◆	$46-$58	476
28 / p. 451		Quality Inn North	◆◆	$70-$80	476
29 / p. 451		Econo Lodge	◆◆	$50-$60	475
30 / p. 451		Homewood Suites by Hilton	◆◆◆	$149	475
31 / p. 451		Cabot Lodge of Jackson North	◆◆◆	$88-$155	475
32 / p. 451		Drury Inn & Suites-Jackson, MS	◆◆◆	$75-$135	475
		RIDGELAND - Restaurants			
24 / p. 451		The Trace Grill	◆	$5-$17	476
25 / p. 451		Cock of the Walk	◆◆	$10	476
26 / p. 451		The Parker House	◆◆◆	$19-$36	476
27 / p. 451		Deja Vu	◆◆	$9-$22	476
28 / p. 451		Little Tokyo	◆◆	$6-$17	476
29 / p. 451		Shapley's	◆◆◆	$18-$35	476
30 / p. 451		Amerigo	◆◆◆	$7-$29	476
31 / p. 451		AJ's Seafood Grille	◆◆	$12-$37	476
		FLOWOOD - Lodgings			
35 / p. 451		Country Inn & Suites By Carlson	◆◆◆	Failed to provide	444
		CLINTON - Lodgings			
38 / p. 451		Days Inn	◆◆	Failed to provide	442
		CLINTON - Restaurant			
34 / p. 451		Archestratus Grill	◆◆	$13-$27	442
		RICHLAND - Lodgings			
41 / p. 451		Executive Inn & Suites	◆◆	$45-$59	475
42 / p. 451		Best Western Richland Inn & Suites	◆◆	$75-$85	475

Spotter/Map Page Number	OA	PEARL - Lodgings	Diamond Rating	Rate Range High Season	Listing Page
45 / p. 451		Comfort Inn Airport	2 Diamonds	$65-$95	472
46 / p. 451	AAA	**Super 8 Motel**	2 Diamonds	$46-$66 SAVE	473
47 / p. 451		Econo Lodge-Airport	2 Diamonds	Failed to provide	472
48 / p. 451	AAA	**Best Western Airport Inn**	2 Diamonds	$70-$75 SAVE	472
49 / p. 451		Holiday Inn Express-Airport	2 Diamonds	Failed to provide	473
50 / p. 451		Hampton Inn-Airport	3 Diamonds	Failed to provide	473
51 / p. 451		Fairfield Inn & Suites	3 Diamonds	Failed to provide	472
52 / p. 451		Jameson Inn of Pearl	3 Diamonds	$54-$120	473
53 / p. 451	AAA	**Country Inn & Suites By Carlson**	3 Diamonds	$89 SAVE	472
54 / p. 451		La Quinta Inn & Suites Jackson Airport (Pearl)	3 Diamonds	Failed to provide	473
		PEARL - Restaurant			
37 / p. 451		El Charro	2 Diamonds	$6-$12	473

JACKSON pop. 184,256 (See map and index starting on p. 451)

WHERE TO STAY

BEST WESTERN JACKSON NORTH *Book great rates at AAA.com* **Phone:** 601/956-8686 **5**

Small-scale Hotel

Property failed to provide current rates

Location: I-55, exit 102, just w. 593 Beasley Rd 39206. Fax: 601/956-8680. **Facility:** 60 one-bedroom standard units, some with whirlpools. 4 stories, interior corridors. *Bath:* combo or shower only. **Parking:** on-site. **Amenities:** high-speed Internet, voice mail, irons, hair dryers. **Pool(s):** small outdoor. **Leisure Activities:** exercise room. **Guest Services:** coin laundry. **Business Services:** business center.

SOME UNITS

CABOT LODGE MILLSAPS *Book great rates at AAA.com* **Phone:** (601)948-8650 **12**

SAVE

Small-scale Hotel

All Year 1P: $79-$129 2P: $79-$129 XP: $10 F18

Location: I-55, exit 98A northbound; 1 mi w on Woodrow Wilson Blvd, then just s. 2375 N State St 39202. Fax: 601/948-8650. **Facility:** 204 units. 203 one-bedroom standard units. 1 one-bedroom suite ($129). 6 stories, interior corridors. *Bath:* combo or shower only. **Parking:** on-site. **Terms:** package plans, small pets only ($40 fee). **Amenities:** voice mail, irons, hair dryers. **Pool(s):** outdoor. **Leisure Activities:** exercise room. **Guest Services:** complimentary evening beverages, valet and coin laundry, wireless Internet. **Business Services:** meeting rooms, business center. **Cards:** AX, DC, DS, MC, VI. **Free Special Amenities: expanded continental breakfast and high-speed Internet.**

SOME UNITS

FEE

CLARION HOTEL **Phone:** 601/366-9411 **10**

fyi

Large-scale Hotel

All Year 1P: $79-$119

Under major renovation, scheduled to be completed November 2006. **Last rated:** ♦♦♦ **Location:** I-55, exit 102A, s on west frontage road. 5075 I-55 N 39206. Fax: 601/366-6688. **Facility:** 222 units. 192 one-bedroom standard units. 30 one-bedroom suites. 2-6 stories, interior/exterior corridors. *Bath:* combo or shower only. **Parking:** on-site. **Terms:** weekly rates available, package plans, pets ($25 extra charge). **Amenities:** video games (fee), voice mail, irons, hair dryers. **Pool(s):** outdoor, wading. **Leisure Activities:** exercise room. **Guest Services:** valet and coin laundry, wireless Internet. **Business Services:** conference facilities, PC. **Cards:** AX, DC, DS, MC, VI.

SOME UNITS

ASK FEE

COMFORT INN SOUTHWEST *Book great rates at AAA.com* **Phone:** (601)922-5600 **23**

SAVE

Small-scale Hotel

5/1-8/31 1P: $69 2P: $69
12/1-4/30 & 9/1-11/30 1P: $64 2P: $64

Location: I-20, exit 40 eastbound; exit 40A westbound, just se. 2800 Greenway Dr 39204. Fax: 601/922-0768. **Facility:** 76 one-bedroom standard units, some with whirlpools. 2 stories (no elevator), exterior corridors. *Bath:* combo or shower only. **Parking:** on-site. **Terms:** [CP] meal plan available. **Amenities:** high-speed Internet, irons, hair dryers. **Pool(s):** outdoor. **Business Services:** fax. **Cards:** AX, CB, DC, DS, JC, MC, VI. **Free Special Amenities: expanded continental breakfast and high-speed Internet.**

SOME UNITS

COURTYARD BY MARRIOTT *Book great rates at AAA.com* **Phone:** 601/956-9991 **2**

Small-scale Hotel

Property failed to provide current rates

Location: I-55, exit 103, just e to Ridgewood Rd, then 0.3 mi s. 6280 Ridgewood Court Dr 39211. Fax: 601/956-9994. **Facility:** 117 units. 111 one-bedroom standard units, some with whirlpools. 6 one-bedroom suites. 3 stories, interior corridors. *Bath:* combo or shower only. **Parking:** on-site. **Amenities:** voice mail, irons, hair dryers. **Pool(s):** small outdoor. **Leisure Activities:** whirlpool, exercise room. **Guest Services:** valet and coin laundry, wireless Internet. **Business Services:** meeting rooms, PC.

SOME UNITS

DAYS INN COLISEUM *Book great rates at AAA.com* **Phone:** 601/352-7387 **15**

Motel

All Year 1P: $55-$65 2P: $65-$75 XP: $5 F12

Location: I-55, exit 96B (High St), e to Greymont, then just ne. 804 Larson St 39202. Fax: 601/352-7387. **Facility:** 46 one-bedroom standard units, some with whirlpools. 2 stories (no elevator), exterior corridors. *Bath:* combo or shower only. **Parking:** on-site. **Terms:** [CP] meal plan available. **Amenities:** high-speed Internet, safes, irons, hair dryers. **Pool(s):** small outdoor. **Guest Services:** coin laundry. **Cards:** AX, DS, MC, VI.

SOME UNITS

ASK

THE EDISON WALTHALL HOTEL *Book at AAA.com* **Phone:** (601)948-6161 **21**

Classic Historic Large-scale Hotel

All Year 1P: $99 2P: $99 XP: $10 F17

Location: I-55, exit 96A (Pearl St), 0.8 mi w; between West and Lamar sts; downtown. 225 E Capitol St 39201. Fax: 601/948-0088. **Facility:** Near State Capitol and Governor's mansion. 203 units. 191 one-bedroom standard units. 12 one-bedroom suites ($110-$195), some with kitchens. 8 stories, interior/exterior corridors. **Parking:** on-site. **Terms:** cancellation fee imposed, pets ($10 extra charge). **Amenities:** high-speed Internet, irons, hair dryers. **Pool(s):** heated outdoor. **Leisure Activities:** whirlpool, exercise room. **Guest Services:** gift shop, valet laundry, area transportation, barber shop. **Business Services:** conference facilities, business center. **Cards:** AX, CB, DC, DS, MC, VI.

SOME UNITS

ASK FEE

EXTENDED STAYAMERICA JACKSON-NORTH *Book at AAA.com* **Phone:** (601)956-4312 **9**

Motel

All Year 1P: $54-$64 2P: $59-$69 XP: $5 F17

Location: I-55, exit 100, just n. 5354 I-55 N 39211. Fax: 601/956-7135. **Facility:** 108 one-bedroom standard units with kitchens. 3 stories, exterior corridors. *Bath:* combo or shower only. **Parking:** on-site. **Terms:** office hours 7 am-9 pm, pets ($75 fee). **Amenities:** irons, hair dryers. **Pool(s):** outdoor. **Guest Services:** coin laundry, wireless Internet. **Cards:** AX, CB, DC, DS, MC, VI.

SOME UNITS

ASK FEE

(See map and index starting on p. 451)

FAIRVIEW INN

Phone: (601)948-3429 **13**

SAVE

Bed & Breakfast

All Year [BP] 1P: $100-$275 2P: $115-$350 XP: $15 F

Location: I-55, exit 98A, 0.8 mi w to State St, then 0.4 mi s. Located in a residential area. 734 Fairview St 39202. Fax: 601/948-1203. **Facility:** Modern amenities enhance 10 new units in this B&B set in a stately mansion and featuring spacious accommodations. Designated smoking area. 18 units. 17 one-bedroom standard units, some with whirlpools. 1 one-bedroom suite. 3 stories, interior corridors. *Bath:* combo or shower only. **Parking:** on-site. **Terms:** check-in 4 pm, 3 day cancellation notice-fee imposed. **Amenities:** high-speed Internet, voice mail, irons, hair dryers. **Dining:** 5:30 pm-9 pm, Sun 11 am-2 pm; closed Mon-Wed. **Leisure Activities:** *Fee:* massage. **Guest Services:** valet laundry, wireless Internet. **Business Services:** meeting rooms, fax. **Cards:** AX, CB, DC, DS, MC, VI. **Free Special Amenities: full breakfast and local telephone calls.**

SOME UNITS / VCR /

HAMPTON INN & SUITES *Book great rates at AAA.com*

Phone: 601/352-1700 **19**

Small-scale Hotel

Property failed to provide current rates

Location: I-55, exit 96B (High St), just sw. 320 Greymont Ave 39202. Fax: 601/352-9988. **Facility:** 111 units. 80 one-bedroom standard units. 31 one-bedroom suites with efficiencies. 7 stories, interior corridors. *Bath:* combo or shower only. **Parking:** on-site. **Amenities:** high-speed Internet, voice mail, irons, hair dryers. **Pool(s):** heated outdoor. **Leisure Activities:** exercise room. **Guest Services:** sundries, complimentary evening beverages: Mon-Thurs, valet and coin laundry, wireless Internet. **Business Services:** meeting rooms, PC.

SOME UNITS / VCR /

HAMPTON INN NORTH *Book great rates at AAA.com*

Phone: (601)956-3611 **7**

Small-scale Hotel

All Year [BP] 1P: $85-$109 2P: $91-$113 XP: $6 F18

Location: I-55, exit 102 (Briarwood Dr), just w. 465 Briarwood Dr 39206. Fax: 601/956-4999. **Facility:** 119 one-bedroom standard units. 4 stories, interior corridors. *Bath:* combo or shower only. **Parking:** on-site. **Amenities:** video games (fee), dual phone lines, voice mail, irons, hair dryers. *Some:* high-speed Internet. **Pool(s):** small outdoor. **Guest Services:** valet laundry, wireless Internet. **Business Services:** business center. **Cards:** AX, CB, DC, DS, MC, VI.

SOME UNITS ASK / /

HILTON JACKSON *Book great rates at AAA.com*

Phone: 601/957-2800 **1**

Large-scale Hotel

Property failed to provide current rates

Location: I-55, exit 103 (County Line Rd), just e. 1001 E County Line Rd 39211. Fax: 601/957-3191. **Facility:** 273 units. 262 one-bedroom standard units. 11 one-bedroom suites, some with whirlpools. 14 stories, interior corridors. *Bath:* combo or shower only. **Parking:** on-site. **Amenities:** video games (fee), dual phone lines, voice mail, irons, hair dryers. *Some:* CD players. **Dining:** Huntington's Grille, see separate listing. **Pool(s):** outdoor. **Leisure Activities:** whirlpool, exercise room. **Guest Services:** gift shop, valet laundry, area transportation, barber shop, wireless Internet. **Business Services:** conference facilities, business center.

SOME UNITS / /

HOLIDAY INN EXPRESS HOTEL & SUITES *Book at AAA.com*

Phone: 601/948-4466 **17**

Small-scale Hotel

Property failed to provide current rates

Location: I-55, exit 96B (High St), just sw. 310 Greymont Ave 39202. Fax: 601/352-9368. **Facility:** 107 units. 76 one-bedroom standard units. 31 one-bedroom suites. 5 stories, interior corridors. *Bath:* combo or shower only. **Parking:** on-site. **Amenities:** voice mail, irons, hair dryers. **Leisure Activities:** exercise room. **Guest Services:** coin laundry, wireless Internet. **Business Services:** meeting rooms, PC.

SOME UNITS / /

JACKSON FAIRFIELD INN *Book great rates at AAA.com*

Phone: (601)957-8557 **3**

Small-scale Hotel

All Year 1P: $65-$95 2P: $65-$95

Location: I-55, exit 102, just w, then just s on Frontage Dr. 5723 I-55 N 39206. Fax: 601/957-8557. **Facility:** 79 one-bedroom standard units. 3 stories, interior corridors. *Bath:* combo or shower only. **Parking:** on-site. **Amenities:** irons, hair dryers. **Pool(s):** small heated indoor. **Leisure Activities:** whirlpool, exercise room. **Guest Services:** valet laundry, wireless Internet. **Cards:** AX, CB, DC, DS, JC, MC, VI.

SOME UNITS ASK / /

JACKSON INN & SUITES

Phone: (601)899-9000 **8**

SAVE

Small-scale Hotel

All Year 1P: $74-$90 2P: $84-$100 XP: $10 F18

Location: I-55, exit 102A northbound; exit 102 southbound, s on west service road. 5411 I-55 N 39206. Fax: 601/899-8613. **Facility:** 103 units. 61 one-bedroom standard units. 42 one-bedroom suites, some with whirlpools. 3 stories, interior corridors. *Bath:* combo or shower only. **Parking:** on-site. **Terms:** small pets only ($35 fee). **Amenities:** dual phone lines, voice mail, irons, hair dryers. **Pool(s):** small heated indoor. **Leisure Activities:** whirlpool, exercise room. **Guest Services:** coin laundry. **Business Services:** meeting rooms. **Cards:** AX, DC, DS, MC, VI. **Free Special Amenities: full breakfast and local telephone calls.**

SOME UNITS FEE / VCR /

JAMESON INN *Book at AAA.com*

Phone: (601)206-8923 **4**

Small-scale Hotel

All Year [ECP] 1P: $54-$120

Location: I-55, exit 102, just w. 585 Beasley Rd 39206. Fax: 601/899-0108. **Facility:** 67 units. 65 one-bedroom standard units. 2 one-bedroom suites. 3 stories, interior corridors. *Bath:* combo or shower only. **Parking:** on-site. **Terms:** cancellation fee imposed, small pets only ($10 fee). **Amenities:** voice mail, irons, hair dryers. **Pool(s):** small outdoor. **Leisure Activities:** exercise room. **Guest Services:** wireless Internet. **Business Services:** meeting rooms, business center. **Cards:** AX, DC, DS, MC, VI.

SOME UNITS ASK FEE / /

(See map and index starting on p. 451)

LA QUINTA INN JACKSON (NORTH) Book great rates at AAA.com Phone: (601)957-1741 6

Small-scale Hotel All Year [ECP] 1P: $64-$74 2P: $70-$80 XP: $6 F18

Location: I-55, exit 102A northbound, just ne on Frontage Rd. 616 Briarwood Dr 39211. Fax: 601/956-5764. **Facility:** 144 one-bedroom standard units. 2 stories (no elevator), exterior corridors. **Parking:** on-site. **Terms:** small pets only. **Amenities:** video games (fee), voice mail, irons, hair dryers. **Pool(s):** outdoor. **Guest Services:** wireless Internet. **Business Services:** meeting rooms. **Cards:** AX, CB, DC, DS, MC, VI. *(See color ad p 386)*

SOME UNITS

OLD CAPITOL INN Phone: (601)359-9000 18

Bed & Breakfast All Year 2P: $135-$225 XP: $10

Location: I-55, exit 96A (Pearl St), just n; downtown. 226 N State St 39201. Fax: 601/355-5587. **Facility:** Most of the rooms are suites in this inn featuring a courtyard and a rooftop garden. Designated smoking area. 24 units. 2 one-bedroom standard units. 22 one-bedroom suites, some with whirlpools. 3 stories, interior corridors. *Bath:* combo or shower only. **Parking:** on-site. **Terms:** age restrictions may apply. **Amenities:** irons, hair dryers. **Pool(s):** small outdoor. **Leisure Activities:** whirlpool. **Guest Services:** complimentary evening beverages, valet laundry. **Business Services:** meeting rooms, fax (fee). **Cards:** AX, MC, VI.

SOME UNITS

FEE

QUALITY INN & SUITES Book great rates at AAA.com Phone: (601)969-2230 22

Small-scale Hotel All Year 1P: $80-$100 2P: $90-$109 XP: $10

Location: I-55, exit 96B (High St), just w, then just s. Located opposite the coliseum and fairgrounds. 400 Greymont Ave 39202. Fax: 601/714-5856. **Facility:** 130 units. 115 one-bedroom standard units, some with whirlpools. 15 one-bedroom suites ($125-$150). 4 stories, exterior corridors. *Bath:* combo or shower only. **Parking:** on-site. **Terms:** cancellation fee imposed, [CP] meal plan available, small pets only ($25 fee). **Amenities:** voice mail, irons, hair dryers. **Guest Services:** valet and coin laundry. **Cards:** AX, DS, MC, VI. ***(See color ad below)***

SOME UNITS

FEE FEE

RED ROOF INN FAIRGROUNDS Book at AAA.com Phone: (601)969-5006 16

Motel

1/28-11/30	1P: $42-$58	2P: $48-$63	XP: $5	F18
12/1-12/31	1P: $46-$55	2P: $51-$60	XP: $5	F18
1/1-1/27	1P: $42-$53	2P: $48-$58	XP: $5	F18

Location: I-55, exit 96B (High St), e to Greymont, then just ne. 700 Larson St 39202. Fax: 601/969-5159. **Facility:** 116 one-bedroom standard units. 3 stories, exterior corridors. *Bath:* combo or shower only. **Parking:** on-site. **Terms:** small pets only. **Amenities:** video games (fee), voice mail. **Cards:** AX, CB, DC, DS, MC, VI.

SOME UNITS

REGENCY HOTEL & CONFERENCE CENTER Book great rates at AAA.com Phone: 601/969-2141 20

Small-scale Hotel All Year 1P: $89-$129 2P: $89-$129 XP: $10 F5

Location: I-55, exit 96B, just w, then just s. Located opposite the coliseum and fairgrounds. 400 Greymont Ave 39202. Fax: 601/355-1704. **Facility:** 143 units. 139 one-bedroom standard units. 4 one-bedroom suites ($195-$350). 2 stories, interior/exterior corridors. *Bath:* combo or shower only. **Parking:** on-site. **Terms:** [BP] meal plan available, small pets only ($25 fee, with prior approval). **Amenities:** high-speed Internet, voice mail, irons, hair dryers. **Dining:** 6:30-9:30 am, 11-2 & 5-9 pm, Sat 6:30 am-9:30 & 5-9 pm, cocktails. **Pool(s):** outdoor. **Leisure Activities:** exercise room. **Guest Services:** valet and coin laundry, wireless Internet. **Business Services:** conference facilities, business center. **Cards:** AX, DC, DS, MC, VI. **Free Special Amenities: local telephone calls and newspaper.** *(See color ad below)*

SOME UNITS

FEE FEE

(See map and index starting on p. 451)

RESIDENCE INN BY MARRIOTT Book great rates at AAA.com Phone: 601/355-3599 14

Property failed to provide current rates

Small-scale Hotel

Location: I-55, exit 96C, just e. 881 E River Pl 39202. Fax: 601/355-5127. **Facility:** 120 units. 99 one-bedroom standard units, some with efficiencies. 21 one-bedroom suites with efficiencies. 2 stories (no elevator), exterior corridors. *Bath:* combo or shower only. **Parking:** on-site. **Terms:** check-in 4 pm, pets ($75 fee). **Amenities:** high-speed Internet, voice mail, irons, hair dryers. **Pool(s):** small outdoor. **Leisure Activities:** whirlpools, jogging, exercise room, sports court. **Guest Services:** sundries, complimentary evening beverages: Mon-Thurs, valet and coin laundry. **Business Services:** meeting rooms, fax (fee).

SOME UNITS

FEE

SLEEP INN AIRPORT Book great rates at AAA.com Phone: (601)936-0007 11

All Year	1P: $85-$102	2P: $90-$112	XP: $5	F17

Small-scale Hotel

Location: I-55, exit 98B northbound, 4 mi e to jct Airport Rd. 4351 Lakeland Dr 39232. Fax: 601/936-0625. **Facility:** 90 units. 85 one-bedroom standard units. 5 one-bedroom suites ($102-$112). 4 stories, interior corridors. *Bath:* combo or shower only. **Parking:** on-site. **Terms:** [ECP] meal plan available. **Amenities:** voice mail, irons, hair dryers. **Pool(s):** small outdoor. **Guest Services:** complimentary evening beverages: Mon-Thurs, valet laundry, wireless Internet. **Cards:** AX, CB, DC, DS, JC, MC, VI.

SOME UNITS

ASK

WHERE TO DINE

BEAGLE BAGEL CAFE **Lunch:** $6-$8 **Dinner:** $6-$8 **Phone:** 601/956-1773 2

American

Location: I-55, exit 103, 1.4 mi e on County Line Rd; in Promenade shopping area. 898 Avery Blvd 39157. **Hours:** 6:30 am-8 pm, Sun 8 am-6 pm. Closed major holidays. **Features:** This friendly neighborhood cafe with many local regulars features sandwiches made with your choice of 23 different kinds of bagels and a great selection of fillings. Chicken salad is the specialty, as are the homemade cream cheeses. Casual dress. **Parking:** on-site. **Cards:** AX, DS, MC, VI.

BRAVO! **Lunch:** $9-$17 **Dinner:** $14-$30 **Phone:** 601/982-8111 9

Italian

Location: I-55, exit 100 northbound, just e on Northside Dr; in Highland Village, south plaza upper level. 244 Highland Village 39211. **Hours:** 11:00 am-10 pm, Sun-9 pm. Closed major holidays; also Mon. **Features:** Voted the metro Jackson restaurant of the year by the local convention and visitors bureau, Bravo! serves novel Italian dishes prepared with fresh ingredients. The interior captures the mood of Napa Valley via a design that incorporates huge murals and an exposed kitchen. Wine choices are extensive. Casual dress; cocktails. **Parking:** on-site. **Cards:** AX, CB, DC, DS, MC, VI.

BROAD STREET BAKING COMPANY & CAFE **Lunch:** $5-$10 **Dinner:** $5-$10 **Phone:** 601/362-2900 11

American

Location: I-55, exit 100 (Northside Dr), just s on W Frontage Rd. 4465 I-55 N 39206. **Hours:** 7 am-8 pm, Fri & Sat-9 pm, Sun-3 pm. Closed major holidays. **Features:** If homemade bread sounds good to you, the real thing smells and tastes even better. The welcoming cafe uses a centuries-old French manner of breadmaking to resurrect traditional European recipes and formulas. Different breads baked daily add pizazz to sandwiches. Casual dress; beer & wine only. **Parking:** on-site. **Cards:** MC, VI.

CHAR **Lunch:** $8-$28 **Dinner:** $8-$30 **Phone:** 601/956-9562 10

American

Location: I-55, exit 100 (Northside Dr) northbound, just e; in Highland Village. 4500 I-55 N/142 Highland Village 39211. **Hours:** 11 am-10 pm, Fri & Sat-10:30 pm. Closed major holidays. **Features:** Popular with the local crowd, an elegant supper club ambience is the setting for delicious prime rib, steak, seafood and the chef's daily specials. Casual dress; cocktails. **Parking:** on-site. **Cards:** AX, DC, DS, MC, VI.

DENNERY'S **Lunch:** $12-$15 **Dinner:** $18-$35 **Phone:** 601/354-2527 20

American

Location: I-55, exit 96B (High St), just sw. 330 Greymont Ave 39202. **Hours:** 11 am-9 pm, Sat 5 pm-10 pm. Closed major holidays; also Sun. **Reservations:** accepted. **Features:** A city favorite for decades, the restaurant presents a broad and varied menu that includes some Greek-influenced dishes. The Greek rotunda-shaped dining room has a flowing fountain as its center. Casual dress; cocktails. **Parking:** on-site. **Cards:** AX, CB, DC, DS, JC, MC, VI.

EL RANCHERO MEXICAN RESTAURANT **Lunch:** $4-$6 **Dinner:** $7-$10 **Phone:** 601/321-8797 15

Mexican

Location: I-55, exit 98C northbound; exit 98B southbound, 0.7 mi w on SR 25 (Lakeland Dr), then just s. 2741 Old Canton Rd 39216. **Hours:** 11 am-9 pm, Fri & Sat-10 pm. Closed: 11/22, 12/25. **Features:** Guests can nibble on freshly prepared Mexican food while sipping sangria on the patio. Casual dress; beer & wine only. **Parking:** on-site. **Cards:** AX, CB, DC, DS, MC, VI.

GIOVANNI'S **Lunch:** $8-$17 **Dinner:** $8-$17 **Phone:** 601/956-9550 3

Italian

Location: I-55, exit 103, 0.6 mi e. 1189 E County Line Rd 39211. **Hours:** 11 am-1:30 am, Sun-11:30 pm. Closed: 12/25 & Easter. **Features:** In a strip mall, the small Italian restaurant presents a menu that runs from baked ziti to pizza. Popular with the locals, a small bar in the back schedules karaoke on Mondays. Casual dress; cocktails. **Parking:** on-site. **Cards:** AX, DS, MC, VI.

HAL & MAL'S RESTAURANT AND BREWERY **Lunch:** $5-$12 **Dinner:** $8-$24 **Phone:** 601/948-0888 19

Seafood

Location: I-55, exit 96A (Pearl St), just w to State St, 0.4 mi s to Tombigee St, just e, then just n. 200 S Commerce St 39201. **Hours:** 11 am-10 pm, Fri & Sat-10:30 pm. Closed major holidays; also Sun. **Features:** Located in a converted warehouse, this popular restaurant and brewery is a fun place for everyone from singles to couples to families. Festive music and brightly colored hand painted murals enhance the appeal. Casual dress; cocktails; entertainment. **Parking:** street. **Cards:** AX, DS, MC, VI.

(See map and index starting on p. 451)

HUNTINGTON'S GRILLE **Dinner:** $18-$44 **Phone:** 601/957-1515 (4)

American

Location: I-55, exit 103 (County Line Rd), just e; in Hilton Jackson. 1001 E County Line Rd 39211. **Hours:** 5 pm-10 pm, Fri & Sat-10:30 pm. Closed major holidays; also 12/24 & Sun. **Reservations:** suggested. **Features:** In the setting of an Old English hunting lodge, the restaurant specializes in steak and seafood. Also on the menu are New Zealand elk and Colorado lamb. An extensive wine list is presented. Dressy casual; cocktails. **Parking:** on-site. **Cards:** AX, CB, DC, DS, MC, VI.

LA CAZUELA MEXICAN RESTAURANT **Lunch:** $4-$7 **Dinner:** $7-$12 **Phone:** 601/353-3014 (17)

Mexican

Location: I-55, exit 96C (Fortification St), just w. 1401 E Fortification St 39202. **Hours:** 11 am-10 pm, Fri & Sat-10:30 pm. Closed major holidays. **Features:** Although not near the Mexican border, the restaurant prepares hearty traditional meals made from fresh ingredients. Meat-filled tamales are large, and fajitas are sizzling and spicy. Casual dress; cocktails. **Parking:** on-site. **Cards:** AX, DS, MC, VI.

MIKHAIL'S NORTHGATE **Lunch:** $7-$10 **Phone:** 601/982-3838 (8)

American

Location: I-55, exit 99, 1 mi w on Meadowbrook, then just n. 4330 N State St 39206. **Hours:** 7 am-3 pm. Closed: 11/22, 12/25; also Sun. **Features:** Breakfasts come with everything from biscuits and eggs to ham and sausage. Lunch specials feature Southern specialties, such as fried chicken and cornbread. Casual dress. **Parking:** on-site. **Cards:** AX, MC, VI.

NAGOYA JAPANESE CUISINE & SUSHI BAR **Lunch:** $7-$9 **Dinner:** $10-$19 **Phone:** 601/977-8881 (5)

Japanese

Location: I-55, exit 103, just w; in Junction Shopping Center. 6351 I-55 N, Suite 131 39213. **Hours:** 11 am-2:30 & 5-10 pm, Fri & Sat-10:30 pm, Sun noon-3 & 5-10 pm. Closed: 11/22. **Features:** Located in a strip mall, this restaurant offers authentic Japanese cuisine for lunch and dinner; choose from a hibachi grill or sushi bar dining experience. Casual dress; cocktails. **Parking:** on-site. **Cards:** AX, DS, MC, VI.

NICK'S **Lunch:** $9-$18 **Dinner:** $19-$34 **Phone:** 601/981-8017 (13)

American

Location: I-55, exit 98B, 0.8 mi e. 1501 Lakeland Dr 39216. **Hours:** 11 am-9:30 pm, Fri-10 pm, Sat 5:30 pm-10 pm. Closed major holidays; also Sun. **Reservations:** suggested. **Features:** Fresh seafood and an award-winning wine list are key elements of this dining experience. Nick's provides a warm and cozy atmosphere, the walls hung with artwork, camelback sofas and big chairs in the lounge. Private parties of up to 50 diners are welcome. Casual dress; cocktails. **Parking:** on-site. **Cards:** AX, DC, MC, VI.

OLD VENICE PIZZA CO **Lunch:** $7-$16 **Dinner:** $7-$16 **Phone:** 601/366-6872 (7)

Italian

Location: I-55, exit 100 (Northside Dr), 0.5 mi e on E Frontage Rd, then just s. 1428 Old Square Rd 39211. **Hours:** 11 am-10 pm. Closed major holidays. **Features:** A favorite of the local crowd, the restaurant serves large and tasty portions of Italian food. Casual dress; cocktails. **Parking:** on-site. **Cards:** AX, DS, MC, VI.

PAN-ASIA **Lunch:** $7-$15 **Dinner:** $10-$23 **Phone:** 601/956-2958 (1)

Regional Asian

Location: I-55, exit 103, 1.4 mi e on County Line Rd; in Promenade shopping area. 862 Avery Blvd 39157. **Hours:** 11 am-2 & 5-9:30 pm, Fri & Sat-10 pm. Closed major holidays. **Features:** Plans are to move this restaurant to the other side of the adjacent Honda dealer and convert this space into an Asian cuisine restaurant. Diners should call in advance to verify. Casual dress; cocktails. **Parking:** on-site. **Cards:** AX, DS, MC, VI.

QUE SERA'SERA' **Lunch:** $6-$15 **Dinner:** $6-$25 **Phone:** 601/981-2520 (14)

Cajun

Location: I-55, exit 98A (Woodrow Wilson), 0.8 mi w, then 0.5 mi n. 2801 N State St 39216. **Hours:** 11 am-11 pm, Sun-10 pm. Closed: 11/22, 12/25. **Features:** Guests appreciate the casual atmosphere and patio seating while sampling Cajun flavors in dishes from breaded artichoke hearts to shrimp Creole. The red beans and rice dish has won awards in the South. Casual dress; cocktails. **Parking:** on-site. **Cards:** AX, MC, VI.

SCHIMMEL'S **Lunch:** $7-$16 **Phone:** 601/981-7077 (16)

Steak & Seafood

Location: I-55, exit 98A northbound, 1 mi w on Woodrow Blvd, then 0.3 mi n. 2615 N State St 39216. **Hours:** 11:30 am-2 & 5:30-10 pm, Sat-9 pm. Closed: Sun. **Reservations:** suggested. **Features:** Guests arrive to valet parking at the fine-dining steak and seafood restaurant. The large dining room is between the lounge and a large wine cellar. The lounge, which opens earlier than the dining room, presents a limited menu. Casual dress; cocktails; entertainment. **Parking:** valet. **Cards:** AX, DS, MC, VI.

STEAM ROOM GRILLE **Lunch:** $6-$12 **Dinner:** $15-$30 **Phone:** 601/899-8588 (6)

AAA

Steak & Seafood

Location: I-55, exit 99, 1.2 mi e on Frontage Rd; between Northside and Briarwood drs. 5402 I-55 N 39211. **Hours:** 11 am-10 pm, Sat from 3 pm. Closed: 11/22, 12/25 & Easter; also Sun. **Reservations:** accepted. **Features:** The local favorite is well known for hand-cut steaks and fresh seafood, including straight-from-the-tank lobsters. Casual dress; cocktails. **Parking:** on-site. **Cards:** AX, DS, MC, VI.

THAI HOUSE RESTAURANT **Lunch:** $8-$15 **Dinner:** $8-$15 **Phone:** 601/373-8154 (21)

Thai

Location: I-55, exit 92A southbound, just w, then just n. 2665 I-55 S 39204. **Hours:** 11 am-2 & 5-9 pm, Fri-9:30 pm, Sat 4 pm-9:30 pm. Closed major holidays; also Sun, Mon. **Reservations:** accepted. **Features:** The restaurant offers authentic Thai cuisine in a great Thai atmosphere; floor seating is available in the back room for the adventurous diner. This is a perfect place for a Thai food lover. Casual dress. **Parking:** on-site. **Cards:** DS, MC, VI.

TWO SISTERS' KITCHEN **Lunch:** $9-$14 **Phone:** 601/353-1180 (18)

Regional American

Location: I-55, exit 96C (Fortification St), 1 mi w, then 0.4 mi s; center. 707 N Congress St 39202. **Hours:** 11 am-2 pm, Sun from 10:30 am. Closed major holidays; also 11/21-11/24, 12/24-1/1 & Good Friday. **Reservations:** not accepted. **Features:** The early 1900s cottage opens only for lunch and serves some of the best Southern cooking in town. Buffet service offers changing main dishes—such as fried chicken, country-fried steak and catfish—with just about any side dish Mama ever cooked. Casual dress. **Parking:** on-site and street. **Cards:** DC, DS, MC, VI.

(See map and index starting on p. 451)

WALKER'S DRIVE-IN **Lunch:** $7-$10 **Dinner:** $21-$29 **Phone:** 601/982-2633 (12)

American

Location: I-55, exit 98A (Woodrow Wilson), 0.8 mi w, then 0.6 mi n. 3016 N State St 39216. **Hours:** 11 am-2 & 5:30pm to close, Mon-2 pm. Closed major holidays; also Sun, 1st week in Jan & July. **Reservations:** accepted. **Features:** The converted drive-in now houses a restaurant marked by upscale service and Chef Emerson's innovative foods. Creative seafood dishes reflect California influences. Try grilled jumbo shrimp with red pepper sauce or Colorado lamb. Casual dress; cocktails. **Parking:** on-site. **Cards:** AX, DS, MC, VI.

KOSCIUSKO pop. 7,372

WHERE TO STAY

AMERICAS BEST VALUE INN *Book great rates at AAA.com* **Phone:** (662)289-6252

Motel

4/27-9/30 [CP]	1P: $55	2P: $59	XP: $4	F12
12/1-4/26 & 10/1-11/30 [CP]	1P: $51	2P: $55	XP: $4	F12

Location: Just sw of jct SR 35 and Natchez Trace Pkwy. 1052 Veterans Memorial Dr/Hwy 35 Bypass 39090. Fax: 662/289-4007. **Facility:** 51 one-bedroom standard units. 1 story, exterior corridors. **Parking:** on-site. **Terms:** small pets only ($5 extra charge). **Amenities:** high-speed Internet, irons, hair dryers. **Pool(s):** outdoor. **Guest Services:** wireless Internet. **Business Services:** meeting rooms. **Cards:** AX, CB, DC, DS, MC, VI. **Free Special Amenities: continental breakfast and high-speed Internet.**

SOME UNITS

FEE

DAYS INN *Book great rates at AAA.com* **Phone:** (662)289-2271

Small-scale Hotel

5/16-9/15	1P: $54-$58	2P: $56-$58	XP: $5	F12
4/1-5/15	1P: $52-$54	2P: $54-$58	XP: $5	F12
12/1-3/31 & 9/16-11/30	1P: $48-$52	2P: $52-$56	XP: $5	F12

Location: Just sw of jct SR 35 and Natchez Trace Pkwy. 1000 S Veterans Memorial Dr/Hwy 35 Bypass 39090. Fax: 662/289-4076. **Facility:** 38 one-bedroom standard units. 2 stories (no elevator), exterior corridors. **Parking:** on-site. **Amenities:** irons, hair dryers. **Pool(s):** outdoor. **Guest Services:** wireless Internet. **Cards:** AX, DC, DS, MC, VI. **Free Special Amenities: continental breakfast and high-speed Internet.**

SOME UNITS

MAPLE TERRACE INN **Phone:** (662)289-5353

Historic Bed & Breakfast

All Year	1P: $85	2P: $100-$110	XP: $10	F

Location: Natchez Trace Pkwy, exit Mile Marker 160, then just w to N Huntington st. 300 N Huntington St 39090. Fax: 662/289-5348. **Facility:** Built in 1912, this home offers a blend of Colonial Revival, Arts and Crafts and Prairie styles just off the Natchez Trace parkway. Smoke free premises. 4 one-bedroom standard units. 2 stories (no elevator), interior corridors. **Parking:** on-site. **Terms:** 3 day cancellation notice-fee imposed, weekly rates available. **Amenities:** hair dryers. *Some:* irons. **Guest Services:** complimentary laundry, wireless Internet. **Cards:** AX, DS, MC, VI.

ASK

LAUREL pop. 18,393

WHERE TO STAY

HAMPTON INN *Book great rates at AAA.com* **Phone:** (601)425-4455

Small-scale Hotel

All Year	1P: $89-$120	2P: $89-$129

Location: I-59, exit 95B, just w. Located in a commercial area. 309 S 16th Ave 39440. Fax: 601/425-4485. **Facility:** 53 one-bedroom standard units, some with whirlpools. 3 stories, interior corridors. *Bath:* combo or shower only. **Parking:** on-site. **Terms:** [BP], [CP] & [ECP] meal plans available. **Amenities:** high-speed Internet, dual phone lines, voice mail, irons, hair dryers. **Pool(s):** small outdoor. **Leisure Activities:** exercise room. **Guest Services:** complimentary evening beverages, valet and coin laundry. **Business Services:** meeting rooms, fax (fee). **Cards:** AX, CB, DC, DS, MC, VI.

SOME UNITS

ASK

MAGEE pop. 4,200

WHERE TO STAY

COMFORT INN *Book great rates at AAA.com* **Phone:** (601)849-2300

Small-scale Hotel

All Year	1P: $50-$90	2P: $50-$90	XP: $6	F12

Location: US 49 at US 28 W. Located behind gas station. 5441 Simpson Hwy 28 W 39111. Fax: 601/849-2300. **Facility:** 50 one-bedroom standard units. 2 stories (no elevator), interior corridors. **Parking:** on-site. **Terms:** [CP] meal plan available. **Amenities:** high-speed Internet, irons, hair dryers. **Pool(s):** small outdoor. **Guest Services:** coin laundry, wireless Internet. **Cards:** AX, DC, DS, MC, VI.

SOME UNITS

ASK

MCCOMB pop. 13,337

WHERE TO STAY

COMFORT INN *Book great rates at AAA.com* **Phone:** (601)249-0080

Small-scale Hotel

3/31-9/30 [ECP]	1P: $91-$110	2P: $110-$125	XP: $10	F18
12/1-3/30 & 10/1-11/30 [ECP]	1P: $81-$110	2P: $91-$110	XP: $10	F18

Location: I-55, exit 17, just ne. Located in a commercial area. 107 Scott Dr 39648. Fax: 601/249-0080. **Facility:** 55 one-bedroom standard units, some with whirlpools. 2 stories (no elevator), exterior corridors. **Parking:** on-site. **Terms:** 3 day cancellation notice. **Amenities:** high-speed Internet, irons, hair dryers. **Pool(s):** small outdoor. **Guest Services:** valet laundry. **Business Services:** business center. **Cards:** AX, CB, DC, DS, JC, MC, VI.

SOME UNITS

ASK

HAWTHORN INN & SUITES *Book great rates at AAA.com* **Phone:** (601)684-8655

AAA SAVE

Small-scale Hotel

All Year 1P: $90 2P: $90

Location: I-55, exit 18, just off interstate. 2001 Veteran's Blvd 39648. Fax: 601/684-9570. **Facility:** 75 units. 73 one-bedroom standard units, some with whirlpools. 2 one-bedroom suites ($100-$110). 3 stories, interior corridors. **Parking:** on-site. **Terms:** weekly rates available, small pets only ($125 fee). **Amenities:** voice mail, irons, hair dryers. *Some:* DVD players. **Dining:** 4 pm-midnight; closed Sun. **Pool(s):** small outdoor. **Leisure Activities:** limited exercise equipment. **Guest Services:** complimentary evening beverages: Wed, valet and coin laundry, wireless Internet. **Business Services:** meeting rooms, business center. **Cards:** AX, CB, DC, DS, MC, VI. **Free Special Amenities: full breakfast and high-speed Internet.**

SOME UNITS

FEE

MERIDIAN pop. 39,968

WHERE TO STAY

BEST WESTERN OF MERIDIAN *Book great rates at AAA.com* **Phone:** (601)693-3210

AAA SAVE

Small-scale Hotel

6/1-11/30	1P: $57-$70	2P: $57-$70	XP: $5	F12
12/1-5/31	1P: $56-$69	2P: $56-$69	XP: $5	F12

Location: I-20/59, exit 153, just sw. 2219 S Frontage Rd 39301. Fax: 601/693-3210. **Facility:** 122 one-bedroom standard units. 2 stories (no elevator), interior/exterior corridors. **Parking:** on-site. **Terms:** small pets only ($10 fee). **Amenities:** irons, hair dryers. *Some:* high-speed Internet. **Pool(s):** small outdoor. **Guest Services:** valet and coin laundry, wireless Internet. **Business Services:** meeting rooms, PC. **Cards:** AX, CB, DC, DS, MC, VI. **Free Special Amenities: local telephone calls and high-speed Internet.**

SOME UNITS

FEE

BUDGET 8 MOTEL **Phone:** 601/693-3461

Motel

Property failed to provide current rates

Location: I-20/59, exit 153, 0.5 mi sw. 2325 S Frontage Rd 39301. Fax: 601/693-3461. **Facility:** 28 one-bedroom standard units, some with whirlpools. 2 stories (no elevator), exterior corridors. *Bath:* combo or shower only. **Parking:** on-site. **Amenities:** irons. *Some:* hair dryers. **Guest Services:** coin laundry. **Business Services:** fax (fee).

SOME UNITS

COMFORT INN *Book great rates at AAA.com* **Phone:** (601)693-1200

Small-scale Hotel

6/1-8/31	1P: $95-$123	2P: $100-$124	XP: $5	F18
12/1-5/31 & 9/1-11/30	1P: $85-$113	2P: $90-$118	XP: $5	F18

Location: I-20/59, exit 154, just s. Located opposite the mall. 701 Bonita Lakes Dr 39301. Fax: 601/485-3138. **Facility:** 52 units. 51 one-bedroom standard units, some with whirlpools. 1 one-bedroom suite ($101-$124) with whirlpool. 3 stories, interior corridors. *Bath:* combo or shower only. **Parking:** on-site. **Amenities:** voice mail, irons, hair dryers. **Pool(s):** small outdoor. **Guest Services:** coin laundry, wireless Internet. **Business Services:** business center. **Cards:** AX, CB, DC, DS, MC, VI.

SOME UNITS

DAYS INN *Book great rates at AAA.com* **Phone:** (601)483-3812

Motel

All Year	1P: $55-$65	2P: $59-$69	XP: $5	F12

Location: I-20/59, exit 154 westbound; exit 154B eastbound, just n to Frontage Rd, then just e. 145 Hwy 11 & 80 E 39301. Fax: 601/485-5570. **Facility:** 115 one-bedroom standard units. 2 stories (no elevator), exterior corridors. **Parking:** on-site. **Terms:** package plans, pets ($5 extra charge). **Amenities:** high-speed Internet, hair dryers. *Some:* irons. **Pool(s):** outdoor. **Guest Services:** coin laundry. **Cards:** AX, CB, DC, DS, JC, MC, VI.

SOME UNITS

FEE

ECONO LODGE *Book great rates at AAA.com* **Phone:** 601/693-9393

Motel

Property failed to provide current rates

Location: I-20/59, exit 153, 0.5 mi sw. 2405 S Frontage Rd 39301. Fax: 601/693-9393. **Facility:** 33 one-bedroom standard units. 2 stories (no elevator), exterior corridors. **Parking:** on-site. **Terms:** pets ($10 extra charge). **Amenities:** hair dryers. **Business Services:** fax (fee).

SOME UNITS

FEE

HAMPTON INN OF MERIDIAN *Book great rates at AAA.com* **Phone:** 601/483-3000

Small-scale Hotel

All Year [CP]	1P: $130-$145	2P: $140-$155	XP: $10	F18

Location: I-20/59, exit 154 westbound; exit 154B eastbound, just n to Frontage Rd, then just e. 103 US Hwy 11 & 80 39301 (PO Box 5497). Fax: 601/693-2466. **Facility:** 116 one-bedroom standard units. 4 stories, interior corridors. **Parking:** on-site. **Amenities:** video library, dual phone lines, voice mail, irons, hair dryers. *Some:* DVD players. **Pool(s):** outdoor. **Leisure Activities:** exercise room. **Guest Services:** valet laundry, wireless Internet. **Business Services:** meeting rooms, business center. **Cards:** AX, DC, DS, MC, VI. ***(See color ad p 462)***

SOME UNITS

HILTON GARDEN INN **Phone:** 601/485-3506

Small-scale Hotel

All Year	1P: $115-$185	XP: $10	F18

Too new to rate, opening scheduled for July 2006. **Location:** I-20/59, exit 154 westbound; exit 154B eastbound, just n to Frontage Rd, then just e. 109 US Hwy 11 & 80 39301 (PO Box 5497). Fax: 601/485-2914. **Amenities:** 133 units, coffeemakers, microwaves, refrigerators, pool. **Terms:** 21 day cancellation notice. **Cards:** AX, CB, DC, DS, JC, MC, VI. ***(See color ad p 462)***

HOLIDAY INN EXPRESS HOTEL & SUITES *Book at AAA.com* **Phone:** (601)581-4777

Small-scale Hotel

All Year 1P: $99-$115

Location: I-20/59, exit 153, just s. 1399 Roebuck Dr 39301. Fax: 601/581-5090. **Facility:** 76 one-bedroom standard units. 3 stories, interior corridors. *Bath:* combo or shower only. **Parking:** on-site. **Terms:** [ECP] meal plan available. **Amenities:** high-speed Internet, dual phone lines, voice mail, irons, hair dryers. **Pool(s):** heated indoor. **Leisure Activities:** whirlpool, limited exercise equipment. **Guest Services:** valet and coin laundry. **Business Services:** meeting rooms, business center. **Cards:** AX, CB, DC, DS, JC, MC, VI.

SOME UNITS

HOLIDAY INN NORTHEAST *Book great rates at AAA.com* **Phone:** 601/485-5101

Small-scale Hotel

5/23-7/31 1P: $98-$105
12/1-5/22 & 8/1-11/30 1P: $89-$98

Location: I-20/59, exit 154 westbound, just n to frontage road, then just e; exit 154B eastbound. 111 US 11 & 80 39302 (PO Box 5248). Fax: 601/693-2497. **Facility:** 103 one-bedroom standard units. 2 stories (no elevator), exterior corridors. *Bath:* combo or shower only. **Parking:** on-site. **Terms:** pets ($25 fee). **Amenities:** high-speed Internet, voice mail, irons, hair dryers. **Pool(s):** small outdoor. **Leisure Activities:** limited exercise equipment. **Guest Services:** complimentary evening beverages: Mon-Thurs, valet and coin laundry. **Business Services:** meeting rooms, business center. **Cards:** AX, DC, DS, MC, VI. ***(See color ad below)***

SOME UNITS

FEE

JAMESON INN *Book at AAA.com* **Phone:** (601)483-3315

Small-scale Hotel

All Year [ECP] 1P: $54-$120

Location: I-20/59, exit 154 southbound; exit 154A northbound, just s. Located at Bonita Lakes Mall. 524 Bonita Lakes Dr 39301. Fax: 601/483-2675. **Facility:** 59 units. 58 one-bedroom standard units. 1 one-bedroom suite with whirlpool. 2 stories (no elevator), exterior corridors. *Bath:* combo or shower only. **Parking:** on-site. **Terms:** cancellation fee imposed, small pets only. **Amenities:** *Some:* dual phone lines, irons, hair dryers. **Pool(s):** small outdoor. **Leisure Activities:** exercise room. **Guest Services:** wireless Internet. **Business Services:** PC, fax (fee). **Cards:** AX, DC, DS, MC, VI.

SOME UNITS

MICROTEL INN & SUITES *Book at AAA.com* **Phone:** (601)553-8100

Small-scale Hotel

All Year 1P: $60-$120 2P: $70-$130 XP: $10 F18

Location: I-20/59, exit 154 westbound, 0.4 mi s to Bonita Lakes Dr, then just sw; exit 154A eastbound, just s. Located at Bonita Lakes Mall. 518 Bonita Lakes Dr 39301. Fax: 601/553-0996. **Facility:** 79 one-bedroom standard units. 3 stories, interior corridors. *Bath:* combo or shower only. **Parking:** on-site. **Amenities:** high-speed Internet, dual phone lines, irons, hair dryers. **Leisure Activities:** exercise room. **Guest Services:** coin laundry, wireless Internet. **Business Services:** meeting rooms, PC, fax (fee). **Cards:** AX, CB, DC, DS, MC, VI.

SOME UNITS

MOTEL 6 *Book at AAA.com* **Phone:** 601/482-1182

Motel

Property failed to provide current rates

Location: I-20/59, exit 153, 0.5 mi sw. 2309 S Frontage Rd 39301. Fax: 601/483-9247. **Facility:** 88 one-bedroom standard units. 2 stories (no elevator), exterior corridors. *Bath:* shower only. **Parking:** on-site. **Pool(s):** small outdoor. **Guest Services:** coin laundry.

SOME UNITS

RODEWAY INN *Book great rates at AAA.com* **Phone:** (601)482-4400

Motel

All Year 1P: $50-$110 2P: $50-$110 XP: $5 F18

Location: I-20/59, exit 154B eastbound; exit 154 westbound, on northeast frontage road. 146 Hwy 11 & 80 39301. Fax: 601/482-3400. **Facility:** 30 units. 27 one-bedroom standard units. 3 one-bedroom suites, some with whirlpools. 2 stories (no elevator), exterior corridors. **Parking:** on-site. **Terms:** [ECP] meal plan available. **Amenities:** irons, hair dryers. **Guest Services:** coin laundry, wireless Internet. **Business Services:** fax (fee). **Cards:** AX, DS, MC, VI.

SOME UNITS

FEE

SLEEP INN *Book great rates at AAA.com* **Phone:** 601/485-4646

SAVE

Motel

All Year 1P: $60-$76 2P: $70-$76

Location: I-20/59, exit 153, just sw. 1301 Hamilton Ave 39301. Fax: 601/485-3722. **Facility:** 55 one-bedroom standard units. 2 stories (no elevator), interior corridors. *Bath:* combo or shower only. **Parking:** on-site. **Terms:** [CP] meal plan available. **Amenities:** voice mail, irons, hair dryers. **Pool(s):** small outdoor. **Leisure Activities:** exercise room. **Guest Services:** coin laundry, wireless Internet. **Business Services:** PC, fax (fee). **Cards:** AX, CB, DC, DS, JC, MC, VI. **Free Special Amenities: expanded continental breakfast.**

SOME UNITS

SUPER 8 MOTEL *Book great rates at AAA.com* **Phone:** 601/482-8088

SAVE

Motel

All Year 1P: $60-$65 2P: $65-$70 XP: $5 D10

Location: I-20/59, exit 154 westbound; exit 154B eastbound, on northeast frontage road. 124 Hwy 11 & 80 39301. Fax: 601/482-1961. **Facility:** 67 one-bedroom standard units. 2 stories (no elevator), exterior corridors. **Parking:** on-site. **Terms:** 1-3 night minimum stay - seasonal, weekly rates available, package plans. **Amenities:** high-speed Internet, irons, hair dryers. **Guest Services:** coin laundry, wireless Internet. **Business Services:** fax (fee). **Cards:** AX, DS, MC, VI. **Free Special Amenities: continental breakfast and high-speed Internet.**

SOME UNITS

WHERE TO DINE

BARNHILL'S BUFFET **Lunch:** $5-$9 **Dinner:** $7-$10 **Phone:** 601/485-3335

American

Location: I-59, exit 153, just n on US 11. 2220 N Frontage Rd 39301. **Hours:** 10:45 am-8:45 pm, Fri-9 pm, Sat 7 am-9 pm, Sun 7 am-8:45 pm. Closed: 12/25. **Features:** Casual dress. **Parking:** on-site. **Cards:** AX, DS, MC, VI.

CRESCENT CITY GRILL **Lunch:** $7-$17 **Dinner:** $7-$17 **Phone:** 601/553-3656

Cajun

Location: I-20/59, exit 154A eastbound; exit 154 westbound, just s. 519 Azalea Dr 39305. **Hours:** 11 am-10 pm, Fri & Sat-11 pm. Closed major holidays. **Features:** In a bustling commercial area, the grill presents a Cajun/Creole menu that emphasizes seafood. Casual dress; cocktails. **Parking:** on-site. **Cards:** AX, DS, MC, VI.

THE HUNGRY HEIFER **Dinner:** $6-$25 **Phone:** 601/483-2509

American

Location: I-20/59, exit 153, 1.2 mi nw on 22nd Ave, then 0.5 mi se. 1310 14th St 39301. **Hours:** 4 pm-10 pm. Closed major holidays; also Sun. **Reservations:** accepted. **Features:** Popular with the after-work crowd, the eatery serves choice steaks and seasonal wild game and seafood, with a healthy infusion of live music. Casual dress; cocktails. **Parking:** on-site and street. **Cards:** AX, DC, DS, MC, VI.

MOSS POINT pop. 15,851

WHERE TO STAY

BEST WESTERN FLAGSHIP INN *Book great rates at AAA.com* **Phone:** (228)475-5000

SAVE

Small-scale Hotel

All Year 1P: $60-$110 2P: $70-$110 XP: $10 F

Location: I-10, exit 69, just s. 4830 Amoco Dr 39563 (PO Box 1280, ESCATAWPA, 39552). Fax: 228/475-0601. **Facility:** 78 one-bedroom standard units. 2 stories (no elevator), exterior corridors. *Bath:* combo or shower only. **Parking:** on-site. **Terms:** small pets only ($6 extra charge). **Amenities:** dual phone lines, irons, hair dryers. **Pool(s):** small outdoor. **Guest Services:** valet laundry. **Cards:** AX, CB, DC, DS, MC, VI. **Free Special Amenities: expanded continental breakfast and newspaper.**

SOME UNITS

FEE

COMFORT INN *Book great rates at AAA.com* **Phone:** 228/474-3600

Small-scale Hotel

Property failed to provide current rates

Location: I-10, exit 69, just s. 6801 Hwy 63 39563. Fax: 228/474-2080. **Facility:** 82 one-bedroom standard units, some with whirlpools. 3 stories, interior corridors. *Bath:* combo or shower only. **Parking:** on-site. **Amenities:** voice mail, irons, hair dryers. **Pool(s):** small outdoor. **Leisure Activities:** exercise room. **Guest Services:** valet and coin laundry.

SOME UNITS

HOLIDAY INN EXPRESS Book at AAA.com **Phone:** 228/474-2100

Small-scale Hotel

Property failed to provide current rates

Location: I-10, exit 69, just s. 4800 Amoco Dr 39563. Fax: 228/474-0084. **Facility:** 102 units. 96 one-bedroom standard units, some with whirlpools. 6 one-bedroom suites with efficiencies. 3 stories, interior corridors. *Bath:* combo or shower only. **Parking:** on-site. **Terms:** small pets only ($10 extra charge). **Amenities:** voice mail, irons, hair dryers. *Some:* dual phone lines. **Pool(s):** outdoor, wading. **Leisure Activities:** whirlpool. *Fee:* game room. **Guest Services:** valet and coin laundry. **Business Services:** meeting rooms.

FEE SOME UNITS FEE

QUALITY INN Book great rates at AAA.com **Phone:** (228)475-2477

SAVE

Small-scale Hotel

All Year [ECP] 1P: $59-$79 2P: $79-$109 XP: $10 F12

Location: I-10, exit 69, just s. 6800 Hwy 63 N 39563. Fax: 228/475-8990. **Facility:** 114 one-bedroom standard units. 2 stories (no elevator), exterior corridors. **Parking:** on-site. **Amenities:** high-speed Internet, voice mail, irons, hair dryers. **Pool(s):** outdoor. **Leisure Activities:** exercise room. **Guest Services:** valet laundry. **Business Services:** meeting rooms. **Cards:** AX, CB, DC, DS, MC, VI. **Free Special Amenities: expanded continental breakfast and high-speed Internet.**

SOME UNITS

WHERE TO DINE

BARNHILL'S BUFFET **Lunch:** $5-$9 **Dinner:** $7-$10 **Phone:** 228/474-2986

American

Location: I-10, exit 69, just s. 6706 Hwy 63 39563. **Hours:** 10:45 am-8:45 pm, Fri-9 pm, Sat 7 am-9 pm, Sun 7 am-8:45 pm. Closed: 12/25. **Features:** Casual dress. **Parking:** on-site. **Cards:** AX, DS, MC, VI.

NATCHEZ pop. 18,464

WHERE TO STAY

COMFORT INN Book great rates at AAA.com **Phone:** (601)446-5500

SAVE

Small-scale Hotel

3/11-4/15 [CP]	1P: $80-$90	2P: $90-$100	XP: $10	F18
4/16-10/31 [CP]	1P: $65-$75	2P: $71-$81	XP: $6	F18
12/1-3/10 & 11/1-11/30 [CP]	1P: $60-$70	2P: $65-$75	XP: $6	F18

Location: 1 mi ne on US 61, 84 and 98. Located in a commercial area. 337 D'Evereux Dr 39120. Fax: 601/446-5500. **Facility:** 50 one-bedroom standard units, some with whirlpools. 2 stories (no elevator), exterior corridors. *Bath:* combo or shower only. **Parking:** on-site. **Amenities:** high-speed Internet, irons, hair dryers. **Pool(s):** outdoor. **Guest Services:** wireless Internet. **Business Services:** PC. **Cards:** AX, CB, DC, DS, JC, MC, VI. **Free Special Amenities: continental breakfast and high-speed Internet.**

SOME UNITS

DAYS INN OF NATCHEZ Book great rates at AAA.com **Phone:** (601)445-8291

SAVE

Small-scale Hotel

All Year 1P: $59-$85 2P: $64-$90 XP: $5 F17

Location: Just se of jct US 61, 84 and 98. Located in a commercial area. 109 US Hwy 61 S 39120. Fax: 601/442-4861. **Facility:** 121 one-bedroom standard units. 2 stories (no elevator), exterior corridors. **Parking:** on-site. **Terms:** pets ($5 fee). **Amenities:** hair dryers. **Pool(s):** outdoor. **Leisure Activities:** game room. **Guest Services:** sundries, coin laundry, wireless Internet. **Business Services:** fax (fee). **Cards:** AX, DC, DS, MC, VI. **Free Special Amenities: expanded continental breakfast and high-speed Internet.**

SOME UNITS

FEE

THE DR'S INN **Phone:** 601/442-3561

SAVE

Historic Bed & Breakfast

All Year [BP] 1P: $125 2P: $125 XP: $30 F12

Location: 0.4 mi n of jct Washington and Martin Luther King sts. Located in a historic residential area. 507 Washington St 39120. Fax: 601/442-4785. **Facility:** Spacious bedrooms, modern conveniences and Southern hospitality combine at this comfortable B&B in historic Natchez. Smoke free premises. 4 one-bedroom standard units. 2 stories (no elevator), interior corridors. **Parking:** street. **Terms:** age restrictions may apply. **Amenities:** hair dryers. **Guest Services:** complimentary evening beverages. **Cards:** AX, MC, VI. **Free Special Amenities: full breakfast and local telephone calls.**

ECONO LODGE Book great rates at AAA.com **Phone:** (601)442-3686

SAVE

Motel

All Year 1P: $50-$60 2P: $55-$65 XP: $5 F15

Location: Just n of jct US 61/84. 271 D'Evereaux Dr 39120. Fax: 601/442-0834. **Facility:** 59 one-bedroom standard units. 2 stories (no elevator), exterior corridors. *Bath:* combo or shower only. **Parking:** on-site. **Terms:** package plans. **Amenities:** irons, hair dryers. **Guest Services:** coin laundry, wireless Internet. **Business Services:** PC, fax (fee). **Cards:** AX, DS, MC, VI. **Free Special Amenities: full breakfast and local telephone calls.**

SOME UNITS

ISLE OF CAPRI CASINO-NATCHEZ **Phone:** 601/445-0605

Small-scale Hotel

All Year 1P: $85-$129 2P: $85-$129 XP: $10 F12

Location: US 84/65, exit just before the Mississippi River. 645 S Canal St 39120 (53 Silver St). Fax: 601/442-9823. **Facility:** 143 units. 137 one-bedroom standard units. 6 one-bedroom suites ($195-$209). 6 stories, interior corridors. **Parking:** on-site. **Terms:** cancellation fee imposed, package plans. **Amenities:** video games (fee), voice mail, irons, hair dryers. **Pool(s):** outdoor. **Leisure Activities:** whirlpool, exercise room. **Guest Services:** gift shop, area transportation. **Business Services:** meeting rooms. **Cards:** AX, DS, MC, VI.

SOME UNITS

ASK / /

LINDEN **Phone:** 601/445-5472

AAA SAVE

Historic Bed & Breakfast

All Year [BP] 1P: $120-$145 2P: $120-$145 XP: $40

Location: 1.5 mi e, just off John A Quitman Pkwy. 1 Linden Pl 39120. Fax: 601/442-7548. **Facility:** This antebellum home dating from 1800 features canopied beds and a wide porch. Smoke free premises. 7 units. 6 one- and 1 two-bedroom standard units. 2 stories (no elevator), interior/exterior corridors. *Bath:* combo or shower only. **Parking:** on-site. **Terms:** 7 day cancellation notice-fee imposed, package plans. **Free Special Amenities: full breakfast and local telephone calls.** *(See color ad p 465)*

SOME UNITS

/ /

MONMOUTH PLANTATION *Book great rates at AAA.com* **Phone:** (601)442-5852

AAA SAVE

Historic Country Inn

1/1-11/30 [BP]	1P: $170-$295	2P: $170-$295	XP: $50
12/1-12/31 [BP]	1P: $165-$285	2P: $165-$285	XP: $50

Location: 1.3 mi e on State and John A Quitman pkwys. Located in a historic residential district. 36 Melrose Ave 39120. Fax: 601/446-7762. **Facility:** Guest rooms are furnished with period antiques at this restored antebellum home that was once owned by Mexican War General John A. Quitman. Designated smoking area. 30 units. 15 one-bedroom standard units, some with whirlpools. 14 one- and 1 two-bedroom suites, some with whirlpools. 3 stories (no elevator), interior/exterior corridors. **Parking:** on-site. **Terms:** office hours 8 am-10 pm, age restrictions may apply, 7 day cancellation notice-fee imposed, package plans. **Amenities:** voice mail, irons, hair dryers. **Dining:** restaurant, see separate listing. **Leisure Activities:** fishing, croquet court, walking trail. *Fee:* massage. **Guest Services:** gift shop, complimentary evening beverages, valet laundry, wireless Internet. **Business Services:** meeting rooms, business center. **Cards:** AX, CB, DC, DS, MC, VI. **Free Special Amenities: full breakfast and local telephone calls.** *(See color ad below)*

SOME UNITS

/ VCR /

FEE

NATCHEZ EOLA HOTEL *Book great rates at AAA.com* **Phone:** (601)445-6000

AAA SAVE

Historic Large-scale Hotel

3/1-5/31 & 10/1-11/30	1P: $128-$145	2P: $128-$145	XP: $10	F12
12/1-2/28 & 6/1-9/30	1P: $98-$118	2P: $98-$118	XP: $10	F12

Location: Corner of Main and Pearl sts. 110 N Pearl St 39120. Fax: 601/446-5310. **Facility:** This restored hotel, dating from 1927, has many balcony rooms. 131 units. 128 one-bedroom standard units. 2 one- and 1 two-bedroom suites ($300-$500), some with whirlpools. 7 stories, interior corridors. *Bath:* combo or shower only. **Parking:** on-site. **Terms:** cancellation fee imposed. **Amenities:** voice mail, irons, hair dryers. **Dining:** 2 restaurants, 6:30 am-2 & 5:30-10 pm, cocktails. **Leisure Activities:** exercise room. **Guest Services:** gift shop, valet laundry. **Business Services:** meeting rooms. **Cards:** AX, CB, DC, DS, MC, VI. **Free Special Amenities: room upgrade (subject to availability with advance reservations) and high-speed Internet.** *(See color ad p 465)*

SOME UNITS

/ /

RIVERSIDE B & B **Phone:** 601/446-5730

Bed & Breakfast

All Year 1P: $90 2P: $90

Location: S from Oak St; between Clifton and Linton aves; entrance by service alley. Located in a residential area. 211 Clifton Ave 39120. **Facility:** Once a gatekeeper's home and now restored, this B&B dating from 1858 overlooks the river and is decorated with period antiques. Smoke free premises. 3 units. 2 one-bedroom standard units. 1 one-bedroom suite ($120-$160). 2 stories (no elevator), interior corridors. *Bath:* combo or shower only. **Parking:** on-site. **Terms:** age restrictions may apply, 7 day cancellation notice, [BP] meal plan available.

SOME UNITS

/ VCR /

WHERE TO DINE

THE CARRIAGE HOUSE RESTAURANT **Lunch:** $7-$15 **Dinner:** $8-$16 **Phone:** 601/445-5151

Traditional American

Location: High St at Pearl St; on grounds of Stanton Hall, on Commerce St side. 401 High St 39120. **Hours:** 11 am-2 pm; also 5 pm-8 pm 3/12-4/13 & 10/22-11/5. **Reservations:** accepted. **Features:** Located in Stanton Hall's carriage house, this restaurant features hearty, southern-style cooking such as fried chicken, biscuits and pecan pie. A dinner theater is hosted during Natchez's fall pilgrimage, which lasts from late September through mid-October. Casual dress; cocktails. **Parking:** street. **Cards:** AX, DS, MC, VI.

THE CASTLE RESTAURANT AND PUB **Lunch:** $8-$13 **Dinner:** $15-$37 **Phone:** 601/446-8500

Regional American

Location: Jct US 61, 84 and 98, 1.5 mi w on US 84 and 98, then 1.5 mi n; in Dunleith Plantation. 84 Homochitto St 39120. **Hours:** 7:30-10 am, 11-2 & 6-9 pm, Fri-10 pm, Sat 7:30 am-10 & 6-10 pm, Sun 7:30 am-10 am. Closed: 12/25. **Reservations:** suggested. **Features:** Within the brick walls of the Dunleith Plantation's former carriage house, the restaurant offers an interesting medley of New Orleans Cajun and traditional Southern cooking. This place's red fish, speckled trout and crab cakes have contributed to its solid reputation. Also delicious is grilled filet mignon served on a bed of Yukon Gold creamed potatoes with a mushroom port wine Bordelaise sauce. Dressy casual; cocktails. **Parking:** valet. **Cards:** AX, DS, MC, VI.

COCK OF THE WALK **Dinner:** $11-$18 **Phone:** 601/446-8920

Seafood

Location: Between Jefferson and Franklin sts; behind post office; downtown. 200 N Broadway St 39120. **Hours:** 5 pm-close. Closed: 1/1, 11/22, 12/25; also Sun. **Features:** On the banks of the mighty Mississippi, the family-friendly restaurant serves good old-fashioned seafood on cast-iron skillets and tin miners' plates. Don't miss the yummy fried dill pickles and skillet bread. Casual dress; cocktails. **Parking:** on-site. **Cards:** AX, DS, MC, VI.

KING'S TAVERN **Dinner:** $12-$21 **Phone:** 601/446-8845

American

Location: Jefferson and Rankin sts; center. 619 Jefferson St 39120. **Hours:** 5 pm-10 pm. Closed: 1/1, 11/22, 12/25. **Reservations:** accepted. **Features:** Built in 1789 at the end of the famed Natchez Trace and operated as a tavern, stage stop and mail station, the city's oldest building was renovated in 1972 to house what is now a popular restaurant. The historic essence of the building was maintained—be sure to ask the staff about the resident ghost. The menu's featured item is hickory-smoked prime rib. Casual dress; cocktails. **Parking:** street. **Cards:** AX, MC, VI.

LA FIESTA GRANDE RESTAURANTE MEXICANO **Lunch:** $5-$8 **Dinner:** $6-$12 **Phone:** 601/445-0720

Mexican

Location: On US 61/84/65, 1 mi se of Mississippi River Bridge. 288 John R Junkin Dr 39120. **Hours:** 11 am-10 pm, Fri-11 pm, Sat from noon, Sun noon-10 pm. Closed major holidays. **Features:** Guests can enjoy good Mexican food, authentic music and friendly service at the popular eatery, which is just a mile from the mighty Mississippi River. Casual dress; cocktails. **Parking:** on-site. **Cards:** AX, MC, VI.

MAGNOLIA GRILL **Lunch:** $7-$9 **Dinner:** $13-$20 **Phone:** 601/446-7670

Regional Seafood

Location: Natchez Under the Hill at Mississippi River. 49 Silver St 39120. **Hours:** 11 am-10 pm. Closed: 1/1, 11/22, 12/25. **Reservations:** suggested. **Features:** Set by the banks of the mighty Mississippi, the restaurant serves simple but scrumptious food, including such local favorites as boula boula, a soup with turtle, crab and sherry; crabmeat-stuffed mushrooms; and the diet-busting barbecue shrimp. Cooked in hot spicy butter, it's ideal for dipping toasted French bread. Delicious homemade desserts and spectacular sunsets are a memorable way to round off a meal. Casual dress; cocktails. **Parking:** on-site. **Cards:** AX, MC, VI. **Historic**

MONMOUTH PLANTATION *Menu on AAA.com* **Dinner:** $45 **Phone:** 601/442-5852

American

Location: 1.3 mi e on State and John A Quitman pkwys; in Monmouth Plantation. 36 Melrose Ave 39120. **Hours:** dinner seating at 7:30 pm; 2 seatings in season. **Reservations:** required. **Features:** The setting is that of an intimate, elegant dinner party hosted in the main house of a beautiful plantation. After strolling in the 26-acres of gardens, settle down to a five-course meal featuring favorites such as grilled quail with a hot pepper glaze. Dressy casual; cocktails. **Parking:** on-site. **Cards:** AX, CB, DC, DS, MC, VI. **Historic**

(See color ad p 466)

PEARL STREET PASTA **Lunch:** $6-$9 **Dinner:** $8-$15 **Phone:** 601/442-9284

Italian

Location: Just s of jct Main St; downtown. 105 S Pearl St 39120. **Hours:** 11:30 am-2 & 6-10 pm. Closed major holidays; also Sun. **Reservations:** accepted. **Features:** Continental influences punctuate good Italian dishes at the cozy and romantic spot. Casual dress; cocktails. **Parking:** street. **Cards:** AX, DS, MC, VI.

OCEAN SPRINGS pop. 17,225

WHERE TO STAY

BEST WESTERN CYPRESS CREEK *Book great rates at AAA.com* **Phone:** (228)875-7111

Small-scale Hotel

All Year 1P: $99-$159 2P: $99-$159 XP: $10 F15

Location: I-10, exit 50, just nw. 7921 Lamar Poole Rd 39532. Fax: 228/875-7186. **Facility:** 90 one-bedroom standard units, some with whirlpools. 4 stories, interior corridors. *Bath:* combo or shower only. **Parking:** on-site. **Terms:** 7 day cancellation notice, [CP] meal plan available. **Amenities:** high-speed Internet, voice mail, irons, hair dryers. **Pool(s):** small outdoor. **Leisure Activities:** exercise room. **Guest Services:** area transportation-casinos. **Business Services:** meeting rooms, business center. **Cards:** AX, CB, DC, DS, JC, MC, VI. **Free Special Amenities: expanded continental breakfast and high-speed Internet.**

SOME UNITS

COMFORT INN BILOXI/OCEAN SPRINGS *Book great rates at AAA.com* **Phone:** (228)818-0300

Small-scale Hotel

12/1-6/1 & 9/1-11/30 1P: $99-$149 2P: $99-$149 XP: $10 F12
6/2-8/31 1P: $89-$149 2P: $89-$149 XP: $10 F12

Location: I-10, exit 50, just nw on service road. 7827 Lamar Poole Rd 39532. Fax: 228/872-2980. **Facility:** 84 one-bedroom standard units, some with whirlpools. 3 stories, interior corridors. *Bath:* combo or shower only. **Parking:** on-site. **Terms:** [CP] meal plan available, pets ($25-$50 fee). **Amenities:** high-speed Internet, voice mail, irons, hair dryers. **Pool(s):** small outdoor. **Leisure Activities:** whirlpool. **Guest Services:** coin laundry, area transportation-casino. **Cards:** AX, DC, DS, MC, VI. **Free Special Amenities: continental breakfast and high-speed Internet.**

COUNTRY INN & SUITES *Book at AAA.com* **Phone:** (228)818-0901

Small-scale Hotel

All Year 1P: $89 2P: $99 XP: $10 F10

Location: I-10, exit 50, just ne on SR 609. 13900 Wilford Seymour Rd 39564. Fax: 228/818-0902. **Facility:** 64 units. 44 one-bedroom standard units, some with whirlpools. 20 one-bedroom suites ($135-$155). 2 stories, interior corridors. *Bath:* combo or shower only. **Parking:** on-site. **Terms:** [ECP] meal plan available. **Amenities:** high-speed Internet, dual phone lines, voice mail, irons, hair dryers. **Pool(s):** small outdoor. **Leisure Activities:** exercise room. **Guest Services:** coin laundry, area transportation. **Business Services:** meeting rooms. **Cards:** AX, DS, MC, VI.

GULF HILLS HOTEL AND CONFERENCE CENTER *Book at AAA.com* **Phone:** (228)875-4211

Small-scale Hotel

All Year [ECP] 1P: $109-$139 2P: $109-$139 XP: $10 F18

Location: I-10, exit 50, 2.3 mi s on SR 609, 0.5 mi w on Shore Dr, then follow Fairway Dr. Located on Gulf Hills Golf Course. 13701 Paso Rd 39564. Fax: 228/875-4213. **Facility:** 53 units. 52 one-bedroom standard units, some with efficiencies. 1 one-bedroom suite ($300-$500) with whirlpool. 2 stories (no elevator), exterior corridors. *Bath:* combo or shower only. **Parking:** on-site. **Terms:** 3 day cancellation notice-fee imposed, package plans. **Amenities:** dual phone lines, voice mail, irons, hair dryers. *Some:* DVD players (fee), CD players, high-speed Internet. **Pool(s):** outdoor. **Leisure Activities:** *Fee:* golf-18 holes, 10 lighted tennis courts. **Guest Services:** coin laundry. **Business Services:** meeting rooms. **Cards:** AX, DS, MC, VI.

HAMPTON INN BILOXI/OCEAN SPRINGS *Book great rates at AAA.com* **Phone:** 228/872-6370

Small-scale Hotel

Property failed to provide current rates

Location: I-10, exit 50, just sw. 13921 Big Ridge Rd 39532. Fax: 228/872-8387. **Facility:** 71 units. 69 one-bedroom standard units. 2 one-bedroom suites. 3 stories, interior corridors. *Bath:* combo or shower only. **Parking:** on-site. **Amenities:** video games (fee), high-speed Internet, voice mail, irons, hair dryers. **Pool(s):** small outdoor. **Leisure Activities:** exercise room. **Guest Services:** coin laundry. **Business Services:** meeting rooms.

HOWARD JOHNSON EXPRESS INN *Book great rates at AAA.com* **Phone:** (228)872-0440

Small-scale Hotel

5/21-9/3 [CP] 1P: $80-$140 2P: $80-$140 XP: $10 F17
12/1-5/20 & 9/4-11/30 [CP] 1P: $60-$130 2P: $60-$130 XP: $10 F17

Location: I-10, exit 50, just se. 7412 Tucker Rd 39564. Fax: 228/872-0320. **Facility:** 78 one-bedroom standard units. 3 stories, interior corridors. *Bath:* combo or shower only. **Parking:** on-site. **Amenities:** high-speed Internet, voice mail, irons, hair dryers. **Pool(s):** small outdoor. **Guest Services:** coin laundry. **Business Services:** meeting rooms. **Cards:** AX, CB, DC, DS, JC, MC, VI. **Free Special Amenities: continental breakfast and high-speed Internet.**

QUALITY INN **Phone:** 228/875-7555

Small-scale Hotel

3/2-7/31 1P: $90-$110 2P: $90-$110 XP: $5 F
12/1-3/1 & 8/1-11/30 1P: $80-$100 2P: $80-$100 XP: $5 F

Location: I-10, exit 50, 0.4 mi s on SR 609. 7304 Washington Ave 39564. Fax: 228/875-6550. **Facility:** 64 one-bedroom standard units, some with whirlpools. 2 stories (no elevator), exterior corridors. *Bath:* combo or shower only. **Parking:** on-site. **Terms:** cancellation fee imposed, [CP] & [ECP] meal plans available, package plans, small pets only ($20 fee). **Amenities:** high-speed Internet, dual phone lines, voice mail, irons, hair dryers. **Pool(s):** small outdoor. **Leisure Activities:** whirlpool. **Guest Services:** coin laundry, area transportation. **Cards:** AX, DC, DS, MC, VI.

RAMADA LIMITED *Book at AAA.com* **Phone:** (228)872-2323

Small-scale Hotel

All Year [ECP] 1P: $79-$139 2P: $99-$159 XP: $10 F16

Location: I-10, exit 50, just n. 8011 Tucker Rd 39532. Fax: 228/872-2833. **Facility:** 70 one-bedroom standard units, some with whirlpools. 2 stories (no elevator), exterior corridors. *Bath:* combo or shower only. **Parking:** on-site. **Terms:** cancellation fee imposed, 7% service charge, small pets only ($10 extra charge). **Amenities:** high-speed Internet, voice mail, irons, hair dryers. **Pool(s):** small outdoor. **Leisure Activities:** exercise room. **Guest Services:** coin laundry, area transportation. **Cards:** AX, CB, DC, DS, JC, MC, VI.

SUPER 8 MOTEL *Book at AAA.com* **Phone:** (228)875-2288

Small-scale Hotel

All Year 1P: $49-$125 2P: $49-$125 XP: $5 F18

Location: I-10, exit 50, just ne. 13838 Wilfred Seymour Rd 39565. Fax: 228/875-6188. **Facility:** 92 one-bedroom standard units, some with whirlpools. 2 stories (no elevator), exterior corridors. *Bath:* combo or shower only. **Parking:** on-site. **Terms:** [CP] meal plan available. **Amenities:** safes (fee). *Some:* high-speed Internet, irons, hair dryers. **Pool(s):** small outdoor. **Guest Services:** coin laundry. **Business Services:** meeting rooms. **Cards:** AX, DS, MC, VI.

WHERE TO DINE

AL FRESCO ITALIAN BISTRO **Lunch:** $6-$9 **Dinner:** $13-$35 **Phone:** 228/818-9395

Italian

Location: 1 mi s from jct US 90. 708 Washington Ave 39564. **Hours:** 11 am-9 pm, Fri & Sat-10 pm. Closed: 1/1, 12/24, 12/25. **Reservations:** suggested. **Features:** Located on a quaint little downtown street alongside other restaurants and shops, the pleasant little bistro offers pizza, fun pastas such as BBQ chicken rigatoni and the more traditional Italian dishes. On a nice summer evening, opt to dine in "la bella cortile," the beautiful courtyard. Casual dress; cocktails. **Parking:** street. **Cards:** AX, DS, MC, VI.

AUNT JENNY'S CATFISH RESTAURANT **Lunch:** $8-$13 **Dinner:** $8-$13 **Phone:** 228/875-9201

American

Location: From US 90, just n on SR 609 (Washington Ave). 1217 Washington Ave 39564. **Hours:** 11:30 am-close, Sat from 4 pm, Sun noon-8 pm. Closed: 11/22, 12/25 & Easter; also Mon. **Features:** Guests can sample all-you-can-eat catfish and Southern fried chicken in a lovely setting surrounded by centuries-old, moss-draped oaks. The dining area looks out onto the beautiful bay. Casual dress; cocktails; entertainment. **Parking:** on-site. **Cards:** DS, MC, VI.

BAYVIEW GOURMET **Lunch:** $6-$9 **Phone:** 228/875-4252

American

Location: From US 90, just s on SR 609 (Washington Ave), then just e; across from Chamber of Commerce. 1010 Robinson St 39564. **Hours:** 8 am-3 pm, Sun 7 am-1 pm. Closed major holidays; also Mon & Tues. **Features:** Offering a large selection of fresh salads and home-cooked soups, the Bayview Gourmet is a real treat. Not to be missed are tomato basil soup and the crabber burger, an overflowing crab cake on whole wheat with tasty Creole sauce. Casual dress; cocktails. **Parking:** on-site. **Cards:** AX, CB, DC, DS, MC, VI.

MANHATTAN GRILL STEAKHOUSE **Dinner:** $14-$27 **Phone:** 228/872-6480

Steak House

Location: From US 90, just s on SR 609 (Washington Ave); in historic downtown. 705 Washington Ave 39564. **Hours:** 5 pm-10 pm. Closed major holidays; also Sun. **Reservations:** accepted. **Features:** In historic downtown, the restaurant builds its menu on succulent steaks, pasta and seafood. Patrons can sit back, relax and enjoy charming town views. Casual dress; cocktails. **Parking:** on-site. **Cards:** AX, MC, VI.

MARTHA'S TEA ROOM **Lunch:** $6-$10 **Phone:** 228/872-2554

American

Location: From US 90, just s on SR 609 (Washington Ave); in historic downtown. 715 Washington Ave 39564. **Hours:** 11 am-2 pm. Closed major holidays; also Sun. **Reservations:** accepted. **Features:** In the historic part of town, the charming cottage offers delicious homemade breads and desserts. Many health-conscious choices are included among a good selection of dishes and unusual sandwiches. A displayed collection of teapots contributes to the quaint atmosphere. Casual dress. **Parking:** on-site. **Historic**

MCELROY'S ON THE BAYOU **Lunch:** $7-$26 **Dinner:** $11-$26 **Phone:** 228/818-4600

Seafood

Location: On US 90, 0.7 mi e of Biloxi/Ocean Springs Bridge. 705 Bienville Blvd 39564. **Hours:** 7 am-10 pm. Closed major holidays; also Tues. **Reservations:** accepted. **Features:** This family restaurant located just over the Bridge boasts an attractive location, friendly, and efficient service. Their Cajun inspired dishes compare to some of the best in New Orleans. Casual dress; cocktails. **Parking:** on-site. **Cards:** AX, DC, DS, MC, VI.

PHOENICIA GOURMET RESTAURANT **Lunch:** $8-$15 **Dinner:** $13-$35 **Phone:** 228/875-0603

Mediterranean

Location: From US 90, just s on SR 609 (Washington Ave), then just e; in historic downtown. 1223 Government St 39564. **Hours:** 10:30 am-3 & 5-9 pm, Fri & Sat-10 pm, Sun 10 am-4 pm. Closed major holidays. **Features:** The unassuming restaurant prepares a variety of delicious and health-conscious Mediterranean dishes. Soft music and courteous, professional service enhance the experience. Casual dress. **Parking:** on-site. **Cards:** AX, MC, VI.

SALVETTI BROS CABARET/RISTORANTE **Dinner:** $8-$16 **Phone:** 228/875-0120

Italian

Location: On US 90, 1.3 mi w of SR 57. 4505 Bienville Blvd 39564. **Hours:** 3:30 pm-10 pm. **Reservations:** accepted. **Features:** Relocated from the historic district to a new location on US 90, the congenial family restaurant is now larger and has a lounge. The menu includes many old favorites as well as some new temptations. Casual dress; cocktails. **Parking:** on-site. **Cards:** AX, DS, MC, VI.

THE SHED BBQ **Lunch:** $4-$15 **Dinner:** $4-$15 **Phone:** 228/875-9590

Barbecue

Location: I-10, exit 57, just n; in Camp Journey's End. 7501 Hwy 57 39565. **Hours:** 11 am-9 pm, Fri & Sat-10 pm. Closed: Mon, Tues & week of Christmas. **Reservations:** not accepted. **Features:** The festive and casual joint prepares "fall-off-the-bone" baby back ribs and barbecue brisket in huge portions. Homemade Southern iced tea tops off the meal and leaves patrons satisfied. Live music adds to the atmosphere on weekends. Casual dress; beer only. **Parking:** on-site. **Cards:** DS, MC, VI.

OLIVE BRANCH pop. 21,054

WHERE TO STAY

COMFORT INN *Book great rates at AAA.com* **Phone:** (662)895-0456

Small-scale Hotel

All Year 1P: $74-$79 2P: $79-$84 XP: $5 F14

Location: US 78, exit 2, SR 302, just w. 7049 Enterprise 38654. Fax: 662/895-9555. **Facility:** 63 one-bedroom standard units, some with whirlpools. 2 stories (no elevator), interior corridors. *Bath:* combo or shower only. **Parking:** on-site. **Terms:** [ECP] meal plan available, pets ($10-$20 extra charge). **Amenities:** high-speed Internet, voice mail, irons, hair dryers. **Pool(s):** small outdoor. **Leisure Activities:** exercise room. **Guest Services:** valet laundry. **Business Services:** PC. **Cards:** AX, CB, DC, DS, MC, VI.

SOME UNITS

FEE

HAMPTON INN *Book great rates at AAA.com* **Phone:** (662)893-7600

Small-scale Hotel

All Year 1P: $109-$149 2P: $109-$149 XP: $7 F12

Location: Just w of US 78 on SR 302. 6830 Crumpler Blvd 38654. Fax: 662/893-3799. **Facility:** 77 one-bedroom standard units, some with whirlpools. 3 stories, interior corridors. *Bath:* combo or shower only. **Parking:** on-site. **Terms:** package plans. **Pool(s):** small heated indoor. **Leisure Activities:** whirlpool, exercise room. **Guest Services:** valet and coin laundry, wireless Internet. **Business Services:** meeting rooms, business center. **Cards:** AX, DC, DS, MC, VI.

ASK

HOLIDAY INN EXPRESS HOTEL & SUITES *Book great rates at AAA.com* **Phone:** (662)893-8700

AAA SAVE

Small-scale Hotel

All Year 1P: $89-$109 2P: $89-$119 XP: $10 F18

Location: US 78, exit 4, just e. 8900 Expressway Dr 38654. Fax: 662/893-8701. **Facility:** 80 units. 79 one-bedroom standard units, some with whirlpools. 1 one-bedroom suite. 3 stories, interior corridors. *Bath:* combo or shower only. **Parking:** on-site. **Terms:** cancellation fee imposed, pets ($10 extra charge, in designated units). **Amenities:** high-speed Internet, dual phone lines, voice mail, irons, hair dryers. **Pool(s):** small outdoor. **Leisure Activities:** picnic area, grill, exercise room. **Guest Services:** sundries, valet and coin laundry, wireless Internet. **Business Services:** meeting rooms, business center. **Cards:** AX, CB, DC, DS, JC, MC, VI. **Free Special Amenities: expanded continental breakfast and high-speed Internet.** *(See color ad below)*

SOME UNITS

FEE

SUPER 8 MOTEL OF OLIVE BRANCH *Book great rates at AAA.com* **Phone:** 662/893-8930

AAA SAVE

Small-scale Hotel

All Year 1P: $60 2P: $60 XP: $5 F10

Location: US 78, exit 6 (Bethel Rd), just se. 11064 Business Center Dr 38654. Fax: 662/893-8950. **Facility:** 65 one-bedroom standard units, some with whirlpools. 2 stories (no elevator), interior corridors. *Bath:* combo or shower only. **Parking:** on-site. **Terms:** cancellation fee imposed, [CP] meal plan available, package plans. **Pool(s):** small heated indoor. **Leisure Activities:** whirlpool. **Guest Services:** coin laundry, wireless Internet. **Cards:** AX, DC, DS, MC, VI.

SOME UNITS

WHISPERING WOODS HOTEL AND CONFERENCE CENTER *Book at AAA.com* **Phone:** (662)895-2941

Resort Large-scale Hotel

All Year 1P: $99-$139 2P: $109-$149 XP: $10 F18

Location: US 78, exit SR 302, 3.6 mi e. 11200 E Goodman Rd 38654. Fax: 662/895-6442. **Facility:** Nestled in the northern pines, this resort provides a retreat from the bustle of nearby Memphis, with expansive facilities and 18-hole golf course. 181 units. 175 one-bedroom standard units. 6 one-bedroom suites ($239). 4 stories, interior corridors. *Bath:* combo or shower only. **Parking:** on-site. **Terms:** 3 day cancellation notice-fee imposed, small pets only ($100 fee). **Amenities:** voice mail, irons, hair dryers. **Pool(s):** outdoor. **Leisure Activities:** sauna, 4 lighted tennis courts, bicycles, jogging, exercise room, basketball, horseshoes, volleyball. **Guest Services:** valet and coin laundry, wireless Internet. **Business Services:** conference facilities, PC. **Cards:** AX, DS, MC, VI.

SOME UNITS

ASK

FEE

WHERE TO DINE

COLTON'S STEAK HOUSE & GRILL **Lunch:** $6-$21 **Dinner:** $9-$21 **Phone:** 662/890-4142

Steak House

Location: US 78, just e SR 302 (Goodman Rd). 8051 Goodman Rd 38654. **Hours:** 11 am-10 pm, Fri & Sat-11 pm. Closed major holidays. **Features:** Casual dress; cocktails. **Parking:** on-site. **Cards:** AX, DS, MC, VI.

KYOTO JAPANESE STEAKHOUSE & SUSHI BAR **Lunch:** $10-$25 **Dinner:** $12-$25 **Phone:** 662/895-8780

Japanese

Location: Just w of US 78 on SR 302. 6399 Goodman Rd 38654. **Hours:** 11 am-2 & 5-9:30 pm, Fri-10:30 pm, Sat 5 pm-10:30 pm. Closed major holidays. **Features:** Watch your meal come to fruition as a shrimp flies through the air and onto your plate! For the less adventurous, standard tables are available with a sushi menu as well as typical entrees. Casual dress; cocktails. **Parking:** on-site. **Cards:** AX, DS, MC, VI.

OXFORD pop. 11,756

WHERE TO STAY

DOWNTOWN OXFORD INN & SUITES *Book at AAA.com* **Phone:** 662/234-3031

Property failed to provide current rates

Small-scale Hotel

Location: Downtown; just n of town square. 400 N Lamar Blvd 38655 (PO Box 647). Fax: 662/234-2834. **Facility:** 100 units. 64 one-bedroom standard units. 32 one- and 4 two-bedroom suites. 2 stories, exterior corridors. *Bath:* combo or shower only. **Parking:** on-site. **Amenities:** high-speed Internet, voice mail, irons, hair dryers. **Pool(s):** outdoor. **Leisure Activities:** exercise room. **Guest Services:** valet and coin laundry, wireless Internet. **Business Services:** meeting rooms.

SOME UNITS

HAMPTON INN *Book great rates at AAA.com* **Phone:** (662)232-2442

All Year [ECP] 1P: $104-$109 2P: $114-$119 XP: $10 F17

Small-scale Hotel

Location: SR 6, exit W Jackson Ave, 0.8 mi ne. 110 Heritage Dr 38655. Fax: 662/513-0340. **Facility:** 80 one-bedroom standard units. 5 stories, interior corridors. *Bath:* combo or shower only. **Parking:** on-site. **Terms:** cancellation fee imposed. **Amenities:** high-speed Internet, dual phone lines, voice mail, irons, hair dryers. *Some:* DVD players, CD players. **Pool(s):** heated indoor. **Leisure Activities:** whirlpool, exercise room. **Guest Services:** valet and coin laundry. **Business Services:** meeting rooms, business center. **Cards:** AX, DS, MC, VI.

ASK SOME UNITS

WHERE TO DINE

AJAX DINER **Lunch:** $6-$9 **Dinner:** $6-$9 **Phone:** 662/232-8880

Southern

Location: Downtown. 118 Courthouse Square 38655. **Hours:** 11:30 am-10 pm. Closed major holidays; also Sun. **Features:** Down-home cooking makes up the menu at the comfortable eatery. Specialties include tasty fried catfish, chicken and dumplings and homemade meatloaf. Casual dress; cocktails. **Parking:** street. **Cards:** MC, VI.

CITY GROCERY **Lunch:** $8-$17 **Dinner:** $19-$28 **Phone:** 662/232-8080

American

Location: Center. 152 Courthouse Square 38655. **Hours:** 11:30 am-2:30 & 6-10 pm, Thurs-Sat to 10:30 pm. Closed: Sun. **Reservations:** suggested, for dinner. **Features:** Casual elegance is a hallmark of the fine-dining establishment. The eclectic menu includes such items as Basque chicken, Virginia veal, Peking duck and other seafood and steak entrees. Visitors to the storefront building on Oxford's Square are reminded of what it must have been like to dine out in the "Old South". Casual dress; cocktails. **Parking:** street. **Cards:** MC, VI.

DOWNTOWN GRILL **Lunch:** $8-$11 **Dinner:** $17-$29 **Phone:** 662/234-2659

Southern

Location: Downtown. 110 Courthouse Square 38655. **Hours:** 11 am-2 & 5-9 pm, Fri & Sat-10 pm. Closed major holidays; also Sun. **Reservations:** accepted. **Features:** The upscale eatery prepares a good mix of Southern and traditional fare. Overlooking the well-known Courthouse Square, the restaurant invites guests to have a drink and enjoy music from the upstairs piano bar or have a relaxing meal in the cozy downstairs dining room. Dressy casual; cocktails. **Parking:** street. **Cards:** AX, DS, MC, VI.

TWO STICK SUSHI BAR & GRILL **Lunch:** $7-$8 **Dinner:** $10-$12 **Phone:** 662/236-6639

Sushi

Location: Just w of jct Lamar St; downtown. 1007 Harrison Ave 38655. **Hours:** 11:30 am-2 & 5-10 pm. Closed: 1/1, 11/22, 12/25; also Sun. **Features:** Located downtown "on the square," this restaurant is popular with students and locals, featuring very fresh sushi and tempting entree selections and live music regularly. Casual dress; cocktails. **Parking:** on-site. **Cards:** AX, MC, VI.

The following restaurant has not been evaluated by AAA but is listed for your information only.

ADEN'S GRILLE **Phone:** 662/234-3855

fyi

Not evaluated. **Location:** 1007 College Hill Rd 38655. **Features:** The restaurant serves steaks and seafood; casual dining with a large bar.

PASCAGOULA pop. 26,200

WHERE TO STAY

LAFONT INN *Book great rates at AAA.com* **Phone:** 228/762-7111

AAA SAVE

Small-scale Hotel

All Year 1P: $79-$99 2P: $79-$99

Location: I-10, exit 69, 3.5 mi s on SR 63, then 2 mi w on US 90. 2703 Denny Ave 39567 (PO Box 1028, 39568-1028). Fax: 228/934-4324. **Facility:** 192 one-bedroom standard units, some with efficiencies. 2 stories (no elevator), exterior corridors. *Bath:* combo or shower only. **Parking:** on-site. **Terms:** cancellation fee imposed, pets (in designated units). **Amenities:** high-speed Internet, voice mail, irons, hair dryers. **Dining:** 6-10 am, 11-2 & 5-9 pm, cocktails. **Pool(s):** outdoor, wading. **Leisure Activities:** sauna, whirlpool, 2 lighted tennis courts, playground, exercise room, horseshoes. **Guest Services:** coin laundry. **Business Services:** meeting rooms. **Cards:** AX, DC, DS, MC, VI. **Free Special Amenities: local telephone calls and high-speed Internet.**

SOME UNITS

/ VCR /

SUPER 8 MOTEL *Book at AAA.com* **Phone:** (228)762-9414

Motel

7/1-9/30 [CP]	1P: $130-$140	2P: $140-$170	XP: $10	F10
4/1-6/30 [CP]	1P: $120-$130	2P: $130-$160	XP: $10	F10
12/1-3/31 & 10/1-11/30 [CP]	1P: $110-$120	2P: $120-$150	XP: $10	F10

Location: I-10, exit 69, 3.5 mi s on SR 63, then just w on US 90. 4919 Denny Ave 39581. Fax: 228/762-7536. **Facility:** 42 one-bedroom standard units, some with efficiencies (no utensils) and/or whirlpools. 2 stories (no elevator), interior corridors. *Bath:* combo or shower only. **Parking:** on-site. **Terms:** cancellation fee imposed, pets ($50 deposit, $15 extra charge). **Amenities:** high-speed Internet, dual phone lines, irons, hair dryers. **Pool(s):** small outdoor. **Leisure Activities:** whirlpool, exercise room. **Guest Services:** coin laundry. **Business Services:** business center. **Cards:** AX, DS, MC, VI.

SOME UNITS

ASK FEE / /

PEARL pop. 21,961 (See map and index starting on p. 451)

WHERE TO STAY

BEST WESTERN AIRPORT INN *Book great rates at AAA.com* **Phone:** (601)936-2060 48

AAA SAVE

Motel

All Year 1P: $70-$75 2P: $70-$75

Location: I-20, exit 48, just n. 257 Pearson Rd 39208. Fax: 601/932-1341. **Facility:** 50 one-bedroom standard units. 2 stories (no elevator), exterior corridors. **Parking:** on-site. **Terms:** [CP] meal plan available. **Amenities:** high-speed Internet, irons, hair dryers. **Pool(s):** small outdoor. **Guest Services:** wireless Internet. **Business Services:** PC. **Cards:** AX, DC, DS, MC, VI. **Free Special Amenities: local telephone calls and high-speed Internet.**

SOME UNITS

/ /

COMFORT INN AIRPORT *Book great rates at AAA.com* **Phone:** (601)932-6009 45

Motel

5/1-10/31	1P: $65-$90	2P: $70-$95	XP: $5	F18
12/1-4/30 & 11/1-11/30	1P: $60-$85	2P: $65-$90	XP: $5	F18

Location: I-20, exit 48, just n. 235 S Pearson Rd 39208. Fax: 601/939-6922. **Facility:** 79 one-bedroom standard units. 2 stories (no elevator), exterior corridors. *Bath:* combo or shower only. **Parking:** on-site. **Terms:** [ECP] meal plan available. **Amenities:** high-speed Internet, irons, hair dryers. **Pool(s):** small outdoor. **Guest Services:** coin laundry, wireless Internet. **Business Services:** business center. **Cards:** AX, CB, DC, DS, MC, VI.

SOME UNITS

ASK / /

COUNTRY INN & SUITES BY CARLSON *Book great rates at AAA.com* **Phone:** (601)420-2244 53

AAA SAVE

Small-scale Hotel

All Year 1P: $89 2P: $89 XP: $5 F17

Location: I-20, exit 48, just sw. 3051 White Blvd 39208. Fax: 601/420-2266. **Facility:** 61 units. 50 one-bedroom standard units, some with whirlpools. 11 one-bedroom suites ($99-$119). 3 stories, interior corridors. *Bath:* combo or shower only. **Parking:** on-site. **Amenities:** high-speed Internet, dual phone lines, voice mail, irons, hair dryers. **Pool(s):** small heated indoor. **Leisure Activities:** whirlpool, exercise room. **Guest Services:** coin laundry. **Business Services:** meeting rooms, PC, fax (fee). **Cards:** AX, CB, DC, DS, JC, MC, VI. **Free Special Amenities: continental breakfast and early check-in/late check-out.**

SOME UNITS

/ /

ECONO LODGE-AIRPORT *Book great rates at AAA.com* **Phone:** 601/932-4226 47

Motel

Property failed to provide current rates

Location: I-20, exit 48, just n. 232 S Pearson Rd 39208. Fax: 601/932-4571. **Facility:** 44 one-bedroom standard units, some with kitchens (no utensils). 2 stories (no elevator), exterior corridors. **Parking:** on-site. **Pool(s):** small outdoor. **Business Services:** fax.

SOME UNITS

/ /

FAIRFIELD INN & SUITES *Book great rates at AAA.com* **Phone:** 601/936-3434 51

Small-scale Hotel

Property failed to provide current rates

Location: I-20, exit 48, just n. 407 Riverwind Rd 39208. Fax: 601/664-1919. **Facility:** 78 one-bedroom standard units. 3 stories, interior corridors. *Bath:* combo or shower only. **Parking:** on-site. **Amenities:** high-speed Internet, dual phone lines, voice mail, irons, hair dryers. *Some:* CD players. **Pool(s):** small outdoor. **Leisure Activities:** whirlpool, exercise room. **Guest Services:** valet and coin laundry, wireless Internet. **Business Services:** meeting rooms, PC, fax.

SOME UNITS

/ /

(See map and index starting on p. 451)

HAMPTON INN-AIRPORT Book great rates at AAA.com Phone: 601/932-7676 50

Property failed to provide current rates

Small-scale Hotel

Location: I-20, exit 48, just n. 1234 Phillips St 39208. Fax: 601/932-7637. **Facility:** 64 one-bedroom standard units. 4 stories, interior corridors. *Bath:* combo or shower only. **Parking:** on-site. **Amenities:** high-speed Internet, voice mail, irons, hair dryers. **Pool(s):** outdoor. **Leisure Activities:** whirlpool, exercise room. **Guest Services:** valet and coin laundry, wireless Internet. **Business Services:** meeting rooms, business center.

SOME UNITS

HOLIDAY INN EXPRESS-AIRPORT Book at AAA.com Phone: 601/932-4141 49

Property failed to provide current rates

Small-scale Hotel

Location: I-20, exit 48, just n. 1226 Phillips St 39208. Fax: 601/932-6753. **Facility:** 55 one-bedroom standard units, some with whirlpools. 3 stories, interior corridors. *Bath:* combo or shower only. **Parking:** on-site. **Amenities:** high-speed Internet, voice mail, irons, hair dryers. **Pool(s):** outdoor. **Guest Services:** valet laundry. **Business Services:** meeting rooms, business center.

SOME UNITS

JAMESON INN OF PEARL Book at AAA.com Phone: (601)932-6030 52

All Year [ECP] 1P: $54-$120

Small-scale Hotel

Location: I-20, exit 48, just nw. 434 Riverwind Dr 39208. Fax: 601/939-6025. **Facility:** 65 units. 64 one-bedroom standard units. 1 one-bedroom suite. 3 stories, interior corridors. *Bath:* combo or shower only. **Parking:** on-site. **Terms:** cancellation fee imposed, small pets only ($10 fee). **Pool(s):** small outdoor. **Leisure Activities:** exercise room. **Guest Services:** valet laundry. **Business Services:** meeting rooms, PC. **Cards:** AX, DC, DS, MC, VI.

SOME UNITS

ASK FEE

LA QUINTA INN & SUITES JACKSON AIRPORT (PEARL) Book great rates at AAA.com Phone: 601/664-0065 54

Property failed to provide current rates

Small-scale Hotel

Location: I-20, exit 48, just s. 501 S Pearson Rd 39208. Fax: 601/664-9755. **Facility:** 65 one-bedroom standard units. 3 stories, interior corridors. *Bath:* combo or shower only. **Parking:** on-site. **Terms:** small pets only. **Amenities:** high-speed Internet, irons, hair dryers. **Pool(s):** small outdoor. **Leisure Activities:** exercise room. **Guest Services:** coin laundry, wireless Internet. **Business Services:** PC, fax (fee).

SOME UNITS

SUPER 8 MOTEL Book great rates at AAA.com Phone: (601)718-1860 46

All Year 1P: $46-$60 2P: $50-$66 XP: $5 F17

Motel

Location: I-20, exit 52, just n. 111 Airport Rd 39208. Fax: 601/718-1868. **Facility:** 52 one-bedroom standard units, some with whirlpools. 2 stories (no elevator), exterior corridors. **Parking:** on-site. **Terms:** cancellation fee imposed, [AP] meal plan available. **Amenities:** *Some:* irons, hair dryers. **Guest Services:** wireless Internet. **Cards:** AX, DS, MC. **Free Special Amenities: continental breakfast and local telephone calls.**

SOME UNITS

WHERE TO DINE

EL CHARRO **Lunch:** $5-$10 **Dinner:** $6-$12 **Phone:** 601/936-3500 37

Mexican

Location: I-20, exit 48, just n. 136 S Pearson Rd, Suite A 39208. **Hours:** 11 am-9:30 pm, Fri & Sat-10 pm. Closed major holidays. **Features:** With several locations throughout Mississippi, the popular restaurant offers typical Mexican favorites. Casual dress; beer only. **Parking:** on-site. **Cards:** AX, DS, MC, VI.

PHILADELPHIA pop. 7,303

WHERE TO STAY

DANCING RABBIT CLUB HOUSE **Phone:** 601/663-0011

Property failed to provide current rates

Country Inn

Location: Jct SR 15, 2 mi w. 1 Choctaw Trail 39350. Fax: 601/656-4779. **Facility:** Stay in the heart of two awarding-winning golf courses; each guest room overlooks more than 700 acres. This is a golfer's dream getaway spot. 8 units. 7 one-bedroom standard units. 1 cottage with whirlpool. 2 stories (no elevator), interior corridors. **Parking:** on-site. **Terms:** check-in 4 pm, age restrictions may apply. **Amenities:** voice mail, irons, hair dryers. **Leisure Activities:** *Fee:* fishing, golf-36 holes. **Guest Services:** gift shop, valet laundry. **Business Services:** meeting rooms, fax.

DELUXE INN & SUITES Book at AAA.com **Phone:** 601/656-0052

4/1-10/31	1P: $50-$149	2P: $50-$149	XP: $5	F17
12/1-3/31 & 11/1-11/30	1P: $44-$149	2P: $44-$149	XP: $5	F17

Small-scale Hotel

Location: Jct SR 15 and 16. 1004 Central Dr 39350. Fax: 601/656-0442. **Facility:** 44 one-bedroom standard units. 2 stories (no elevator), exterior corridors. **Parking:** on-site. **Terms:** cancellation fee imposed, [CP] meal plan available, package plans, pets ($10 extra charge). **Amenities:** irons, hair dryers. **Pool(s):** outdoor. **Guest Services:** wireless Internet. **Business Services:** fax. **Cards:** AX, CB, DC, DS, JC, MC, VI.

SOME UNITS

FEE

GOLDEN MOON HOTEL & CASINO Phone: 601/650-1234

Large-scale Hotel

Property failed to provide current rates

Location: From jct SR 15, 2 mi w. 13541 Hwy 16 W 39350. Fax: 601/650-1368. **Facility:** Enjoy contemporary, vibrant, luxurious, "out of this world" guest rooms, luxurious bathrooms, numerous restaurants and shops at this happening casino. 571 units. 427 one-bedroom standard units. 144 one-bedroom suites, some with whirlpools. 26 stories, interior corridors. *Bath:* combo or shower only. **Parking:** on-site and valet. **Terms:** check-in 4 pm. **Amenities:** CD players, high-speed Internet, voice mail, safes, irons, hair dryers. **Dining:** Bistro 24, see separate listing. **Pool(s):** small heated indoor/outdoor. **Leisure Activities:** saunas, whirlpool, exercise room. *Fee:* waterslide, fishing, golf-36 holes. **Guest Services:** gift shop, valet laundry. **Business Services:** conference facilities.

SOME UNITS

SILVER STAR HOTEL & CASINO Phone: 601/650-1234

Large-scale Hotel

Property failed to provide current rates

Location: From jct SR 15, 2 mi w. 13541 Hwy 16 W 39350. Fax: 601/650-1368. **Facility:** Offering very nice accommodations, this large, upscale casino features plenty to do including a full service spa, salon, fine dining and shopping. 496 units. 408 one-bedroom standard units. 85 one- and 3 two-bedroom suites, some with whirlpools. 12 stories, interior corridors. *Bath:* combo or shower only. **Parking:** on-site and valet. **Terms:** check-in 4 pm. **Amenities:** voice mail, safes, irons, hair dryers. **Dining:** Phillip M's Restaurant, see separate listing. **Pool(s):** outdoor. **Leisure Activities:** exercise room, spa. *Fee:* waterslide, fishing, golf-36 holes, game room. **Guest Services:** gift shop, valet laundry. **Business Services:** conference facilities.

SOME UNITS

WHERE TO DINE

BISTRO 24 **Lunch:** $5-$10 **Dinner:** $6-$12 **Phone:** 601/650-1234

American

Location: From jct SR 15, 2 mi w; in Golden Moon Hotel & Casino. 13541 Hwy 16 W 39350. **Hours:** 24 hours. **Features:** Located on the casino floor, this 24-hour restaurant offers a variety of menu items and a fully stocked bar. Casual dress; cocktails. **Parking:** on-site and valet. **Cards:** AX, CB, DC, DS, JC, MC, VI.

PHILADELPHIA HOUSE OF PANCAKES **Lunch:** $5-$14 **Dinner:** $5-$14 **Phone:** 601/650-3689

American

Location: On SR 15, just e of jct SR 16; in Canal Place Plaza. 280 Canal Pl 39350. **Hours:** 6 am-11 pm, Fri & Sat 24 hrs. Closed: 11/22, 12/25. **Features:** As the name suggests, pancakes are the order of the day at this roadside restaurant, just off the highway. Whether diners are in the mood for a greasy spoon breakfast of eggs, bacon, grits and hash browns or want to try a sandwich, they can be guaranteed quick service and great value. Casual dress. **Parking:** on-site. **Cards:** AX, DS, MC, VI.

PHILLIP M'S RESTAURANT **Dinner:** $22-$52 **Phone:** 601/650-1234

Continental

Location: From jct SR 15, 2 mi w; in Silver Star Hotel & Casino. 13541 Hwy 16 W 39350. **Hours:** 5 pm-10 pm, Fri & Sat-midnight. **Reservations:** required. **Features:** You're sure to hit the jackpot at this intimate and luxurious restaurant; upscale in everyway, it features delicious food, superb service and an extensive, award-winning wine collection. Dressy casual; cocktails. **Parking:** on-site. **Cards:** AX, DS, MC, VI.

PICAYUNE pop. 10,535

WHERE TO STAY

COMFORT INN *Book great rates at AAA.com* **Phone:** (601)799-2833

AAA SAVE

Small-scale Hotel

All Year [CP] 1P: $89-$119 2P: $99-$129 XP: $15 F12

Location: I-59, exit 4, just nw. 550 S Lofton Dr 39466. Fax: 601/799-2833. **Facility:** 51 one-bedroom standard units. 2 stories (no elevator), exterior corridors. *Bath:* combo or shower only. **Parking:** on-site. **Amenities:** high-speed Internet, irons, hair dryers. **Pool(s):** small outdoor. **Guest Services:** coin laundry. **Business Services:** PC. **Cards:** AX, CB, DC, DS, JC, MC, VI.

SOME UNITS

DAYS INN *Book great rates at AAA.com* **Phone:** 601/799-1339

Small-scale Hotel

Property failed to provide current rates

Location: I-59, exit 4, just nw. 450 S Lofton Ave 39466. Fax: 601/799-5766. **Facility:** 50 one-bedroom standard units, some with whirlpools. 2 stories (no elevator), exterior corridors. *Bath:* combo or shower only. **Parking:** on-site. **Terms:** small pets only ($5 extra charge). **Amenities:** hair dryers. *Some:* irons. **Pool(s):** small outdoor. **Leisure Activities:** exercise room. **Guest Services:** valet laundry. **Business Services:** PC.

SOME UNITS

FEE FEE

PONTOTOC pop. 5,253

WHERE TO STAY

DAYS INN *Book great rates at AAA.com* **Phone:** (662)489-5200

AAA SAVE

Motel

All Year 1P: $50-$55 2P: $50-$55 XP: $5

Location: Just n of jct SR 6 and 15. 217 Hwy 15 N 38863. Fax: 662/489-8418. **Facility:** 56 one-bedroom standard units. 2 stories (no elevator), exterior corridors. **Parking:** on-site. **Terms:** package plans, pets ($10 extra charge). **Amenities:** hair dryers. *Some:* irons. **Pool(s):** outdoor. **Guest Services:** coin laundry, wireless Internet. **Business Services:** meeting rooms. **Cards:** AX, DC, DS, MC, VI. **Free Special Amenities: continental breakfast and local telephone calls.**

SOME UNITS

FEE

RICHLAND pop. 6,027 (See map and index starting on p. 451)

WHERE TO STAY

BEST WESTERN RICHLAND INN & SUITES *Book great rates at AAA.com* **Phone:** 601/936-7004 42

Motel

4/1-9/15	1P: $75-$85	2P: $75-$85	XP: $10	F12
12/1-3/31 & 9/16-11/30	1P: $60-$65	2P: $60-$65	XP: $10	F12

Location: I-20, exit 47, 3.5 mi s on US 49. 101 Roland Dr 39218. Fax: 601/936-0870. **Facility:** 36 one-bedroom standard units, some with whirlpools. 2 stories (no elevator), exterior corridors. **Parking:** on-site. **Terms:** [CP] meal plan available. **Amenities:** irons, hair dryers. **Pool(s):** outdoor. **Guest Services:** coin laundry, wireless Internet. **Business Services:** PC. **Cards:** AX, DC, DS, MC, VI.

SOME UNITS

EXECUTIVE INN & SUITES **Phone:** (601)664-3456 41

Small-scale Hotel

All Year [CP]	1P: $45-$55	2P: $49-$59	XP: $5	F

Location: I-20, exit 47, just s. 390 Hwy 49 S 39218. Fax: 601/664-3401. **Facility:** 49 one-bedroom standard units, some with whirlpools. 2 stories (no elevator), exterior corridors. *Bath:* combo or shower only. **Parking:** on-site. **Terms:** weekly rates available, pets (dogs only, $5 fee, $20 deposit). **Amenities:** hair dryers. **Pool(s):** small outdoor. **Cards:** AX, DC, DS, MC, VI.

SOME UNITS

FEE

RIDGELAND pop. 20,173 (See map and index starting on p. 451)

WHERE TO STAY

CABOT LODGE OF JACKSON NORTH *Book at AAA.com* **Phone:** (601)957-0757 31

Small-scale Hotel

All Year	1P: $88-$155	2P: $88-$155	XP: $8	F17

Location: I-55, exit 103 (County Line Rd), just ne. 120 Dyess Rd 39157. Fax: 601/957-0757. **Facility:** 208 one-bedroom standard units. 3 stories, interior corridors. **Parking:** on-site. **Terms:** package plans. **Amenities:** voice mail, irons, hair dryers. **Pool(s):** small outdoor. **Leisure Activities:** exercise room. **Guest Services:** complimentary evening beverages, valet laundry, wireless Internet. **Business Services:** meeting rooms, business center. **Cards:** AX, DC, DS, MC, VI.

SOME UNITS

DAYS INN AND SUITES RIDGELAND/MADISON *Book great rates at AAA.com* **Phone:** (601)956-9726 26

AAA SAVE

Small-scale Hotel

5/1-8/15	1P: $68-$109	2P: $68-$109	XP: $5	F17
2/1-4/30 & 8/16-11/30	1P: $64-$99	2P: $64-$99	XP: $5	F17
12/1-1/31	1P: $59-$89	2P: $59-$89	XP: $5	F17

Location: I-55, exit 103 (County Line Rd), just e to Ridgewood Rd, then just n. 150 Centre St 39157. Fax: 601/956-9727. **Facility:** 51 units. 49 one-bedroom standard units, some with whirlpools. 2 one-bedroom suites ($59-$149). 3 stories, interior corridors. *Bath:* combo or shower only. **Parking:** on-site. **Terms:** cancellation fee imposed, [CP] meal plan available. **Amenities:** high-speed Internet, irons, hair dryers. **Pool(s):** small outdoor. **Leisure Activities:** exercise room. **Guest Services:** coin laundry, wireless Internet. **Cards:** AX, DS, MC, VI. **Free Special Amenities: continental breakfast and early check-in/late check-out.**

SOME UNITS

DRURY INN & SUITES-JACKSON, MS *Book at AAA.com* **Phone:** (601)956-6100 32

Small-scale Hotel

All Year [BP]	1P: $75-$125	2P: $85-$135	XP: $10	F18

Location: I-55, exit 103 (County Line Rd), just w. 610 E County Line Rd 39157. Fax: 601/956-6100. **Facility:** 176 units. 136 one-bedroom standard units. 40 one-bedroom suites ($100-$150). 7 stories, interior corridors. *Bath:* combo or shower only. **Parking:** on-site. **Amenities:** high-speed Internet, voice mail, irons, hair dryers. **Pool(s):** small heated indoor/outdoor. **Leisure Activities:** whirlpool. **Guest Services:** complimentary evening beverages, valet and coin laundry, wireless Internet. **Business Services:** meeting rooms, PC. **Cards:** AX, CB, DC, DS, MC, VI.

SOME UNITS

FEE

ECONO LODGE *Book great rates at AAA.com* **Phone:** (601)956-7740 29

Motel

All Year	1P: $50-$60	2P: $50-$60	XP: $7	F17

Location: I-55, exit 103 (County Line Rd), just e, then just n. 839 Ridgewood Rd 39157. Fax: 601/896-0142. **Facility:** 52 one-bedroom standard units. 3 stories (no elevator), exterior corridors. **Parking:** on-site. **Terms:** pets ($10 extra charge). **Amenities:** irons, hair dryers. *Some:* high-speed Internet. **Guest Services:** coin laundry, wireless Internet. **Cards:** AX, CB, DC, DS, JC, MC, VI.

SOME UNITS

FEE

HOMEWOOD SUITES BY HILTON *Book at AAA.com* **Phone:** 601/899-8611 30

Small-scale Hotel

	1P
All Year	1P: $149

Location: I-55, exit 103 (County Line Rd), just e to Ridgewood Rd, 0.4 mi ne, then just e. 853 Centre St 39157. Fax: 601/899-8612. **Facility:** 91 units. 85 one- and 6 two-bedroom suites with efficiencies. 3 stories, interior corridors. *Bath:* combo or shower only. **Parking:** on-site. **Terms:** pets ($100 fee). **Amenities:** high-speed Internet, dual phone lines, voice mail, irons, hair dryers. **Pool(s):** small outdoor. **Leisure Activities:** exercise room. **Guest Services:** sundries, complimentary evening beverages: Mon-Thurs, valet and coin laundry, area transportation, wireless Internet. **Business Services:** meeting rooms, PC, fax (fee). **Cards:** AX, DC, DS, MC, VI.

SOME UNITS

FEE

(See map and index starting on p. 451)

QUALITY INN NORTH Book great rates at AAA.com Phone: (601)956-6203 28

All Year 1P: $70-$80 2P: $70-$80 XP: $5 F17

Small-scale Hotel

Location: I-55, exit 103 (County Line Rd), just ne. 839 Ridgewood Rd 39157. Fax: 601/957-9981. **Facility:** 78 one-bedroom standard units. 3 stories, exterior corridors. **Parking:** on-site. **Terms:** small pets only ($10 fee). **Amenities:** high-speed Internet, irons, hair dryers. **Pool(s):** outdoor. **Guest Services:** coin laundry, wireless Internet. **Business Services:** meeting rooms. **Cards:** AX, CB, DC, DS, JC, MC, VI.

SOME UNITS

ASK FEE

RED ROOF INN RIDGELAND Book at AAA.com Phone: (601)956-7707 27

All Year 1P: $46-$53 2P: $51-$58

Motel

Location: I-55, exit 103 (County Line Rd), just ne on Frontage Rd. 810 Adcock St 39157. Fax: 601/956-7865. **Facility:** 108 one-bedroom standard units. 2 stories (no elevator), exterior corridors. *Bath:* combo or shower only. **Parking:** on-site. **Terms:** small pets only. **Amenities:** video games (fee), voice mail. **Business Services:** fax (fee). **Cards:** AX, CB, DC, DS, MC, VI.

SOME UNITS

WHERE TO DINE

AJ'S SEAFOOD GRILLE **Lunch:** $9-$15 **Dinner:** $12-$37 **Phone:** 601/956-2588 31

Seafood

Location: I-55, exit 103 (County Line Rd), just ne; in North Regency Square Plaza. 900 E County Line Rd, Suite 107 39157. **Hours:** 11 am-2 & 5-close, Sat from 5 pm. Closed: 1/1, 12/25; also Sun. **Reservations:** suggested. **Features:** The eatery offers a casual atmosphere in which to enjoy well-prepared seafood dishes in large portions. Don't miss out on the bread pudding for dessert! Dressy casual; cocktails. **Parking:** on-site. **Cards:** AX, DC, DS, MC, VI.

AMERIGO **Lunch:** $7-$12 **Dinner:** $7-$29 **Phone:** 601/977-0563 30

Italian

Location: I-55, exit 103 (County Line Rd), 2 mi e, then 0.3 mi n. 6592 Old Canton Rd 39157. **Hours:** 11 am-10 pm, Fri & Sat-10:30 pm. Closed major holidays. **Features:** This is a bustling restaurant specializing in pasta, seafood and veal with daily specials. There is a full bar and cocktail area, and a good variety of wines to choose from. You will receive a friendly welcome, and the staff is knowledgeable and prompt. Casual dress; cocktails. **Parking:** on-site. **Cards:** AX, CB, DC, DS, MC, VI.

COCK OF THE WALK **Lunch:** $10 **Dinner:** $10 **Phone:** 601/856-5500 25

American

Location: I-55, exit 105A, e on Natchez Trace to Ross Barnett Reservior exit, s to Rice Rd, then 1.2 mi e. 141 Madison Landing Cir 39157. **Hours:** 5 pm-9 pm, Sat 4 pm-9:30 pm, Sun 11:30 am-9:30 pm. Closed: 11/22, 12/24, 12/25. **Reservations:** accepted. **Features:** The rustic dining room is decked out in a Western motif with tin mugs, tin plates and pails holding the cutlery. A nice waterfront view, a fun atmosphere and good, friendly service make up for the limited menu of only fried catfish and chicken dinners. Locals flock here. Try a fried dill pickle. Casual dress; cocktails. **Parking:** on-site. **Cards:** AX, CB, DS, MC, VI.

DEJA VU **Lunch:** $9-$11 **Dinner:** $9-$22 **Phone:** 601/899-8690 27

Regional American

Location: I-55, exit 103 (County Line Rd), 2.2 mi e, 1 mi n on Old Canton Rd, then just e. 810 Lake Harbour Dr 39157. **Hours:** 11 am-10 pm, Fri & Sat-10:30 pm, Sun 10 am-9 pm. Closed: 11/22; also Mon. **Features:** The friendly staff welcomes patrons to the locally popular eatery, where Cajun foods share menu space with dishes prepared in more traditional styles. Try redfish d'Iberville with crab and artichokes and for dessert, the delightfully light orange crepes. Casual dress; cocktails. **Parking:** on-site. **Cards:** AX, MC, VI.

LITTLE TOKYO **Lunch:** $4-$6 **Dinner:** $6-$17 **Phone:** 601/991-3800 28

Japanese

Location: I-55, exit 103 (County Line Rd), 1.4 mi e; in Promenade Shopping area. 876 Avery Blvd 39157. **Hours:** 11 am-2 & 5-9:30 pm, Fri & Sat-10:30 pm, Sun 11 am-2 pm. Closed: 7/4. **Reservations:** accepted. **Features:** Two dining rooms and a large sushi bar make up the popular Japanese restaurant. Local magazines have lauded the sushi creations. Casual dress; cocktails. **Parking:** on-site. **Cards:** AX, CB, DC, DS, MC, VI.

THE PARKER HOUSE **Lunch:** $7-$15 **Dinner:** $19-$36 **Phone:** 601/856-0043 26

American

Location: I-55, exit 105B, 0.7 mi se on Jackson St. 104 SE Madison Dr 39157. **Hours:** 11 am-2 & 5:30-10 pm, Sat from 5:30 pm. Closed major holidays; also Sun. **Reservations:** suggested. **Features:** Fine dining, friendly owners, a cozy dining room, and an eclectic blend of continental cuisine take you back to a time of classical elegance. Share an unforgettable meal with someone special at The Parker House and you'll soon become one of their many regulars. Dressy casual; cocktails. **Parking:** on-site. **Cards:** AX, CB, DC, DS, MC, VI.

SHAPLEY'S **Dinner:** $18-$35 **Phone:** 601/957-3753 29

American

Location: I-55, exit 103 (County Line Rd), 0.5 mi e, then 0.3 mi n; in Center Park North. 868 Centre St 39157. **Hours:** 5 pm-9:30 pm, Fri & Sat-10 pm. Closed major holidays; also Sun. **Reservations:** suggested. **Features:** A very popular restaurant with local residents, Shapley's specializes in steak, some priced by size. Also a house specialty are their hot, hand-rolled tamales. The unusual decor is accented by painted partitions placed around each table for privacy. Casual dress; cocktails. **Parking:** on-site. **Cards:** AX, DC, DS, MC, VI.

THE TRACE GRILL **Lunch:** $5-$7 **Dinner:** $5-$17 **Phone:** 601/853-1014 24

Regional American

Location: I-55, exit 105A, 0.9 mi e on Jackson St, then just n on Ridgeland Rd (US 51). 554 A Hwy 51 N 39157. **Hours:** 11 am-8:30 pm, Sat-3 pm. Closed major holidays; also Sun. **Features:** Located near the Old Natchez Trace, this grill has long served great food with southern flair. Fried green tomatoes or fried okra accompany ribs, chicken, meatloaf or country steak for a hearty meal sure to please. Casual dress. **Parking:** on-site. **Cards:** MC, VI.

SENATOBIA pop. 6,682

WHERE TO STAY

DAYS INN & SUITES *Book great rates at AAA.com* **Phone:** (662)562-5647

Small-scale Hotel

All Year 1P: $45-$55 2P: $55-$61 XP: $5 F16

Location: I-55, exit 265, just se. 513 E Main St 38668. Fax: 662/560-0922. **Facility:** 51 one-bedroom standard units. 2 stories (no elevator), exterior corridors. *Bath:* combo or shower only. **Parking:** on-site. **Terms:** small pets only. **Amenities:** irons, hair dryers. **Pool(s):** outdoor. **Guest Services:** wireless Internet. **Business Services:** fax (fee). **Cards:** AX, CB, DC, DS, JC, MC, VI.

SOME UNITS

SOUTHAVEN pop. 28,977

WHERE TO STAY

COMFORT INN *Book great rates at AAA.com* **Phone:** (662)342-5847

Small-scale Hotel

All Year 1P: $55-$79 2P: $60-$89 XP: $5 F18

Location: I-55, exit 291, just e, then just s. 8792 Hamilton Rd 38671. Fax: 662/342-6915. **Facility:** 61 one-bedroom standard units. 2 stories (no elevator), exterior corridors. **Parking:** on-site. **Terms:** [BP] meal plan available. **Amenities:** high-speed Internet, irons, hair dryers. **Pool(s):** small outdoor. **Leisure Activities:** whirlpool. **Guest Services:** coin laundry. **Cards:** AX, CB, DC, DS, MC, VI.

SOME UNITS

COMFORT SUITES SOUTHAVEN *Book great rates at AAA.com* **Phone:** 662/349-0100

AAA SAVE

Small-scale Hotel

12/1-11/13 [ECP] 1P: $119-$179 2P: $119-$179
11/14-11/30 [ECP] 1P: $99-$129 2P: $99-$129

Location: I-55, exit 289, just e. 7075 Moore Dr 38671. Fax: 662/349-0063. **Facility:** 73 units. 70 one-bedroom standard units. 3 one-bedroom suites with whirlpools. 4 stories, interior corridors. *Bath:* combo or shower only. **Parking:** on-site. **Amenities:** high-speed Internet, dual phone lines, voice mail, irons, hair dryers. *Some:* DVD players. **Pool(s):** outdoor. **Leisure Activities:** whirlpool, exercise room. **Guest Services:** complimentary evening beverages: Mon-Thurs, valet and coin laundry. **Business Services:** meeting rooms, business center. **Cards:** AX, CB, DC, DS, JC, MC, VI. **Free Special Amenities: full breakfast and high-speed Internet.**

SOME UNITS

COURTYARD BY MARRIOTT **Phone:** 662/349-6640

fyi

Small-scale Hotel

All Year 1P: $129-$169 2P: $129-$169

Too new to rate, opening scheduled for August 2006. **Location:** I-55, exit 289, just ne. 7151 Hungry Fisherman Dr 38671. Fax: 662/349-6360. **Amenities:** 85 units, coffeemakers, microwaves, refrigerators, pool. **Cards:** AX, DC, DS, MC, VI.

FAIRFIELD INN AND SUITES BY MARRIOTT *Book great rates at AAA.com* **Phone:** (662)349-6640

Small-scale Hotel

All Year [CP] 1P: $114-$139 2P: $114-$139

Location: I-55, exit 289, just ne. 7149 Hungry Fisherman Dr 38671. Fax: 662/349-6360. **Facility:** 92 one-bedroom standard units. 3 stories, interior corridors. *Bath:* combo or shower only. **Parking:** on-site. **Amenities:** voice mail, irons, hair dryers. *Some:* CD players. **Pool(s):** outdoor. **Leisure Activities:** whirlpool, exercise room. **Guest Services:** valet and coin laundry, wireless Internet. **Business Services:** meeting rooms. **Cards:** AX, CB, DC, DS, MC, VI.

SOME UNITS

HAMPTON INN *Book great rates at AAA.com* **Phone:** (662)349-8855

Small-scale Hotel

All Year 1P: $114-$139 2P: $114-$139

Location: I-55, exit 289, just ne. 390 Goodman Rd W 38671. Fax: 662/349-8866. **Facility:** 86 one-bedroom standard units. 3 stories, interior corridors. *Bath:* combo or shower only. **Parking:** on-site. **Amenities:** video games (fee), voice mail, irons, hair dryers. **Pool(s):** outdoor. **Guest Services:** valet laundry, wireless Internet. **Business Services:** meeting rooms, fax. **Cards:** AX, DS, MC, VI.

SOME UNITS

HOLIDAY INN EXPRESS *Book great rates at AAA.com* **Phone:** (662)393-2881

AAA SAVE

Small-scale Hotel

11/1-11/30 1P: $99 2P: $99 XP: $10 F18
12/30-10/31 1P: $96 2P: $96 XP: $10 F18
12/1-12/29 1P: $89 2P: $89 XP: $10 F18

Location: I-55, exit 291, 0.4 mi e. 340 Stateline Rd 38671. Fax: 662/393-2517. **Facility:** 56 one-bedroom standard units, some with whirlpools. 3 stories, interior corridors. *Bath:* combo or shower only. **Parking:** on-site. **Amenities:** high-speed Internet, voice mail, safes, irons, hair dryers. **Pool(s):** small outdoor. **Leisure Activities:** exercise room. **Guest Services:** valet laundry. **Business Services:** meeting rooms, business center. **Cards:** AX, CB, DC, DS, JC, MC, VI. **Free Special Amenities: continental breakfast and high-speed Internet.**

SOME UNITS

MAGNOLIA INN & SUITES **Phone:** (662)280-5555

AAA SAVE

Small-scale Hotel

All Year [CP] 1P: $55-$75 2P: $65-$85 XP: $5 F10

Location: I-55, exit 287, just w. 5069 Pepper Chase Dr 38671. Fax: 662/280-5500. **Facility:** 27 one-bedroom standard units, some with efficiencies (no utensils) and/or whirlpools. 1 story, interior corridors. **Parking:** on-site. **Terms:** cancellation fee imposed, weekly rates available, package plans. **Amenities:** irons, hair dryers. **Guest Services:** wireless Internet. **Cards:** AX, DC, DS, MC, VI. **Free Special Amenities: continental breakfast and local telephone calls.**

SOME UNITS

RESIDENCE INN BY MARRIOTT — **Phone:** 662/349-6640

fyi — Small-scale Hotel

All Year — 1P: $149-$189 — 2P: $149-$189

Too new to rate, opening scheduled for August 2006. **Location:** I-55, exit 289, just ne. 7153 Hungry Fisherman Dr 38671. Fax: 662/399-6360. **Amenities:** 78 units, coffeemakers, microwaves, refrigerators, pool. **Cards:** AX, DS, MC, VI.

WHERE TO DINE

DANVER'S — **Lunch:** $3-$8 — **Dinner:** $3-$8 — **Phone:** 662/349-9001

American

Location: I-55, exit 289, just e. 115 Goodman Rd 38671. **Hours:** 6:30 am-10 pm, Fri & Sat-11 pm, Sun 7:30 am-10 pm. Closed major holidays. **Features:** The popular burger joint is an area must. In addition to delicious burgers, it offers a tempting salad bar. Everything is reasonably priced. Casual dress. **Parking:** on-site. **Cards:** AX, MC, VI.

HUNAN OUTSTANDING CHINESE CUISINE — **Lunch:** $5-$10 — **Dinner:** $6-$12 — **Phone:** 662/349-8680

Chinese

Location: I-55, exit 289, just e; in South Lake Center. 35 C Goodman Rd W 38671. **Hours:** 11 am-9:30 pm, Fri & Sat-10:30 pm. **Features:** Plenty of traditional Chinese food as well as sushi are available on the daily buffet, all for an excellent price. Casual dress. **Parking:** on-site. **Cards:** MC, VI.

LA HACIENDA MEXICAN RESTAURANT — **Lunch:** $6-$10 — **Dinner:** $7-$15 — **Phone:** 662/349-4484

Mexican

Location: I-55, exit 289, just e; in South Lake Shopping Center. 175 B Goodman Rd 38671. **Hours:** 11 am-10 pm. Closed major holidays. **Features:** This family-friendly restaurant, featuring mounds of chips and salsa continuously flowing to the tables, is sure to satisfy a craving for Mexican food. Casual dress; cocktails. **Parking:** on-site. **Cards:** AX, DS, MC, VI.

STARKVILLE pop. 21,869

WHERE TO STAY

DAYS INN & SUITES *Book great rates at AAA.com* — **Phone:** (662)324-5555

Small-scale Hotel

All Year — 1P: $85-$95 — 2P: $105-$125 — XP: $10 — F

Location: SR 12, 1.5 mi w of jct US 82. 119 Hwy 12 W 39759. Fax: 662/323-4615. **Facility:** 60 one-bedroom standard units. 2 stories (no elevator), exterior corridors. **Parking:** on-site. **Terms:** 2 night minimum stay - seasonal, [CP] meal plan available, small pets only ($7 extra charge, with prior approval). **Amenities:** voice mail, irons, hair dryers. **Pool(s):** outdoor. **Business Services:** meeting rooms, fax (fee). **Cards:** AX, CB, DC, DS, JC, MC, VI.

ASK FEE SOME UNITS

MICROTEL INN & SUITES *Book at AAA.com* — **Phone:** 662/615-0700

Small-scale Hotel

All Year — 1P: $64-$129 — 2P: $64-$129 — XP: $5 — F

Location: On US 82, east end of town. 1121 Hwy 82 39759 (1121 Hwy 82 E). Fax: 662/615-0702. **Facility:** 73 one-bedroom standard units. 3 stories, interior corridors. *Bath:* combo or shower only. **Parking:** on-site. **Terms:** 7 day cancellation notice. **Amenities:** high-speed Internet, voice mail, irons, hair dryers. **Pool(s):** small outdoor. **Leisure Activities:** exercise room. **Guest Services:** valet laundry, wireless Internet. **Business Services:** meeting rooms. **Cards:** AX, DC, DS, MC, VI.

SOME UNITS ASK

WHERE TO DINE

BARNHILL'S BUFFET — **Lunch:** $5-$9 — **Dinner:** $7-$10 — **Phone:** 662/615-5491

American

Location: Jct US 82, 1 mi s on SR 12. 409 Hwy 12 E 39759. **Hours:** 10:45 am-8:45 pm, Fri-9 pm, Sat 7 am-9 pm, Sun 7 am-8:45 pm. Closed: 12/25. **Features:** Casual dress. **Parking:** on-site. **Cards:** AX, DS, MC, VI.

TUNICA pop. 1,132

WHERE TO STAY

AMERICAS BEST VALUE INN *Book at AAA.com* — **Phone:** (662)363-0030

Small-scale Hotel

All Year — 1P: $65-$199 — 2P: $65-$199

Location: Just n of jct US 61; near casinos. 4250 Casino Center Dr 38664. Fax: 662/363-1636. **Facility:** 100 one-bedroom standard units. 2 stories (no elevator), interior/exterior corridors. *Bath:* combo or shower only. **Parking:** on-site. **Amenities:** voice mail, irons, hair dryers. **Pool(s):** heated outdoor. **Leisure Activities:** exercise room. **Business Services:** meeting rooms. **Cards:** AX, DS, MC, VI.

SOME UNITS

BALLY'S SALOON GAMBLING HOTEL — **Phone:** 662/357-1500

Small-scale Hotel

Property failed to provide current rates

Location: Off US 61. 1450 Bally Blvd 38664 (PO Box 215, ROBINSONVILLE). Fax: 662/357-1756. **Facility:** This modest lodging offers complimentary casino transportation. 238 units. 232 one-bedroom standard units with whirlpools. 6 one-bedroom suites with whirlpools. 2 stories (no elevator), interior corridors. *Bath:* some combo or shower only. **Parking:** on-site. **Terms:** check-in 4 pm. **Amenities:** voice mail, hair dryers. **Pool(s):** outdoor. **Leisure Activities:** whirlpool, exercise room. **Guest Services:** sundries, coin laundry, area transportation. **Business Services:** meeting rooms.

SOME UNITS

BEST WESTERN TUNICA NORTH Book great rates at AAA.com **Phone:** 662/363-6711

Small-scale Hotel

Property failed to provide current rates

Location: Jct US 61 and SR 304. 7500 Casino Strip Resort Blvd 38664. Fax: 662/363-0011. **Facility:** 80 one-bedroom standard units. 3 stories, interior corridors. *Bath:* combo or shower only. **Parking:** on-site. **Amenities:** irons, hair dryers. **Pool(s):** outdoor. **Guest Services:** wireless Internet.

SOME UNITS

COTTAGE INN Book great rates at AAA.com **Phone:** 662/363-2900

Cottage

All Year 1P: $50-$150 2P: $50-$150

Location: Off US 61. 4325 Casino Center Dr 38664. Fax: 662/363-2971. **Facility:** 19 units. 11 one-bedroom standard units, some with whirlpools. 8 cottages, some with whirlpools. 1 story, exterior corridors. **Parking:** on-site. **Amenities:** *Some:* irons, hair dryers. **Business Services:** fax (fee). **Cards:** AX, DC, DS, MC, VI. **Free Special Amenities: continental breakfast and local telephone calls.**

SOME UNITS

FITZGERALDS CASINO/HOTEL TUNICA Book at AAA.com **Phone:** 662/363-5825

Large-scale Hotel

Property failed to provide current rates

Location: Off US 61. 711 Lucky Ln 38664. Fax: 662/363-7150. **Facility:** Try your luck at this themed casino hotel, which features leprechauns and four-leaf clovers as part of the decor. 507 units. 455 one-bedroom standard units. 52 one-bedroom suites, some with whirlpools. 9 stories, interior corridors. *Bath:* combo or shower only. **Parking:** on-site. **Terms:** check-in 4 pm. **Amenities:** voice mail, irons, hair dryers. **Pool(s):** small heated indoor. **Leisure Activities:** whirlpool, limited exercise equipment. **Guest Services:** gift shop. **Business Services:** conference facilities.

SOME UNITS

GOLD STRIKE CASINO RESORT Book great rates at AAA.com **Phone:** (662)357-1111

Large-scale Hotel

All Year 2P: $59-$249 XP: $10 F18

Location: Off US 61. 1010 Casino Center Dr 38664. Fax: 662/529-2010. **Facility:** Some rooms with river view. 1133 units. 1083 one-bedroom standard units, some with whirlpools. 50 one-bedroom suites. 31 stories, interior corridors. **Parking:** on-site and valet. **Terms:** check-in 4 pm, cancellation fee imposed, package plans. **Amenities:** voice mail, irons, hair dryers. *Some:* safes. **Dining:** 4 restaurants, 24 hrs, cocktails, entertainment. **Pool(s):** heated indoor. **Leisure Activities:** whirlpools, theater, stage shows, exercise room. *Fee:* massage. **Guest Services:** gift shop, valet laundry, tanning facility. **Business Services:** conference facilities, fax. **Cards:** AX, CB, DC, DS, JC, MC, VI. (See color ad below)

SOME UNITS

GRAND CASINO TUNICA *Book at AAA.com* **Phone:** 662/363-2788

Large-scale Hotel

Property failed to provide current rates

Location: Off US 61, follow signs. 13615 Old Hwy 61 N 38664. Fax: 662/357-3355. **Facility:** The hotel offers upscale lodging and a nearby casino. 188 units. 154 one-bedroom standard units. 34 one-bedroom suites with whirlpools. 6 stories, interior corridors. *Bath:* combo or shower only. **Parking:** on-site. **Terms:** check-in 4 pm. **Amenities:** video games (fee), voice mail, hair dryers. *Some:* irons. **Pool(s):** heated indoor. **Leisure Activities:** exercise room. *Fee:* golf-18 holes, massage. **Guest Services:** wireless Internet. **Business Services:** conference facilities.

SOME UNITS

HOLLYWOOD CASINO RESORT HOTEL **Phone:** 662/357-7700

Large-scale Hotel

Property failed to provide current rates

Location: 6.8 mi w of US 61 and SR 304. 1150 Casino Strip Resort Blvd 38664 (PO Box 218, ROBINSONVILLE). Fax: 662/357-7800. **Facility:** Delight in viewing Hollywood memorabilia from the past and present that decorates this casino hotel, including the Batmobile. 494 units. 437 one-bedroom standard units. 57 one-bedroom suites, some with whirlpools. 8 stories, interior corridors. *Bath:* combo or shower only. **Parking:** on-site and valet. **Amenities:** video games (fee), voice mail, irons, hair dryers. *Some:* dual phone lines, safes. **Pool(s):** heated indoor. **Leisure Activities:** whirlpool, limited exercise equipment. *Fee:* golf-18 holes. **Guest Services:** gift shop. **Business Services:** meeting rooms.

SOME UNITS

KEY WEST INN TUNICA *Book at AAA.com* **Phone:** 662/363-0021

Motel

Property failed to provide current rates

Location: US 61, 0.3 mi n of SR 304. 11635 Hwy 61 N 38664. Fax: 662/363-1396. **Facility:** 44 one-bedroom standard units. 2 stories (no elevator), exterior corridors. **Parking:** on-site. **Terms:** small pets only ($10 extra charge). **Amenities:** hair dryers. **Guest Services:** coin laundry, wireless Internet. **Business Services:** fax (fee).

SOME UNITS

FEE

WHERE TO DINE

FAIRBANKS STEAKHOUSE **Dinner:** $27-$39 **Phone:** 662/357-7700

Steak House

Location: Just n of jct US 61; in Hollywood Casino. 1150 Casino Strip Resort Blvd 38664. **Hours:** 5 pm-10:30 pm, Sun 4:30 pm-10 pm. **Reservations:** suggested. **Features:** Although it's inside the casino, the steakhouse evokes the feeling of being in a Civil War-era gentlemen's club. Soft music, dark paneling, gracious staff and, best of all, delicious food are hallmarks. Dressy casual; cocktails. **Parking:** on-site and valet. **Cards:** AX, DC, DS, MC, VI.

THE HOLLYWOOD CAFE **Lunch:** $3-$6 **Dinner:** $5-$11 **Phone:** 667/363-1126

Southern

Location: On Old US 61, just s of jct SR 304; in Casino Strip Resort Blvd. 1130 Old Commerce Rd 38664. **Hours:** 11 am-2 pm, Fri also 5 pm-10 pm, Sat from 5 pm. Closed major holidays; also Sun. **Features:** Home-style Southern cuisine is served in the small, simple cafe. The menu consists of black Angus burgers and such favorites as meatloaf and batter-fried fish. Hushpuppies are a must try, and a long list of vegetables and delicious cakes also should be considered. Friendly service and a casual atmosphere round out the down-home dining experience. Casual dress. **Parking:** on-site. **Cards:** MC, VI.

N'AWLINS LOUISIANA CUISINE **Dinner:** $15-$25 **Phone:** 662/357-5500

Creole

Location: In The Horse Shoe Casino. 1021 Casino Center Dr 38664. **Hours:** 6 pm-11 pm, Fri-midnight, Sat 5 pm-midnight. Closed: Wed & Thurs. **Reservations:** accepted. **Features:** This is as close to real New Orleans food as it gets. The food here is exactly what you've been wanting for; their award-winning chef will treat you to dishes that will not disappoint. Enjoy a relaxing environment with a welcoming staff. Casual dress; cocktails. **Parking:** on-site and valet. **Cards:** AX, DS, MC, VI.

TUPELO pop. 34,211

WHERE TO STAY

AMERIHOST INN-TUPELO *Book great rates at AAA.com* **Phone:** 662/844-7660

AAA SAVE

Small-scale Hotel

All Year	1P: $69	2P: $69	XP: $6	F

Location: On SR 145, 0.4 mi n of McCullough Blvd. 625 Spicer Dr 38804. Fax: 662/844-3009. **Facility:** 61 one-bedroom standard units, some with whirlpools. 2 stories (no elevator), interior corridors. *Bath:* combo or shower only. **Parking:** on-site. **Terms:** cancellation fee imposed, pets ($25 deposit). **Amenities:** voice mail, safes (fee), irons, hair dryers. **Pool(s):** small heated indoor. **Leisure Activities:** sauna, whirlpool, exercise room. **Guest Services:** valet laundry, wireless Internet. **Business Services:** meeting rooms. **Cards:** AX, DC, DS, MC, VI. **Free Special Amenities: continental breakfast and high-speed Internet.**

SOME UNITS

FEE

COMFORT INN *Book great rates at AAA.com* **Phone:** (662)842-5100

Small-scale Hotel

All Year [CP]	1P: $72-$90	2P: $77-$95	XP: $5	F18

Location: Jct McCullough Blvd and SR 145, 1.3 mi s to McCullough Blvd, w to N Gloster St, then 0.3 mi n. 1190 N Gloster St 38804. Fax: 662/844-0554. **Facility:** 83 one-bedroom standard units. 2 stories (no elevator), exterior corridors. **Parking:** on-site. **Terms:** cancellation fee imposed, pets ($25 deposit). **Amenities:** high-speed Internet, irons, hair dryers. **Leisure Activities:** exercise room. **Guest Services:** valet laundry, wireless Internet. **Business Services:** meeting rooms, PC. **Cards:** AX, CB, DC, DS, JC, MC, VI.

SOME UNITS

ASK

FEE

COURTYARD BY MARRIOTT *Book great rates at AAA.com* **Phone:** (662)841-9960

Small-scale Hotel

All Year 1P: $104 2P: $104

Location: On SR 145, 0.4 mi n of McCullough Blvd. 1320 N Gloster St 38804. Fax: 662/841-9907. **Facility:** 93 units. 90 one-bedroom standard units, some with whirlpools. 3 one-bedroom suites. 3 stories, interior corridors. *Bath:* combo or shower only. **Parking:** on-site. **Amenities:** high-speed Internet, voice mail, irons, hair dryers. **Pool(s):** outdoor. **Leisure Activities:** whirlpool, exercise room. **Guest Services:** sundries, valet and coin laundry, wireless Internet. **Business Services:** meeting rooms, business center. **Cards:** AX, CB, DC, DS, JC, MC, VI.

SOME UNITS

JAMESON INN *Book at AAA.com* **Phone:** (662)840-2380

Small-scale Hotel

All Year [ECP] 1P: $54-$120

Location: US 45, exit Barnes Crossing, 1 mi sw. 879 Mississippi Dr 38804. Fax: 662/840-8317. **Facility:** 60 one-bedroom standard units. 2 stories (no elevator), exterior corridors. *Bath:* combo or shower only. **Parking:** on-site. **Terms:** cancellation fee imposed, small pets only ($10 extra charge). **Amenities:** irons, hair dryers. **Pool(s):** small outdoor. **Leisure Activities:** exercise room. **Guest Services:** wireless Internet. **Business Services:** PC. **Cards:** AX, DC, DS, MC, VI.

SOME UNITS

ASK FEE

MICROTEL INN & SUITES *Book at AAA.com* **Phone:** (662)840-2111

Small-scale Hotel

All Year [ECP] 1P: $49-$69 2P: $55-$75 XP: $6 F12

Location: Just w of jct SR 145. 1532 McCullough Blvd 38804. Fax: 662/840-0077. **Facility:** 58 one-bedroom standard units. 2 stories (no elevator). *Bath:* combo or shower only. **Parking:** on-site. **Terms:** package plans. **Amenities:** irons. *Some:* hair dryers. **Guest Services:** wireless Internet. **Cards:** AX, CB, DC, DS, MC, VI.

SOME UNITS

ASK

THE MOCKINGBIRD INN BED & BREAKFAST **Phone:** 662/841-0286

Bed & Breakfast

Property failed to provide current rates

Location: On SR 145, just n of jct SR 6. 305 N Gloster 38804. Fax: 662/840-4158. **Facility:** Have a relaxing stay in one of the comfortable guestrooms, each with a different international flair. Smoke free premises. 8 units. 7 one-bedroom standard units, some with whirlpools. 1 cottage with whirlpool. 2 stories (no elevator), interior corridors. *Bath:* combo or shower only. **Parking:** on-site. **Terms:** age restrictions may apply. **Amenities:** *Some:* DVD players, irons, hair dryers. **Business Services:** fax.

SOME UNITS

SLEEP INN & SUITES *Book great rates at AAA.com* **Phone:** (662)840-7737

AAA SAVE

Small-scale Hotel

All Year 1P: $72-$90 2P: $72-$90 XP: $10 F17

Location: McCullough Blvd to N Gloster exit. 1721 N Gloster St 38804. Fax: 662/840-7735. **Facility:** 66 one-bedroom standard units. 4 stories. *Bath:* combo or shower only. **Parking:** on-site. **Terms:** cancellation fee imposed. **Amenities:** high-speed Internet, voice mail, irons, hair dryers. **Pool(s):** small outdoor. **Leisure Activities:** exercise room. **Guest Services:** valet and coin laundry, wireless Internet. **Business Services:** meeting rooms, business center. **Cards:** AX, CB, DC, DS, JC, MC, VI. **Free Special Amenities: continental breakfast and high-speed Internet.**

SOME UNITS

SUPER 8 MOTEL *Book great rates at AAA.com* **Phone:** (662)842-0448

AAA SAVE

Motel

All Year 1P: $51-$53 2P: $51-$63 XP: $5 F17

Location: US 78, exit 81, just sw. 3898 McCullough Blvd 38801 (PO Box 505, BELDEN, 38826). Fax: 662/842-0448. **Facility:** 49 one-bedroom standard units, some with whirlpools. 2 stories (no elevator), exterior corridors. **Parking:** on-site. **Terms:** [CP] meal plan available, pets ($10 extra charge, in limited smoking units). **Amenities:** *Some:* irons, hair dryers. **Pool(s):** small outdoor. **Guest Services:** coin laundry, wireless Internet. **Business Services:** fax (fee). **Cards:** AX, DS, MC, VI. **Free Special Amenities: continental breakfast and high-speed Internet.**

SOME UNITS

FEE

WHERE TO DINE

BARNHILL'S BUFFET **Lunch:** $5-$9 **Dinner:** $7-$10 **Phone:** 662/844-0755

American

Location: Jct Main St, 1 mi s. 803 S Gloster St 38801. **Hours:** 10:45 am-8:45 pm, Fri-9 pm, Sat 7 am-9 pm, Sun 7 am-8:45 pm. Closed: 12/25. **Features:** Casual dress. **Parking:** on-site. **Cards:** AX, DS, MC, VI.

IV'S RESTAURANT **Lunch:** $8-$11 **Dinner:** $20-$29 **Phone:** 662/407-0096

AAA

South Continental

Location: Just sw of jct W Main St and US 145. 150 S Industrial Rd 38801. **Hours:** 11 am-2 pm & 5-10 pm, Sat from 5 pm. Closed: Sun. **Reservations:** accepted. **Features:** This hot spot plates up Southern cuisine at its finest; enjoy this eatery, locally owned and operated by a true Southerner whose beautiful and inquisitive dishes will make your mouth water. Dressy casual; cocktails. **Parking:** on-site.

VANELLI'S GREEK & ITALIAN RESTAURANT *Menu on AAA.com* **Lunch:** $7-$11 **Dinner:** $7-$18 **Phone:** 662/844-4410

AAA

Italian

Location: On SR 145 (Gloster St), 0.4 mi n of McCullough Blvd. 1302 N Gloster St 38804. **Hours:** 11 am-10 pm, Fri & Sat-11 pm, Sun-9 pm. Closed: 12/25. **Reservations:** accepted. **Features:** Vanelli's serves up a tasty combination of Greek and Italian cuisine; selections include chicken, steak, pizza, pasta and gyros. A well-stocked salad bar, spacious booths and fast, friendly service are the reasons customers keep coming back. Casual dress; cocktails; entertainment. **Parking:** on-site. **Cards:** AX, CB, DC, DS, MC, VI.

VICKSBURG pop. 26,407

WHERE TO STAY

AMERISTAR CASINO HOTEL — **Phone:** (601)638-1000

AAA SAVE · Large-scale Hotel

All Year — 1P: $69-$119 — 2P: $69-$119

Location: I-20, exit 1A, just n. Located in a commercial area. 4155 Washington St 39180 (4116 Washington St). Fax: 601/630-4657. **Facility:** 149 one-bedroom standard units, some with whirlpools. 8 stories, interior corridors. *Bath:* combo or shower only. **Parking:** on-site. **Terms:** cancellation fee imposed. **Amenities:** video games (fee), high-speed Internet, voice mail, irons, hair dryers. **Dining:** 3 restaurants, 24 hours, cocktails. **Pool(s):** outdoor. **Leisure Activities:** whirlpool. **Guest Services:** area transportation-casino & bus station, wireless Internet. **Business Services:** meeting rooms. **Cards:** AX, DC, DS, MC, VI.

SOME UNITS

ANCHUCA — **Phone:** 601/661-0111

Bed & Breakfast

Property failed to provide current rates

Location: I-20, exit 4B, follow signs; in historic downtown. Located in a quiet residential area. 1010 1st East St 39183. Fax: 601/661-0501. **Facility:** Separate cottage rooms are available at this Greek Revival-style 1830 home featuring shady, brick-lined gardens, a pool and period furnishings. Smoke free premises. 7 units. 5 one-bedroom standard units. 2 one-bedroom suites, some with kitchens. 2 stories (no elevator), interior/exterior corridors. *Bath:* combo or shower only. **Parking:** on-site. **Terms:** age restrictions may apply. **Amenities:** video library, hair dryers. *Some:* CD players, irons. **Pool(s):** heated outdoor. **Guest Services:** complimentary evening beverages: Thurs-Sat, valet laundry, wireless Internet. **Business Services:** meeting rooms.

SOME UNITS

ANNABELLE BED & BREAKFAST — **Phone:** 601/638-2000

AAA SAVE · Bed & Breakfast

All Year — 1P: $99 — 2P: $99 — XP: $25 — D16

Location: I-20, exit 1A, 2.3 mi n on Washington St, just w. Located in a historic residential area. 501 Speed St 39180. Fax: 601/636-5054. **Facility:** Adorned with ornate iron grillwork, this brick home dating from around 1868 is decorated with well-preserved antiques and offers views of the river. Smoke free premises. 6 units. 5 one-bedroom standard units, some with whirlpools. 1 one-bedroom suite ($150) with kitchen (utensils extra charge). 2 stories (no elevator), interior/exterior corridors. **Parking:** on-site. **Terms:** 7 day cancellation notice, package plans, small pets only ($25 fee, with prior approval). **Amenities:** irons. **Pool(s):** outdoor. **Guest Services:** gift shop, wireless Internet. **Cards:** AX, MC, VI. **Free Special Amenities: full breakfast and local telephone calls.**

SOME UNITS

FEE

BATTLEFIELD INN — **Phone:** (601)638-5811

AAA SAVE · Small-scale Hotel

All Year — 1P: $69 — 2P: $79 — XP: $5 — F16

Location: I-20, exit 4B, 1 mi ne. 4137 I-20 N Frontage Rd 39183-3498. Fax: 601/638-9249. **Facility:** 117 one-bedroom standard units, some with whirlpools. 2 stories (no elevator), interior/exterior corridors. **Parking:** on-site. **Terms:** [BP] meal plan available, package plans, pets ($10 extra charge). **Amenities:** voice mail, irons, hair dryers. **Dining:** 6 am-9:30 & 5-9 pm, Sat & Sun 6 am-10:30 & 5-10 pm, cocktails. **Pool(s):** outdoor. **Leisure Activities:** miniature golf, playground, basketball. **Guest Services:** complimentary evening beverages, valet and coin laundry, wireless Internet. **Business Services:** meeting rooms, PC. **Cards:** AX, CB, DC, DS, MC, VI. *(See color ad below)*

SOME UNITS

FEE

BEST WESTERN VICKSBURG — *Book great rates at AAA.com* — **Phone:** (601)636-5800

AAA SAVE · Small-scale Hotel

5/16-8/15	1P: $70-$85	2P: $70-$95	XP: $10	F12
12/1-5/15 & 8/16-11/30	1P: $65-$75	2P: $65-$75	XP: $10	F12

Location: I-20, exit 3, just w on NW Frontage Rd. Located in a commercial area. 2445 N Frontage Rd 39180. Fax: 601/636-1102. **Facility:** 63 one-bedroom standard units, some with whirlpools. 2 stories (no elevator), exterior corridors. *Bath:* combo or shower only. **Parking:** on-site. **Terms:** [BP] meal plan available. **Amenities:** high-speed Internet, irons, hair dryers. **Pool(s):** small heated indoor. **Leisure Activities:** sauna, exercise room. **Guest Services:** coin laundry, wireless Internet. **Business Services:** business center. **Cards:** AX, CB, DC, DS, MC, VI. **Free Special Amenities: full breakfast and high-speed Internet.**

SOME UNITS

CEDAR GROVE MANSION **Phone:** (601)636-1000

Country Inn

All Year 1P: $100-$260 2P: $100-$260 XP: $10 F3

Location: I-20, exit 1A, 2.3 mi n on Washington St, then w on Klein; to gated entrance. Located in Historic Garden District. 2200 Oak St 39180. Fax: 601/634-6126. **Facility:** Furnished with antiques, this restored 50-room antebellum mansion overlooking the river was originally a bride's wedding gift from her father in 1840. Designated smoking area. 33 units. 19 one-bedroom standard units, some with whirlpools. 11 one- and 3 two-bedroom suites, some with kitchens and/or whirlpools. 1-4 stories (no elevator), interior/exterior corridors. *Bath:* some combo, shower or tub only. **Parking:** on-site. **Terms:** 3 day cancellation notice-fee imposed, [BP] meal plan available, package plans, pets ($50 deposit, in designated units). **Amenities:** video library, voice mail, irons, hair dryers. *Some:* CD players. **Dining:** The Cedar Grove Mansion and Restaurant, see separate listing. **Pool(s):** small outdoor. **Leisure Activities:** lighted tennis court, croquet, exercise room. **Guest Services:** gift shop, valet and coin laundry. **Business Services:** meeting rooms. **Cards:** AX, DS, MC, VI. **Free Special Amenities: full breakfast and early check-in/late check-out.**

SOME UNITS

FEE

COMFORT INN *Book great rates at AAA.com* **Phone:** (601)634-8438

Small-scale Hotel

All Year 1P: $85-$105 2P: $85-$105 XP: $5 F18

Location: I-20, exit 4A eastbound; exit 5B westbound, 0.5 mi s of National Military Park. Located in a commercial area. 3959 E Clay St 39180. Fax: 601/630-0415. **Facility:** 80 one-bedroom standard units, some with whirlpools. 2 stories (no elevator), exterior corridors. **Parking:** on-site. **Terms:** [CP] meal plan available. **Amenities:** irons, hair dryers. **Pool(s):** outdoor. **Leisure Activities:** sauna, whirlpool. **Guest Services:** wireless Internet. **Business Services:** PC. **Cards:** AX, CB, DC, DS, JC, MC, VI.

SOME UNITS

THE CORNERS BED & BREAKFAST **Phone:** 601/636-7421

Bed & Breakfast

Property failed to provide current rates

Location: I-20, exit 1A, 2.3 mi n on Washington St, just w. Located in a historic residential area. 601 Klein St 39180. Fax: 601/636-7232. **Facility:** Boasting a brick-walled garden and glassed-in veranda, this 1873 home facing the Mississippi River features both Greek Revival and Victorian elements. 14 units. 13 one- and 1 two-bedroom standard units, some with whirlpools. 2 stories (no elevator), interior/exterior corridors. *Bath:* combo or shower only. **Parking:** on-site. **Terms:** small pets only. **Amenities:** *Some:* irons, hair dryers. **Business Services:** meeting rooms.

SOME UNITS

ECONO LODGE *Book great rates at AAA.com* **Phone:** 601/630-0100

Small-scale Hotel

All Year 1P: $60-$100 2P: $60-$100 XP: $5 F15

Location: I-20, exit 1C, on northeast frontage road. 1675 N Frontage Rd 39180. Fax: 601/630-0100. **Facility:** 30 one-bedroom standard units. 2 stories (no elevator), exterior corridors. **Parking:** on-site. **Amenities:** hair dryers. **Pool(s):** small outdoor. **Guest Services:** wireless Internet. **Cards:** AX, DS, MC, VI.

SOME UNITS

ECONO LODGE OF VICKSBURG **Phone:** 601/634-8766

Motel

Property failed to provide current rates

Location: I-20, exit 4B (Clay St), just n. 3330-A Clay St 39183. Fax: 601/638-3295. **Facility:** 49 one-bedroom standard units. 2 stories (no elevator), exterior corridors. **Parking:** on-site. **Terms:** pets ($10 fee). **Amenities:** irons, hair dryers. **Guest Services:** coin laundry. **Business Services:** fax.

SOME UNITS

FEE

HAMPTON INN & SUITES *Book great rates at AAA.com* **Phone:** 601/636-6100

Small-scale Hotel

Property failed to provide current rates

Location: I-20, exit 4B (Clay St), just n. 3330 Clay St 39183. Fax: 601/634-1962. **Facility:** 123 one-bedroom standard units, some with whirlpools. 5 stories, interior corridors. *Bath:* combo or shower only. **Parking:** on-site. **Amenities:** DVD players, voice mail, irons, hair dryers. **Pool(s):** heated indoor. **Leisure Activities:** whirlpool, exercise room. **Guest Services:** sundries, complimentary evening beverages: Mon-Thurs, valet and coin laundry, wireless Internet. **Business Services:** business center. *(See color ad p 483)*

SOME UNITS

HAMPTON INN & SUITES OF VICKSBURG **Phone:** 601/636-0804

Motel

All Year 1P: $109-$179 2P: $119-$189 XP: $10 F18

Location: I-20, exit 4B (Clay St), just n. 3332 Clay St 39180. Fax: 601/636-7307. **Facility:** 131 units. 118 one-bedroom standard units. 13 one-bedroom suites. 4 stories, exterior corridors. *Bath:* combo or shower only. **Parking:** on-site. **Terms:** [BP] meal plan available. **Amenities:** video library, voice mail, irons, hair dryers. *Some:* DVD players, high-speed Internet. **Pool(s):** small outdoor, wading. **Leisure Activities:** limited exercise equipment. **Guest Services:** complimentary evening beverages: Mon-Thurs, valet and coin laundry, wireless Internet. **Business Services:** meeting rooms, business center. **Cards:** AX, CB, DC, DS, MC, VI.

SOME UNITS

HOLIDAY INN EXPRESS *Book at AAA.com* **Phone:** (601)634-8777

Small-scale Hotel

All Year 1P: $119-$150 2P: $119-$150

Location: I-20, exit 4A eastbound; exit 5B westbound, just s. 4330 S Frontage Rd 39180. Fax: 601/634-8300. **Facility:** 75 one-bedroom standard units, some with whirlpools. 3 stories, interior corridors. *Bath:* combo or shower only. **Parking:** on-site. **Amenities:** high-speed Internet, voice mail, irons, hair dryers. **Pool(s):** outdoor. **Leisure Activities:** exercise room. **Guest Services:** valet and coin laundry, wireless Internet. **Business Services:** meeting rooms, PC, fax. **Cards:** AX, CB, DC, DS, JC, MC, VI.

SOME UNITS

JAMESON INN *Book at AAA.com* **Phone:** (601)619-7799

Small-scale Hotel

All Year [ECP] 1P: $54-$120

Location: I-20, exit 4A, on southeast frontage road. Located next to the outlet mall. 3975 S Frontage Rd 39180. Fax: 601/619-0072. **Facility:** 59 units. 58 one-bedroom standard units. 1 one-bedroom suite with whirlpool. 2 stories (no elevator), exterior corridors. *Bath:* combo or shower only. **Parking:** on-site. **Terms:** cancellation fee imposed, small pets only ($10 fee). **Amenities:** hair dryers. **Pool(s):** outdoor. **Leisure Activities:** exercise room. **Guest Services:** wireless Internet. **Business Services:** PC. **Cards:** AX, DC, DS, MC, VI.

SOME UNITS

FEE

MOTEL 6 #4189 *Book at AAA.com* **Phone:** 601/638-5077

Small-scale Hotel

Property failed to provide current rates

Location: I-20, exit 4B (Clay St), just ne. Located adjacent to national battlefield. 4127 N Frontage Rd 39183. Fax: 601/638-6004. **Facility:** 58 one-bedroom standard units. 2 stories (no elevator), interior corridors. **Parking:** on-site. **Terms:** small pets only (must be attended). **Amenities:** *Some:* high-speed Internet. **Pool(s):** outdoor. **Guest Services:** wireless Internet.

SOME UNITS

QUALITY INN & SUITES **Phone:** 601/636-0804

fyi

Small-scale Hotel

5/28-9/2 [CP] 1P: $75-$140 2P: $75-$140

12/1-5/27 & 9/3-11/30 [CP] 1P: $65-$130 2P: $65-$130

Too new to rate. **Location:** I-20, exit 4B. 3332 Clay St 39183. **Amenities:** 148 units, coffeemakers, microwaves, refrigerators, pool. **Cards:** AX, DC, DS, JC, MC, VI. *(See color ad p 483)*

RAINBOW HOTEL CASINO *Book great rates at AAA.com* **Phone:** (601)638-7111

AAA SAVE

Small-scale Hotel

All Year 1P: $79 2P: $79 XP: $5 F

Location: I-20, exit 1A, 1.4 mi s. Located next door to the Rainbow Casino. 1350 Warrenton Rd 39180. Fax: 601/630-9046. **Facility:** 89 units. 88 one-bedroom standard units, some with whirlpools. 1 one-bedroom suite with whirlpool. 2 stories (no elevator), interior corridors. *Bath:* combo or shower only. **Parking:** on-site. **Terms:** [ECP] meal plan available. **Amenities:** high-speed Internet, voice mail, safes (fee), irons, hair dryers. **Pool(s):** heated indoor. **Leisure Activities:** whirlpool, exercise room. **Guest Services:** wireless Internet. **Business Services:** PC. **Cards:** AX, DS, MC, VI.

SOME UNITS

WHERE TO DINE

BEECHWOOD RESTAURANT & LOUNGE **Lunch:** $5-$19 **Dinner:** $5-$19 **Phone:** 601/636-3761

Steak & Seafood

Location: I-20, exit 4A eastbound; exit 5B westbound, 0.5 mi se. 4451 E Clay St 39180. **Hours:** 11 am-10 pm, Fri & Sat-midnight. Closed major holidays. **Reservations:** accepted. **Features:** The comfortable, popular restaurant serves tasty, reasonably priced home-cooked meals. Casual dress; cocktails. **Parking:** on-site. **Cards:** AX, DS, MC, VI.

BORRELLO'S **Lunch:** $5-$10 **Dinner:** $10-$25 **Phone:** 601/638-0169

Italian

Location: I-20, exit 1A, 3.5 mi n; in historic town center. 1306 Washington St 39180. **Hours:** 11 am-10 pm; Sunday brunch. Closed: 12/25. **Reservations:** suggested. **Features:** In a beautifully restored 1840s building, the restaurant specializes in Italian cuisine with a Creole influence. Dressy casual; cocktails. **Parking:** street. **Cards:** AX, DC, DS, MC, VI.

THE CEDAR GROVE MANSION AND RESTAURANT **Dinner:** $12-$40 **Phone:** 601/636-1000

American

Location: I-20, exit 1A, 2.3 mi n on Washington St, then w on Klein St to gated entrance; in Cedar Grove Mansion Inn. 2200 Oak St 39180. **Hours:** 5 pm-10 pm. Closed: 12/25. **Reservations:** suggested, weekends. **Features:** Experience intimate dining in a historic antebellum mansion that still has a cannonball lodged in one parlor wall. There are six dining rooms to choose from, each room with its own unique atmosphere. A recommended entree is the Raspberry Forest Salmon. Dressy casual; cocktails. **Parking:** on-site. **Cards:** AX, DS, MC, VI.

FARRADDAYS' RESTAURANT **Dinner:** $18-$32 **Phone:** 601/636-5700

Regional American

Location: I-20, exit 1A, 0.7 mi n. 3990 Washington St 39180. **Hours:** 5 pm-10 pm, Fri & Sat-midnight. **Reservations:** accepted. **Features:** In the Isle Capri Casino, the restaurant displays Mississippi Cajun decor. On the menu are items ranging from Angus beef steaks to boiled crawfish. Patrons can order a $13.99 three-course meal between 5 and 7 p.m. Casual dress; cocktails. **Parking:** on-site. **Cards:** AX, DS, MC, VI.

GOLDIE'S TRAIL BAR-B-QUE **Lunch:** $5-$13 **Dinner:** $5-$13 **Phone:** 601/636-9839

Barbecue

Location: I-20, exit 1A, just n. 4127 Washington St 39180. **Hours:** 11 am-9 pm, Fri & Sat-10 pm. Closed major holidays; also Sun. **Features:** In operation since 1960, the barbecue joint serves such favorites as spare ribs and sliced beef platters with its legendary Texas-style sauce. Casual dress; beer only. **Parking:** on-site. **Cards:** AX, MC, VI.

ROWDY'S FAMILY RESTAURANT **Lunch:** $6-$12 **Dinner:** $8-$14 **Phone:** 601/638-2375

American

Location: I-20, exit 5B, just s. 60 Hwy 27 39180. **Hours:** 11 am-9:30 pm, Fri & Sat-10 pm. Closed major holidays. **Reservations:** accepted. **Features:** Open, airy with lots of windows, this casual family eatery sports a wildlife theme. The atmosphere is busy, but cozy, and you will be treated with Southern charm and hospitality. They specialize in catfish, and serve pecan pie as their signature dessert. Casual dress; beer only. **Parking:** on-site. **Cards:** AX, MC, VI.

RUSTY'S RIVERFRONT GRILL **Lunch:** $6-$21 **Dinner:** $6-$21 **Phone:** 601/638-2030

Traditional American

Location: I-I-20, exit 4B; in the historic downtown district. 901 Washington St 39183. **Hours:** 11 am-2 & 5-9:30 pm. Closed major holidays; also Sun & Mon. **Features:** Popular with the locals, the cozy restaurant is a fixture in the historic district. Casual dress; cocktails. **Parking:** on-site. **Cards:** AX, DS, MC, VI.

WALNUT HILLS ROUND TABLE **Lunch:** $8-$13 **Dinner:** $9-$24 **Phone:** 601/638-4910

Regional American

Location: I-20, exit 4B (Clay St), 2 mi w, then just n. 1214 Adams St 39183. **Hours:** 11 am-3 & 5-9 pm, Sat from 5 pm, Sun 11 am-2 pm. Closed major holidays. **Features:** The converted old house in historic downtown is a great spot in which to enjoy Southern home-cooked food, such as fried chicken, liver and onions and red beans and rice. Diners may opt for "shared dining" with other guests at large tables with center turntables. Casual dress; cocktails. **Parking:** on-site. **Cards:** AX, DC, DS, MC, VI.

WINONA pop. 5,482

WHERE TO STAY

WESTERN INN & SUITES **Phone:** (662)283-3900

Motel

All Year 1P: $65-$95 2P: $70-$99 XP: $10 F10

Location: I-55, exit 185, just se on US 82. 301 SE Frontage Rd 38967. Fax: 662/283-3900. **Facility:** 39 one-bedroom standard units, some with whirlpools. 2 stories (no elevator), exterior corridors. *Bath:* combo or shower only. **Parking:** on-site. **Terms:** 3-4 night minimum stay - seasonal, 14 day cancellation notice. **Amenities:** high-speed Internet, irons, hair dryers. **Pool(s):** small outdoor. **Guest Services:** wireless Internet. **Cards:** AX, CB, DC, DS, JC, MC, VI.

SOME UNITS

YAZOO CITY pop. 14,550

WHERE TO STAY

COMFORT INN *Book great rates at AAA.com* **Phone:** (662)746-6444

AAA SAVE

Small-scale Hotel

All Year 1P: $62 2P: $62 XP: $5 F12

Location: US 49 E, 1.8 mi n of jct US 49 W. 1600 Jerry Clower Blvd 39194. Fax: 662/746-6448. **Facility:** 50 units. 48 one-bedroom standard units. 2 one-bedroom suites ($120-$130) with whirlpools. 2 stories (no elevator), interior corridors. **Parking:** on-site. **Amenities:** irons, hair dryers. **Pool(s):** heated outdoor. **Guest Services:** coin laundry, wireless Internet. **Business Services:** meeting rooms. **Cards:** AX, DC, DS, MC, VI. **Free Special Amenities: continental breakfast and high-speed Internet.**

SOME UNITS

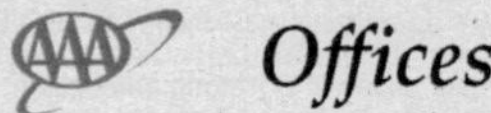

Offices

Cities with main offices are listed in **BOLD TYPE** and toll-free member service numbers in *ITALIC TYPE.* All are closed Saturdays, Sundays and holidays unless otherwise indicated. The type of service provided is designated below the name of the city where the office is located:

- ✚ Auto travel services, including books/maps, marked maps and on-demand Triptik maps
- ● Auto travel services, including books/maps, marked maps, but no on-demand Triptik maps
- ■ Provides books/maps only. No marked maps or on-demand Triptik maps available
- ▲ Travel agency services

NATIONAL OFFICE: 1000 AAA DRIVE, HEATHROW, FLORIDA 32746-5063, (407) 444-7000

ALABAMA

BIRMINGHAM—AAA ALABAMA, 2400 ACTON RD, 35243. MON-FRI 8-6, SAT 9-2. (205) 978-7000. *(800) 521-8124.* ✚▲

BIRMINGHAM—AAA ALABAMA, 2001 PARK PL TOWER #100, 35203. MON-FRI 8:30-5. (205) 323-4494. *(800) 521-8124.* ✚▲

DECATUR—AAA ALABAMA, 1605 BELTLINE RD SW #D-9, 35603. MON-FRI 8:30-5. (256) 353-4924. *(800) 521-8124.* ✚▲

DOTHAN—AAA ALABAMA, 3850 W MAIN ST, 36305. MON-FRI 8:30-5. (334) 793-6080. *(800) 521-8124.* ✚▲

FLORENCE—AAA ALABAMA, 102 S PINE ST, 35630. MON-FRI 8:30-5. (256) 764-9173. *(800) 521-8124.* ✚▲

HUNTSVILLE—AAA ALABAMA, 2625 MEMORIAL PKY SW, 35801. MON-FRI 8:30-5, SAT 9-2. (256) 539-7493. *(800) 521-8124.* ✚▲

MOBILE—AAA ALABAMA, 718 DOWNTOWNER LOOP W, 36609. MON-FRI 8:30-5. (251) 342-5550. *(800) 521-8124.* ✚▲

MONTGOMERY—AAA ALABAMA, 6901 VAUGHN RD, 36116. MON-FRI 8:30-5. (334) 272-1650. *(800) 521-8124.* ✚▲

OXFORD—AAA ALABAMA, 653 SNOW ST, 36203. MON-FRI 8:30-5. (256) 832-3101. *(800) 521-8124.* ✚▲

TUSCALOOSA—AAA ALABAMA, 312 MERCHANTS WALK #5A, 35406. MON-FRI 8:30-5. (205) 759-1202. *(800) 521-8124.* ✚▲

LOUISIANA

BATON ROUGE—AAA MISSOURI, 5454 BLUEBONNET RD #M, 70809. MON-FRI 8:30-5:15, MON 8:30-7, WED 8:30-7 (FEB-OCT). (888) 718-7968. ✚▲

METAIRIE—AAA MISSOURI, 3445 N CAUSEWAY BLVD #201, 70002. MON-FRI 8:30-5:15 (FEB-OCT), MON & WED 8:30-7 (FEB-OCT). (504) 838-7500. *(800) 452-7198.* ✚▲

SHREVEPORT—AAA MISSOURI, 6570 YOUREE DR #500, 71105. MON-FRI 8:30-5:15, MON & WED 8:30-7. (318) 797-0262. *(877) 415-3071.* ✚

SLIDELL—AAA MISSOURI, 1300 GAUSE BLVD #D-4, 70458. MON-FRI 8:30-5:15 (FEB-OCT), MON & WED 8:30-7 (FEB-OCT). (985) 781-7068. *(866) 325-2371.* ✚

MISSISSIPPI

RIDGELAND—AAA MISSOURI, 900 E COUNTY LINE RD #220, 39157. MON-FRI 8:30-5:15. (601) 957-8484. *(800) 596-2227.* ✚

Metric Equivalents Chart

TEMPERATURE

To convert Fahrenheit to Celsius, subtract 32 from the Fahrenheit temperature, multiply by 5 and divide by 9. To convert Celsius to Fahrenheit, multipy by 9, divide by 5 and add 32.

Celsius °		Fahrenheit °
100	BOILING	212
37		100
35		95
32		90
29		85
27		80
24		75
21		70
18		65
16		60
13		55
10		50
7		45
4		40
2		35
0	FREEZING	32
-4		25
-7		20
-9		15
-12		10
-15		5
-18		0
-21		-5
-24		-10
-27		-15

ACRES

1 acre = 0.4 hectare (ha)   1 hectare = 2.47 acres

MILES AND KILOMETRES

Note: A kilometre is approximately 5/8 or 0.6 of a mile. To convert kilometres to miles multiply by 0.6.

Miles/Kilometres		Kilometres/Miles	
15	24.1	30	18.6
20	32.2	35	21.7
25	40.2	40	24.8
30	48.3	45	27.9
35	56.3	50	31.0
40	64.4	55	34.1
45	72.4	60	37.2
50	80.5	65	40.3
55	88.5	70	43.4
60	96.6	75	46.6
65	104.6	80	49.7
70	112.7	85	52.8
75	120.7	90	55.9
80	128.7	95	59.0
85	136.8	100	62.1
90	144.8	105	65.2
95	152.9	110	68.3
100	160.9	115	71.4

LINEAR MEASURE

Customary	Metric
1 inch = 2.54 centimetres	1 centimetre = 0.4 inches
1 foot = 30 centimetres	1 metre = 3.3 feet
1 yard = 0.91 metres	1 metre = 1.09 yards
1 mile = 1.6 kilometres	1 kilometre = .62 miles

LIQUID MEASURE

Customary	Metric
1 fluid ounce = 30 millilitres	1 millilitre = .03 fluid ounces
1 cup = .24 litres	1 litre = 2.1 pints
1 pint = .47 litres	1 litre = 1.06 quarts
1 quart = .95 litres	1 litre = .26 gallons
1 gallon = 3.8 litres	

WEIGHT

If You Know:	Multiply By:	To Find:
Ounces	28.000	Grams
Pounds	0.450	Kilograms
Grams	0.035	Ounces
Kilograms	2.200	Pounds

PRESSURE

Air pressure in automobile tires is expressed in kilopascals. Multiply pound-force per square inch (psi) by 6.89 to find kilopascals (kPa).

24 psi = 165 kPa   28 psi = 193 kPa
26 psi = 179 kPa   30 psi = 207 kPa

GALLON AND LITRES

Gallons/Litres				Litres/Gallons			
5	19.0	12	45.6	10	2.6	40	10.4
6	22.8	14	53.2	15	3.9	50	13.0
7	26.6	16	60.8	20	5.2	60	15.6
8	30.4	18	68.4	25	6.5	70	18.2
9	34.2	20	76.0	30	7.8	80	20.8
10	38.0	25	95.0	35	9.1	90	23.4

NATIONAL PARKS PASS

The *National Parks Pass*, valid for 1 year from its first use in a park, and allows unlimited admissions to all U.S. national parks that charge an entrance fee. The **$50** pass covers all occupants of a single, private, non-commercial vehicle at parks where the entrance fee is per vehicle. At parks with individual entry fees, the pass covers the pass holder, spouse, parents and children.

As a result of a partnership with the National Park Foundation, AAA members may purchase the pass for **$48**, either through AAA's internet site (www.aaa.com) or by visiting a participating AAA office. Members may also phone the National Park Foundation at **(888) 467-2757** or purchase the pass online at www.nationalparks.org. Non-members may purchase the pass through participating AAA offices for the full **$50** price or online at www.nationalparks.org.

For an upgrade fee of **$15**, a Golden Eagle Hologram sticker can be added to a *National Parks Pass*. The hologram covers entrance fees not just at national parks, but at any federal recreation area that has an admission fee. Valid for the duration of the *National Parks Pass* to which it is affixed, the Golden Eagle hologram is available at National Park Service, Fish and Wildlife Service and Bureau of Land Management fee stations.

GOLDEN PASSPORTS

Golden Passports, available in three types, offer benefits and significant savings to individuals who plan to visit federal recreation sites.

*The Golden Eagle Passport**, available for a **$65** annual fee, is valid for entrance only to all federal recreation areas that have an entrance fee. Sites include those operated by the National Forest Service, National Park Service, Bureau of Land Management and the U.S. Fish and Wildlife Service. The passport admits all occupants of a single, private, non-commercial vehicle at locations where entrance is on a per vehicle basis. At locations where a per person fee is charged, the pass covers the pass holder, spouse, parents and children.

Citizens or permanent residents of the United States who are 62 and older can obtain *Golden Age Passports** for a one-time **$10** fee. Proof of age is required.

*Golden Access Passports** are free to citizens or permanent residents of the United States (regardless of age) who are medically blind or permanently disabled. Medical documentation is required.

Both *Golden Age* and *Golden Access Passports* cover entrance fees for the holder and accompanying private party to all national parks and sites managed by the U.S. Fish and Wildlife Service, the U.S. Forest Service and the Bureau of Land Management, plus a 50% discount on federal recreation use fees. When a per person fee is imposed, the pass covers the pass holder, spouse and children.

***Each of the Golden Passports must be purchased in person at a Federal Recreation Site, with proof of identification.**

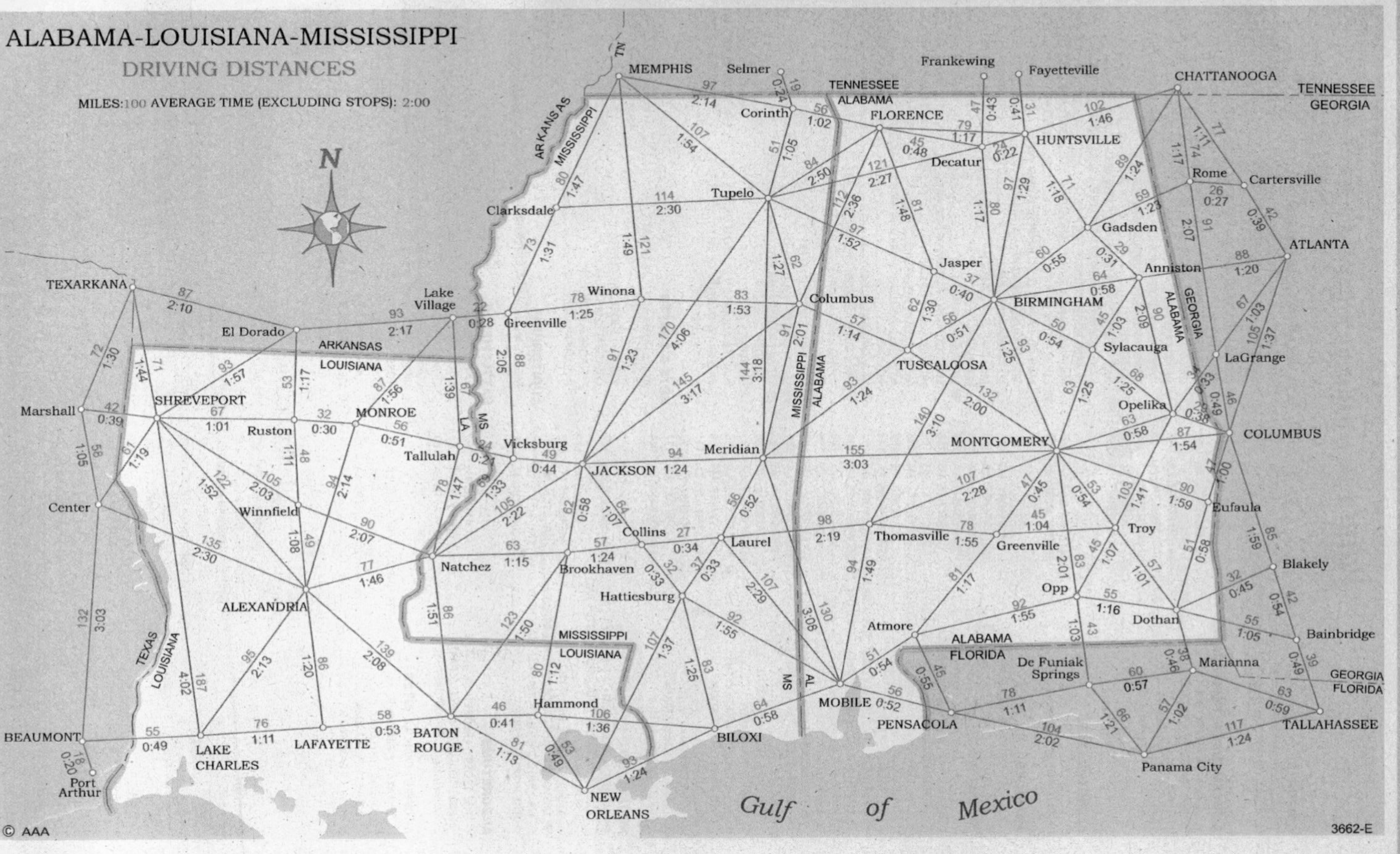
ALABAMA-LOUISIANA-MISSISSIPPI
DRIVING DISTANCES
MILES:100 AVERAGE TIME (EXCLUDING STOPS): 2:00
N
TN
MEMPHIS
Selmer
Frankewing
Fayetteville
CHATTANOOGA
TENNESSEE
GEORGIA
TENNESSEE
ALABAMA
ARKANSAS
MISSISSIPPI
Corinth
FLORENCE
Decatur
HUNTSVILLE
Rome
Cartersville
Clarksdale
Tupelo
Gadsden
ATLANTA
Jasper
Anniston
TEXARKANA
Lake Village
Winona
Columbus
BIRMINGHAM
Greenville
El Dorado
ARKANSAS
LOUISIANA
ALABAMA
GEORGIA
Sylacauga
LaGrange
TUSCALOOSA
MISSISSIPPI
ALABAMA
Opelika
Marshall
SHREVEPORT
MONROE
LA
MS
Ruston
Tallulah
Vicksburg
MONTGOMERY
COLUMBUS
JACKSON
Meridian
Center
Winnfield
Eufaula
Collins
Laurel
Thomasville
Greenville
Troy
Natchez
Brookhaven
Hattiesburg
Blakely
ALEXANDRIA
Opp
Dothan
Atmore
MISSISSIPPI
LOUISIANA
ALABAMA
FLORIDA
Bainbridge
TEXAS
LOUISIANA
De Funiak Springs
Marianna
GEORGIA
FLORIDA
MS
AL
MOBILE
PENSACOLA
Hammond
TALLAHASSEE
BEAUMONT
LAKE CHARLES
LAFAYETTE
BATON ROUGE
BILOXI
Panama City
Port Arthur
NEW ORLEANS
Gulf of Mexico
© AAA
3662-E

Points of Interest Index

Index Legend

NB........national battlefield
NBP........national battlefield park
NC........national cemetery
NF........national forest
NHM........national historic(al) monument
NHP........national historic(al) park
NHS........national historic(al) site
NL........national lakeshore
NME........national memorial
NMO........national monument
NMP........national military park
NP........national park
NRA........national recreation area
NR........national river
NS........national seashore
NWR........national wildlife refuge
PHP........provincial historic(al) park
PHS........provincial historic(al) site
PP........provincial park
SF........state forest
SHM........state historic(al) monument
SHP........state historic(al) park
SHS........state historic(al) site
SME........state memorial
SP........state park
SRA........state recreation area

GEM: Points of Interest Offering a *Great Experience for Members*®

BATTLE RE-ENACTMENTS

BEACHES

BIRTHPLACES & CHILDHOOD HOMES

BOARDWALKS

BRIDGES

BRIDGES, COVERED

BUILDINGS, PUBLIC; CAPITOL; CITY HALL

BUTTERFLY HOUSES

CANYONS

CARILLONS

CAROUSELS

CASINO & RIVERBOAT GAMBLING

CAVES

CEMETERIES

CHILDREN'S ATTRACTIONS

CHURCHES, CATHEDRALS & BASILICAS

EXHIBITS & COLLECTIONS-ANIMALS & BIRDS

EXHIBITS & COLLECTIONS-ART

EXHIBITS & COLLECTIONS-AVIATION

EXHIBITS & COLLECTIONS-CIVIL WAR

EXHIBITS & COLLECTIONS-DOLLS & TOYS

EXHIBITS & COLLECTIONS-HISTORICAL

EXHIBITS & COLLECTIONS-INDIAN

MUSIC HALLS & OPERA HOUSES

NATURAL BRIDGES

NATURAL PHENOMENA

NATURE CENTERS

NATURE TRAILS

OBSERVATORIES

PAINTINGS

PARKS, CITY; STATE; PROVINCIAL

PARKS, NATIONAL

PERFORMING ARTS ORGANIZATIONS

PIERS

PLANETARIUMS

RACETRACKS-AUTO

RACETRACKS-DOG

RACETRACKS-HORSE

RAILROADS

RAILROADS-LOCOMOTIVES & CARS

RANCHES

RECREATION-SUMMER ACTIVITIES

RECREATION-WINTER ACTIVITIES

RESEARCH ORGANIZATIONS

RESTORED VILLAGES & SETTLEMENTS

THEATERS-BUILDINGS

THEATERS-PLAYS, DRAMAS & MUSICALS

TOWERS

TRAILS-SUMMER RECREATION

TREES

VIEWS

VISITOR CENTERS

VISITOR INFORMATION

WALKING TOURS

WATERFALLS

WATER PARKS

WAX MUSEUMS

WILDERNESS AREAS

WILDLIFE SANCTUARIES

WINERIES

ZOOLOGICAL PARKS & EXHIBITS

ZOOLOGICAL PARKS & EXHIBITS-CHILDREN'S ZOOS

SAVE Attraction Admission Discount Index

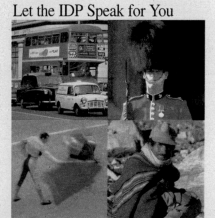

Bed & Breakfast Lodgings Index

Some bed and breakfasts listed below might have historical significance. Those properties are also referenced in the Historical index. The indication that continental [CP] or full breakfast [BP] is included in the room rate reflects whether a property is a Bed-and-Breakfast facility.

ALABAMA

ACCOMMODATIONS

LOUISIANA

ACCOMMODATIONS

MISSISSIPPI

ACCOMMODATIONS

Country Inns Index

Some of the following country inns can also be considered as bed-and-breakfast operations. The indication that continental [CP] or full breakfast [BP] is included in the room rate reflects whether a property is a Bed-and-Breakfast facility.

ALABAMA

ACCOMMODATION

LOUISIANA

ACCOMMODATIONS

MISSISSIPPI

ACCOMMODATIONS

Historical Lodgings & Restaurants Index

Some of the following historical lodgings can also be considered as bed-and-breakfast operations. The indication that continental [CP] or full breakfast [BP] is included in the room rate reflects whether a property is a Bed-and-Breakfast facility.

ALABAMA

ACCOMMODATIONS

RESTAURANTS

LOUISIANA

ACCOMMODATIONS

RESTAURANTS

MISSISSIPPI

ACCOMMODATIONS

Historical Lodgings & Restaurants (cont'd)

Resorts Index

Many establishments are located in resort areas; however, the following places have extensive on-premises recreational facilities:

ALABAMA

ACCOMMODATIONS

LOUISIANA

ACCOMMODATION

MISSISSIPPI

ACCOMMODATION

Comprehensive City Index

Here is an alphabetical list of all cities appearing in this TourBook® guide. Cities are presented by state/province. Page numbers under the POI column indicate where points of interest text begins. Page numbers under the L&R column indicate where lodging and restaurant listings begin.

Comprehensive City Index (cont'd)